# A History of Twentieth-Century Germany

# A History of Twentieth-Century Germany

ULRICH HERBERT

TRANSLATED BY
BEN FOWKES

OXFORD
UNIVERSITY PRESS

OXFORD
UNIVERSITY PRESS

Oxford University Press is a department of the University of Oxford. It furthers the University's objective of excellence in research, scholarship, and education by publishing worldwide. Oxford is a registered trade mark of Oxford University Press in the UK and certain other countries.

Published in the United States of America by Oxford University Press
198 Madison Avenue, New York, NY 10016, United States of America.



CIP data is on file at the Library of Congress
ISBN 978-0-19-007064-9

1 3 5 7 9 8 6 4 2

Printed by Sheridan Books, Inc., United States of America

Originally published as Geschichte Deutschlands im 20. Jahrhundert.

# Contents

## PART TWO: 1919–33



## PART THREE: 1933–45

## PART FIVE: 1973–2000

# Preface

The image of Germany has changed, but the country's murderous past has not been forgotten. In spite of all the differences in detail, Germany is still initially associated in most other countries with Hitler and the Nazis. When the subject of Germany comes up in films or novels, it is as a rule in the context of the Second World War or National Socialism. In those Eastern and Western European countries which suffered most under German occupation, the Germans continue to be among the least popular European nations, for reasons it is not difficult to comprehend.

And yet, at the same time the present Federal Republic is almost everywhere regarded as a stable, though somewhat boring, Western democratic state. The peaceful reunification of the country in November 1989 has in many respects made a deep impression. Surveys of public opinion have shown that things like Germany's commitment to ecological concerns and its acceptance of millions of refugees are viewed positively, although of course there are also diametrically opposed positions held on these matters.

In general, however, people actually have very little knowledge of present-day Germany, and what they do know tends to be associated vaguely with subjects like prosperity, social policy, football or fast cars. There seems to be a practical disconnect between the deeply-rooted and persistent memory of the Nazi period and this German present. A much less disturbed but also rather less interesting present has apparently edged its way into people's minds alongside Germany's catastrophic twentieth-century history, and it is evidently not easy to connect the two things together.

The situation was different in earlier decades. World-wide public perceptions of the history of Germany in the previous century, indeed perhaps of the whole of German history, were so much overshadowed, indeed dominated, by the massive crimes, inconceivable in their monumentality and frightfulness, which were committed during the Nazi dictatorship, that preceding years and decades were viewed as their historical background and the times that followed as their aftermath. The core question of contemporary German history was therefore: how did it come to this? 'This' was understood above all to mean the Nazi seizure of power, in 1933, and then later on the beginning of the systematic mass murder of the Jews of Europe, in 1941.

Contemporaries, both the protagonists themselves and observers from abroad, had also posed this question. For a long time the dominant conviction was that the coming to power of the Nazis was to be attributed to aberrations in Germany's more distant past. These were alleged to constitute a *Sonderweg*, or special path, stretching back into the eighteenth century or even earlier. This idea, that the development of a German 'spirit of subservience' could be traced back to Frederick the Great or possibly even Martin Luther, soon turned out to lack substance. On the other hand, the thesis that problematic structures had taken shape in Germany in the course of the nineteenth century, and that they had favoured the establishment of the Nazi dictatorship after 1933, appeared to be more convincing. To put it briefly, this thesis was based on the view that owing to Germany's historically conditioned *Kleinstaaterei*, the nation-state could only arise, and industrialisation only take place, with the belatedness this necessitated. The German bourgeoisie had therefore been unable to develop a liberal, democratic self-awareness, or it had developed this only incipiently. As a result, the movement of liberal nationalism was defeated along with the 1848–49 revolution, mainly owing to the resistance of the nobility and the King of Prussia. The consequence was the emergence of a semi-feudal and authoritarian state, with which the bourgeoisie rapidly came to terms, partly because it feared the rising workers' movement. According to this thesis, the overpowering influence of the old elites on the landed estates, in the military, and in the government administration had prevented the coming of democracy and parliamentary rule to Germany, and at the same time nationalism had become an ever more important way of binding the masses to the state. The democracy of the Weimar Republic, which replaced the Empire after defeat in the First World War, was therefore only able to draw support from a rapidly shrinking section of the population, and was finally destroyed by an alliance between the old elites and a nationalist mass movement.

Some aspects of this interpretation retain their persuasive force, but there are two arguments which have invalidated it as a whole. Firstly, the concept of a *Sonderweg* presupposes the existence of a norm from which there could be a deviation, in this case Germany's deviation from the development of the big Western democracies. But neither in France nor in Great Britain did conditions reflect such a norm of 'Westernism'. This is true whether one looks at the limited franchise, at the massive social contradictions, or, in the French case, at the deep chasm that separated the supporters of the republic from its opponents at the turn of the century, not to mention the colonial policies of the European states, which were the complete antithesis of any value-oriented conception of 'Westernism'.

Secondly, the *Sonderweg* theory presented a distorted picture of the German Empire. It was impossible, it was true, to overlook the defects of the political system as regards the role of parliament or the influence of the military. But these were offset by remarkable advances of a kind only achieved much later in other countries, such as universal male suffrage, the well-entrenched rule of law and social policy, in which Germany was a world pioneer. Moreover, the extreme right by no means exerted a determining influence in Germany before 1914. And if one bears in mind that throughout the period between 1919 and 1930 the democratic parties always possessed a clear electoral majority, the collapse of the Weimar Republic was, it seems, not unavoidable. Even in the spring of 1933 more than half of the population voted against the National Socialists.

During the post-war decades, both the Federal Republic and the GDR were long viewed primarily from the perspective of the Nazi state. Thus for many observers in the West, the East German state counted as a 'second German dictatorship' in continuation of the Nazi regime, as a repetition of that regime under different circumstances, and at the same time as a specific bureaucratic variant of communist rule within the Soviet Union's sphere of influence. On this view, what the Nazi state and the SED state had in common was a rigid rejection of democracy, liberalism, freedom and human rights.

West German society, too, was long suspected of being nothing more than a successor of the *Volksgemeinschaft* of the National Socialists. The number of National Socialist officials who were able to continue their careers in the Federal Republic was also too large for this suspicion *not* to arise, and the impression was confirmed by constantly repeated scandals over personnel appointments. Moreover, although the fear that the drive towards expansion and world hegemony lived on in the German national character, and might possibly find expression at any time, was not voiced openly by the country's western neighbours and allies, the feeling still existed. In 1989, after the fall of the Berlin Wall, the first thing the British Prime Minister said was a reference to a 'Fourth Reich', and in 1993, when outrages were committed against foreign asylum-seekers, world opinion placed them in the context of the pogroms of 9 November 1938.

Thus the shadow of the Nazi regime hung over the whole of Germany's twentieth-century history. The period before 1933 was regarded as a preliminary to the dictatorship, while the period afterwards was viewed in the light of its consequences.

After 1989, however, when the reunification of Germany failed to produce the boastful nationalism which Mrs. Thatcher was not alone in expecting, the initial reaction of the outside world was one of irritation. When German foreign policy turned out to be marked rather by reticence, as in the case of the Gulf Wars of 1991 and 2003 or the war over Libya in 2011, and the German government persistently refused to take up the leading political role in Europe indicated by the country's economic strength, there was great amazement.

Indeed, some people even called upon the Germans to exercise greater leadership, to become more engaged militarily and greeted Germany's rejection of these demands with an angry response.

It had become obvious that the history of the Nazi period was no longer an adequate guide to understanding Germany. Other questions now came to the forefront: how could it have come about that within less than forty years the Federal Republic had become not only prosperous but as democratic, liberal and civil as the average Western society? To find an answer to this question is made more difficult by the fact that according to all the major parameters, West German society has developed in consonance with the other Western European countries since the 1950s. If one looks on the contrary for specific cultural, political and social features of West Germany as compared with the rest of Europe, leaving aside the debates over Germany's past, it is not easy to find anything which can stand up to a more detailed examination.

This applies even in the sphere of economic development. After the country's reunification and the unprecedentedly expensive reconstruction of the ailing regions of East Germany the German economy displayed a considerable shortfall in modernisation, and at the beginning of the new century Germany, with its five million unemployed, was regarded as the 'sick man on the Rhine', and certainly no longer as the economic Hercules its European neighbours had learned to fear. Admittedly, the (comparatively moderate) neoliberal thrust, which led after 2003 to a restructuring of the labour market and the tax system, and still more the tremendous appetite of foreign countries, above all China, for German products, entailed fresh growth and tremendous export surpluses, but these developments also increased the gap between rich and poor to a degree hitherto almost unknown in the country. The crises that followed, particularly those resulting from the world financial crisis and the euro crisis, threw the Federal Republic into a condition of turbulence, both domestically and in foreign policy. But Germany did not differ in this respect from other European countries, though the opportunity was repeatedly taken to criticise it as the new European hegemon, owing to its significant influence in the European Union, which was based both on its size and its economic strength. At the height of the Greek government-debt crisis, Greek demonstrators marched in condemnation of the European Union's 'policy of austerity' with placards on which Angela Merkel was depicted wearing an SS uniform with a swastika sign. But attempts of this kind to brand the German Chancellor's policy as a continuation of Hitler's were almost universally regarded as utterly absurd.

It would not, I think, be too daring to derive the following prognosis from the above observations: Germany's past will in the future continue to be perceived as its key feature. From the end of the nineteenth century onwards, for more than a hundred years, right up to the fall of the Berlin Wall and reunification, Germany has stood at the centre of international crises. Now, however, perceptions of German history have begun to be less dramatic, and the country has as a result moved out of the centre of international interest, becoming comparable with countries like New Zealand or Canada. According to some opinion surveys, Germany is now even regarded, seventy-five years after the end of the Second World War, as one of the most respected countries in the world, a view which reflects not just its prosperity, economic strength and political stability, but also a liberalism in domestic politics, noted by many observers, which is perhaps highly unexpected in the German case, given the country's past history.

The present work is chiefly concerned with the twentieth century. In its German version, it was completed at the end of 2013. One or two small changes have been incorporated into the English edition. The book constitutes an attempt to recount the frequently fractured, contradictory and complex history of the country, and to explain this history in a convincing manner, without reducing the story of Germany's century to one or two strong theses. To write a national history, particularly in the German case, in a global and transnational age, is somewhat anachronistic, it should be said. It is clear that the national framework is not an adequate basis for understanding German twentieth-century history, because even a cursory inspection would demonstrate that many important developments are not nationally specific but pan-European or even global phenomena. How could one possibly use the categories of the nation-state to explain historical manifestations of supranational dimensions—ranging from imperialism and the world economic crisis of the 1930s to the youth rebellion of the 1960s—when fundamental common processes, in their numerous variants, are patently involved?

Europe is indubitably our present. But our past continues to be rooted in the national. There are good reasons for this, for just as in all other European countries so also in Germany personal experiences and social traditions, political choices, cultural orientation and everyday familiarity are related to a person's country of origin and residence.

The history of Germany and German society is therefore recounted here for its own sake, but it is also narrated in the context of Europe-wide developments and global interconnections. It is hoped that it will be possible in this way to free national history from its self-referential character without neglecting the innate momentum and the specific traditions of the country.

Whether the author has been successful, and whether he has been able to communicate his objective to the readers of the English-language edition, will be for those readers to decide. It only remains for me to thank the publishers for including this voluminous book in their programme, and the Stiftung Geisteswissenschaften International for awarding the book the German translation prize for the year 2015 and thereby laying the groundwork for the English-language edition. Above all, however, I should like to thank Ben Fowkes for his wonderful translation, and Larissa Wegner for her expert work in proofreading and correcting the text.

Ulrich Herbert,
Freiburg, March 2019

# Introduction

The twentieth-century history of Germany is marked by its division into two epochs, each of which could not be more markedly different from the other. The first half of the century was characterised by wars and catastrophes on a scale the world had never seen before. Germany occupied the central point in these events, and it has been associated ever since with the most frightful crimes in human history. The second half of the century, by contrast, led finally to a degree of political stability, freedom and well-being which, in 1945, had appeared to be utterly unattainable. The problem of how the two halves of the twentieth century are historically related in the German context represents the first unifying theme in the argument of this book. If a symbolic date has to be assigned to mark the transition from one epoch to the other, it should perhaps be the summer of 1942, when 'Aktion Reinhard' set in motion the systematic murder of almost all Polish Jews and the mass deportation of Jews from Western Europe to Auschwitz. How the economic and cultural blossoming of Germany from around the turn of the century could lead to such a bloody nadir is one question. The other question is how the German nation found a way out of this apocalypse over the sixty years that followed.

Nevertheless, as little as fifteen or twenty years before the summer of 1942, ordinary people could not even have suspected where events were leading. Nor could the anti-Semites and the National Socialists, who were relatively few in number at that time. This fact circumscribes the question, 'How could it have come to that?', by illuminating the openness of the historical process and the manifold byways and detours of history. The First World War was avoidable as late as June 1914. At the Reichstag elections of 20 May 1928, the National Socialists obtained no more than 2.6 per cent of the vote. As late as the autumn of 1939, the fate of the European Jews was still uncertain. Any attempt to unravel the problems of the present by reference merely to the facts of the past without consideration of the multiple possible alternative paths that events could have taken will only ever offer a partial teleology, one that unduly overlooks those historical developments that were cut short, ended in failure or simply petered out.

The course of events between the turn of the century and the apocalypse of mass murder was not predetermined, although the propulsive forces in that direction were plainly visible. Nor was there anything inevitable about the recovery of liberty and well-being after 1945, which occurred firstly in the western part of Germany, then in the whole country. Bearing in mind Germany's industrial potential, it was not out of the question that an economic boom could take place, although in view of the level of mass destruction at the end of the war, few people believed this was possible. But that it would once again be possible to awaken a sense of democracy, the rule of law and human dignity within such a nation and its leadership, and to give this a lasting character, appeared to be almost out of the question. The slow transformation which we can trace in the Federal Republic from a society moulded by National Socialism into an increasingly western and liberal society is one of the most remarkable developments of the century. Indeed, the more clearly we see the actual weight of the burden imposed by the personal and psychological legacy of the Nazi dictatorship, the more remarkable it becomes.

The second half of the century was divided in its turn. This was a division between East and West. As a result, people who lived in the eastern part of Germany only had an opportunity at the end of the century to share in the freedom and well-being of the West Germans. After 1945, people in the West fared much better than their counterparts in the East, even if this was not of their own doing, but resulted rather from the vagaries of fate and the decisions of the Occupying Powers. It soon appeared as if the Germans in the East of the country had to bear the consequences of the war by themselves. In this context, the history of the GDR was related more strongly to the year 1945 than that of the Federal Republic, as a product of the occupation policies of the victorious power, the Soviet Union, but also as a reaction by the German communists to fascism and war. The present book is in no sense a comparative history of the two German states, but it is impossible to deny that their relations, entanglements and antagonisms play as great a role here as the differences and similarities between them.

Without a doubt, the first strand of argument followed here bears an exclusively German signature. German history in this century differs from the history of all other countries, and cannot simply be subsumed under European history. Nevertheless, it is *also* a part of European history, hence the second major strand of the book's argument is in conflict with the first, because it encompasses the caesura of the year 1945.

This second strand of our argument is intimately connected with the rise of industrial society in the two decades before the First World War and the repercussions of that fundamental transformation for the economy, the society, the culture and particularly the politics of twentieth-century Germany. After the turn of the century, the immanent tendencies of industrialisation were no longer restricted to specific groups and a minority of regions, as they had been in previous decades. Instead, they transformed the lives of almost *all* people. Moreover, this took place within the lifetime of one generation, and its impact was more far-reaching than had ever been seen before.

The intensity and the dynamic force of these changes confronted contemporaries with extraordinary challenges. The political, social and cultural movements which emerged in the decades that followed, each of which adopted highly radical positions, should be understood above all as attempts to react and respond to these challenges, which were perceived as previously unimaginable advances, but at the same time as symptoms of a profound and existential crisis of bourgeois society. Subsequent decades were moulded by the reaction to these tremendous changes, expressed in the search for a way of ordering politics and society which would promise to combine security with dynamic development, equality with continuing growth.

The First World War, the inflation and particularly the world economic crisis all eroded the legitimacy and persuasiveness of the liberal capitalist model in Germany. It found that it was faced with competition from radical left-wing and right-wing alternatives, which set the principle of unity against plurality, and countered diversity with dichotomies which were based on the categories of class or race. Large stretches of twentieth-century German history can be understood as the narrative of this competition between rival social and political models. At the same time, National Socialism and Communism did not embody 'anti-modern' social formations but rather proposals for a different way of organising the modern world, in which the liberal triad of the free economy, open society and belief in universal human values was disrupted in ways specific to each movement. Both movements should be understood as shorthand solutions to the dynamic changes that had taken place since the turn of the century. These responses were rendered more radical by the experiences of the First World War and the fierceness of the confrontation between the two competing proposals for a new social order.

After the Second World War, the principles of liberal and democratic capitalism were reactivated by the victory of the West, especially the USA, with its superior military and economic strength. In Germany, as over the whole of Europe, these principles developed a power of attraction which could hardly have been imagined during the 1930s. But it was only in the 1950s, when the free market economy and the liberal system had proved to be stable and successful, that liberalism really gained the upper hand. As the 'social market economy', it was clearly in competition with the Soviet conception of socialism dominant in the GDR, and it was closely bound up with the global confrontation of the Cold War.

In West Germany, as in most other Western European societies, a model gradually took shape in which capitalism was integrated with the social state. Liberal ideas were combined with ever broader conceptions of planning, and a focus on the nation-state by no means excluded an involvement in European integration. All this was understood in terms of an explicit and coherent narrative of progress, which continued throughout this time to be focused on the challenges presented by the industrial society which had emerged during the late nineteenth century. Classical industrial society reached its zenith in the 1960s, but it increasingly declined in strength and prestige after that date. Until then, heavy industry and mass industrial employment had occupied an unchallenged position, but their dominance now began to be challenged. The model of industrial progress reached its limits, both in the West, where mines, steelworks and shipyards began to close, and in the GDR and the other lands of the Soviet Empire. In the latter case, the social and political order was completely oriented towards heavy industry and mass employment, and the erosion of classical industrial society led to collapse. The liberal capitalism of the West, on the other hand, proved to be more flexible, and after the 1970s it successfully adapted to the new conditions of the post-industrial era. Since then, a painful process of transformation has allowed the beginnings of a new economic structure to emerge, characterised by the provision of services, the globalisation of the economy and the return of traditional market-based models, with an outcome, however, which is by and large unknown.

This, the second strand of our argument, makes it possible to grasp the years between 1890 and 1990, the years of 'high modernity', as a historical unity, despite the frequent political disruptions experienced in this period, and to relate the very diverse individual developments in economics, politics, society and culture with one another. This allows us to decipher the associations between the first and second halves of the century without relying exclusively on the two world wars, the Nazi dictatorship, the GDR regime and the triumph of socially renewed and democratic capitalism.

It will already be clear from this short sketch that we are dealing here with transnational processes; and that our decision to concentrate on the history of Germany is in considerable need of justification. Until a few years ago, the situation was different, because the interest of the public and of modern historians in this country was almost self-evidently directed towards contemporary German history. The sequence of German Empire, First World War, 1918 Revolution, Weimar democracy, National Socialist dictatorship, Second World War, Holocaust and finally division and eventual reunification of Germany contained such a wealth of dramatic and large-scale events with such far-reaching consequences (and unexplained connections) that, as a rule, twentieth-century history meant German history. There is no doubt that Europe's twentieth century cannot be understood without a detailed knowledge of German history. And, even if one approaches all attempts to construct a historico-political identity with the deepest suspicion, especially when they proceed from the fiction of naturally given units, one still possesses a living cultural attachment to the country in which one grew up and where one resides, and to its history.

But it is anachronistic to regard a concentration on national history as a matter of course, even if the manifold attempts that have been made to escape from German history and its consequences by asserting a European or universal identity can be recognised as an evasion of responsibility. The constant use of categories such as 'industrial society', urbanisation, imperialism, migration or 'Cold War' shows that the history of the twentieth century cannot be decoded nationally. This point applies specifically and emphatically to Germany.

This leads us back to the two overarching strands of argument which span the present work, and which also make it clear that Germany's twentieth century cannot be summarised if we have recourse to a single thesis. Such an approach would be at variance with the multiplicity and contrariety of the movements involved, as well as the opaque and above all the contingent character of the developments investigated here. But there are some guiding threads we can follow for considerable periods of time: the abovementioned issue of the relation between industrial society and the political order is one such, and there are several others, such as the rise and decline of radical German nationalism, the relation between the culture of modernity and mass society, the dynamics of violence and war, the relation between the Self and the Other, and the tendency of developed industrial societies to converge. In this context, the attempt will be made to integrate the different fields of study, classically defined as politics, society, the economy and culture, and to demonstrate the connections between them. Culture will be understood here in the broad sense, as the reflection and the working out of social processes in the arts, science, public debate and ways of life.

In any case, the contradictory diversity of the twentieth century can also be gleaned from the author's failed efforts to choose a catchy title for this book. Alternative titles under consideration all failed, needless to say, because they inevitably led to a one-size-fits-all approach. There was perhaps one exception: the author would have liked to have given the book the title *The Years That You Know*, following the title of a book written in 1972 by Peter Rühmkorf, in which he combined his memories of the 1960s with all sorts of poems and fanciful reflections. But the title is protected by copyright, since the book was reprinted in 2000, and, in any case, it would doubtless be somewhat impertinent to make such a takeover bid. This is why the present book is now drily entitled *A History of Twentieth-Century Germany*, which is after all a precise description of what is being attempted here. *The Years That You Know*, however, would have addressed the complex relationship of the Germans to their own twentieth century—a contemporary history which never fades from view. It is true that when this book came out, the beginning of the Second World War already lay seventy-five years in the past, but for anyone who follows newspapers and television programmes, not a single day has gone past without a mention of that war, the post-war years or the period of Nazi rule. The First World War began over one hundred years ago, and in the jubilee year of 2014 the title pages of the weekly magazines were full of it, and there were probably more than a hundred books published on the subject by the time the year had ended. The events symbolised by the number '1968' are far from being regarded as entirely in the past; even now, every undesirable development in West German history is certain to be explained with a reference to them. Even people who know almost nothing, or at least very little of relevance, about these events have an opinion on the subject. Contemporary observers of the history of Germany in the twentieth century are therefore of a very special kind, almost independently of their generation, and we need to take account of them, albeit from a largely critical point of view. The purpose of the book is not to present novelties of a suspiciously sensational character. The advantage of the historical view is rather that chronological separation and the use of a variety of perspectives allow new connections to be laid bare. It is also possible to reveal long-term processes and changes in conditions of life, political mentalities and cultural orientation, the meaning of which was often entirely opaque to contemporaries.

The book is articulated in five sections, with the years 1918, 1933, 1945, 1973 and 1990 marking the breaks between them. The external structure conforms to these politically important dates, but the course of the argument as a rule does not. Chapters that provide a cross-sectional view have been included in each section. In these chapters, individual years or time intervals are examined more closely, independently of the course of political events. The years in question are 1900, 1926, 1942, 1965 and 1989–90.

Since work on the manuscript has taken much longer than planned, owing to a number of interruptions, the author has been forced into a constant chase after history, or, more precisely, the writing of history, because his own presentation had to be corrected, expanded, or accented differently, owing to the way new studies of the period constantly kept appearing. Certainly, no one who has written a work of contemporary history could possibly have coined the aphorism that one must imagine Sisyphus to have been a happy man! In some respects, indeed, work done on later phases of the twentieth century has led the presentation of earlier phases to undergo modification. The assertion that history is a construct has never appeared more persuasive to the author than on those occasions. And yet a return to the sources, and to the statements by contemporaries that they contain, has repeatedly brought him back to the view that the history presented here really did happen and that it is the historian's professional obligation to fulfil the responsibility that arises from this.

# PART ONE
# 1870–1918

# 1

# Germany around 1900

## Progress and Its Costs

In September 1913, on the occasion of the twenty-fifth anniversary of Emperor William II's accession to the throne, a review of the economic development of Germany was presented by one of the leading German economists, Karl Helfferich, who was also a member of the board of management of the Deutsche Bank and the central executive committee of the Reichsbank. He wrote a book with the title *Germany's National Wealth 1888–1913*, in which he described the rapid rise of the German economy: the growth of industry; the innovations in technology and science; the expansion of transport, communications and trade; the increase in income per head; and the improvement in the standard of living of much of the population. Helfferich concluded his sober description with a reference to the broader social and political context:

> In the development of scientific and practical technology, in the establishment of an economic organisation connecting together all forces and instruments in an effective manner, in the rise in the production and transportation of goods, in the growth and strengthening of our world economic position, in the improvement of people's income and financial circumstances and in the rise in the standard of living of our population while it proceeds to grow in a healthy fashion, in all these areas of progress Germany has raised itself up to a level never before reached in the whole of its previous history, and proved itself to be the equal of the first and most powerful of its rivals in the peaceful competition between the nations.

Germany's ascent, 'compressed into such a short space of time, hardly has its equal in the history of the nations'. It was therefore entirely legitimate to take pride in this immense achievement, Helfferich went on, especially as the Germans had been accustomed over previous decades 'to stand on the sidelines and humbly bow the knee in the face of other nations' superiority'. The effects of this attitude could still be felt today, he said, for the Germans were characterised on the one hand by a lack of healthy self-confidence, internal equilibrium and self-assurance, and on the other hand by attacks of 'vain presumption and superficial arrogance'. The successful and rapid ascent of Germany and in particular 'the big shifts in the internal structure of the population, namely changes in the relation between town and country, in professional and social structure and in financial circumstances' had led to 'a condition of tension' which was liable to threaten 'the foundations of the moral and physical health of large parts of the population'. It had led above all to 'class struggles and class hatred' but also to 'indolence, flabbiness, greed and a thirst for enjoyment'.[1]

This accurately reflects the state of mind of the German elites and considerable sections of the German population in the years after the turn of the century. On the one hand, there was a pride in what had been achieved, which increased still more when the overwhelming economic expansion of the previous twenty-five years was compared with the situation of other European countries, thereby underlining the magnitude of Germany's rise to a position of one of the leading industrial nations of the world. On the other hand, there was also reason for lamentation. The new epoch was marred by the emergence of unwanted accompanying phenomena such as social contradictions, cultural tensions, and, in politics as in society, a constant alternation between overweening pride and feelings of inferiority.

## A Booming Economy

In *Germany's National Wealth*, Helfferich was reflecting on a period which, if we consider it from our present standpoint, was a phase of historically unparalleled and almost unbroken expansion, lasting more than twenty years, by which Germany was transformed within a generation from an agrarian into an industrial state, thereby altering its structure and physiognomy to an extent never seen before in the whole of its history.

The phenomena of tremendous economic growth, rising industrial production and growing income per head were common to the whole of Europe in the last third of the nineteenth century. In fact, the highest rates of increase in GNP between 1860 and 1910 were found in a number of smaller European states—Belgium, Denmark, Sweden and Switzerland. Among the larger states, however, Germany was always one of the countries with the highest rates of growth, whichever yardstick one chooses to apply, and in the two decades before and after 1900 it rose to become one of the three leading economies in the world. The others were the USA and Great Britain.

Not the least of the reasons for this astounding achievement was that, in the previous years, the leading industrial nations had enormously expanded the markets for their products. Technical improvements in the transport of commodities by land and sea, the acceleration of communications brought about by the telegraph and the telephone, and the intensification of trading relations between the industrial countries and towards the colonised parts of the world had internationalised the process of economic exchange. It had become 'globalised', to use the word current since the 1980s, a decade when international interconnectedness reached a yet higher level of intensity and frequency. Constant comparisons between the economic, technological, scientific and cultural achievements of the 'progressive' countries were also a feature of analyses made in these decades around 1900, as a way of expressing the 'peaceful competition' between nations. Under such a model, evidence of denser forests or larger items of rolling stock was viewed as a sign of the superiority of the nation in question.[2]

In Germany, it was above all the speed of industrialisation which proved particularly astonishing. Industrial production rose six-fold between 1870 and 1913. In the 1860s, Germany's share in world industrial production had amounted to a mere 4.9 per cent, while Great Britain's share was almost 20 per cent. In 1913, however, Germany's share was 14.8 per cent. This was higher than Great Britain's share (13.6 per cent) although considerably lower than that of the USA (32 per cent), the other great economic growth story of those years. In the sphere of international trade, too, by the year 1910 Germany was one of the three leading nations, alongside Great Britain and the USA.[3]

In Germany, the process of growth was marked by great unevenness. It varied by time, region and economic sector. Its chief feature, however, was the rapidity with which these far-reaching changes were accomplished. This is what gave the process described here the spectacular dynamism which had already impressed contemporaries and distinguished developments in Germany from simultaneous processes in other countries, where the transition from the industrial revolution to large-scale industrialisation often extended over a relatively long period. As late as 1867, more than half of the employed population of Germany, or rather the German Confederation, were involved in the agricultural sphere (8.3 million people, or 51.5 per cent). Only 4.3 million people (27 per cent) worked in industry, handicrafts and trade, and they were concentrated in a few places (the big cities, Silesia and the Rhineland.) By 1913, the total number of employees had increased considerably. This was true of agriculture as well, a sector in which 10.7 million people now worked, but agricultural employees now constituted only a third of all those in employment. The number of employees in the secondary sector, on the other hand, had almost tripled over the same period, and it now stood at 11.7 million, which corresponded to 37.8 per cent of the total.[4]

These changes are still more striking when measured in monetary terms. In 1873 the value of all goods produced had stood at 16.3 billion Marks. Industry, handicrafts and mining accounted for a third of this sum. By 1900 the total value had doubled (to 33.1 billion Marks) and by 1913 it had tripled (to 48.4 billion Marks). In the meantime, the share of industry, handicrafts and mining in the total had risen to 44 per cent.

In face of such numbers, developments in the agricultural sphere give an impression rather of crisis, and contemporary observers were already warning of a decline in farming or even its complete collapse, although those who held this view were mainly agrarian lobbyists. Two tendencies were of decisive importance in this context: one was the expansion of agricultural production itself. This doubled in value between 1873 and 1913 and the number of people employed in the sector increased by more than a quarter. New techniques of production such as the use of artificial fertiliser, for instance, or the introduction of threshing machines, played an increasing role, although in Germany the mechanisation of agriculture proceeded more slowly than in the USA. Productivity and yields per hectare increased, and agricultural production rose by 73 per cent between 1873 and 1912. Finally, in agriculture too, a focus on the market became the order of the day. Moreover, agriculture looked not just to the national but to the world market. This was made possible above all through the opening up of transport links such as railway lines, roads and canals.

In relation to the economy as a whole and the industrial sector in particular, however, the agricultural sector declined in importance, and within a short period it had lost its formerly dominant position in the German economy. The share of agriculture in the total value of production fell from 37 per cent in 1875 to 23 per cent in 1913, while its share of employment also fell, as we have seen, from more than a half to a third. Nevertheless, some 18 million people were still making their living from agriculture even after the turn of the century.[5]

The coal, iron and steel industries, the leading sectors of the first phase of industrialisation, continued to form the basis for rapid industrial growth. The amount of bituminous coal mined rose from 8 million tonnes in 1865 to 114 million tonnes in 1913, and the number of people employed in this sector rose from roughly 40,000 to almost half a million. Pig iron production had averaged 1.6 million tonnes a year between 1870 and 1874; thirty years later, between 1900 and 1904, it was 8 million tonnes, and just before the war it had risen to 14.8 million tonnes.[6]

But it was the new industries which were the most prominent hallmarks of the new century. The extraordinary dynamism and intensity of growth which characterised this period was seen most clearly in the chemical and electrical industries, the leading sectors in the second phase of industrialisation. Germany quickly became the world's leading producer of chemicals. Its chemical industry had a 28 per cent share in the world export trade, 250,000 employees (1907) and annual rates of growth of over 6 per cent. Here, three developments stood out in particular: the growth of the electro-chemical industry, which made possible the production of aluminium; the manufacture of synthetic dyestuffs; and the rise of the pharmaceutical industry. German manufacturers were particularly successful in the last two of these areas, and they soon joined together in gigantic, vertically integrated chemical concerns. Between 1900 and the First World War, Germany's share in the production of dyes for the world market fluctuated between 80 and 90 per cent.

The electrification of public and private lighting, the use of electric motors and the spread of electrically driven trams and underground trains offered the electrical engineering industry tremendous opportunities for growth. Two large firms, Siemens and AEG, which had their main factories in Berlin, were the most active in this area. As in the case of chemicals, the close connection between science, technology and the electricity industry was of decisive significance: it meant that new discoveries, for instance, in the area of high voltage technology, could be quickly put into practice in the industrial field. By 1910, all the big towns and cities and large parts of the countryside were already connected to the electrical grid. At this time, German firms accounted for a third of world electrical engineering production. Growth rates were correspondingly high, standing at nine per cent in 1890 and 16 per cent in 1900.[7]

## The Reinvention of the World

Alongside the explosive growth of industry, this epoch was characterised above all by the systematic connection between science and technology. Its results changed the lives of contemporaries, and their perceptions, in ways previously thought impossible. Never before and never since has a scientific worldview changed so dramatically in such a short time and with such an impact as in the three decades before the First World War. In the field of chemistry, there were big advances in chemical synthesis, such as the synthesis of indigo (1880), of rubber (1909), and of ammonia from nitrogen and hydrogen by the use of catalysts (1908). This facilitated the development of artificial materials, which now began their triumphant progress through industry and everyday life. At the same time, the chemists succeeded in making the breakthrough into systematic pharmacology, thereby beginning the development of modern pharmaceutical chemistry. In physics, the development of the theory of electromagnetism, the discovery of the electron and finally research into radiation were all of great significance. A particularly spectacular moment was the discovery of X-rays by Conrad Röntgen, a phenomenon which could not be explained by means of the current physical theories. In this context, the quantum theory developed by Max Planck had already indicated the limitations of classical mechanics. Questions about the formation and the splitting of the atom now began to be raised. Hence, the period around 1900 also saw the birth of nuclear physics. The theories of Charles Darwin had already gained acceptance in the field of biology; in the wake of this advance, causal explanations of the mysteries of life as being immanently present in nature itself drove out theological and metaphysical approaches. Cell research and the theory of evolution opened up the new science of genetics. Biochemistry and behavioural research made their appearance, and they revolutionised traditional conceptions of life and human nature.[8]

But as far as the public were concerned, the most sensational changes were in medicine, for after all it was the new potential for medical treatment which had the most direct impact on people's lives. The basis of this revolutionary development was the victory of scientific thought in the medical field: if illnesses originated in chemical and physical changes, it must be possible to prove the connection with the methods of natural science. This was the starting point for the differentiation of medicine into individual specialisms, and the creation of a systematic science of medicine soon resulted in outstanding successes. Thus, in the field of physiology and cell research, the classification of hormones, vitamins and blood groups could now be undertaken. The discovery of microorganisms allowed the pathogens that caused many illnesses to be identified and successfully fought with the help of antibodies. In the 1870s and 1880s, with the discovery of the agents responsible for anthrax, tuberculosis and cholera, a triumphant onslaught began on diseases which affected large numbers of people. This was followed by campaigns against gonorrhoea, typhus, diphtheria, pneumonia and syphilis. And, finally, the improvement in techniques of anaesthesia made it possible to carry out operations unthinkable until then: gall bladders, kidneys and appendixes could now be removed surgically.

The tremendous growth of the natural sciences was a phenomenon common to all industrial countries. Scientists in Great Britain, Germany, France, Italy and the USA maintained close links with one another, and the successes of scientific and medical research at that time, which contemporaries found almost inconceivable, owed a great deal to this international cooperation. Even so, these successes were also often interpreted in nationalistic terms. It was claimed that they demonstrated the excellence not just of the scientists responsible but also of the nations to which they belonged. This applied particularly to Germany, and the development of natural and medical science did in fact proceed there with extraordinary intensity. Almost half of the significant scientific discoveries in the medical field between 1860 and 1910 (249 out of 556) have been ascribed to German specialists. In physics too, the German contribution was roughly as significant as it was in medicine, and this was soon reflected in the number of Nobel prizes awarded, for the Nobel Prize was also an expression and an instrument of the competition between the industrial nations for prestige, influence and market share.[9]

These astounding German successes in the scientific field were mainly grounded in the system of school and university education, which had been extended systematically since the middle of the nineteenth century with the aim of counteracting the economic backwardness of the German states, especially in comparison with Great Britain. The foundation of the German Empire led to an intensification of these efforts, which were pursued even more strongly after the turn of the century. Between 1873 and 1914, expenditure on the universities by the federal states that made up Germany rose by almost 500 per cent. The number of high school students doubled over this period, while the number of university students registered a fivefold increase.

The basic principle adopted by the German universities was the primacy of research. Scientists' careers were determined by their research achievements, and research into fundamentals occupied pride of place. Technological applications, it turned out, could not readily be planned. They emerged rather as side effects of pure research, which was pursued without any practical objective. This approach was the basis of the pre-eminence of the German university system around the world, and it was emulated by the founders of universities both in the USA and in Russia. In the 1880s, moreover, the existing universities were supplemented by Technical Universities, which served to train the very large number of technical experts now required in branches of the economy such as mining, and mechanical, electrical and civil engineering. This increase in the number of scientifically educated specialists had a particular impact on the new, leading sectors of chemicals and electrical engineering, and it formed the basis for an intensification of product-oriented industrial research. The third pillar of this educational edifice was the research institute. The first big research establishments were founded around the turn of the century. They were examples of close cooperation between science, industry and the state. They received immense sums of money, were constructed as special establishments devoted to particularly promising research fields, and they were often given the title 'Emperor William Institutes'.[10]

The successes of scientific research were reflected above all in the technological innovations which transformed everyday life so profoundly and, to some extent, perplexingly. This applied particularly to the rapid spread of electrical lighting, which had become cheap and relatively safe to utilise since the introduction of the tungsten filament lamp. The night-time illumination of streets, squares and houses represented one of the most significant changes to the way life was perceived and conducted in cities from this time onwards. Alongside this revolution in the urban environment there was the increasing ubiquity of the electric motor, which was an essential element in household electrical appliances and also the power source for the trams which now began their rapid spread over Germany's cities. By 1900 there were already roughly 3,000 kilometres of tramlines in Germany. This was as much as in all other European countries combined together, a statistic which was immediately calculated and triumphantly made public. The internal combustion engine was also developed at this time, thereby beginning the success story of the automobile, although not in fact in Germany. It is true that functionally adequate prototypes were first developed there, by Benz, Otto and Daimler, but Germany did not possess an adequate market for such an invention. Until the early 1950s, motoring remained the privilege of the property-owning upper strata of the country. In the USA, by contrast, more than 1.2 million motor vehicles were already in use by 1913, and in Great Britain there were 250,000, as against a mere 70,000 in Germany.

At the turn of the century, the symbol of individual travel was rather the bicycle, which now experienced a real boom, and rose to become a means of mass transport, as well as dominating the first modern phase of mass sporting activity. Office and communication technology experienced similarly rapid advances at this time: the typewriter and the telephone came into use first in private firms, then in the state bureaucracy and private households. By 1895 there were already 100,000 telephone lines in Germany, in 1904 there were more than half a million, the greater part of them in Berlin, and by 1915 there were 220 telephone lines for every 1,000 inhabitants. The entertainment industry, finally, was also revolutionised. Improvements in photographic technique allowed the first moving pictures to be produced, and from being initially displayed in annual fairs they were subsequently shown in fixed locations, or 'moving picture theatres'. These soon exerted their spell on a mass public. By 1914, there were already roughly 2,500 cinemas in Germany.[11]

## The Dynamic of Social Change

The economic, scientific and technological changes we have mentioned were accompanied by a rapid process of social change. At the turn of the century, the German population was experiencing an unprecedented degree of geographical mobility. In 1907, only half of all Germans still lived where they were born. The rest had changed their place of residence at least once; the working population much more frequently. This trend began with the tremendous increase in population which had already been apparent since the middle of the century and had accelerated since the 1870s. Between 1871 and 1910 the population grew from 41 to 64 million. This was an increase of more than a half (56 per cent), somewhat higher than the European average of approximately 45 per cent. The population of France, on the other hand, only increased by 6 per cent during this period, a phenomenon interpreted in that country as a sign of weakness and degeneration.

Until the early 1890s, the sizeable increase in Germany's population was attributable first and foremost to a reduction in infant mortality. After that date, the main causal factor was an accelerated decline in the overall death rate, resulting from improved living conditions and better medical care. In the first phase of industrialisation, starting in the mid-nineteenth century, the increase in population led to a worsening of living conditions, because corresponding employment opportunities were yet to be made available, particularly in the countryside. The response of the people to this pressure on livelihoods was a great wave of emigration. Between 1880 and 1895 almost two million Germans left the country, most of them settling in North America. After 1895, however, the rapid economic development of the German Empire began to give rise to a considerable demand for labour, above all in the newly emerging industrial agglomerations of Berlin, Silesia, Saxony and the Ruhr. Now the stream of emigrants changed direction, strengthening migratory movements within the country which had already been apparent since the 1870s. Internal migration generally proceeded from East to West, from country to town, and from agricultural to industrial regions. This movement was driven by poverty and under-employment in the countryside, and people were enticed into industrial employment by better wages, greater security of employment and the greater measure of individual freedom in the towns, which was often given as the primary motive for moving.

The majority of the migrants were young, unmarried men. Many of them were recruited by the big firms, the mining companies above all, which promised them work and a place to live in the industrial areas. On arrival, most of them did not settle down immediately but frequently changed where they lived and worked. It has been calculated that the average German who lived in an urban area relocated as many as four times a year. Many country dwellers also moved back to the countryside at times of economic depression, returning to the towns when work again became available.[12]

The gigantic migratory movements of the time were also the most important trigger for urbanisation. 'Urbanisation' refers, firstly, to the growth in the urban population, which had already been apparent since the 1860s but accelerated from the 1890s onwards. Towns dominated by mining and heavy industry experienced particularly rapid growth. Between 1875 and 1910, the number of inhabitants of Duisburg increased from 37,000 to 229,000. The increase in Essen was from 54,000 to 294,000, and in Leipzig the population grew from 127,000 to 589,000. The biggest increase—in numerical terms—was in Berlin. Here, the number of inhabitants grew from 966,000 to over 2 million. In percentage terms, the increase was more rapid in neighbouring suburbs such as Schöneberg and Charlottenburg, which were soon to be incorporated into the city. Charlottenburg's population jumped from 25,000 to 305,000 over this period. In 1871, there were only eight cities in Germany with more than 100,000 inhabitants, comprising a national total of just 2 million people. In 1920 there were forty-eight cities in this category, with a total of roughly 13 million inhabitants, a fifth of the country's population. Of course, roughly half the population still lived in rural communities or small towns in 1910. Thus the German Empire continued to be dominated by the rural and small-town milieu, but its predominance was no longer overwhelming. Now the big industrial towns were equally important.[13]

The word 'urbanisation', however, also refers to the victorious advance of the new metropolitan way of life, which differed radically from the traditionalism of the small towns and villages. The big city became the symbol of the age. Indeed, the very foundation of German society was reforged in the big cities. The face of urban society no longer bore the imprint of groups like the nobility, the clergy and the 'burgher estate' (*Bürgerstand*), legitimated by the Estates tradition of the past, but instead consisted of the various classes, which were defined by their position in the market society of capitalism. By the turn of the century, the social hierarchy had also come to be determined in the same way.

The topmost social stratum comprised the small group of the so-called big bourgeoisie, consisting of not more than one to two hundred thousand persons. Beneath this thin upper crust were the economic bourgeoisie proper, consisting of entrepreneurs in industry, trade and handicrafts. They made up roughly 3–4 per cent of the population. Below them were the educated bourgeoisie (*Bildungsbürgertum*), a group which comprised only about 1 per cent of the population at the turn of the century. This group was on the increase, owing to the entry of members of the academic profession into state service: they joined the bureaucracy, the legal and medical systems and the educational institutions. At the same time, there was also a considerable increase in the number of people with an academic education employed in the industrial sphere, such as engineers, chemists and architects. The *Mittelstand*, the so-called 'lower middle class', was much less homogeneous. It comprised not just the 'old' *Mittelstand*—such as small traders, artisans, middle-ranking officials and officers in the armed forces—but also the rapidly growing army of salaried employees in the industrial and service sectors, the 'new' *Mittelstand.* All these groups, taken together, made up the 'bourgeoisie' (*Bürgertum*). They constituted roughly 8–10 per cent of the population, barely 5 million people.

The social differences between these various groups were nevertheless immense, as was the symbolic distance that separated them. One of the new super-rich entrepreneurs such as Krupp, Thyssen or von Stumm-Halberg was worlds away from a master craftsman, a town official or a schoolmaster: not just materially, but in social behaviour, from their attitude to marriage to their mode of social intercourse. And yet there was a bond that encompassed and united all these groups, namely their common relation to bourgeois culture, and the high value they placed on humanistic education and the norms of bourgeois morality. This is what allows us to refer to them in their totality as 'the bourgeoisie'.[14]

The second class defined by the market, the working class, was also an extremely heterogeneous entity. If one takes the narrower group, which consisted of dependent workers employed in industry, trade and transport, one arrives at 24 per cent of the population in 1882 and roughly 33 per cent in 1907. If we also include agricultural workers, domestic workers and servants, the lower strata of pre-industrial times, the proportion rises to 50 per cent. On the other hand, if we take the Prussian income statistics and count all who were below the poverty line of an income of 900 Marks a year, this amounts to almost two thirds of the whole society. The same order of magnitude is also reached when the share of wage labourers in the total number of economically active people is measured. This rose from 56 per cent in 1875 to 76 per cent in 1907.

Even if the narrowest definition is taken as a basis, the group that results is itself not socially homogeneous. Individual groups of workers differed far too widely from one another for this. Regional origin is one distinguishing mark. The original inhabitants had been moulded by very different previous experiences and their attitudes were very different from those of the incomers from the East. Another distinguishing mark was social origin. Most of the workers were the children of members of the lowest strata. But ever greater numbers of children of artisans, peasants or small-scale independent producers and traders were entering the working class. The 'proletarianisation' of the lower *Mittelstand* was a widespread phenomenon, and a subject of anxious debate. Different levels of training also created substantial distinctions between individual groups of workers. What it meant to be a 'skilled worker' could not be defined exactly, but a trained metalworker's conditions of employment, for instance, were much better than those of an unskilled 'labourer', the first to be laid off during an economic downturn, who was often offered only short-term employment when the next opportunity arose.

Differences between workers in large and small enterprises were also considerable. But the biggest difference of all was between men and women and young and old workers. Young male workers were best paid and had the best social position, while poverty remained the widespread fate of workers in old age. In 1907, between 15 and 20 per cent of employed workers were female, though the proportion naturally varied greatly between different industrial sectors. The women were mostly unskilled or semi-skilled and earned distinctly less than men doing the same job.

But these considerable variations and differences were outweighed by a number of common features: the hours of work were long; the work was, as a rule, physically exhausting, dirty and dangerous; and living arrangements in the cramped dwellings of the big cities were oppressive. Loss of employment signified impoverishment for the whole family. Despite the system of social insurance that was gradually being introduced, for the workers an inability to work because of accident or sickness remained well into the twentieth century a risk as terrifying as it was real and life-threatening.

The increasing prevalence of wage labour also contributed to the unification of the working class. Partial payment in-kind continued to exist in the countryside for a long time, but, in the towns, it rapidly lost all significance. In the long run, the income of workers began to improve: the average nominal annual wage rose from 506 Marks (1870) to 711 Marks (1890) and then to 1,163 Marks (1913), though here too there were big differences between the individual branches of industry. Real wages also rose. They increased by 50 per cent between 1871 and 1890, and by 1913 they had risen by 90 per cent. These were considerable increases, but wages in Germany still remained significantly below those enjoyed by workers in France, Great Britain and the USA.

As a result of this rise in income, the worst distress of the working population was on the whole alleviated, and still further improvement seemed likely in the longer term. In 1892 in Prussia and in 1895 in Saxony, three quarters of the taxpaying citizens had been assessed as earning below the taxable limits of 900 and 950 Marks of annual income, respectively, and they were therefore living in poverty. But by 1912 this proportion had fallen from three quarters to a half.[15] Even so, that meant that at least every second person continued to live in poverty.

The gap between rich and poor widened considerably in the years of rapid industrialisation. In 1854 in Prussia, a fifth of the total income went to the wealthiest 5 per cent of the population; by 1873, this figure had increased to a quarter, and in 1913 it was a third. In contrast to this, the share of the poorest 25 per cent of the population fell from 8 per cent to 7 per cent over the same period of time. These figures were by no means unusual in the international context: in Great Britain, 5 per cent of the people, the top earners, received almost half the total income. But, in Germany, it was the rapid increase in income differences and in the share of income received by the top earners that drew people's attention.[16] One of the greatest concerns of the time in Germany was the apparently inexorable widening of the gap between rich and poor and the concomitant growth in social divisions. Conservatives and socialists were at one in criticising the 'social dismemberment of the nation' by modern capitalism, although their objectives were entirely different.

Well into the first half of the twentieth century, the social structures prevailing in rural areas continued to look very different from those that had taken shape in the towns. Even taking into account regional divergences, a three-way division between big landowners, peasant farmers and agricultural workers predominated in the countryside. Big landownership, which was particularly widespread in the economically backward districts of the north-east of the country, had its origin in part in the manorial estates (*Rittergüter*) held by the nobility. While the legal and social privileges traditionally attached to these estates had gradually been eroded since the Prussian reform era, they had not disappeared completely. In many respects, they lasted into the twentieth century, despite the movement towards civil equality. These inequalities permeated the tax system, the legal system, the institutions of rural self-government and also the position of day labourers, housemaids and servants. Rural Germany, above all the region to the east of the River Elbe, remained the domain of manorial rule. This was not identical with the rule of the nobility, however. As early as the 1860s a majority of the manorial estates were in bourgeois hands, and, by 1880, the proportion had risen to two-thirds.

Many estates had sunk deeper and deeper into debt since the 1870s, partly owing to the difficult crisis of adaptation facing agriculture, but also because of mismanagement and excessive consumption of luxuries by the estate-owning nobility. This led to their sale, often to wealthy bourgeois. In order to avoid economic ruin, many estate-owners now began to adapt themselves more wholeheartedly to modern capitalist economic principles, turning into agricultural entrepreneurs; though this was of course a very lengthy process. At the same time, however, the new bourgeois estate-owners adopted or imitated the style of life of the 'Junkers'—and assumed some of their privileges. Many of them strove to obtain titles. This was a trend seen in many Western European states at that time, but the German nobility reacted by reinforcing the barriers that separated them from the newly rich social climbers. In Germany, therefore, the number of newly ennobled families remained relatively small.

Although the economic weight of agriculture had declined, the nobles retained their special social position. As landowners, the nobility continued to dominate the countryside, often in connection with their role as District Administrators (*Landräte*), in other words members of the regional state bureaucracy, which was continuously increasing its influence. Above all, though, the nobles were grossly overrepresented at the top of the administration, in the diplomatic service and in the army leadership. Almost all the army generals were members of the nobility. At the beginning of the new century, the social prestige and political influence of the nobility were, paradoxically, higher than they had been at the beginning of the age of industrialisation.[17]

Around the turn of the century, there were altogether 5.5 million owners of land in Germany, or more than 10 million if their families are included. Less than 0.5 per cent counted as big landowners; all the others were peasant farmers. There were only approximately 250,000 well-off peasant proprietors, each holding 20 to 100 hectares of land, while the number of middle-ranking peasants, with up to 20 hectares of land each, was estimated at roughly a million. These two groups dominated the social hierarchy of the village and they differed markedly from the more than 4 million small and dwarf ('parcel-holding') peasants, who were unable to live from the yield of their land or could only eke out a miserable existence from it. For most of this group, farming was a subsidiary occupation in addition to their work as day labourers on the lands of the nobility and the richer peasants, or in a nearby town.[18]

The agricultural workers, finally, stood below the rural proprietors and their families. There were roughly 6 million of them, if we include their families, and they lived in needy, indeed in poverty-stricken, circumstances. At the beginning of the new century, some of them continued to be dependent on the owners of the manorial estates, although this 'semi-free' status as tenants (*Insten*), crofters (*Kätner*) or cottagers (*Häusler*) was becoming increasingly rare even in the back-country of East Elbia. Most of them were day labourers, hence formally free wage labourers, although here the principle of market-based wage labour was only gradually making inroads. There were also servants, in other words, men and women who were employed on the manors and farms as a permanent live-in labour force rather than as day labourers. The rural proletariat and the parcel-holding peasants increasingly regarded their dependence on peasant farmers or estate-owners as oppressive. It was this, as well as the poor living and working conditions, which made migrating to the towns and securing a job in industry such an appealing prospect.

Town and country gradually became mutually interdependent. The most important factors in this process were market relations, the state administration, railways, taxes, military service and compulsory education. Even so, right into the twentieth century the village remained a world of its own, marked by sharply delineated and almost insurmountable social hierarchies. Here there was little chance of rising in the social scale, high levels of social control prevailed, and the culture was deeply imbued with traditional norms.[19]

If we look at the social structure of Wilhelmine Germany as a whole, we see a divided society. On the one hand, there was a rapidly expanding class society of a capitalist kind—urban and industrial, and marked by tremendous growth and a high degree of transformation in all areas of life. On the other hand, we see an agrarian society, increasingly influenced by the dynamism of industry, but still clearly characterised by an inherited Estates structure and the survival of traditional norms, which also shaped how new developments were perceived. Both situations existed simultaneously and were superimposed on each other: the sharp class antagonisms and social inequality typical of industrial societies stood alongside the Estate-based divisions and highly marked privileges enjoyed by the nobility, the military, the bureaucracy and the big landowners.

If a comparison is drawn with the rest of Europe, it becomes apparent that these features were not specific to Germany. In this long phase of transition from a society under predominantly agrarian determination to a predominantly industrial society, the simultaneous existence of traditional and modern formations is the rule rather than the exception. The fashionable dominance of an aristocratic style of life in the upper strata of bourgeois society, the continuing impact of rural norms and traditions, the stubborn independence of rural modes of life, are all found in other industrialising countries of Europe at this time, as well as in the southern United States.

One's attention is therefore repeatedly drawn to what was the most outstanding peculiarity of Germany's development: the immense rapidity of the economic, social and cultural transformations of the decades around the turn of the century. In Germany, the friction between traditional and modern attitudes was greater, the potential for conflict higher, and the changes experienced far more intense.[20]

## Enthusiasm for Progress and a Crisis of Direction

The modern metropolis was the symbol of this dynamic of forced transformation, and the modern metropolis was represented by Berlin. 'It is a new city, the newest I have ever seen' wrote Mark Twain, who came from America to visit Germany in 1892. 'Chicago would seem venerable beside it, for there are many old-looking districts in Chicago, but not many in Berlin. The main mass of the city looks as if it had been built last week.'[21] Contemporaries were particularly impressed by the building mania that took hold of Berlin around the turn of the century. Whole new districts of the city sprang up within a few years, transport links were doubled and redoubled, life was conducted at a breathless pace.

Visitors reacted with confusion; this was felt even more strongly by those who had been drawn into the city from the countryside. 'What an idea of Berlin we got!' wrote the agricultural worker Franz Rehbein on his first journey by train from Pomerania into the capital city of the German Empire.

> We had been told wondrous things about the city, about its size, its houses reaching up into the sky and its fairytale lighting. The number of station lights now increased rapidly. We took turns to stick our heads out of the carriage windows and look in the direction of the sea of lights in the capital. Exclamations of surprise and astonishment followed: There were probably not as many lights in the whole of Hither Pomerania as we could see shining towards us on our journey into the city.[22]

The baker's apprentice Jessaia Gronach had a similar experience when he travelled from Galicia to Berlin for the first time in 1906:

> Here I did not come into a city, here a city came over me. Here I felt invaded, attacked, pulled in all directions by a new rhythm, new people, a new language, new manners and customs. I had to keep hold of myself, open my eyes wide, and tense my muscles, in order not to be overrun, crushed, squashed.[23]

During these decades, Berlin embodied the breakthrough into the modern era in a fashion matched only by London and New York. The ceaseless building activity, the construction of ever larger and more magnificent new shopping palaces, the spread of modern means of transport and communication, all these advances were symbolic of the far-reaching optimism of everyday life. It was firmly believed that the discovery of nature's secrets and the mastery of technology would lead to unlimited progress. Werner von Siemens, one of the most famous inventors and entrepreneurs of his age, summed up this happy certainty about the future in these words:

> Our activities in research and invention lead people to a higher cultural level, ennoble them and make them more accessible to the search for ideals . . . and the dawning age of natural science will satisfy their needs, lessen their infirmities, increase their enjoyment of life, and make them better, happier and more contented with their fate.[24]

And just as at night towns could be made as light as day and traversed within minutes in electrical trains running through tunnels kilometres in length, just as hitherto incurable illnesses could be overcome and products made out of artificial materials, so also the laws of collective social life would soon be discovered, allowing a reshaping of the foundations of state and society, based on the principles of rationality, predictability and technological reasoning. That, at least, was the widely held conviction of the time.

But the marvels of technology and the benefits of social organisation were only one aspect of the way the new epoch was perceived. For, at the same time, the new cities, and Berlin in particular, stood for the social distress of the industrial workers, their wretched housing conditions, and the growing antagonism between rich and poor. The 'social question' was at the forefront of public debate in the German Empire at the turn of the century, and although it was adopted as a unifying cause by the workers and the working-class movement, which was pushing for improvements in social conditions, it was of equally central importance to the bourgeoisie and the nobility, who viewed demands for social improvement as a threat not just to their privileges but to the state and the community in general. The bourgeoisie saw the tearing asunder of society and the struggle between the social classes that accompanied it as the major curse of the modern age, and it was not long before people began to construct an ideology that emphasised the importance of the national community in order to combat tendencies towards class division.

The new urban agglomerations were accompanied by the destruction of the landscape. They concentrated hundreds of thousands of people in a confined space, produced mountains of rubbish and noxious odours, and led to marked changes in people's living conditions and perceptions. Speed, organisation, planning, an increased division of labour and an altered sense of time and space demanded a degree of rapid action which was often perceived as excessive. 'Audiences last five minutes, telephone conversations last one minute, the rotary printer acts in one second and the movements of the bicycle wheel are measured in fifths of a second': these are the new units of time by which human life is now determined, wrote the cultural historian Karl Lamprecht in 1912. To suffer from excessive stimulation of the senses—'nerves', 'neurasthenia'—became the fashionable sickness of the age. 'The haste, restlessness and discomfort of social existence, class and racial hatred, and the drive to change economic and social conditions at any price' were the reasons for this sickness, as was confirmed by the representatives of the appropriate new scientific disciplines—neurologists, psychologists and psychiatrists.[25]

It was not just the environment that was changing, but the people themselves. New forms of behaviour were necessary if one wanted to make one's mark in the factory, the town, the tenement house or the street. Gender roles began to change, as did the relation between the generations. New leisure activities emerged, which influenced the way the world was experienced and the governing tastes of the masses. But there was as yet no sign of any new guidelines corresponding to the changed conditions, and this made the search for them all the more intense.

At the turn of the century, the sense of loss and anxiety grew into a manifest crisis of direction, which became one of the characteristics of the epoch. The new industrial world was exposed to ever sharper criticism. This was voiced most eloquently and most vociferously by members of the bourgeoisie, above all the *Bildungsbürgertum*. It is one of the paradoxes of the period that in a phase during which the most outstanding fields of activity of the bourgeoisie—the capitalist economy and modern science—flourished as never before, that same bourgeoisie began to suffer from grave doubts, distancing itself ever more emphatically from the cultural changes brought about by its own success. It was among the bourgeoisie that opposition to materialism and the power of money, to 'cold' intellectualism, to the division of labour and specialisation, to alienation and 'massification', was most widespread, and this opposition developed into a protest movement against the cultural concomitants of modernity more generally.[26]

Criticisms of this kind were not necessarily associated with a rejection of technology, industry and science as such. It was by no means regarded as certain that the emergence of the capitalist form of economic organisation inescapably involved specific changes in the spheres of culture and society, from the division of the community into classes to the creation of 'mass society' and the enticements offered by the big city. To that extent, we can also understand these manifold critiques of modernity as an endeavour to accept aspects of the new era that were regarded as positive but to reject the accompanying phenomena that were felt to be harmful.[27]

The critique of modernity also reflected the declining significance of the authority which had traditionally provided direction and meaning to life, namely religious belief. It is true that religious affiliation and church-based ties continued to be the most important cultural factors in Germany. It was regarded as self-evident that a person had to belong to one of the two branches of Christianity, and religious ties were in fact strengthened by the confessional divide and the resultant rivalry between Protestants and Catholics. But, at the same time, the hold of the churches on everyday life was gradually becoming looser and religious norms were losing their compulsory character. This process was clear to see, particularly in the towns, and it increased the need to make sense of the world, and to establish a new order and a new security.[28]

The reconstruction of the world through technology, science and capital in those years doubtless went hand in hand with growing insecurity, a loss of confidence, a loosening of relations (even private ones), and economic insecurity and social instability; yet it also meant greater opportunities for many people, with a chance for some to climb the social scale and the prospect of a considerable long-term improvement in living standards even for the working-class population, in view of the prosperity of the industrial economy. The atmosphere at the turn of the century was therefore marked by two opposing states of mind: optimism about progress and pessimism about the future. There was both relief at the freedom offered by the waning of the old conventions and anxiety about the way that new currents were infiltrating the customary social sphere.

The commonest and most widespread reaction to these challenges was to keep a firm grip on traditional and inherited values. This attitude was most pronounced in the private spheres of family and sexuality, child-rearing and modes of living. The nineteenth century had witnessed the victory of the bourgeois model of the family. This had three main characteristics: the unconditional rule of the husband over wife and children, a gender-based division of roles, whereby the husband was active in professional and public life while the wife was responsible for running the house and bringing up the children, and finally the idealised unity between marriage, love and sexuality. After the end of the century, however, the basic assumptions of private life began to change. Among the lower social strata—above all, the new groups of urban industrial workers, who generally had fewer responsibilities tying them to conventional roles—ambiguous marital and familial relationships were frequent, as were illegitimate children and single mothers. The growing use of the expression 'young people' referred to an age-group straddling childhood and adulthood. This was felt to be a new phenomenon, with its own way of life and a new sense of self, and it was often anxiously repudiated. Moreover, many women, particularly among the bourgeoisie, longed to overturn traditional gender roles and break free from the limitations of family life and child-rearing. This aspiration frequently came up against aggressive male resistance. Prostitution and homosexuality, phenomena which surfaced more visibly and on a larger scale in the big cities than in the discreet niches they had occupied in provincial towns, were regarded as symptoms of the way that modernity was undermining moral values and an assault on the family, marriage and normality. The big city was referred to as 'the great whore of Babylon'.[29]

A powerful counter-movement therefore emerged, which found expression both in public declarations, articles and social commentaries, and in legislation. Both the Reich Criminal Code (*Reichsstrafgesetzbuch*) of 1871 and the Civil Code (*Bürgerliches Gesetzbuch*) of 1900, which unified and reorganised the different laws of the German federal states, were used to ward off these threats, and give written expression to the traditional ideals of family and morality. In the treatment of homosexuality, therefore, the greater severity of the Prussian legislation was adopted rather than the more liberal traditions of the South German states. Indeed, in some respects, the Prussian provisions were themselves made increasingly draconian. The aim of the divorce laws was to protect the institution of marriage even against the personal wishes of married couples, and they accordingly imposed further restrictions on the grounds for divorce. The legal position of the husband in relation to his wife was strengthened, as he was entrusted with a kind of guardianship over his partner. A wife's ability to conduct business was already limited, yet here too the Civil Code worsened the position. The illegitimate child and its mother were subjected to considerable legal discrimination. The prohibition of abortion continued to be backed up by legal penalties, and the ambit of the law was extended still further.[30]

Repressive lawmaking of this kind should be understood primarily as a reaction to changes in traditional structures and a weakening of their hold, or the fear that this would happen. In the fight against the feared destruction of the family, marriage and the moral law by the big city, the industrial proletariat and mass society, as well as by the endeavours of women and young people to gain their independence, traditional norms and the notions of right and wrong that were handed down with them were to be fixed from top to bottom and firmly secured against all possible alterations. There were two reasons for this reaction: firstly, it was in the political interest of those groups which were in general against any change in society and sought to formalise existing power relations by establishing stable normative structures. Secondly, the shoring up of traditional values at a time of extreme social and cultural change also corresponded to the needs of all those who sought a definitive list of norms in order to be able to deal with the panoply of new experiences that were flooding into society. The latter group undoubtedly comprised the majority of the people, irrespective of political divisions.

But there were also forces working in the opposite direction, which attempted to reform the sphere of private life and adapt to the new reality. Deviations regarded as criminal were now at least a subject of public debate, in politics and scientific discourse. They were no longer merely pushed aside and suppressed. Repressive methods of education and the suffering caused by the rigid enforcement of norms of sexuality became big literary themes. Nakedness and sexuality were now frequently presented in a positive way, as elements of a direct and natural life. A movement for sexual reform also arose. This called for changes in legal norms, as applied to family law, the treatment of homosexuality, or the approach to illegitimacy. The first steps towards a loosening of moral codes were perceptible: for example, the famous bathing machines, which women who visited a spa were forced to use to avoid the eyes of the curious when they took the waters, now gradually disappeared. Clothes were less strictly regulated, and relations between the sexes began to become more relaxed, although this only happened in the big cities, and even there only in restricted social circles.

The close association between an enthusiasm for progress and a search for security in traditional values was also apparent in other spheres of activity, architecture being one such example. The showpiece buildings of the new Berlin were constructed in the peculiar style known as Historicism. Neo-Renaissance, Neo-Baroque and Neo-Romanesque dominated the skyline: there were towers, domes, statues, castle-like constructions, ornamentation and inscriptions which were allegedly historical but served completely mundane purposes. An inclination towards ostentation, magnificence and monumentalism was especially evident. Railway stations resembled cathedrals, town halls resembled Hohenstaufen fortresses, department stores resembled castles out of a fantasy past. The principal rule was that everything should aspire to a definite 'old German' look. This was a young society, in a newly founded nation-state, a state which had never existed before in that form. Yet the more insecure people felt about the future, the more vehemently did they swear by tradition. It was above all buildings with especially 'modern' purposes, such as banks, insurance buildings and railway stations, which were given pseudo-historical accoutrements. The newly built 'Aschinger' in Berlin, a cheap restaurant where more than 4,000 people could eat at the same time, took this historical masquerade to new heights. As a French journalist noted in astonishment, 'The façade was in the style of a medieval cathedral, the walls were heathen burial-chambers, the basements, taken from the Thousand and One Nights, were veritable Indian cave-dwellings, and the halls could have served as throne rooms for the kings of the Goths'.[31]

This architectural combination of technological modernity and monumental, pseudo-historical drapery demonstrated how proud people were of what had been achieved, and how uncertain they were of how to deal with it. This was symbolised in a curious way in the behaviour of the German Emperor William II, who represented the country during this period of dramatic transformation. William's enthusiasm for modern technology was legendary, as was his condemnation of the phenomena that accompanied the new epoch, from parliamentarism to modern art. His orientation towards an idealised past was expressed just as much in his preference for a romanticised Middle Ages as in his richly ornamented and constantly changing uniforms. The bombastic style of the monarch, his inclination towards the grand and impressive gesture, showed that he was a parvenu who was uncertain about how to handle his newfound wealth. The more dynamic the transformations of the present, the more he sought out artificial symbols of his roots in the past and in tradition. In this sense, William personified the emblematic, 'modern' type of contemporary German: the social climber and careerist who thirsted for respectability and prestige and yet remained one of the *nouveaux riches*, possessing neither roots in the soil nor the calmness of self-confidence, the lack of which he compensated for with a snappy military bearing and a typically Prussian abruptness exaggerated ad nauseam, combined with arrogance, the mentality of a subaltern and a bellowing chauvinism. That is of course a caricature, but William was often perceived in this way, particularly when his diplomatic mishaps and embarrassments started to happen more frequently. The period was admittedly marked by other characteristic figures: the witty, ironic *littérateur*, the working-class leader who was both respectable and revolutionary, the enthusiast for the youth movement, or the gnarled business patriarch. But William expressed much of the spirit of the epoch through his restlessness, his archetypal combination of arrogance and feelings of inferiority, and his strident emotionalism.[32]

After all, the conduct of the monarch corresponded with the collective psyche of the German people, who took pride in the rapid rise of the country as expressed in pageantry and grand gestures, while seeking security and authority in compensation for the loss of the many traditions which had provided a firm foothold. Deep-rooted needs of this kind bound the bourgeoisie to the state and its representatives. Since the defeat of the revolution of 1848–9, the strength of state institutions and the weakness of parliamentarism had been fundamental structural features first of Prussian, and then of Prusso-German society. Then, when the German nation-state had been founded from above, a feat made possible by three deliberately planned and victorious wars, this basic authoritarian structure was supplemented by the primacy of the military, which continued to operate even decades after the victories of the 1860s and beyond. In no other industrial state of the period did members of the military caste attain such a level of social prestige. From then on, the manners of the military practically set the trend, in the field of education as much as in social intercourse. The dominance of the military, like the existence of an authoritarian state, offered a dependable stability, and in a world which was literally breaking loose from its moorings, it promised security, constancy and reliability.[33]

Hence the search for familiar landmarks to counteract the disorientating speed of social change was one of the dominant features of the epoch. The workers' movement offers a further example of this. It came into existence as a defensive association of the new urban wage labourers in order to represent the workers' social and political interests vis-à-vis the entrepreneurs and the state, namely: to obtain a certain basic security of existence through improved wages and the beginnings of social insurance and to obtain political representation in the parliaments in order to protect the interests of the workers, who were at first highly under-represented there. At the same time, the socialist workers' movement, in Germany as elsewhere, shared the general enthusiasm for the economic, technological, scientific and cultural progress of the age. The socialists were convinced, after all, that if only greater political and social justice could be achieved, economic progress would eventually also benefit the broad masses of workers. The social democratic workers of Germany were convinced that the future belonged to them.[34]

As far as the present was concerned, however, the organisations of the workers' movement were above all places of refuge, which offered security and companionship in a new and unfathomable world. The first trip made by the abovementioned apprentice baker Jessaia Gronach, who felt all but crushed after his arrival in Berlin, led him to the trade union headquarters, located on the Berlin Engelufer, where he was given a friendly reception. The bakers' trade union offered him assistance and gave him the feeling that he was among friends:

> I received information, a waiting number for my certificate, financial support, advice about a place to sleep, and food . . . Yes, I was scared! Berlin! I had a healthy respect for this giant of a city, but Engelufer 12 was friendly, called me colleague and comrade, and offered me its hand. My heart began to fill with self-confidence.[35]

This way of integrating workers into familiar social and cultural surroundings, into the 'social and moral milieu', became very important in the decades after 1900. The most significant example of this is the close bond the socialist workers' movement offered, with its many clubs and organisations for dealing with life's problems and taking care of the worker's day-to-day needs. The effects of this bond went far beyond the movement's political objectives. Similar developments took place in the case of Roman Catholic workers. They benefited from the social and cultural associations run by the Church and from the political activities of the Centre Party. The Polish minority, too, built a dense network of cultural, social and political institutions, so as to provide security and a point of orientation to their compatriots, who lived predominantly in the Ruhr district.

Migrants, whether German or Polish, only accepted their new, unsettling surroundings by stages, and the greater the transformation in their accustomed way of life, the more closely they banded together in the private sphere, living according to the traditional values of the society from which they came. This led to a characteristic gulf between the world the new arrivals now inhabited and the cultural orientation they drew on for protection. Private cultural and mental reassurance was chiefly implemented through rules and conceptions relating to the family, marriage and sexuality, as well as through definitions of normality. These rules gained a large part of their legitimacy from the existence of allegedly centuries-old traditions and values inherited from past generations. In many cases, the old values were idealised images of a tradition that was now under threat. It had to be restored and firmly anchored as a bulwark against the onslaught of the new world by the use of severe sanctions. But the idealised character of the old values did not impair their effectiveness.[36]

The interaction between social upheaval and a renewed focus on traditional values was particularly marked in the youth movement. This was initially a part of the much broader contemporary movement for 'life reform' (*Lebensreform*). The life reformers felt the world of the Wilhelmine Empire to be restrictive and oppressive, and they strove to find a new and distinctive path of their own, to search for freedom, nature and the primitive, and to break free from the shackles of convention. The impact of these aspirations was felt as strongly in the fields of housing and urban development as it was in education and sexual politics. But the youth movement was much broader than this, and its objectives were also more diffuse than those of the life reformers. It exerted a great deal of influence, which lasted for several decades.

Its origins date back to the endeavours of high school students in the major cities around 1900 to free themselves not just from ties to the city, mass society and industrialism but also from parents, regarded by many as narrow-minded and authoritarian, and schools, where learning was crammed down their throats. They aspired to join with kindred spirits to find a way back to nature, comradeship and a life unfettered by convention. The main features of this rapidly growing movement among middle-class youth were walking tours through what was characterised as a primal natural world, a simple life far from civilisation, a habit of sleeping by camp fires under the open sky, a glorification of folkways, midsummer celebrations following old Germanic customs, and enthusiasm for a romantically imagined Middle Ages. The movement reached its zenith in 1913 when thousands of members assembled on the summit of the Hoher Meißner and, in an emotion-laden ceremony, swore to 'shape their lives by their own decision, on their own responsibility, and with inner truthfulness'.[37]

Activities of this kind may often have been limited to weekend or Sunday excursions into the surrounding woods, and they soon took on strange forms. Nevertheless, the youth movement's critique of civilisation expressed a widespread discontent with the modern, growth-obsessed mass society of Imperial Germany and a deep yearning for simplicity, immediacy and a point of orientation. These emotions were felt by many people who, weary of civilisation, fled from the cities to indulge in a cult of sunlight, 'life', health and nature. They often had connections with the youth movement, which soon found a diverse range of imitators.

It was the ideal of 'youth' itself which occupied centre stage in this very varied movement. The decision to commit oneself to one's own youthfulness was seen as the real act of liberation. This becomes more comprehensible if it is borne in mind that in previous decades the role model for German society had been the mature older man. The Austrian writer Stefan Zweig, who was born in 1881, recalls in his memoirs that his school years were a period during which he did nothing but run the gauntlet of punishments for not having grown up yet. During the 1880s and 1890s, he laments, 'youth was a hindrance in all careers and age alone was an advantage'. Thus,

> in that age of security, everyone who wished to get ahead was forced to attempt all conceivable methods of masquerading in order to appear older . . . Men wore long black frock coats and walked at a leisurely pace, and whenever possible acquired a slight *embonpoint,* in order to personify the desired sedateness; and those who were ambitious strove, at least outwardly, to belie their youth, since the young were suspected of instability.[38]

This was a time of change, during which people looked for guidance to what was old and familiar, but the youth movement rebelled against this, seeking out new and more up-to-date examples to follow. These were found, paradoxically, in yet older and more original-seeming myths, the myths of the Middle Ages, in Romanticism, and an archaic nature-mysticism. Thus, the youth movement expressed two opposed phenomena: an increase in insecurity caused by the rapid and dynamic changes around the turn of the century and a rejection of the current ways in which people were reacting to those changes. At the same time, the myth of youth reflected the country's altered demographic structure. Never before had the proportion of young people in the total population been as high as it was at this time, and that was particularly evident in the new urban centres, with their extremely strong contingent of recently arrived workers.

The avant-garde artists were even stronger supporters of radical change than the adherents of the youth movement, with which they were associated in various ways. The radicalism of their works and their mode of life expressed the extent and depth of the social changes that were under way. It also mirrored the inner turmoil of the epoch. For, on the one hand, they sought and found in their texts and pictures new and 'modern' forms of expression, unknown until then and appropriate to the new age; while, on the other hand, their works expressed a distinct hostility towards the new urban and industrial world which was often more extreme than the experiments of the 'life reformers' or the youth movement's search for meaning. Needless to say, there were also intermixtures and transitions of all kinds to be seen. This was characteristic of the cultural life of Germany at the turn of the century, particularly in Berlin, a city which was an extraordinary kaleidoscope, bursting with dynamism. If we look beyond the multiplicity of literary styles and the unending series of shifts from one aesthetic school of thought to the next, certain clear trends are visible. The main emphasis was no longer placed on the social dislocations brought about by capitalism, as it had been in the heyday of Naturalism, a trend which lasted until the 1890s, but on the cultural impact of industrialism, which was regarded as destructive.

The artistic currents which turned away from Naturalism came in many different forms: Decadence, Impressionism, Symbolism, Neo-romanticism, Art Nouveau, Secessionist *Stilkunst* and finally Expressionism. What all of them had in common was a rejection of direct social and political involvement. The problems of the great bourgeois ego now took centre stage. The autonomous artistic personality was pained by the unreasonable demands of the new mass society, and by its banality, and withdrew into a realm of pure and ideal art. This was intended to provide a basis for renewing the world through the celebration of spiritual and aesthetic values, and through a concentration on the individual and the community instead of on the masses and society. The new artists established a cult of the autonomous ego, of youth, of 'life' and of art itself, in opposition to the conventions of bourgeois civilisation, with its emphasis on rationality, achievement, utility and technological advance.[39]

This new artistic attitude can be seen in an almost pure form in the works of the lyric poet Stefan George, who was at the centre of an esoteric circle of devoted young men. He preached a radical aesthetic of absolute art, and he 'opposed the epoch's lack of spirituality, search for a great man, mania for progress, egalitarian phrase-making, levelling of all that is great, liquidation of values, liberal-democratic mediocrity, and prescribed points of view' as well as 'the rule of "society", its banal rationalism, and its emphasis on individualism', to quote the list of his views drawn up by Thomas Nipperdey. But the literature of the George circle was also to a great extent 'modern' insofar as it swiftly identified the emerging tendencies of the time, seized on them, and did so in new artistic forms which were appropriate to the epoch and were felt by contemporaries to be entirely revolutionary. In other words, this was a modern uprising against modernity.[40]

These ideas were, of course, the preserve of small, avant-garde minorities, as were the attempts made to establish new ways of living in communities and rural communes or to propagate a new sexuality. But young people, particularly from the middle classes, were enormously influenced by them. Not a few of those born at the turn of the century were deeply and lastingly impressed by the cult around Stefan George. The radical critique formulated by George and his circle of what the new world had brought forth moulded a whole generation's ways of thinking and feeling.

This is also significant because certain sections of the reform movement and the new artistic avant-garde moved on from cultural criticism to more strongly politicised forms of protest against modernity. They began to take a negative attitude towards competition, conflict and the separate representation of the interests of social groups and political parties. They were committed instead to achieving a harmonious 'organic life'. What was understood by this was a life without alienation and free from any connection with the market, utilitarian thinking or pragmatism. This would, of course, need the support of a strong, authoritarian state: they would 'turn inwards, protected by the power of the state', as Thomas Mann put it much later on.[41] The critique of 'trivialisation' and merely external technical progress, of materialism, alienation and loss of meaning also played its part here. The tendency which prevailed in this milieu was to draw a sharp contrast between the autonomous personality and the rise of 'mass society', and to deplore the absence of tragedy and profundity. This culminated in an approach which contraposed community and culture to society and civilisation, and thus clearly contained the elements of a line of thought which was opposed to liberalism and directed against the principles of the Enlightenment.[42]

## Radical Answers to the Crisis of Bourgeois Society

The radical transformation the world underwent in the two decades preceding the First World War was perceived as a crisis of bourgeois society and a threat to it. This led, particularly in Germany, to the emergence of responses of an equally radical character, as reflected in the rise of the grand political ideologies which in the course of the rise of mass society mobilised more people than ever before. Modern ideologies are ways of interpreting the world. They explain complex relationships in an approachable and plausible manner, emphasise obvious causal factors, and, in this way, offer a guide to action and a firm basis for conduct. In the period of time treated here, modern ideologies filled the gap left by the decline of religious attitudes. They were also a reflection of the modern participatory society, in which the mobilisation of supporters in previously unheard-of numbers—through elections, through political actions such as demonstrations and strikes, and through the means of communication and the powerful mass political and social organisations which were emerging—became a political factor of the first rank.

The socialist workers' movement was an example of this confluence of ideology, political action and mass involvement. It was both a social support organisation and a political party, and it gave its adherents self-confidence and a sense of security through the conviction that with Marxism they possessed an explanatory framework through which they could both analyse the processes of change they had just experienced and make reliable predictions about future development.

The success of Marxism in its popularised form depended above all on its ability to explain workers' experiences of exploitation, discrimination and persecution as part of an eternal struggle between the exploiting and exploited classes, which ran through the whole of human history. In this way, the theory seemed to have acquired historical legitimacy and profundity. With the help of Marxism, the social and political discrimination experienced by the working class could be explained and the possibility of changing the situation demonstrated.

The efforts of the authorities to resist proletarian subversion by proclaiming states of emergency and bringing in troops confirmed the Marxist analysis of the class state and class justice and strengthened the socialist workers' conviction that their theories were justified and that they correctly described not only the present and the past but also the direction of future development. They were convinced of the irreconcilability of class antagonisms and the necessity of socialism, and looked forward to the utopia of a classless society devoid of both exploitation and social contradictions. This theory, which was a mixture of persuasive analysis of the present and political religion, gave rise to optimism and deep-seated convictions, and it laid the foundation for the close solidarity and spirit of sacrifice of the German workers' movement, which lasted for over a century.[43]

Contradictions which could not be explained by Marxist theory, on the other hand, were negated. It was true that a considerable section of the new working class had suffered impoverishment, which was at its worst between the 1850s and the 1880s. But, in the 1890s, there were clear indications of a slow but constant improvement in social conditions. Similarly, according to the ideal of internationalism upheld in the workers' movement, it was social and not national differences which dominated society under capitalism. But in actual fact, the socialist workers were increasingly gripped by ideas of national unity and patriotic feelings for the Fatherland.

Meanwhile, practical politics soon softened the revolutionary perspective of the workers' movement, a tendency which became more pronounced the more the Social Democrats enjoyed social and political success in the society of Imperial Germany. Even so, the SPD still held onto its fundamental revolutionary convictions, at least officially. One reason for this was that radical rhetoric about the eventual achievement of an ideal society offered a vision of salvation and therefore provided an important motivation for the workers to engage enthusiastically in the struggle and maintain their sense of solidarity. Moreover, the increasing strength of the movement led the state and the political Right to take increasingly tough measures against it. Such actions by the authorities tended to undermine any suggestion that reform could succeed or that the political and social system of the Empire could be altered incrementally.

The intensification of political conflict after the turn of the century led finally to the emergence within the party of a radical, revolutionary wing, which consistently placed its faith in a violent overthrow of the system and the establishment of a dictatorship of the proletariat in line with Marx's theory. This was the starting point for the development of communist parties, not just in Germany but elsewhere too, for the Marxism developed in Germany proved to be highly exportable, becoming the theoretical foundation of emerging socialist workers' movements in the whole of the industrialising world. This applied particularly to Russia, for in their analyses of capitalism, the Russian revolutionaries constantly referred back to the situation in the developed capitalist countries of the West, Germany above all.[44]

The strength of Marxist movements in Germany does not of course prove that social contradictions or the political oppression of the workers were particularly pronounced there. The opposite was rather the case: a comparison with the other developing industrial nations of the West, not to mention a comparison with the backward despotism of Tsarist Russia, entirely favours Germany, for several reasons, not least because of the early moves made by the German state towards introducing the elements of a social policy. What strikes the observer is rather that *fin-de-siècle* Germany was a laboratory for modernity, thanks to its particularly successful and rapid economic, social and cultural development. In the twenty-five years between 1890 and the start of the First World War, the country experienced the effects of a transformation which was rapid and, to some extent, unchecked. The brakes were off, so to speak, and all possible reactions and responses to the situation were played out in all variants and at breakneck speed. In the hothouse atmosphere created by Berlin's explosive growth, the newest variants of scientific, technological, infrastructural, but also cultural and ideological accomplishment emerged extremely quickly. Expressionism and life reform, radical nationalism and radical Marxism, the youth movement, modern anti-Semitism and Zionism, the *völkisch* movement and the predecessors of the world communist movement, were all invented and tested out here almost simultaneously and sometimes in the same place.

Nationalism was the most dynamic and widely distributed of all these movements and ideologies. It had been an opposition movement in Germany until the establishment of the Empire in 1871. It had been closely linked with the struggle for liberal freedoms, democracy and parliamentarism. Moreover, at that stage, it had not been tied to a nationally defined state, being rather a cultural and linguistic phenomenon, which, however, soon created an identity by self-demarcation from non-German groups and peoples. When its narrower goals had been attained, through the establishment of the Little German (*kleindeutsch*) nation-state and the proclamation of the German Reich, it mutated into imperial nationalism (*Reichsnationalismus*), thereby becoming the crucial mode of integration for a young, extremely heterogeneous and disunited 'nation', which now needed to unite an amorphous and accidental structure by surrounding itself with forces of cohesion. What was 'German' was, in the first instance, defined by drawing a line separating what was German from what was not, thus setting up a front against the Poles in the East and the French in the West. Very soon this external demarcation was combined with an internal one, against people who did not want the nation-state to take precedence as the primary or indeed the sole unifying bond, namely the Social Democrats, with their commitment to internationalism, and the Roman Catholics, with their connection to the papacy in Rome. Moreover, the new German nationalism was also quick to exclude the only non-Christian minority in the country, the Jews. This led in the 1880s to the growth of anti-Semitic parties of a traditional kind, ostensibly Protestant in character, which soon disappeared, however, making way for other variants of the same approach.[45]

Nationalism was able in this way to bundle together many, if not all, of the grievances and anxieties of the epoch. It combined regret over social fragmentation and political conflict, glorification of unity as opposed to multiplicity, resignation in the face of the complexities of the modern world, a yearning for simple explanations, anxiety over the anarchic tendencies of freedom, and a search for prospects of salvation with quasi-religious stability. At the same time, however, it also provided fresh experiences: the intoxication of a mass meeting, the newly awakened thirst for power and the pursuit of national expansion.

The foundation of the nation-state from above stripped German nationalism to a considerable degree of its critical anti-authoritarianism. It lost its revolutionary impetus and rapidly became one of the dominant aspects of the culture of the new German Empire, which, like all young nation-states, directed its initial efforts at creating the oldest possible traditions for itself, to demonstrate that it was a 'natural' association, not simply an expression of political aspirations. This was one of the reasons why constant references to the German Empire of olden times were a lasting phenomenon of everyday culture. The cult of the German Middle Ages, the Teutons, the Migration of the Peoples (*Völkerwanderung*) and the Wars of Liberation was repeatedly called on to suggest historical depth and thereby provide legitimacy. Its effects spread far beyond the *Bildungsbürgertum*, the social stratum that was particularly receptive to nationalism.

The new Reich German nationalism was a combination of pride in the almost unbelievable rise of Imperial Germany and enthusiasm over its economic successes and the 'international standing' the country had achieved. At the same time, however, nationalism became a way of escaping from the crisis of modernisation. In view of the anxieties over social status evoked by the rapidity of the transformation process, the crisis-ridden and unpredictable oscillations of the economic conjuncture, and the unhappiness produced by the consequences of urban civilisation and cultural modernity, identification with the nation offered people a feeling that they belonged naturally to a sizeable, successful association, which could overcome inner conflicts and compensate for the impairment of identity, the loss of direction and the concern felt over the future.

Soon, the new nationalism started to turn its attention to the outside world as well: the rise in Germany's economic strength required, it was thought, a corresponding increase in its external power. The start of the new century saw the emergence of mass nationalist organisations, which agitated for the 'Germanisation' (*Germanisierung*) of the Prussian part of Poland, the expansion of the German colonial Empire, and the enhancement of Germany's 'international standing' (*Weltgeltung*). These groups were extremely effective. Moreover, the ideological underpinnings of nationalism also began to mutate. The establishment of the German Reich by Bismarck had been directed against Greater German (*Großdeutsch*) aspirations, and involved abandoning the perspective of a pan-German state structure, but the period after the turn of the century saw the return of such objectives. The Little German Reich was no longer big enough. People now began to speak of a German '*Volk*' (folk), which was still scattered over various states and thirsted for unity.

The manifest connection between the anti-modern movement and *völkisch*-nationalist tendencies could already be seen in Paul de Lagarde and Julius Langbehn, two earlier protagonists of anti-liberal cultural criticism, whose main works appeared in the 1880s and 1890s, gaining a wide readership. Both of them preached against the soulless materialism of advancing modernity, advocating instead a religion of spirituality and idealism which would draw its strength from the '*Volk*'. What they meant by the '*Volk*' was not the 'mass of the people' in the republican sense of the conceptual opposite to 'authority', but the members of a 'nation'. The category '*Volk*' was at first understood culturally, but its meaning increasingly changed so that it began to signify a biological, 'racial' characteristic determined by descent. With this transition, an 'organic' category of natural origin had been found which could be associated with the yearning for what was primitive and genuine and opposed to 'mechanistic' categories of modernity such as 'class' or 'society'.[46]

This notion was also reflected in the new law on German citizenship. With the continuation of the economic boom there was a further influx of foreigners, particularly Polish workers, into the farmlands of eastern Germany and also into various industrial sectors. In response to this, it was established by law that a German was a person of German descent. It was not sufficient simply to be born in Germany. When the law was discussed in the German parliament, the Reichstag, the German Conservatives stressed that 'descent, blood, is the decisive requirement for the acquisition of citizenship. This provision is an excellent method of maintaining and preserving German racial (*völkisch*) character and German individuality.'[47]

This definition of German nationality based on 'blood' and 'race' was also directed against the German Jews. The new anti-Semitism that emerged here was no longer derived from religious differences and the traditional Christian animosity toward the Jews, but increasingly from the Jews' postulated biological—'racial'—otherness, which was derived from the assumed biological unity of the German *Volk*. This was clearly different from traditional anti-Semitism, which continued to rest on Christian anti-Judaism, and it first drew political attention in the 1880s in the form of a number of anti-Semitic currents and parties. But while this political anti-Semitism appeared to decline in significance after the turn of the century, social anti-Semitism began to spread, and indeed it spread in social strata in which it had never previously played a big role, in particular among the *Bildungsbürgertum*, the intellectuals and the artists, where it was combined with a critique of the civilisation and culture of modern society.[48]

A very typical example of this approach was Ludwig Klages, one of the fashionable philosophers of the later years of the Empire. In his early twenties, he came under the influence of Munich's Bohemian circles, and their star attraction Stefan George, and he soon formed part of the group of so-called 'cosmics'. These were people who turned against the modern-day world, seeing it as the locus of a decline which would culminate in an apocalypse. They regarded themselves as the chosen ones, as pioneers, entirely separate from the 'insignificant' masses. In modern society, declared Klages in his early writings, people no longer lived their lives as human beings, but 'merely existed, whether as slaves of their "profession", exhausting themselves mechanically in the service of the big firms, or as slaves of money, unthinkingly devoted to the numerical delirium of stocks and shares, or finally as slaves of the frenetic entertainments of the big city.' These were conventional *topoi* of cultural criticism, but in Klages's *episteme* they were combined with an invocation of the harmonious but vanished world of the '*Volk*', with its festivals, songs and costumes. This had been replaced, he said, with 'the gifts of "progress" . . . schnapps, opium and syphilis.' People now had to put up with 'smoking chimneys, the racket of street noise and nights as light as day' as well as popular songs, melodies from operettas and cabarets. Primal life, the life of nature, had disappeared.[49]

But it was the influence of the Jews, an ethno-religious group which was alien to the *Volk* and derived nothing from its tradition, that had played a decisive part in the alienation of humanity from 'life': 'We consider the forces and creations with which the modern world imagines it has outdone the old one, including the much-praised progress and uniformity of civilisation, to be in essence machinations of Judaism', wrote Klages in 1900.[50] Later, Klages also expressed his anti-Semitism in psychological terms: in his view, the Jew was a type of 'modern hysteric', characterised by features such as 'a craving for admiration', 'vanity', 'crude external display' and 'boastful arrogance'. This finds expression in 'the rising flood of literature', 'advertisements', 'noisy newspaper campaigns' and 'the saturation of party life with highly personal gossip'. 'Here one sees the impact of a vivacity which is new and tenacious but entirely lacking in higher qualities and is carried along by the element of a degenerate Semitism, irresistibly striving to rise in society.'[51]

Indefatigable purveyors of mystical notions like Klages saw the Jews as an appropriate target for their fixation on decay and degeneracy. Similarly, a not insignificant part of the artistic avant-garde and the youth movement became influenced by *völkisch* ideas in the years before the First World War, incorporating anti-Jewish convictions into this mixture as well. But these notions were never dominant. In face of the multiplicity of politico-cultural movements around this time; anti-Semitism was far from being a determining factor in cultural life. What is much more significant here is the way the critique of modernity could easily be associated with anti-Semitic sentiment. Indeed, it also proved capable of making links with movements of other kinds.

There were many attempts to confront aspects of modernity which were deemed to be irritating and threatening, especially where they contravened bourgeois norms of behaviour, such as the actual or supposed rise in criminality, prostitution, homosexuality, 'youthful depravity' and also mental disturbance. One of the most influential examples of this was the spread of concepts of Social Darwinism and racial hygiene. Darwin's teaching, in its popularised form, appeared to provide a convincing explanation for these disturbing phenomena. Moreover, it seemed to have a sound scientific basis, which was particularly important for an age which believed in progress and scientific advance. According to Darwin, natural selection was necessary in order to negate the imbalance between an excess of offspring and the resources available. In the struggle for existence, only those who were most adapted to their situation survived, and this was the necessary condition for a constant improvement and development of the species to a higher level. This insight, according to which the reason for the evolution of organisms should be sought in 'natural selection', was later extended by Darwin himself to human beings, and then brought to Germany by Ernst Haeckel.[52]

This was the point of contact through which the Darwinian model was transferred from biology into the sphere of human society, but with a significant caveat. Now it was no longer the best adapted who survived the struggle for existence, but the strongest. The principle of selection, it seemed, had determined the rules of human association since time immemorial. In modern times, however, the conditions for the struggle for existence had ceased to exist, because there were no longer famines, as a result of the modernisation of agriculture, for instance. At the same time, through medicine, welfare and social assistance, modern civilisation also supported people who would previously have been defeated in this struggle and 'selected' for their weakness. Through these developments, human beings had been exempted from the need to conduct a 'struggle for existence' and the natural law of selection had been set aside. As a result, the number of weak individuals had now increased considerably, so that the basis of evolution, the survival of the strongest, was rendered ineffective. The further and higher development of mankind, or, as the case might be, a *Volk*, was therefore threatened, or indeed prevented, precisely by the impact of state assistance for the needy and the weak, which had developed out of the bourgeois tradition of humanity and presumed equality, and the Christian view of the human being as God's creation.

This line of thought was plainly related to the progress of medicine and the movement for public hygiene in the struggle against the mass infections then prevalent. For, just as it had become possible during these years for the causes of bodily illnesses to be discovered through scientific analysis, allowing their successful treatment, so, according to this line of thought, it ought to be possible to use scientifically exact means to combat the causes of undesirable social developments.

These notions emerged at the end of the nineteenth century in various different guises, and they were applied to a range of different groups which were seen as 'inferior', namely 'the feeble-minded', the physically disabled from birth, 'habitual criminals', and even the 'unloved' and the 'ugly'.

Thus, the Munich doctor Wilhelm Schallmayer conducted a study demonstrating that the modern social system supported precisely those population groups which possessed particularly undesirable inherited predispositions and also produced large numbers of children. He also argued that medicine to a large extent nullified the mechanisms of 'natural selection' by successfully combating the most prevalent illnesses. This had worsened the hereditary characteristics of the Germans as a whole. In order to combat this, the birth rate must be increased, people with bad hereditary characteristics should be compulsorily sterilised and people with particularly good characteristics should be encouraged to produce more children, perhaps through tax incentives and social assistance.[53]

Ideas of this kind were not restricted to the political Right. Alfred Grotjahn, who wrote the health section of the SPD's Görlitz Programme, said that workers who suffered from 'tuberculosis, sexual ailments, diseases of the mind, insanity, or epilepsy' or were 'deaf and dumb, crippled, alcoholic, infirm, or severely injured' should be separated from the rest and placed in asylums.[54]

In many Western countries, racial hygiene and 'eugenics' were widespread aspects of socio-biological thought among social scientists, physicians and criminologists at the beginning of the twentieth century. This applied to Britain, the Scandinavian countries and above all the USA, where the Galton Society's postulates of racial hygiene, advocated particularly by the eugenicist Charles B. Davenport, gained a certain amount of influence over American immigration policy.

Conceptions of this kind admittedly also met with determined resistance, both from humanistically oriented groups, which were also present in the workers' movement, and from the Christian churches, though in the latter case this opposition was intertwined with other notions. The churches saw social hygiene and racial anthropology as a part of the cultural modernity they fulminated against in their attempt to preserve traditional values and moral guidelines. The attempt to fight the 'pathological symptoms' of modernity with equally modern means can therefore be seen as an exaggerated expression of the social and cultural contradictions of the turn of the century.

In conclusion, the developments outlined here should be compared with those in other European countries. This comparison needs to stress first of all what all the industrialising societies of Europe had in common. In France, the Netherlands, Austria, Italy and Great Britain, we find the same search for familiarity and a fixed point of orientation in face of a rapidly changing environment, though its forms varied from one country to the next. The critique of modernity, life reform movements, the workers' movement, anti-Semitism and radical nationalism also seem to have developed even more strongly than they did in Germany in some other European countries, namely France, Russia and Austria.[55]

What was specific about Germany was the intensity and rapidity of these processes. This explains both the radical character of the ideologies that emerged and the attempt made to give artistic expression to them. In most other countries, it seems, there were countervailing forces which weakened these movements, slowed down the transformation or limited it to specific regions or social strata. In France, for example, great swathes of the countryside were, for a long time, completely unaware of the modernisation transforming the towns, or at least they had far less knowledge of what was happening than was the case in remote rural areas of Germany. In Great Britain, the change from an agrarian to an industrial society had begun almost fifty years earlier, and it was completed over a much longer period of time, stretching from the early nineteenth into the early twentieth centuries. Modernisation in Russia was limited to a few islands of development in a sea of rural backwardness. It quickly became apparent that, since the final years of the nineteenth century, the mantle of the laboratory of modernity had passed from Great Britain to

Germany. The course of German development was correspondingly diverse, dynamic and crisis-ridden.

This phase of German history has exerted an extraordinary degree of fascination right up to the present day. The society was bursting with vitality and a sense of novelty. Germany had developed in a very short time from a country which was, in many respects, backward and permeated by agricultural influence into a continentally dominant economic power, leading the world in almost all economic, scientific and technological spheres. It had also proposed, tested and discussed almost all possible cultural and political reactions to these fundamental changes within a period of twenty-five years. The ideological arsenal of the gigantic political movements which stamped their mark on the face of the twentieth century took shape in Germany, as did the grand designs of cultural modernity, as well as the movements that opposed them.

The yearning of the majority for security and fixed points of reference when faced with such dynamic transformations is entirely understandable. Confronted with wholly novel surroundings, which were often perceived as hostile, they harked back to tradition, returning to cultural values which offered the stability and reliability of a past actually experienced or merely imagined. But, at the same time, this reversion to tradition can also be understood as the prerequisite for a gradual process of integration, which extended over many generations. Beneath the shelter of a continuing adherence to traditional values, people could adapt themselves by stages to the new situation. The period of rapid change which started in 1890 should therefore be understood as a phase in a long-term learning process during which people adapted their behaviour and learned how to deal with the emerging modern industrial society. It could already be foreseen that this would involve extraordinary crises, failures and constantly renewed approaches to a solution, though how profound these crises would be could not yet be predicted and had not yet been decided.

Right into the second half of the twentieth century, the standard of prosperity and success for a German community was set by the experience of the German Empire. To quote one of its fiercest present-day critics, it was characterised by

> a high degree of legal security, rights of political participation equalled by only a few countries in the West, social policy achievements matched only by Austria and Switzerland, freedom for uncompromising criticism, some opposition successes, a liberty of expression limited only rarely by the intervention of the censorship, educational opportunity, social mobility, increasing well-being [and] perceptibly improved opportunities for living one's life and participating in society.[56]

At the same time, however, extraordinary tensions had accumulated in this society, unavoidably so in view of the above-mentioned developments. How these tensions would be resolved was still an open question, which depended on very many factors. The first of these was the configuration of political forces which had taken shape in Germany. This would determine whether it would be possible in the medium term to establish a structure of political and social compromise capable of settling the social, cultural and political crises that were constantly recurring. The second factor was the state of the economy. The relative tranquillity of Imperial German society was clearly founded upon the assumption that economic growth would continue, and that the situation of the lower social strata in particular would improve. Thirdly, and most importantly, the country's continuing prosperity was dependent on whether German society would have sufficient time at its disposal to pass through these processes of learning and transformation.

# 2
# The New Reich

## Bismarck's Legacy

When Reich Chancellor Bismarck was dismissed by the young emperor William II on 20 March 1890, the main feeling in the country he had founded and ruled with an iron fist for twenty years was that a burden had been lifted. 'It is good that we are rid of him, and many things will now be dealt with better, more honourably and with greater clarity than before' remarked Theodor Fontane, breathing a sigh of relief.[1] The greatness of Bismarck's political achievement was largely unquestioned. But the internal tensions which had grown up under his rule were regarded as equally great. The political system, completely tailored as it was to the requirements of the all-powerful Reich Chancellor, clearly needed an urgent overhaul, in order to be able to confront the dynamic transformations that had taken place in the economy, in the society, and in domestic and foreign politics. It was hoped, erroneously as it turned out, that without Bismarck the job would be done more easily.

The problem of a German nation-state had been posed since the beginning of the century. It was solved with the sword by the foundation of the German Empire in January 1871, after the failure of all other attempts, in particular the one of 1848–9 to solve it by bourgeois revolution. The German Reich was created by princes, civil servants and soldiers, not by burghers, peasants and workers. This was reflected both in the constitution and political structure of the new state and in the way the social system was organised. The apparatus of political rule consisted of four constitutional organs—the Kaiser, or Emperor, the Chancellor, the Reichstag, or parliament, and the Bundesrat, or federal council—a party system with five relatively stable party groupings—the Conservatives, the National Liberals, the Left Liberals, the Centre Party and the Social Democrats—and finally two centrally important elite groups: the ministerial officials and the officers of the armed forces.

The role of the Kaiser was initially embedded within the federal framework. As King of Prussia he was intended to act above all as the holder of presidential power in the *Bund,* or the federation of states that made up Germany. But, after a few years, he began to be regarded as the symbol of the new nation-state. The monarch's authority in regard to government and legislation was limited. He could, it is true, dissolve the Reichstag, and appoint and dismiss the Chancellor as well as all other members of the government. In addition to this, he had a number of special prerogatives, which extended the range of his authority, especially in times of crisis, and granted him a degree of power which was exceptional in Europe: he could declare war and make peace and through his power of command over the Prussian army he had sole authority over the German armed forces, which were therefore subject neither to the Reichstag, nor the Bundesrat, nor the Chancellor. This fact itself demonstrates the special role of the military in Germany. The power of the anti-parliamentary forces was based on the special position of the monarch and the military. Even as late as 1910 one of the spokesmen of the Prussian Conservatives could make this remark: 'The King of Prussia and German Emperor must at any moment be in a position to say to a lieutenant: "Take ten men and close the Reichstag!"'.[2]

The Reich had a 'Reich leadership' but no government. This saying expresses the fact that there was only one minister: the Chancellor. He made the main decisions and determined the government's policy, and his overall power was considerable, since he functioned simultaneously as Prime Minister of Prussia, which was by far the largest federal state. But he was also in a position of dual dependence. He was subordinate to the Emperor, who could appoint and dismiss him, and also to the Reichstag. The parliament did not, it is true, possess the right to elect him or to vote for his removal. But the Chancellor had to persuade the Reichstag to pass the laws and above all the budget. To that extent, the Chancellor's position was contradictory: it was too strong for a democratic parliamentary system and too weak for a constitutional dictatorship.

The Bundesrat, the body representing the federal states, had in name a strong position: like the Reichstag, it had to give its agreement to all legislation, in particular the budget, and it could propose laws and issue ordinances with the force of law. But in fact this simply served to conceal the special role of Prussia, which, as the largest individual state in the Empire, set the direction of the Bundesrat and also provided its chairman, in the shape of the King of Prussia. The three-class electoral system continued to be in force in Prussia. It was linked to the taxes paid by each individual, and this favoured the big landowners of the eastern region. As a result, the dominant position of Prussia also meant that the big landowners east of the Elbe had a strong political influence on the country as a whole.

The position of the monarch, the Chancellor and the Bundesrat, the supremacy of Prussia and the special position of the military were all indications of the authoritarian character of the new state. But, at the Reich level, this was somewhat counterbalanced by the introduction of a strong parliamentary element, the Reichstag, which was a concession to the bourgeoisie and the liberals, who as the strongest political grouping had played a part in the foundation of the Empire. This body was initially elected every three years, then after 1888 every five years, on the basis of a decidedly democratic franchise, which gave all males over twenty-five years of age the right to vote. A franchise as wide as this was not introduced in Britain and France until fifty years later. All the laws required the agreement of the parliament, which also had to approve the budget every year, and in addition could call on the Chancellor to appear before it to state the government's position. The Chancellor was thus compelled to obtain a majority in the Reichstag. This was the starting point for a gradual parliamentarisation of the Empire, something which Bismarck had wanted to prevent at any cost. Important areas of competence were, of course, excluded: the parliament could elect neither the Chancellor nor the ministers, who were described as 'State Secretaries'. Above all, it could not decide on the largest item of the budget, military expenditure, though it is true that the Reichstag did succeed in gradually extending its competence over this area. Right until the end of the Empire, however, the financing of military expenditure remained a major cause of dispute.

The Constitution of the German Empire was a compromise. It was an expression of power relations at the beginning of the 1870s, which were characterised by a coalition between Conservatives and Liberals on the basis of the politics of nationalism. But the most important question was as yet undecided: should the new German Empire be ruled in the bourgeois-parliamentarian manner or as a constitutional monarchy of an authoritarian kind? The conflicts arising from this uncertainty were perceptible early on: conflicts between Prussia and the Reich, between the Emperor and the Chancellor, and above all between the Emperor, Chancellor and Bundesrat on one side and the Reichstag on the other. It had also not yet been decided to what extent this structure would be federal, and how much power would fall to the Reich.

This initially seemed to be a side issue, for the main task of the new nation-state was to create a unified economic and legal area and remove obstacles to communication, building on what the North German Confederation had already achieved. This was, after all, why it had been founded, and in these fields of activity the new system proved to be extraordinarily successful.

The new German state was faced with numerous domestic opponents, despite all the elation produced by the nation's military victory over France. Four major opposition groups can be identified: firstly, those who had hoped for a Great German solution, which would have meant that Prussia's dominant position was less highly marked. This group included many liberals from the south German states. The second group consisted of the majority of Roman Catholics, who now found themselves in a minority position in a Protestant-dominated country. Then there were the Social Democrats. In 1871, they were not yet a formidable movement and in any case they were definitely not anti-national;

but they were driven into fierce opposition by the thoroughly undemocratic and militaristic character of the Bismarckian Empire. The fourth group of opponents consisted of the non-German minorities, who inevitably feared marginalisation or perhaps even discrimination in a state which was now explicitly German. This applied of course to the inhabitants of Alsace-Lorraine, the provinces which had been separated from France after the war and incorporated into the new Reich, but it also applied to the Danes; and above all to the Poles, whose yearning for the restoration of their fatherland, divided into three parts since 1795, was reinforced by the foundation of the German nation-state.

In contending with these opposing forces, one of the chief tasks of the new nation-state was internal integration. Until the end of the century, this was essentially promoted, and indeed achieved up to a point, by three factors: the modernisation of the administration and the country's infrastructure, the tremendous upsurge of the economy and the emergence of a Reich nationalism, which absorbed the strong national-liberal traditions of previous decades and recoded them on an authoritarian basis.

With regard to modernisation of the infrastructure and the administration, the most important prerequisites were already put in place during the first ten years: freedom of trade was implemented over the whole of the Reich, weights and measures were standardised, a single currency was introduced, the criminal law was harmonised, a strong and independent judicial system was organised, central offices for post and telegraph, statistics, health and other branches were established, and a start was made with reforming local ordinances at district and province level, which were often still feudal in character. The legislation of the 1870s laid the foundation for the extraordinary economic growth of subsequent decades.[3]

The growing importance of a modern centralised state, with its far-reaching jurisdiction over the economy, law and administration, was one of the preeminent features of the period between 1871 and 1890 and doubtless a success story. But it met with resistance from those groups which were interested in maintaining the existing structures and feared the impact of modernity on their traditional world. Resistance was strong among the rural population, particularly in the backward East. Here, the anxiety of the peasant strata about the way the liberal market economy was disrupting the foundations of their existence joined hands with the interest of the estate-owners and the big farmers in maintaining their hold over the countryside. This happened in all European countries in the phase of transformation from the agrarian to the industrial state, but in Germany the agrarians had long enjoyed a particularly strong political influence, quickly giving rise to a structural conflict which lessened the internal political flexibility of the Reich, and at the same time led the interests of agriculture to receive disproportionate consideration.[4]

The liberal reforms also met with resistance from the Roman Catholics. This happened wherever the state bureaucracy penetrated into areas of life previously reserved for the Church alone. This affected above all the supervision of schools, the education of priests and the marriage contract. When the Catholic Church mounted an attack on these reforms, through its political representative the Centre Party, and with the support of the Pope in Rome, Bismarck unleashed a strongly anti-Catholic campaign, helped by the National Liberals, who played a particularly active part in this conflict. Priests, politicians from the Centre Party, Catholic associations and Catholic newspapers were placed under immense pressure. For Bismarck, of course, the result of this conflict between State and Church, known as the *Kulturkampf*, was a disaster. The Centre Party and the clergy were able to preserve their essential rights and they withstood Bismarck's attacks without suffering any damage. In fact, they were considerably strengthened by the episode. This was also true of the Catholic milieu in general. It now became increasingly separate, self-absorbed and emphatically aware of its own traditions. Its cohesion continued to grow. It became clear that the Catholic third of the population, in its majority, encountered Germany's accelerated modernisation with distrust, rejection and energetic resistance, and it was supported in this by the Vatican, which had already issued Encyclicals condemning the modern world in general and rationalism in particular.[5]

In the years after the foundation of the German Empire, the bourgeoisie, the majority of which was National Liberal in opinion, took a largely optimistic view, and the progress of the economy appeared to confirm its support for fundamental change. This attitude did not change substantially even after 1873, when business conditions, stable until then, began to lose their sparkle. Turnover, prices and profits all went into decline, and the mining industry in particular fell into a crisis caused by overproduction and speculation. This led to greater rationalisation, and increases in productivity, which had a positive impact on German industry in the medium term. For contemporaries, however, this was the first crisis of the kind, and there was neither a basis in economic theory for its explanation, nor a store of experience on how to deal with it.

## The End of the Liberal Era

The shock of the so-called *Gründerkrise* (founders' crisis) of the years 1873 to 1879 led to a far-reaching reorientation of large sections of the bourgeoisie. Criticism of the principles of liberalism became more strident; the free market economy, which was largely independent of the state, and freedom of trade were the main objects of attack, but the political maxims of the liberals were also a target. The call for the state to intervene more decisively in the economy became louder: the aim of such intervention would be to protect the national market against foreign competition, which was now being felt more strongly, and to lessen the inherent risks of industrial capitalism for German manufacturers. This too was by no means a uniquely German phenomenon. The call for protective duties reverberated in other countries too. In France, for example, the flag of protectionism was raised as emphatically as it was in the German Empire. But these protective measures had a particularly powerful effect in Germany, because high import duties were imposed not only on industrial goods but on agricultural products as well. The result was that food prices were kept high for longer, which tended to prevent any attempt at a thorough rationalisation, precisely in the sector where it was most necessary, namely agriculture.

Another source of conflict was the treatment of Social Democracy. Until 1875, there had been two separate workers' parties in Germany, but in that year they joined together to form a single Social Democratic party, which adopted the name Socialist Workers' Party of Germany (*Sozialistische Arbeiterpartei Deutschlands*, SAPD). The Social Democrats rejected the Bismarckian state structure as authoritarian and undemocratic, and as a result they were stigmatised and combated as enemies of the Reich (*Reichsfeinde*). As in the case of the Catholics, this campaign forced the organised workers further back into their milieu. This veritable universe of associations, cooperatives, newspapers and trade unions soon developed into a rival world, sealed off from bourgeois society. At the same time, Social Democracy's political importance increased constantly. As early as 1877, the united party obtained 9.1 per cent of the vote, and in heavily industrialised areas such as Saxony and Berlin the figure was almost 40 per cent. This very early and successful growth of a socialist-oriented workers' party is one of the specific features of German history; in no other country was a comparable development to be observed at this time. There were two reasons why this happened. One was the particularly rapid spread of market capitalism and the emergence of a class of wage labourers associated with it. The traditional forms of organisation of the artisans who had now become wage labourers could thus be transferred to the new situation, so that the industrial workers were able to come together in political parties and trade unions at a very early stage. The growth of German Social Democracy was also a reaction to the political alliance the liberals had made with the conservative politician Bismarck in order to found the Reich, which had led to the loss of German liberalism's ability to integrate elements of the left, thus creating the necessary prerequisite for the early emergence of a radical left-wing workers' party.[6]

The existence and spread of such a radical alternative to the existing order of state and society called forth deep anxiety among the German bourgeoisie, and for more than half a century this provided an underlying ground bass to the domestic political mood. In the early summer of 1878, two unsuccessful attempts were made to assassinate the German Emperor, and the fear of revolution in bourgeois circles grew to such an extent that the liberals gave up their resistance to the emergency law against the SAPD which Bismarck had long demanded. This now provided a basis for the suppression of the party and the persecution of its leaders.

Yet even the anti-socialist law still reflected the ambiguous character of the German Empire's political constitution. From a democratic perspective, it was a repressive, authoritarian instrument without any constitutional justification, on the basis of which roughly 1,500 people were prosecuted for political reasons and sent to jail. Nevertheless, from the perspective of an absolutist conception of the state, the anti-Socialist Law was a half measure, for it allowed the Social Democrats to retain their seats in parliament and the active and passive franchise. Moreover, it was temporary, so that every time it was extended there was a protracted debate over its advantages and disadvantages. If, for example, the anti-socialist law is compared with the suppression of the French Commune in 1871, which led to the death of more than 1,000 people, and was followed by merciless persecution for years afterwards, it becomes evident that far more radical options were entirely conceivable at that time.[7]

In its effects, finally, the oppressive anti-socialist law actually benefited its victims. It was only under persecution that the SAPD (later SPD) was constituted as a solid political and also cultural entity. The mystique of working-class solidarity had its origins in the anti-socialist law and in the strikes that took place and were sometimes bloodily suppressed, above all, the strike of the Ruhr miners at the end of the 1880s. It was also during this phase that the radical teaching of Marx and Engels gained its position as the party's obligatory doctrine. The anti-socialist law seemed to confirm that emancipation from exploitation and oppression was not to be expected from the German state. The hopes of the organised workers were therefore directed towards its overthrow through revolution. It is true that the workers did not possess a precise or an especially violent conception of this, but in view of the oppression they had suffered, they no longer thought that change could successfully be achieved within the existing social order, even if the SPD's constantly growing share of the vote at each Reichstag election appeared to contradict this conviction.[8]

The anti-Socialist law marked the end of the 'liberal era'. Although Chancellor Bismarck's protective duties were harmful to trade, he was able to push them through the Reichstag in the summer of 1879 with the votes of the conservative parties and the Centre Party. After the ending of the *Kulturkampf*, which was a Catholic success, the 'black–blue' coalition with the conservatives offered an alternative to cooperation with the liberals, for there were strong forces in the Centre Party which largely agreed with the Prussian Conservatives in defending the interests of agriculture and the rural population and rejecting liberal, 'modern' ways of living.

Thus Bismarck's parliamentary majority had shifted to the right. But it was precisely with this majority that he now implemented his social policy, which was directed above all against two domestic political opponents. It was intended to take the wind out of the Social Democrats' sails by freeing the workers from the worst of their misery. At the same time, it would demolish the liberal principle that the state should not intervene in economic affairs, which Bismarck considered was one of the reasons for the rise of a radical workers' party. His social security laws diverged from the existing principles of poor relief, and they established for the first time that the individual had a legal claim to assistance both when reaching old age and when incapable of continuing to work as a result of sickness or accident. The insurance contributions for this were divided between the employer and the employee, while in the case of old-age insurance the state also had to contribute.

Only much later was a comparable system of social welfare established in the other countries of industrialising Europe. This is a further indication that in Germany the social antagonisms arising out of industrialisation were regarded as particularly harsh and intolerable evils, for the actual degree of poverty was no greater there than in other European industrial countries. From that time onwards, the German conception of the tasks of the state included the notion that it was responsible for the welfare of its citizens and for a certain level of social protection. This became one of the cornerstones of German political thinking.[9]

But, in view of his reliance on the conservatives and the Centre Party, Bismarck was unable to gain a parliamentary majority for a reform of the finances, which was urgently necessary owing to the entirely inadequate financial basis on which the Reich had been set up. The need to depend on parliamentary majorities was regarded by rigorous opponents of parliamentarisation in government circles as an intolerable imposition. Bismarck endeavoured to counteract this dependence by restricting the jurisdiction of the Reichstag, by dissolving it, and by almost openly threatening a *coup d'état*, but without much success.

The political situation did not change until the mid-1880s, when the party landscape took on a new colouring. Political liberalism suffered a split: the Left Liberals seceded from the National Liberal Party. As a result, the latter group moved to the right and together with the conservatives they formed a more stable parliamentary basis for Bismarck's policies until the end of the 1880s. For a short period, this provided the Chancellor with enough votes to put into effect a number of his objectives, such as the further strengthening of the armed forces, the forced Germanisation of the eastern provinces of Prussia, which were inhabited predominantly by Poles, the improvement of the finances of the Reich by imposing taxes on consumption, and the renewal of the anti-socialist law. In 1887, however, the National Liberals objected to a further increase in grain duties, which was extremely steep (they were raised from the 1879 figure by a multiple of five). The Centre Party had to be asked to help, so that once again the Chancellor had lost his stable parliamentary majority.

But now the death firstly of the Emperor and then of the Crown Prince, followed by the accession to the imperial throne of the very young William II, created further political upheaval. Whereas Bismarck wanted to renew the anti-socialist law, limit the scope of social policy and continue the struggle to reduce the Reichstag's responsibilities, the new monarch placed his faith in a policy intended to increase the integration of the workers into society. In addition, the defeat of the conservatives and National Liberals at the elections of 1890 meant that there no longer seemed to be sufficient parliamentary backing for the Chancellor's policies. Bismarck's removal from office was a direct result of this.

But the sense of relief at Bismarck's resignation rested on false hopes. For it soon became apparent that the difficulties that had confronted the old Chancellor derived less from his personal character than from the architecture of the political system. There were two ways of quickly and permanently addressing the much bemoaned inability of the Reich to take decisive action. One option was to risk a thoroughgoing parliamentarisation and liberalisation of the system of government. But the existing relationship of forces blocked the way to this solution, since it would have met with fierce resistance from the Crown, the bureaucracy, the military, the big landowners and the conservatives, and there was no united phalanx of advocates to support it. The other option was a consistent retreat from parliamentarism and the installation of an authoritarian government. This would presumably have led to an increase in Germany's decision-making capacity, but it would also have introduced onto the scene a vast array of opposing forces—the Social Democrats, the Left Liberals, sections of the Centre Party and the National Liberal Party, and finally the overwhelming majority of the population. In short, in Germany it was clearly already too late for a dictatorial constitution, while, in view of the relationship of forces, it was perhaps still too early for a parliamentary democracy. Bismarck's technique of government was to tack between these two polar opposites, and it would soon become apparent that his successors chose to pursue exactly the same course.

On the other hand, the new German Reich had proved itself to be an enormous success in almost all areas of trade, business, science, infrastructure and administration. Within twenty years, a nation-state has arisen which was increasingly unified in the political, economic and cultural sense. The national economy had weathered the long, crisis-ridden years of the early 1870s and the late 1880s which saw the transition from agricultural to industrial primacy astoundingly well. The country had constructed a remarkable infrastructure, a modern legal system, and an incomparable educational and scientific system. Its future prospects were undoubtedly excellent. It was also clear that the political structure, in contrast, displayed clear deficiencies. But other Western European countries also found it very difficult to change their political order to meet the new challenges presented by the development of industrial society. This applied to their voting arrangements, the structure of their political parties, their social policy and their legal systems.[10] In many of these spheres of activity, the Germans had developed sound models; it was not yet certain, however, whether these models would also be able to function if there was a further acceleration in the speed of change.

## The New Course

The middle classes strongly approved of the departure of Bismarck. In view of the quickening dynamism of the industrial economy and the many changes this involved, they now hoped for a fresh start. It was clear to everyone that decisive moves in economic policy were inevitable, particularly with regard to agriculture and the level of tariffs; this was also true of tax policy, where it was necessary to secure for the Reich an income to match its rapidly growing responsibilities, as well as domestic policy, where there was a need to defuse the increasing confrontation between the state and the political and social elite on one side and the organised working class on the other. Of course, different political and social groups had rather differing expectations as to what had to be done.

The new government of Reich Chancellor Count Leo von Caprivi made a large number of very promising attempts to overcome the stagnation of Bismarck's later years. The anti-socialist law was not renewed, and fresh measures of social policy were at last introduced, after a lengthy period of stagnation. In particular, the safety regulations that protected people at work were improved. In the countryside, a reform of local government ended the unrestricted rule of the owners of manorial estates over rural districts and communes. A start was made in Prussia with the introduction of a modern tax system on the basis of a progressive income tax and a wealth tax. In addition, the government concluded a series of trade treaties with Germany's European neighbours so as to make sure that the export of German industrial goods was not hindered by the existence of tariff barriers. Taken as a whole, therefore, these were highly energetic attempts to modernise German politics and administration.

But, before long, the reaction against these measures made itself felt. In concluding the trade treaties, the government had been obliged to make certain reductions in the duties on the importation of agricultural goods. The vigorous protests of the agrarians that followed this decision showed the narrowness of the government's room for manoeuvre. An ever-sharper confrontation between agrarian interests and government policy developed out of these protests, and this soon culminated in the adoption of a stance of total opposition by the conservatives. The German Conservative Party moved in a clearly right-wing direction, and its agitation now had unmistakable anti-Semitic undertones. The agrarian opposition movement acquired a mass basis through the establishment of the *Bund der Landwirte* or Agrarian League, and this organisation was an important factor in German domestic politics from then onwards.

Political reform continued to be stymied, however. The government was unable either to integrate the Social Democrats into the political system or to create a stable parliamentary majority. It was also unable to settle the antagonism between Prussia and the Reich. Two personal factors also came into play: for one thing, Emperor William II began to intervene increasingly actively in the conduct of government policy. It is true that this primarily took the form of a series of uncoordinated and random interventions by the court, often about symbolic rather than substantive issues. But, for a whole decade, it was almost impossible to achieve anything against the Emperor's will. Moreover, the aged Bismarck was also intriguing against the government's policies, and his activities struck a chord with his ultra-conservative landowning neighbours.

After only four years, therefore, Caprivi's 'New Course' came to an end. His successor, Chlodwig zu Hohenlohe-Schillingsfürst, did not fare much better. Attention continued to be focused on the struggle against Social Democracy although nobody was able to find any more innovative ways of conducting it. The Emperor now pressed for the workers' party to be forced to retreat, marginalised and suppressed, and he was enthusiastically supported in this by a broad front, ranging from the conservatives to the National Liberals. But when the provisions of the so-called *Umsturzvorlage*, or Bill against Subversion, were revealed, they demonstrated the true nature of the anti-socialist front's objectives. For the bill was so vaguely and aggressively formulated that it would hit not just subversive socialist and anarchist activities but liberal tendencies in art and science. In fact, anyone who was described as the enemy of respectability, morality, order and tradition would fall victim to it. Such a storm of protest arose in response to this that the bill failed to pass the Reichstag. A similar disaster befell the government a year later, when it tried to force through a penal law against striking workers.

The failure of the 'Bill Against Subversion' was clear evidence of the limits on the power of the old forces, and also of the influence of public opinion, which now gradually began to emerge, through opinions expressed in newspapers, party meetings and demonstrations. Defeats of this nature led some of the Emperor's entourage to revert to the idea that after all it would perhaps be a better plan to do away with the Reichstag completely, force through a new, authoritarian constitution, and possibly declare a state of emergency. But they had neither the determination nor the means to accomplish such a coup, especially as they might have to reckon with a civil war if that came to pass. Thus the functional defects of the Empire's system of government continued to be as unmanageable as the political stalemate, which rendered decisive moves in one direction or the other quite impossible.

But these problems were offset by the obvious material successes of the Empire: the country could bask in gigantic figures for economic growth, magnificent achievements in science and technology, and a construction boom never previously experienced. It is true that people were generally aware of the intrigues that marred domestic politics, but these did not stand at the forefront of public interest. In any case, the intractable situation at home now led the rulers of the country to place their faith increasingly in foreign policy. It seemed that political successes on a grand scale could be achieved more easily abroad than at home, and without incurring any irritating criticism from parliament and the public.

## Reich and *Weltreich*

Abroad too, though, contradictions abounded. Just as in domestic policy the new German nation-state had been obliged to create the prerequisites for social integration, so too in foreign policy it had to attempt to lay to rest the growing unease felt by the European powers over the rise of this new contender in the centre of the continent. The European equilibrium of forces which had existed since the Congress of Vienna had been disturbed by the emergence of a new German nation-state. This was evident even from the population figures: before the foundation of the German state Prussia had no more than 16 million inhabitants. The German Empire now numbered 41 million. This gave it the second largest population in Europe, after Russia. When Germany then set out to become the strongest country on the continent in economic terms, this altered the structural balance of European power relations. In Germany itself, this was the source of manifold hopes and aspirations, but in other countries it increased fears of German supremacy. In order to counteract these anxieties, Bismarck initially pursued a defensive policy of appeasement, attempting to create a certain degree of balance in the new European constellation of forces.[11]

That this balance was never achieved was in large part the fault of the Germans themselves. The annexation of Alsace-Lorraine in 1871 placed such a heavy burden on the Franco-German relationship that no lasting compromise with Germany's western neighbour could be achieved, even far into the future. The separation of these provinces from France against the declared will of the great majority of the population was a constant stimulation to French nationalism and it pushed French foreign policy in a revanchist direction. The German Empire was therefore repeatedly forced to forge groupings and alliances which were either aimed directly against France or sought to prevent other powers from allying with her.

Nevertheless, international politics long continued to be imbued with the traditional practices of classical diplomacy, in which crises were provoked and resolved, alliances were entered and abandoned, in whatever way governments considered sensible, without being controlled or even molested by public opinion or mass political organisations. By the 1890s at the latest, however, the foundations of international politics had shifted, with the result that the traditional methods of conducting foreign policy proved to be increasingly anachronistic and incapable of performing their function. In this context, we need to emphasise the following three developments: firstly, owing to its rapid growth, industrial capitalism clearly moved beyond the framework of the nation-state. The products of industry were in search of new export outlets, the development of new means of transport allowed the volume of foreign trade to rise to previously unimagined heights, and the financial markets became internationally interdependent. This led to a strengthening of the connections between the European states, but by the same token areas of friction also increased.[12]

Secondly, the threat posed to the traditional structure of the European powers by the constantly increasing influence of nationalism grew greater and greater. This threat had a particular relevance for the big multinational states, namely the Ottoman, Russian and Austro-Hungarian empires, where the calls of the various national minorities for independence resounded at varying volumes. Where they were loudest, they endangered those empires' unity and even their very existence. In this way, the number of potential centres of conflict in Europe increased considerably, and actual conflicts soon emerged. This applied particularly to the Balkans, where the endeavours of the South Slav peoples to secure independence came up against the interests of two competing great powers—Russia and Austria-Hungary. Overwhelmingly in the last quarter of the nineteenth century, the upsurge of organised nationalism secured greater and greater influence over the direction of foreign policy. Nationalism therefore became an important, and indeed soon a decisive, factor in international relations, especially in times of crisis.[13]

Thirdly, in the 1880s overseas expansion became a feature of European foreign policy. After hesitant beginnings, this movement grew rapidly in the 1890s and beyond. In the twenty-five years that followed, overseas expansion intensified, becoming a veritable frenzy of imperialism, which hardly any major nation was able to avoid. The thirst for colonial possessions had its origins in economic factors, or at least factors regarded as economic. Since the 1870s, the industrialising states of Europe had repeatedly suffered apparently uncontrollable conjunctural crises, which were associated with overproduction, falling prices, bankruptcies, unemployment and social tensions. In view of this, the possession of export markets outside Europe appeared to be a tried and tested means of countering such visitations. In economic terms, this view had little validity: outlets in the other industrially developed countries, and internal markets within the country in question, proved to be far more significant. Moreover, the contribution of the overseas spheres of influence and possessions of the European powers in relation to the acquisition of raw materials and opportunities for investment was also greatly overestimated. Rational commercial calculations clearly played a subordinate role in this process. But until then people had had little experience of world economic links of this kind, and, undeniably, the prospect of large profits was a tempting one.[14]

But soon political and ideological rather than economic aspects determined imperialist ambitions. Industrialisation had brought about such an extraordinary increase in power through the technological and scientific possibilities associated with it, and such a heightening of national self-confidence, especially in connection with the nationalism that fed on it, that the urge to expand overseas must also be understood as an expression of the sense of progress and destiny that had been unleashed in Europe. Whereas aspirations for expansion within the European continent were always associated with the danger of a great war between the European countries, the race for the last regions of the world not yet ruled by Europeans became the preferred way of conducting the competitive struggle between the European powers, who ceaselessly made comparisons with each other, economically, cultural and militarily. The acquisition of colonies became a yardstick of prestige and success.

The urge to expand overseas was closely linked with the widespread conviction of the superiority of the 'white man' over Africans and Asians, whose 'backwardness' appeared to furnish a justification of European supremacy. The various doctrines asserting a natural hierarchy among the races, which had already existed in the pre-modern era, were now given the appearance of scientific backing. They gained adherents everywhere in Europe, and, what was more important, the colonies provided an area in which they could be put into practice.

Germany occupied an unusual position in this respect, in that it began to acquire colonies relatively late. Moreover, in Germany's case, these colonies were of very slight economic utility, while the politically motivated goals of colonial expansion were particularly pronounced. Initially, Bismarck had aimed merely at securing informal zones of influence, and it was only under pressure that he agreed to the acquisition of overseas possessions. Hence, in the 1880s and 1890s, many areas were placed under formal German rule relatively quickly. These colonies lay scattered around the world, in East, West and Southwest Africa, and in Asia and the Pacific, and even in the long term they offered little hope of rich pickings either through the exploitation of raw materials or access to new export markets. Non-economic considerations had played a determining role from the outset, and they continued to do so. The acquisition of overseas possessions served above all to raise the nation's prestige, and in addition it offered a national task about which 'Germans could be enthusiastic', as Bismarck himself put it. There was, moreover, an increasingly influential view in the country that it was better to relieve the pressure of Germany's lamented 'overpopulation' through emigration to her 'own' overseas territories, rather than to foreign countries such as the USA or Canada. This would be a way of reducing or completely removing the social tensions and dangers of 'mass society'. There were also widespread hopes that imperialism would satisfy the nation's need for its international importance to be recognised and that it would overcome internal divisions.

While such visions of the colonial empire provided a basis for far-reaching hopes about the future, foreign policy on the continent of Europe turned out to be a laborious and complicated affair. Since a return of Alsace-Lorraine or even a change in the province's status appeared impossible in view of the rising nationalist movement in Germany, an understanding with France would be out of the question for a long time. Germany had therefore to seek an agreement with the other three great powers of Europe. She only succeeded in the case of Austria-Hungary. Relations with Russia had been worsened by Bismarck's economic policies, while as far as Great Britain was concerned, one major obstacle to an improvement of relations was the German conservatives' fear that this would raise the standing of liberalism and parliamentarism in the Reich. Moreover, the system of support and reinsurance treaties which Bismarck had developed to provide security to Germany proved to be less a well-planned and thought-out foreign policy shelter for Germany than a system of expedients without any long-term stabilising effect. The danger of a simultaneous confrontation with France and Russia, resulting in a war on two fronts, was neither exorcised, nor was it reduced, by the efforts of Bismarck's successors. They were unable either to achieve a *rapprochement* with Great Britain or to weaken the ties between France and Russia.

There were therefore unmistakable symptoms of crisis in the field of European power politics. Even so, disagreements between the powers did not seem insurmountable, and as long as the European balance of power remained relatively intact and the tensions and crises which repeatedly emerged could be resolved without military conflict, there was for the moment no need to expect any large-scale conflict to erupt in Europe

But the rise of mass nationalist organisations since the 1890s had transformed the balance of forces in domestic politics. This also had an impact on the direction of foreign policy, as soon became apparent. In France, just as in Great Britain, Austria-Hungary and the German Empire, broad sections of the population had become politicised. A large number of leagues and associations were established to promote special interests, while electoral participation increased and the membership of political parties increased. This process ran parallel with a tremendous expansion of the newspaper press, as a result of which a much greater part of the population than just a few years previously took part in political events.

On the German Right, it was above all the Pan-German League (*Alldeutsche Verband*) and the East Mark Association (*Ostmarkenverein*) which influenced the course of politics outside the parliament and the parties. Both of these groups had relatively few members, but they were regarded as influential, particularly among the bourgeoisie. The Pan-Germans spearheaded the forces favouring an aggressive foreign and colonial policy, combined with a domestic policy directed against Social Democrats, Left Liberals and Jews, while the objective of the East Mark Association was to 'Germanise' the Polish-inhabited areas of the eastern part of the Reich.

The veterans' associations were much larger. Their umbrella organisation, the *Kyffhäuserbund*, had more than 2.5 million members in the autumn of 1910, who were mainly small craftsmen, officials, office employees, and workers. This was not a violent or a radical movement, but it did form the popular basis for militarism in Germany; it could always be mobilised on special occasions, such as days of national commemoration and the erection of memorials to dead soldiers, and it provided support for the constantly increased armaments programmes and the expansion of the armed forces.[15]

The temporary success of the anti-Semitic parties, on the other hand, turned out to be a reaction to the economic uncertainties of the early 1890s. In the Reichstag elections of 1898 their share of the vote rose to 3.7 per cent, only to decline again in later elections. This decline, however, was merely an expression of the fact that hostility to the Jews as the sole element in a party's programme was not sufficient to secure long-term success. Anti-Semitism itself did not disappear. At this time, it began to penetrate into the programmes of several national associations, such as the German National Association of Commercial Employees (*Deutschnationaler Handlungsgehilfenverband*) and the Agrarian League (*Bund der Landwirte*). Anti-Semitism also gained ground in the big political parties, particularly among the German Conservatives, who now explicitly took up the cudgels against 'the constant increase of destructive Jewish influence on the life of our people' and the Jews' 'un-German infringement of the principles of fidelity and good faith in business affairs'.[16]

Alongside the political groupings, economic associations also became more vociferous at this time. In 1907, there were 500 of these in industry and trade alone, all attempting to exert an influence on political decisions and public opinion. But it was the agriculturalists who were most successful. Their Agrarian League numbered more than 300,000 members and was a lobby group as effective as it was aggressive, coming out equally radically against liberalism, Social Democracy and industrial modernity. From the 1890s onwards, the political debate in Germany was increasingly dominated by movements of this type, which campaigned against the economic, social and cultural effects of modernisation.[17]

It should not be overlooked, however, that the trend towards mass organisation on the political Right was above all a response to the challenge from the Left: the importance of well-organised mass movements for the business of politics was unmistakable, given the success of Social Democracy and the growth of trade unions, which by 1913 counted more than three million members. It was evidently impossible to win further influence with parties made up of local dignitaries and associations of functionaries. Organisations of a new type, which could mobilise tens of thousands of supporters, were more promising opponents of the workers' movement, the rise of which appeared to be irresistible. By the turn of the century, at the latest, the growth of the SPD vote at the Reichstag elections (it rose from 10 per cent in 1887 to 31 per cent in 1903) had become the central problem of German domestic policy, and almost all the political efforts made in both the bourgeois and the conservative camps were aimed at finding a solution. If the growth of the SPD continued, and in the given state of affairs they had to reckon with this possibility, how could a parliamentary majority be constructed without calling on this party, which continued to be ostracised?

The answer lay in what was called *Sammlung* ('gathering together'). Behind this slogan, coined by the Prussian Finance Minister Johannes von Miquel, there lay the conviction that only close cooperation between conservatives and liberals could halt the further advance of socialism. In order to achieve a closer cooperation between the bourgeoisie and the agrarians which would also be politically effective, the resultant 'cartel of the state-supporting and productive estates (*Stände*)' had to iron out the sharp antagonisms which existed between agriculture and industry and between free-traders and protectionists. In this context, the fundamental problem continued to be the same as it had been twenty-five years earlier: agriculture was under severe pressure to rationalise because of the tremendous competition arising from the import of cheap grain from abroad.

To increase the productivity of agricultural enterprises to the extent required to make them capable of withstanding foreign competition, far-reaching changes in both the form of the enterprise and the way farming was conducted would have been necessary. But this would have brought the traditional social structures in the countryside and the power of the East Elbian 'Junkers' to the verge of collapse. A fierce battle was waged against these proposals by the farmers, who were led by the big estate-owners and represented by the conservative parties and associations. By making imported grain dearer, agrarian pressure groups did in fact succeed in at least slowing down the drive towards rationalisation. This in turn led to protests from the liberals and large parts of industry, whose export opportunities were reduced by these protectionist measures.

The deep divergences of interest which surfaced here were temporarily smoothed over in 1902 by a compromise, negotiated by the new Chancellor, Count Bernhard von Bülow: a further increase in customs duties, but a moderate one, was combined with improvements in social policy and the renewal of the trade treaties with other European powers which were being urgently demanded by industry and criticised by the agricultural interest. This was entirely in line with the policy of balancing the interests of agriculture and industry at the expense of the consumer, which had been customary since Bismarck's time. But it did not provide a sufficiently stable basis for the desired cooperation between the 'state-supporting forces' in the fight against the increasing strength of Social Democracy.

A much broader vision was required, and this was found in a foreign policy project which appeared to open up such bold, global horizons that the enthusiasm it unleashed would ease the path to unity despite divergences over economic policy. The answer was to build a modern battle fleet for the nation.

## Building the Fleet and 'World Policy'

Germany was not the only country to hatch such a vision. The rivalry between the European powers over worldwide influence, to be secured through expansion, had already, brought about a renewed focus on the military and political significance of naval armaments. This was demonstrated both by the result of the Sino-Japanese naval conflict (which the Japanese won, chiefly thanks to their modern cruisers) and, to an even greater extent, by the global domination of Great Britain, whose military strength and worldwide presence depended first and foremost on its fleet. In line with this, the Americans and the Japanese, along with the Russians, endeavoured to buttress their claims for worldwide influence by constructing modern fleets and above all by building large armoured vessels.[18]

It was only to be expected, in view of Germany's economic expansion, that that country too would follow the trend. But there was a difference. Whereas the other great powers were satisfied with a limited building programme involving a few squadrons, partly for financial reasons, because battleships were extremely expensive items, Germany possessed the ambition and above all the resources to operate on a grand scale. There were various motives and objectives associated with this.

For one thing, the aim was to conduct 'world policy' (*Weltpolitik*), or, in other words, to create a worldwide empire after the British model, with colonies and possessions on every continent. According to the dominant opinion at the time, the world would be divided between a small number of world powers within the next few years, and a country which fell behind in the race would become a second- or third-rate power. The consequence of this view was a policy of expansion, the establishment of strategic strongholds, and the acquisition of colonies. A strong navy was needed to achieve this. It is true that commercial interests were linked with this policy, and they were energetically promoted, but they remained rather vague and imprecise. In this respect too, Germany did not differ from other countries.

There was another factor at work, though: if Germany wanted to conduct a 'world policy', it would inevitably come up against Great Britain at every step of the way. For this reason, the German objective, from very early on, was to build a battle fleet which would be, if not a match for Britain's, at least a close rival in size and striking power, either, as was officially affirmed, to deter that country from aggressive action towards the Reich, or to reach a position whereby Germany's interests could be secured despite British opposition, if necessary by force. This objective could not easily be achieved on the world's oceans; but the North Sea was a different matter. The Imperial Naval Secretary (*Staatssekretär im Reichsmarineamt*), Alfred von Tirpitz, who now rose rapidly to become one of the most important political figures in Imperial Germany, had already asserted bluntly that naval equality with Britain in the North Sea could and should be achieved quickly: 'Our fleet must be organised in such a way that it can reach its highest degree of fighting capacity between Heligoland and the Thames.'[19] The decision to build a battle fleet, which was made in 1898 and repeatedly confirmed after that, made it clear to the world that Germany felt strong enough even to challenge Great Britain, with all the risks that evidently entailed. Germany's inflamed nationalist rivalry with Britain, which at first related to steel production and the share of each country in world trade, as well as the number of Nobel prizes achieved and the number of telephone lines connected, now extended as far as military strength and territorial gains.

In addition to 'world politics' and opposition to Britain there were also solid domestic political reasons for building the fleet. On the one hand, as mentioned previously, it provided a basis for the 'policy of gathering together' (*Sammlungspolitik*). The conservatives were sceptical rather than supportive of the fleet, which they regarded as a 'middle-class type of weapon'. They immediately demanded compensation. This was the significance in domestic politics of the tariff of 1902: protective tariffs in return for battleships. On the other hand, building the fleet was explicitly intended as an instrument in the fight against Social Democracy. 'World policy' and the fleet were necessary, as Tirpitz declared quite openly, 'also in no small degree because the great new national task and the economic benefits connected with it will provide a strong antidote to educated and uneducated Social Democrats.'[20] Enthusiasm for the German fleet and Germany's self-assertion as a great power, with a global reach, were intended to promote popular identification with the Emperor and the Reich, even among the poorer strata of society, and thus stop the rush to Social Democracy. In order to stir up this enthusiasm, the Naval Office now itself applied the modern methods of mass agitation and propaganda it so detested when the Left used them. Its most important instrument in this campaign was a new nationalist mass organisation, the 'Navy League' (*Flottenverein*), expressly founded by heavy industrialists and ship-builders in cooperation with journalists, party leaders from the liberal and conservative parties, and representatives of the Naval Office, for the sole purpose of stimulating 'enthusiasm for the fleet' among the public.

Their efforts were crowned with success. At the end of the first year after its foundation in 1898, the Navy League numbered almost 80,000 members, and in later years it served as a reservoir for numerous nationalist societies and associations. By 1913, more than 1.1 million people had joined. The fleet, it turned out, was the ideal projection of bourgeois wishes, and at the same time an expression of the strengthening economy of the new German nation-state. Unlike the largely aristocratic and Prussian-dominated army, the fleet was the triumph of bourgeois ideals. It combined modern science and technology with the prospect of worldwide trading connections. And it was clearly also calculated to dispel the apprehensions of the cultural critics: it promised modernity without its disquieting accompaniments, namely the big city, the masses and critical attitudes. It was modernity in the form of organised military technology.

It now became customary, above all in the *Bildungsbürgertum*, to declare one's commitment to the fleet. The typical figure of the 'fleet professor' agitating impetuously for Germany's proper place in the world became well known, indeed it was also lampooned. Moreover, even 'big names' in the intellectual sphere such as Erich Marcks, Gustav von Schmoller, Karl Lamprecht and Max Weber were enthusiasts for the fleet. 'World policy' had many things to offer, they believed: the world would be civilised with the help of German virtues, a world empire would be created, exactly like the British one, and some of them even hoped that the Prussian Conservatives would lose their dominant position and the stalemate in domestic politics could be ended.

Expansionist nationalism had thus developed a dynamic thrust which could no longer be halted by diplomatic considerations. Quite the reverse, in fact: competition with Great Britain practically became a craze among the German bourgeoisie. England's bloody colonial war against the Boers in South Africa produced the first spike of anti-British agitation and emotion in German public opinion. We began this book by quoting Karl Helfferich's statement that the Germans had been accustomed over previous decades 'to stand on the sidelines and to bow the knee in humility before other nations' superiority.'[21] Now his words found expression in a new manifestation of national pride: At last we can draw level with Great Britain, at last we can assert ourselves and see the German Empire acting as a great power, indeed as a world power! This dream of plebiscitary imperialism intensified each time the keel of a new battleship was laid down.

The reality was more prosaic. None of the objectives connected with the fleet building programme was attained: Great Britain countered the arms race Germany had set in motion by developing a new and far superior kind of battleship, so that the Germans were forced to raise the stakes again. In the First World War, in any case, the fleet would turn out to be largely worthless in military terms. It also caused a dramatic worsening of relations with Britain, which henceforth regarded Germany as its main future opponent and set about improving its poor relations with France and Russia. The hope that fleet-based imperialism would help to weaken the Social Democrats also came to nothing. The SPD made further gains in the elections of 1903.

The gigantic fleet-building programme also devastated the finances of the Reich, which were in any case chronically in deficit, because expenditure on the military budget had risen constantly for almost thirty years. This was the end of bourgeois 'gathering' (*Sammlung*), for although a reform of the finances, which would have involved introducing a modern tax on income and wealth, had been urgently needed for years, it met with emphatic resistance from all the possessing classes. It was one of the inescapable anachronisms of the later German Empire that this country, one of the most dynamic and modern in the world, did not possess a secure foundation for its tax revenues. Every new fleet-building programme, and every expansion of the land army, in an arms race which had now escalated considerably, increased the severity of this problem, which was only temporarily glossed over by imposing higher taxes on consumption, taking out loans, or employing special short-term measures.

For years, 'world policy', fleet-building and colonial policy had been the subjects of vehement criticism and no less vehement rebuttal. But the real truth about German imperialism only came into full view in the course of the year 1904, when two groups of indigenous inhabitants of German Southwest Africa, the Herero and the Nama, began an uprising against their German colonial masters, which soon spread, and in which the Africans at first enjoyed considerable success. There were several reasons for the rising, including the destruction of the local farmers' herds of cattle, the impoverishment associated with this and the dissolution of traditional social structures, but it was also a reaction to the forcible recruitment of a labour force for German companies and excesses committed by German settlers.

The government put down the rising with a 20,000-strong contingent of troops. The almost unbelievable brutality with which the German troops acted here against the insurgent tribes in the first war of the new German Empire stood in contradiction to the peaceful nature of Imperial German society, both internally and externally, as compared with other industrial countries. This contradiction at first appeared to be inexplicable. For the German troops did not limit themselves to the military defeat of the opponent. They conducted a veritable war of extermination, aimed at eradicating the insurgents, who were driven into the waterless Omaheke Desert, where most of them perished. More than 60,000 Herero lost their lives in this campaign, amounting to almost 80 per cent of the indigenous population.[22]

These actions clearly had several roots: the radicalisation of German nationalism, the associated racist feeling of superiority over the 'savages', the devastating impact on the troops of the Emperor's rabble-rousing speeches and a bourgeois public opinion intoxicated with ideas of world supremacy. In this case, a great power with colonial ambitions but without colonial experience was endeavouring to compensate for its uncertain grasp of the problems and obstacles that emerged by increasing the severity and brutality of its actions against 'indigenous' opponents. It was also characteristic of the prevailing mood that these gruesome atrocities only gained greater attention from the Reichstag when the mismanagement of the German colonial authorities became obvious and the financial burdens this commando action had placed on the imperial budget came under criticism.

When the Centre Party and the Social Democrats refused to vote for any further money to finance the struggle against the 'Hottentots', as the rebels were called in Germany, Chancellor Bülow felt that this was a favourable moment for action: he dissolved the Reichstag, ordered new elections and organised a campaign against the 'enemies of the Reich' (*Reichsfeinde*), whipping up nationalist and imperialist emotions to a pitch which outdid all previous election campaigns in ferocity. The new mass organisations of the nationalists could now be used as a powerful basis for agitation, headed by the Imperial League for the Fight against Social Democracy (*Reichsverband zur Bekämpfung der Sozialdemokratie*), which had been founded a few years earlier, along with the Navy League and the Colonial and Defence Leagues. The aim of this 'Hottentot election', as it was soon called, was to check the rise of the Social Democrats by winning over the masses, and at last to bestow upon the Chancellor what had been urgently needed since Bismarck's time: a stable parliamentary majority.

## Stability and Crisis

The fact that von Bülow's calculation was to a certain extent successful must be counted as one of the most decisive occurrences in the domestic politics of the late Empire. For the first time the 'state-supporting forces' had succeeded in reducing the voting strength of the Social Democrats and the number of deputies elected by them, even if the decline in support was slight and was the result above all of a high level of turnout and disadvantageous constituency boundaries. And yet, in conducting a consistently nationalist agitation against the Social Democrats the government seemed to have finally found an effective means of stopping their almost irresistible rise. An alliance between the conservatives, the National Liberals and the Left Liberals was now on offer as a basis for government policy. This was the so-called 'Bülow bloc', a new version of Bismarck's 'cartel', which was held together above all by imperialism and opposition to socialism.

But this alliance was not stable enough to provide the government with reliable and lasting support. The degree of domestic policy consensus uniting the parties that supported the Bülow government turned out in practice to be insufficient. The conservatives continued to obstruct any reform of the anachronistic three-class electoral law in Prussia, an urgently needed measure which was decades overdue. The desire for unity was not even strong enough to allow a minor reform of the finances, which was a long-running issue in German domestic politics. The fundamental question at issue was this: who ought to bear the cost of the massive rise in armaments expenditure? Excise duties hit everyone equally and therefore the better-off suffered less. The liberals advocated raising tax receipts by supplementing the traditional method of increasing excise duties with a very moderate inheritance tax and thus placing some of the burden on landowners. This was flatly rejected by the conservatives and the Agrarian League. The result was instead a new version of the 'black–blue' preventive majority, made up of the conservatives and the Centre Party, in other words 'the rule of clerics and Junkers', as the ancient historian and liberal Theodor Mommsen bitterly remarked.[23] The new majority made an agreement to take the inheritance tax plan off the table and increase excise duties still further. In addition, they invented a tax on securities and cheques, which did not hit landed property and bore for the most part on the bourgeoisie. With this, cooperation between the two liberal parties and the conservatives was at an end. Bülow resigned, having failed in almost all policy areas, both at home and abroad.

The collapse of the 'Bülow bloc' demonstrated the impracticability of the repeated attempts to find a broad basis in the Reichstag for the government's policy by including both conservatives and liberals. The political system itself was clearly to blame for this. The parties and factions in the Reichstag were not an integral part of the government's activities. They neither chose the government nor elected the Chancellor. As a result, they were also not compelled to enter into any compromises to show they were capable of ruling. Instead of this, it was expected that the parliamentary factions would vigorously and uncompromisingly uphold the interests of party members, electors and lobbyists, without considering the need to organise parliamentary majorities to achieve their goals.

Short-term political alliances could therefore be formed for specific purposes, but solid structures of political cooperation could not be constructed in this manner. Conservative-liberal cooperation was based on their common front against Social Democracy and their support for imperialism and strengthening German power. There was no common ground in relation to domestic reforms. On the contrary: after the failure of the financial reform and the collapse of the Bülow government, bourgeois criticism of the 'Prussian Junkers' became more acrimonious than ever.

The basis for cooperation between the conservatives and the Centre Party was no less fragile: the conservatives bent all their efforts towards preserving the status quo and they rejected all attempts to change the political, social and economic power relationships inherited from the past. They were particularly opposed to financial reforms, and to attempts to democratise the Prussian electoral law, limit the role of the monarch and reduce the dominant position of the Prussian nobility, the military and the top civil servants. The fundamental conservative attitude of resistance to any change did, it is true, often coincide with the position of the Centre Party, which aimed first and foremost to protect the traditional cultural and ethical norms of Catholicism from the transformative pressure exerted by the dynamic modernisation of those years. But no positive goals or reform projects ever emerged from this defensive alliance.

The liberals, on the other hand, and with them the middle classes, were in an ambiguous position. In domestic politics, they stood in fierce opposition to the black–blue alliance which was trying to block reform. But a parliamentary majority excluding the Centre Party and the conservatives would only have been possible with the support of the Social Democrats, and this hardly even entered into consideration. Cooperation with the SPD, which stood for social revolution and consistently rejected Germany's 'world policy', was unthinkable for most liberals. There were, admittedly, certain areas where this negative attitude had begun to crumble. In Baden, for instance, cooperation between liberals and Social Democrats, known as a front 'from Bassermann to Bebel', was actually established. But this approach could not be transferred to the national level, because cooperation with the Social Democrats over foreign and defence policy was absolutely out of the question for those liberals who enthusiastically supported nationalist 'world politics'.

The Social Democrats too were hardly ready for this sort of cooperation. They were subjected to unflinching hostility from many sides: from the Crown, the government, the other political parties, the nationalist associations, the employers' organisations and the overwhelming majority of the press. This had resulted in a sense of cohesion, and disconnection from the world outside, which made them regard 'solidarity' as the most valuable party quality. Even so, a number of different tendencies developed within their ranks. These can be classified, somewhat crudely, as Right, Left and Centre. The Right consisted above all of the leaders of the Free Trade Unions, which, with almost 3 million members, were far bigger than the party itself. Their chief concern was to improve the workers' situation in areas such as wages, working hours, social insurance and housing. A strong representation of the SPD in the Reichstag was an important requirement for achieving these trade union goals. More far-reaching political objectives, as envisaged in the party programme, such as the establishment of socialism after the collapse of the existing economic and social system, were of less interest to the trade union leaders.

A Left faction began to crystallise more clearly within the party after the turn of the century. For this group, the fierce hostility of the German government towards the SPD and the trade unions, as well as its nationalism, militarism and imperialism, were proof enough of the correctness of what Karl Marx and Friedrich Engels had predicted: fundamental change could not be achieved through reforms within the political system of the Empire. These views gained fresh impetus from the revolution of 1905 in Russia and the emergence of the left radical 'majority' faction of Russian Social Democracy (the 'Bolsheviki'). In Russia, 'revolution' was no longer merely the subject of theoretical discussion but had been placed on the agenda as political practice. The SPD was generally unclear about what revolution might look like in Germany. For some Social Democrats, it was seen as the winning of a parliamentary majority and a democratic transformation of state and society; for others, it was rather the French Revolution of 1789 or indeed the Paris Commune which supplied the model.

The Centrists, finally, who dominated the party leadership, occupied a middle position. They stood for a compromise, continuing to adhere to the revolutionary rhetoric of the party programme, with its martial ring, but in practice following a moderate reforming course, directed at parliamentary success and social and political advance. This inclusive approach—radical in theory, moderate in practice—was blatantly contradictory and great pains needed to be taken to bridge the conflicting positions within the party. The aim of the Centrists was to prevent Social Democracy from falling to pieces. It could easily be foreseen, however, that at times of crisis the party's precarious unity would not survive for long.[24]

In view of the inability of the parties to cooperate in any consistent way to achieve the government's political objectives, it was not surprising that the new Chancellor, von Bethmann-Hollweg, unlike his predecessor von Bülow, did not try to construct a new 'bloc', but hoped rather to assemble majorities on a case-by-case basis. He failed, however, the first time he tried to do something relatively significant, which was a renewed attempt to change the Prussian electoral law. The Prussian law of the time divided voters into three taxation classes. It was one of the most striking symbols of the pre-democratic conditions that prevailed in the biggest federal state. But the three-class system also operated in other parts of the Reich, in bourgeois Hamburg, for instance, because it corresponded with the liberal belief that only a person who was economically independent had the right to participate in politics.

The SPD gained almost a quarter of the votes cast in the Prussian elections of 1908, but it received only 1.5 per cent of the deputies in the Prussian Diet, whereas the German Conservatives, with 14 per cent of the vote, received more than a third of the seats. Chancellor von Bethmann-Hollweg did not want to change this state of affairs fundamentally, but he did want to make a symbolic offer to the bourgeoisie. He proposed that academically qualified citizens and long-serving officials (and army officers) should have their status raised slightly, and also that the third class should no longer comprise 82 per cent of the electors but only 76 per cent.

It was hardly surprising that a sham reform of this kind was greeted by a storm of protest. But the fact that the protests were largely organised by the Left Liberals, who had in the meantime united together to form the Progressive People's Party and were a factor of growing significance in the later Empire, indicates that certain shifts had taken place within the middle-class camp.

Numerous proclamations were made about electoral reform, signed by well-known personalities. According to one of them, issued in November 1909, 'the domination of the agrarian conservatives over Prussia, and thereby over Germany', as manifested in the three class suffrage, must finally be broken.[25]

The Social Democrats also organised big demonstrations, at which hundreds of thousands of their supporters protested against the Prussian electoral system. This sparked off a debate on fundamental principles in the party. The Left, represented above all by its leading member Rosa Luxemburg, called for the use of strikes in the future not only in disputes over wages and working conditions but for political goals as well. The political mass strike, according to Luxemburg, was an up-to-date instrument in the struggle to achieve the social revolution, and it promised success.[26]

The party leadership rejected this view, but the SPD's demonstrations and marches and the radical tone adopted by its left wing caused long-lasting apprehensions in both the bourgeois and conservative camps and further strengthened anti-Social Democratic feeling. On the issue of the franchise itself there was no progress at all. The conservatives refused to accept even the slightest change in the Prussian electoral system, and the bourgeois movement to reform the franchise gave up the fight, while the Chancellor withdrew his reform bill and thenceforth steered clear of proposing any legislation which was likely to meet with conservative opposition.

Was the German Empire still governable? Substantive reforms were clearly incapable of commanding a majority in the Reichstag, whether they related to the franchise, to financial policy, to the constitutional position of the Emperor and the parliament, or to Alsace-Lorraine. All attempts to alter the system were wrecked by the veto power of the forces that opposed them. The political system was manifestly no longer able either to give direction to the social, economic and cultural forces unleashed over the previous twenty-five years, or to control foreign policy, and it could no longer react appropriately to the immense changes that were transforming German society.

To offer a somewhat oversimplified synopsis, around 1910 in Germany there were three possible ways of emerging from this political stagnation:

1. The overwhelming majority of the German middle classes continued to consider the Empire to be the most successful sociopolitical formation in modern Europe, despite all its contradictions and blockages. The National Liberals, parts of the Centre Party and the Left Liberals therefore placed their faith in the prospect that the explosive force of social divisions could gradually be lessened, and the rise of the SPD curbed, by further rapid economic progress and the accompanying processes of social improvement, as well as by greater stress on social policy and a

successful 'world policy'. In this way, parliamentary control would gradually be exerted over the authoritarian constitutional system, though it would not necessarily be democratised. To achieve this, it was only necessary to make sure that there were no major cataclysms in political life and in social relations.

2. The conservatives, on the other hand, continued to flirt with the idea of an authoritarian regime, of the kind they had favoured ever since the 1870s, in which the Crown, the military, the nobility and the top-level officials (*Ministerialbeamten*) would recover their dominant position; the Reichstag would lose its authority; and an aggressive foreign policy would be pursued. In view of the relationship of forces that had arisen in the meantime, this programme could only be carried out with the help of a *coup d'état*, and would be opposed by the vast majority of the population. The prerequisites for the conservative approach were entirely absent in 1910.
3. The Social Democrats, finally, were theoretically in favour of revolution and socialism, but in practice supported parliamentarisation and reform. Behind this, however, lay two increasingly incompatible options: on the one hand the position of the Left, who looked forward to a crisis involving the intensification of the contradictions, which would lead to a breakdown of the whole system and a revolution on the model of Russia's 1905 revolution, which would establish either a democratic, parliamentary republic or a socialist republic. On the right wing of the SPD, on the other hand—and also among a section of the Left Liberals after the 1910 débâcle over the Prussian electoral law—increasing numbers of people held the view that any more far-reaching changes could only be achieved by a new majority, to be formed by an alliance between the bourgeoisie and the working class. To gain a majority in elections by this method would certainly take a considerable time, and it would also take time to propagate a readiness to choose such an option among both liberals and Social Democrats. Once this had been achieved, however, the parliamentary majority would be able to set in motion an accelerated process of internal transformation, which would finally lead to a democratic system of government and a smoothing out of social contradictions.

The Reichstag elections of 1912 appeared to confirm hopes and fears to an equal extent. The SPD, with almost 35 per cent of the vote, could celebrate a real triumph. The number of SPD deputies increased from 43 to 110, which meant that the party had obtained not only the largest number of votes, but also the largest number of seats and was now the biggest party group in the Reichstag. Now no parliamentary alliance could achieve a Reichstag majority without the Social Democrats, whether it was a black–blue *bloc* or a liberal–conservative coalition. But a Left Liberal and SPD majority continued to be as distant a prospect as before. Thus the SPD held an important position in parliament but was not strong enough to take the situation in hand itself. There was just one area where a parliamentary majority could be achieved without the Social Democrats: arms policy. In every other sphere, the government and the Reichstag had only a limited capacity to take action.

Within the SPD, the results of the 1912 elections confirmed the opinions of all those who had backed the idea that the party would obtain a parliamentary majority in the foreseeable future. Reichstag Deputy Gustav Noske, for instance, was certain of victory: 'You can almost calculate the day when we shall have behind us a majority of the German people', he proclaimed.[27] There was, in fact, every reason to make this prognosis, and the fury of the political Right was correspondingly great. If it was necessary to reckon with a Social Democratic majority at the latest after the next elections, due in 1917, all attempts to hold back the workers' party which remained within the context of the current constitutional system were manifestly in vain.

## Radical Nationalism

Considerations of this kind led to moves in the direction of a fourth option. Forces which were critical of the Chancellor for his readiness to make compromises, and demanded a radical break with the system, began to assert themselves increasingly on the Right after the 1912 elections. It was significant that the traditional boundary lines between the imperial government and the new mass nationalist movements now began to erode and the outlines of a new Right appeared above the horizon, one which advocated radical action against both Social Democracy and the cultural accompaniments of modernity, and favoured an overheated nationalism which now became *völkisch* (ethnic nationalist) at its periphery. According to the *völkisch* movement what characterised a German was no longer residence, culture or language, but descent. The targets of its agitation were firstly foreigners living in Germany, above all Polish seasonal workers; but it was also directed against a group of German citizens whom it intended to exclude in this way from the German people: the Jews.

Some weeks after the elections of January 1912, the leader of the Pan-German League, the Mainz lawyer Heinrich Claß, published a book under a pseudonym with the title 'If I were the Emperor'. This aroused considerable attention: in the course of two years it went through four editions.[28] In it he gathered together all the current sentiments and demands of the extreme Right. Arguing from the result of the 1912 Reichstag election—'the Jewish election' as he called it—he asserted that people of wealth and education in Germany felt threatened and disenfranchised and were disappointed by the government's policies. The tremendous economic boom of recent decades had led to the loss of a sense of belonging and attachment to the homeland. Industrialisation and urbanisation had made possible the rise of Social Democracy and weakened healthy popular energy. The rise of large-scale industry had destroyed the lower middle classes (*Mittelstand*). Habits of dissipation and luxury had penetrated into the upper social strata, while art was dominated by decadence and 'Americanisation'.

This jeremiad was in line with the widespread contemporary critique of modernity, but when Claß began to set out the reasons for these developments and to derive his own policy proposals, he went well beyond customary views. He viewed the entry of foreign seasonal workers into the rural districts of East Prussia and even into German industry as one of the reasons for the crisis, believing that the racial stock of Germans was in danger of being obliterated through interbreeding with these largely Polish workers. In addition, the Jews had played a fateful role in recent decades. The years of high industrialisation had been a 'great time' for the Jews, because 'their instincts and their mentality' were directed towards 'gain'. It was the Jews who 'with their lack of scruples, their avarice, and their indifference to right and wrong, honour and dishonour' had introduced 'the elements of haste, ruthlessness and immorality' into economic life. As a result, they dominated areas of activity which were particularly characteristic of the new industrial society, namely 'advertising, the theatre, journalism' and also 'the legal profession, the universities and medicine'.

It was already too late for the kind of moderate changes attempted by the government, he added. 'Only a catastrophe' could create the conditions for renewal: a great war was necessary to overcome the danger from within. If it ended in victory, a national Reichstag would be elected, and this would then institute a constitutional change whereby universal and equal suffrage would be abolished and replaced by a voting procedure which would privilege businessmen, big landed proprietors, high officials and the academically educated, as well as the commercial *Mittelstand*. If the outcome of the war was a defeat ('a possibility which will not terrify the brave, since a people of 65 million cannot be crushed entirely; this would only be a temporary misfortune') the present disruption would be intensified and turn into chaos 'which can only be restored to order by the powerful will of a dictator.'

If a war does not occur 'we shall have to stick it out, and seek the assistance of a coup d'état'. It would in any case be necessary to suppress Social Democracy, expel all socialist agitators from the country, destroy the trade unions and prohibit the non-nationalist press, but, most of all, drastic measures against the Jews would be needed. All Jews in Germany would have to be regarded as foreigners in a legal sense and they would be made to pay taxes at a double rate. Further Jewish immigration would need to be prevented, and descent not religion would be the decisive factor here. Jews would be excluded from taking public office, doing military service or pursuing the professions of lawyer, teacher or theatre director, and they must also, according to Claß, be deprived of the franchise.

All the elements of the revolt against the political and cultural effects of modernity came together in the anti-Semitism propagated here. Not without reason, the Jews were regarded as having been particularly successful in meeting the challenges of the new epoch. Proportionately more of them belonged to the bourgeoisie, they were particularly keen on education, and like most religious or ethnic minorities they were highly successful and very focused on social advancement. In 1901, 7.3 per cent of non-Jewish children in Prussia achieved an educational qualification above the elementary level, whereas for Jewish children the figure was 56.3 per cent. At the turn of the century, the Jews were extremely well-represented in the modern industrial economy, the banking system and the academic professions. Their average income was roughly five times as high as that of non-Jewish Germans. Those Jews who were not religiously oriented had hardly any connection with pre-modern traditions, and it was easier for them to find their bearings in the new situation than it was for many non-Jewish Germans, especially members of the *Bildungsbürgertum*, who tended to look to the past. For the anti-Semites, the Jews were a combination of all their aversions and their anxieties, and they ascribed whatever phenomena of modernity they regarded as negative to the activities of this very small minority.[29]

In its mixture of radical nationalism, anti-Semitism, anti-socialism and anti-liberalism, as well as the way it gravitated towards war and *coup d'état*, the Mainz lawyer's pamphlet was an outline indication of the programme of the New Right. This movement had begun to crystallise since the late 1890s with the formation of mass nationalist organisations in which the Pan-German League acted as a kind of coordinating centre. There were also *Mittelstand* associations. These joined together after the Reichstag election to form the League of the Reich German *Mittelstand* (*Reichsdeutscher Mittelstandsverein*). This in its turn played a leading part in the foundation of the 'Cartel of the Productive Estates' (*Kartell der schaffenden Stände*), in which the Agrarian League, the Central Association of German Industrialists (*Centralverband Deutscher Industrieller*) and the Association of Christian Peasant Leagues (*Vereinigung Christlicher Bauernvereine*) joined together for the 'protection of national labour' and the fight against Social Democracy. The camp of the New Right also included many student associations (*Burschenschaften*), which had refused to admit Jewish students to their ranks for many years, and various new and old anti-Semitic groups such as the German League (*Deutschbund*), the Wagner Clubs, the Gobineau Associations and the Imperial Hammer League (*Reichshammerbund*). The membership of these radically anti-Jewish associations was not large, but thanks to their links with the mass organisations and the conservative parties their ideas enjoyed a definite degree of support.

With the arrival of these groups, a new element stepped forth onto the political stage, and its importance constantly increased. Unlike the conservatives, these groups took no account of the imperial government or the Chancellor, and they advocated an uncompromising course towards war with no concern for diplomatic negotiations.[30]

## Before the War

A paradigm shift had taken place in the foreign affairs of Europe since the turn of the century. By building the fleet and pushing forward with 'world policy', the German Empire had placed itself in a position of antagonism towards Great Britain, the sole real world power at that time, without the backing of a strong alliance. In the years that followed, this antagonism dominated the course of events in Europe. Britain reacted to the German challenge by settling its disputes with France and Russia, and in less than five years it developed its ties with both those powers into an alliance which, though informal, was so solid that it forced Germany into the isolation it had itself set in motion earlier and now regarded as 'encirclement'. Moreover, Britain showed that it was still well able to maintain its lead in the arms race fuelled by Germany's naval policy, despite Berlin's expectations. The worsening of foreign policy tensions also led to an intensification of anti-German nationalism in England and anti-English nationalism in Germany. This process stirred up emotions which in turn made it increasingly difficult to pursue a foreign policy aimed at compromise.[31]

Even so, there is no direct line of development leading from here to the outbreak of war in the summer of 1914. On the contrary, the system of crisis management by the great powers, which had already made possible the maintenance of European peace throughout a period of forty years, continued to prove its worth. Every successfully defused regional conflict was taken as further proof that the foreign policy system was functioning. The system did, it is true, have one problematic aspect: the ability of the participating states to achieve their aims in these conflicts depended on how long they were prepared to bear the risk of war before the opposing side gave in. That gave rise to the danger that, at some point, the opportunity to withdraw at the last moment would be missed, with devastating consequences.[32]

Moreover, on the German side there was as little sign of a straightforward foreign policy as there was of a clear definition of the country's interests. Germany's focus seemed to be not so much on *being* a great power as on *behaving* like one. By indulging in acts of self-assertion and threats of force Germany strengthened the impression gained by the other European powers that it was aiming at world power and hegemony.

Even so, the final break came about not in Germany but in Austria-Hungary. In 1908 the latter country had annexed Bosnia and Herzegovina. A conflict between the Tsarist Empire and the Danube monarchy had long been smouldering in the Balkans on account of the Slavs who lived there. Matters became more urgent when Russia, which had suffered a severe military defeat at the hands of Japan in the autumn of 1905, directed its expansionist aims back to the west, particularly to the Balkans. The Austro-Hungarian thrust towards Bosnia and Herzegovina therefore threatened to precipitate a war with Serbia and Russia. Ultimately, this could only be avoided by Germany's decisive intervention on behalf of its alliance partner Austria-Hungary. The Germans thereby placed Russia under considerable diplomatic pressure, which compelled Serbia in turn to beat a retreat. But Germany's move was risky, because it could have led to a war with those two countries. Russia in fact recoiled from choosing such a path, and the German leadership's manoeuvre had a successful outcome. But at what a cost! Russo-German relations deteriorated, French and British fears that Germany was seeking to assert its hegemony increased yet further and as a result the political isolation of the German Empire was made even worse.[33]

Germany's attempt to isolate France and attack its colonial policy was likewise a move both risky and contradictory. In 1905, in order to weaken the Anglo-French alliance, Chancellor von Bülow staged a crisis in Morocco, the sole outcome of which was that the alliance became stronger. Six years later, the adventure was repeated by Secretary of State Kiderlen. Germany again intervened powerfully against France's advance into Morocco, admittedly with the goal of eventually accepting French control of the country if France handed over certain colonial areas in another part of Africa in compensation. One aim was to fulfil the considerable expectations of the German public, which was pressing for an extension of Germany's 'world policy' and the acquisition of further overseas possessions. But Germany itself had no substantial interests whatsoever in Morocco. The dispatch of a gunboat to Agadir in 1911 was intended to underline Germany's claims militarily and to force France to give way. But, in actual fact, and against Germany's intentions, a serious conflict very rapidly developed out of this which conjured up the spectre of a European war after Great Britain had placed itself entirely on France's side.

The results of Kiderlen's policy stroke, which had taken much effort to stage, were exceedingly meagre: France offered the German Empire an exchange of

African possessions—Togoland for parts of the Congo—and received in return a free hand in Morocco. Once again, a German thrust had strengthened the Anglo-French alliance and increased suspicion of Germany's foreign policy objectives.

The impact of these events on domestic politics was even more fateful. Expectations were already great, and the action taken by the Foreign Office and the Chancellor raised them still further. When the result of the negotiations became known, the feeling of disappointment fed into a storm of protest by all political forces, with the exception of the Social Democrats, against the allegedly weak-kneed policies of the government. The frustration of the colonial enthusiasts was vented in furious attacks on the 'arrogant' British Empire ('perfidious Albion') and they loudly expressed their readiness to accept even the grave risk of a war so as to ensure Germany's 'international standing'. It ought no longer to be accepted in future, wrote the chairman of the National Liberals, Bassermann, to the State Secretary for Foreign Affairs, that

> doors are slammed in the face of the Germans by our world market competitors in areas which are still free. This must drive a nation like Germany, which has to expand if it is not to drown in its own population surplus, into a position where finally war is the only remaining option, as the last resort.[34]

This mood of nationalist exasperation reduced the government's room for manoeuvre in foreign policy yet further, though in view of the threatening situation it endeavoured to smooth relations with Great Britain to a certain extent. In particular, it decided to pursue any further overseas expansion only in consultation with London. This augured well for a future agreement, but despite this, the discussions on disarmament and détente were unsuccessful. Germany was not prepared to limit its armaments to any substantial degree, and Britain was not prepared to give Germany a solid assurance that it would remain neutral if a conflict occurred, because it did not want to give the German Empire a free hand for a policy of hegemony over the Continent.

The failure of these negotiations gave the hardliners on the Right a further stimulus. The Pan-German League, for instance, now openly put forward the idea that the German Empire would have to fight for its 'place in the sun', by force of arms if necessary. It was pointed out again and again in this context that the German Empire could never have been founded in 1871 without victory in the wars against Denmark, Austria and France. In the spring of 1912 Friedrich von Bernhardi, a writer on military matters who was widely read at the time, had the following to say: 'We fought and struggled in earlier great wars for our national unification and at the same time for our position as a European power. Today we stand before a greater decision, as to whether we will also develop into a world power.' War, he continued, is 'the basis of all healthy development' and, in that sense, it is 'not only a biological necessity but also an ethical imperative and as such an indispensable element of civilisation.' In relation to the present situation, he drew the conclusion that 'there is no way in which we can avoid a war for world power, and what is important here is not to postpone it as long as possible but to bring it about under the most favourable possible circumstances.'

This was also how the conservative press saw the situation. As *Die Post* wrote on 26 August 1911: 'There is a widespread conviction that a war can only be advantageous, because it will clarify our precarious political situation and have a healing effect on many political and social conditions.' A hostile interjection made during a speech to the Reichstag by the chair of the SPD, August Bebel, when the Morocco crisis was being debated summarised this attitude in pointed fashion: 'Things get better after every war!'[35]

Between 1912 and 1914 the international atmosphere deteriorated dramatically. This was primarily the result of three factors: first, competition between the imperialist powers, the focus of which was increasingly shifting from overseas territories to the European continent; second, the effects of nationalism, which was destabilising the supranational empires of Central and Eastern Europe, thereby bringing about an explosive situation in the Balkans in particular; and third, the arms race, which, apart from increasing foreign policy tensions, also had an impact on the development of domestic politics. The governments of Great Britain and Germany both tried to work against these tendencies and end the resulting crises by compromise and agreement, so as to avoid a European war. But their attempts proved to be half-hearted and inadequate.

The crisis in the Balkans began to escalate when a number of small states, including Serbia, reacted to the disintegration of the Ottoman Empire by forming an alliance to rob Turkey of her remaining European possessions. The alliance partners declared war on Turkey in October 1912 and quickly overran almost the whole area they coveted. Austria-Hungary regarded the rise of Serbia as a danger to its own possessions in the Balkans, because it gave added impetus to the endeavours of the South Slavs to secure their national unification. The conflict between the two quickly escalated when Russia gave her support to Serbia, and there was a danger that it would result in a full-scale war.

Anglo-German crisis management again prevented this from happening. Even so, during the crisis Germany confirmed that it would fulfil its alliance duties in case of an attack on Austria-Hungary, while Britain made the same statement about France. The German war party in turn saw this as a demonstration that the attempted *rapprochement* with Britain had failed, and the General Staff (*Heeresleitung*) was asked to examine the chances of success in a preventive war. The chief of the General Staff, Helmuth von Moltke, himself regarded war as unavoidable and pressed for an early start because Germany's prospects would worsen as time went on in view of increasing Russian military strength: 'The sooner, the better' he averred. On the other hand, the head of the Imperial Naval Office (*Reichsmarineamt*), von Tirpitz, called for 'the great fight' to be 'postponed for eighteen months' because the fleet was not yet ready for combat.[36] This meeting had no direct consequences, but the record makes it clear that the military leadership had now moved to a unanimous position in favour of war, and it shows the internal pressure the government was under in conducting its foreign policy.

Shortly after this, there was a new armed confrontation between the victorious Balkan states over the spoils of the previous war. In this second Balkan war, Bulgaria was defeated and Serbia was able to expand its territory still further. It is true that the German government was able once more to prevent an Austrian intervention and to localise the crisis. But it proved increasingly difficult to work with the traditional methods of great power diplomacy against crises exacerbated by the dynamic force of South-East European nationalism, and the only way of achieving success would have been through joint action by all the great powers. The crises themselves, however, tended to increase antagonisms between the two blocs, particularly between Russia on one side and Austria-Hungary and Germany on the other.

Between Germany and Great Britain, in contrast, a compromise seemed possible in the long run. But moves towards reconciliation were thwarted by the constant rivalry over armaments. In June 1913, the Reichstag voted to increase Germany's military strength by 136,000 men. This was a reaction to the Russian decision to increase its peacetime military establishment. France replied by reintroducing a three-year period of military service. At the same time, weapons systems were being modernised everywhere and strategic plans were being brought up to date.

In addition to this, there was a further upsurge of nationalism. In Germany, it was chiefly anti-Russian feeling which increased. By spring 1914 it had reached almost hysterical levels. The German government, for its part, placed its faith in improved relations with Great Britain, though it came up against increasing resistance from the military men, who were openly demanding a preventive war against Russia. Chancellor von Bethmann-Hollweg was keen to achieve a compromise with the British. But, when it became known that Britain and Russia had made a secret agreement for joint naval operations in case of a war with Germany, his position was shaken, and von Moltke's advocacy of a preventive war gained further ground. In this situation, wrote Bethmann on 16 June to the British Prime Minister, 'any kind of conflict of interests between Russia and Austria-Hungary, even a quite insignificant one, may ignite the torch of war.'[37]

Two weeks later, on 28 June 1914, that is exactly what happened. The heir to the Austrian throne, the Archduke Franz Ferdinand, and his wife, were shot by Serbian nationalists. This happened in Sarajevo, the San Andreas Fault of European power politics, the boundary between the Western European and Slav worlds, the point at which the nationalisms of the Balkan peoples and the spheres of influence of the Austro-Hungarian and Russian Empires collided. To that extent, it was not an accident that this political murder triggered the First World War; the initial explosion took place at the most dangerous location in Europe.

It was assumed in Austria that the Serbian government was involved in the assassination. That view was not without justification, as it later turned out. And since Serbia, which had grown into a regional power through its victories in the Balkan Wars, supported the independence aspirations of the Slav peoples living in the Imperial and Royal Austrian monarchy, Vienna now appeared to have been given an opportunity to extinguish this source of mischief either politically or militarily. The Danubian Monarchy was in danger of collapsing, and it was calculated that action against Serbia would strengthen it internally and externally, as well as weakening Russia, Serbia's protector. In pursuing these goals, Vienna received support from Berlin, without which a conflict with Serbia was unthinkable.

The German government's thinking was similar: Russia's aggressive foreign policy, its economic strength, its armaments and not least its rapidly increasing population had led in Berlin to an enormous strengthening of the belief that Russia posed a threat. Moreover, the alliance system between Great Britain, France and Russia continued to convey the feeling of isolation and 'encirclement' which had determined German foreign policy since 1904 at least.

After its experiences with the crises of previous years, the German leadership endeavoured once again to profit from the situation, but not to let the crisis escalate into a war. That method had succeeded in 1908 and 1912, so why should it not function in the same way this time? Bethmann-Hollweg's ostensible aims were to defeat Serbia, to weaken Russia, to inflict a diplomatic defeat on the alliance system of the 'Triple Entente' so as to loosen it, or indeed dissolve it altogether, and to strengthen Austria-Hungary, Germany's sole remaining alliance partner. But the German government was also under domestic pressure to achieve a success, because the war party was now openly calling for a preventive war, which must be fought while Germany still had the military and economic advantage over Russia.

In formulating his strategy, the Chancellor had also reckoned with the possibility of failure. It was not that he desired war, or worked deliberately towards it, as has long been assumed. But if necessary—if Russia did *not* give way to German pressure, if the Triple Entente was *not* weakened, if England and France did *not* pull back there would be nothing for it but to go to war. The above list of conditions itself shows the risk Bethmann was prepared to take. The German leadership did not possess the kind of strategy aimed at the unconditional preservation of peace which might perhaps have involved placating Austria, making a settlement with Russia and seeking a compromise with Britain. In the German view, an alternative course of this kind simply did not exist. It would have called into question the status of the German Empire as a great power, put a stop to its world political ambitions, and weakened, or perhaps even destroyed, the foundations of its policy of strength, expansion and aggrandisement. In the intellectual universe of the political leaders, such an outcome was inconceivable. Moreover, there was a widespread tendency to think in terms of victory or capitulation, and to determine questions of foreign policy by characterizing outcomes in terms such as honour and disgrace, pride and shame. Germany, it was thought, had a right to a position of hegemony over the European continent, indeed it had a right to be a world power alongside Britain, because of its achievements, its greatness and its importance. This claim was under question by envious neighbours; Germany had therefore to fight for its place or lose its right to the respect of the world.

Such were the surrounding circumstances when the news of the Sarajevo murder reached Vienna. After that, events followed in rapid succession: the Vienna government wanted to make an example of Serbia, and it was powerfully supported in this by the German Empire. Austria-Hungary thereupon formulated an 'unacceptable' ultimatum to Serbia. The Serbs unexpectedly accepted most of its terms, but Vienna broke off diplomatic relations with Belgrade in any case. Serbia then mobilised its army. The German government rejected British mediation proposals and also refrained from exerting a calming influence on Austria-Hungary, which was the only way in which the Vienna government could have been persuaded to change its mind. On 28 July, Austria-Hungary declared war on Serbia.

What it had been possible to avoid in previous crises had now taken place. And whereas the German leadership had, until then, followed the line that the crisis should only be taken up to the threshold of war and used for Germany's advantage, while war itself was to be avoided if at all possible, its aim now was different: to present the outbreak of war, which could clearly no longer be prevented, as a result of Russian policy, and thus to make it appear as if Germany were defending itself against a Russian attack. In relation to the Entente powers this did not succeed, but at home the strategy was effective, in that a large part of the German population regarded Russia as the aggressor, especially when on 30 July the Russian government began to mobilise. Thus, the firm conviction spread in Germany that the war was the result of a plot long prepared against the country by the Entente, and in particular by Great Britain.[38]

Germany's declaration of war on Russia on 1 August was followed within a few days by declarations of war by the other powers involved. From that point onwards, the course of events was determined by military considerations.

The European security system had preserved the peace for almost fifty years. What were the reasons for its failure? There are four points to be made here.

1) There was no longer a functioning system by which different international interests were balanced against each other. The connection between Great Britain and Germany, which until then had helped to prevent dangerous regional conflicts from exploding, although often only at the last minute, had been destroyed by the increasing rivalry between the two powers. On the contrary, the long history of successful crisis management now promoted a tendency to take risks, so as not to be the first to be forced to give way.

2) Most of the military men still thought the results of a European war could be calculated in advance. On both sides, people thought in terms defined by the previous war, as is always the case with armed conflict: they looked back to the wars of German unification or the colonial wars of the late nineteenth and early twentieth centuries. Many people believed that the war would be short, if only because modern industrial economies could not withstand long wars. The war would have a clear victor, and the distribution of power in Europe would be re-adjusted.[39] But the American Civil War, the Crimean War and the Russo-Japanese War had already shown what a modern, mechanised war looked like. These wars had also shown that the number of victims would be far higher than in previous wars, and that the war would also affect the civilian population.

The chief of the German General Staff, von Moltke, who had insistently called for a preventive war for years, did not attempt to conceal that the impending war would be

> a people's war, which will not be settled with a decisive battle, but will be a long, wearisome struggle with a country which will not be overcome until the whole strength of its people has been broken, and which will exhaust our own people to the uttermost, even if we are the victors.

In the coming 'world war' Europe would 'tear itself apart' and 'the civilisation of almost the whole of Europe' would be destroyed 'for decades.'[40] Such prophecies were not believed, and they did not terrify people. No one had yet had burned into their consciousness the fact that world war would be a frightful experience with millions of dead and the use of weapons of mass destruction, as a result of which the risk of the victor's own annihilation would be so great that it no longer seemed possible to wage war. Experiences of this kind, and of the Second World War to follow, proved sufficiently salutary to prevent the Cold War from bursting into flames, on the occasion, for instance, of the crises over Berlin or

Cuba. This explains why the actions of the governments of the European great powers before 1914, particularly the governments of Germany and Austria-Hungary, appear so frivolous in retrospect.

3) In 1914, domestic factors determined the shape of foreign policy and also the conduct of war to a much greater extent than had been the case in the nineteenth century. Governments, monarchs and military leaders no longer had an absolute say in these matters. They were closely tied to the newly emerging mass movements, the most powerful of which turned out to be nationalism. And where rulers joined up with nationalist movements, the chances of restricting their dynamism were reduced almost to nil. The rapidly growing importance of the mass media, the politicisation of public associations, and the increasing impact of parties and leagues on politics and public opinion bestowed much greater foreign policy influence upon those who knew how to direct and accelerate such currents. This trend occurred in all the industrialised countries of Europe, and it was most strongly present where the impulse towards modernisation was at its most powerful.

4) Although the dynamic of change since the end of the nineteenth century should be seen as a factor in the movement towards war, it must not be forgotten that war was itself regarded by at least one strand of public opinion as an exit from modernity, as a response to its challenge. In Germany at least, the Right, represented most strongly by the Pan-Germans, hoped that a war would confirm or resuscitate their favoured proposal for a return to an ordered society, which was to rid the country of the damaging cultural effects of the new age, effects which included everything from socialism to urbanism to modern art, and to move to a new social structure in which industry, science and modern technology would be combined with authoritarian rule, a traditional social order and conceptions of culture and morality handed down from the past. The cry 'Things get better after every war' therefore applied not just to the foreign policy arena but to the situation within the country as a whole.

# 3
# The Power of War

## The War Begins

A war on two fronts against an alliance of three great powers was exactly what the government in Berlin had always wanted to avoid. Now, exactly that had transpired. Moreover, the starting conditions were difficult. Germany's most important alliance partner, Austria-Hungary, was regarded as weak, and her other allies, Italy and Romania, did not even enter the war at first. This itself was a reason why Germany had to risk everything to arrive at a military decision before the structural superiority of the Entente took effect on the battlefield. When the war started, the Central Powers and the Entente each had roughly 3 million soldiers at their disposal. By the summer of 1918, however, the proportions were different: the Central Powers, including the Ottoman Empire, which entered the conflict in October 1914, had mobilised roughly 19 million soldiers, whereas the Entente had been able to mobilise almost 37 million.[1]

It was not just for military reasons that a short war was considered a necessity; political and economic motives also played a part. Politicians as well as businessmen were convinced that the German economy could not survive a long war without suffering lasting damage. This also applied to the world economy, through which the wartime opponents were bound together in many ways. But the greatest fear of the German leadership, particularly the Chancellor, Theodor von Bethmann-Hollweg, who had been in office since 1909, was that the internal situation of the German Empire, which was precarious in any case, would become highly unstable if the war lasted a long time and did not end with a German victory. There were many reasons for anxiety: the fear of internal disturbances if things started to go badly at the front, the fear of civil war, and even the fear that the government would be forced into making reforms at home. These would all remain important considerations, constantly operating on German military and domestic policy throughout the war.[2]

German military strategy had already been worked out decades earlier. It had been moulded by two requirements: the need to avoid a two-front war, in the East and the West, and the need to seek a quick decision. The war plan developed many years before 1914 by the chief of the German General Staff, Count Alfred von Schlieffen, aimed to ensure that Germany would mobilise much more quickly than Russia. As a result, time would be gained, and this would allow the whole of the army to be engaged first in the west, and then in the east. But in order to bypass the strong French fortifications on the German border, von Schlieffen wanted to attack France not from the east but from the north, after the German army had passed through Belgium. In this way, the French army would be defeated in a gigantic battle of encirclement and Paris would quickly be seized. While this was happening, only weak German units would remain in the east, where they would ward off any Russian advance. Then, after the victory in the west, they would join up with the main bulk of the army and attack and defeat the Russians. Von Schlieffen's successor, von Moltke, had, it is true, repeatedly modified this plan, but its fundamental character remained the same, even though it involved violating the neutrality of Belgium, an act which would almost certainly bring Great Britain into the war.

But most of the assumptions behind the Schlieffen Plan turned out to be entirely mistaken. Russia's troops did not require weeks and months to be mobilised but only a matter of days; Austria's troops were not strong enough to beat off Russia's units in Galicia; and, above all, it soon appeared that, thanks to advances in military technology, particularly the new rapid-firing weapon, the machine gun, as well as heavy artillery and the howitzer, the military advantage no longer lay with the attacker: it had shifted to the defender.[3]

Thus Germany's military leaders were under enormous time pressure from the outset. Belgium refused to give the German army the right to pass through its territory unmolested; on the contrary, the Belgians strongly resisted the first German onslaught. The conquest of Liège in particular was delayed, which threatened to bring the whole advance to a halt. In the German army, this resistance was blamed on the activities of armed Belgian civilians, the '*francs-tireurs*' they had learned to know and fear in the war of 1870–1 against France. As time went by, these suspicions turned out to be almost entirely unjustified, but the fear of Belgian sharp-shooters grew into a veritable hysteria. Army commanders issued orders to use the utmost severity against even the slightest sign of resistance from the civilian population of Belgium, since any other course would endanger the success of the planned invasion of France. The consequence of this, it has been estimated, was that brutal excesses were committed against over 5,000 Belgian civilians. The German army also destroyed large parts of the city of Louvain, including its renowned library. The German leadership was discredited by these wartime atrocities. Great Britain, which had after all based its decision to enter the war on Germany's attack on Belgium, now felt itself vindicated. From then on, Britain fought the war against Germany under the watchword of a struggle of freedom against barbarism.[4]

In the east, too, the strategy of the Central Powers proved to be problematic. Thanks to the Russians' rapid mobilisation, weak detachments of German troops were faced with two Russian armies of more than 600,000 soldiers. They overran German positions and invaded East Prussia. On the southern front, too, the Russian army demonstrated its superiority to the Austrians and Hungarians and penetrated deep into Austrian Galicia. Two German army corps therefore had to be sent from the Western Front to the east in order to strengthen the Central Powers' forces there. In addition, General Ludendorff, a particularly energetic and ruthless military leader, was transferred to the east, where he assumed command of the army, together with the higher ranking General von Hindenburg, who had been brought out of retirement. By the end of August, the German units were in a position first to defeat the Russian armies near Tannenberg and then a few days later to defeat them at the battle of the Masurian Lakes, and to expel them from German territory.

There was a great sense of relief over this victory. The confidence in final success which had generally been felt at the start of the war now seemed to be justified once again. General von Hindenburg was celebrated as the victor of Tannenberg and the saviour of the Reich. Parents named their children after him, and big wooden statues of Hindenburg were erected in towns and villages. Nails could be driven into these statues, in exchange for donations to the Red Cross. While the reputation of Emperor William II declined, and he was increasingly forced into the background, Hindenburg gained in charisma and authority.[5]

In the west, too, the German army was now advancing on all fronts, and it soon penetrated a long way into French territory. It proved strong enough to force its opponents to retreat, but not sufficiently strong to win a decisive victory. Moreover, it became apparent that, because the front now extended over a great distance, it was almost impossible to coordinate the five advancing Army Groups with the means of communication then available, and the leaders of each Army Group were increasingly left to their own devices. The German forces failed to achieve their intention of surrounding and destroying the French and British formations from the west and then encircling Paris. The First Army, which was on the right wing, was therefore ordered to cease its advance westwards and turn directly towards Paris instead. This marked the practical abandonment of the Schlieffen Plan.

The German formations had reached the area between the rivers Aisne and Marne, and their spearheads were only 60 kilometres from Paris when on 5 September the commander-in-chief of the French forces, General Joffre, ordered the counter-attack which led to the Battle of the Marne. After four days, the Germans were forced to withdraw behind a secure line further north, along the banks of the river Aisne. The German offensive had thus been brought to a standstill. Further thrusts were made in the area of Rheims and Soissons in the weeks that followed, but they brought no success to the German troops;

the attempt to take Ypres, in the west of Belgium, and to defeat the British Expeditionary Corps stationed there, was equally unsuccessful. On 15 November, German troops finally reached the Channel coast near Nieuport. Both sides now began to secure the positions they had reached, and to fortify them with an almost impregnable system of trenches, barbed wire obstacles and artillery emplacements. After that, the whole of the Western Front became static, along a length of more than 700 kilometres. For almost four years, the war in the west would be conducted solely on this narrow strip of land stretching from the North Sea to the hills of the Vosges.

After four months, there was no more talk of a quick victory or any suggestion that Germany's troops would be back home before Christmas. It was true that the German armies in the west were deep in enemy territory, but the failure of Germany's military strategy was unmistakable. Nevertheless, the reports from the war fronts that reached the public told only of victory, and the confidence of the population remained unshaken. But this divorce between reality and propaganda, between the real situation and the popular mood, contained hidden dangers. Popular expectations of success continued to rise, and this increasingly deprived the German government of the political room for manoeuvre which would have allowed it to end the war without securing a triumphant victory.

## The Spirit and Ideas of 1914

The beginning of the war in August 1914 was accompanied by tempestuous manifestations of patriotism in Germany, as indeed in all the countries which participated in the fighting. The jubilant words inscribed on the wagons of the departing troop trains are themselves an indication of the exuberant overconfidence of the time: '*Ist Frankreich erledigt, wird den Russen gepredigt!*' ('We'll finish the French, then we'll start on the Russians'). The widespread sense of unity in face of a war that seemed to have been forced upon the nation frequently degenerated into frenzied war hysteria.[6]

The German government's strategy of portraying the Reich as the innocent victim of an attack thus succeeded in convincing a large part of the population. 'Envious people have forced us into justified self-defence. They are pressing the sword into our hands', proclaimed the Emperor on 31 July from the balcony of Berlin Castle. And a Darmstadt schoolboy formulated the same idea in a German language essay written in August: 'The world conflagration has been caused by the hatred, envy and vindictiveness of our foes . . . Our cause is a just one before God. We did not want a war.'[7]

Enthusiasm for the war was particularly prevalent among middle-class youth. Indeed it was almost alarming. More than 180,000 young men, many of them students at high school and university, volunteered for military service. This was more than the military authorities were in a position to register and train. The *Wandervögel* generation and the German youth movement regarded the war as an opportunity to experience an 'overwhelming, intoxicating adventure' and to break out of the tedious conventionality of everyday life. The poet Ina Seidel wrote these verses at the start of the war, under the title 'German Youth 1914':

We knew not why we flourished
Youth seemed a curse and a bore,
A feast which did not nourish—
One drank—one left—and nothing more.
Our blood coursed so thick and heavy
And we tired of firing blanks
The paths we followed were too level
And we had no reason to give thanks
That is why we celebrate
While the drums rumble and exhilarate
That is why we are drunk without wine
O to be young and let the sun shine![8]

During the war, versification became a veritable passion among the young, and it is estimated that more than a million war poems had been written by 1918. The end of a self-satisfied, boring and unheroic age was celebrated in verses like Seidel's, as well as the lived experience of comradeship, injury, heroism and death and the search for grand, uncomplicated feelings.

But jubilation over the war was not universal. It was more a feature of the towns than the countryside, it was expressed more vociferously by middle-class people than by workers and peasants, and the young felt it more powerfully than the old. In the working-class quarters of the big industrial cities, the war was greeted with scepticism and uneasiness, according to police reports on the popular mood. 'A heavy feeling of sorrow has taken hold of many of our peasant families, because fathers who often have very many children must leave home, their sons, horses and carts are required by the military authorities, and the harvest is still waiting', wrote the *Münchener Neueste Nachrichten* on 4 August 1914. Manifestations of patriotic enthusiasm for the war were countered by the SPD's large-scale anti-war demonstrations, which took place all over the country. In Berlin, almost 100,000 people took part in a prohibited peace demonstration held on 28 July in Treptow Park. In the summer of 1914, pacifism was a powerful force in Germany, as it was in France as well. But its influence clearly declined when mobilisation started. German propaganda against Tsarist Russia met with widespread agreement.

The warlike hysteria of the time was combined, particularly in the bourgeoisie, with the hope and expectation that the manifold contradictory challenges of the modern epoch would fade into the background in the face of the impending struggle for existence, that decades of disagreement about what kind of internal organisation Germany should have would come to an end, and that all social, political and religious antagonisms would vanish. These hopes found expression in the Emperor's speech of 1 August: 'I no longer see any parties or different religions; today we Germans are all brothers and nothing but brothers.'[9]

Soon, however, these patriotic declarations went one step further, raising more fundamental questions. They moved on from rejection of what were seen as unjust reproaches from abroad to an assertion of Germany's moral, political, military and economic superiority. A lecture by the legal historian and scholar Otto von Gierke, who spoke in September 1914 about the purpose and meaning of the war, may serve as an example of innumerable proclamations of this kind. For Gierke, as for many others, the point of departure was the war of 1870–1. That war had made Germany united, great, strong and rich. But those successes had been put at risk in many ways: by party conflicts, by the special interests of capital and labour, and by the 'excessive admiration of what is alien' which the renown of the French Revolution had given rise to. Above all though, Germany had lost its moral strength by 'overrating material possessions', by 'an unhealthy thirst for pleasure which had choked off the healthy joy of living', by 'frivolity and sensuality', by 'increasingly lax moral principles as regards relations between the sexes', and by the abandonment of God and religion. Now, in August 1914, a splendid miracle had happened: the magnificent upsurge of the German people's soul in response to the war which the country had been forced to fight. 'All our divisions, all our party quarrels, all our petty selfishnesses' now lay in the past. Everyone now had the feeling of being a part of the whole, never before had a people felt one with the state like this, never had it trusted its leadership so unwaveringly. A victorious end to the war would therefore mean the 'rule of a rejuvenated German culture'. The new state and the German legal order guaranteed by it would be strengthened, as would the monarchy. The military spirit of the state and the 'severe discipline' of its institutions would be confirmed. Faced with the democratic republic favoured by the French and the 'shadow monarchy under the yoke of a parliament' favoured by the British, the popular character (*Volkstümlichkeit*) of the German constitutional and legal system, with its bond between the monarchy and the people's freedom, would prove to be superior. Once Germany had secured a victorious peace, this would signify to the outside world 'the unleashing' of Germany's 'world-conquering strength'. But most importantly, morality would again become the cornerstone of German life:

> German culture is moral culture. Its superiority is rooted in the unfathomable depths of its predisposition towards morality . . . May its purity never again be troubled by the hurly-burly of the thirst for enrichment, the degeneration caused by sensual enjoyment, the luxuriant growth of a wanton search for sensation and the superficial arrogance of ability and knowledge.[10]

Such notions were extraordinarily widespread, and they were by no means restricted to the radical Right. The endangered German military monarchy could be saved through a victorious war, and a society could be created in which modern technology and science would be combined with a traditional value system, and the romantic idea of a united national community no longer split apart into interest groups would triumph. But many people went even further. It was postulated that the confrontation between Germany and England was, primarily, a struggle between two ideas, two concepts of social organisation. This view was expressed most clearly in a work by Johann Plenge, a political and economic theorist from Münster. He gave the book the title '1789 and 1914'. Plenge's basic idea was that modern society was too complex and diverse to be governed according to the principles of liberalism, individualism and the free play of economic forces. This had resulted in acute social tensions, moral decline, the loss of true freedom and the withering away of the state. The appropriate answer to these challenges was a corporative state socialism of the kind developed in Germany since 1871. Its leading idea was organisation. In this system, individual interests would not stand against each other but would be united by a common ideal. The 'spirit of 1914' had demonstrated this unity, which had found expression in the 'ideas of 1914'. The source of freedom was not an absence of social bonds but organisation. Just as the ideas of the French Revolution of 1789 had dominated the nineteenth century, so the ideas of the German revolution of 1914 would dominate the twentieth century. This revolution was 'the revolution which would build up and join together all the state's forces in the twentieth century, in contrast with the eighteenth-century revolution of destructive emancipation'. 'We are the twentieth century', he added. 'However the war ends, we are the nation which will set an example. Our ideas will determine the purpose of life for humanity.'[11]

This was no longer reactionary romanticism; it was a different conception of modernity. On this view, nationalism and socialism would merge together, and individual freedom would be restricted in the interest of collective freedom. The unified direction of economy and society, instituted by the state and organised on a semi-military basis, would be shown to be plainly superior to civilian and democratic principles. The correct answer to the challenge of modernity was not democracy and liberalism but army methods and organisation.

Before the war started, ideas like this had only been put forward in esoteric political circles or books written by nationalist extremists. Now they found their way into the writings of respected academics. The war radicalised people's ideas. Moreover, these theories also gave rise to far-reaching claims for territorial expansion after a German victory. It was no surprise that it was again Claß and the Pan-German League who led the way with the series of war aims memoranda which would determine the shape of domestic political debate for years to come. Demands for extensive territorial gains both in the east and the west were connected here with the assumption, already widely shared years earlier, that the inhabitants of the conquered regions would have to be deported so that German soldiers could be settled there and jobs could be created for the German *Mittelstand.*

Similarly far-reaching ideas, although without the deportation element, were worked out by the Ruhr industrialist August Thyssen and the leader of the Centre Party, Matthias Erzberger. Finally, in September 1914, the Chancellor's secretary, Kurt Riezler, made a summary of the government's war aims. This was followed by a veritable blizzard of memoranda. The plans put forward envisaged the extension of German territory in various different directions, but they were all aimed at creating an unassailable German hegemony over the Continent. To this end, France would need to lose important regions in the west, particularly the iron ore district of Longwy-Briey, as well as the whole coast of Flanders, in some versions. Belgium would become a vassal state of the German Empire, and the border of Russia would be pushed back further to the east, in which connection different variants of dependence on the Reich were discussed for the Baltic states. These plans also included the idea of a Central European economic area, which was intended to secure Germany's supremacy in Europe both politically and economically. The latter conception was rendered popular by Friedrich Naumann's book *Mitteleuropa,* which appeared in 1915 and became a bestseller.

One of the main contradictions in German policy was the way the government combined aggressive war aims with a constant reassertion that in going to war it had, after all, only reacted to the attacks of its opponents. Even so, in the debate over war aims, the conviction that Germany was the victim of foreign aggression was in effect taken to be a justification for large-scale annexation proposals.[12]

This debate reached a climax in the spring of 1915, when the most important economic associations and, following them, a large number of professors, some of them very prominent, adopted the essentials of the Pan-German annexation programme: extensive territorial gains in both east and west, the expulsion of the indigenous population in the east, and worldwide colonial expansion on a vast scale. More than a thousand individuals prominent in German intellectual life, including 352 professors, supported these demands.

Shortly afterwards, a considerably smaller, more moderate, group of intellectuals, including Gerhard Anschütz, Albert Einstein, Adolf von Harnack, Max Planck, Gustav von Schmoller, Ernst Troeltsch, Max Weber and Alfred Weber, appended their signatures to another memorandum, which was critical of annexations in the west, but emphatically demanded them in the east.[13]

Germany's motive in going to war had not, however, been to make concrete territorial gains. This was also true for the Entente Powers. The demand for annexations was only raised in the course of the war, though it should be said that Germany called for them considerably earlier than France or indeed Great Britain, whose main demands were the restoration of Belgian independence and a return to the European balance of power. But none of the Powers aimed at a permanent peace settlement which would restore the pre-war status quo. It was not territorial gains or simply great power interests which occupied the foreground in these proposals. The aim was rather to eliminate the opponent militarily, economically and politically for an extensive period, and to dismantle the opposing social system in a similarly comprehensive fashion. The nineteenth century had shown that compromises could be reached over great power interests, if a due balance was maintained between successes and risks. But, when war aims were combined with nationalist emotions, tailored to proposals for reordering political and social systems and supported by mass organisations, they developed an impetus of their own. This was an all-or-nothing war, and it hardly seemed possible to bring it to an end in any other way than by complete victory.[14]

The widespread sense of national unity in face of external danger gained strong support from the surprising decision of the SPD Reichstag fraction on 4 August 1914 to agree to the war credits and the policy of '*Burgfrieden*' (party truce) which followed from that decision. As late as the last week of July 1914, no one had thought that the Social Democrats would vote for the war credits. It was considered probable that the majority of them would abstain, while a minority might possibly vote against. One of the reasons for the swing of opinion in the SPD parliamentary group was that many Social Democrats had also been infected by the national euphoria of the July days. Another factor was the expectation that the party's organisations would be subject to repression by the authorities, or even complete prohibition, after a state of emergency had been declared, if it consistently opposed the war. In view of the SPD's experiences under the anti-socialist law, this was an important argument. But what was decisive for the SPD was Russia's general mobilisation on 30 July. In the eyes of the majority of the SPD party executive, a war against autocratic Tsarism was legitimate, not only for national reasons, because this was a war of self-defence, as Chancellor Bethmann-Hollweg stressed repeatedly, but also on political grounds, because it was a war against a reactionary and 'backward' state.

In taking the view that their country was defending itself, the German Social Democrats were by no means exceptional among the working-class parties of Europe. The French and British labour movements were equally convinced that their countries were innocent, and had been attacked by the enemy. The German *Burgfrieden* had its counterpart in the French *Union sacrée*. There, as in Germany, the immense current of national unity overcame the presumed solidarity of the international working class.[15]

Shortly after the war broke out, the chair of the SPD, Hugo Haase, addressed the Reichstag, describing it as a result of the arms race and the imperialist policies of the great powers. Social Democracy had always fought against these policies and would continue to do so, he said. He justified the decision of his parliamentary group to vote for the war credits in spite of this in these words:

> There is much, if not everything, at stake for our people and its democratic future . . . in case of a victory of Russian despotism. This danger must be averted, and the civilisation and independence of our country must be preserved. We shall therefore put into practice what we have always preached: we shall not leave our Fatherland in the lurch in the hour of danger.

This was a reply to the Chancellor, who had just invoked the unity of the Fatherland in a similarly emotional fashion by declaring:

> 'Our army is in the field, our fleet is ready to fight, and behind them stands the whole German people!' (*Lively and continuous cheers and applause from all sides of the house, and on the platform—the Reichstag rises to its feet*)). Bethmann-Hollweg (addressing the Socialists): 'The whole German people, united to a man!' (*Renewed jubilant applause for several minutes*).[16]

For many Social Democrats, who had endured disparagement and discrimination throughout their lives as 'unpatriotic fellows' (*vaterlandslose Gesellen*), this ostentatious acceptance into the bosom of the nation was a moving and long hoped-for event. The SPD deputy Konrad Haenisch found that he was able now 'for the first time . . . from the bottom of his heart, with a good conscience and without having to worry that he would be betraying the cause, to join in a rousing rendering of the song *Deutschland, Deutschland über alles*'. This filled him with a feeling of relief, that he could finally be 'what he was anyway, notwithstanding all rigid principles': namely, German.[17]

With this, the ground had been laid for '*Burgfrieden*'. Petty vexations directed against the SPD and the trade unions had continued to exist everywhere in Germany until then. The government now made efforts to bring these to an end. The SPD, for its part, not only voted for the war credits, it also approved the far-reaching War Enabling Act (*Kriegsermächtigungsgesetz*) by which the Reichstag largely divested itself of its powers, handing them over to the Bundesrat. Bethmann-Hollweg calculated that domestic political conflicts could be, as it were, held in suspension for the duration of the war. The Reichstag would only assemble every six months, simply to confirm the war credits. In return for taking this conciliatory attitude, many of the SPD leaders hoped that the constitutional reforms they had long demanded, such as the ending of the three-class electoral system in Prussia, could now finally be implemented. The trade unions also supported the war effort, not least by declaring that they would abandon the strike weapon, in the hope that they would be recognised by the entrepreneurs as legitimate representatives of the workforce. Nevertheless, neither the SPD nor the trade unions received a binding commitment from the government in return for their conciliatory attitude.

The Left of the SPD, on the other hand, had suffered a complete defeat. It had been forced to accept the majority decision in favour of war credits, and indeed for the sake of party unity the deputies of the Left had also voted for them. The Left had not succeeded in bringing about a united international front of socialists, although as late as 1 August, emissaries from the SPD had travelled to Paris, where they learned that the French workers, like the Germans, would enter the war, notwithstanding all their pacifist demonstrations. In Brussels, the International Socialist Bureau had to look on helplessly as most of the European workers' parties joined the national defence fronts of their governments. The European workers' movement was further away from acting collectively against war than it had ever been.[18]

Both for the German workers' movement and the international workers' movement, therefore, the fourth of August signified the start of a split. The German Social Democrats were never able to achieve a united attitude towards the war. The number of deputies who opposed the war credits in the SPD parliamentary group's preliminary internal discussions constantly increased as the war progressed. The ratio between supporters and opponents was seventy-eight to fourteen in August 1914, but by March 1915 there were already twenty-three deputies who opposed the war credits, and by December 1915 that number had risen to forty-four. The opponents of war who gathered together in this group formed the kernel of the partly pacifist and partly revolutionary left wing which would leave the party in the next few years and build its own political formations, first as the Independent Social Democratic Party of Germany (USPD), then as the Communist Party of Germany (KPD).[19]

## War of Attrition

After the failure of the Schlieffen Plan, the winter of 1914–15 saw sharp disagreements within the military and political leadership about the future course of the war. The new commander-in-chief, General Falkenhayn, who had replaced the luckless Moltke in the autumn, called for a separate peace with Russia, so as to be able to defeat England and France in the West. Hindenburg and Ludendorff, on the other hand, demanded a massive blow against the Russian army, so as to be able to attack in the west after it had been annihilated. In actual fact, however, a stronger German involvement in the east was inescapable in any case, owing to Austria-Hungary's military weakness, particularly after the fall of the great fortresses of Przemyśl and Lemberg (Lviv). If they did not want to risk the collapse of the Imperial and Royal Monarchy, which it was feared would happen if the Russians advanced any further, a sizeable German offensive would have to be mounted in the east to relieve the situation. The German forces in the east, which had in the meantime increased in number to 600,000 men, were able in May 1915 to break through the Russian lines on a broad front between the towns of Tarnów and Gorlice, south-east of Kraków. In the course of the battles that followed, both sides suffered heavily, but the Russians suffered more than 750,000 dead and wounded, withdrew completely from Galicia and were finally forced back 400 kilometres to the east. After a further offensive in September, the Central Powers gained control of the whole of Poland, Lithuania and Latvia. Their victories on the eastern front during the summer of 1915 would turn out to be their greatest military successes during the whole of the war.[20]

This was what Berlin had expected the war to look like to the German people: a heroic struggle, a clever military strategy and great victories! This was the way not only to win a war, but to save the hard-pressed nation. The sacrifice of the individual for a higher cause was expressed symbolically in the 'Langemarck Myth', which originated in November 1914, when rows of very young and badly trained volunteers, schoolboys and students for the most part, were literally mown down by British and French machine guns during a series of German attacks on enemy positions near Ypres. The story was spread by German propagandists that the 'heroes of Langemarck' had marched enthusiastically to their death with the anthem '*Deutschland, Deutschland über alles*' on their lips. The aim was to use the idealism and self-sacrifice of the young men who died for the fatherland as an example to the whole German people, and to overcome the social and political fissures in Germany by emphasising the experience of war and national solidarity.[21]

But a completely different kind of war from this had developed in the west. The trench system had grown to cover more and more territory. Eventually, there were approximately 40,000 kilometres of trenches, and they proved to be almost impregnable. The front lines had frozen; the war had become positional. In the course of 1915 the troops of the Entente undertook various offensives, both small-scale and large-scale: in February and March in Artois and Champagne, in May and June around Arras, and around Neuve-Chapelle in Flanders, finally in autumn in Champagne again. When the attacks were on a large scale, they opened with hours (and ultimately days) of bombardment by heavy artillery. Before the beginning of the Arras offensive, more than 2 million shells were fired at the German positions. After this, several waves of infantry attempted to occupy the opponent's trenches. It turned out, however, that despite the massive use of hand grenades and mortars, entrenchments could only be conquered at the cost of tremendous losses. Most of the attacking soldiers were wounded or killed by defenders firing from fortified positions, or, alternatively, they bled to death on the barbed wire fences, which were often a metre high, so that when the opponent mounted a counter-offensive it was an easy task to annihilate the attacker's exhausted troops.

The numbers of dead and wounded reached astronomical levels. A war of attrition had begun, of an order of magnitude which broke all previous records. 'What a sight I was faced with!' wrote an Alsatian soldier after a battle on the Western Front.

> In front of us lay dead and wounded Frenchmen, as far as the eye could see. The dead Germans were also still there, but the wounded had been taken away . . . It was horrible to look at the dead. Some of them lay on their faces, and some on their backs. Blood, clutching hands, glazed eyes, distraught faces. Many still held their guns tightly in their hands. Others were clutching earth or grass which they had ripped out in their final agony.[22]

Poison gas was used as a weapon of war for the first time. It was the German side which took the initiative in this respect, on the Western Front in the spring of 1915. Gas was regarded as a particularly dastardly weapon owing to its invisibility, and it unleashed panic and terror among the soldiers. In actual fact, the proportion of soldiers who perished from poison gas inhalation was relatively small. The vast majority of the killed and wounded—more than three quarters of them—were hit by artillery fire. Roughly 16 per cent were hit by rifle shots. The main feature of this war was not man-to-man combat, but hours and hours, even days, of heavy artillery fire, which the soldiers had to undergo helplessly. Only towards the end did the war cease to be positional, with the introduction of armoured vehicles, or 'tanks' as they began to be called. This new weapon ended the massive losses caused by artillery bombardment.

The reality of war did not, as had been hoped, lead to the disappearance of social distinctions. On the contrary: the class divisions of German society were more clearly visible in the army than at home. The privileges, prerogatives and arrogance of the officers magnified the social distinctions and associated tensions of Wilhelmine society. The soldiers often feared and hated their officers more than the enemy.

The war on the Western Front was anonymous, the opponent was invisible, and the mechanisation of death and the process of getting killed led to a decline in the individual's fighting spirit.

> We were subjected to heavy fire, which drove you from one hole to the next; we heard the cries of pain and the groans of the wounded, who had to perish miserably because to carry them back was out of the question. Shellfire by day and by night. Often 10 to 20 shots rained down on us in a single second, buried us and then dug us out again. Our lieutenant cried like a child; the way they lay there, with a foot off, an arm off, or completely torn to pieces. God, that was frightful.[23]

This experience was no longer comparable with previous wars. In the summer of 1914 the German soldiers, just like the British and French soldiers, had taken the field thinking that they were involved in a cabinet war of the nineteenth century: it would last a few months, there would be many victims, but the risk could be calculated, and it formed part of the traditional experience of life and death. But now they experienced an apocalyptic killing machine, which within a single day snatched away more men than had been killed in the course of a whole war in earlier times. There was no visible opponent, nor was there any opportunity to influence your own fate by being stronger or more careful, and the compensation of heroism was absent, for that was associated with individual combat.

There were some exceptions: aircraft pilots, for example, the 'knights of the air', were soon surrounded with admiration. Every child knew their names, because in their spectacular aerial duels they were waging an archaic fight of one man against another. But the soldiers of the so-called 'storm troops' were also honoured as heroes. They still conducted 'killing as a handicraft'. These were usually small units which went on reconnaissance beyond their own lines, and attacked the enemy's forward positions. Individual motivation played a great role here. The soldiers and officers of these commando groups, who sought to carry on the fight in a direct fashion, and literally hunted down individual enemy soldiers, brought the whole company into danger and were strongly disliked by the ordinary soldiers of both sides. But they offered a suitable subject for the home front's fantasies of heroism and in this way they contributed to the way modern warfare was predominantly portrayed, underlining its chief features: contempt for human life, ice-cold gallantry devoid of all morality and an aestheticisation of violence, all of which exerted considerable fascination after the war, particularly in Germany.[24]

In general, the war seemed to be going well for the Central Powers in 1915. In the east, they had achieved great victories, though not enough to force a decision. In the west, the enemy's offensives had been repulsed, though the German side had also suffered considerable losses. In addition, the efforts of the French and British to gain a foothold in South-East Europe had not been successful. British troops had attempted to occupy the Straits of the Dardanelles, which ran between the Mediterranean and the Black Sea, against Ottoman opposition, with as little success as the French had had when they tried to land in Salonica (Thessaloniki). The Central Powers, on the other hand, who now included Bulgaria, mounted an offensive against the Serbian army in September and October 1915, which ended with the latter's complete defeat, followed by the occupation of the country.

It was not clear, however, how the war could be continued in the longer term, and above all it was not clear how it could be brought to an end. The German leadership's plan to make a separate peace with Russia turned out to be a non-starter. Moreover, Italy's entry into the war on the side of the Entente had opened a new front in the south, and the Austrian army's best troops were tied to this front. It continued to be the fixed conviction of the German General Staff under Falkenhayn that the war would have to be won in the west. The strategy worked out for the year 1916 was directed towards this end: a powerful offensive at Verdun, the strongest French fortress, would induce the French side to mass its troops at that point, and then they would be 'bled dry', as Falkenhayn put it, in a gigantic battle of attrition. High German losses were factored into the calculation, but it was envisaged that the enemy's losses would be many times greater, with the result that France's 'national strength' (*Volkskraft*) would be broken.

These tactics, however, ended in a complete fiasco. The Germans were neither able to inflict a decisive defeat on the French, nor were the losses of the opposing side much greater than Germany's. Over the course of the year 1916, a total of over 700,000 soldiers lost their lives or were wounded in the 'meat-grinder' of Verdun, and 40 per cent of them were German. The second great battle of attrition of 1916 assumed dimensions which were even more appalling. This was the battle which British troops began on 1 July in the north of France, on the river Somme. British confidence that it would be easy to overcome the German lines after the most powerful artillery bombardment of the entire war—there was a heavy gun set up every 18 metres over a total length of 20 kilometres—turned out to be a fatal miscalculation. Sixty thousand British soldiers fell on the first day of the offensive. At the end of November, it had to be called off. The Entente had won 12 kilometres of territory, and it had lost more than 600,000 men, while German losses were approximately 450,000.[25]

In view of the frightful consequences of these battles of attrition, it now appeared that the Social Darwinist calculation of the German side that the French could be 'bled dry' because of their inferior 'national strength' was beginning to work in reverse. It was not just that the Entente's superiority in regard to economic and military resources now became more plainly apparent. Germany had, in the meantime, suffered such losses that even the constant extension of conscription could no longer provide an adequate supply of fresh troops.

Not the least of the reasons for this was that Germany's numerous strategic obligations in various parts of the European continent became ever more pressing. In summer 1916, at the height of the battle of Verdun, the Russian army began a big offensive against Austria's positions in southern Galicia. This was quickly successful, and the front was shifted 160 kilometres to the west. As a result, real signs of dissolution appeared in the Austrian army, and more than 200,000 soldiers deserted. The German side was admittedly able to stop the Russian advance by shifting large troop detachments to the east, but this meant taking them away from the Western Front.

By August 1916, when Romania entered the war on the side of the Entente, Germany's strategy had failed definitively. The principle of a battle of attrition, applied at Verdun, had proved to be a ghastly error of judgement. Large-scale offensives on the Western Front held no promise of success. In the east, the Russian army had not been beaten; the Austrian army, on the other hand, was evidently at the end of its tether. Germany lost 1.2 million men in 1916, and victory was further away than ever.

In this situation, Falkenhayn was forced to resign. He was replaced by Hindenburg and Ludendorff, the two generals who had so far been most successful. Together they made up the third OHL (Supreme Army Command). The appointment of Hindenburg and Ludendorff also marked a pronounced shift in the balance of power in the German leadership from the civilians to the military men, with the political backing of the extreme Right.[26]

## The War Economy

This was a war of a completely new and unexpected magnitude. As a result, Germany's military plans and preparations rapidly became worthless. The same was true, to an even greater extent, of the government's approach to the economy. There had been just as little attempt to plan for a war economy before 1914 in Germany as in Britain or France. Everyone reckoned on a short war, so no one was prepared to undertake any extensive remodelling of the national economy for wartime purposes. Not until November 1914 did the chimera of a short war dissipate; only then did the extent of the problems which demanded immediate solution become clear, especially in Germany. Firstly, military supply requirements increased exponentially. But since the import of raw materials was severely affected by commercial blockade operated by the British navy, entirely new organisational structures were now necessary. Secondly, millions of workers were sent to the front, and, by the end of the war, almost 14 million men had been called up, 85 per cent of the able-bodied male population. They had to be replaced by others, since production requirements had risen considerably, above all in the defence industries. Thirdly, new ways of financing these extraordinary efforts had to be found. And, fourthly, the British blockade of Germany's seaports caused such a drastic reduction in food imports that new methods had to be found to feed both the civilian population and the soldiers.

Every great power that participated in the First World War faced this problem of making the transition to a war economy. These were new challenges, and there were no precedents to follow. It was therefore necessary to strike out on new paths, and create new institutions and administrative structures, although a fair proportion of these eventually proved to be useless, as in the case of the German military administration itself, which proved to be dysfunctional shortly after the beginning of the war, despite the country's pride in the efficiency of its bureaucracy. A military institution, the so-called General Command, was given authority over the civilian departments during the war. It was not divided into the same geographical districts as the civilian offices, with the result that respective competences were unclear, inconsistent objectives were set, and contradictory instructions were issued. That remained the case until the end of the war, but it is hard to say what alternatives were available. The German military state proved to be unwieldy and its system of organisation has been described as 'polycratic', but this was no less true of the British administration, and it was even more clearly the case in France. It should also be noted that Germany was able to hold its own for four years against an adversary which eventually possessed overwhelmingly superior strength. This speaks for rather than against the ad hoc organisational structures that had been created.

There is no doubt that the influence of the state on the economy grew everywhere during the war, and many people saw this as a model with a promising peacetime future. One particularly clear example was the increasing role of the state in supplying the war economy with raw materials. To secure their optimal distribution, the biggest industrial enterprises joined with the authorities to create new institutions, which purchased the available raw materials and divided them among the individual war firms. These hybrid state–private institutions, known as 'War Raw Materials Companies' (*Kriegsrohstoffgesellsch aften*), were coordinated by a central office in Berlin, the War Raw Materials Department (*Kriegsrohstoffabteilung*), which in the first months of its existence was directed by the man who invented the idea, Walther Rathenau, the head of the General Electricity Company (AEG). Rathenau's system proved to be flexible and fairly effective, although it was common knowledge that it allowed the biggest producers of war materials to issue themselves with their own contracts, as it were, and to make quite extraordinary profits. Average share dividends rose by over 10 per cent during the war years, and in the big armaments firms profit margins of 100 and 200 per cent were seen in the four years of the war. This remained a constant source of irritation right through the war, especially as the government did not succeed in trimming the exorbitant war profits by taxing these firms.[27] Labour supply also remained a critical issue until the end of the war. The men who had been called up were at first replaced by unskilled workers. In addition to this, whole gangs of workers were transferred from firms unconnected to the war effort to those that were. As long as that was organised through a semi-free labour market, the employees could take advantage of the big rise in the demand for workers by insisting on higher wages. But, early in the war, attempts were already being made to prevent this by organising changes in the place of employment on an official basis, and later on, workers who moved from one firm to another without permission were threatened with being immediately called up and sent to the front.[28]

Right from the start, however, the employment of women in industry was also encouraged. Even so, female economic activity did not increase during the war any faster than it was already doing before the war started, either in Germany, Great Britain, France or Austria. In Germany, the number of economically active women rose by 17 per cent over the four years of war, but in the two decades before the war the rate of increase had always exceeded 20 per cent. A more significant feature of the situation was rather a pronounced shift of the female labour force from industries that were not war-related to those that were. In Berlin after 1917, female workers formed the majority of the employees in the engineering, metal-working and chemical industries. But most of them had already been economically active beforehand. Maidservants, for example, now preferred to enter into factory employment, where they earned considerably more money than they had done 'in service'.

For most women, however, gainful employment was neither possible nor desirable. For one thing, there was no public provision for childcare. Moreover, women's wages were only half as much as men's, and working conditions were sometimes so atrocious that they avoided taking up employment in a factory, if at all possible, especially since state support for 'warriors' wives' was sufficient to feed the family. There were also ideological objections: the conviction that female labour, especially in industry, was something unnatural often prevailed over the urgent need for workers. Female labour was felt to be an attack on gender roles and on the traditional family structure, which was one of the foundation stones of the inherited canon of values. In war too, it seemed, it was so indispensable to maintain these norms that even urgent military requirements ought not to force their abandonment.[29]

Another way of gaining an extra labour supply for the war economy was to bring in foreign workers. To begin with, prisoners of war were an obvious target. Roughly 1.6 million out of the 2.5 million prisoners who fell into German hands were set to work, half of them in agriculture and a third in industry, especially coalmining. Foreign civilians living in Germany also came under consideration; but to bring them into the labour force was much more difficult than making use of prisoners of war. Initially, seasonal workers who came from the Russian part of Poland and were already employed in eastern Germany were prevented from going home and put to work, predominantly in agriculture. This happened even against their wishes, although a formal ordinance providing for forced labour was not issued at first. But from 1915 onwards, strenuous efforts were made to recruit workers from the occupied regions of Eastern Europe, above all from the General Government of Warsaw. The dividing line between forced deportation and 'voluntary migration' became increasingly blurred, with the signing of labour contracts by a total of roughly 250,000 workers from Russian Poland up to the end of the war.

In Belgium, too, the German authorities started the compulsory recruitment of workers, but here, unlike in Poland, they were under the eyes of the outside world. Between October 1916 and February 1917 roughly 61,000 Belgian workers were taken to Germany. While the authorities were taking these deportation measures, a further 17,000 Belgians signed up 'voluntarily'. At least, this was the official view. In practice, however, compulsion proved to be a disaster both organisationally and in terms of domestic and foreign policy. The authorities succeeded neither in bringing a sufficient number of Belgian workers to Germany nor in effectively employing a significant section of the already deported forced labourers. Numerous protests from neutral countries, such as Spain, Switzerland, the Netherlands and the USA, as well as from the Vatican, confirmed the picture of German militarism held by international public opinion and contributed to the worsening of Germany's diplomatic isolation.

On the other hand, little attention was paid to Germany's treatment of Polish workers. There were neither international protests, nor did the opposition within Germany express any criticism. This was a clear demonstration that the war had rapidly raised the threshold of tolerance for injustices committed in civilian life. When the deaths of thousands of soldiers at the front were announced every week, the forced employment of enemy civilians apparently stirred up no emotions, the more so as the employment of hundreds of thousands of prisoners of war in Germany led to a blurring of the distinction between a civilian and a military labour force.[30]

The financial costs of this war were on a completely unprecedented scale. In order to be prepared for the war, the German Empire had built up a monetary reserve of 225 million Marks, which was held under guard like a medieval war-chest in the Juliusturm, part of the fortress of Spandau. After the war started, however, this sum of money proved to be completely inadequate in view of the costs actually incurred. In fact, it was just enough to cover two days of war. The First World War cost the German Empire a total of between 156 and 200 billion Marks, depending on the basis used to make the calculation. Germany's total national wealth before the war amounted to roughly 40 billion Marks. As Walther Rathenau wrote in retrospect in the summer of 1918, 'a month's worth of war expenditure would have done away with all the poverty in the world. Another month would have given human beings long-lasting security. A third month would have turned the towns into paradises. A fourth would have freed research from all material problems. A fifth would have done the same for art.'[31]

There were three ways of raising the extraordinary sums of money needed to finance the war: taxes, loans and the printing of money. The tax-raising route was admittedly sound and effective, but it presupposed an efficient tax system and a corresponding degree of acceptance by the public. Neither of these conditions was adequately present in Germany, or indeed in the other countries engaged in the war. For to produce the necessary amount of money, a greater amount of direct taxation would have been needed than before, particularly taxes on income and turnover. The 'Bülow bloc' had already failed to achieve this five years earlier, because the Conservatives and the Agrarian League could not reach agreement over taxes on income, property or inheritance. Germany entered the war without having a secure basis for its tax receipts because the representatives of conservative interests had torpedoed any attempt to introduce a modern income tax system, which would have graduated the tax burden according to income and wealth. It was decided that the war would instead be paid for by Germany's defeated opponents. This policy was explained by Karl Helfferich, the Imperial Treasury Secretary, in these words:

> We do not want to add to the tremendous burdens borne by our people during the war by imposing taxes, as long there is no urgent necessity to

> do this . . . The future standard of living of our people must remain free and clear of the immense burdens caused by the war, as far as this is at all possible. It is the instigators of this war who deserve to shoulder the lead weight of billions of debts; they, not us, should be obliged to carry this burden around for decades.[32]

Only towards the end of the war were there changes in this policy, whereby a tax on turnover and a war profit tax were introduced, though at very low rates. Altogether, Germany financed only 17 per cent of its war expenditure with taxes. The figure for Great Britain, in contrast, was 26 per cent.

Wartime spending was financed overwhelmingly by means of the so-called War Loans. The state issued the appropriate securities, guaranteeing repayment at a good rate of interest after the end of the war. There were altogether nine such loans in Germany up to 1918, always in connection with big patriotic campaigns and symbolic actions for the salvation of the fatherland, and the government had some success in persuading the population to subscribe: more than 7 million people subscribed to the seventh War Loan, which was issued in March 1917. In total, the loans brought in the immense sum of 97 billion Marks, which was roughly two-thirds of the money needed to finance the war. Loans of this type functioned like long-term securities. They were therefore dependent on a favourable interest rate and the confident expectation of a big profit at the end. But because this profit would only eventuate if the war ended in victory, the government was obliged, if only for financial reasons, to make sure that the German people continued to have high hopes of victory, notwithstanding the actual course of events at the front. They succeeded to an astonishing degree, although already by the autumn of 1916 the amounts subscribed were insufficient to fill the gap in the country's finances.

That is why the third method of raising money became increasingly important: direct indebtedness and the printing of money associated with this. The legal limit on state indebtedness had already been removed when the war started. Ever larger debts were therefore incurred as it continued. Since it had become impossible to borrow money from abroad, the basis of the state's debts, apart from the war loans mentioned above, was first and foremost the issue of extra notes by the Reichsbank. Since these additional quantities of money were not balanced by any corresponding increase in value, prices rose. This was the starting point for spiralling rates of inflation—the constantly accelerating price increases ultimately leading to a progressive decline in the value of salaries, pensions and rental income. In effect, this loss of value worked like a tax increase: the population was defrauded to pay for the requirements of the war. The people themselves had absolutely no idea of why this was happening, and as rage and bitterness over inflation grew, so the search for those responsible became intensified. The fact that it was their own government that had set in motion the devaluation of money remained hidden from most Germans, even after the end of the war. This was a truly calamitous development.

By the end of the war, the German Empire had piled up debts of more than 150 billion Marks, half of which were short-term loans. The burden of interest payments alone amounted to roughly 90 per cent of the ordinary income of the Reich. It was now realised that if Germany were to lose the war, thereby becoming unable to impose its costs on defeated opponents, this gigantic mountain of debt would collapse onto the Germans themselves. This is what took place during the hyperinflation of 1921 to 1923, when a large part of the private monetary wealth of the population was destroyed. Only then were the costs of the war paid.[33]

Lastly, there was the problem of food. The British Royal Navy began in August 1914 to set up a blockade of all trading vessels carrying goods for the Central Powers. The spring of 1915 marked the closing of the ring blockading the parts of the North Sea which lay outside the range of the German fleet. Roughly a third of Germany's annual food requirements had been imported from abroad before the war started. These imports were now no longer available. Germany's agricultural production also declined considerably after 1914—by the end of the war it had fallen by more than 30 per cent. The main reason for this was a shortage of labour. Even the use of foreign workers and prisoners of war did not entirely counterbalance this. In the first winter of the war, therefore, a clear shortage of food supplies was already noticeable, especially in the towns, and this worsened in subsequent years. It soon became the most urgent domestic problem of all.

Here too the German leadership's room for manoeuvre was limited. If the market economy were allowed to function in its usual way, the considerable reduction in supply would quickly cause prices to rise so much that only the wealthier sections of the population would be able to feed themselves adequately. And, in fact, food prices did begin to rise significantly as early as autumn 1914. As a reply to this, the government now attempted to take various steps to organise the distribution of available food supplies, with the result that a black market very quickly came into being, at which all commodities could be obtained, but only at market prices, which made them unaffordable for the working population. Despite this, almost half the available food supplies were soon being sold on the black market.

In the winter of 1915–16, a catastrophic shortage of food could only be averted by short-term imports from Romania. After this, the whole food sector of the economy was placed under the control of a central authority, on the model of Rathenau's War Raw Materials Department. This move naturally met with fierce resistance from the peasants and above all the big landowners, who did not want the government to be able to dictate prices. It should be added that the bureaucratisation and centralisation of food distribution sometimes had absurd consequences. Foodstuffs which were in short supply, and therefore needed to be distributed fairly, disappeared from the market completely as soon as it became known that they would be rationed. The peasants received better prices for pork than for potatoes, and they therefore fed the potatoes to their pigs, with the result that there was a potato shortage. In 1915, popular protests against this led the state to order the slaughter of an estimated 9 million pigs, a third of the total stock. As a result, a severe meat shortage developed a year later. This turn of events demonstrates what an impenetrable mixture of conflicting interests, excess demand and corruption was involved here. The central authorities were unable either to achieve a fair distribution of the available foodstuffs or to limit the growth of the black market. Market forces, it appeared, could not be defeated with state ordinances, and the unexpected side effects of these measures often far exceeded any benefits they were originally intended to achieve.[34]

The food shortage was at its worst in the winter of 1916–17. Large sections of the working population went hungry. They froze too, for it was the coldest winter in living memory, and fuel was also rationed. The official food rations scarcely covered more than 50 per cent of a person's daily calorie requirements, and inferior 'ersatz' products of all kinds (by the end of the war there were more than 11,000 of them) were not much help. People living in the towns were forced to feed themselves on turnips, since even potatoes, traditionally the main source of nourishment for ordinary people, had now become scarce. In January and February 1917, the food crisis triggered protests in many big towns, which finally developed into veritable food riots. According to a report by the Berlin Chief of Police,

> the shortage of foodstuffs is a continuous source of discontent among the workers and the less wealthy groups of consumers. They hold stubbornly to the view that a more robust approach to the producers of food would lead to the discovery of rich quantities of foodstuffs which are being wrongfully held back from the market.[35]

These protests were directed firstly against the state, which was after all responsible for the distribution of provisions, but also against 'profiteers', such as food merchants who held onto their supplies, bakers who offered their bread on the black market rather than in shops, and peasants who sold their potatoes at twice the price to schnapps dealers. Rationing and the black market led to a steep rise in the number of criminal offences, since it was hardly possible to feed oneself adequately while staying within the law. There were increases in all kinds of theft, infringements of the rationing regulations and incidents of vandalism. Manners also became coarser: in 1917 proceedings were taken against a total of 1,256 women for threatening policemen or other officials with violence.[36]

In some areas, hunger disturbances involved so many people that army units were brought in to suppress them. In April 1917, moreover, there were mass strikes in many towns, directed above all against the catastrophic state of food supplies. This showed the degree to which the situation was now coming to a head. Nothing else demoralised the population during the war as much as did hunger.[37]

Another reason why the rapid worsening of the mood on the 'home front' was of great concern to the German leadership was the outcome of the gigantic battles of Verdun and the Somme in 1916. The lesson of these battles was that it was not so much the number of soldiers as the superiority and modernity of the available war supplies which determined defeat or victory, and that this would increasingly be the case as time went on. For the OHL to be able to continue the war with some prospect of success, it would undoubtedly need a considerable increase in arms production. The first measures of the new military leadership under Hindenburg and Ludendorff were accordingly aimed at a rapid and dramatic increase in the production of war materials: munitions production was to be doubled, the output of rifles and artillery pieces was to be tripled, coal production was to be increased by a million tonnes and iron ore production by 800,000 tonnes. This 'Hindenburg Programme' planned by the OHL also included drastic measures of labour mobilisation, so as to bring about a significant increase in the number of workers employed in the arms factories. A wide-ranging system of compulsory labour service was introduced, which included women as well. Conscription was formally extended to cover all men between seventeen and sixty years of age. The aim was to assimilate the position of workers in the factories to that of soldiers in the field, and thus to give the factory owners a quasi-military power of command over their workers. There was of course a danger that this would increase the workers' discontent yet further and endanger the foundations of the *Burgfrieden*. Hence in order to place these far-reaching measures on a broad social foundation, the Chancellor ordered that the new regulations be established not by government ordinance but by law, so that the political parties and the Reichstag would be associated with the OHL's proposals.

The importance of the Reichstag grew in proportion to the increased need of Germany's political and military leaders to secure the agreement or at least the passive acceptance of broad strata of the working population during the war.

This became increasingly evident as the fighting continued, and for the first time it offered the opportunity for the Social Democrats, the Centre Party and the Progressive Party to cooperate more extensively with one other. This cooperation was to prove valuable during the negotiations with the generals and the representatives of industry which now took place.

These negotiations resulted in a compromise. The 'Law on Patriotic Auxiliary Service' (*Hilfsdienstgesetz*), passed on 5 December 1916, introduced labour conscription for all males aged between seventeen and sixty. No one wanted to risk applying this to the millions of women who were not economically active, so great was the fear of a further increase in discontent and revolt both at home and on the war front. To make it possible to move workers where necessary to enterprises of particular importance to the war effort, severe restrictions were placed on the individual's right to choose his workplace. In compensation for this, committees of workers and employees, with parity of representation, were set up in the bigger firms, to arbitrate on disputed cases.

The establishment of joint committees was actually a subsidiary aspect of the programme for a massive increase in armaments capacity. In the long run, however, it unintentionally turned out to be the most important sociopolitical innovation of the whole wartime period. It gave the trade union organisations an institutionalised share in management in return for agreeing to the compulsory mobilisation of the male population for arms production. The trade unions had shared the burden of this war, and until 1917 they had renounced industrial action in any form. Now they were accepted as equal partners of the entrepreneurs, in a formal sense as well. This was a success for the corporatist ideal. Indeed, it was a revolution in German social policy. On the other hand, the Hindenburg Programme had established the principle of increasing production without regard to cost, and this in effect meant that the profits of the big 'armaments combines' (a concept which now emerged for the first time) rose as rapidly as the debts of their only customer, the state.

Taken as a whole, however, the Hindenburg Programme was more damaging than useful to the German leadership. None of its goals was achieved. Less steel was produced in February 1917 than in summer 1916. Total armaments production did not rise significantly until the spring of 1918. The intended massive extension of the reservoir of labour was a failure. As mentioned above, the attempts made to fill the gaps in the labour force by bringing in forced labourers from Belgium and Poland had ended in an economic and political fiasco. The main results of the Hindenburg Programme were disorganisation and the squandering of money, raw materials and labour power. But above all, it became crystal clear that the demands of this war far exceeded Germany's human and industrial resources.[38]

## Political Confrontation at Home

In the spring of 1915, the British fleet succeeded in closing the ring around Germany. The country was now fully blockaded. The question of how to break through therefore became increasingly important. Germany's High Seas Fleet was clearly no match for the Royal Navy, and during this time it lay passively at anchor in various harbours, to the despair of German fleet propagandists. Nevertheless, a few German ships managed to sink a significant number of British merchant vessels. In this connection, the U-boats proved to be so successful that the High Command of the German navy announced in the middle of February 1915 that from that time onwards every merchant ship in British waters would be subject to U-boat attack. To take this step involved considerable diplomatic risks, because it was contrary to the international laws of maritime warfare. It was true that the British blockade was also a breach of maritime law, but world opinion did not view a blockade of goods deliveries as seriously as it did the sinking of merchant ships carrying hundreds or thousands of civilian passengers. The USA took centre stage in this controversy, not least because it was in its economic interest to continue selling large quantities of civilian and military products to Britain.

On 7 May 1915, a German U-boat sank the British passenger-steamer *Lusitania.* A total of 1,198 passengers lost their lives as a result, including 120 US citizens. The German government's line was that the ship was carrying large quantities of weapons and ammunition, a claim that was in fact true, despite the denials from the USA which ultimately swayed world opinion. The US government now presented the German leadership with the stark alternative of either ending the U-boat war or accepting the risk that the USA would enter the war on the enemy's side. From that point onwards, the question of the U-boat war was a major point of dispute between those who placed their faith in complete victory, irrespective of the risks, and those who were looking for an opportunity to extricate the country from the war as quickly as possible while Germany could still get out with its head held relatively high. The specific point at issue was whether Germany should conduct 'restricted' submarine warfare, operating according to international maritime law, or 'unrestricted' submarine warfare, in which all merchant ships would be attacked, even those sailing under a neutral flag. That would probably mean the entry of the USA into the war. When presented with this choice, the German government backed down and withdrew its U-boats.[39]

For the country's hungry population, however, any measure that promised to end the war, and with it the food shortage, was bound to be popular. Awareness of that fact encouraged the navy leaders, the representatives of the armaments industry and the political Right to put pressure on the Chancellor in favour of a resumption of the U-boat campaign. Only in this way, they said, can we bring the conflict to a rapid and victorious conclusion. At the beginning of 1916, therefore, German U-boats again began to attack merchant shipping. More passengers lost their lives, among them American citizens, and again the German government withdrew its submarines in response to American threats.

In summer 1916, though, when the course of events on the battlefield made it apparent that Germany would be unlikely to force a decisive victory on land, the agitation in favour of an unrestricted U-boat war increased considerably. The German Admiralty presented a calculation that the U-boats could sink 600,000 nautical tons of shipping every month, so that within five months it would be possible to force Great Britain to its knees and end the war with victory. The campaign for the unrestricted use of U-boats thus followed the pattern of thought characteristic of the Hindenburg Programme, which was being developed at the same time, namely that if all reservations were finally laid aside, and everything staked on one card, victory would be won very quickly. This example of wishful thinking was replete with illusions and grotesque miscalculations. Its advocates did not even fear US intervention: by the time the Americans arrived in Europe, they said, the war would long have been over, and in any case, the U-boats could also sink American troop transports!

The pressure on the German government was now so strong that Chancellor Bethmann-Hollweg thought the only way out was to accelerate Germany's diplomatic attempt to enter peace discussions, with American mediation. Since the armies of the Central Powers had succeeded in autumn 1916 in conquering Romania and occupying Bucharest, the favourable moment to start peace negotiations from a position of strength appeared to have arrived. Bethmann had several objectives. On the one hand, he wanted to discover the conditions for a negotiated peace and prepare the German public for an end to the war that might not satisfy all of Germany's wishes. On the other hand, a failure of the negotiations could also be used as an opportunity to declare unrestricted submarine warfare and in this way bring the war to an end by military means.

In actual fact, however, no serious negotiations at all took place. The Central Powers accompanied their offer of talks with a maximum programme containing so many demands for territorial expansion, including German rule over Belgium and the annexation of the iron ore regions of northern France, that the Entente powers had no difficulty in rejecting it. In any case, they were under no compulsion to negotiate. It is true that their short-term military position was worse than Germany's, but the longer term prospects were much more favourable to the Entente than to the Central Powers. The American President, Woodrow Wilson, declared that he was prepared to act as a mediator in peace negotiations, yet the German side replied immediately by again formulating war aims so excessive that the Allies needed no further reason to refuse to enter into any such negotiation.

The German response, on 1 February 1917, was to resume unrestricted submarine warfare. This decision was jubilantly welcomed by a large part of the German public, which was firmly convinced that a victorious peace was now in the offing. In the course of the year 1917 over 1,000 allied ships were sunk, and by spring at the latest the predicted rate of 600,000 nautical tons a month had been exceeded. But none of the expectations attached to this success was fulfilled. The British side was easily able to compensate for these losses, and the United Kingdom's food supplies were never endangered. On the contrary, by using new tactics, the Royal Navy succeeded in causing German losses to rise rapidly. Moreover, the United States now entered the war, as could have been foreseen. With this, the outcome of the war had now, in effect, been decided, not so much on account of the American soldiers, who only intervened actively on the battlefield in 1918, as because of the resulting inequality of resources. In 1918 the USA's total production of coal, iron and steel was twice as much as that of all the warring European powers taken together. Not only the German navy leaders and the political Right, but also a considerable proportion of the population, attached their wishes and hopes to the effectiveness of an unrestricted U-boat campaign, which proved, in the event, to be a catastrophic mistake from the German point of view.

The change of fortunes which appeared to be heralded by the internal collapse of Tsarist Russia in the spring of 1917 was therefore a completely unexpected bonus for the Central Powers. In Russia, as in almost all the warring states, domestic disturbances had been on the increase since the autumn of 1916. The failed western offensive of the Russian army, and to a much greater extent the growing discontent of the workers in the armaments factories, faced as they were with deprivation and hunger, created a dangerous situation, which led to the explosion of March 1917. A hunger demonstration in Petrograd escalated into a revolt. A 'Workers' and Soldiers' Council' was set up, the spark of revolution spread quickly to other cities, above all Moscow, and within a few days the government was overthrown and the Tsar abdicated. A provisional government made up of representatives of the middle-class parties took control, but it had to share power with the Petrograd Workers' and Soldiers' Council, which issued a call for a 'peace without annexations or contributions'.[40]

These words captured the spirit of the age. They soon spread throughout Europe, and they met with broad agreement, particularly from workers. This created conflicts within the biggest European workers' party, the SPD, because its support for the German government's war policies was increasingly rejected in its own ranks. One of the main problems in this context related once again to war aims. In preceding years, the political Right, along with the industrialists and the OHL, had remained consistently committed to victory and annexations, and the SPD had just as consistently rejected annexationism. The Chancellor, meanwhile, had tacked from side to side, avoiding any clear declaration of intent, because he could not rule either against the Right or against the SPD. Events in Russia put an end to this prevarication, because the language now being heard from Petrograd forced the German government to adopt a clear position.

This was essentially true for the SPD as well. The longer the war lasted, the stronger the pressure from the opposition within the party, which rejected the policy of support for the war. In spring 1916 the oppositionists set up their own organisation, the Social Democratic Working Group (*Sozialdemokratische Arbeitsgemeinschaft*). The first mass demonstration for peace took place on 1 May 1916, and the political line of the party leadership, which was to support Bethmann-Hollweg against Hindenburg and Ludendorff despite his vacillations over war aims, met with increasingly vehement criticism.

The long-running issue of constitutional reform was another controversial area. In August 1914, Bethmann-Hollweg had wanted to postpone until the end of the war any discussion of the SPD's demands for a government controlled by parliament and the abolition of the anachronistic three-class Prussian franchise. But now these questions appeared on the agenda once more. Three simultaneous developments proved to be of long-term significance. Firstly, the big parties in the Reichstag, except the Conservatives, started to move closer to each other. The SPD, the Centre Party and the Progressive People's Party, and on some points even the National Liberals, entered into an informal alliance aimed at domestic reform. Secondly, the political Right reacted by hardening its position. From then on, it utterly rejected any form of 'rotten peace' and any change in the distribution of power at home, and it began instead to set up a new organisation on this basis. Thirdly, in reaction to developments in Russia, the Left Social Democrats finalised the political break begun earlier: a new party, the Independent Social Democratic Party of Germany (USPD), was founded, combining opponents of the war and radical leftists.

With these three developments, the political spectrum which was to characterise the structure and dynamics of German domestic politics for some time into the future had now taken shape. There was a heterogeneous political centre, which stood in varying degrees for parliamentarism, a constitutional and democratic state (not necessarily a republic), an active social policy and a compromise peace. This was, in essence, a constitutionalist movement, and its influence grew constantly, although it was plain from the broad range of its phalanx of supporters, which included Social Democrats, Catholics and various brands of Liberal, that it had no solid structure as yet.

Set against this movement there was a radical Right, which on the basis of extreme nationalism committed itself to an authoritarian government, a pre-modern model of society, and the rule of traditional elites, in particular the military, as well as extensive annexations and a 'victorious peace', after which it expected to receive broad support for its social and political objectives.

The picture on the political Left was not especially clear at this time. The USPD consisted first and foremost of those who rejected the SPD leadership's policy of supporting the war. It was the war, rather than the internal party debates before 1914 around reform, revolution and the mass strike, which had split the SPD. Not until the October 1917 Revolution in Russia did revolutionary forces emerge within the USPD which wanted to replace parliamentarism and bourgeois democracy with a dictatorship of the working class. Even then, these forces continued to be in a minority.

After the resumption of unrestricted submarine warfare, it was no longer possible to move towards an early peace settlement. On the contrary, the war aims laid down once again in April 1917 by the German government included far-reaching annexations. As a result, an ambiguous peace offer announced by the Emperor at the same time left the Allies with little option but to reject it. The big parties in the Reichstag, however, now began to reach agreement on a joint policy of domestic reform and intensified efforts to secure an early peace. The 'Peace Resolution' of July 1917 was the first fruit of this development. It called for a 'peace of mutual agreement and lasting reconciliation between the nations', which would be 'incompatible with the forced acquisition of territory and acts of political, economic and financial oppression'.[41]

This was a real historical watershed. The resolution had been passed without the agreement of the Chancellor and of course against fierce resistance from the OHL. It reset German politics. The constitutionalist movement of the parties of the Reichstag majority had gained its first significant success. Moreover, it now created an informal executive for itself in the shape of the 'Inter-party Committee' (*Interfraktioneller Ausschuss*), which exerted more and more political influence as time went on. The attitude of the National Liberals, however, remained hesitant: they could agree on domestic reforms, but on war aims they continued to back a 'victorious peace', including annexations. Their attitude prevented the Reichstag majority from confronting the OHL, and in particular the powerful figure of Ludendorff, in a strong and unified manner.

The wrath of the latter was directed first and foremost against the Chancellor, because he had been unable to prevent the passing of the peace resolution and the increase in the parliament's power. Bethmann-Hollweg's ambiguous course on the war aims question had already been subjected to harsh criticism by the military leadership and the political Right. But, as long as he was needed to keep the Reichstag and the political parties in check, they had accepted him. Now, however, Ludendorff pressed the Emperor to dismiss Bethmann and replace him with someone more acceptable to the OHL. An appropriate replacement was soon found in the little-known figure of Georg Michaelis, the Prussian State Commissioner for Food Supply, though he was replaced a couple of months later by the Bavarian Centre Party politician Count Hertling. As this shows, the source of power did not lie with the Chancellor, still less with the Emperor, who was, to a great extent, under the tutelage of the military, but was shared between the military leadership around Hindenburg and Ludendorff, on one side, and the majority parties of the Reichstag, on the other.

The Right reacted to the rise of the Reichstag and the Peace Resolution of July 1917 by founding a new political party: it gathered together its forces, which until then had been split into a large number of leagues and associations, and it created the first mass nationalist party, in the shape of the German Fatherland Party. It had roughly 2,000 local associations and almost a million members. The fight for power and influence would no longer be fought within clubs of local dignitaries (*Honoratioren*) and traditional circles, but in the political marketplace. It was entirely self-evident, the Fatherland Party's leaders assured their supporters, that the word 'party' was only used temporarily, because they were after all engaged in a fight against parliamentary 'trafficking'. The Fatherland Party was therefore founded as an anti-party with just one objective: to secure a 'victorious peace' which would include the annexation of extensive territories. Once that was achieved, and the war ended, the party would dissolve itself.

The Fatherland Party combined a radical, expansionist, and militarist nationalism with a programme aimed at maintaining the existing structures of power and wealth, rejecting cultural modernity and ruling out any idea of a republic. At the same time, it functioned as the political lever of the OHL, which used this mass organisation as an instrument of propaganda and mobilisation both at home and within the army.[42]

In this context, the significance of anti-Semitism began to grow once again. At the beginning of the war it seemed to have disappeared almost completely, especially as many German Jews would not allow themselves to be outdone by anyone in their patriotic fervour. When two Jewish entrepreneurs, Walther Rathenau and Albert Ballin, took up leading positions in the state-organised system of war capitalism, this was often seen as an expression of the successful integration of Jews in Germany. But these appointments intensified the fury of the anti-Semitic groups, and when Germany started to suffer military reverses, the anti-Jewish campaign regained its strength, sparked off by the rumour that the Jews had managed to avoid serving at the front, which spread rapidly, and had such an impact that in October 1916 the government ordered a so-called 'census of Jews', intended to check whether these reports were correct or not. The result of the 'census of Jews' was of no assistance to its anti-Semitic advocates, as it showed instead that the proportion of Jews called up for military service was higher than the average for the whole population. Moreover, there were more front soldiers, soldiers killed in action, and decorated soldiers among the Jews than among the generality of arms bearers. For this reason, the document remained unpublished. Nevertheless, or perhaps precisely for that reason, the decree ordering a census of Jews encouraged a further intensification of anti-Semitic agitation, and the number of incidents of harassment against Jewish soldiers and officers in the army also increased. The Jews themselves regarded the census as discriminatory and humiliating, and they also saw it as an attempt to reverse the process by which they had been granted equal rights and encouraged to integrate. The 1916 'census of Jews' can in fact be seen as a turning point in the modern history of German Jewry.[43]

The immigration of the so-called 'Eastern Jews' (*Ostjuden*) gave a further impulse to the anti-Semitic campaign. Even before the war, thousands of Jews had come to Germany from Russia, owing to the increasing persecution and the pogroms they had suffered there. Most of them were firmly rooted in the culture of Jewish Orthodoxy. The actions of the German war economy administrators themselves brought about a considerable increase in the number of Russian Jews arriving in the country from 1915 onwards, because they recruited Jews, including those of explicitly 'Orthodox tendency', from the Russian part of Poland now occupied by the German army, to work in German armaments firms. Indeed, from the start of 1916, this recruitment was generally carried out by force.

As a result, by 1917, the number of *Ostjuden* who had entered Germany was 30,000. But, by that time, the anti-Semitic agitation had increased to such an extent that the authorities stopped recruiting them. The German police authorities complained that the *Ostjuden* represented a potential source of unrest which was difficult to control, particularly in the cities. In addition to this, they were a threat to health. As a result of their 'ineradicable dirtiness', they were 'particularly liable to carry and spread typhus and other communicable diseases'. The Eastern Jews were a favourite target of anti-Semitic agitation during the war, and even more so after it had ended.[44]

Domestic political controversy in Germany from summer 1917 until the end of the war was dominated by the confrontation between the Reichstag and the third OHL, along with its ally, the now united Right. The Budget Committee of the Reichstag became a kind of ersatz parliament, in which all important questions were fiercely debated. The disagreement over war aims and annexations was directly linked to the struggle over the further development of Germany's internal political structure. The Reichstag majority took its stand on a 'peace of mutual agreement' without annexations, which should be followed by fundamental internal reforms, in particular, the reform of the electoral and tax systems. For the Right and the military leadership, the war had been regarded right from the outset as an instrument for reversing the way domestic politics had developed in the pre-war years, and it had been welcomed as such. This continued to be the case: Ludendorff was convinced that a military victory, a marked extension of the area of German influence and the resultant frenzy of nationalist triumphalism would obliterate the phalanx of domestic political opponents and disrupt the informal coalition of Reichstag parties. At the same time, it would provide plebiscitary backing and sufficient mass support for the traditional forces, and in this way prevent any further slide in the direction of democratisation and cultural modernisation.

## The Effects of the October Revolution

In the autumn of 1917, Germany's troops were further away than ever from the victory envisaged by Ludendorff. The pressure of Allied troops on the Western Front was increasing, although the Allies' summer offensives did not lead to a breakthrough. But they had, in the meantime, achieved such a clear superiority over the Central Powers as regards military technology and troop strength that a victory for the German Empire and its allies now seemed highly unlikely.

The fact that this state of affairs changed yet again can be traced back once more to the unfolding events in Russia. After the February Revolution, the Russian Provisional Government had announced that it would fulfil its obligations as an alliance partner, and it had continued military operations, but this announcement met with clear opposition from both the urban and the rural population, and of course from the Petrograd Soviet. There were soon unmistakable signs of disintegration in the Russian army. The peasant soldiers in particular started to desert because they expected that the development of the revolution would lead to a radical land reform and they wanted to go home to participate in it. Among the political parties, the Bolsheviks were the only ones to call for an immediate and unconditional end to the war. At the same time, they came out in favour of a far-reaching redistribution of the land. This was the main reason why they gained more and more support. On 7 November 1917, they mounted an uprising in Petrograd, which has entered into history under the name of the 'October Revolution'. Within a few days, they were able to overthrow the Provisional Government and install their own regime. They quickly succeeded in taking control of all the important central locations, although at this stage their power was far from firmly established.

The priorities of the new rulers around Lenin were to spread the Revolution over the whole Russian Empire and to disentangle Russia from any foreign involvement, and so, on the very next day after the Bolshevik seizure of power, the new government formulated an all-embracing offer of peace without annexations or contributions on the basis of the right of nations to self-determination. This peace proposal, which was directed to all the European countries engaged in the war, was also combined with an appeal to the working class in all the industrialised countries to bend its efforts towards 'freeing mankind from the horrors of war'.[45]

With this, a completely new way of doing politics had entered the history of Europe and the world. Nevertheless, the seizure of power in Russia by this party of the extreme Left was essentially a result of conditions in the country itself. The Russian Empire covered an immense territory inhabited by a tremendous number of different national groups, divided by ethnicity and religion, and held together after a fashion by a corrupt bureaucracy and a despotic monarchy. Moreover, it was a peasant country at a low level of development, with a few islands of industry, the economic dynamism of which contrasted sharply with the situation in the countryside. In the Bolshevik revolution, the revolutionary energies of the urban working class had combined with the radicalism of the peasant movement, with its central demand for land reform and land redistribution, under the leadership of a small stratum of intellectuals, whose cultural and political horizons had been moulded by the socialist workers' movements of Central and Western Europe.

The energy and momentum of the October Revolution radiated out in three different directions. As a peasant revolution, it was directed against the power relations that traditionally prevailed in the Russian Empire, namely the rule of the big landowners and the despotism of the Tsars. As a movement for the right of national self-determination, it was a definite threat to the multi-ethnic empires of Europe, including, besides the Russian Empire, the Austro-Hungarian and Ottoman Empires; but it was also a threat to the colonial empires of the industrialised European countries, above all Great Britain and France. As a proletarian revolution, finally, the theoretical foundations of which had been taken over by the Bolsheviks from the Marxists (although Russia was far from being a fully industrialised society with a capitalist bourgeoisie at the helm), the October Revolution offered permanent backing to the socialist movements of the industrialised countries and challenged both liberal-capitalist political systems and semi-parliamentary and authoritarian ones. After the October Revolution, the theory of international Marxism ceased to be merely a romantic idea, and began to offer to the various socialist and workers' parties of Europe a vision of its practical implementation.

With Russia's withdrawal, there was one fewer great power involved in the war. This suddenly seemed to offer conditions under which a political compromise could be brought about between the Entente and the Central Powers. Even a quick end to the war seemed a possibility. The peace initiatives of the American President, Woodrow Wilson, now assumed great importance. In

January 1918, making reference to the Soviet demand for a 'peace without annexations or contributions', he proposed the outlines of a lasting European peace, whose foundations would be disarmament, free trade, the return of all occupied territories and the right of national self-determination. This was a liberal-democratic model, an alternative both to the autocratic military monarchies of Central Europe and the principles of the Bolshevik revolution as described by Lenin. For Germany, Wilson's 'Fourteen Points' meant on the one hand the return of all occupied territories in east and west, including Alsace-Lorraine. On the other hand, however, they offered Germany an opportunity to emerge undefeated from the war, because with Wilson's programme a lenient peace without winners or losers would have been possible. The Allies seemed ready to entertain such a solution for a brief period, because after the loss of Russia and the resulting increase in Germany's strength, the likelihood that this sanguinary conflict would last far longer than expected was once again magnified.

But a peace settlement of this kind contradicted the objectives of the military leaders of Germany and their allies on the extreme Right, especially as Wilson's offer was plainly addressed to the forces behind the German peace resolution of July 1917 and not to the political and military leadership of the Reich.[46]

The military leaders of Germany, who were by now conducting policy increasingly independently, had a different vision from President Wilson's. They saw the exit of Russia from the war as a final opportunity to gain a free hand in the east and place extensive areas of territory under German domination. This was also the guiding principle pursued in the peace negotiations with the Bolsheviks at Brest-Litovsk, where the German delegation behaved in a brusque and arrogant fashion. Its aim was to push the German sphere of influence as far as possible towards the east, so that it extended from the Baltic through Poland and White Russia into Ukraine. The Russian side broke off negotiations in reaction to these demands. Shortly afterwards, on 18 February, the German army resumed its offensive. Within a few days, it had occupied a great swathe of the western territories of the Russian Empire, without meeting any noteworthy resistance. On 1 March, German troops conquered Kiev. The new Bolshevik system was in danger of collapsing.

In this situation, Lenin bowed to force: on 3 March, the Bolsheviks accepted a dictated peace, which detached vast areas from the western part of the Russian Empire. It lost Poland, Ukraine and Finland as well as Livonia, Estonia, Courland and Lithuania. It lost a third of its population, railway network and cultivated land, more than a half of its industry and almost 90 per cent of its coal resources.

Despite this, the German army continued its drive to the east. Thirty divisions advanced from Ukraine to southern Russia as far as the Donets basin, Crimea and further towards Transcaucasia. In August 1918, three months before the end of the war, the Russian government had to make further concessions in a supplementary treaty: the renunciation of rights over the Baltic, the recognition of Georgian independence from Russia, the delivery of all the country's gold reserves to Germany, and the payment of 5 billion Marks of reparations. Russia also had to grant Germany the right to exploit the coalfields of the Donets basin.[47]

The eastern boundary of Germany's military advance of summer 1918 corresponds approximately to the limit reached in autumn 1942. For almost a year, the German army was the sole ruler in the areas under occupation. The dictatorial government of *Oberost* (the German administration of the conquered territories in the east) did not just aim at ensuring the stable control and economic exploitation of these territories. There was more. Various plans for the long-term Germanisation of the east were worked out, and further expansion eastwards and the complete destruction of Bolshevik Russia were also considered. Control over the east thus also offered a perspective for a possible German victory in the whole of Europe. Both German strategists and German soldiers had now gained the impression that the east was easy to conquer, and that no resistance was to be expected. It was obviously easy to establish a new political and national order in the areas under German supremacy. The immense region between the eastern border of Germany and the 'Muscovite' lands practically offered itself as the basis of a new German colonial empire, this time on the continent of Europe. These experiences had far-reaching long-term effects.[48]

As Ludendorff had foreseen, the parties of the Reichstag were unable to resist joining in the celebrations over Germany's unexpected victory in the east. Only the USPD voted against the Treaty of Brest-Litovsk; the SPD abstained, and all the other parties voted in favour. There was a renewed upsurge in hopes of a possibly rapid victory, and this pushed questions of suffrage and tax reform into the background. For the annexationists, the treaty was a triumph. Even their wildest dreams had been exceeded. There was of course no longer any question of a negotiated peace with the Allies, for after their actions in the east, who could possibly believe that the Germans desired peace?

At the same time, however, the negotiations at the beginning of January with the Russian delegation also had an impact on Germany's internal conflicts. There had already been numerous strikes in the course of 1917, which had various causes and motives, such as the shortage of food supplies, the lack of any domestic reforms and the increasing agitation of the Fatherland Party for annexations and a 'victorious peace'. But in January 1918 another reason emerged: the rapid spread of the fear that a peace settlement with Russia would be wrecked on the ever more extreme annexationist demands of the

German military. This had already led to disturbances and mass strikes in Vienna, and, on 28 January, workers in the big German armaments factories started a strike, which began in Berlin but spread rapidly to many other cities. In all, roughly half a million workers took part in these strikes. Significantly, they were organised by the USPD or by small left-wing cells such as the Revolutionary Shop Stewards (*Revolutionäre Obleute*), while the leaders of the free trade unions and the SPD were taken completely by surprise. These events already reflected the example of the October Revolution, and the self-confidence of the radical Left, which had increased as a result. A Workers' Council was elected in Berlin, and representatives of the SPD and the trade unions were unwillingly compelled to join it so as not to lose their influence over the movement. The demands of the strikers were clearly political: they wanted peace without annexations, the participation of representatives of the workers in future peace negotiations, the lifting of the state of siege, better food supplies and a reform of the electoral system. This was the biggest political mass strike that had ever taken place in Germany, and, to that extent, it was a clear warning sign for the parties of the Reichstag majority, the government and the German military leadership.

After a few days, the strikes were quickly and brutally suppressed. Ringleaders, mainly USPD members, were arrested, meetings were prohibited, and workers from the striking factories were called up for military service. These strikes played a very significant part in the way the internal political situation subsequently evolved. For one thing, they offered the Army High Command and the Fatherland Party an argument to fall back on in case the war ended in defeat. They could say that the German army and the German government had not failed. It was rather the striking workers, as well as the SPD, the trade unions and the Reichstag majority, which had left the front-line troops in the lurch. This argument, which was later to be called the 'Stab in the Back Legend', was already being prepared in January 1918.

In addition to this, the January 1918 strikes saw the emergence of a 'third force', alongside the majority parties of the centre, and the Army High Command and the extreme Right, which would in future play an important role in Germany's internal conflicts: a spontaneous workers' movement, which was increasingly independent of SPD and trade-union control.[49]

## The March Offensive and the German Collapse

The unexpected end of the war in the east offered the Germans the opportunity to prepare an offensive in the west. Thanks to the movement of troops away from the Eastern Front, Germany now had numerical superiority in the west, for the first time since early in the war. It is true that almost half a million German soldiers were still needed in the east to make yet further advances and occupy the conquered territory. These units would be lacking during the operations in the west. It was very clear, from the beginning, that by mounting this western offensive, which began on 21 March 1918, the German military leadership had staked everything on one outcome: they wanted to bring the war to a victorious end in the west as well as in the east by throwing all their strength into one last, gigantic effort, before the arrival of American soldiers at the battlefield *en masse*. And, in fact, in the first two weeks of the offensive, Germany's forces achieved considerable success, making large territorial gains. After further offensives in April and at the end of May, German troops had penetrated as far into French territory as they had in autumn 1914. It seemed as if the decisive breakthrough was about to take place. But, while the British army lost 160,000 men and the French some 80,000, the German army lost more than 300,000, either dead, wounded or taken prisoner. In addition, thanks in part to the arrival of fresh US troops, the Allies were able to compensate for their losses, whereas the German army was at the end of its strength. There were insufficient reserves and reinforcements, and German military equipment was inferior to that of the Allies, particularly as regards 'tanks', which now demonstrated that they were a particularly effective weapon. The number of deserters also rose steeply, with whole detachments surrendering their arms.

On 15 July, the Germans mounted another big offensive, on the Marne. It was the last one. The collapse of Germany's troops had already started when the Allies made their counterstroke, between Soissons and Rheims. This collapse is historically associated with the day of 8 August 1918, when British troops overran German positions near Amiens, and made large subsequent advances because the German units no longer had anything to set against the weight of the allied attacks. Finally, on 26 September, the allied detachments began a coordinated offensive, which drove the German units far to the rear of their prepared fallback lines. The theatre of operations continued to be located on Belgian and French territory, but the German army had been beaten.[50]

The German public learned nothing of these developments. On the contrary, the victories announced in the spring had rekindled hopes of a victorious end to the war, particularly among the middle classes, and the OHL and the government continued to propagate their slogans of victory and perseverance throughout the summer. By the end of July, however, the military leadership was already aware that the situation was very difficult, and, needless to say, they blamed this on the failings of the 'home front'. Walter Nicolai, the head of the Military Secret Service, remarked in August 1918 that the 'two-front war against the east and the west' had now become 'a two-front war against the external enemy and the internal one'.[51]

The military reverses were also disguised, or even hidden, from the party leaders of the Reichstag majority. Not until the end of August did the military inform leading German politicians of the actual situation. Their reaction was one of absolute dismay. The bourgeois politicians in particular, who, even days earlier, had been dreaming of an impending victory, after the advances in the east and the continuous propaganda from the OHL, now reacted with bewilderment and disbelief to the reports from the front.

Among the rank and file soldiers, on the other hand, and the vast majority of the population of the big cities, any illusions about a victorious peace had already been exploded long before. The mood at the front as well as at home was marked by war-weariness, exhaustion, a decline in discipline, disappointment, apathy and a mood of protest. 'Three quarters of the lower ranks here want the end to come. They don't care how that happens' noted a soldier in a letter written at the beginning of August 1918 about the attitude of his comrades. 'The mood of the population' according to an official report made to the Prussian Ministry of War during the same month, 'has reached depths never yet seen in the course of the war. It has been shown once again how dangerous it is to arouse exaggerated hopes of victory and peace among the people which are subsequently unfulfilled.' And this is what Kurt Riezler wrote in his diary about the mood in Berlin at the end of August 1918:

> Practically everything has changed. The change of fortunes at the front has had an immense impact. People who were previously the biggest loudmouths are now the ones who tremble the most. The bourgeoisie has a double fear: of revolution and of defeat. Everyone talks about the former, with the exception of the Social Democrats. No-one dares to speak of the latter, and even the most level-headed have no idea what it might signify. Everything is terribly sad.[52]

Unprecedented political developments came thick and fast in the few weeks between the beginning of September and the beginning of November 1918. There were four active forces which largely determined the course of events at this time. The first one was the constitutionalist movement, in other words, the Left Liberals, the Social Democrats and the Centre Party. Their main objective was to end the war as soon as possible, roughly on the lines of the Peace Resolution of 1917. At the same time, they wanted a rapid parliamentarisation of the Reich to be put in place, and an appropriate constitution to be worked out. The second power factor in the situation was the OHL, in association with the right-wingers around the Fatherland Party and the Emperor, though his behaviour was ambiguous and his political influence was in progressive decline.

The OHL intended, above all else, to preserve an army capable of fighting internal and external foes so as to restore stability to the existing structures of social and political power.

The third active player in these events was of increasing importance but hard to identify clearly, recognizable as much by its unpredictable nature as any other defining characteristic. It could not even be given a clear name. Was it the public? The working class? The population? It had become apparent since the January strikes, at the latest, that the actions of the politicians were increasingly influenced, even directed, by the mood in Germany, however it was perceived and measured. This mood was characterised by a clear desire for an immediate peace, in which context President Wilson's 'Fourteen Points' were increasingly seen as an appropriate guideline. If the military leadership again rejected the opportunity for a quick peace that had been available after the Treaty of Brest-Litovsk and again sought to intensify the conflict, this would undoubtedly have led to an explosive situation within the country. That was also the main reason why the bourgeois parties now pressed the SPD leadership to enter the new government that was on the point of being formed. This was the only way, it was thought, to calm the unrest in the working population and make possible an orderly post-war transition to a parliamentary system. The entry of the SPD into office was especially urgent now because every delay in bringing about the end of the war brought an increase in the influence of the USPD on the Left.

The fourth protagonist in the events of these weeks between military defeat and revolution turned out to be perhaps the most important one: President Wilson of the USA. His successive replies to German requests for an armistice played a decisive role in determining Germany's internal evolution. Wilson expressed a readiness to grant acceptable armistice conditions, but combined this with a demand for a complete transformation of power relationships within Germany. He insisted in particular on the complete democratisation of the country and the removal of the military leadership from office.

The Reichstag majority's endeavours to bring about a new government resting on parliamentary support turned out to be difficult and time-consuming. It was generally thought that the country should seek an armistice, but it was not clear how this could happen. There was no agreement either on the shape of the new government or the person of the future Chancellor. The reports on the military situation had thrown the Conservative and National Liberal politicians into a state of complete perplexity. Should they now give the rudder a sharp wrench to the right and stake everything on a national dictatorship, as some were proposing? Should they extend the idea of a 'total war' and unleash a 'people's war' by calling up every man who was capable in any way of bearing arms? This was what Walter Rathenau himself called for. Paul von Hintze, the State Secretary for Foreign Affairs, was of the opinion that a revolution from below could only be avoided by staging a 'revolution from above', in which a government would be established to allow the participation of 'the broadest possible circles', the Social Democrats in particular. Only in this way, he said, could the shock of defeat be overcome and a rising by the workers prevented.[53]

Under these conditions, it was again the OHL which seized the initiative. Once it became clear that the Central Powers were faced with the immediate prospect of complete defeat, and that any further continuation of military operations threatened to destroy the German army in the west, the military leadership directed its main efforts towards preventing the war from encroaching on the territory of the Reich itself and keeping the army intact, in order to be prepared for the conflicts which were expected to break out at home. In addition, the OHL and the politicians of the Right felt that it was absolutely essential to avoid being saddled with responsibility for the defeat and the armistice negotiations. On 29 September, therefore, Ludendorff and Hindenburg called on the government to conclude an armistice immediately and start peace negotiations: 'Not only can the war no longer be won; it is rather that we are faced with an immediate and definitive defeat. . . . Our own army is unfortunately already heavily contaminated with the poison of Spartacist-socialist ideas. The troops can no longer be relied on.' After the expected Allied breakthrough, 'the army in the west will lose its last foothold, flood back in complete dissolution over the Rhine and carry the revolution into Germany.' The government would therefore have to approach the American President without delay, in order to achieve the most favourable possible armistice on the basis of his 'Fourteen Points'. These negotiations should, however, now be conducted by the parties of the Reichstag majority, the military leaders considered, in order, as Ludendorff put it, 'to bring into the government those groups mainly responsible for the situation we now find ourselves in. We shall therefore now see these gentlemen enter the Ministries. They should make the peace which must now be made. Let them eat the soup they cooked up for us!'[54]

The strategy of the military leadership also left open the possibility of obtaining an adequate respite, after which the army would again be in a position to continue the fight, so as at least to achieve favourable peace conditions. But the most important motives behind this plan were of a domestic nature: the military leaders wanted to shift responsibility for the defeat away from themselves and lay it onto the very people who had warned for years that Germany could not win this war. In this way, the Reichstag parties and the workers' movement would bear the stigma of defeat and revolution, and the Reich and the monarchy would be saved. As the Bavarian liaison officer at the OHL noted,

> it is pretty good news that the parties of the left will now have to take upon themselves the odium of these peace negotiations. The storm of indignation

> will then be directed against them. Later on, we hope to jump into the saddle again and continue ruling according to the old formula.[55]

This war, according to the official version adopted by the OHL, was lost by the politicians, not the military. 'Just as Siegfried was felled by the cunning sword-thrust of the grim Hagen, so did our exhausted front collapse' was how Hindenburg later put it. And he added:

> The front endeavoured to imbibe new life from the dwindling sources of the homeland's energy, but in vain. It then became our task to preserve the strength of what remained of our army so that the fatherland could later be rebuilt. The present was lost. The future remained the only hope.[56]

When all else had failed, a compromise candidate was chosen as the new Chancellor. This was Prince Max von Baden, a man with a reputation as a liberal. His government had to perform two essential tasks with the utmost urgency. The first was to send a request for an armistice to the US President and no-one else, so that Wilson's relatively mild 'Fourteen Points' could be used to define the basis of the negotiations. The second was to place the government on a parliamentary basis and democratise the constitution as quickly as possible.

Max von Baden's government was the first legitimate democratic government in German history, and it was also the first government in which the Social Democrats were represented. This was a remarkable turn of events. But its significance was hardly perceived by the German public, because the key personnel in the government and the administration were almost the same as before. Above all, the power of the military leadership was unbroken. The working-class population in particular suspected that the OHL would again torpedo a peace which was within Germany's grasp, as it had done at Brest-Litovsk. The workers' mistrust was fed by the OHL's own actions, like the decision in mid-October to call up the young men of the 1900 class as well as many previously exempt armaments workers.

The American President also demonstrated how suspicious he was of the German military leadership in the first two Notes he sent in reply to the German armistice offer of 3 October. He was not prepared to negotiate with Germany's military leaders, he said. There could only be peace when the German government had freed itself from the influence of militarism. This approach was entirely consistent with the 'Fourteen Points', in which he had outlined the vision of a liberal, democratic Europe without military monarchies.[57]

The majority parties of the Reichstag reacted to Wilson's demands by accelerating their attempts to parliamentarise the government and institute democratic reforms. They were, of course, unable to encroach on the power of the OHL, and, for that reason, the reforms met with little response from the population. Ludendorff, on the other hand, saw that Wilson's Notes endangered his tactic of preventing the military collapse of the German army by a quick armistice and by this means continuing to control future developments. The military leadership was not prepared to accept subordination to a parliamentary government. A confrontation between military and civilian rule had become inescapable.

In his third Note, sent on 23 October, President Wilson raised his demands still further: before an armistice could be agreed, 'the power of those who ruled Germany until now', namely the German military authorities and the King of Prussia, would have to be destroyed irrevocably. This Note brought the struggle for political power within Germany to its height. It thwarted the OHL's calculations. Ludendorff and Hindenburg reacted accordingly: they demanded the immediate abandonment of the negotiations with Wilson and a resumption of hostilities. The American President's demands, the OHL declared in an Army Order of 24 October, signified capitulation, and they could not be accepted. The country was therefore compelled 'to continue the resistance with all the means at its command'. This confirmed the widespread distrust of the military leadership's policy, which was felt particularly by the workers.[58]

After the Army Order of 24 October time was of the essence. If the new government wished to prevent the disappointed masses from rising in revolt, it would have to act quickly, and it did so. The first step it took was to demand the dismissal of Ludendorff, and it was able to prevail on William II to take this decision. The most influential figure in the silent military dictatorship was thereby removed. The government then started to move more energetically towards a thoroughgoing reconstruction of the Reich's constitution. All the changes that had been discussed for decades and repeatedly rejected could now be implemented. From now on, under the new rules, the Chancellor had to possess the confidence of the parliament, and even the Prussian franchise would be altered within a few weeks. The movement for constitutional democracy was on the way to victory.

The German public was not particularly impressed by these measures. Ludendorff had been overthrown, but the Emperor was still in place, though President Wilson had demanded his removal (at least that is how most Germans perceived it). William II now decided to leave Berlin and travel to Spa, where the headquarters of the army was located. Hence there was now also a territorial separation between the military monarchy and parliamentary democracy. Various envoys from Berlin attempted to force the Emperor to abdicate, so as to clear the way to an acceptable peace, but they failed. Both the military leadership and the Emperor rejected the idea of abdication, preferring a continuation of the war to a peace which would deprive them of their power.

It was not by chance that it was in the German navy that these developments reached crisis point, because this institution had stood at the centre of the dispute over the future direction of German domestic and foreign policy ever since the turn of the century. In his second Note, President Wilson had demanded the immediate cessation of unrestricted submarine warfare. The fleet was the showpiece of the German military monarchy; but it had lain inactive in port throughout almost the whole of the war. Now the German navy leaders were being asked to give up the U-boat, the only naval weapon which had proved effective in the war, even if the consequences had ultimately turned out to be calamitous. In military eyes, Wilson's demand was an attack on the 'honour' of the German navy, indeed, on the honour of the armed forces as a whole. When the government agreed to end the U-boat war despite these objections, the German Admiralty issued an order to the High Seas Fleet to leave harbour and attack the British fleet in the Thames Estuary and on the Flemish coast so as to force it into a 'fight to the finish'. The German Admiralty, unlike the government, did not want to bow to the dictates of the victors, even if its plan was completely senseless in military terms. It therefore did not inform the government of the action it planned. People began to talk about the 'admirals' rebellion'.[59]

The crews of the German battle fleet now started to hear rumours that a fatal voyage was being planned and that the Admiralty wanted in this way to prevent an armistice and eliminate the new government. The suspicion that the military leadership had decided once again not to seize the chance of peace but to torpedo it hardened into certainty. The military structures of command and obedience, ingrained over decades, collapsed with lightning speed. On 29 October, when the order to get under way was actually given, the crews of some ships in Wilhelmshaven prevented it from being carried out. When the Admiralty responded by ordering the arrest of more than 1,000 mutineers, disturbances spread among almost the whole fleet. Earlier in the war, in summer 1917, an outbreak of disobedience in the High Seas Fleet had been brutally suppressed by order of the Commander-in-Chief, Admiral Scheer; five sailors were condemned to death, and two were executed. The consequences of this could now be seen: in Kiel the sailors tried to force the liberation of their comrades by demonstrating. On 3 November, the naval authorities gave the order to open fire on the mutineers. Eight men were killed as a result. Now there was no stopping the revolt. The sailors assembled on dry land, disarmed their officers, freed the prisoners by force, brought the town of Kiel under their control and formed a Soldiers' Council. A mutiny against unilateral action by the German Admiralty and an attempt to free prisoners had turned into a revolt, which spread within the next few days to become a revolutionary movement embracing almost the whole area of the Reich.[60]

By 9 November, uprisings were in progress from one end of Germany to the other. Governments and mayors resigned from their posts and Workers' and Soldiers' Councils seized power. The fact that this process took place so rapidly everywhere and with almost no violence demonstrates how far the imperial authorities' loss of legitimacy had already progressed. The fury of the revolutionaries was directed first and foremost against those 'who were until now the rulers in Germany', to use Wilson's formulation, in other words, the military leaders and the ruling kings and princes. These were the people they suspected of wanting to prevent the peace which was imminent. The King of Bavaria was the first to abdicate; he was followed within a few days by all the remaining German princes.

For the abdication of the Emperor, however, they had to wait. The Chancellor sent an emissary to William to urge him to renounce the throne. William replied that he had no intention of abdicating 'because of a few hundred Jews and a thousand workmen'. As late as 8 November, he was contemplating the idea of a final struggle by Germany as Europe's advance post against Bolshevism. This was a vision pregnant with future possibilities: 'The struggle is now against Bolshevism in Europe. It is not out of the question that the English will yet offer me military assistance to suppress Bolshevism in Germany.' After the conclusion of the armistice negotiations, he announced, he would come to Berlin with his troops and, if necessary, blow the whole town to smithereens.[61] Troops of this kind were, however, no longer available. Even units hitherto fiercely loyal to the Emperor were defecting to the side of the revolution, and for a few days the representatives of the old order vanished from sight under the onslaught of the workers' and soldiers' revolution.

William II's abdication was finally announced without his consent by the Chancellor on 9 November. It was the end of the German Empire. Two days later, on 11 November 1918, a German delegation led by the Centre Party politician Matthias Erzberger signed the armistice agreement, which was based on the conditions set by the Entente. The First World War had ended.

## The First World War in German History

In the historiography of twentieth-century Europe, the First World War has been given the character of a dividing line between two epochs, and there are indeed weighty reasons for regarding it as one of the greatest turning points in the modern history of the continent. Only with the First World War did the nineteenth century really come to an end. With the fall of the German Empire, the Habsburg Dual Monarchy also collapsed, while a year previously the rule of the Russian Tsar had already been ended by the February Revolution, and the Ottoman Empire was also about to disappear. The end of the war saw the collapse of four monarchically ruled empires, whose chief features were the predominant role of pre-modern forces, the prominent position of the military and the oppression of national minorities. All four had now suffered enormous territorial losses, and a number of small nation-states emerged in East Central Europe from the inheritance of three of these empires. And, although barely any of these new states could be described as stable, a return to the idea of multinational empires was never mooted, although many elements of the imperial tradition can still be recognised in the history of the Soviet Union. Even so, the age of the multinational empire had passed. The future belonged to the nation-state.

It is very clear that the Bolshevik Revolution of 1917 marked an epochal watershed which would determine the physiognomy of the twentieth century almost to its end. It entailed the rise, after the First World War, of that far-reaching political and social dichotomy between the western lands of liberal capitalism on the one hand and communist Russia on the other, which meant that they would compete with each other on a global scale. But it also set off a conflict within the western countries between Left radical workers' movements and a liberal, pro-capitalist bourgeoisie. This was therefore a worldwide conflict between rival powers which assumed the structural form of a social antagonism.

The end of the First World War was also associated with a decline in the dominant role of Europe. The rise of the USA was correlated with the decline of the European powers, both militarily and economically. The period after the First World War marked the beginning of the end of European colonial rule and also the start of the European economies' dependence on the USA, which was the new hegemonic power of the Western world.

Moreover, the First World War can also be seen as the conclusion of that long phase, lasting from June 1815 to July 1914, in which the atmosphere was relatively peaceful, interrupted only by a small number of military conflicts. During that period, bourgeois society had taken shape in Europe, with national, liberal and social movements at its core. When the First World War arrived, it created completely new underlying conditions, unlimited violence of a previously unknown magnitude and extension, a decline in social civilisation, challenges to the liberal inheritance of the nineteenth century, the destruction of inherited political structures and the conversion of war from a struggle over state interests into a fight between worldviews, which increased the readiness of the contending parties to make the conflict a total one.

These new conditions laid the basis for several decades of dictatorship, civil war and revolution, expulsion and genocide, and economic collapse and political catastrophe. This was an epoch which ended in 1945 in Western Europe but not until 1990 in Eastern Europe, when the power of the Soviet Union collapsed. In this sense, then, the First World War was, in the words of the American diplomat George F. Kennan, 'the great seminal catastrophe of this century'.[62]

This interpretation, which leads to the concept of the 'short twentieth century', has its merits. But there are many arguments against it, in relation to Germany. For one thing, the decision to unleash the First World War was also connected with the attempt of the three European military monarchies to use a war to prop up their own position, which was already unmistakably eroding, and to renew their vanishing legitimacy. The empires of Russia, Germany and Austria-Hungary had already been hard hit since the end of the nineteenth century by the onslaught of nationalist movements and liberal forces aiming to achieve democracy and parliamentary rule. Their power was clearly limited and their end could be foreseen. Their collapse was certainly accelerated by the First World War, but it did not bring it about.

Another point to note is that, if one dates the twentieth century from 1917 to 1990, making it coextensive with communist rule in Russia, the contradiction between communist and liberal societies, which started with the October Revolution, is thereby rendered the characteristic feature of the epoch. Under this frame of reference, the existence of Right radical regimes, and in particular the rule of National Socialism, is presented as a phenomenon subordinate to the principal contradiction. To assume that the antagonism between communism and bourgeois rule is the primary contradiction of the era is to follow the Marxist conception that contradictions between different 'forms of bourgeois rule', including therefore the contradiction between democracy and National Socialism, are of second-order significance. This would compel one to interpret the Nazi regime, its war against the Soviet Union, and the Holocaust, as subordinate aspects of history, or as a side effect of the conflict between East and West, a view which, in Ernst Nolte's more extreme interpretation, renders the murder of the Jews a kind of putative self-defence measure by the German bourgeoisie, as the representative of the European bourgeoisie in its fight against Bolshevism.[63]

In order to avoid such a disastrously reductive approach, it is necessary to draw on the triad of liberal democracy, radical nationalism and Bolshevism to explain the events of the twentieth century, and not to reduce them to two sets of bilateral antagonisms. But, to seek out the historical location at which the radical ideological movements of the twentieth century arose, one must go back before the October Revolution and the First World War, because the destabilisation of the societies of Western Europe had already been set in train during the phase of high industrialisation and the fundamental transformation processes associated with it that took place at the turn of the century. All the big political mass movements which made such an indelible mark on the twentieth century originated at this time. With the coming of the October Revolution, the conflict between capital and labour became the definitive emblem of the new century. But it had already taken shape in the final third of the previous one. The formation of the German workers' movement, as a programmatic and organisational response to this conflict, had largely been completed by the 1890s. Radical anti-liberal and anti-Semitic nationalism, the rise of which can also be observed at this time, had already turned into a powerful movement long before the Bolshevik revolution.

Thus the point of rupture at which a phase of relative calm turned into one of all-embracing dynamic change does not lie between 1914 and 1918 but in the period of rapid transformation over the three preceding decades. It was at that time that the preliminary conditions arose for the phase of civil wars and catastrophes which to a large extent determined the course of the first half of the twentieth century in Europe. The outbreak of the First World War, and the previously unknown level of violence that characterised it, were the consequence and expression of processes of radical change and the dissolution of boundaries to violent action which had already been experienced.

In that sense, then, there is a contradiction between the theses of a 'short' and a 'long' twentieth century. But, if one takes both arguments together, it becomes apparent that it was in the course of the First World War, and above all its final stages, that processes already laid down earlier and in train for more than twenty years combined and finally prevailed.

In Germany, there were two contrasting lines of development. Before 1914, German society was certainly marked by multiple contradictions and transformation processes. Their impact, however, had been softened until then by a high level of economic prosperity, which offered individuals the prospect of social advancement, at least in the long term, and created a potential for the redistribution of wealth which had a calming effect in spite of glaring social inequality. In addition, social and cultural conflicts were mitigated by the legitimacy of an authority which, even though it clashed sharply with the desiderata of extensive popular participation and liberal reform, functioned effectively and guaranteed legal security, welfare and also symbolic greatness, as expressed in the primary role of military and colonial expansion. The basic assent which the social order of the empire had enjoyed from the overwhelming majority of its citizens, even those who opposed the Wilhelmine political system, was a result of these achievements, and they were long remembered.

When the foundations of the social order began to crumble, the confidence of the citizens in their state also began to disintegrate. During the war, decades of accustomed economic prosperity were replaced by years of hunger and shortage. Social inequality had never been more clearly apparent, both at the front, in the relationship between officers and men, and at home, with the black market. The financial resources for a compensatory social policy were no longer available. Usury, profiteering, hunger protests and strikes had by now considerably loosened people's commitment to an entrenched social order, and the military defeat destroyed the symbolic greatness of the traditional society.

Almost all Germans were agreed at the end of the war that new ways of ordering society and new forms of governance were necessary. But there was very little accord over what these should be.

# PART TWO

# 1919–33

# 4

# Revolution and Republic

## The Revolution and the Movement for Constitutional Democracy

The German Revolution of 1918–19 took place against the background of the events in Russia, where an open civil war had been raging since the summer of 1918, in which anti-revolutionary forces of many different political tendencies were fighting the new regime on all fronts, supported by the troops of the Western powers, who feared that the revolutionary impulse would spread in their direction. The nations at the periphery of the empire had declared their independence, and the multinational Russian state appeared to be disintegrating. The economy was sinking into chaos, production figures were falling dramatically and galloping inflation had led to the development of an immense black market. The ferociously conducted civil war extended further and further into Russia, and as it did so it endangered the supply of food to the towns, leading eventually to famine conditions, and the death of some 2 million people. The nominal rulers of Russia were the Soviets of Workers, Peasants and Soldiers, as was laid down in the first Soviet Constitution, issued in July 1918. That constitution also envisaged the holding of free elections to a National Assembly. But, in practice, the Bolsheviks prevented elections from being held and turned the Soviets into powerless institutions, and, in the course of the years of civil war, they eliminated all their competitors and established a one-party dictatorship resting on the Red Army and the terror of the secret police.[1]

All political camps in Germany based their perceptions and evaluations of the course of the Russian Revolution on these developments.[2] On the extreme Left, the Russian Revolution was regarded as proof that a radical transformation of conditions in state, society and economy was possible, if only it was pursued consistently. At the same time, the onslaught of counter-revolutionary troops and the civil war were seen as confirmation that the revolution could only be made safe if the former authorities were completely deprived of power. To achieve this, fundamental changes in the state apparatus, the armed forces and the economy were necessary, and the undivided power of the workers and soldiers was a prerequisite. This was only possible in practice if authority was concentrated in a few hands. General elections should not be held, because if they were, bourgeois parties might gain the upper hand, thereby endangering the revolution. The October Revolution thus became a blueprint for the revolutionary left in Germany and the whole world, and in March 1919, with the foundation of the Communist International, the instrument was also created for the transformation of the societies of the industrialised countries along Russian lines.

Members of the Majority SPD had a diametrically opposed perception of the Russian Revolution. They were convinced that a revolution would unleash the inner momentum of the radical forces and endanger the economy and food supplies of the population. It could turn into a civil war and ultimately lead to a dictatorship. In view of the unmistakable parallels between the situation in Russia in autumn 1917 and that in Germany a year later, maximum effort should be directed towards demobilising the army as quickly as possible, converting the economy back to a peacetime basis in order to secure essential supplies for the population, ensuring the return of millions of soldiers to their places of work and feeding the millions of war-wounded soldiers and bereaved relatives. This required a strong economy, first and foremost, and a functioning administration, as well as stable and democratically based political conditions. It was also the only way to deal with the extraordinarily hazardous challenges of foreign policy, in particular, the negotiation of an acceptable peace treaty. In the eyes of Friedrich Ebert, who had chaired the SPD since 1913, there was nothing more dangerous in such a situation than to engage in sociopolitical experiments founded on radical and utopian ideals. Moves in the direction of socialism could be undertaken at some point in the future, when the government had won adequate parliamentary majorities. What was at issue now, however, was the maintenance of order, security and food supplies and also the preparation of elections to a constituent National Assembly.

Among the middle classes, finally, the October Revolution confirmed all the fears they had harboured for many years about socialism. The newspapers were full of reports of Bolshevik atrocities, famine and civil war, and they spread a sense of impending danger which people on the political Right applied to all forms of socialism. For the time being, however, fear of the 'commune' was so pronounced both in bourgeois circles and among the conservative elite that Ebert and his majority Social Democrats were regarded as virtually the last secure bulwark against this danger.

Friedrich Ebert had been appointed Chancellor of the German Reich by Prince Max von Baden in a manner which was constitutionally somewhat curious. He presided from 9 November 1918 onwards over a transitional government, the 'Council of People's Representatives' (*Rat der Volksbeauftragten*), confirmed in office on 10 November by a full assembly of the Berlin Workers' and Soldiers' Councils. The People's Representatives' first main aim was to rein in the revolutionary dynamism to which they owed their existence. In order to establish order, security and welfare, four fundamental decisions were taken in the first few days of the revolution, which moulded its later development for a long time to come.

The first decision was to maintain the continuity of official functions: the police, the hospitals, the financial institutions and the ministerial bureaucracy were asked to continue their work. There were no purges of personnel for political reasons. 'A failure of organisation at this difficult time' said Ebert 'would deliver Germany over to anarchy and the most terrible misery.'[3] The new government needed bourgeois specialists and without them, it would not be in a position to take necessary, and sometimes far-reaching, measures of domestic and foreign policy. A democratisation of the administration, which was entirely possible given the power relations prevailing in November 1918, was not a priority for the SPD in view of the other tasks it faced.

The second decision concerned the economy. The Auxiliary Service Law of December 1916 had already introduced corporatist structures into German industry. The preparations made after autumn 1918 for impending demobilisation had led in addition to especially far-reaching agreements between the representatives of the employers and the trade unions. These were now extended. The employers accepted the regulation of labour conditions by wage contracts (*Tarifverträge*) with the trade unions, the Eight-Hour Day, and Factory Councils (*Betriebsräte*). The trade unions, for their part, accepted something they had not in fact questioned at any point, namely, the principle of private property in the means of production. In view of the imminent entry of millions of soldiers into civilian economic life, as well as the threat of unemployment and the problem of maintaining a supply of food, the demand for the socialisation of the large enterprises, particularly in the mining industry, which was first raised on isolated occasions and then reasserted more vociferously by some Social Democrats in the course of the next few months, was not a priority objective for the trade unions. In view of the attitude of the trade union leadership, therefore, there was no longer any need to fear a Russian-style revolution against private property.[4]

The third major decision concerned the military. Consideration had already been given to the creation of a separate fighting force with republican loyalties to defend the new government, because there were justified doubts about the political reliability of the troops of the imperial army (Reichswehr) led by the officers of the OHL. On the other hand, the establishment of a force of new, republican troops involved the danger of a confrontation between the old army and the new one. Ebert thought it was urgently necessary to make sure of the loyalty of the old Reichswehr by inducing the OHL to recognise the new government. In this he succeeded: as early as 10 November, he concluded an agreement with General Groener, Ludendorff's successor as First Quartermaster General, whereby the OHL recognised the Council of People's Representatives as the lawful government and agreed to support it. In return, Ebert agreed that the OHL was still the supreme military authority in the country, and confirmed the principles of military discipline. From the outset, this decision was hotly disputed by the Workers' and Soldiers' Councils, because by accepting the authority of the OHL Ebert had brought back onto the scene precisely those forces against which their revolutionary uprising had mainly been directed. Ebert, on the other hand, regarded the agreement as an opportunity to avoid a confrontation between the Reichswehr and the pro-republican forces, which he thought might lead to a civil war as in Russia and end in catastrophe. It is this fear which largely explains the immense caution with which Ebert and the new government went about their activities.[5]

Caution was also the watchword of the fourth major decision, which concerned the role of the Workers' and Soldiers' Councils and their relation to the parliamentary democracy sought after by Ebert and his government. It was already apparent on 9 November that the SPD would not be able by itself to steer the revolution towards the establishment of a parliamentary democracy. It would need the assistance of the USPD, which had great influence in the big factories, particularly in the capital city. As we have seen, the USPD arose as a movement against the Majority SPD's policy of maintaining the wartime 'party truce'. Its sociopolitical profile, however, was extremely inconsistent. Its strong left wing, based above all on groups such as the 'Revolutionary Shop Stewards' (*Revolutionäre Obleute*) in the big Berlin factories, aimed to go beyond the party's pacifist programme towards a continuation of the socialist revolution. For the majority of the party's members, however, the end of the war had lessened the differences that divided them from the Majority SPD. This was reflected in the coalition between the two social-democratic parties which led on 9 November to the establishment of a Council of People's Representatives in which each party was equally represented. Even so, there were two highly sensitive points on which the parties had developed widely divergent positions: the relation of the government to the Reichswehr, and the future of the Council movement.[6]

The future of the Council movement was decided in December at a General Congress of Workers' and Soldiers' Councils, which was now the supreme revolutionary authority. Once again, it was developments in Russia which decided the issue. In Russia, said Max Cohen, the main speaker for the Social Democrats, the Bolsheviks had only introduced the system of Councils (or Soviets) so as to prevent free elections and install a dictatorship. Even a socialist transformation, he said, required the agreement of the majority of the people: 'No greater amount of socialism can be introduced than is wished by the majority of the people.' Moreover, in a highly developed industrial society, socialist experiments were extraordinarily dangerous. The events in Russia spoke for themselves, he said: 'Russia is freezing and starving.' A peasant society could recover from this. But an industrial society might be damaged permanently. 'Once Germany's industry has been destroyed, it will never recover.'[7]

The overwhelming majority of the delegates to the Congress of Councils agreed with this position (by 400 votes to fifty). The Councils had sprung up as institutions of the revolutionary transition, and they were regarded as such. The rejection of the Council system also signified a decision in favour of holding elections to a National Assembly. The road to parliamentary democracy lay open.

On the whole, the course followed by Ebert and the Majority Social Democrats proved entirely successful. They were able to canalise the dynamism of the revolution and reconnect it in a relatively short time with the objectives of the movement for constitutional democracy. They successfully completed the demobilisation of the soldiers, reintegrated a large number of them into the production process and set in motion the transition from a wartime to a peacetime economy. Moreover, the introduction of women's suffrage, and the establishment of the Eight-Hour Day and the right to make collective wage contracts were social and political reforms of tremendous scope.

But these successes were paid for with far-reaching concessions. In the field of administration, the primacy of continuity meant that even fierce opponents of democracy and the working class remained in office and in power. The government reintroduced the hated disciplinary regulations into the army against the wishes of the Soldiers' Councils, so that even the officers against whom the sailors had mutinied in October once again had the power to issue orders. The decision to call off socialisation also applied to branches of industry which even bourgeois specialists regarded as 'ripe' for state ownership, the coalmines in particular, the owners of which were some of the most vehement opponents of the workers' movement. The influence of the East Elbian landowners was not destroyed, though they more than any other social group represented the old, pre-democratic social order. The government did not even attempt to alter the foundations of their social and political power.

The events of 9 November 1918 had raised the hopes of the workers to great heights, but the measures (or rather the cautious restraint) of the Council of People's Representatives disappointed them, even if they largely approved of Ebert's political line. He lost the support of the small left wing of the revolutionary movement, which now openly began to oppose the government's course of political and social continuity, and to call for a dictatorship of the proletariat. The course followed by the left wingers finally led to the formation of a new organisation, consisting of parts of the Left of the USPD, the Revolutionary

Shop Stewards and the Spartacus Group around Karl Liebknecht and Rosa Luxemburg, which had a strong public presence but little mass influence. At the end of 1918 a Communist Party of Germany (KPD) on the Bolshevik model emerged from these groups.[8]

Tensions between the Majority SPD and the radical Left increased sharply after the Council Congress which took place in mid-December. Around Christmas 1918, the conflict turned violent. A left-wing military unit (the 'People's Naval Division') occupied the Berlin Palace, taking a Social Democratic politician hostage, in order to obtain the payment of wages. The Majority SPD saw the Left radical movement through the prism of the Bolshevik revolution, and the Ebert government was accordingly prepared to proceed against its opponent by force of arms, if it should become apparent that the Russian events were about to be repeated in Germany. In line with his agreement with General Groener, Ebert called on the Reichswehr for assistance, giving it *carte blanche* to do as it thought fit. This intervention of the Reichswehr against the supporters of the revolution was at first unsuccessful, but even so, it had great symbolic significance, for the government had openly made an agreement with the military authorities against the revolutionary forces. The result of this was the break-up of both coalitions: that between the two social democratic parties and that between the constitutionalist and revolutionary movements. After Christmas 1918, the split in the German workers' movement was an accomplished fact: Social Democracy, with its constitutionalist and parliamentary orientation, was now opposed by a revolutionary communist movement which aimed at establishing a proletarian dictatorship.

The elections of 19 January 1919 to the National Assembly marked the definitive victory of Ebert's approach over that of the Left opposition. The results showed that the German people increasingly supported the constitutionalist parties, but they also demonstrated a certain amount of continuity with the 1912 elections. Having gained roughly 45 per cent of the vote, the two workers' parties (Majority SPD 37.9 per cent; USPD 7.6 per cent) stood 10 percentage points higher than the level reached by the SPD alone in 1912, but they were still at a considerable distance from securing an absolute majority. The DDP (German Democratic Party), the successor of the Left liberal Progressive Party, obtained 18.5 per cent (an increase of 6.2 per cent), the Centre Party 19.7 per cent (an increase of 3.3 per cent). The constitutionalist parties had thus achieved an absolute majority, gaining three-quarters of the seats in the National Assembly. Their political line had thus been impressively confirmed and legitimated. In contrast to this, the DNVP (German National People's Party), which had been formed by a merger between the two conservative parties and various anti-Semitic groups, did significantly worse, with 10.3 per cent, than its predecessors had in 1912, when they secured roughly 15 per cent of the vote. The National Liberals, now reorganised under the title of 'German People's Party' (DVP), had an even more disappointing result: they obtained 4.4 per cent instead of the 1912 figure of 13.6 per cent. The radical Left, therefore, had been chosen by less than 8 per cent of the voters, and the Right, if it is appropriate to combine the DNVP and the DVP under this heading, had only received 15 per cent of the vote. Taken together, these results showed unmistakably that the electorate was committed to parliamentary democracy.[9]

The National Assembly elected Friedrich Ebert as the President of the Reich and Philipp Scheidemann, also a Social Democrat, as its first head of government. The Assembly began its constitution-making labours on 2 February 1919, not in Berlin, for fear of possible excesses by the revolutionary groups, but in distant Weimar. The strategy of the movement for constitutional democracy had been successful, and its perspective for the future was clear: a new and democratic constitution should be created, but this also had to take into account the doubts entertained about Western parliamentarism, chiefly among Centre Party members and Left Liberals, but also in parts of the SPD. It was also calculated that a democratic Germany created in this way would be able to negotiate an acceptable peace settlement with the Allies. In addition, it was expected that the restoration of calmer conditions and legal stability would contribute to stimulating the economy. More far-reaching reforms would then also be possible, including the reconstruction of the finances in particular, but also a substantial expansion of state-financed social policies and the modernisation of German society.

These hopes were frustrated, however. The Allies refused to make a mild peace settlement, the Versailles Peace Treaty strengthened the obstructive attitude of the political Right, and the lack of social reform increased working-class unrest and encouraged the radical Left to engage repeatedly in attempted uprisings.

The new constitution, passed half a year later, was largely drafted by the liberal academic and Professor of Constitutional Law Hugo Preuß. It reflected the country's positive, as well as its negative, experiences with the constitutional practice of the German Empire. Many of its aspects, such as the rule of law, universal, equal male and female suffrage, a parliament with strong powers, and the responsibility of the government to the Reichstag, were the fruit of decades of criticism of conditions in the Empire, and the majority of the constitution-makers quickly agreed on these points. The financial reform of 1920, which at last allocated to the Reich the means of financing its considerably increased expenditure, also belongs within this context. But Preuß's original intention of reducing the power of the individual states (*Länder*) that made up Germany, and in particular splitting up Prussia, was abandoned, partly under pressure from the states themselves but also because it was feared that to divide Germany into smaller fragments would be to pander to the interests of the Entente powers, particularly France.

The constitution also reflected a widespread suspicion of parliamentarism and political parties. This was reflected in the immense powers granted to the president, who was elected by direct vote and thus obtained his own personal political legitimacy. The role of the president, it was considered, was to express the unity between the people and the state and to counterbalance the conflict of opinions and the strife between the parties. In part, this attitude reflected the reservations of the constitution-makers towards Western-style parliamentarism. But the great importance assigned to the president and the inclusion in the constitution of Article 48, which granted the president almost dictatorial powers during a state of emergency, should also be understood as a reaction to the uprisings and disturbances of the spring of 1919. The insertion of elements of direct democracy such as provisions for a 'people's initiative' (*Volksbegehren*) and a plebiscite (*Volksentscheid*) also expressed the widespread discomfort with a purely parliamentary, representative system which had long been felt on the Right, but was also propagated by the Left in the winter of 1918–19, not least in its adoption of the Council idea.

Here, as on other issues, the Wilhelmine Empire cast a long shadow. The new republic replaced something which had not proved successful before 1914 with new and fundamentally democratic regulations. But it became apparent as early as the debate on the republic's emblem that the bourgeois centre, despite its alliance with the Social Democrats, wanted the new form of the state to maintain continuity with the old one. It is true that the SPD was finally able to push through its proposal that the national colours should be 'Black-Red-Gold', but the bourgeoisie's attachment to the familiar 'Black-White-Red' of the Empire was so great that the flag of the German merchant fleet continued to bear the old colours, though with a tiny black-red-gold insertion. That decision had a certain amount of symbolic significance: Germany was a democratic, reformed and modernised kind of empire, without an emperor but with a strong and directly elected president. This was a system which reflected widely held opinions, even those of people who in principle took a positive attitude towards the republic.[10]

## The Left Rises in Revolt

After the surprisingly rapid collapse of the old authorities in November 1918, and the defeat of the Left at the Congress of Councils held in December, the elections to the National Assembly were expected to end the revolution and stabilise the republic. This turned out to be a misconception. Instead the opposite took place: the next four years were characterised by repeated attempts at a forcible seizure of power by radicals from both the Left and the Right of politics. This sequence of events began early in 1919 and continued until 1923. It should be noted that under the Empire, until 1914, a resort to violence had not been a widespread feature of domestic political conflict in Germany. The escalation which occurred after 1918 could be traced back, firstly, to the experience of massive violence during the war, and secondly to the fact that large quantities of weapons continued to circulate, which served to arm the semi-official *Freikorps* units, the Red Workers' Armies and the local militias (*Einwohnerwehren*). But the brutality of the years after 1918 also reflected the ideological character of the conflicts, in which it was no longer differences of interest or political disagreements which were at stake, but rival worldviews (*Weltanschauungen*). The fight over the future ordering of society increasingly assumed the characteristics of a civil war, directed towards securing the complete victory of one fundamental political position over the other. The aim was no longer to establish a compromise or to strike a balance between different interests.[11]

The rising tension in the country first exploded as early as January 1919, a few days before the elections to the National Assembly. On one side there stood the Majority SPD with its course towards constitutional reform, while on the other side a radical left-wing movement, committed to the rule of the Councils and socialist revolution, was in process of formation. On 4 January, armed left-wing groups occupied the Berlin newspaper district, and in particular the building that housed the SPD newspaper *Vorwärts*. Completely misinterpreting the situation, Karl Liebknecht, speaking on behalf of the Communist Party of Germany (KPD), which had been founded three days earlier, proclaimed the occupation of the *Vorwärts* building to be the signal for an uprising to overthrow the Ebert–Scheidemann government. The Council of People's Representatives, warned by its earlier fiasco at the Berlin Palace, now placed its faith in a massive military attack, which was carried out both by armed Republican detachments and by units of the Reichswehr, and ended with the bloody suppression of the rising.

The parallel between the 'Spartacus Uprising' and the events in Russia in 1917 should be noted. It was an attempt by the radical Left to swing round the political rudder with a military insurrection before the elections to a National Assembly, at which a victory by the working-class parties was rather uncertain, and to set up a dictatorship of the proletariat in whatever form was possible. The suppression of the January Uprising already gave an indication of the other threat to the republic, from the newly awakened forces of the Right, which was in fact much greater. The well-known leaders of the Spartacus League, Rosa Luxemburg and Karl Liebknecht, were murdered after the military operations had ended. The culprits were the officers commanding troop units assembled together from volunteers, and described as 'Free Corps' (*Freikorps*). They had placed themselves at the disposal of the government in its effort to suppress the communist uprising, and soon began to fight the revolutionary workers on their own account. The *Freikorps* detachments contained many soldiers and officers of the Reichswehr who feared having to return to a civilian life to which they were unaccustomed. There were also students, who had been too young to take part in the war and now wanted to make up for their lack of patriotic front-line experience by fighting the Bolsheviks. Supporters of the new, militant right-wing extremism gathered together in these units.[12]

For many of the workers, on the other hand, the revolution offered the hope that there would now be a lasting improvement in their material living conditions, after the years of privation suffered during the war. When these hopes were dashed, the workers' dissatisfaction increased rapidly. The big centres of industry in the Ruhr and Central Germany in particular were a simmering cauldron of discontent. Wage increases, shorter working hours, the establishment of a system of Factory Councils and the socialisation of key industries were the central demands of big strike movements, which put the government under severe pressure. The risings in the Ruhr and Central Germany were brought to an end by negotiation and compromise, but in Berlin in March 1919 there was a renewed military confrontation. A strike in Berlin, led initially by the Revolutionary Shop Stewards and the USPD, later came under the leadership of the KPD, and its goals were chiefly political. It demanded the implementation of everything the Left had failed to achieve in January: the recognition of the authority of the Workers' and Soldiers' Councils, the establishment of a revolutionary army, the removal of the Army High Command's powers and a close alliance between Germany and Soviet Russia. This strike too, which was supported at the outset by the trade unions and by both Social Democratic parties, broadened out after a few days into an attempt at an armed uprising by communist groups, which was finally suppressed by the Armed Forces Minister Gustav Noske with the help of Reichswehr troops. The battles of March 1919 in Berlin resulted in almost 1,000 deaths.[13]

Bavaria (or more precisely Munich) was a fourth centre of disturbances in 1919, alongside Berlin, the Ruhr and Central Germany. Here there had been numerous assassination attempts against representatives of the republic. The Bavarian revolutionary leader Kurt Eisner was one of the victims. A group of Independent Social Democrats and left-wing intellectuals replied to Eisner's murder on 7 April 1919 by announcing the deposition of the Social Democratic state government of Bavaria, proclaiming a 'Council Republic' and forming a government with a somewhat bizarre composition. The troops the official Bavarian government immediately sent into action in reply were defeated by the quickly assembled 'Red Army' of the Munich Council Republic, at a cost of twenty dead and more than a hundred wounded. The putsch mounted by the *literati* of Schwabing now turned into an attempted communist insurrection that was in direct contact with the Russian Revolutionary leaders. A few days later, the government of the Reich responded by sending to Munich a sizeable military force, consisting of more than 30,000 men. This drowned the short-lived Council Republic in blood. The death toll was more than 600, and many of the supporters of the Munich republic were murdered after the fighting had ended.

The middle classes were profoundly shocked by the adventure of the Munich Council Republic. Their worst apprehensions were confirmed when it was seen that a big German city could be ruled for weeks by a small, dilettantish group of radical left-wing *literati* and anarchists. As a result, the ideas of socialism and rule by the Councils were linked with a sense of threat and insecurity even in the minds of those contemporaries who had sympathised with the republic. The men of the *Freikorps* who had been utilised to defeat the Council Republic were characterised as much by their radical right-wing attitudes as by their brutality, yet they were celebrated as liberators. An almost fanatical hatred for Bolshevism and for left-wing intellectuals now took hold of the bourgeoisie, particularly in Bavaria. And since some of the leaders of the Munich Council Republic were Jewish, the experience of Council rule was associated with an image of Jewish communism and thus gave considerable encouragement to anti-Semitic obsessions which were already present in the population.[14]

## Versailles and Its Consequences

During these weeks, while the Germans were concentrating entirely on domestic political events, such as the Berlin March uprising, the Munich Council Republic, and the strikes on the Ruhr, and worrying about the increasing depreciation of the currency, the representatives of the Entente were negotiating in Paris over the transition from war to peace. There were three main topics: the territorial reorganisation of the European continent, the setting up of the League of Nations and the treatment of defeated Germany.

The dissolution of the Central European empires presented the Entente with the task of reorganising the European state system. The map of Central Europe would no longer be made up of multinational entities; it would consist instead of independent nation-states. Finland, Hungary, Czechoslovakia, the Baltic states, Poland, Yugoslavia, Bulgaria and Romania were either newly created as nation-states or had undergone drastic territorial modifications. Wherever the majority nation was faced with ethnic minorities, it was decided to guarantee an appropriate form of minority protection. In disputed cases a plebiscite would decide whether a given region should belong to one state or the other. These new nation-states ought also to be ruled according to the principles of parliamentary democracy, it was said, in part because this would also be the best way of regulating the coexistence of different ethnic groups.

In a few instances, this attempt to reorder the continent of Europe turned out to be logical and long-lasting, but most of the time it missed its target. For one thing, the national minority problems which had contributed to the collapse of the multi-ethnic empires of Russia and Austria-Hungary were in fact made worse by the decision to define minority groups in ethnic terms. National conflicts between majority and minority populations in the new nation-states were not attenuated or regulated but rather repeatedly rekindled by this decision. The emergence within a few years of authoritarian regimes, which were as a rule nationalist as well, in almost all the states of East Central and South-East Europe, was closely linked with these situations of national conflict. It became apparent that in the region between the Baltic Sea and the Crimea, where ethnic and religious population mixtures were present on a much greater scale than in Western Europe, a clear demarcation of nation-states, organised on the Western European model, would quickly lead to severe conflicts. In 1923, after the Greco-Turkish war, a forced exchange of populations was agreed. Some two million Greek Orthodox inhabitants of Turkey were driven out of the western districts of that country, where they had lived for thousands of years. In return, almost half a million Muslims had to leave the eastern districts of Greece and emigrate to Turkey. This was a foretaste of the new approach to solving perceived problems with minority groups: the creation of ethnically pure nation-states by the forcible expulsion of national minorities on a massive scale.[15]

The American government, under President Wilson, wanted to avoid future conflicts between the powers by creating a League of Nations, which would also guarantee the territorial integrity of the newly created states and arbitrate in disputed cases. However, when the American Congress voted against the entry of the USA into the League of Nations, thereby torpedoing President Wilson's conception of a new and peaceful world order, the League was deprived of the strong hand of the nation which was by now the greatest economic power in the world, and the only one which could have lent sufficient weight to its endeavours.

There were two competing positions among the Allies over the future of Germany. France, which had now fought two wars against that country within a few decades, and each time predominantly on its own territory, had several demands. It wanted both financial compensation for the damage it had suffered, and extensive security guarantees: Germany was expected to hand over to France large territories in the west, stretching as far as the River Rhine, and radically to reduce its military forces. It would also have to compensate France financially. In making these demands, the French politicians were under pressure from a public with a strongly nationalist outlook, which reacted with a storm of indignation to every concession made to the Germans. Great Britain, for its part, was also interested in receiving considerable reparation payments from Germany, and here too an upsurge of nationalist feeling played a role, but British politicians were keen to avoid endangering the continental balance of power once again, and were therefore unwilling to concede too much to France's aspirations for great power status. After months of negotiation, agreement was finally reached on a compromise. It involved the return of Alsace-Lorraine and Eupen-Malmedy, but France would not acquire Germany's territories on the left bank of the Rhine. In the east, regions with a predominantly Polish population were separated from Germany, but in this case the Allies' initial peace proposals were changed, in that there would now be plebiscites in areas of mixed population. In addition, Germany was to be thoroughly demilitarised: it would have to hand over its air force, its U-boats and its High Seas Fleet. The maximum size of the German army was set at 100,000 men. Germany lost its colonies, and it was intended to burden the country with a substantial level of reparations for many decades. In order to give legitimacy to the demand for reparations, it was put on record in a special article of the treaty (Article 231) that Germany alone bore the guilt for causing the war. On the other hand, the country was not split up, as foreseen under the French proposals, nor was its economy destroyed. It could therefore be predicted that, as the European nation with the largest population and the strongest economy, Germany would soon be able to recover its great power status.[16]

But considerations of this kind played no role in the reception by German public opinion of the peace conditions, which were presented to the country's delegation on 7 May 1919. The mood in Germany after the terms of the Versailles Treaty became known was one of resentment and consternation, shared by all political camps. The government itself set the tone. In its first press release on the subject, on 8 May 1919, it stated: 'The peace conditions signify nothing other than the complete economic annihilation of Germany.' The liberal press struck a similar note: 'The lunacy of conquering materialism has reached its apogee in this document. If this or a similar proposal were actually to be put into effect, it would be time to despair of humanity' wrote the *Frankfurter Zeitung* on 9 May 1919.[17] The employers' associations and the trade unions issued a joint declaration that the treaty was nothing but a 'death sentence for Germany's economy and the life of its people'. Never in human memory, they said, had a crime comparable to the one now planned ever been committed against such a great, hard-working and civilised people as the Germans.[18] German scholars used similar language: 'Our misfortune is boundless, a whole lifetime is not sufficient to exhaust it' wrote the national-liberal historian Hermann Oncken. 'One could examine history since Charlemagne in vain to find a parallel to this enslavement of a defeated people' he added.[19] On 21 June the ships of the German fleet, which were interned in the British naval base of Scapa Flow, were deliberately scuttled, while students and *Freikorps* members entered the Berlin arsenal and burned the French banners which had been captured in the war of 1870–1 and kept there ever since. These two acts serve to indicate the combination of disappointment, powerless fury and refusal unflinchingly to recognise the reality of defeat, which characterised the mood of Germany in the early summer of 1919.

The war had never reached German soil, hence Germany's national energies had not been exhausted. A denial of reality and a posture of radical resistance could therefore already be observed between November 1918 and May 1919, during that 'dreamland of the armistice period', to use Ernst Troeltsch's frequently quoted expression. This applied particularly to the Rhineland, where the entry of French troops in November 1918 was received with astonishment and horror. Only a few days earlier, when German soldiers were returning from France, many of the locals felt as if they were observing military manoeuvres: 'The bearing of the soldiers who marched through was exemplary' a resident of Mainz recalled. 'There was nothing to indicate that a detachment which had held out heroically at the front for more than four years and obtained incomparable victories was returning home because it was forced to march back over the Rhine by the conditions of a ruinous armistice.' The citizens who gazed admiringly at the marching columns found it difficult to believe that this proud army had lost the war. In their perception, these troops were returning 'as heroes, as unbeaten, undefeated heroes.'[20] This denial of reality continued for some time, and in this connection it proved to be particularly fateful that both the Council of People's Representatives and the Scheidemann government refrained from publishing an unvarnished analysis of the disastrous policies of the cabinets of the Wilhelmine Empire.

Thus many people continued to feel that it was out of the question either to speak of Germany's guilt for the war or to admit that the country had suffered a total defeat. And, after all, had not Germany fulfilled, and even gone beyond, Wilson's political demands, by making a revolution which deprived the emperor and the military leaders of their power? As a result, most politicians, and with them the majority of the population, proceeded on the assumption that the peace negotiations would be conducted on the basis of Wilson's 'Fourteen Points', and not go beyond them. Not only were completely unrealistic expectations constructed in this way; the conditions for a broad national movement of protest were also created. 'Perhaps the most fateful consequence of the Versailles Peace Treaty', wrote the historian Martin Broszat, 'was that from 1919 onwards it largely blocked all self-criticism of prewar Wilhelmine imperialism and of the monarchy's wartime record.'[21]

It was not a radical nationalist, but the president of the National Assembly, the Centre Party deputy and later Chancellor Konstantin Fehrenbach, who on 12 May 1919, addressing a rally held at the University of Berlin, exhorted his audience to work for the revision of the Versailles Treaty. This is what he said:

> This treaty . . . eternalises war. And now I turn to our enemies in a language they too understand, and I say: *Memores estote, inimici, ex ossibus ultor* [Remember this, enemies, an avenger will arise from the bones of the fallen.] German women will bear children in the future too, and those children will smash the chains of slavery and wipe away the shame the enemy intends to inflict on our German countenances.[22]

Chancellor Philipp Scheidemann was no different, although his frequently quoted exclamation, 'What hand would not wither that binds itself and us in these fetters?',[23] could not conceal the fact that the government had absolutely no clear political options. Contemporaries capable of calmer reflection, such as the chairman of the Centre Party in the National Assembly, Matthias Erzberger, had long recognised that the German government would have to sign the treaty. In contrast to this, the Scheidemann government itself contributed to the nationalist agitation that led to its own demise.

The parties of the bourgeois centre, the DDP and the DVP foremost among them, quickly took steps to extricate themselves from responsibility for signing the treaty. It was already clear at the time that this behaviour was a result of the agitation over Versailles and a precautionary reaction to the expected reversal of public opinion. In this situation, it was of negligible significance that the German Nationalists and the DVP were generously prepared to attest to the 'patriotic motives' of those who wanted to vote for the acceptance of a peace treaty, for there was no realistic alternative, either political or military, to accepting the ultimatum.

Right from the outset of the public discussion of the peace conditions in May and June 1919, the Right agitated without restraint against the government and particularly against elements who were denounced as the promoters and wire-pullers of the decision to sign, Matthias Erzberger emerging as a particular target. This campaign was based on two myths. First, there was the belief that Germany was innocent of the outbreak of the First World War, and second, there was the 'Stab in the Back Legend', which was already circulating in summer 1918, and which Hindenburg 'officially' presented to the world in November 1919, when he addressed the parliamentary Investigation Committee the National Assembly had set up to clarify the events surrounding the collapse of the German Empire.[24] These two legends served thenceforth as the basis for a German nationalist view of recent history, which proved to be extraordinarily successful. In this version, the true patriots were not those who soberly weighed up the advantages and disadvantages of signing and feared the possibly catastrophic consequences of a total occupation of Germany for the living conditions of the population and the continued existence of the Reich, but those who had decided to take up the struggle against the Western Powers, notwithstanding all the associated risks. From then onwards, a pose of heroism, combined with hollow prophecies of revenge, counted as proof of a person's noble, idealistic patriotism.

## The Kapp Putsch and the War on the Ruhr

The Treaty of Versailles entered into force on 1 January 1920, including the provisions which governed the trial of German war criminals and the reduction of the German army to 100,000 men. The reduction in troop numbers was a direct blow to the *Freikorps* members, who were still under arms, but it also hit thousands of Reichswehr officers, who had hoped in vain that the government would circumvent these regulations. The bitterness aroused by this provided an opportunity to put into effect an idea the Right had been weighing up for some time, namely the overthrow of the November Republic. This long-meditated putsch was set in motion by a number of right-wing politicians, among them Wolfgang Kapp, who had been one of the leaders of the Fatherland Party, and Colonel Max Bauer, Ludendorff's closest colleague in the OHL. It found support first and foremost in the *fronde* of the East Elbian landowners and in large parts of the Reichswehr, not least General von Lüttwitz, who was in command in Berlin. The military implementation of the putsch was largely in the hands of *Freikorps* units, including in particular the Ehrhardt Naval Brigade, which had the reputation of being the most ruthless and violent of them all. On 13 March, it marched into Berlin.

This was a putsch by the old Right. It was described by the liberal theologian Ernst Troeltsch as 'the coup d'état of the praetorian guards, the Junkers and the Pan-Germans', and its objectives consisted of little more than the re-establishment of the conditions that had prevailed when the third OHL was still determining the fate of the country.[25] The conspirators had not even prepared a list of ministers. It was only initially surprising that the attempted putsch collapsed so quickly, for there were several important factors working against it. The putschists were not actively supported by the Reichswehr leadership, although most of the generals did refuse to send in Reichswehr units against the troops engaged in the mutiny ('Reichswehr does not fire on Reichswehr' was the saying). This demonstrated once again how dependent the government was on the attitude of the military. Moreover, support for the putschists by the authorities and the civil service was very slight outside East Elbia. Even the parties of the Right held back. The DVP and its leader Stresemann were ready to support Kapp and von Lüttwitz if he succeeded, but not unreservedly. They decided to wait. The decisive factor, however, turned out to be the response of the trade unions. While the government itself fled first to Dresden and then to Stuttgart, the trade unions proclaimed a general strike, which paralysed the whole country and the capital within a short time, and compelled the putschists to abandon their enterprise. The Ehrhardt Brigade had to withdraw from Berlin, though not without opening fire on demonstrators who were protesting against its presence, killing twelve and wounding thirty.[26]

This episode showed once again that the working class was united against the old forces of the Fatherland Party and the army leadership. The strike was supported in equal measure by the Social Democrats, the Independents (USPD) and the Communists. But, as soon as the Kappist uproar had died away, their paths again diverged. In return for saving the government, the trade unions extracted concessions on all the points that had been at issue since November: the punishment of the putschists, the resignation of Reichswehr minister Noske and two other ministers, the socialisation of the coalmines, the democratisation of the administration and the formation of loyal security units staffed by workers. In practice, however, almost none of these provisions was put into effect, apart from the ministerial resignations.

For the workers themselves, meanwhile, the general strike was the starting point for more far-reaching actions, especially in the Ruhr area. After the experiences of the previous spring, when their strikes had come to an end with almost no result, and the government had not fulfilled any of their demands, a clear process of radicalisation had occurred among the workers of the Ruhr. The bulk of the skilled workers, particularly in the central and western parts of the region, were inclined towards the Independents and the Free Trade Unions. But the unskilled workers, particularly in the new industrial agglomerations, were more inclined towards the Syndicalist radicals of the Free Workers' Union, who demanded the immediate implementation of their demands and placed their faith in direct military action. Armed 'action committees' had already been formed everywhere at the beginning of the general strike against Kapp, and these had defeated the advancing *Freikorps* units in the first battles. They joined together to form the 'Red Army of the Ruhr', which eventually comprised more than 50,000 men and within a few days had taken control of the whole Ruhr district between Duisburg and Hagen. After the collapse of the Kapp putsch, the government made a number of concessions to the workers of the Ruhr in an attempt to persuade them to lay down their weapons, but without success. The insurgents then restarted their general strike, with the support of more than 300,000 workers. The government replied by ordering troops to march into the Ruhr district. These included *Freikorps* units which had supported the putsch against the government only a few days earlier. What followed was the most frightful slaughter of the whole civil war period. Many more than 1,000 dead were counted on the side of the workers, while the *Freikorps* lost roughly 250 men. And once again, as before, the majority of the workers who lost their lives were shot after they had been taken prisoner.[27]

The struggles of March 1920 had manifold and long-lasting political results. For the Right, the inglorious end of the Kapp putsch signified that a military operation of this kind had little prospect of success against a militant workers' movement, and might well degenerate into an all-embracing civil war. A regime consisting of the Fatherland Party, the OHL and the big landowners could not count on broad support from either the workers or the bourgeoisie. The lesson of the Kapp adventure was that different methods and different people were needed to overthrow the republic from the Right.

A promising path in this direction appeared to be opening up in Bavaria. There the army command had forced the resignation of the Social Democratic prime minister with an ultimatum, and enthroned a right-wing government, supported by bourgeois and conservative forces. In the months that followed, Bavaria became a stronghold of anti-republicanism. The state was converted into a 'cell of order' (*Ordnungszelle*) and there were soon indications that preparations were being made to overthrow the Reich government.

Events in Prussia moved in the opposite direction. Here the SPD, led by the energetic Prussian prime minister, Otto Braun, entered into a Grand Coalition with the Centre Party, the DDP and the DVP. It was Otto Braun who, after the experience of the Kapp putsch, set to work to democratise the administration, not least the police force. He thereby ensured that Prussia would remain loyal to the republic, becoming a strongpoint for pro-republican forces.[28]

Among the workers, however, the defeat of the Red Army of the Ruhr left behind traumatic memories. The attempt to achieve power by direct action, by a military uprising, had failed, and this also brought to an end the anarchical movement of mostly young, unskilled workers who had fought for their interests without having any ties to political parties or trade unions and had now been shot down by the soldiers of the *Freikorps*. From then on, the Ruhr was dominated by the Social Democratic, Communist or Catholic workers' organisations. The period of mass working-class uprisings had come to an end.

What tremendous changes had taken place in the political landscape in the course of a year! In January 1919, in the elections to the National Assembly, the parties of the movement for constitutional democracy had secured a dazzling success. Now, a year later, they stood with their backs to the wall, and radical forces of the Left and the Right were on the offensive. The first ordinary parliamentary elections, held in June 1920, shone a glaring light on this change. The share of the vote obtained by the three parties of the 'Weimar coalition', namely the DDP, the Centre Party and the MSPD, fell from 76 to 43 per cent. The actual number of votes they received almost halved, from 22 million to 12 million. The share of the parties to the Right and Left of them increased dramatically: the DNVP's share rose by half, to 15 per cent, the DVP tripled its share to almost 14 per cent, and the USPD rose from 7.6 per cent to almost 18 per cent. The bourgeois voters had sheared off to the Right; the working-class voters had sheared off to the Left.

After the 1920 elections, the USPD began to disintegrate. Its revolutionary wing had already rejected the pro-republican tendencies of the party leadership some time before this. In October 1920, the majority of the party agreed to merge with the KPD. As a result, the KPD was converted from a small cadre organisation into a mass party. Two years later, the pro-republican section of the USPD united with the Majority SPD. The influx of former members of the USPD led the reunited SPD to revert to a more strongly left-wing course. Thus, the development which had already appeared in outline at the beginning of the First World War now found organisational form: three political camps had come into existence, marked off from each other relatively clearly. A unified radical Left, which unconditionally followed the example of the Soviet communists and was also led from Moscow, stood opposed to a Right which was still in a state of great ideological and political ferment and a centre which continued to be made up of the forces of constitutional democracy, sometimes in association with the former National Liberals of the DVP, and sometimes without them.

## Reparations and the Policy of Fulfilment

It was laid down under the Versailles Treaty that Germany would be obliged to pay the victorious allies a considerable amount in reparations. The level and the duration of the required payments, however, had not been fixed. From then onwards, for the next decade, this was one of the dominant themes of German and international politics. After this war, which was on a larger scale than had ever been seen before, public opinion in the victorious countries, and particularly in France, demanded reparations on a similarly large and unprecedented scale for the damage inflicted during the hostilities. France and Great Britain were heavily in debt to the USA as a result of the war; it was therefore in the paramount interest of both countries to repay those debts as far as possible with the proceeds of German reparations payments. Whether the German economy would be in a position to provide these payments was not something that initially concerned them. To hand over sums of money of the amount required, Germany would have had to produce, and in particular to export, at its highest possible capacity. But the national industries of the victorious countries wanted to protect themselves from unwelcome German imports by tariffs and prohibitions, so that it remained extremely unclear where the money was expected to come from. Moreover, transfer payments of such quantities had never been made before. No one therefore had any experience of the impact that payments of this magnitude would have on the world economy and the financial policies of the powers.

But, above all, Germany's currency had been systematically wrecked during the war, because, as stated earlier, the imperial government had financed it not with taxes but predominantly with loans. The debts of the German Reich had risen between 1913 and 1919 from 5 billion Marks to the immense sum of 144 billion. This, by itself, already made the adoption of a new financial policy inescapable. But post-war German governments continued to borrow money and depreciate the currency even after the armistice, because this would make it easier to finance wages, salaries and the immense range of social benefits which stretched all the way from support for war victims to unemployment assistance. This was a way of avoiding social unrest, and counteracting revolutionary tendencies among the workers. Moreover, a fall in the value of the currency meant a fall in the prices of German export goods, so that, owing to the 'lubricating effect of inflation', Germany experienced growth and full employment rather than suffering the economic crisis which affected most other European countries between 1919 and 1922.[29]

The reparations themselves were a further reason for continuing an inflationary policy, because they were largely financed by contracting more debts. In April 1922, after lengthy negotiations, the Allies finally arrived at a figure of 132 billion Gold Marks, to be paid over a period of roughly forty years. This was an enormous figure, exceeding anything previously known to history. Germany's reaction to this demand, on the other hand, again displayed unequivocal vehemence. People on the political Right were particularly vociferous in calling for its rejection. But the consequence of this would have been the occupation of the Ruhr by France and possibly the separation of the western part of the Rhineland from Germany. It was therefore the parties of the 'Weimar coalition' who again surrendered to the inevitable and voted in favour of the acceptance of the ultimatum, in the hope that it would be possible to persuade the Allies of the impracticability of this payment plan once they saw that Germany was seriously, but vainly, endeavouring to fulfil their demands.[30]

This 'policy of fulfilment' formulated by Chancellor Wirth and Foreign Minister Rathenau now offered a further target for the agitation of the radicals on the Right, whose attacks on leading politicians became more and more violent, leading finally to a wave of political assassinations. In August 1921 Matthias Erzberger, one of the most prominent politicians of the Centre Party, fell victim to a murder of this kind. The culprits were two former *Freikorps* officers, who after its dissolution had joined a secret organisation with the name 'Organisation Consul' (OC), which planned and carried out murderous attacks on representatives of the republic. A year later an attempt was made to kill Philipp Scheidemann with prussic acid, and on 24 June 1922 two former officers, members of the 'Organisation Consul' and the German *Völkisch* Defensive and Offensive Association (*Deutschvölkischer Schutz- und Trutzbund*), shot the Foreign Minister, Walther Rathenau.

By targeting Rathenau, the assassins were striking a quintessential representative of the enlightened German bourgeoisie. During the war, he had not only been one of the most important organisers of the German war economy, but also an ardent advocate of a 'victorious peace' with annexations. As late as October 1918, he had called for an armed 'People's War' against the Allies. After the November Revolution, however, he supported the republic though at the same time he opposed the Versailles Treaty. He planned the 'policy of fulfilment' and sought to achieve a political *rapprochement* with Russia. He was at once Foreign Minister, self-confident German Jew and brilliant political intellectual. Both in his thirst for action and his contradictions, Rathenau was one of the symbolic figures of the new state and one of its most capable thinkers.[31]

In any case, the murder of Rathenau led to a more emphatic reaction on the part of the government, which now officially proclaimed that the main enemy was on the Right. A Law for the Protection of the Republic was quickly passed, but it was of very limited use, because it was only applied with maximum severity to workers and communists, whereas it was either not applied at all to the political Right, or with remarkable leniency. In addition, Bavaria refused to implement the law; and the inability of the government of the Reich to impose its laws on a state which openly defied the constitution was a further demonstration of its practical weakness.

## A Topsy-Turvy World

Meanwhile, the devaluation of the Mark proceeded by leaps and bounds. By February 1920 the cost of living, when compared with a base year of 1913, had risen by a factor of eight, and by January 1922 by a factor of twenty. This figure reached 1,120 in January 1923, 376,512 in July, 15 million in September and 1.2 billion in December. But hyperinflation had very different effects on the various social groups. Anyone who possessed wealth in the form of money, savings, life insurance, interest on capital or public loans was almost completely expropriated. Members of the *Bildungsbürgertum* were pre-eminent among the losers. They traditionally tended to possess few material assets (*Sachwerte*), and they now lost the whole of their monetary wealth as well as the war loans subscribed to during the war in fulfilment of their patriotic duty. The recipients of wages and salaries suffered a decline in real income, but the impact of the inflation on them was chiefly an indirect one, exerted through the economic crisis. By 1923, the real weekly wages of skilled workers had fallen to 50 per cent of their pre-war level, the real monthly salaries of higher officials to 38 per cent.

Those who possessed material assets, on the other hand, enjoyed considerable advantages, as their wealth was not reduced by inflation. Debtors also benefited, since their debts were practically wiped out. The inflation was also particularly advantageous to the state, because it was able in this way to redeem almost all its internal obligations at a real value of zero. Shopkeepers, farmers and even artisans also gained from the inflation for the same reason. It was entrepreneurs who made the greatest gains, however, because their fixed assets remained unchanged or even increased as the value of money fell, especially as it was ridiculously easy for the owners of foreign currency, like Hugo Stinnes, the Ruhr industrialist who rose to become one of the richest men in Germany during the period of inflation, to buy up real estate, factory installations and whole commercial enterprises. This greatly accelerated the process of industrial concentration.

From the economic angle, the inflation had an ambivalent effect. Without a fall in the value of money, the post-war boom and the demobilisation of the troops would not have been possible. Moreover, the state was almost free of debt after 1923, and that is what made it possible at least for a short period to institute generous social policies. On the other hand, large sections of the *Bildungsbürgertum*, the class that upheld the state, were almost expropriated, while it is not even possible to calculate the losses incurred abroad when currency was converted.[32]

But the inflation was also of long-term significance because of its impact on the psychology and the political attitudes of the public, particularly when it is placed in the context of the unbroken chain of dramatic and devastating experiences suffered during the decade between 1914 and 1924: a war of a magnitude never previously experienced or even imagined; a disastrous defeat which was in addition felt to be unexpected, undeserved and inexplicable; a revolution which brought with it an almost unending series of attempted risings, revolts, political murders and coups; a dictated peace which imposed on Germany extensive territorial losses and billions in reparations payments extending into the 1980s; and the occupation of the Ruhr by France and the attempt to oppose the Allies, which was as futile as it was costly. The drumbeat of revolutions, catastrophes and humiliations continued for so long and was so intense that hardly any of those who experienced it survived this whirlpool of change, passion and insanity without being damaged, particularly when one bears in mind the heights from which the Germans had fallen. And the deeper they fell, the more harmonious, fortunate and splendid did the pre-war world of the German Empire appear in retrospect.

While the risings and the putsch attempts were only directly experienced by a section of the population, namely the inhabitants of Berlin, the Rhineland, Saxony and Munich, the inflation changed the lives of everyone, and it did so in a manner which stood the world on its head and turned absurdity into reality, as a contemporary report in the *Berliner Illustrierte Zeitung* made plain:

> The crazy numbers, the uncertain future, the way today and tomorrow come into question again overnight. The epidemic of worry, the extreme neediness . . . What rises along with the dollar? Hatred, despair and want. . . . The day's emotions follow the day's exchange rate. A fall in the dollar sets off an outburst of scornful laughter: 'Butter is cheaper! Instead of 1 million 600,000 marks it now costs only 1 million 400,000 marks.' But that is no joke: those are realities, seriously written with a blue pencil, hung up in a shop window, and seriously read.[33]

It was not just the political and social order which was destroyed by war, defeat, revolution and inflation; the fixed landmarks of private life were also destroyed. Norms and values which had previously been firmly established were robbed of their meaning. This was a 'witches' sabbath of devaluation'. Respectable bourgeois families, which had lived 'prudently' for years, saved their money and subscribed to war loans, lost all their wealth overnight, while the beneficiaries of inflation, the speculators and the 'profiteers' became rich just as quickly. The fundamental principles of 'loyalty and trust' no longer counted, long-held plans for the future faded away, along with institutions and values, and concepts like integrity and modesty seemed to be suffering the same fate.[34]

In addition to its exchange value, money also lost its function as the tacit regulator of social relations. One might feel social hierarchies to be unjust and scandalous and want to change, or even to overthrow them. But that money itself became uncertain, that it practically dissolved, and that the firm connection between the possession of money and social status was lost, was for contemporaries an experience as extraordinary as it was deeply disturbing. Savings accounts and life insurance policies which had been inherited or acquired over decades could disappear within a few weeks through no fault of the individual. This was not just incomprehensible to the people directly afflicted; it posed a palpable threat to everyone.

The economic and political mechanisms which led to the fall in the value of money and the rise in prices were actually not understood by most of those concerned, and this magnified their sense of insecurity. For example, between 1919 and 1922 the number of savers making deposits at the Munich Savings Bank continued to rise, although savings accounts lost more and more of their value in the years after the war. Even in 1923 there were more deposits than withdrawals. People who were shrewd, on the other hand, withdrew their money and bought items which retained their value. But who could know what still had value and what did not?

The incomprehensibility of these events increased the vehemence with which people sought to explain them, and to uncover the guilty parties, the people behind the process. They looked at the farmers, who lived magnificently from the black market, at the traders, whose storage depots grew constantly, and at foreigners and tourists, who rose to be the real kings of the market, thanks to their foreign currency. But, above all, they pointed a finger at the profiteers, the black marketeers and the speculators, all of whom became a byword for the beneficiaries of the inflation, and very obviously had acquired great wealth in a short time without any effort. 'I can never forget the fat man' wrote Kurt Tucholsky in 1920 'who sat on the esplanade, in the big hall, before a large table loaded with coffee, sugar, milk and cakes. "Yes" he said, while he endeavoured to stuff a whole pancake into his mouth at one go, "Look: take the Bolsheviks for instance . . .! Those people don't even work!" He, at any rate, was working.'[35]

Even the relation between work and basic social security, as a fixed element in planning one's life, had become uncertain. The 'veterans of honourable labour, to whom Germany owes its greatness, are in want, they are starving and freezing' wrote an anonymous resident of Munich at the end of 1923 to the authorities,

> while very young boys, overfed cattle-dealers, speculators in timber, and food profiteers, who also know how to conceal their dark business from any kind of tax inspection, travel in luxury in elegant automobiles and revel through the night in cabarets and wine-soaked nightclubs with their idle female hangers-on, whose only interest is in dressing in ever more ridiculous outfits.[36]

It was therefore tempting to explain the inexplicable through the workings of networks and secret organisations, through conspiracies and private arrangements. It was not a great leap from that position to anti-Semitism, because the observation that Jewish merchants and traders gained from the inflation led to suspicion and resentment. It is true that non-Jewish merchants also profited, but they were not so easily identifiable, whereas a textile dealer, originating perhaps from Galicia, who prospered during the inflation, offered to those looking for it stark evidence to justify the suspicion that the unprecedented inflation was bring directed by hidden forces. It was precisely the 'modern' type of personality, who was unattached to tradition and family origins, who found his feet in the new epoch and profited from it. Individuals like this were identified with the Jewish element by many people, even by such a generally sober observer as Thomas Mann, who characterised the typical speculator in this way: 'The man, blond, Jewish and elegant, in his mid-thirties, with a monocle and fat, white, manicured hands, dressed in a quilted jacket and Lackhaus shoes, splendid as the type of the cultured international capitalist profiteer.'[37] Thus the period of inflation became a kind of incubation phase for the new anti-Semitism, a time in which what had until then been regarded more as rumour and gossip appeared to have solidified into certainty. A Reichswehr report sent from Bavaria as early as the spring of 1920 states that 'the hatred of the broadest circles is directed to a heightened extent against the Jews, who have gained control of the greater part of commerce, and who, according to everyone's opinion, have enriched themselves at the expense of their fellow human beings in the most unscrupulous manner.'[38]

The experience of the inflation also increased the mistrust and resentment felt towards liberalism and capitalism as such. Unlike anti-Semitism, which served the Right as a means of explanation and a useful outlet, the popular anti-capitalism which arose out of the inflation was widespread on the Left and also in the political centre. Thus, the experiences of the early 1920s also loosened emotional and intellectual ties to the liberal economic and social system, even among the social representatives and political champions of that system, namely the bourgeoisie, and in particular the *Bildungsbürgertum*.

The yearning for a just society, and for the restoration of an orderly moral framework, which was a reaction to the privations and the glaring injustices of the inflation period, was widespread and multifaceted. Political radicalism and esotericism, religious reawakening and extreme nationalism, utopias of salvation through communism and a nature-oriented romanticism which derived from the pre-war Youth Movement: all these tendencies found more adherents than ever before during those years. Prophets and heralds of salvation were particularly prominent in this environment. There were bizarre figures like the 'Messiah of Thuringia', 'John of the Youth', or the Berlin swindler Max Klante, who founded a free cooperative and promised that anyone who invested in it would receive an interest rate of 600 per cent a year. A quarter of a million people followed this holy man of the inflation, until he was unmasked as a fraudster and arrested.[39]

The yearning for a simplicity and clarity which would cut through the thicket of interests and beneficiaries, parties, leagues and associations provided a powerful motivation, and it crystallised in the call for a great individual who would bring an end to these chaotic conditions. 'Again and again the call resounds for a dictator who will proceed with the utmost severity against the racketeering which reaches into the highest circles', according to the Reichswehr report from Bavaria quoted previously.

> Broad circles view an energetic offensive against big capital, which has gradually brought everything under its influence, as the only possible salvation. Whether this can be done through Bolshevism, through state bankruptcy or through ruthless action against international banking capital, which has profited from the war and the revolution, in other words along the lines of a *völkisch* movement, is the subject of lively and varied discussions.[40]

## The Crisis Becomes Total

These fateful developments—risings and coups, assassinations and political violence, demands for reparation and inflation—finally culminated in 1923 in a fundamental political crisis of a kind Germany had never yet experienced: a crescendo of emergencies, which was not followed, as many expected, by the republic's collapse, but by its stabilisation, at least for the moment.

The occupation of the Ruhr by French and Belgian troops on 11 January 1923 was ostensibly a reaction to arrears in German reparations deliveries. In reality, it reflected France's quest to weaken Germany's dominant economic position in Europe permanently and if possible to gain further accessions of territory, perhaps by supporting separatist groups in the Rhineland. These groups aimed to set up an independent Rhineland state which would be friendly to France, but their ideas received almost no response from the local inhabitants. On the contrary, all strata of the population of the Ruhr responded to the German government's proclamation of 'passive resistance' against French occupation with a broad wave of strikes and protests. They refused either to work for, or to cooperate with, the French occupiers.

The occupation of the Ruhr, and the '*Ruhrkampf*', brought about a further upsurge in nationalist feeling in Germany, and the public proclamations of all the political parties were full of solemn affirmations of the 'rediscovered' unity of the nation in its defensive struggle against an external threat and repeated appeals to the 'spirit of 1914'. The Berlin government had, of course, to pay the wages and salaries of the striking workers and office employees, but, in addition to this, tax receipts now ceased to come in from the economic heart of the country, and there were no more deliveries of coal. The government's obligations could only be met by increasing the amount of money in circulation, and the degree of depreciation, which was already a cause of anxiety, now very quickly reached absurd heights. The political test of strength with France thus turned rapidly into a financial débâcle. Germany's national debt eventually amounted to over 100,000 billion Marks, and all wealth held in monetary form, including all savings accounts, became valueless. The effects of passive resistance were catastrophic: Germany's currency was destroyed, the economy almost reached a standstill, unemployment rose and considerable sections of the population were deprived of their savings. The disastrous balance sheet of the *Ruhrkampf* reads as follows: 132 dead, 180,000 expelled from their homes, and an economic loss of between 3.5 and 4 billion Gold Marks. The population did not, however, blame this in the first instance on its own government, but rather on the French, because they were the ones who had started the 'Ruhr conflict'. The decision of 26 September to discontinue passive resistance was therefore not only a result of a belated insight into its failure; it also meant capitulation by Germany and the abandonment of its policy of obstructing the Versailles Peace Treaty and the associated reparations obligations.[41]

The disastrous outcome of the first six months of 1923 also provided an opportunity for the republic's radical opponents to make another attempt to overthrow it. On the Left, the new leadership of the KPD, which was entirely committed to obeying the instructions of the central headquarters of the Communist International ('Comintern'), based in Moscow, switched its course towards immediate revolution. This was a grotesque misreading of the actual situation in Germany. In March 1921 a rising had been set in motion on Moscow's instructions in the Central German industrial district of Merseburg-Halle. It was suppressed after a few days, but it cost 180 deaths and led to the imprisonment of over 4,000 workers. The leadership of the Comintern and with it the leadership of the KPD regarded the crisis of autumn 1923 as a fresh opportunity for an uprising, which was intended to bring about the socialist revolution in Germany without further delay. In the states of Saxony and Thuringia, the KPD joined the Social Democrats in government coalitions, and they also established armed workers' detachments there. These units were waiting for the signal for action, which was supposed to be given by a hurriedly called conference of Factory Councils in Chemnitz. But the conference had no intention of letting itself become involved in such an adventure. When the Reich government reacted by proclaiming a state of emergency, sending troops to Saxony and deposing the head of the Saxon government, the order for an uprising was rescinded. But the news of this decision did not reach Hamburg in time, and a few hundred communists provoked a short-lived rising there. It was crushed by the Hamburg police alone; although the *Freikorps* had been alerted, there was no need for them to intervene. The German October, which was intended to bring revolution to Germany on the Russian model, and to recruit millions of German workers into the Red Army, as the Moscow leadership imagined, ended as a sanguinary farce.[42]

The situation was different in Bavaria. Nationalist feelings were strong, and the abandonment of passive resistance in the Rhineland had inflamed them still further. The Bavarian government, which was extremely right wing, had ceased to obey instructions from Berlin. The leadership of the Reichswehr had sent troops against the state government of red Saxony without hesitation; but it was not prepared to support a similar executive action by the Reich against Bavaria. In view of the hyperinflation, the separatist movements in the Rhineland and the attempted uprising by the communists, the collapse of the republic seemed to be merely a matter of time.

By the summer of 1923, preparations for a fresh attempt at a right-wing putsch were well under way. The plan was to start in Munich, and with the support of the Reichswehr to put a dictatorial right-wing regime into the saddle. Unlike at the time of the Kapp putsch of March 1920, a model for the conquest of power now existed, in the shape of Mussolini's 'March on Rome' the year before. It was envisaged that a large number of radical right-wing groups, paramilitary organisations and ethnic nationalist (*völkisch*) parties, which had all joined together into 'Patriotic Associations' under the dominant influence of Ludendorff, would take part in the often invoked 'march on Berlin'. But the proposed 'national revolution' was repeatedly delayed, not least because the French government had quite unequivocally threatened military intervention if a right-wing dictatorship were set up in Germany. Moreover, plans for a *coup d'état* were based on the assumption that the Reichswehr would also take part, so as to avoid a repetition of the experience of the Kapp putsch. The army command, however, and its new Chief, Hans von Seeckt, had not yet given a clear statement of their intentions.

Among the numerous *völkisch*-nationalist groups in Munich there was one that was particularly strident and radical in its agitation. It also had a ringleader who was both an able speaker and a good organiser, namely the thirty-four-year-old Adolf Hitler, who led the National Socialist German Workers' Party (NSDAP). This party was already strongly established in Bavaria but hardly known in the rest of Germany. As all the other groups were hesitating, Hitler decided to take matters into his own hands. With a few loyal followers, he burst into a meeting in the Bürgerbräu Cellar in Munich, declared himself head of a provisional national government and at gunpoint forced two leading members of the Bavarian Right who were present at the meeting, namely the former Bavarian prime minister Gustav von Kahr and the local Reichswehr commander Lieutenant-General Otto von Lossow, to proclaim their support for his 'national revolution'. Kahr and Lossow, however, had absolutely no intention of allowing themselves to be outmanoeuvred by this inexperienced newcomer, or of entering into an undertaking which would be futile without the support of the Reichswehr. This amateurish putsch by the National Socialists, which the former wartime dictator Ludendorff had also joined, ended the following day at the Feldherrnhalle in a hail of police bullets.

This event, however ludicrous it seemed, was nevertheless of some importance for German politics. For one thing, this was the first time there had been an open confrontation between the old and the new Right. With the 'Hitler putsch', the *völkisch* radicals, who until then had always been visible in the streets, but were never a significant factor in national politics, stepped into the limelight of national and international public awareness. With his appearance in the Bürgerbräu Cellar, when he jumped onto the table holding his pistol and proclaimed the revolution, Hitler demonstrated the difference between the young, radical *völkisch* movement, which pressed unhesitatingly for immediate action, and the Pan-German dignitaries, who preferred to wait for developments and would only strike when success was certain.

On the other hand, however, Hitler's reckless conduct had discredited the whole plan of a 'march on Berlin'. His attempted putsch had been bloodily crushed by the armed forces of his own allies. The Reichswehr, which might well have been won over to a right-wing dictatorship if von Seeckt had headed it, now distanced itself from the project. The Bavarian conspirators around Kahr and Lossow had been made to look foolish. This was a disaster which weakened the Right for many years, and put an end to its hope of coming to power quickly with a putsch and a march on Berlin, following the example set by Mussolini.[43]

There was a particular reason why Hitler usurped the leadership of the Bavarian putschists with such frantic haste: by November, the crisis of the republic had already come to an end. As early as August 1923 Chancellor Cuno's short-lived cabinet of officials had been replaced for the first time by a Grand Coalition, consisting of the SPD, the DDP, the Centre Party and the DVP, after the Social Democrats had overcome the distrust they felt towards the DVP chairman Stresemann owing to his attitude during the Kapp putsch. Despite the series of severe crises which continued unabated throughout the autumn of 1923, this alliance between the parties succeeded not only in ending the pointless charade of passive resistance but also in bringing the hyperinflation to a halt by issuing a new currency, the 'Rentenmark', and in this way re-establishing the former rate of exchange with the dollar.

This brought to an end the nightmare of the bottomless fall in the value of money. The consequences of the hyperinflation were now clearly visible: all possessions held in the form of money, all savings accounts and all war loans had become worthless. The payment of reparations had to be resumed, but this time without the 'lubricant' of inflation, hence drastic cuts in the budget became necessary. Roughly 400,000 state employees were dismissed at this time.

The currency reform finally laid the foundation for a realistic test of the German economy's productive capacity, which had been impossible to calculate precisely until then given the effects of hyperinflation. The agreement of the Allies to this audit of Germany's economy was the first step towards cooperation. Great Britain in particular pressed France to take up a more realistic attitude towards Germany and its ability to pay, and in any case, France's German policy had suffered a fiasco, with the failure of the occupation of the Ruhr to produce any results. In fact, only eight more years would elapse before it was agreed at the Lausanne Conference that Germany's payment of reparations could come to an end. Until then, however, reparations remained a lasting source of discord in German domestic politics.

In the summer of 1923, no one would have dared to predict not only that Germany would survive the crisis but also that the republic would emerge from it stronger than before. Various interconnected factors were of decisive importance in this context, and sheer chance also certainly played a role. For one thing, domestic and foreign threats actually cut across each other: on the Right, and above all in the Reichswehr, the fear that the French would occupy the whole of Germany was greater than the will to risk another putsch. Only the ultra-radicals in the *völkisch* associations, and the NSDAP in particular, were ready to run such a risk and then possibly to wage a guerrilla war against the French. Moreover, the threat from the Left had declined to a manageable level. Whereas the Ruhr conflict of 1920 had mobilised tens of thousands of armed workers, the attempted communist risings of 1921 and 1923 were militarily weak. In the years that followed, the KPD was mainly preoccupied with its own problems and the process of internal Stalinisation. It only returned to its previous status as a serious political actor after the onset of the world economic crisis, which drove millions of unemployed workers to lend it their support.

At the other end of the political spectrum, a certain amount of disillusionment spread among right-wingers after the failure of the Munich adventure. On several occasions since the war, the radical Right had attempted a 'quick solution', through which they would triumph over internal and external enemies and achieve a 'revision of Kiel and Versailles'. This turned out to be impracticable both in 1920 and in 1923. By the beginning of 1924, it seemed clear that there was no likelihood either of an early end to the Weimar Republic, or of a resurrection of Hitler's party, which was disintegrating after the November débâcle and would soon be prohibited everywhere in Germany.

Nevertheless, the camp of radical nationalism had expanded continuously since 1919, and the crises of 1923 had further consolidated its position. 'Year by year, in proportion as this [state] becomes stronger' wrote Friedrich Meinecke, commenting on the mental state of people on the political Right,

> the hopes which once flamed up explosively, for example at the time of the Kapp putsch, become weaker. People are becoming accustomed to the existing state of affairs, since it cannot be changed in the foreseeable future. But according to my observations attitudes have nevertheless hardened; people are more rigidly and bitterly hostile towards the new epoch than ever before.[44]

All the apprehensions of the pre-war era, all the prophecies about the impending destruction of the bourgeois world, were confirmed, and even outdone, by the decade between 1914 and 1924. Parts of the *Bildungsbürgertum* and people of conservative inclinations were already inclined to view the new age with scepticism and antipathy; now, however, their scepticism developed into a firm conviction, bolstered by experience. A very long phase of calm and stable development in all areas of activity, the economic and political and well as the social and cultural, would therefore be needed to restore confidence in the future viability of a republican Germany.

## A Precarious Stabilisation

The political structure of the Weimar Republic continued to be unstable between 1924 and 1929; but the period of civil war and attempted uprisings had come to an end for the moment. Economic stability had been restored, though it was still fragile. The centre of the political stage was now occupied for several years by the attempt to find reasonably sustainable solutions to the many problems faced by German post-war society and to build parliamentary majorities for them. The first issue was Germany's position in relation to the great powers, and, closely bound up with this, the question of reparations; the second was how to organise the relationship between capital and labour, particularly in regard to the expansion of social policy; and the third was the interplay of compromise-building and opposition on principle in the shaping of government policy.

The emotional charge was taken out of the sensitive and complex subject of reparations by the establishment of a committee under the direction of the American financier Charles G. Dawes, which had the task of constructing a plan for the execution of reparation payments. This was an important step because it meant the return of the USA to a close involvement in European politics. The plan worked out by the Dawes Committee offered Germany a breathing space for economic recovery by setting the country's annual payments at roughly 2.5 billion Marks, but postponing the first payment for four years. France promised to withdraw from the occupied Ruhr district in return for the payment of reparations. In April 1924, this agreement was accepted by all the powers involved. Accordingly, the dispute over reparations which until then had been permeated with nationalist passions now became to a certain extent a question of financial calculation. In addition to this, the German market again became of interest to American capital. American credit flowed to Germany and offered the German side the chance to meet its need for hard currency. This not only bound the German economy closely to the American financial market, but also led to a degree of international financial circulation, which had until then not existed in this form. American credit went to Germany, the credit was used to pay reparations to Britain and France, and those countries in turn used what they received from Germany to liquidate their debts to the USA, which provided further credit to Germany with the capital that flowed to America from Britain and France. In this way, almost the whole of the European financial system depended on the USA. Any disturbance in the American financial market would therefore inevitably have a decisive impact on the European economy. At the same time, the emerging policy of reconciliation between the European powers required this circulation process to function properly. If its basis was altered, the European political compromise was also endangered.[45]

After the old order had been shattered and its underlying conditions destroyed by the First World War, the paramount policy objective of the great powers was to establish a strong new system to preserve peace in Europe. The peace treaties of the years immediately following the war had been devised in such a way as to produce such a system, but they could only function if the main European conflict—that between France and Germany—was at the very least neutralised. Any hope of achieving this aim was initially dashed by the renewed confrontation over the French occupation of the Ruhr. By the end of 1923, however, the most extreme version of French policy towards Germany had failed, as had Germany's policy of a complete refusal to pay reparations. Both sides therefore needed to make a new start. Fresh opportunities beckoned.

German foreign policy, the course of which was set by Gustav Stresemann between 1923 and 1929, had two essential elements. The move towards reconciliation with France was one of them. It was only surprising at first glance that the compromise with France was achieved not by a Social Democrat but by the chairman of the DVP, who had come to prominence as a nationalist and an annexationist, because Stresemann differed from the Social Democrats in enjoying in advance a certain degree of confidence among nationalist hardliners. This gave him greater political room for manoeuvre. He was ready to recognise the security interests of his western neighbour, and he aimed to negotiate an international guarantee of Germany's western borders. That meant the abandonment of any German claim to Alsace-Lorraine, and the renunciation by the French of any aspiration towards a border on the Rhine. In view of the disastrous course of Franco-German relations in the preceding fifty years, this was a remarkable change of approach, and it led in 1925 to the sensational Locarno Agreement.

Just oneyear later, Stresemann and the French Foreign Minister Aristide Briand tried to take a further leap forward. They agreed that in return for an advance payment of reparations (which appeared possible, given Germany's good economic situation) France would withdraw earlier than planned from the occupied parts of the Rhineland. The Saar would be returned to Germany, as would Eupen-Malmedy, the strip of territory on Germany's border that had fallen to Belgium under the Versailles Treaty. It was, however, still too early for such a far-reaching compromise to be accepted. Neither their government colleagues nor public opinion could be won over to such an option, in either country. But Stresemann's policy of reconciliation still registered some successes: in 1926, Germany became a member of the League of Nations; in 1927, France and Germany concluded a trade agreement; and, in the same year, allied military supervision of Germany came to an end. A year later the Briand-Kellogg Pact outlawing war was signed. This was a highly symbolic act, coming as it did ten years after the end of the First World War. In the course of the years 1929 and 1930, the troops of the Allies left the Rhineland, and the Young Plan determined the final total of reparations (112 billion Marks) and the timescale for payment (fifty-nine years). Finally, Briand and Stresemann even held discussions about the prospects for European unification, which Briand tended to see in political terms, whereas Stresemann envisaged an economic union.[46]

Bearing in mind the lengthy confrontation between France and Germany during and after the war, hardly anyone would have thought in 1923 that this process of reconciliation was possible. It emphatically refutes any form of determinism. For, if such a development was possible in Franco-German relations, why should not something similar occur in other areas, in domestic policy for example, notwithstanding all the heavy burdens which had their origin in the calamitous post-war years?

Stresemann's policy of reconciliation in the west, however, was combined with the second element in his policy, which looked to the east. In the east, he aimed at a revision of Germany's borders rather than reconciliation with the country's neighbours. This was his response to the separation of East Prussia from Germany by the Polish 'corridor' and, more generally, to the problem of the Germans who lived outside Germany, in the countries of East and South-East Europe, and particularly in Poland. The explosive problem of the relation between majority and minority populations in the new nation-states was particularly acute in Poland, and, in the conflict around Upper Silesia in 1921, it spilled over into violence for the first time. According to the Treaty of Versailles, this region, jointly inhabited by Germans and Poles, which also included the Upper Silesian industrial district, was originally supposed to go to Poland. But, after a plebiscite, the region was divided into two, a decision which led again to the presence of national minorities in both areas. The dispute finally culminated in an armed conflict between Polish irregulars and German *Freikorps* troops.

The long-term goal of German policy was to revise the border between Germany and Poland, something which could only be achieved if the Polish state remained weak politically and economically. Foreign Minister Stresemann bent his efforts towards precisely this objective. It is true that, in the Locarno Treaties, Germany gave assurances that it would pursue its policy by exclusively peaceful means, but it did not give a boundary guarantee to Poland as it had done to France. As Stresemann emphasised in an internal memorandum, without mincing his words: 'It will not be possible to achieve a peaceful solution of the Polish boundary question unless Poland's economic and financial distress has reached its utmost severity and brought the whole of the Polish body politic to a state of powerlessness.' Here, unlike in the west, there could be no compromise and no negotiation: 'We can only be satisfied by the unlimited restoration of sovereignty over the areas in question.'[47]

Not the least of the reasons for Germany's intransigent policy was the difficult situation facing German minorities in the areas attached to Poland after 1918. They were humiliated and mistreated by Polish nationalists. Moreover, while Germany had lost the war in the west, it had won the war in the east, and the discrepancy between the immense stretches of territory the Germans had added to their country after Brest-Litovsk and the few eastern territories remaining to Germany in the east after the war was felt to be in particular need of revision. Above all, the modern Polish state had only existed for a few years, while many of the areas which were now Polish had been Prussian or German for more than a hundred years, so that, in German eyes, the legitimacy of Poland's claims was inferior to the security needs of the French in the west.

German foreign policy support of German minorities naturally had consequences for the future, for it further inflamed ethnic conflicts in East Central Europe, and in Germany too the Association for Germanism Abroad (*Verein für das Deutschtum im Ausland*, VDA), one of the biggest and most influential associations in the republic, kept the issue continually on the boil. While the policy of reconciliation between France and Germany was welcomed in the west, and Briand and Stresemann were eventually even awarded the Nobel Peace Prize, German revisionism in the east acted as a constant factor of destabilisation and disturbance in the whole of East Central Europe.

While the foreign policy compromise was taking shape between France and Germany, conditions within the latter country started to settle down, although the fundamental conflicts had been postponed rather than solved. The relationship between capital and labour was a particularly difficult issue. This question had stood at the centre of the debate over how German society should best be organised ever since the turn of the century. One side wanted the capital–labour relationship to be regulated through the market, while the other side raised the demand for social security, to be organised by the state. In 1918 the principle of social partnership had won the upper hand, with the establishment of the Central Association for Cooperation (*Zentralarbeitsgemeinschaft,* ZAG). The employers had accepted the trade unions as representatives of the workers in wage negotiations, and the trade unions had guaranteed the existence of private property in the means of production. At the same time, increases in mass strikes and disturbances by the workers after the ZAG compromise had indicated that it was necessary to pacify them by guaranteeing substantial increases both in wages and in social welfare payments. This requirement applied as much to the various different kinds of bourgeois cabinet in office between 1924 and 1928 as it had to the earlier governments under Social Democratic leadership. But, already by the mid-1920s, the conflict between the constitutionally embedded principle of the social state and the implementation costs this entailed for both the state and private enterprise had poisoned the atmosphere.[48]

Among other things, this conflict also affected the agreements over working hours and wage levels, which were the most important social achievements of the November Revolution. The employers criticised these landmark decisions of the immediate post-war era, and they attempted to extend working time beyond the eight hours fixed in 1918, and to push through reductions in wages and social benefits. In the long-running conflict that emerged from these endeavours, the employers succeeded to some extent in undermining the Eight-Hour Day, but only in exceptional cases and not right across the board. In any case, it was obviously becoming more and more difficult to conclude negotiated agreements between the two sides as regards both wages and working hours. In 1923, therefore, it was decided that in cases where the employers and the trade unions could not agree, state arbitration committees should be established, and that their decisions would be binding for both sides. The decisions of the state arbitrators were, as a rule, compromises. But the employers increasingly regarded compulsory arbitration as a relic of the revolutionary period, and they considered that the wage levels set by these arbitrators were much too high. It was a fact that, at least after 1927, wage increases considerably outpaced rises in productivity. On the other hand, the starting level of wages during the post-war crisis was especially low; not until 1927 did the real weekly wage again reach its 1914 level.

Disputes over wages therefore intensified rapidly at this time. In 1928, almost half of all contractually agreed wages were set by state arbitration procedures. Finally, at the end of 1928, the Ruhr industrialists refused to accept state arbitration of the wages of ironworkers in the region, and they locked out the whole workforce of over 230,000 people. This marked the definitive end of the social and economic compromise of 1918, and heavy industry in particular now decided to rely on open confrontation with the state and the trade unions. It was the heavy industrialists' conviction that a radical improvement of the economy could only be achieved by cutting back on wages and social benefits, lengthening working hours and severely restricting the influence of the working-class movement. From the end of 1928 onwards, it was being openly asserted that these measures also required changes in Germany's constitution, in particular a reduction in the powers of the parliament, the political parties and the workers' organisations.[49]

But it was the instability of the political system that continued to be the most important problem. Even contentious questions such as foreign policy and reparations in a changed Europe or the readjustment of relations between capital and labour appeared soluble if governments with the ability to take long-term decisions could be installed in office. But this had already become impossible in the later years of the Wilhelmine Reich, owing to reciprocal obstruction by the different social forces. By 1914, it had become almost impossible to get substantial reforms through the Reichstag. The war and the conflicts of ideology and interest exacerbated by it further increased the difficulty of finding the appropriate political instruments to manage the dynamic social, economic and cultural changes which had been unleashed in the country. Above all, it proved almost impossible to forge alliances between the different parties and social camps which possessed a sufficient degree of common ground and were also in a position to translate this into political practice.

The widely held thesis that the Weimar Republic was a 'democracy without democrats' can therefore only be accepted with reservations. The Majority SPD's early decision to seek an alliance with the Left liberal bourgeoisie and political Catholicism had contributed to the fall of the Empire and led relatively quickly, after a short phase of revolutionary upheaval, to a parliamentary democracy which was supported by three quarters of the population in the first post-war election. This majority had, it is true, already collapsed by 1920, and the characteristic three-way division into Left Radicals, Centre parties and Right Radicals had emerged, but it should not be overlooked that, until 1930, the pro-republican camp, which stretched from the SPD to the DVP, always had an absolute majority. The thesis of the accelerated collapse of the two liberal parties only applies to the period after the outbreak of the economic crisis in 1929. It is true that they never again reached the proportion of votes secured during the revolutionary period (22 per cent) but, until 1928, they were able to hold steady at roughly 15 per cent. Their rapid collapse into insignificance only began after that date.

Throughout the Weimar Republic, there were just three coalition options with any political consistency: a 'Weimar Coalition', a coalition of working-class parties, and an alliance between the bourgeois parties of the middle (the DDP and the DVP) and the Centre Party of political Catholicism. None of them was ever able to obtain a majority in the Reichstag. Consequently, government coalitions always had to embrace a wider political spectrum, which meant including either the SPD to the left or the DNVP to the right. This led to a significant increase in the range of political opinions represented by the parties involved in coalition negotiations. Compromises were therefore more difficult to achieve. After other options had been ruled out, only two remained viable. One was a centre-right government stretching from the DDP to the DNVP. Here, there was a high degree of consensus over social and economic matters: budgets should be brought back into balance, wages should be reduced, and above all social benefits should be cut back. But no common basis could be arrived at in the foreign policy sphere, because the DNVP and the right wing of the DVP rejected the Versailles Treaty and also did not want to engage in any negotiations with the Allies over the reparations payments. The other possible option was a Grand Coalition all the way from the SPD to the DVP. Here, there was a considerable level of agreement on foreign policy issues, but no solid common ground on social and economic matters. Under Weimar, no election result was ever able to resolve this dilemma. The parties therefore had to collaborate with each other on a case-by-case basis, and rule with changing majorities. As a result, cabinets were usually short-lived, and the governmental system was characterised by continuous instability.[50]

Further difficulties arose from the fact that the party groups in the Reichstag were under heavy pressure from their respective party organisations, and were liable to withdraw from the government even over relatively insignificant issues, when government decisions contradicted their own party position. Ideological ties thus took precedence over political pragmatism. This situation was a legacy of the long decades of imperial rule, during which the parties had no hope of entering government. Moreover, most of the parties were connected with entrenched groups, socially and culturally defined, and it was their interests that were given primary consideration. Thus, the Social Democrats looked to the skilled workers, the DNVP to the Protestant–Agrarian–Conservative milieu, the Centre Party to the Roman Catholic section of the population, and the DVP to heavy industry. If the interests of their clientele were in danger, they preferred to leave the government rather than continue the search for a compromise. The party groups in the parliament therefore always preserved a critical distance from the governments they themselves supported, and the electors also rewarded their party representatives for oppositional rather than governmental activities.

This dilemma was particularly acute for the Social Democrats. Between 1920 and 1928, they did not participate directly in any national government, with the brief exception of their membership of the Stresemann Cabinet between July and November 1923. There were, it is true, repeated attempts to form a coalition which included the Social Democrats, but such a government could only obtain a parliamentary majority with the help of the DVP, the party of heavy industry. The Social Democrats, however, had a programme of a more strongly left-wing character after their 1922 merger with the remainder of the USPD and they wanted to avoid a coalition with the DVP, as the government that resulted would be more likely to cut social benefits than extend them. The SPD leaders feared, not without reason, that this would alienate their own voters, driving them towards the KPD, their rival on the left.

This, then, was the fundamental political constellation of the Weimar Republic. The result was that, over the fourteen years of the republic's existence, the SPD was only in government for a total of three years and seven months. Throughout by far the greater part of this period, the party served to provide a voting majority for an ever-changing kaleidoscope of bourgeois cabinets on all foreign policy questions but kept its distance from the task of shaping domestic policy in order to avoid being forced into compromises which would lead to alienation between the party's leaders and its rank-and-file membership. Thus, an alliance between the working class and the bourgeoisie, which was the only possible way of stabilising the Weimar Republic, never came to pass.

After the death of Friedrich Ebert in 1925, the seventy-seven-year-old Paul von Hindenburg was elected president, after a second round of elections, in which he narrowly defeated the candidate of the forces of the centre, the Centre Party politician and former Chancellor Wilhelm Marx. The highest office in the Weimar Republic was now occupied by a man who stood for the Wilhelmine era and the third OHL, represented the milieu of the East Elbian landowners and supported agricultural protection, Protestant nationalism, anti-republicanism and the interests of the military. Hindenburg's victory expressed the desire of a section of the electorate to return to the glorious past, of which the victor of Tannenberg was the quintessential representative, but it also indicated a critical attitude towards the republic, the political parties and the culture of modernity. In that sense, Hindenburg's election was a severe defeat for democratic forces, even though the new president promised to adhere loyally to the Weimar constitution.

Of course, a strong president independent of the parties was not inevitably a threat to democracy, as can be seen from the example of the USA. Moreover, the extensive powers afforded to the president by the constitution, in particular the article that provided for the issuing of emergency ordinances, did not inevitably mean that there was a danger of constitutional dictatorship. After all, Friedrich Ebert had also made much use of this instrument to rule the country, and with great success, especially during the crisis of 1923. But Hindenburg's election made it clear that the possibility of a right-wing anti-republican majority existed in Germany. Many of those who promoted his candidacy emerged from the milieu of those who had supported the Kapp putsch, and they saw his election as offering the chance to change the constitution by lawful means, and create an authoritarian presidential government. East Elbian landowners, military men like Kurt von Schleicher, who was the new head of the Armed Forces Department of the Reichswehr Ministry, conservatives at the top of the civil service, and the entourage of the former imperial house: all these groups were aware that a man from their own circle was again in power, and they did everything they could to solidify his position and make the office of the president of the Reich a power hub able to compete with the Chancellor and the parliament. [51]

Notwithstanding these manifold encumbrances and structural weaknesses, the Reichstag elections of 1928 unmistakably but also surprisingly demonstrated the continuing viability of the republic. The SPD obtained almost 30 per cent of the vote, while the DNVP lost practically half its supporters. The share of the vote received by the three parties of the centre did admittedly fall slightly, but as a whole the pro-republican forces were clearly in the lead, with 58 per cent of the vote.

On the extreme Right, the re-founded NSDAP remained a splinter party, with 2.6 per cent. The years of stabilisation had given the republic a second chance, despite all the handicaps that burdened it.

# 5

# Germany around 1926

## Between War and Crisis

### The Economy between Crises

Under the Versailles Treaty, Germany had forfeited 13 per cent of its territory and roughly 10 per cent of its population, including parts of the industrial region of Upper Silesia. It had lost 80 per cent of its iron ore deposits, almost a quarter of its coal and 17 per cent of its area of cereal cultivation. In addition to this, there were considerable reparation payments to be made, of an amount not precisely indicated at first, though in fact they worked out at roughly 1.5 billion Marks a year. If one adds to this the loss of export markets and the effects of internal disturbances as well as the hyperinflation, it is all the more surprising that the German economy recovered relatively quickly after 1923, the year of chaos, and was almost able to repeat the successes of the pre-war economic boom. An important reason for this was that German industrial installations had not been damaged during the war, unlike those of France or Belgium. On the contrary, they had grown in scale and in part undergone modernisation in order to meet continuing orders for the supply of armaments. German industry therefore had an enormous amount of capacity and productive power to draw upon, provided the necessary external conditions were in place.

The most important of these conditions, apart from access to international and above all European markets, was the availability of adequate means of investment. The financial resources of German investors were not enough by themselves, but the Reichsbank, which was under the supervision of the western powers, set very high interest rates. These rapidly made Germany a favoured location for foreign, particularly American, depositors, who could obtain interest payments in Germany which were twice as high as in the USA. The money which flowed from the USA to Germany for this reason amounted to roughly 13 billion Marks. This underpinned the incipient boom, imbuing it with increasing momentum. Of course, the high level of interest payments, which almost reached 10 per cent a year, and the short-term character of the foreign credits, constituted dangerous burdens on the future economic development of the country. But in comparison with the economic catastrophes Germany had just survived, the risk involved was plainly the lesser evil, and, in that sense, there was no genuine alternative.[1]

Five years after the end of the war, the German economy was already back at its 1913 level. The average annual growth of industrial production between 1924 and 1929 was 7.9 per cent, and the economy as a whole grew by roughly 4 per cent a year. From 1926 onwards, as much coal was again produced as before the war, while in 1927 the production of iron and steel was already 40 per cent above the 1913 level. Between 1925 and 1929, the rates of increase achieved in many branches of production could only be compared with the boom years of the pre-war era: in steel, the rate of increase was more than 7 per cent, in metallurgy it was 6.7 per cent and in the refining of oil it was 17 per cent. Rates of investment also increased. At 11.1 per cent, the share of investment in the Net National Product lay only two percentage points below its pre-war level, while the amount of public and private capital investment almost doubled between 1924 and 1928, increasing from 7.5 to 13.7 billion Marks. By 1929, the amount of goods exported had again reached its pre-war level, and industrial exports had a particular hand in this achievement. The gross wage bill was roughly 30 per cent higher in 1929 than it had been in 1913, and labour productivity had risen by almost 100 per cent. German industry led the world in some important areas of activity, above all mechanical engineering, steel, coalmining, chemicals and electrical engineering. The Vereinigte Stahlwerke and IG Farben were among the biggest and most productive enterprises in the world, and the German electrical engineering industry accounted for half the world's exports and a third of the world's production.

Alongside these remarkable successes, there were also trends in the opposite direction. After the war, in Germany as in all European industrial countries, the economy was characterised by stagnation and retarded growth. One reason was that the industrial nations of Europe which had traditionally led the world were now exposed to competition: big industrial agglomerations had arisen in the USA, Canada and Japan, and they had filled the supply gaps that emerged in the European countries during the war. In 1913, Europe was responsible for 57.6 per cent of the world's production of industrial goods; by 1928, this figure had fallen to 47.1 per cent. Over the same period, the USA's contribution rose from 32 to 39 per cent. The Europeans also became less important on the world market as a whole: between 1913 and 1927–9, the British share declined from 13.9 to 11 per cent, the French share from 7.2 to 6.5 per cent and the German share from 13.2 to 9.1 per cent.

The twenty-year phase of pre-war expansion was now replaced, after 1919, by a long-term crisis of adaptation for the new industrial economies of Europe. During the first phase of rapid industrialisation, before 1890, the coal and iron industries had served as the engines of rapid growth, and during the second phase the electrical and chemical industries had performed the same function. After the war, however, no leading sector could be discerned, and this is one reason why there was no driving force available to provide a powerful and long-lasting push towards industrial growth. Not until the 1950s did a new, long-term growth dynamic emerge with the rise of modern consumer society. A new leading sector then arose, in the shape of the motor vehicle industry, whose success already indicated a reorientation towards consumer durables. In addition, the First World War had disorganised financial systems both nationally and internationally, it had reduced national and international trade and it had burdened the national budgets of every combatant country with the immense task of caring for the war-wounded and the dependants of the millions of men who had lost their lives.

If one considers the average rate of growth over a fairly long period, one arrives at an average European figure of just one per cent per annum between 1913 and 1929, though within this there were considerable divergences between the different national economies: the growth rate was 3.3 per cent in the Netherlands, 2.1 in France, 1.5 in Italy, 0.7 in Great Britain and 0.5 in Germany. The industrial production statistics give a still clearer demonstration of the tendency of growth to decelerate: in Germany, by 1929, industrial production was only 13 per cent higher than in 1913, while industrial production worldwide had risen by 42 per cent and the growth figure for the USA was a remarkable 70 per cent. In that sense, therefore, the picture is mixed: the surprisingly strong and rapid recovery of the German economy after the currency reform should be set against its clearly inadequate growth and the strength of the competition faced by the country on the world market.

What counted after 1924, however, was the positive aspect, in comparison with the dreadful wartime and post-war years. The majority of people in Germany were directly affected by the improvement of the economy that followed. Most significant was the rise in real wages. In 1927, they again reached the pre-war level, and in 1928 and 1929 they exceeded it. Indeed, in some branches, such as coalmining and the iron and steel industries, they were considerably higher than they had been before the war. But this hardly compensated for the utter destitution of the preceding ten years, especially as the workers, who continued to comprise almost half of the population, were largely excluded from any chance of social advancement. The inflation had also led to a levelling-out of wages and salaries, and wage differentials between skilled and semi-skilled workers had started to become blurred. There continued to be striking differences between the wages of the workers and the salaries of office employees and state officials, though they were now slightly less pronounced. State officials earned less in relative terms than they had under the Empire. There was a noticeable reduction in the gap which separated them from office employees, even though a reform of state officials' salaries in 1927 brought about material improvements for them, and a more pronounced differentiation in pay scales.

Members of the *Bildungsbürgertum,* however, felt that they had suffered a painful and undeserved degradation, caused not so much by the decline in their real income as by a loss of status, and a blurring of the distinction between themselves and the lower middle classes and the proletariat, especially as this was associated in many cases with the loss of financial assets during the years of inflation. Taken as a whole, though, by 1928 they had again attained the level of real income enjoyed during the pre-war years, the time that had persisted in their collective memory as a period of unparalleled prosperity.[2]

In other fields, by contrast, the upsurge of economic growth was less perceptible: before 1914, unemployment had been a short-lived problem, but now it remained consistently high, at 7–9 per cent. In 1926, when the business cycle passed through a brief but severe crisis of adjustment, it almost reached 17 per cent. One reason for this was the considerable rise in the number of people of working age: the large birth cohorts of the years between 1900 and 1914 now crowded into the labour market, at a rate of between 400,000 and 500,000 people a year. Economic growth was not rapid enough to absorb this additional labour force, so that between 1924 and 1929 roughly 10 per cent of male juveniles were unemployed.[3]

The other great economic problem of those years, alongside unemployment, was the state of agriculture. Whereas the years after 1924 had seen a clear expansion of industry and also services, the agricultural sector was unable to find its way out of the continuous crisis into which it had fallen since the gigantic industrial upsurge of the 1890s. Before the foundation of the German Empire, more than half of the employed population was involved in agriculture; by 1920 the proportion had fallen to 30 per cent. Moreover, this branch of the economy now generated no more than 16 per cent of the gross domestic product (GDP), and a further decline was in progress. From this point of view, Germany occupied an intermediate position among European industrial countries. Agriculture was clearly more important in France, with 41.5 per cent of the employed population and a 35 per cent share in GDP, and the same was true of agriculture in Italy (56 and 48) and indeed in the Soviet Union (86 and 38). In the Netherlands (23 and 12) and in Great Britain (7 and 6), on the other hand, the contribution of the agrarian sector to the economy was already considerably less than it was in Germany.

The rapid decline of agriculture was bound up with similar problems in almost all industrial countries: European agriculture could only overcome overseas competition by increased productivity, specialisation, the rapid introduction of technology, and the improvement of harvest yields. In Great Britain, the process of readjustment had already led by the middle of the nineteenth century to a drastic reduction in the country's agricultural output. By the beginning of the twentieth century, British agriculture, with a share of less than 7 per cent in employment and GDP, was already almost insignificant economically. In the countries of continental Europe, on the other hand, this transition was more difficult and occurred at a slower pace. Firstly, it was only possible to increase productivity, improve yields and introduce modern technology with a considerable outlay of capital. After the war, however, capital was not available in most places. Secondly, any country which wanted to concentrate on the lines that were profitable, and to import the other agricultural products, would have to abandon the idea of national agricultural self-sufficiency in times of crisis. This was scarcely imaginable in post-war societies such as France, Germany or Italy, with their strongly inflamed nationalism. Moreover, the all-embracing modernisation and capitalist transformation of agriculture it involved was not consistent with the positions of political and social power which the overwhelmingly conservative agrarian lobbies were defending all over continental Europe.[4]

In Germany, where the rise of industry and agriculture's loss of importance since the end of the nineteenth century had occurred particularly quickly, the representatives of the agricultural interest were well organised, and they attempted, with great success, to prevent a modernisation of agriculture which would orient it towards the world market. One result of their endeavours was the introduction of protective duties and agricultural subsidies. Another result was the preservation of the formal and informal power of the big landowners, particularly in the eastern part of the country. It continued to be the case that less than 5 per cent of Germany's agriculturalists owned almost 50 per cent of the area capable of cultivation.

At the same time, the first post-war years continued to provide positive results for the owners of agricultural land. One positive aspect was that the prices of agricultural products rose significantly. Between 1913 and 1927, wheat increased in price by 40 per cent; beef by 21 per cent. This clear improvement in income was not a result of greater purchasing power on the part of consumers but of protective duties, which rendered imported foreign produce considerably more expensive. Another positive aspect was that highly indebted farmers, particularly the East Elbian landowners, were able in the course of the hyperinflation to expunge their debts almost completely. As a result, at the beginning of 1924, German agriculture was largely free of debt, for the first time for many decades. This was a particularly favourable starting point, as can be imagined. But only a few years later, a large proportion of Germany's agricultural enterprises, particularly the manors in the east of the country, were already deep in debt again.

Some were in this position by 1928, most by 1930. This was an obvious indication of their utter lack of economic efficiency. In addition, by 1927 Germany was feeling the effects of a worldwide agricultural crisis, which was a result of continuing agricultural overproduction. The crisis quickly pushed down wheat prices by 40 per cent. In response, Germany's agricultural associations made great efforts to prevent market-driven consolidation by obtaining financial assistance from the government. They succeeded, and a number of state relief funds were established for heavily indebted agriculturalists, funds which by 1931 contained more than two billion Marks.

This did nothing to change the condition of German agriculture, which continued to be extremely critical. The income of the farmers, at roughly 1,100 Marks annually, was clearly below the average income of employees in general. Roughly half the farmers earned considerably less than they had done before the war. High tax burdens, falling prices on the world market, and a clearly inferior productivity in comparison with Germany's European and international competitors led to a further worsening of the situation in rural areas after the mid-1920s, and led to the emergence after 1928 of a large-scale and sometimes violent protest movement, mainly concentrated in Schleswig-Holstein, which had a plainly anti-republican and anti-Semitic character.[5]

Excessive dependence on foreign credits, insufficient amounts of investment, the burden of reparations, the continuously high level of unemployment, the permanent crisis of agriculture: all these problems stood in the way of any radical improvement in Germany's economic performance during the middle years of the Weimar Republic. Moreover, the phase of stabilisation, which lasted only five years, was far too short to promote a return to optimism and confidence in the future after the decade of war and its sequel. There was a crisis of adjustment in 1926; although it was brief, it was severe enough to underline the uncertainty and vulnerability of Germany's economic situation.

It therefore made sense for all the major economic actors to seek out counter-strategies and a more long-term way of protecting themselves against fresh crises, either by directly influencing the state, as the big landowners did with success, or by forming conglomerates and cartels, with the help of which heavy industry endeavoured to reduce its operational risks. Many enterprises were able to achieve market domination in this way by engaging in mergers and takeovers, particularly in the steel (Vereinigte Stahlwerke) electrical (Siemens and AEG) and chemical industries (IG Farben). These gigantic concerns were able to compete on the world market with the large British and American firms, and they could also exert a dominant influence on the domestic market. Where this was not possible or the time was not ripe, the big firms of a given sector made agreements over prices, products and the distribution of contracts. These 'cartels' gained greater and greater influence in almost all branches of industry, including coal supply, chemicals, steel and electrical and mechanical engineering. A count has demonstrated that there were more than 3,000 cartels during this period. By introducing elements of planning and coordination, the cartels attempted to remove the crisis-ridden instability of industrial capitalism and the dependence of the market economy on the vicissitudes of the business cycle, the world market and the flow of international finance.[6]

Industrial enterprises also endeavoured to raise their productivity by transferring the experience gained in the wartime economy, with its standardised assembly methods and mass production of war materials, to the task of peacetime production. Reports from the USA about new manufacturing methods also gained influence in Germany, particularly the ideas of Frederick W. Taylor about the subdivision of work processes into uniform and measurable units, and the conveyor belt system perfected by the car manufacturer Henry Ford, which allowed the fabrication of products in series on a mass scale ('Fordism'). It naturally took several years before managers could actually put such methods into practice, as in the case of mining for instance. The scientific and organisational prerequisites for mass production were created by the foundation in 1924 of the Committee of German Industry for the Establishment of Norms, followed a year later by the German Institute for Technical Work Training (*Deutsches Institut für technische Arbeitsschulung*, or DINTA). To introduce new methods inevitably took time. In contrast, agreements between producers with a view to reducing commercial risk had an immediate effect, and because of this, they rapidly became widespread.[7]

## Governance through Welfare Policy

The state too was searching for strategies to protect the economy against conjunctural risk. The lesson of the crisis years was that self-regulation by the free market did not prevent economic catastrophe. After all, it was pointed out, the German war economy only reached its full capacity when the state took a hand in organising it. Did not the example of the inflation also demonstrate that the only effective way of countering the destructive forces of the market was decisive action by the state? Confidence in the state had risen greatly in the whole of Europe during the war and afterwards (paradoxically, it has to be said, in view of what we now know of the economic and political context), and confidence in market forces had declined. This was particularly the case in Germany. The legitimacy of the state now depended far more than it had before the war on whether it was capable of warding off conjunctural disturbances by intervening in the economy and mitigating the impact of crises on the population.[8]

This was the main reason for the massive rise in state expenditure during the 1920s. In 1913, it had amounted to 17.7 per cent of the Gross National Product, but it stood at 25 per cent in 1925 and 30.6 per cent in 1929. In a demilitarised Germany, arms expenditure was modest enough to be discounted, so this money was essentially spent on subsidies and social security, as well as outgoings for public services and infrastructural projects. The purpose of the subsidies was to maintain or stabilise endangered branches of the economy, agriculture above all, but also parts of industry, as, for example, when industries in nationally sensitive regions such as Upper Silesia and the Rhineland threatened to fall into foreign hands.[9]

The biggest items of expenditure were social security payments. It was in the Weimar Republic that the requirement to conduct social policy was first anchored in the constitution. It lay at the heart of the government's concerns under the republic and it occupied the centre of public attention and political conflict. It was one of the basic elements in the new state's legitimacy. The agreements already worked out just after the war through the Central Association for Cooperation (ZAG), formed the groundwork of the system. Under these agreements, trade unions, factory councils and negotiated wage contracts were recognised, and thus the cornerstones of German corporatism were in place. Public support for the victims of the war was also organised very early on. It is true that the pensions paid, and the support services provided, for wounded ex-soldiers, and for the widows and orphans of those who had died in the war, remained at a low level, but they were still sufficient to prevent explosive disturbances emerging from this corner of society during the Weimar years, which was by no means a foregone conclusion in view of the millions of wounded and bereaved people in Weimar Germany.

Initially, the Weimar state did not create a new system of social insurance, but it did increase the number of people insured and the amount of benefit they received. In the late 1920s, however, with the introduction of unemployment insurance, a completely new mechanism was established, until then largely untested internationally. It was a response to a level of long-term mass unemployment which had never been experienced before the First World War, and it was an extraordinary, epoch-making achievement by the Weimar state, given its financial weakness. Yet the size of the reserve fund that was envisaged was calculated on the basis of the amount of unemployment experienced in previous years. After 1929, in the course of the world economic crisis, unemployment attained dimensions never previously known or considered possible, and the system imploded.[10]

Alongside the insurance system, the greatest and at the same time the most visible projects of public welfare policy were state-promoted housing developments and the extension of the urban infrastructure. More than

2 million new dwellings were built with state assistance in the Weimar years. This amounted to roughly 80 per cent of all newly built apartments, as compared with barely 10 per cent before the war. The quality of the houses was improved, and rents were stabilised or even reduced. In spite of these remarkable achievements the accommodation of the working population continued to be of a low standard. In 1927, only 7 per cent of the workers' flats were newly built. More than half the inhabitants of the towns lived in small dwellings consisting of one to three rooms, and a quarter of these also contained subtenants or night-lodgers. The building of houses had been neglected during the boom years of the pre-war decades and this now placed an enduring burden on the public purse at a time of much greater economic difficulty.

In view of the multiplicity and magnitude of the state's social tasks, it was not surprising that state expenditure on social security increased almost tenfold in proportion to the pre-war period. It rose from a billion Marks in 1913 to more than 9 billion Marks in 1929, and this increase was not backed by correspondingly high rates of economic growth or national income. The burden of taxation and social contributions rose accordingly, a development accompanied by vehement criticism on the part of business, because it meant a decline in profit margins and investment levels.

State assistance was needed above all in times of crisis, when the state was particularly short of cash. But it was exactly then, when the state was suffering from a shortfall of tax receipts, that it became less able to satisfy needs which had now become much greater, because it did not have adequate relief funds at its disposal. It would have needed a long phase of stability and growth to allow it to save the necessary financial means to pay for social assistance in case of emergency. As there had never been any long and stable phase of this kind since the foundation of the republic, the Weimar state did not have the means to give effective assistance when those in need of help felt the full impact of the economic crisis.

The Weimar Republic's social policies created considerably improved living and working conditions, for the poorer social groups in particular, and they also went some way towards reducing the most glaring social differences. Nevertheless, the main social policy objectives could only be achieved in part. For a number of years, conflicts of interest between the employers and the workers were to some extent smoothed over, and sharp confrontations were avoided, by the establishment of a system of a corporatist type. But this only operated properly as long as the economic situation facilitated concessions and the political situation compelled compromise. When the world economic crisis set in, however, and not only the amount of available goods but also the power of the trade unions melted away, the employers' side cancelled the agreements made in 1918.

The arrival of the crisis, and the reduction in social security benefits, led to deep disappointment among the social groups affected, but it also placed a question mark over the legitimacy of the whole political system. It must nevertheless be pointed out that, despite these eventual cuts in benefits, the Weimar years saw the creation of a standard from which it was impossible to retreat in the future, even when, as after 1933, most of the rights of social co-determination were removed. Henceforth, in addition to the avoidance of crisis and an economic policy directed towards smoothing out conjunctural fluctuations, an effective social policy was the most important criterion of success and failure for all governments. At the same time, it also became clear how difficult it was to strike a balance between economic efficiency and social security. Here the economic interests of the different social classes and interest groups collided directly with each other. It was therefore no accident that the last Weimar government to enjoy parliamentary legitimacy came to grief on an issue of social policy.

## Classes, Genders and Generations

The war, the post-war turmoil and the inflation had destabilised the structure of German society. The nobility had lost its political power, but it had been able to preserve the strongholds of its economic and social influence. The *Bildungsbürgertum* had been deprived of its wealth during the inflation and its privileged social position was also under threat. Since 1923, its previously firm ties to the bourgeois-liberal and nationalist parties had become looser; and the resentment of local officials and professors, secondary school teachers and lawyers towards the new republic had become even stronger.

New tendencies showed themselves most clearly in the so-called *Kleinbürgertum* (lower middle class). The 'old *Mittelstand*'—small traders and artisans in particular—had declined in numbers and importance. The new group of office employees had grown larger: its share of the labour force grew from 12.6 per cent in 1907 to 16.5 per cent in 1925. This increase was an expression of the rise in the number of office jobs in the big firms, and also the expansion of the state bureaucracy. The office employees were distinguished from the artisans or the owners of small businesses by their lack of independence. From the workers, on the other hand, they were separated by a set of carefully preserved privileges and status symbols: they received a monthly salary rather than the worker's daily or weekly wage packet, and they had a right to longer holidays. They performed office work in a clean environment instead of doing physical labour in dirty factory premises, they had their own insurance funds, and they had their own professional organisations, meticulously kept separate from the Free Trade Unions which organised the workers. Attitudes to marriage and consumption, housing, savings and leisure activities clearly illustrated their orientation towards the bourgeoisie and their cultural distance from the workers, although in many respects they were actually not very different from them, in terms of income level, for instance, or job security. In the interwar period, the male or female office worker (a third were women) was regarded as the 'modern' type of employee par excellence. He or she was associated with the big city, the big firm and modern technology, enjoyed a wider choice of consumer goods, and had a characteristically urban attitude towards leisure. Though attributes of this kind were in fact restricted to comparatively small groups located in the big cities, the status of office employee was in many respects a desirable goal for a large part of the working-class population, at least among the younger generation. Roughly a quarter of all office employees came from working-class families and these people were therefore seen as proof that social ascent was an achievable reality within two generations.[11]

The political attitudes of the office employees were by no means uniform. The largest employee organisation, the German National League of Commercial Employees (*Deutschnationaler Handlungsgehilfenverband*), was a centre of anti-Jewish nationalism throughout the Weimar Republic. But, in 1920, almost half of the organised office employees were members of the *AfA-Bund* (Cooperative Union of Free Salaried Employees' Associations), which was close to the SPD, and even in the late 1920s a third of them were still members of that organisation.

The working class, on the other hand, had not increased in size since the war, and the movement of migration from east to west had almost ceased. In fact, in times of crisis the opposite happened: the unemployed returned from the industrial districts to their original homes in the countryside. Roughly 45 per cent of all employed persons were workers—53 per cent of the men and 30 per cent of the women. The number of unskilled workers had increased greatly during the war, in the course of rationalisation and the introduction of more simplified methods of production. This was only partially reversed in the post-war period. Skilled workers continued to earn much higher wages than semi-skilled, but the differences were less than they had been before. A skilled worker in coalmining, who in 1913 still earned almost half as much again as his unskilled colleague, earned only 27 per cent more in 1927. If real incomes are compared internationally, an industrial worker in Berlin lay somewhere in the middle: he earned more than his colleagues in Warsaw, Prague, Milan and Vienna but less than those in London, Amsterdam or Copenhagen, not to mention workers in the US city of Baltimore, whose real wages were almost three times as high.

Finally, a comparison of income differentiation in Germany between 1913 and 1928 shows the impact of the war and its aftermath. In 1928 the average annual income of a worker was 1,825 Marks, which was in nominal terms 66 per cent more than before the war (real wages first returned to their pre-war level in 1927). Commercial employees earned 2,600 Marks (30 per cent higher than in 1913), while officials received 4,050 Marks (48 per cent higher). The self-employed, on the other hand, a category which also includes farmers, earned 14 per cent less than in 1913. Taken together, then, workers continued to earn a much lower income than other broad social groups, but the differences had declined somewhat. During the world economic crisis, however, this tendency would again go into reverse.[12]

There were clear changes in these years in women's employment. This initially happened for demographic reasons: the above-average birth-rate of the years around 1900 made itself felt in the labour statistics. At the same time, the proportion of women in gainful employment increased. Thus, in 1925, there were 1.5 million more women in full-time employment than in 1907. Roughly one woman in three now went to work. During the same period, the number of jobs available in industry and the service sector rose, and the number in domestic service and agriculture declined. The 1920s saw a further acceleration of the trend already apparent during the war, whereby industrial undertakings increasingly placed unskilled and semi-skilled women in sectors where articles were manufactured in series and on a conveyor belt system. Almost three quarters of the women employed in industry worked in these sectors. They earned roughly half as much as the men employed in identical positions.

At the same time, the essential pattern of male and female employment proved astoundingly resilient. In most cases, a woman's phase of gainful employment was short. It was the interval between leaving school and getting married. Moreover, it was not only customary for a woman to give up her job after marriage, it was also regarded as worth aiming for, since it meant that the husband's earnings and social status were high enough to make it unnecessary for the wife to continue in employment (only 20 per cent of women workers were married). The wives of artisans, shopkeepers or farmers represented an exception, as they continued after the marriage to 'lend a hand' on the farm or in the shop, and they show up in the statistics as 'family members helping in the business'. As late as 1925, this category included more than a third of all women in employment.

By and large, women continued to be denied promotion into the small group of top earners, although equality between the sexes was laid down for the first time by the Weimar Constitution. The proportion of girls who received high school education did increase considerably, but as a rule they only proceeded as far as the one-year school-leaving certificate awarded at the end of the tenth class. Women were admitted to university from 1908 onwards, and by 1931, 16 per cent of students were female. Around this time, there were roughly 12,000 women in employment in professions requiring academic training, working mainly as doctors, lawyers and schoolteachers. Most of them worked in the cities; they were seldom seen in the provinces. In short, there was a certain amount of movement away from the traditional pattern of gender roles in the area of employment, though at a glacial pace.[13]

The so-called 'new woman' of the interwar years was exemplified, above all, by female shopworkers and office workers. The number of sales assistants, clerical assistants and shorthand typists had tripled since 1907, and these roles in commercial employment proved of particular interest to younger women. They promised a higher status and better working conditions than a job as a sales assistant, though the salary was no better: roughly half the female employees earned less than 100 Marks a month, which was not much more than subsistence level. Approximately 90 per cent of them were unmarried and under twenty-five. They too followed the prevailing gender norms of employment, marriage and a return to domesticity.

Even so, the office employee symbolised the new, modern type of woman, praised, ridiculed or spurned in many magazines and also in the utterances of politicians, but always the subject of vigorous discussion. The office worker, who was predominantly young and in tune with big city living, embodied a new phenomenon: a certain kind of female independence, which contrasted strikingly with the Wilhelmine image of a woman, with its archetypical farmers' wives, care-worn working-class women with many children to care for, and conservative bourgeois 'ladies' of a better class, who were entirely uninvolved in the world of work. This was also reflected in their appearance: whereas before the war the fashionable image was that of the rather mature lady, with her hair artistically pinned up, a broad-brimmed hat, and often a gathered skirt, now hair was short and bobbed, figures were boyish, clothes were knee-length and smooth, and the general image was smart and casual. 'Short, flat, geometrical and rectangular—a woman's clothing follows the pattern of a parallelogram.' That was the comment of a Paris contemporary. The most popular fashions stressed the youth and independence of the new woman, allowing her to radiate an erotic appeal further accentuated by make-up and jewellery. These images spread rapidly through the medium of street hoardings and the advertisement pages of magazines and journals, which were becoming increasingly important at this time.[14]

Women now began to appear in public in entirely new roles. They engaged in athletics, they skied, they drove cars, they played tennis and they rode bicycles. Cilly Aussem, who won the ladies' singles title at Wimbledon in 1931, embodied this type of woman, but the most famous example was the actress

Marlene Dietrich: a bold and sophisticated woman, who smoked and wore trousers. She became a popular idol, at least until 1930, when she moved to the USA, choosing to settle there because political developments in her homeland were becoming increasingly disquieting.[15]

For most of the women of the twenties, idols like Dietrich were as far removed from the reality of their everyday lives as was the new pattern of gender roles from their previous experience. But even if such exemplars were regarded as unattainable, their existence still offered new perspectives, which placed the situation of the average woman in a different context. The new gender roles also coloured the way family life was viewed. By the end of the 1920s, the average number of children per couple had fallen below 2.0. With the growth of state-provided social benefits, particularly old-age pensions, the establishment of a family was no longer the only way to provide care from one generation to the next. Family planning, and birth control and prevention, themes which were hardly discussed publicly before the war except within communities of life reformers, now increasingly occupied the centre of attention. The number of abortions also increased (though possibly this only reflected improvements in the availability of evidence for estimating this.) But the campaign by working-class parties, women's associations and sexual reformers for the relaxation or abolition of the laws that prohibited the practice met with such strong resistance from the Catholic Church and the conservative and right-wing parties that it failed to achieve its objective.[16]

Even so, the discussion of birth control, sexuality and family planning occupied a much larger space in the public sphere than before the war. Books providing sex education and advocating sexual reform did a roaring trade. It was hardly possible to imagine a greater difference between this and the embarrassed silence over these themes twenty years earlier, which reflected the prevalence of inhibitions, taboos and double standards. 'It is quite possible that there is no sphere of public life', wrote Stefan Zweig in retrospect, 'in which a series of factors . . . have brought about so complete a change within one generation as in the relationship between the sexes.'[17]

The nature of housework also began to change. One has, of course, to bear in mind the limited scale of this development. Only 7 per cent of the houses were newly built. The overwhelming majority of the population and almost all working-class people continued to live in cramped circumstances, mostly in old buildings without baths, which conformed to the standards of the 1880s and 1890s. But running water, electricity and gas-fired heating were increasingly the norm in bourgeois households and newly built dwellings in general. Electrical devices for the home—vacuum cleaners, electric irons, spin dryers, semi-automatic washing machines and refrigerators—began to spread among the population. The automation of the household made housework easier for women, but it also reflected a slight rise in the number of professionally active housewives, and to a much greater extent a fall in the number of maidservants. Above all, however, household electrical devices were enormously attractive to most people, who were initially unable to afford them, and in this way they offered new horizons for consumer desires, which burned no less strongly for their short-term unattainability.

The automation of the household went hand in hand with the demand for the rationalisation and modernisation of housework, and at the same time for a 'progressive' mode of private life informed by scientific knowledge. According to this, it was not the number of children but their health that was important. This had a bearing on standards of hygiene just as it did on attitudes to disease and goals of upbringing. Accordingly, 'positive population policy' led not only to the establishment of marriage counselling centres and courses to improve the care of infants, but also to campaigns for better healthcare and improved nutrition. Every European industrial country had policies of this kind, and pronatalist and social reforming motives played a role in them all.

These initiatives, which were usually promoted by the state but often also by reform-oriented leagues and associations, were frequently influenced by experience around the turn of the century, when more intense scientific and political efforts, in the field of medicine, for example, had made it possible in a relatively short period to restrain the spread of the major epidemic diseases. Reformers began to ask: why should this not be possible in other spheres, in dealing with big social problems for instance? 'Architects would solve the housing question as well as all the other woes of urbanisation; lawyers and educationalists would together teach criminals to mend their ways; medical research and public-health programmes would abolish illness; and psychologists and social workers would abolish "asocial" behaviour', writes the historian Detlev Peukert. The aim of this movement, he notes, was to realise 'the dream that the social question could finally be solved.'[18]

These reforming endeavours were based on an optimistic picture of humanity and an assumption that people were capable of learning and ready to seek enlightenment. They should be seen as a further attempt to solve the problems produced by the rise of modern mass society by means of science and technology, modern methods of state intervention in the social and private spheres, and the establishment of new norms and standards for a normal, healthy and comfortable life. To pursue this course was to offer the state authorities and the governing political forces tremendously increased opportunities to intervene in individual private lives, but in view of the basically liberal attitude of the reforming forces this development was not initially regarded as particularly threatening.

The existence of the 'new youth' was also postulated alongside the idealised picture of the 'new woman'. This too reflected real social and demographic changes. Since the 1880s, the self-image of German society had been radically rejuvenated. The 'young person' (*der Jugendliche*) entered the picture. This was someone of an intermediate age between childhood and adulthood, who was searching for his or her own way of living and mode of self-expression and who rapidly became the subject of social, political and artistic fantasies. The lyrical tone of glorification which was so typical of the pre-war years and the youth movement continued to be heard, but the conditions in which young people started their adult lives had now become much more difficult. The children born in the especially fecund period around the year 1900 now began to pour into the labour market, and they often failed to find work. Youth unemployment was a new phenomenon, until then unknown in German industrial society, and its effects were a cause of anxiety. 'Loafers' (*Eckensteher*), 'Young Hooligans' (*Halbstarken*), 'Unruly Cliques' (*Wilde Cliquen*)—these words express the fear which was commonly felt by the bourgeoisie of the post-war years that a whole generation of predominantly urban working-class youth would fall into bad ways. This prompted the emergence of a separate academic discipline, under the name of 'social pedagogy', which concerned itself with this new phenomenon and looked for ways to help young people who had 'lost their way', to educate, improve, and discipline them. Apart from such endeavours, however, the post-war society of the Weimar Republic clearly had little to offer young people who were faced with doors that were closed and chairs that were already occupied. The resulting remoteness of the young from the 'senile republic' was a phenomenon frequently observed by contemporaries.[19]

The differences and conflicts between the generations as a whole were also much discussed, and many observers were convinced that the profound changes of the epoch not only found expression in the transition from one generation to the next but could also be explained by it. 'Sons without fathers' became a fertile subject of debate. These were young men who had grown up during the war years while their fathers were fighting at the front. The war itself had played the role of father to this generation, wrote Günter Gründel, who had been in the nationalist youth movement: 'Hunger, misery and privation; youth training; coal shortages; and then again and again hunger and privation . . . Finally: the collapse of the paternal world and everything in it that had previously been valued. Revolution and the "revaluation of all values"'. But this then placed a question mark over 'even the last remnant of what had been valued until then, at least implicitly: liberty, the fatherland and almost all the ideals and values that their elders had constantly talked about'. With this, the 'definitive bankruptcy of the whole of the older generation's world' reached its culmination.

The publisher Peter Suhrkamp, though himself inclined towards liberalism, wrote in a similar vein:

> The fathers, by the way, were for the most part in the war. After the war, the children of these parents, since they were either left to themselves or ran away, got caught up in all the hysteria and unpleasantness of the crisis. But they didn't suffer much harm from their experience. They reacted to the epoch, surrendered to it, made use of it. They were always clever, sharp and capable.

This paean of praise for the first modern generation of young people, who had grown up quickly and become independent in the absence of parental authority, was obviously somewhat stylised. But it did demonstrate the anxiety felt over the effects of a period which had brought about upheavals and transformations of such magnitude that children's formative lives now differed tremendously from their experience in the years of security before the war, and it was impossible to predict how they would turn out.[20]

Three major aspects of the development of young people in the Weimar years should be given particular prominence here. First, there was the role played by the various offshoots of the youth movement, who had now become differentiated into countless 'tribes' (*Stämme*), 'leagues' (*Bünde*) and 'gangs' (*Meuten*) but continued to have certain core elements in common: walking tours, nature, the critique of the city, autonomy and the principle of comradeship. The nationalistically inclined youth movement was by far the strongest tendency. It was organised in numerous large and small groups, often divided only by their commitment to different ringleaders or idols, but united by their orientation towards the *Volk*, the nation and Germanism (*Deutschtum*). But there were other tendencies too. The spectrum extended all the way from the scouts and the politically neutral associations to the aggressive *völkisch* youth leagues (*völkische Jugendbünde*).

The second aspect was their politicisation. Many of the nationalistically inclined groups functioned as youth sections of national parties or leagues. This applies to the *Jungstahlhelm* (Young Steel Helmets), the youth sections of the *Jungdeutscher Orden* (Young German Order) and the *Jungnationaler Bund* (Young Nationalist League) of the DNVP. Later on, the *Hitlerjugend* (Hitler Youth) was the most prominent example. The fact that the parties now had their own youth leagues was itself an expression of the growing significance of the mystique of youth in the political arena. The distinguishing marks of these leagues were selectivity, military discipline and orientation towards a leader, to whom 'fealty' (*Gefolgschaft*) was owed. At the same time, many youth groups combined the romantic aspects of the pre-war years and the soldierly ideals of the front-fighter myth with the feeling that the political questions of the present could best be tackled not by the 'elders' but by young people, who, rather than pursuing their own interests, had a sense of obligation to the ideals of the community. In this context, the unity of youth was contrasted with pluralism and public in-fighting; military organisation with self-determination and individualism, as in a typical proclamation of the period: 'It feels like the running of the spring tide when I feel the marching rhythm of the boys' brigade, when I know that hundreds are marching with me, thousands. Soldiers with a common goal: German Boyhood.'[21]

The Social Democrats, the Centre Party and the liberals also tried to respond to the cult of youth, and they founded their own youth organisations: here too there were walking tours, campsites and a mixture of scouting activities and paramilitary training, although ideological divergences were considerable. The Social Democratic 'falcons' were committed to the republic and socialism and they were closely linked with the party milieu, while the various Catholic youth groups trained the rising generation to keep a critical distance from democracy and the modern environment. Both lines of approach enjoyed much success among the young, but it was apparent early on that it was, above all, the parties of radical extremism which profited from the wave of youth. The communists and the National Socialists not only had younger members than all other parties, they also received the votes of most young people in the elections of 1930 and beyond. The myth of the young had become politicised; youthful political radicalisation grew out of this development.[22]

Apart from the youth movement and its politicisation, a further important aspect of young people's lives was an interest in leisure and consumption, in sport and technology, in life in the big city and entertainment, and in dance music and the cinema. In the beginning, all this was entirely non-political. The chaos of war and its aftermath had increased the need for entertainment, diversion and amusement (*Amüsemang*), and it had also to some extent freed young people from the disciplinary shackles of the parental home and the schoolroom.[23] But these activities soon implied a political statement as well, though it was often unintentional. The nationalist youth associations continuously criticised the entertainment industry of the cities and the desire of the young to dance, and indeed their uniformed marches, excursions and rituals of self-denial offered a counter-programme against all forms of urban hedonism. There were some young people and adults from middle-class families who rejected such tendencies and developed what was tantamount to a political programme out of their veneration of modern technology, motor cars, sport, dance music and, above all, America. In 1930, the journalist Hans A. Joachim described this state of mind:

> We set great store by America. America was a good idea; it was the land of the future. It was at home in its century. . . . Technology, that glorious field of endeavour, had appeared to us in the shape of tanks, mines and poison gas and other instruments for destroying human lives for quite long enough.

> In America technology was at the service of human life. The sympathy we expressed for the lift, for the radio tower, for jazz, was demonstrative. It was an affirmation. It was a way of turning swords into ploughshares.[24]

Explicit statements of this kind were rare, but enthusiasm for modernity, as symbolised by America, was extremely widespread.

## The Culture of the Metropolis

At the end of the 1920s, only a third of the German population still lived in villages and rural communes. More than a quarter lived in towns of more than 100,000 inhabitants, and every fifth person lived in a city of more than 500,000. In 1910, there had been only seven cities with more than half a million inhabitants: Berlin, Hamburg, Cologne, Munich, Leipzig, Dresden and Breslau [Wrocław]. In 1939, there were eleven: the seven already mentioned plus Essen, Frankfurt-am-Main, Düsseldorf and Dortmund. Berlin, through the incorporation of its suburbs, had by 1920 become one of the biggest cities in the world. In area it was the second largest, behind Los Angeles, and in population (at 4.3 million) it was third behind London and New York. It was larger than Hamburg, Cologne, Munich and Leipzig put together. Nevertheless, it did not occupy the same prominent position as London did in Great Britain or Paris in France, if only because of the particularism of Germany's federal states.

By the turn of the century, Berlin had already become the main focus of all the thoughts, sentiments and programmes which were bound up with the city and city life. Berlin was unique in its outward physical appearance: the immense factories of big firms such as Borsig or Siemens; the tenements and housing districts of the workers; the incessantly growing motor car traffic, and the new rapid trains (*S-Bahnen*) and underground trains (*U-Bahnen*); the palaces of consumption, amusement and sport; and the centres of light entertainment, vice and criminality. Berlin was also the main arena of activity for the modern professions and social groups such as journalists, scientists, and intellectuals, as also for female office employees and independent women in general. It was in addition the city of revolution and counter-revolution, of avant-garde artists, of writers and of people who were trying to change the world.

Berlin was generally perceived as a kind of large-scale social experiment. Processes that elsewhere took place over long periods happened there instantaneously and in parallel. That is how the journalist Josef Räuscher saw it in 1930: 'Berlin is nothing other than the most advanced post, the experimental station with the most modern equipment, for testing out whether and in what way Germans are mentally capable of coping with civilisation in its most up-to-date manifestation.'[25] Just as in Germany the move from an agrarian to an industrial state had taken place particularly quickly, so Berlin had been transformed within a generation into one of the most modern cities in the world, in which the contrasts were so clear, and the contradictions so glaring, that new political movements, economic theories, artistic upheavals, revolutionary pamphlets, unique technological innovations and exaggerated fashions seemed to emerge unceasingly out of these confrontations.[26]

But it was not just that Berlin was modern. It *wanted* to be modern, the most modern city in the world, if only to compensate for the fall into the abyss that had happened in 1918. In actual fact, there were far fewer motor cars in Berlin than in other world-class metropolitan centres, since motoring by private individuals spread more slowly in Germany than in Britain and France, and of course the USA. But, as the architect Hans Stimmann put it, 'a world-class city had to have motor-car traffic, if possible on several levels. People knew this was true of Paris, London and above all American cities like New York, Chicago and Los Angeles. It also had to have white-gloved traffic policemen or, still more modern, crossings regulated by traffic lights' even if they were actually completely unnecessary.[27] In 1926, Kurt Tucholsky gave a biting and accurate description of this somewhat parvenu-like endeavour to deck oneself out with the insignia of the American metropolis: 'All this hype fits in with the New German's strong urge to have the same feelings as he imagines the Americans have. He is quite happy to abandon the attempt to be a character, provided he can live in a place with a "Ssity" and a "Brodweh". That really gives you a lift!'[28]

Berlin stood for 'Americanisation', which was one of the catchwords of 1920s Germany. It stood for the victory of technology and for the industrial dynamism symbolised by Henry Ford, whose book *My Life and Work* sold more than 200,000 copies in Germany during the period. It stood for the new mass consumption, the rejection of tradition in favour of utility, new gender roles, a successful entertainment industry aimed at the tastes of the masses and a levelling-down of social hierarchies. 'Americanism' was used as a byword for cultural modernity, and a description of everything previously unheard-of and new. The literary historian Georg Bollenbeck has made this point with striking effectiveness: 'When the son listens to jazz music and fails his Latin examination, when the wife bobs her hair and makes erotic demands, when the boss introduces new production methods and accelerates the work tempo—all this can be classed as Americanism.'[29]

The American entertainment industry was at the heart of the process. Charlie Chaplin, the star of the American silent film, enjoyed tremendous popularity in Germany. His visit to Berlin in 1931 drew larger crowds than had ever been seen for any other actor. The cinema now became the most important form of modern leisure entertainment. The number of cinemagoers multiplied many times over, and the introduction of talking pictures at the end of the 1920s brought in still more people. The films made by German studios, particularly UfA (*Universum Film A.G.*), were seen by a mass public, and they created 'stars' like Heinz Rühmann, Heinrich George, Hans Albers, Lil Dagover, Adele Sandrock and Luis Trenker. The masses were also gripped by the new entertainment music. The 'dance craze' took off. People participated enthusiastically in fashionable dances like the Foxtrot and the Charleston. Jazz bands sprang up like mushrooms after rain. By 1925, there are said to have been more than 30,000 in the country.

> Dance musicians and orchestras burned their old music scores in embarrassment, got hold of red frock coats, painted their faces black, put on yellow stockings and blue shoes, bought children's trumpets, cowbells, guitars and toy pistols and cheerfully got themselves hired in their hundreds as the "Original Yazz Band" or the "Shimmy Band". The slogan "No pub without its jazz band" was faithfully followed. And the public arrived in their thousands.

These are the words of a music critic, writing in 1922, who was already somewhat amused by the phenomenon.[30] Berlin established itself as an entertainment metropolis. The main attractions, apart from the dance halls, were the revue theatres, with their revue girls, who were soon famous everywhere. In Berlin alone, more than 10,000 spectators went to these theatres every day. The gramophone record began its victorious career at the same period, along with the popular hit tune, which was mostly sentimental and slushy, though there were also some saucy lyrics, such as those of the 'Comedian Harmonists', who soon rose to become Germany's most well-known vocal group. Approximately 30 million gramophone records were sold in Germany in 1929. Moreover, these products of mass culture were, as a rule, no longer regionally limited. There was now a nationwide public, which was immensely enlarged by the spread of wireless broadcasting in the late 1920s and early 1930s. The number of radio sets in Germany increased from 10,000 in 1924 to 4.3 million in January 1933.[31]

These miracles of the new mass culture exerted an almost immeasurable fascination, for at this time they still possessed the aura of the new, the unfamiliar, and the sensational. It must have seemed like a miracle to contemporaries that they could hear the same voice and the same piece of music on the radio everywhere in the country at the same time, or that living individuals appeared to be singing, talking and moving around on the cinema screen. Admittedly, there was plenty of criticism of cinemas, hit tunes and mass entertainment from the very beginning, but the Jeremiahs of cultural pessimism could make no headway against the general approbation, indeed enthusiasm, with which these innovations were greeted. 'Then we went to see a comedy film with Pat and Patachon, and laughed our troubles away', as a young textile-worker wrote in a report to her trade union. She continued: 'You can say what you like, the cinema may be kitsch, but it makes you forget your worries, and anyway I like a good laugh.'[32]

But even the cinema was overshadowed by the attraction of sport, both in terms of the games played around the nation to tone up and strengthen the individual's physique, and the mass sporting events which had a magnetic effect on the spectators. In Germany in 1930, there were already roughly 6.5 million members of sports clubs, almost a million of them women. Football, cycling and swimming were the main activities. The German Football League (*Deutscher Fußballbund*) included roughly 7,000 clubs in 1929, with more than a million members. Tens of thousands of spectators watched the matches played for the German Football Championship, and from the late 1920s onwards, hundreds of thousands of people listened to the commentaries on the radio. The same was true of the six-day bicycle races, and, to an increasing degree, professional boxing, particularly after the heavyweight Max Schmerling achieved his first victories and became a popular idol.

The popularity of sport cannot be understood without reference to the new cult of the body that emerged at the time. The young, athletically hardened body became the ideal figure, for both men and women, as Stefan Zweig noted enthusiastically:

> It was just in the swimming pools that the transformation was most noticeable; whereas in my youth a really well-built man attracted attention among the thick necks, the fat bellies and the sunken chests, now persons athletic, lithe, browned by the sun and steeled through sport vied with one another . . . The women threw off the corsets which had confined their breasts, and abjured parasols and veils since they no longer feared air and sunshine. They shortened their skirts so that they could use their legs freely at tennis, and were no longer bashful about displaying them if they were pretty ones.[33]

There was to some extent a conflict between the gradual expansion and spread of modern mass culture over the whole country and the traditional regional cultures, which were strongly embedded in Prussia east of the Elbe, in the Rhineland and in Bavaria. But modern mass culture was also in conflict with the 'socio-moral milieux', which were particularly characteristic features of the socialist workers' movement and Catholicism, and no doubt the national camp as well. In some cases, these milieux were also linked to regional cultures. The close connection they provided with a network of organisations firmly bound together by basic political and ideological convictions and by repeated rituals which created a sense of community offered the individual not only material assistance and a solid and reliable framework in a world which was clearly out of joint, but also a convincing explanation of the upheavals that were taking place. Solidarity, and a feeling of community and warmth, arose from the social milieu, but this was also bound up with constant supervision, narrow attitudes and excessive traditionalism. In the 1920s, these limitations led to criticism from the younger generation, which had a tendency to break away, especially as the tempting offerings of mass culture now presented alternatives. Nevertheless, the network of social democratic organisations expanded strongly in the Weimar years, and both the workers' movement and the Catholic movement built up their own associations, in sport for example, in competition with the existing bodies, which were mainly dominated by the nationalists. These new associations proved very successful. In the post-war world, the need for integration into the narrower framework of the milieu was felt by many people: they viewed it as protection against a multiplicity of crises and insecurities, the more so as the state social security system turned out to be insufficiently reliable when put under stress. When those social (and also political) pressures were set aside, though, it became obvious that the long-term dominance of modern mass culture could hardly be denied, as much among young workers and Catholics as among other groups.[34]

But it was not just mass culture that was new and extraordinary. In the years before the war, the artistic avant-garde had often replied to the challenge of modernity by combining the new, revolutionary art forms with harsh criticism of the new urban and industrial world. The contradiction between the individual genius and the demands of mass society was reflected in Expressionism, which emphasised the primacy of nature, youth and art as against technical progress and economic thinking. After a devastating war, however, this became more difficult. As in the political field, so too in art, many stylistic forms and creations were tested out, praised, then torn apart and replaced by others. There was a constant search for new, appropriate answers to the constantly changing challenges of the present, challenges which succeeded each other with the same frantic rapidity as the different artistic styles.

In this context, it is worth mentioning the attempt to combine revolution and art in the environment provided by the Munich Council Republic. Various poets of an expressionist tendency composed verses encouraging revolution. Yet more mischievous, and in their own way more radical, were the Dadaists. They had already started to react to the catastrophes of the present with mockery and derisive cynicism while the war was raging, and after the mass slaughter was over they put forward the idea of the futility of art and formal artistic excellence. The first Dadaist journal, issued by George Grosz and the brothers John Heartfield and Wieland Herzfelde, bore the splendid name 'Everyone his own football'. The Dadaists called for the immediate regulation of sexual relations by the introduction of a central Dada sex office, they appeared dressed in military uniforms, wearing grotesque masks, they rode on Iron Crosses and they organised 'happenings' such as a race between a typewriter and a sewing machine. The main target of their satire was the way of thinking and the mode of life of the nationalist-minded intellectual bourgeoisie and conservative society in general, and they hit the mark with great success. But they also infiltrated the sphere of everyday life, showing how art could shine a spotlight on the commonplace, particularly in the case of Heartfield's photomontages.

The Dadaist way of perceiving the city, technology and mass culture, as impartial as it was critical, was also characteristic of the 'New Matter-of-Factness' (*Neue Sachlichkeit*), an artistic movement which coolly rejected the high-flown emotionalism of the Expressionists, advocating instead a plain and simple vision of reality. Precise factual description, acceptance of technology and rejection of ideology formed a common basis for the movement, although no uniform artistic style developed out of it, as is clear when one contemplates such diverse writers as Egon Erwin Kisch, Erik Reger, Hans Fallada, Kurt Tucholsky, Alfred Döblin and Siegfried Kracauer, who all fall under this rubric. What they had in common was less an artistic programme than an attitude of sober pragmatism and an acceptance of modernity as it existed and could be both criticised and enjoyed. They were all unmistakably antagonistic towards both the agitational art of the Left and the nostalgic style of the Right, tendencies which were both starting to take hold at this time. But '*Sachlichkeit*' also became the slogan of the young adherents of the 'new Right', who replaced the nationalistic pathos of the veterans' associations and the political parties of the local elites with an icy vision of the folk, the race and the nation and declared that their own anti-Semitism was not emotional but rational.[35]

If we take a look at high culture, we can see how closely the decades before and after the First World War belong together. The many devastating catastrophes and changes in the economy, politics and society between the 1890s and the early 1930s formed the seedbed for the multiplicity of suggestions and proposals which were discussed and tested in the artistic and intellectual spheres during the period. An enormous potential was unleashed, revealing an ability to create and reconfigure the landmarks of culture arguably unparalleled in recent history. In the course of a few years, artists and writers passed through the whole repertoire of possible artistic responses to the new epoch.[36]

The culture of modernity had now established itself in Germany, although predominantly as an urban phenomenon. It had followed defeat in war, revolution, civil war and inflation and it emerged in a strife-torn society which was struggling to find direction and focus. Modernity was therefore seen by many not as an answer to the problems of the epoch but as the problem itself. The hostile response to it, which intensified in the course of the 1920s, took a correspondingly violent form.

## Cultural Critique and Alternative Visions

After all, Berlin was not Germany. The artistic avant-garde hardly penetrated beyond the capital's boundaries. Experimental silent films were only shown in Berlin. There was hardly any perceptible reflection of functionalist 'New Building' in the nationwide statistics on construction. 'The province, where it is at its most intimate' wrote Kurt Tucholsky in 1920,

> lives from its aversion towards Berlin and its secret admiration for the city . . . There the bourgeois rules in his most evil shape. There the old-style officer rules. There the official of the old regime rules. And how they rule! Not a trace of comprehension has made its way into the provinces. No breath of air from the new age has swept in. There everything is still as it was in the old days.[37]

In actual fact, this claim was only half correct. Certainly, the 'golden twenties' turned out on closer inspection to be a chimera, a Berlin invention. But the concept did serve as an image, albeit a distorted one, of what was new, and as a projection of the wishes and anxieties of the provincials about the changes the new age would bring for them as well. The travelling cinema now visited the village twice a month. Increasingly, reports about national sporting events appeared in the local newspapers. At weddings, operetta music was played on the teacher's gramophone, to general amusement. And, of course, the new tractors and radio sets, the mechanised harvesters and telephones, and not least the new methods of treatment employed in the local district hospital, bore witness in the countryside too to the fact that radical changes had occurred in daily life.

Many things, however, did not change, or if they did, they changed much more slowly: the rhythm of the agricultural year, the customs of the region, the isolation of the rural areas, the paramount importance of piety and the Church, the social hierarchies in the village and the family. Most people therefore had a dual experience: they were firmly anchored in the traditions of their own world, yet they sensed the phenomena of change which were occurring predominantly outside it, although a few individual elements and messages penetrated into their own lives. It was only where people saw their own social and economic situation as reasonably stable that they were in a position to open up to the new age.

Where that was not the case, the new age had an unsettling and threatening effect, and might well be seen as a cause of the difficulties they faced, as symbolised by Berlin, which represented the myth of modernity. The Swabian writer Ludwig Finckh wrote a polemical pamphlet against the 'spirit of Berlin', which he considered to be the repository of everything he feared and despised: industry, politics, public opinion and modern culture. Berlin could not provide a secure future, either: 'The new Reich must have a new capital city . . . Somewhere in the heart of Germany, in woodland, or in open country'. 'The spirit of the German *Volk*' wrote the influential *völkisch* author Wilhelm Stapel, 'is rising up against the spirit of Berlin. What the present day needs is a revolt of the countryside against Berlin.'[38]

The new everyday culture of modernity was the neuralgic point and the main target of the fundamentalist critique, which was now practised in particular by the new intellectual Right, a group which soon received the somewhat imprecise collective name of the 'conservative revolution'. The basis of the conservative argument continued to be the opposition between community and society, between culture and civilisation, between German profundity and Western superficiality and numerous other variants of these Germanocentric dichotomies. According to the credo that emerged from this critique, the dissolution of traditional bonds had allowed the rule of technology, industry and the city to take hold. This had separated people from their values and their customs and destroyed their culture. Moreover, the adoption of foreign influences (before 1914 voluntary, and after 1918 as a result of Germany's defeat by the West) had allowed the establishment of the principles of liberalism, capitalism and individualism, and these had destroyed the traditional German values of commitment, hierarchy, honour, loyalty and duty.

The mass culture of the city, according to the bestselling authors of radical cultural criticism during this period, such as Stapel, Spengler, Jung and Moeller van den Bruck, was the intensified expression of this loss of values, and this lay at the core of the alienation of the *Volk* from its cultural roots. 'Cinema, Expressionism, Theosophy, boxing contests, nigger-dances, poker and racing', wrote Oswald Spengler, demonstrated 'the sterility of civilised man'. Genuine culture had been replaced by marketing and soulless diversions, and genuine artists had been replaced by intellectuals and journalists. People no longer looked to the great examples of German culture, according to Spengler, but to America. But America did not have any genuine culture. The fashions that had overflowed from there to Germany were nothing more than 'childish vanity lived out as civilisation' and 'America's domination of the world' only demonstrated the 'spiritual self-abandonment of the peoples of ancient culture'.

The critics lashed out against films and popular songs as well as votes for women, trade unions and birth control. They attacked modern art, popular sport, pacifism and jazz bands. New forms of dance were a particular target of the cultural critics: 'The adoption of the cult of negro dancing', that 'dance form which comes from America and derives from a barbaric blood-stock', is itself proof, wrote Edgar Jung, that, 'we can no longer speak of a land of high culture, even though Gothic cathedrals were once built on its soil.' The fear spread rapidly through the population that 'negro bands', as well as dark-skinned dancers like Josephine Baker, so famous in the twenties, would start the process of cultural collapse by 'mixing the races'.

There was also anxiety that orderly relations between the sexes would be undermined by the new type of woman who was appearing in advertising and images from popular culture. According to the journalist Fritz von Haniel: 'The emancipation of women, the hardening and deliberate training of the body through sport, the unceasing profanation of the female body by eccentric dances, revues and the advertising-bustle, the whole unfortunate "girl-cult", have degraded women into a kind of ornament made of flesh.' It was a widespread view among Conservatives and also Catholics that American feminism was nothing other than a way of 'subverting the will of the divine Creator': 'It is not the independent, unwomanly, inherently mawkish American woman, but the German mother, as Schiller portrays her in the "Lied von der Glocke", a woman according to God's will as pictured in the Bible, who is worthy of respect.'[39]

Despite the nationalistic tone of these words, the fundamental cultural critique of modernity by traditionalists was by no means restricted to Germany. It was the common property of conservative and nationally minded intellectuals in Europe throughout the decade. One could also read in Johan Huizinga that progress was 'a phase in a continuing and irreversible process' of self-destruction; one could read in T.S. Eliot that the 'moloch of the city' was a symbol of alienation, hedonism, materialism and decadence, and a 'breeding-ground of apathy and delirium'; and one could read a critique of liberalism and individualism as well as of America and Americanism in José Ortega y Gasset.[40]

What was specifically German (and Austrian), on the other hand, was the way the critique of modernity was combined with the humiliating experience of defeat in the First World War, which was interpreted as a victory of the principles of the West over the contrasting ideals of the Germans. This is why cultural critique in Germany was so strongly charged with nationalist sentiment, and why the phenomena of modernity were regarded as variants of alien rule. Thus the mainstream criticism of modernity joined hands with a fundamental rejection of the democratic republic and a search for revenge for the defeat of 1918. It was from this source that it derived its political dynamism and destructive power.

This did not necessarily imply a rejection of technology, industry and science, however. Even the Wilhelmine predecessors of the conservative revolutionaries of the twenties did not find it difficult to combine their critique of urbanism and mass culture with an enthusiastic acceptance of the blessings of industrial modernity, all the way from the new methods of medical treatment to the imperial war fleet. In the 1920s, however, an alternative model of social order gradually took shape within the movement against cultural modernity, which is somewhat imprecisely described by the phrase 'reactionary modernism'. The acceptance of technical progress and industrial society which began to prevail on the Right, particularly among the younger generation, could be readily combined with a rejection of liberalism, the republic, and Americanised culture as well as with an advocacy of dictatorship and a worship of *Volk* and race.

The radical Left, on the other hand, interpreted the contradictions and the dynamic changes brought about by industrial society as an expression of the eternal class struggle which was currently being fought between the bourgeoisie and the proletariat and was manifestly entering its decisive phase. The war, the social misery of the wartime and post-war years, the period of inflation and unemployment, could all be convincingly and simply explained in this way. The republic, the legal apparatus of the state and parliamentarism could all be repudiated as mere instruments for suppressing the workers. But the Marxist interpretative framework also offered an outlet for expressing irritation with the phenomena of cultural modernity, which could immediately be explained as reflecting the decadence and shallowness of American capitalism.

But what the Marxists and the conservative intellectuals had most of all in common was the critique of 'alienation', seen as a process of differentiation, division of labour and destruction of tradition, which had done away with the condition of unity and wholeness believed to have been widespread in earlier times. Among intellectuals of both the Left and the Right, the critics of cultural modernity were on the whole in a clear majority over its advocates. Only a few social scientists and intellectuals, such as Max Weber, expressed approval of the phenomena that accompanied modernity, and accepted bureaucratisation, individualisation, rationality and liberty, though they did not overlook modernity's darker side.

The right-wing and left-wing versions of the rejection of liberal capitalism, parliamentary democracy and modern mass society coincided in the view that this model of the social order had clearly failed, and could only be overcome by a revolutionary upheaval of the same radicalism and potency as modernity had itself displayed. They considered that this in itself provided a special historico-political legitimacy to their readiness to act unconditionally and ruthlessly. On this view, in order to cope with the immense dynamism of industrial society, there was an obvious need for radically different models of social order, which would be based on an understanding of history and nature. This would allow the past to be explained and the future to be totally reshaped, in accordance either with the category of class or with that of ethnicity. The approaches which emerged from these ideas no longer involved anti-modern conceptions. They were instead radical proposals for a different kind of modernity.[41]

## Perspectives for the Future

In 1926, the future of the Weimar Republic was still an open question, but not all the options were still equally realistic. The economic situation was difficult, although far less catastrophic than it had been three years earlier. Provided the international business outlook remained stable, the conditions for a slow but sustained growth of the German economy were favourable, despite all the country's burdens, especially as economic relations within Europe had started to return to normal.

The prospects for a relaxation of tensions in foreign policy appeared to be improving in Germany and Austria, as well as in France. There was therefore a good chance of an early settlement of the question of reparations, which had constantly reignited domestic and foreign tensions in the European countries and repeatedly threatened to destabilise the financial markets.

In Germany, living conditions continued to be difficult for a large part of the population. As in most of the other countries which passed through this process, the transition from an agrarian to an industrial society involved considerable social costs for the rural population and it endangered social peace. On the other hand, the agrarian lobby continued to possess a high degree of political influence, and as a result any further movement towards shrinking the agricultural economy would involve the payment of an enormous amount of compensation.

Sections of the industrial working class continued to be sceptical towards the republic. Only a long-lasting economic boom would produce a noticeable increase in the living standards of the workers and their families and lead to their political integration. A predominantly politically motivated loyalty to democracy and republic, on the other hand, could only be expected from Social Democratic workers and parts of the Catholic workers' movement. For the other groups of workers, social conditions and social security were of paramount importance, irrespective of the form taken by the state or the government. The overwhelming majority of the bourgeoisie observed an expectant attitude towards the Weimar state, and not just for economic and social reasons. Economic and governmental liberalism had come under suspicion through the experience of inflation, and perhaps even earlier. Middle-class *attentisme* was heightened by the nationalism aroused by Germany's defeat and stirred up anew by the Versailles Treaty, along with the fear of Bolshevism and revolution.

Even so, the successes of the new state did have some impact on attitudes, as was demonstrated by the elections of 1928, at which the radical parties at either extreme were marginalised. It could be predicted that a continued upward trend in the economy would further stabilise the republic and ultimately make it less receptive to radical alternatives. But, without this economic stabilisation, a return to the state of affairs between 1919 and 1923 and a renewed upsurge of the radical forces of opposition was likely, to say the least.

# 6
# The Destruction of the Republic

## The Crisis of the Parliamentary System

In spite of the clear gains made by republican forces at the Reichstag elections of 20 May 1928, it proved to be very difficult to form a government. Even relatively minor problems such as how ministerial positions should be allocated or whether a warship ought to be built led some parties to threaten to withdraw from the government before it had taken office. Only by making a tremendous effort was the designated Chancellor, the Social Democrat Hermann Müller, able to form a 'Grand Coalition'. It included both the party of the industrialists, the DVP, and the party associated with the trade unions, the SPD. It also included the other liberal party, the DDP, and the Centre. The coalition was held together by its approach to foreign affairs; as far as domestic policy was concerned, the parties' programmes hardly coincided at all.

It still proved possible to establish a government with a stable majority, but a certain weariness with cooperation and compromise building was unmistakably apparent in day-to-day political life, and there were increasing complaints about the inadequacies of the parliamentary system. The main reason for this attitude was that a political culture based on public discussion and the balancing of rival interests against one another did not enjoy a long tradition in Germany, and in addition, it was widely regarded as inefficient. The feeling also increasingly gained ground that the fundamental political decisions made after 1918 on relations between capital and labour, dictatorship and democracy and the military and civilian spheres had turned out to be impermanent. So why enter into compromises, when the last word had probably not been said about the way things should be organised? It was clear that the conflicts of the post-war years had not led to a generally accepted long-term outcome, but rather to a provisional suspension of hostilities. This was apparent from the fact that forms of political organisation other than parliamentary democracy continued to be sought out, not only on the extreme Right and Left but in the middle-class camp as well.

The very prospect of having to form coalitions with the SPD strengthened the reservations of the middle-class parties about the parliamentary procedures of building a majority and finding compromises. In Stresemann's DVP, suggestions for a 'reform of parliamentary democracy' were put forward, according to which the rule of the parties would be ended by handing over the task of governing to 'individuals with a sense of responsibility'. At the end of 1928, the Centre Party elected Prelate Ludwig Kaas as its chairman. Kaas wanted to replace the party state by an authoritarian constitutional system, and he declared that the 'call for leadership on the grand scale' was resounding 'more enthusiastically and impatiently in the soul of the German *Volk*' than ever before.[1] In the DNVP, meanwhile, the previous chairman, von Westarp, who had led his party towards some degree of reconciliation with the republic, was replaced by the industrialist and Pan-German Alfred Hugenberg, who ended this tentative *rapprochement* with the Weimar system and pushed the party back onto a course of radical nationalism and cooperation with *völkisch* groups.

There were already indications before the beginning of the economic crisis that large-scale industry was about to end the social and political compromise of 1918–19. The so-called 'Ruhr Iron Dispute' in autumn 1928 marked a turning point in the conflict over social policy and began the transition to an offensive against the Weimar Constitution's principle of state involvement in social affairs. When the Social Democrats won the Reichstag elections of 1928 and a Social Democrat was again able to become Chancellor, this increased the fear felt by heavy industry in particular that the 'trade union state' would again be expanded and further financial burdens would be imposed in the name of social policy. In response, discussions were held as to whether it would be possible to install a form of government independent of parliament, and how this could be done.

In July 1927, unemployment relief was transformed into unemployment insurance. This obliged the employers to increase their social contributions. During the winter of 1928–9, the number of people unemployed rose to almost 3 million, owing to a significant conjunctural downturn. This placed an excessive financial burden on the newly established 'Reich Office for Labour Exchanges and Unemployment Insurance' (*Reichsanstalt für Arbeitsvermittlung und Arbeitslosenversicherung*), and the state had to take a hand. The government's financial situation, which was precarious in any case, was thereby rendered still worse. This in turn increased antagonisms within the governing coalition of Social Democrats and middle-class parties. Leading industrialists now started to intervene directly in politics. Their demands, supported within the government by the DVP, were stiff: a cut in taxes on capital and production, an increase in income tax and taxes on consumption, a reduction in social contributions, and radical limits on the level of social insurance. This was an open declaration of war on the working class and the SPD.

In rejecting a government led by the Social Democrats, the representatives of industry were in line with the intentions of Reich President Hindenburg, who was under pressure from his ultra-conservative entourage to stop cooperating with the party. The decisive factor here was that the continuing agrarian crisis had driven the agriculturalists deeper and deeper into debt, and they renewed their call for massive state support, something which could not be expected from an SPD-led government. An important part was now played by Major-General Kurt von Schleicher, Office Chief in the *Reichswehr* ministry, who was close to the president. He encouraged him to force the SPD out of the government and rule if necessary without a parliamentary majority, with the help of emergency decrees, using Article 48 of the constitution, just as President Ebert had done with success in the crisis years of the early 1920s.[2]

Material interests were therefore at stake here: the workers wanted improved social security, the agrarians wanted more state subsidies, and industry wanted lower social contributions and taxes, all this at a time when the economic situation had already begun to worsen. These conflicts could no longer be smoothed out within the Grand Coalition. Moreover, after the elections of 1928 there was no prospect of constructing a coalition on any other basis. And so the search began for ways of ruling without a parliamentary majority.

But there was one important obstacle to the removal of the Müller government: foreign policy. At the beginning of 1930, after long negotiations over the question of reparations, the Young Plan was signed. This brought considerable financial advantages to Germany, and the industrialists did indeed see it in this way. But it had already been the target of furious agitation by the parties of the Right, who had joined together in 1929 to mount a campaign against reparations and for a popular referendum against the plan. The NSDAP formed part of this coalition for the first time, a move which visibly increased its standing. For the leading strata of German conservatism, the destruction of the Grand Coalition and the acceptance of the Young Plan by parliament were now two competing objectives: if the Müller government were to be immediately dissolved, the Young Plan would be endangered. If a right-wing government independent of parliament were to come to power, it would have to accept the Young Plan in any case and thus lose credibility in the eyes of its own supporters. The removal of the Grand Coalition government was therefore postponed until after the Young Plan had been adopted.

## The World Economic Crisis

On 24 October 1929, there was a collapse in share values on the New York Stock Exchange. Within a short time, this sparked off an economic crisis, which was limited initially to the USA but soon had a worldwide impact of a volume and amplitude quite unprecedented hitherto. It was easy to understand the short-term causes of the US stock exchange crash. A large amount of money had been invested, particularly in industrial assets, by speculators who were confident that the boom of the 1920s would continue. This had led to a considerable expansion in productive capacity. When the first signs of a crisis of overproduction became visible and the equity values of the big industrial undertakings began to fall, a panic broke out among shareholders. People who were able to do so endeavoured to sell their shares as quickly as possible, without incurring any losses. This led within a few weeks to the collapse of the American stock market.[3]

The long-term causes of this collapse, in contrast, only became clear later. Firstly, what was involved was a classical crisis of cyclical overproduction in the USA, encouraged by a high level of speculation and unstable financial and equity markets. The second reason was a change in the direction of the world economy. Previously, it had been oriented towards Europe, but after the war it was oriented towards the USA. The European–Atlantic financial circuit had created a precarious interdependence between the European and American economies, in that German reparations to France and Britain enabled these countries to liquidate their American debts, and short-term private American credits were then returned to Germany. In September 1929, the Dow Jones Index reached 381, its highest ever level. By the spring of 1930, it had fallen below the 60 mark, and in response to their massive losses, American banks withdrew from Europe roughly $12 billion of the capital they had invested there. Most of the short-term credits had flowed to Germany, but three-quarters of this money had been used to make long-term investments there and could not be turned back into liquid form very quickly.

It was the big industrial countries which were hit hardest by the crisis. Between 1928 and 1932, national income fell by more than 50 per cent in the USA, 39 per cent in Germany, and 18 per cent in France and Great Britain. Industrial production fell by 54 per cent in Germany, 47 per cent in the USA, 46 per cent in Poland, 39 per cent in Austria, 38 per cent in the Netherlands, 36 per cent in Czechoslovakia, 33 per cent in Italy and around 31 per cent in Belgium and France, though the effects of the decline varied according to each individual country's level of industrialisation.

Most states reacted to the crisis by protecting their own national economies. Tariff barriers were as much a part of these measures as restrictions on foreign currency trading and devaluation. The volume of world trade rapidly began to fall, and the end of the gold standard as the symbol of a global trading system began to seem a likely outcome. The collapse of world trade led to a steep fall in the prices of agricultural products, which in turn led to a worldwide agricultural crisis. This then dragged the largely agricultural countries of East Central and South East Europe into the vortex of decline. Peasant households fell into debt, and rural unemployment increased rapidly. This was less visible than unemployment in the towns, but it probably affected more than half the rural population in Poland, Hungary and Bulgaria, and it brought with it widespread and long-lasting impoverishment.

In the USA, the crisis was initially limited to particular sectors of the economy. It extended its grip by stages, worsening sharply after 1931. In Europe, on the other hand, the impact of the crisis was felt more rapidly and on a broader scale, particularly in Germany, which was more strongly connected with the USA in terms of finance and foreign trade than any other European country because there had been an extreme shortage of capital there after the war. This was initially apparent in the sphere of investments, which by 1930 were worth only 60 per cent of their 1928 value. Other indicators also illustrate the extent and duration of this economic crisis: the production of investment goods fell by more than 50 per cent between 1929 and 1932, and share values fell by 55 per cent. By 1932, Germany's Gross National Product had fallen by more than a third, and there was a similar fall in private consumption.[4]

The most politically explosive number, though, was the figure for unemployment: in the USA in 1933 roughly 25 per cent of the labour force was unemployed, in Belgium and Sweden the figure was 23 per cent, in Great Britain 20 per cent—though that country had already experienced continuously high unemployment throughout the previous decade. In France, the recession did not set in until the global agricultural crisis struck in 1931, owing to that country's lower level of industrialisation. Unemployment in France was clearly lower than in Germany. Given the absence of precise statistics in this case, any analysis has to depend on estimates but the figure was roughly 10 per cent. There may also have been roughly 2 million short-time workers. But, as there was no state support for the unemployed in France, the social consequences of the depression there were all the more severe.

It was in Germany that the number of unemployed workers rose most rapidly. There, 1.9 million unemployed were reported in 1929, in 1930, the figure was already 3.7 million; in 1931, 5.1 million; in 1932, 5.3 million; and finally in 1933, 6.0 million out of a labour force of roughly 13 million. Thus, every third worker was without employment, and among trade union members, the proportion was almost 50 per cent. But since there were probably a large number of people who were not covered, or no longer covered, in the statistics, the total number of those capable of work who did not receive a wage can be assumed to have been more than 8 million, an average of one unemployed person per family. Roughly 3 million short-time workers should also be added to this figure. Even for people who were still in employment, the results of the crisis were devastating: average wages and salaries fell between 1928 and 1932 by one-third, and the salaries of state employees were reduced by roughly the same amount. There was also a similar fall in income from property.

Workers in heavy industry who were less than thirty years old are reported to have suffered the highest unemployment levels, and the proportions were even higher among those under twenty-one. Another reason for this was that, when the crisis struck, members of the large population cohorts born between 1905 and 1912, who reached the age of gainful employment in the 1920s, were dismissed first, before the older family men. In 1932, probably half of young males under twenty years old were unemployed or on short-time working, and those who still lived with their parents could not claim unemployment benefit. The long-term effects of this trend were already described as depressing and indeed ominous by contemporaries, as, for example, in a report published in the Social Democratic journal *Freies Wort* in spring 1931:

> There they stand at the street-corners, hands in their pockets, hand-rolled cigarettes in their mouths, dissatisfied with themselves and with the world. Young men with old men's faces; faces from which every trace of optimism and youthful joy in life has been banished; faces which express a bottomless, irreconcilable, and therefore dangerous, hatred for this social order and for the whole of the surrounding world.

An investigation into the children of the unemployed reported as follows: 'The most depressing experience we are having with many of these children is their indifference to their own future. They are hardly interested in what profession to choose. They appear to have decided that their destiny is the profession of unemployment.' In Berlin in January 1933, 63 per cent of young people under the age of twenty-five were without work; and in 1933 across the whole country 1.7 million young unemployed people were counted.[5]

In this crisis, the social policy provisions made by the Weimar state proved to be inadequate. The state was unprepared to deal with such a level of unemployment, which had never been encountered before. Moreover, because the phase of prosperity in previous years had been relatively short, there had been no time to lay down long-term reserves. Average benefit levels were therefore reduced because of the state's lack of financial resources. In 1927, average benefit payments were still over 80 Reichsmark (RM) a month, but by summer 1932 they had fallen to 43.46 RM. Furthermore, this level of payment only lasted for six months. After that, still smaller sums were then paid for thirteen weeks from the 'Crisis Fund' (*Krisenfürsorge*), and at the end of that period the unemployed were left to depend on welfare payments from their local community. At the beginning of 1933, more than 5 million out of the 6 million unemployed were no longer in receipt of state unemployment benefit. Some 1.4 million lived from the Crisis Fund, almost 2.5 million lived from their local communities, and roughly 1.2 million received no support at all.[6]

Moreover, the authorities were instructed to apply extremely restrictive criteria in disbursing unemployment benefit, 'Crisis Assistance' and locally funded 'welfare payments', in view of the difficulties the public institutions had in meeting their financial needs. This led to the introduction of humiliating procedures and generated in the needy feelings of fury and resentment towards the authorities. This, in turn, increased doubts about the Weimar Republic even among people who, after all, had profited from it. These doubts were strengthened still further in the summer of 1931, when the American banking crisis, which set off a crisis in the German banking system, signalled a second and far severer phase of development. This seemed to show that people were wrong to hope that this crisis, like previous conjunctural downturns, would only last for a short while.

In order to measure the psychological effects of the catastrophe one needs to bear in mind that the traumatic experience of hyperinflation and expropriation lay only six years in the past. The boom years, which had done little more than provide a brief respite between the inflation and the world economic crisis, now appeared in retrospect as a mirage. For many Germans, the years after 1918 increasingly resembled a continuous succession of crises and catastrophes, and the conclusion they drew was to reject Weimar. The juncture established in 1919 between the republic, democracy and capitalism was clearly incapable of dealing appropriately with the immense forces of industrial society which had been awakened. Thus a whole generation experienced the perception that the world economic crisis marked the collapse of the liberal capitalist way of organising society. This had an impact which lasted for several decades.

These developments did not, of course, take place in Germany alone. The world economic crisis encapsulated all the critical symptoms of the years after the First World War and created a degree of instability previously unknown in that form across the whole European continent. Democracy and the market economy were now called into question in all European states. Anti-liberal forces gained a significant amount of ground in the countries of Western Europe, while in almost all the states of East Central and South-East Europe, systems of right-wing authoritarianism emerged in the next few years. Various variants of dictatorial rule were tried out, from military dictatorships to regimes modelled on Italian Fascism. What they had in common, apart from their rejection of constitutional rule, parliamentary democracy and liberal capitalism, was the decision to abandon the economic system of liberalism and international free trade and replace it with a nationalist economic policy. This was oriented towards the domestic market or to trading zones cordoned off by tariff barriers from the world market, with the state functioning as the central authority for planning and regulation. After all, in the Soviet Union, the Bolshevik dictatorship was driving its industrialisation policy forward in the same way, namely, in isolation from world trade, and it was using state planning and not the principles of the market. This, it appeared, was the model of social organisation which held most promise for the future.[7]

In the first few years after 1919, a large majority of the German people had voted in favour of the Weimar system and the parties of the Weimar coalition on which it rested. But both among the socially dominant groups and in the broader strata of the population, there was a feeling that the hopes and promises associated with this system had been largely betrayed. The world economic crisis therefore 'hastened the final crisis of the republic' on two levels at once, to quote Detlev Peukert's formulation: '"Below", the masses whose hopes for the future had been blighted by the crisis had become radicalised, while "above" the old élites and the politicians of the right believed the moment had come when they could dismantle, once and for all, the structures established in 1918.'[8]

## The Radical Left

Most observers of developments in Germany, both at home and abroad, were convinced that mass unemployment would mainly benefit the forces of radicalism. It was thought that the young, mostly unskilled, workers, who had been hit harder by unemployment than any other group, would turn to the Communist Party. The ruling Social Democrats were also apprehensive about this. The KPD did in actual fact increasingly become the party of the young unemployed, who looked to the example of the Bolshevik Soviet Union in their radical rejection of the republic. The reorganisation of the party on the model of the Soviet Communist Party meant that democracy within it was dismantled, to be replaced by the absolute rule of the Central Committee. Ernst Thälmann, a Hamburg docker who was both unpretentious and popular, soon became the party leader. This was a logical choice, since he had far less in common with democracy and bourgeois society than his predecessors, who had all emerged from the left-wing intelligentsia.[9]

From the communist viewpoint, any distinction between a Social Democratic government and a government of *völkisch* nationalists could be ignored. They were both regarded by the communists as variants of bourgeois rule, which had to be removed as soon as possible by a mass uprising and a communist seizure of power. The support given to the communists by young workless proletarians was understandable, in view of their desperate situation and their disappointment over the defeat of the post-war uprisings, to which the Social Democrats had made a considerable contribution through their decision to call in the aid of the *Freikorps*. Most of them found it inconceivable that a lasting improvement to their situation could be brought about through parliamentary democracy, even during the greater economic stability of the mid-twenties. The Soviet example, in contrast, seemed to show how a determined minority of revolutionary workers could make the revolution here and now and establish the dictatorship of the proletariat. They accordingly favoured any development that appeared to be conducive to the collapse of the bourgeois Weimar Republic. But the very high rate of fluctuation among the members of the KPD, as well as those who voted for it, leads to the presumption that support for the communists should be understood as an expression of protest and a yearning to be radical rather than an indication that they agreed with the political goals and methods of the Bolsheviks.

Many left-wing intellectuals, on the other hand, were confident that the KPD actually belonged to the democratic camp and was simply more consistent in pursuing its objectives than the SPD, which spent its time in making a great variety of compromises and coalitions. This turned out to be a complete misapprehension. The communist sympathies of many intellectuals expressed their rejection of the everyday world of mass society and Americanism, which was seen as alienated, cold, dishonest, shallow and commercialised. They also shared the right-wing intellectuals' aversion towards parliament and a state run by political parties, as well as towards compromises and the balancing of rival interests. Their absolutist approach and their tendency towards the grand gesture expressed both an angry discomfort with the complexity of modern society and a contempt for the principle of majority rule by the mass of the people.[10]

Thus, the rise of the KPD substantially weakened democracy. When a presidential election was held in 1925 to replace Ebert, the communist candidate Thälmann maintained his candidacy in the second round, despite having no chance of success. As a result, the democratic candidate Marx did not receive the necessary number of votes to defeat Hindenburg, the successful candidate of the right. Between 1924 and 1933, the permanent reservoir of votes for the KPD remained at around 12 per cent. This figure was only significantly exceeded in one single year, 1932. In essence, the communists remained a small party throughout the period of the Weimar Republic. They were roughly equal in size to the liberals. This made their self-identification as a mass revolutionary party, aiming at the seizure of power, look even more bizarre. But the picture was distorted by their strong support in Berlin, where they received 18 per cent of the vote in elections to the city council in 1925 and almost 25 per cent four years later, while in the final years of the republic they were highly visible almost every day, with their demonstrations and violent clashes with the Nazis. This made them appear much more ubiquitous and powerful than was evidenced by their results in national elections. Hence the KPD was very much overestimated up to the end of the republic. It was regarded as a serious national threat, both by the liberals and Social Democrats and by the right, who for their part repeatedly used the communists' threat of revolution as an opportunity to draw up plans for a state of emergency and a military dictatorship.

## The Radical Right

All attempts by the right to achieve a 'quick solution', in other words to carry out a putsch or a military *coup d'état*, had failed during the post-war years. What was clearly needed in order to overthrow the republic and establish the 'national state' was a longer period of preparation and new political and organisational concepts.

In summer 1925, a report to the Prussian Ministry of the Interior distinguished three groups within the right-wing movement. Firstly, the largest group. This consisted of the Young German Order, along with the Stahlhelm, whose members were estimated at roughly 1 million. Secondly, the 'Patriotic Leagues' (*Vaterländische Verbände*), with their innumerable individual groups, which could be regarded as within the sphere of the DNVP. Thirdly, the *völkisch* and national-socialist organisations, which included the German *Völkisch* Freedom Party (*Deutschvölkische Freiheitspartei*), the *Völkisch* Bloc (*Völkischer Block*) and the NSDAP as well as numerous splinter groups.[11]

The 'national camp', as it was frequently described from that time onwards, was not a disciplined political bloc, but rather a milieu, a permanently feverish state of mind, constantly engaging in demonstrations and secret meetings. It consisted of associations which were repeatedly being founded and dissolved, and were defined rather by moods and personalities than by programmes and parties. This milieu become progressively more active after the mid-1920s in forming reciprocal links and contacts. In addition, it received support from numerous seemingly non-political networks. This kind of organisational structure exemplified the national camp's rejection of the party system, which was regarded as an element of parliamentary democracy alien to the German political tradition. The *bündisch* (federative) idea expressed in this way met with broad agreement, stretching all the way from the national camp to the bourgeois middle parties.

In this semi-public structure of clubs and informal associations, the leaders of the Patriotic Leagues, the *völkisch* circles, the student fraternities and the *bündische* (federalist) youth movements came into contact with radical right-wing intellectuals in the orbit of Arthur Moeller van den Bruck, Ernst Jünger or Martin Spahn, and also leading representatives of the Reichswehr, the ministerial bureaucracy, the big landowners and industry, as well as representatives of conservative and right-wing parties ranging as far afield as the Centre and the DVP. In this environment, there were continuous discussions about the purposes and policies of a nationalist dictatorship, although no unity or clarity was achieved for a long time over how the dictatorship would proceed in concrete terms. The main problem was the relationship between the dictatorship of the elite and the role of 'mass society', and this remained unsettled for the time being.[12]

University students played an important part in this movement, because the overwhelming majority of them had already adopted an attitude of radical opposition to the republic in the first years of Weimar. In the 1923, elections to the General Students' Committee (AStA, or *Allgemeiner Studentenausschuss*) the 'University Ring of Germans by Race', which was *völkisch* in orientation, gained more than two-thirds of the votes, on a turnout of over 60 per cent. In retrospect, it can be said that the fact that young intellectuals sided with its fiercest enemies was one of the heaviest burdens weighing on the first German republic. For this group, members of the old Right were also a bunch of powerless, reactionary figures with no political vision. Whereas the old right desired a return to the authoritarian nation-state based on something like a division of society into Estates, the young radical Right had no precise vision as yet regarding their aims or their route to victory. The future would show which variants of radical nationalism would ultimately prove to be most successful.

The Right did not possess a developed political programme of the kind that played such a great role on the Left. It did, however, hold a series of firm convictions and aims, which were shared by almost all the right-wing groups. The most salient of these was an attraction to military activities. The demobilisation of the Reichswehr and the dissolution of the paramilitary leagues after the Versailles Treaty had catapulted hundreds of thousands of young men into a civilian life they did not know and treated with disdain. Military organisation, a clear structure of command and obedience, as well as the security of integration into a community of soldiers, offered considerable attractions. Many of these young men therefore flocked to join the various catchment organisations of militarism. They joined the traditional veterans' associations, the defence leagues like the 'Stahlhelm: League of Front Soldiers', which by itself had more than 400,000 members, the successor organisations of the *Freikorps* and the *Einwohnerwehren*, or the numerous small-scale soldiers' federations and circles, one of which was the SA (*Sturmabteilung*, or Storm Division) of the NSDAP. All these organisations offered weapons training, marches in uniform, flag consecrations, torch-lit processions and, in increasing measure, violent clashes with political opponents. The paramilitary leagues of the Right rapidly became a threat to the republic, especially as they had considerable arsenals at their disposal.

The parties of the centre and the Left reacted to this massive influx by establishing their own militarily organised and uniformed leagues. In February 1924 the SPD, DDP and Centre Party jointly inaugurated an organisation called the 'National Flag Black-Red-Gold' (*Reichsbanner Schwarz-Rot-Gold*). This was a republican fighting league, which had 250,000 members in 1931, yet it was fundamentally defensive in its objectives and avoided violent conflict with its political opponents, unlike the 'Red League of Front Fighters' (*Rote Frontkämpferbund*), founded in the same year by the KPD, which had a much more militant demeanour and engaged in actual battles with the right-wing leagues after 1930, particularly with the SA.

The notion of the superiority of life in a soldier's uniform over existence as a civilian was inherited from the German Empire and of course the First World War. Its attractiveness, however, was not just ideologically determined. On the contrary, the paramilitary leagues also gathered together young men who had been unable to find a place in the new society and compensated for the insecurity of their civilian existence by binding themselves to a community which did not just give them backing but also bread—and a uniform.[13]

The foreign policy views of the Right were dominated by two objectives: the first was the revision of the Versailles Treaty (by military means); the second was the eastward expansion of the territory directly or indirectly ruled by Germany. The objective of treaty revision was directed first and foremost against France, but it went beyond revision to the restoration of Germany's position as a great power, indeed a world power. The plan for eastward expansion was directed against Poland. The intention was to gain an area of settlement for the growing German population, to use this to strengthen the peasant element in the German *Volk* and to mitigate the disastrous social effects of the movement of people towards the big industrial cities.

Unlike the majority of conservative nationalists, the radical *völkisch* groups, particularly the small Munich-based NSDAP led by Adolf Hitler, regarded the war of revenge against France and the reincorporation of parts of Poland into Germany merely as a stepping stone. The experiences of the final phase of the First World War in the east, mentioned earlier, when German troops advanced into large areas of Ukraine and White Russia, had given birth to the idea of a great continental empire in the east: 'What India was for England, the territories of Russia will be for us.'[14] Germany's expansion to the east would have to extend a long way into the western regions of the Soviet Union. The NSDAP and similar groups also had visions of the possible recovery of the German colonies in Africa, but these would obviously be difficult to defend in wartime, and their economic value was doubtful. In contrast, territorial expansion towards the east on the model of what had been achieved in the spring of 1918 offered the prospect not only of obtaining almost infinite resources, but of providing a long-term guarantee of Germany's position as a world power. 'Living space (*Lebensraum*) in the east' was one of the central ideas in Hitler's writings, and he made no secret of the fact that he would not be satisfied with a mere revision of Germany's 1918 borders. 'Germany will either be a world power or nothing at all' as he stated categorically in what has been called his 'Second Book', written in 1926, and expansion to the east was needed to achieve this. In the search for new living space for the German *Volk*, he added, 'we can primarily have in mind only Russia and her vassal border states.'[15]

The central reference point in the ideology of the radical Right was the '*Volk*', which was seen as comprising a specific mixture of historical, cultural and biological characteristics. This was based on the theory that it was not individuals or classes that were subjects of history, but peoples (*Völker*), who were manifested through individuals endowed by tradition and genetic code with differing abilities and qualities. In addition, social developments were essentially, though not completely, derived from biological and genetic rather than social factors. But the '*völkisch* substance' of the German *Volk* was threatened from two directions.

The first danger came from within. As a result of the development of modern civilisation, unhealthy and degenerate elements of the race were no longer weeded out by natural selection but unnaturally protected, and their numbers accordingly multiplied disproportionately. On this basis, different forms of social deviation could be explained biologically; that is to say, they could be derived from the genetic, 'blood-related', essence of the individual, with the result that anyone who wanted to remove the disturbing phenomena of modernity, from urban criminality to mental illness and 'asocial' tendencies, would have to remove the carriers of the genetic disposition to this kind of behaviour from the 'body of the *Volk*' and prevent its inherited substance from being subjected to fresh negative influences.

The second danger, which came from without, was the threat of a mixture of the German people with other peoples or races. In this context, the concept of a 'race' could be interpreted, roughly speaking, as 'biologically determined potential for development'. Jewry (*Judentum*) represented the biggest danger here, because it was endowed with particularly harmful genetic characteristics, both biologically speaking and on the basis of its history (as a people without land or a state, the Jews were subject to a compulsion to assimilate). The Jews had already penetrated a long way into the German *Volk* and its inherited substance, and everywhere in Europe they formed the basis for political internationalism, whatever form it might take, and thereby for the fight against German racial and national self-preservation. They were also considered to be responsible for criminality and degenerative trends in the various countries of the European continent, and indeed all over the globe. Both developments—the internal and external endangerment of the German people—were already well under way. The consequences could be observed in the internal decay and the external impotence of the German *Volk* since 1918.[16]

If the German *Volk* wanted to deal successfully with its internal problems and at the same time carve out for itself the outstanding place in Europe and the world which corresponded to its real value, it would have to eliminate the elements within its own people (*Volkstum*) which were degenerate and furthermore eliminate the elements of an alien and parasitic people, the Jews, which had penetrated society from outside. According to this way of thinking, the Jews were the sole element that epitomised the two dangers equally—the threat from outside and the one from within. The reasons for the extraordinary decline of Germany during and after the war, and what lay behind it, were distilled in the symbolic conception of the Jews.

The First World War and the post-war years therefore functioned as the empirical confirmation of everything the radical Right had long asserted before the war. They had claimed that internationalist forces within the country and universalist great powers in the world at large posed a tremendous threat to Germany and the Germans, and that Jewry (*Judentum*) was the 'racial' expression of the link between the two. Theories of eugenics and natural selection were increasingly popular after the First World War. They were not restricted to nationalist and *völkisch* enthusiasts, however. Many anthropologists and population experts held similar views.

An extremely influential book with the title *Permission to End Valueless Lives. How and to What Extent it May be Given* was published in 1920 by Karl Binding, a Professor of Law at Leipzig, and Alfred Hoche, a Professor of Psychiatry at Freiburg. The authors were shocked by the number of victims of the world war, and deeply impressed by the theory of 'negative selection', and in their book they demanded that the mentally ill in particular no longer be nursed in hospices but killed. There was, they said,

> absolutely no reason, either from a legal, a social, an ethical or a religious standpoint, not to permit the killing of these people, who are the ghastly antithesis of a genuine human being and awaken horror in almost every person who comes into contact with them. . . . In epochs of superior morality—our own epoch however, is no longer heroic—these poor people would be delivered from themselves by official order.

The prerequisite for a measure like this, the two authors conclude, is for the community to emancipate itself from outmoded ethical principles and apply new standards of value:

> There was a time, which we now regard as barbarous, when it was a matter of course to get rid of those who were born unfit to live, or became so. This was followed by the current phase, in which the preservation of even the most worthless existence counts as the highest moral imperative. But a new time will come, in which a superior morality will prevail, and the demands of an exaggerated humanitarianism and an overestimation of the value of existence as such, which are now continually put into effect at the cost of heavy sacrifices, will no longer be accepted.[17]

This passage also indicates the political character of these ideas: they involved a radical rejection of the political and philosophical principles of equality and the protection of the weak, along with an unconditional prioritisation of the interests of the community over those of the individual.

Racial hygiene was introduced into the curriculum in the 1920s at almost all German universities. In 1927 the Kaiser Wilhelm Institute for Anthropology, the Principles of Human Heredity and Eugenics was founded. The racial anthropologists received a tremendous boost from Darwin's theory and the discovery, or rediscovery, of Mendel's laws of heredity. Until then, the concept of a race had largely been based on observation. Now this new discipline of population genetics appeared to offer the opportunity of using biology to demonstrate variations in the races and differences in their intrinsic value. This was done by combining objective biological differences with standards of value and social qualities, thus equating 'race' with intelligence, cultural level and mental characteristics. The Social Darwinists approached all those who deviated within a society in a similar way to the racial anthropologists when they examined the relations between the various human races. In this context, other groups such as nations and cultural regions were also subsumed under the category of race, in view of the absence of any other scientific foundation. With the aid of scientific categories, anything deviant, alien or unsettling was defined as 'less valuable'. Thus, a feeling that society was under threat was converted into a state of objective biological danger.

Socio-biological thinking was widespread at the end of the Weimar Republic in the relevant branches of science, though it also met with emphatic rejection, particularly in regard to the 'destruction of valueless lives' recommended by Binding and Hoche. But there were some people, including eminent legal scholars, who viewed the call for the incurably sick to be 'helped to die' more positively. In this context, the argument that the 'custody' and care of the mentally ill and the physically disabled, as well as the cost of imprisoning or providing social benefits for the 'asocials', imposed an intolerable financial burden on society clearly met with wide agreement, especially when it was bolstered by the assertion that disabilities or 'asocial behaviour' could be transferred by genetic inheritance to the next generation, which meant that the cost of supporting such people would rise continuously.[18]

The view that many of the disturbing trends of the present, from alcoholism and 'asocial behaviour' to criminality, could be traced back to biological factors was a core element in the right-wing radicalism of those years. With this argument, the greatest evils of the contemporary world could be ascribed to specific causes, defined biologically or racially. The conviction that this was in line with the conclusions of modern natural science gave these opinions an almost unshakeable solidity, especially as they could be employed very flexibly in the political struggle, and potentially used against all political opponents.

It was not surprising that there had been a tremendous upsurge in anti-Semitism since the period of defeat and revolution in the winter of 1918–19. In the strenuous search for the instigators and the guilty parties responsible for the misfortunes of the fatherland, both the communist revolution in Russia and the western liberal civilisation of the victors were seen as forces of universalism and internationalism, and thereby as the polar opposite of the nationalist and '*völkisch*' direction of German thought. Both of these hostile forces, it was thought, were represented by, indeed led by, the Jews, a group of people who were internationalist and universalist by definition. Were not the leading bankers in the USA, as also in Britain, France and Germany, Jewish themselves? Were not the leading representatives of the left-wing parties and the revolutionary groups—from Leon Trotsky to Rosa Luxemburg and the ringleaders of the Munich Council Revolution—also Jewish? Anti-Semitism gained plausibility and mass support from these arguments, and the assumption that the Jews had profited more than other groups from the new tendencies of the epoch and that they held the decisive positions, both in the capitalist civilisation of the West and in the Bolshevik revolution of the East, now appeared for many people as an established fact. Anti-Semitism thus became the master key that could be used to explain almost all the antagonisms of modern life, especially in a Germany torn apart by defeat, coups, and attempted uprisings.[19]

At the end of the war, the Pan-German League attempted to incorporate and utilise these attitudes by founding numerous anti-Semitic groups and parties. These sought to outdo each other in radicalism and vociferousness in the period of uncertainty that obtained between 1919 and 1923, and they also amalgamated with earlier and later groupings of the radical Right. The German *Völkisch* Protective and Defensive League (*Deutschvölkischer Schutz- und*

*Trutzbund*) was the largest and most important of these in the early Weimar years, with almost 200,000 members (1922) organised in more than 600 local groups. Its methods of social agitation were unsurpassably crude and primitive, but that did not make it any less successful.[20]

It was of particular significance that the 'radical', or racially anti-Semitic, tendency made early inroads in the universities, with the activities of the 'German University Ring'. These groups did not call for the expulsion of all Jews from Germany through pogroms and outrages, but by legislation against aliens and action by the state. This, they thought, would enable the 'Jewish Problem' to be 'solved' quickly, and both radically and 'matter-of-factly' (*sachlich*)—a maxim which met with agreement far beyond the narrow circles of the *völkisch* movement.

The German National People's Party (DNVP) was also plainly anti-Semitic. In fact, the radical anti-Semitism of the right wing of the party was notorious. Even in Stresemann's DVP, anti-Semitism was not a rare occurrence. It was also present in the nationalist ex-servicemen's leagues such as the *Stahlhelm* and it was particularly widespread in the Protestant Church. In 1924, the *Stahlhelm* introduced an 'Aryan paragraph' for its roughly 400,000 members. By this, Jews, even highly decorated war veterans, were excluded from membership. The same rule was in operation in the Young German Order, with 200,000 members, the German National League of Commercial Employees (*Deutschnationale Handlungsgehilfenverband*), with 400,000 members, the *Reichslandbund*, which had a million members, the German *Burschenschaften*, the German League of Gymnasts and many other organisations.

But what was most characteristic of these years was a passive kind of anti-Semitism. This received fresh encouragement as a result of developments during the First World War and afterwards, but it did not express itself in open hostility or street rioting. That the Jews represented a foreign body in the German *Volk;* that they possessed particularly unpleasant qualities; that they were in league with Germany's wartime enemies; that they controlled the press; that they had enriched themselves during the war, the inflation and the economic crisis; and that their great success was inexplicable and without doubt undeserved, were all widespread convictions, and these ideas were combined with a passionate desire to take revenge for a defeat to which many were still unreconciled. This brand of anti-Semitism was neither fanatical nor aggressive; it strongly disapproved of 'rowdy anti-Semitism' and kept its distance from it, and it was not directed at a particular goal or a particular 'solution'. But there was always enough passive anti-Semitism in the air to allow even harsh measures against the Jews to be accepted, notwithstanding some criticism of 'excesses', provided that these measures were put into effect by the government, using 'lawful means', rather than by bawling anti-Semitic thugs.

Nevertheless, until 1933, the anti-Semites always faced a large group of opponents in Germany. In the course of the Weimar years, there were many genuine waves of indignation against anti-Semitism to be observed in all the newspapers, including those of the reputable Right as well as the Left. These occurred after the brawls in the Jewish quarter of Berlin, for instance, after the murder of Rathenau, after the repeated desecration of Jewish cemeteries in 1924–5, and after attacks on Jews by members of the SA, in particular the riot on the Kurfürstendamm organised by the Berlin NSDAP.

Still more important than this was the relative security afforded to the Jews by the Weimar Republic as a *Rechtsstaat,* or state governed by laws. There were, it is true, court judgments that showed distinct sympathies with the anti-Semites, but these always led to scandals, and were the exception rather than the rule. Recourse to the courts in cases of excesses, slanders or propaganda smears remained the most important counter-measure the Jewish organisations could take against the anti-Semites, and the Central Association of German Citizens of Jewish Faith (*Central-Verein deutscher Staatsbürger jüdischen Glaubens*) never tired of utilising this instrument, not unsuccessfully.

The use of the courts in self-defence was also related to the hope, indeed the conviction, of many German Jews that, from the historical point of view, anti-Semitism was a survival from a dark past which was gradually dying out. Most German Jews tended towards moderation in politics, and their optimism about the future paralleled the way the Left, and particularly left-wing intellectuals, evaluated anti-Semitism. In *Die Weltbühne,* for example, anti-Semitism and anti-Semites were the subject of caustic satire, or, at best, contemptuous head shaking. Liberals tended to conflate the most dangerous aspects of the radical Weimar Right with militarism and its link with the traditional elites. Organised hatred of Jews, on the other hand, appeared rather to be an anachronism which would certainly be overcome in the near future. For example, Arnold Zweig wrote in 1919, also in *Die Weltbühne,* that in the eyes of the anti-Semites the Jew was a 'horrifying but amusing fairy-tale beast' and the Aryan Siegfried would not rest until

> the judaized world had been cured by the essence of Germanism. In short: we are dealing here with the age-old adolescent dreams of immature, overindulgent enthusiasts for Dahn and Wagner, who are ecstatic if they can fight against a phantom of their own creation and lie repulsively about their own nature.[21]

Most liberal and left-wing intellectuals had no sensitivity and also no analytical categories for the power and suggestiveness of the ideologies of the radical Right.

After the Reichstag elections of 1930, and the rise of National Socialism, this scenario changed. Now the Hitler movement, which was unquestionably the most radical of the anti-Semitic parties, was at the heart of politics. It has, it is true, often been pointed out that, after 1930, the NSDAP did not place anti-Semitism as ostentatiously at the centre of its propaganda as it had done before. But, at the same time, nobody who voted for, or sympathised with, Hitler's party could fail to see that by doing so they were giving support to the most anti-Jewish group that had ever emerged in Germany. Some people may have accepted this as part of the package because they expected the election of the Nazis to bring improvements in their social condition or in Germany's international standing, or for other reasons. But many probably also believed the assertion that the Jews were guilty of causing Germany's misfortune and that an improvement would only come about if they were removed from the scene.[22]

## The Rise of the NSDAP and the Disempowerment of Parliament

Out of all the numerous Right radical parties and *völkisch* groups, it was, ultimately, the NSDAP that won the upper hand. This was chiefly because they alone had an outstanding leader, who could unify the party and inspire the masses with enthusiasm.[23] After the failed putsch of 9 November the party had at first ceased to play any part in events. Hitler, who had risen in the meantime to nationwide fame because of his Munich activities, was brought before a court and condemned to five years of imprisonment. But he was only subjected to a few months of jail time, in very comfortable conditions, because the judges had repeatedly confirmed during the trial that his motives in attempting to mount a coup were honourable. He had, meanwhile, become the undisputed head of the NSDAP, and he was without doubt the most gifted figure within the nationalist camp, politically, organisationally and oratorically, and also the most unscrupulous. The Right had a chronic yearning for a leader who could master the incomprehensible confusions of modern life and overcome the menagerie of political parties at a single stroke, and bring clarity and unity, on the model of Napoleon or Alexander, or at least Mussolini. Hitler deliberately worked to create this image. He no longer presented himself as the propagandist and prophet of the leader to come; he donned the robe of national messiah in person. During his short period of imprisonment, he put his party on ice, because in view of the stabilisation of the Weimar system no new upheavals were to be expected in the immediate future, and he started to write a book in which he summarised the current positions of the radical *völkisch* Right. What Hitler wrote could be read in analogous form in very many pamphlets and programmatic writings of the time. But, since no other radical nationalist author was also the ringleader of a *völkisch* group and a rousing popular speaker, his ideas and concepts gained much greater attention.

The NSDAP did not enter the two Reichstag elections of 1924, and those *völkisch* groups which did enter were relatively unsuccessful. After his release from prison, Hitler began to rebuild the party and make it entirely a vehicle for his own personality. The failure of the putsch of 1923 had shown the extreme right that its previous line of approach, directed towards a violent *coup d'état*, had hardly any prospect of success. After his short period of imprisonment, Hitler pointed his refounded party in a new direction: henceforth he no longer placed his faith in the forcible seizure of power by a small minority. He relied instead on gaining mass support and mobilising the party for elections. This strategy was reinforced by the construction of a 'modern', or bureaucratically organised, party apparatus, with regional branches all over the country, alongside the paramilitary SA. Thenceforth the SA was subordinated to the party, serving as both a social reservoir for unemployed and radicalised young men, and an instrument for terrorising political opponents. The main methods used by the NSDAP in its second attempt to conquer power were not political manoeuvres by executive committees or debates on matters of political principle but semi-military organisation, mass advertising and above all huge rallies and marches.

Some right-wing intellectuals and national-conservative groupings criticised the party's new approach. Edgar Jung, for example, claimed that the heart of the NSDAP's dilemma was that it was attempting to destroy the age of the masses with the help of a mass movement, and was thus 'capitulating to mass intoxication' instead of restoring the rule of the intellectual elite.[24] But in fact, the success of Hitler rested on doing precisely that. The party programme of the NSDAP was provocatively brief and unspecific; Hitler took no part in any of the discussions about it. This vagueness allowed commitments to be avoided, so that the party could react to whatever interests, anxieties or needs existed among a range of socially and politically heterogeneous groups, without contradicting its own programme. The NSDAP reflected the widespread embitterment and hatred felt towards the political and social establishment which ran the Weimar Republic, and it did this through its radical and abrasive *habitus*, through the fanatical determination it put on display, through its unconditional rejection of the republic and the liberal system in general, and through its refusal to enter into any kind of compromise except in order to take power.

Hitler himself symbolised this air of radicalism, fanaticism and programmatic flexibility. In retrospect, his political style appears ridiculous, but it evidently absorbed and articulated the state of mind of sections of the population to a considerable degree. As the 'Führer', Hitler embodied the yearning to abolish social conflicts by creating a supreme personal authority regarded as sacrosanct and infallible. The search for a Führer had long been a nationalist obsession. The Führer was expected to lead the state and the people to national unity and social justice out of the deepest humiliation and confusion, to restore political and cultural order in the country, and simultaneously to overcome the division of the nation into social classes, end party conflicts, facilitate economic recovery and expunge the shame of the war that had been lost. Germany was not the only country to suffer from such fantasies of redemption. The tendency to focus on a supreme individual who would rid the nation of conflicts and disagreements played an important role in almost all the authoritarian regimes and movements of the time, from Lenin and Stalin on the Left to Mussolini, Piłsudski, and later Salazar, Franco and the authoritarian dictators of East Central Europe on the Right.[25]

The concept of 'charismatic rule' indicates that there is an ascertainable interaction between the desire of the masses for a 'leader' and the emergence of outstanding individuals who can satisfy this desire. It is doubtful whether this was true for all the European dictators and junta chiefs of the period, or even for the majority of them. To that extent it is also doubtful whether 'charismatic rule' can really be regarded as a category which characterises a general phenomenon. But there can be no doubt that it applies to Hitler. In any case, the stylisation of Hitler as the Führer, the revered genius who stood above all mundane conflicts of interest, made a considerable contribution to the unity of the party, and became the decisive characteristic that distinguished the NSDAP from other nationalist groupings in Germany. From the very beginning a semi-religious yearning to believe was plainly visible in Nazism. The Führer, Hitler's loyal follower Josef Goebbels wrote in 1926, 'is the fulfilment of a mysterious longing', a 'liberator of the masses', who 'preaches faith in the depths of despair' and accomplishes 'a miracle of enlightenment, bringing faith to a world of scepticism and despair.' The Führer, wrote Rudolf Hess in 1927, 'must never leave his listeners the freedom to think a different view is right . . . The great popular leader is similar to the great founder of a religion: he must communicate to his listeners an apodictic faith. Only then can the mass of followers be led where they should be led.' The prominence given to Hitler, as the party's leader and genius, was certainly one of the most important reasons why this, and no other Right radical grouping, succeeded in Germany in the late 1920s. The 'Führer' created simplicity and clarity in an unfathomable situation, he appeared to soar above the petty struggles of other parties and associations for their own particular interests, and he imbued his supporters with an unconditional faith in their own cause.[26]

Thus, between 1925 and 1928, the National Socialists grew into a well organised and vigorous party, with roughly 100,000 members and an extensive network of party sections and local associations. Even so, they only obtained 2.6 per cent of the vote at the Reichstag elections of 1928. In response to this, Hitler abandoned the path he had previously followed of appealing predominantly to the nationalistically inclined working class, and widened his range of targets to include office employees, artisans and, above all, farmers, whose difficult situation in North-West Germany and elsewhere first drew them in the direction of right-wing radicalism, and then pushed them in large numbers towards the NSDAP itself. From the winter of 1928–9 onwards, the NSDAP was the fastest growing force in the 'national camp', thanks to the way it combined organisational professionalism and unconditional radicalism in public with a positively opportunistic flexibility which allowed it to represent the mutually contradictory interests of various different social groups.

But the development of the NSDAP into a mass party cannot be attributed either to the reconstruction of the party organisation, or the cult of Hitler, or the marches of the SA. It was caused rather by the impact of the world economic crisis, which increasingly moved into the foreground of all political plans and debates after the spring of 1930. This was made clear as early as the Saxon Diet elections of June 1930, at which the NSDAP was able to increase its share of the vote from 5 to 14.4 per cent. The NSDAP also made clear gains in Mecklenburg-Schwerin, Baden and Thuringia, and in each of these places the main losers were the DNVP and the parties of the middle.

It was precisely in this tense situation of economic crisis that the Müller government resigned. Two weeks after the 20 January 1930 agreement over the Young Plan, which reduced Germany's reparations obligations and allowed the country's financial position to be calculated on a more long-term basis, the DVP withdrew from the government coalition. Müller's decision also reflected the weariness of large parts of the SPD with the constant arguments within his coalition, whose members now no longer had anything to bind them together.

In response, President Hindenburg appointed Heinrich Brüning as Chancellor, thereby handing over the leadership of a government which had no parliamentary majority to an exponent of the conservative wing of the Centre Party. Brüning accordingly formed an emergency cabinet, without holding discussions with the party factions or establishing any coalition ties. He hoped, with the support of President Hindenburg, to be able to restore the economy and the finances of the state to good health without taking account of the views of either the parties or the federal states (*Länder*). The more long-term perspective of this change of system was the complete abandonment of the parliamentary form of government, a plan which was referred to in coded fashion by the phrase 'reform of the Reich' (*Reichsreform*). What kind of role the parliament would continue to play in all this became clear a few weeks after Brüning had come into office. In July 1930, the Reichstag rejected one of the government's emergency decrees, as was its constitutional right. Hindenburg dissolved parliament on the spot, using a fresh emergency ordinance to reissue the ordinance that had been rejected. With this, a decision of parliament had been declared null and void by the arbitrary action of the head of state. This was not only an illegal act, it was also a breach of the constitution, and it clearly indicated that the transition from a parliamentary democracy to a presidential dictatorship had now taken place.

Fresh elections were thus in the offing, and in view of the economic and constitutional crisis there could be no doubt that the radical forces would gain greater support. Even so, the shift in voting allegiances that took place on 14 September 1930 came as a sensation. The NSDAP secured eight times as many votes as it had done two years earlier, and with 18.3 per cent it became the second strongest party (behind the SPD). The DNVP was the big loser, receiving 7 per cent instead of the 14.2 per cent it had gained in the 1928 elections. The voting share of the radical nationalist camp, taken together, had risen from 16.8 to 25 per cent. The KPD also improved its vote, and its 13.1 per cent share was greater than that of the Centre Party. The vote for the two liberal parties fell by more than 5 per cent, while the two Catholic parties, the Centre Party and the *Bayerische Volkspartei* (BVP, Bavarian People's Party), held on to their share of the vote. The parties of the Weimar coalition obtained only 40 per cent of the vote, thereby losing their overall parliamentary majority. A purely middle-class government, even with the inclusion of the DNVP, was a very distant prospect. Even a continuation of the Grand Coalition was no longer possible.

The 6.4 million people who voted for the NSDAP could be divided into three basic groups: roughly a third of them were previous non-voters, a point already apparent from the very high turnout, which was 82 per cent. A third had previously supported the DNVP, showing the clear shift in the balance of forces within the right-wing camp. The rest had previously voted for other parties, over the whole of the political spectrum. It should also be noted that this election, and all subsequent ones until 1933, both at local and national level, displayed an extraordinarily high level of fluctuation. Party membership also fluctuated. A large proportion of those who voted for Hitler for the first time in 1930 were certainly not firmly attached to the ideology of National Socialism. But, by voting for this sensational, uncompromising and decidedly un-bourgeois party, they could express their despair and also their readiness to abandon the established parties of the republic entirely if help did not arrive quickly.

Analyses of the social structure of the roughly 120,000 members of the NSDAP have made clear the incorrectness of the theory often put forward by contemporaries that the NSDAP was the party of the 'old *Mittelstand*'. It is true that artisans were over-represented in the party (9.1 per cent of party members, as against 5.5 per cent of all employees), the same being true of farmers (14.1 per cent as against 6.7 per cent) and office employees (25.6 per cent as against 15.9 per cent), while workers were plainly under-represented (28.1 per cent as against 45.1 per cent). But in numerical terms the 34,000 workers still formed the biggest group of party members, and this trend increased in subsequent years, both among voters and members. The NSDAP had more supporters and voters in the Protestant north-east of the country than in the Catholic south or the working-class strongholds. The highest proportion of members to the overall population could be seen in Kiel, Königsberg, Cassel and Wuppertal; the lowest proportion in Dortmund, Augsburg, Gelsenkirchen and Cologne. As time went on, however, the National Socialists were able to push their way into all social strata and gain voters and adherents in all confessions, regions and age groups, among men as much as among women. Admittedly, the core of the Social Democratic and Catholic electorate largely remained true to its political or ideological convictions, but among voters who were not firmly rooted in their traditional milieu the National Socialists achieved success everywhere.[27]

The elections of September 1930 made the Hitler party an important factor in German politics. Any government which wanted to avoid relying on the SPD would be impossible *without* the NSDAP. On the other hand, no bourgeois or conservative politician wanted to govern *with* it, since the party was regarded as both untrustworthy and unpredictable, especially as Hitler himself had made it clear to everyone that he had no interest in entering a coalition with anyone else, but desired to rule alone. Nevertheless, from that time onwards, the political operators around Hindenburg and the army leadership, whose activities would have a decisive influence over German politics in the next two and a half years, increasingly focused their attention on the NSDAP. In social, and indeed even in personal terms, these were roughly the same forces which had supported the third Army Supreme Command (OHL) at the end of the war and had come out in opposition to the movement for constitutional democracy. The difference was that, alongside these forces of the 'reaction', a further force had emerged on the Right, the NSDAP, the attitude of which increasingly determined the manoeuvres of those who supported 'reform of the Reich'.

For Brüning too, the formation of a coalition government with parliamentary backing was no longer on the agenda. In agreement with the Reich President and the army leadership, he stopped conducting coalition negotiations, preferring instead to continue governing through emergency ordinances by the grace of Hindenburg. His supreme goal was to end the payment of reparations. He therefore had no wish to give priority to combating the catastrophic economic situation. He intended rather to make use of it both to put the state's finances on a sound footing with the aid of a rigorous policy of saving and deflation, and to present the First World War victors with clear evidence of the obvious inability of the Reich to pay and the impossibility of fulfilling their demands. This objective was shared by the army leadership, the top industrial leaders, the big landowners and the civil service, and the influence of these groups grew constantly, while the parliament was almost eliminated from decision-making, and in fact now sat very rarely.[28]

Admittedly, there seemed to be little alternative to Brüning's policy. To reduce public expenditure, especially on social welfare, and to wait until the crisis had passed and private investors restarted their activities was the strategy adopted by almost all the governments of crisis-ridden Europe. There was no serious discussion, either in France, Britain or Germany, of a policy of state intervention, involving anti-cyclical increases in state expenditure to reinvigorate the economy. All parties in Germany, not least the Social Democrats, warned against an increase in expenditure and the fall in the value of the national currency this would bring with it, because the misery of hyperinflation was still fresh in their memory. It was only later, in reaction to the world economic crisis, that some governments discovered these instruments of economic policy, which they started to apply after the mid-1930s, although in very different ways, with the 'New Deal' in the USA and the rearmament policy of National Socialist Germany.[29]

Brüning's policy of reducing government expenditure and pursuing deflation had catastrophic effects on the German population. The number of people unemployed, in short-time work or receiving reduced wages rose rapidly, and the state's ability to compensate for this with measures of social policy began to dry up. The hyperinflation of 1923 had expropriated large parts of the *Mittelstand*, but now the crisis hit all social strata equally: workers, commercial employees, state officials, farmers, the urban population, the rural population, men, women. The reason for people's hopelessness and despair in this situation was not solely the rapid deterioration in social conditions. It was rather the growing impression that the politicians were no longer attentive to the interests of the unemployed and the poverty-stricken and that they had not taken appropriate measures in response to their growing impoverishment.

The ability of the trade unions to act was very much impaired by mass unemployment, and they had to look on almost powerlessly while the employers sought to take advantage of the economic crisis by dismantling the system of social benefits. The Social Democrats had already lost their share of power in the Reich, but until July 1932 they did their best to defend their control of the Prussian state government, the last bastion of democracy in Germany, headed by Prime Minister Otto Braun. The SPD, like the Centre Party, was able by and large to hold on to its supporters in the years of the crisis. But large parts of the working class, the *Mittelstand*, and the peasantry, who belonged neither to the organised workers' movement nor to the Catholic social milieu, moved to the extreme Right or the extreme Left, in order to give themselves a voice and a hearing in response to the misery that was either threateningly close or already being experienced.

Brüning did not need an active parliamentary majority to carry on his policies, but he could still be overthrown by a majority decision of the Reichstag. He therefore endeavoured to secure passive support. He tried the extreme Right first, but his advances were brusquely rebuffed by the NSDAP. There then followed the grotesque turn of events by which it was precisely the Social Democrats who were prepared to tolerate Brüning and thus supported a government established with the explicit purpose of breaking the power of Social Democracy and the trade unions. For the SPD leadership, there were two decisive arguments in favour of this course. Firstly, they hoped in this way to shore up the Prussian government coalition, which consisted of members of the SPD, the Centre Party and the DDP. Secondly, the rise of the NSDAP meant that there was now a radical right-wing alternative to Brüning, which made his policies appear to be the lesser evil. The decision to support Brüning was therefore understandable, and in view of the threatening alternatives, perhaps even unavoidable. Of course, the SPD thereby acquired the reputation of being jointly responsible for Brüning's harsh deflationary policies, which were constantly worsening Germany's distress. This was bound to have a devastating impact on the party's election results, and that is indeed what happened.[30]

Most big industrialists were at first entirely in favour of Brüning's policy. But soon voices were raised against him, complaining that his approach had worsened the crisis in domestic politics, favoured the rise of the Communists and led to a further increase in state influence over the economy. Moreover, the president and the big landowners resented Brüning's dependence on the Social Democrats. Paul Reusch, the head of the steel firm Gutehoffnungs-Hütte, declared

> that Herr Brüning has failed to meet the expectations we placed in him and lacks the courage to break with the Social Democrats. He must therefore be fought with the utmost vigour by the leaders of the economy and by the National League (of German Industry), and industry should state quite openly that it distrusts him.[31]

Instead of Brüning's semi-parliamentary form of government, these groups now favoured the complete abolition of parliament and the establishment of an authoritarian elite dictatorship, which would press ahead with dismantling social benefits and ending state interventionism, possibly in cooperation with the right-wing bloc stretching from the Stahlhelm to the NSDAP, which presented itself to the public in October 1931 under the name of the 'Harzburg Front'.

There were some obstacles to this plan. Brüning's endeavours to obtain a revision of the reparations payments were on the point of reaching a successful conclusion, and this would be put at risk by the formation of a cabinet standing still further to the Right. At the same time, the role of the NSDAP was still extremely unclear. The 'socialist' elements of the National Socialists' economic programme were regarded with deep distrust by industry and the big landowners, even though leading National Socialists endeavoured to provide an industry-friendly interpretation of the relevant passages. It was therefore too early for the creation of a 'bloc of the Right', as the former leader of the DNVP, Count Westarp, commented in October 1931:

> Anyone who is not sure that the right-wing opposition is capable of governing . . . must regard the price to be paid for such an attempt as too high at present . . . The attempt to form a right-wing government led by the National Socialists—in practice the German Nationalist leadership hardly comes into consideration any more, unfortunately—must and can be made, but only after an agreement with our creditors, a revision of the tribute and the beginning of better conditions.[32]

Thus, two prerequisites for the fall of Brüning and his replacement by a government of the Right were still missing: the successful conclusion of the reparations negotiations in Lausanne, and at least a reduction of the risk that a right-wing government might be brought down by the workers' movement, the political strength of which rested in the meantime almost exclusively on its participation in the Prussian government. By the end of April 1932, these two prerequisites were in place: the reparations negotiations in Lausanne had almost reached a conclusion, and the parliamentary majority of the 'Prussia coalition' had been destroyed by the Prussian Diet elections held on the 24th.

## Variants of Dictatorship

The fall of Brüning followed. His departure was the joint work of the leading groups in industry, agriculture and the armed forces, along with the camarilla around Hindenburg. The opportunity they sought was provided by a landowners' protest against Brüning's proposal for the compulsory expropriation of landholdings which were no longer able to get out of debt. The main instigator of the Chancellor's fall was Kurt von Schleicher, who was supported by the army leadership. His ultimate objective was to establish an authoritarian and anti-parliamentary regime ruled by the president and including the

NSDAP. This would be tantamount to merging the military and civilian sectors of the government, thereby creating a dictatorially led 'army state'.

The plan to 'insert' the National Socialists into the government was not without its critics. It was true that Hitler had made a good impression on the big industrialists who heard him speak at the Düsseldorf Industrial Club on 26 January 1932, when he emphasised the 'struggle against the trade unions' and the 'role of the individual'. But the socialist phrases used in National Socialist propaganda, and anxieties about the inherent revolutionary momentum of the party's mass following, above all the members of the SA, led some people to suggest that direct participation in the government by the NSDAP ought to be avoided if at all possible and to favour instead a presidential regime which would lack parliamentary backing, but enjoy the toleration of the right-wing parties. This would, it was thought, lead more quickly to 'federal reform' (*Reichsreform*) and an about-turn in economic and social policy.[33]

The Papen cabinet, which was appointed on 1 June 1932, accorded well with this approach. It came into office at a moment when the negotiations over the question of reparations were about to be concluded. On 20 June 1931, the American President Herbert C. Hoover had proposed a year's suspension of the payment of German reparations and inter-allied war debts. Following on from this, it was agreed at the Lausanne reparations negotiations that Germany should make a final payment of 3 billion Gold Marks, which would fall due in 1935. With the conclusion of this agreement in Lausanne, Germany's reparations payments were in practice abolished. This was a favourable result for Germany, and it derived from the realisation particularly in the USA and Great Britain that the recovery of the world economy would not be possible until the international financial obligations arising from the First World War had been settled. In return for this agreement, the German delegation abandoned the demand raised by the right-wing opposition at home for the removal of the war guilt and disarmament articles from the Versailles Treaty. As a result, the German Right opposed the Lausanne Treaty.

The conclusion of the reparations negotiations removed the foreign policy pressure on the new German cabinet. Now the most important demands of the 'Reich reformers' were rapidly implemented. By making it possible to reduce wages below the level fixed by wage contracts, the Papen government destroyed a cornerstone of the working-class movement's post-1918 achievements in the sphere of social policy. At the same time, it reduced the level of unemployment benefit by almost a quarter and reduced the period of entitlement from twenty weeks to six. Finally, the Papen cabinet took the offensive against the last bastion of German Social Democracy: the Prussian government. Since the SPD's electoral defeat in April 1932, it had been impossible to form a new government there; the Social Democratic Prime Minister Otto Braun and his colleagues were only in office as a caretaker government. They faced a continuous increase in the number of street battles between the National Socialists, the Communists and the Prussian police, which took place in an atmosphere reminiscent of civil war. On 20 July 1932, the Reich government used this situation as an excuse to take over the Prussian government itself, an act which was unconstitutional and almost amounted to a *coup d'état*. The SPD leadership felt that there would be no point in resisting the 'Papen putsch', because the trade unions hardly had a base from which to mount a general strike, given that 6 million workers were unemployed, while the Reichswehr was ready and determined to intervene militarily against any armed resistance by the Prussian police or the *Reichsbanner*.

After 20 July 1932, there was hardly any prospect of a restoration of democratic conditions in Germany. The SPD and the workers' movement were no longer a decisive force in German domestic politics, and without them the country lost the political and social support base which since November 1918 had at least placed some limits on the influence of the old elites and the political right. The issue in subsequent months was no longer whether the parliament and the workers' parties would be deprived of all power but how this might be accomplished.[34] The formation of the Papen government now seemed to offer the right approach for a long-term solution, as Paul Reusch wrote in August 1932:

> We shall only make progress in Germany when the parties are excluded in the future from taking part in the formation of governments. The work of reform which needs to be undertaken is so immense that for the present there can be no thought of allowing the parties in the Reich and in Prussia to have access to the government in any way.[35]

Thus, the project of establishing a dictatorship of the elite unrestricted by parliament seemed to be proceeding according to plan. But it was now undermined by the very side from which it hoped to receive support: the NSDAP. The level of support the Hitler movement had achieved was already clear in March 1932, with the elections to the office of Reich president. In the second round, Hindenburg had been supported by the SPD, in the absence of any alternative. He did, it is true, win a conclusive victory over Hitler, with 53 per cent against the latter's 37 per cent of the vote. But, if Hitler were to achieve a similar result in parliamentary elections, it would be impossible to avoid giving him the office of Chancellor, sooner or later, especially as the NSDAP went on to win all the Diet elections that took place in the following weeks and months. It obtained 36.3 per cent in Prussia, 32.5 per cent in Bavaria, 40.9 per cent in Anhalt, 48.4 per cent in Oldenburg, 44 per cent in Hesse and 49 per cent in Mecklenburg-Schwerin.

Relying on these successes, Hitler had made the calling of new elections a condition for tolerating Papen's government. The results of these elections, which were held on 31 July 1932, were politically revolutionary. There was a very high poll, and the NSDAP received 37.4 per cent of the vote, which meant that their share had more than doubled since 1930, and they now became by far the strongest party in the Reichstag. The Communists too, with 14.5 per cent, also made gains at these elections. The two extreme parties, taken together, had 52 per cent. This gave them an absolute majority in the Reichstag. There could not have been a plainer repudiation of democracy and the republic by the majority of the population. The Catholic parties alone were able to keep their share of the vote. All other parties suffered losses: the SPD fell to 21.6 per cent, the same result as in 1920. The liberal parties were pretty well pulverised, and the DNVP, with 5.9 per cent, shrank to the position of a minor political grouping.

The elections did not produce any clear majorities, however: the two right-wing parties taken together only made up 43 per cent, while the Weimar coalition achieved 36 per cent, as did the two workers' parties (which were in any case completely hostile to each other). Only a coalition between the Centre Party and the NSDAP could have produced a parliamentary majority, but this possibility was quickly shelved after discussions at the state level proved relatively unsuccessful.

The NSDAP was now too strong for the role of a junior partner. It therefore pulled out of the plan to tolerate a Papen cabinet, and demanded the chancellorship of a future government. This made the whole project of an emergency government tolerated by the Right a non-starter, as was shown with utter clarity by Papen's devastating defeat in the Reichstag on 12 September, when 512 deputies voted against him and only forty-two in favour. The first time the Reichstag sat after the elections, therefore, fresh elections were announced for November 1932.

It had now become obvious that it was impossible to carry out an authoritarian policy in this form without a mass basis. But what alternatives were still available? Political decisions were being taken by an ever smaller group of politicians and lobbyists, whose most important members were Hindenburg and his advisers, the army leadership, and individual representatives of large-scale industry and the DNVP. Three requirements served as a basis for their deliberations: no return to parliamentarism, the elimination of the workers' movement and the continuation of the Papen government's economic and social policies.

The first option was to continue the Papen plan: a presidential government without a parliamentary majority. But this would force them to postpone the holding of Reichstag elections, and Hindenburg recoiled from openly breaching the constitution. Papen, however, initially advocated this solution, with the support of the DNVP, but he abandoned it when it became clear that if fresh elections were not scheduled the NSDAP and the Centre Party would institute legal proceedings against the president.

If, despite this, it was decided to follow the unconstitutional route, the situation would unquestionably take on the features of a civil war, and the government would have to call on the Reichswehr to intervene. As a consequence, this would have meant a military dictatorship, and that was the second option. Strong elements in the army leadership favoured this course, and until January 1933 the military option never entirely disappeared from the discussion, especially as it had already been tested successfully in some East European countries, such as Poland. In the last resort, however, military intervention in domestic politics seemed to the army leaders themselves to be too hazardous. After all, they saw their task as, first and foremost, to rearm the country, and then in the medium term to revise the results of the First World War. The solution under discussion might possibly force the military into a long and bloody confrontation with millions of organised industrial workers. Apart from that, they would have to reckon with the possibility that at least sections of the NSDAP membership who were excluded from a share in power might also have to be forcibly repressed by the army. The military leadership understandably recoiled from the prospect of fighting both the Right and the Left.[36]

The third possibility was a parliamentary government under the leadership of the National Socialists. This variant was of topical interest because of the contacts between the NSDAP and the Centre Party which followed the July 1932 elections. It made the industrialists and landowners apprehensive, however, because a 'black–brown coalition' of this kind might reverse their achievement in depriving the parliament of power, and lead to a 're-parliamentarisation' of the country. But, in any case, the areas of conflict between the two potential partners turned out to be too great for an agreement to be reached, as the initial consultations had already shown.

The fourth option, government by a 'right-wing bloc', would have lacked a majority, and it would therefore depend on presidential support. The offer made by Papen and Hindenburg to the NSDAP after the July elections envisaged the setting up of a presidential government, with NSDAP ministers serving under Papen as Chancellor. On 13 August, Hitler rejected this offer and uncompromisingly demanded that he be appointed head of a presidential cabinet. That signified the demise of the fourth option.

Now a number of new ideas were brought forward. One suggestion was to undermine the Hitler party by a quasi-parliamentary manoeuvre. The idea of gathering together all middle-class parties in a single movement had repeatedly arisen in earlier decades, but it had never been able to overcome the traditional party structures. This time too, the idea of collecting a big 'movement' around the DNVP which might be able to produce a majority was nothing more than a speculation, especially because a mass right-wing party already existed: the NSDAP. The notion of a majority party of the Right in which the traditional elites would have the final say was quickly exposed as an anachronism.

There therefore remained only the variant that had already failed, namely a Papen government without parliamentary backing. The Reichstag elections of November 1932 appeared to offer this possibility once again, because the NSDAP suffered a clear loss of support, falling back to 33.1 per cent. Two parties gained in the elections: the DNVP, now on 8.3 per cent, and the Communists, whose vote, at 16.9 per cent, was only 3 per cent behind that of the Social Democrats. There continued to be no workable majority in the Reichstag. The two extreme parties, taken together, continued to have an absolute majority, and this ruled out all coalitions based on the parties of the centre. Moreover, now not even a black–brown coalition possessed a majority. At least the almost irresistible rise of the Hitler party seemed to have been halted. The 'Fascist' solution of the crisis, following the Italian model, was to hand over the leadership of a right-wing presidential regime to a radical nationalist mass movement. This was evidently no longer as urgent as it appeared after the July elections.

## The Decision for Hitler

The result of the November elections strengthened Hindenburg and the business organisations in their endeavour to stabilise the Papen government in the longer term. Of course, a regime of this kind could not be kept afloat against both the working-class movement *and* the National Socialists. A new approach was needed, and this was put forward by the most powerful of the numerous political intriguers of the final months, Kurt von Schleicher, who had been promoted in the meantime to the position of Armed Forces Minister. His scheme was intended to make sure that the presidential regime continued to develop into an authoritarian elite dictatorship under the control of the armed forces, and at the same time to keep the NSDAP leadership around Hitler out of the government, because its extravagant demand for absolute power and its economic and political objectives aroused the suspicions of industry. By peeling off the 'sensible' elements from the NSDAP, so as to include the Right radical mass movement alongside parts of the trade unions in the ruling cartel, it would be possible to create a 'mass support point' for the dictatorship he envisaged, and this would also obviate the need for the forcible intervention of the Reichswehr.[37]

This complicated construction, which Schleicher called a 'diagonal front' (*Querfront*), was not as out of place as it may appear in retrospect. At least, it was no stranger than the proposal Papen had made in November, namely to abolish the Reichstag, proclaim a state of emergency, use the Reichswehr and the police to suppress all political parties and paramilitary organisations, and set up an authoritarian, non-parliamentary, system. On 3 December 1932, immediately after he was appointed Chancellor, Schleicher started to make contact with both the left wing of the NSDAP and the trade unions. He did not, however, succeed in splitting Hitler's party. The grandiose plan fell apart as quickly as it had emerged.

By now, time was running out. Since the economic situation appeared to be improving after the end of 1932, the whole plan to destroy parliamentary democracy was in danger of collapsing. In December 1932, Paul Reusch wrote to Schleicher with a warning:

> It is precisely now, in the midst of the crisis, that the decisive incisions must be made in the state organism. The will to reform cannot be put on ice indefinitely! If the financial pressure has been lifted so far away from our state organism by an improvement of the economic situation that it can again catch its breath, the strongest incentive towards the implementation of a reform on a truly grand scale will have been irreversibly removed.[38]

From the point of view of Hindenburg's advisers, there were now only a few possibilities left. Schleicher's approach, which was to work towards the suspension of the Reichstag and the establishment of a military dictatorship with more generous social policies, was unwelcome to most of the business organisations, chiefly because they were put off by his socialist phraseology. He also lost the backing of the chiefs of the armed forces because of the danger of civil war associated with his approach. To dissolve parliament and call fresh elections, on the other hand, was seen as too risky a course, for in the light of the impending improvement in business conditions there was a danger that this would bring about a renewed strengthening of the working-class parties, leading either to the restabilisation of the Weimar system or even to power-sharing with the Communists.

All that was left, therefore, was the Papen variant, which enjoyed the support of the majority of the leading conservative groups, but with one important difference: after the failure of Schleicher's attempt to split the NSDAP, any cooperation with that party would require the acceptance of Hitler's demand to lead the government. Hitler's presence admittedly guaranteed the stability of the government, but, at the same time, there was a danger that the inherent dynamism of the National Socialist mass movement would change the proposed government partnership of the NSDAP with the old elites into the sole rule of that party, and indeed that, under certain circumstances, its socially revolutionary and anti-capitalist elements, particularly the SA, would take an independent role.

If it turned out to be possible to build into the coalition sufficiently strong safeguards against any tendency within the NSDAP towards independent action, this risk appeared manageable. Papen had in fact already been working on precautions of this kind since the middle of December. The plan to 'box in' the NSDAP had already been suggested on many occasions. It was now put into effect, but in the version with Hitler as Chancellor, which had originally been rejected. It was felt that with Papen as Vice-Chancellor and the DNVP chair Hugenberg as 'economic dictator'—and taking into account both Hitler's repeated declarations in support of the continued existence of an independent capitalist economy and the small number of NSDAP representatives in the proposed Hitler–Papen cabinet, as well as the continued authority held by President Hindenburg—the risk of the NSDAP's asserting an independent position, though not entirely removed, was at least calculable, unlike the other available options.

Since the beginning of January, Papen had been working to prepare the overthrow of Schleicher. The final impulse for the latter's fall was provided by vehement complaints about his policies made to Hindenburg by the big landowners, followed by their decision in favour of a Hitler–Papen government. Hindenburg refused to give Schleicher the authority he wanted for yet another dissolution of the Reichstag, which meant that he faced defeat the next time it met. This led him to hand in his resignation. The way was now clear for Hitler. On 30 January 1933, the new cabinet took the oath to Hindenburg. It contained only three National Socialists: Adolf Hitler as Chancellor, Hermann Goering and Wilhelm Frick. There were nine conservatives. This government, like the previous ones, lacked a parliamentary majority. It functioned as a presidential cabinet, just as the cabinets of Brüning, Papen and Schleicher had done.

Nevertheless, this new cabinet was something different, because Hitler, unlike his predecessors Papen and Schleicher, had the backing, not just of the wire-pullers around Hindenburg, but of a mass party of millions of devoted adherents equipped with a gigantic paramilitary force. The NSDAP was a movement of extraordinary dynamism, ruthlessness and lust for power, explicitly aimed at removing the surviving remnants of parliamentary democracy and constitutional rule and at the persecution and liquidation of its opponents. On the evening of 30 January, the National Socialists came out onto the streets in mass marches and torchlight processions to stage the 'national uprising', which is how they perceived the appointment of Hitler as Chancellor of Germany.

Barely three years elapsed between the resignation of the Müller government and the coming to power of Adolf Hitler. These years were marked by economic collapse, social impoverishment and political disaster. The increasingly frequent and violent clashes between the SA and the communists, which the police were ultimately unable to control, further strengthened the impression of an untenable situation. This feeling that the whole system needed to be overthrown accorded well with the intentions of the two radical parties. They did their best to strengthen it, the communists because in boundless over-estimation of their own strength they thought a revolutionary situation was ripening in their favour, and the National Socialists because they were aware that their assistance would only be called for in a situation of extreme emergency.

But the decisive role in Hitler's path to power was played by the incessant endeavours of the army leaders, the big economic interest groups, the right-wing parties and the advisers of the president to bring into being an authoritarian dictatorship of the elite which would be unconstrained by parliament. After all the other possibilities had been explored and rejected, the NSDAP was seen as an ally in attaining this goal, an ally which was certainly unloved, but acceptable nevertheless. In contrast to the military dictatorships installed in other European countries during the 1920s, the assistance of a radical right-wing mass movement, as in Italy, was the more promising path to follow, because it did not negate mass society but integrated it: it was the plebiscitary legitimation of a dictatorial regime. According to Heinrich August Winkler: 'Where a strong socialist industrial working class already existed, a right-wing counter-movement also had to get its support from the masses. When sections of the "power élite" wanted to make use of these masses, they could not be fastidious.'[39]

The 'government of national concentration' which was formed on 30 January 1933 therefore reflected the calculations made by two political forces. First, the calculation of the conservative right-wingers, who regarded the new configuration of political power as a government of the old elite which unlike its predecessors had gained a lasting stability through its alliance with the nationalist mass movement; and second, the calculation of the National Socialists, for whom 30 January 1933 signified the 'seizure of power'. By obtaining Hindenburg's permission to dissolve the Reichstag and issue instructions for fresh elections to be held, the Nazis also secured the opportunity to use the instruments of a governing party to unleash the street-level momentum which turned the Hitler–Papen cabinet into a government of 'national revolution'.

Seen from this angle, the 'seizure of power' by the Nazis resulted from the attempt by the conservative elites to install a government independent of parliamentary restrictions. From a somewhat broader perspective, it was a consequence of the fact that, after the renewed collapse of the German economy, a growing section of German society had lost confidence in the Weimar political system, and in the Weimar combination of parliamentary democracy, state legal and social protection and liberal capitalism—and was determined to seek out more radical alternatives which promised greater advantages.

In that sense, the historical background to the 'seizure of power' extends beyond the Weimar years to the late nineteenth century, the period when, after rapid industrialisation and the far-reaching changes that followed, the search began for a social order that could offer adequate support throughout this process of transformation. This was a time when social currents set on radical alternatives to traditional bourgeois society also made their appearance. Prior to 1914, this desire for a new direction had grown within the dynamic and unstable but also extraordinarily successful society of imperial Germany. Thus the forces of political disintegration could have been curtailed if Germany's road to war had not itself ultimately been due to precisely those centrifugal forces.

But the escalation of radical nationalism during the First World War and after Germany's incomprehensible and unaccepted final defeat was followed by a civil war which was sometimes implicitly, and at other times, explicitly manifested in violence, and which received further nourishment by repeated outbreaks of crisis, so that it could not even be contained by the forces of stabilisation at work between 1924 and 1929. Thus the 'seizure of power' by the Nazis signified the end of this conflict over the way industrial society should be organised, between the movement for constitutional democracy and its nationalist opponents—a conflict which had defined the contours of German domestic politics since 1917, if not before.

But the traditional categories of 'reaction' and 'restoration' would be an inadequate framework to explain the events that now unfolded. January 1933 signified a fundamental rejection, not just of Weimar, but also of a law-governed state, parliamentary democracy, and liberal capitalism, and of their political and cultural manifestations, at least in the forms in which they had been promulgated since the turn of the century and entrenched after 1918. This was by no means a renunciation of 'modernity', of industry, mass society and technology. It was, rather, a radically different form of modernity, in which people rejected the principles of democracy, liberalism, universality and human rights, without having any clear vision of the goal towards which they were now heading.

# PART THREE

# 1933–45

# 7
# The Dynamics of Violence

## 'Seizure of Power'

Almost a year after Hitler had been appointed German Chancellor, the French ambassador in Berlin, André François-Poncet, made this comment on the situation in Germany:

> At the end of the year 1933 National Socialist Germany stands there with its customs, its institutions, its vocabulary, its new form of greeting, its slogans, its fashions, its art, its laws and its festivals. Nothing is missing. The *Reichsparteitag* (Reich Party Congress) in Nuremberg, the '*Reichsparteitag* of victory' at the beginning of September, showed a Germany which was ready, complete, triumphant.

The ambassador's field of vision was no doubt limited to political developments at the top of the state and the party, and the fascination of the mass processions and the propaganda of the new regime certainly also played a part in convincing him. But he was a liberal nationalist of the old school, and a sober observer who had good relations with all the political camps in the capital city. He did not overlook the 'violence of the government against the Churches and the Jews' or the 'outrages committed by its militiamen', although excesses of this kind did not surprise him in view of the abrupt nature of the change in Germany's political direction. As he explained: 'This revolution is astounding not only for the pace at which it has proceeded, but also for the ease with which it has taken control all over Germany and the slight amount of resistance it has faced.'[1]

In less than a year, the new regime under Hitler succeeded in undertaking a complete change of system, which contained all the elements of a revolution. His policies were evidently regarded as very successful by the overwhelming majority of the population. This sequence of events was of such immense weight and emotional intensity that it was already perceived by contemporaries inside and outside Germany as a radical turning point, marking the dividing line between two epochs.

The central concept under which the new Hitler government summed up its programme on 1 February 1933 was '*Volksgemeinschaft*' (Community of the

*Volk*). The term itself had been one of the chief watchwords of the critics of modernity over the previous fifty years, whatever their political tendency. Their critique was directed against industrial society's class divisions and religious conflicts, which in their view were tearing apart the community. They also opposed political parties and parliamentary democracy, which was based on disunity and competing interest groups. William II's famous assertion on 1 August 1914, 'I no longer see any parties or different religions; today we Germans are all brothers' was an expression of this critique and the yearning for unity that underlay it.

This was not a specifically German phenomenon. Social unrest had greatly increased all over Europe after the war. There were strikes and revolutionary uprisings; but there were also conflicts in the newly established nation-states between rival ethnic groups. This situation had favoured the rise of authoritarian regimes in Spain, Italy, Poland, Hungary and Yugoslavia, as well as in Greece and Bulgaria. Those regimes all stressed the need to overcome internal divisions and create national unity, and they promised to intervene with force if necessary to achieve their objectives. Here, as also in the metropolitan cities of the western democracies, class conflicts within society were seen as regrettable manifestations of an unnatural state of affairs. The utopias of the radical Left, too, envisaged the ending of class struggles by revolution and the establishment of an equality free of conflict. In Germany, though, class conflicts and internal divisions were particularly pronounced, and national and social antagonisms had been very much intensified by defeat in war.

This was the basis for the social agitation of the National Socialists. The first section of Hitler's government declaration was devoted to evaluating the legacy of the democratic era. The previous governments of the 'November parties', he said, had driven the nation to rack and ruin, left behind a place of devastation, destroyed the 'peasant estate', created an army of millions of unemployed and contributed to the growth of 'spiritual, political and cultural nihilism'. The supreme task of the government, therefore, was to 'restore the spiritual unity and strength of will of our people, irrespective of all divisions into estates and classes'. The main political tasks were to end mass unemployment and the agricultural crisis, to reform the relations between the Reich, the states and the municipalities, to continue implementing social policies, and in foreign affairs to restore Germany's equal rights. But first it was necessary to 'overcome communist subversion' and thereby get rid of 'class lunacy and class struggle'.[2]

This programme, enveloped as it was in the emotional and piously elevated language customary at the time, entirely followed the lines set by previous governments. Schleicher and von Papen had also announced the 'reform of the Reich', the abolition of the party system and parliamentary democracy, the fight against the communists, the recovery of Germany's position in the world, rearmament, and the ending of the economic crisis. Behind closed doors, however, Hitler formulated his objectives in a much clearer and more brutal fashion, issuing these directives to the heads of the armed forces on 3 February: 'Complete reversal of the present domestic pol. conditions in G.', 'root and branch eradication of Marxism', 'Anyone who refuses to be converted must be brought to heel', 'All means must be used to strengthen the will to arms', 'The strictest possible authoritarian national leadership is required. The cancerous disease of democracy must be removed', 'Building up the defence forces (*Wehrmacht*) is the most important requirement for achieving the goal, the recovery of pol. power.' To eliminate domestic opponents, to establish an authoritarian regime, to rearm and win back foreign policy strength with the option of an early war: these were the essential objectives Hitler revealed in this speech. Even so, they differed at most stylistically from the publicly declared aims of the national-conservative Reich reformers.[3]

The major difference between Hitler's policies and those of the preceding cabinets was rather that his policies were driven and pushed forward by a mass movement which was both radical and thirsty for action, and which saw his appointment as German Chancellor as a 'seizure of power' by the National Socialist party under its leader, rather than the beginning of another presidential government. Already in previous years, the dynamism deriving from this relation between the leader and his followers had constituted a clear distinguishing mark between the National Socialist movement and other groups of right-wing radicals. This dynamism now continued to operate at the governmental level, and ensured the constant acceleration and unlimited character of the political upheaval.

As would soon become apparent, the objectives formulated by Hitler on 1 February were in line with the fundamental convictions of a section of the population which extended far beyond the group of radical right-wingers. All political camps, with the exception of Social Democracy, were fundamentally agreed that the 'system' of the Weimar Republic had failed, and that a new order was needed in the economic sphere as well as in relation to social and political institutions, although there were immense divergences in the way this new order was understood. Moreover, the political agony of the years of crisis since 1929 had heightened the yearning for political leadership, for drastic measures and hard decisions, to such an extent that anything seemed better than a continuation of the pain. 'We may well make plenty of mistakes' said Goering in March 1933 'but we will at least take action and keep our nerve.'[4]

Both the conviction that Weimar had failed and the yearning for decisive leadership provided favourable conditions for the political revolution the National Socialists now set in motion. Those who held that the changes Hitler brought about were by and large correct, even if they might have reservations about individual aspects of policy, were the former supporters and electors of a group stretching all the way from the political Right to elements of the bourgeois liberal and Catholic camps. The other group, above all the supporters of the working-class parties and the core elements of political Catholicism, greeted the activism of the Hitler movement with resignation and fury, but also with a grudging admiration, because they had nothing of equal value to set against the energy, the brutality and the youthful enthusiasm of the Nazis.

The new regime succeeded within roughly eighteen months in establishing an organised system which in essence fulfilled the political and ideological objectives the radical Right had aimed at since roughly 1917. This period culminated on 2 August 1934 when the offices of Chancellor and president were joined together in the person of Hitler, who was now 'Führer and Reich Chancellor'. It only took a few months for the principles of liberalism, democracy and constitutionalism to be cast aside almost completely. Domestic and foreign policy were affected as much as was the economy, society and culture, and the fact that everything happened simultaneously and at a breakneck speed contributed considerably to the effectiveness of the transformation.

Hitler's first movein the political sphere was to obtain Hindenburg's agreement to the holding of fresh elections. These would be 'the last elections for a long time' in von Papen's opinion. He, like most of the national-conservatives, considered that it would be completely unnecessary to hold any more elections after this one.[5] For Hitler and the NSDAP, the new elections, in which their control of state power would be a useful asset, offered the possibility of obtaining a majority in the Reichstag. This would then make it easier to implement far-reaching and permanent changes in the constitution. To achieve this, however, they had to proceed in line with the existing constitution at least to some degree, both in order to be sure of the loyalty of the civil service and to gain the agreement of the president. In the meantime, Hitler made use of the opportunities offered by his position as Chancellor.

The initial scenario here was the attempted communist uprising that was expected or perhaps only postulated. This war game had already been played out repeatedly during the Weimar years in emergency and civil war planning. The emergency ordinance of 4 February, which had already been drafted under Schleicher, gave legal backing for the prohibition of communist meetings and demonstrations and the suppression of communist and social democratic newspapers. This was the first step in the direction of complete dictatorship. At the same time, Goering, as Acting Prussian Minister of the Interior, organised the political intimidation of the other side, appointing 50,000 men from the SA, SS and Stahlhelm as 'auxiliary policemen' and authorising the use of firearms against communists.[6] With this there began a reign of terror of an extent never previously considered possible against the opponents of National Socialism, particularly the communists, who were now regarded almost as outlaws and were harassed and persecuted everywhere by the new forces of law and order.

The second step was taken with the so-called 'Reichstag fire decree'. On the night of 27 February, the Reichstag was set on fire, and only a few hours later Marinus van der Lubbe, a Dutch bricklayer's apprentice, was arrested as the arsonist. Nobody believed that he had acted alone. On the Left they were absolutely convinced that the Nazis themselves had set fire to the building, which was the symbol of the parliamentary rule they hated, in order to justify violent measures against their opponents. On the Right, in contrast, there was an equally firm conviction that the burning of the Reichstag was intended as the signal for the long-awaited communist uprising. The Nazi leaders greeted the news of the fire with delighted and almost incredulous surprise. In fact, the idea of exploiting such a provocative act as a pretext for taking forcible action against the Left was by no means alien to them. Now, however, a purely fortuitous event had come to their aid. Nothing could have been more convenient.

The Papen cabinet had already prepared a draft emergency decree to cover the case of a civil war caused by a communist uprising, under the name of the 'Ott Simulation Exercise', which set aside basic legal rights and gave the government dictatorial powers. On 28 February, this draft decree was issued almost unaltered by the president, as an 'Emergency Decree for the Protection of the People and the State'. The provisions of what soon became known as the 'Reichstag fire decree' henceforth formed the basis for a kind of permanent state of emergency. The decree in fact liquidated the rule of law in Germany. Over the next few months, it was used to justify the removal of all major legal rights, the introduction of 'protective police custody', and, stemming from that, the concentration camps, the arbitrary arrest of political opponents and the prohibition of all undesirable parties and groups. On the night of 1 March, the police and the SA made a series of raids in which thousands of communist leaders were arrested, more than 1,500 in Berlin alone. These arrests also included many of the party's parliamentary deputies. The KPD's offices were closed, and its newspapers were prohibited. A further 7,000 communists were arrested in the weeks that followed, among them the party leader, Ernst Thälmann. Most of them were taken to prison, although, particularly in the provinces, many were also sent to quickly erected 'wild' camps all over the country, where the SA imprisoned and mistreated their political opponents. At the same time, the National Socialists made use of the opportunity to arrest some of their most prominent left-wing intellectual opponents, including Erich Mühsam, Carl von Ossietzky and Egon Erwin Kisch.[7]

This first wave of terror did not meet with any explicit opposition from the German population, apart from members of the working-class parties. Ever since the attempted coups and uprisings of the post-war years, the fear of a communist revolution had created a firm bond between all bourgeois and nationalist forces. In the Catholic press, for instance, under the headline 'No More Moscow', one could read that the emergency decree had at last struck a blow against

> Bolshevism, the deadly enemy of Germany, the focus of Germany's sickness, the ulcer which has poisoned and infected German blood for years. . . . Against murderers, arsonists and poisoners there can only be the most vigorous defence, and only the death penalty can deal with terror. The fanatics who wanted to turn Germany into an Asiatic robbers' cave must be rendered harmless. . . . More than parties are at stake here. Germany is at stake, indeed the whole of Western culture, built upon Christianity, is at stake.[8]

The election campaign for the Reichstag elections of 5 March 1933 was conducted in an atmosphere of street terror directed principally against the workers' parties by the Nazi paramilitaries. The result was a death toll of more than fifty opponents of National Socialism. Eighteen Nazis were also killed. Over the course of these weeks, the National Socialists worked themselves into a state of propagandistic intoxication, giving the impression, as the American Ambassador Frederic M. Sackett wrote, 'that in Germany there is only one great party'.[9] In actual fact, however, in an election with a very high level of participation (almost 89 per cent) the Nazis only obtained 43.9 per cent of the vote, and thus were well short of an absolute majority. The DNVP suffered slight losses (down from 8.9 per cent to 8.0 per cent).

It was not a surprise that the KPD lost votes, after the general indignation over their alleged responsibility for the Reichstag fire and the wave of persecution that followed it. With 12.3 per cent, it fell back to approximately the same position as after the 1930 election. There were roughly 5 million communist voters, who could be said to belong to the narrower circle of communist support, and they continued to be true to their party even after the persecution of the previous few weeks. The SPD, with 18.3 per cent instead of 20.4 per cent, suffered only slight losses. It had lost votes to the NSDAP, but these were counterbalanced by gains from the KPD. The two Catholic parties had also largely held their ground (the Centre Party and BVP together received 13.9 per cent instead of their previous 15 per cent of the vote). Taken together, therefore, Catholic and Socialist support had remained relatively stable, suffering only slight losses. The liberal parties, in contrast, had now become almost insignificant. The DVP received 1.1 per cent, and the left liberal DDP, which had presented itself to the electors under the name 'German State Party' (*Deutsche Staatspartei*), received no more than 0.8 per cent. The National Socialists made gains in all directions: they gained the support of people who formerly voted for the bourgeois parties, the numerous small right-wing parties, the Social Democrats and the KPD, as well as first-timers and people who had previously abstained from voting.

Three conclusions could be drawn from the March elections. Firstly, the NSDAP had won a great victory. It had hoovered up almost the whole of the middle-class vote, and taken many votes from the Left as well. There was a clear mandate for a right-wing, authoritarian, and nationalist government. Secondly, 56.1 per cent of the electors had *not* voted for the NSDAP, and it could only reach a majority together with the DNVP. The electorate had therefore not voted in favour of exclusive domination by the Hitler party. Thirdly, however, if the votes in favour of the parties unambiguously hostile to the constitution (NSDAP, DNVP and KPD) were counted together, more than 64 per cent of the electors, almost two-thirds, therefore, had unmistakably voted against the Weimar Republic, whereas the forces behind the constitutionalist revolution of 1918 and the Weimar coalition of 1919 had shrunk to 30 per cent. One result of the vote was therefore clear: the electors wanted the republic to come to an end.

Meanwhile the votes the Nazis had obtained in March were sufficient for their purposes. Together with the DNVP, they had an absolute majority, and they now began to make use of it. Within a few weeks, they succeeded in destroying the constitutional structure of the Weimar Republic, and, to the constant accompaniment of resounding mass processions and propaganda rallies, they established a dictatorship in name as well as in fact. First, they deposed those state governments which were not yet National Socialist. A model for this was offered by Papen's removal of the Prussian government a year earlier. First, the Nazi paramilitaries provoked clashes with their opponents. Then, the Reich Minister of the Interior could proclaim a state of emergency and use that to justify appointing a Reich commissioner.

This process was completed with astonishing ease. In Hesse-Darmstadt, for instance, local Nazi party offices had been sending reports to the Reich Minister of the Interior since the middle of February that clashes with the communists were disturbing public order. The day after the Reichstag elections, the Minister of the Interior appointed a Reich commissioner and placed the elected prime minister of the state under house arrest. Noisy demonstrations and the raising of swastika flags over government buildings accompanied these castling manoeuvres on the political chessboard, giving the impression of a 'seizure of power' from below. The conquest of power took place in the same way in the towns and municipalities. Here too, SA units arrested Social Democratic or Catholic mayors or town councillors and compelled them to resign.[10]

Although the Nazis had only obtained just under 44 per cent of the vote in the Reichstag elections, during the next two weeks they succeeded in taking over the conduct of business in all the federal states and almost all the municipalities.

This was an indication of just how overwhelming an impression was created by the onslaught of the brown battalions on state power, as well as how irresistible was the violence and intimidation of the NS paramilitaries given the impotence and paralysis of their opponents. The communists had already been removed from the scene as a political opposition in the first few days after the Reichstag fire. They were not prepared for organised resistance against a right-wing dictatorship, because in the previous months they had chiefly directed their attention to the struggle against Social Democracy (the 'Social Fascists'), a party they regarded as the 'main support of the bourgeoisie', in line with the position of the Stalinised Communist Party of the Soviet Union. Moreover, almost all political forces to the Right of the SPD supported the Nazis in their fight against the communists, and an attempt by the KPD at an organised uprising would very probably have brought the Reichswehr into the field against it as well.

The Social Democrats had been strengthened rather than weakened by their respectable showing at the March elections, but their leaders were obliged to contemplate the interplay of government policy and terror in the streets as well-nigh powerless onlookers. Open resistance against the new regime was a hopeless undertaking, and it also contradicted the political self-image of the party, which was committed to legality and non-violence. In any case, most leading Social Democrats assumed that the Hitler cabinet, like other presidential governments before it, would collapse in a few months. In March 1933 this conviction seemed entirely realistic, and many foreign observers had a similar opinion. Why would this bunch of nationalist hooligans and dilettantes, failed sectarians and racialist fanatics succeed in doing something neither the Left liberal nor the conservative elites had been able to achieve, namely, solve the economic crisis, stabilise political conditions and restore a calm and confident atmosphere? If this were true, why risk a possibly armed resistance, which could not succeed in view of the existing relationship of forces, but would cost many sacrifices and risk the very existence of the party?[11]

But the main reason for the manifest inactivity of the workers' parties was the terror of the Nazi paramilitaries, which reached unprecedented dimensions. In March 1933, in Prussia alone, roughly 20,000 communists were taken into 'protective custody', and this figure does not even include people who were imprisoned in the SA's own camps, which were now springing up everywhere. As Rudolf Diels, the first chief of the Berlin political police after the Nazi takeover, commented later: 'No Red Front man who had ever thrashed, or even cold-shouldered, an SA man during the "Time of Struggle" was able to escape the private vengeance of the victorious brownshirts.'[12]

The 'fight for the annihilation of Marxism' was the watchword under which the conservative nationalists in the government also supported the escalating terror of the Nazi militia, thereby accepting the destruction of all legal safeguards. The brutal momentum of the National Socialist movement led some of Hitler's conservative and bourgeois nationalist partners to doubt whether the dynamic forces that had been set in motion could really be 'contained' in the way they expected. But their fears were calmed by the dramatic spectacle staged in Potsdam on 21 March to celebrate the opening of the newly elected Reichstag. Hitler, dressed in civilian clothes, made obeisance to President Hindenburg, whose uniform was adorned with military decorations. There was a festive service, involving the laying of wreaths, an organ concert and the singing of the chorale '*Wir treten zum Beten*' ('We Gather Together in Prayer'). All this was intended to symbolise the merging of the old Prussian and Wilhelmine traditions with the young 'national movement'. The spectacle was the brainchild of Joseph Goebbels, who had just been appointed Minister of Propaganda. The Protestant clergyman Otto Dibelius preached a sermon in which he explicitly approved the actions of the National Socialists against their opponents:

> When the state exercises its office against those who subvert the foundations of law and order, and particularly against those who with cutting and hateful phrases seek to undermine marriage, pour scorn on religious belief, and besmirch the idea of dying for the fatherland, it is doing its duty in God's name. . . . When the history of a state makes a new beginning this always somehow involves the application of force. For the state is power. New decisions, new directions, changes and revolutions always mean the victory of one side over another. And if the life and death of the nation are at stake, the power of the state must be strongly and uncompromisingly engaged, whether externally or internally.[13]

The spectacle in Potsdam was impressive. It was intended, on the one hand, to demonstrate to the public at home and abroad that the German people had 'recovered its unity', and on the other hand, to prepare for the session of the Reichstag held two days later, at which the deputies had to vote on an 'Enabling Act' which would officially bring an end to the republic and establish a dictatorship.

To pass this law, a two-thirds majority was needed, in both the Reichsrat (Federal Council) and the Reichstag. As far as the Reichsrat was concerned, the sending of pro-government commissioners to take charge of the federal states had already solved the problem. In the Reichstag as well, a numerical two-thirds majority was ensured in advance by manipulating the voting figures: the votes of the communist deputies, most of whom were in prison, were recorded as 'abstentions', and the same method was applied to Social Democrats who were absent. One of the most unbending Social Democrats, Carl Severing, who had spent many years as Prussia's Minister of the Interior, was arrested on the way to the Kroll Opera, where the meeting was to be held.

Four hundred and forty-four deputies voted 'Yes'. Not one single deputy from the bourgeois, Catholic or Conservative parties voted 'No'. The Social Democrats alone, with their ninety-four votes, opposed the Enabling Act. With this vote, the Reichstag had confirmed its own (and the president's) disempowerment. For four years—a period which was regularly extended, at the end simply by decree—the government could promulgate laws, even unconstitutional ones, and make treaties with foreign powers at its own discretion. 'An historic day' declared the *Völkischer Beobachter*, triumphantly.

> The parliamentary system has capitulated to the new Germany. For four years Hitler will be able to do everything he considers necessary: negatively the extermination of all the corrupting forces of Marxism; positively the establishment of a new Community of the Volk (*Volksgemeinschaft*). The great undertaking is begun! The day of the Third Reich has come.[14]

Until August 1934, when Hindenburg died and Hitler took over the office of president and declared the National Socialist revolution at an end, the national dictatorship envisaged in the Enabling Act was built up in stages, but with astounding rapidity. The Reichstag was deprived of power and, following the same pattern, the state parliaments and town and city councils were dissolved and then reconvened as bodies whose job was to rubber-stamp decisions already arrived at elsewhere. But this was only the beginning. By summer 1933, all parties apart from the NSDAP had been dissolved or forced into self-dissolution, the trade unions had been crushed, all the major interest groups had been reconstituted under National Socialist domination, and the most influential institutions, with few exceptions, had declared their loyalty to the aims and methods of the 'national revolution'.

This happened very quickly and met with little resistance, indeed many of those affected approved of the changes and accepted them, for two reasons. The enormous energy displayed by the National Socialist formations in pushing them through was certainly one, but another was the crippling anxiety which spread rapidly among the opponents and potential victims of the Nazis, further intensified by reports of what was happening in the SA's concentration camps and the cellars of police headquarters.

This by itself does not explain the almost universal and simultaneous collective 'self-coordination' (*Selbstgleichschaltung*) of most of the social institutions of the country, a process which affected the sports clubs and the Philharmonic Orchestra, the research institutes and the universities as well as the professional associations, the youth groups and also the nationalist parties and groupings. Nor does it explain why more than 3 million Germans decided to join the NSDAP between January 1933 and the end of 1934, thereby tripling its membership. Many of these people were certainly opportunists and careerists, but they too were reacting to a basic social trend which could be felt everywhere in those months. It is also not enough to refer to Hitler's charisma, for most Germans still knew him as the somewhat ridiculous putschist of 1923 and as a fervent street agitator. The aura of the utterly infallible 'Führer' only emerged over time, and the degree of its effectiveness undoubtedly varied according to age group.

The essential concept of the 'national revolution', namely the elimination of the forces of political, social and cultural pluralism and the establishment of national 'unity', met with agreement even on the part of many of those who lost both voice and influence as a result of this process. People of this kind clearly bought into the popular belief that, by bringing to an end the 'fragmentation' and 'disunity' of the German *Volk,* the National Socialists had overcome what were considered to be the principal reasons for Germany's decline. The slogans most commonly recited in those weeks and months, alongside the 'destruction of Marxism', were 'restore unity' and 'overcome the fatal division of the German people'. The call for the unity of physical and intellectual labour, of men and women, of rich and poor, of South Germans and Prussians, of Catholics and Protestants, of Liberals and Socialists, was much more than mere propaganda. It expressed people's discomfort with the complicated game of politics, with the alternating collaboration and mutual hostility of social and political interests and with the wearisome search for compromises and temporary coalitions which found expression in the division of powers, the political parties, the economic interest groups and not least the many competing voices of public opinion, and made life in modern industrial society so difficult and incomprehensible for many. From this perspective, therefore, the rejection of pluralism and institutionalised conflicts of interest which the Nazi government was now putting into practice was not perceived as the usurpation of power by a single party but as the victory of the natural, national, unity of a *Volk* over the artificial social and political fragmentation it had suffered in the modern state, dominated as it was by parties and pressure groups. The desire for unity was bound up with the expectation that the nation would regain its strength and be delivered from the continuous economic, political and social crisis that had now lasted for twenty years. The emphatic ruthlessness and uncompromising radicalism employed by Hitler in achieving his aims was therefore taken by roughly half the population as an indication that he might well be successful.

The Nazis presented the destruction of the free trade unions on 2 May 1933, and the prohibition of the SPD in June, as two blows struck against the bastions of the class struggle, and therefore against the division of the German nation into social interest groups, and that is how these measures were perceived by many people. Even the demolition of the traditional structures of the workers' movement was garnished with the slogan of national unity: the establishment in 1933 of the First of May as the official holiday of national labour expressed this idea, as did the creation of the German Labour Front as the symbol of the 'national unity of all producers' a year later.[15]

With the churches, it was more difficult to reach an agreement. It was true that the National Socialists had enjoyed great sympathies among the Protestants long before 1933, and it was not surprising that the Nazi 'German Christians' obtained two-thirds of the seats in church elections held in summer 1933 and so were able to elect their candidate Ludwig Müller as 'Reich bishop' (*Reichsbischof*). The evangelical youth clubs, which with more than a million members were the largest youth association in Germany, were in any case nationalist in tendency, and in December 1933 they merged with the Hitler Youth. But there were also tendencies in the other direction, working against the politicisation of religion. A counter-movement to the 'German Christians' emerged in the shape of the Confessing Church, which was joined by roughly a third of the clergy. Remarkably, the National Socialists thereupon lost interest in pushing the coordination (*Gleichschaltung*) of Protestantism any further, especially because critics of their intervention in church affairs restricted themselves to internal ecclesiastical matters and did not oppose the policy of the new regime in other respects.[16]

With the Catholics it was different. There were, it is true, several points on which they agreed with the objectives of the Nazi government, such as their rejection of modern 'asphalt culture' (*Asphaltkultur*) as well as their support for an authoritarian regime. But the Catholic Centre Party, however nationalist it might now wish to appear, had played as big a part in founding the Weimar state as had the Left liberals and the Social Democrats, and the Nazis therefore eyed it with as much mistrust as they did the interlocking sociocultural networks of the Catholic milieu, with its youth associations, welfare institutions and trade union organisations.

It was the more surprising, therefore, that the Vatican was now prepared to treat these networks as a bargaining counter in political horse-trading. By the agreement ('Concordat') of July 1933 between the German government and the Vatican, Hitler conceded to the Catholics the recognition of Catholic religious education and the retention of Catholic schools. He also permitted Catholic organisations to continue their activities in so far as they had purely religious purposes. These were all aims that the Catholics had long pursued in Germany, and they had finally been achieved, in what now appeared to be a favourable moment. In return, a few weeks after the signing of the Concordat, the numerous cultural and political organisations of Catholicism, including the Centre Party itself, were wound up on instructions from Rome. German Catholicism thus abandoned its political and social structures in order to preserve its core operation of providing pastoral care.

The Nazi regime, however, gained enormously in international credibility and legitimacy through this agreement with the Vatican, and it also benefited greatly from being accepted by Roman Catholics within the country. Nevertheless, political Catholicism continued in later years to be regarded as dangerous by the Nazi leaders, and it was frequently attacked, particularly at the municipal level, where the solidarity of the Catholics often remained firmly rooted, resisting pressure from the NSDAP and the state.[17]

## Safeguarding the Dictatorship

By the autumn of 1933, almost all Germany's political and social institutions and organisations had been brought into line or prohibited by the new regime. The long sought-after 'Community of the Volk' (*Volksgemeinschaft*) seemed to have been established, at least politically. As a result, the NSDAP had tremendously extended its responsibilities and jurisdiction and, in many fields, it stood alongside the state's administrative apparatus, indeed it had replaced it in some respects. The completely unabashed demands now made for state sinecures and pension settlements by Nazi activists from the 'time of struggle' (*Kampfzeit*) were criticised and resisted by the top civil servants, who were largely conservative nationalists. It also became apparent that the elimination of institutionalised conflicts of interest had not led to the disappearance of the divergent interests themselves. Since parties and associations, and a functioning public opinion, no longer existed, clashes between rival interests were soon transferred to the institutions of the regime—government departments, and party offices and authorities. Furious jurisdictional wrangles now started; they remained a characteristic feature of the regime right up to its collapse in 1945. But it was not conflicts of competence or the number of institutions jealously guarding their prerogatives which distinguished the Nazi regime from a parliamentary state. Conflicts of competence and inter-departmental struggles are a widespread phenomenon in democracies as well. It was rather that there were no longer any institutionalised and legal routes for communication or forums for the pursuit of disagreements and the building of compromises, such as serve in democracies to prevent conflicts of interest from escalating. All these institutions had been swept away in the course of the 'national revolution' as symbols of discord and replaced by proclamations of the unity of the

*Volk*. This meant that there was no longer any regular mechanism for balancing interests against each other. The government's actions ceased to be reliable or predictable, and which groups gained the upper hand depended on fortuitous configurations of power in the state.

To a certain extent, this situation was counterbalanced by the prominent position of Hitler himself. He increasingly began to play the role of an actual sovereign. Soon a cabinet in the proper sense of the word no longer existed. Instead, the ministers had to reach agreement with each other on proposals which they laid before the Chancellor, who then made the decision by himself. From the outset, cabinet meetings were very rare, but, from 1938 onwards, they did not happen at all. The ministers had a duty of obedience towards the Führer and Chancellor. Anyone who wanted to predict which department would be victorious where there was a difference of opinion would need to know how Hitler thought, felt and reached his decisions. Access to the Führer thus became the decisive source of power, and instead of checking the persuasiveness of the arguments advanced or the numerical strength of the relevant interest group people tried to work out how the Führer would decide.

Hitler's outstanding position within the regime was also a consequence, a function of the yearning for unity and the desire to push differences of interest into the background. Accordingly, the decisions of the Führer now replaced the examination of arguments and the search for compromise, and all the endeavours of the ministers, party officials and civil servants were directed towards gaining his support.[18]

Hitler's power rested on three pillars: the loyalty of those who directed the economy, the administration and the army, the support of roughly half the population and the brute strength of his 'movement', in which the SA retained the outstanding role it had played in the 'seizure of power'. By the spring of 1934, the membership of this party army had expanded to almost four million, thanks to the inclusion of the former 'national defence associations', particularly the largest one, the 'Stahlhelm'. It was now larger than the NSDAP itself. In previous years, the SA had fought most of the street battles, and it saw itself as the core element of National Socialism. Its chief, Ernst Röhm, made his demands on that basis: the SA, he said, should be regarded as the 'cornerstone of the coming National Socialist state', and it was its task above all 'to complete the National Socialist revolution and create the National Socialist Reich',[19] 'side by side with the armed forces' as 'the third power factor of the new state', alongside, not trailing behind, the army and the police.[20] In actual fact, once the phase of the 'seizure of power' had passed, the SA had no real function. This was in stark contrast to the high expectations its members attached to their association. Leading figures of the economy and the administration feared 'brown

Bolshevism' and Röhm's repeated calls for the 'continuation of the revolution' strengthened their apprehensiveness. The top generals of the Reichswehr were even more concerned. Röhm's plan to make his 4 million–strong association into a kind of specifically National Socialist army, which would gradually replace the old Reichswehr, was regarded by the army leaders as a threat to their existence, and in view of the mere 100,000 men in the current army, they were right to be worried.[21]

On 17 June 1934, Hitler's most high-ranking conservative alliance partner, Vice-Chancellor von Papen, gave a speech criticising conditions under the Nazi dictatorship. With hitherto unprecedented severity, he denounced the 'selfishness, lack of character, insincerity, lack of chivalry and arrogance hidden beneath the cloak of the German revolution'. From Hitler's perspective this was tantamount to opening a 'second front' against the Nazi state. Papen's opposition seemed to be a serious threat to the new regime; but it also offered Hitler a chance to rebuff the claims to power of both the SA and his conservative critics, and to bind the traditional rulers of Germany more closely to the dictatorship. On 30 June, therefore, with the support of the Reichswehr, Hitler unleashed a carefully prepared 'action' by the SS against both the SA leadership and a number of conservative critics and former competitors, in which at least eighty-nine men were murdered, including Röhm, the former Chancellor of Germany von Schleicher, General State Commissioner von Kahr, Hitler's former rival during the failed putsch of November 1923, and Gregor Strasser, his adversary within the party.[22]

The so-called 'Röhm Action' was an important turning point in the history of the Nazi regime, because it marked the transition from the phase of the 'seizure of power', during which Hitler still had to share authority with the various groupings of the 'national movement', to the full National Socialist dictatorship, in which inconvenient obligations of this type no longer existed. The opposition within the party, in the shape of the SA, had now been dealt with in such a drastic fashion that, right to the end of the regime, no organised oppositional current again surfaced within the Nazi movement.

Moreover, the hurriedly invented attempts at a legal justification of the action demonstrated the regime's intention to act on a legal basis at least in appearance. This continued, as before, to be of great importance in persuading the elites and indeed considerable sections of the population to accept the new government. Thus the murders were sanctioned after the event by a 'Law on Measures for the Emergency Defence of the State' to which the cabinet gave its retrospective blessing on 3 July 1934, and the German Nationalist Minister of Justice Gürtner explained conveniently that the draft did not create new law, but simply confirmed existing law. Hitler was congratulated by the cabinet for his actions, and in a message to the army Reichswehr Minister Werner von Blomberg explicitly thanked him 'for the resolute and courageous action through which he had protected the German people from civil war', despite the fact that two of Hitler's victims had been German generals. President von Hindenburg also sent a congratulatory telegram. A few days later, Hitler gave a speech to the Reichstag, in which he openly and aggressively accepted responsibility for the murders: 'In this hour I was responsible for the fate of the German nation and thereby the German people's supreme judge.' The well-known nationalist constitutional lawyer, Carl Schmitt, who had previously been a close associate of von Papen but had now swiftly changed sides, seconded Hitler in an article in the *Deutsche Juristenzeitung*: 'The Führer is protecting the law against the worst abuses when at the moment of danger he directly creates law by virtue of his Führer quality as the supreme judge.'[23] This interpretation, by which the division of powers was abolished in the person of the Führer and all legal restrictions on his actions were removed, was also reflected a month after Hindenburg's death in the law uniting the offices of president and Chancellor. Hitler ordered a plebiscite to be held on 19 August so as to provide popular legitimacy for this measure. Nearly 90 per cent of the electorate voted in favour, although the election process was marred by violence and manipulation. It was asserted that this vote represented a confirmation by the people not just of the unification of the two highest offices of state and Hitler's appointment as 'Führer and Chancellor' but also of the murderous acts of 30 June.[24]

The murders of 30 June also changed the role of the Reichswehr in the power structure of the Nazi state. It was true that the competition from the SA had been eliminated and the monopoly position of the Reichswehr as the nation's bearer of arms was no longer disputed, but at what a price! By helping to prepare for the action of 30 June, which cost the lives of two generals, among other people, the Reichswehr made itself an accomplice of the Nazi leadership, surrendered its independence and irrevocably bound itself to Hitler. As early as 2 August 1934, the Reichswehr generals took the next logical step, and swore a new oath, to Hitler personally, in line with a proposal made by von Blomberg.

Finally, the 'Röhm Action' also signified the beginning of the rise of the SS to become one of the most powerful institutions of what was now called the 'Third Reich'. The SS was originally a small subsidiary organisation within the SA, established chiefly for Hitler's personal protection, but its '*Reichsführer*', the agricultural economist Heinrich Himmler, succeeded in constructing an independent and constantly growing power position for himself by gradually assuming control of the political police in the individual German states.

## Anti-Jewish Policies

Whenthe NSDAP came to power this was the first time an extreme anti-Semitic party had taken over the government of a European country. The party, like its Führer, had left no doubt in previous years that it regarded the small Jewish minority in Germany as responsible for a large part of the problems faced by Germany, particularly since the advent of industrial society and even more so since the First World War. According to the January 1933 issue of the *Nationalsozialistische Monatshefte:* 'Without eliminating Judaism and overcoming its delusional ideas' there will be 'no healing the German *Volk* . . . no liberation from the rule of inferiors, no deliverance from the phrases which serve as a cloak for anti-national tendencies.' The 'fight against Judaism' therefore signified an 'attack on the enemy's central headquarters'.[25] It is true that the NSDAP leaders toned down their extreme anti-Semitism somewhat between 1930 and 1933, in order to secure votes from outside the anti-Semitically inclined circles of the population, but the party's adherents firmly expected that sharp measures would be taken against the Jews after the seizure of power.

The Jews themselves also expected and feared this. Many of them, it is true, initially underestimated the significance of 30 January 1933, but the *Jüdische Rundschau* immediately recognised the implications of what had happened:

> As Jews we stand before the fact that a power hostile to us has taken over governmental authority in Germany. . . . National Socialism is an anti-Jewish movement, its programme is more anti-Semitic than that of any previous party, and it owes a large part of its agitational success to its unscrupulous Jew-baiting.[26]

Discriminatory measures against Jews did in fact increase everywhere in Germany directly after Hitler's appointment as Chancellor, and soon there were also violent assaults against individual Jews. These increased after the Reichstag fire. SA units attacked well-known left-wing leaders as well as Jews in Munich on 9 and 10 March 1933, on the instructions of the local Nazi party leadership. The business premises of Jewish firms were vandalised, and Jewish businessmen were mistreated. 'Before my very eyes' reported a witness

> an SA detachment whipped a man forward in front of them, in broad daylight. He had neither shoes, socks, coat, or trousers. Just a shirt and some torn underwear. Around his neck there hung a placard with the inscription: 'I am the Jew Siegel and I will never complain about the National Socialists again.'[27]

On the same day, Hitler issued a declaration expressing his disapproval of these outrages. Goering, however, who as Prussian prime minister bore direct responsibility, explicitly refused to provide police protection for Jewish businesses. At first, the regime did not follow a clear line in its anti-Jewish policy. The National Socialists were united in wanting to humiliate Jews, force them out of influential positions, seize hold of their property and induce them to leave Germany by violence and the threat of violence, but the long-term perspective remained unclear. In any case, though, whatever form this took it would be the most radical solution imaginable. A dynamic process in which different agencies strove to outbid each other set in right at the start. As was noted in reports sent from Germany to the exiled SPD leadership, 'state offices, party authorities, courts and the police compete to persecute and torment the defenceless Jews. If any official body shows any sign of exercising leniency, the party press immediately steps in to denounce negligent judges, officials and folk comrades (*Volksgenossen*), with *Der Stürmer* leading the charge.'[28] Where the Jews were concerned, once a given level of radicalism had been attained, it was now hardly possible to step back from it.

When reports of the measures oppressing the German Jews and depriving them of their rights started to appear more frequently, a reaction began among Germany's European neighbours and to a much greater extent in the USA. At the end of March 1933, a big protest meeting was held in New York against the anti-Jewish policy of the Hitler regime. This aroused worldwide attention, because exact descriptions were given there of numerous outrages against Jews, and an overall picture of their situation started to emerge. This was an inconvenient development for a German government which was struggling to secure international recognition. For the Nazi movement itself, on the other hand, it was a proof that world Jewry was working against Germany, and it was used as a pretext to proclaim a national anti-Jewish boycott, at the beginning of April. This offered party members and Nazi paramilitaries the opportunity to slake their thirst for anti-Jewish action. SA guards paraded in front of Jewish shops, department stores and medical and legal practices. Attacks on Jewish cultural establishments, anti-Jewish street demonstrations and violent assaults on Jews were reported from almost all the towns of Germany.

Even so, the actions of 1 April 1933 were not a complete success. 'The attitude of the public towards yesterday's extraordinary scenes was largely passive in nature' wrote the London *Times* two days later. 'Spontaneous and active anti-Semitism is not widespread among the mass of the people.'[29] Violent attacks on Jews and Jewish institutions were largely greeted with disapproval by the non-Jewish population. The attitude to official and apparently legal anti-Jewish actions was different, however. There were very few objections made to these, even if they threatened the economic existence of the Jews.

The Jews were inundated by a flood of discriminatory decrees and special legal regulations during the first weeks and months after the Nazi takeover. On 7 April 1933 the law for the 'Restoration of a Professional Civil Service' provided for the immediate and compulsory retirement of politically obnoxious officials, particularly Jewish ones. In the universities the authorities began to force out Jewish scholars and scientists. The same fate was suffered by Jewish judges, prosecutors and solicitors, who were either subjected to restrictions or completely prohibited from practising their profession. On 25 April, the proportion of new admissions of Jews to the schools and universities was limited to 1.5 per cent; all the rest must be 'of German blood'. On 21 May, Jews were excluded from military service. The web of discriminatory measures was drawn ever tighter. It was gradually extended to cover all areas of activity and life, and by the start of the war more than 1,400 specifically anti-Jewish decrees had been issued.[30]

Moreover, local municipalities and individual German states often developed their own anti-Jewish initiatives. Without any legal foundation, Jews were prohibited from entering hotels or restaurants, Jewish shops were simply closed and Jewish businesses were boycotted. There were harsh interventions into fundamental rights alongside petty provisions which appeared ridiculous, but covered matters now also subject to strict regulation. Civil servants and administrators of associations seemed to be competing to outdo each other in zealotry, ingenuity and malice. Thus, as early as March 1933, the city of Cologne forbade Jews the use of its sports facilities. At the beginning of April, the German Boxing Association barred Jews from membership. On 19 April, the authorities in the state of Baden forbade the use of the Yiddish language in cattle markets. On 24 May, the German Gymnastic Association, followed gradually by almost all other clubs and associations, demanded that its members submit proof of Aryan descent (*Ariernachweis*) for all four grandparents. The word 'Aryan' (meaning German and not Jewish) now began to be used increasingly in official ordinances. On 17 September 1933, the Prussian authorities restricted the right to organise private lotteries to Aryan entrepreneurs. Only 'Aryan press illustrators' were allowed to make photographic slides. Jews were prohibited from acting as jockeys or gentleman riders. In July 1934, in Bad Kissingen, Jews were forbidden to use the municipal swimming baths, and in Saxony they were no longer recognised as dental technicians.[31]

Central government offices often reacted to far-reaching ordinances issued at the local or regional level by dissociating themselves from them or mitigating their application. But a few weeks later, further government decrees appeared, legalising what was already being practised at the local level. This interaction between grass-roots radicalisation, subsequent mitigation by party or government offices and ultimate legalisation was characteristic of the regime's Jewish policy and played an important part in increasing its severity, but also in easing its acceptance. For, in comparison with noisy and mostly violent street actions, an official decree appeared as a procedure which was at least legal, and to that extent acceptable, even if it contained regulations which would have been unthinkable a few weeks earlier.

The regime's leading figures did not possess an overall plan for their policy towards Jews, but it would also be wrong to assume that the individual steps they took were purely spontaneous and that a gradual radicalisation took place. 'The legal measures taken by the government until now' wrote Günther Gercke, a 'Racial Research Specialist in the Ministry of the Interior', in May 1933,

> represent a cleansing operation. . . . The whole of the *Volk* thereby gains enlightenment on the Jewish question, it learns to understand that the community of the *Volk* is a community of blood, it grasps the racial idea for the first time . . . . All proposals which are aimed at securing a lasting situation, a lasting regulation, for the Jews are not solutions to the Jewish question, because they do not separate the Jews from Germany. And that is what is essential . . . . We must build our state without the Jews. They can only remain here as stateless aliens and they can never receive a permanent legal position. Only in this way will we be able to compel Ahasver to take up his staff for the last time.[32]

The aim of these acts of discrimination and violence was therefore to drive the Jews out of Germany, and it was a strategy which proved effective. By the end of 1933, 37,000 Jews had left, followed in the next two years by 23,000 and 21,000 respectively. These annual amounts remained roughly static in the first few years of the Nazi regime. By the end of 1937, a total of 125,000 Jews had emigrated, amounting therefore to roughly a quarter of the total Jewish population.[33] The Zionist organisations, whose objective was to build a Jewish state in Palestine, were given support in order to accelerate the process of emigration. The 'German Jewish' organisations, on the other hand, which wanted to strengthen Jewish assimilation, were persecuted.

At the same time, outrages against the Jews in particular towns and rural districts repeatedly served as a relief valve for energetic Nazi militiamen, and in the spring of 1935 assaults of this kind again increased considerably. There were large-scale actions against Jewish shops on the Kurfürstendamm in Berlin, in which members of the Hitler Youth played a prominent part. To be sure, criticisms of these disorders from business associations increased in proportion to the harmful effects they had on their economic interests.[34]

The Gestapo, led by Reinhard Heydrich, and the SD, the security service of the SS, also led by Heydrich, were responsible for domestic political intelligence. These organisations now worked out a method by which all Jews could be induced to emigrate as quickly as possible while at the same time the economic interests of the Reich were protected. 'The Jewish question' according to a memorandum dated 9 September 1935, 'should not be solved by using force, by mistreating individuals, by damaging personal property or other isolated actions.' Instead 'the principle of equal treatment should be abandoned in the sphere of the private economy' so that 'the economic dominance the Jews have exercised until now can be broken'. The immigration of Jews into the cities would have to be prevented, mixed marriages between Germans and Jews forbidden, and sexual relations between Germans and Jews made a punishable offence. In addition to this, the identification documents of Jews would have to be provided with a special distinguishing mark. But street actions against the Jews were also entirely to be welcomed: 'The most effective means of removing a feeling of security from the Jews is the anger of the *Volk,* which breaks out in riots' is how a report from the Jewish Department of the SD put it at the end of 1936. 'Although this method is illegal, it has had a lasting impact, as the Kurfürstendamm riot demonstrated.'[35]

The Nuremberg Laws, promulgated very hastily in September 1935 on Hitler's initiative, were a response to this pressure. A new 'Law on Reich Citizenship' ended the equal citizenship previously enjoyed by German Jews. Henceforth, only people of 'German blood' could be 'citizens of the Reich'. The 'Law for the Protection of German Blood and German Honour' made marriages between Jews and Germans, as well as sexual relations between unmarried Jews and non-Jews, punishable offences. On the basis of this law, in the following months and years, Jewish men were persecuted and condemned to hard labour all over Germany for actual or alleged relations with 'Aryan' women, a procedure frequently combined with the public denunciation of one or both participants. Precisely who counted as Jewish and who did not remained unclear even after this law, however. The race researchers asserted that the definition of a Jew should be based on objective criteria, based on the proportion of Jewish blood in a given individual, but no actual method of establishing this existed. It was therefore laid down that someone who had at least three Jewish grandparents (as defined on a religious basis) should count as a Jew by race.

Someone who had two Jewish grandparents counted henceforth as a '*Mischling*', or person of mixed Jewish blood. This entirely new category affected roughly 150,000 people, who now also suffered discrimination. What was to happen to this group of people remained unclear up to the end of the Nazi dictatorship. Roughly 50,000 marriages between Jews and non-Jewish Germans now counted as 'mixed marriages' and even the partners in these unions had no clear idea of how the authorities proposed to treat them. Many of them got divorced, because they could not stand the pressure. If they remained together, the non-Jewish partner suffered professional and personal disadvantages. After 1941, marriage with an 'Aryan' saved the lives of spouses who were Jewish, because they were exempted from deportation. But none of them could have known or expected this in advance.[36]

Two and a half years after the National Socialists took power, therefore, the German Jews had been relegated to the position of a population group with inferior legal rights. These measures, and still more far-reaching ones announced for the future, were aimed at reversing the emancipation of the Jews which had taken place a hundred years earlier, at depriving them of opportunities for an economic existence and at driving them out of Germany completely within a very short space of time. Only a few years before, nobody outside the narrow circle of *völkisch* activists would have been able to imagine this turn of events.

The constant outrages and deeds of violence by the Nazi paramilitaries, seconded openly and frequently by units of the Hitler Youth, could still be regarded as the excesses of a minority of political fanatics, but the Nuremberg Laws established racial anti-Semitism as the foundation of the state's administrative activity, and thus legalised the break made by the Nazis with the fundamental principles of equality before the law and human rights. For the Jews themselves, these laws signified not only ever-increasing discrimination, but also almost total isolation. 'In relation to social life' noted the Hamburg SD with satisfaction at the end of 1937 'one is already justified in saying that the Jews are in an invisible ghetto'. 'One no longer feels oneself to be part of the German people', explained a German Jew to investigators who reported back to the exiled SPD, adding: 'One feels like a spiritual exile from one's own country.'

And yet the mood of many Jews fluctuated greatly during those years. 'All of a sudden it seems as if some measure by the regime has destroyed all hope', observed the Hamburg SD, 'but then people believe they can perceive signs that the official persecution of the Jews will not be carried any further. Many Jews do not have the courage to brace themselves to take the decisive step and burn all their bridges.'[37] This was particularly true of the elderly and the less well-off. By the summer of 1941, approximately 270,000 Jews had left Germany. But an equal number remained within the country, until emigration was forbidden and deportations to the death camps began.

The economic aspects of hostility to the Jews had already been prominent since the coming of modern anti-Semitism. To ascribe the contradictions and aporias of modern capitalism to the activities of a small group, which had proved particularly successful in industry, trade, banking and the free professions and appeared to possess considerable influence over market forces through secret channels, was so seductively simple an explanation of the otherwise inexplicable fluctuations of the economic conjuncture and the capital markets that it was accepted even by people who did not regard themselves as in any sense anti-Semitic. The idea of secret Jewish influence had gained strength in the crisis years of the Weimar Republic, first during the inflation of 1923 and then again after 1929 and the coming of the world economic crisis.

It was therefore unsurprising that the fury of the anti-Semites was directed above all against Jewish shops and businesses. But from the very beginning, the economic squeeze on the Jews was also associated with corruption, theft and self-enrichment. In this context it was mostly party functionaries, but often also colleagues or competitors of Jewish shopowners or artisans who endeavoured by denunciation and violence to profit from their economic dispossession. By the end of 1935, roughly a quarter of all Jewish enterprises had already been liquidated, or transferred to non-Jewish owners, in this way, before the regime itself started to issue the appropriate decrees to bring Jewish businesses into 'Aryan' hands, and to divert private wealth and the proceeds of sales of Jewish property into its coffers. A contribution of 25 per cent was levied on the assets of emigrants. This was the '*Reichsfluchtsteuer*' (Reich Flight Tax), and it reached such proportions that in 1938 the Exchequer received more income from the Flight Tax than from the Income Tax. In addition to this, those wishing to emigrate and transfer their capital had to face a deduction of 20 per cent at first, which was increased to 68 per cent, then a year later to 81 per cent, and finally set at 96 per cent in 1939.[38]

The authorities were more cautious, however, in their treatment of the big Jewish businesses, especially because the closure of such enterprises would have involved the loss of many jobs. It was only after 1936, when the economic situation had begun to improve noticeably, that this restraint ceased to operate. Now the big banks and insurance companies also involved themselves in the 'De-Judaization of the German economy'. All large-scale enterprises were now taken away relatively quickly from their Jewish owners. The Jewish directors of banks, insurance companies and industrial firms were gradually dismissed. A veritable 'Aryanisation industry' grew up, in which trustees, 'emigration agents', brokers and solicitors organised the expropriation of Jewish enterprises, making big profits out of this activity. There were roughly 100,000 Jewish firms in 1933, and by the summer of 1938 70,000 of them had been 'Aryanised' or shut down. The historian Frank Bajohr has examined how the process worked in Hamburg, and he has shown that after 1938 '"Aryanisation" became a "competition in self-enrichment" in which Nazi party members in particular were able to gain possession of lucrative undertakings. In this phase, the character of "Aryanisation" was determined by corruption and nepotism.'[39]

The spoliation of the German Jews after 1933 was one of the biggest acts of expropriation in German history, and it has much in common with other property revolutions in the twentieth century. Admittedly, in the Soviet Union after 1917 and the countries of the Eastern Bloc after 1945 the capitalist system as a whole was destroyed. In Germany, on the other hand, a part of the economy defined by racial criteria was cut out, while the economy as a whole was certainly constricted and regimented by government instructions, but still retained its private character. Hence the policy of robbing the Jews did not just break the law; it was an infringement of the principles of the capitalist property system and commercial credibility. But, because of the opportunity to get richer, to remove competitors and to take over big and to some extent world famous firms, the beneficiaries disregarded all commercial principles, especially as the robberies, committed by the state's economic and financial authorities themselves, were concealed by a veil of legitimacy, albeit an extremely threadbare one. Thus, Hitler announced in August 1936 in his Memorandum on the Four Year Plan that 'Jewry as a whole' must be made responsible for 'all the damage inflicted on the German economy and thereby on the German *Volk* by individual exemplars of this criminality.' The policy of 'de-Judaizing the German economy' was thus declared to be a defensive measure, a way of exacting 'compensation', in other words an attempt by the Germans to call to account those who were allegedly responsible for the past crises and catastrophes suffered by the German economy.[40]

The persecution of the Jews, which was reported in great detail in the major newspapers of the USA, Britain and France, was greeted with remarkable indifference in Germany itself until 1938. One reason for this was the repressive apparatus of the regime, which had been greatly extended in the meantime. Nobody was prepared to enter into an argument with the Gestapo or the activists of the Nazi Party over their actions against a group which most Germans regarded with reserve and many with dislike. The leaders of the SPD in exile, for example, who were far from being anti-Semitic, wrote in their January 1936 report that workers who were inclined towards socialism were certainly 'resolutely opposed to the outrages'. But many of them felt it was right 'that the rule of the Jews should be broken once and for all, and that the Jews should be assigned a particular field for their activity.' Most of the workers 'did not agree with the harsh methods . . . but their view was: "It doesn't hurt most of the Jews".' The attitude of the Catholics was similar. The Archbishop of Munich, Cardinal Faulhaber, wrote to a priest who had found the persecution of the Jews disturbing that what the Nazis had done was certainly unchristian, but there really were other problems to consider: 'For the church authorities, there are much more important current problems . . ., especially as we can assume, and we have already experienced this, that the Jews are capable of helping themselves.'[41]

Another reason why the persecution of the Jews did not occupy the centre of attention was that, during those years, as major events came thick and fast, an atmosphere of urgency and permanent mobilisation developed. This atmosphere was constantly stoked by the regime through ostentatious pieces of political theatre, and it served to obscure the discrimination, persecution and loss of rights suffered by political opponents and Jews. In the light of the regime's success in dealing with the economy and reducing unemployment, alongside its foreign policy achievements, these events were considered as collateral damage, regrettable but unavoidable. 'Most revolutions are accompanied by a reign of terror', wrote the British ambassador in Berlin to the Foreign Secretary in London. In comparison, the German revolution had taken place 'on the whole with leniency, and though there is no doubt that many innocent men have been murdered, incarcerated or maltreated, and that Germany's good name as a civilised country has suffered severely in foreign countries, the transition might have been much more sanguinary.'[42]

## Transforming the Function of Terror

Control of the political police was one of the essential prerequisites for the rapid and well-nigh complete elimination of all opposition forces in the country. The head of the SS, Heinrich Himmler, succeeded within a short time in converting the separate political police forces of the individual states, among them the 'Gestapo', which was the Prussian political police force, into a single unified and tightly organised apparatus of oppression. The SS was distinguished from the other party institutions and above all from the SA by its elite image and by its strong focus on racialist biological ideals and technocratic efficiency. When Himmler was entrusted with the construction of a system of concentration camps independent of government control for the persecution of the opponents of the Nazi state, the SS finally became a new power centre within the regime, and its name henceforth came to symbolise the Nazi terror.

The political police force was later combined with the SD, or Security Service, a subordinate organisation of the SS, which had originally been set up as an intelligence service. The head of the SD, Reinhard Heydrich, was in charge of both institutions. This ensured that the persecution of the regime's opponents would follow the maxims and the political and ideological aims of the National Socialists. At the same time, the boundaries between state institutions and political organisations became blurred. It is true that the existing state administration and the general police force, of which Himmler became the head in 1936, continued to be subject to constitutional principles; this was intended to strengthen the confidence of the public in the legality of the police's actions. But this rule did not apply to the political police force. This was independent of legal control and its measures drew their legitimacy directly from the supreme power of the Führer.[43]

The most important instrument used by this very specific combination of police authority and ideological sect for the suppression of the regime's opponents was the concentration camp (*Konzentrationslager*, KZ), and the names of the first 'KZs', the biggest of which by far was Dachau, quickly acquired a terrifying notoriety.

Thus, just a few years after the start of Nazi rule the 'camp' had already become a customary phenomenon of everyday life, and the term was not restricted to places for the punishment of opponents of the regime. There were already tens of thousands of young men in the camps for unemployed workers run by the National Labour Service, and there were also camps for people who worked on the autobahns, and later on the so-called 'West Wall' erected on the French border. The camps reflected the notion that the adversities and challenges of modern life could best be overcome with military organisation, in other words, by militarising both work and life. Even refresher courses for students, doctors and lawyers were now organised 'in camps', schoolchildren went to holiday camps in summer, and sportsmen and women went into sport camps. The camp system was always intended to express the provisional, collective and military element which characterised the notion of a 'camp'. Daily life in these places was everywhere dominated by words such as: camp organisation, camp seniority, camp overseer, strict regime, roll call, and *Essenfassen* (chow down). These words linked camp life with an ideology which emphasised the military, natural, unspoiled, collective and healthy element, as opposed to the individualistic conveniences offered by civilian life in the modern world.[44]

This background is of some significance for the understanding and perception of the concentration camps. The notion of a 'camp' not only had a certain resonance of the provisional and the unofficial, which clearly distanced it from the traditional Prussian prison, but it also had an undertone of improvement and education, which was reflected, for example, in the words '*Arbeit macht frei*' (Work Makes You Free) inscribed on the camp entry gates. From the start, however, those words turned out to be merely camouflage. Reports of murder, torture and terror in the concentration camps soon made them synonymous with Nazi terror as a whole.

The first phase of the dictatorship, until the early summer of 1934, saw the emergence everywhere in Germany of camps of various sizes, or other prison-like establishments, in which the political opponents of the National Socialists were confined.[45] At first, the political opponents of Nazism were by far the majority of the people forced into concentration camps, the communists above all, but also Social Democrats, trade unionists or even government officials who had played a prominent part in prosecuting National Socialists before 1933. The camps also held priests, writers, journalists and others whom the Nazis found objectionable for one reason or another.

The orgy of violence which accompanied the suppression of the National Socialists' opponents during this phase came as a resounding shock to both German and international public opinion, because such excessive and brutal proceedings in a civilised country like Germany had previously been regarded as inconceivable. Germany was still measured by democratic criteria, and in this context the new concentration camps represented something unprecedented, although the violence which came to light here was not particularly different from developments in other contemporary dictatorships (such as Italy under Mussolini, or Greece under Metaxas, not to mention the Soviet Union under Stalin).

In 1936, the political police were amalgamated with the criminal police to form the 'security police'. This increased the level of persecution. The boundary between criminal and political offences became porous, and political or criminal wrongdoing was increasingly seen as conditioned by hereditary or racial factors. The socio-biological paradigm that lay behind these notions was not, of course, a specifically Nazi invention. It had already existed long before 1933, with broad support within the relevant academic professions. But it had also met with considerable criticism and opposition. Both its scientific seriousness and its ethical implications were impugned. Attempts to apply the theory in practical terms had therefore largely been excluded before 1933. Even plans to allow voluntary sterilisation for eugenic reasons never got beyond the stage of pre-parliamentary discussion, unlike in some other Western countries.[46]

This equilibrium between supporters and opponents of eugenics was overturned by the Nazi seizure of power. Advocates of racist thinking were now promoted to decision-making positions, while their critics were either muzzled or fell silent voluntarily. At the same time, what had previously only been contemplated was now put into practice, a practice which underwent continuous radicalisation. 'Racial policy' and the 'social question' now increasingly coalesced. Social problems, it seemed, could be solved by eliminating everyone who was regarded as having caused those problems. 'Vagrants', 'drinkers', 'prostitutes', 'the subnormal', 'the work-shy', 'homosexuals', and 'habitual criminals' were persecuted, because their behaviour deviated from what was felt to be normal and because they were regarded as harmful to the 'folk community' for two reasons: firstly, because they damaged the community and were a burden to it, and secondly, because their harmful behaviour was seen as innate, inherited, and capable of being passed on to the next generation. The same view was taken of those who were 'mentally ill', a concept which was quickly given broader application.

The head of the NSDAP's Office for Racial Policy, Dr Walter Groß, who was born in 1904, was one of the leading Nazi racial theorists. In 1934 he explained the connection between social and racial factors in a programmatic statement of the fundamental position adopted by the new state on racial questions. Two things had destroyed races in the past, and threatened to do the same to the German *Volk* today: the 'qualitative deterioration of the inheritable worth of a *Volk*', and its 'mixture with alien races'. 'Qualitative deterioration' could only be stopped by the restoration of 'that brutal and ruthless, but utterly just, and, if you like, divine, natural order, which consists in the constantly repeated eradication of everything that does not at least reach a good average level.'[47]

Academics in various disciplines saw that there was an opportunity here to get rid of 'hopeless cases' and concentrate primarily on those people whose deviations from the norm appeared to be correctable. The rapid reduction in the resources available for social security caused by the world economic crisis gave much encouragement to these attitudes. The first step was taken already in the early summer of 1933 with the 'Law for the Prevention of Hereditarily Diseased Offspring'. This law provided for the sterilisation of individuals who suffered from 'hereditary feeble-mindedness'. This condition was understood to include 'every degree of feeble-mindedness which can be diagnosed as clearly abnormal in the medical sense.' By 1945, more than 400,000 people had been sterilised on this basis. The procedure also resulted in the death of 5,500 women and 600 men.[48]

A law against 'dangerous habitual criminals' which provided for 'measures for their protection and cure' was also adopted, after the abandonment of the plan originally entertained of including habitual criminals in the 'Law for the Prevention of Hereditarily Diseased Offspring'. It was true, said the official commentary, that in principle there could be 'no doubt that criminal tendencies are also hereditary', but the specialists in racial hygiene and criminal biology had not yet been able to arrive at a definitive and reliable definition of individuals who could be regarded as having an inherited predisposition towards criminality.[49]

The range of those affected by these provisions was considerably extended by adding people 'with a predisposition' towards criminality to the category of criminal offenders. The introduction of the concept of the 'asocial' individual was of particular significance in this context. Since 1934, numerous institutes and scientific departments had been working to determine what constituted 'asociality'. Criminal biologists and 'gypsy researchers' played an important role here, because 'gypsies' lay at the heart of the attempts being made to prove a causal link between deviant social behaviour, heredity and ethnic affiliation.

In Germany, as in most other European countries, the groups described as 'gypsies' had been regarded since the late eighteenth century as backward and defective creatures whose behaviour could, and must, be altered by state action, education and punishment. Modern racism, on the other hand, regarded the 'gypsies' as hereditarily inferior creatures. They were 'primitive people without history or civilisation', declared the German neurologist and psychiatrist Robert Ritter. He laid the intellectual basis for National Socialist policy towards the Roma, and he later exerted considerable practical influence on it. In his opinion, 'gypsies' could not be changed by education. They could only be 'rendered harmless'. Previous attempts by police and social administrators 'to solve the gypsy problem' had failed, and 'new paths' must therefore be taken 'in full awareness of their racial characteristics'.[50]

In the spring of 1937, Ritter's research institute began to investigate the 'gypsies' and systematically to collect data on them. In pursuing this project, he collaborated closely with the Reich Criminal Police Office (*Reichskriminalpolizeiamt*, RKPA), which was involved not only in 'liquidating criminality' but also, in particular, in 'fighting against crime with preventive measures', directed not least against the Roma and the Sinti. Beginning in 1938, therefore, more than 2,000 German and Austrian 'gypsies', stigmatised as 'asocial', were placed in the concentration camps of the Reich. Anyone who did not pursue a wage-earning occupation counted as 'asocial'.

Thus, 'asociality' became a collective term for all modes of living that looked unusual, and were felt to be offensive or 'unnatural', but could not be placed in a definite legal category. 'Asocial' behaviour was seen as the expression of an individual predisposition which was in the majority of cases inherited and therefore incapable of improvement.

The organisational expression of this approach was the above-mentioned combination of the criminal police and the political police into a single unit, the security police, headed by Heydrich, and the establishment of new concentration camps in Sachsenhausen and Buchenwald. This went hand in hand with a remarkable widening of the definition of police responsibilities. The police force became a 'doctor operating on the German nation', in other words, 'an institution which carefully supervises the political state of health of the German nation, recognises any symptom of sickness in good time, establishes the sources of damage—whether they have arisen through internal disintegration or through poison administered intentionally from outside—and removes them by all appropriate means.'[51]

The gigantic dimensions of the new camps already indicated the sheer size of the population that was destined for incarceration, and how far-reaching the coming war on 'asociality' was expected to be. In the subsequent raids and 'actions' of the criminal police, the rubric 'asocial' incorporated vagabonds, beggars, gypsies, pimps and all such persons as have 'received repeated convictions for resisting arrest, wounding, fighting, trespassing and the like, and have shown thereby that they do not wish to conform to the orderly society of the folk community'. This signified a shift in the focus of activity of the National Socialist security authorities from fighting against political opponents to combating undesirable social and 'socio-biological' elements. After 1937–8, the proportion of people locked up for political opposition to National Socialism declined, and the number of people imprisoned for 'socio-biological' reasons increased. On 1 July 1938, only 21 per cent of the 7,723 prisoners in Buchenwald were registered as 'political prisoners', with 59.3 per cent classified as 'unwilling to work for the Reich', 13.8 per cent counted as 'habitual criminals', and 5.1 per cent described as 'bible students' (*Bibelforscher*), which was the usual name for Jehovah's Witnesses. On the eve of the Second World War there were over 21,000 concentration camp inmates, roughly a third of them 'politicals'.[52]

In the late 1930s, the concentration camp gradually came to characterise Nazi rule. For one thing, it was the physical expression of an extralegal punishment system which was distinguished from the traditional legal norms which applied to the life of the citizen. With its help, actual and potential opponents of National Socialism could be isolated, suppressed and humiliated. But, in proportion as the regime became more firmly established and perceptible resistance died out, this function of the concentration camp became less significant.

At that point, the camp's second function came to the forefront: as a place of socio-biological exclusion, through which the separation between the worthwhile and the worthless elements of the population could be accomplished. This change of function represented a quantitatively and qualitatively new and historically unprecedented phenomenon, informed by a vision of society from which conflict had been removed, because the carriers of a hereditary predisposition to deviant behaviour, felt to be socially 'harmful', had been weeded out, prevented from reproducing, and finally 'eliminated'.

Within three years of the 'seizure of power', therefore, the Nazi system of repression had undergone a drastic change, largely unperceived by the general German population: its main purpose was no longer the pursuit of political opponents but the exclusion from the German 'Community of the Volk' of elements that were alien to it.

## The Arms-Related Boom and the 'Battle for Labour'

In almost all the industrialised countries, the world economic crisis had led to the breakdown of the nation's economy. The steep fall in share prices had destroyed an immense amount of wealth, and the number of business bankruptcies had risen tremendously. Governments had failed to meet the task of lessening the suffering of their populations, which were being tormented by unemployment and poverty.

Liberalism in economic policy and in particular as regards the world economic system had been severely discredited by the collapse of economies based on industrial capitalism. The main targets of criticism were the worldwide interdependence of commercial and financial relationships, the dependence of the European economies on the USA and the convertibility of currencies. Only through these factors, it was said, had the crisis been able to spread to such an extent. Plans for the isolation of national markets from the international economic system now began to win support. Large economic areas, following the model of the British Empire or the hegemony exercised by the USA over the American continent, seemed to be a more effective guarantee of stable economic growth in the industrial countries than the liberal principles of the world market.

The countries with the strongest economies therefore started to move towards economic isolation. In Germany, the Brüning government abolished the convertibility of the Reichsmark (RM) in July 1931 and introduced a quota system for foreign currency. The British government adopted similar measures in the same year, the French government in 1936. The United States also followed an autarchic policy for the national economy, by disentangling it from the world market with a series of measures which included the abandonment of the gold standard and the devaluation of the dollar in the spring of 1933, the introduction of protective tariffs and foreign exchange controls, and the sale of goods at dumping prices.

But it was not just in international trading relations that the world economic crisis seemed to have refuted the liberal, anti-statist version of the capitalist economic system. The same applied in the domestic sphere. The market was obviously not in a position to find its own way out of the catastrophic economic situation in the industrialised countries. The conviction that the state alone could do this gradually won the upper hand. The anti-democratic forces which were gaining ground everywhere in Europe were without exception statist and anti-liberal in inclination. The forces of liberalism had lost influence, and they almost sank into political insignificance in Germany as they did in France, Austria, and the Scandinavian countries as well as in the countries of East Central and Southern Europe, which were now largely ruled by right-wing and authoritarian regimes.[53]

More than a third of the German population, numbering almost 20 million people, lived in poverty in the autumn of 1932, existing on state support. With its emergency decree of December 1931 'to safeguard the economy and the finances and to protect internal peace' the Brüning government had already got rid of free collective bargaining and market-based price formation. Now prices and wages could be regulated by the state. The first state job creation programme followed, in May 1932. Papen issued another programme in August

1932, and Schleicher issued a third one in December. The National Socialists copied these efforts, giving their 'Immediate Economic Programme' a central role in the electoral contests of 1932. The presidential cabinets had previously invested a few hundred million RM in job creation, but the National Socialists proposed to multiply this figure many times over, and in fact the job creation programme implemented by the Hitler government after June 1933 involved the expenditure of more than 5 billion RM. Over the next three years, approximately 3.5 billion RM were spent, at first mainly on the repair and improvement of buildings, then after autumn 1933 on national autobahns, for which the plans had already been made in the 1920s. In this connection, as the sociologist Rudolf Heberle noted in 1934, the new regime was very successful in presenting its measures as 'completely new, original National Socialist schemes, even when the plans for them were already lying in the desk drawers of the Brüning government'.[54]

There is no doubt that the job creation measures contributed to the reduction of unemployment during this period of gradual improvement in economic conditions, which started at the beginning of 1933. But the impact of the propagandistic presentation of the programme was probably greater, as it presented the universal impression that a fresh start was being made, that sleeves were being rolled up and that vigorous efforts were being made to overcome the economic crisis. The feeling of verve and dynamism this campaign generated was augmented by the peculiar mixture of military and agricultural messages conveyed by the images of columns of marching of workers carrying their shovels like weapons; though in fact, the overwhelming majority of the unemployed sought and found their jobs in industry, not agriculture. It was not just the situation of the economy, but the popular mood, that improved, and the main reason for this was the decision of the new regime not to allow any further fall in wages, which had already suffered a tremendous decline during the crisis, falling by more than 30 per cent since 1929.

The number of unemployed workers in Germany had already begun to fall in spring 1933, and by summer this decline was proceeding much more quickly: the number fell from almost 6 million in January 1933 to 3.8 million a year later. The average annual figure for 1933 was 4.8 million, and by 1934 this was already down to 2.7 million. Nothing strengthened the stability of the Hitler regime in the pre-war years as much as this rapid reduction in the number of people out of work. The unemployment rate had become the decisive indicator of the state of the economy, and because the crisis evolved at different speeds in each industrialised country, and the proportion of people unemployed had in fact fallen more slowly in France, Great Britain and particularly in the United States than it had in Germany, the rapid recovery of the German economy was felt to have been caused largely by domestic economic developments, or at least it was wholeheartedly ascribed to the economic policy of the Hitler government.[55]

Such a view was not completely mistaken, although since 1934 at the latest it was not the columns of workers engaged in building roads or draining the marshes who were responsible for this rapid transformation, but the rearmament programme, which was historically unprecedented in its size and the speed with which it was executed. In one of the first cabinet meetings he held, on 8 February 1933, Hitler left nobody in any doubt that rearmament was the most important goal, and that job creation too had the main purpose of making Germany 'capable of bearing arms again'. During discussions over the budget, he rejected the demands of the individual ministries, and stressed that 'any publicly promoted job creation measure must be judged by asking whether it is necessary from the standpoint of making the Germans an arms-bearing people again. This idea must always and everywhere have precedence.' The supreme principle must be: 'Everything for the armed forces (*Wehrmacht*). Germany's position in the world will be decisively determined by the condition of Germany's armed forces. The position of the German economy in the world also depends on this.'[56]

A few days earlier, in his speech of 3 February to the army and navy leaders, referred to earlier, Hitler had explained his objectives even more forcefully. A reorientation of economic policy towards increasing exports and, thereby, a return to the world market, was no longer possible, he said, if only because other countries would not allow it. Only when Germany again had a strong army and could use it to assert its political influence would it be possible to think again about 'conquering new export possibilities'. A better option, though, was 'the conquest of new living space (*Lebensraum*) in the East, and its ruthless Germanisation'. If this was done, Hitler calculated, they would not need to renew their links with the world market. But all that was a matter for the future. What was certain was that 'the present economic conditions can only be changed by using political power and through struggle.'[57]

From 1934 onwards, German rearmament was pursued on a broad scale and at tremendous speed. The government planned to increase the size of the army to 300,000 men. It also started to build up an air force (*Luftwaffe*). In May 1933 a special ministry was set up for this purpose under the direction of Hermann Goering. It was also decided in 1934 that the navy would be expanded significantly beyond the limits fixed by the Versailles Treaty. National expenditure for the armed forces, including payments not publicly disclosed, rose exponentially, from 1.9 billion RM in 1933 to 4.1 billion RM a year later, and this rapid growth continued in subsequent years: by 1936 the sum had reached 10.3 billion, in 1937 it was 11.0 billion and in 1938, finally, it was 17.2 billion. The proportion of public expenditure invested in the armed forces shot up from 4 per cent in 1933 to 18 per cent in 1934, and by 1938 it had reached 50 per cent. Government spending as an overall amount rose by 70 per cent between 1933 and 1935, and more than half of this increase was accounted for by the armed forces. Private consumption and private investment remained at a considerably lower level than in the period before the crisis (it was lower by 7 per cent and 22 per cent, respectively). By 1938 the share of state expenditure in the national income had risen to 35 per cent (as against 30 per cent in France, 23.8 per cent in Britain and 10.7 per cent in the USA) and 74 per cent of this expenditure was on armaments. In other words, in 1938 more than a quarter of Germany's total national income was spent on armaments. 'A reallocation of total national production on this scale in such a short space of time', concludes the economic historian Adam Tooze, 'had never before been seen in any capitalist state in peacetime.'[58]

The explosive surge of armaments expenditure set off a similarly explosive surge in economic growth. Unemployment fell from 10.3 per cent in 1935 to 1.9 per cent in 1938. A shortage of labour was reported in some branches of the economy as early as 1936, and from 1937 this applied to almost every area. The idea of an 'economic miracle' emerged, which was the main factor behind the growing popularity of the regime in general, and Hitler in particular.[59]

In view of the tremendous increase in state expenditure, private investment and private consumption inevitably lagged behind. Issues of this kind receded into the background at first, owing to the politically decisive comparison that was made with the utterly hopeless situation before 1933. Even so, it was essential to find a way of financing the post-1933 explosion of state expenditure. Tax increases, the tried and tested method, were unpopular and, in any case, they would not suffice to cover the expenditure by themselves. Moreover, they would have attracted much undesired attention to German rearmament, both at home and abroad. Hjalmar Schacht, who was both president of the Reichsbank and Minister of Economics, was the man who made the decisions on economic policy during the early phase of Nazi rule. He discovered another way of financing rearmament which was as unobtrusive as it was effective: the armaments industry sent its invoices to a dummy company, which was set up by four big firms, and which was given the name *Metallurgische Forschungsgesellschaft* [Society for Engineering Research], or 'Mefo' for short. The 'Mefo' bills were in turn discounted by the Reichsbank.

This indirect way of financing arms expenditure had two advantages. It prevented the extent of Germany's rearmament from quickly becoming known abroad, because the Mefo bills were not mentioned in the state's instructions to the armaments firms. It also concealed the fact that the Nazi state was financing its armaments policy by loading an enormous amount of debt onto the state budget: in 1938 only slightly over half the state's expenditure of 30 billion RM was covered by tax receipts. Roughly a third of the 62 billion RM spent on rearmament between 1933 and the beginning of the war was financed by open or concealed credit. The hope that had originally been entertained that debts incurred while kick-starting the economy could be cancelled out by a big flow of tax receipts once the economy was booming proved to be illusory. Despite this, the concentration on rearmament was intensified after 1936. The Nazi leadership considered that victory in war, not increased tax receipts, would wipe away these debts.

The regime had thus taken three fundamental economic policy decisions early on in its career: to turn away from liberalism in world trade, to continue and intensify state intervention in the economy and to start a gigantic programme of rearmament, financed by debt. The problems associated with these decisions quickly became apparent. Firstly, there was a danger of massive wage and price increases because of the boom in armaments manufacturing, the rising level of employment and the increasing scarcity of consumer goods. That meant inflation, and in Germany it immediately awakened memories of the traumatic experiences of 1922–3. The Nazi government attempted to deal with this danger by imposing an all-embracing and rigidly administered price freeze, which was followed by a freeze on wages and salaries. It did in fact succeed in containing wage and price increases in this way. But this only postponed, rather than solving, the basic problem of a lack of financial backing for the rapid increase in state expenditure. The bill for this was picked up during the war by the people of the occupied countries of Europe, and later on by the people of Germany. Just as they had paid at the end of the First World War, Germans also had to pay at the end of the Second World War, through the currency reform of 1948, which reduced the value of private savings accounts and monetary wealth by a ratio of 1:10.[60]

Secondly, the abandonment of free trade inevitably resulted in severe dislocation for an economy such as Germany's, which was both strongly export-oriented and dependent on imports. On the other hand, it was desirable to reduce import dependency for military and diplomatic reasons. Most military observers were of the opinion that the Entente's economic blockade in the First World War had succeeded largely because the German economy was greatly dependent on imports. If Germany wanted to revise the results of that war by military force, the creation of a 'blockade-proof' area of influence on the Continent was an essential prerequisite. This calculation gave additional political impetus to anti-liberal economic conceptions.

The third problem was as follows: owing to the arms-related expansion of the economy since 1934–5, Germany was particularly dependent on the import of industrial raw materials and food supplies. These, however, had to be paid for with foreign currency, which in turn could only be acquired by exporting an increased quantity of industrial goods. But these industrial goods were needed for the rearmament programme. This was a vicious circle the regime initially endeavoured to break by ceasing to service its debts. Foreign debt amounted to more than 28 billion RM, which had to be serviced in foreign currency; meanwhile, export receipts were falling and the recovery of the economy led immediately to an increase in import requirements. As early as June 1933, therefore, the German government announced a moratorium on the payment of all long-term foreign debts. In normal times, a step like this would have meant a refusal by other nations to grant any further credit and the insolvency of the debtor. But the times were far from normal. When, a few days later, the World Economic Conference in London failed to lead to any concrete result owing to the disunity of the Western powers, there was no longer any immediate question of the restoration of the system of multilateral world economic relations, and Germany's cessation of foreign debt payments was just one more unsolved problem among many.

This situation did not, however, do anything to alter Germany's chronic shortage of foreign currency, which took on such dimensions in the course of 1934 that it posed a serious danger to the continuance of the rearmament programme. The government responded by placing all foreign exchange transactions under state supervision, and by using a tightly meshed network of surveillance and investigation offices to exert control over them. At the same time, it started to introduce a barter system into the country's international trading activities. The suppliers of important raw materials or food supplies were not paid in foreign currency. Instead the imports were set against deliveries of exported commodities. This 'clearing system' was applied particularly to trade with the countries of South-East Europe. An additional advantage of the new system was that, because the economies of these countries thereby became more tightly bound to Germany, this helped to create a large 'blockade-proof' economic region under German domination.[61]

Another way out of the import dilemma was to encourage the manufacture of 'ersatz materials', following the example set in the First World War, when a shortage of saltpetre, which threatened the war effort, was countered by Fritz Haber's invention of synthetic ammonia for use in the production of dynamite. This time too, there was some success in lessening Germany's import dependence: petrol was produced from coal, synthetic rubber ('Buna') and artificial fibres like rayon and artificial silk were manufactured, and the mining of German iron ore of inferior quality was promoted. Even so, the basic problem had still not been solved: 'Buna' for example was able to supply only 5 per cent of Germany's rubber requirements, and even the 'Hermann Goering Works' in Salzgitter, which the regime had built up from scratch at great speed, was only able to compensate for the loss of imported steel to a very slight extent.

In addition, the production of ersatz materials of this kind was extremely expensive, and in normal times completely unprofitable. But normal meant 'at market prices', and these no longer counted. The priority was now to reduce import dependency at any price, in areas of importance to armaments production above all.

Within a few years after the establishment of the Nazi dictatorship, a complete change of course in economic policy had thus been accomplished. Both the principles of multilateral world trade and the system of liberal market economics with minimal state intervention had been abandoned. At the beginning of 1936, it appeared as if by doing this the Nazis had chosen the right path. Germany's economic recovery was recognised and admired in neighbouring countries: its unemployment rate was lower than that of any other big industrial nation, its rate of growth was tremendous and inflationary tendencies had been banished. In the USA, in contrast, the unemployment rate continued at almost 24 per cent, and it was uncertain whether the US economy would ever be able to recover from the effects of the world economic crisis. The difficulties faced by liberal capitalism and liberal democracy in responding to the new challenges confronting the economies and societies of modern industrial nations appeared to suggest that these methods were inferior to the system of authoritarian dictatorship and state interventionist *Grossraumwirtschaft* (large-area economy) that had been established in Germany.

## Rearmament and Foreign Policy

Yet another thorny problem was associated with the radical course towards rearmament. How would the Western powers react when they realised that Germany was rapidly arming itself in defiance of its treaty obligations? And in what way would they confront Germany? Hitler was never in any doubt that the Reich would face the same opponents as it had faced during the First World War. Immediately after he came to power, he made clear that if Germany proceeded to engage in large-scale rearmament it would have to reckon with the opposition of the Western powers, particularly during the first, the transitional phase of the process: 'The most dangerous period is when we are building up the armed forces. We shall see then whether France possesses any statesmen. If it does, it will not allow us any time and will launch an attack immediately.'[62] If the French had marched into German territory with the aim of compelling the German government to observe its treaty obligations, that would doubtless have meant the end of the Hitler government. Hitler's willingness, despite this, to take such a course while fully aware of the risk involved, marked him out from the heads of government in neighbouring states, who carefully calculated the prospects of success and the dangers of failure, the effort their actions cost and the expected gain from them. That is precisely what Hitler did not do. He was ready, from the outset, to run incalculable risks and play all or nothing. This gave him an advantage over his opponents, who, unlike him, were not prepared to stake the fate of the whole country to obtain a short-term advantage. But this advantage only lasted until it became more dangerous for his opponents to keep out of the way than to react. Then the military and economic strength of the other side, which would undoubtedly also include the USA, would be many times greater than Germany's. The foreign policy agendas of Germany and the European powers evolved according to this strategic framework between February 1933 and September 1939, and even beyond.

The main objective of Hitler's foreign policy during the phase of rearmament and what was called 'the recovery of Germany's capacity to bear arms' was to survive the dangerous period of transition without suffering too much damage. The immediate objective was to revise the Versailles Treaty as quickly as possible and extend Germany's area of informal influence on the European continent. The more distant goal was to extend the area of formal German rule, particularly by expanding into Eastern Europe.

Hitler estimated that the period of maximum risk would last between three and four years. During that time, he pursued a fairly consistent policy of appeasement towards both east and west. This was linked with a gradual expansion of his room for manoeuvre and a policy of ensuring his legitimacy within the country by holding plebiscites. In his first big foreign policy speech, therefore, he stressed in emotional language Germany's desire to preserve peace and its readiness to observe all treaties, including the Versailles Treaty. Because we have an obligation as National Socialists to our own people, he emphasised, 'this attitude also leads us to respect the national rights of other peoples, and our desire to live with them in peace and friendship lives in the depths of our hearts.'[63]

This 17 May 1933 'speech for peace' made quite a big impression internationally, which was confirmed when the German government extended the Treaty of Friendship and Non-Aggression with the USSR, an action glaringly at odds with the bloody persecution of communists within Germany. Hitler was also ready to reach an agreement with Poland, which was a surprise even to the officials of the German Foreign Office, who had been working since 1919 to secure a revision of the country's eastern borders. In making the Non-Aggression Pact of January 1934 with Poland, Germany by no means abandoned the possibility of future boundary changes, but the agreement to renounce the use of force went considerably beyond earlier concessions Germany had made to its eastern neighbour.

In view of these active demonstrations of Germany's peaceful intentions, there was no strong reaction from the western powers to Hitler's sensational October 1933 announcement of withdrawal from the Geneva disarmament negotiations. Great Britain had previously suggested that Germany's rearmament activities alone should be subject to supervision, which the German side abruptly rejected as another case of discrimination, and Hitler used this as a pretext for withdrawing from both the Geneva Conference and the League of Nations. The kind of supervision proposed would have immediately revealed the extent of German rearmament. But since under the British proposal international supervision would be limited to Germany, the German reaction had a certain plausibility. Hitler had no need to fear any harsh, possibly military, punitive measures, especially because he had confirmed the territorial status quo in the west, so as to dispel French and British doubts on that score, and had shown an interest in improving Germany's relationship with both countries. At the same time, he dissolved the Reichstag and ordered fresh elections, to be held in conjunction with a plebiscite on the government's policy. Relief over the relaxation of foreign policy tensions (which had been created by Hitler in the first place); the plebiscite, which resulted in an overwhelmingly favourable vote and appeared to legitimate the regime by signalling support for a kind of authoritarian democracy; and the Chancellor's apparent will to peace were all mutually reinforcing factors, and they turned the German government's risky foreign policy manoeuvre into a domestic political success.

And the successes did not stop there. In January 1935, 90.8 per cent of the voters in the territory of the Saar, which had been separated from Germany by the Versailles Treaty, supported its reunion with the Reich. These free elections, conducted under the supervision of the League of Nations, with a turnout of 98 per cent, meant a remarkable boost to Hitler's personal standing. He could now point out that the people of the Saar, who had been free to choose between the French republic and National Socialist Germany, had unequivocally decided in favour of both Germany and National Socialism.

The triumph of the Saar vote was followed two months later by the reintroduction of conscription. This was a clear breach of the provisions of the Versailles Treaty, and the Western powers would have been within their rights to impose sanctions and even to intervene militarily. Nevertheless, there was no sign of a firm response from them, although it had been feared in Berlin that military reactions would follow. On the contrary, the British government had, in the meantime, come round to the view that the provisions of Versailles concerning Germany were in many respects outdated, and that Germany's desire for rearmament should be regarded as legitimate within certain limits. Great Britain's main concern was therefore to direct and limit the rearmament process. The navy was of particular concern, given the memory of the role played by German naval armaments in the origins of the First World War, and the United Kingdom very much desired to arrive at an agreement with Germany on this issue. For the British side, this was a conclusive argument: only a few months after Germany's announcement of the restoration of conscription and its repudiation of the disarmament clauses of the Treaty of Versailles, Britain concluded a bilateral naval agreement with Hitler by which the size of Germany's fleet could be increased, though only up to a maximum limit of 35 per cent of Britain's naval forces.

From the British point of view, this treaty promised to avoid any repetition of what had occurred before 1914, and to guarantee British naval superiority. Needless to say, the German side was at first in no position to exceed the 35 per cent limit. But, for Hitler, it was more important that one of the signatories of the Versailles Treaty had accepted its ineffectiveness in the area of rearmament, and conceded to Germany the right to rearm. This provided renewed justification for Hitler's combination of rearmament and conciliation. The Anglo-German Naval Agreement of 1935 also signalled that the system of multilateral European security policy under the auspices of the League of Nations, which had been envisaged in 1919, was now regarded as out of date, and would be replaced by bilateral agreements between individual states.[64]

This erosion of the post-war order was confirmed in the next few months by other international developments. Three events need to be highlighted here: Italy's war in Abyssinia, the entry of German troops into the demilitarised Rhineland and the Spanish civil war. In autumn 1935, Fascist Italy attempted to create an empire in Africa by military means, in line with the ruling geopolitical doctrine that possession of an empire is what defines a Great Power. This represented a qualitative change in international behaviour. Abyssinia (later called Ethiopia) was a member of the League of Nations and the war was conducted by Italy with modern weapons and enormous brutality against this medieval-looking empire which was ruled by Haile Selassie, its 'Negus'. Italy's action not only cost hundreds of thousands of victims, but was a blatant infringement of existing international law. On 9 May 1936, the 'Duce' triumphantly celebrated the 'restoration of the Roman Empire' in front of his supporters. The failure of France and Great Britain to intervene already indicated the new relation of forces in Europe: the two right-wing dictators, who were continuing to move closer together, announced in November 1936 that they had formed an alliance, which they described as an 'axis'. They could no longer be impressed by threats of sanctions or intervention. As Goebbels wrote in his diary after the Italian victory: 'You see: one needs force to achieve anything. Everything else is nonsense.'[65]

The same calculation was made when on 7 March 1936 German troops entered the demilitarised Rhineland. This was without doubt Hitler's riskiest step so far, because the demilitarisation of the land on the left bank of the Rhine was not only provided for by the 'dictate of Versailles', which had been discredited in the meantime, but it was a part of the Locarno Treaties, which had been voluntarily signed by Germany. As one of the generals who participated in these events stated during his trial at Nuremberg, the German leadership felt 'like a gambler who in playing roulette has staked the whole of his possessions on red or black'. Hitler himself proceeded on the assumption that the Germans would not be able to resist a French invasion, and that they would have to 'withdraw again with their tails between their legs'.[66] In France, however, where the generals considerably overrated the strength of the German *Wehrmacht*, it was thought that the Germans could only be opposed if a general mobilisation was proclaimed. But a step of this nature would no doubt be interpreted in Europe as a repetition of July 1914, with incalculable consequences. A new war with Germany over the Rhineland? After all, as they said in London, all the Germans had done was to march into Germany. Great Britain's vital interests appeared to be unaffected by this. France therefore also held back from military action.

In addition, Hitler did everything he could to restrain the Western powers from intervening militarily. He offered a new multilateral security system, a demilitarised zone on both sides of the German border to the west, a pact of non-aggression with France and all Germany's western and eastern neighbours, the renunciation of further territorial demands and even a return to the League of Nations. None of this was meant seriously, as Hitler informed the people around him. But it worked: there were sharp protests, and the League of Nations condemned Germany's action, but no military intervention took place.

March 1936 was an important milestone in National Socialist policy. The Rhineland was again in German military hands, and the Ruhr was now shielded from French attack. Defensive positions on Germany's western border could be strengthened. In foreign policy, Hitler's readiness to take risks had made the cautious and indecisive attitude of France and Great Britain appear foolish. He had also won a victory over conservative nationalist critics in his own ranks, whose warnings against his reckless policy gambles now seemed to have been refuted. The international security system of the post-war years had broken up, and bilateral agreements were the order of the day. This made it easier for the German *Reich* to return to the club of the Great Powers and to pursue a policy of rearmament that no longer needed a careful disguise.

In domestic politics Hitler used this opportunity to once again dissolve the Reichstag and organise a plebiscitary confirmation of his foreign policy through 'fresh elections'. A tremendous propaganda campaign began, and an outburst of patriotic frenzy was put on display, while the glorification of the 'Führer' reached new heights both in form and content. Decorated streets, organised demonstrations and also spontaneous celebrations proclaimed the significance of the events of the preceding weeks. Large sections of the German population saw it as almost a miracle that Hitler, by boldly pressing ahead, had succeeded in throwing off the shackles of the Versailles Treaty, against all predictions. People who had feared the coming of war reacted in many cases by enthusiastically supporting the 'Führer', who seemed to be successful at everything. The result of the elections was announced as a 98.8 per cent vote in favour of the Nazis.

Reports of the falsification of the election results and the arrest of those who had called for people to abstain or vote against the Nazis indicated exactly how this almost unanimous vote had been produced. Even so, there is no doubt that the overwhelming majority of Germans approved of Hitler's foreign policy. This included many workers, as even the exiled SPD noted in March 1936: 'Everyone is impressed by the firm line the Führer has taken in occupying the Rhineland. Many are convinced that Germany's foreign policy demands are justified and cannot be overlooked. The last few days have brought a further increase in the Führer's personal reputation, even among the workers.' 'You can say what you want against Hitler, but he is certainly a remarkable fellow' is how another informant recorded the general attitude. 'Something like this impresses the philistines, but it also impresses some of the workers and even some socialists.'

But this admiration and relief was at the same time bound up with an increasing fear of a warlike outcome. As a report for SOPADE from Westphalia put it: 'In all circles of the population, even the National Socialists, the main theme of discussion is the danger of becoming embroiled in a war.' The connection between the occupation of the Rhineland and rearmament was also understood: 'Anyone who looks at things attentively can see that the whole of the so-called job creation and stimulation of the economy is a big swindle. These are state orders, nothing else. This will eventually come to an end if war does not happen.'[67]

The events of March 1936 also changed Hitler's position within the system of National Socialist rule. The propaganda machine, which Goebbels was now operating with the skill of a virtuoso, stepped up its volume with every foreign policy coup. Hitler appeared as a leader of genius, sent by destiny, who was giving back both bread and dignity to the Germans. The presentation of Hitler as the saviour of the *Volk* and the fatherland now took on an almost mythical air, cheered on emphatically by his supporters. Even foreign observers were affected by these transports of ecstasy. Denis de Rougemont, a Swiss journalist, wrote this account of Hitler's visit to Frankfurt am Main on 11 March 1936:

> A hundred thousand people surged against the walls of the auditorium. A few women fainted and had to be carried away, which created a certain amount of elbow-room. Seven o'clock. No-one became impatient, no-one made jokes . . . But then a murmur passes through the swaying crowd of people.

> Trumpets can be heard from outside. The arc lamps down below in the hall are switched off, while arrows of light pass across the ceiling and move towards a door on the first floor. A floodlight reveals a small man, in brown clothing, at the threshold, bare-headed and smiling ecstatically. 40,000 people and 40,000 arms rise up in a single movement. The man moves forward very slowly under the deafening thunder of rhythmical shouts of 'Heil', and greets the crowd with a slow gesture reminiscent of a bishop's blessing. . . . The people stand upright and motionless and bellow rhythmically while they stare at this point bathed in light, this face with its ecstatic smile, and tears run down their cheeks in the darkness. Suddenly everything goes quiet. . . . Hitler, looking upwards, vigorously stretches out his arm, and the gloomy sound of the Horst Wessel song rises from the stalls. 'Comrades, shot by red front and reaction, are marching with us side by side' . . . Now I sense what one can well name holy terror. I thought I was taking part in a mass meeting, a political demonstration. But they are celebrating their cult! And a liturgy is being performed, the great sacred ceremony of a religion. I do not belong to it, and I am being overwhelmed by it. . . . I am alone, and they are a community.[68]

In Hitler, the widespread yearning for a charismatic leader found a destination which rose to ever greater heights. Führer worship now became the defining aspect of German domestic politics. There are clear indications that Hitler himself now became convinced of his own infallibility, particularly once the reoccupation of the Rhineland had been safely accomplished. References to providence and divine inspiration henceforth became regular *topoi* in Hitler's speeches and his thinking. 'I go the way providence dictates, with the surefootedness of a sleepwalker' he told an enthusiastic audience on 14 March 1936. And at a Nuremberg rally, amidst the thrilled jubilation of his supporters, he had this to say: 'That you have found me . . . among so many millions is the miracle of our epoch! And that I have found you, that is Germany's fortune!' His conviction that he was acting in accordance with history, and his certainty that no rival was a match for him, increased Hitler's readiness to run even greater risks in the future.[69]

An opportunity soon presented itself. The underlying framework of European politics had been reshaped by the brutal action of Italy in Abyssinia, the rise of National Socialist Germany and developments in East Central and Southern Europe, where by 1938 there was no longer any democratically governed country in existence except Czechoslovakia. States still under liberal and democratic rule, which included France, Great Britain, the Benelux countries, Switzerland, the Scandinavian lands and Czechoslovakia, were aggressively confronted by authoritarian, right-wing dictatorships of various kinds, ruling under the aegis of the two 'Axis powers', National Socialist Germany and Fascist Italy.

The role of the Soviet Union was at first unclear. As long as Moscow proceeded on the assumption that a proletarian revolution was on the agenda in the countries of Western Europe, above all Germany, the Social Democrats were regarded as the communists' main enemy. But once the outlines of a bloc of authoritarian European states, right wing in orientation, became clearly perceptible, and the anti-Soviet thrust of Hitler's Germany became unmistakable, the Soviet communists executed a volte-face, and began to call for the formation of alliances with Social Democratic and bourgeois forces in order to fight 'Fascism' in Europe.

In the spring and early summer of 1936 'Popular Front' governments, including both communists and Social Democrats, were formed on this basis in France and Spain. This appeared to confirm Hitler's warnings about the advance of Bolshevism in Europe. Then, on 17 July 1936, part of Spain's armed forces, led by General Franco, endeavoured to overthrow the left-wing government there with a military putsch, thus setting off the Spanish Civil War. It was logical for Italy and Germany to line up with the military rebels against the Spanish republic and support them with arms and troops.

The almost immediate response to this in the capital cities of the West was the growth of a movement of solidarity with the Spanish republic, and a large number of volunteers, overwhelmingly left-wingers, joined the 'International Brigades', so as to provide military support to the fight against Franco. France finally decided to assist the Spanish government; the Soviet Union followed suit somewhat later. Thus the regional conflict in Spain quickly became a proxy war between the representatives of two rival international camps: on one side the right-wing dictatorships, on the other the liberal democracies and the communist USSR. There were certainly also economic and diplomatic motives behind the engagement of the Great Powers in this war, but this was an ideological conflict first and foremost, in which the stakes were rival social systems and the domination of Europe. It was in those terms that Hitler explained Germany's intervention in Spain: 'If Spain really goes communist, France in the present situation will also be bolshevized in due course.' The victory of Bolshevism in France, he continued, would be followed by the bolshevisation of Europe and the downfall of Germany.[70]

Within as little as three years, therefore, the political constellation in Europe had changed completely. The territorial and political remodelling of Europe in the Paris treaties of 1919 had largely been reversed, and the international security system had almost been destroyed, to be replaced by hastily signed and unstable bilateral agreements. The League of Nations was powerless, and an effective disarmament treaty had not been concluded. Germany had instead plainly broken her international treaty obligations by introducing military service and marching into the Rhineland, without suffering any consequences, and

Italy had waged a victorious imperialist war against a member of the League of Nations, remaining equally unpunished. The war in Spain, finally, had created a new battle line, across which the Great Powers confronted each other in a proxy war. The Great Power configuration which had now emerged was predominantly defined politically and ideologically, as a struggle between social systems and a fight for European hegemony.

## The Workers, the Farmers and the Middle Classes

During the first two or three years of the dictatorship, the attitudes of the Germans were divided. The supporters of the Right were triumphant and welcomed every step taken by their government and every speech by their Führer with joy and satisfaction. But the largest group in Germany was made up of people who were as yet neutral. They had decided to postpone judgment until later. It was worth persevering with Hitler, they thought, in view of the privations and disappointments of earlier years; it remained to be seen whether he succeeded or not. The supporters of the republic, and particularly the workers' parties, on the other hand, suffered under the terror of the Nazi paramilitaries and the vindictiveness of the winning side. But they believed that this government would prove to be as unstable as its predecessors had been and that the nightmare would quickly come to an end. It soon became clear that their predictions were entirely mistaken.

After the Nazis had taken over the government, many Social Democratic and communist cadres had hoped that even after their organisations as such had been crushed, the solidarity of the working class could be maintained at least in the neighbourhoods and the factories. But this hope too was in vain. The Nazis were entirely unable to suppress the solidarity of the workers inside the proletarian social milieu, but this ceased to have a political character. The defeat of 1933 also weakened the prestige of the working-class movement. This applied particularly to the KPD, which had been prophesying a proletarian revolution only a few months before. Now it was not even capable of protecting working-class districts against the raids of the SA. The links between the small number of political activists and the workers in the neighbourhoods and the factories had largely been broken, and as early as the beginning of 1935 the Gestapo could proceed on the assumption that the Marxist organisations no longer offered any noteworthy resistance.

The decisive factor in the attitude of the working class proved to be the reduction in unemployment and the improvements in working conditions. By 1935 the problem of unemployment had largely been overcome, and after 1936 there was a shortage of labour. By 1938 the economy was already overheating, and the number of people without work had fallen to 400,000. For most workers, the experience of long-term stability in employment was something new, which they had not known for decades. This had a great impact on the way they perceived and evaluated the situation.

With wages, the situation was different. They had been frozen at the low level they reached during the world economic crisis, owing to the price and wage stop introduced by the Nazi government. The destruction of the trade unions and the ending of freely negotiated wage contracts meant that the workers no longer had any instruments with which to improve their situation on their own account. Even so, real incomes rose as a result of rearmament-related boom conditions, and, in some branches, they reached the pre-crisis level between 1936 and 1939, although this was usually achieved rather through longer working hours than by wage increases.

The armaments firms were urgently in need of an extra labour force, because the boom conditions had led to a shortage of labour, and this soon brought about renewed population flows, both from country to town and from one factory to another. The authorities attempted to restrict the mobility of labour, so as to prevent employers from poaching workers and workers from making 'wild' moves from one job to another. The government had already militarised a part of the labour market in 1933 by setting up the 'National Labour Service' (*Reichsarbeitsdienst*). This was intended to keep workers in their current place of employment. During the rearmament boom the application of this method of restricting mobility was extended, and in February 1939 compulsory labour service was introduced for all workers. Industrial work was thus stripped of its character as a private economic activity carried on by civilians. It would in future be regarded as a 'service' on the same lines as military service.

In the years before 1939, the development of the economy by and large brought benefits to the working class, but these were often counterbalanced by shortages of food and accommodation. The workers, who continued to constitute roughly 60 per cent of the population, also remained socially disadvantaged in comparison with the other social strata, which profited more quickly and to a greater extent from the rising prosperity. But the comparison with the pre-1933 situation was the decisive factor, because it threw into relief the improvements that had taken place since then.[71]

The regime compensated for the social inequality which continued after 1933, and to some extent even increased, by mounting an intensive propaganda campaign in praise of egalitarianism. The stylised presentation of the 'honest worker' and 'German socialism' was as important in this regard as the mobilisation of resentment against 'the reaction', 'the bosses' and other privileged groups, or those thought to be so, above all the Jews. The employer became the 'works leader' (*Führer des Betriebs*) and the workers and office employees became his 'retinue' (*Gefolgschaft*). This postulated equality was also reflected in changes of designation and sociable factory evenings—the social hierarchy, however, remained intact.

Nevertheless, the egalitarian propaganda of the Nazis was not without impact. There were constant street collections by the 'Winter Relief Fund' (*Winterhilfswerk*), there were staged 'one pot meals' (*Eintopfessen*) shared by the political leaders with building workers or people with large families, and on the First of May, now renamed the 'Day of National Labour', elaborate spectacles were staged, at which workers, office employees and the management had to participate in joint parades, followed afterwards by joint beer-drinking sessions. All these things contributed to the impression that the workers were very much respected under the new regime and that 'the community of the *Volk*' (*Volksgemeinschaft*) was perhaps more than just a Nazi slogan.

But a merely ideological compensation for the deprivation of political rights would have been totally ineffective in the absence of any tangible social improvements. It was therefore the regime's social policy achievements which had greater resonance. Foremost among these were the improvements in family support, the loans given to recently married couples, the organised leisure activities and the greater availability of consumer goods. The promotion of the 'People's Car' (*Volkswagen*) was also a part of this effort: in Germany, the production of motor cars for the masses had failed to keep pace with that of the Western countries, but now the prospect of being able to possess a motor car, perhaps in the not-too-distant future, after a lengthy period of saving, seemed to be moving from a utopian dream to a tangible reality. In actual fact, though, the investments of the Volkswagen savers later disappeared into the regime's war chest.

The introduction of holidays with a minimum length of six days a year proved to be extraordinarily popular, not least because of the offer of cheap package tours. A state mass tourism organisation following the Italian model was established for this purpose. This was called 'Strength Through Joy' (*Kraft durch Freude*, KdF) and in 1938 it organised 10.3 million holiday trips. The famous steamer voyages to Madeira (without the chance to visit the island itself, owing to a lack of foreign currency) were unattainable for most; but many people could afford short organised trips in the immediate neighbourhood or for short distances. The word 'holiday' had until then referred to a luxury enjoyed by the upper classes; now, holiday travel became a concrete possibility, a piece of tangible evidence to support the belief that things would continue to improve.

The war put an abrupt end to these emerging hopes for a better life, which were in essence aspirations for a consumer society. But the desire had been awakened, and it persisted until it was satisfied, at least in the West, in the 1950s and 1960s.[72]

The regime's social policy continued that of its predecessors, but it was not simply a continuation of the tradition that had operated since Bismarck. Instead, a concern with effective delivery of services and an insistence on social equality were combined with *völkisch* and racial criteria. The aim of these social policies was to provide encouragement to those members of the *Volksgemeinschaft* who had shown their 'value' by their social behaviour and performance at work. Their living and working conditions were to be improved, their families were to be supported and they were encouraged to have more children, in order to raise the amount of 'valuable' material present in the 'body of the *Volk*'. At the same time, individuals of 'inferior value' who were a burden on the 'body of the *Volk*' would be investigated, segregated and excluded from social policy benefits, in line with the requirements of Nazi ideology. The ruthless approach of the police authorities and the administrators of the war economy towards 'slackers', 'the work-shy' and 'asocials' shows the close connection between the imposition of social discipline and persecution for reasons of 'racial hygiene'.[73]

On the whole, in the first three years after 1933, the Nazi regime succeeded in gaining the support of at least part of the working class. Alongside the fall in unemployment, the increasing emphasis on social policy and the propaganda in favour of social egalitarianism, what proved particularly effective was Hitler's success in foreign policy and the perception of him as a man who never failed to get what he wanted. Hence, explicit rejection or indifference towards the regime and its policies was increasingly replaced by a combination of positive attitudes towards some government measures and a rejection of others. This meant that the fundamental antagonism towards Hitler and opposition to his dictatorship which before 1933 had characterised at least the part of the working class organised in the socialist camp had now largely disappeared.[74]

In the agricultural sphere, the starting point for Nazi policy was different from that in industry. Everywhere in Europe the transition from an agrarian to an industrial society had given rise to considerable social and political dislocation. Since the 1870s, and in Great Britain much earlier than this, large sections of the agricultural workforce had been absorbed by industries which were growing and prospering. The severe economic crisis of the years after 1929 interrupted this trend and led voices to be raised once again in criticism of industry and in favour of separating agriculture from industrial capitalism, with its dynamism and associated risks. In Germany, the farmers' protests of the late 1920s and the constant attempts of the big landowners east of the Elbe to persuade the state to write off the debts owed by their uneconomic properties were striking expressions of this trend.

Once in power after 1933, the Nazis were faced with a dilemma. The desire to strengthen the peasantry, as the 'blood source' of the German *Volk*, lay right at the core of their political convictions. But both the priority given to rearmament and the goal of freedom from the risk of blockade required a substantial increase in German agricultural production, so as to reduce the amount of food that had to be imported. Moreover, with the onset of the armaments boom after 1935, the process of emigration from the countryside to the industrial towns gathered strength once again, and agriculture was therefore more than ever deprived of its urgently needed labour power.

In a market-driven economy this would have increased the pressure to make agriculture more productive by increasing the use of machinery. But, under Hitler, the rearmament programme involved directing all investments towards industry, which meant in turn that the mechanisation of agriculture was only possible to a limited extent. Nevertheless, it still proved possible to increase the value of agricultural production by 20 per cent between 1928 and 1938, and to reduce the importation of foodstuffs in roughly the same proportion. A considerable degree of state intervention in the agricultural sector helped in achieving this. All the separate agricultural associations were brought together in 1933 to form a 'National Food Corporation' (*Reichsnährstand*), which controlled production, prices, marketing and foreign trade and directed them according to the objectives set by the course towards war. This in fact led to considerable increases in production, despite continuing migration from the countryside, although at the beginning of the war the government was still far from achieving the 'self-sufficiency' that was its aim.

At the same time, roughly a fifth of all agricultural enterprises were allocated a special status. A law already promulgated in September 1933 declared that approximately one million mainly medium-sized enterprises were 'hereditary farms'. They could no longer be sold and had to be bequeathed undivided to the eldest son. These 'hereditary farms' were in a sense given to the peasant 'clans' as permanent fiefdoms, with the intention of exempting them completely from the capitalist market in land. This was entirely in line with the agrarian romanticism preached by the cultural critics of previous decades, but it was hard to reconcile with the regime's objective of a streamlined, efficient and highly productive agricultural sector. The contradictions arising from this were not resolved, but they were partially obscured during the war by the mass recruitment into German agriculture of forced labourers from foreign lands.

In the longer term, the exponents of National Socialist agrarian policy planned a complete and systematic change in the structure of the rural economy. Small farms would be broken up, the backwardness of the agricultural sector in comparison with industry would be ended by mechanisation and scientific farm management, and the superfluous rural population would be settled in East Central Europe, the only place where Germany's 'shortage of space' could be alleviated. In 1936, such plans would have appeared insanely ambitious, but it only took three years before the first steps were taken to put them into effect.[75]

The relationship of the Nazis with the middle classes was also contradictory. On the one hand, they presented themselves as strongly anti-bourgeois, and their demands for a 'community of the *Volk*' (*Volksgemeinschaft*) and a 'national' socialism terrified the entrepreneurs and the educated bourgeoisie. But even more than the political aspects, it was the plebeian style of the brown-shirted paramilitaries which met with indignant rejection on the part of middle-class Germans.[76] On the other hand, the National Socialists were, in many respects, also a product of the bourgeois critique of civilisation, which had been nurtured since the turn of the century in the anti-urban fantasies of the *bündisch* (federative) youth movement and in the militaristic style of the veterans' associations or the radical critique of modernity put forward by the intellectual advocates of the 'conservative revolution'.

If one takes as an example the German professorate, the group which 'lay at the core of the educated bourgeoisie' (Wehler), these connections with Nazism rapidly become apparent. The National Socialists had made inroads into the universities earlier and more easily than into society as a whole. One reason for this was the strong support for *völkisch* radicalism among the students, but another reason was that the overwhelming majority of university professors were strongly nationalist, conservative and anti-republican in attitude. The coordinates of their political vision of the world were clearly apparent: opposition to Weimar and Versailles, a conviction that the results of the First World War had to be revised, if necessary by force, the demand for a strong government independent of parliamentary control, hostility towards the cultural modernity of the West and a wish to reinstate elite structures and counter the levelling tendencies of the democratic and social state. A virulent anti-Semitism and a tendency to think in biological categories was also widespread, though not universal. Broad areas of intersection with the positions of the radical, *völkisch* Right, to which the National Socialists also belonged, were clearly apparent. Nevertheless, German university professors kept their distance from the views of the radical Right, if only because many of them had strong reservations about the 'crude anti-intellectualism' and rowdiness of the Nazis, which was sharply at odds with the orderly world of the educated German bourgeoisie.[77]

The educationalist Eduard Spranger was one of the more prominent university teachers who kept the Nazis at arm's length. Yet it was he who drew up the Würzburg Declaration of the German University Association, issued on 22 April 1933, which contained this statement:

> For the universities of our fatherland, the rebirth of the German *Volk* and the rise of the new German Reich signifies the fulfilment of their yearning and the confirmation of their passionately felt hopes. . . . With the cessation of the regrettable antagonisms between classes, the hour has again come for the universities to draw spiritual nourishment from the deep unity of the German people's soul, the manifold endeavours of which were previously oppressed by misery and foreign dictation, and consciously to direct it towards the tasks of the current epoch.[78]

The Nazi seizure of power therefore inspired 'passionately felt hopes' among university professors. But that phrase could have various meanings. Many accepted the political overturn, but at the same time stressed the autonomy of the university and of scholarship. In the humanities, above all, there was a widespread conviction that the Nazi victory would finally bring an end to the culture of modernity, perhaps through a symbiosis between Christianity and the *völkisch* state or a return of the Bismarckian empire. In line with this view, many works of scholarship now laid the foundations for a thoroughgoing legitimation of the National Socialist regime.

One prerequisite for this relatively untroubled adaptation to Nazi rule was of course the rapid removal of Jewish and politically dissident university teachers. In the first two years after the Nazis came to power, between 15 and 20 per cent of the academic staff were dismissed from the universities; by 1938 this figure had reached almost 30 per cent, including roughly a fifth of the full professors. The proportions involved varied very much from place to place, thus providing an indication of the relative numbers of pro-republican or Jewish lecturers previously employed at each one. More than 32 per cent of the academic staff were dismissed from the universities of Berlin and Frankfurt am Main, 24 per cent from Heidelberg, and roughly 20 per cent from Breslau (Wrocław), Freiburg, Göttingen, Hamburg and Cologne. In contrast to this, 4 per cent were dismissed from Rostock and only 1.6 per cent from Tübingen.[79]

This tremendous wave of dismissals and expulsions proceeded without any loud disturbances or objections. The anti-Semitic activities of the students, who at many universities organised campaigns against Jewish professors, were one reason for this. A greater role, however, was probably played by the widespread attitude of indifference and rejection towards Jewish colleagues displayed by the German professorate. Another reason was the shortage of university posts. In 1931 there were 2,000 openings for university professors, but 3,000 qualified applicants without a permanent position, and in view of the economic crisis they would hardly be able to find adequate employment outside the universities. The proportion of active Nazis among them was far higher than it was among the employed professors. The NSDAP hoped that the appointment of younger lecturers, which would mean an influx of new blood, would lead to a rapid increase in its influence at the universities. Max Planck, when asked by Otto Hahn in July 1933 to take part in bringing together as many colleagues as possible to protest against the treatment of their Jewish colleagues, made this reply: 'If 30 professors stand up today and state their opposition to the government's actions, 150 people will come along tomorrow and declare their solidarity with Hitler because they want to have their jobs.'[80]

But by accepting without protest the dismissal of almost a third of their colleagues on political and racial grounds the German professors had made themselves the accomplices of the regime, and they could no longer oppose it from the high ground of moral authority and independence. We know from surviving correspondence that many university teachers observed the fate of their Jewish as well as their socialist and pacifist colleagues with anger and regret. But in view of their support for the successes of the National Socialists in dealing with the economy and in foreign affairs, these attitudes were of little significance.

And yet, there had already been plenty of opportunities to discern the implications of National Socialist cultural policies. The proscription and banishment of the elite of German intellectual life—from Thomas and Heinrich Mann to Alfred Döblin and Bertolt Brecht, Kurt Tucholsky, Carl von Ossietzky, Hermann Broch, Alfred Kerr, Anna Seghers, Robert Musil, Franz Werfel, Carl Zuckmayer, Arnold and Stefan Zweig, Erich Maria Remarque, Erich Kästner and Arthur Schnitzler, followed by renowned university teachers such as Karl Mannheim, Hermann Heller, Hans Kelsen, Wilhelm Röpke, Joseph Schumpeter, Ernst Cassirer, Max Horkheimer, Karl Löwith, Karl Popper and Paul Tillich—had already begun in the first weeks and months of the regime, and reached its first grisly culmination on 10 May 1933 with the book-burning ceremony. Twenty-four Nobel laureates were driven into emigration, among them Thomas Mann, Albert Einstein, Max Born, Fritz Haber, Paul Hertz, James Franck, Erwin Schrödinger and Otto Stern.

But there were others who stayed, and made their peace with the regime. Gerhart Hauptmann, for example, enjoyed being proclaimed the prince of German poets by the Nazis. Werner Krauss, Wilhelm Furtwängler and Richard Strauss were also part of this group, which provided the new state with the cultural reputation that was so important for its acceptance by the educated bourgeoisie. A further group actually went over to the National Socialists. This included Martin Heidegger, the most famous philosopher of the epoch, and the poet Gottfried Benn, one of the pioneers of Expressionism, who now proclaimed his turn towards the *Volk* in powerful language:

> I declare my entirely personal support for the new state, because it is my *Volk* that is striking out on its path . . . The city, industrialism, intellectualism, all

> the shadows the epoch has thrown over my thoughts, all the powers of the century to which I surrendered myself in producing my work: there are moments when the whole of this tortured life sinks below the horizon, and nothing remains but the open country, the distance, the seasons, the soil, all simple words, and the *Volk*![81]

The rejection of cultural modernity, of the avant-garde, Expressionism, experiments with form, and socially critical left-wing art: these were all issues over which National Socialism and bourgeois anti-modernism could join hands. Hitler never tired of repeating that the National Socialists would 'wage a relentless war of purification' against 'every single element that has caused our cultural disintegration' and against '"works of art" which in themselves cannot be understood but require a bombastic set of instructions to justify their existence, so that they eventually discover someone intimidated enough to tolerate such stupid and impudent nonsense with patience.'[82] The new German art which was intended to counter this found expression in literature, as well as painting and architecture. There were racially oriented still lives, there were pictures glorifying peasant labour, there were stylised warriors and idealised mothers—but what met with the greatest approval was the heroic pathos of architecture. The 'House of German Art' in Munich, the New Reich Chancellery in Berlin and above all the new Party Congress site in Nuremberg displayed an intimidating aesthetic which featured a combination of archaising classicism, monumentalism and ostentatious sacramentalism. In general, the mixture of grandiose mass demonstrations and liturgical and religious themes was characteristic of the regime's self-presentation.

But this turn towards a mythical past was only one part of the regime's cultural efforts. There was also a more pragmatic side, in which continuity and traditionalism were emphasised. Tried and tested styles, traditional artistic repertoires and classical art forms were cultivated. The suppression of avant-garde modernism gave the impression of a 'purification', but the actual result was to create a culture of uninspired and conventional mediocrity.

At the same time the trend towards modern mass culture, against which the bourgeois protagonists of cultural criticism had fulminated so vehemently since the end of the nineteenth century, continued to assert itself. In fact, it was accelerated by the rearmament-led boom in the economy. The public flocked to performances of dance music and popular hits, to operettas and revues, rather than to *Thingspiele* (the outdoor theatre productions favoured by the Nazis) or readings of war poetry. Sound films and radio broadcasts increasingly occupied the centre of attention. American films attracted a mass public and, at the same time, under the careful encouragement and supervision of Propaganda Minister Goebbels, who was a cinema enthusiast, many German films were produced, most of them undemanding entertainment pictures. These were often big hits with the public.[83]

Here we again see the paradox which was also evident in other areas of Nazi policy: on the one hand, specifically National Socialist aims and guidelines were put into effect, as in the case of the 'Hereditary Farm Law' (*Reichserbhofgesetz*) or the glorification of racially oriented heroism in the artistic sphere. On the other hand, we see the continuation of the trend towards industrial modernity, further accelerated by the dynamic growth of the economy, which gave rise to the formation of a broad range of cultural offerings for the masses, some of which were completely contradictory to the critique of modernity which was the main concern of the *völkisch* ideologists. The tensions created by this antinomy increasingly characterised politics and everyday life in the Third Reich, and they manifested themselves even more strongly after the war had started. Nevertheless, it was possible in practice for both these elements to coexist. In the cultural sphere, for example, blood-and-soil romanticism rubbed shoulders with American short stories, while Speer's monumental architecture sat alongside purely functional industrial buildings, the cult of classical music coexisted with hit songs, and romantic films with runic intimations. What was most important, however, was that the nation gained the impression of a return to 'normality', after the extreme experiences of the previous decade. But this was a peculiar kind of normality: without the Left, without avant-garde artists, without class struggle—and without Jews.

## The Course Is Set for War

The Third Reich put on one of its greatest ever theatrical performances in the summer of 1936. The Berlin Olympic Games, like the Winter Olympics held shortly before in Garmisch, were celebrated with extravagant pomp. A great effort was made to ensure their success. The anti-Semitic campaign was temporarily suspended. Signs bearing the legend 'Jews are not wanted here' were removed, as were the display cabinets holding copies of *Der Stürmer*. Foreign guests were given courteous service. The grandees of the Reich organised opulent parties, Goering and Ribbentrop in their villas, Goebbels on the Pfaueninsel (he had 2,000 guests), and foreign visitors were highly impressed. As the American journalist William Shirer noted in his diary: 'I'm afraid the Nazis have succeeded with their propaganda. First, they have run the games on a lavish scale never before experienced, and this has appealed to the athletes. Second, they have put up a very good front for the general visitors, especially the big business-men.'[84] Could Hitler and his regime perhaps still be tamed, after their first few years of wild behaviour? Did the openness to the world displayed in the Olympic Games perhaps mean the return of a recovered Germany to the international arena? 'Everyone went into ecstasy' was the French ambassador's comment on world reaction to the Berlin Olympics.[85]

In fact, the main purpose of this Olympic showcase was to improve the standing of the Nazi regime abroad, which had been severely hit by the occupation of the Rhineland and the reports about the persecution of the Jews. But it also had a domestic aim. It was a celebration of '*Volksgemeinschaft*' (the community of the *Volk*) and of what the regime had already achieved. It also served as a compensation for the conditions of life in the Reich, which in many ways continued to be meagre and difficult. The economic problems caused by the unrestrained rearmament policy were becoming more severe, and they reached a climax in autumn 1936. In 1937 William Shirer reported retrospectively that he had seen 'long lines of sullen people before the food shops', adding that 'there is a shortage of meat and butter and fruit and fats, whipped cream is *verboten*, men's suits and women's dresses are increasingly made out of wood pulp, gasoline out of coal, rubber out of coal and lime' and that 'there is no gold coverage for the Reichsmark or for anything else, not even for vital imports.'[86]

The situation of the German economy had now become so serious, owing to the extreme character of the rush towards rearmament, that there were unmistakable symptoms of crisis. As a result, there was a considerable division of opinion within the regime over its future course. Financial resources for the continuation, let alone the expansion, of the rearmament drive were no longer available: the Reichsbank's reserves of foreign currency had largely been exhausted by now, and the 'clearing system' was no longer effective. Germany was deeply in debt to most of its trading partners, above all Romania, which was an irreplaceable source of energy supplies. There was only enough raw material to cover a few more months; Germany was now living from hand to mouth for its supplies of rubber, iron ore, lead and zinc. On top of that, industry was desperately in need of a larger workforce, and since wages were far higher there than in agriculture, 1.4 million people abandoned farming between 1933 and 1939. This made it still harder to produce enough food. Germany's agricultural sector was further away than ever from its hoped-for wartime self-sufficiency.

Above all, though, there was a shortage of foreign currency for the import of raw materials. This could only be procured by selling German products abroad, in other words, through exports. But to raise production for export, it was necessary to cut down on arms production. Hjalmar Schacht, the Economics Minister and head of the Reichsbank, saw only one way out of this difficult situation: to devalue the Reichsmark, increase exports and reduce the tempo of rearmament. A memorandum from the mayor of Leipzig, Carl Goerdeler, went further. Only devaluation and an intensification of exports could bring the overheated economy back into balance; the prerequisite for this was of course the re-entry of Germany into the world economy, which made necessary a *rapprochement* with the Great Powers of the West, above all Britain and the USA. These proposals involved nothing less than the abandonment of Germany's disproportionate stress on rearmament and its isolation from the world economy, and they implied an admission that National Socialist economic policy had failed, because the dynamic growth in armaments it had set in motion had ruined the state's finances.[87]

Hitler, however, saw things very differently. In a memorandum he composed in August 1936, while the Olympic Games were in progress, he explained the objectives of his regime and the conclusions that followed from them as regards Germany's future economic and political course. The starting point, he said, was the threat of Bolshevism, which was so immense and so dangerous that if Germany wished to survive, it would have to prepare for war as quickly as possible. Accordingly, further rearmament could not be done 'too swiftly, or on too large a scale'. Everything else must be subordinated to this criterion. In order to procure raw materials, they would have to emphasise synthetic products more strongly, irrespective of cost. The provision of food to the population in case of war would also have to be guaranteed. They would have to economise on foreign currency. But it was Jewry that was responsible for the shortage of foreign currency, and the Jews must be made liable for this. Hitler refused either to allow exports to be increased or arms production to be throttled.

His alternative to the liberal world economic system was therefore not a different economic system but war. The cost of increased armaments ought no longer to be relevant, as it would be recovered by victory in war, and the same was true of raw materials. One would temporarily have to make do with ersatz materials, and acquire the foreign currency needed by reducing private consumption still further and by expropriating the Jews. Hitler's summary was this: 'I. Germany's armed forces must be ready for action within four years. II. The German economy must be ready for war within four years.'[88]

This decision accelerated the course of events in the next few years to such a degree that those responsible for conducting policy were not entirely able to maintain control. In order to coordinate the economic preparations for war, a gigantic organisation was set up, called the 'Four Year Plan Authority'. Goering was now the strong man of economic policy, having been appointed head of this organisation after Schacht's resignation from the post of Minister of Economics. He described his task in this way: 'All our measures have to be conducted as if we were under the threat of an approaching war.'[89]

What was most important, however, was to gain access to new sources of finance, since there was now hardly any money left for the policy of frenzied rearmament. The acquisition of raw materials was also a priority, because the production of synthetic materials was only moving forward slowly and, in any case, these could never be more than a stopgap. What was needed to improve Germany's starting position effectively was an expansion of territory, while staying below the threshold of war, if possible. Germany's potential opponents in war, particularly Britain and France, had now themselves begun to rearm more strenuously, so that the country would soon lose the lead it had gained in the years 1936 and 1937. Moreover, the Western powers would be able to count on the support of the USA, a factor the German leadership was also aware of. In that case, though, Germany would be significantly inferior to the West in the long run, from the point of view of both resource availability and productive capacity.

That is why the great war would have to come soon, in the period 1943–5 at the latest, as Hitler told his generals in November 1937. After that time, the relation of forces would develop to Germany's disadvantage. Also, an army as big as Germany's could not be financed and kept inactive for longer than that. If the circumstances of foreign policy were to change, however, it would be possible to strike before 1943. Then Austria and Czechoslovakia could be conquered first, and this would allow Germany's economic base to be broadened considerably. 'Germany's problem could only be solved by means of force, and this was never without attendant risk', he emphasised, against the objections of the leaders of the armed forces, who pointed out the incalculable risks he was running, and the material superiority of the West.[90]

The entry of German troops into Austria in March 1938 was in line with Hitler's logic. Through the 'Anschluss' with Austria Germany gained 1.4 billion RM in gold and foreign currency, more than 600,000 as yet unemployed workers, big supplies of raw materials and six Austrian army divisions in full readiness for action. It also worsened the strategic position of Czechoslovakia, France's last ally in the region and its only surviving democracy. South-East Europe had been earmarked as an area for the expansion of the German war economy, and it now lay completely within the German sphere of influence. Along with these economic and strategic advantages, the position of Hitler's regime in Germany and its reputation abroad were strengthened by his triumphal entry into Austria, by the enthusiasm of more than 500,000 Viennese, who cheered the 'Führer' as he passed, and last but not least by the result of the plebiscite of 10 April 1938, which delivered a 'Yes' vote of 99.7 per cent. The Western powers recognised the inclusion of Austria in the German Reich a few days later. The Nazi leaders took this to mean that resistance to Germany's further expansion was not to be expected for the time being. This spurred them on to take further aggressive steps.

As with Hitler's previous foreign policy coups, the initial reaction of the German population was a feeling of uneasiness and tension. This only changed when it turned out that everything had gone well and the Allies had not intervened. The atmosphere now was first one of relief, and later enthusiastic admiration. The words 'Hitler, a genius!' could be read in the German newspapers. 'Hitler, who succeeds in everything' was the resigned comment in the SOPADE reports. When he celebrated his 49th birthday ten days later, Germany experienced a climax of Hitler worship. 'The jubilation around Hitler's birthday celebrations in the whole of Germany was so tremendous' noted the American *Time Magazine* angrily and sarcastically

> that Dr. Wilhelm Frick, the Minister of the Interior, felt compelled to pronounce the words 'Adolf Hitler is Germany, and Germany is Adolf Hitler' Lorry-loads of birthday presents were brought into the Reich Chancellery, where the non-military part of the birthday celebrations took place. The Führer received flowers by the ton, cakes by the hundred, a set of tape-recordings of his Anschluss speeches, a set of foreign-language editions of *Mein Kampf* and a baby lion.[91]

In Austria, however, the terror had already begun. What had required months and years in Germany was completed there in days and weeks. From 11 March 1938 onwards, members of working-class parties all over the country were attacked, beaten and locked up in camps by Nazi paramilitaries. For Jews, it was much worse. They were publicly humiliated in a way rarely seen as yet, even in Germany. 'Already on the very same day, the anti-Semitic rabble saw that their time had come', reported a Jewish doctor on what happened in Vienna.

> Jews were beaten bloody, spat at and insulted in the streets. Large numbers of Jews with broken ribs, battered skulls and knocked-out teeth came to the outpatients' departments of the Jewish hospitals. Just to give one example: one afternoon, the Jews in the Hauptallee, whatever their age or sex, were herded together, and forced to do leapfrogs and cry out 'Perish the Jew' or 'I am a Jewish sow'. They had to run the gauntlet and so on. The humiliation of Jews was the order of the day. Old men and women, respected rabbis, doctors and lawyers were forced to sweep the streets or clean cars.[92]

Since the reoccupation of the Rhineland, a reference to the right of self-determination had been the strongest and most effective argument on the German side. In Great Britain in particular there were powerful forces which regarded the treatment of Germany since the First World War as a breach of this right, and therefore had a certain degree of understanding for the Austrian 'Anschluss'. It would hardly have been possible to persuade the British population to wage war against a country simply because it was bringing its own people 'back to the Reich' with their agreement. 'Appeasement' of Hitler seemed to the Western powers to be the appropriate way of preventing a new war. In any case, neither Britain nor France was prepared for war. They had only just started rearming, and thus if there really had to be a new war with Germany, it would be best for it to happen as late as possible.

The German side, on the other hand, was under time pressure. Immediately after his extremely successful stroke against Austria, Hitler instructed the Wehrmacht to start preparing for an invasion of Czechoslovakia. But, for the present, a military solution was only the last resort. A suitable way of altering the status quo was offered by the difficult situation of the Germans in Czechoslovakia, who with 28 per cent of the population were the second largest national group in the country, after the Czechs with their 46 per cent, and were organised in the Sudeten German Party. The German minority in Czechoslovakia enjoyed full civic equality but suffered disadvantages in the areas of language policy and appointments to the civil service and also in the cultural sphere. The German side began to use this as a lever to exert such strong pressure on Czechoslovakia that on 20 May 1938 the Prague government mobilised its troops, in fear of a German attack. When London and Paris responded to this by reaffirming their obligation to defend the country, and the Soviet Union added its voice as well, Europe seemed to be on the point of entering a large-scale war. In actual fact, it had not been Hitler's intention to invade immediately. Germany now moderated its tone, but it continued to exert pressure on its neighbour. Hitler issued a directive to the army on 30 May, stating: 'It is my unalterable decision to smash Czechoslovakia . . . by military action' and he fixed 1 October 1938 as the deadline for this.[93]

An instructive dispute about Germany's future course now developed among the leaders of the country around this question. 'The military do not want to march, because they have a clear view of the consequences of a war waged against us by a coalition of opponents', noted State Secretary of the Foreign Office von Weizsäcker.[94] The Foreign Office and most of the leading military men, as well as economic specialists such as Schacht and von Krosigk, were opposed to an early invasion of Czechoslovakia, because this would involve the risk of a war with France and Great Britain. The Reich was neither economically nor financially prepared for such a war, they said. Moreover, the generals of the Wehrmacht feared that a war started in the current circumstances would end in defeat. The conflict went so deep that Chief of the Army General Staff Ludwig Beck, together with numerous other Wehrmacht generals, considered for a while the possibility of mounting a military coup. He finally resigned from his position instead. These differences of opinion, however, did not relate to the fundamental foreign policy goals of the Reich. The need to make territorial conquests in Europe, by military means if necessary, was undisputed. Beck was entirely convinced 'that Germany needs greater living space (*Lebensraum*), both in Europe and the colonial regions. In Europe this can only be acquired by war.'[95] The critics occasionally included Goering, who as head of the Four Year Plan was only too aware of Germany's economic problems. None of them disputed that a war of revenge against France was probably inevitable. What they objected to was the decision to take the risk *now* of a large-scale war which Germany might well lose because its economic and military foundations were not yet sufficiently stable.

For Hitler, on the other hand, the risky gambles of the previous years had been the key to success. Even in conflicts of lesser importance, which the conflict over 'Sudetenland' undoubtedly was, he was ready to risk a large-scale war, which in case of defeat would mean, as von Weizsäcker formulated it, 'not only the end of the Third Reich but *finis Germaniae*' while his adversaries in Paris, London and Prague, who were aware of their responsibilities, shrank back from the prospect. This gave him the strategic advantage once again.[96]

In autumn 1938, the crisis again became acute, after Hitler had attacked the Czechoslovak government in strident tones, openly threatening the use of force. Disturbances broke out in 'Sudetenland' in response to Hitler's speech, and they assumed the character of an uprising. Now events came thick and fast: Czechoslovakia mobilised, France called up its reserves, Britain placed its fleet on a war footing and Europe was again faced with the prospect of war. In this situation, the United Kingdom gave way to the pressure of the Germans, who were supported by Italy, and signed the Munich agreement of 29 September 1938, by which areas of Czechoslovakia with a majority German population were to be annexed to Germany. On 1 October, the Wehrmacht began to occupy the area evacuated by the armed forces of Czechoslovakia.

Germany had enjoyed a complete triumph. Without needing to take military action, the Reich had acquired an area of almost 30,000 square kilometres and more than 3.5 million inhabitants, containing important industrial centres and significant deposits of raw materials such as lignite, tungsten and uranium ore. This meant a considerable expansion in the material basis for the intended war.[97]

The Munich Agreement had a decisive impact on the European diplomatic framework, and political observers all over the world reacted to it with deep concern. 'The negative effects of the Munich Agreement are already fully in operation' was the verdict pronounced by the World Jewish Congress in an internal analysis of the situation made in October 1938.

> Czechoslovakia is rapidly becoming an anti-democratic state, which will in practice be forced to become a vassal of Germany. Yugoslavia, Bulgaria and Turkey are increasingly coming under the dominant economic, and therefore

> also political, influence of Germany. Romania will also find it difficult to escape from the growing pressure of the Third Reich. Poland lives in panicky fear of Germany and it will . . . increasingly accommodate itself to Germany's wishes. All the small states of Europe are terrified of the future and are consumed by panic over Germany's hegemony. Europe is about to experience a difficult and bitter winter.[98]

The results of the Munich Agreement can be summarised in five points. Firstly, it sealed the fate of the new European order created by the Paris peace treaties of 1919, in which the principle of nation-states with guaranteed rights for ethnic minorities was enshrined. For the future, this signified the possible disintegration of the states of East Central Europe, most of which were ethnically mixed. Czechoslovakia, which had been created at the end of the First World War by the Western powers in the course of the dissolution of the imperial and royal Austrian monarchy, had now been robbed of its most economically important regions. Henceforth, its hold on existence was precarious.

Secondly, by their appeasement policies, the Western powers had lost their credibility as protectors of the other states threatened by Germany. Great Britain's weakness had become transparently obvious, and this threatened to damage its reputation as a world power. Admittedly, Prime Minister Chamberlain had been celebrated in London after his return from Munich as the peacemaker who had avoided a possible world war. Further concessions, however, were not to be expected in the future, and in any case they would have been impossible to implement in Britain for domestic political reasons.

Thirdly, the composition of the rival camps in the coming confrontation was already implied in the 'Anti-Comintern Pact' directed against the Soviet Union, which was joined by Japan in addition to Germany and Italy. At the same time, however, Britain and France had negotiated the Munich Agreement with Germany and Italy unilaterally. Czechoslovakia was only there to take instructions, and the Soviet Union had not even been invited to the conference. The Soviet leadership drew the conclusion from this that in case of a conflict the Western powers would come to an agreement with Hitler's Germany, and make common cause with Hitler against the Soviet Union. Stalin's logical response to this danger was to explore various alliance options, partly with the West but also partly with Germany.

Fourthly, as regards German domestic politics, it had been shown that the Nazi regime could not be entirely certain of receiving backing from the German population for its risky policy of expansionism. Reports from local party offices and the secret services bore witness to the apprehensive and dejected mood in the country and the increasingly widespread rumours about an impending war, even within the NSDAP. A Bavarian NSDAP District Leader reported that it had recently become clear that 'the necessary unconditional trust in the Führer was lacking among many Party members, who could not be counted on if things became serious.'[99] Admittedly, it was possible after the Munich triumph to observe a typical mood swing from tense anxiety to relief and enthusiasm. But there was no trace of any enthusiasm for war among the German people as a whole. In later years, the regime's doubts about the attitude of the population repeatedly led it to take careful account of the popular mood and to intensify political surveillance.

Fifthly, the Sudeten crisis and the Munich Agreement freed the regime from its previous concerns about protest and resistance both at home and abroad. Notwithstanding all the objections, Hitler's risk-taking strategy had again prevailed and proved to be successful. Neither the conservative diplomats and economists nor the sceptics within the Nazi movement had anything to set against Hitler's aura of success. Beck's military colleagues, having failed to act in the summer of 1938, now fell into line with Hitler, who had demonstrated his superior strategic grasp with such virtuosity. They waited for a further six years, until it was too late, before they risked another attempt to overthrow him. It seemed as if the course of events had refuted the views of the conservative nationalists, and they largely ceased to play a role in correcting the accelerated radicalisation of German policy. Hitler's foreign opponents also seemed to have given up the fight at the moment of danger. Hitler no longer had to take account of the negative diplomatic consequences of his actions. What could possibly scare him, after he had weathered two episodes of mobilisation and achieved all his goals? As a result, the dynamic of force intensified as the force of resistance diminished.

## The Night of Broken Glass

Hitler's foreign policy successes also reduced any need to take account of possible diplomatic consequences or economic disadvantages arising from the country's policy towards the Jews. The regime's anti-Jewish measures had been briefly interrupted by the Nuremberg Laws and the 'Olympic Peace' of summer 1936. But, from the beginning of 1938 onwards, the anti-Semitic campaign was again intensified. The ruthlessness with which the Austrian Jews were persecuted and deprived of their rights reached such a pitch that, as the American ambassador observed, 'the present anti-Jewish campaign is being carried out more thoroughly than anything that has happened since the beginning of 1933, and goes far beyond what was merely the party's summertime exuberance as manifested in 1935.'[100]

The 'solution of the Jewish question in the economy' lay at the heart of the new campaign. By now, of course, a large part of the Jewish population in Germany was living on its savings, and the majority of Jewish firms had already been 'Aryanised', whether by official action or in the form of unofficial or 'wild Aryanisations', whereby Jewish enterprises were compelled to abandon trading by local banks and firms, acting in concert. But when attempts were made to snatch the remaining firms from their Jewish proprietors, especially larger firms, which had not been very much affected so far, some people raised serious objections. In July 1938, the Ministry of the Interior proposed to issue a law providing for the immediate, complete and compulsory removal of Jews from the German economy and the confiscation of their property. The Finance Minister, however, protested against this, pointing out the resultant loss of tax revenue, while the Reichsbank also objected, on the ground that the measure would endanger the capital market. It was also known that corruption and self-enrichment by officials was flourishing. In Austria, Goering remarked critically, 'De-Judaizing the economy' was evidently regarded as the party's most essential field of activity, and 'as a system for the maintenance of inept party comrades'.

The objective of Germany's Jewish policy, according to Heydrich, the head of the Security Police, must be firstly 'to create emigration opportunities while avoiding as much as possible the expenditure of foreign currency' and secondly 'to secure funds for the support of the remaining Jews by drawing on foreign and domestic Jewish resources'. These ideas soon turned out to be impracticable, however. Either the emigration of the Jews was the regime's main objective, in which case it would have to let them keep the resources they needed to be accepted abroad. Or it took away everything from the Jews, which was a course it was inclined to take in view of the precarious economic situation. But then there would not be enough countries prepared to accept the penniless Jews who emigrated. In practice, the regime followed both policies simultaneously. Persecution of Jews, and discrimination against them, was intensified in order to induce them to emigrate. But expropriation was also increased, so as to get hold of their wealth. The effect was that the movement of emigration came to a standstill.[101] The situation the Jews were in was further worsened by the results of the international conference held in summer 1938 in Évian, which showed that the readiness of most countries to accept Jewish refugees from Germany was extremely limited. The USA, for example, stuck to its quota of 27,370 immigrants from Germany and Austria, while most of the other countries closed their borders completely.[102]

The stalemate which resulted from these contradictions in autumn 1938 made the direction in which the regime's anti-Jewish policy would develop uncertain and relatively open: would it move towards a slow 'elimination' of the Jews, above all, the bigger Jewish firms, from German economic life, which would stretch out over a number of years, or would it opt for their rapid and radical exclusion from the economy, even at the cost of damaging the latter?

In October 1938, the regime started to remove Jews of Polish nationality from Germany. Within two days, 17,000 Polish Jews, most of them male, were arrested in Germany, collected together in holding camps, and then transported by train to the Polish border, so that they could be deported. But the Polish border guards forcibly prevented the Jews from crossing over, so that the deportees had to be accommodated in no man's land in improvised internment camps. The operation was eventually broken off, and the Jews had to be brought back again to their homes. This failure confirmed that no promising plan was available for the forced emigration of the Jews, and it heightened the expectation among the authorities as well as in the party that a different way of proceeding against them would be chosen at the next opportunity.[103]

This opportunity arrived just a few days later. On 7 November 1938, a German diplomat in Paris was shot by a young Polish Jew, whose parents had been among those previously transported to the Polish border. A day later the diplomat died of his wounds, and Hitler and Goebbels ordered the Gauleiters who had gathered in Munich to celebrate the 15th anniversary of Hitler's attempted putsch to start 'operations against the Jews on the largest possible scale. These should end with an appropriate destruction of Jewish property, and everyone would have a completely free hand.' These are the words recorded by the Gauleiter of Vienna, Odilo Globocnik.[104]

Having received these instructions, SA and party people banded together all over the country that very evening. With the support and encouragement of members of the Hitler Youth, onlookers and other 'comrades' who had hurried to the scene, they began to plunder Jewish businesses, drag Jews out of their homes and mistreat them, destroy Jewish institutions and set fire to synagogues. More than 100 people lost their lives. Plundering took place all over the country, and more than 800 cases were officially reported, in many of which children and Hitler Youth members participated. In Berlin, the big jeweller's shop Markgraf, on Unter den Linden, was robbed, and jewels to the value of 1.7 million RM were stolen. Fur shops and draperies suffered the same fate. 'Now the anger of the people is raging' wrote Goebbels contentedly in his diary. 'I drive to the hotel. I hear the noise of shattering windows. Bravo! Bravo! . . . The whole nation is in uproar.'[105]

These stage-managed pogroms led to worldwide indignation and protest. Western newspapers reported the barbaric acts in detail, the USA recalled its ambassador from Berlin and the French *chargé d'affaires* in Berlin predicted that 'the violence and cruelty which are an inherent part of National Socialist ethics will condemn Germany itself to be judged by the law of the sword, with which it wants to subdue its enemies.'[106]

The reaction of the German population was similar. Almost all the local party offices reported that the 'Action' had been greeted with popular incomprehension and rejection. The Bielefeld Gestapo, for instance, received exclusively negative replies to a questionnaire it sent to local police stations. According to its report, the operation had called forth 'head-shaking and icy silence' from the people. 'The population were gloomy and depressed. Here and there clear indications of sympathy could be noted.' 'The overwhelming majority of the population have not understood the operation against the Jews, and they condemn it, pointing out that things like this ought not to happen in a civilised country.' This was the consistent tenor of the replies.[107]

But there was no open criticism either from the churches, the army leaders or the conservative nationalists in charge of the economy. Indeed, at a conference held on 12 November von Krosigk, the Minister of Finance, one of the spokesmen of the conservative nationalists in the government, explicitly stated his approval of the radical course adopted by Heydrich and Goering: 'What must always be the determining factor, is that we should not keep the whole of the social proletariat here. It will always be a frightful burden to keep hold of them. . . . Consequently, the goal must be as Heydrich puts it: bring out what can be brought out!'[108]

The internal reports from the party organisation, on the other hand, referred mainly to the criticisms made of the public character and the 'disorderliness' of the action, and the repeated condemnation of the 'unnecessary destruction of valuable property'. This could also be a camouflaged form of criticism. But, at the same time, the next step was already announced here: from now on, the houses, furniture, and businesses of the Jews should not be destroyed but taken away from them undamaged.[109]

Despite these criticisms, the leading Nazis were not unhappy with the operation. The anti-Jewish policy, which had previously been at a standstill, was extended and pushed forward in succeeding months. On the same day as the pogroms took place, Hitler ordered 'that the economic solution should now be put into effect', and this was the purpose of the above-mentioned conference of 12 November, which was scheduled by Goering, and attended by representatives of all government departments, local authorities and National Socialist organisations which were involved in any way with the regime's Jewish policy, particularly in the economic field. While Goering lamented the millions of Marks of damage done by the actions of 10 November and examined the question of 'de-Judaizing' the economy, Goebbels proposed that synagogues be turned into 'parking places' and that Jews be forbidden from visiting circuses or beaches, using sleeping compartments on trains, or entering Germany's woodlands.[110]

But the period of merely symbolic harassment of the Jews had evidently come to an end, and these petty and malicious proposals met with little agreement: in future, action would take place on a much broader scale. The Jews would now be expropriated completely, and thereby pushed into emigrating. On the same day, 12 November, Goering announced the imposition of a 'contribution': the Jews would have to pay one billion RM as 'atonement', and in addition they would have to meet the cost of repairing the damage done to their own property. The Nazi leaders did not hesitate to admit how welcome the money of the Jews was in view of the country's extremely critical economic situation. As Goering told the Reich Defence Council: 'Gentlemen, the finances are looking very critical. But now a certain alleviation has taken place owing to the billion the Jews have had to pay.' Even so, the regime's financial problems were by no means solved by this method.[111]

The night of 9 November had far-reaching political consequences. Internationally, the pogroms had aroused considerable attention, and they had removed any doubt about the violent character of the Nazi regime even among observers who had nourished a certain sympathy for the 'new Germany'. Domestically, too, everyone had been shown what was to be expected from the National Socialists: acts of violent assault, arson, pillage and murder had taken place in public, and henceforth no one in the country could maintain that he or she had been unaware of the persecution of the Jews. On the contrary, from that time onwards, it required a special effort to avoid paying anxious attention to their subsequent fate.

After repeated internal criticisms, the regime's anti-Jewish policy was now centralised under Heydrich's Security Police and the Security Service (SD). The impression thus arose that operations against the Jews would henceforth no longer be conducted by drunken gangs of SA men but by state officials, in due legal form, smoothly and without any public furore. At the same time, the tempo was accelerated; the radicalism of the regime's measures increased dramatically.

In the months that followed 9 November 1938, the authorities took a number of far-reaching steps in quick succession, aimed at the 'economic liquidation of Jewry'. These included the above-mentioned confiscation of one billion RM as 'atonement' for the Jews' 'sins', the 'Decree for the Exclusion of the Jews from German Economic Life', which rapidly led to the 'Aryanisation' of the remaining large Jewish enterprises, and a host of other specific measures which rendered the German Jews completely destitute within a few months.[112] The establishment of the Reich Central Office for Jewish Emigration allowed expulsion to be organised more quickly. The Law on Jewish Rental Arrangements was a step towards concentrating Jewish families in 'Jewish houses', and the Reich Association of Jews in Germany was set up as a compulsory body through which all Jewish cultural activities were placed under the control of the Security Police. In order to increase the Jews' 'willingness to emigrate', the Gestapo sent almost 30,000 predominantly wealthy Jewish males to concentration camps—11,000 to Dachau, 9,800 to Buchenwald and between 6,000 and 10,000 to Sachsenhausen. The incarcerated Jews were treated with tremendous brutality in order to force their emigration. In Dachau alone, 185 of those imprisoned since November were dead within a few weeks. 'I would not wish to be a Jew in Germany' was Goering's cynical comment at the 12 November conference.[113]

The German authorities thus made it plain even to the doubters among the Jewish community that it was not just their social position but their life which was in danger, and the terror these measures inspired caused the number of emigrants to rise rapidly in the next few months. In order to gain release from the concentration camps, Jews had to present emigration papers and agree to the 'Aryanisation' of their property. Between December 1938 and the beginning of the war, approximately 80,000 Jews fled from Germany, most of them completely destitute and in pitiable circumstances. They attempted to get to Palestine, France, England, Cuba, the Netherlands, Switzerland or the USA, and eventually even tried to reach Japanese-occupied Shanghai. But many of them failed to obtain a visa, had insufficient money to pay for the journey or fell foul of bureaucratic hurdles. Those who did manage to make it, after their Odyssey through the maze of domestic and foreign bureaucracy, had been forced to leave all their possessions behind them. Some, such as the refugees on the steamer St Louis, even arrived back in Germany after being shuttled for weeks between Cuba and Florida.

The proportion of young people among the emigrants was disproportionately high: in 1939, 75 per cent of the Jews who remained behind were over forty years old. Most of them were impoverished, having been expelled from their jobs. Often, they were driven out of their homes as well and accommodated in designated 'Jewish houses'. Only 16 per cent of them were reported as being in employment. The treatment of those Jews who still remained in the Reich was now first and foremost a police problem, because these impoverished, isolated and unemployed people soon appeared to fit the distorted image which had been put over by anti-Semitic propaganda of the dirty, workshy and criminal Jew, who should be treated accordingly. Isolation and pauperisation, predicted the SS newspaper *Das Schwarze Korps* on 24 November 1938, would force the Jews into a miserable existence, as a result of which they would all inevitably 'sink into criminality'.

> At such a stage of development, we would therefore be faced with the harsh necessity of rooting out the Jewish underworld in the same way as we are accustomed to rooting out criminals in our orderly state: with fire and sword! The consequence of this would be the real and final end of Jewry in Germany, its complete annihilation.[114]

During those weeks at the end of 1938, threats of this kind could often be heard, as well as announcements of the Jews' downfall and prophecies of their extermination. Thus Goering, for instance, proclaimed after the November pogroms: 'If the German Reich enters into conflict with a foreign power at some point in the foreseeable future, it goes without saying that our very first thought in Germany will be to undertake a grand settlement of accounts with the Jews.'[115] Remarks of this kind signified that boundaries were being crossed. By explicitly formulating what was intended in terms their own supporters could understand, the meaning of which was only concealed from outsiders for form's sake, the Nazis extended the sphere of what could be thought and uttered. Moreover, in view of perspectives of this kind, possible objections to recent intensifications of anti-Jewish policy, which had previously still been regarded as unimaginable, now almost had an air of pedantry.

These rhetorical excesses reached a climax on 30 January 1939, when Hitler explained to the Reichstag the basis and the purpose of his regime's anti-Jewish policy. First of all, he gave a justification for the 'Aryanisation' of Jewish property: 'What this people possesses today it has acquired through the most vicious manipulations at the expense of the Germans, who are not quite so crafty. We are only getting back what this people owes us.' If the Western powers are not ready to accept the Jews, it will not be possible to solve the Jewish problem in Europe, because 'Europe will never be at rest until the Jewish question has been cleared out of the way. . . . The world has enough settlement areas.' But if Jewry is not thrown out and settled in some other part of the world, 'it will sooner or later fall victim to a crisis of unimaginable dimensions.' Hitler then goes on to give undisguised utterance to the threat he has just made implicitly: 'If international Jewish finance within Europe and outside it should succeed once more in plunging the nations into a world war, the result will not be the Bolshevisation of the world and thereby the victory of Jewry but, on the contrary, the annihilation of the Jewish race in Europe.'

Hitler's 'prophecy' of 30 January 1939, which he repeatedly referred to in subsequent years, contained three essential features. Firstly, he explained the decline of Germany and the crises set off by the rise of modernity in politics and culture by the activities of the Jews. Secondly, he stressed the role of the Jews in causing the war which Germany had long been preparing for. Thirdly, by making these statements, he revealed the ultimate goal of his anti-Jewish policy to the supporters of the Nazi regime. This does not mean that they were already aware at this point of the direction that policy would take in the future. It was rather that once the notion of the 'annihilation of the Jewish race in Europe' had been stated openly, it developed its own dynamic. Now no National Socialist functionary was able to retreat from this notion when speaking of the Jews.[116]

## On the Eve of War

Immediately after the army had marched into 'Sudetenland', Hitler gave orders for the next stage of German expansion. This involved three regions: Memelland, a small stretch of territory at the edge of the Baltic state of Lithuania, which had belonged to East Prussia until 1918 and had been autonomous since 1924; Danzig (Gdańsk) which had enjoyed the protection of the League of Nation since the Versailles Treaty as a 'Free City'; and, by far the most important, Czechoslovakia, or rather what was left of it after the Munich Agreement. This was, however, an industrialised and well-armed state, and unlike in the cases of Austria and 'Sudetenland', the German side could not count on being greeted by the majority of the population as liberators. An invasion would presumably lead to a war in which Germany would suffer serious losses, and an intervention by the Western powers could not be ruled out.

Hitler therefore decided to use the internal tensions between Czechs and Slovaks as a lever with which to the split the country in two. Germany supported the separatist movement in Slovakia and pressed the Slovaks to declare independence. They finally did this on 14 March 1939. The Czech government would have liked to resist. But Hitler had been working towards this situation. The German government now summoned the Czech president Dr Emil Hácha to Berlin and put him under such strong pressure, both politically and physically, that he finally signed a document of surrender by which he 'confidently placed the fate of the Czech people in the hands of the Führer and of the German Reich.' In formal terms, therefore, this was a request for German aid. On the morning of the next day, 15 March 1939, Wehrmacht units marched into Prague, and on 16 March Hitler visited the city to proclaim the 'Protectorate of Bohemia and Moravia'.

While the Sudetenland, like Austria, was annexed to Germany, and Slovakia was made a formally independent state, dependent in fact on Germany, the Czech part of former Czechoslovakia was declared to be a German 'protectorate'. The fact that the Czech region retained its own administration, and the autonomous status granted to Slovakia, were intended to demonstrate to the outside world that the peoples in the German sphere of domination would keep a certain degree of independence. On the other hand, the notion of a 'Protectorate' was reminiscent of colonial traditions, and it was comparable to the position of Algeria within the French colonial empire.

By incorporating 'Czechia', Germany obtained a considerable increase in economic and military potential. The Czechs had enough ammunition to arm twenty divisions, and their military equipment alone had a value of 77 million RM. The highly developed defence industry of a country which had previously been one of the ten most important industrial states in the world, and the

Czechs' extensive reserves of gold and foreign currency provided the extremely overheated German war economy with an enormous increase in strength, without the need to fire a single shot.

March 1939 meant more than just one further step on the road of German expansion. Before the march into Prague, the world had continued, despite all its criticism, to make allowances for Germany's policy of treaty revision and expansion on the ground that in the cases of the Rhineland, the Saar, Austria and 'Sudetenland' these were areas inhabited overwhelmingly by Germans. But there was no justification of this kind for the march into what was described as 'Rump Czechia'. It was clear to everyone that this was an act of pure violence, in which military, power-political and economic motives were paramount. The regime therefore no longer sought to legitimate its expansionism by talking of 'bringing home' fellow Germans, but by asserting the right of a Great Power to act in its own sphere of influence as it wished, in the same way the British did in India; the French in North Africa; and the USA in Central and South America. According to a highly regarded lecture by the Berlin jurist Carl Schmitt, there was no such thing as a 'law of nations', conceived as a universal principle of order, independently of actual power relations. It was purely an instrument for maintaining the status quo, and therefore served the interests of the Western democracies. Moreover, the Monroe Doctrine of 1823 showed that the USA acted purely in its own interests in its own vast region. Germany wanted nothing more for itself in regard to East Central Europe.[117]

This manner of theoretically underpinning German expansionism proved to be helpful in warding off British and American criticism of Germany's actions. On 20 April 1939, Hitler referred to the Monroe Doctrine in his reply to President Roosevelt's letter urging Germany to end its policy of expansion. After all, he said, Germany did not ask what aims America was pursuing in its foreign policy 'let us say, for example, towards the states of Central or South America.'[118] But, in reality, the German conception went far beyond such an analogy to the Monroe Doctrine. As Hitler had emphasised three months earlier, 'the next war will be purely a war between rival world-views, i.e. it will be quite deliberately a war between races and peoples.' [119] What that meant was intensively discussed by Nazi intellectuals during these months. In the *völkisch* conception, wrote the SS jurist Werner Best, there was no 'law of nations'. What counted was the interest of one's own people and there were no limitations on a people's activities apart from its own strength. 'In its behaviour towards other peoples, no people (*Volk*) can let itself be bound by rules which are alleged to be valid regardless of its own life-purposes.' It was therefore a matter for the Germans alone whether they accepted the presence of other peoples in their region or 'they felt that their collaboration was undesirable', and 'the artificial conservation' of other peoples in their region was by no means the task of the Germans.[120]

After the march into Prague and the occupation of Memelland shortly afterwards, the Western powers were no longer under any illusions about the character of German policy. Now they were only interested in gaining time, so as to push forward as far as they could with their own war preparations. In addition, there was no longer any support from public opinion for a continuation of the policy of appeasement, either in Britain or in France.

Poland's turn came next. For a long time, it had been unclear what role that country would play in Germany's further expansion: was it to be a junior partner in a German attack on the Soviet Union or was it to be a target in its own right? The Poles had reacted with hesitation in autumn 1938 to Hitler's attempts to involve them in an alliance, because this would have meant taking part in a front against the USSR. Warsaw wished to avoid this at all costs in view of its past experiences with its two dominant neighbours. The Poles much preferred to put themselves under the protection of the Western powers. After the German army had marched into Prague, Great Britain in fact gave protection to Poland by guaranteeing its territorial integrity. For Hitler, this decided the issue, and he ordered the leaders of the Wehrmacht to prepare for a war with Poland. They should be ready to attack at any time from 1 September 1939 onwards. This time, however, Berlin did not count on a lack of resistance. 'There will be war', Hitler announced, although he hoped to be able to strike at an isolated enemy, with no intervention from Britain and France, two powers he had perceived to be irresolute and toothless at the Munich Conference and after the occupation of Prague.[121]

A war was now in the offing, this was clear. But diplomatic options also continued to be available. The most important of these related to the Soviet Union. Relations between Great Britain and the USSR could hardly have been worse at that point, but in view of the threat from Germany, Britain and France now made a concerted effort to come to an agreement with Stalin, because it was calculated that this would perhaps intimidate the Germans and lead them to recoil from entering a large-scale conflict. The Soviet side, however, was convinced after the Munich experience that the Western powers would join Hitler's Germany in a military onslaught against the USSR if the prospects looked favourable. Stalin therefore also tested out the option of making an alliance with Germany. For the Germans, in turn, an alliance with the Soviet Union would avert the danger of a war on two fronts. The months between March and the end of August 1939 were thus characterised by a 'race for Moscow', a race Hitler finally won, because he could make the Soviet side a better offer than the Western powers. If Stalin decided in favour of an alliance with the West and against Germany, it would be vital for the Red Army to have the right to march through Poland for an attack on Germany. But the Polish government did not want to guarantee this without reservation because they feared for the continued existence of their country. Hitler, in contrast, offered to divide the area between Germany and the Soviet Union with Stalin. The western part would fall to Germany, while the eastern part, and the Baltic lands as well, would fall to the Soviet Union. A Treaty of Non-Aggression sealed the alliance between the two countries, and its territorial provisions were laid down in an additional protocol which remained secret.[122]

When, on 23 August, the alliance between the two dictators became known, the news was greeted with astonishment and horror, not just by the Western powers but by the adherents of both regimes. The National Socialists had for the previous twenty years repeatedly described the fight against 'Jewish bolshevism' and the destruction of the Soviet Union with the aim of acquiring living space (*Lebensraum*) as their most important political goals. Similarly, 'German fascism' was for the Communists the most radical variant of capitalism and imperialism and the chief political and ideological enemy, and it was difficult to justify making an alliance with it.

But this was a superficial view. In terms of power politics, the German–Soviet Pact was entirely in the interest of both states. Stalin gained time to take precautions against an attack on the Soviet Union, which would certainly take place, in his opinion. It might come from Germany, or from the Western powers or from all of them simultaneously, he thought. By assigning eastern Poland and the Baltic states to the USSR the Pact also allowed Stalin to win back regions Russia had lost in 1917 and which it continued to claim. Germany, for its part, was able not only to expand its sphere of influence in Europe and consolidate its dominant position on the Continent, but also to avoid a simultaneous war against three Great Powers in the east and the west, a war it would probably be unable to win at this point. But Hitler's chief gain from the pact with Stalin was a free hand to conduct his war against Poland.

Within his own circle, Hitler repeatedly implied that the real war, the war for living space (*Lebensraum*) against the Soviet Union had only been postponed by the Pact. At first, however, Berlin hoped once again to isolate the war against Poland because the new alliance would deter the Western powers from intervening. This time, however, Hitler was wrong.

Whereas the 1914–18 war was followed by decades of disagreement over who had launched this first great world war, and why they had done so, in 1939 nobody was in any doubt. The Nazi regime had from the very first moment set its course towards revising the results of the First World War by force, and, in addition, it had also harboured much more far-reaching objectives, namely, to achieve German domination over continental Europe, gain an economically self-sufficient hinterland in Eastern and South-East Europe, conquer living space on the territory of the Soviet Union and establish Germany as a world power. It should not be overlooked that these objectives were in many respects a continuation of the policies of the war party during the First World War, because the latter had aimed at a victorious German peace involving extensive acquisitions of territory in both west and east, as well as a radical liquidation of the cultural and political accompaniments of industrial modernity. The Right had proved far too weak after 1918–19 to bring such projects to fruition. It was only fifteen years later that it succeeded, at its second attempt, in overthrowing a republic which was still supported at the end by roughly a third of the population, and then, from the very first days of the nationalist dictatorship, embarking on the transformation of the situation within Germany and making plans for a war of revenge.

These striking elements of continuity need to be recognised if one is to explain other changes which also made their mark on developments after 1919. Since, contrary to expectations, there was no way back to the rule of the old elites, a new political formation took shape, which was characterised by a close connection between a mass movement and a dominant leader, and which soon neutralised or eliminated all restraining or modifying elements, including parties and associations, domestic public opinion, parliamentary democracy, the independence of the judicial system, the workers' movement, the churches, the conservative nationalist alliance partner, the special position of the military, and finally foreign public opinion and the attitude of the Great Powers. As a result, the violent dynamic inherent in the National Socialist movement surged forward both at home and abroad. It can readily be seen that, once the war had started, all existing reservations and countervailing forces ceased to operate.

# 8

# The Destruction of Europe

Germany's attack on Poland on 1 September was followed two days later by declarations of war on Germany by Britain and France. On 6 September the British dominions of India, New Zealand, Australia and Canada also joined the war. With this, the German–Polish border conflict became the great war Hitler had long been working for. It was a war of the dictatorships against the democracies. On one side stood Germany, which had made an agreement with the Soviet Union, and Mussolini's Italy, which had declared its neutrality, but was firmly aligned with the Reich. On the other side stood the Western European powers along with their colonies and dominions and also the USA, which maintained an attitude of strict non-involvement, but did not hesitate to declare its sympathy with the Western European powers.

The declaration of war on Germany did not mean that Britain and France were ready to begin military operations. The governments of the two Western powers regarded Poland's situation as hopeless, given Germany's military strength, and they shrank from taking a direct role in the conflict. They sought rather to gain time, particularly in view of their lack of preparedness. France needed to reorganise its land forces, while Great Britain needed to strengthen its air force. Hence, they avoided intervening in the war between Germany and Poland. This allowed Hitler to send most of his forces against the Poles, leaving only a small number of troops to guard Germany's western borders.

The German army was therefore able to inflict a complete defeat on Poland within a few weeks. The German attack was conducted with great ferocity: systematic bombing raids were made on big cities for the first time in history. They caused immense loss of life among the civilian population. But, despite the Wehrmacht's rapid success, this was not just a 'weekend outing', as had been the case in the Rhineland, Austria and the Sudetenland, but a real war. The eventual death toll was approximately 66,000 on the Polish side, and 10,000 on the German.

On 17 September, the Soviet Union fulfilled its part of the secret agreement with Germany by occupying the eastern part of Poland. The areas Stalin occupied were almost identical with the areas Poland had taken from the Soviet Union in 1921 as a result of the Polish–Soviet war. The city of Warsaw surrendered on 27 September 1939, on 28 September Germany and the USSR signed a 'Treaty of Friendship and Boundary Demarcation' on the division of the booty, and by 6 October the military operations had come to an end. There was no capitulation by the Polish government, and no peace treaty. Poland was subjugated and partitioned. By the end of the war, roughly 5.5 million out of the 35 million people who lived in Poland in 1939 had lost their lives. At approximately 16 per cent, this was a greater proportional loss than any other country suffered during the Second World War.

It soon became apparent that war was the element most natural to National Socialism. Now, at last, it was no longer necessary either to do the wearisome job of weighing up opposing interests or to perform the difficult task of organising a modern and multifaceted industrial society. What was at stake now was victory or defeat, triumph or extinction. All now seemed to be subordinate to a single goal, namely victory. That simplified everything and made all actions legitimate. Opposition, objections and reservations were now obsolete, and in a situation of existential threat, the most radical proposal usually gained the upper hand. Until the war, written laws, international obligations and informal rules of behaviour had still been taken into account. Now, all these reservations were abandoned if it was deemed to be in Germany's interests to do so. The Nazi leaders accordingly took four fundamental decisions during the first six months of the war which had the effect of predetermining the main lines of future development. These decisions related to Germany's occupation policy in Poland, the persecution of the Polish Jews, the introduction of forced labour on a mass scale and the murder of the mentally and physically disabled.

## Occupation Policy

Germany's war aims with regard to Poland were of a completely different kind from those applied in March 1939 during the occupation of 'Czechia'. There was no question of Poland's continued existence as a state. The yardstick used here was the position before the First World War, when Poland was still divided between its more powerful neighbours. Nor was any attempt made to secure the cooperation of any Polish collaborationists, in running the government bureaucracy, for instance.[1]

After 1919, the conflict between rival nationalisms in the western regions of the new Polish state had radicalised the local Germans just as it had the local Polish population. The motivating forces here were revenge and hatred. Since the early 1930s, the situation had calmed down somewhat, but at the beginning of 1939 the conflict intensified again, chiefly stoked up by the vehemently anti-Polish propaganda issued by the German government, which was intended to prepare the population for the approaching war.

The strategic motive for the attack on Poland lay mainly in Hitler's conviction that the Polish threat 'from the rear' had to be removed in view of the planned war against the Western powers. But this motive was combined from the beginning with the idea that Poland could be converted into a largely agrarian satellite, a German colony with a predominantly peasant population. Elements of Hitler's conception of 'living space', which originally referred to the far-flung territories available in the Soviet Union, were now applied to Poland. What was at stake in the conflict with Poland, Hitler emphasised in May 1939, was not Danzig at all: 'For us it is a matter of rounding out our living space in the East.'[2]

Ideas of this type were being put forward and justified exactly at this time by scholars researching the German national heritage. Thus the Königsberg historian Theodor Schieder wrote a draft memorandum stating that in this region the German and Polish national groups should be separated from each other 'by population shifts on the largest possible scale'. In order to make room for the settlement of German 'returnees' from Eastern Europe, the Poles would have to be expropriated and forced to move elsewhere. At the same time, the 'building of a healthy national organisation' required 'the de-Judaization of rump Poland' and the 'removal of Jewry from the Polish towns' because otherwise 'the disintegration of the Polish nation' could make it 'the focus of yet more dangerous disturbances'.[3]

The German approach became more radical when the conflict between Poles and Germans in the western districts of the country culminated in the events of 3 and 4 September 1939. Roughly 450 Germans in Bromberg (Bydgoszcz) and more than 4,500 in the whole country fell victim to murders and lynchings carried out by Polish irregulars and fleeing regular troops.[4] On 7 September Hitler spoke for the first time about the need for a 'national land-clearance' in Poland. What he meant was explained by the head of the Security Police and the SD, Heydrich, in the following terms: the western parts of Poland must be incorporated into the Reich and 'Germanised'. 'The leading population stratum in Poland must as far as possible be rendered harmless. The low-level Poles that remain will not receive any special schools, but will be suppressed in one way or another.' The Polish workers would be used as seasonal and migrant labour and gradually shifted from the west to the east. To achieve objectives of this kind would require a hitherto unknown form of occupation policy. As Hitler announced to the top leaders of the party and the armed forces: 'The methods will be inconsistent with methods we use elsewhere . . . Lower standard of living. Our sole interest is that the density of the population provides us with a cheap labour force. In summary: an immensely tough, but focused struggle for the nation, which will rule out any legal restrictions.'[5] Admittedly, enormously extensive plans for resettlement, expulsion and exploitation had been put forward during the First World War, not least in the European colonies, but the magnitude of what was now envisaged was something unknown until then in European history.

Shortly before the war started, special 'task forces' (*Einsatzgruppen*) had been assembled, consisting of members of the Gestapo, the Criminal Police and the SD. They entered Poland behind the Wehrmacht, and they had the job of putting into effect the political goals of the Nazi regime, which were: '(1) the physical liquidation of all Polish elements which a) had played any kind of a leading part on the Polish side in the past, or b) might in the future be supporters of a Polish resistance. (2) the removal or resettlement of all "resident Poles" and "Congressers" from West Prussia. (3) the transplantation of Poles valuable racially or in other respects to the centre of the "Altreich" (i.e., Germany before its territorial expansion).'[6] The first of these measures was directed against the political and intellectual elite of the country, above all the nobility, the clergy, the teachers and the professors, and they were now seized and shot as hostages. The intention was to deprive the Poles of leadership, so that in future they could serve the Germans as a population of labourers. The second and third points indicated the regime's racial objectives: to drive all Poles out of the formerly West Prussian districts, and to begin a racial audit, so as to find 'valuable' Poles who could be Germanised in the Reich.

The *Einsatzgruppen* were joined in their massacre of the civilian population by units of the regular army, who mainly shot people presumed to be partisan fighters. At the same time, another group, the rapidly assembled 'Ethnic German Self-Protection Force', which consisted essentially of ethnic German political activists from western Poland, also began to murder 'objectionable' Poles. As a result of these measures, a total of roughly 20,000 Polish civilians were killed over a mere eight weeks of German military administration.

The attitudes of the army leaders towards this explosion of violence were not uniform. On the one hand, most generals supported the taking of radical measures against the Poles. The agreements on the deployment of the *Einsatzgruppen* were made between the Quartermaster General of the army and the head of the Security Police, Heydrich. At the same time, though, parts of the Wehrmacht leadership had definite reservations about this kind of occupation policy. In November 1939, for instance, Major Hellmuth Stieff wrote to his wife: 'The wildest inventions of atrocity propaganda pale into insignificance in comparison with the acts of criminality committed by an organised band of murderers, thieves and plunderers, tolerated allegedly at the highest level.' The military commander in Poland, Colonel-General von Blaskowitz, openly informed the Wehrmacht leadership of his objections: 'It is misguided to slaughter tens of thousands of Jews and Poles, as is happening at present, because in view of the huge population this neither destroys the Polish national idea nor gets rid of the Jews.' Blaskowitz also pointed to the future implications of the German leadership's instructions:

> When high officials of the SS and the police call for violence and brutality, and publicly commend this, it will very soon be only the men of violence who call the shots. Unwholesome characters of similar inclinations will join together surprisingly quickly to give vent to their bestial and pathological instincts. This is currently happening in Poland. There is hardly any possibility of keeping them in check, because they inevitably, and rightly, feel that every act of cruelty has been officially authorised and justified.[7]

But objections of this kind referred only to the violent excesses of the police units, not the behaviour of the troops. Moreover, the Wehrmacht leadership, around Franz Halder, the Chief of the General Staff and Walther von Brauchitsch, the Supreme Commander of the Army, never gave any backing to these protests and they were therefore largely without result. On the contrary, at the end of October, in order to be able to continue this barbaric ethnic policy undisturbed by the objections of the military, who were regarded as 'too soft' for 'Polish deployment', the Nazi leadership withdrew the occupied Polish districts from the jurisdiction of the Wehrmacht and placed them under the civil authorities.[8]

Hitler had already explained his views on the future structure of the conquered Polish region at the end of September:

> He wanted to divide the territory now established into three strips: 1 Between the Vistula and the Bug the entire Jewry (also from the Reich) along with all elements in any way unreliable. At the Vistula an impregnable Eastern Wall, even stronger than in the West. 2 Along the previous border a broad belt of Germanisation and colonisation. . . . 3 In between, a Polish state structure. Whether the belt of settlement could be pushed forward after some decades was a matter for the future.[9]

On 6 October 1939, Hitler announced to the Reichstag that the 'ethnographic picture' in the German-occupied territories would be 're-modelled'.[10] This referred first of all to the German–Soviet population exchange which had been agreed with the Soviet Union at the end of September. All the German-speaking minorities in the eastern parts of Poland which had now been occupied by the Soviet Union would be moved towards the west. A place would be found for them in the parts of western Poland now incorporated into Germany by resettling most of the currently resident Polish population in the east. At the beginning of October, therefore, the Polish territories occupied by Germany were divided into two large sections, roughly equal in size. The western districts, with approximately 10 million inhabitants, were attached to the Reich as the two provinces (*Reichsgaue*) of Wartheland and Danzig-West Prussia. Eastern Upper Silesia was attached to the province of Silesia, and the districts north of Warsaw were attached to the province of East Prussia.

Warsaw itself, which lay only a few kilometres from the new border of the German Reich, was included in the other half of German-occupied Poland, which with its 12 million inhabitants was placed under German administration as a 'General Government' (*Generalgouvernement*). All important industrial areas were excluded from this Polish 'rump state'. This was intended to be purely agricultural in character, its purpose was to provide a supply of labour to be employed in the Reich, and it was administered by a German 'government' under the lawyer Hans Frank, who certainly had no intention of conducting his administration according to traditional models of occupation policy. 'Authoritative for the activities of the General Government', he declared right at the start, 'is the wish of the Führer that this area should be the first colonial territory of the German nation. In the General Government, the German point of view must prevail.'[11]

Himmler was made 'Reich Commissar for the Consolidation of Germandom' (*Reichskommissar für die Festigung deutschen Volkstums*, RKF) and given the task of implementing Hitler's plans for ethnic remodelling. He presented an initial proposal at the end of October. According to this, one million people would be removed from the incorporated Polish territories by February 1940, more than half of them Jews. But it soon became clear that these figures were unrealistic. The transfer of more than 80,000 Poles into the General Government, which was pushed through within a few days at the beginning of December, created such unbelievable chaos that Himmler ordered it to be halted temporarily. Even so, despite the frightful conditions suffered by the deportees, and despite the technical problems arising from the effort to transport so many people in goods wagons, a further 42,000 people, almost all non-Jewish Poles, had been deported into the General Government by the middle of March. By the end of 1940, roughly 320,000 Poles in the incorporated territories had been robbed of their possessions and brought into the General Government. That figure had probably risen to about 750,000 by the end of the war.

Himmler's idea of taking a large number of Germans from the Soviet Union, and later also Romania, South Tyrol and other regions, and settling them in the incorporated territories turned out to be somewhat unrealistic. In fact, only about 60,000 Germans had been relocated there by the end of 1940. But, of course, the impending arrival of 'ethnic German' settlers always gave an extra impulse to the violent and brutal eviction of Poles from house and home in order to make way for the new occupants.

The plan to settle Germany's 'recovered eastern territories', as they were described officially, with millions of 'ethnic Germans' from other parts of Europe or indeed the world also turned out to be impossible to implement even in the longer term. In order to Germanise the Polish territories incorporated into the German Reich, which were inhabited by more than 8 million Poles, the Polish population was sifted according to racial criteria so as to pick out those who were able to become German, as Heydrich had announced. The Germans brought from the USSR to settle in the incorporated territories were also subjected to racial screening. Departments of the Main Office for Race and Settlement (RuSHA) were set up for this purpose within the *Einsatzgruppen* of the Security Police, and they had already started work by the spring of 1940.

The fate of the people subject to screening was determined by the results of a case-by-case examination of all Poles in the region according to a system established in advance which was relatively easy to operate. This involved a division into four categories: German by blood, Germanic, Mixed and Racially Inferior. Non-Jewish Poles, however, received a separate classification system in the shape of a 'German people's list', which made a rapid decision possible as to whether to remove them from the list or to 're-Germanise' them. These non-Jewish Poles were divided into four categories, according to language, cultural and political orientation and 'overall racial impression'. The first group consisted of 'Citizens of the Reich', who immediately received full rights. The second group were 'Citizens of the State' who received German legal status initially on a temporary basis. The legal status of the third group was yet lower, but they could still hope to attain 'Citizenship of the Reich' in the long term. Taken together, these three groups amounted to 3.5 million people. The fourth group covered roughly 6 million Poles who did not count as 'capable of becoming German' and they were now described as 'protected subjects'. They would either be put to forced labour in the Reich, or shifted across the border into the General Government.[12]

## The Polish Jews

The occupation of Poland brought more than 2 million Polish Jews under German control. This was the largest Jewish population group in Europe. The responsible authorities were by no means prepared for this. It is true that German researchers on 'ethnic questions' had repeatedly pointed to the dangers that arose from the Jews who were living in Poland. Thus, the head of the Institute for the Eastern European Economy at the University of Königsberg, Theodor Oberländer, called for the 3.5 million Jewish citizens of Poland to be deprived of their rights and segregated, while the social and ethnic historian Werner Conze stressed the alleged connection between Jewry and Bolshevism and proposed the 'de-Judaization of the cities and market towns'.[13] But, at the beginning of the war, there were still no concrete plans as to how to deal with the Jews of Poland.

The Polish Jews had to endure a real explosion of violence after 1 September 1939. The Orthodox were the main victims. Their appearance and language were perceived as strange, and they were often described by German soldiers as 'dirty', 'degenerate', 'sly' and so on. They were terrorised and mistreated by *Einsatzgruppen* and Ethnic German Self Protection groups, but also by units of the Wehrmacht. Many, therefore, tried to escape from persecution by fleeing into the Soviet-occupied part of the country. Roughly 200,000 Polish Jews had succeeded in doing this by mid-October 1939, when the Soviet authorities closed the border.

Jews in the German-occupied part of Poland were immediately placed under special regulations. They were forced to wear a special distinguishing mark on their clothing, and in the larger towns and cities they had to form 'Jewish Councils' (*Judenräte*)—a form of local government introduced by the Germans—they were put to forced labour, and they were robbed. In the first few weeks of the war, robbery took the form of uncoordinated and often spontaneous thefts committed both by German officials and private individuals. From November, the expropriations were organised systematically. They largely followed the pattern already established in Germany itself, but in Poland they took place much more rapidly and with greater brutality. In addition, the Jews were compelled at the outset to pay 'contributions' to finance Germany's occupation costs. As a result of all these measures, by January 1940 Poland's Jews had been by and large expropriated and completely deprived of their rights.[14]

In December 1939, the German authorities introduced forced labour for all Jews between the ages of fourteen and sixty. The purpose of this measure was not purely economic. Like the forced labour in the concentration camps of the Reich, it also served as an instrument of humiliation. An NSDAP report with the title 'The Jew at the Eastern Border' asserted that the Jews had done 'just as little really heavy and dangerous physical labour in Poland as they had anywhere else in the world'. The newsreel pictures shown in Germany of 'Jews loading stones onto devastated Polish highways' had been greeted with 'much laughter' but they were 'completely genuine'. Jewish doctors and lawyers were shown carrying stones, and Orthodox Jews cleaning out pigsties. These pictures were supposed to be evidence of 'genuine German humour'.[15]

The institutionalisation of forced labour for Jews gave rise to plans to use them in gigantic construction projects. They could be used to make roads or erect border fortifications. For example, forced labour camps were set up in the district of Lublin for the construction of an 'Eastern Wall', and more than 20,000 Jews were put to work on the project.

Measures of this kind, which often tended to be imposed on the spur of the moment, had a far lower priority in the incorporated districts of western Poland than the actual deportations. When Reinhard Heydrich presented the leaders of the *Einsatzgruppen* on 21 September with his Hitler-approved guidelines on Polish policy, he also indicated how the Polish Jews would be dealt with in future. Within a year, he said, the German authorities must remove all Jews from the western districts of Poland, resettle them in the 'rump state' of Poland, which had been shifted to the east, and concentrate them there in urban ghettoes. He made a distinction between 'the final goal (which will take longer) and the separate stages by which the final goal is to be reached'. The Jews must first be driven out of the incorporated districts as quickly as possible into a small number of towns in the General Government with good transport facilities, and then concentrated in special closed districts of each town, until it is possible to start the 'overall measures which have been planned (the final goal, therefore)' which must be kept strictly secret.[16] This plan took on concrete form on 13 December, when instructions were given for the 'second stage of the plan' to be put into effect. This was 'to round up all Jews in Germany's eastern provinces, without regard to age or sex, and expel them into the General Government of Poland.' Up to 600,000 people were affected.[17]

The deportations, chiefly in the direction of Radom and Lublin, began in January 1940. They took place in a completely unorganised fashion, without regard to weather or food supplies, and it was also absolutely unclear how the Jews would be accommodated in the General Government. The authorities were forced to revise their plans repeatedly and reduce the numbers targeted. It also proved impossible to accomplish the planned deportation of Jews from Germany itself. In order to make space for German immigrants from the territories occupied by the Soviet Union, a thousand Jews were removed from the towns of Stettin (Szczecin) and Schneidemühl (Piła), in the Reich, and brought to the district of Lublin. This operation, which took place practically in public, received a considerable amount of attention in the international press. Also, General Governor Hans Frank, who was based in Cracow, objected to these 'inward transfers' because, he said, there was not enough space for these people in the General Government. The transports from Germany were therefore halted temporarily in March 1940.[18]

Now the deliberations on what to do with the Jews from the incorporated districts centred increasingly on the plan for a 'Jewish reservation' which was to be established in the area around Lublin. As early as the end of September 1939 there were discussions in the Reich Security Main Office (*Reichssicherheitshauptamt*, RSHA) about establishing a 'Reich Ghetto behind

Warsaw and around Lublin' in which to accommodate 'all the political and Jewish elements which have to be expelled from the future German provinces'. Frank at first agreed with this idea of converting at least the eastern part of the General Government into a 'Jewish reservation', expressing himself with great openness about the fate of the deportees:

> We'll make short work of the Jews. It will be a pleasure to be able at last to come to grips with the Jewish race physically. The more that die, the better; any blow that lands on him [the Jew] is a victory for the Reich. The Jews should feel that we have arrived. We want to put between a half and three quarters of all Jews east of the Vistula.[19]

The head of the Resettlement Department of the RSHA in Berlin, Adolf Eichmann, now began to transport several thousand Jews from eastern Upper Silesia to a camp in the west of the Lublin district, near the small town of Nisko on the river San. But after the army leaders had spoken out against the resettlement of Jews in an area bordering the Soviet Union this plan was also dropped. Henceforth, Himmler informed his colleagues, not just the region of Lublin, but the whole of the General Government should be regarded 'as a reservoir for elements which are racially of no use to Germany'.[20]

Even so, the plan to deport all Jews from the incorporated territories into the General Government proved to be unworkable. By the end of 1940, 110,000 of the 600,000 Jews in these territories had been removed; as had roughly 20,000 of the 350,000 German Jews who still lived in Germany proper. Meanwhile, out of the approximately 30,000 German Sinti who were persecuted by the German authorities and also slated for deportation, roughly 2,800 had been removed by that time.

It was therefore clear by at least March 1940 that the deportation of all Polish Jews, in whatever direction, could not be accomplished, at least in the short term. In response to this, as Heydrich had already announced in September 1939, the German authorities gradually started to establish closed areas, or Jewish ghettoes, in all the larger towns of the incorporated districts and the General Government, and in many of the smaller ones too, and in the course of the next few months a considerable proportion of the Jewish population was concentrated in these places. Miserable and overcrowded conditions soon began to prevail in them. The ghetto of Łódź, for instance, received not only Jews from the city itself but also from the surrounding districts, so that more than 160,000 people had to live in an area of no more than four square kilometres.

This 'Ghettoisation' was the fruit of improvisation rather than long-term planning. It was only an interim solution, until it became clear what the final destination of the deported Jews would be, and where they would be resettled. The hurriedly delineated Jewish areas of the towns were not at all suitable for the accommodation of large numbers of people, and soon everything was in short supply: food, lodging and jobs as well as medical and sanitary care for hundreds of thousands of human beings. Starvation and epidemic diseases spread, along with black marketeering and food smuggling. This in turn gave the German authorities the opportunity to take further, still sharper, measures against the Jews, since the catastrophic conditions in the ghettoes, which they themselves had caused, provided fresh confirmation for them that Jews brought with them epidemics, illicit trading and criminality. This was the situation the SS had foretold in November 1938: if the Jews are pushed into poverty, they will inevitably offend against the law, and then we can exterminate them as criminals.[21]

The conviction that Ghettoisation was purely a temporary measure, which would soon or at least in the foreseeable future be followed by a final decision as to the destination of the Polish Jews, proved to be a factor of tremendous significance in escalating the situation, because the Germans who ran the Polish provinces now followed a cynical logic: the organisation of the ghettoes should be so evidently transitional that the bad, and soon execrable, living conditions in the 'Jewish residential districts' pointed unmistakably to the 'unsustainability of these circumstances', which urgently needed to be brought to an end by the expected removal of the Jews. In that sense, the decision to resettle, deport and 'ghettoise' hundreds of thousands of human beings, without making appropriate arrangements for their accommodation or sustenance cannot be understood simply as a decision made with inadequate organisational preparation, which then led to chaotic conditions and in reaction to these to ever more radical proposals by the authorities. On the contrary, the creation of 'unsustainable' conditions and insurmountable constraints, to which the security forces would have to react with correspondingly 'severe measures', was not just a result of the policy but part of the plan.[22]

## The War Economy and Labour Deployment

As mentioned in Chapter 7, three fundamental economic policy decisions had already been made in the mid-1930s. The third of these, which was to engage in a gigantic programme of rearmament, gave Germany a favourable starting-point. It meant that the country's arms production was three and a half times as great as Britain's. Hitler possessed by far the biggest, and the most well-armed and battle-ready, army in Europe, he had the best and most up-to-date air force, and owing to the expansion of Germany's territory through the annexation of

Austria and 'Czechia', he had an armaments industry of much greater capacity than before, which could now grow even larger thanks to the raw material deliveries the Soviet Union agreed to make after the Nazi–Soviet Pact of 1939.

In the longer term, however, the Western powers were clearly superior to Germany in economic potential and resources. Indeed, they were superior many times over, if the potential of the USA was added. In aircraft production the ratio between Germany on one side and Britain and the USA together on the other was 8:14 in 1939; a year later it was 10:28. As far as tanks were concerned it was 13:10 in 1939 and 9:33 in 1942. It was therefore easy to calculate when Germany would lose the lead it had attained in the summer of 1939, because by then 23 per cent of the country's national income was being expended for military purposes, as against 17 per cent in France, 12 per cent in Britain and no more than 2 per cent in the USA.

The impact of this imbalance would be felt more strongly as time went by. In that sense, Hitler's decision to wage war in 1939 against the Western powers followed a certain bellicose logic. As he wrote retrospectively to Mussolini in the spring of 1940: 'How could our armaments have been improved upon in two or three years? . . . As far as the relative strength of the German Wehrmacht was concerned, there was scarcely any room for a substantial change in our favour.'[23]

Germany would probably be unable to survive a long war, because its reserves of raw material were too exiguous, its shortage of foreign currency was too severe, and its structural inferiority was too evident. But it could triumph in a short war, if it was able to bring into play all its forces at once and once again stake everything on a single card. In March 1940, Hitler ordered his generals to conduct the war in such a way 'that it can be ended in 1940 with a great military victory. From 1941 onwards, time works against us (USA-potential).'[24] In order to achieve this goal, all reserves had to be mobilised and all production not relevant to military requirements had to be set aside.

A considerable amount was achieved in this respect. Between January and July 1940, the output of the German arms industry almost doubled. This was only possible because of energetic efforts to transform the industrial structure, a reorganisation of the arms industry's administration which began in spring 1940 and, above all, the shutting down of industries in the consumer goods sector, the adaptation of production to the supply of military goods and large-scale transfers of labour to the arms industry. These changes naturally had consequences for the standard of living and conditions of existence of ordinary Germans.

The people of Germany reacted to the news that the war had started with depression rather than enthusiasm. 'When the war broke out there was terrible anxiety among everyone' reported a SOPADE observer from south-west

Germany. 'People pictured "modern war" as a horrific affair, and they had a great fear of air attack.' 'Nowhere was there real enthusiasm' said a report from the west of the country. 'Even so there was plenty of excitement, bragging and loud posturing, especially among the Nazis.' Even critically inclined people were 'uncertain in their evaluation of Germany's military prospects. Until now Hitler had always been successful, and no-one could know how things would turn out this time.'

As with earlier military adventures, confidence grew in proportion to the number of victories announced: 'Now there is no more fear of the war. It now appears much less terrifying . . . "Perhaps we shall win after all" and "This time we shall certainly get some colonies."'

The Germans' main concern, apart from the announcements from the Front, was the supply of food, for memories of the hungry winters of the First World War were still fresh. It is remarkable, the report goes on, that 'there is much more discussion of questions of nourishment than of politics. Everyone is harassed by the worry: "How do I get hold of my rations?"' According to another observer the cynical view was expressed 'that this war will not last as long as the last one, because there is already not enough to eat.'[25]

The regime had succeeded until 1939 in neutralising the German working class politically, and even in partially integrating some of its members. The responsible authorities were well aware that this was due not just to Hitler's foreign policy successes but above all to the National Socialist 'economic miracle'. Whether it would be possible to maintain people's loyalty and confidence in the leadership of the regime, despite the war and the expected increase in the burdens they had to bear, was therefore a very important question.

The first cuts in social benefits were announced at the beginning of the war. Even before it started, the standard of living in Germany was already lower than in France, Great Britain or the USA. The working population of Hamburg and Duisburg were less well fed, and their living conditions were poorer, than their counterparts in Birmingham or Lyons. To that extent, the lives of ordinary Germans were not altered fundamentally at the beginning of the war by the introduction of rationing first of basic foodstuffs and soon afterwards of textiles and other consumer goods. But rationing also contributed to a sense that things were being distributed fairly, for the absence of fairness had been a major subject of criticism during the First World War, quite apart from the low level of the rations themselves. In addition, the Nazi authorities succeeded throughout the war in avoiding any substantial fall in food supplies. Owing to the blockade of the North Sea mounted by Britain from the start of the conflict, this feat was not achieved with the agricultural resources of Germany and its allies alone, but rather through the exploitation of the occupied territories, whose inhabitants had to endure great privations in order to make sure that the Germans in the

Reich were provided for. To give the 'homeland' (*Heimat*) preferential supplies of food remained one of the paramount goals of the Nazi regime until the end of 1944, and alterations, or indeed reductions, of the ration led regularly to increasing discontent, to which the Nazi authorities paid great attention.[26]

Apart from food rationing, reductions in wages and noticeable increases in working hours were also announced by the government in September 1939. In addition, extra payments for working overtime, on Sundays and at night, were all cancelled, and taxes on alcohol and tobacco were increased. But the expectation that the outbreak of war and an appeal to patriotism would dampen reactions of discontent among the workers turned out to be erroneous. There was an increase in people who reported sick, there were cases of 'laziness' and there were other signs of increasing working-class dissatisfaction. Moreover, criticism of the wartime tax increases was also voiced at the top of the Nazi party and in local branches. As Rudolf Hess wrote to Goering: 'The Führer, and all of us along with him, have not fought for two decades to win the confidence of the workers for this to be jeopardised at the most critical moment on account of more or less theoretical considerations.' As a result, between November 1939 and spring 1940, the 'September decrees' were largely rescinded.[27] The objective of these decrees had been to absorb purchasing power so as to make it possible to reduce the production of consumer goods. They did not work. On the contrary, real wages continued to increase until 1942 despite the official pay freeze. The regime also gave up on the idea of drastically increasing taxes. It is true that a wartime supplement of 50 per cent was added to the taxes after 4 September 1939, but this only applied to annual incomes of over 2,400 RM, and 60 per cent of the population were below this limit. Even the recipients of higher incomes only had to bear a relatively insignificant burden. An income of 10,000 RM was taxed at 13.7 per cent, whereas in Great Britain the tax burden was half as much again.[28]

There was therefore still plenty of purchasing power. The shops, however, stocked fewer and fewer unrationed goods, in other words items which could be acquired without ration cards. Private and public housebuilding was also drastically reduced. Since there was little to buy and nothing to invest in, the savings ratio rose steeply. Between January 1939 and January 1941, savings deposits increased by 100 per cent. This development was certainly linked to the hope of a better life after the war, and to that extent it demonstrates a certain degree of optimism. But what was important for the Treasury was that these savings provided immense sums of money with which to finance the war: in 1941 alone, they amounted to 14 billion RM.[29]

In addition to a lack of foreign currency and a shortage of raw materials, the greatest problem faced by the German war economy was the inadequate supply of labour. An acute shortage of workers had already begun to emerge in 1937.

Now, though, after the Wehrmacht had called up approximately 4 million men for military service, this shortage became a very serious matter indeed. An effective increase in productivity by the introduction of new machinery, the construction of modern factories and more efficient management was a long-term goal, and the new Minister of Armaments and Munitions, Fritz Todt, made efforts to achieve this. In the short term, however, there was no advantage to be drawn from these measures. People employed in the consumer goods industry were admittedly transferred to an even greater extent into war production, but at the same time the armaments firms, where the pay was better, exerted a strong pull on those employed in other branches, particularly on the land. Agriculture was already suffering from a shortfall of almost a million workers when the war broke out.

One way out of this dilemma was to employ more women in the arms factories. The proportion of women in paid employment was already relatively high in Germany in 1939. It stood at one third, in comparison with Great Britain's 25 per cent. Of course, the greater part of Germany's female employees, more than 6 million people, worked in agriculture. To increase the number of women working in industry was one option, which would have made necessary the introduction of obligatory labour service. But the echoes of the disputes over the use of female labour conscription in the First World War were still reverberating in the ears of the German authorities. Even when the Supreme Army Command (OHL) had introduced labour conscription for all men aged between seventeen and sixty, by the draconic Law on Patriotic Auxiliary Service (*Hilfsdienstgesetz*) of 1916, it had not dared to apply this to the millions of women who were not in paid employment, because of the fear that this would produce dissatisfaction and disturbances both at home and at the Front. Twenty-five years later, the authorities still recoiled from taking such a step. Franz Seldte, the Minister of Labour, made this comment: 'There are probably still certain reserves among female workers . . . However, in falling back on female labour, there are numerous reasons why caution is necessary.'[30]

Since the shortage of labour had already reached alarming levels by 1939, the only option left was once again to make use of a foreign workforce. The German authorities had gained extensive experience of this method during the First World War, and as there was no longer any reason to worry about inhibiting factors such as parliamentary control, public criticism or foreign interference, this way of procuring labour was an obvious solution. Moreover, there were already 500,000 foreign workers in Germany in the summer of 1939, especially Czechs from the 'Protectorate' and Poles, who were working to bring in the harvest on the estates of East Elbia, in line with a tradition of seasonal employment. There were also a few thousand Italian workers employed on the massive construction sites of the Volkswagenwerk and the Salzgitterwerk, who had been brought in to the accompaniment of much propaganda by German and Italian workers' organisations.

Even so, the Nazi party had strong objections to the mass deployment of foreign workers in Germany, particularly Poles, because it was thought to offend against the fundamental racial principles of the National Socialist movement. German soil must be tilled by people of German blood, was the position taken up by District Leaders and Farm Leaders, and the dangers of a 'mixture of bloods' were called to people's attention in threatening tones. But in view of the desperate situation in the labour market, there was no realistic alternative, and, in any case, it was very clear that the involvement of foreigners in the German economy which was now starting had not only economic but also political reasons. In the language of the party ideologists: the decision to employ foreigners demonstrates 'how much we prefer to sacrifice our values by allowing a temporary alien intrusion into particular professions rather than to endanger the biological strength of the German *Volk* through increasing the employment of women.'[31]

Roughly 300,000 Polish prisoners-of-war had fallen into German hands, and they were very quickly put to work, mainly in agriculture. At the same time, a massive campaign for the recruitment of Polish workers was started in occupied Poland, first in the territories incorporated into the Reich and then in the General Government. The government hoped to continue the long German tradition of employing Poles in agricultural labour. But it soon became clear that very few Poles were reporting voluntarily for work in Germany, with the result that, by the beginning of 1940, the German authorities had already gone over to increasingly severe measures of forcible recruitment. They started literally to ensnare a workforce by imposing labour obligations on whole Polish age cohorts, by collective repression, by police raids, and by surrounding cinemas, schools and churches. By April 1940, roughly half a million Polish workers had been brought into the Reich in this manner. The vast majority were put to work on the land.

Even so, the Nazis continued to regard the so-called 'Polish deployment' (*Poleneinsatz*) as an infringement of their nationalist principles. 'It would be better if we didn't have them—we know that—but we need them', observed Himmler in February 1940. The 'political danger to the *Volk*' arising from this would have to be countered with correspondingly harsh measures. An extensive network of repressive regulations was therefore developed for Polish workers in Germany. They had to live in barracks (something which soon turned out to be impracticable in the countryside, however); they had to pay a supplementary tax; they were not allowed to use any public facilities (whether trains or baths); they could not attend German religious services; they had to work longer hours than Germans; they were obliged to wear a distinguishing mark—the 'Polish

P'—on their clothing. Contact with Germans outside the work situation was forbidden; sexual congress with German women was punished by the public execution of the Polish participant. It was also determined 'in order to protect German blood' that at least half of the Polish workers who were recruited should be female. This catalogue of measures was in many respects entirely without precedent, as far as its extent and severity were concerned, although it was reminiscent of forms of labour compulsion in the colonies of Africa which were much discussed in Western Europe during the 1920s.

For the German authorities, however, the 'Polish deployment' proved to be generally successful. They succeeded in bringing a large number of Polish workers to Germany—almost 700,000 by May 1940—in most cases against their will. They also succeeded in installing a two-class society in the German Reich, with a hierarchy defined by national or rather *völkisch* criteria.[32]

## 'Euthanasia'

The coming of war freed the Nazi regime from the constraints and obstacles which had continued to exist until 1939. This applied to the conduct of military operations as much as it did to occupation policy or the deployment of labour. What had seemed impossible, indeed unthinkable, in previous years, or even previous months, was now put into practice in the activities of the *Einsatzgruppen* as well as in the mass expulsion of Poles and Jews from their homes or the bringing of hundreds of thousands of foreign workers into the Reich for forced labour. The point applies even more strongly to the most characteristic sphere of National Socialist social and population policy, 'racial hygiene'. It was in this field that the fourth of the above-mentioned fundamental decisions was made, also right at the start of the war.

After the 'Law for the Prevention of Hereditarily Diseased Offspring' was issued in summer 1933, and those who suffered from 'hereditary feeble-mindedness' began to be sterilised, there were repeated attempts to introduce further and more comprehensive measures. The initiative often came from the medical profession itself. Gerhard Wagner, the head of the Reich Doctors' League, had already called on Hitler in 1935 to make a 'Führer decision' in favour of 'the eradication of unworthy lives'. It could be said that there was a certain trend in this direction. There had already been vigorous discussions in some parts of the country as to whether 'the present system of care for the mentally ill in hospitals and nursing homes' continued to accord with 'National Socialist principles'. There was also talk of a 'final solution of the institution question'.[33]

Hitler had reacted negatively to Wagner's initiative, but his reasons were illuminating: it was 'prudent to wait', he said. But he also indicated that 'if there is a war' he would 'take up this question of euthanasia and put it into effect', because then 'the attention of the whole world will be turned to military operations, and in any case the value of human life will count for less.' Then it would be possible 'to free the people from the burden of the mentally ill . . . more easily.'[34]

Some institutions had already anticipated this decision. The Department Head of one Prussian mental institution declared in 1936 that he 'could no longer see it as the task of a National Socialist to provide maintenance for completely idiotic children', and there were an increasing number of cases in which the food rations of the mentally disabled were reduced, in order to achieve a 'natural reduction' in the number of patients.[35] A combination of medical and economic arguments was used in this context. In view of the shortage of resources, it was said, it was impossible to justify the enormous expense of caring for the incurably mentally ill who had no prospect of recovery. These resources should go to sick people who were curable. On the other hand, it was absolutely clear to the Nazis and to the doctors who argued in this way that actions of this kind went against the fundamental values of Christianity and humanism, and would meet with vehement criticism from the population, and in particular from the churches. But it was calculated that this situation would change when the war started, and in fact the war did make it possible here too to put into effect what had until then been regarded as a utopian proposal.

The initiative again proceeded from the doctors, in the shape of the 'Reich Committee for the Scientific Investigation of Severe Hereditary and Congenital Diseases'. One of the experts on this committee recommended the parents of a handicapped child to petition Hitler to give his permission for the child's life to be ended. This individual case soon had tremendous ramifications, because Hitler showed considerable interest in it, and in January 1939 the doctor he assigned to the case, Karl Brandt, had the child killed, after conducting an investigation. A practice of 'child euthanasia' developed within a short time on this basis. There was nothing in writing at first, and the process was set in motion and organised by the 'Chancellery of the Führer' and the Health Department of the Ministry of the Interior purely on Hitler's oral instructions. In August 1939, it was ordered that all newly born babies who were handicapped had to be reported to the authorities. This information was then sent on to the above-mentioned Reich Committee, its members examined the documentation, and they then sent children they considered as unworthy to live to 'Special Children's Departments' to be killed.

The procedure tested out here was extended in summer 1939 to all inmates of psychiatric institutions, both children and adults. The initiative for this evidently came from Hitler himself. He presented the two officials responsible for 'child euthanasia', Karl Brandt and Philipp Bouhler, with a memorandum he had written empowering them to act, which was to be submitted to a group of experts for examination. Some weeks later, in October 1939, Hitler signed a secret decree, which was backdated to 1 September in order to emphasise its connection with the outbreak of war, previously referred to by him as making this possible. The decree consisted of a single phrase:

> Reich Leader Bouhler and Dr. Brandt are given the responsibility to extend the authority of certain doctors, whose names are to be determined, in such a way that they can, after the most critical evaluation of the nature of their illness, grant a merciful death to those whose sickness is incurable, as far as can reasonably be established.[36]

A special organisation was set up to implement this secret order. It was responsible to the Führer's Chancellery, and it was directed by the economic specialist Viktor Brack. The 'euthanasia' programme was given the name 'Aktion T4' after its headquarters in Tiergartenstrasse 4, Berlin. The first step, just as in the case of the 'child euthanasia' programme, was to make a systematic investigation of all mental institutions to uncover suitable inmates, whose condition would then be the subject of expert reports from a much larger group of doctors. If the experts gave a negative opinion, the sick were transported to one of the six institutions earmarked for this purpose and murdered in gas chambers, using previously constructed apparatus. Any gold teeth were then extracted from the mouths of the dead, and after that the bodies were sent to be cremated. Family members, most of whom were entirely unaware of what had happened, were informed about the death of their relatives and presented with an urn containing their ashes.

With this, the regime had not just reached a further stage in the escalation of violence; it had crossed a boundary. The National Socialist state had begun to murder thousands of its own citizens. Leaving aside periods of civil war, this was a historically unprecedented event.

The Health Department of the Ministry of the Interior had worked out a set of criteria to ensure uniformity in the choice of those to be killed. Most of the patients to be delivered to the killing institutions were those who were not capable of work, and whose diagnoses included schizophrenia, epilepsy, senility, paralysis, syphilis, feeble-mindedness and encephalitis. But patients who had lived continuously in a mental institution for at least five years were also to be reported to the authorities, as were all those detained as 'criminally insane'. The way heredity, incurability, incapacity to work and 'asocial' tendencies were combined in this list lays bare the close association between criteria of racial hygiene and economics which was characteristic of Nazi racial policy in general, but which could already be found in the euthanasia discussion after the First World War.

One group of patients, however, was not covered by these selection criteria: Jewish inmates. Unless they were foreign nationals, they were included almost without exception in the 'euthanasia action'.

By August 1941, a total of 70,273 disabled people had been murdered as part of 'Aktion T4'. With these large numbers, it was inevitable, despite the secrecy and the exclusion of the normal authorities from the process, that the fate of the patients sent 'on a journey' would become known both to those who worked in the asylums and to the public. The Bishop of Limburg, Antonius Hilfrich, wrote to the Ministry of Justice about rumours swirling around a mental institution in the neighbouring town of Hadamar:

> Several times a week buses arrive in Hadamar containing a considerable number of such victims. Schoolchildren in the neighbourhood know these buses, and they say 'Here comes the murder van again.' After the arrival of these vehicles, the citizens of Hadamar look at the smoke rising from the chimney and the constant thought of these poor victims is upsetting to them. The repulsive odours are particularly unpleasant, if the wind is in a certain direction. . . . You can hear old people saying things like: 'No, I'm not going near any state-run hospital: after the feeble-minded it will be the turn of the old next, as useless mouths.'[37]

Moreover, many of the victims had still been in contact with their relatives, who now started to investigate their whereabouts, turning to mayors or priests for advice. This soon gave rise to a noticeable degree of unrest, which was reinforced by the open protests of representatives of both Christian confessions, including the bishop of Württemberg, Theophil Wurm, the director of mental institutions in Bethel, Pastor von Bodelschwigh and finally, and most spectacularly, the bishop of Münster Count Clemens von Galen, who threatened from the pulpit on 3 August 1941 to lodge an accusation of murder against those responsible.

Hitler thereupon ended the process as informally as he had started it, by giving an oral instruction for 'Aktion T4' to be brought to an end. Here it became apparent that, under certain circumstances, public opposition, and protests by the churches or other influential groups could have an impact on the decisions of the regime's leaders, Hitler in particular. The war against the Soviet Union, which had just begun, and the particularly attentive observation of the mood of the German population which was linked with that event, may have played a role in the decision to end 'Aktion T4'. The victims were not completely isolated and marginalised, as the Jews were a little later, and their murder was in no way connected with military operations at the faraway eastern front. Hitler had calculated that the killing of the mentally ill could be carried out more easily during the war, because then public attention would be concentrated on the military events and anyway 'the value of human life' would not be 'of such weight' during a war. It turned out that in this case he was mistaken.

But Hitler's decision did not end the murder of the disabled by the state; it simply altered the methods. 'Child euthanasia' continued to take place, and adult patients continued to be killed in hospitals and nursing homes, but now largely by overdosing them with medicaments and systematically depriving them of nourishment. In addition to this, another action had already started. This was 'Aktion 14f13', started on 3 April 1941. The code '14f13' concealed the selection and killing of roughly 20,000 inmates of *Konzentrationslager* (KZ, concentration camp) who were not capable of working. The final step in the process was taken at the end of 1943 when Karl Brandt, who was in charge of matters of health and sanitation, was instructed to close the hospitals and nursing homes for the mentally disabled, and to move the patients out and kill them, so as to make space for wounded soldiers.[38]

As we noted earlier, the Nazi racial theorist Dr Walter Gross had in 1934 recommended the murder of the mentally ill, the 'asocials' and all people who were incapable of working, and were therefore regarded as 'useless' Germans, because it would restore the 'brutal and ruthless, but utterly just, and, if you like, divine order of nature'. This policy remained one of the essential features of the regime until the end.[39] In this context, the economic and medical aspects of the programme were inseparably linked with elements of racist ideology. Repeated references to the 'usefulness' of these actions, such as in this case the provision of infirmaries for wounded soldiers in the buildings of former nursing homes whose residents had been removed and killed beforehand, already presupposed a distinction between people with a greater, and those with a lesser, right to life.

The 'euthanasia actions' were in addition directly interconnected as regards both method and personnel with the mass murder of the European Jews, which began in 1941. The experience of mass killing with poison gas acquired through 'Aktion T4' offered a technical basis for the establishment of the gas chambers, and those who managed the murder of the sick later took part in organising the murder of the Jews. Irmfried Eberl, Franz Stangl and Christian Wirth, who commanded, respectively, the death camps of Treblinka, Sobibor and Belzec, are examples of this. But the way Hitler's orders for these initial murders were given and transmitted also makes it possible to recognise the methods employed in later decision-making. First, there were initiatives from below, from the circle of specialists directly involved in the matter. Then there was a decision by Hitler, given as an instruction to people who enjoyed his confidence, rather than as a decree transmitted to ministries and public authorities through official channels. After that, a special organisation was set up with the task of carrying out the murders, while secrecy was carefully maintained, although in practice this was not completely feasible. Finally, after protests, the location of the murders was shifted to special areas not accessible to the German public.

It is evident that 'Aktion T4' crossed the line between individual acts of murder, for which the regime was already responsible, and systematic mass murder. The decisions of the years that followed involved ever more extensive killing operations with ever greater numbers of victims. But this turn towards the principle of the mass murder of civilians as a part of Nazi social policy had already been introduced and put into effect in the first few months of the war. It was timed to take advantage of the special circumstances of wartime, but it was not brought about by the war itself.

As was noted at the beginning of this chapter, four fundamental decisions were made in the first few months of the war, relating to occupation policy, treatment of the Jews, the use of forced labour and the murder of the sick. They were all made at the same time, within a few days or weeks, by the same very limited circle of individuals in Hitler's intimate entourage. They were in direct association with each other and they set in motion an explosion of violence of a hitherto unprecedented extent.

There were objections and protests raised against these measures both within German society and by the military leadership. The killing of the mentally disabled affected the Germans themselves, and by that fact it broke through the dividing line between the Self and the Other which the Nazis had propagated and which continued to be accepted. The protests were so persistent that Hitler largely put an end to the operation, in so far as it affected citizens of the Reich. The objections of a few military men to Germany's actions in Poland, on the other hand, did not find the same broad support, since here it was Poles, not Germans, who were affected. There were almost no protests either from the military or from civilian authorities against the deportation and ghettoisation of the Polish Jews, the legal and economic isolation of the Jewish population and the murders associated with this policy. The more intense persecution of the Jews within the territory of the Reich also did not lead to any perceptible discontent or criticism. The German population had been subjected to years of anti-Jewish indoctrination and they had gradually accustomed themselves to the terror meted out to the Jews. The result was that, even before the war, action taken against the Jews was clearly regarded as unavoidable and not particularly worthy of attention. In addition, when the war started, the regime strengthened the apparatus of surveillance and repression at home, so as to strangle at birth any possible manifestations of discontent.

Moreover, the abrogation of the September Decrees and the maintenance of a relatively high level of food supply indicated that Germany's leadership was ready to pay careful attention to the material interests of the German population even during the war. As a result, the great agitation and disquiet in Germany at the beginning of the war was followed, by Christmas 1939 at the latest, by a widespread feeling of reassurance that things were returning to normal, and rumours began to circulate that Britain and France did not want to continue the war and might possibly make an agreement with Germany.

From then onwards, this gulf between the endeavour to continue living in Germany almost 'as in peacetime' under war conditions, and the explosion of violence in the occupied territories in the east, as well as towards marginalised groups in the country itself, was to form an essential feature of the course of the war, especially as each side of this antithesis conditioned and facilitated the other.

## Hegemony

The victory over Poland had not brought the war to an end, although it might at first have looked like it. Some of the Nazi leaders hoped that Britain and France might still give way, after they had failed to march in strength into western Germany in September 1939. But the brutal proceedings of the Germans in Poland produced a further hardening of the will to resist, particularly in Britain.[40]

Even so, almost four months elapsed before military operations started in the west. This interval was greatly to the advantage of the Western powers, because it allowed them more time to reduce the German lead in armaments. The German side, on the other hand, was in a hurry, because it had to be borne in mind that by autumn 1940 at the latest, after the American presidential elections, the USA would make sure that Britain and France attained a clear military ascendancy by delivering increased arms supplies. 'We must achieve victory during this year', Hitler told Goebbels. 'Otherwise the material superiority of the opposing side will be too great. In addition, a war lasting many years would be difficult to tolerate psychologically.'[41] In practice, however, Hitler postponed the date of the western offensive again and again. One reason for this was that he continued to hope for a signal from London that the British would be prepared to make a peace settlement which would give the German Reich hegemony over the European continent, while Great Britain retained its overseas empire. Moreover, there was no clear German strategy, and the rearmament programmes the Nazis had set in motion were not yet complete. Rearmament in the air was aimed at a war beginning in 1942, while for the navy the preferred date was 1943.

For the war in the west, the leaders of the Wehrmacht, quite in line with the traditions of William II's army, had envisaged a repetition, with modifications, of the Schlieffen Plan which had failed so spectacularly in 1914. This involved marching into France through Belgium and the Netherlands, and waging an encirclement battle in northern France, followed by the capture of Paris. But, since they were aware that the Allies had prepared for precisely that eventuality, all the indications pointed to a war of position and a long period of hostilities. Hitler therefore decided in favour of a variant which was much riskier, but promised in case of success to avoid a lengthy war. According to Hitler's plan, the main mass of German troops would be sent through the narrow valleys of the Ardennes, behind the opponent's back. This method would allow the French units to be taken by surprise and defeated in short order. The purpose of this manoeuvre was to reach the Channel coast quickly, so as to gain a favourable jumping-off point for the invasion of Great Britain.

As it turned out, however, the offensive against the Western powers started in Northern Europe. German troops marched into Denmark and Norway so as to make sure of Swedish iron ore deliveries to Germany, most of which were sent by ship from the Norwegian port of Narvik. The invasion of Denmark succeeded without meeting any opposition, but in Norway the German units met with fierce resistance from Norwegian and also French and British troops. The two Western powers did indeed withdraw their forces from Norway after Germany invaded France, but the German navy suffered severe losses in the Norwegian campaign and incurred long-lasting weaknesses as a result.

The German advance in the west began on 10 May 1940, and Hitler's strategy met with the desired success. The thrust through the Ardennes remained unnoticed, and the French were quickly encircled and defeated. The Netherlands capitulated as early as 15 May, and on 20 May, German troops reached the French section of the Channel coast. Belgium capitulated on 28 May, on 14 June the Germans marched into Paris, and on 22 June, six weeks after the beginning of the campaign, the armistice was signed in Compiègne, in the very same railway carriage where the armistice had been signed on 11 November 1918 after Germany's defeat in the previous war. Goebbels wrote in his diary: 'The shame has now been erased. One feels reborn.'[42]

Germany had won an overwhelming victory. The French army, once the strongest in Europe, had suffered a crushing defeat. Ninety thousand soldiers had been killed on the Allied side, while Germany had lost only 30,000. In addition, 1.9 million Allied soldiers had been taken prisoner or were missing in action. France, Belgium, the Netherlands and tiny Luxemburg were in German hands, as were Denmark and Norway. German troops ruled Europe from the Atlantic to the Bug, from Biarritz to Narvik.

There was unlimited jubilation and relief in Germany. When the news of France's capitulation arrived in Berlin 'traffic came to a halt in the streets. Women kissed each other and wept. Strangers embraced. The radio played "Deutschland, Deutschland über alles" over and over again.'[43] The trauma of the 1918 defeat had been overcome, the confidence of the Germans in the energy and genius of their Führer reached unbounded heights. 'A previously unattained level of inner unity and close solidarity between the Front and the homeland has taken shape among the whole German people under the impression of the great political events and in the wake of the military successes', reported the SD. 'Everyone gazes gratefully and confidently upon the Führer, and upon his Wehrmacht, as it dashes from victory to victory.' Reports from the provinces on the public mood were no different: 'One can assert with confidence that the whole nation is now imbued with a trusting confidence in the Führer of an extent which has never been seen before', ran one SD report, and according to another: 'In face of such greatness all pettiness and grumbling are silenced.'[44]

The leaders of the Wehrmacht were also full of admiration for Hitler's strategic abilities, and Keitel's description of Hitler as 'the greatest commander of all time' was not just a courtier's flattery but indicated the complete submission of the officer corps to the Führer. There would no longer be any jokes about the dilettante corporal.

Historians were enthusiastic as well. The Munich Professor Karl Alexander von Müller, writing in *Historische Zeitschrift*, praised Hitler's brilliant strategy, thanks to which Germany's troops had conquered 'Norway, the Netherlands and Belgium in thrusts of breathtaking audacity, speed and precision' and then gone on to march into Paris. 'France has been thrown to the ground and prised away from the English alliance. Isolated and alone, the island of Britain lies open to German attack.'[45] Even Friedrich Meinecke, one of the few German professors to adopt a critical attitude towards Hitler and National Socialism, wrote this enthusiastic encomium on 4 July 1940:

> Joy, admiration and pride in this army has to be the dominant initial impression, even for me. And the reconquest of Strasburg! How could one's heart not beat faster! It was after all an astounding achievement of the Third Reich, and perhaps its greatest positive achievement, that it was able in four years to build up an army of millions which has proved capable of such an accomplishment.[46]

The conviction that the war would soon come to an end was admittedly disturbed by anxiety over the impending confrontation with Britain, because the

British army had succeeded in bringing its defeated expeditionary force across the English Channel to safety. This meant that it would be possible for Great Britain to continue the fight against Germany, and the triumphant mood of the Germans was soon diluted by the fear that the war would not end as quickly as they had first thought. Since Great Britain refused to back down and a peace offer by Hitler met with no response, the German leadership was in a quandary about how to proceed. An invasion of the British Isles was an immensely costly undertaking, and its military outcome was extremely doubtful. Hitler therefore repeatedly postponed the planned operation, finally abandoning it altogether. Instead, the German side endeavoured to break the morale of the population and to weaken the country so greatly with heavy air attacks that either the prospects for an invasion became more favourable, or the British government was finally compelled to come to terms with Germany and recognise its hegemony on the Continent.

The 'aerial battle for England' was accompanied by a great deal of noisy propaganda, but for the Germans it ended in disaster. The German attacks on the British cities, particularly London, caused severe damage and kept the population in a state of anxiety and terror for months. But the Luftwaffe did not succeed either in undermining British morale or in reducing the level of the country's arms production. On the contrary, the Royal Air Force, after suffering a number of initial setbacks, succeeded in winning the upper hand, and in its turn started to bombard German cities, beginning on 25 August 1940 with Berlin. While the German Luftwaffe flew 783 missions over Great Britain (333 of them over London alone) in October 1940, the Royal Air Force attacked German territory 601 times in the same month, and with increasing frequency. Between August and October 1940 1,733 German and 915 British aircraft were shot down in the air offensive over England. The Germans did not achieve their objective of bringing Great Britain to its knees.

But this confronted the German leadership with an exceedingly difficult strategic problem. There were three options. One was to wait. Germany's superiority would soon become overwhelming because of the alliance with the Soviet Union and the deliveries of Soviet raw materials and armaments which were arriving in ever-increasing quantities, and a victory over Great Britain would no longer be difficult after some time had elapsed. That was one argument that was presented. But it was precisely time that the Germans were short of, in view of the entry of the USA into the conflict, which was expected to happen within a year. Moreover, there was a danger that by taking this course Germany would become increasingly dependent on the Soviet Union. The second option was to continue the war against Britain at the periphery of Europe: British strongpoints and possessions in the Mediterranean could be attacked, the British could be defeated in North Africa, at the Suez Canal and in the Near East, and this would deter the USA from coming into the war. But a struggle for the Mediterranean would take a long time, the planned cooperation of Spain and Turkey was dubious, and the outcome of such a struggle was uncertain. Even so, this variant was considered seriously, and the navy leaders continued until the end of autumn 1940 to view this as the most promising course of action.

The third option was a war against the Soviet Union. On the one hand, this was a natural response, since Hitler had always placed a war for living space in the east, the destruction of the Soviet Union and the ending of 'Jewish rule' over that country as the very heart of his conception of foreign policy. On the other hand, to attack the Soviet Union before winning the final victory over England meant engaging in a war on two fronts. In the First World War the simultaneous fight in east and west, and later the entry of the USA into the war, had been considered to be among the most important reasons for Germany's defeat. This fact alone suggested caution. Hitler's calculations, however, were entirely different. He proceeded on the assumption that Great Britain had set its hopes on two things: the USA would enter the war and the Soviet Union would change sides. It was in fact true that the British government was making strenuous efforts to achieve a change in Soviet policy in favour of the West. Hitler feared that the Soviet Union might one day give way to these entreaties and thereby worsen Germany's position considerably. 'Stalin is flirting with Britain to keep her in the war, and tie us down, with a view to gaining time and taking what he wants, knowing he cannot get it once peace breaks out', he told his generals. On 21 July, therefore, two days after Britain had rejected his peace offer, Hitler prepared his top commanders for the possibility of a war against the Soviet Union: 'Our attention must be turned to tackling the Russian problem and drawing up plans for this.' Ten days later he stated his plans more precisely: 'With Russian smashed, Britain's last hope would be shattered. Germany then will be master of Europe and the Balkans. Decision: Russia's destruction must therefore be made a part of this struggle. Spring 1941 . . . Five months to finish the job.'[47]

Hitler's decision was not a surprise to the leaders of the Wehrmacht. They had already started making preparations in this direction. Instead of a landing in Britain, which would probably result in heavy losses, they assumed that in this way they could both deprive the British government of its hope that the war could be continued successfully and deter the USA from entry. The prognostications of Hitler and his generals were based on an extraordinary underestimation of Soviet strength and an overestimation of their own capacity. But, after the splendid victory over France, Hitler and the whole of his regime imagined themselves to be invincible. No plan was too grand, no objective too chimerical, no opponent too powerful. Hitler was more than ever convinced that he could achieve anything.

Right from the start, therefore, the planning operation was permeated with an exuberant optimism. It was assumed that the war against the Soviet Union, like the campaigns against Poland and France, would last no longer than a few months. In belittling the fighting strength of the Red Army, the Germans were of course in agreement with many international observers. After Stalin's sanguinary purge of his top generals, and particularly after the heavy losses suffered by the Red Army in the Winter War against tiny Finland, a victory for Germany's troops, which had, after all, defeated the armies of Britain and France within a few weeks and occupied seven European countries, appeared to be a matter of course. When that had been achieved, Germany would be almost unbeatable on the Continent, and it would also be a world power in the economic sense on the basis of its control over the resources of almost the whole of Europe. In this situation, the country would be able to force Great Britain to its knees and also isolate the USA.

But a final decision had not yet been made. Hitler's attempt to bring together a worldwide alliance against Great Britain met with little success. Neither France's new head of state, Marshal Pétain, nor Spain's dictator General Franco were ready to take part in an alliance with Nazi Germany. The only agreement Hitler could make was with Italy and Japan. This was the Tripartite Pact, which was directed above all against the USA. The Soviet Union, on the other hand, while it continued to be a reliable supplier of raw materials, was prepared neither to join the Tripartite Pact nor to abandon its strategic interests in Finland, Turkey and above all the Balkans. This became clear during a visit by Soviet Foreign Minister Molotov to Berlin in autumn 1940.

The Balkans were strategically of great importance to Germany, partly because the British had interests there, and partly on account of the oil supplies from Romania, which were indispensable to the further conduct of the war. A close alliance with Romania, which became closer still in September 1940, after General Antonescu had seized power, secured for the Reich a quasi-monopoly of Romania's oil resources. Romania and Hungary, followed soon afterwards by Slovakia, also joined the Tripartite Pact. Yugoslavia, however, did not do so at first, nor did Bulgaria, although it remained firmly aligned with Germany.

German domination had now extended to the south-eastern part of the continent, and the Germans possessed significant strategic advantages over the British there, because although the latter ruled the eastern Mediterranean with their navy, they did not control the mainland. The situation in Greece was uncertain, however. Mussolini very much overestimated the strength of his armed forces, and he marched his troops into Greece at the end of October 1940 with the aim of extending Italy's sphere of influence and gaining control over the Mediterranean, though he also no doubt wished to enhance Italy's position vis-à-vis its practically all-powerful alliance partner Germany. The Italian forces met with strong resistance from the Greek army, which also had British support. This compelled the German leadership to prepare for a possible intervention in Greece, above all to protect the Romanian oilfields from British air attack. Thus the war between Britain and Germany continued to extend into peripheral regions, although there was no sign of a decisive outcome anywhere, not even in North Africa, where German troops were supporting Mussolini's forces, and fighting with varying degrees of success against the British expeditionary corps. Hitler and the leaders of the Wehrmacht were both equally convinced that a favourable decision in the struggle against Great Britain would only be possible after a German victory over Russia.

Hitler made the definitive decision to go to war with the Soviet Union by mid-November 1940 at the latest, after the divergence of strategic interests between Germany and the Soviet Union unmistakably came to the surface during the visit of Soviet Foreign Minister Molotov to Berlin. On 18 December he issued

> Directive No. 212 for 'Operation Barbarossa': the German Wehrmacht must be prepared, also before the ending of the war against England, to crush Soviet Russia in a rapid campaign (Operation Barbarossa). . . . If the case arises, I shall give the order for the invasion of the Soviet Union eight weeks before the intended beginning of operations. Preparations requiring a longer starting period should begin immediately, in so far as they have not already begun.[48]

Hitler set mid-May 1941 as the earliest possible invasion date. The actual start of the war against the Soviet Union was then postponed for five weeks, partly because of dramatic developments in the Balkan peninsula. In Belgrade, the pro-German government of Yugoslavia, under Hitler's pressure, had declared its adherence to the Tripartite Pact in March 1941. Only a few hours later, however, it was overthrown by a putsch mounted by Serbian officers, and replaced by a government which was friendly to Great Britain, and, more importantly in this context, to the Soviet Union. This caused Hitler to react immediately by combining his intervention in Greece in support of the hard-pressed Italians, which he had planned in any case, with a simultaneous attack on Yugoslavia. On 6 April, German troops marched into both countries and were rapidly victorious. The Yugoslav army surrendered on 17 April; the Greek army four days later, whereupon 344,000 Yugoslav, 223,000 Greek, and 22,000 British soldiers were taken prisoner.

Hitler had once again conducted a 'Blitzkrieg', although after this it would never be repeated. Germany ruled the European continent and appeared almost invincible. The plan to inflict an indirect but devastating defeat on the

British by securing a rapid victory over the Soviet Union, and thereby conclude the war victoriously within the next few months, seemed to be working perfectly, even though the 'Balkan campaign' had not only led to considerable losses of men and material but also compelled extra Wehrmacht units to be stationed in both countries as an occupation force. Moreover, in Yugoslavia, the Wehrmacht was exposed to the attacks of a rapidly growing partisan movement, which soon gained its first successes in the trackless and mountainous countryside. Despite this, Nazi Germany stood at the summit of its power and self-confidence in the spring of 1941.

## War Plans

The circumstances and objectives of German military planning underwent an almost complete transformation in the course of 1940. Previously, Hitler had seen a victory over Great Britain as the prerequisite for starting the—also ideologically motivated—war against the Soviet Union which he had announced more than twenty years earlier. Now, however, the situation was reversed: the attack on the Soviet Union was intended to be the means of forcing Britain to surrender. In view of the alternatives, Hitler's decision in favour of the 'Russia campaign' was understandable, at least in the view of the generals of the Wehrmacht, who bore equal responsibility for the plan and worked it out in detail. Once again, it was the riskiest of all possible variants and it further intensified the extreme time pressure which already weighed upon the German side.

The Wehrmacht therefore prepared itself for a short 'Blitzkrieg' campaign lasting only three months: it expected to defeat the Soviet Union by the end of 1941. Large reserves of personnel were not established, and arms production was not concentrated entirely on the campaign in the east. On the contrary, attention was shifted in July 1941 from the production of weapons for the war in the east to preparations for the war against Great Britain. If the war were to last longer than the prescribed three months, this would lead to the collapse of the whole house of cards the German leadership had built up since the victory over France. It was above all this threatening prospect which forced the war planners to gamble on achieving a quick victory by all possible means, without any regard for the civilian population or the rules of international law.

This attitude was linked with the political and ideological objectives of the war. To defeat the Soviet Union would mean not only defeating a European Great Power but liquidating a hostile political system along with the social strata that upheld it, an expression that in Nazi ideology had both a political and a racial connotation. Since the rule of communism was regarded as the political expression of the rule of the Jews, the slogan 'destruction of Bolshevism' always also had as its undertone 'the destruction of Jewry', even if the consequences of this equivalence only came to the surface gradually. The German side was convinced that the elimination of the thin, predominantly Jewish leading stratum of Bolshevik rule would be enough to bring about the collapse of this 'colossus with feet of clay'.

In the longer term, the German war leaders aimed at establishing a German colonial empire in Eastern Europe. The analogies with European colonialism in Asia, America and Africa were visible everywhere, though more in German perceptions than in actual practice. Hitler at least never wearied of alluding to British rule in India or the conquest of the American West. He planned, he said, 'to Germanise this country by the immigration of Germans, and to look upon the natives as Redskins'.[49] The inhabitants of the Soviet Union were disparaged by Hitler; as Slavs, they were assigned to an inferior racial level. Accordingly, they should be treated not as European civilians but as indigenous colonial peoples, and their fate should be determined not by the laws of war and international agreements but by considerations of utility.

These strategic, political and ideological perspectives were reflected in far-reaching economic objectives, which loomed ever larger in the war preparations made between January and June 1941. The conquered areas of the Soviet Union were to function as a resource base for the Reich, to deliver agricultural products, raw materials and labour and at the same time to offer living space on a grand scale for German settlement. Here, the colonial perspectives of the German leaders' thinking can be seen in their clearest form.

Himmler, as the Reich Commissar for the Consolidation of Germandom (RKF) had already commissioned a group of high-ranking experts to elaborate long-term plans for the settlement of the parts of the Soviet Union which were to be conquered. Their director, Professor Konrad Meyer, born in 1901, was a recognised specialist in regional planning and agricultural sciences. Since 1939, he had also been in charge of the 'Planning and Soil' section of the RKF, which was responsible for resettlement planning. He gathered together a team of specialists from a number of different disciplines, among them the leading geographer and regional planner Walter Christaller, the landscape planners Erhard Mäding and Franz Doubek, the financial experts Felix Boesler and Max Rolfes and the constitutional lawyer Reinhard Höhn. This group now proceeded to work out a reconstruction programme for the period after the conquest of the east. At the beginning of June 1942, after some preliminary studies, they presented a 'General Plan East' which envisaged the rationalisation of agriculture, the transformation of the settlement structure and the construction of a large number of roads and canals on a twenty-five-year timescale. This was a modernising and civilising project. Dirty, inefficient single farmsteads inhabited by impoverished peasants and communicating by pathways deep in mud were to be replaced by a modern system of large and medium-sized rural centres with roads, canals, electricity and hospitals which would raise stock and till the fields according to the most up-to-date and scientific agricultural methods.

It is impossible to overlook the contradiction which came to the surface here. On the one hand there were plans for a radical modernisation of Eastern European agriculture, with large-scale cultivation, thorough mechanisation and extensive resettlement by more than 3 million Reich German and ethnic German small peasant families, whom it was intended to remove from their areas of origin and resettle forcibly in Eastern Europe. On the other hand, however, there were widespread notions that it was desirable to restore a traditional German peasantry, bound to its native soil, as the blood source of the nation, and this view had already found expression in the Hereditary Farm Law (*Reichserbhofgesetz*).

There was, of course, one prerequisite for the various plans for settlement, reconstruction and agricultural improvement, and the team of experts made this clear in detail: Eastern Europe had to offer a 'space empty of human beings'. But this situation had yet to be created. According to the plans worked out by the experts, most of the indigenous population would have to be expelled and resettled elsewhere. It was intended to remove 80 per cent of the Poles, two-thirds of the Ukrainians and three-quarters of the Belorussians from their homelands. These were megalomaniac notions, involving unprecedented population shifts. But, measured against the vast dimensions and the fascination of this project of radical modernisation and ethnic reorganisation of the whole of Eastern Europe as far as the Ural Mountains, the fate of the indigenous population appeared as a secondary consideration which could be ignored.

What of the Jews who lived in these regions? They were already absent from these plans. Even at this early stage, the experts were already proceeding on the assumption that, when the plans were put into effect, the Jews would have vanished from the scene.[50]

By the end of February 1941, planning for the war against the Soviet Union was already complete in its basic outlines. On 30 March, Hitler explained the character and aims of the coming war to the generals of the Wehrmacht: 'Clash of two ideologies' noted Halder, the Chief of the General Staff, during the two-hour speech.

> Crushing denunciation of Bolshevism, identified with 'asocial' criminality. Communism is an enormous danger for our future. We must forget the concept of comradeship between soldiers. A communist is no comrade before or after the battle. This is a war of extermination. . . . We do not wage war to

> preserve the enemy. . . . Extermination of the Bolshevist commissars and of the Communist intelligentsia. . . . We must fight against the poison of disintegration. This is no job for military courts. The individual troop commanders must know the issues at stake. They must be leaders in this fight. The troops must fight back with the methods with which they are attacked. Commissars and GPU men are criminals and must be dealt with as such. . . . This war will be very different from the war in the west. In the east, harshness today means lenience in the future.[51]

Even by his standards, Hitler's address to the generals was imbued with a peculiar brutality: no one in the audience could be in doubt that a war of annihilation was being planned. But unlike in the case of the French campaign or the war against Poland, no objections were raised. The generals shared Hitler's views on how the war should be waged.

As early as the middle of March, the High Command of the Wehrmacht (OKW) announced that 'in order to prepare for the political administration', Himmler, as *Reichsführer SS* (Reich Leader of the SS), would receive by order of the Führer the 'special powers which are required for the final struggle between two opposed political systems'.[52] With this, the *Einsatzgruppen* of the Reich Security Head Office (RSHA) were removed from the Wehrmacht's jurisdiction. There had been friction over this issue during the war against Poland, but in any case, the problem no longer existed, because the proclamations and instructions of individual military leaders were now even harsher than Hitler's pronouncements.

The procedure announced by Hitler on 30 March was implemented point by point in the weeks that followed in orders and instructions issued to individual offices and troop detachments. On 13 May, for instance, a 'Decree on Jurisdiction' was issued, setting out the judicial powers of the Wehrmacht over the indigenous population in the occupied areas of the Soviet Union. Suspicious or even merely undesirable persons were not to be put before a court but immediately shot by the troops. The shooting of groups of hostages was explicitly permitted. In addition, German soldiers who took action against the civilian population were explicitly exempted from prosecution. By this decree, the troops were given unrestricted authorisation to commit murder.[53]

From the beginning,the German leaders were united in the view that in the Soviet Union those who 'upheld the idea of hostile resistance' should be eliminated, in other words killed. In Poland, a year earlier, this strategy had been directed against politicians, intellectuals, scientists and the upper ranks of the clergy, with the aim of extinguishing Polish nationalism. In the Soviet Union, however, it was above all the Bolshevik functionaries, the 'Judaeo-Bolshevik intelligentsia' in Hitler's words, who were to be liquidated. On 6 June, finally, the troops received the order either to shoot the political commissars immediately, or to segregate them after prisoners had been taken and then to 'finish them off'. By summer 1943 roughly 10,000 men had been murdered directly by the Wehrmacht on the basis of what has come to be called the 'Commissar Order' (*Kommissarbefehl*) and probably about the same number were murdered in this period by the *Einsatzgruppen* of the SS.[54]

But the annihilation plans of the German leadership assumed an even more horrifying aspect in the economic sphere. Two major objectives stood out: firstly, the Soviet Union, as a colonial appendage of the Reich, was expected to deliver raw materials and agricultural produce, in such quantities as to make a repetition of the First World War blockade impossible. Russian corn and oil would make Germany economically impregnable. That was the plan. But the prerequisite for this was that the food and raw materials produced by the occupied Soviet areas would be used exclusively for German purposes. Secondly, the dimensions of the war against the Soviet Union were also completely different geographically from those in previous wars. If, as planned, the German thrust was to extend to Moscow and Leningrad and in the south as far as the Black Sea, the front would stretch out over almost 3,000 kilometres and be 1,500 kilometres distant from Germany's eastern border. This would pose considerable supply problems, particularly in relation to the provision of food for the troops. This gave rise to the requirement that the Wehrmacht units should mainly live off the land.

But both of these objectives, economic exploitation and living off the land, faced a significant obstacle: the Soviet population. This combination of circumstances led the German leadership to call, at first hesitantly, and then more and more insistently, for the Soviet civilian population to be largely deprived of access to food supplies. On 2 May 1941 a discussion between Goering and the most important representatives of the civilian departments and Wehrmacht sections responsible for wartime economic planning arrived at the following conclusions:

> 1. The war, which is now in its third year, can only be continued if the whole Wehrmacht is fed by Russia . 2. Umpteen million people are likely to starve if what we need is taken from the land. 3. What will be most important is the recovery and removal of oil-bearing seeds, oil cakes and then corn. The troops will doubtless use up the fat and meat that is available. 4. The population must only be allowed to return to industrial employment in agricultural deficit areas.[55]

Three weeks later, on 23 May 1941, these succinct instructions were developed in more detail in the 'Guidelines on Economic Policy for the Economic

Organisation East, Agriculture Group'. The document began by noting that Russia had previously produced considerable agricultural surpluses and exported them to Europe. Now, however, as a result of the great increase in the population and the Soviet policy of industrialisation, individual consumption in the cities had grown so much that there were no more export surpluses available. But since 'it is absolutely vital for Germany to have these surpluses, consumption must be reduced accordingly.' The most appropriate way of achieving this would be to cease the delivery of food from the agriculturally based South to the agricultural deficit areas of the North and the towns located there, with the following result: 'The population of these areas, particularly in the towns, will have to expect extreme starvation.' Even if the German side were to try to stem the tide of hunger, this would change nothing:

> Tens of millions of people in this region will be superfluous, and they will have to die or emigrate to Siberia. Any attempt to save the population from dying of hunger by drawing on surplus food from the Black Earth region can only take place at the expense of Europe's own supplies. It would work against Germany's ability to last out the war and undermine Germany's and Europe's immunity to a blockade. We must be absolutely clear about this.[56]

It was therefore intended to return the territory of the Soviet Union after its conquest by Germany to the situation of around the year 1860. There would be no industry and roughly 30 million fewer inhabitants than there were in 1941. The orders of magnitude named in this document—'umpteen millions', 'tens of millions of people'—are a clear indication that here very imprecise notions about the economic future of the country were combined with an uninhibited and unlimited readiness to exterminate the opponent. In fact, most of the assumptions underlying these plans were entirely erroneous. Firstly, there was no clear geographical separation between the Soviet Union's areas of agricultural surplus and deficit; secondly, the urban population did not just live in the north of the country; thirdly, the objective of complete deindustrialisation turned out very soon to be completely unrealistic; and fourthly, the amount of agricultural produce that could actually be brought from the Soviet Union to Germany was entirely unclear, since the Wehrmacht itself was planning to live off the land. This is how the historian Christian Gerlach summarises the insane calculations of the German war planners: 'In the eyes of the German leadership, the more uncertain the surpluses were, the more brutally they would have to be extracted from the country.'

The 'hunger plan' was the brutal consequence of a war which completely overstretched Germany's resources; it seemed to those in authority to be an inherent necessity, indeed an act of self-defence. The readiness to exterminate which derived from this belief was therefore not the abstract expression of a racist doctrine, but rather the result of using racist criteria to assign priorities to the survival of different groups in view of the obvious shortage of resources. 'Hunger planning' had its most drastic impact in the treatment of the groups on the bottom rungs of this hierarchy: the Jews, the Soviet prisoners of war and the inhabitants of the cities of 'Great Russia', as in the siege of Leningrad, for instance. Here, the ideas of the wartime planners were put into practice with frightful results, so that millions of human beings did in fact die of starvation.[57]

## Barbarossa

Most Germans were completely taken by surprise by the news that a war with the Soviet Union had started. As in the case of September 1939 and Hitler's other military campaigns, they reacted with dismay and anxiety, but this time the feeling was combined with the fear that this war would probably last a very long time. 'We are all utterly dejected. Hitler is a madman! What on earth will happen?' recorded one man in his diary. 'One thing the invasion of Russia would certainly mean is a lengthening of the war by many years and perhaps a tremendous increase in the number of victims' wrote another. Many people made historical comparisons with Napoleon Bonaparte's defeat in Russia, saying that they feared history would repeat itself. And unlike what had happened in the previous wars, the announcement of the first big victories did not cause this mood of uneasiness to subside.[58]

Germany's strategy in this war was to deploy a force of 3 million soldiers, surprise the opponent completely, and destroy his army in gigantic battles of encirclement. The army was divided into three groups. Army Group North advanced from East Prussia via Riga towards Tallinn and Leningrad, Army Group Centre advanced from the General Government via Minsk to Smolensk, with Moscow as its objective, and Army Group South advanced via Kiev in the direction of Rostov-on-Don. In the first five weeks, German troops stormed forward towards the east with almost irresistible force, triumphantly winning immense stretches of territory, capturing hundreds of thousands of prisoners and acquiring enormous quantities of military equipment.

The German attack took the Soviet leadership, under Stalin, by surprise. It had neither ordered the necessary military preparations nor prepared the population for the impending danger. Initial signs of disintegration rapidly appeared in the Red Army. The disorderliness of the retreat and the high number of deserters bore witness to the military chaos and the soldiers' disorientation. It took several weeks before the Soviet leadership was again fully capable of functioning. The Red Army suffered big defeats at Białystok and Minsk on 9 July and at Smolensk on 5 August, and hundreds of thousands of its soldiers fell into captivity. Eventually, the Soviets did succeed in filling the gaps, slowing down the German advance, and in inflicting on the German army the first defeats of the Second World War.

The German offensive started to falter at the beginning of August, and despite considerable territorial gains, the Wehrmacht was no longer able to continue its advance on all three fronts simultaneously. The Red Army's capacity for resistance was a shock to the German leaders. 'We underestimated the Russian colossus', conceded Halder. 'At the outset of the war we reckoned with about 200 enemy divisions. Now we have already counted 360. . . . And if we smash a dozen of them, the Russians simply put up another dozen.'[59] A few days earlier, the Germans had been counting firmly on victory within a few weeks, and planning had already started for the transfer of unnecessary divisions to the west for the attack on Great Britain. Now, they had to reckon with the failure of the Blitzkrieg strategy.

At the beginning of September 1941, therefore, Hitler decided to make a concentrated thrust in the direction of Ukraine, with Army Group South, so as to capture Kiev, conquer the industrial region of the Donets basin and make certain of the agricultural resources of the area as well as the Caucasian oilfields. This decision, which was taken predominantly for economic reasons, was resisted by the generals, who begged to be allowed to advance immediately with Army Group Centre towards Moscow so as to destroy the main fighting force of the Red Army and capture the Soviet capital. The advance into Ukraine did, it is true, prove to be extraordinarily successful for the Wehrmacht. On 19 September, Kiev was taken, Kharkov followed shortly afterwards, and Rostov-on-Don on 21 October. More than 600,000 Soviet soldiers were taken prisoner. This was one of the greatest German victories of the whole war. The German Reich now ruled over almost the whole of Ukraine and it could utilise both its industrial potential and its agricultural produce. German propaganda proclaimed that the war in the east was almost over, and on 9 November 1941 Hitler told his party comrades in Munich: 'Never before has a gigantic empire been shattered and defeated in a shorter time than the Soviet Union on this occasion.'[60]

At the same time, however, Germany's losses had risen tremendously. By mid-September, 400,000 men had been killed or wounded, and only half of that number could be replaced by fresh troops. The Soviet side, in contrast, had begun to raise new divisions and transfer considerable reserves from the Far East to the western front. It also succeeded, by dint of enormous effort, in dismantling large industrial establishments in the west of the country in advance of the German approach, and rebuilding them to the east of Ukraine.

At the beginning of October, the Wehrmacht made a tremendous effort to take Moscow and so bring the war to a victorious end. It failed in this objective. The Germans did in fact succeed by 20 October in breaking through the Soviet defensive positions and capturing almost 700,000 Soviet soldiers. But the German advance now became bogged down because of exhaustion, supply difficulties and tremendous losses. The final straw was the inclement weather. Heavy autumn rains were followed by freezed winter cold. On 5 December, the army was ordered to desist from further attacks. By the end of 1941, the Wehrmacht had lost almost a million dead, wounded and missing: roughly a third of its initial strength. Its military equipment, particularly tanks and aircraft, had been decimated. The Red Army began its first counter-offensive on 5 December, and it forced the Wehrmacht approximately 150 kilometres back towards the west. The German plan to bring the Red Army to its knees by the end of 1941 had ended in failure.[61]

A week later, on 11 December, the USA entered the war; the European war had become a world war. The Germans were now threatened with the war on two fronts, east and west, which they had been determined to avoid after the experience of the First World War. Hitler's all-or-nothing gamble had failed.

Before the war with the Soviet Union started, the soldiers of the Wehrmacht had already been told, and this was reinforced emphatically in orders of the day issued by the army commanders, that this war would need to be conducted differently from those against France or Norway. The Commander in Chief of the 17th Army, Colonel-General Hoth, reminded his men that this was a war between two ideologies:

> The German sense of honour and race, and the centuries-old German tradition of soldiering, are in battle against Asiatic ways of thinking and primitive instincts whipped up by a small number of mainly Jewish intellectuals such as fear of the knout, failure to respect moral values, levelling down, and readiness to throw away their own worthless lives. We are ever more strongly imbued with our faith that now is an epochal turning-point in which the leadership of Europe has been transferred to the German *Volk*, thanks to its racial superiority and its achievements. We clearly recognise our destiny, which is to save European culture from the advance of Asiatic barbarism. . . . Sympathy and softness towards the population is completely out of place. . . . The enemy's local government authorities should be left to deal with any food supply problems that may arise. Any trace of active or passive resistance or any kind of machination by Jewish Bolshevik agitators is to be immediately and mercilessly eradicated. The soldiers themselves must understand the necessity of harsh measures against elements which are alien to the *Volk*.[62]

Orders of this kind were not exceptions. They were issued frequently.

But according to everything we know, this war enjoyed no greater popularity among the soldiers than among the German people as a whole. Optimism and arrogance were mixed with the fear of a long, hard war with a high number of casualties. Half of the German army which invaded the Soviet Union consisted of men who had passed part of their adult life in the period before Hitler seized power. At least half of these, in turn, had not supported the Nazis in the closing years of the Weimar Republic. Even so, hostility towards the Soviet Union and Bolshevism was extremely widespread among them. Their first impressions after marching into the country confirmed, and even strengthened, their prejudices. 'We are deep in Russia, the so-called paradise, as it has been called' wrote a soldier to his family just after the beginning of the war.

> Russia invites the soldiers to desert and go over to this paradise. But there is utter misery here, people have been placed for decades under a kind of pressure one can hardly imagine. We would all prefer to die rather than suffer the kind of misery and torture these people have suffered.

'Here in Russia' wrote a sergeant on 17 July, 'the communist system rules. The individual owns almost nothing. A cow, a few fields for vegetables, and woe to him who wants to get richer, in other words to increase his holding. Financial penalties, forced labour, and exile. You can just imagine how most of these tormented people welcomed our arrival.'

The limitless poverty of the rural population, the utterly primitive character of their dwellings, and the neglect and the decay which could be seen everywhere, were in sharp contrast to the proclaimed utopia of a communist society, and they made a deep impression on the soldiers, especially when they compared them with conditions back in Germany. The people of the Soviet Union were frequently described as passive, crude, dirty, primitive, and apathetic. This applied particularly to the Red Army soldiers who were taken prisoner: 'We often meet with prisoners, individually or *en masse*. They are apathetic, brutish and their clothing is in rags, but they are often treacherous', remarked a sergeant of the 6th Infantry Division on 15 October. A soldier who belonged to a battalion of engineers wrote as follows:

> Now we have a clear idea of what the fate of our wives and children would have been if these Russian hordes who are now in captivity had been able to penetrate into our fatherland. Here I have the opportunity of contemplating and observing these uncultivated persons who come from many different races.

Culture and civilisation on one side; barbarism and savagery on the other: these were the colonial war categories with which the German soldiers sought to make sense of this alien and disturbing world. 'The primitiveness here is quite beyond words. There is no yardstick for comparison' noted a lieutenant on 25 October. 'It is a very peculiar feeling for us to hear dance music on the radio occasionally. . . . One then realises that, good God, they even have music, dancing and theatre, but here . . . there is only dirt and decay. That is the Soviet paradise.' But the conclusions drawn from these acutely felt differences between two civilisations were not uniform. According to a letter sent from a field post office on 1 August: 'These are people who need a lot of good training to become human beings. The character and temper of the Russians belongs more to the Middle Ages than to modern times.' This kind of evidence that the tradition of a civilising mission continued to operate can be found as frequently in letters from the eastern front as the ferocious wish to annihilate the enemy, which sometimes repeated Nazi political propaganda word for word: 'These are no longer human beings. They are wild hordes, who have been trained in bestiality by the Bolsheviks for the last twenty years. We cannot allow ourselves to feel sympathy for these people.'

The picture the German soldiers had of the land they were invading was marked by racism, fear of Bolshevism, colonial arrogance and anti-semitism:

> No newspaper could describe what we have seen. It borders on the unbelievable, even the Middle Ages could not equal what has happened here. And when one reads *Der Stürmer* in Germany and looks at the pictures, that is a mere token of what we see here and what crimes the Jews have committed.[63]

These reports were balanced, not always, but often, by dreams of a splendid future for the individual concerned: 'This region, which has an excellent climate—comparable to that of Italy—is a precious treasure-house of colonies', wrote a soldier to his wife in February 1942. And he continued: 'It must be marvellous down there on the Black Sea, where palm trees flourish in an almost tropical climate. A farm down there—a big horse-breeding farm, a nice house, work and effort, and I'd be bound to succeed with you by my side.'[64]

German units had already started to murder Jewish men and communist functionaries in the first few days after the war began. In most cases, no distinction was made between these two groups. Detachments of the Wehrmacht cooperated closely in this activity with police and SS units. The violence increased when advancing German troops found thousands of corpses in almost all the larger towns of the border region. In eastern Poland, the Baltic region and Ukraine, the Soviet secret service, the NKVD, had not only organised large-scale population evacuations before they retreated but also killed almost all the political prisoners who were confined in corrective institutions. Many of these prisoners were supporters of anti-communist and in particular nationalist movements, and as a result the arrival of the Germans was followed by terrible acts of revenge against communists and especially against Jews by nationalist groups which now emerged into the open.

In the occupied territories, German troops lived off the land from the beginning. Requisitioning, free quarter and large-scale plunder were the order of the day. 'Everywhere our people go in search of additional horses and take them away from the peasants', noted a German general as early as the second day of the invasion. 'There is tremendous howling and wailing in the villages. This is what is called "liberating" the population.'[65] It was no surprise, therefore, that resistance against the German conquerors grew quickly. On 3 July, Stalin ordered partisan units to be set up. The first resistance actions were reported in mid-August in the immense terrain to the rear of the German units, which they had been unable to secure properly owing to the rapidity of their advance. These groups of partisans were at first numerically weak and badly armed, but the Germans were unprepared for them. This led in turn to an increasingly harsh reaction from the Wehrmacht. The taking and shooting of hostages was a particular feature of this. The military authorities would seize numerous civilians as a guarantee against attacks on the troops. If there was an attack on the occupying power, one hundred hostages were killed for each dead German. This practice spread within a few months to the whole of the German-occupied area in Europe, and many people were killed as a result, particularly in Serbia and France.

After October 1941, the struggle against the partisans gave rise to ever more extensive reprisals. By the end of December, it is estimated that more than 60,000 people had been killed in anti-partisan operations. The more violent the behaviour of the German occupying power, the greater was the influx of supporters into the resistance groups. This applied particularly to individuals who were in serious danger of being killed, such as Jews and Red Army stragglers. Moreover, the oppressive and bloodthirsty actions of the German troops meant that they lost any support from the indigenous population, although at the beginning they had frequently received a friendly, and sometimes an enthusiastic, welcome, particularly in the Baltic lands and Ukraine, because the local people were happy to have escaped the Soviet regime. Despite the population's increasing antagonism, the Germans succeeded in putting large numbers of Soviet citizens to work for their own purposes. By the end of the war, more than a million people were involved. Many of them had been forced into cooperating. The motives of those who cooperated voluntarily were generally better access to food and a certain degree of protection from reprisals. A large proportion of these 'Hiwis', who were usually assigned to specific Wehrmacht units, failed to survive the war.[66]

But it was Germany's starvation policy which produced the highest death toll among the Soviet population, away from the field of battle. One of the major goals of Germany's conduct of the war was the destruction and depopulation of the large towns and cities. The flight of residents from towns under bombardment in rear areas was systematically promoted in many parts of the battlefront. According to an order issued on 20 October 1941 by Army Group South, 'the chaos in Russia will be all the greater, the more the population of the towns of Soviet Russia flees to the interior of the country. Before towns are seized, therefore, they should be destroyed by artillery fire and their population induced to take flight.'

Leningrad and Moscow, however, would not be captured, Hitler decided. He wanted rather to 'level them to the ground, and make them uninhabitable, so as to relieve us of the necessity of having to feed the populations through the winter. The cities will be razed by the air force.' Halder made a word-for-word record of Hitler's remarks on the desired consequences of this measure: 'A national catastrophe, which will deprive not only Bolshevism but also Muscovite nationalism of their centres.' It was intended to destroy not just communist rule, but the 'Great Russian' population as well.[67]

As a result of this strategy, Leningrad was not conquered but surrounded. After the expected capitulation, the aim was to leave the population of the city to fend for itself without food supplies over the winter. The survivors would then be driven out, and the city completely destroyed. But, in this case, the Germans did not manage to surround the city completely, with the result that the Soviet authorities were able to continue supplying it at least in part across the ice of frozen Lake Ladoga, and it was not forced to capitulate. The German blockade of the city continued until January 1944, and during this period more than 700,000 residents of Leningrad starved to death, more than 600,000 of them during the first year of the blockade. The Security Police's 'Report on Events in the USSR' of 18 February 1942 gives the following information:

> In the course of January, the civilian population started to die on a genuinely mass scale. . . . At the beginning of January the number of victims who died of hunger and cold every day was given as 2 to 3 thousand. At the end of January it was rumoured in Leningrad that every day 15,000 people were dying, and that 200,000 people had already died of hunger in the previous three months. Even this number is not all that great, seen as a proportion of the total population.[68]

The question of the balance between supplying the troops and feeding the local population increased in acutenessin proportion as the Wehrmacht advanced further to the east and the south-east, and its lines of supply became longer and longer. In order to keep food supplies in the German Reich at the high level that was demanded, and to make sure that the army had sufficient reserves, an 'order of priorities for the supply of provisions in the occupied eastern regions' was laid down as follows: 'a) the Wehrmacht b) the homeland c) the civilian population in the occupied eastern regions d) prisoners of war.' But Goering had already issued an order in mid-September that 'only those who work for us should be provided with appropriate sustenance', adding: 'Even if we wanted to feed all the other inhabitants, this would not be possible in the newly occupied eastern regions.' The food rations were accordingly set so low that 'non-workers' as well as 'children and Jews' fell below the starvation level, and in practice even these rations were often not distributed.[69]

These instructions led to a catastrophic famine, which was in line with the calculations and predictions of those who had planned the German war economy. From October onwards, the big cities of the east suffered mortality on a mass scale, and this worsened steadily over the winter, particularly in zones scheduled to be 'stripped bare', which units of the Wehrmacht had plundered completely, leaving nothing behind. In Kharkov, a city of more than half a million inhabitants, supplies of food had either been entirely consumed or taken away by the Red Army. The Wehrmacht fed only a small proportion of the inhabitants with its own supplies, but it also prevented people from attempting to acquire food in the surrounding countryside. Famine therefore started within a few days of the German occupation. By the end of 1942, some 30,000 residents of the city had died of hunger.

It is hardly possible to put a precise figure on the number of civilians who died of hunger in the occupied region. Estimates range from a few hundred thousand to millions. The higher figures take into account the indirect effects of the famine as well.[70]

The people who suffered worst of all from the German leadership's starvation policy were the Soviet prisoners of war. On both sides of this conflict, which was fought with merciless severity, the life of a prisoner of war was worth very little. On both sides, prisoners were often simply shot after the battle had ended, and news, or rumours, of this practice led to its reciprocal escalation. As far as we can judge from the information at our disposal, on the Soviet side the background to this was not a plan to murder prisoners but above all a shortage of food, as their own people also suffered from hunger. On the German side, on the other hand, the deaths of Soviet prisoners of war were planned. The war economy planners repeatedly reminded the authorities that there was not enough food for the masses of prisoners, since the needs of the Wehrmacht, the German population and Soviet civilians who were working for the Germans had priority. Moreover, even before the war, Hitler had explicitly rejected the idea of bringing Soviet prisoners to the Reich as forced labourers. In view of the quick war which was expected, it did not seem necessary to do this, and in addition, the presence of Red Army men on the territory of the Reich was seen as both a political and a racial danger. There was therefore no overriding economic incentive to preserve the labour power of the prisoners. General Quartermaster Wagner therefore made it clear on 13 November that: 'Non-working prisoners in the prisoner-of-war camps must starve.' But even where prisoners were set to work, the Economic Staff for the East (*Wirtschaftsstab Ost*) had the impression 'that many of them will not survive this winter.'[71]

Along with starvation, other factors such as the way they were transported and accommodated and the lack of medical attention also contributed after September to a level of mortality among the prisoners of war which was greater than any yet known and which counts alongside the murder of the Jews as the greatest and most terrible crime committed by the Germans during the Second World War. More than 50,000 prisoners had died by spring 1942 in the camp of Pskov, some 20,000 in Roslavl, and the same number in Smolensk, Viaz'ma, Bobruisk, Gomel, Mogilev, Orsha, Vitebsk, Kiev, Kirovograd, Zhitomir, Khorol, Kharkov and many other places. Roughly as many people died in each of these camps as died in the big concentration camps of the Reich. At the end of October 1941, a German private described his daily experience in a letter to a comrade: 'At the front we've taken more than 100,000 prisoners and you can imagine how things are going here. Every day that goes by around a thousand deaths, and on 18 and 19 October over 1,700. You can guess what happening. Some are shot, and the others die.'[72]

By the end of October 1941, it was reported that about 600,000 Soviet prisoners of war had died in German hands. In the middle of December, Goebbels was proceeding on the assumption that by then roughly 900,000 prisoners were already dead. In February 1942, the German labour administration calculated that out of the 3 million Soviet prisoners, roughly 2million were dead or no longer capable of work. By the end of the war, 2.7 million of the 5.7 million Red Army men who had been taken prisoner had lost their lives.[73]

## Changing Course towards a Long War

Despite the setback before Moscow in autumn 1941 and the considerable superiority in arms production of the Allies, who now included the USA, Nazi Germany was able to continue fighting for almost three and a half more years. This is one of the most astounding aspects of the war, and it requires some explanation. Three factors played a decisive role here: Speer's transformation of the arms industry, the way the war was financed and the exploitation of the occupied territories.

Germany's economic preparations for the war against the Soviet Union had already reached their zenith in June 1941. Since it was expected that the war would last for five months at most, preparatory measures for the air and sea war against England had already begun at this time, and the army was not given any more weapons. Even after the Moscow debacle, many weeks elapsed before the German leadership began to understand that the German economy needed to be completely reorganised, to enable the country to conduct a long war of attrition instead of the planned Blitzkrieg and to achieve a massive expansion in arms output. Fritz Todt, who had been 'Reich Minister for Arms and Ammunition' since spring 1941, had already attempted in autumn 1941 to start restructuring the ponderous and uncoordinated apparatus of the war economy. But it was the shock of failure which created the conditions for a thoroughgoing change of approach. Around the turn of the year, the course was set for a long land war. Post-war planning was to be delayed, and all forces were to be concentrated on increasing arms production.[74]

It was surprising that Albert Speer, who took over Todt's position after the latter's death, was able to achieve these goals relatively quickly, because until then he had only been marginally involved in the arms economy and industrial production. But he did possess an enormous talent for organisation, and he also had Hitler's confidence, which was of vital significance for his position within the government apparatus. Speer directed his chief efforts towards rationalisation and standardisation, and he accelerated the move towards continuous mass production, on the pattern set in the USA, where weapons, tanks and aircraft were produced in only a few models, in very large numbers and in a few gigantic factories. With this aim in mind, he increased the autonomy of the armaments industries, created for the first time a uniform authority to direct the whole field of war production, in the shape of the Central Planning Office (*Zentrale Planung*) and closed a large number of small-scale enterprises. Between 1942 and 1944, he achieved a threefold increase in Germany's armaments production by these methods. As early as 1942, Germany produced 15,000 aircraft, which was almost 50 per cent more than in the previous year. Of course, even these enormous increases in production were inadequate in view of the immense quantities of military hardware the Allies were able to produce: the Soviet Union was already producing 27,000 aircraft in 1942, the British Empire 23,000 and the USA 48,000.[75]

Speer's comprehensive measures of rationalisation brought about a thoroughgoing modernisation of German industry, which continued to have an impact even after 1945, and they transformed both production and management methods. They were peculiarly contradictory to the sociopolitical proclamations of the regime, because it had always promoted the private businessman as the Führer of the enterprise and mounted fierce polemics against the soulless capitalism of the Western democracies. By increasing working hours, by going over completely to assembly-line production, which until then had not been introduced across the board in Germany, and by introducing the two-shift system, Speer and his colleagues hoped to end Germany's clear inferiority in productivity as compared with British and American industry. They only succeeded in making a start in this direction, however, because there was insufficient time to make a lasting improvement in the skill levels of the workers.

In order to pay for the war, the regime had to obtain financial resources from its citizens, either by raising taxes or by incurring debt, perhaps in the form of government bonds. There were political objections to both courses of action. The German leadership considered that to raise taxes would cause discontent, and as always Hitler tried to avoid imposing such explicit burdens on the German population. The experience of the First World War was an argument against issuing government bonds, because the memory was still fresh among the population that all the money they had contributed to these investments had been lost at the end of the war. The National Socialist state therefore adopted a different way of financing the war, relying on the fact that private households were relatively wealthy, because taxes were low and real wages were high, not least on account of the longer working hours. At the same time, private consumption was very much restricted, because almost all food was rationed, extra taxes were imposed on travel, beer, tobacco and visits to the cinema and the theatre, and private building activity was severely limited. Thus, there were not many opportunities to spend the money that had been earned. In 1941, the level of consumption in Germany was 18 per cent lower than in 1938, and the year 1938 had itself not yet surpassed the level of 1932, the worst year of the world economic crisis. There were therefore considerable increases in the amount Germans saved. Between 1938 and 1941, savings doubled, and in 1941 the inflow of savings amounted to over a billion RM a month, while withdrawals remained constant, or even fell. Since private investment activity was greatly reduced, these resources largely went to the state as credits, amounting to 12.8 billion RM in 1941, and thus became a fundamental element of war finance.

This form of 'silent war finance' proved to be extremely advantageous to the regime. It did not have to raise direct burdens on the citizen, and the question of war finance did not become a public theme of discussion as in the First World War, when appeals to subscribe to government bonds required a great deal of propagandistic exertion. It is true that, after 1941, the savings banks advertised increasingly for 'iron savings', but only a very small number of Germans would have been aware that their own savings were being used directly to finance the war, especially as the restrictions and rationing affecting their daily lives left few other possibilities open than to deposit their money in the bank. Moreover, the constant growth in people's savings promised a better life after the war—a victorious war, it went without saying—and here the interests of the people and the leadership coincided. At the end of the war, the German Reich had debts of 451.7 billion RM, and three years later the citizens of Germany had to pay those debts. The currency reform of 1948 meant a 90 per cent reduction in the value of private savings. That was how the debts the state had incurred to finance the war were liquidated.[76]

It turned out, however, that the savings deposits of Germany's citizens were not in fact an adequate basis for financing the war. Since the beginning of the war, the gap between the Reich's income and its expenditure had become ever wider. In 1939, it was still possible to raise 30 per cent of the total expenditure of 89.58 billion RM from ordinary income; by 1943–4, this proportion had fallen to 15.3 per cent, and in the final year of the war it stood below 10 per cent. In addition to increasing state indebtedness, the war was also financed from the resources of the countries occupied by, and allied to, Germany. Even before the beginning of the war, it was stated categorically that: 'in order to cover the extra demands on the Wehrmacht we must draw on the economic strength of the Protectorate (of Bohemia and Moravia) and of the other regions which will be conquered in the course of the campaign.'[77]

The utilisation of the occupied territories for the Reich's own purposes assumed many different forms. It stretched from the confiscation of the military equipment of the defeated country and the exploitation of the raw materials available there to the employment of the defeated country's own industry in German armaments production. German firms also acquired majority shareholdings in industrial enterprises by agreement, under conditions which were especially favourable to the German side owing to the wartime situation, or they acquired them by force.

In this context, cooperation between the German occupying power and the countries of Western and Northern Europe proved to be more profitable than the colonial forms of exploitation practised in the East. France in particular became a favourite target for German economic interests. Large quantities of raw materials such as copper, tin, nickel and oil were confiscated by the Wehrmacht, as well as the overwhelming majority of the locomotives and wagons owned by the French, Belgian and Dutch railway companies.

In addition to this, the occupied countries, and some friendly countries too, had 'occupation costs' to pay. As a result, by the end of 1943 almost 25 billion RM had flowed from France to Germany. The total income received by the Reich from the above-mentioned sources in the course of the war was roughly 90 billion RM. The figures for each country were: France 31.6 billion RM, Italy 12.0 billion, the Netherlands 10.1 billion, Belgium 5.3 billion, Greece

3.8 billion, Norway 6.9 billion and Denmark 2.4 billion. Taking together the income derived from all the occupied territories, the proportion contributed to Germany's finances by the countries of Western and Northern Europe was roughly 65 per cent.

The vouchers distributed to German soldiers so that they could go shopping in the occupied regions, the 'Reich Credit Cash Vouchers' (*Reichskreditkassenscheine*), which were a form of requisitioning, also played a role. The vouchers proved very attractive. In Paris, it was reported, German soldiers emptied the shops which sold fashionable clothing, and in Belgium 'long processions of soldiers bent under the weight of their innumerable purchases were a daily spectacle.'[78] The national bank of the relevant country was obliged to change the Reich Credit Cash Vouchers into its own currency. In this way, direct confiscation or requisitioning was avoided, but even so, it was the economies of the occupied countries which had to bear the burden.

They were also burdened with indirect loans, which had their origin in the clearing system. Under this system, the imports and exports of two countries were balanced against each other, and any deficit remained on the books as a debt. The effect of this practice was that the Reich became more and more indebted to the occupied and friendly countries. By 1944, this debt amounted to more than 20 billion RM, of which, 8.5 billion RM were owed to France, 4.9 to Belgium, and 1.4 to Denmark[79]

The reason why the exploitation of the eastern regions proved to be on the whole less profitable was that political considerations had priority. In Poland, only a part, and in the occupied territories of the Soviet Union, very little of the economy was systematically brought into operation and utilised in Germany's interest. Poland's national income fell by 40 per cent after the German invasion, and many factories were plundered or closed down. After 1941, however, the officials in charge of the war economy directed Polish industrial production more systematically towards serving Germany's industrial needs. This applied particularly to the extraction of coal and oil and the production of armaments. A large proportion of this material went directly to the Wehrmacht and was not exported into the Reich.

In addition, the General Government had to make payments into the German exchequer. These were described as a 'Contribution by the General Government for its Military Protection' and increased twenty-fold between 1941 and 1943. The General Government paid a total of 5.5 billion RM to the Reich in the course of the war, part of it in kind. Moreover, the whole of the assets possessed by the Polish state were transferred to the German Treasury, since it was not intended that a Polish state would exist in the future.[80]

The exaggerated expectations of the war economy planners for the Soviet territories were not fulfilled. The German economic authorities extracted less from the Soviet Union during 1941 than Stalin had promised to deliver to the German Reich at the beginning of that year, and only a little more than the army of Imperial Germany had carried off from the occupied east in 1917–18. This was partly a result of the Soviet 'scorched earth' policy put into effect when the Red Army retreated in the summer of 1941, with the aim of leaving behind as little as possible of value for the conquerors. But it also reflected the way the German war economy had been planned, because no long-term exploitation of the industrial facilities of the Soviet Union had originally been envisaged. This attitude changed rapidly under the pressure of military events, and the Hermann Goering Works, for example, started to take over steel works and arms factories in the occupied Soviet Union as well. After all, 58 per cent of Soviet steel production and 64 per cent of Soviet coal production was by now in German hands.[81]

It was above all food that the German regime had hoped to import from occupied Soviet territory. But, in practice, the food supplies denied to the local population went almost exclusively to the Wehrmacht. The expectation had been that large quantities of agricultural products would be taken from the Soviet Union and sent to Germany. This did not happen. It was different in the General Government. Although the policy of robbing and plundering the country long held sway, the yield from the harvest began to rise as early as 1940, and after two good harvests, the German authorities were able to move considerable amounts of grain from the General Government into the Reich: 383,000 tonnes were exported in 1940–1 and over a million tonnes in 1942–3. This made a considerable contribution to mitigating the German food supply crisis of spring 1942, which had been serious enough to cause a reduction in the food ration.

In August 1942, in reaction to this crisis, Goering addressed an assembly of the top representatives of the various German occupation authorities. He called upon them to reduce the rations in their areas:

> I see people eating like pigs in all the occupied territories, while our own *Volk* is suffering from hunger. God knows, you have not been appointed to work for the good of the populations entrusted to you but to extract the uttermost amount from them, so that the German *Volk* can live. . . . I have reports lying in front of me about what you intend to deliver. That amounts to absolutely nothing, when I think of the countries you are responsible for. It is a matter of indifference to me when you say your people are collapsing with hunger. Let them, as long as no single German suffers the same fate.[82]

These short-term exploitation strategies were completely inconsistent with the attempts made particularly in the occupied countries of the west to set in motion a kind of European economic cooperation, so as to keep the German war machine running. In the Netherlands alone, the Central Office for Commercial Orders supervised 20,000 firms which produced goods for German customers largely without a hitch. French and Belgian entrepreneurs frequently reported on their close cooperation with German business partners. As the Belgian banker Baron Paul de Launoit wrote: 'The economic area Ruhr-South Holland-Belgium-Lorraine-Luxembourg-North France is, as regards coal and iron, a natural economic region . . . Coal and steel industrialists ought to break through state borders and co-operate in economic matters'; and a French official emphasised that in these acts of economic cooperation the German entrepreneur did not always

> desire hegemony or domination, but on the contrary he wanted to secure himself against all eventualities. In fact some of them are uncertain about a German victory or the duration of the Nazi regime, or they act as bourgeois, who are seeking to connect with other bourgeois, so as to influence social conditions in their own country.[83]

Germany's overall occupation policy, which involved murdering hostages, deporting Jews and persecuting political opponents, ensured that this sort of cooperation did not get very far during the war. Four years of German occupation were not long enough to have a really lasting impact on the European economy. Even so, there were indications that the elites of the occupied lands of Western Europe were reflecting on the possibilities and the advantages of a greater integration of the European economies, including the German economy, under different and fairer conditions than prevailed during the German occupation. But this was a vision for the future, not the present.

In the course of the year 1942, the Nazi regime succeeded to an astonishing extent, and relatively quickly, in reorienting its economy and its finances towards a long-lasting war, and in mobilising the necessary resources. The more intensive exploitation of the conquered countries of Europe, both through the exertion of control over agricultural and industrial production and through the operation of a rigid fiscal policy, was a decisive aspect of this reorientation. The relation of economic forces undoubtedly changed still further to Germany's disadvantage during this year as well, but the decline was kept within limits. The war could certainly no longer be won by the Germans in this way, but it could be prolonged.

# 9
# Germany in 1942

## Genocide and *Volksgemeinschaft*

### Helene Holzman

Helene Holzman, née Czapski, was born in Jena in 1891. She grew up in a middle-class household and became an artist. She spent some time as a pupil of Max Beckmann. In the 1920s, she moved with her husband, who was a bookseller, to Kaunas in Lithuania, where he had been stationed as a German soldier during the wartime occupation. They ran a bookshop there. They had two children, Marie and Grete. Max Holzman was Jewish, while Helene Holzman counted in Nazi terminology as a so-called Half Jew (*Halbjüdin*).[1]

In summer 1940, the Red Army occupied Lithuania. The Holzmans' bookshop was closed and expropriated by the Soviet authorities. Thousands of Lithuanians were sent to Siberia because they were 'bourgeois', including many middle-class Jews. The Holzmans, too, were on the NKVD's list, but they were spared deportation. A year later, in June 1941, the Germans marched into Lithuania. The Lithuanian nationalists were their willing accomplices. A savage bloodbath started immediately after the entry of the Wehrmacht. Hundreds of Jews were hunted down and slaughtered in the streets by the Lithuanian nationalists. A few days later, the commander of a German *Einsatzkommando* (Task Force Command), Karl Jäger, had 3,000 Jewish men shot in a fortress in the town, known as the Seventh Fort. Max Holzman was very probably one of the victims. By the end of October, the German occupation authorities had murdered more than a third of the 45,000 Jews who lived in Kaunas.

Here are some extracts from Helene Holzman's notes on these events, written immediately after her liberation:

> They pushed their way into the Jews' houses and drove all those living there onto the market square or into the synagogue. Sick people and babies were carried. The people were told that they were required for work elsewhere and would be resettled temporarily. They were asked to bring with them the items of clothing they needed. Utterly appalling scenes had already unfolded in

the streets, the squares [and in the] synagogues. The Jews were battered with cudgels and rifle butts, the articles they had brought with them were snatched away, children were separated from their mothers, they were spat upon and jeered at. Then they were driven out of the town in a single group.

In many places, Jewish engineers and their assistants had been fetched a few days earlier and instructed to dig wide pits in the woods, or out in the open, on the pretext that they were wells that needed digging. After they had finished their work they were shot on the spot. The Jews were led to these pits. They had to pile their bundles in a heap and take off their outer clothing. Groups of them were then driven half-naked to the edge of the pits and machine-gunned. First came the sick and the old, then women and children, and finally the men. The wounded were stabbed or beaten to death. In many places the slaughter lasted the whole day. The unlucky ones had to witness how the others were butchered before their own turn arrived. The dead lay in the pits on top of each other, in layers. When the pits were full up, the Jews were forced to cover them with soil, after the corpses had been sprinkled with calcium chlorate, for 'hygienic reasons'. Little children were thrown alive into the pits and then covered over. Some men defended themselves, leapt at the throats of their executioners and pulled them along with them into the ghastly mass grave

It was always Lithuanian partisans, 'volunteers', who implemented the Germans' instructions. The German police and the Wehrmacht directed and supervised the operation. If the Lithuanians started slacking, they were encouraged with alcohol. In many places these scenes were filmed by German cameramen. In taking these pictures, care was always taken that only Lithuanian murderers appeared on the screen. The Germans later tried to falsify the evidence by saying that the slaughter had been organised on the initiative of the Lithuanians, who were expressing the 'justified anger of the people against the Jewish exploiters'. All this took place in broad daylight.[2]

The Holzmans' older daughter, Marie, was also arrested. She had visited German soldiers in the field hospitals and tried to convince them of the need for peace. She was shot three months later.

In autumn 1941, the mass extermination operations in Kaunas were temporarily suspended, because there was a need for Jewish workers, mainly to rebuild the city's airfield. It had originally been envisaged that Soviet prisoners of war, of whom there were more than 10,000, would do this work, but they starved to death in August and September, so the Jews were now called upon to make the airfield operational again.

Helene Holzman did everything she could at least to save the life of her younger daughter, Grete. She herself was in very great danger owing to her uncertain status as a 'Half Jew' and the wife of a Jew. After Marie had been arrested, she and her younger daughter left their home, as it was now unsafe, and were given accommodation by two Russian women, who helped many of the townspeople who were persecuted and in danger of being killed. The risk was enormous: anyone who hid Jews was shot by the Germans, and there were informers everywhere. Despite this, a few friends, some of them previously unknown to each other, gradually constructed a secret network of helpers: the two Russian women, a woman doctor, a woman writer, a female German student from Freiburg and Helene Holzman and her daughter. They smuggled food into the ghetto, which had been set up and sealed off in the meantime, they offered refuge to individuals, and they supplied them with food ration cards and papers which another friend, the violinist Vocelka, evidently knew how to forge excellently.

They even succeeded in bringing out of the ghetto two friends of the Holzmans, the composer Edwin Geist and his wife Lyda, and hiding them. In this case their efforts were in vain. After a few weeks, Edwin Geist was seized and killed. When the Gestapo was about to fetch Lyda as well, she committed suicide.

Life in semi-legality started to become more difficult and dangerous. Helene Holzman always carried poison, in order not to fall alive into the hands of the German and Lithuanian killers. Hope began to emerge again with the news of the German defeat at Stalingrad, because it made them think that an end to the situation, and survival, was still possible. In spring 1944, however, the Germans restarted the programme of mass murder. At the end of March, 'a horrible operation began', wrote Helene Holzman. They assembled together all the children and old people of the ghetto, 1,300 people in all, and shot them.

> The children were fetched. The German police went from house to house, accompanied by Ukrainians. . . . All children up to twelve years of age were seized and loaded onto lorries. The mothers were compelled to bring the smallest children to the vehicles themselves. Big police dogs sniffed their way through the houses, the floors, the outhouses. They were trained to drag the children out. Women who refused to give up their children, and who thronged around the lorries wanting to pull their [children] out again were bludgeoned to the ground. Some were shot. Many parents wanted to suffer death along with their children: 'You pigs still have to work. This rubbish here has to be got rid of.' The children were dragged from their beds completely unclothed. They were thrown so crudely into the vehicles that many suffered serious wounds. They screamed piteously, and the bigger children tried to get away. These scenes of indescribable misery were accompanied by the sound of loud radio music, booming out from the vehicles. Never before has the world seen such perfidious cynicism.[3]

At the beginning of July 1944, the Red Army's offensive brought it close to Kaunas. The German terror again cast its shadow over the town. The Kaunas ghetto, which had in the meantime been converted into a concentration camp by the SS, was dissolved. Those residents who were still alive were transported to Dachau and Stutthof. The Red Army marched into the town on 1 August. For Kaunas, the war was now at an end. Helene Holzman and her daughter had survived. But only approximately 9,000 of the 200,000 Jews of Lithuania lived to experience the end of the war.

## Retribution

German occupation policies varied considerably from country to country. It made a difference, for instance, whether the territory in question was ruled by a military commander—as in Belgium and France—or by a civilian administration, in which the Nazi Party had the final word, as in the regions into which the occupied Soviet Union was divided, the General Government or the Netherlands. The administration of the occupied lands did not follow any thoroughgoing system. Decisions were made ad hoc, and in large part they were improvised. The disparity between east and west was unmistakable: the severity of the occupation varied according to the racial classification and cultural prestige of the population. But the endeavour to seek out as many Jews as could be found in a given region, and make them disappear in some as yet unspecified manner, was given the same high priority in all occupied countries.

The German occupation had three objectives, which were to some extent in competition. The first objective was to secure the area using the smallest possible number of military and police personnel, in most countries with the help of the indigenous local bureaucracies, which took over the bulk of the administrative tasks. The second was to utilise the region to the maximum extent to serve the economic interests of the Reich. And the third was to identify and expropriate, and finally to deport and murder all the Jews of the country in question. The rule of a movement or party akin to the Nazis was not a necessary requirement. Hitler understood more clearly than many of the leading German occupation officials and military men that the rule of the Germans rested on force alone, and that collaborationist elements in the occupied countries were very much in the minority. In case of a German withdrawal, they would be exposed to the fury of their fellow countrymen. That would make them obedient, he thought. In Denmark, for instance, he said that they should set up a 'puppet government' the members of which must be constantly made aware that 'if German troops eventually marched away, they would be hanged from the nearest lamp-post.'[4]

In Poland and the Soviet Union, the idea of setting up a collaborationist administration above the town council level was almost entirely abandoned. There, unlike in the rest of Europe, Germany was interested in creating a colonial hinterland, from which most of the indigenous population would be expelled, so as to allow the settlement of German families. Even in areas of the Soviet Union where at least at the beginning of the war both the population in general and the elites in particular were ready to collaborate, such as the Baltic lands and parts of Ukraine, the German rulers rejected any form of political autonomy. The establishment of a Russian or Ukrainian government was not envisaged even as a long-term goal.

The generals of the Wehrmacht regarded their way of waging war in the west as 'fair', and in accordance with the laws of war, unlike the war in the east. This also applied to Germany's occupation policies, especially as the number of troops stationed in the countries of Western and Northern Europe was soon reduced, and the occupation force was predominantly made up of older men. Members of the Wehrmacht regarded it as a stroke of good luck to be stationed in the Netherlands, Denmark, Norway and particularly France. For a long time, they could live there in almost 'peaceful conditions'. Theatres and cinemas were open and well attended, food and even luxury goods were available in large quantities and under the voucher system even ordinary soldiers could afford to buy what they wanted. Air raids, too, which made life increasingly difficult in Germany, occurred rarely or not at all in the occupied west.

France was divided into two parts after the German victory of summer 1940. The northern half and the coastal regions were ruled by a German general, the 'Military Commander in France'. A French government was established in the south, under Marshal Pétain, 'the hero of the First World War'. Its capital was in the town of Vichy, and it collaborated with the Germans. The German Military Commander in France after October 1940 was General Otto von Stülpnagel, a typical representative of the Prussian military caste, conservative and correct within the narrow limits of his view of the world. Under him, there was a French administration, which ruled the country under the supervision of a small number of German officers and military officials. There were only about 200 of them in Paris, and fewer than 1,000 for the whole of Occupied France.[5]

For most of the officers and bureaucrats who belonged to the German military administration located in Paris, in the Hotel Majestic, Germany's victory over France was something like the fulfilment of modern German history. Their view of politics was characterised by an insistence on the social supremacy of the military, intense nationalism and an orientation towards an authoritarian model of state and society. In terms of foreign policy their views were dominated by the prospect of European hegemony and a desire to avenge Germany's defeat in the First World War. The restoration of German military strength after 1933 and above all the quick victories gained by Germany after 1939 tied them firmly to Hitler. At the same time, however, they remained condescendingly aloof from the so-called 'party fellows'.

In summer 1941, however, when the war against the Soviet Union began, armed resistance started to increase in France, taking the form of assassinations and dynamite attacks. The German military administration reacted first by intensifying surveillance, and unmasking and destroying resistance groups. Von Stülpnagel reacted to the attacks of 4 August 1941 by ordering the imposition of the death penalty for 'communist subversion' and he instructed the French police to undertake a large-scale arrest operation, in the course of which more than 4,000 people were seized. The crackdown was directed against those who supported the communists. Jews of French nationality were also arrested on this basis, among them 200 intellectuals and local notabilities. The military authorities decided not to take any further measures for the moment, so as not to endanger the smooth cooperation that had so far existed with the French administration and the population at large. The German military administrators repeatedly stressed that they wanted if at all possible to avoid 'Polish conditions'. Nevertheless, after a further attack on 21 August 1941, all French prisoners held by the German authorities were, for the first time, declared to be collective hostages. On 3 September, another attack, resulting in an assassination, led the Military Commander to order the shooting of three imprisoned communists on that basis.

Now, however, Hitler and Keitel intervened in the affair and gave orders that when the next attack took place at least 100 people must be shot for each dead German, with the justification that 'political relations between Germany and the country in question . . . should not determine the line of conduct of the military occupation authorities.'[6] For the German officers in Paris, on the other hand, political relations with the country in question, or, more precisely, their own political and cultural evaluation of those countries, provided a yardstick for their line of conduct in the occupied areas. What was customary and accepted practice among German occupation officers in Serbia and Russia at that time met with protests from German occupation officers in France. In any case, when further attacks occurred a little later, 98 hostages were in fact executed on orders from Hitler's headquarters, a measure which attracted a great deal of attention and gave rise to much outrage both in France and internationally.

To avoid the recurrence of such mass shootings, the Military Administration proposed to respond to further attacks by proceeding against the Jews instead. In France, it was the Military Commander's administrative staff who were responsible for 'Jewish policy' and they had already laid down harsh rules on the subject in August 1940. In agreement with the French authorities, decrees ordering the registration of Jews, discrimination against them and the theft of their property were issued in quick succession. It should be noted that the officers in charge of the Paris Military Administration did not generally regard themselves as radical anti-Semites. However, their traditional conservative anti-Semitism, which varied in strength according to the individual, proved to be completely adequate to the task in hand.

Jews had already formed the majority of the victims of the first mass arrests after the attacks of 4 August 1941. For most officials of the Military Administration, there was no doubt at all that there was a connection between communism, attempted assassinations and Jewishness, especially as some of the first assassins to be picked up were in fact Frenchmen of Jewish descent.[7]

The officers of the German administrative staff therefore proposed that, in the future, Frenchmen who had been declared hostages would not be shot, but instead a large number of people would be deported 'to do forced labour in the east'. Apart from communists, this group would include Jews, particularly foreign Jews who had immigrated to France after 1918 and would presumably not be able to count on much solidarity from the native French population.

On 28 November, news came of a further attack, in which three German soldiers were killed. The Military Administration now attempted for the first time to apply its new policy. Instead of shooting the 300 French hostages, as demanded by Hitler, it proposed to the OKH (Army High Command) the execution of 'fifty Jews and communists' plus the 'imposition on the Jews of Paris of a penalty of one billion Francs' as well as the 'internment and deportation to the east of Jews who had come to attention in a criminal or anti-German context.' The number of people the authorities had in mind was 1,000.[8]

Only a few days later, further attacks were made, also resulting in deaths. In response, on 12 December 1941, 743 mainly well-off Jewish males, most of them French citizens, were arrested and brought to the concentration camp of Compiègne, which was run by the Germans. From there it was intended to transport them 'to the east'. To make up the number to 1,000, 300 largely Jewish inmates of the camp at Drancy were added.

But this attempt to avoid the mass shooting of French hostages which Hitler had ordered by replacing it with a mass deportation of Jews 'to the east' did not achieve the desired effect. Hitler and Keitel did agree to the proposal to deport 1,000 Jews, but this was to be *in addition* to shooting a hundred hostages for every one dead German, not *instead* of it. Von Stülpnagel thereupon resigned as Military Commander. There was tremendous indignation among his administrative staff members over Hitler's behaviour in the hostage question, fuelled by a combination of factors: the officers' code of honour, reservations about legality, moral scruples, political and ideological reflections on the future of Europe and the cultural and 'racial' status of the French, and finally, concerns over the further development of Franco-German relations. It can be seen, in retrospect, that the order to shoot French hostages *en masse* increased the aloofness felt by many officers towards the Nazi regime and prepared the way for the participation of many of the officers associated with von Stülpnagel in the attempted rising of 20 July.

Nevertheless, the proposal to deport large numbers of French Jews 'to the east' instead of shooting hostages was ultimately accepted, and deportation rapidly became the official practice. On 23 March 1942, the first transport departed from Compiègne towards Auschwitz. This date marks the beginning of the mass deportation of French Jews to the death camps.

The officers on the staff of the Military Commander were manifestly ready to enter into conflict with the leadership of the regime and even with Hitler himself when orders from Berlin wounded their sense of self and their honour as soldiers and at the same time stood in contradiction to their opinions about policy, in this case concerning the correct way of administering the occupation in Paris. The German military had no such objections to make against corresponding orders in the countries of Eastern and South-East Europe. Appreciation of French culture and of the French in general clearly played a decisive role here, as well as the attitude connected with this, which was to treat peoples regarded as being on an equal footing with the Germans in culture and civilisation differently, in other words in a more civilised way, from peoples or groups felt to be inferior. There was thus no fundamental divergence between the Berlin leadership and the Paris Military Administration over the treatment of Jews, any more than there was over measures against communists. In the latter case, indeed, the military often took the initiative. Communists counted as enemies of Germany and agents of the Soviet Union, and they should be treated as such. The treatment of the French Jews was of secondary importance in the eyes of the protagonists in this dispute. If 'toughness' absolutely had to be demonstrated, it was best exerted against a group they disliked in any case, which was not counted as French, had already suffered immense discrimination, lacked any advocates, and was assumed to include the instigators of the outrages, or even to constitute the heart of the anti-German opposition itself. This latter aspect was obviously the decisive one, as it removed the decision to start the deportation of the Jews from the purely ideological context and based it on the pursuit of supposedly objective and rational goals.

In the Soviet Union, in contrast, these culturally motivated reservations or obstacles did not exist. Before the German Sixth Army had captured the Ukrainian capital, Kiev, in mid-September 1941, the retreating Red Army had covered large areas of the city with mines or fitted delayed action explosives. There were big explosions on 24 September, followed by others on subsequent days. A large part of the city caught fire, and numerous German soldiers, probably hundreds, were killed. The response of the officers of the Sixth Army was to reach automatically for measures of retribution. But, here, standards of behaviour differed from those in France. The Sixth Army had already carried out similar revenge attacks in previous weeks in the course of its advance into the Soviet Union. In this connection, a division of labour grew up in the course of time between units of the Sixth Army and Special Commando 4a, which consisted of approximately sixty police and SS men. 'Irregulars' or saboteurs were shot by the Wehrmacht units, but the responsibility for collective measures of punishment was handed over to the Special Commandos. The job of the Wehrmacht units in such killing operations was to secure the area. Voluntary participation of Wehrmacht soldiers in the executions frequently carried out by the Special Commandos was forbidden, in order to prevent the troops from 'becoming barbarised'.

From July 1941 onwards, these 'collective measures' mainly involved the shooting of Jews, and from August at the latest the Special Commandos started to murder not just the male inhabitants of the places chosen but the Jewish population as a whole. The Supreme Command of the Sixth Army pointed out to the soldiers that 'necessary executions' were being carried out 'against criminal, Bolshevik, primarily Jewish, elements'.[9] These actions remained within the legitimating category of retribution, even though this piece of rationalisation had long since been rendered out-of-date by facts on the ground.

After the devastating explosions in Kiev, the collaborationist sections of the Ukrainian population blamed the whole thing on the Jews, as usual. Some commanders of the Sixth Army responded by agreeing to conduct a large-scale 'measure of retribution' against the Jews of Kiev. A propaganda company of the Sixth Army printed 2,000 wall posters containing a proclamation calling upon all the Jews of the city to assemble together on the morning of 29 September in one of the city squares.[10]

A survivor has reported on what happened next:

> Many people thought they were to be sent to provincial towns. Families baked bread for the journey, sewed knapsacks, rented wagons and two-wheeled carts. Old men and women supported each other. Streams of people flowed into the endless human current on Lvov Street, while German patrols stood on the sidewalks. The town fell silent. Lvov Street led to Melnik Street, which led to a barred road through naked hills to the sheer ravines of Babi Yar. An entire office operation with desks had been set up in an open area. Thirty to forty persons at a time were separated from the crowd and led under armed guard for 'registration'. Documents and valuables were taken away. Then the Germans forced everyone to strip naked. No exceptions were made. Their clothing was gathered up and carefully folded. Rings were ripped from the fingers of the naked men and women, and these doomed people were forced to

stand at the edge of a deep ravine, where the executioners shot them at point-blank range. The bodies fell over the cliff.[11]

Members of the Special Commando murdered 33,771 Jews in this way on the 29th and 30th September 1941. After the 'action' had come to an end, a detachment of military engineers dynamited the edges of the mass graves in the ravine, so that the corpses were buried by the fall of earth. This was a sensational and terrible event; news of it spread around Europe like wildfire. Only a few days later, they were already talking about Babi Yar in the officers' clubs in Paris. And, in spring 1942, even the isolated and beleaguered Jewish Professor of Romance Languages Victor Klemperer, living in Dresden, noted in his diary that there were reports of 'ghastly mass murders of Jews in Kiev'.[12]

The road travelled by the Sixth Army finally came to an end in Stalingrad. But its development from summer to autumn 1941 shows how military calculation, enmity towards Jews, growing ruthlessness in face of unforeseen difficulties and the drive to take revenge for attacks and resistance actions rapidly combined together, culminating in the murder of tens of thousands of Jewish victims of all ages. In France, the Wehrmacht was proud of its honour and independence and had shown that it was even ready to confront Hitler over breaches of the military code of conduct; in the Soviet Union, however, it was to a large extent fused with the Nazi regime. This did not mean in the least that the Wehrmacht's officers all saw themselves as National Socialists. A combination of partial disagreement with the Nazi leadership in some areas and concurrence in others can practically be regarded as a distinguishing mark of the attitude of German elites during the Third Reich. In many cases, officers who actually accelerated measures of extermination in various ways, as well as some of the organisers of mass murder in the occupation administrations of Eastern Europe, did not regard themselves as National Socialists because, for example, they did not agree with the government's policy towards the churches or they despised the Nazi party because of its plebeian image.

The slide towards barbarism and brutality and the loss of inhibition which can be observed here quickened its pace once the war with the Soviet Union had started. The decisive factors here were the time pressure resulting from military setbacks, problems with the supply of food, the threat from the Soviet partisan movement, and the identification of Jews with communists. What emerged from this maelstrom was the conviction, constantly renewed by events, that only by operating with complete ruthlessness, taking ever harsher measures, stamping out any tendency to restraint or moderation, and abandoning previously acquired standards of behaviour, was it possible to triumph over these dangers. Shielded by this conviction, they were able to justify their actions in Babi Yar and elsewhere, if indeed they still felt it was even necessary, after everything that had already happened in the first few months of the war against the Soviet Union.

## The Final Solution

If one bears in mind the almost unending series of vexations, the deprivation of rights, the expropriation, the persecution and the violence the Jews had to suffer first in Germany and Austria, then in Poland and finally in the whole area of German domination in Europe, the beginning of systematic mass murder in autumn 1941 almost appears in retrospect as a logical step, the culminating blow the regime had long been seeking to strike. For a long time, therefore, historians writing of these monstrous murder operations concluded that it had been the National Socialists' intention right from the start to kill all Jews. This view fails to recognise, however, that the German leadership found it absolutely impossible to imagine the extent of such a gigantic slaughter of a whole people in 1933, 1937 and even in 1939, just as in summer 1939 no one dared to think that, only a year later, three-quarters of the continent would be under German rule and that therefore almost 4 million Jews would live under German domination. It was only the explosion of violence during the war that led to a constantly worsening climate of ruthlessness and brutalisation which gradually dissolved existing reservations against, for example, the systematic murder of women and children, and made ever more radical solutions appear conceivable and therefore also capable of achievement.

Nevertheless, in the minds of most of those responsible, this gradual extension and aggravation of actions against the Jews was borne along by their firm conviction that the Jews, as representatives or agents of both the liberal, universalist West and the Bolshevik, internationalist East, constituted the polar opposite of National Socialist Germany, and that ways of driving them out of the area of German control must be found.

Since the mid-1930s, there had been discussions in the German leadership about how to get rid of the German Jews. One of the regime's objectives was to force the Jews to emigrate; but there was also another one, which was to take possession of their wealth. These two objectives contradicted one another. The beginning of the war meant that the search for a 'solution of the Jewish question' was intensified, and that solution now had to include all Jews in German-occupied Europe. The German authorities repeatedly had to implement provisional, short-term solutions. The idea now began to emerge of working towards a 'final solution of the Jewish question' which would soon make such provisional solutions superfluous. This search for a 'final solution' lasted until roughly October 1941. It took contradictory forms, and by no means followed a linear path. Motives and justifications changed, and it was developments at the front which exerted the strongest influence on the decisions that were made. The murder of the Jews was not an event dissociated from other developments, whether military, political or economic; it was directly bound up with them. It cannot be traced back to ideological elements alone, but equally it cannot be understood without them. It is helpful in this context to conceive 'ideology' not as a closed body of doctrine which directly suggests certain actions but as a view of the world which interprets and helps to explain events and experiences and allows a hierarchy of objectives to be established.

The 'final solution' was a process which took place during the war in a number of phases and individual steps, and in operations which usually escalated but were also sometimes put into reverse. Moreover, it did not occur simultaneously and with identical effect in every region of German-occupied Europe. Even so, it is still possible to gain a clear picture of the individual steps along the way and the crucial decisions that were taken.[13]

In Poland, the anti-Jewish policy was quickly intensified and made more systematic in the first months of the German occupation: acts of mistreatment and discrimination against the Jews were followed by the imposition of forced labour, mass deportation and assignment to ghettoes. In the early summer of 1940, after the victories in the west, persecution of the Jews also began in the regions of Western and Northern Europe occupied by the Wehrmacht. Except in Denmark, it followed the usual model set by the course of events in Germany after 1933, although the process was much quicker. The discovery and registration of the Jews was progressively followed by numerous measures of discrimination and persecution aimed at isolating them. Foreign Jews in these countries, many of them refugees from Germany and Austria, suffered particularly under these persecutions, especially as they were not protected by the indigenous authorities, or less protected than Jews who had long since become citizens of the country in question. At the same time, economic harassment was also intensified, and finally the expropriation of Jewish property and wealth was put into effect and the Jews were separated from the rest of the population in particular districts and camps, mostly organised with the use of regulations on compulsory labour. The resentment against Jews, and particularly foreign Jews, which existed in most countries, tended to accelerate this process.

After the beginning of the war, emigration became more difficult for those Jews who still lived in the Reich, many of them very old people. Even so, a further 20,000 managed to leave the country. Those who remained behind were subject to regulations of constantly increasing severity: many were made to do forced labour, whether in armaments factories or in snow-sweeping gangs. Many had to leave their homes and were placed in 'Jewish Houses'.

Approximately 100,000 Jews who lived in Vienna were forced to concentrate together in certain specific districts.

The German leaders, however, still had no clear idea as to what should now happen to the Jews in the Reich, in Western Europe and in Poland. The 'overall problem of the approximately three and a quarter million Jews in the area under German rule' wrote the head of the Security Police and the SS, Reinhard Heydrich, to Foreign Minister von Ribbentrop, two days after the victory over France, could 'no longer be solved by emigration'. They now had to look instead for a 'final territorial solution'.[14]

The victory over France appeared to provide an appropriate territory: the African island of Madagascar, a French colony which now seemed to have come into German hands. Himmler had already announced on 25 May 1940, in the elated atmosphere of the impending victory over France, that he hoped 'to see the very notion of a Jew completely obliterated' by the 'possibility of a great emigration of all Jews to a colony in Africa or elsewhere'.[15] The Madagascar idea quickly spread among the Nazi leaders, and a few weeks later it assumed concrete form for the first time. At the beginning of July 1940, the Foreign Office presented an initial draft. Technical details of the mass deportation were already being calculated, such as the number of Jews to be resettled each year and the amount of maritime tonnage needed for the purpose.[16] But resettling millions of human beings by ship was completely unthinkable without the previous overthrow of Britain's rule over the seas, so this option was no longer pursued after autumn 1940. One result of the discussions over the Madagascar Plan, however, was to place the planning process in a broader European context.

By summer 1940, after attempts to settle ethnic Germans in the parts of Poland annexed to the Reich and to push large numbers of Poles and Jews from there into the General Government had largely failed, the resettlement policy had come to a standstill. At the same time, however, the individuals who held power in the occupied countries and regions were vying with each other to expel large numbers of 'their' Jews as quickly as possible. But Hans Frank, the German ruler of the General Government, fought with all his might against allowing any further deportations into his territory. His best argument was that 'intolerable conditions', namely overcrowding, food shortage, plague and above all the black market, prevailed in the Jewish districts of the larger towns. In fact, the greater the problems in the ghettoes became, the more loudly was the call for a solution raised.

Hitler's decision to prepare for war against the Soviet Union gave a fresh impulse to the policy of resettlement and deportation. He instructed Heydrich, possibly as early as December 1940, to prepare a 'total solution' of the Jewish question. By now the number of Jews in the 'European economic area' had risen to 5.8 million. After victory over the Soviet Union these people would have to be resettled either in the Pripet Marshes, east of the General Government, or in the Soviet forced labour camps in the Arctic region. In both cases it was already assumed in spring 1941 that, as under the Madagascar Plan, a large proportion of the Jews would die in their new abode in the not too distant future. Further deportations into the General Government were therefore stopped, and as early as May 1941 German officials in Western Europe were informed that 'any further emigration of Jews' should be 'prevented, in view of the final solution which is no doubt about to come.'[17] The victory which was expected to come soon in the east seemed to be the solution to all the problems identified by the deportation authorities and the racial theorists. There were only a few more months to wait. In the meantime, the situation in the Polish ghettoes grew increasingly catastrophic. Food supply difficulties increased and the number of deaths rose rapidly. In Warsaw, for instance, the death toll rose from 898 in January 1941 to 5,550 in July.

In summer 1941, with the advance of the Wehrmacht into the Soviet Union, a further 2.4 million Jews fell into German hands. Barely a million had succeeded in fleeing eastwards before the arrival of the German forces. The *Einsatzgruppen* had received orders from Heydrich to liquidate the leading stratum of Bolshevism immediately after the invasion. According to the Nazi view, this referred in particular to Jews. From the very first days of the war, therefore, and wherever they went, the *Einsatzgruppen* murdered all male Jews of military age.[18] They received the support of groups of local nationalists and radical anti-Semites, particularly in the Baltic lands. These groups took a frightful revenge on the Jews, whom they blamed for the misdeeds of the Soviet secret police. Sometimes they clubbed them to death in the street. There were daily reports of massacres, which assumed ever greater proportions. On 7 July 1941, a police battalion from Lübeck murdered 3,000 Jewish men in Białystok. During the summer of 1941, the Hungarian authorities began to deport thousands of Jews across the border to Ukraine. By the end of August, 26,000 Jews had ended up in the Ukrainian town of Kamenets-Podolsk. Now several SS and police units entered the town. Within three days, they had shot 23,600 Jews. In addition, Jewish soldiers of the Red Army who fell into the hands of the Wehrmacht were killed almost without exception. There were probably more than 50,000 of them.

Meanwhile, the situation in the Polish ghettoes had worsened still further. Since the *Einsatzgruppen* and other police and SS units in the Soviet Union had already shot tens of thousands of Jews, the German authorities in Poland now started to consider more radical proposals. The director of the SD section in Posen (Poznań), Rolf Höppner, wrote to Eichmann on 16 July that in view of the state of affairs in the ghetto of Litzmannstadt (Łódź) the office of the Governor, Artur Greiser, was looking for new solutions, for example, the construction of a camp for 300,000 Jews. But even that would ultimately be inadequate:

> This winter there is a danger that it will not be possible to feed all the Jews. It should seriously be considered whether the most humane solution would not be to finish off Jews who are not capable of working with some sort of quick-acting means. This would in any case be more agreeable than letting them starve to death. . . . Apart from this, the proposal has also been made to sterilise all Jewesses who can still conceive children, so that the Jewish problem can be completely solved within this generation.[19]

Utterances of this kind are an indication of the terms in which the responsible people in the occupation authorities and resettlement agencies considered the future during those weeks, although they continued to start from the assumption that the Jews would later be deported to the Soviet Union to do forced labour. Indeed, Hans Frank now obtained a commitment from Hitler that the General Government would only function as a transit camp for the Jews and not a permanent resting place. The basis of this view of the future was a highly optimistic evaluation of the military situation. It is probable that Goering's 'authorisation' of 31 July 1941 to Heydrich to 'move the Jewish problem towards the most favourable possible solution corresponding to contemporary conditions, in the form of emigration or evacuation' also coincides with this phase, when it was assumed that the Jews would be deported to the Soviet Union after the victory which would soon occur.[20]

In the Soviet Union, the destructive rage of the Germans was initially directed largely against Jewish males of military age. The presumed connection between Jewry and Bolshevism played a predominant role here. In Serbia too, almost all Jewish men were murdered during this period, not in this case by the *Einsatzgruppen* of the Security Police and the SD, but by units of the Wehrmacht.[21] After Himmler's visit to the Eastern Front at the end of July 1941, however, the murder programme was extended to include women and children. An SS unit sent this telegraphic confirmation of Himmler's instructions: 'Express order from the Reichsführer SS. All Jews must be shot. Drive Jewish women into the marshes'.[22] The paramount justification for murder was now no longer purely political. Food shortages and the victims' inability to work were emphasised more strongly. 'Useless mouths' must not be fed, people who cannot work must not be dragged along by the healthy, it was said. With this, every boundary had now been broken through. For the first time, the Jewish population of whole districts was completely annihilated, whether for a concrete reason, as happened at Babi Yar, or for no reason at all. More than 600,000 Jews were murdered in the occupied areas of the Soviet Union between June 1941 and March 1942 by the *Einsatzgruppen*, the *Waffen-SS*, the police and the Wehrmacht.

The authorities now started to take harsher measures against Jews still living in Germany. From 1 September 1941 onwards, they had to wear a yellow star fixed to their clothing. They were concentrated in particular houses and they were forced to wait there until the authorities decided what to do with them. In the middle of September, Hitler decided that, in contrast to what had been planned initially, the German Jews would be deported to the east during the war. It is possible that the decisive impulse was provided by the intervention of the Gauleiter of Hamburg, Karl Kaufmann, who asked him 'to have the Jews evacuated, so that at least some of the people who have been bombed out of their houses can be assigned a new place to live.'[23]

Here, as at many other junctures, it can be seen that action taken against the Jews by the responsible German authorities was connected with an attempt to solve some urgent problem of a more general nature. The authorities were struggling against Jewish Bolshevism, the food shortage, the labour shortage, epidemic diseases, the black market, the partisans, and, particularly in the Reich itself, the housing shortage. In each case, the argument was that the survival of the Jews had a lower priority than the particular objective being pursued, whether it was to economise on food, to acquire a labour force for Germany's needs, to combat disease and black marketeering, or to release accommodation either for Germans or for the indigenous population of the area.

It would, however, be wrong to believe that the reason for the deportation and, ultimately, the murder of the German Jews was the need to make more accommodation available, any more than that the reason for the murders which were just beginning in the east was a shortage of food supplies or the spread of infectious diseases. It was rather that National Socialist anti-Semitism found its specific expression in the fact that the persecution of the Jews was based on matters of population, health or food policy and political, military, and public protection objectives, so that the figure of 'the Jew' as spy, idler, spreader of infection, partisan or communist appeared almost to provide evidential support for the correctness and necessity of the persecution.

It had become clear by the middle of October 1941 that it would no longer be possible to count on a German victory over the Red Army by the end of the year. The idea of deporting Polish Jews, or indeed all European Jews, to northern Russia, which had been considered, was therefore no longer realistic. There are clear indications that the German leadership and especially Hitler reoriented their thinking during these days and weeks. Until then, it had still been possible for the Jews of Western Europe to emigrate. That was now prohibited.

In eastern Galicia, which had been part of the territory of the Soviet Union between 1939 and 1941, and was now attached to the General Government, systematic mass shootings of Jews started in October. This happened, for example, in Stanislau (Ivano-Frankivsk), near the Hungarian border. It had been intended to establish a ghetto there. But, because the section of the town earmarked for this purpose was too small for the number of Jews living there, the local office of the Security Police decided to shoot a large proportion of them. On 6 and 12 October 1941, a total of between 11,000 and 12,000 Jews were shot at the edge of the town.[24]

There was now no more discussion of camps in the Arctic region of Russia. Instead, preparations were begun in the General Government to build installations where a large number of people could be killed quickly. The construction of the first of these centres for the extermination of human beings began at the start of November 1941 in Belzec in the vicinity of Lublin. Specialists from 'Aktion T4', whom the ending of the 'Euthanasia programme' had now made available for 'operations in the East', had already arrived in Lublin in September. The severe nervous strain suffered by the members of the murder units involved in the mass shootings in the Soviet Union and Poland had occasioned much internal criticism, and as a result it was decided that the killings would be done with gas from now on, both at Belzec and at another extermination camp, Chełmno (Kulmhof), near Łódź.[25]

Hitler also commented more frequently on the coming settlement with Jewry at this time, usually referring back to his 'prophecy' of January 1939. On 25 October, he remarked to Heydrich and Himmler:

> This race of criminals has the two million dead from the world war on its conscience, and now hundreds of thousands more. Let no-one say to me: we can't send them into the swamps! Who's worrying about our people? It's good if the fear that we are exterminating Jewry precedes us.[26]

The *Einsatzgruppen* shot hundreds of thousands of Soviet Jews in October and November 1941. Hundreds of thousands of Soviet prisoners of war died at the same time in camps and transit stations run by the Wehrmacht owing to the policy of starvation. In Leningrad and many other regions, the civilian population was subject to starvation, and again the death toll was in six figures. In Poland and the Warthe district the number of dead in the ghettoes increased week by week. Altogether, in the six months between June and December 1941, more than 1.5 million people in Poland and the Soviet Union died of hunger or were killed by German units off the battlefield.

In view of this situation, as well as the rapidly rising losses on the Eastern Front, which were of very great importance for the German leadership, it clearly did not mark a fundamental change of policy when the Jews in the area of German rule were not, as originally planned, transported to Siberian labour camps to end their lives there but instead immediately taken to the General Government to be killed in the extermination camps set up since November 1941.

The key decision was made at the beginning of December at the latest. On 11 December, Germany declared war on the USA. In Hitler's eyes, this meant a repetition of the international constellation of the First World War, under which the intrigues of the Jews had pushed the USA into war against Germany. And, as had often happened before, Hitler reacted with furious murder threats against international Jewry. As many of his listeners noticed, he was unusually explicit in an address delivered to the top leadership of the NSDAP the next day, on 12 December. Goebbels made a summary of his comments:

> With regard to the Jewish question, the Führer is determined to make a clean sweep of it. He prophesied that if the Jews brought about another world war, they would experience their annihilation. That was not empty talk. The world war is here. The annihilation of Jewry must be the necessary consequence. This question is to be viewed without any sentimentality. We are not here to have sympathy with the Jews, but only to have sympathy with our German people. If the German people has again now sacrificed around 160,000 dead in the campaign in the East, the originators of this bloody conflict will have to pay for it with their own lives.[27]

After his return from Berlin, Hans Frank reported back to the officials of his government in Cracow about this address by Hitler and the conclusions to be drawn from it. He was completely explicit: 'As far as the Jews are concerned' he said

> and this I will tell you quite openly: they must be done away with, in one way or another. And I must say, as an old National Socialist, should the Jewish brotherhood in Europe survive the war, this war would only be a partial success. My attitude towards the Jews will therefore be based only on the expectation that they should disappear. They must go. At any rate, a great Jewish migration will begin. But what is to be done with the Jews? Do you think that they will be housed in settlement villages in the *Ostland* [eastern territories]? We were told in Berlin: why all this bother? We can't do anything with them in the *Ostland* or in the *Reichskommissariat* [Ukraine] either; liquidate them yourselves. The Jews are particularly harmful gluttons as far as we are concerned. We cannot shoot these 3.5 million Jews, we cannot poison them, but we will nevertheless be able to intervene in ways which will lead in some way to successful annihilation, and this in connection with the great measures to be discussed in the Reich.[28]

It is not completely certain whether Hitler's speech of 12 December, which was, after all, only one of a whole series of similar addresses at this time in which Hitler threatened the Jews with annihilation, can be interpreted as 'the fundamental political decision to murder all the Jews of Europe'. He was only repeating what he had already said on many occasions since the summer of that year, although the phrases recorded by Goebbels ('The world war is here. The annihilation of Jewry must be the necessary consequence') did signify a more drastic approach and a greater sense of urgency. But, in the context of the time, Hitler's speech was understood by the high-level functionaries who were present as a confirmation of what the Reich Security Main Office (RSHA), the resettlement experts and the German occupation authorities had long regarded as unavoidable, and as an instruction to act immediately to kill at least all Jews in the German area of control who were not able to work.[29]

The Wannsee Conference was initially convened by Heydrich for 8 December 1941, but it was then postponed until 20 January 1942. It served three purposes. Firstly, to inform the relevant departments of the new line of policy and to co-ordinate the measures that followed from it, namely the deportation of the Jews of Poland and Western Europe immediately, rather than after the war, and to the extermination camps in the General Government rather than to the north of Russia. Secondly, the RSHA wanted to make sure that the other government departments knew it had overall control of the matter. Thirdly, and finally, the meeting was supposed to clarify the question of 'half Jews' and German Jews living in mixed marriages, which had long been a subject of dispute.

The deportation programme presented in the Wannsee villa related to all European Jews, including those in countries not under German occupation. The essential element in it was a differentiation between those Jews who were capable of working and those who were not:

> Under proper direction, and in the course of the final solution, the Jews must now be put to work in the East in the appropriate manner. Jews who are capable of working are to be taken there in big work gangs, with the sexes separated, to construct roads. No doubt a high proportion of them will fall by the wayside through natural wastage. Those who may possibly remain alive must be dealt with in an appropriate manner, since this group will no doubt contain the elements most capable of resistance, who therefore constitute the results of a natural selection and can be regarded if they are set free as the germ cell of a new Jewish structure.

Here, therefore, it was laid down that labour deployment was also a route to death, albeit an indirect one.[30]

Between January and July 1942, the German authorities began to prepare for the deportation of the Jews from all the areas they occupied. In particular, further extermination camps were constructed. Belzec and Chełmno were followed in spring by Auschwitz, near Cracow, and Sobibór in the south-east of Poland. Finally, in the summer, the camp of Treblinka was set up north-east of Warsaw. More of the Jews of Western Europe were now put in transit camps, such as Drancy in France, Westerbork in the Netherlands and Mechelen in Belgium, where they were to wait to be transported eastwards. Hitler had already ordered the first deportations from the Reich and the Protectorate of Bohemia and Moravia in October 1941. Nineteen thousand Jews from all over the Reich as well as from Prague were brought to Łódź, and on 8 November the first transport left for Minsk, where Polish Jews had already been killed to make room for the German Jews who were about to arrive. Some transports also went to the Baltic region. The German Jews arrived there at the end of November, and they were shot immediately. The shootings took place on 29 November in Kaunas and a day later in Riga.

Systematic deportations started in Western Europe in summer 1942. On 11 June 1942, the heads of the Security Police and the SD in France, Belgium and the Netherlands arranged with Eichmann to begin the deportation of specified numbers of Jews. Fifteen thousand Jews from the Netherlands, 10,000 from Belgium and a total of 100,000 from France were to be deported to the east. Four days later, however, this number was reduced, because it was seen as unrealistic. Now only 40,000 Jews were to be sent eastwards during the next three months.[31]

From that time onwards, the transport trains started to roll regularly. On 22 June 1942 a train containing 1,000 Jewish men and women left the camp at Drancy, near Paris, on its way to the east. It was followed on 25 June by another one. In the Netherlands, the first transport left Westerbork on 15 July 1942 with 1,135 Dutch Jews on board. The first train from Belgium for the east left Mechelen on 4 August 1942 with 998 Jews. Most of the Jews deported from Western Europe were shipped to Auschwitz, where a big concentration camp was attached to the extermination site. As soon as they stepped onto the station platform, the Jewish arrivals were examined to establish their ability to work. Those who could work, usually less than a third of the total, were assigned to the camp and put to forced labour. The remainder, as a rule old people, women and children, were immediately sent to the gas chambers and killed.

In the General Government, the authorities had already started to clear the first ghettoes of their inhabitants by the middle of March 1942. They developed a registration system for this purpose, by which the Jews were placed in three categories: important to the war effort, capable of work and not capable of work. The Jewish Councils introduced by the Germans were obliged to choose who was to be deported. The deportees were then sent to the nearest extermination camp and killed there. This wave of deportation, which lasted from mid-March to mid-July 1942, cost the lives of roughly 110,000 people, the vast majority of whom had been classified as 'not capable of work'.

Then, in mid-July, the decision was made to kill *all* Polish Jews within the next few months, whether they were capable of working or not. Himmler issued the relevant order on 19 July 1942, according to which 'the resettlement of the whole Jewish population of the General Government' had to be 'put into effect and concluded by 31 December 1942'.[32] After that, the systematic murder of all Polish Jews began. The SS named this 'Aktion Reinhard' in internal memoranda, in memory of Reinhard Heydrich, who had died in Prague on 4 June 1942 after being wounded in an attempt on his life by the resistance movement. The murder operations were at their height between July and the end of November 1942. Ghetto after ghetto was cleared out, the inhabitants were forced to assemble together and then sent by train to the nearest extermination site, where they were killed in the gas chambers on the day they arrived. The number of people whose deportation was postponed because they were employed in factories of military importance became smaller and smaller. By the beginning of 1943, only 300,000 Jews still lived in the General Government, most of them in forced labour camps close to important military enterprises. Even these camps were finally dissolved, and the labour camps in the district of Lublin were also dissolved, on 3 and 4 November 1943. In the 'Harvest Festival Operation', which was the name given to the dissolution of the last of the forced labour camps, police and SS units shot approximately 43,000 people.

With this, the 'final solution of the Jewish question' in Poland was concluded, as far as the German authorities were concerned. Fewer than 100,000 out of over 3 million Polish Jews survived the end of the war.

In the period up to March 1943, roughly 1.3 million Polish Jews were murdered, overwhelmingly in the camps of Belzec, Sobibór and Treblinka. Auschwitz was envisaged as the place of extermination for the Jews of other parts of Europe. It was originally a camp for Soviet prisoners of war, but it was rebuilt from the end of 1941 and equipped with large gas chambers, in which mass killings could be carried out using the poisonous gas Zyklon B. The first transports with Jews from eastern Upper Silesia, Slovakia, France, Belgium and the Netherlands arrived there in spring 1942. In summer, Jews began to be transported from the Reich, Romania, Norway and Croatia. Later arrivals came from Bulgaria, Hungary, Greece and the south of France. By the end of 1943, roughly 840,000 Jews had been murdered at Auschwitz.

The Jews were the largest group to fall victim to Nazi extermination policy, but they were not alone. The fate of the Sinti and the Roma is similar in many respects to that of the Jews. Until 1938, the 'gypsies' were persecuted along with others under the rubric of 'criminal' or 'asocial'. Later on, however, they fell under a specific regulation as 'gypsies by their racial nature'. Now, therefore, they were to be persecuted not because of their behaviour, but on the basis of their racial classification.[33]

The case of the Sinti and the Roma, like that of no other persecuted group, demonstrates the intertwining of traditions of stigmatisation and harassment, the ascription of biological origins to social divergence, and modern racism. The association of 'asociality' and 'spying' with 'gypsies' acted as a practical confirmation of the racial diagnosis of a hereditary tendency in this direction. The deviant behaviour of a long despised and persecuted minority was diagnosed with the help of the racist paradigm as the expression of unchangeable, inherited characteristics, and the Nazis felt this provided them with a justification for creating a *Volksgemeinschaft* (folk community) which was free of such elements. The autumn of 1941, when the systematic deportation of the German Jews started, also saw the deportation of 5,000 Roma from Burgenland into the ghetto of Łódź, where they were placed in a separate section. The grounds given for deportation were particularly varied in this case. They were allegedly 'thieves by profession', 'do-nothings', 'work-shy', 'loafers' and 'criminals' and they were also the bearers of a 'gypsy sexual morality' which was particularly dangerous to the German *Volk*.[34] Some of the Burgenland Roma died in the ghetto; the remainder, like the Jews, were killed by gas early in 1942 in the extermination camp of Chełmno. After the start of the war with the Soviet Union, 'gypsies' who were discovered either by Wehrmacht units or by *Einsatzgruppen* were killed in large numbers. Here too, asociality, theft and espionage were cited as the main grounds for extermination. Unlike in the case of the Jews, however, the *Einsatzgruppen* did not go looking for 'gypsies' but rather murdered them if they happened to meet them while hunting for Jews. It is probable that more 'gypsies' were murdered by German military units in the Soviet Union and the General Government than ended their lives in the concentration camps.

Finally, on 16 December 1942, Himmler ordered that all Sinti and Roma should be deported as 'gypsies' to the concentration camp at Auschwitz, where a special 'gypsy camp' was set up. As a result, Sinti and Roma from Germany, Austria, the Protectorate of Bohemia and Moravia, the Netherlands, Belgium and the north of France were brought to Auschwitz. By summer 1944, when the 'gypsy camp' at Auschwitz-Birkenau was closed, 19,300 of the 22,600 inmates had died. By 1945, the lives of a total of 200,000 Sinti and Roma had been violently brought to an end in the area of German domination.[35]

By the end of 1943, the German authorities had succeeded in seizing, deporting and killing Jews in almost all the countries either occupied or allied with them. The proportion of Jews who were killed in each country depended on various factors: the efficiency and strength of the German occupation authorities and the German police, the geographical conditions, the degree of Jewish integration into each society and the readiness of indigenous bureaucracies to collaborate. Thus almost 70 per cent of the Jews who lived in the Netherlands were murdered by the Germans, whereas in France only 20 per cent were murdered. In Romania, it was overwhelmingly indigenous forces which did the killing, whereas in Bulgaria the authorities protected the longer established sections of the Jewish population from persecution. In Denmark, the anti-German resistance succeeded in keeping almost all the 5,000 Jews who lived there out of the grip of the Germans and sending them to Sweden by boat. But these were exceptions. In general, the German authorities were able to proceed against the Jews with the utmost consistency and brutality in the areas under their domination.

At the beginning of 1944, there was only one large Jewish community which remained largely untouched, that in Hungary. But, on 19 March 1944, German troops marched into the country to prevent it from following Italy's example and abandoning the German alliance. This meant that Adolf Eichmann and his colleagues could start preparing for the deportation of the Hungarian Jews. Two months later, on 14 May 1944, the first train set off for Auschwitz. In the weeks that followed, roughly 12,000 Jews a day were deported to Auschwitz from Hungary. By mid-July, the total number of deportees had reached 438,000, 320,000 of whom were killed in the gas chambers immediately after their arrival.[36]

The murder of the Jews was an event of truly monstrous dimensions. According to the most recent calculations, the number who lost their lives through violence was around 5.7 million. It should be noted that the widespread conception that this was an 'industrial' mass murder is only partly correct. Less than half the murdered Jews died in the gas chambers. The others were killed in entirely conventional ways: they were shot or beaten to death, they died of infectious diseases, and they died of hunger or physical debility. It is still impossible to give a precise overall figure for the number of deaths during the Second World War which resulted from Germany's extermination policies. Roughly a million non-Jewish civilians of Polish nationality should be added to the 5.7 million Jews and the 200,000 Sinti and Roma who lost their lives. We should also add a further 2.8 million Soviet prisoners of war and 3 to 4 million Soviet civilians as well as half a million non-Jewish civilians in other countries occupied by Germany and in Germany itself. One should therefore proceed from an order of magnitude of between 12 and 14 million in estimating the total number of civilians who were killed in the area ruled by Germany, excluding deaths in military operations.[37]

What did the Germans themselves know of these mass murders? The forcible deportation of Jews from the German cities after autumn 1941 and the sale by auction of the possessions of the deportees took place openly and in public. Placards hung everywhere bearing the inscription: 'The Jews are our misfortune. They wished for this war in order to destroy Germany. German folk comrades (*Volksgenossen*), never forget this!'[38] A part of German society welcomed, indeed rejoiced at, the deportations, and when the Jews were marched in columns through the townships to the stations, they were not seldom accompanied by yelling children and youths. After the war, one deportee recalled his experience when being conveyed to the Frankfurt railway station: 'Along the whole of the route we were cursed and jeered at by a howling mob. "Kill them" they shouted, "Why waste expensive coal on the transport train?"'.[39] These people were a minority, no doubt, but a vociferous one.

Most of the population adopted a reserved attitude to the deportation and did not react at all. There was a very clear difference between this response and the considerable attention paid by the German population to information about the murder of the sick. Even so, silence cannot be interpreted unreservedly as consent, especially as any public expression of sympathy for the Jews drew the attention of the police. There were one or two rare cases of public criticism. The Minden SD reported as follows on what the critics were saying:

> One can be sure that very many Jews will not survive the journey. It is pointed out in this context that the Jews now being evacuated were after all people who had lived in the area for a very long time. They are of the opinion that for many Jews this decision is too harsh.[40]

But, as long as nothing, or very little, was known of the subsequent fate of the deportees these attitudes remained exceptional.

After the end of 1941, however, the flow of information about events in Eastern Europe increased, particularly through reports from soldiers on leave from the front. The most accurate information about the mass murders, especially in Poland and the Soviet Union, was no doubt possessed by people who were active in the German civilian and military institutions that administered the occupation of Eastern Europe. They were able to observe the conditions in the ghettoes, the mass shootings and the trains transporting Jews to the extermination sites, and some were directly involved. There were some tens of thousands of these people, and if one adds Germans involved in the arrest and deportation of Jews in the occupied countries of Northern, Western and Southern Europe and members of the responsible authorities in Berlin and the regional offices of the Gestapo, it is clear that more than 200,000 Germans had precise information about the mass murder of the Jews.

The degree of knowledge among the soldiers on the Eastern Front and in the rear echelons varied from unit to unit. But, if one bears in mind the speed with which rumours spread about mass executions such as those in Babi Yar, people had to make a certain amount of effort to expunge such information from their minds. Members of the Wehrmacht in the east had a precise picture of the violent treatment of the Soviet civilian population and the death of millions of

Soviet prisoners of war, but the policy of starvation and the destruction of vast swathes of land in the struggle against the partisans was seen as a part of the war effort. The slaughter of tens of thousands of Jews, mainly women, children and old people, was already surrounded by an aura of the sinister and the horrific, and it was felt to be better to keep quiet about this, or to avoid thinking about it.

The reports of soldiers on leave from the front were reinforced by the media. On 16 November 1941, exactly at the time that the decision to exterminate the Jews was made, Joseph Goebbels published a leading article in the weekly paper *Das Reich* under the heading 'The Jews Are Guilty'. This article was also transmitted over the radio and distributed as a special supplement with a large print run. Goebbels referred in it to Hitler's 'prophecy' of 30 January 1939 that a new world war would lead to the 'destruction of the Jewish race in Europe', and he proclaimed: 'We are now living through the fulfilment of this prophecy, and Jewry is faced with a fate which is hard, admittedly, but very much deserved. . . . World Jewry is now undergoing the gradual process of extermination it intended for us.'[41] Moreover, the BBC reported repeatedly on the mass killings of Jews in Poland in its German-language broadcasts, and from autumn 1942 onwards it gave increasingly precise details.

The German population could easily have accessed concrete information about the murder of the Jews. This can be seen from the notes compiled by an engineer from Celle in 1942. He collected numerous indications that tens of thousands of Jews were being murdered by German units in the east. His information came from soldiers on leave from the front, German newspapers and BBC reports. 'The Jew is being eradicated' was the title of an article in the *Niedersächsische Tageszeitung* about a speech made by Hitler on 25 February 1942. Soldiers reported that 'thousands of Jews were shot in Poland last autumn.' They explained how this was done: 'First they had to dig graves for others, then a day came when they dug their own grave and were shot from behind.' A former colleague reported on what he saw as a soldier in Vilnius: 'The Jews from France and other countries were brought to Poland, and there some were shot and others were gassed.'[42]

But to collect information like this and assemble it together to make an overall picture, a person had to be especially interested in the matter and to feel the need to gain more knowledge about it. Anyone with sufficient persistence could acquire quite precise knowledge about what was happening in Eastern Europe and could also make a good guess about the number of victims of these mass murders as early as autumn 1942. Few people took this step, though, if only because the rumours were so horrifying that it was easier to repress or disbelieve them than to dig deeper. But, above all, the Germans were so strongly focused on their own fate, thanks to the reports from the front and the regular bombing raids, and so worried about what would happen to their families, that it was easy to ignore rumours about the mass killing of Jews in Eastern Europe.

In answering the question as to what the Germans knew about the mass murders and how they reacted to them, we can perhaps distinguish between three groups. The hardline National Socialist Jew-haters, and there were plenty of these, were the first group. They intensified the killing where they could, and they endeavoured to increase the number of those deported, strengthen the pressure on the Jews, and worsen conditions in the ghettoes. Moreover, many Germans profited from the persecution, deportation and murder of the Jews, through 'Aryanisation', through taking over houses and furniture or through taking the job a Jew had been forced to leave. The second group, which was small, attempted to lessen the suffering of the Jews in whatever way they could, and gave assistance to those they knew personally.

Most Germans, on the other hand, formed the third and largest group. They had had little or no contact with Jews even before the beginning of the war. The Jews, especially those from the east, were an alien group of human beings, whom they often saw as sinister, hearing the many stories that were whispered about them or spread by Nazi propaganda. It was not necessary to believe these stories, they said, but there was clearly no reason to become more closely involved with the Jews. In fact, one sometimes gains the impression that even the reports about the violent death of the Jews which trickled through to Germans during the war actually confirmed the aura of strangeness and foreignness which clung to them.

These attitudes can also be found among Germans who would in no way have regarded themselves as National Socialists. To illustrate this point, consider the case of Franz Josef Schöningh, who was born in 1902.[43] He studied economic history, and then became a journalist for *Hochland,* which was a periodical aimed at Catholic intellectuals. He finally rose to be its chief editor. Even after 1933, he continued to be regarded as a definite opponent of the National Socialists, which is one of the reasons why, under the American occupation after the war, he was designated as one of the three founding editors of the *Süddeutsche Zeitung.* In 1941, to avoid military service, he used his contacts to obtain a position in Galicia, in the 'General Government' as a Deputy District Chief, a post which corresponded to the office of District President (*Landrat*) in Germany. His first appointment was to the district of Sambor, near the old Polish border. Here he was responsible for 'Population and Welfare', which included, as he wrote to his wife, 'the delicate matter of Jewish resettlement'. In March 1942 he was transferred to the district of Tarnopol, where he continued to administer 'Population and Welfare' but was now also responsible for maintaining links with the German police authorities. The Ukrainian Auxiliary Police Force was also assigned to him. Its job was to assist operations against the

Jews by blocking the roads and by digging trenches for the bodies of those who were shot. During Schöningh's period of office in Tarnopol, up to June 1943, 12,000 Jews were deported from the town's ghetto to the extermination camp at Belzec. On 23 March 1942, 630 Jews, among them Jewish children from the local orphanage, were murdered by the SS in the middle of Tarnopol, in front of the ruined synagogue.

Schöningh was officially concerned in these events: he was involved with the preparation of lists of those to be deported, with the establishment of police roadblocks, with the allocation or the denial of jobs and places to live. But he clearly repressed any thought of his own participation in these events or his responsibility for them, even while the events were actually proceeding. He kept himself fully supplied with food, alcohol and all the accoutrements appropriate to his official position; he went on hunting trips as often as he could. His official colleagues regularly indulged in lively celebrations in the castle of Myskowice, not far from Tarnopol. Schöningh made no secret of his scorn for the Nazis, but since the administration for which he was partly responsible evidently functioned better than most other district administrations, he suffered no disadvantages from this. He experienced the end of the war in his hunting lodge in Bavaria, in the proud awareness that he had never fought for Hitler and the Nazis as a soldier.

As far as we know, he did not see himself as an anti-Semite. On the contrary: it has been established that when he was in Galicia he helped two Jewish acquaintances by providing them with false papers, which saved their lives. He almost never spoke about the so-called 'Jewish operations', which he witnessed every day, either before or after 1945. But it is clear that he was entirely convinced that because he had distanced himself mentally from National Socialism he was merely a passive observer of these occurrences, even when he was a direct participant. On one day in July 1942, some Jews whom the authority he headed had itself picked out to be transported to a death camp were passing in front of his office. He happened to see them, and he wrote to his wife: 'Today some figures passed by in front of me, and when I saw these figures I thought I must be dreaming.'[44]

Like many Germans, Schöningh's main objective was to get through the war unharmed, and either to ignore or to accept the unpleasant phenomena that unavoidably accompanied it. He regarded the persecution of the Jews as one of these accompanying phenomena. But, because he saw the Jews as a lost people who were irrevocably destined to die, his own conduct seemed to him to have no influence whatever on their fate. What was crucial in determining his attitude was that, like most Germans, he perceived the Jews as aliens, who did not belong to the community, and that it was his own privileged position as a German *Volksgenosse* that protected him from suffering a similar fate.

## Forced Labour

One of the factors which decisively contributed to Germany's ability to continue the war for several years after the winter of 1941–2 was the 'labour deployment' of foreign workers. Polish workers had already been recruited in spring 1940. They were followed in the summer by roughly a million French prisoners of war who were brought to Germany to be put to work, after some French prisoners and all Belgian and Dutch prisoners had been released. In summer 1941, around 3 million foreigners were working in Germany, predominantly in agriculture and construction.

But the shift to a full wartime economy in the winter of 1941–2 meant that the number of workers needed by German industry increased considerably. Between December 1941 and March 1942, more than a million extra German soldiers were inducted into the Wehrmacht, although in October 1941 the German armaments industry had already announced that it needed another 800,000 workers. Until then, only 17 per cent of the industrial workers had been called up for military service, while the figure specifically for coalminers was as low as 11 per cent. Now the proportion of industrial workers called up rose to more than 25 per cent, reaching 40 per cent, its highest point, in 1944.[45]

Only at this point was the large-scale labour deployment of Soviet prisoners of war envisaged. Previously, this had been explicitly forbidden on the orders of the Führer. At the beginning of November 1941, it was decided to allow the employment of prisoners in the Reich, but the authorities did not succeed in actually putting a large number of them to work. The ministerial official whose task it was to organise the deployment of the prisoners reported as follows in February 1942:

> The present difficulties in labour deployment would not have arisen if a timely decision had been made to deploy Russian prisoners of war on a large scale. We had 3.9 million Russians at our disposal, but now there are only 1.1 million left. 500,000 Russians died in the months from November 1941 to January 1942 alone. We are hardly likely to be able to increase the number of Russian prisoners currently employed (400,000).[46]

With the appointment of Gauleiter Sauckel, a man regarded as politically influential, as 'General Plenipotentiary for Labour Deployment', the 'deployment of foreigners' was reorganised. The enlistment of as many foreign workers as possible in as short a time as possible now become a political task of the highest priority. A veritable hunt for civilians began in the occupied regions of the Soviet Union, and immense numbers of them were brought to Germany to work—1.4 million just between April and the end of November 1942. It was principally the arms factories and the mining industry that were in urgent need of a workforce, to be able to deliver the quantities of arms that were now demanded by the Wehrmacht.

Just as in the case of the earlier 'Polish deployment', the employment of Soviet forced labourers in the Reich was regulated by an all-embracing system of repression and discrimination, but it was far more radical than the rules applied earlier to the Poles. The new workers from the Soviet Union, called 'Workers from the East' (*Ostarbeiter*) were forced to wear a label with the word 'Ost' (East) written on it, they had to live under guard in camps surrounded by barbed wire, and they were very much at the mercy of the Gestapo and the army units standing guard in the factories.

By now, a veritable universe of labour camps had grown up within the Reich. There were camps for foreigners all over the larger towns and cities and also in the countryside. In Berlin, there were several hundred, and the total for the Reich as a whole was probably more than 30,000. About 400,000–500,000 Germans occupied various functions, from camp chief to 'foreign labour commissioner', and were directly involved in the organisation of 'foreign labour deployment'.

The conditions of existence of the various groups of foreign workers varied according to their position in a strict national hierarchy, which was regulated down to the smallest detail. Workers from the occupied parts of Western Europe and the so-called 'friendly' countries had to live predominantly in labour camps, but they received the same food rations as Germans in a comparable situation and they were also subject to the same working conditions. Workers from the east, and above all the 'Russians' were in a much worse position. However, the situation of foreigners engaged in forced labour did vary from factory to factory and from camp to camp. Foreign workers in agriculture generally fared distinctly better than those in industry, but in industry too there were striking differences between different enterprises in regard to the treatment of foreign workers and the amount of food they received, especially after the end of 1942. This in itself demonstrates the great extent to which the individual enterprise was able to use its own judgment and act in the way it thought fit.

Wages were also subject to a detailed grading system. Civilian workers from all countries other than the formerly Polish or Soviet lands received the same wages as German workers, male or female, in comparable jobs, at least nominally. Polish workers were also supposed to receive the same wages, but they had to pay a special 15 per cent tax, the 'Polish contribution', which was introduced by the German labour authorities on the remarkable ground that this payment compensated for the fact that Poles, unlike Germans, were not liable for military service. Soviet workers, on the other hand, received a fixed wage 40 per cent lower than that of a German worker. But the labour authorities reported that many firms paid no wages at all to their Soviet civilian workers, because they regarded them as 'civilian prisoners' and treated them accordingly. The employment of foreign forced labour was not restricted to the big firms. It extended over the whole economy (administrative positions excluded), from the small peasant farm or the locksmith's workshop with six employees, to the railway network, the municipalities and the big arms factories.

In September 1944, there were 7.6 million foreign workers in the Reich. Of these, 5.7 million were civilians and just under 2 million were prisoners of war. Taking into account the considerable amount of fluctuation in personnel, it is probable that roughly 11 million foreigners from almost twenty European countries were brought to Germany for 'labour deployment' during the war. In autumn 1944, there were 2.8 million workers from the Soviet Union, 1.7 million from Poland and 1.3 million from France employed there. More than half the Polish and Soviet civilian workers were women, averaging under twenty years of age. In September 1942, roughly 15 per cent of all people employed in the Reich were foreign workers, either civilians or prisoners of war. Two years later, this figure had risen to 24 per cent. In arms-related branches of industry the proportion was higher, sometimes exceeding 40 or even 50 per cent, and if the manufacturing process was physically exhausting the proportion rose to 70 or 80 per cent.

The need to increase war production, though, was not the only maxim followed by the Nazi regime in its calculations. This is shown particularly by the development of the work deployment of concentration camp inmates. At the beginning of the war, the holding capacity of the concentration camps was expanded considerably. The number of inmates rose quickly: within a short time, it had doubled. The majority of the concentration camp population was now no longer composed of Germans but of nationals of the countries occupied by Germany, above all Poles, French, Czechs, Yugoslavs, Dutch and Belgians. From 1940 onwards, German inmates of the camps were in a minority. In addition, the German Security Police had set up camps and places of confinement of various kinds all over the countries occupied by the Wehrmacht. Soon, more prisoners were locked up in them than in all the concentration camps in Germany itself. After 1942, prisoners from the Soviet Union and Poland formed by far the largest group of foreign inmates. Over half of them had been brought to Germany for forced labour as civilian workers or prisoners of war, and delivered to concentration camps by the Gestapo for real or alleged offences. In the final year of the war, the number of inmates in the concentration camps rose to 524,000, of whom more than 90 per cent were non-Germans.[47]

The importance of prisoners' labour was already on the increase before the war broke out. The SS ran its own production facilities in the concentration camps, which were mainly used for the manufacture of basic building materials for the construction of the National Socialist towns that were planned. In this phase of their history, the concentration camps were not involved in arms production, or at least it was only just starting. Their productivity also remained extremely low. Death rates reached very high levels. Four per cent of the inmates of KZ Dachau died in 1938; by 1942 the figure was 36 per cent. In Buchenwald, the mortality rate rose from 10 per cent in 1938 to 19 per cent in 1941, and in Mauthausen, the worst of all the concentration camps in the area of the German Reich, it increased from 24 per cent in 1939 to 76 per cent in 1940.[48]

When the German arms industry was reorganised at the end of 1941, the SS also made efforts to give priority to arms production in the concentration camps. But there were two obstacles: the concentration camps were not prepared for such a rapid change of direction, and the Head Office for Business and Administration (WVHA) newly established by the SS did not have enough business expertise to be able to conjure up a centre for large-scale arms production from nothing.[49]

In spring 1942, the SS began to employ concentration camp inmates in larger numbers for arms production, especially in the construction of the IG Farben Works near Auschwitz. Even so, it cannot be said that labour deployment had primacy in the concentration camps. This was partly due to the fact that a pressing need for the employment of concentration camp inmates in the arms industry did not arise, in view of the mass deportation of Soviet workers to Germany which was beginning at this time. The second half of 1942 saw the death of 57,503 of the 95,000 registered KZ inmates, over 60 per cent of the total.

In September 1942, Hitler finally decided that the SS should henceforth place its KZ inmates at the disposal of industry, on loan, and that industry for its part should integrate them into the existing production processes. This established the principle that private industry would borrow prisoners from the concentration camps, and from that time on this was the method used to put them to work.

In order to strengthen its involvement in war production, it was now very much in the interests of the WVHA to increase the number of prisoners as quickly as possible. The number of people incarcerated in all the concentration camps grew from 110,000 in September 1942 to 203,000 in April 1943. By August 1944, the number of inmates had already risen above 500,000, and at the beginning of 1945 it was over 700,000. The monthly death rates of the inmates continued to be extraordinarily high, and they only began to fall in 1943. There was thus a fall from 10 per cent in December 1942 to 2.8 per cent in April 1943. The number of KZ inmates was greatly increased in order to meet the increased demand for KZ workers from both private and SS-controlled firms, but the working and living conditions of the prisoners in the camps did not change.

From the start of the year 1939, Jews within the German Reich area had been enlisted systematically for forced labour, first in 'closed labour deployment' as unskilled workers, predominantly in road-building, then after 1940 mainly in industry. But, from spring 1941 onwards, the drive to set the German Jews to work as forced labourers in Germany came into conflict with the regime's goal of deporting all Jews from the Reich. In summer 1941, there were still some 50,000 Jews doing forced labour in arms factories. Their places of work, many of which were classified as 'important to the arms industry', did not offer any secure protection against deportation, but merely a postponement, the length of which was graduated according to the importance of their activity to the war economy. In summer 1943, finally, the last surviving group of 'armaments Jews', who were employed in particularly important factories in Berlin, was deported to Auschwitz.[50]

The two Nazi objectives of labour deployment and genocide also came into conflict in the concentration camps 'in the East'. Roughly two-thirds of the Jews who were deported from all over Europe to Auschwitz were classified as incapable of work and immediately killed after their arrival. The remainder were registered as KZ inmates and initially employed in construction, then, later on, also in the arms factories. The survival rate of the Jewish KZ inmates was extremely low. Once they had been 'worked to a standstill' they were killed. This usually happened after only a few months.

Even in Germany's desperate military and economic situation after the setbacks on the Eastern Front, it was not the requirements of labour deployment and arms production which counted but the political and ideological goals of the regime in dealing with its political and racial enemies. This was demonstrated by its treatment of the KZ inmates and the Jews. The deportation of the Berlin 'armaments Jews', the closure of the factories and workshops in the Polish ghettoes and the treatment of the inmates of the concentration camps were not the result of errors in planning, conflicts between rival agencies or severe problems of food supply. They followed rather from the goals and attitudes of the leaders of the regime.

## *Volksgemeinschaft* during the War

The 'community of the folk' (*Volksgemeinschaft*) was the National Socialist ideal of social and political order. It involved downgrading social conflicts of interest and pursuing a policy of social integration. Nazi propaganda postulated the equality of all Germans along with the marginalisation of 'elements alien to the race and the *Volk*'. When the war began, this conception of a *Volksgemeinschaft* standing against a world of external foes gained a new foundation, which rapidly solidified in the era of military success. But this internal cohesion became precarious after the setbacks on the Eastern Front in the late summer of 1941, the beginning of Allied bombing raids on German cities and the defeat at Stalingrad. There had been almost a decade of constant successes and triumphs for Hitler, both within the country and outside it, but now the Germans were confronted for the first time with defeats and a worsening of their own situation. Different mechanisms of integration were therefore needed to preserve social cohesion and loyalty to the regime.[51]

Large sections of the German population perceived the Nazi seizure of power as bringing about a kind of tranquillity, after long decades of crisis. Even people who did not support the Nazis politically could appreciate and take advantage of the progress the economy was making, the rapid fall in unemployment and the cessation of internal disturbances, despite being aware of the methods by which this calm atmosphere had been established. It was therefore not surprising that, even after the outbreak of war, people's main endeavours were directed towards preserving this 'normality' as long as possible, along with the prospect of future stability associated with it.

Such aspirations, however, were constantly thwarted by the incessant flow of life-changing events and the wholesale changes introduced repeatedly by the regime, for which a state of emergency was the elixir of life. Constant friction therefore arose between the yearning for normality, on the one hand, and the permanent state of mobilisation, on the other. Antinomies had already been perceptible in the pre-war years, but after the war began, they became almost a characteristic feature of German life: the visit to a concert and the air-raid siren, family solidarity and children's evacuation, Latin lessons and Hitler Youth Afternoons, leave spent at home and deployment in the east.

For the leadership, it was extremely important to keep the 'mood' of the people as positive as possible, and to lighten their burdens. The taxation policy already referred to was specifically directed at achieving this. The upper income groups were taxed more heavily than the rest, although the burden was light in comparison with many other countries, and two-thirds of the population were entirely exempted from income tax. Another policy of the same kind was the generous provision made for soldiers' families, by which they received roughly 70 per cent of their last peacetime income. This was a much higher proportion than in Great Britain (38 per cent) or the USA (36 per cent), although it is true that real wages in Germany were considerably lower than in those countries. According to the plans drawn up by the regime in autumn 1939, the population was supposed to feel the effects of the war as little as possible.[52]

Ordinary Germans therefore reacted with consternation to the restrictions necessitated by the change in the fortunes of war after 1941. What was happening at the front was now followed much more attentively, and concern for one's own relatives, who were fighting on the Eastern Front, was now at the forefront of people's minds. The 'arrival of hospital trains from the east', for instance, aroused great interest. 'The sight of the wounded was now greeted with "more compassion"', it was reported.

> It was often said that the soldiers were terribly thin and their uniforms were so torn that they could scarcely be recognised any more as German soldiers. These descriptions, and experiences with the hospital trains, have contributed considerably to increasing the worry and depression felt about the soldiers on the Eastern Front.[53]

The number of dead and wounded increased rapidly. The war no longer had anything 'unreal' about it.

It was the supply of food which had the greatest influence on the 'mood' of the German population, as is shown not least by the agitated reports of the SD regarding the reaction to a temporary cut in rations in spring 1942: 'The announcement that the food ration is being reduced has had a well-nigh "devastating" impact on much of the population, to an extent greater than hardly any other event during the war.' The workers above all 'completely lack any understanding of the need for the new measures.' The mood of this section of the population, it was reported, had 'reached a nadir not seen so far at any point in the course of the war. The military reports of recent days have been pushed into the background completely by the announcement that the food ration is being reduced.'[54] This reduction in rations was rescinded in autumn 1942, and Goering explicitly stated, in the speech in which he announced this, that the improvement in Germany's food supplies was only possible because German troops in the east had conquered an immense amount of territory 'and indeed these are the most fertile areas we know of in the whole of Europe.' Next time, he explained, alluding to the German policy of starving the inhabitants of the occupied regions of the Soviet Union, there would be no cuts in rations in Germany: 'The German people have absolute priority when hunger has to be assuaged and food provided. If the opponent's measures lead to difficulties in supply, the point everyone should be aware of is this: people may go hungry, but this will absolutely not happen in Germany!' Here, therefore, the connection between Germany's policy of starvation in the Soviet Union and the food supply situation in the Reich was blatantly proclaimed. At the same time, Goering announced special supplements for particular groups: 50 extra grams of meat for the residents of areas threatened by air attack, a Christmas supplement of 'meat, flour and other nice things, we hope' for everyone, and 'by order of the Führer' a parcel for every German soldier travelling home on leave, containing flour, peas, sugar, butter 'and a big dried sausage'.[55]

Special allowances of this kind were ostentatiously presented for propaganda reasons as gifts from the Führer to his people, as an expression of his selfless efforts on behalf of those particularly in need, although they actually just made it obvious that these supplies had to remain restricted to a small number of groups. Many companies attempted to procure additional food supplies, or 'peacetime commodities' for their employees, not least to prevent their workers from moving to a rival firm, because of the increasing competition between employers over this scarce resource. This was not permitted officially, but it increasingly became current practice, and despite all prohibitions, individual companies conducted campaigns to entice workers away from their existing employers with extra pay or special rations. This kind of behaviour was seen more and more, and it was referred to ironically as 'organising something through the back door'. Individuals, firms, municipal bureaucracies and whole Wehrmacht units endeavoured to acquire additional goods in whatever way they could, often semi-legally, or illegally. The use of 'connections' in the occupied territories made this a good deal easier.

In spite of the regime's efforts to give the people an immediate share in the fruits of victory, life in Germany remained bleak.

> 'People on the streets, in the shops and on public transport looked down at heel', wrote the Swiss journalist Konrad Warner on the situation in Berlin during the war. 'They were both weary and constantly in a hurry. They queued to get a few vegetables or potatoes, to obtain a cigarette voucher or to have their ration books stamped. They queued at the cinema to get a seat, and they queued in the shops to get a bottle of wine. Sometimes they queued without knowing what was on offer. They hoped it was something they could perhaps exchange, if they could not make use of it themselves.'[56]

In face of such wretchedness, the reports of soldiers from occupied France or Denmark, telling of fully stocked shelves and freely purchasable goods, resembled news from another world. And, when the bombing raids on German towns became more frequent, as they did after summer 1942, it began more and more difficult to hold on doggedly to the level of security and 'normality' that had been achieved earlier.

It was, above all, children who suffered under the war conditions, as Warner observed:

> They had to help with the shopping and do some of the housework, they had to go to school and homework needed to be done, while in addition they were loaded with tasks by the youth organisations. They had to collect paper,

> bottles, and scrap metal, they had to take part in exercises and marches, they were roped into courses and meetings which provided 'political training', and the events of the war and their impact on family and household, the air attacks and the deaths of neighbours, fathers and brothers burdened their spirits to an increasing degree. They matured astonishingly early. They became grim, and also brutal, and when one looked at them, the word 'youth' lost its optimistic ring.

The situation of children and young people during the war was contradictory, and it cannot be reduced to a common denominator. They were, on the one hand, more under the grip of the Nazi authorities than any other generation, and they had grown up holding the Third Reich's view of the world. Although the influence of non-Nazi teachers in the schools had never been completely obliterated, it had been greatly reduced. Education was saturated with National Socialist doctrine, and militarisation was a particular feature of the state schools. In March 1939, membership of the Hitler Youth was made obligatory for all schoolboys between the ages of fourteen and eighteen, and in 1940 the age groups between ten and fourteen were added. The periods of schooling became ever shorter, and the 'services' to be done for the regime became ever greater. In bringing in the harvest, in the 'land year' for girls, and in the semi-military task of helping with anti-aircraft batteries or air-raid warnings in the later years of the war, children were largely removed from the traditional channels of their upbringing, particularly from their parents, and parents who wanted to counter these influences needed to have very firm political and ideological convictions.

On the other hand, membership of the Nazi organisations, the multiplicity of 'camps' and 'excursions' and the evacuation of children from the towns and cities did not automatically produce the attitudes and modes of behaviour desired by the political leaders. On the contrary, there were increasing complaints about young people's lack of respect, their independence and their tendency to run wild, both from the Nazi organisations and from conservative parents. Young people lost their ties to their original milieu, their notions of morality became looser, and middle-class, Catholic and Social Democratic parents became more and more anxious about the attitudes and behaviour of their sons and daughters during their absences from home, which often went on for weeks or even months.

This early independence of youth in a time of war might express itself in different ways, however. It could lead to a rejection of tutelage and authority, as with the 'wild cliques' of proletarian origin, or the bourgeois 'Swing Boys', but it could also produce extreme fanaticism, as with some units of the Hitler Youth, which literally fought to the last bullet, on the model of the SS, in the final phase of the war. For most young people, however, the experience of having to fend for yourself early in life led to a concentration on survival and the day-to-day concerns of wartime existence, as well as to a pronounced indifference to politics.[57]

The importance of the 'second economy' increased as the supply situation worsened. Foraging trips, illicit slaughtering, hoarding and black marketeering all increased after the middle of the war. This was to be expected, in fact, it was almost inevitable in view of the prevailing market conditions. '"Organisation" trumps everything these days', commented René Schindler, a Swiss visitor to the Reich.

> Everything that is urgently needed for living must be 'organised'. . . . Tobacco has the best exchange rate, particularly among the rural population, who have the readiest access to the so-called 'peasant currencies'. A pound of 'black' butter costs about 150 Marks at present, but you can get it for 20 foreign cigarettes, which have been put into circulation by prisoners of war, or for 35 German cigarettes.[58]

The existence of the black market was not a sign that the population distrusted the Nazi regime. But the Darwinian laws of the black market strengthened the feeling of a struggle of all against all, especially for the workers, who were largely cut off from gaining extra provisions through the 'second economy' because most of them had nothing to exchange.

The bleaker life became, the more the regime attempted to put into effect the equality implied by the notion of the *Volksgemeinschaft*, at least in propaganda terms. Dreams of the vast territories of the east, and hopes of a life of abundance after the war had been won, which would allow the differences between rich and poor to be offset, had long made it possible to ignore some of the troubles and injustices of the present. But now the war had continued longer than expected, and how it would end seemed more uncertain. Questions of social justice began to be raised more emphatically, as the SD worriedly pointed out. The regime reacted with measures such as improving workers' protection against dismissal and continuing the payment of wages during ill health. It also called for equality of treatment between workers and office employees in matters of retirement insurance. The population welcomed its efforts.

Even so, criticism of the real and alleged privileges of the 'better circles' of society continued to gain strength as the war went on. While the population of the industrial towns is suffering from reduced rations and air attacks, reported the SD, 'the "world of polite society" is taking winter sports holidays', and it satirised the behaviour of young women in the winter sports resorts, who with their 'ski attire and their sunburned faces' had a 'downright provocative' impact 'on working-class folk comrades'. After spring 1942, the SD regularly reported on the 'bitterness' of the workers, who denounced the ability of 'many members of the so-called better social circles to procure all kinds of scarce goods thanks to their connections and their deep pockets, in addition to the provisions they are entitled to.' The point made here, that the rich were not entitled to higher food supplies than the rest, demonstrates that the continuing existence of social distinctions was increasingly felt to be unacceptable.[59] This did not at all mean that the conditions of life of rich and poor had come any closer together. On the contrary, the fury of the poor was increased by the way inequality continued to exist while the propaganda of the regime proclaimed the equality of all *Volksgenossen*.

The NSDAP played a more and more significant role as the war continued. At the beginning of the war, almost two-thirds of the population were attached in some way to the party, or to the ever-increasing variety of groups existing under the party umbrella. The biggest participation rates were to be found in mass organisations like the German Labour Front, the Hitler Youth, the National Socialist Women (*NS-Frauenschaft*) and the National Socialist Public Welfare (*NS-Volkswohlfahrt*). These party associations, characteristically described as 'party agencies', inserted themselves between the state authorities and the population, and acted in part in collaboration with, in part alongside, the state agencies, but also often replaced them. A network of membership and maintenance, discipline and control was thereby created, which. contributed both to the preservation of 'normality', as with the provision of assistance after air raids, and to the mobilisation of society for the war. Not least, the party offered privileges in all walks of life. Without the agreement of the party, a young person could not secure an apprenticeship, and a bombed-out family could not get a new place to live. The appointment, promotion and dismissal of all higher officials required the involvement of the party leadership. The party issued political evaluations, and it could obtain or block the provision of state welfare. And it could arrange for a '*uk-Stellung*', in other words a declaration that a worker's presence in the factory was 'indispensable', which meant that he could not be taken away and put into the Wehrmacht. After the war with the Soviet Union began, this was the most effective control instrument of all, and the highest privilege.

By these methods, the party created a gigantic army of officials, who faithfully served the regime and its Führer, and in return received quasi-sovereign functions, even if they were completely lacking in administrative competence. There were more than 28,000 Local Branch Heads (*Ortsgruppenleiter*), who were unpaid but often possessed a great deal of influence. The symbols of power were important to them: they were allowed to carry a service pistol and they wore a uniform. The Hitler Youth Leaders also wore a uniform. These were sixteen- or seventeen-year-old youths who acted as a 'Hitler Youth Patrol', a kind of youth police. The same applied to female NSV (National Socialist Public Welfare) officials, who helped their neighbours, but could also instruct them in racially aware living and check up on their political attitudes. Wartime German society was a society of privileged uniform-wearers, and for many Germans, not just for the young, this acquisition of 'official' authority, this devolution of the power of command, was clearly one of the most attractive aspects of the regime, and it compensated at least in part for the continued existence of real social differences. But what these 'service functions' promised above all was privilege. The holders were quicker to receive goods in short supply, they could influence the service roster of the Hitler Youth and they could also prevent or accelerate their own evacuation. Anyone who held an 'office' or had 'connections' did better than those who did not. The corruptibility of party officials was proverbial; hardly anything refuted the slogan of the *Volksgemeinschaft* as powerfully as the arrogant bearing of the 'golden pheasants', as they were colloquially called. But the noisy grumbles about brown functionaries also diverted attention away from the fact that the whole of German life during the war was characterised by a quest for privileges, preferences and favours of all types. The search for distinction and privilege was the inevitable corollary of the demand for equality.[60]

Many Germans also experienced indirect social advancement through the presence of millions of rightless foreigners. This could be seen in the streets, where gangs of prisoners of war were set to work, under guard, to clear away rubble or to assist in building work. In the factories, German workers were generally regarded as being in charge of the labour force from Eastern Europe, and in large enterprises where the proportion of foreigners was particularly high, Germans were generally only there as instructors or supervisors. It is true that there was also increased pressure on the German workers, but foreigners suffered far more from the growing severity of punishments for 'idling at work' and 'breaching labour contracts'.

Even so, German and foreign workers also potentially had interests in common, and the number of cases of German readiness to assist 'alien workers' is not small. On the whole, Germans were neither helpful towards foreigners nor did they actively mistreat them, demonstrating instead a lack of interest and a matter-of-fact indifference, which increased as the war continued and their own worries worsened. Thus, an attitude soon emerged towards foreigners which implicitly presupposed inequality, while the instrumentalisation of the individual as an active factor in racist politics was no longer regarded as something peculiar.

In Germany, the year 1942 was already marked by serious bombing raids. At the end of March there was an attack on Lübeck, and half the town was levelled to the ground. On 30 May, it was the turn of Cologne. This was the first attack by more than 1,000 bombers, and in it almost 500 people were killed, 5,000 wounded and 45,000 rendered homeless.[61] As early as May 1940, during the German invasion of France, British aircraft had flown the first big sorties against Hamburg and the Ruhr district, and from then onwards nightly air-raid warnings and falling bombs were the war's constant accompaniment for the urban population. Since the Allies were not yet in a position to conduct a land war on German soil, British strategy, apart from operations in the Mediterranean, concentrated on the air war, which was also a reprisal for German attacks on British cities, which had cost the lives of 24,000 people by mid-1942.

The strategic air war had two objectives: one was to destroy industrial installations, transport links and infrastructure, the other was to undermine the morale of the German population. Since daylight air attacks were too risky, because of German anti-aircraft defences, most of the attacks were made at night. By the end of 1942 the Royal Air Force had 2,000 heavy bombers, and a year later this number had already risen to 13,000.[62] The German side did, indeed, construct an effective system of air defence in a relatively short time, and in 1941 alone it shot down more than 1,000 British bombers. But air defence duties forced almost a third of Germany's fighter planes to remain at home, and the anti-aircraft batteries which were now set up all over the country also tied down a significant amount of manpower.

Month by month, and year by year, the intensity of the attacks increased. In January 1943, British and US representatives, meeting in Casablanca, agreed to coordinate their aerial activities. The British would fly at night, and the Americans would fly by day at a very high altitude. After this decision, town after town was systematically attacked and destroyed, week by week. The air attacks reached a terrible climax in summer 1943, when Hamburg was attacked continuously for two days and nights. The city suffered serious destruction in a gigantic firestorm. More than 30,000 people were killed, and 125,000 wounded. Altogether, approximately 600,000 people in Germany lost their lives by air attack during the war (including 40,000 foreign workers and prisoners of war), and nearly a million were wounded.

The economic impact of the attacks was considerable. The Allies succeeded in disrupting arms production to an increasing degree after summer 1942, and partially paralysing it after 1944 by attacking the aircraft industry and targeting hydrogenation plants, ball-bearing factories and railway junctions. The most lasting impact of the bombing raids, however, lay in the almost total destruction of Germany's town centres and the infrastructure that supported the basic living requirements of a large part of the population. Roughly 30 per cent of Germany's total housing stock was damaged or destroyed by the bombing. In Cologne, Dortmund, Duisburg and Kassel the proportion was two-thirds, and in Düren and Paderborn more than 90 per cent.

'People abroad have in general no conception of the purely organisational problems which result from the air attacks', noted the Swedish journalist Arvid Fredborg, who was based in Berlin.

> The bombing raids destroy food supplies, which must be replaced. Clothes, furniture and household items use are rendered useless. The housing shortage is made worse. Hundreds of thousands of people have to be evacuated, and the necessary means of transport have to be provided for this. Official documents go astray and can only be replaced in a makeshift fashion. Important books go up in flames. Tens of thousands of window-panes are smashed. Power lines are torn up, telephone poles are snapped, gas mains rupture, and the sewage system sinks into chaos. The transport system collapses, railway carriages, trams and buses are destroyed, and the rails are torn out of the ground.[63]

All these hardships imposed an enormous burden on the population. There was a widespread fear of nighttime attacks, of death, of being wounded, of being buried under debris, especially as the construction of shelters had been neglected before 1941. Exhausting nights spent in air-raid shelters made people jumpy and irritable, and in this situation the fact that Jews and workers from the east were forbidden to go into air-raid shelters was hardly even noticed. People were forced by the destruction of their apartments and houses to move to other quarters. They often had to make do with temporary accommodation. From autumn 1940, the authorities started to move people from particularly endangered cities to rural parts of Central and Eastern Germany. Whole schools, together with their pupils and teaching personnel, were transferred to 'air secure' districts, a move which met with energetic protests from some parents, who feared, not without reason, that their children would become alienated from them as a result. Firms altered their working hours and locations. In many factories, the employees had to work during the day and do air raid duty during the night.

The air raids gave rise not only to feelings of hopelessness and anxiety but also to anger and bitterness against the superior enemy, and there is something to be said for the idea that the bombing campaign aroused solidarity with the Nazi regime rather than undermining it. In large parts of the population, however, the determining factor was fear of a defeat of Germany at the hands of the Soviet Union, and this was the most important point for Nazi propaganda to latch onto in the second half of the war. 'Many people react with deep embitterment, which makes them still more unyielding', observed Fredborg on the impact of the air attacks; 'Others, in contrast, sink into despair. . . . Of course, if the attacks coincide with bad news about politics or food supplies, attitudes can certainly change.'[64]

## The Popular Mood and Mass Culture

The increase in the burden borne by the Germans as the war went on led the regime's leaders to devote still greater attention than previously to keeping up their spirits. 'To keep our people in a good mood is also important for the war effort', wrote Goebbels in February 1942, and he considered that not just the provision of plentiful material goods but also a broad palette of cultural offerings had a contribution to make. This applied, first, to the classical arts. More than a quarter of the state's subsidies for cultural purposes went to the theatre. In 1940, there were 220 state-run theatres and 120 private theatres in Germany, with seating for 250,000 people and 40,000 employees. Never before had so many people visited a theatre. Audience figures rose by a third between 1938 and 1940, reaching a total of 40 million. Directors such as Hilpert, Gründgens, George and Klöpfer were stars of the cultural scene and they enjoyed the admiration of theatregoers as much as the support of the Nazi leaders. In the theatre, said Goebbels, the German *Volk* comes into contact with 'a spiritual and artistic way of expressing its being and its character as a *Volk*'. Henceforth, he added, the people and the theatre 'are two concepts which supplement and condition each other'. Schiller, Goethe, Kleist, and also Gerhart Hauptmann, were the playwrights performed most often, while plays by Nazi-influenced dramatists like Dietrich Eckart and Hanns Johst were rarely staged.[65]

Similar efforts were made to promote classical music. During the war, Germany supported 181 permanently active orchestras, which employed over 8,900 musicians altogether. The great theatre directors had their parallel in conductors such as Eugen Jochum, Herbert von Karajan, Karl Böhm and, first and foremost Wilhelm Furtwängler. These were all admired leaders of the culture industry, who conducted almost every day before capacity audiences. Particular attention was paid to Richard Wagner and the Bayreuth festival. In 1940, Hitler ordered that the festival should be continued during the war, although the operas should no longer be performed before middle-class spectators in dinner jackets but before workers and soldiers, who were brought to the Green Hill of Bayreuth at the state's expense. This, wrote an SD agent enthusiastically, is 'a magnificent attempt to bring the simplest of our national comrades into contact with the greatest and in part the most difficult works of German art.' It was, he wrote, 'a top-ranking cultural accomplishment'.[66] The notion of *Volksgemeinschaft* was given dramatic expression here, in that Bayreuth, the incarnation of the high culture of the German bourgeoisie, was symbolically opened up to the masses in order to strengthen their appreciation of higher things. For the middle classes, equally, this stress on classical culture offered the opportunity to immerse themselves in the world of art and higher spiritual values and withdraw for a while from their mundane wartime daily life. By making this possible, the Nazi state created cohesion and an illusion of normality.

Nevertheless, the main concern of most Germans once the war had started was to get on in life, and to keep a firm grip on the 'normality' of a steady job, a fixed income and a certain amount of hope for the future. They had finally reached this position after decades of privation, and did not want it to be destroyed by the circumstances that accompanied the war. An intense zest for life, a thirst for enjoyment and a preference for shallow entertainment were observed everywhere, not least by party comrades who were scandalised by this behaviour. The number of holiday trips continued to increase after the beginning of the war, and the spas and seaside resorts reported bigger bookings. The restaurants and the bars were full, and the dance halls and cabarets were sold out. People tried to block out the war, as far as possible. Even in the big classical theatres, operettas, comedies and lighter pieces increasingly prevailed. In the Münchner Kammerspiele theatre, for instance, two-thirds of the programme consisted of 'comedy pieces'. The public demanded light fare, entertainment and humour, and that was what it got. Works of a 'basically pessimistic or depressing nature' were to be taken out of the repertoire.[67]

For the broader public, however, it was not the theatre and the concert hall but the cinema and the radio that were of central interest. In 1942, a billion entry tickets were sold, in a total of 7,000 cinemas: the number of cinemagoers had increased fivefold since 1933. There were also many mobile cinemas which served rural areas, and, to an increasing degree, the soldiers at the front. The number of films produced by the German film company UfA rose to more than sixty a year, the overwhelming majority of them light entertainment films, above all comedies. Here are the titles of some of the films shown in the 1941–2 season, which were greeted with enthusiasm by the public: *Everything for Gloria*; *After All, Women are Better Diplomats*; *The Main Thing is to be Happy*; *Love Costs Nothing*; *The Secret Countess*; *Seven Years of Good Fortune*; *We're Making Music*. But, until spring 1941, it was American productions which really drew in a mass audience: Mickey Mouse and Laurel and Hardy films were much in demand, and Clark Gable, Errol Flynn and Olivia de Havilland were big stars in Germany as well as elsewhere. In contrast to this, the political films commissioned by the Ministry of Propaganda, such as 'Ohm Krüger', 'Jud Süss' or, later on, 'Kolberg', which were supposed to bring a specifically National Socialist message to the people, were rarely seen, in comparison with the ever-widening flow of love films and musicals, although they were not entirely ignored.

The radio was also very popular. Like the press, it was completely controlled by Goebbels. He made radio programmes the most important propaganda instrument during the war, alongside the 'weekly newsreels' shown by the cinemas. New broadcasts, special announcements, speeches by Hitler and above all the Wehrmacht report and 'air warnings' were listened to by a very large number of people, who could be reached by no other medium. Here too, though, political matters were not exactly given pride of place: 126 of the 190 hours of broadcasts per week were devoted to entertainment and hit songs. This reflected the demands of the soldiers, who listened to the radio in their quarters. Broadcasters inevitably had to take their wishes into account. The programmes were dominated by sentimental love songs, and genuine hits like 'Lili Marleen' or 'Davon geht die Welt nicht unter' [Still the World Does not Collapse]. Swing music, long opposed by the Nazis, was now played on the radio, and became more and more popular, even though it was performed in blander German versions and under the programme title of 'Snappy Tunes'. The SD reported disgustedly in summer 1942 that 'respectable light music conforming to German taste' had been 'so clearly boycotted' by the youthful public, and 'jazz music' had been demanded 'so insistently that the bands were gradually giving in to this pressure, and the wilder, the hotter, and the more jazzed up the music on offer, the more frenetic is the applause of young people of this sort.'[68] The regime did occasionally take action against such 'excesses', but evidently this was mainly to mollify its own adherents.

In short, what served to keep the Germans satisfied was tolerated, within limits, even when it contradicted the ideological foundations of the regime. This very much exasperated the educated middle classes, whose power to define culture was being undermined by the continuing rise of mass entertainment. 'The level to which we have sunk is like something from the *Decline of the West*', wrote schoolmaster Martin H. during the war to a colleague, complaining that on the radio they only played 'the music that is made there for the hoi polloi'. 'It is always the same: either this abominable tootling called jazz or slushy sentimentality', he added furiously. 'And think what a hoard of good music our people still possessed until a few decades ago, through its folksongs!' Thus, the hegemony of popular culture extended its reach in Germany even during the war years, at the same time as it did in Great Britain and France, though some years later than in the USA. Radio, film and, within limits, the gramophone record and the illustrated magazine, became the main media, and this applied to the whole country, rather than being restricted to a few big cities, as had still been the case in the 1920s.[69]

After the end of 1942, and despite the regime's vigorous efforts, the mood of the German population started to change, declining into a state of indifference and apathy, particularly in the heavily bombarded cities. This development found expression in a restriction of the social horizon to the individual's own existence and a growing lack of interest in all social events. People concentrated on their own life and survival and had little awareness of more general issues.

This was accompanied by a severe degree of de-politicisation, the impact of which lasted beyond the war and into the post-war era. 'The attitude of a large part of the population', reported the SD in summarising the situation on the third anniversary of the start of the war in autumn 1942,

> is often marked by a certain degree of resignation, which where it is more pronounced even extends to indications of war-weariness. The increasing difficulty of obtaining provisions, three years of restrictions in all spheres of daily life, the enemy air raids which are constantly increasing in severity and extent, and concern for the lives of family members at the front

were factors which 'increasingly lead people to desire an early end to the war'.[70]

But this increasing war-weariness could very well be combined with hopes for 'revenge' and for 'the final victory'. Moreover, the critical remarks about the Nazi regime and its functionaries which were now more frequently registered by the SD were not necessarily in contradiction to continuing loyalty. In this connection, the people's lasting attachment to the Führer played a great role, despite all the general disillusionment, for after his earlier successes, Hitler was thought to be capable of almost anything. Fear of the Red Army also bound many people strongly to the regime and led them to hope that the war would end victoriously. It is also noticeable how frequently the party offices and the SD reported on remarks made by the population to the effect that 'the terror attacks are a result of the measures taken against the Jews' and that 'we would not have had to suffer so much from the terror attacks if we had treated the Jews better.' Remarks like this indicate a further source of loyalty: the knowledge, or at least the sneaking suspicion, about what was happening 'in the East', led not only to a fear of being made jointly responsible for this, but also to the conviction that the Jews somehow stood behind Germany's wartime opponents.[71]

Thus, many Germans were swayed simultaneously, and to an equal extent, by, on the one hand, war-weariness and increasing de-politicisation, and on the other hand, trust in the Führer and 'strength through fear' (*Kraft durch Furcht*). The loss of unambiguous reference points and values, such as right and wrong, good and evil, can to that extent be understood as a process of growing moral indifference, as an expression of the continuing revaluation of values advocated and practised since 1933. From a more long-term perspective, it was also the result of the unending succession of catastrophic experiences and radicalisations since the First World War, through which any certainty about where the individual belonged and which set of rules to follow was seriously undermined.

But contrary developments were also in evidence. The number of people who believed neither in Hitler nor in the final victory seemed to be growing again, and in many places greater attention was paid to those who had not sided with the Nazis, and whose authority now increased. This was also accompanied by a surge in the prestige of the churches. They were again full of Sunday worshippers, as National Socialist observers noticed with concern. In face of the growing risk to life from the air raids and the fear of the consequences of the military defeat that was beginning to appear on the horizon, people increasingly returned to religion. There was an unmistakable decline in the cohesive force of the Nazi movement and its ideology, but the authorities were strong enough to prevent these overwhelmingly private attitudes from finding expression in public.

During the war, the state of mind and behaviour of the population had increasingly ceased to be determined by social and political allegiances. Even regional ties had lost part of their strength. There were many reasons for this: the progressive destruction of urban neighbourhoods, the upheavals in the workforce because of military service and the deployment of foreign labour, the years spent by soldiers in socially mixed Wehrmacht units, the involvement of women in wartime duties, the evacuations and the introduction of rationing. All these factors distanced the experiences of individuals from their socially determined predispositions, and rendered other considerations far more important, such as whether one was drafted into the Wehrmacht or declared an 'indispensable worker'; whether one was sent to the Western Front or the Eastern Front; whether one was wounded or not; whether a husband or father was killed in the war or not; whether one's family lived in a small town or an industrial region; at the edge of the town or in a bomb-endangered city centre; whether one was bombed out or not, whether the children were evacuated; whether one had to take in bombing victims or refugees or one had oneself to be accommodated by strangers; whether one had connections who could get hold of provisions or provide access to privileges; and whether one was a skilled black market trader or not. Those were the criteria which now primarily determined the fate of the individual and moulded the individual's experience. As a result, membership of a class or a social milieu increasingly lost its significance, though not entirely. Communities of fate grew up instead, groups of people whose condition was dependent on a range of geographical, military and political factors, and, last but not least, on the vagaries of fortune.

# 10
# Downfall

## Retreat

Between the turning point of the war, in the winter of 1941–42, and its end in May 1945, military events came thick and fast. Hundreds of battles were fought, as well as thousands of lesser engagements. The dead could be counted in millions. But more than half of the soldiers who died during the Second World War fell during the final eighteen months. It might appear, in retrospect, as if the victory of the Allies could already have been predicted at the end of 1941, in view of the relationship of forces and the respective arms-producing capacities of the contending parties. But, in fact, until late summer 1942 it seemed almost inconceivable that the Wehrmacht could be defeated. The period between autumn 1942 and late summer 1943 marks the real turning point in the war, when the initiative passed into the hands of the Allies. From then onwards, the Wehrmacht was in retreat, although it took a further one and a half years before National Socialist Germany ceased to exist.[1]

The dominant military event of the period between the late winter of 1941 and the late summer of 1942 was the second German offensive in the east, which displayed an extraordinary parallelism to that of the previous year. The aim of this second offensive, according to Hitler's instructions, was 'to wipe out the entire defence potential remaining to the Soviets.'[2] The main thrust was to be directed southwards, towards Stalingrad, a centre of arms production on the river Volga, and towards the Caucasus, with the aim of capturing the oilfields of Maikop. The German military leadership was unanimously of the opinion that the Wehrmacht would not be in a position to mount a third operation of this magnitude, in view of the shortage of reserves. Once again, then, everything was staked on one card. But it took until June before the starting point of the previous year was again reached, so this offensive, like the one the previous year, was too late in starting. Even so, the Wehrmacht once again achieved extraordinary successes. It advanced southwards over more than 1,000 kilometres of territory; Rostov-on-Don was occupied, and so was the eastern coast of the Black Sea.

On 21 August 1942, soldiers of the Wehrmacht raised the German flag over Mount Elbrus, the highest mountain in the Caucasus. That was the point in the war when the area of German control reached its greatest extent. It now stretched from the Channel Islands to the Crimea, from the Pyrenees to Leningrad, and from the North Cape to Egypt. But the portents of defeat were already unmistakable. The Wehrmacht had almost run out of reserves; the troops were exhausted and had suffered heavy losses. The front was completely overextended, as were the supply lines. The southern front now stretched out over more than 2,000 kilometres. In addition to this, there was chaos in the military leadership, for Hitler reshuffled his generals after every major setback, he prohibited any attempt to save particular Wehrmacht units by retreating, and he intervened in tactical questions or over details of military technique. Above all, the Wehrmacht was unable to capture the strategically important city of Stalingrad, in which a bitter street-to-street struggle began, lasting for month after month. At the end of August, the German advance came to a standstill everywhere. Hence the second offensive by the Wehrmacht had still not delivered victory over the Red Army.

This meant that the strategic initiative was now in the hands of the Allies. In Africa, a British offensive which began on 23 October 1942 compelled the German units to begin a retreat. At the beginning of November, British and American troops landed in Morocco and Algeria, and on 19 November the Red Army began an offensive against the German 6th Army in Stalingrad, which resulted in its encirclement and eventual destruction. Ninety-one thousand men became prisoners of war, 40,000 were airlifted out of the city and roughly 100,000 either fell in battle or lost their lives to the cold weather or through starvation. In May 1943, German and Italian units in North Africa were forced to capitulate, and as a result 250,000 men were taken prisoner. May was also the month when the decision to call off the so-called 'Battle of the Atlantic' waged by the German submarine fleet signified defeat in the fight to cut the maritime supply lines of the Allies. In the east, however, German troops succeeded in re-establishing a firm front line and limiting their retreat.

At home, Germany's arms production had risen uninterruptedly since the appointment of Speer, but now the Royal Air Force succeeded in restricting its growth by repeatedly bombing the Ruhr district, the heart of the German arms industry. This has been described as a 'turning point in the history of the German war economy.'[3] The capitulation of the German-Italian Army of Africa opened the route to Southern Europe for the Allies. On 10 July 1943, the Americans and the British landed in Sicily, rather than in France, as the Soviet Union had demanded in the hope that the opening of a 'Second Front' in the west would bring an urgently needed respite in the east. The British and American generals thought it was too early for an operation of this kind, which required much greater military strength. But the British, in particular, were already thinking about what would happen after Germany's defeat, and they felt that a military presence of the Western Allies in Southern and South-East

Europe might be able to limit the expected post-war increase of Soviet influence in that region. After the fall of Mussolini, the landing on the Italian mainland, and the surrender of Italy on 8 September 1943, followed by the thrust of early autumn to the north of Naples, the Western Allies succeeded in advancing a long way into what the Germans had named 'Fortress Europe'. At that point, however, the Western advance stalled and a static front line developed, a situation which lasted for over nine months.

In the meantime, the Wehrmacht had disarmed the Italian army. The 600,000 Italian soldiers who did not want to continue the fight on Germany's side were transported to the Reich, where they were conscripted as forced labourers in conditions analogous to those suffered by Soviet prisoners of war.

In the East, on 5 July 1943, the Germans mounted a fresh summer offensive. For the third time, they tried to force the Red Army to its knees. But the German units were defeated in the battle of Kursk, the greatest tank battle in history, and when the Soviet counter-offensive began on 17 July 1943, the German army started a retreat which lasted for almost two years, occasionally brought to a halt but always accompanied by heavy losses, until it ended with the battle for Berlin in April 1945. By now, the German detachments had shrunk to less than half their former strength. Even so, they were repeatedly compelled by the German military leadership, and ultimately by Hitler, to hold onto 'firm footholds' or 'fortress positions' at any price. This admittedly delayed the Soviet advance in several places, but not everywhere, and it caused German losses to rise dramatically.

When retreating, the German units operated according to the 'scorched earth' principle; they destroyed the whole infrastructure of the regions they passed through, obliterating thousands of villages, and they also compelled vast numbers of the indigenous population, probably amounting to more than two million people, to retreat along with them. The aim was for the advancing Red Army to be confronted with a land both devastated and empty of human beings. The behaviour of the German units was marked by a combination of military logic, an ideologically motivated desire to kill and a mania for destruction. These motives can hardly be separated retrospectively. For the German troops, as Himmler put it in April 1943, there was now only one question: 'How do we take away as many people as possible from the Russians, dead or alive?' His reply was: 'We do that by killing them or by taking them into captivity and really putting them to work, and by making sure that we have the firmest possible control over an area we capture, while an area we abandon, a space we leave to the enemy, is left empty of people.' By March 1944, the German army had been driven back to the eastern border of pre-war Poland.[4]

The phase from April until December 1944 was marked by Allied offensives and German retreats as far as the boundaries of the Reich. Western forces landed in Normandy on 6 June 1944 and in the neighbourhood of St Tropez on 15 August. These events visibly signified the end of German rule in Western Europe. By the end of June, the British and the Americans had already brought 1.5 million men to France. They liberated France, Belgium and Luxemburg within five months, as well as Italy as far north as Florence. Beyond that city, the slowly retreating German troops held on until the end of the war in the region of the 'Republic of Salò', which was ruled by Mussolini, the overthrown Italian dictator who had been reinstalled there by Germany.

In the east, meanwhile, on 22 June 1944, the third anniversary of Germany's attack on the USSR, Soviet troops began their summer offensive, codenamed 'Bagration'. In the course of this offensive, the German Army Group Centre, located in White Russia, was destroyed. This was by far the most serious German defeat of the whole war. It was here, and not during the Normandy landing of the Western Allies, that the decisive event of the war took place, because the strongest element of the Wehrmacht had now been ground to pieces. In the weeks that followed, Soviet troops rapidly advanced to the west. By October 1944, they had already reached the German border.

It was now clear that both the Soviet Union and the Western Powers were increasingly thinking about the post-war situation. In the Pacific theatre, the USA was fighting a war against Japan which was extremely costly in human lives. Its main interest lay in defeating Germany as quickly and comprehensively as possible. The Red Army, on the other hand, called a halt to its advance just outside Warsaw, and refused to support the uprising begun at that time by the Home Army of Polish nationalists against the German occupier. The Warsaw rising was then bloodily suppressed by the German forces. The Soviet Union was not interested in promoting the rebirth of the conservative nationalist Poland of the interwar period. After all, it had an ally of its own in the shape of the small Polish Workers' Party, which it wanted to hoist into power. The political configuration of the post-war years was already being announced here.[5]

Despite its defeats, the Wehrmacht once again demonstrated its fighting strength with a counter-offensive in East Prussia in October 1944 and with the 'Ardennes Offensive' in the west in the region around Luxemburg in December 1944. At this point, the Allies were still far from attaining their agreed war aims, namely, the conquest of the whole of Germany, the complete destruction of the Wehrmacht and the unconditional capitulation of the Reich.

## Terror and Total War

After the stunning defeat in Stalingrad, if not earlier, it was apparent to everyone that Germany could also lose this war. The Nazi regime reacted to this threatening situation firstly by mobilising its last reserves and raising the level of war production still further, secondly by campaigning to turn the conflict into a Europe-wide 'total war' and thirdly by intensifying the policy of repression domestically as well.

At the beginning of 1943, the Wehrmacht's losses were running at 150,000 men a month. It was calculated that at least two million extra soldiers were required, and this meant that it was impossible to avoid large-scale extra recruitment. In addition to this, the war economy needed an extra 1.5 million workers in summer 1943 to increase arms production and continue the 'armaments miracle' achieved by Speer.[6] To get anywhere near that figure, an additional labour force had to be found for the armaments industry. The simplest method was to recruit more foreign workers; here, the interned Italian soldiers had an important role to play.

It turned out to be more difficult, however, to increase the number of German women in industrial employment and to mothball parts of the economy which were not relevant to the war, with the aim of transferring the personnel employed there into the arms industry. In 1942, the proportion of women in employment continued to be lower than it had been before the war. It was thought that this could be raised considerably by the introduction of stricter registration regulations. In 1943, Sauckel reported, 3.6 million women were investigated to determine their capacity for work, and 1.6 million were found capable of employment. But half a million of these were again released with a doctor's certificate, and 700,000 were only given half-time work, so these efforts only had a slight impact.[7]

The fundamental question as to whether an increasing number of German women ought to be drawn into working in the armaments industry continued to be disputed within the Nazi leadership. Goebbels demanded that, as in Stalin's Soviet Union, 'we should strike with an iron hand to ensure that female idlers are finally made to do important war work', but Hitler was strongly opposed to ideas like this, because 'our long-legged, slim German women are not to be compared with squat, primitive and healthy Russian women.' Goering, for his part, said that women from the lower classes were after all used to working; the job of the others was to have children: 'If a thoroughbred is harnessed to the plough it gets exhausted more quickly than a work horse. Consequently, one can never impose a universal obligation on women to work.'[8]

Since the regime was unable to agree on a definite course of action, the number of women in employment only rose by about 400,000 between 1941 and 1943, reaching a total of 14.8 million. This figure continued to include 1.3 million domestic servants. But the regime did succeed in transferring larger numbers of women who already had long experience in employment from office work and the consumer goods industry to the armaments sector. In addition, the authorities drew on large numbers of women and girls to engage in all kinds of services. All females born in 1927 were called up in 1944 to do women's labour service; young women were employed as Red Cross sisters, in the intelligence services, and as air-raid wardens. They even operated anti-aircraft batteries. At the end of the war, the Wehrmacht was being assisted by roughly 500,000 women.

The only way of implementing these harsh measures without their leading to a decline in the political loyalty of the population was to make it plain that they affected everyone to the same degree, including the 'better circles of society'. It was above all middle-class women and girls, reported the Reich women's leadership, who were evading their obligation to work:

> These are people who live by the old selfish principle: we have earned this, now let us think about ourselves, after a few years we shall be able to have a child, and then perhaps one more. . . . Here the kitchen cupboard is coupled with the second child, and the bathroom mirror or the radio set with the third one. It is difficult to win these people's support for ideas of selflessness and making a useful contribution to the community.[9]

Imposing compulsory service on 'women painted like Red Indians, cavorting in slacks', as an SD report put it,[10] would not produce any significant gain, but if the war was to be made 'total', it had to have an egalitarian character to be politically defensible. Thus, compensation was offered for the heavier burdens laid on the population through compulsory registration, the mothballing of factories, 'combing out operations' and increasing the hours of work by the propagation of the idea of 'German war socialism' and by campaigns against the 'better-off'. 'In the People's War of the present' wrote Goebbels 'the psychology of wartime leadership plays a decisive role.' The 'image of our civilian life', therefore, ought not to 'contrast provocatively with the war itself.'[11]

At the beginning of 1943, the Armaments Ministry started a nationwide closure of firms which did not contribute to the war, particularly the producers of consumer goods. In practice, it was mainly smaller enterprises which were affected. Their personnel were then sent to the factories that produced war materials. The larger enterprises, which were efficient and modern, were better fitted to increase war production rapidly. Tens of thousands of smaller firms were closed down, temporarily, as it was claimed, although in fact most of them closed for ever.

But this decision to lay hands on small enterprises and on independent handicraft workers and traders turned out to be highly problematic in political terms. The Nazi leaders were informed that the middle classes were beginning to fear 'that National Socialism was increasingly adopting Bolshevik methods'; many people prophesied 'a "decline of the middle class (*Mittelstand*)," which would be replaced by a centralised economy of a state capitalist type, and only a small top layer of society would reap the benefit of this.' These fears inevitably disturbed the Nazi leaders, because they were felt by their own supporters. As the perspective of a German victory and an imperialist peace became more unrealistic, the population increasingly began to ask 'what form their life would take, when they emerged from this war as "survivors", to use the Führer's own words.'[12]

The regime reacted to the worsening popular mood which followed the devastating air attack on Hamburg and the exit of Italy from the Axis in summer 1943 by organising another wave of violence, symbolised by Heinrich Himmler's appointment as Minister of the Interior. After 1943 there was a rapid increase in the number of people punished for 'defeatism' and 'pessimism'. Listening to foreign radio stations was now punished more frequently, usually after denunciations, which now spread almost like an epidemic. The number of death sentences shot up, from 926 in 1941 to 5,336 in 1943. In 1943, for the first time, the People's Court of Justice (*Volksgerichtshof*) sentenced more people to death than to imprisonment. In January 1943 the jurisdiction of this, the highest special court in Germany, was extended to cases of 'undermining the will to fight', which were construed to include critical remarks about the regime and sceptical statements about the course of the war. Roughly half the people accused under this heading were condemned to death during the final year of the war. It is true that more than three-quarters of the Gestapo's activities continued to be directed against foreign workers, who were regarded as by far the greatest danger to internal security. But by mid-1943 at the latest the terror of the regime was once again felt very distinctly by the German population as well.[13]

While making strenuous efforts to strengthen the war economy, the Nazis combined this with an all-embracing campaign to propagate the idea of 'total war'. The growing fear of the consequences of a defeat at the hands of the Soviet Union played a central part here. To achieve the desired effect of a terror of Bolshevism, said Propaganda Minister Goebbels, all that was needed was to portray conditions on the Eastern Front in a fairly realistic manner: the Red Army had won an important battle at Stalingrad, and it must be clear to everyone that 'if we are defeated, everyone's throat will be cut, whatever the individual German's attitude to National Socialism.'[14] But if every man and every woman immediately engaged themselves fully in the war, irrespective of the individual's social position, a quick victory would still be possible: this was the central message of the propaganda campaign which reached its zenith with Goebbels' speech of 18 February 1943 at the Berlin Palace of Sports.[15]

But this also marked a remarkable change in the war aims that were being propagated. Until then, the war in the east had largely been presented as a fight for living space (*Lebensraum*). Now, however, it was reinterpreted as a struggle in defence of European civilisation against the rule of Bolshevism. 'Europe against Bolshevism' was from then onwards the central slogan of the war in the east. 'What would have become of the German *Volk* and Europe, had the German Wehrmacht not raised its shield before Europe at the last minute on June 22, 1941!', proclaimed Hitler in his speech of 30 January 1943, the tenth anniversary of his seizure of power. It had only been possible to ward off Bolshevism because 'since 1941 the greater part of Europe has rallied to Germany in the struggle against the threat from the east.'[16] In view of the danger from the east, announced the Propaganda Ministry the next day, it was now of prime importance 'for the European peoples to forget everything that divides them. Family feuds must be deferred until after the war. Now the imperative is to keep the fire from consuming their common house.'[17] In view of Germany's war policy of the preceding ten years, the notion of 'family quarrels' was of unsurpassable absurdity. Even so, it was not without effect within the country, in spite of the daily destruction of German towns and industrial centres by British and American bombers, because the return to an emphasis on the cultural similarities of the (Western) European countries appeared to offer a positive outlook for the future, if, as was increasingly likely, the verdict of war did not go in Germany's favour. Germany as the hegemon of a Europe united against the Bolshevik threat from the east: that was the perspective for the post-war order the regime hoped to achieve after the defeat in Stalingrad. Ideas of this kind were no more than propagandist illusions in view of current German practices in the occupied countries of Europe. But even after the end of the war there were rumours, to which many Germans lent a willing ear, that the Western Powers now wanted to march against the Soviet Union, side by side with the Wehrmacht.

## Perspectives of Resistance

Even before the war with the Soviet Union, it was already apparent that Germany would not be able to count on the support of the countries of Western and Northern Europe for the creation of a new order in Europe under its leadership, while the views of East Central Europe hardly came into consideration. In any case, plans for a Europe under German domination had never got beyond the stage of grandiose and half-baked memoranda, and they contained far too many contradictions for it to be possible to speak of a German foreign and European policy which offered even a halfway realistic prospect apart from the conquest of other countries and the use of force. Hitler wanted

German occupation policy in the west as well as the east to concentrate on two objectives: military pacification and economic exploitation. In face of this insistence, more far-reaching political goals, which were put forward by German administrators in the occupied lands, and were sometimes fairly ambitious, had very little purchase on reality. 'Herr Abetz is the only one doing any collaboration', remarked Goering in August 1942 about the German ambassador in France, who was regarded as a Francophile.

> I don't do collaboration. My version of collaboration with the French gentlemen is this: if they deliver supplies to us until they themselves are unable to carry on any further, if they do that voluntarily, I will say, I collaborate. If they gobble everything up themselves, then they are not collaborating.[18]

For a long time, the population, the elites, and the different political parties of the occupied lands of Western Europe did not adopt a uniform attitude towards the occupying power. They knew that they would probably have to reckon with the Germans for an indefinite length of time, in view of their strength, and so the predominant feeling in the first half of the war was a readiness to cooperate, though it varied on a scale running from an *attentisme* which scarcely concealed rejection, at one end, to benevolent and occasionally enthusiastic cooperation at the other. In many countries, sections of the bourgeoisie combined a relatively positive attitude towards Germany, which represented a 'sense of order' and industrial progress, with fierce hostility towards the Left in their own country and to workers' organisations in general. Nevertheless, there were considerable variations from one country to the next. In the Netherlands, collaboration functioned relatively smoothly at the administrative level, but neither the population nor the political parties, the social elites and the royal house left any doubt about their blunt rejection of the occupation. The same was true of Denmark and Norway. But it was only when the occupiers began to reveal the shape of future occupation policy by their reprisals, their deportation of the Jewish population and their conscription of the men of the country to work in Germany, that this attitude of rejection stiffened. As the aura of the German army's invincibility began to disappear, rejection changed into a patriotically motivated resistance, which was seldom given open support by broad strata of the population, but did nevertheless meet with increasing sympathy.[19]

Apart from collaboration and resistance, there was also in the majority of cases yet a third element in the situation: the exile governments. They played a part in influencing the relationship of political forces, and they increasingly occupied the foreground as the end of the war came nearer, since this raised the question of political legitimacy and the outlook for the post-war order. The relations which existed between these three forces and the occupying power were full of tensions, and varied considerably from country to country. Their structure ultimately determined the course of post-war development.

The French example offers a particularly clear picture of the relation between resistance and collaboration. Resistance against Germany was, above all, a phenomenon of the second half of the war, when the prospect of a German defeat began to emerge. The resistance was limited to two groups of people: first, members of organisations which fought against the Germans for political or ideological reasons—above all the Left and the Gaullist Nationalists—and second, people who were defending themselves against direct oppression or repression, such as the workers who fled to the *maquis* so as not to be sent to Germany, and, not least, the Jews. The traditional French elites, and the majority of the population, on the other hand, had come to terms with the Germans after their invasion of summer 1940, and indeed not only in the area controlled by Marshal Pétain but also in the occupied zone. In addition, a certain proportion of the bourgeois Right also had political reasons for its readiness to cooperate with the Germans, although it is hard to give a precise figure of its size. This group's partial ideological agreement with the goals of National Socialism, such as its widespread anti-Semitism and its sharp rejection of the policies of the socialist Left, very much contradicted the traditions of French nationalism. In fact, the occupiers' modern methods of administration, economic management and no doubt also military leadership were more attractive to this group than the ideological conceptions of National Socialism. But these elements of acceptance, admiration and also pure orientation towards profit were not inevitably bound up with explicit political attitudes. They could just as easily go hand in hand with hopes for a rapid German defeat or even with active participation in the resistance.[20]

It was the occupying power itself which determined the forms and methods of resistance to it. In addition, it is also evident that in France, as also in the Netherlands, Denmark and Italy, the endeavour to avoid involvement—on either side—and to be left in peace were the obvious and preferred forms of behaviour for most people. Indeed, this was often the only alternative to collaborating with the occupiers or becoming one of the persecuted.

The pro-National Socialist puppet regimes and the Nazi parties in the occupied Western countries played a relatively minor role. In almost all Western countries, there was a small layer of explicit Nazi supporters. But, even during the time when Germany appeared almost invincible, they nowhere obtained any noteworthy support from the population as a whole, differing in this respect from parties in countries allied to Germany such as Italy, Romania, Hungary and also Croatia. This situation was in fact entirely in line with the views of the German leadership: Hitler never left it in any doubt that German rule in the west rested exclusively on military strength and that the regimes constructed by indigenous Nazi parties were without value for Germany. Rather the reverse: the fear was that if governments of this kind were in too strong a position, they would raise unwelcome demands in the post-war era. Thus, the German occupation authorities as a rule concentrated their efforts on cooperating with the representatives of the traditional elites, particularly those who ran the administration and the economy. Their help was needed to keep Germany's occupation costs as low as possible.[21]

It was Hitler's wish that more long-term political objectives, stretching perhaps beyond the end of the war, should not be taken into account in the fight against the developing resistance movements in the Western countries. In September 1941, Keitel described the resistance against the German occupation forces as exclusively a 'mass movement under unified direction'. What was involved here, he said, was a communist revolt in all the areas occupied by Germany. The yardstick to be applied in this case was not political or cultural relations between Germany and each particular country but the struggle against international communism. The Führer's instructions, therefore, were to intervene to suppress the resistance movement as quickly as possible in the same manner in both east and west, and that meant 'using the severest measures'. 'The standards for the actions of the military occupation authorities are not set by political relations between Germany and the country in question.'[22] Hence the German security police fought the resistance groups with terror and reprisals, a method which constantly increased the rage and bitterness of the population. Admittedly, the liberation movements in these countries did not succeed in causing serious difficulties for the German occupiers, but they did tie down considerable forces and worsen the security situation.[23]

Politically, the individual resistance movements were very heterogeneous, but three main tendencies can be distinguished among them: bourgeois nationalism, which combined together patriotic currents and was usually explicitly anti-communist; Western democracy, which drew much of its support from traditions of Left liberalism and social democracy; and communism, represented by groups which were at first relatively small in most countries but rapidly became more important owing to the activism of their adherents and the support of the Soviet Union. In their varied composition, the national resistance groups reflected not only the political traditions of each country, but also the breadth of the Great Power coalition against Hitler. As long as the Germans were the main opponents, and appeared almost invincible, the political and ideological contradictions within this alliance remained in the background. After German power began to erode and people started to reflect on the shape of the post-war order that would follow the defeat of Hitler's empire, differences within the resistance movements became more significant.

Only the partisan movements in the Soviet Union, Yugoslavia and, after autumn 1943, Italy, were serious factors in military terms. In the other countries, the importance of the national resistance movements lay predominantly in other fields. There, the conditions were created (in sharp opposition to the elites which were cooperating with the occupiers but also in part in a kind of unspoken division of labour with them) which made it possible for the country in question, after victory over Germany, to claim to be a victor rather than a collaborator with the vanquished regime. This was of great importance for countries which had been allied with Germany, such as Italy, or whose governments had cooperated with the Germans, while always keeping their distance from them, such as Denmark.

In most of Europe, a large proportion, often the largest proportion, of active resisters and of those who gave their lives for the resistance, were communists. There were a number of reasons for this. The traditional opponents of communism in these countries—the elites and the bourgeoisie—were compromised to a considerable extent by their closeness to the German occupiers, and this state of affairs strengthened the convictions and energy of the communists. The fight against 'German fascism' thereby acquired a character of internationalism and class struggle, which increased the attractiveness of communist anti-fascism to young people and intellectuals as well as to the working class. But it was of equal importance to the communists that, in the struggle against the German occupiers, they could recover the identity as revolutionary fighters for justice and freedom which they had lost in their role as the Soviet Union's auxiliaries. To fight against the most brutal right-wing dictatorship in history gave them far greater moral legitimacy than to attempt the overthrow of democratically elected governments in Western Europe or to purge alleged deviationists in their own ranks as they did in the Soviet Union or during the Spanish Civil War.

At a certain point, the antagonisms between the various components of the resistance movements ceased to be merely the source of regionally limited conflicts and began to come to the fore. If one wants to give a precise date for this, it was probably the outbreak of the Warsaw Uprising in August 1944.[24] The decision of the Red Army to remain ostentatiously on the eastern bank of the River Vistula, while the rising of the Polish Home Army was put down on the orders of SS Obergruppenführer Erich von dem Bach-Zelewski, indicated that the European resistance movement was split. It demonstrated that the Soviet side would not support resistance groups which were opposed to communism; it would even fight against them. In other countries too, particularly Greece and Yugoslavia, the antagonisms that had long smouldered between nationalist and pro-communist resistance groups now came to a head. Before the end of the war they had already reached the stage of armed conflict. Thus, in many European countries, fighting began to take place on two fronts simultaneously: on the one hand, against the supporters of National Socialism and those who collaborated with the Germans, and on the other hand, against the communists' drive for power, which was orchestrated from the Soviet Union.

As Eric Hobsbawm has put it, the most important element of the European resistance movements was their myth: 'Except to some extent in Germany itself, the legitimacy of postwar régimes and governments essentially rested on their resistance record.'[25] This is what gave the resistance movements a political significance for decades after the war, which went far beyond any contribution they had made to weakening the German occupation forces. In Germany itself, in contrast, by 1936 at the latest, the resistance of the working-class movement had been completely crushed by the security apparatus of the Nazi regime. Any activist and sympathiser with the communists, any Social Democrat, any trade unionist, and, to a lesser extent, any member of a Christian group, who was not in prison, concentration camp or exile, aimed to keep out of the way and simply to survive, in most cases in isolation. After the summer of 1941, and even more strongly after the German defeat at Stalingrad, the amount of activity by left-wing opponents of the regime recorded by the Gestapo began to increase again. It is true that, until spring 1945, it was still able to keep a constant check on these activities. But this period did see the restoration of political associations, connections were re-established and personal contacts renewed, and this made it possible for social democrats and communists, Christian opponents of Hitler, liberals, and trade unionists, to reappear in public relatively quickly and to become politically active in the first days and weeks after the end of the war.

But the most efficacious forms of opposition and resistance emerged not in the camp of the declared enemies of National Socialism but in the ranks of the elite and the followers and coalition partners of the National Socialists. These people were first and foremost officers, high officials, professors, a few priests and numerous members of the nobility, who met in various groups and circles which sometimes combined together and sometimes acted independently, and became increasingly opposed to the policies of the regime the longer the war lasted. Four groups can be distinguished, roughly speaking: the group around Carl Friedrich Goerdeler and Ludwig Beck; the Kreisauer Circle around Helmuth James Graf von Moltke and Peter Graf Yorck von Wartenburg; the officers of Army Group Centre around Henning von Tresckow; and, finally, the military group around Claus Graf Schenk von Stauffenberg. This opposition movement, which has been described with the basically but not entirely accurate portmanteau expression of 'conservative nationalists', comprised a small number of active participants, perhaps a few hundred, and it was largely isolated within the population and even within the professional and social milieu of the protagonists. But, since this was the last direction from which the Gestapo expected an attack to come, and since the code of conduct followed by noble officers, high officials and middle-class professors offered a certain degree of protection against denunciation, these groups were able over a period of several years not only to hold internal discussions both in private and by circulating memoranda and holding meetings about the aims and principles of a different Germany, but also to forge concrete plans for overthrowing the regime. These led finally to the failed assassination attempt on Hitler on 20 July 1944, and after that, of course, to the death of almost all the people who had participated in these groups.

If Hitler had been killed at that point, it is probable that there would have been a civil war between hostile and loyal Wehrmacht units, which would perhaps have shortened the war and thus saved the lives of millions of people. In that sense, the preparations for a putsch and the attempted assassination were far more than merely symbolic actions. For the conspirators, though, this consequence of their plot, at this late stage in the war, was no longer the decisive factor. Their thinking was nationalist in character, and their paramount endeavour was to transmit to later generations the message that a different Germany from Hitler's had actually existed.[26]

Most of the members of these conservative nationalist opposition circles had originally taken a positive attitude towards National Socialism, welcoming it as a liberation movement which offered hope for the future. Many of them had also taken up top-level positions within the regime. Their view of the world was imbued with that deep resentment against modern mass society, the growth of urbanism, party democracy, parliamentarism and 'bureaucratisation' which had already been the leading idea of large parts of the middle classes and the conservative elites before the First World War, and had gained strength in the subsequent period. The Third Reich appeared to be the materialisation of their hopes, and they therefore supported it. Developments like the erosion of the justice system or the persecution of the churches by the Nazis were criticised by the conservative nationalists, but in view of Hitler's successes they were accepted as the inevitable by-products of a 'youthful' movement, especially after the war started.

After the victories of summer 1940, criticism of Hitler's hazardous military adventures against France and Great Britain had fallen silent, and the military leadership and the state bureaucracy had jointly participated in the war against the Soviet Union, the operations directed against civilians and prisoners of war, and the persecution of the Jews. When the flow of military success dried up, and the Reich, the Wehrmacht and the people were threatened by defeat, there was a renewed upsurge of critique and discontent among the conservative nationalists. Now National Socialism was no longer seen as the political alternative to liberalism but as itself the expression of the deplorable and materialistic 'age of the masses', and at a further remove as the conclusion of the long process of dissolution the Christian West had undergone since the sixteenth century. Party rule and mass agitation, egalitarian propaganda and mass culture, phenomena which had spread ever more vigorously during the Nazi regime, represented exactly those tendencies of modern industrial society against which they had previously entered the lists.

The conservative nationalists now started to become more strongly opposed to Hitler's conduct of the war and to reject Nazi occupation and extermination policies. Even those who had formerly supported the regime became increasingly antagonistic to the Nazi system. 'The treatment of the occupied countries', wrote von Stauffenberg,

> is an essential aspect of the whole miserable situation. The beginning of the end of the military development was the Russian campaign, which began with the order to kill all commissars and continued with the decision to let prisoners of war die of hunger and to conduct manhunts with the aim of getting hold of civilian workers.

Stauffenberg did not mention the murder of the Jews and the war against the partisans, although the policy of the regime towards the Jews played a considerable part in strengthening the critical attitude of many members of the conservative nationalist resistance. It is true that most Wehrmacht officers were themselves anti-semitic, and the opposition's plans for the future after a successful putsch did not envisage a complete end to discrimination against the Jews, but rather an end to the killing. But indignation over the 'planned extermination of human beings', about which the conspirators had far better information than the broader public, after all, was without doubt an important factor, although it did not trigger the decision to resist. What was decisive for the conservative opponents of National Socialism was the threat of military defeat, which was equated with the end of Germany: 'If the present course is continued the inevitable result will be defeat and the destruction of [Germany's] hereditary human reserves (*blutsmässige Substanz*)', wrote von Stauffenberg.

> The fate that hangs over us can only be averted by removal of the present leadership. . . . After a change of government let the most important objective be that Germany should still be a power-factor that can be deployed in the interplay of forces, and that the Wehrmacht in particular should remain a viable instrument in the hands of its commanders.[27]

As regards domestic politics, ideas of returning to a state governed by the rule of law, and establishing a federation of European states, were at the centre of the thinking of some of the conspirators, the Kreisau Circle in particular.

But most of the plans discussed by the conspirators for renewing the state and society in Germany were in fact a recapitulation of old ideas, such as the well-known views of the German Nationalists and the young conservatives of the 1920s, which involved a society of Estates, in which the elite would rule without parliaments, political parties or publicity, and a harmonious order would exist without the excrescences of capitalism or the culture of modernity. Class struggles and religious divisions would have been overcome in this new order, which would be based on the community of the folk. This would be a society neither capitalist nor communist, but German. Many of these notions were identical with the proposals for 'Reich reform' which had been developed during the era of presidential rule under Papen and Schleicher: a 'personal socialism' of inner dignity, a renewal of society on a Christian basis, and a combination of a people's movement with authoritarian leadership without free or equal elections.

For most of the conspirators, a return to the Weimar situation was completely unthinkable, if we leave aside a few personalities from the social democratic and trade union movements such as Julius Leber and Carlo Mierendorff, who in any case played only a marginal role in the movement. There was also, it is true, some element of economic liberalism present, with Goerdeler for instance. But the idea of a democratic future on Western lines was not to be found among the conspirators, or at least only the beginnings of such an idea were present. Western democracy had been discredited, even within parts of the labour movement.

New ideas that might shape the future were thus not a feature of the 20 July conspiracy. On the Left, too, the workers' movement had been destroyed in Nazi Germany and remained largely crippled, so that the development of new programmes took place almost exclusively in exile. In Moscow, the remnants of the KPD leadership were preparing for the establishment of a communist dictatorship after the victory of the Red Army. The foundation of the National Committee for a Free Germany (*Nationalkomitee Freies Deutschland*), which was formed of soldiers and officers of the Wehrmacht who had ended up in Soviet captivity, made people more strongly aware of the possibility of a communist alternative, quite apart from the propaganda warnings issued by Goebbels.

The exile groups in the SPD milieu, on the other hand, were mainly concentrated in the West, above all in Great Britain, Scandinavia and the USA, and they invested considerable effort into drawing lessons from the traumatic defeat of 1933. Unlike their party comrades who had remained in Germany, they were able to profit from the debates and social changes which were taking place in the democratic and pluralist societies of the host countries. The essential elements of their new thinking were rejection of any perspective of social revolution for post-Nazi Germany, sharp opposition to Stalinism and Soviet communism, and the conception of a social democratic people's party which would reach beyond the industrial working class and no longer have a class orientation. Over foreign policy, they differed: ideas of neutrality and of reliance on Western Europe and the USA were both put forward. Pluralist democracy and trade union unity, on the other hand, were largely uncontroversial objectives.[28]

The impulse towards a reshaping of Germany after the fall of Hitler, which would overcome the lines of conflict drawn in the Weimar years, therefore came from outside: from the victorious armies of the Allies, who brought with them their own political systems and concepts of social order, and from the German émigrés, who had gained new experiences and new insights while in exile. In the bunker atmosphere of besieged Germany, people's minds were concentrated on the war and on survival, and it was hard for them to develop ideas of how things ought to progress, as long as they were not sure whether they would progress at all.

The National Socialists, for their part, were expecting resistance from a different quarter entirely: from the millions of foreigners in the country. Every important decree issued on this subject had a preamble referring to the danger of a 'Bolshevik rising' among the foreigners, and after spring 1943 preventive military and police measures were taken in view of possible revolts by this group. In summer 1943, when the 20 July conspirators started to make plans for a takeover of power once Hitler had successfully been assassinated, they wanted to mobilise all military forces available in the Reich, which would be used to deprive the Nazi Party and the SS of their power. To that end, they produced a scenario which would allow troop movements and the appropriate logistical dispositions of the Reserve Army to take place without giving rise to suspicions on the part of the regime's leaders or the security police. The starting point of this was the assumption that there would be internal disturbances in Germany created by an uprising of the foreign workers and prisoners of war, who by then numbered roughly 6 million. The alleged precautions against eventual revolts by aliens, to which the conspirators gave the name 'Valkyrie', were so much in line with the expectations of the political and military leaders of the regime that the preparations for the planned *coup d'ëtat* could be organised in relative safety under this cover.[29]

Among the mass of the people, in contrast, there were no signs of unrest after 20 July, let alone any readiness to revolt. The security police's reports on the popular mood bear witness to the general sense of relief and joy that Hitler had survived the assassination attempt without suffering any serious wounds. 'Almost without exception, attachment to the Führer is now deeper and confidence in his leadership is now stronger', was the unanimous verdict from all regions of Germany. The action of the conspirators was also rejected by people who were not National Socialists, 'because they are convinced that only the Führer can control the situation, and his death would have led to chaos and civil war.'[30] The Führer myth had admittedly been damaged by military disasters and bombing raids, but it was still powerful.

## War in Germany

In December 1944, Hitler ordered his troops to begin a surprise offensive in the West against the armies of Britain and the USA. This heralded the final act of the European war. German formations did actually succeed for several days in overrunning the positions of the Western Allies. They pressed forward almost as far as Dinant, 120 kilometres west of the German border. The aim was to reach Antwerp quickly, cut off the Allied troops from their supply bases and, after the Western Allies had thus been decisively weakened, to concentrate forces on the Eastern Front and defeat the Red Army as well. But the Germans lost more than 90,000 men and an enormous quantity of military reserves in the Ardennes offensive.

Even so, it did delay the advance of the Western armies into Germany by roughly four weeks. This delay turned out to have fateful consequences. For the race between the Allies to win as much territory as possible within the area of the German Reich was intended to underpin their respective negotiating positions during the 'Big Three' discussions about the division of Germany which were scheduled to take place at Yalta on 4 February 1945. Owing to the Western offensive mounted by the Germans, the Soviet side were able to gain a big lead in the race to grab land.[31]

The Soviet winter offensive began on 12 January 1945. The 570,000 men on the German side were faced by 1.5 million Red Army men. In some sections of the Front, the ratio between German and Soviet strength was 1:20. The German leadership had no plausible strategy to oppose the advance of the Soviet armies onto German soil. Attempts to convert particular places into 'fortresses' and to hold them at any price only led to an increase in the number of casualties on the German side, while the Red Army simply swung round these fortified positions. Within two weeks, it had stormed forward 300 kilometres to the west. Warsaw was conquered on 17 January; on 21 January, the Soviets advanced into East Prussia, which was part of the Reich; and, by 29 January, they were outside Königsberg. When they reached the Oder, the Red Army units were held up for a few weeks. But they were able to establish a bridgehead over the river near Küstrin early in February.

During this period, on 8 February, the Western Allies also began their delayed onslaught on the Reich. They finally conquered Cologne on 6 March. The British army now turned north, while the Americans went to the east and the south. French troops under the supreme command of General de Gaulle attacked the south-west of the country, conquering Karlsruhe on 4 April, and they advanced as far as the Swiss border. American troops took Nuremberg on 20 April, and Munich ten days later. Here, a German resistance group had attempted to achieve a peaceful surrender, but in vain.

The final battle for Berlin began on 16 April, and it culminated in two weeks of house-to-house fighting, in the course of which more German civilians died than as a result of all the bombing raids on the city during the whole of the war. Hitler, who had withdrawn with a few faithful followers into the bunker of the Reichskanzlei, now only controlled a few units in the city area. He shot himself on 30 April, in order to avoid the fate of Mussolini, who had been executed two days earlier at Lake Como, following which his corpse had been publicly hanged in Milan. A week later the Wehrmacht capitulated.

In the final phase of the war, the violence which Germany had brought upon the countries of the European continent had turned against the German population itself to an extent never previously experienced. It was inflicted both by the institutions of the Nazi dictatorship and by the enemy troops who were now conquering the country piece by piece. The towns of Germany were attacked and devastated by fleets of Allied bombers until the very last moment. Dresden, which had been spared until then, experienced the heaviest conventional bombing raid of the war on 13 and 14 February. The British bomber squadrons no longer faced any German anti-aircraft defences. On the first night, they set the city on fire, and on the second night they dropped bombs to prevent the fires from being put out. The following morning, the American air force again attacked the city. Dresden was completely destroyed over an area five kilometres long and seven kilometres wide. Between 25,000 and 30,000 people died in the inferno. Most of them burned to death.[32]

In the east, the civilian population fell victim to the frightful thirst for revenge felt by the Soviet troops, who had marched for almost two years for more than 1,500 kilometres through areas of the Soviet Union which had first been occupied by the Wehrmacht and then largely destroyed when it retreated. Now, when they crossed the German border in East Prussia, they entered an undamaged and opulent land. As early as October 1944, when Soviet troops briefly overran the eastern corner of the region around Gumbinnen, they had shot twenty German civilians in Nemmersdorf, before they moved away from the place again. This crime, which was exploited on a grand scale by National Socialist propaganda, heightened the widespread fear of the Russians, and as early as autumn 1944 German civilians began to flee westwards. They did this secretly, as the rulers of Nazi Germany, in line with the strategy of a 'people's war', were not prepared to organise any evacuations.

When the Red Army finally entered German territory in January 1945, the population suffered a series of bloody excesses, involving plundering, pillaging and mass rape. Heinrich Graf von Einsiedel, a German officer who was a member of the National Committee for a Free Germany, had advanced into the country alongside units of the Red Army, and he described what he and other National Committee representatives observed: 'They had seen how the Russian soldiers burned down towns and villages; had watched them shoot prisoners and civilians, rape women and turn Army hospitals into death houses. . . . They had witnessed an orgy of extermination such as no civilised land could ever have experienced before.' It is hard to put a figure on the number of Germans who lost their lives as a result; 24,500 are known for certain to have died, but the total number of people murdered during these excesses was probably more than 90,000. The number of women who were raped in Berlin alone was around 100,000, and for the whole of Germany the total is estimated to have been up to one million.[33]

But it was not just reports of the outrages committed by Soviet soldiers or the years of anti-Bolshevik propaganda that caused anxiety to people who lived in the eastern parts of the country. As the SD reported, critical views were already being voiced after the news of the massacre in Nemmersdorf, to the effect that

> every thinking person seeing these sacrificial victims thinks immediately of the atrocities we have committed on enemy territory, indeed even in Germany. Have we not slaughtered Jews in their thousands? . . . By doing this we have shown our enemies what they are allowed to do to us if they are victorious.[34]

All over Europe, wherever the Red Army penetrated, hundreds of thousands of Germans fled into the Reich. They fled from Slovakia, Croatia, Yugoslavia and Romania, but above all, they fled from Germany's eastern regions. Between January and May 1945, more than 7 million Germans set out westwards from East and West Prussia, Danzig, Farther Pomerania, East Brandenburg and Silesia. There were terrible scenes: people froze to death, they were shelled by Allied low-flying aircraft, or they fell victim to Soviet troops if they were overtaken by them. In East Prussia the refugees tried to reach the ports so as to take ship for the West. In Danzig, hundreds of thousands of soldiers and refugees were surrounded, and they waited day after day to be embarked on board ship. There were 200,000 waiting in the small town of Pillau alone. The navy was able to evacuate a total of roughly 1.5 million people by sea; but German ships were torpedoed again and again by Soviet submarines. The cruise ship Wilhelm Gustloff, for instance, was sunk with the loss of 5,300 lives. Altogether, 20,000 refugees died owing to the sinking of evacuation vessels.

When the refugees arrived in the West, they often had neither accommodation nor provisions. A considerable number of those who had fled earlier, more than a million people, tried to return home in spring 1945. Their efforts were mostly in vain, because in the meantime the decisions taken at Teheran and Yalta had been confirmed and extended at the Potsdam Conference of the victorious Allies, held in July 1945. The Soviet Union insisted on shifting its boundary with Poland westwards to the line proposed but never implemented after the First World War. This removed an area of roughly 180,000 square kilometres from newly restored Poland. In compensation, it was decided that Poland would receive parts of East and West Prussia, Pomerania and Silesia, which covered some 100,000 square kilometres, and were inhabited almost exclusively by Germans. The victorious powers agreed that, just as the Polish population in the eastern part of the country, which had been added to the Soviet Union, would be sent westwards for 'resettlement', so would German populations 'or elements thereof, remaining in Poland, Czechoslovakia and Hungary' have to be transferred to Germany. It was added that 'any transfers that take place should be effected in an orderly and humane manner.'[35]

In practice, an 'orderly and humane' transfer was out of the question. At the Potsdam Conference the 'Big Three' had decided that systematic 'resettlement' of the Germans would not begin until November, but in fact the new administrations of Poland and Czechoslovakia started to seize and expel the German inhabitants as quickly as they could immediately after coming into office.

The expulsions were often conducted with an extraordinary brutality to which the recollections of many of the victims bear witness:

> Without regard for the exhaustion of the older people after a sleepless night, we were driven further and further along the highway. We were hardly even allowed a short meal break. Shots were always fired at us from behind, accompanied with cries of 'Keep moving, you German pigs!' At midday, in baking heat, we arrived at Raigern. Here our rucksacks were again searched, and everything of the slightest usefulness was taken away. After that it was on again towards Pohrlitz. Many children and sick people were unable to go any further, but with kicks and blows from rifle butts they were forced to go on until they collapsed in the ditches out of sheer exhaustion. Even after that no mercy was given. . . . We suffered cruelty after cruelty. Our ranks became ever thinner. Despite the burning heat we were not even allowed to refresh ourselves with water. Mothers were not even allowed to give suck to their babies. That is the reason why so many infants died during the journey.[36]

In Czechoslovakia, the Germans now had a taste of the forms of discrimination and repression the German occupiers had inflicted on the local population for years. They had to wear a yellow armband with the letter N (standing for 'Němec', or 'German'), the food rations they were given were the same as those they had previously allotted to the Jews. The manner of their expulsion also reinforced this parallel: the Germans had to appear within a few hours at the station, with no more luggage than they themselves could carry, and they were transported to the west in goods wagons—though in this case towards freedom rather than death.

In this way, then, an exodus of Germans started, which lasted for months, and sometimes for years. Roughly 12.5 million refugees and expellees flooded into the newly established occupation zones of Germany. The number of those who lost their lives is hard to ascertain, and it was immediately a subject of political dispute. Detailed evidence can be produced for the death of 500,000 Germans who fled from, or were driven out of, the countries of Central and South-East Europe, while the fate of a further 1.5 million people is uncertain. This number includes the 600,000 German civilians who were deported to the Soviet Union as forced labourers. Almost nothing is known of their fate; it is likely that about half of them died in captivity.

The political rationale of the expulsions went back to the discussions at the Paris peace negotiations after the First World War, when, as described earlier, the creation of new, ethnically homogeneous nation-states on the Western European pattern had turned more than 25 million people in Europe into 'minorities'. The population exchange between Greece and Turkey, by which more than 2 million people were driven out and resettled, indicated a new way of solving the minority problem: the forcible expulsion of national minorities on a mass scale to create ethnic homogeneity. With his policy of 'ethnic cleansing', Hitler adopted this principle and radicalised it in the extreme. He began by expelling Poles and bringing in ethnic German settlers, and continued by deporting the European Jews, for whom there were finally no more settlement areas available.

The notion that ethnic separation and extensive population exchanges could end the conflicts between ethnic groups also dominated the post-1945 discussions of the Allies about the impending expulsion of the Germans from East Central Europe. President Roosevelt, for instance, asserted that 'the Prussians will be removed from East Prussia in the same manner as the Greeks were removed from Turkey after the last war'. The British Labour politician Clement Attlee was of the opinion that the Germans were 'not entitled to appeal on the basis of the moral laws that they have disregarded'. The shifting of population, he continued, 'may be very, very painful, but it may be far better than a long drawn out sore of populations under peoples whom they hate'.[37]

The expulsion of the Germans and the separation of the eastern regions from Germany were in fact intended first and foremost as acts of moral and material retribution for the endless series of German crimes over the previous six years. But there is no doubt that these motives were also connected with the traditional conflicts between rival nationalisms in Central Europe, which dated back much earlier than 1939 or 1914. This applied in particular to the question of the existence or non-existence of a Polish state between Russia and Prussia, or later Germany. And the idea of removing a lasting source of discord by expelling the Germans from East Central Europe and thereby creating ethnically stable and homogeneous states certainly seemed to be an obvious approach, seen from the perspective of the time. But the hundreds of thousands, perhaps millions, of deaths, which the expulsion of the Germans cost, mainly after hostilities had ended, could not be justified in this way.

## The End

In line with the idea of a 'people's war', improvised formations of both the young and the old were established in great haste in September 1944, by the Nazi Party, not by the Wehrmacht. These people were badly armed, and almost untrained, and most of them had no uniforms. They were known as the *Volkssturm* (people's militia), and they were now thrown into action against the troops of the Allies. While in the west these units often dissolved at their first contact with the enemy, in the east they fought fiercely against the Red Army, in some cases in combination with the Hitler Youth—and with correspondingly high casualties. A total of 3.2 million German soldiers died in battle during the war, but more than half of that number died in the final year of the war, and more than 800,000 died just in the period between January and May 1945.[38]

The collapse of the Führer state was accompanied by the disintegration of the bureaucratic hierarchy and the military command structure. The resulting decentralisation of decision-making power led to a further increase in arbitrary actions. Any soldier in the Wehrmacht or the *Volkssturm* who tried to avoid fighting was cruelly punished. In the final months and weeks of the war, itinerant courts martial were established. These ordered public hangings for soldiers suspected of desertion without taking much time to consider the evidence.[39] The experience of violence became ubiquitous, and, more importantly, the individual found it almost impossible to predict when and where it would occur. This was true both for soldiers and civilians, and it was no longer restricted to those 'alien to the community' or political opponents, as it had been until a few months previously. Moreover, there was a dramatic increase in the number of people who thought they were entitled to use terror to force the population to carry on to the bitter end.

At the beginning of April 1945, Himmler, who had in the meantime become the commander of the Reserve Army, ordered that all male persons found in a house displaying the white flag should be shot. This meant that members of the Wehrmacht were now authorised to kill German civilians without consulting their superior officers. Party functionaries, municipal officials and finally even air-raid wardens now acted as accusers or executioners, actuated by a mixture of 'the desire to settle scores, intoxication with their own power and aggressive desperation', as the historian Klaus-Dietmar Henke has put it. Civilians who called for their locality to capitulate when foreign troops drew near, or even people who simply expressed doubt about Germany's final victory, were hanged, with cardboard signs around their necks bearing the words: 'Condemned to death for cowardice.'[40]

But the National Socialists no longer exercised unlimited power everywhere. In the town of Harburg, which was part of Hamburg, a man criticised a uniformed party official in public after a severe bombing raid: 'You brown party dogs gobble up everything for yourselves, you have your own safe bunkers where nothing can happen to you.' The man was warned, but nothing happened to him. The authorities had lost all respect here, and the bitterness of the people was so great that they no longer worried about the possible consequences of their remarks.[41] On 23 April 1945 in Regensburg, on the other hand, when there were protests against the planned evacuation of the town, the district leader of the NSDAP ordered a number of people to be arrested, and three to be shot, including the cathedral dean. Here, the representatives of the party and the Wehrmacht still had the ability to take action, and they exerted their untrammelled power literally until the last second of the war. Then they put on civilian clothing and disappeared from view. Four days later, the Americans occupied the town.[42]

The foreign workers were particularly affected by this reign of terror during the final weeks of the war. Right from the start of the conflict, the authorities had regarded the millions of 'alien workers' as a danger to Germany's security, but in the last phase of the war fear of this group grew into a veritable psychosis. The living conditions of foreigners became worse and worse, particularly those who lived in industrial cities endangered by aerial bombardment. After bombing raids, which severely affected the camps of foreign workers, mostly located close to the factories, the authorities made efforts to assist victims who were German, but as a rule they did nothing for the foreigners. This meant a sharp increase in the number of foreign workers wandering through the cities without accommodation or food. These people now tried somehow to ride out the storm, and make their way towards the rural areas, which were not so dangerous. In the cities, this led to the emergence of a mixture of indigence, self-help, theft of food supplies and the formation of illegal networks. The Gestapo was no longer able to keep control. At the beginning of November 1944, the RSHA allowed subordinate officials to carry out executions of foreigners without consultation, As a result, there was a rapid increase in measures of persecution, participated in not just by the police but by soldiers, party officials and ordinary 'national comrades'. Over a number of weeks after February 1945, some cities witnessed a veritable war waged by the Gestapo against 'gangs of foreigners', as in Cologne for instance, or in the Ruhr area, where tens of thousands of foreigners were trying to escape from encirclement and flee to the east.

The months of March and April 1945 saw massacres of foreigners everywhere in Germany. The final official act carried by members of the Gestapo or the regular police force before they threw their uniforms away was often the shooting of groups of foreigners who were awaiting the arrival of the Allies at the edge of town, in woodland or among the ruins of buildings. Various motives were involved here. Justification was found in real or assumed acts of plunder or sabotage, in the 'protection of the population' against the vengeful fury expected of foreign workers, particularly Soviet workers, after the arrival of the Allied troops, and 'revenge' for the bombardment of German towns; but often it reflected an apocalyptic mentality: if we are doomed to be defeated, we will at least kill as many of our enemies as we can beforehand, even if they are defenceless *Ostarbeiter*. Thus, the British, American and Soviet troops found fresh mass graves all over Germany, in which sometimes hundreds of foreign workers lay buried, slaughtered in the closing minutes of the war. The precise number of forced labourers murdered in these final massacres is unknown, but it is estimated to have been between 10,000 and 30,000.[43]

But it was concentration camp inmates who suffered the most dreadful fate. Towards the end of the war, the SS camp universe increased tremendously in size. In January 1945, there were more than 700,000 officially registered inmates. It is difficult to judge exactly how many of these people were Jews, but estimates put the number at 250,000. In summer 1944, the German authorities had changed their policy, deciding to spare some Jews temporarily, and to transport them into the Reich so that they could be put to work in the armaments industry. This measure also affected 100,000 of the Hungarian Jews who had been taken to Auschwitz. Most of the prisoners were distributed over more than 600 satellite camps attached to the main ones. Roughly 150,000 prisoners were living in Auschwitz and its satellite camps in autumn 1944, most of them Jews, but there were also non-Jewish Russians and Poles.

Himmler decreed in June 1944 that the most exposed camps should be cleared when the enemy approached the area, and the inmates transferred to concentration camps in the rear. If a camp was in danger of falling into the hands of the enemy and evacuation no longer seemed possible, the inmates were to be killed.[44] With the advance of the Red Army in the east and the entry of the armies of the Western Allies into West and South Germany, this command was put into effect. This mainly happened in a great hurry and with an unprecedented amount of organisational chaos. The power of command was transferred to lower ranks in the SS, and these people were now faced with the task of bringing tens of thousands of prisoners into the heart of the Reich, usually on foot. This had to be done as quickly as possible to prevent them from falling into the hands of the enemy. In some cases, prisoners who were sick and incapable of walking were left behind while still alive, but mostly they were killed. Any prisoner who could not keep moving on these marches of misery, which lasted for days and sometimes weeks, was either shot or beaten to death. More than half of the evacuated prisoners lost their lives on these journeys, either through murder or through exhaustion and sickness.

The SS had set up a concentration camp in the town of Bergen-Belsen, in Lower Saxony. Now most of the survivors from the concentration camp evacuations were brought there. Typhus spread rapidly in the overcrowded camp, and more than 35,000 inmates died in Bergen-Belsen during the last four and a half months of the war. Thousands of evacuated camp inmates were also transferred to the Thuringian camp of Dora-Mittelbau in the final weeks of the war. This camp was an inferno of brutality and death. On arrival, the survivors were crammed into the galleries of the tunnel built for the production of V2 rockets. There was neither food nor accommodation available. Finally, the inmates who were still alive were evacuated from there and transported to Bergen-Belsen, where most of them died of typhus. A smaller group of inmates from Dora were evacuated towards the town of Gardelegen. There the local Nazi Party district leader declared that the prisoners were a danger to the German population. With the help of members of the Wehrmacht and the Reich Labour Service, he separated out a group of roughly 1,000 prisoners and placed them in a barn. The barn was then set alight and the prisoners burned to death.

Approximately 300,000 of the over 700,000 inmates of concentration camps registered in January 1945 lost their lives. Many were slaughtered by the camp guards when the liberators were only a few kilometres from the gates. The surviving prisoners were not safe until the arrival of Allied troops, and thus the American, Russian and British soldiers were confronted with the frightful sight of heaps of corpses and sick and emaciated people. The pictures that were taken soon went around the world and provided a sense of the reality of National Socialist rule. It was, however, a long time after liberation before many former prisoners were able to accustom themselves to living in freedom, as Primo Levi wrote (he himself had been imprisoned in Auschwitz):

> Liberty. The breach in the barbed wire gave us a concrete image of it. To anyone who stopped to think, it signified no more Germans, no more selections, no work, no blows, no roll-calls, and perhaps, later, the return. But we had to make an effort to convince ourselves of it, and no one had time to enjoy the thought. All around lay destruction and death.[45]

## After the Third Reich

The Third Reich set out to create a radical alternative to the bourgeois liberal society which was regarded in almost the whole of Europe as having failed after the world war and the world economic crisis. This view was held more strongly in Germany than elsewhere, firstly because modern industrial society had triumphed particularly quickly and decisively there, and secondly because defeat in the First World War had led to an extreme intensification of national and social antagonisms.

Yet National Socialism had not come to power at the end of the Weimar Republic through elections, but through the concentrated efforts of a section of the traditional elite, which had allied itself with a collective movement of militant, radical nationalists in order to defend its power and influence against the democratic and social republic. That alliance had allowed the elites to hold onto power at the price of their own integration into the National Socialist system. The result, however, was that the elites became dependent on the National Socialist regime, rather than the reverse. In this context, the terror of the early years of Nazi rule fulfilled a function, because it destroyed the power bases of political opponents, eliminated the political structures of the Weimar Republic and intimidated potential dissidents.

The objective of creating a unified, single will was accomplished in the new state by the leadership of the Führer, and social unity was secured through the '*Volksgemeinschaft*' concept. The intention was to restore national greatness by rearming and conducting a war of revenge. The state led by Hitler replaced the division of powers and the balancing and compromising of interests with a single will, exerted hierarchically, from the top down. The civilian principles of pluralism and compromise were replaced by the military principles of command and obedience, which seemed to accord better with the challenges of modern industrial society than the complicated balancing of interests and evaluation of possible outcomes characteristic of liberal democracy.

The idea of *Volksgemeinschaft* involved the repudiation of modern society, with its social and religious antagonisms, the rejection of a state run by political parties, and a critique of modern culture, but it also offered the vision of a harmonious national community. This was an idea which had been widely shared by people of many political persuasions since the turn of the century, and it was not a specifically German phenomenon. By the 1930s, it was possible to speak of a hegemony of the idea of national communities. Over almost the whole of Europe in the years before and after the First World War, this notion was used to counter the class struggle politically and ideologically. The National Socialists responded to the desire for a '*Volksgemeinschaft*' by espousing equality, solicitude for the poor and the extension of the benefits of the welfare state, just like other contemporary movements, but in their case the approach was founded on racial exclusion and political oppression. The organisation of society according to ethnic and racial criteria rather than according to social hierarchy meant that the great mass of privileged '*Volksgenossen*' was set against the small group of people to whom responsibility for the problems of modernity was attributed, and who therefore had to be excluded: namely, people who were 'alien to the community' ('*Gemeinschaftsfremde*'), disabled, or, in particular, Jewish.

The paramount goal of the National Socialists, apart from establishing a hierarchical community on a racial basis, was to restore national greatness by waging a war of revenge. Here, Hitler's objectives differed from those of his conservative nationalist alliance partners because his concern to secure 'living space' in the East and establish a continental empire was alien to their way of thinking. The rapid and complete reorientation of economic and financial policy towards war preparations meant that the German economy quickly recovered its strength, but it also led resources to become hopelessly overstretched, and this turned the war of conquest from an option into a necessity. The remarkable success of Germany's policy of treaty revision was founded on the unlimited readiness of the dictator to take risks, and it was therefore soon possible to foresee that this situation would come to an end. But Hitler's successes gave the regime an enormous reputation among the population, and along with economic prosperity, they provided the foundation for the spread of the Führer myth.

For the Germans, the most important experience of the Nazi period proved to be the arrival of economic stability, after twenty-five years of uninterrupted crisis. It was the National Socialist 'economic miracle' and the associated improvement of living conditions as much as the cessation of street-fighting that helped to bind large sections of the population to the regime. Even people who continued to oppose Hitler and knew how he had achieved his successes were able to profit from the prosperity and stability brought by the Nazis. Nothing played a greater role in consolidating political loyalty towards the National Socialists than the economic stabilisation of the country.

This feeling was also bound up with the social advancement enjoyed by many during the war. It was members of the Wehrmacht and the party apparatus who benefited most from this, but leadership positions were also available on a smaller scale, such as in the organisations run by the Hitler Youth. The war thus accelerated the replacement of one generation by another, but it also gave rise to experiences of social and cultural alienation. Military service, wartime captivity, evacuation and expulsion cut individuals loose from the social, political, religious and, to some degree, regional allegiances which had previously held them in a tight grip, and despite the collective character of these experiences people suffered them predominantly as isolated individuals.

When the war began, the socially egalitarian implications of the *Volksgemeinschaft* receded into the background. On the contrary, Nazi society came to be built overwhelmingly on favouritism and corruption. With the destruction of all formal structures, Germany turned into an El Dorado of arbitrary actions and the illegitimate pursuit of personal advantage. These tendencies increasingly determined the course of people's lives, and they reached their peak in the boundless tyranny exercised by the Germans in the occupied eastern regions. The idea of the '*Volksgemeinschaft*' owed its continuing vitality not to a sense of equality but to an experience of favourable treatment which resulted from a racially grounded inequality.

The quintessential characteristic of the Nazi state was the rule of force, and the coming of the war extinguished everything that might have inhibited this. At the same time, the Nazi regime was in no position, either politically or ideologically, to construct a realistic vision of a Europe unified under its aegis, although there were elements in the occupied countries which were ready to make terms with the Nazis. Nazi terror was too brutal, and Nazi economic exploitation was too unlimited, for this to happen. The murder of tens of thousands of disabled people in Germany was an early and almost public revelation of the readiness of the regime to commit mass murder. The resettlement policy in Poland, the persecution of the Jews, the colonialist policy of annihilation and starvation in the Soviet Union, and finally the decision to set in motion a genocide of all the Jews of Europe, mark out the stations of a murderous policy the dimensions of which exceeded all previous atrocities. In this context, a kind of complicity developed between the Nazi leaders and sections of the German population, who were unable right to the very end to free themselves from this connection. The process finally ended in an inferno of violence which eventually rebounded upon the German people as well.

The scale of destruction, the number of people murdered, killed in battle, mutilated and wounded, the number of homeless people, refugees and orphans at the end of the war: all this was without historical precedent. Large parts of

Europe had been devastated from the Atlantic Ocean to the Crimean Peninsula. The fury of the Allied bombing campaigns, the collapse of the fronts and the violence of the final months of the war now disabused the Germans themselves of any illusions about its outcome.

Nothing more was left of the National Socialist alternative to the system of liberal capitalism. A German state no longer existed, and the Germans now faced a completely uncertain future.

# PART FOUR

# 1945–73

# 11
# Post-War

## Zero Hour

The war had been total; and so was the defeat. The Allies now put into effect the provisions they had agreed to impose in 1943: unconditional capitulation of the Wehrmacht, all soldiers in German uniform to be disarmed and taken prisoner, the occupation of the whole of Germany and its division into occupation zones, a complete takeover of power by Allied troops. The Germans should feel that they had lost the war. Legends or doubts about defeat such as had arisen after 1918 should not be able to emerge again.

In many places, the transfer of power took place within a few hours, or even minutes. This was a unique and dangerous moment. Until the morning of the day in question, officers of the Wehrmacht and the SS were still in command, members of the Hitler Youth were still moving anti-tank weapons into position and party officials were still threatening to kill anyone who wanted to surrender. At midday, the Nazi officers all suddenly disappeared. This was succeeded by a power vacuum (dubbed 'no man's time') which lasted a few hours and was marked by a tense and anxious silence. Then the first foreign soldiers entered the town, followed soon by more and more of them. They moved quickly: they ordered exits to be blocked, arrested any Nazis they could get hold of, appointed politically uncontaminated persons to head the local administration, and put up posters announcing to the Germans what they must and must not do. Among the Germans there was a reversal of roles: people previously ostracised and persecuted now stepped forward, taking over important and responsible posts. The previous holders of power were either taken into custody or went into hiding.

Never before in modern German history had there been a more decisive, or a more significant, turning point than this moment. Despite all the elements of continuity and restoration which made themselves felt sooner or later, a sharper break was hardly imaginable, whether in politics, society, culture or law. To that extent, the concept of the 'zero hour' (*Stunde Null*), which was already being applied at the time, had its justification.[1]

Just a few hours before, the people of Germany were still divided into different social groups, as they had been throughout the previous twelve years.

They were slotted into a hierarchy of roles from anti-aircraft artillery assistant to officer in the SS, or from RAD man to NSDAP Local Group Leader, and uniforms of all kinds had made these distinctions visible to everyone. Then, suddenly, everyone appeared to be equal. Party uniforms were nowhere to be seen. Pictures of Hitler disappeared. Flags were burned, uniforms were hidden, documents were destroyed, medals were buried. A Hamburg schoolgirl noted in her diary on the morning of 2 May 1945:

> On the way to Borgweg Station I looked around to see whether anyone still had a party badge on. Wherever I looked I couldn't see any. It was strange, no-one wept or even looked sad, although the beloved, honoured Führer, whom the total idiots almost regarded as a god, was no longer alive and could no longer wield the knout.[2]

The active agents now became passive instruments, subjected to the orders of the Allies. But this inversion didn't simply appear to efface the differences between the formerly powerful and the formerly powerless or between the victims and the perpetrators. It also implied a process of impoverishment in a wrecked environment which was similar for everyone. The population appeared to be united and equal in misfortune: cold, hungry and under foreign rule. In many respects, this picture was accurate: astonishment, disorientation, despair, relief and anxiety for the future mingled together to produce a widespread feeling of shock and exhaustion. As a young Berliner noted in his diary in spring 1945:

> Tens of thousands, covered in dust and dirt, shovel the rubble, and dig in the ruins. In long human chains they throw bricks and masonry to each other, items which are then tossed into the vaults of the department stores and the office buildings. The barricades, which were piled up weeks earlier by other hands, are now torn down. Berlin is clearing itself up. These men and women, encrusted with a flour-like dust, have no name, no rank and no meaning.[3]

And here is how Ursula von Kardorff described her impressions of the railway station in Halle shortly after the end of the war: 'Horrifying images. Piles of rubble, among which there wander beings who no longer appear to belong to this world. Returning soldiers in torn, padded uniforms, covered in ulcers, creeping along on home-made crutches. Living corpses.'[4] That is the usual picture of the German people immediately after the war, united in hardship and deprivation. It is highly memorable, and it is accurate for many people.

But not for everyone. 'How the average German of today lives in the occupied areas depends very much on where he lives', reported an American intelligence officer in April 1945 after an inspection tour of the western part of the

Rhineland. In the cities there was destruction and misery, but the rural population were much better off. And in the middle-class suburbs and the spa towns, wealthy Germans continued to live unscathed by all these events. There the shelves of the shops were fully stocked, people were well clothed, and they seemed 'to radiate health and wealth and not to have come into contact with the horrors of the war.'[5]

Already during the war years, noticeable social shifts had been apparent, based on the difference between those who had suffered severely from the effects of the war and those who had not. These tendencies continued and were intensified after 1945. The lives of people bombed out of their homes in the cities, of the refugees who had left the eastern regions and moved westwards, of those who returned home from evacuation or captivity, of the foreign prisoners of war and the 'alien workers', and of the liberated concentration camp inmates and the surviving Jews differed fundamentally from the lives of people who had not suffered those experiences. It was soon apparent that the events of the war had accentuated traditional social differences, rather than abolishing them.

According to surveys made by the American secret service, there were above all three areas which caused the Germans the greatest concern in the years between the end of the war and the 1948 currency reform: uncertainty as to the fate of their relatives, the destruction of their homes and workplaces, and hunger, along with the rise of the black market.

During the war, 18 million soldiers had been conscripted into the Wehrmacht. By the end, more than a third of them were dead or missing, and more than 10 million had become prisoners of war. Owing to the chaotic situation during the final years of the war and the early post-war period, it was often impossible for months, or even years, to find out anything about their whereabouts. Moreover, for a long time it was difficult to obtain reliable information about the fate of the 12 million Germans who had fled or been expelled from the eastern regions. Roughly 2 million of them were dead or missing, but often it was not until years afterwards that their identities could be established. There was even less information available about the 600,000 civilians who had been taken to the Soviet Union along with roughly 2.1 million prisoners of war.

Within the area of the Reich, roughly 8 million Germans from towns and cities endangered by bombing had been evacuated to the countryside and rehoused. They were mostly children, women and old people, but there were also 'factory transfers' in which all those who worked in industrial enterprises of importance to the war effort were moved. To return to the ruined towns was at first impossible, and even later on it was extremely difficult, so that a long time often went by before the evacuees could return home. In April 1947, two years after the end of the war, 3 million people were still classified as 'evacuees'.[6] Not until the early 1950s did this compulsorily mobilised society recover a degree of stability, and in many families worries over missing relatives lasted even longer.

At the end of the war there were between 8 and 10 million foreign prisoners of war, forced labourers and concentration camp inmates on German soil. After the liberation, the lives of these people, now described as 'displaced persons' (DPs), changed rapidly. Many of the civilians and soldiers of Western European origin were 'repatriated' very quickly, either by the Allied occupation forces or by their own efforts. DPs who came from Eastern Europe were in a much more difficult situation. Former forced labourers carried out widespread acts of revenge and looting after the liberation. This caused anxiety and terror to the Germans, but it also disturbed the Allied authorities. At first, many Poles remained in Germany, because they did not want to return to a homeland which was now under communist rule, and they were waiting for a passage overseas.

Many of the prisoners of war and civilians from the Soviet Union were also scared of repatriation. This applied particularly to the soldiers of the Vlasov Army, who had fought on the German side, and were likely to face a death sentence if they returned home. But the Soviet authorities also suspected all the civilian forced labourers and the prisoners of war of collaboration, simply because, in Stalinist eyes, their very presence in the enemy camp had compromised them. Nevertheless, the Western Allies had agreed at Yalta to the Soviet Union's demand for the return of all its citizens, and so the DPs from the USSR were repatriated even against their will. In fact, many of them when they returned were fated to suffer years of discrimination, which lasted until the final years of the Soviet Union, assuming that they managed to survive their 1945–6 sojourn in the 'filtration camps' run by the Soviet secret police, the NKVD. In August 1945, there were 2 million DPs in the three Western occupation zones of Germany, and at the end of 1948 there were still 438,000.[7]

The Jewish DPs, who had survived the Holocaust and the death marches and now lived in reception centres in Germany, were in a particularly difficult situation. At the end of the war, there were roughly 60,000 Jews in the Western zones, but by the end of 1946 a further 100,000 had arrived from Eastern Europe, mainly from Poland. They were, it is true, given medical treatment and material assistance by the Allies, but the future fate of most of them, particularly the old, was shrouded in uncertainty. Many remained in the living quarters or the camps to which they had been assigned for months and even years. There they waited for the opportunity to emigrate to Palestine or the USA, or to return to their homes in Poland, Hungary and elsewhere. Many of them, however, were completely traumatised and for a long time in no condition to make any decisions about their future life. In spring 1947, there were still roughly 70,000 Jewish DPs in Germany.[8]

If one takes all these groups together, by the start of the post-war era 30 million Germans and 10 million non-Germans had been 'uprooted', in other words, they were not in their original homes. This was more than half of the 75 million inhabitants of the four occupation zones. Their geographical distribution was very uneven, however. Because of the destruction of the towns, the flow of refugees was redirected to rural areas. In Mecklenburg-Vorpommern and Schleswig-Holstein, the 'uprooted' constituted roughly 50 per cent of the population, while the proportion in Hamburg and Bremen was only 7 per cent, and in Berlin it was 2 per cent, although in the case of Berlin the count did not include non-Germans.[9]

The influx of refugees and expellees from the East greatly increased the population of Germany's four zones. The overall increase was 10 per cent, but in the Western zones it was more than 20 per cent. This placed an additional burden on accommodation and the necessities of life, which were already in short supply. One hundred and thirty German towns had been targeted by bombing raids during the war. Almost 30 per cent of the dwellings in the four occupation zones had been destroyed. The towns of the Ruhr area, the Rhineland, and the North German coast as well as the industrial centres of South and Central Germany had suffered particularly badly. The housing situation was catastrophic there, and that is how it remained for a long time, especially for the approximately 1.5 million people who lived in the emergency shelters which shaped the face of urban Germany right into the 1950s. The country was crippled by the destruction of transport links and the general infrastructure. The railway network had been in large part destroyed, and the same was true of water pipes, power supply cables, and telephone lines.

Industrial installations, in contrast, were much less damaged than their external appearance indicated. It is true that some factories were completely wrecked, but many other factories could be brought back into operation relatively quickly. The IG-Farben Works in Hoechst, for example, and most of the coalmines in the Ruhr area, were reported by American economic officials to have suffered no damage. The management of the Krupp Works in Essen told the Americans that: 'steel production on the Ruhr could be raised within four months to two thirds, or even three quarters, of the wartime level, if coal, transport and a workforce were made available.' According to the surveys made by the Americans, the bombing raids had not even destroyed 10 per cent of Germany's machine tools. There was enormous potential here, but for the moment it was impossible to make use of it.[10]

In thc first days and weeks after the end of the war, the food situation was still relatively good, because the German authorities' warehouses were full, and many Germans had made provision for the uncertain situation that would follow the end of the war. Within a few weeks, however, the situation altered dramatically. For one thing, the delivery of foodstuffs from the parts of Europe formerly occupied by the Wehrmacht had now come to an end. More important, though, was the loss of roughly a quarter of the country's agricultural land owing to the cession to Poland and the Soviet Union of territory in eastern Germany. In addition to this, the first two harvests of the post-war years were inferior to those of previous years, and even after the repatriation of the DPs there were 10 per cent more people in the four occupation zones than there had been in 1939. Germany's agricultural production now accounted for only a third to a half of its average food requirements, and the supply shortfall was correspondingly serious.

All the Allied military authorities therefore retained control of foodstuffs and other scarce commodities, as well as keeping the rationing system imposed by the Nazis. 'Calories' and 'vitamins' became words familiar to everyone. Even so, until 1948 it proved impossible to feed the population continuously at the minimum required level, and in the winter of 1946–7 much of the population in all four zones went hungry. Children and young people were most seriously affected by this. Many of them grew up without parents or in broken relationships. They were only entitled to receive 1,500 calories a day, and so the number who fell ill rose sharply.

The occupying powers therefore had to bring in additional food supplies from their own reserves. For the British, French and Soviet military authorities this constituted an enormous burden, which was not easy to explain to their own people. Without such relief efforts as the American CARE packages or the 'Soli Packages' of 'People's Solidarity' in the East, the German nutritional balance would have been even worse.[11]

Just as during the war years, the combination of price control, shortage of goods and increased demand led inevitably to the spread of a second economy based on the black market, which was further reinforced by the decline of the German Reichsmark, which lost its purchasing power. It was increasingly replaced by other standards of value, such as foreign currency, or the new currency substitute, cigarettes. The use of the latter soon spread almost like an epidemic. The black market grew rapidly, and in 1946–7 it accounted for about 15 per cent of total commodity circulation, though the proportion was even higher for articles of daily use which were in particularly short supply. Bombed out families, refugees and DPs, who possessed absolutely nothing, were forced to rely on the black market to procure what they urgently needed. Almost everything was available on the black market, not least because large quantities of goods from the stocks held by the Allied armies came onto it illegally, while many vital items could not be obtained in exchange for German currency, or only in inadequate amounts. The managers of firms tried to acquire additional food supplies for their employees. Works Councils also became involved in the 'grey market'. In many firms, the workers therefore demanded the payment of part of their wages in kind, and this inflated the black market yet further. Town-dwellers began to make regular trips into the surrounding countryside, where they sought to exchange jewellery or household goods with the farmers for food. This brought many of the latter a degree of prosperity, and it generated an equal amount of envy and resentment.

Poverty, shortages and the black market altered moral attitudes. Offences caused by hunger increased. The level of criminality rose. In Berlin, there was a tenfold increase in the number of thefts, and also robberies and gang attacks took place more frequently. There was a decline in moral values which, however, was only a continuation of what had been kept secret from those in power during the war but was already a widespread phenomenon all over the country. The farmers, the retail traders and anyone who had anything at all to exchange profited from the black market. As in the war, the black market increased social inequality, often to an extreme degree. Those who gained were the efficient and the sly, the astute and the unscrupulous, the people with connections to the occupying power—in short, all those who were best able to cope with the circumstances of the market, with its rapid price fluctuations and changing requirements. This was a way of 'getting in training for the market' which at least in the West could also be understood as a preparation for capitalist enterprise. That was one side of this development. The other side was that the black market was also a paradise for racketeers and fraudsters, and this experience also had more long-term effects. Ten years after the end of the war, election posters could be seen in West Germany with the spectre of the black market prominently displayed.[12]

For most Germans, the first two years of the post-war era were dominated by concern for their own existence and survival. Help and solidarity were not to be expected. At most, support and protection were offered by the individual's own family. Politics was an entirely subordinate matter. 'All over Germany there is apathy, weariness and a feeling of helplessness, and the Germans are more concerned with the problems of daily life than with politics', wrote American intelligence officials.[13] But the concentration on survival also made it possible to forget and repress the past. The Nazi period had only just ended, but it already seemed to have receded into the far distance. 'Newspapers that are only a few weeks old appear strangely unreal, and they make one shudder' wrote a Berlin actress in her diary as early as 4 May 1945.[14]

What the Germans did not see was that their situation in post-war Europe was not exceptional. In practically the whole of Eastern Europe, people went hungry, particularly in the western areas of the Soviet Union, where the destruction had been complete, in parts of Poland, in the Balkans and in Greece, where the German withdrawal had been followed by a civil war. Food rationing was also a post-war phenomenon common to all European countries, and in fact it lasted longer and was more extensive in victorious Great Britain than in West Germany. Even so, the depressing and often desperate situation of the Germans was increasingly seen by occupying soldiers and foreign observers as something exceptional, as a portent, because the sight of these bombed-out, starving and freezing masses differed so much from the image of the fanatical Hitlerite German which had terrified the world for six years. 'It was simply impossible to harbour any feelings of enmity towards these unhappy creatures', wrote an officer of the British occupation about his impression of Berlin in 1946.[15]

## The Hour of the Allies

Cooperation in war and victory painstakingly achieved had created a firmer bond between the three allied powers, the USA, Great Britain and the Soviet Union than might have been expected, given the difference in social systems. Wartime cooperation also offered the basis for the considerable degree of consensus over post-war planning which marked the meetings of the heads of government and the foreign ministers until 1945. The unconditional surrender of Nazi Germany, the complete occupation of the country, its demilitarisation, the destruction of its war potential and the punishment of the guilty: all these aims were as uncontroversial among the three Great Powers as was the conviction that Germany would have to pay compensation for the immeasurable damage it had done. The most important steps in the political field after the end of the war were also taken by mutual agreement. This applied to the direct takeover of government in the whole of Germany by the Allies, the division of the country into four occupation zones under the orders of the respective supreme commanders of each zone, the establishment of a joint supreme governing body, the Allied Control Council, and the division of Berlin into four occupation sectors. It was intended that Germany would remain subject to Allied rule for a long period, and would have no means of exerting direct political influence. As a whole, the German policy of the Allies at the end of the war was not without its tensions, certainly, but the sense of consensus prevailed at first, while disagreements only gradually became more significant.[16]

From the outset, the question of Germany's future was bound up with the deliberations over the setting up of a new system of international cooperation. This endeavour was shaped above all by the view put forward emphatically by the USA and President Roosevelt that after two devastating world wars, a new structure must finally be established so as to make it possible to achieve the grand, utopian goals of humanity, namely peace, economic progress, social justice and the worldwide abolition of hunger and disease. The founding of the United Nations was therefore not just an attempt to repeat in a better way what Wilson had started, and failed to achieve, with the League of Nations. It was more than this. The attempt to establish an 'international community' independent of all interest-related power politics was also guided by a future-oriented idealism. Now, it was thought, after the most frightful war ever fought, the occasion and the opportunity were present to establish the prerequisites for a lasting peace in which justice would prevail.[17]

The model and the point of departure for this was the wartime cooperation between the Allied Great Powers, joined by the end of the war by almost half the nations on earth, against Nazi Germany, which was seen as the incarnation of evil. This view of the conflict had the effect of creating unity and setting a standard. There was also the associated question of how Germany could be prevented in future from posing a danger to its neighbours and to world peace. One proposal, repeatedly modified, was for the country to be divided. The idea was not completely outlandish in view of the fact that Germany had only existed as a nation state for seventy-five years. The plans of the American Secretary of the Treasury Henry Morgenthau for the partitioning and deindustrialisation of the country therefore temporarily gained a hearing from both Roosevelt and Churchill. The dismantling of industry proposed by Morgenthau was also linked with political and security objectives: Germany would lose all its heavy industries, and the industries of the Ruhr area would be completely dismantled. It was calculated that in this way the desires of the European Allies for reparations would be satisfied, the economic balance in Europe would be altered to Germany's disadvantage, and Germany would lose the means to commit any further aggression.

But a dismembered and deindustrialised Germany would be in no position to pay reparations, hence the occupying powers would have to bear the costs themselves on behalf of the population living in their respective occupation zones. This powerful objection won the day, with the result that plans for partition had already been swept aside before the end of the war. There were, however, clear differences of opinion between the Allies about reparations. Although the Western politicians accepted that the Soviet Union possessed a legitimate claim to the lion's share of reparations because of the large-scale destruction it had suffered, they also had to consider the liabilities of their own countries and the wishes of the electorate at home. Then there was the question of the loans granted by the USA to its wartime partners, amounting to a total of $42 billion. Most of this money had been lent to the Soviet Union. After the victory, the American public expected to be freed from these burdens and not to have to finance countries in distant Europe any longer. For this reason, the US government stopped providing economic assistance to the Soviet Union on the very day of the German surrender. The Soviet government was unprepared for this blow, and it had lasting effects. Stalin regarded it as an attempt to put the Soviet Union under pressure, and it strengthened his decision not to give up anything he had laid his hands on. Mutual mistrust therefore increased.

It has long been a subject of dispute, both in the political sphere and in historical research, whether in expanding westwards the Soviet Union harboured aggressive intentions such as the export of communism or what was involved here was rather a defensive policy aimed at guaranteeing what had been achieved. This discussion, which concentrated above all on the motives of Stalin and the Soviet leadership, has been permeated by the assumption that the Soviet side had clearly defined foreign policy aims. More persuasive, however, are the indications suggesting that Stalin's actions were tentative and not free of contradiction, that they proceeded from considerations of security and reparations, and that he was increasingly provoked by the policies of the Western powers, which he viewed with increasing suspicion.[18]

The expansion of the Soviet Union into East Central and South-East Europe met with sharp criticism, particularly from Great Britain, and especially with regard to Poland and Greece, where Soviet and British interests were in direct conflict. Great Britain had entered the war not least on account of Poland, and it had strongly supported that country and its exiled government during the war years. London was therefore strongly opposed to simply abandoning Poland because the interests of the Soviet Union required this.

For the Soviet Union, on the other hand, expansion to the west offered the opportunity to surround itself with a belt of neutral, or, where possible, dependent states, and thereby to gain protection from any renewed attack from the West. The Soviets had already declared in 1941 that in their view the parts of eastern Poland obtained in the Polish partition of 1939 belonged to their country, had been illegally appropriated by Poland in 1920, and would not be given back. The idea of compensating Poland for the loss of its eastern territories at Germany's expense was therefore already under consideration. But, before the Potsdam Conference of the 'Big Three' had made a decision on the matter, the Soviet side, in collaboration with the communist administration it had established in Poland, had already created facts on the ground: the flight of the German population from the advance of the Red Army was now followed by the expulsion of the remaining Germans by Soviet and Polish military units. In this way, Poland's westward shift was prepared, and it was made permanent by the 'transfer' of the Polish population from the eastern areas which were now Soviet to the western areas which had been cleared of Germans. The Great Powers meeting in Potsdam were still wrestling in mid-July 1945 with the question of how to reconstruct Europe; but, by then, millions of people, Poles as well as Germans, had already been transferred westwards.

It was these developments in Poland, but also reports about the ruthless actions of the Red Army in Germany, which led to a transformation of the public mood in the USA and Great Britain. This change had already started in the first few months after war ended. During the war, the soldiers of the Red Army, and also Stalin himself—'Uncle Joe'—had been very popular in the West, owing to the years of sacrificial struggle against the Germans. Now, however, this began to change. The number of newspaper articles critical of the Soviet Union increased in Britain and the USA, and when Churchill spoke about the 'iron curtain' which had been lowered on the borders of the area occupied by the Red Army, the phrase was rapidly taken up all over the West. In September 1945 54 per cent of US citizens still believed that cooperation with the Soviet Union could continue; but by February 1946 the figure had fallen to 34 per cent.

The worsening of the atmosphere between the Western Allies and the Soviet Union was followed by a worsening of their mutual relations. The fear again arose in the Soviet Union, as it had in summer 1939, that Germany had entered the West's sphere of influence, and would now make common cause with the West against the USSR. The politicians of Britain and America, for their part, increasingly saw it as their paramount objective to prevent Western Europe from falling into the Soviet sphere of influence. And Western Europe meant, above all, Germany.

For the Germans, and particularly for the West Germans, this was a remarkable piece of good fortune, as would soon become clear. For, in this way, the conflict between Nazi Germany and the Allies, the catastrophic impact of Germany's policies of war and annihilation, and the resulting consequences for the Germans, were overlain and supplanted within barely two years by the new world conflict between the Western democracies and the Soviet dictatorship. As a result, Germany's role and importance altered quite miraculously. The country was rehabilitated 'with unnatural rapidity' and transferred from the role of beaten and ostracised foe to that of 'partner on probation'.[19]

It was, unsurprisingly, the reparations question which ignited the crucial disagreements between the Allies at Potsdam. For the Soviet negotiators, reparations were of absolutely paramount importance in view of the devastation of their country and the ruin of their agriculture, industry and infrastructure in the areas formerly occupied by the Wehrmacht. Arguments like that of the British Chancellor of the Exchequer, who said that one could only take as much from the Germans as they could give without becoming impoverished, therefore cut very little ice with the Soviets. The Yalta Conference had agreed a figure of $20 billion, $10 billion of which would go to the USSR. This had been regarded by the Soviet side as a remarkable, though partial, success. But the Western powers feared that, in view of the Soviet Union's tremendous reparation needs, the German economy would quickly become so exhausted that it would be unable to provide any further reparations to anyone, with the result that the USA would have to support Germany (and possibly other European countries as well) as it had after the First World War and thus indirectly pay reparations itself. The Soviet side naturally rejected the American proposal to avoid naming fixed amounts but instead to establish quotas, according to which the Soviet Union would receive 50 per cent of the reparations which the Germans could actually pay in each case, because if the German economy failed to grow this would mean 50 per cent of nothing.

The compromise that was finally found, coupling together questions of reparations and territorial changes, would have a lasting impact on German and European post-war history. Under this agreement, the victorious powers would not share reparations quotas or receive fixed amounts of reparations. Instead, each Allied state would take its reparations requirements from its own occupation zone. Since approximately a third of Germany's industrial potential lay within the territory occupied by the Red Army, inclusive of the parts of eastern Germany now assigned to the USSR, this proposal appeared to accommodate the interests of the Soviet Union. In addition, the Soviet Union would also receive a part of the reparations taken from the west of Germany, particularly from the Ruhr, the industrial heart of the country, whose economic strength acted as a guarantee of Germany's reparations potential. From now on, control of the Ruhr area was one of the permanent themes of negotiations between the Allies, though without any tangible results.

The Western powers calculated that by distributing reparations according to occupation zones they could prevent the gigantic reparations requirements of the USSR from spilling over onto them. In order to persuade Stalin to accept this idea, the Western Allies agreed in return not only to the westward shift of Poland together with the mass population movements that were taking place in association with this, but also to a Soviet sphere of influence which would stretch from Finland to Yugoslavia. This was a clear demonstration of the importance they ascribed to the question of reparations.

These concessions, of course, did no more than recognise what the Soviet Union already possessed on the ground. In retrospect, the contours of a divided Germany and a divided Europe were already apparent at this point. Nevertheless, the situation at the time was, in many respects, much more open than this suggests, partly because a willingness to cooperate continued to exist despite the first setbacks. This was shown later in 1945 by the implementation of the Potsdam Agreements over the treatment of Germany. Not least, France was now included as the fourth occupation power. That country had not participated in the Potsdam Conference, though it had accepted its results, with some reservations. France's occupation and reparations zone was carved out of the British and American zones, and the interests of France would exert a strong influence on further developments.

## Reshaping Germany

The long-term elimination of the potential danger posed by Germany to its neighbours was less a military than a political goal. Moreover, it could only be attained by political means, and whatever version was adopted it signified a fundamental reshaping of German society. In this context, five central tasks needed to be accomplished: the destruction of the German military, the punishment of those responsible for National Socialism and its crimes, structural reform of the economy, the rebuilding of political life and the democratisation of German society.

It could be foreseen that these objectives, stated in such broad and general terms, would be fulfilled in very different ways in the three Western zones and the Soviet Occupied Zone (SBZ). But there were also differences between the French and American zones, for instance, so that the extent of the divergence between East and West only became fully apparent in the course of time.

It was obvious that the German military complex had first to be destroyed, especially as the American military had long considered the Wehrmacht rather than the Nazi government as exercising the real power in the German Reich. A German guerrilla movement, announced by the Nazis under the name 'Werewolf', and feared by the Allies, turned out to be largely chimerical. Demilitarisation thus went ahead surprisingly quickly and smoothly, and the transfer of almost 11 million German soldiers into prisoner of war camps was achieved without any great difficulties, at least in the three Western zones. Their fate, however, differed substantially according to which hostile power had taken them prisoner. In the weeks preceding the final surrender, whole Wehrmacht formations had attempted at the last minute to evade the Red Army in whatever way possible and to get captured by the British or the Americans. Considering what the Wehrmacht had done in the Soviet Union during its retreat, the German soldiers did not expect that captivity in Russia would lead to anything other than hunger, disease, forced labour and death. This expectation was also confirmed, although many returnees later reported on many occasions that, although they were treated badly in Russia, their fate was no worse than that of the local population, who were also suffering from starvation. To be taken prisoner by the British, or still better by the Americans, on the other hand, was regarded as a guarantee of survival, even though conditions in the rapidly constructed mass prisoner of war camps of the Americans and the British were equally bad during the first days and weeks of captivity, and indeed in the *Rheinwiesenlager* (Rhine Meadow Camps) there were a considerable number of fatalities. Two years after the end of the war, there were still 435,000 German prisoners in the British, 640,000 in the French, and 14,000 in the American camps. There were still 890,000 German prisoners of war in the Soviet Union at that time. Altogether, approximately one million German soldiers lost their lives in Soviet captivity. The death rate among German prisoners in Soviet hands was 35 per cent, while for those in French hands it was 2.6 per cent and for those in British and American hands it was less than one per cent.[20]

Before the war ended, a large proportion of the German prisoners in Allied hands still believed in victory, and in many prisoner of war camps the National Socialists had initially taken control, and opponents of the Nazis or even merely battle-weary soldiers were regarded as defeatists. This situation changed after the surrender of Germany. There were no longer any indications that militarism continued to exist, or that there were groups intending to take up the struggle again, as had been seen in Germany after 1918. The former Wehrmacht soldiers were too demoralised and war-weary for that to happen, and according to the reports of the Allied intelligence services they yearned above all to return home and re-enter civilian life. Long years of excessive strain, and a weariness with life in uniform and the exclusively male environment in which some of the soldiers had lived uninterruptedly since they were inducted into the Reich Labour Service in 1935 all now took their toll.

Another aspect of their experience was, if possible, yet more decisive. It is true that many soldiers returned from the Soviet Union, sometimes after long years of captivity, with very mixed feelings. They frequently combined sympathy for the Russian population with contempt for the Soviet system. But the experiences of soldiers in British and American camps were very different: there they were usually treated correctly and also well accommodated and well fed, after the initial difficulties had been overcome. Most of the German prisoners took little interest in the political re-education courses, but they took advantage of the offers of cultural education and self-improvement, and they were often impressed by the relaxed and casual approach of the American GIs, particularly in camps in the USA. But, more than anything else, it was the living conditions which surprised the German prisoners: provisions were completely adequate, and in North America the sheer profusion of food, clothing and consumer goods of all kinds was astounding. A greater contrast to the austere living conditions in Germany during the war could not be imagined. And the difference between life in the camps and the situation that confronted them after they returned to devastated Germany was still greater. That left a powerful impression.

The implementation of what was described as 'denazification' turned out to be very difficult, because it involved making a judgement about what National Socialism actually was and who should be made chiefly responsible for its policies, and the Allies had very different views about this. It was by and large undisputed that the Nazi perpetrators who were directly responsible for the crimes of the regime should be punished as quickly as possible, and in the country in which the crimes had taken place. This affected people who had occupied leading positions in the regional administrations of the Nazi empire and in the party organisation, as well as those who had either taken leading positions, or directly executed orders, in the SS, the RSHA, the WVHA, the Security Police, the *Einsatzgruppen* and the concentration camps, as well as the German occupation authorities in the occupied countries, especially in the east.

By the end of the war, many leading National Socialists were already dead, some had committed suicide, while others had lost their lives in the turmoil of the final phase of the war. Anyone who had survived was confronted for many years with severe repressive measures by the occupying powers, involving a sliding scale of penalties. Automatic arrest, internment camp, tribunal proceedings, civil and military trials and a whole catalogue of punitive measures were the most important instruments in the attempt of the Western occupying powers to punish those responsible for Nazi crimes and to neutralise them politically. And, in fact, the overwhelming majority of those who had occupied leading positions in the 'Third Reich', or had played an active part in one of the institutions and organisations classified in the Nuremberg trials as 'criminal', and found themselves in the West at the end of the war, spent the first few months or years after the German surrender in an internment camp run by one of the three Western Allies. They made up a total of 250,000 people, half of whom were still in internment in summer 1946, a number which had fallen to roughly 40,000 a year later. In the British zone, most of those who were interned for a lengthy period, around 25,000 people, were also put before a tribunal which could impose long sentences (although this rarely happened). The Western powers handed over some 6,000 incriminated individuals to third countries, half of them countries in Eastern Europe, particularly Poland. Criminal proceedings were opened before Allied military tribunals against 5,200 persons. Four thousand were convicted, and 668 of these were condemned to death. By 1949, roughly the same number of people had been convicted by German courts for Nazi-era crimes against German nationals. If one bears in mind in addition that those released from internment had subsequently to undergo a denazification procedure and also to put up with tremendous disadvantages in their daily life, particularly in their professional occupations, it becomes clear that, despite all the loopholes, errors and omissions, the Western powers enjoyed partial success for many years in their endeavour to remove Nazi officials and to exclude them from public life in West Germany.[21]

The long-term significance of these developments lay less in the results measurable in judicial statistics than in the experiences the National Socialists were compelled to undergo. It is true that the whole process ended pretty well for most of the more prominent Nazis. But they did not know this in advance. The Allied intelligence branches reported unanimously that in the internment camps the National Socialists practically vied with each other in their opportunism, their denials of responsibility and their refusal to accept the evidence. It was reported in 1946 from the internment camp of Neuengamme that 95 per cent of the internees regarded their past National Socialism as an error. At the beginning, the predominant emotions had been bitterness, disappointment and defiance, but this attitude gave way to a pressure to adjust which was imposed by the conditions of existence and soon internalised. This preserved the individual's life and soon afterwards his or her freedom, but was associated with a loss of political identity and personal history.[22]

The prosecution of National Socialist criminals was in fact less problematic than the question of German society's responsibility for Nazi policies. On this issue, particularly in the USA, there were two contrasting explanatory approaches, which differed immensely in the answer they gave to the question of who was responsible for the dictatorship and its crimes. One approach stressed the responsibility of the traditional German elites, and followed the analysis of Franz Neumann, who had emphasised the role of the leading groups in the military, industry, large-scale agriculture and the government bureaucracy in his study of the Third Reich. A policy of denazification, therefore, should above all be directed at permanently weakening, indeed breaking, the influence of these groups on politics, the economy and society.[23]

The practical consequences of this approach were reflected in the agenda of the war crimes trials. At the Trial of Major War Criminals held jointly by the four Allies in Nuremberg, representatives of the German social elite had sat in the dock beside the political leadership of the Nazi regime, although the choice of protagonists was partly determined by chance, owing to the haste with which the trial was prepared. Thus, the Essen firm of Krupp was chosen as representing the involvement of heavy industry in the Nazi system, though it would have been more accurate to regard it as a symbol of the German armaments industry during the First World War. The whole of the Third Reich's apparatus of persecution, including the SS, was represented by one person: Ernst Kaltenbrunner, Heydrich's successor. But, in view of the historical significance of the trial, these were matters of subordinate importance. What was decisive was that the responsible figures of the Nazi regime who were available were convicted in a public and fair trial, and the mass crimes of National Socialism were revealed to the world to a hitherto unknown extent, not least because more than 200 people were present at the proceedings and later reported on them, including Alfred Döblin, John Dos Passos, Ilia Ehrenburg, Hans Habe, Erich Kästner, Erika Mann, Peter de Mendelssohn, Willy Brandt and also Markus Wolf.[24]

This targeting of the elite, with its tendency towards social criticism, was still more pronounced in the so-called Follow-Up Trials conducted in Nuremberg by the Americans alone. In one trial, the representatives of three giant firms, in the shape of the owners and managers of Krupp, IG-Farben and Flick, were charged with employing forced labour and plundering the occupied regions. In the 'trial of the doctors', the charge was experiments on human beings and euthanasia murders. In the 'Wilhelmstraße trial', the role of leading ministerial officials in the biggest Nazi crimes was examined, and in the proceedings against leading military men and SS generals the crimes of the Wehrmacht and the *Einsatzgruppen* were the subject of the charges. The Follow-Up Trials took place relatively late in the day, however. The judgment in the Wilhelmstraße trial was not rendered until April 1949, when the interest of German and international public opinion in the crimes of the Nazis had already died away considerably. In West Germany, there was a widespread feeling that the actual Nazi criminals had already been convicted in the main Nuremberg trial, and that the Americans were now only interested in revenge.[25]

According to the alternative approach, it was not so much the elites who were the main support of the German dictatorship as the close bond between the Nazi leadership and the German people. This view was in line with the conviction that National Socialism had been first and foremost a modern mass movement. It was therefore necessary to filter out all active National Socialists from the German population and re-educate the Germans in a democratic sense. The practical consequence of this approach was the denazification programme, in the course of which all adult Germans in the US zone had to complete a questionnaire, in which they were obliged to give exhaustive information on their lives during the Nazi period. In the first two post-war years, many people were dismissed from their jobs as a result, particularly among the public services.[26]

There was, from the outset, considerable criticism of this bureaucratic process, not only from the German side, as was only natural, but also from within the occupation administration. Nevertheless, the denazification procedure had a beneficial effect, at least in the first two years after the war. Firstly, the Nazi past of individual Germans, which had previously appeared almost impossible to bring to light, now became a plainly visible mark of distinction between perpetrators, victims and the many people who stood somewhere in the middle. Secondly, denazification made it possible to prevent the important state positions, such as judge, teacher, civil servant, or mayor, from being filled by the old elites immediately after the end of the war, as had happened after

1918. It is true that, a few years later, a large proportion of those dismissed from the public service would be reappointed in West Germany, something which could scarcely have been imagined in 1945 or 1946, but the intervening years represented for most of them a clear break in their professional career, which might well have put them at a severe disadvantage.

It was remarkable, however, that the US administration chose to start the denazification programme with the easy cases, which could be dealt with rapidly, whereas the guiltier individuals were not examined until after 1947, when the programme had already been largely handed over to the German authorities. The judgments of the latter were increasingly mild, not least because of the changing political climate, with the result that it was precisely those Nazi officials who bore an especially heavy burden of guilt who profited from this general de facto amnesty during the Cold War, and mainly got off scot-free.

The course of events in the tribunals in the British zone was not very different. Important members of the NSDAP, the SS and the Security Police, of the rank of *stellvertretender Gauleiter* (Assistant District Leader), *Kriminaldirektor* (Director of the Criminal Division), *Standartenführer* (SS Standard Leader) and above were condemned to an average fine of 4,000 Marks or two years in prison, including the period already spent in internment. The mildest approach was taken by the military authorities in the French zone. There, even high-ranking Nazis remained unmolested if this suited the pragmatic interests of the French occupiers.

Thus the denazification process sometimes turned into its opposite: a procedure for removing National Socialists from influential positions in political, economic and cultural life gradually became a way of freeing former Nazis from the stigma attached to their earlier activities. It was therefore not surprising that the questionnaires and the denazification procedure met with outraged condemnation from most Germans. This was not entirely unjustified, since the proceedings often dragged on endlessly owing to the concern of the occupation authorities to avoid any appearance of a hasty verdict. Moreover, it was sometimes hard to draw a line between political convictions and punishable behaviour. Finally, the obvious amateurism of the '*Spruchkammern*' (the German civilian courts handling denazification) also generated mockery and bitterness among the Germans. The victors were held up to scorn for what appeared to be their foolishly arrogant claim to sit in judgment over a civilised people. With the gradual worsening of the Cold War, and the accompanying change in attitudes towards the prosecution of former Nazis, criticism of denazification escalated in West Germany into a veritable campaign. This lasted into the late 1950s and was supported by a broad social consensus. As early as the end of the 1940s, it was the firm conviction in West Germany, shared by many people, that far more people had been convicted than were actually guilty. It was therefore demanded that both denazification and the prosecution of Germans for war crimes should cease as soon as possible.

Nevertheless, a purely negative verdict cannot be given on the denazification process. Despite all its inadequacies and injustices—which were probably unavoidable in view of the complexity of this large-scale experiment conducted on a whole society—it still made a considerable contribution to exposing the responsibility of German society and its leading groups for National Socialist policies, naming and isolating active National Socialists and those who had taken part in Nazi crimes, and keeping them out of office and away from public influence at least for a certain length of time. Thus, for most Germans, their own experiences, the information campaigns of the Allies, denazification, or perhaps simply an instinct for political accommodation, had the result of imposing a taboo on the National Socialist system of government, even if that did not prevent some parts of the ideological and political legacy of the dictatorship from continuing to have an impact.[27]

In the SBZ, on the other hand, the denazification process proceeded quite differently. There the Soviet Military Administration (SMAD) instituted a radical purge. All National Socialists were removed from public service and higher-level professional positions. More than half a million people lost their jobs as a result. More than 16,000 members of the SS, the Gestapo and the NSDAP were put before the courts, 12,000 were convicted, and 118 were condemned to death. In the SBZ, denazification was carried out more quickly, more decisively and more thoroughly than in the West. But, from the very beginning, it was combined with the radical political upheaval which gave the German communists control of the state institutions, particularly the police force and the judicial system.

At the same time, this process was shrouded in a mysterious aura of silence and rumour. In the first few months after the end of the war, tens of thousands of people were fairly randomly locked up in the internment camps of the Soviet occupying power under the heading of 'denazification'. Many thousands lost their lives in these camps. The victims included, apart from probable Nazis, many people who were interned for other reasons: politically unwelcome elements of all colours. From 1946 onwards, these people were largely Social Democrats who opposed the unification of the KPD and the SPD or young persons suspected of belonging to the 'Werewolf' organisation. Altogether, 122,000 Germans were detained in 'Special Camps'. More than 42,000 of them lost their lives, and a further 13,000 were taken to the Soviet Union. These 'purges' in the SBZ soon became a 'denazification' policy in name alone. They were, from the start, a part of the 'democratic and anti-Fascist revolution', in other words, the process of establishing a new order under the direction of the SMAD at the conclusion of which the communists held sole power.[28]

After the founding of the GDR (German Democratic Republic), the denazification process there was completely transferred into German hands, as it was in the West. The Special Camps the Soviets had run were dissolved and 3,400 still untried inmates were handed over to the GDR authorities. It was now in the interest of the leadership of the SED (Socialist Unity Party) both to emphasise that anti-fascism was the foundation of their state and to demonstrate to their own population that the denazification process was regarded as complete. Anyone who took the side of socialism would henceforth have nothing more to fear. In a legally unacceptable summary trial in the Saxon town of Waldheim, the former inmates of the Special Camps, most of whom had no defence counsel and no previous knowledge of the charges, were convicted in the course of a few weeks. Only a hundred were found not guilty. Almost 3,000 were condemned to more than ten years in prison, 157 of them were members of the SPD, while fifty-seven were members of the KPD. Thirty-one people were condemned to death, and of these twenty-four were actually executed.[29]

In view of the differences between the respective political and economic systems of the victorious Allies, it was not surprising that the reform of the economic structure that had been agreed between them would vary considerably in each of the four zones. The Allies all agreed that Germany's economic power, and above all its ability to produce armaments, should be destroyed for a long time to come. In practice, however, the difference between the approach of the Soviet Union and that of the other occupying powers led within less than three years to economic and social circumstances in the Eastern zone widely different from those prevailing in the three Western zones.

Three ways of limiting German economic power were discussed in the West: dismantling, deconcentration and socialisation. Initially, the dismantling of whole industrial installations occupied the centre of attention. An 'industry limitation plan' was compiled in March 1946 in the US zone. Under this, Germany's industrial capacity would be reduced to roughly 50 per cent of the 1938 level. That would have signified the destruction or dismantling of more than 1,500 factories. But the disadvantages of this procedure rapidly became apparent: the dismantling of machine-tool factories and chemical plants and the removal of much of Germany's coal-producing capacity compromised the ability of the country to supply the population from its own resources, not to mention its ability to pay reparations. Moreover, owing to the deepening conflict with the Soviet Union, the view soon began to assert itself, particularly within the US administration, that it would be better to fight the new enemy than punish the old one and that it would be better to use Germany's industrial potential than to destroy it. As a result of this change of course, which was adopted by Britain as well, and much later on by France, the number of factories scheduled for dismantling was reduced. Even so, by 1949 more than 600 industrial installations had been dismantled in the Western zones of Germany. These measures did not in fact have any decisive economic significance. But the Germans themselves, particularly the workers, felt that the dismantling of factories was a serious problem, because here their future was at stake, as no-one imagined they could have any future if Germany ceased to have a strong economy.[30]

The deconcentration process had a more radical effect than the dismantling of factories. This had been agreed upon in Potsdam by the victors in the conviction that it was the big industrial combines and the monopolies above all which had supported the Nazi system. 'De-cartelisation' concentrated on three branches of the economy: heavy industry, the chemical sector and the banks. Particularly severe measures were taken against the twelve coal, iron and steel combines, which accounted for 90 per cent of Germany's steel, and half of its iron. They were split up into twenty-eight separate and independent enterprises. The chemical giant IG Farben was divided in 1953 into three large firms and a large number of smaller enterprises. The three big banks were divided into some thirty individual institutions. These were measures which considerably altered the structure of the West German economy. They proved to be largely unsustainable, however. By the mid-1950s, large enterprises had already arisen in all three branches. They had well-nigh complete market dominance, owing to the growth of cross-connections and linkages between different firms. Later on, however, they increasingly came under the pressure of international competition because of the liberalisation of world trading relations.

The demand for the socialisation of key industries had a long tradition in the German working class movement, but it eventually failed to enjoy great priority, in view of the threat of mass unemployment and problems of food supply, just as happened after the First World War. Although the State Diet of North Rhine-Westphalia decided by a majority to socialise the Ruhr coal mining industry, the British occupation authorities withheld their agreement, because for them increases in production and efficiency ranked ahead of political demands. The situation was similar in the US zone. When the socialisation of key industries and state control of the banks were written into the constitution of the state (*Land*) of Hesse, against the wishes of the United States, and this was confirmed by more than 70 per cent of the electors in a referendum, the Americans suspended the operation of the relevant article, stating that this was a matter for the future federal government to decide.

Calls for socialisation were also not particularly popular among the working class itself. The big strikes and hunger demonstrations in the spring of 1947 and at the start of 1948 were related not to this, but to shortages of food and the necessities of life, and only a quarter of the population regarded socialisation as desirable. Twice as many thought an increase in the influence of the state on the economy would be more likely to have harmful consequences. This was no surprise, in view of people's experience with state restrictions on prices and wages, and the system of controls and rationing, which had dominated German economic life since the early part of the war and brought with it miserable living conditions. Apart from this, the almost immeasurable wealth of the Americans, the impact of which could be admired every day on the black market, led Germans to form the impression that the economic system of the USA was superior. When asked in which country of the world the workers were best off, 47 per cent of West Germans named the USA, 10 per cent Germany, and only one per cent Russia. These figures were a clear indication that even at the outset there was little basis in the Western zones of occupation for a socialist transformation of the economy. In addition, the approaching confrontation with Soviet communism promoted an anti-socialist frame of mind, the effects of which were increasingly felt by the SPD. In this respect, the predominant attitude towards changes in economic organisation in the Western zones of occupation between spring 1947 and summer 1948 was extremely ambivalent, despite all the rhetoric about socialism.[31]

The Soviet Union, in contrast, began immediately after the end of the war to dismantle German industry extensively and systematically. In the SBZ, some two-thirds of heavy industry and up to 80 per cent of vehicle and aircraft production capacity was dismantled and taken to the Soviet Union. The bitterness of local workers over the dismantling process was increased by cases in which these installations were not transported to Kiev, say, or Rostov on Don, but left to rust away within Germany, in the port of Rostock, for example. Moreover, some 200 additional factories, representing a quarter of the zone's industrial capacity, were converted by the occupation authorities into 'Soviet Joint-Stock Companies' (SAGs). These continued to produce goods, but were now under Soviet management. The total value of the factories dismantled by the Soviet Union is difficult to calculate, but, in any case, it was many times the amount of $10 billion which had been agreed between the Allies as its entitlement. The result of this radical policy of de-industrialisation was that the starting conditions for a revival of the economy in the SBZ were much worse than in the West. For the Soviet government, however, that was not the decisive factor. Nor was it swayed by the fact that the SMAD would now no longer be able to count on the approval of large sections of the German population, not even the workers, whose workplaces had been destroyed by the dismantling of the factories. The supreme priority for the Soviet Union was the delivery of reparations, and if the standard of living of the Germans was considerably reduced as a result, that was not the first concern of the Soviet authorities. After all, it would continue to be much higher than the Soviet population's.[32]

As in the case of denazification, the economic reforms in the Eastern zone were conceived as the first step on the road to a socialist economic order. From the communist perspective, the Nazi government had been supported primarily by the big industrial combines, and thus demands for placing the economy under state control and abolishing private industry were logically justified as a way of punishing 'Nazi criminals and war criminals'. In 1946 a referendum was held in Saxony under this slogan, and 77 per cent of the voters agreed to the demand for expropriation. This result was taken as the basis for a wave of nationalisations which now started in the whole of the Eastern zone. Within two years, more than 10,000 firms were expropriated without compensation. By mid-1948 the nationalised firms, taken together with the SAGs, accounted for more than 60 per cent of the zone's industrial production. With these measures, the establishment of a socialist economy was already predetermined before the foundation of the GDR, irrespective of any political decisions.[33]

The second decisive economic policy measure taken by the SMAD in the early post-war period was land reform. It had originally been envisaged that there would also be land reform in the west of the country, but, owing to German objections, only a few attempts were made in this direction. In the SBZ, on the other hand, well-off farmers with more than a hundred hectares of land, along with former leading National Socialists, were expropriated, also without compensation. Large agricultural enterprises were nationalised, and a total of 3.1 million hectares of land was divided between some 500,000 agricultural workers, landless peasants and expellees. In this way, more than 200,000 new peasant properties were created. These were overwhelmingly small and medium enterprises. From the communist point of view, of course, this was merely the first step. But all attempts to induce the peasants to combine together to form cooperatives met with vigorous protests from the newly established proprietors, and the first agitational campaigns mounted against 'rich peasants' did not lead to much success, either. Hence the collectivisation of agriculture was postponed for the time being.[34]

It was not to be expected that the four occupying powers would have much in common in their endeavours to democratise German society. There was indeed agreement on the great urgency of reforming those institutions which had been centrally involved in the nationalist indoctrination of the population and the functioning of the dictatorship. This referred particularly to the educational system, the civil service and the mass media. As far as the schools were concerned, the tripartite system, which involved a very early separation of the gifted from the less able, was regarded as a bastion of class society and the high school (*Gymnasium*) as a stronghold of nationalist indoctrination. All four occupying powers therefore made efforts to introduce comprehensive schools of various kinds and to reform the content of the courses and the method of teaching. This was only possible, of course, if there was a corresponding change within the teaching body, especially as this was the profession with the highest proportion of NSDAP members (more than 70 per cent). It was relatively simple to put into effect a fundamental change of this kind by dismissing teachers with a Nazi past, but the authorities would then have few trained teachers at their disposal.

Here too, it was the Soviet Military Administration which took the most drastic measures. It introduced comprehensive schools by decree. In them, pupils started with eight years of elementary education, after which they could choose either three years of vocational school or four years of high school. Thousands of new teachers were trained in crash courses in order to compensate for the teacher shortage consequent on the dismissal of all the former Nazis. The new teachers all had to be 'anti-fascists' of working-class origin. In this way, the schools were successfully restructured in a very short space of time, although they were under the close supervision of the military administration and the education that was provided was explicitly ideological in orientation. Thus denazification was thoroughly put into effect in the schools, but there could be no question of democratisation.

In the West, change was more difficult to achieve. The occupation authorities were quick to adumbrate far-reaching school reform plans, which were aimed at establishing community schools for pupils up to the sixth or eighth school year, coeducation, and abolishing tuition fees. But, from the very outset, they met with determined resistance from the German side. The educated bourgeoisie (*Bildungsbürgertum*) regarded the *Gymnasium*, with it stress on humanism and antiquity, as the cornerstone of the German educational tradition and also as a guarantee of Germany's intellectual rebirth. This resistance against the school reforms was also an expression of the indignation provoked by the proposed 're-education' of the Germans. Germany had been defeated, certainly, and was also perhaps burdened with guilt. But the requirement set by the Allies that the Germans should be 're-educated' was seen as the arrogance of the victors, whose claims to moral or even cultural supremacy were greeted with scorn even by people who did not contest the need for a thoroughgoing transformation of the country.

Despite such opposition, it would have been possible to implement the school reforms planned by the Western Allies in the first two post-war years, but only by fiat. However, owing to the escalating confrontation with the Soviet Union the occupation authorities in the West were increasingly inclined to proceed by agreement with the German side. The debate over the school reforms dragged on into 1948, and at that late stage the introduction of the school reforms by decree against the wishes of German parliamentary representatives—who had been elected in the meantime—would have contradicted the democratic postulates of the Western occupying powers and undermined the establishment of the partial state of West Germany which was taking shape at that point. The reform was therefore postponed.[35]

Parallel developments occurred in the university sector. British and American occupation officers encouraged comprehensive structural reforms and they also negotiated with the rectors of the universities about 'the modernisation of courses, changes in the composition of the student body and the democratisation of the universities'. The student representatives also regarded a radical reform of the universities as 'one of the most urgent needs in the area of German cultural policy', according to a leading figure in the Socialist German Student Federation (SDS), Helmut Schmidt (Hamburg). But university reform, he noted, had come up against the resistance of 'exceptionally strong conservative elements in the universities themselves'. In fact, a reform which would have restricted the influence of the full professors could only have been carried out by overriding the opposition of the German universities. Nothing was done. Moreover, a thorough purge of the professorate also failed to take place, with the result that continuity of personnel was almost completely preserved in the universities, leaving aside one or two exceptional examples.[36]

Attempts to reform the public services suffered the same fate. Originally, the Americans had intended to disband the professional civil service, because they saw it as a stronghold of militarism and state-worship, and they regarded the servants of the state as enjoying unjustifiable privileges in comparison with the employees of private companies. The proposal was the subject of long discussions, but it was first postponed and then abandoned, in view of the solid front of resistance presented by the officials, whose cooperation was urgently needed by the Allied military administrators. The German civil service, with the many privileges it enjoyed as a separate estate, remained in existence, and a few years later it offered numerous ex-National Socialists the opportunity to return to public employment.[37]

The process of reforming the mass media had a different outcome. At the end of the war, all German newspaper offices and radio stations were closed down by the Allies. The occupation armies issued their own newspapers and bulletins, and they also organised radio broadcasts themselves. In order to make sure that continuity with the Nazi era did not prevail in the sphere of the press, the military governments issued licences to suitable, politically reliable individuals, whereas in the Soviet zone they were issued to the political parties which had quickly been authorised. In the Western zones, an entirely new press system emerged in this way. It later turned out that this was an intervention with lasting effects, which restructured and moulded the West

German newspaper industry for many decades. In mid-1946, there were already thirty-five newly established newspapers in the US zone, among them the *Neue Zeitung*—which was for a long time the flagship of the new, democratic press—the *Frankfurter Rundschau*, the *Süddeutsche Zeitung*, and the *Stuttgarter Zeitung*. In the British zone, there was *Die Welt*, and somewhat later the journalistically innovative *Der Spiegel*, which would soon be very influential. The administrators of the Western occupation zones achieved a similarly successful transformation in dealing with the radio. This was newly established as an institution which was semi-official but nevertheless remained independent of the state and ensured the representation of many different opinions by a rigorous system of federalisation.

In this sphere too, the reforms in the Soviet zone were linked with the objective of extending communist power. The newspapers, like the radio, were from the beginning consistently oriented towards the Communist Party line. Pluralism was institutionalised, but only in appearance. The disbandment of the old civil service also allowed the most important positions in the government and the administration to be occupied by new people who were politically reliable and had received instruction on their new activities in crash training courses. A rapid fall in social status for some was thus combined with rapid social advancement for others, and a broadly based circulation of elites began, which, while allowing considerable social mobility for workers and clerical employees, also quickly led to a wave of emigration from the SBZ into the West by a large number of former officials and administrative specialists.[38]

In summary, the Western Allies were only able to put into effect their plans for social reorganisation in part. De-militarisation was achieved quickly and completely, the press and the radio were shaped entirely afresh, Nazi criminals were punished, Nazi elites were removed from power and influence, even denazification was achieved at least to some extent. But the Western Allies only managed to destroy the industrial power of the big combines to a very limited degree. The same was true of reforms of the school system, the universities and the civil service. Changes which had not already been implemented in the first months of the occupation hardly had any chance of being realised later, because, in the shadow of the approaching Cold War, the occupation authorities took greater and greater account of German public opinion. For the Soviet military administration this played no role. The reforms it set in train were not directed at democracy and pluralism but at adaptation to the Soviet system. The overall result of these divergent Allied policies was quickly perceptible: as early as a year after the end of the war, the institutional structures and the circumstances of life in the Western and Eastern zones of occupation clearly differed considerably.

## Political Reconstruction

Under the Potsdam Agreement, political power in Germany was to be exercised centrally, by the Allied Control Council. But, in practice, the four occupation zones soon developed a political life of their own. It was unanimously agreed that political life ought to start first at the level of the municipalities and the states (*Länder*), and that the activities of democratic parties and trade unions ought to be permitted within that context. But it was an open question whether, and when, a central German administration would come into existence, and above all whether there would be a German government covering the whole country. It was agreed in theory that this would happen, but in practice particularism had its own internal dynamic.

The eastern occupying power and the three western ones differed with regard to their understanding of democracy more than on any other subject. Even so, both camps regarded the establishment of a multi-party system as indispensable. The Soviet Military Administration was in a particular hurry to do this, but unlike the Western powers it acted strictly from the top down. As early as 10 June 1945—even before the beginning of the Potsdam Conference!—German political parties and trade unions were permitted to function in the Soviet zone. Alongside the communists, this included the SPD and the bourgeois parties. The KPD (Communist Party of Germany), which visibly enjoyed the support of the Soviet administration, initially stepped forward with a very moderate programme, in which the word 'socialism' was not mentioned once. There was no question of 'imposing the Soviet system' on Germany, the party said. It was committed instead to a 'parliamentary and democratic republic' and to 'the development of free trade and private entrepreneurial initiative on the basis of private property'. It was necessary 'simultaneously with the destruction of Hitlerism' to carry through to completion 'the task of Germany's democratisation, the task of bourgeois-democratic transformation, which had been begun in 1848.'[39]

Most members of the party had far more radical views than this, and many also assumed that it was now time, in view of the experiences of past history, to end the 'division of the workers' movement' into social democrats and communists and to create a joint organisation. In the SPD too, there were supporters of the 'unity of the working class', but many party members had strong reservations about joining the communists.

At this time, however, the KPD leadership was pursuing a different strategy. 'It must look democratic, but everything must be under our control' was the guideline issued by Walter Ulbricht, the leader of the group of cadres sent back to Germany at the end of the war from their Moscow exile. The conquest of power took place according to the same pattern as in the other countries which had come under Soviet influence: the formation of a voting bloc, with the distribution of seats determined in advance, usually on a parity basis, as in Bulgaria in November 1945 or in Romania a year later. In the SBZ, a 'United Front of Democratic Anti-Fascist Parties' had already been formed in July 1945. It was composed of an equal number of representatives of the four most important political groupings: the KPD, the SPD, the CDU and the Liberals, and though its original purpose was only to serve as a coordinating committee, bodies with the same structure were later installed at all levels. It is possible that the Soviet authorities already regarded this as a move towards a 'parliamentary democratic republic' with free elections which bourgeois parties were permitted to contest. Like the construction of central administrative bodies, mentioned below, the establishment of this party system was intended as evidence that the USSR's policy was meant to provide a template for the whole of Germany. But, in actual fact, neither electoral results nor the size of a party's membership had any significance here. The representatives of the other parties could achieve nothing against the wishes of the KPD. Thus, the 'United Front' was the basis for a gradual takeover of power by the Communist Party.[40]

The SMAD also set up central German-run administrative bodies in July 1945, much earlier than the Western powers in their zones. These were intended as ancillary organs, and were subdivided into separate departments. The chairs and vice-chairs of most of these administrative bodies were communists, who had thus taken control of the most important power centres in the Soviet zone within a few months after the end of the war, although they had been disappointed in their expectations of victory in the first local elections, and in fact received fewer votes than the SPD. The newly founded individual states (*Länder*) and their prime ministers, appointed by the SMAD, were less important than the central administrative bodies, and at the local level too, the influence of the 'United Front' and the determining role of the KPD in it was perceptible from the beginning.

The course of development in the Western zones was slower and more sinuous. The US military governor, Lucius D. Clay, repeatedly expressed the conviction that the political life of the Germans should start from the ground and develop upwards. The first elections in the three Western zones took place at a local level at the beginning of 1946. It was there that the formation of the new political parties and the emergence of suitable political leaders was expected to take place. Most Diet elections were not held until spring 1947. The configuration of the individual states (*Länder*) had already been altered in advance of this. The new federal structure followed ideas already put forward unsuccessfully in the Weimar years.[41]

The smoothness with which the fundamental forms of parliamentary democracy were brought back into action in the Western zones was astonishing. But in their zone the Soviet authorities were able just as quickly to put into effect the plan of a communist power centre behind a parliamentary façade. This indicates how little room for manoeuvre the German people already had at this stage, and how little influence was possessed by the new German politicians, who were almost exclusively veterans from the days of Weimar democracy. The shaping of new forms of government and new administrative structures was primarily a matter for the occupying powers, and only the worsening of the conflict between East and West allowed the German representatives to gain a significant role vis-à-vis the military governments.

The system of licensing political parties allowed the Western military governments to intervene extensively in Germany's political life. They excluded radically right-wing parties and parties with National Socialist affiliations, a move which was met with understanding in all quarters. They initially refused to license any expellee parties, which was a sign of how apprehensive they were about the growing stream of German refugees. But, on the whole, their decisions on which parties to permit were in line with the trends that had emerged among the Germans themselves. This applied both to the re-establishment of old parties and the formation of new ones. Moreover, a similar basic political structure, with national variations, had taken shape in most of the countries of Western Europe, namely a communist party, a socialist party, a Christian unity party, a bourgeois-liberal party and, except in Germany, a nationalist party. Monarchist and agrarian movements, on the other hand, had become less significant, as had parties linked to a specific confessional milieu.[42]

It was, to be sure, predominantly older Weimar politicians who now spoke for the Germans, but a very different party landscape was already visible in the first post-war months, especially among the middle-class groupings. Changes in the two workers' parties were less dramatic. The SPD was reconstituted with surprising rapidity. Party members were swiftly collected together again on the basis of the old membership lists, and the exiled leaders of the party returned to Germany. As early as summer 1945, local SPD branches could be seen again almost everywhere. The SPD at first gravitated around three political centres. In addition to the exile leadership, which returned to Germany from London in January 1946, and the executive of the Berlin SPD, known as the Central Committee, a new centre had grown up in Hanover around the former Reichstag deputy Kurt Schumacher, who had been released from almost ten years' imprisonment in a concentration camp. The London exile leadership soon joined Schumacher's group. The SPD's first party programme was much further to the left than the tactically restrained line of the KPD. The key slogan of the SPD was 'democracy in the state and the community, socialism in the economy and society', and, in view of the success of the party at the first Diet elections, it seemed that it would soon be possible to achieve these aims.[43]

The reconstructed Communist Party was dominated from the very beginning of the post-war epoch by a group of cadres around Walter Ulbricht. They had been trained in exile in Moscow and had prepared at length for the task they had to accomplish after the entry of the Red Army into Germany. They were joined by communist prisoners who had been released from Nazi concentration camps, whereas KPD supporters who returned from exile in the West had less influence and were eyed with distrust by the functionaries who had been in Moscow. After the communists in the Soviet zone had firmly established their claim to power by means of the anti-fascist united front and by taking over key positions in the central administration, they changed their strategy. Early in 1946, when the results of the first local elections turned out to be extremely disappointing, they set their sights on a merger with the SPD. The Berlin Central Committee of the SPD was rather undecided about its response to this suggestion, but the West German SPD around Schumacher was bitterly opposed. When a direct vote was held by the West Berlin SPD, 80 per cent of party members rejected the idea of unification with the KPD (the election was prohibited in the eastern sector of the city). Nevertheless, the communists were able to push through the merger in the Eastern zone, with the help of the SMAD and parts of the Berlin SPD around Otto Grotewohl, who supported the unification of the parties as a historically necessary act. The merger of the two parties to form the 'Socialist Unity Party of Germany' (SED) took place in the SBZ on 19 and 20 April 1946.

There were also elements of the SPD in the West which had been in favour of a closer association with the communists, and if possible a merger in the long term. But, under the prevailing circumstances, this rapid amalgamation of the two parties was nothing other than a forced merger. Moreover, it was a merger with a party blemished by its character as an auxiliary organ of the Soviet occupying power. The hostility of the Social Democrats of West Germany to the SED increased considerably when they discovered the extent of the persecution of social democratic critics in the SBZ by the Soviet Military Administration and the communists. In summer 1946, some social democratic prisoners found they had been brought back to the very same concentration camps from which they had been liberated the previous year. These now served as internment camps for the SMAD.

The forced unification of the SPD in the east with the KPD and the foundation of the SED had far-reaching consequences for the future development of post-war Germany. Firstly, Schumacher's SPD, with its unswerving anti-communism now made even stronger by experience, became a constitutive element in the developing West German state. For the SPD, the unity of all democrats had priority over the unity of the workers' movement, as had already been the case before 1933. Secondly, the SPD was now no longer allowed to function in the Soviet zone, and it thereby became a purely West German party. As a result, the confrontation between East and West was transferred from the level of the occupying powers to relationships within Germany. Henceforth, a unification of the four zones into a single German state presupposed either the dissolution of the SED or a fusion of the West German SPD with the communists. Both options seemed highly unlikely.[44]

It was among the middle-class parties that the biggest changes took place after 1945. The emergence of the Christian Democratic Union (CDU) and its Bavarian offshoot the Christian Social Union (CSU) marked the success of a new formation which did indeed have parallels elsewhere in Europe but was still somewhat surprising in view of the distinctive features of the German situation. On the one hand, for Protestants and Catholics to join together in a single party was by no means a matter of course, even seventy-five years after the *Kulturkampf*, although in view of past historical developments it was logical. A role was played in this respect by the old yearning for a united middle-class party of the centre, which had repeatedly come to the surface ever since Bülow's *Sammlungspolitik*. On the other hand, Protestant conservatism had been discredited by its cooperation with the National Socialists, and the hardly less inglorious role of the Catholic Centre Party in the final phase of the Weimar Republic also gave occasion to reflect on the need for a new formation in the political centre. To establish this party under a Christian banner was an obvious step, since for post-1945 conservatives the Christian religion counted as almost the sole place of political refuge largely untouched by the stain of Nazism.[45]

But the new coalition party did not just call for an end to the religious divide; it also wanted to go beyond class divisions, though this aspiration took many different forms. There were powerful forces in the Union which supported Christian socialism, particularly in the Rhineland, which rapidly became the strongest party region, and in Berlin, where Jacob Kaiser, among others, called for extensive measures of socialisation. But, at the same time, the Union was also a rallying point for determined opponents of any form of socialism. It contained supporters of a centralist view of the state, reminiscent of the Prussian past, side by side with other people who were inclined towards federalism. Lastly, the Union was far from united about its economic policy aims. Its members included advocates of a social economy, supporters of the market economy and people who still held to the idea of a state organised into Estates (*Stände*). 'This party is socialist and radical in Berlin, clerical and conservative in Cologne, capitalist and reactionary in Hamburg and counter-revolutionary and particularist in Munich.' This was the apt comment made in the French periodical *L'Ordre*. The new party's programmatic diversity was the price that had to be paid to establish a middle-class coalition, but it was also a possible breeding ground for future splits.[46]

But the diversity of the CDU–CSU (the 'Union') could also be of advantage if a strong and persuasive leadership figure emerged who was able to reconcile the contradictions. The right person was soon discovered in the shape of Konrad Adenauer, who had been mayor of Cologne between 1917 and 1933. He had gained political legitimacy at home and abroad during the Nazi period through his oppositional stance, for which he was repeatedly imprisoned. He was a veteran Centre Party politician, and his political experience, his instinct for power and his Christian values made him an ideal candidate for the vacant position of leader of the middle-class camp. Adenauer was deeply rooted in Catholicism, but extremely mistrustful of large-scale political or ideological projects and wary of his nation's tendency to be seduced by them. His political temperament was that of an authoritarian democrat, and he set more store by the strength of state institutions than by public participation and public opinion. He soon reached the view that the growing strength of Soviet communism was much more dangerous than the threat of vanquished Nazism. Unconditional alignment with the Western Allies, particularly the USA, was therefore a very important part of his policy.

Adenauer quickly took control of the CDU, the creation of which had largely been his own work, although the success story of the Union appears to run more smoothly in retrospect than it did at the time. It was not at all clear at first whether Adenauer would be able to hold the party together in view of the immense range of political positions that needed to be integrated. His success in accomplishing this owed much to the precise and sceptical evaluation of Germany's situation and of international politics in general which he had worked out soon after the war ended, and in which he proved to be almost clairvoyant. In October 1945, barely half a year after the war ended, Adenauer pointed out that Russia had 'the eastern half of Germany, Poland, the Balkans, apparently Hungary, and part of Austria' in its grip, that it was refusing to cooperate with the West and that in the part of Europe it ruled it was operating entirely as it thought fit. In that part of Europe 'economic and political principles completely different from those in the rest of Europe' now prevailed. 'This has made the division of Europe into the East, the Russian sphere, and Western Europe a fact.' It was therefore in the interest of France and Britain 'to combine Western Europe together under their leadership, to establish political and economic stability in the part of Germany not under Russian occupation, and to restore it to good health.' The French and Belgian desire for security could 'only be satisfied adequately and in the long term by the economic interdependence of West Germany, France, Belgium, Luxemburg and Holland.' If Britain also wanted to join in, 'this would bring us a long way closer to the highly desirable final goal of the unification of all the Western European countries'. There were very few politicians at that time who possessed such a clear vision of the world situation and future developments. This, far more than his tactical finesse, was the reason for Adenauer's superiority, and it would make him the dominant figure in West German politics for almost twenty years.[47]

The newly founded liberal party, the Free Democratic Party (FDP), was a combination of the various liberal tendencies which had already separated from each other in the early days of the German Empire, and had found political expression under the Weimar Republic in the DDP, the DVP and to some extent in the DNVP. It differed from the CDU primarily because it rejected any religious orientation. It was worlds away from the SPD. Like the CDU, the new FDP was also very heterogeneous at first, and it remained in this condition, because it lacked the unifying bond of a single worldview and a relationship to a particular milieu. In this party, the national liberals of the north and the west faced the Left liberals of the south and the south-west. What kept the two halves of the party united was their strong support for federalism. If we leave aside its opposition to the trade unions and to any enhancement of social policy, its ideas of political order only developed gradually. Alongside this, however, the provincial branches of the FDP, especially those of a national liberal tendency, soon developed into catchment organisations for former National Socialists. The FDP's opposition to war crimes trials and denazification, cautiously expressed at first, became a characteristic, indeed a determining element in its political practice after 1948, and this lasted into the 1960s.[48]

When the first Diet elections were held in the states that made up the Western zones of Germany, the above-mentioned division of the political spectrum into four groups was clearly confirmed by the level of electoral participation, which was around 70 per cent. A basic political structure emerged, consisting of two large parties, the CDU and the SPD, and two small parties, the FDP and the KPD. This structure would prove to be fairly stable. The first state elections in the Western zones were held at different times, but if they are taken together, we see that the Union, with 37.6 per cent, was slightly ahead of the SPD, with 35 per cent, while the liberals and the communists obtained around 9 per cent each. If these results are compared, say, with 1932, the differences look enormous. But, if they are compared with the last elections held before the world economic crisis, the degree of continuity is striking: in 1928, the DNVP, the Centre Party and various small centrist parties together obtained 38.6 per cent, close to the 37.5 per cent obtained by the Union in 1947. The SPD had 29.8 per cent in 1928 and 35 per cent in 1947. The DVP and the DDP, taken together, had 13.6 per cent in 1928, while the FDP now had 9 per cent. And the KPD had received 10.6 per cent in 1928 and now received the same as the FDP, 9 per cent.

This continuity is an indication that, after the catastrophes of Nazism and war, many Germans had now returned to their starting point prior to the Nazi disaster. But it could also be assumed that the first post-war elections marked a transitional stage, and that they did not reflect a firm political choice. Indeed, how could such a choice have been made? Prospects for the future were too uncertain, and it was also unclear what elections of this type actually signified for the future, and what kind of future this would be.

## The Cold War and the Division of Germany

The political agenda of the Allies did not involve either the retention of Germany's territorial unity or its long-term division. Priority was rather given to the interests of the four powers themselves, at first in alliance within the context of the Potsdam Agreement, then increasingly divided into two camps, the East and the West. The French, though, had from the outset views which were peculiar to them alone, centred on security and reparations, which frequently put them at odds with Great Britain and the United States. Certain decisions had been made in advance, such as the division into four zones of occupation, which were also intended to supply reparations for each occupying power in its own zone, but apart from that each of the four powers was determined to retain what it now held in its own hands. The emergence of the East–West confrontation and the decision to divide Germany into two states were therefore parallel processes, which passed through four phases between May 1945 and June 1948, although there were also cross-currents throughout the period, following other rhythms and obeying a different logic.

In the first phase, between the making of the Potsdam Agreement in summer 1945 and the end of the Paris Reparations Conference in July 1946, the wish to reach agreement dominated the negotiations between the four victorious powers. It is true, as already indicated, that a feeling of mistrust gradually developed between the Western powers and the Soviet Union, but the desire to rule Germany jointly still predominated, as was demonstrated not least in the Nuremberg trial of the major war criminals.

The second phase began with the Paris Conference. Here the divergences between the powers emerged more sharply, and they continued to be largely economic in origin. The American proposal to make the four zones a single economic unit, so as to be able to proceed with the reconstruction of the German economy, was rejected by France and the Soviet Union. For both powers, the extraction of reparations from their respective zones (and control over the Ruhr) was more important than the restoration of German economic strength.

The agreement to combine the British and American zones into 'Bizonia' was therefore at first purely a pragmatic decision. The precarious economic situation worsened in the winter of 1946–7. Cold, hunger and undernourishment characterised the German condition, as they did almost everywhere in ruined Europe, not only because production facilities and infrastructure had been destroyed but also because of political instability. These difficulties were felt in France, the Benelux countries and Italy as much as they were in the parts of East Central and South-East Europe which were disputed between East and West. Moreover, and this is what proved to be the decisive factor, the links between the European national economies had been severed. Exports and imports were unable to get back on their feet, and the driving force of European economic strength was absent owing to the de facto collapse of the German industrial economy.

The merger of the British and American zones of occupation on 1 January 1947 was of far-reaching political significance, because it shaped the outlines of a division of Germany. Economically, on the other hand, it was only a small step, though not without importance. A reconstruction of the economies of the European countries on an isolated national basis could not lead to a healthy outcome, in either the short or the long term, and in any case it could not happen unless the German economy was again set in motion. That was the essential conclusion of the analysis of the European situation undertaken by the US administration around the turn of the years 1946–7. A much more coordinated reconstruction of Europe was therefore needed, which would include Germany, and a generous financial stimulus would have to be provided to overcome problems of liquidity, which were immense.

The third phase of the process lasted from March to June 1947. This was marked by a worsening of Great Power tensions, which from the US point of view were a result of the Soviet Union's endeavours to expand its European empire. The Soviet Union had imposed its system of government on the countries occupied by the Red Army, without paying any attention to the results of elections. In Yugoslavia, Tito's partisan forces had founded a communist republic aligned with the Soviet Union; in Iran, communist groups in the north of the country had proclaimed autonomous republics. In France, the communists had become the strongest party in parliamentary elections, and the US government thought the Soviet Union was engaged in expansionist penetration of Turkey as well. The scenario of a communist-dominated Europe seemed to be becoming a reality.

This trend of events reached a dramatic climax in March 1947 with the withdrawal of British troops from participation in the Greek civil war, in which a communist guerrilla movement was fighting with growing success against the British-supported army of the conservative Greek government. When Great

Britain ceased its assistance to Greece and Turkey, largely for financial reasons, the moment had come for the USA to change course and adopt a much harder line. With President Truman's speech to the American Congress on 12 March 1947 cooperation between Second World War Allies now turned into open confrontation between Cold War opponents. According to Truman, two ways of life were now confronting each other:

> One way of life is based upon the will of the majority, and is distinguished by free institutions, representative government, free elections, guarantees of individual liberty, freedom of speech and religion, and freedom from political oppression. The second way of life is based upon the will of a minority forcibly imposed upon the majority. It relies upon terror and oppression, a controlled press and radio, fixed elections and the suppression of personal freedoms.

On these grounds, he announced that, in future, the USA would give political and economic support to every country that was resisting 'attempted subjugation by armed minorities or by outside pressures.'[49]

The dispute over the shape of political systems in industrial societies had dominated the European scene since the end of the nineteenth century and with the October Revolution it had taken on worldwide dimensions. Now the rivalry between the democratic capitalism of the West and the socialist dictatorships of the East would make this dispute the matrix of world history for the next fifty years. The demise of National Socialist Germany meant that one radical alternative to the liberal system had been defeated. It had also lost any legitimacy it possessed. The other alternative, however, namely Soviet communism, had gained considerably in political prestige as an ally of the West in the victorious war against Germany, and also because of the devastating losses the country had suffered in the process, although an examination of the situation within the USSR showed that this was a dictatorship comparable in its frightfulness with the Nazi regime. Even so, this view of the USSR only started to be dominant in the West when cooperation between the USA and the Soviet Union was replaced by the political and ideological antagonism invoked by Truman in 1947. From then onwards, the central feature of US foreign policy was the 'containment' of Soviet expansion, and this context now required a different approach to the German question.

'World communism is like a malignant parasite, which feeds only on diseased tissue.' This is what George F. Kennan, the US ambassador in Moscow, wrote in an analysis dated 22 February 1946. Communism, he said, spreads wherever poverty and chaos prevail. The only way to counter communism was to end the economic distress of the European countries by providing generous assistance. This was the essence of the offer made by US Secretary of

State George C. Marshall to the governments of Europe in his speech of 5 June 1947, which soon acquired worldwide renown. He offered extensive American credits to restore 'the confidence of the European people in the economic future of their own countries and of Europe as a whole. The manufacturer and the farmer . . . must be able and willing to exchange their products for currencies the continuing value of which is not open to question.'

This offer of comprehensive financial support was bound up with three requirements, which gave America's assistance an explosive political impact. Firstly, Marshall explicitly stated that

> before the United States Government can proceed much further in its efforts to alleviate the situation and help start the European world on the way to recovery, there must be some agreement among the countries of Europe as to the requirements of the situation and the part those countries themselves will take.[50]

Economic and financial assistance would therefore not be given to the European countries on a piecemeal basis, but only on condition of political and economic coordination, and above all the restoration of European economic and commercial contacts.

Secondly, this offer of help was directed to all European countries, hence also to those within the area of Soviet domination, and to the Soviet Union itself. But the free market and free economic exchange relations were diametrically opposed to the economic and political principles of the Soviet Union, and it was clear that the American offer had political objectives as well. Nevertheless, the offer was tempting enough for the Soviet Union at least to examine it, and thus the Soviet government accepted the invitation to a joint conference on American aid, which was soon dubbed the 'Marshall Plan' after its author's name, though its official title was the 'European Recovery Programme', or ERP.

Thirdly, Germany was also one of the European countries which were offered assistance, although as a state it did not in fact exist. The strategic core of Marshall's initiative was that the German economy would be restored to activity by extensive economic aid. This would serve both to preserve Germany from sliding into communism—the nightmare of all Western politicians—and to stimulate the European economy, something which was not possible without the impetus Germany could provide.

Between July and September 1947, the Organisation for European Economic Co-operation (OEEC) was set up in Paris. This put in place the necessary prerequisites for the implementation of the Marshall Plan. West Germany, as represented by the military governors of the three Western zones, also joined the OEEC, and it was thereby integrated, as a national economy rather than a national community, into the Western European state structure, which was in process of formation, even before it was founded as a state. This decision itself highlighted the country's current condition and its prospective future. The amount of Marshall Plan money which now began to flow towards Europe was of considerable significance, although it was not the decisive factor. Great Britain received $3.2 billion, France $2.7 billion, and Italy $1.5 billion. West Germany received only $1.4 billion and was expected to repay the money, unlike the other recipients. In 1949, the ERP provided less than 7 per cent of the capital invested in West Germany. The Marshall Plan was nevertheless of inestimable value as a signal of America's readiness to support the economies of the European nations, and as a basis for their economic and political stability. It was also 'a key event in European history, because it tied the West German economy firmly to Western Europe.'[51]

Thus the Marshall Plan became an important instrument in the American struggle to win the West Europeans, and, not least, the West Germans, for the West in political terms as well. With this aim in view, the publicity activities of the ERP were as lavish as the aid itself. Countless leaflets, books and posters and more than two hundred short films explained the beneficial effect of the Marshall money. Goods which had been provided with the help of ERP money were labelled accordingly. These efforts were crowned with success. The newspaper *Die Welt* had this to say about the Americans' plans: 'On the horizon of free Europe the silver lining of economic recovery became visible on 1 April 1948. We welcome the warm-hearted decision of the great nation on the other side of the Atlantic.' According to the *Frankfurter Rundschau:* 'No political propaganda can persuade us to see American aid as anything other than the only way to achieve a normal life for Germany.' The proportion of the people surveyed who were aware of the Marshall Plan had risen by 1948 to 76 per cent (91 per cent in Berlin). Of those questioned, 85 per cent were convinced that the plan would improve their lives.[52]

Not quite three years after the end of the war, therefore, Germany had gone from being a defeated enemy which had to be punished to a potential partner. Whereas, two years previously, the Western powers had wanted to shrink the economic foundations of the country for decades to such an extent that it would no longer be able to present a danger to its neighbours, now American money was to be used to make possible its rapid economic recovery, which would save the continent from communism. Seldom in Europe's recent history has there been a more abrupt change of direction by policy-makers.

The fourth phase, from the advent of the Marshall Plan in June 1947 to the currency reform of June 1948, began when the Soviet delegates to the Marshall Plan conference in Paris rejected American aid for themselves and the countries in their area of control. This decision consummated the division of Europe, and thereby also that of Germany. In the months that followed, all efforts were concentrated on the consolidation and stabilisation of the two camps, with the result that each of them assumed the rigidity of a 'bloc'.

The specific steps to be taken towards the foundation of West Germany were discussed at the Six Power Conference held in London between February and June 1948, in which the Benelux countries also participated along with the three Western occupiers. The French opposed the plan at first, but eventually gave their agreement, in view of the worsening of the East–West conflict. The conference concluded on 7 June 1948 by calling upon the military governors of the Western zones to summon a constituent assembly for the western part of Germany.

The fact that these proceedings took place simultaneously with the dramatic dénouement of the currency reform and the Berlin blockade lent the events a flavour of world crisis and emergency. The act by which the West German state was constituted was therefore perceived by both the Germans and the Allies as part of the context of the new international confrontation rather than in national terms as the foundation of a state and an act of constitution-making.

## Summer 1948

Up to that point, all decisions had been taken by the Allies, in fact essentially by the US government, and the German politicians had been informed and consulted, but little more than that. Now the Germans were gradually given a larger share of responsibility. The establishment of Bizonia had already produced central governing bodies with German directors. These individuals functioned as government ministers, but were obliged to conform to the instructions of the military governors. A body called the Economic Council (*Wirtschaftsrat*), which was drawn from the parliaments of the *Länder* on a proportional basis, served as a parliament for Bizonia. A basic parliamentary structure thus emerged, with the directors serving as a shadow government. This lacked a direct electoral mandate, but it had a strong enough electoral basis to allow it to prepare an administrative structure and provide the personnel for a new government.

The decisive turning point, however, occurred in the early summer of 1948, when the currency reform, the Berlin blockade and the initial discussions about a West German constitution created the conditions for the advances of subsequent decades, which were the establishment of the economic system, the integration of the country with the West and the formation of a West German political structure.

There is no doubt that the currency reform of June 1948 constituted a profound change. The enormous state debt inherited from Hitler's Reich—at the end of the war it was 452 billion RM, or five times the size of the gross national product—was a heavy burden on any attempt to conduct a fresh economic policy. A radical intervention in the currency field was necessary to bring the quantity of money into line with the level of commodity production, and that, in turn, was the inescapable prerequisite for an economic advance on the basis of the free market. For the SMAD, a currency reform in the Soviet zone was not urgent, because there they were not aiming to establish a market system. On the contrary, they were perfectly comfortable with the system of rationing and food coupons associated with a low level of consumption. Hence the Americans did not even ask the Soviet Union whether they would agree to a currency reform for the whole of Germany.[53]

As we have already shown, in the Western zones the economic prospects for a rapid recovery were not as bad as has long been believed. There was less destruction of industrial potential by bombing raids and post-war dismantling than had been feared, the drive to produce arms during the war had intensified the country's industrialisation, and the necessary supply of skilled labour was available. In fact, there was too much of it, owing to the large number of refugees. In addition, the prospects for a restoration of economic links within Europe, as well as the liquidity of industrial enterprises, had been improved considerably by the foundation of the OEEC and the introduction of the Marshall Plan. But without a stable currency and the liquidation of the financial consequences of the war a full recovery was impossible.

The Americans therefore placed their faith in a fresh start, with rigorous financial discipline, and the currency reform, which had been under preparation since autumn 1947, was accordingly of extreme severity. At a single stroke, the whole of the monetary overhang inherited from the Nazi period was wiped out. The financial assets of ordinary Germans lost 90 per cent of their value, which was an act of expropriation almost unique in history. It meant that the Germans finally had to pay the financial cost of the Second World War. Material assets, in contrast, were not devalued: wealth held in goods, means of production, real estate and also land was largely unaffected. Anyone who did not possess property of this kind and had to depend on what they could earn and what they had saved was deeply affected. All that remained of 1,000 RM was 65 German Marks. But people who owned houses or land, industrial entrepreneurs and tradesmen, did extremely well out of the one-sided decision to devalue financial assets and preserve the value of material assets. The purpose of the measure was to stimulate economic activity and investment and to promote economic circulation.

Social aspects, on the other hand, were a secondary consideration. The Americans rejected German proposals for an equalisation of the burdens imposed by the currency reform which would take into account not just the interests of those who possessed money and material assets but also of the refugees and the people bombed out of their houses. An occupying power was able to do that; a democratically elected government would probably have been overthrown if it had taken such an approach. The German participants in the currency reform therefore hastened to point out that 'all the factually essential counter-proposals of the German technical experts' had been rejected by the occupying powers, and the latter therefore bore 'sole responsibility for the principles and methods of the monetary reform in their zones'.[54]

There was one further important additional step taken on the day after the currency conversion, when it was announced that price controlled rations would largely be abolished. This measure had almost as drastic an impact as the currency reform. But unlike the latter, the ending of state control over prices had been conceived and decreed by the Economic Office of Bizonia and its director, the economics professor Ludwig Erhard. By the Law on the Principles of Price Policy (*Leitsätzegesetz*) agreed on 21 June 1948 the fixed prices of all items were abolished at a single stroke, with the exception of food, rents and some raw materials.

Erhard was supported in his decision by the Scientific Advisory Board of the Economic Council (*Wirtschaftsrat*). In this body, the advocates of a planned economy, who were associated with Social Democracy, had been overcome by the liberally inclined supporters of the Freiburg School of 'Ordoliberalism', who included, apart from the Freiburg professors Walter Eucken and Franz Böhm, the Münster University professor Alfred Müller-Armack, Erhard's closest adviser. All three had kept their distance from National Socialism, and they now championed a conception in which political and economic freedom were closely linked. In their view, a free and capitalist market economy must be combined with a social compromise between group interests, guaranteed by a strong state. This was the 'social market economy', a concept which first emerged in 1949. It was intended to eliminate traditional notions of economic planning and pave the way for free trade and private entrepreneurship. At the same time, however, it was intended to prevent the unrestricted domination of the economically strong and to protect the weaker members of society. The emergence of the social market economy was less a reaction to the directed economy of the post-war years than it was the 'result of a social learning process going back in principle to the end of the great crisis of the early 1930s', and it was already known to elite groups in the administration and economic life as an alternative to both state direction of the economy and a radically pro-market approach.[55]

Erhard's initiative had the support of American officials, especially Lucius Clay. He could rely on the support of a slim majority made up of the middle-class members of the Economic Council. The Social Democrats criticised his plans, but did not attach a great deal of importance to the Economic Council, mistakenly as it turned out. Erhard's course of action was risky, because for more than ten years the German economy had been accustomed to a planned economic system with price controls, and its development had been hedged around with countless limitations and restrictions. To hope that market forces would come to the rescue therefore appeared to be somewhat unrealistic. But the alternative would have been to continue the system of rationing, food coupons and the black market, and considering the dreariness of the post-war years, Erhard's perspective for the future offered at least a glimmer of hope.

When they were actually put into operation, the currency reform and the elimination of price controls had the effect of an economic big bang: the black market disappeared within a few days, the shops became full, and suddenly everything was on sale again, though at prices which were unaffordable for most people. Between June and August 1948 alone, the level of industrial production rose by almost 25 per cent, and by the end of 1949 its value had doubled in Bizonia, whereas before the currency reform it stood at half the 1936 level. The negative effects of the devaluation were however equally apparent: prices rose steeply, in view of the immense demand, and since the wage freeze was not brought to an end until November 1948, the situation of many people worsened in the course of the year, and there was increased resistance to Erhard's drastic measures. Indeed, on 12 November 1948 the trade unions organised a general strike against the abolition of fixed prices, and in public opinion surveys 70 per cent of West Germans indicated their support for the reintroduction of price controls. When prices fell again, at the end of 1949, unemployment grew, and in the following year it exceeded the 10 per cent mark. It took years before the West German economy attained stability, and when it did this was within the framework of the European economic recovery. But it was also easy to see what an enormous impetus had been provided to the economy by the currency reform and the abolition of price controls. The two measures acted as an initial spark, allowing the tremendous economic potential available in the western part of the country to develop. A powerful economic impetus was thereby unleashed. Not until the early 1950s, however, did this set in motion a constant and self-sustaining economic upsurge.[56]

The currency reform and the ending of economic controls marked a decision in favour of a capitalist economic order, oriented towards the free market. This same economic order had lost a considerable degree of legitimacy in Germany and Europe during the 1930s. It was now brought back by the American government (the French and British governments had to tag along, willy-nilly) and West German specialists and politicians joined to make it a reality. Capitalism, therefore, was not imposed on the West Germans from outside. But, without the Marshall Plan and the American-inspired currency reform, different priorities would probably have been set, corresponding perhaps to the French or Italian model of a state-directed industrial economy, as was favoured at the time by the SPD and the trade unions.

The results were spectacular. The currency reform and the freeing of prices provided a tremendous stimulus to growth. But, at the same time, a high level of social inequality was created right at the inception of the new state of West Germany. This inequality fixed the relations of wealth and power in this society for a long time to come. It is true that an attempt was made in the 1950s to lessen inequality by social policy measures, but the fundamental economic system of the new state, in terms of both its underlying impetus and the way this was reflected in society, had been predetermined by the decisions made in 1948. 'For various reasons, a small number of people have been able to make large profits', reported an American committee in 1951 on the social situation in West Germany. 'They will have to watch out that the new republic does not perish through acquisitiveness.'[57]

The Soviet Union rightly understood the West German currency reform as an American refusal to continue the system of joint responsibility for Germany and a decision to establish a separate Western state. The currency reform in the East, ordered by the SMAD in response, simply reproduced what the Americans had done in the West. But now the situation of Berlin became a problem. The city lay in the territory of the SBZ, but it was subject to a special four-power status. In order to prevent the West German currency reform from being applied to West Berlin, the Soviet Union decided to sever all the city's links with West Germany, with the aim of forcing out the Western Allies and incorporating West Berlin into the SBZ. This was 'a large-scale, and somewhat barbaric, attempt at blackmail by starvation.'[58]

The Berlin blockade did in fact seriously endanger the West's project of establishing a state in its part of Germany. To break through the blockade by force would have meant risking an armed conflict. If the West negotiated with the Soviet Union, perhaps over the reversal of the currency reform, this would have perhaps meant the end of the option to establish a West German state, and the outcome would have been uncertain. Under these circumstances, the British and American decision to supply the 2.2 million inhabitants of West Berlin by air was a daring compromise, which required an enormous effort: there were up to 1,300 flights a day into the city for the next ten months. It was also impossible to predict what the outcome would be. That the airlift finally turned out to be successful and that the Soviet Union had to tone down its demands was the result of the tremendous exertions undertaken by the USA, which was by now the unquestioned leader of the West.

The Berlin blockade was a political and psychological turning point for West Germany, but also for the relationship between the Germans and the Western

Allies. Those ten months changed Berlin's image. Instead of being the former capital of the German Reich and the centre of the Nazi terror regime, it became the symbol of the free world. It was also the visible symbol of the American policy which Truman had announced a year earlier, namely to give assistance to every country resisting 'attempted subjugation by armed minorities or by outside pressure'. Berlin thus became a city fighting for its freedom, and in the emotional words of the Mayor of West Berlin, Ernst Reuter, it became a model for the whole world. 'Nations of the world, look at this city!' he said. The blockade and the airlift both demonstrated and accentuated the division of the world into two camps. In the eyes of the West Germans, the aggressiveness and brutality of the Soviet Union was contrasted with the daring assistance of the British and American pilots—the very same pilots who only a few years earlier had reduced Berlin to a pile of rubble.

Probably no other event of the post-war period had a greater effect in strengthening the emotional bond between the West Germans and the Western world than this one. The experience of standing both on the side of freedom and on the side of the stronger power in such a threatening situation laid the basis for their attachment to the West and created the emotional conditions for their acceptance of the half-state founded by the Western Allies. The bond with the West had a dual foundation. One element was the West Germans' uncompromising rejection of the Soviet Union's strong-arm tactics. This allowed a link to be made with the war and the struggle of the Wehrmacht against the Red Army, and it gave them a new and self-confident role as the defenders of Western liberty, which was willingly accepted. The other element was the offer made by the Western powers, and in particular the USA, which was incomparably more attractive than anything the Soviet Union could provide, namely, an early and long-lasting economic recovery, which at that point in time was only a realistic prospect with American assistance. The decision to restore the state in the democratic form clearly rejected by two-thirds of the German population fifteen years earlier was now greeted with majority approval, as was shown by the high level of electoral participation, by the number of votes for the democratic parties, and by public opinion surveys, although there was little active enthusiasm for the democratic system as such.[59]

## Past and Future

There had been a surge of support for the Left everywhere in Europe after the end of the Second World War. In the first post-war elections in France, the communists obtained 26 per cent of the vote, and the Socialists 24 per cent. The results were similar in Italy and Finland. In Czechoslovakia, the communists came out of the elections as by far the largest party, with 38 per cent of the vote. In the Scandinavian countries, the vote for socialist parties varied between 30 and 40 per cent, and for the communists between 10 and 15 per cent. In Austria the Social Democrats won the elections with 45 per cent, and in Great Britain Labour won with 48 per cent. The 1950s would see a weakening of this trend, but in the first post-war years, the Left went from strength to strength. This was not a particularly surprising reaction to the domination of the Right in the interwar period and the war waged by radical right-wing regimes in Germany and Italy.

The Left was also dominant among the intelligentsia. Almost everywhere, the main advocates of the radical Right were either dead, in prison or isolated. Their worldview was imbued with the struggle against cultural modernity and soaked in the intellectual atmosphere of the First World War, which now seemed further away even than the nineteenth century. Their fantasies about the *Volk*, blood, purity, struggle and death were now a thing of the past; they no longer had the capacity to arouse people. Among German intellectuals, and in the newly founded political parties, the question of guilt and responsibility for the National Socialist dictatorship occupied centre stage in all the debates of the immediate post-war years, and the more that was known about the crimes of the Nazis the more intense did the debates become. It was hardly surprising that left-wing positions predominated after the collapse of the dictatorship of the radical Right, especially as the Allies strictly prohibited the dissemination of nationalist views and forbade any attempt to turn the war into a heroic endeavour. The debates of this period, however, did not just concern the immediate past. It was obvious that the future political direction of the country would also be determined by how people analysed the Nazi dictatorship and the reasons for the collapse of the Weimar Republic.

This applied particularly to the communists, who both in Germany and in Europe as a whole now derived their claim to power not, even in part, from their past history of class struggle, but from their actions during the war and the Nazi dictatorship. Anti-fascism became their basis for legitimacy, and this continued to be so right to the end of communist rule. The fact that almost all the top officials of German communism had been opponents of National Socialism and that a considerable number of them had suffered persecution under the Nazis conferred credibility on their anti-fascism far beyond the ranks of the Communist Party. This was also responsible to a certain degree for the forward-looking idealism of the founding generation of SED members, who proceeded from the firm conviction that they were responding to the lessons of history and creating a new Germany which would be 'better' in the moral sense as well, in view of the gradual return of many ex-Nazis to positions of leadership in the west. From the communist angle of vision which underlay this conviction, certain particularly reactionary sections of finance capital had come to power in 1933 with the Nazis, and the Nazi dictatorship had served as their executive organ. But, if capitalism created 'fascism', was it not a logical conclusion from the crimes of the Nazi régime to demand the removal of capitalism? Hence the establishment of a socialist state was ultimately to be understood as the corollary of victory over fascism.

The communist view of history also implied that the German people, above all the German workers, were victims of National Socialism, while the responsibility for it lay exclusively with the elites, particularly big capital. The German people, the SED leaders claimed, had been 'misused' or 'seduced' by those in power. This provided the justification for the imposition of an anti-fascist educational dictatorship.

These fundamental positions were upheld by many left intellectuals, a majority of whom had been in exile during the Nazi period. A large number of them, including Anna Seghers, Bertolt Brecht, Stephan Hermlin, Ernst Bloch, Ludwig Renn, Alfred Kantorowicz and Johannes R. Becher, returned from exile not to West Germany but to the Eastern zone. Becher founded the 'Cultural League for the Democratic Renewal of Germany', a movement which had considerable resonance in the first few years after the war. The intention behind it was to combine German high culture's traditions of bourgeois humanism with the spirit of anti-fascism. 'We want to recover possession of the humanism of the best German minds—the spirit of justice, love of truth and the courage of one's convictions.' This is how Friedrich Wolf formulated the movement's aims in a programmatic way at the end of 1945.[60]

Some of the Jews who returned to Germany also found a new home in East Berlin and Dresden, rather than in Hamburg or Cologne. Their conviction was that only communism could ward off a repetition of the past catastrophe. Thus, the thoroughly bourgeois Professor of Romance Linguistics, Victor Klemperer, made his application to join the KPD at the end of 1945, after he had been very lucky to survive the Nazi period as a Jew married to a non-Jewish woman. This was how he justified it: 'I believe that only a very resolute left-wing movement can get us out of the present calamity and prevent its return. As a university teacher I was forced to watch at close quarters as reactionary ideas made ever greater inroads. We must seek to remove them effectively and from the bottom up. And only in the KPD do I see the unambiguous will to do so.' In line with these views, Klemperer soon joined Becher's League for Democratic Renewal, he also joined the Association of Victims of the Nazi Régime. But his attitude remained ambivalent. 'In my heart of hearts I don't believe in anything, and everything appears to me equally trivial and equally false' he wrote four years later, adding that 'the ghastly similarity to Nazi methods in the propaganda for the Soviet Friendship Society and the hullabaloo over Stalin's birthday cannot be denied.'[61]

The Social Democrats, like the Communists, thought the collapse of the Weimar Republic was a result of the ruthless pursuit of their own interests by the leaders of big business and the military, but they also viewed it as a victory for both right-wing and left-wing enemies of democracy. For most Social Democrats, the idea of a merger with the Communists seemed preposterous, in view of their experiences during the Weimar period, and also during the Spanish Civil War, as well as the reports from the Soviet Union about Stalinist terror. Thus, it was the Social Democratic Left that first invented the concept of 'totalitarianism' as a description of dictatorships of both Right and Left, before it became established on the Right, largely as a means of delegitimising Soviet communism.

The SPD saw itself as the sole unwavering opponent of National Socialism (on a worldwide scale) and it derived a claim to moral and political leadership from this. Its leader, Kurt Schumacher, who had been wounded in the First World War, and whose external appearance testified to the damage his health had suffered in Hitler's concentration camps, became virtually a symbol of German suffering. He stressed that all other political forces, at home and abroad, had either made alliances with the Nazis or compromised with them in some form. The Western Allies had made the Munich Agreement, the Soviet Union had supported the Nazi dictatorship by making the Hitler–Stalin Pact, while 'the failure of the German bourgeoisie and of that part of the workers' movement which had not recognised the value of democracy to the working class' was what constituted 'the German people's share of historical guilt'.[62]

Schumacher's criticisms of the victorious Allies were widely approved outside the ranks of his own party, because they seemed to deprive the Allies' claim to moral superiority of its legitimacy. His belief in the political immaculacy of the SPD also exonerated its members from anything they had experienced or done during the Nazi period and the war. Thus, the party could start to be, or revert to being, a political home even for people who had spent those years in the Wehrmacht or other institutions of the Nazi state, because their commitment to the SPD seemed to make their own private past a kind of resistance activity.

Those Liberals who had not emerged from the German nationalist context interpreted National Socialism as above all a consequence of the lack of a tradition of freedom in Germany. Democracy and liberty, they said, had never been anchored in the German people. After the defeat of the 1848 revolution, socialism and nationalism had inspired the masses, while the liberal movement had never possessed the mass support it had enjoyed in many other countries. As Theodor Heuss emphasised at the beginning of 1946, Britain and America had also experienced an economic crisis, but not a Hitler, 'because they have behind them a history of freedom, which we lack.' On the contrary, as Reinhold Maier, the liberal Prime Minister of Württemberg-Baden, put it, the German people had jettisoned democracy 'with unprecedented frivolity.' They had 'ridiculed and derided our democratic convictions, they called for the strong man, and that is what they received.'[63]

The point of view of the educated German bourgeoisie were given early and prominent expression by Friedrich Meinecke, the Nestor of German historical scholarship, who had opposed the Nazi dictatorship, and distanced himself from it. He had already made his views clear in 1946 in the book *The German Catastrophe*. He described National Socialism as the extreme expression of modernity, and of the fanatical mass movements engendered by mass society. Whereas Germans had previously felt immune from such incursions, feeling all too secure 'in our firmly-grounded, law-governed state, in our comfortable bourgeois order of things, in liberal ideals of personal freedom, self-determination and dignity, which continued to shine despite having grown pale' this world had been rendered fragile, first through the entry of the masses into history after the French Revolution, then by the rise of the two big mass movements of nationalism and socialism which emerged at the end of the nineteenth century. But it was also the spiritual decline of the bourgeoisie itself, which had abandoned prudence and moderation in an increasingly alienated world of technology and unhealthy stimulation, which was part of this development and one of its driving forces. Hence with the revolution of 1918–19, Versailles, and the rise of the forces of right-wing irrationalism catastrophe had approached, to reach its eventual dénouement in the most terrible manner. It would nevertheless be a fallacy, wrote Meinecke, to regard the calamity as being embedded in German history, something that dated back as far as Bismarck, or even Frederick the Great. Hitler's Reich was rather the work of a clique of criminals, who had been in power only briefly, although the consequences had been frightful. Nazism remained external to the German people. But massification and alienation were phenomena affecting all European states in the industrial age. Thus 'the question of the deeper causes of the frightful catastrophe which had burst upon Germany' should be posed more broadly: it was 'a Western and not merely a German problem.' Many of Meinecke's fellow historians shared this point of view. The Freiburg historian Gerhard Ritter also thought that the 'rootlessness of a population which had lost its habitat in modern industrial society', the disappearance of personal ties, and the 'lack of traditions among the masses' which had caused the dictatorship to gain the upper hand were 'European, not just German phenomena.'[64]

Meinecke's analysis had very little in common with the apologetic narratives of the old and new nationalists, which could again be heard loudly after 1948.

His critique of the German bourgeoisie, of the German worship of power, and of German nationalist politicians such as Hindenburg, was trenchant enough for it to be rejected by the Right and the Conservatives. But the claim that National Socialism was an expression of the harmful tendencies of modernity had a direct link with the German bourgeois tradition of cultural criticism since the turn of the century, in which the spread of modern culture, democracy, and technology; the rise of urbanism; the emancipation of women; and Judaism were all equally seen as the expression and motive force of a story of decline. In many authors, harking back to the classics was combined with a 'return to God'; in other words, an attempt was made to interpret the German catastrophe as the result of enlightenment, rationality and secularisation. This perspective appeared to offer a comfortable way out of the dilemma of Germany's entanglement in the Nazi period, and in the years that followed the foundation of the West German state it became increasingly popular.[65]

## Two New States

Debates on the reasons for National Socialism took place later on in the newly formed Parliamentary Council. The result of the debates was that a constitution for the new state emerged, almost every aspect of which was a reaction to the catastrophe of Nazism and war.

With the handing over of the Frankfurt Documents of 1 July 1948 to the prime ministers of the West German federal states (*Länder*), the work of founding West Germany as a state passed into German hands. The three military governors only insisted on a few points, though these were of key importance: the constitution should be federal in character, a central authority should be set up, the rights and freedoms of the individual should be preserved and legitimated by means of a referendum, and the boundaries of the *Länder* should be redrawn. The military governors also announced that they would issue an occupation statute defining the continuing rights of the occupying powers.

This offer by the Western Allies was regarded by the politicians of West Germany as a decidedly mixed blessing. On the one hand, the prospect of the restoration of a German state, with at least partial autonomy, along with political stability and economic prosperity, was certainly enticing. On the other hand, this offer would unmistakably entrench Germany's division into a western and an eastern part. This was a severe encumbrance for the members of the Parliamentary Council, who had almost all been brought up in the tradition of national unity. In discussions with the Western Allies, the Social Democrats expressed strong reservations. They were the most vociferous opponents of any tendency towards a division of the country. In contrast to this, the representatives of the bourgeois parties, particularly the Union, regarded a quick association of the new state with the West as an acceptable solution under the circumstances, because any option involving a united and neutral Germany seemed to them to be risky, because it might open the door to Soviet expansion.[66]

But all parties were at one in insisting that the foundation of a West German state was only a temporary measure, and that the division of the country must not be reinforced by it. The terms 'Basic Law' instead of 'Constitution' and 'Parliamentary Council' instead of 'Constituent or National Assembly' were wrested from the military governors; they indicated that the West German state was to be regarded as temporary. Kurt Schumacher stressed that the decision to establish a West German state had been made by the Western Allies, and they therefore bore the sole responsibility for it. In alluding in this way to the inadequate legitimacy of the Parliamentary Council, the head of the SPD was no doubt correct, because this constituent assembly, which met on 1 September in Bonn, far away from the flashpoints of the Cold War, was dependent on the approval of the occupying powers, and had not been directly elected by the people. It was therefore unsurprising that the discussions which finally led to the passing of the Basic Law of the Federal Republic of Germany on 8 May 1949 attracted little public notice: in an opinion survey, 73 per cent of those questioned showed no interest, or only moderate interest, in the Bonn discussions, and only 21 per cent were 'very interested'. But at the same time, 70 per cent expressed themselves in favour of establishing a West German state. Most West Germans supported the process which had been initiated, seeing no realistic alternative, but they did not ascribe much significance to it.[67]

The draft constitution produced by the Parliamentary Council provided a kind of summation of the varying explanations for the downfall of the Weimar Republic. The catalogue of fundamental rights which introduced the constitution emphasised the outstanding importance of the rule of law, and of the need to protect individuals and minority groups from the unlimited power of the majority in view of the experience of arbitrariness and illegality during the dictatorship. But the constitution also equipped the new state with strong weapons against the enemies of democracy: this implied a rejection of the Weimar relativism about values, which had allowed the Nazis and the Communists to undermine democracy with its own means, accompanied by the scornful laughter of opponents of the republic such as Carl Schmitt. The political parties were allotted an explicit right to collaborate in the formation of the people's political will—this was a reply to the widespread criticism of parties and pluralism in the first republic—and they had to commit themselves to the democratic system (the concept of hostility to the constitution would play an important role in the decisions of the early 1950s to prohibit certain political parties). It was also the unfortunate experience of Weimar that suggested the need to strengthen the role of the parliament and the Chancellor. The Federal President, on the other hand, now simply had the task of representing the country, unlike former President Hindenburg, who had taken a direct part in the formation of governments and was able to dissolve parliament.[68] The Federal Constitutional Court (*Bundesverfassungsgericht*), which started to operate in 1951, was responsible for upholding the provisions of the Basic Law. It represented an innovation in constitutional law in that it had the role of checking whether the organs of the state were acting in a constitutional fashion.

Doubts as to the democratic reliability of the Germans, which were particularly pronounced among Liberals and Conservatives, were reflected in the constitution's strong emphasis on representative democracy and its complete abandonment of referenda. Even the Basic Law was not confirmed by popular vote but by the *Land* parliaments alone. The scepticism of the political elites towards their own people was unmistakable, and for decades this was one of the fixed attitudes (usually unspoken) of German politicians. It was even more prevalent among the bourgeois parties than among the Social Democrats.[69]

Surprisingly enough, there were no big debates on the constitution's social and economic aspects. This was because the Social Democrats preferred politically and ideologically neutral formulations, which would allow them to put their own economic policy into practice after the victory they confidently expected in the first elections to the federal parliament (*Bundestag*). The most contentious issue was rather the relation between the central administration and the federal components of the constitution. Whereas the Social Democrats regarded a strong central government as the indispensable condition for a functioning state, the Liberals and parts of the Union were entirely in favour of the confederative approach favoured by the Western Allies. The final result, after sharp disagreements with the military governors, was a compromise between the central functions of the federal authority and the powers of the *Länder*. In this connection, the idea of establishing a Federal Council (*Bundesrat*) as the body representing the *Länder* triumphed over other proposals which envisaged a return to pre-democratic traditions and the creation of a Second Chamber consisting of non-party personalities to act as a check on the parties.

When the Basic Law had been passed, the new state had to take account of two decrees issued by the Allies, which restricted its independence. The first was the 'Occupation Statute'. In this, the military governors defined their reserved rights, which related to foreign policy, foreign trade and eventual changes in the constitution. The second was the 'Ruhr Statute', which specified that the Ruhr district, because it was the engine of European industrial growth, would in future be controlled by an internationally staffed supervisory authority.

With this decision, a formula had finally been found which combined recognition of France's security interests with the restoration of the Ruhr economy. International control of the Ruhr looked initially like a further restriction on German sovereignty, and indeed that is what it was. But it turned out, in the course of the negotiations over this question, that the coal, iron and steel firms in the area between West Germany, Northern France and the Benelux countries had already cooperated extensively before 1939 and even during the war, and that it would be possible to build on this, under changed political auspices, without formulating the point explicitly. Thus, alongside the cooperation over Marshall Aid which was enforced by the Americans, the Ruhr Statute marked the first beginnings of institutionalised cooperation between the national economies of Western Europe.[70]

The Federal Republic was a child of the Cold War, and without this it would never have come to birth. The West Germans had largely been excluded from the fundamental decisions over the political and economic system in their country. There had been neither a revolution nor a civil war as after 1918. There was neither a Left radical mass movement lining up against the new republic nor a power-hungry military caste hatching plans for a putsch. After 1945, the internal conflict between Left and Right, which had shaken Germany so profoundly after the First World War, had shifted outside the country and taken on a global scale, as a Cold War confrontation between the communist and the liberal capitalist camps. The result of this was the division of Germany, but also a decision in favour of Western democracy and capitalism prescribed from outside, which the Germans merely helped to put into effect. In view of the worsening international situation this seemed to be the best way of making a start, although no German state had ever been brought into existence in such a low-key, unemphatic fashion and with so little future certainty as this one. There was at least the hope of economic stabilisation and military protection by the Americans. The foundation of the West German state was regarded as a provisional measure. It was an act marked by its sobriety and shaped by the catastrophe of the Nazi period and the bleakness of the post-war years. Unlike the German republic of 1919, however, it did not suffer from the pressure of excessive and unrealisable expectations. That was an advantage.

The foundation of a state in the other half of Germany was even more of a makeshift measure than the foundation of West Germany. The change from cooperation to confrontation between the two superpowers of the post-war era has aptly been described by Wilfried Loth as 'a reactive mechanism'. What is meant by this is that, after a certain degree of mistrust had developed between the two powers, every action taken by one power was interpreted as a threat, which must be countered with a correspondingly tough reaction by the other one. There is no doubt that the Soviet Union saw the establishment of Bizonia on 1 January 1947 as a threat. A conflict with the USA was certainly not in its interests at first, if only because of the devastated condition of large parts of the country. Soviet policy towards Germany was directed not towards conflict but towards guaranteeing military security against the West, and towards making sure of reparations deliveries. Its minimum objective was the emergence of a neutral Germany, not hostile to the Soviet Union. But, in fact, the foreign policy pursued by Stalin, particularly his strategy of expansion in Eastern Europe and the Near East, did contribute substantially to a deterioration of relations with the Western Allies. Nevertheless, the Soviets continued to hope until the summer of 1949, and beyond, that an agreement could be reached with the Western Powers to create a united Germany as a buffer state. The attempt made in 1945 to establish a system which would function as a model for the whole of Germany, by holding early elections, permitting political parties to organise and creating a central administration, was obviously based on a misjudgement of the situation. In view of the dismantling of factories, the arbitrary arrests, the suppression of political opponents, the compulsory unification of the SPD with the KPD to form the SED, the conditions in the special camps, and finally the Berlin blockade, the notion that the majority of Germans would embrace the rule of socialism was a piece of wishful thinking far removed from reality.[71]

Stalin's strategy was aimed at keeping the German question open, but, in any case, he intended to prevent the country from falling into the hands of the Western Allies. The creation of Bizonia and the introduction of the American policy of containment marked the failure of this strategy. The Soviet Union, for its part, reacted by consolidating the position in its own sphere of influence. After the quarrel with Tito's Yugoslavia in 1948, separate national roads to socialism were no longer tolerated. From then on, it was necessary to portray the Soviet side as a unified 'bloc' and to make sure that all the regimes in the bloc followed the Soviet model rigidly. This applied very particularly to the SBZ, which the SMAD now rapidly converted into a bulwark against the West.

The SED also started to pursue a more uncompromising policy at this time. It threw aside its bourgeois-democratic mask and began openly to advocate the 'dictatorship of the working class'. In order to destroy the influence of the CDU and the LDP, which were not yet completely adapted to the new regime, two extra parties (a 'national' party and a peasant party) were established from above and provided with a leadership taken from the ranks of the SED. In addition to this, the official but non-party 'mass organisations' were deprived of their autonomy. The Free German Youth (FDJ) the Free German Trade Union Federation (FDGB), the Cultural League, the Women's League and various other organisations were brought into line, and they acted thenceforth as SED transmission belts.[72]

In summer 1948, the SED numbered 1.8 million members. A third of them came from the old SPD. But the principle of parity between former SPD and former KPD members in appointments to leading positions was now abandoned. The proportion of former Social Democrats in the party leadership declined rapidly, and the domination of the communists was soon overwhelming. Many disappointed SPD cadres left the SBZ and travelled to the West. In essence, the slogan that the SED would become a 'party of a new type' meant its Stalinisation. Anyone who disagreed with this policy was accused of 'anti-Soviet agitation' and had to reckon with expulsion from the party and dismissal from state employment, and also in many cases with being placed in a Special Camp. By January 1949, at the latest, this process had been completed, and all the prerequisites for the establishment of a communist dictatorship on the model of the Soviet Union were in place.

After summer 1948 the SMAD and the SED leadership reproduced all the steps taken to found a West German state with some delay, but in an analogous fashion. The 'German Economic Commission' was established in the East as a reaction to the introduction of the Economic Council in West Germany. Shortly afterwards, the 'German People's Council' was commissioned to work out a constitution. This paralleled the activities of the Parliamentary Council in the West. In May 1949, when the Basic Law was adopted in Bonn, the third 'German People's Congress' convened in Berlin as a parliamentary-type body. It had been elected according to the block-voting system, in which the distribution of seats between the parties and the 'mass organisations' was fixed in advance. Two-thirds of the seats went to the SED, and a further 10 per cent were allotted to groups dependent on it, while a total of 22.5 per cent of the seats were given to the CDU and the LDPD. The ballot papers also contained a question: 'Do you want a united Germany and a just peace?' It was possible to answer only 'Yes' or 'No' to this question, and the same was true of the whole list of candidates. Abstentions were counted as 'Yes' votes. In the Eastern zone as a whole, 61.5 per cent of the electors voted in favour, while in East Berlin the figure was 51.6 per cent. Never again did the SED government allow such a high percentage of negative votes to be cast.

In spite of these developments, the Soviet leadership continued to be sceptical, or at least undecided, about the foundation of a separate East German state, for which the SED leadership was pressing. The Soviet view was that a united, but neutral, Germany would serve its interests better than a divided country two-thirds of which would belong to the West. As long as this hope persisted, preparations for setting up a new state were only undertaken half-heartedly. On the one hand, therefore, the SMAD was widening the division between the Eastern and the Western occupation zones. The boundary between these two areas could now hardly be overcome. On the other hand, it continued to call loudly for German unity. The background and early history of the GDR until 1955 was marked by Stalin's contradictory and inconsistent course on this issue.

As late as December 1948, Stalin had advised the German comrades to 'disguise their activities' and pursue 'a cautious policy'. Only after the foundation of the German Federal Republic did the SED leadership get the green light for the creation of a separate state. In response to this, the 'German People's Council' met in Berlin on 7 October 1949, constituted itself the 'Provisional People's Chamber', and accepted the constitution that had been worked out already. This was strongly reminiscent of the Weimar constitution, with the remarkable difference that the parliament was described as the 'highest organ of the republic' and the classic division of powers was abolished. This also meant that there was no independent judiciary. Apart from this the new government looked democratic. Parity between the two working-class parties appeared to be established by the presence of Wilhelm Pieck, who was one of the founder-members of the KPD, as president, and the Social Democrat Otto Grotewohl as prime minister. Indeed, politicians representing the bourgeois parties actually predominated in Grotewohl's cabinet. But in fact these bourgeois-democratic institutions were no more than a façade. The dominant figure in the politics of the new German Democratic Republic was the general secretary of the SED, Walter Ulbricht, who was distinguished above all by the fact that he enjoyed Stalin's full confidence. Born in 1893, he had belonged to the KPD since 1920, and since 1929 he had been a member of its Central Committee. He went into exile in 1933, first to Paris, and then to Moscow, from where he was sent back to Germany by the CPSU in 1945 as a member of the 'Ulbricht Group'. In Germany, he directed the rebuilding of the Communist Party of Germany and its unification with the SPD. He was, first and foremost, a loyal supporter of the Soviet Communist Party and he followed all its twists and turns, before, alongside, and after Stalin. Until the 1960s, there was no indication that he had any independent ideas or plans. But, after all, the chief quality of a reliable communist was that he followed the party line.[73]

It was by no means inevitable that two German states should come into existence at the end of the immediate post-war period. The victorious powers had not set out to do this, and it was not entirely in line with their interests. For the West, the division of Germany was a temporary way out of the economic distress of the post-war years. For the Soviet Union, it meant a temporary end to their hope of receiving a share of the economic resources of the Western zones. But, when the conflicts within the former anti-Hitler coalition increased in severity and the Cold War broke out, long-term strategic goals won priority over short-term interests. Thanks to the new atmosphere of confrontation, the policies towards a defeated Germany which had originally been paramount now played a subordinate role. Thus the territorial reordering of devastated Europe did not occur in a worldwide peace conference, as in 1919, but in the form of a gradual demarcation of the spheres of influence of mutually hostile Great Powers. The task of stabilising and extending their areas of control now occupied the forefront of their preoccupations. This meant a shifting of allegiances. Countries like Czechoslovakia and Poland, which had previously been counted culturally and politically as Western, now belonged to the East. Germany, Austria and Italy, on the other hand, the former Axis Powers, were now part of the West.

But in contrast to the situation at the beginning of the nineteenth century, for instance, when France and Great Britain had confronted each other merely as two world empires, the two contending power blocs now also represented two forms of world organisation. Admittedly, this confrontation had already been inherent since 1917 in the political antagonism between the communist Soviet Union and the capitalist West, but it was only now that it acquired the power-political and global dimensions which shaped the outline of international relations for forty years. In Germany, the complete destruction and far-reaching loss of legitimacy of the Right radical alternative had not brought to an end the political and cultural disagreements over the proper way to order society in the industrial age, which had kept people in suspense since the turn of the century. These disagreements had to a certain degree been transmuted into a global power-political antagonism. Now, with the foundation of the GDR, the communist alternative had been constituted in the form of a separate state, as a dictatorship under Soviet protection and without democratic legitimacy, but even so, not without certain attractive features, the most important of which were the claim to be radically anti-fascist and the promise of social justice in a socialist system.

The Federal Republic, in contrast, was sustained by an alliance of political Catholicism, the democratic workers' movement and the liberals. It inherited to some extent the traditions of the movement during the years after the First World War in favour of constitutional democracy. But the analogy should not be pursued too far: on the one hand because this state was brought into being first and foremost by the Western Allies and the Germans long regarded it as nothing more than a transitional phenomenon, and, on the other hand, because its constitution and structure had been remodelled in reaction to the mistakes of the Weimar Republic, and the old associations no longer possessed their previous binding force.

Thus, the end of the post-war period saw the establishment of two rigid power blocs, and each German state became identified with one of them as the representative of a competing social system. It did not seem at first that this situation would last long. It was not possible to foresee whether the Soviet Union would continue to support its unloved Eastern satellite or abandon it in view of the chance of creating a neutral and united Germany not belonging to the Western bloc. Equally unforeseeable was whether the West German population would accept democracy, capitalism and Western culture more permanently this time than last.

In comparison with the entity established in the East, the state of West Germany, with the Americans at its side, had far better economic prospects and also the advantage of democratic legitimacy. Moreover, it was very clear that the Germans living in the Soviet sphere were having to bear a far greater share of the burdens arising from the catastrophe of Nazism and war than Germans in the West.

# 12
# Rebuilding West Germany

## The Economic Miracle

Between 1950 and 1973, the European economies enjoyed a spurt of growth unparalleled in their previous history. Over a period of some twenty years, there were unprecedented, and almost uninterrupted, increases in the figures for Gross National Product (GNP), real wages, productivity, industrial production and foreign trade. Between 1913 and 1950, the average annual increase in the GNP of the European economies had been 1.4 per cent. Between 1950 and 1973, however, it was 5.6 per cent. It is true that the impact of the boom was not equally strong everywhere, nor did it always occur at the same time. But it affected almost all European countries, just as it did the countries of North America and parts of South America, and also Japan. In Europe the highest percentage growth rates were chalked up by Spain (6.2), West Germany (6.0), France, Italy and Portugal (5.4), Austria (5.3), Finland (5.1) and the Netherlands (5.0). Only the United Kingdom (2.8) remained significantly below the European average for a long time. The figures for the socialist countries (Poland 6.7, Yugoslavia 6.6, GDR 6.2 and Czechoslovakia 5.8 per cent) are probably not as robust as the others because of the unreliability of those countries' statistics, but without any doubt the national economies of East Central Europe did also achieve considerable growth.

If the confrontation between the rival political blocs was one decisive feature of the post-war epoch, this long-lasting economic spurt was the other. It permanently transformed the social structure, standard of living and cultural atmosphere of the European countries. It was also bound up with a considerable intensification of international trade relations, a push towards globalisation which was perhaps still more significant in its effects than the turning points of 1900 and 1985.[1]

The liberal economic policy of the post-war European governments is often singled out as the reason for this economic boom. But the economic policies of European governments were tremendously diverse during the two decades in question. Even if one only looks at the countries of Western Europe, the differences between them are immediately visible. The policy of the post-war governments of Italy was to promote big state-owned industrial concerns, and the French emphasised the role of state economic planning, while the West German market economy was conceived in a neo-corporatist sense and its effects were cushioned by measures of social policy. In each case, economic policy may well have either obstructed or promoted the growth dynamic in individual European countries, but it cannot be regarded as the sole or even the paramount reason for the European economic upsurge.

One important factor was, without doubt, the available economic potential, which could not be fully exploited during the long years of world economic crisis or during the Second World War. But the theory that there was a return to long-term growth tendencies does not explain the extraordinary acceleration in rates of growth after 1950, because similarly high growth rates were not experienced after other great crises, for example, after 1918 or after 1929–32.

On the contrary, the boom conditions that prevailed between 1950 and 1973 were historically exceptional. This is more clearly discernible from a historical distance than it was from a contemporary perspective. The explanation of the boom is that many factors emerged simultaneously after the war, and they reinforced each other owing to the unique political situation at the time. They included the spurt in population growth, the enormous backlog of demand both for consumption goods and investment goods, the liberalisation of international trade and international payments systems, the confidence felt in the superior economic strength of the USA, which was decisive for the investment climate, and finally the Korean War, which from the summer of 1950 unleashed a boom in armaments production.

This economic upsurge was accompanied by profound structural changes. In 1950, Europe as a whole was still predominantly agricultural. Of a working population of roughly 180 million, 36 per cent were employed in agriculture, while roughly a third were employed in the industrial and service sectors respectively. This situation changed fundamentally in the years that followed. By 1980 the proportion of people employed in agriculture had fallen in Italy from 42 per cent to 14 per cent, in France from 36 per cent to 8 per cent, and in the Federal Republic (West Germany) from 22 per cent to 5 per cent.[2]

As in the phase of rapid growth that preceded the First World War, people moved from agricultural regions to industrial towns, where they found work, first in their own country, and from 1960 onwards increasingly beyond its borders. This resulted in a progressive increase in industrialisation and urbanisation and from approximately 1960 a rapid growth in services, but also a rise in real wages and in the standard of living, which was first experienced by the population of the industrialised regions of Western and Northern Europe, though in most countries the effects were not felt until the end of the 1960s.

In the economies of East Central Europe, however, including the GDR, industrial growth did not have a comparable impact on consumption and living standards. There were equally big increases in GNP, industrial production, the level of industrialisation and urbanisation, but the one-sided stress on heavy industry and machine-building was accompanied by a neglect of the sphere of consumption which continued for decades. From the outset, the inadequate provision of consumer goods for the population was one of the most serious shortcomings of the socialist state economies, and this remained the case until they ceased to exist.

The 'economic miracle' was therefore a European, or at least a Western European, phenomenon. But in each individual nation-state it was perceived as a national achievement. This was also true of West Germany. There the economic recovery was felt to be a confirmation of the country's strength and a compensation for the defeats and losses the country had recently suffered. The upsurge in West German economic growth had, of course, been spectacular: in the first five years of its existence the Gross Domestic Product (GDP) of the newly founded Federal Republic grew annually by an average 8.8 per cent, almost twice as big an increase as in Europe as a whole; in 1955, the incredible rate of 12 per cent was achieved. Between 1955 and 1958, the rate was still 7.2 per cent, while in the next four years it averaged 5.7 per cent, declining to 3.6 per cent between 1964 and 1967.[3]

This development could not have been predicted, either as regards Western Europe or the Federal Republic, where the crisis which followed the currency reform and the implementation of liberalism in economic policy in early summer 1948 had at first brought with it rising prices, and then rising unemployment figures, and it was therefore not surprising that the elections to the first federal parliament (*Bundestag*), held in October 1949, were entirely dominated by issues of economic policy.

The crisis which started in 1948 was further intensified by the outbreak of the Korean War in June 1950: the armaments boom it unleashed set off a rise in prices, which particularly affected coal and steel, and the Federal Republic had to buy coal from abroad. This led to a balance of payments deficit, a shortage of foreign exchange and electricity rationing and it even raised the threat of temporary insolvency. Later on, though, the war in Korea produced an upswing in the West German economy. The heavy industries of the Western powers had now shifted over to a considerable extent towards the production of armaments. West German firms, however, were not permitted to do this, and so they concentrated on manufacturing durable consumer goods, for which there was a strong demand both in Europe and overseas. The result was an unprecedented export boom, stimulated particularly after summer 1951 by the classical German export industries of mechanical engineering, electro-technology, chemicals, optical instruments and precision mechanics. In 1950, the export ratio, in other words, the share of exports in total GNP, was still only 9 per cent.

By 1960, it had reached 19 per cent. The domestic market also revived, in order to satisfy the consumption needs of the West German population, which had been piling up for years, and in some cases for decades. The consumer goods industry now expanded so strongly and so quickly that a forced loan of a billion Marks could be imposed on it in 1952, by the Investment Assistance Law, which was introduced to subsidise the investment goods industry.

The government's approach to house-building made an important contribution to this explosive economic boom. Housing was the main focus of the measures taken by the first Adenauer government to promote economic development. There was a tremendous need for accommodation, owing to the destruction wrought by war and the influx of more than 10 million refugees and expellees. By 1960, the country had built almost 5 million new dwellings, of which roughly 3 million were subsidised by the state-run social house-building programme. The construction of private apartments, and, after 1956, private houses, was also strongly promoted by the government. Moreover, the economic effects of these activities radiated out to areas far beyond the house-building sector.[4]

A vibrant domestic market, energetic house building and strong demand from abroad were therefore the main pillars of the West German economic upsurge. Between 1950 and 1960, West German industrial production grew by 150 per cent, unemployment fell from 10.3 per cent to 1.2 per cent, the number of people in employment rose by almost 6 million, and gross wages doubled. Between 1951 and 1958, foreign trade produced a surplus of 44.5 billion German Marks (DM). By 1954, the Federal Republic had already risen to be the third largest trading nation (behind the USA and Great Britain) and, by 1956, it possessed the largest reserves of gold and foreign currency in the world, which was a great surprise to everyone, including economists.

Let us attempt to specify the reasons for West Germany's particularly vigorous economic growth. Five points can be picked out. Firstly, the initial conditions for a rapid reconstruction of the economy were extraordinarily favourable: since the turn of the century, Germany's industries had been the most powerful on the Continent. As indicated earlier, the country's industrial installations had been considerably expanded, and also partially modernised, during the war, and wartime destruction proved to have been far less serious than had been feared. The same thing could be said for the effects of the dismantling of factories after the war.

Secondly, the influx of refugees and expellees provided a large reservoir of labour. These workers were skilled and versatile, and, still more importantly, they were well motivated and keen to get on. This also applied to the 2.7 million refugees who fled the GDR in the years before 1961. Moreover, this was a group in which highly skilled workers were clearly over-represented.[5]

Thirdly, the new system of economic and monetary relations established at Bretton Woods in 1944 had produced the necessary conditions for stable exchange rates and a far-reaching liberalisation of trade. The founding of the World Bank and the International Monetary Fund meant that there were now two institutions in existence able to guarantee the settlement of international payments and to fix a firm rate of exchange between the dollar and other currencies. In addition, the signing of the General Agreement on Tariffs and Trade (GATT) in 1947 made possible a worldwide reduction in customs tariffs. It is true that almost none of the developed industrial countries had a freely convertible currency. Since no one trusted the stability of the currencies of other nations, businesses often had recourse at first to the direct exchange of commodities, which was similar to the clearing procedure of the pre-war epoch. Where trade volumes differed, payment had to be made in hard currency, mainly in dollars. A lasting expansion in international trade could not be achieved in this way. But a decisive step was now taken in this direction by the establishment of the European Payments Union. This functioned as a multilateral instrument for settling the payment of debts. It calculated the account balances arising from trading activities, it adjusted the European currencies against each other and it moved them slowly towards convertibility. The push this gave to the liberalisation of world trade was of benefit to all Western European states, but it was especially advantageous to the Federal Republic in view of its tremendous volume of exports.

The regulation of Germany's foreign debt, which took place in London in 1953, played an important role in this respect. In order to settle the claims of foreign creditors, particularly American firms, which were pressing for the payment of commercial debts that had accrued both before and after the war, the Federal Republic agreed to pay 567 million DM a year for five years, then after that 765 million DM a year until 1988, making a total of 15 billion DM altogether. This was of great importance for the West German economy, because unless these demands were satisfied, the country's creditworthiness could not be restored. Owing to the favourable evolution of West Germany's economic performance, the financial burden was easier to bear than had been expected. The agreement enabled the Federal Republic not only to return to the international market but also to establish the full convertibility of the German Mark. It also allowed it, at least by implication, to postpone the settlement of any reparations claims until the signing of a peace treaty, which was a distant prospect.[6]

Fourthly, Erhard's liberal economic policies ensured enormous profit margins for German enterprises. The paramount influence here was the favourable taxation treatment of entrepreneurial capital formation. Starting in summer 1949, firms were able, right from the opening balance statement, to value their company assets at such a high level that very large deductions could be made from this in the following period. Because of this, there were more self-financing enterprises than in any other European country, and net investment ratios were higher than anywhere else. The evolution of wages also made a contribution to profit margins. Nominal wages did, it is true, grow by an average of 8 per cent, but profit margins were considerably higher than this owing to increases in productivity, hence the share of wages in the total product remained stable or even fell.[7]

The fifth point that needs be stressed is the strong links between the state, the economy, the financial system and the trade unions, which had already been a specifically German phenomenon under both the Wilhelmine Empire and the Weimar Republic. This system of reciprocal involvement affected the way basic economic and social decisions were negotiated between the state, the entrepreneurs and the trade unions, and was particularly reflected in the German system of 'tariff partnership'. In addition, entitlement to social benefits was linked to wages and to the contribution payments taken from them. This was a fundamental principle of German social policy, in contrast to Scandinavia or Great Britain, where social benefits were financed by taxation and uniformly distributed. Finally, the central role of the banks in financing business investment, which linked together the industrial and financial sectors, was also a significant feature of the German system. The effects of this differed from those that arose from the practice of raising resources through a stock exchange listing, which was favoured in the Anglo-Saxon countries, because it was more strongly oriented towards long-term perspectives, whereas shareholders tend rather to hope for short-term gains. The corporatist principle of what was later called 'Rhineland capitalism' contained a strong element of nationally oriented economics and was built on consensus, first and foremost. It proved successful, particularly during the reconstruction phase, in which nationally oriented economics was dominant. Difficulties arose, however, when the West German economy, along with the big German firms, became increasingly internationalised.[8]

If we compare the role of these different factors, it is probable that the most important prerequisite for the rapid rise of the West German economy was its integration into a functioning system of world trade. This again indicates the political conditions required for this to happen. In order to restore international, and in particular intra-European, economic relations, and to bring dynamism into them, what was needed, apart from American guarantees, was the gigantic productive capacity of West German industry. This process could not happen in reverse. German industrial potential would have been largely ineffective without its being embedded in an integrated European economy. The three essential stages in the integration of West Germany into the developing

Western camp, namely the Marshall Plan, the currency reform and the foundation of the West German state, thus proved to be the decisive prerequisites for the economic ascent of the Federal Republic. This was, no doubt, a stroke of luck, because in view of the starting conditions of 1945, a repetition of the disasters of the period between 1919 and 1923 was certainly a possible scenario.

It should be added that the mode of the West German economy's recovery differed from that of the European economy as a whole. Whereas by 1975 the service sector in the six largest Western European economies already accounted for the largest segment of their GNP (53 per cent) while the secondary sector accounted for 41 per cent, in the same year in the Federal Republic the industrial sector, with 48.8 per cent, was clearly still ahead of the service sector, which only took the lead much later than it did in most other European countries. Moreover, the structure of West German industry was not dominated by large-scale firms. Two-thirds of the country's employees worked in firms with a workforce of less than 500, and in turn the majority of these had fewer than 100 employees. Enterprises of this size were more flexible and reacted more quickly to changing market requirements than big firms with gigantic production facilities. In addition, the shift of emphasis towards new branches of production, which had merely been interrupted by the war, continued during the boom of the 1950s and 1960s: there was a movement away from coal, steel and iron towards more innovatory sectors such as mechanical engineering, electronics, industrial chemistry and plastics processing, oil refining and vehicle manufacturing. It was here that most of the new job opportunities were created: the number of employees in the plastics industry alone had increased by 285 per cent by 1960.

Industrialisation reached its highest level ever in West Germany between 1965 and 1970. Almost 50 per cent of the total number of employees worked in industry. At that point, the Federal Republic was probably the most industrialised country in the Western world. None of the big European countries depended on the growth of industry to a greater extent, and for a longer period, than the Federal Republic. This obviously had positive effects on employment, on the standard of living and on the state's opportunities for strategic intervention, owing to the very abundant tax revenue that was generated, though it also created problems, in relation to ecology for instance. But the word 'ecology' was not used around 1960, nor did anyone perceive the long-term impact of hyper-industrialisation on the environment. Moreover, the almost unbelievable success of German industry, particularly in the field of exports, blocked people's view of any shortcomings. As a result, German firms fell far behind in the research and development of new and advanced technologies, such as nuclear energy or aircraft design. Firms in the service sector were also often old-fashioned and insufficiently innovative. These deficiencies were related to the absence of competitive pressure from foreign firms in the areas of finance and communications. But the backwardness of specific sectors did not attract much attention at first, any more than did the stagnant educational level of German employees.

As in all European countries, the growth of the industrial and service sectors was associated with a decline in the significance of agriculture. During the war years, and immediately afterwards, the flight from country to town had temporarily reversed direction, because in that time of hardship it was easier to find food and lodging in the countryside than in the devastated urban areas. But the flight from the land resumed after 1950. The decline of agriculture now proceeded at a historically unprecedented rate. Between 1950 and 1970, the proportion of people employed in the sector declined from 23 to 7 per cent; roughly thirty-five years earlier, when the German Empire came to an end, a third of all employees had been involved in agriculture. Its share of GNP fell from 24 per cent in 1950 to 13.3 per cent in 1960 and 7 per cent in 1973. In these two decades, the countryside lost more than 3 million workers, two-thirds of the total originally employed on the land. There were also structural changes: little by little, the small peasant farms vanished, and large, highly productive enterprises increasingly dominated the rural landscape. In 1949 there were still 1.9 million agricultural enterprises. Twenty-five years later, there were only 900,000. The farms that remained were larger and increasingly rationalised. The productivity of agriculture grew considerably: in 1949, there were roughly 24,000 tractors in Bavaria, while in 1960 there were almost 300,000. 'The combine harvester is coming!', announced a factory for agricultural machinery in its advertising material. 'Do you want to be the last person to get one?'[9] By the mid-1960s, the increase in productivity achieved by the mechanisation of the agricultural sector had already led to overproduction in Germany, as in almost all the countries of Western Europe, and the surplus had then to be absorbed by state subsidies.[10]

The West German state had originally been founded as a provisional solution, but the economic growth of the 1950s and 1960s increased, or one might even say it first established, the population's readiness to accept it. After half a century of catastrophe, and bearing in mind the situation immediately after 8 May 1945, the explosive economic boom came as a complete surprise, and the expression 'economic miracle' indicates how positively overwhelmed the Germans were by this development. In 1951, only 2 per cent of West Germans said that things were better for them than before. Ten years later, in 1960, the proportion had risen to almost 50 per cent. Nevertheless, every fifth West German still thought at that time that life had been better in 1938.[11] By 1960, however, economic stabilisation had also been accompanied by political stabilisation. Both of these developments were equally unexpected.

## Western Integration during the Cold War

The evolution of German foreign policy and the country's fate as a political entity were both dictated in the early 1950s by the three Western powers and the Soviet Union. The starting point was the endeavour of the Western European countries to join together in the face of threats both old and new, and at the same time to form the closest possible bond with the USA. This aspiration was expressed economically by the establishment of the OEEC (April 1948), militarily by the Brussels Pact (March 1948) and politically by the Council of Europe (May 1950). The Brussels Pact in particular was still clearly directed against Germany: the West European states wanted to present a united front against a Germany which was regaining its strength and possibly out for revenge. But the opposite view soon began to prevail: the Cold War, which escalated after the communist coup of February 1948 in Prague, and the West's fear of further Soviet expansion, increasingly came to the fore, accelerating attempts to secure West European integration. But even after the establishment of two separate German states there continued to be suspicion of Germany, not just in France, where security against the neighbour to the east remained the supreme maxim of political wisdom, but also in the rest of Western Europe.[12]

On the other hand, the North Atlantic Treaty Organisation (NATO), which was founded in April 1949, was already directed primarily against the Soviet Union. Germany, at least from the American perspective, had now become a second-order problem. The purpose of NATO, said its first Secretary General, Lord Ismay, was 'to keep the Russians out, the Americans in, and the Germans down'.[13] The priority for the US government was now to bind the Federal Republic as closely and irrevocably as possible to a Europe which was in process of integration. Much rested on this: a neutral, united Germany might possibly have become a risk factor for Europe once again, in view of its large population, its economic strength, its geopolitical situation and its potential military might. If it had become part of the Soviet power bloc, moreover, it was assumed that this would have tipped the Cold War balance in favour of the USSR.

US policy was therefore moulded by two partially contradictory requirements: on the one hand, the need to promote the integration of the Federal Republic into the Western bloc, rapidly, institutionally and irrevocably, and, on the other hand, the need to take account of the anti-German sensitivities of the Western Europeans and build in safeguards against a West German relapse into nationalism. America's policy towards Germany therefore amounted to a process of political barter: to the extent that the Federal Republic integrated politically and economically into the West, and became a stable liberal democracy, the USA was ready, step by step, to concede the elements of sovereignty to the West German government.

Great Britain largely concurred with the USA on this point, but it was more difficult to predict the reactions of the other parties involved, namely France, the West German government and of course the Soviet Union. In the French case, the enormous economic power of West Germany, particularly in the arms-related coal and steel industries, and the potential rearmament of its Eastern neighbour, continued to give rise to considerable apprehension. For this reason, the rapidly changing French governments endeavoured to retard the process by which West Germany gained its sovereignty, and then later, when this method was no longer effective in view of the escalation of the Cold War, to exert control by establishing exclusive bilateral connections with Germany which were, however, not conducted on an equal basis.

The Soviet Union regarded the integration of West Germany into the developing Western bloc as a flagrant shift of power to the advantage of the USA and a serious threat. It seemed to be a repetition of the scenario most feared by Stalin before 1939: a common front of the USA, the powers of Western Europe and Germany against the USSR. It was therefore an urgent priority of Soviet foreign policy towards Europe to prevent this from happening. To achieve this, the USSR was even ready, under certain circumstances, to abandon the GDR and swallow the bitter pill of a united, economically strong and possibly even rearmed Germany, if it did not form part of the potential threat from the West. Whether and to what degree a united and neutral Germany would then drift towards subjection to Soviet hegemony in Europe was, of course, an open question; but while it was a definite option for the Soviet Union, for the West it was a nightmare prospect.

What was certain, however, was that a united Germany of this type would disrupt, and might even prevent, the Western European process of integration and pacification, if only because the countries of Western Europe would want to protect themselves against such a colossus. But these conditions would endanger the rise of the German economy, which had occurred largely thanks to Germany's integration into the world trade network; and thus a repetition of the Weimar experience with a weak economy, instability in domestic politics and foreign policy isolation was a possible or indeed an inevitable outcome.

The leaders of the two big political parties in West Germany, Adenauer of the CDU and Schumacher of the SPD, were broadly in agreement over their principal objective, despite their loudly voiced disagreements over individual aspects of policy towards the German issue: the Federal Republic should become integrated into the West economically, politically and if possible also militarily. They disagreed over how they should behave towards the Western powers and over the relation between Western integration and the reunification of the country. On this issue, Adenauer entirely agreed with the US government: Western integration had priority. Reunification was a secondary matter. For Adenauer, there was no alternative to this approach, in view of the political fickleness of his nation, which he was fond of emphasising, and the massive Soviet threat. A reunited, neutralised Germany would become alienated from the West, domestically it would generate a new nationalism, and it would inevitably enter into the Soviet sphere of influence and control. For Adenauer, therefore, a united Germany was only sensible and desirable as an integral part of the West. But the prerequisites for this would not exist for a long time, and the German Chancellor was therefore primarily concerned to tie the West German republic quickly to the West and thereby regain its sovereign rights as soon as possible. In the light of the current relationship of political forces, this could only happen with American agreement. The Germans would have to make concessions and prove their political reliability, and only then would they gradually be granted sovereign rights. By accepting that this was the basic situation, Adenauer quickly gained the confidence of the USA.

Schumacher, on the other hand, adopted a much more self-confident attitude towards the Western Allies. He too regarded Western integration as an important goal, but he was not so exclusively wedded to it as Adenauer, and above all he did not accept the conditions set by the West. He rejected any policy of making concessions in advance. Instead of this, the Western powers should first grant sovereignty to the Germans, and then the Federal government would decide for the West of its own volition. Thus, for him, reunification took precedence over integration into the West. The prospect of a united and neutral Germany did not terrify him.

An attitude of this kind could most probably only have been taken by an opposition party, because it largely ignored global power relations and exaggerated the room for manoeuvre the West Germans actually possessed. Schumacher's view that Social Democratic Germany should not be made responsible for the policies of the Nazi regime also met with little sympathy in the West. To that extent, Adenauer's line was more realistic, as regards both the perception of Germany in neighbouring European countries and his assessment of the degree of political maturity of his fellow Germans. He was absolutely convinced that a repetition of the Weimar pattern would prevent the pacification of Western Europe for a long time and that the post-war situation, despite all its difficulties, offered an opportunity to bind Germany firmly and irrevocably to the West, although (and this was Adenauer's problem) this would only apply to the Western half of the country, and East Germany would have to be abandoned initially and indeed for a long time afterwards. He could only compensate for this disadvantage by putting out propaganda implying the opposite, and in line with this he constantly and loudly repeated his commitment to reunification, while his actual policy excluded precisely that eventuality.

This led to a paradoxical shift in basic political attitudes. After 1918, the parties of the Right had championed national interests against Versailles, rejected the policy of fulfilment and behaved in an increasingly nationalistic fashion, while the Social Democrats and the parties of the political centre had pursued a policy towards the Western powers of recovering German sovereignty step by step. Now the opposite was the case: the centre Right pursued a course of concessions and prioritised Western integration over reunification, whereas the Social Democrats rigidly insisted on German national interests in dealing with the Western occupying powers, also, no doubt, because they had drawn their own conclusions from the trauma of 1918–19, when they had pursued the policy of fulfilment and gradual revision of the Versailles Treaty but had had hardly anything to set against the wave of nationalist activism, and had therefore been forced to endure the accusation that they were betraying the fatherland. This reversal of roles was an important prerequisite for the Western integration of the Federal Republic, for had the Social Democrats been in government they would have had great difficulty in implementing this course of Western integration against a nationalist camp which would probably have grown rapidly in strength.

This configuration of forces, with some variation, shaped the immense number of conferences and treaty negotiations that took place between 1948 and 1957. Whose interests were dominant had already been demonstrated at the inception of the young Federal Republic: its government and the governments of the individual *Länder* were under the supervision of the Allied High Commissioners, who resided at the Hotel Petersberg, near Bonn. Foreign ambassadors were accredited there and not at the seat of the West German government. The Petersberg Agreement of 22 November 1949, which recorded the results of the negotiations between the High Commission and the federal government that had just been installed, included hardly any concessions by the Western Allies. Rather than bringing to an end the dismantling of the German armaments industry, as was urgently desired by Adenauer, this agreement merely lessened its scope, although at the same time the federal government was made a member of the International Authority for the Ruhr (IAR). The industries of the Ruhr were thereby protected from any further dismantling, but the IAR was also under international supervision, which meant that the German side lost its economic autonomy in this region. Schumacher, for the SPD, thundered that Adenauer had become the 'Allies' Federal Chancellor'. This verdict was not completely wrong, but it failed to recognise that without advance concessions of this kind nothing could be obtained from the Allies, who had adopted a very stiff attitude in the negotiations.

The federal government experienced the same dilemma in its negotiations over entry into the OEEC. The power to make decisions about foreign economic policy was in effect removed from it, but in return it was permitted to re-enter the world trading system. Negotiations over admission to the Council of Europe followed the same pattern. This step was urgently desired by the West German government as an indication of state sovereignty, but it faced the problem that the Saar, a territory provisionally under French occupation, was also intended to become a member of the Council of Europe. This would amount to legitimising the separation of the Saar from Germany, said Schumacher. Nevertheless, Adenauer agreed to it, and he was wise to do so.

If one takes as a starting point for comparison France's earlier and much more far-reaching goals, it becomes clear that the policy of making concessions paid off well for the Federal Republic. France did not succeed either in separating the Ruhr district from Germany or in preventing the foundation of the West German state. Nor could the limits on German steel production be sustained for long, in view of the critical international situation. Even the IAR did not fulfil France's expectations, and, in any case, it disadvantaged the German side so flagrantly that it did not last very long. Above all, though, the American government exerted strong pressure on the French, and they were finally impelled to give up their obstructive policy and themselves contribute to the rapid and definitive integration of the Federal Republic into Western Europe.

If France wanted to take part in shaping the involvement of the Federal Republic with Western Europe, it had to tackle the issue head on. That was the idea at the root of the so-called Schuman Plan, which envisaged the formation of a common market for coal and steel covering France, the Federal Republic, the Benelux countries and Italy. The Schuman Plan was intended to be the first step towards a far-reaching coordination and integration of European economic relations, and should, if possible, also entail political integration. It doubtless reflected French interests first and foremost, in particular the need to guarantee coal deliveries from Germany. But, since it would also mean the cancellation of the discriminatory provisions of the IAR, the German side could only benefit from the plan, which involved the internationalisation of all coal and steel regions in the six affected European countries, instead of just the Ruhr district. Here too the federal government was giving up sovereign rights. These were, however, rights it had never actually exercised, and this made the idea easier to accept, although the SPD continued to reject it.

There is no doubt that by making this agreement of 18 April 1951 to form a 'European Coal and Steel Community' (ECSC), the participants set out in a new and revolutionary policy direction. The fact that it was also in line with specific national interests was a source of strength rather than weakness. European integration, which had begun with the OEEC (an organisation established under American pressure), now seemed to have advanced from the theoretical stage to become a reality, albeit in the form of an authority for economic coordination, performing highly pragmatic tasks. A younger generation, stretching all the way from Pan-Europeans to enthusiasts for the West, who propagated a form of unified European nationalism or a 'Carolingian' Europe imbued with Catholicism, had already put forward ambitious plans for Europe. The ECSC clearly had nothing in common with these ideas. But, from a future perspective, this was in fact rather advantageous.[14]

The invasion of South Korea on 25 June 1950 by North Korean troops, supported by the Soviet Union and China, marked a dramatic change in the global political and military situation. The Korean War confirmed the views of those who perceived a direct line of aggressive expansionism by the Soviet Union, or by communists acting on a world scale, extending from the establishment of Soviet hegemony in East Central Europe to the Prague coup of February 1948, followed by the detonation of the first Russian atomic bomb on 29 August 1949 and the victory of the communists in the Chinese civil war on 1 October 1949, and now culminating in the attack on South Korea. There are good reasons for not interpreting these different events within the rigid framework of an all-embracing Soviet strategy but rather seeing them as a response and a reaction to the inroads of American power. Nevertheless, the sense of a worldwide Soviet threat became a political factor of great significance in Western Europe as well, not least because the communist side actually confirmed the existence of this threat, as in Walter Ulbricht's declaration shortly after the North Korean invasion:

> Korea teaches us that a puppet government such as the one in South Korea, or one could also mention the one in Bonn, will be swept away sooner or later by the will of the people. . . . And the fight will be conducted by the people's patriotic forces with all their strength, so as to liquidate the nests of the war provocateurs, just as is happening in South Korea at present.

In the spring of 1950, three-quarters of the citizens of the Federal Republic still said 'No' when questioned as to whether they were worried that a new world war might break out during the year. In June of that year, however, 53 per cent replied 'Yes'.[15]

It was considered in the West that in such a conflict the Soviet Union would have the advantage, with its considerable preponderance in conventional weapons, especially as Great Britain and France had large military detachments engaged in colonial wars in defence of their territories in Malaya and Indochina respectively. In this situation, therefore, it was not surprising that the idea came up of reinforcing the West's armed forces with German soldiers. Churchill was the first person openly to advocate this, in March 1950. In September 1950 the British and the Americans decided that the Federal Republic should participate in the defence of Europe with twenty army divisions, within the NATO framework. Only on this condition were the Americans prepared to increase their own European troop numbers.[16]

Adenauer, who had previously spoken out categorically against the creation of a German national army, now saw an opportunity to take a big step forward on the issue of sovereign rights, and he drafted out a scheme by which West Germany would declare its readiness 'to make a contribution in the form of a German contingent if an international West European army is created', on condition that the Occupation Statute was abolished and the full sovereignty of the Federal Republic re-established. The people of West Germany, he added, must 'be given sufficient freedom of action and responsibility to make it appear that the fulfilment of these obligations makes sense'.[17]

This, once again, put France in a predicament, because the French were not prepared under any circumstances to accept the creation of a West German national army. The same group of people, around Jean Monnet, the director of the French planning office, who had produced the Schuman Plan in the spring of 1950, now devised a parallel plan for the creation of a European army with German participation. This was put forward on 24 October 1950. It was called the Pleven Plan, after René Pleven, who was the French Minister of Defence at the time. Admittedly, this proposal also clearly discriminated against the German side: the aim here was rather to recruit German soldiers for the defence of the West than to offer the Germans a genuine opportunity to participate. Accordingly, these troops soon became known as 'mercenaries'. Nevertheless, Adenauer was prepared to agree to the proposal, though only on condition that West Germany acquired complete legal equality. The decisive point for him was to couple the creation of the European Defence Community (EDC) with a revision of the Occupation Statute.

The negotiations that now began were conducted under the shadow of an acute danger of war. At the end of November 1950, the Chinese army had intervened in the Korean War with a force of several hundred thousand men, driving the Americans back towards the south of the peninsula. On 16 December, the American President, Harry S. Truman, responded by declaring a national emergency. As a result, the negotiations over the EDC and the revision of the Occupation Statute began to run out of time. This was helpful to the Germans, who thanks to American insistence were now accorded the complete equality they had demanded, within the framework of the EDC. Even so, the result remained unsatisfactory in West German eyes. They were expected to set up an army of more than 400,000, but the proposed revision of the Occupation Statute only contained a small number of Allied concessions in return. There was no mention of sovereignty, and the Allies could at any time declare a state of emergency and restore the state of occupation. The Germans were needed, but not trusted.

For the Soviet Union, on the other hand, the rearmament of West Germany within the framework of the armed forces of the Western powers was an alarm signal. Shortly before the treaties were signed, therefore, it undertook a further attempt to thwart the political and military integration of the country into the Western bloc. It had already reacted to the Pleven Plan by attempting to prevent the Federal Republic's integration into the West and its rearmament with an offer of free elections and the prospect of early reunification. The Western powers, who, like Adenauer, saw this as an attempt by Moscow to torpedo the treaty negotiations, rejected the offer. The Soviet side replied by making more extensive proposals. On 10 March 1952, in a dramatic gesture, Stalin proposed the reunification of the two German states after free elections, a peace treaty and even a German national army, but only on condition that a reunited Germany would be free of all alliances, hence neutral.[18]

The much discussed question of whether this 'Stalin Note' was meant seriously somewhat overlooks the real problem. It goes without saying that the Soviet state meant these proposals 'seriously' in the sense that the military integration of the Federal Republic into the Western bloc represented the most threatening of all possible outcomes for the USSR: an alliance between the opponent defeated in the Second World War at the cost of incredible sacrifices and the USA, a world power, alongside the powers of Western Europe, which confronted the Soviet Union with a sharp hostility verging on military conflict. In a last-minute attempt to prevent such a scenario, the Soviet government was prepared to make considerable sacrifices, perhaps even to abandon the GDR. It is probable that a united, neutral Germany would not have fallen immediately under the power of the Soviets, as politicians in the West, including Adenauer, were quick to predict. In the longer term, however, a closer association of a united Germany with the Soviet Union would have been a realistic possibility, particularly if the USA ever withdrew its forces from Europe.

Adenauer's immediate and very emphatic rejection of this offer was no surprise, for it would have destroyed the foundation of his policy of Western integration. Even so, the Soviet proposals put him in a difficult position, because they compelled him to declare openly that, in his view, Western integration had priority over reunification. The fierce debate on fundamental principles that was triggered in the West German political sphere by the rearmament plans and the rejection of the Stalin Note was conducted over two issues: first, 'Western integration or reunification?', and second, 'For or against rearmament?' Adenauer's call for both 'Western integration *and* rearmament' finally won the day. This victory must be ascribed primarily to the extremely critical foreign policy situation during those months. In view of the Soviet diplomatic offensive, the negotiations with the Western powers were now conducted at an almost frantic pace. On 26 May 1952, the revised Occupation Statute, which was now officially called the 'General Treaty' (also known as the Germany Treaty, *Deutschlandvertrag*), was signed in Paris, while the EDC treaty was signed a day later. The GDR government immediately reacted to this by establishing an exclusion zone 5 kilometres wide along its boundary with the West. The division of Germany was now an accomplished fact.

In France, the notion that the Federal Republic should be an equal member of the EDC had met with little agreement from the outset. The French government had only agreed to this reluctantly and under American pressure. When the end of the war in Korea and the death of Stalin in spring 1953 appeared to show that the immediate danger had passed, the number of French opponents of the treaty increased, and after the French army suffered a devastating defeat in the colonial war in Indochina, nationalist forces gained momentum in the country. The current French government was voted out of office, and, not surprisingly, the EDC treaty was finally rejected by the National Assembly on 30 August 1954.

This rendered obsolete both the EDC Treaty and the General Treaty, and it appeared to endanger the whole of the Federal Republic's painstakingly balanced policy of Western integration. The British and the Americans prevented the policy from collapsing, however, because now their original plan took effect, by which an independent West German army would be established within the NATO framework. This ultimately proved more favourable for the government of the Federal Republic because the General Treaty now needed to be renegotiated, and the new version contained many more sovereign rights than the old one. The reserved rights of the Allies were now largely restricted to the city of Berlin and to questions that affected Germany as a whole.

On the other hand, the failure to create a European army was a bitter blow to those who had hoped that the EDC would advance the process of European integration. It had been demonstrated that integration in the military sphere not only came up against sensitive French security interests but affected core areas of national sovereignty for all Western European states. Because there was still considerable anxiety about a resurgence of Germany, a renunciation of sovereignty of this magnitude was manifestly premature. Deepening cooperation and integration was evidently much easier to secure in the economic sphere, and the ECSC showed that free trade zones and economic cooperation could bring tangible and beneficial results, both for the Germans and the other European participants.[19]

It was primarily the Benelux countries which resumed the initiative towards further integration. They aimed at achieving a more comprehensive economic and customs union on the basis of the ECSC, so as to create a common market, which was a basic requirement for the further growth of the national economies of those three small lands. France, on the other hand, favoured a 'sectoral' solution, in other words the step-by-step integration of specific economic sectors, without a wider economic union. The sectors the French had in mind were transport and energy, above all nuclear energy, which was regarded at this time as the branch of industry with the most promising future. It was, of course, obvious that, in taking this line, France was continuing to pursue its main foreign policy goal, which was to place Germany's economic and military potential under international control.

The federal German government agreed with the Benelux objective of securing economic integration. But it was rather the political aspects which had priority for it. On the one hand, Adenauer's view was that the links of the Federal Republic to the West would be strengthened and deepened by economic interdependence. On the other hand, it was only the political integration of Western Europe that offered even a partial prospect of counterbalancing the dominant position of the two superpowers, the USA and the USSR. Their supremacy became more obvious than ever before in 1956, when the attempt of Britain and France to assert their colonial privileges over the Suez Canal by force of arms led to a military and political disaster which was finally brought to an end by the two superpowers. The 'Suez adventure' should be seen in the context of the process of decolonisation which had unfolded with increasing rapidity since the end of the Second World War, forcing the two biggest European colonial powers onto the defensive and involving them in military rearguard actions all over the globe.

At the same time, the suppression of the spring 1953 rising in the GDR and the 1956 movements in Poland and Hungary showed that the Soviet Union was ready to enforce its domination with an iron hand in the areas occupied by the Red Army and that the Western powers would be obliged to remain inactive spectators if they did not want to risk a third world war.

An obvious reply to these developments was to strengthen European integration. This was especially true for France, which had suffered political isolation after the Suez débâcle, and had a system of government characterised by instability and frequent changes of administration. In this situation, association with the Federal Republic suddenly became one of the few positive aspects of French foreign policy. According to a widespread witticism of the time, France had no more enemies after the war, apart from the Germans, but now it also had no more friends—apart from the Germans. After the Saar referendum, at which the electors had clearly decided in favour of joining the Federal Republic, one of the larger problems between West Germany and France had been eliminated, and in the negotiations over further European integration it was possible relatively quickly to find a compromise acceptable to both countries. According to the agreement they reached, all internal tariffs imposed by member states would be abolished within twelve years and a common market would be created, in which all obstacles to the free movement of goods, services, capital and labour would be removed. The foundation of the European Economic Community was accompanied by the establishment of a European Atomic Energy Authority, which was intended to integrate the different national agencies working in the nuclear sector.

While the European Atomic Energy Authority did not prove to be particularly viable, and soon fell into oblivion, the European Economic Community (EEC) quickly became a model of success: the harmonisation of tariffs was accomplished in less than twelve years, the liberalisation of the flow of goods led to a considerable expansion of trade within the Community, and the Gross National Products of the six members of the EEC experienced significantly greater increases than those of non-members. To that extent, the misgivings of Economics Minister Erhard had been dispelled. He had feared that a small economic union would pursue a protectionist policy towards its neighbours, and this might damage the West German economy, which was geared to worldwide exports. Erhard had spoken out instead in favour of the British proposal for a wider free trade zone covering the whole of Europe and attached to the OEEC. This option had been rejected by Adenauer. For him, the goal of political integration was paramount, and economic considerations were subordinate. He emphasised that the political character of European integration was decisive. European integration ought to produce 'not just technological cooperation for functional reasons, but a community which ensures that the political will moves in a single direction. This would also be in the interest of reunification.'[20]

After the failure of the EDC, European integration ceased to arouse more than limited public interest in Western Europe. The member states were in agreement on the general aim of European unification, but neither the negotiations for the establishment of the EEC nor the signing of the treaties in Rome on 25 March 1957 stirred up much enthusiasm, or indeed any other emotional reaction, in the countries that joined. The treaties were rapidly confirmed in the European parliaments, and without much debate. The only political parties to cast negative votes in the Federal Republic were the BHE, the FDP and the nationalist fringe parties, while the SPD, which after Schumacher's death had gradually begun to adopt Adenauer's policy of integration, voted in support of the treaties, which passed the Bundestag on 5 July 1957 in an entirely unemotional atmosphere.

The correct but restrained interest with which West German public opinion responded to the project of European integration was primarily to be ascribed to the fact that, right from the outset, it was a matter for the elite rather than the broader public. It was manifestly too complex, too novel and too pragmatic to become the subject of political debates and passions. The detailed provisions for gradual tariff reduction hardly lent themselves to controversial exchanges, and the thoroughly bureaucratic character of the authorities that emerged in Brussels aroused indifference rather than engagement. As a result, the historic significance of the integration of countries of Western Europe which had still been at war with each other fifteen years earlier was not perceived as the political sensation it was in reality.

Only in the sphere of agriculture was this different. This sector of the economy was largely given exemption from the otherwise thoroughly liberal economic system of the common market. If agriculture had had to adapt quickly to market conditions, this would have accelerated yet further the already rapid decline in the number of people employed in the sector. National agricultural markets were therefore protected by various exceptions and transitional arrangements, with such success that only a few years later a structural crisis of overproduction forced the European Economic Community to pay out ever-increasing agricultural subsidies. The economic and social problems of European integration were clearly demonstrated here, and conflicts of interest quickly arose between the partners. At the same time, however, though this was obscured by debates over butter mountains and milk lakes, there was an ever-increasing degree of interconnection and coordination between the national economies of the six member states. The process was so successful that within a few years Adenauer's prediction that economic integration would lead to stronger political integration was confirmed.

The economic miracle and Western integration were the characteristic and formative developments of the period between 1949 and 1961 in West Germany. All other fields of politics, society and culture were not just determined but defined by these processes. In stark contrast to the trend of events after the First World War, when tendencies towards an economic upturn were inhibited by political antagonisms and attempts at political reconstruction were thwarted by economic problems, the firm involvement of the West German state in the alliance of Western democracies provided the basis for the development of a stable and democratic republic. At the same time the breathtaking economic success story of the new state provided the popular legitimacy which the Weimar Republic had failed to achieve. The economic miracle and Western integration therefore constituted changes of an extremely profound character. There were, it is true, long-lasting elements of continuity as well: in the composition of elites, in social stratification, in domestic politics, in political philosophy, in culture and in ways of living. But these were felt to be much less significant.

It should not be overlooked, however, that the economic miracle and Western integration were not authentically German creations. Their essential elements had rather been put into operation by the Western Allies, above all the US government. The Americans had taken the decisive steps towards the division of

Germany when it became clear that it would be impossible to achieve a united and democratic Germany which would form part of the group of Western democracies. They had provided the impulse for democratic reconstruction as well as for de-Nazification. Through the currency reform, they had opened the way to a liberal economic system. They had determined essential aspects of the Basic Law for the Federal Republic of Germany before it was drafted. By introducing the Marshall Plan and founding the OEEC, and by exerting various pressures on their European partners, they had laid the foundations of European integration, and by drawing up the Occupation Statute they had created a control mechanism which was intended to prevent any repetition of the aberrations of German politics after the First World War.

To achieve all this, they naturally needed a strong and determined partner on the German side, otherwise a project of this kind would have been impossible to realise. And, in fact, the democratic parties which had re-emerged or been given alternative structures after 1945, in particular the CDU, under the cautious and single-minded leadership of Adenauer, were ready to cooperate closely with the Americans, especially as their influence grew in proportion to the intensification of the Cold War and the increasing need for German military, economic and political assistance.

But the decisive stimulus in politics as in economics did not proceed from the German politicians—since they entirely lacked the means to provide this—rather, it was introduced from outside. In the longer term, this can definitely be regarded as a piece of good fortune. Decades of disputes in German domestic politics over what constitutional and social order was correct, desirable, successful, appropriate or even feasible in an industrial society were now laid to rest by the victors of the Second World War. This was done in a way which excluded the West Germans from participating in decisions on important points, but the consequences of those decisions would turn out to be highly advantageous to them.

It is true that, for a long time, the question of whether the new system of a social and capitalist democracy oriented towards the West would prove stable remained entirely open, but there was no longer a realistic alternative, if one ignores the plan for a reunited and neutral Germany which was debated in the context of Stalin's Note of 10 March 1952 and other Soviet communications. Even a Germany led by the Social Democrats would have been anchored in the Western system, as this was the wish of the SPD leadership, although economic policy would probably have taken a different direction.

Thus, for the western part of Germany, the question of what constitutional and political system to establish had been answered for the time being. The Germans had little room for manoeuvre on this point, even after 1955. Disagreements on domestic policy, with the exception of the debate on rearmament, were no longer about whether the current political and social order was right or wrong, but about the ways in which it should be implemented and developed. When it became clear that the new order had stood the test of time, the fact that the Germans had not installed it themselves ceased to play an important role in people's perceptions, until finally the impression arose, both in the public mind and in the writings of historians, that it was the West Germans themselves who had brought about democracy, the economic miracle and Western integration.

## Internal Stabilisation

The picture revealed by the first Bundestag elections, held in 1949, was one of fragmentation rather than consolidation. Whereas, in the Diet elections of the immediate post-war period, the vote for the CDU–CSU Union had been almost 38 per cent, and for the SPD 35 per cent, both parties now fell back, the Union to 31 per cent, the SPD to 29 per cent. The Liberals increased their vote, as did a number of smaller parties such as the German Party (DP) and the Economic Reconstruction Union (WAV), (both of which were of a conservative nationalist character), the Catholic Centre, and the Bavaria Party which advocated extreme federalism. A little later, a party of expellees which had previously been prohibited by the Allied High Commissioners was set up. This was called the League of Expellees and People Deprived of their Rights (*Bund der Heimatvertriebenen und Entrechteten*) (BHE). Its very name indicated its position on the Right of the political spectrum, because the word '*entrechtet*' (deprived of rights) was understood in contemporary linguistic usage to mean 'victims of de-Nazification'. Unlike these parties, the KPD received fewer votes than previously in the Bundestag elections. It had received 9 per cent in the Diet elections, but now it fell back to 5.7 per cent. It soon became rather an instrument and a victim of the Cold War than an active participant in politics.

The decline in support for the two big political parties reflected uncertainty about the justification for founding a state that covered only part of Germany, and anxieties about the market liberalism of the economic reforms, the success of which was by no means evident until 1951. But it also reflected the rise of a neo-nationalist trend in West Germany. This took the form from 1948 onwards of vehement opposition to de-Nazification and the war crimes trials. The first post-1949 Diet elections continued this trend. The CDU was outstripped in Lower Saxony and Bremen by the DP, and in Hesse by the FDP, while in Bavaria the CSU only just stayed ahead of the Bavaria Party, and also the question of whether large parts of the Catholic milieu would not after all find their way back to the Centre Party did not appear to have been decided yet.[21]

In these circumstances, a grand coalition might perhaps have been the answer, but that would have handed over the role of opposition to the small parties and the special interest groups. The fear that a united nationalist camp might rapidly develop out of the small parties was not unrealistic. But economic policy was the crucial factor here. The SPD had waged the electoral fight just as it had done during the crises that shook the Weimar Republic, with powerful class struggle rhetoric, vehement attacks on the Union as the party of the Church and capital and a focus on social conflict and state control of the economy. The failure of these tactics surprised the SPD, its party chair Schumacher most of all, because in view of the dubious consequences of Erhard's economic policies the party had counted firmly on victory and an opportunity to take over the government. The idea that they could simply recoup the electoral clientele they had been forced to abandon in 1933 proved to be a gross miscalculation. It resulted from the theory that in 1933 the SPD's approach had been insufficiently socialist (this had strengthened the KPD), and insufficiently nationalist (this had helped the NSDAP). But there was no advantage to be gained in the 1949 elections by stressing national interests in opposition to the Western Allies and a socialist orientation in economic policy. Nationalist votes went either to the Union or the small right-wing parties, the rhetoric of the class struggle put off voters outside the narrow core of Social Democratic support, while very few extra votes could be gained on the Left in view of the intensification of the Cold War.

A decade had to elapse before the SPD drew firm conclusions from this turn of events and stopped trying to use the categories of the early 1930s to grasp the changed conditions of the post-war era. In summer 1951, the 'economic miracle' began to gain momentum and as time went on Adenauer's policy of Western integration not only proved successful but received the unmistakable approval of the electorate. This meant that the SPD had failed in both the key areas of its opposition strategy, and the party began to look almost like an anachronism. It was forced to seek an entirely new direction, which it did in 1959 by adopting the Bad Godesberg Programme. This marked the abandonment of the Marxist basis of the SPD's previous policy. A little later, it also came out in favour of Western integration.[22]

The Union reacted to the 1949 election results by joining with the FDP and the DP to form a 'small coalition' of the Centre and the Right. It therefore continued its cooperation with those parties over economic policy in the Economic Council (*Wirtschaftsrat*), but abandoned its previous close collaboration with the SPD in the Parliamentary Council. Alongside Western integration, the 'social market economy' now became the Union's key programmatic message.

This was reflected in the liberal Düsseldorf Guidelines adopted on 15 July 1949, which replaced the Christian Socialism of the earlier Ahlen Programme.

As the first Federal Chancellor, Adenauer was mainly concerned at first with foreign policy and *Deutschlandpolitik* (in other words policy towards the question of German division and the existence of two German states). Since the Occupation Statute had not provided for a German Foreign Minister, the Federal Chancellor took over these tasks and acted as the first and only point of contact with the Allied High Commissioners. All important decisions were taken in partnership with the Commissioners, which placed Adenauer in an exceptional position from the start. This situation favoured the establishment of a form of government entirely focused on one individual, the Chancellor. Public discussions and arguments in parliament, fiercely conducted and sometimes bruisingly acrimonious in nature, were mainly concerned with the issues of Western integration, rearmament and reunification.

In 1952, when the first successes began to be seen in the economic sphere, and in Western integration and the recovery of sovereignty, they were ascribed, logically enough, to the CDU and its Chancellor. This was reflected in the convincing electoral victory of the Union in 1953, when it secured 45 per cent of the vote and half the parliamentary seats. With 28.8 per cent, the SPD did even worse than in 1949. The FDP and the DP suffered slight losses, while the BHE, with 5.9 per cent, entered the political arena for the first time.

The elections of 1953 were strongly affected by the Cold War. The EDC treaty, the war in Korea and in particular the bloody suppression of the popular rising in the GDR occupied the forefront of attention. Moreover, a few days before the elections, the Soviet Union had announced the detonation of its first hydrogen bomb. In the face of such a threat, Adenauer's uncompromising policy of Western integration appeared to be the sole guarantee of protection and security. By now, most West Germans saw the Western option as a question of life and death. No party had hitherto gained 45 per cent of the vote in free elections, not even the NSDAP in 1933. This highlighted the change that had taken place.

Adenauer's style of government was also an important factor in his electoral victory. Democratic governments had as a rule been regarded in Germany since the end of the Empire as highly unstable and lacking in real authority, and the Chancellors of the Weimar period, with few exceptions, had been perceived as weak figures. Now everything was very different: Adenauer conducted his government in a resolute and authoritative manner, using the powerful position deliberately assigned to the Chancellor in the Basic Law. In dealing with the new institutions of the democratic state, which were hardly yet consolidated, his approach was not particularly gentle if his main objectives were at stake, as in the case of the newly established Federal Constitutional Court. But here he soon came up against the limits of his power. The institutional structure of the new state proved to be highly robust, even faced with such a power-hungry Chancellor as Konrad Adenauer.

But, above all, Adenauer's patriarchal demeanour corresponded well to the need for strong leadership which had moulded the political culture of Germany since Bismarck and was clearly marked even among younger people, who had after all mainly been brought up on military lines. No doubt this way of exercising power in a democratic state was not unproblematic, since it preserved and strengthened authoritarianism and the people's faith in the leadership principle. On the other hand, it also made the new state and its institutions more acceptable, and in return it laid the groundwork for a critique of Adenauer's style of government, so that, after less than a decade, voices were increasingly raised in condemnation of his tutelary spoon-feeding of the electorate. In any case, in face of the authoritarian style of political leadership embraced by the Chancellor, the desire for more collaborative forms of governance constantly grew stronger. In the Weimar period, in contrast, exactly the opposite had happened.[23]

Despite his electoral victory of 1953, Adenauer formed a coalition not just with the FDP but also with the DP and the BHE. The main reason for this was the rearmament issue, which occupied the centre of the political debate in the next few years. In order to pass the Law on Military Service, the constitution had to be changed, and that required a two-thirds majority. During the 1950s, the conflict over rearmament and the 'defence contribution' was the dominant domestic political issue in the Federal Republic, and it went beyond the limits of parliamentary discussion. The conflict passed through two phases. In the first phase, which lasted until 1955, the Chancellor was opposed not only by the SPD, the trade unions and the communists (although the latter were already largely marginalised) but also by a broad collective movement consisting of youth leagues and representatives of the churches. The re-establishment of a German national army also met with resistance from many former soldiers, whose experiences in the Second World War had made them pacifists and opponents of military action, independently of their political position on other matters. Nevertheless, after the signing of the Paris Treaties in February 1955, the movement against rearmament quickly lost its ability to mobilise people. Moreover, after the bloody suppression of the anti-communist uprising in Hungary by the Red Army in autumn 1956 the number of people who actively supported rearmament started to increase.

Even so, the strong resistance in Germany to the establishment of a Bundeswehr, combined with the watchful eye of the Western powers, had the result that its mode of organisation broke ostentatiously with all Prussian and German military traditions. In particular, the political past of applicants for the position of officer and above was carefully checked, so as to prevent the emergence of anti-democratic structures, and to make sure that the army was unable to detach itself from government and society and lead an independent life of its own. Other branches of the public service did not possess a monitoring procedure of this kind. This applied particularly to the ministerial bureaucracy, with the consequences one might expect. Given the previous history of the German army, it was hardly surprising that it took a long time before the principle of a democratic army, and the concepts of 'citizens in uniform' and 'developing leadership from within' could be given practical effect. What was surprising was rather that it was possible to implement them at all.

The integration of the Bundeswehr into NATO also raised the question of control over nuclear weapons. The Paris Treaties prohibited the Federal Republic from building them, but at the end of 1956, after the American Defence Secretary had declared that the USA would place tactical nuclear weapons at the disposal of its NATO allies, the West German Minister of Defence, Franz-Josef Strauß, requested that the Bundeswehr also be granted access to these weapons. The federal government planned to arm the Bundeswehr with so-called tactical nuclear warheads. In order to calm public concerns, Chancellor Adenauer described these weapons in an interview as 'artillery at a higher level of development', thereby provoking howls of outrage.[24]

This started the second phase of the pacifist mass movement. It differed from the first not least because a larger number of intellectuals and scientists took part in the protests. The 'Göttingen manifesto', a statement issued by eighteen leading natural scientists, was of particular significance. The signatories included Germany's most prominent nuclear physicists: Max Born, Walther Gerlach, Otto Hahn, Werner Heisenberg, Max von Laue and Carl Friedrich von Weizsäcker. The manifesto criticised the plan to equip the Bundeswehr with nuclear weapons and warned against the military and political consequences of nuclear armaments. This was the opening shot in a campaign described as a 'Fight against Nuclear Death', which was the biggest anti-government mass movement in the Federal Republic to date. It mobilised more than a million people in protest demonstrations, and in some cases led to unofficial strikes. The SPD and the trade unions even began preparations to hold a popular referendum, but this was ruled out by the Federal Constitutional Court as unconstitutional. However, once the NATO Council had decided that the 'right to press the button' enabling nuclear weapons to be used in Western Europe and West Germany would be reserved to the USA, the campaign was broken off.[25]

This episode was significant in several respects. Firstly, it made it clear that the West German government, which like its NATO partners assumed that the Red Army had a considerable superiority in conventional weapons, regarded access to nuclear weapons as part of its policy of restoring sovereignty, though here the Western Allies applied the brakes: the Federal Republic continued to be under their guardianship in a military sense. Secondly, it showed that the SPD's policy towards foreign relations and the question of German unification had become anachronistic. In the election campaign of 1957 it again put forward the idea that reunification had priority over Western integration and it attempted to take advantage of the protest against nuclear armaments. The party was defeated once again, although public opinion surveys showed that more than three-quarters of the population rejected the plan to arm the country with nuclear weapons. Thirdly, the 'movement against nuclear death' also indicated the presence of new elements in the domestic political discussion. The manifesto of the Göttingen professors and the participation of numerous politically unaffiliated groups in the protests showed that in some sections of the population there had emerged a potential for criticism and protest against specific measures by the government which no longer simply reflected the Cold War line-up or the confrontation between West German political parties. But as long as the Cold War conflict between the rival power blocs retained its intensity, the effectiveness of such new approaches remained limited.

## Social Policy

Besides Western integration and the stabilisation of democratic institutions, social policy was the other central issue that dominated the politics of the Federal Republic between 1949 and 1957. Here, the initial starting point was the dramatic and desperate situation of millions of war victims and refugees as well as other destitute people, who urgently required relief. But, after the advent of the social market economy, this issue was also linked with the lack of legal clarity over the relation between capital and labour, which had been at the centre of the country's political disagreements under the Weimar Republic as well. The structure of social policy, and its future development, had to be determined afresh, because the degree of support the new republic received from its citizens was in large measure dependent on this.[26]

Roughly a third of the West German population could be seen in the broader sense as victims of the war: there were 10 million refugees and expellees, 4 million disabled men, widows and orphans, 3.5 million people bombed out of their homes and 1.5 million late returnees from captivity. When the Federal Republic was established, a large number of them still lived in makeshift dwellings. They were either destitute, sick or incapable of working, or all three at once. The government devoted special attention to these groups. Assistance was quickly provided for war victims through the Federal Law on War Pensions

(*Bundesversorgungsgesetz*) and various other measures of support. There was, however, broad agreement that, once these improvised kinds of assistance had been given, a degree of equilibrium should be arrived at, in a fair and systematic way, between those whose health or material situation had suffered from the war and those who had weathered it without incurring much damage.

The Germans had already raised the demand for this sort of equalisation of burdens ('*Lastenausgleich*') in the negotiations with the Allies over currency reform. The Americans had refused to admit any linkage, because they feared that their severe currency measures would be watered down as a result and the West German economy would not get moving quickly enough. With the establishment of the Federal Republic, however, a comprehensive law of this type was in the offing. From the beginning, there were two opposing positions on the subject, and the choice between them was of vital significance. The SPD and the trade unions demanded that the compensation payments should be made independently of the individual's previous income or property. This would also compensate for the injustices of the currency reform. The middle-class political camp, in contrast, regarded the payments as compensation for lost property or physical impairment, which should result in the restoration of the income and property previously held.

The government was able to push through the latter approach. The Equalisation of Burdens Act was passed in August 1950. Under it, compensation payments were made for proven physical and material damage. They were divided four ways. Roughly a quarter of each payment was to go to pensions, a quarter as compensation for loss of household goods, a quarter to housing support, and a quarter for damage to property. The payments were financed by those who had suffered no wartime losses. They had to pay a contribution levied on half their wealth. The effective date for calculating this was the day of the currency reform, 21 June 1948. The payments were spread over thirty years and they remained fixed to the starting value, even in the 1950s when there was a fourfold increase in profit and income. Taken as a whole, the burden amounted to a supplementary tax of between 4 and 6 per cent, which was certainly not a severe imposition on the section of the population which had been spared the consequences of war. This measure did nothing to compensate for the blatant social injustices of the currency reform, nor did it produce any changes in the structure of society. But this unprecedented equalisation process did undoubtedly generate an immense transfer of resources: by 1989 the total amount paid under this heading had reached 140 billion Marks. Thus the equalisation of burdens was of great significance both socially and politically, firstly because it offered appreciable assistance to groups of the population which had been particularly affected by the war, allowing them to integrate into society and recover their former position, secondly because it was seen as a symbol of the mutual solidarity of the West German population, thirdly because it considerably improved the reputation of the young republic among its citizens, and lastly because it involved a clear refusal to intervene in the system of property ownership.

The equalisation of burdens, the provision of support for the victims of war, the survivors' pensions and other social benefits ensured that, by 1953, almost 20 per cent of the national income went on social expenditure. This was the highest proportion in Europe at that time: in Great Britain it was 12.5 per cent, in Sweden 13.5 per cent. But there was also no other country in Western Europe which had such heavy war-related burdens to bear, so many war victims to care for, and so many refugees to compensate. Explosive political problems were bound up with this: the millions and millions of refugees and expellees were generally regarded as a possible source of disturbance and radicalisation. The former soldiers, above all the disabled and the late returnees from captivity, needed housing, care and a chance to work for a living. Once the economic upsurge had begun, the Federal Republic possessed sufficient financial resources to handle these tremendous tasks. Contrary to most predictions, therefore, it succeeded within a few years in integrating most of this group into society.[27]

The economic policy objectives of the trade unions and SPD coincided in many respects in the post-war years, but their priority areas differed. While the Social Democrats focused above all on the socialisation of key industries and the development of a system of central planning for the whole economy, the paramount interest of the trade unions was co-determination (*Mitbestimmung*) of the kind that had been introduced after the war in the iron and steel industry in the British zone of occupation. There the employers had made far-reaching concessions to the trade unions under the pressure of the threatened dissolution of the large conglomerates, with the result that the unions were then able, with the support of the occupying power, to push through parity of representation on the management boards of the big firms. This arrangement expired with the establishment of the Federal Republic, but the trade unions did everything they could to transfer the system to the iron and steel industry over the whole of West Germany and potentially to all other branches of industry as well.

In this they initially enjoyed great success. It was crucial here that Adenauer was convinced in 1950 that he would be unable to achieve either the Schuman Plan or rearmament against the wishes of the trade unions. To ensure their support, he finally offered to continue the system of co-determination in the coal and steel industries, and this was passed into law in April 1951, against the votes of the Liberals. A year later, however, when a new Works Constitution Act (*Betriebsverfassungsgesetz*), which covered all branches of the economy, was under discussion, Adenauer no longer needed to rely on the trade unions, and in spite of massive protests and strike threats the new law did not include a provision for co-determination on a parity basis. It was instead oriented more towards the system of industrial relations adopted under the Weimar Republic and the ideas of industrial partnership found in Christian social teaching.

It also became apparent in these discussions that the readiness of the workers to support a fighting campaign for the extension of co-determination had started to decline considerably with the coming of economic prosperity. The improvement of the individual's life circumstances increasingly took precedence over the need to secure collective working-class rights. The trade unions were therefore the big losers of the first years of the Federal Republic. They were unable either to achieve socialisation, or introduce elements of planning into the economic system, or anchor co-determination in the Works Constitution Act. They reacted to this by gradually changing direction so as to concentrate more strongly on the improvement of wages and working conditions instead of trying to alter the way the economy was run. From the late 1950s onwards, they pursued this new objective with growing success. The basis of the trade unions' growing influence proved to be not co-determination but free collective bargaining, and the consistently favourable economic situation offered a good basis for this.[28]

During the first legislative period, until 1953, the main focus lay on finding a remedy for urgent social needs. In later years, however, the major issue was the future direction of social policy. A complete reform of social insurance had originally been planned. This did not happen, partly because in 1956 the SPD presented an extensive social policy programme, thereby putting the government under pressure in anticipation of the impending electoral contest. Social policy increasingly became a decisive tool for gaining electoral support, and this was never clearer than in the case of the great pension reform of 1957.

In Bismarck's system of social insurance, the old age pension offered only a small supplementary income; for the majority of workers, the approach of old age continued to be associated with the fear of impoverishment. The situation had not altered very much since Bismarck's time: even at the beginning of the 1950s, the pension was 60 DM, less than a third of the average net wage, and at that time some 6 million pensioners lived in conditions of acute material hardship. Only a change of system could bring a fundamental improvement; but the Minister of Finance, the Bundesbank and the employers all raised objections. It was above all reasons of power politics which induced Adenauer to override the votes of his ministers, with the help of the SPD, as often happened in matters of social policy. He was convinced that, in this way, the Union would win the 1957 Bundestag elections, despite the mass protests mounted by the 'movement against nuclear death', which were dominating headlines at the time. According to the new system, pensions would no longer be financed from contributions paid by the insured themselves during their working lives, but from the contributions of the current generation of workers. This would allow the immediate introduction of a tremendous increase in pension payments. They rose by an average of 60 per cent in the year 1957 alone, and there was a further 110 per cent increase from 1957 to 1969. As a result, for the first time ever, millions of retired people received an adequate pension, which functioned as a replacement for the wage, and amounted to more than half of the net income received before retirement. There is no doubt that the pension reform was a decisive factor in Adenauer's triumph at the 1957 elections to the Bundestag.

It also had more long-term sociopolitical implications. Apart from lessening the poverty of the elderly and securing individuals' long-term status, which also made it possible for them to plan their lives in advance, the pension reform also had a specific family policy dimension, because it was concerned solely with people who were economically active, while the role of the housewife was not considered. This stabilised the traditional picture of women and families, a quite deliberate effect given the instability in social relations brought about by the war and its aftermath. The pension reform was also an important factor in the competition between the two German states, because in the GDR poverty in old age had by no means been eliminated (and would not in fact be eliminated until 1989), so that the Federal Republic gained a big lead in social policy in this area.

The pensions system, it should be added, had two essential requirements. The first was continuing economic growth, needed to generate the funds which could then flow via taxes or social contributions into pensions or other social measures. The second was that there should not be a big decline in the birth rate, because otherwise too many pensioners would have to be financed by too small a workforce; this did actually happen from the 1980s onwards. The proposal to combine the pension reform with strong support for families with children failed to win a majority in 1957, with the result that the reform indirectly rewarded childlessness.

Along with the equalisation of burdens, the pension reform set the course of social policy in the 1950s. It was also the prelude to the wide-ranging expansion of social policy in the fifteen years that followed. This development was not unique to West Germany: the welfare state expanded in all the countries of Western Europe, although at varying speeds. Everywhere, the social benefits provided by the state became the fundamental prerequisite for political integration and legitimacy. Attention was drawn from the outset to the drawbacks associated with welfare provision, such as loss of autonomy, dependence on the state, and the strain on the state's financial resources, though the warnings came predominantly from those who were generally sceptical about increases in social benefits, because they encouraged dependency, undermined family ties and weakened motivation. But a gradually extended system of social security became a characteristic feature of Western European countries after the end of the 1950s, unlike in the USA, and the increasing political and social stability of Western Europe in the next twenty years must in large measure be ascribed to this.[29]

By 1957 at the latest, social policy had become the third pillar of the West German social fabric. The other two were Western integration and the economic miracle, but unlike these, social policy resulted from the initiative of the West Germans themselves. Given the catastrophes and the decades of insecurity Germans had experienced, the extension of the social security system was of tremendous importance. Not only did it make it possible for both workers and pensioners to enjoy increased material security, it also offered the overwhelming majority of the population for the first time the chance to make solid plans for the next generation. 'The children should have a better life than us' evolved from being a long cherished dream to a realistic opportunity, and this was seized with enthusiasm.

## The Reintegration of the Ex-Nazis

The rapid successes of the young Federal Republic, its economic progress, its internal stability and also its military weight, changed the relationship of West Germans to the Nazi regime which had fallen in 1945. As the Allies became more inclined to make concessions, so the Germans gained in self-confidence. After the establishment of the Federal Republic, the issue of the reintegration into West German society of former officials and adherents of the Nazi state and also the fate of the imprisoned Nazi war criminals became more and more significant. At the same time, the federal government's move to pay 'reparations' (*Wiedergutmachung*) to the victims of National Socialism, on the analogy of the equalisation of burdens granted to Germans who had suffered from the effects of war and displacement, met with strong resistance even from its own ranks. These were parallel and closely interconnected developments.[30]

At first, in the years after 1945, there had been intensive discussion of the crimes of the Nazis. But after 1948, and to an even greater extent after the founding of the Federal Republic, this issue had faded into the background. The processes of cleansing and de-Nazification which had been operated vigorously by the Western Allies immediately after the war were now rapidly wound down. At the same time, voices started to be raised in the Federal Republic in opposition to Western de-Nazification policies and the view of the war and of National Socialism that underlay them. Attempts were also made to rehabilitate National Socialists who had been punished or forced out of their profession.

The churches played an important part in this process. Both Protestant and Catholic Church leaders had spoken out early on against the prosecution of

Nazi war criminals by the Allies. The Bavarian bishops had emphasised in a pastoral letter that the 'immense army of innocent people' including 'babies and little children, old people and mothers' should be set against the small number of 'murderous associates' of Hitler and Himmler. 'The German people, with few exceptions, had no knowledge of the brutalities committed in the concentration camps against people who were largely innocent.' But any attempt to assign collective guilt to the German people, the bishops declared, must be regarded as just as bad as, if not worse than, what was done in those years.

Fierce protests of this kind against the de-Nazification policy of the Allies were always combined with a rejection of 'National Socialism' in principle. The semantic content of the concept of 'National Socialism' diminished as time went on, however, and it finally shrank to cover a handful of SS leaders and their participation in the murder of the Jews. In this context it proved significant that most Germans had, after all, merely heard about the mass crimes committed in the German death camps, whereas they had personally experienced crimes, or what they considered to be crimes, committed against themselves, from the Allied bombing campaigns to the post-war expulsions, the severe food shortages and the dismantling of factories. Many Germans did not regard themselves as the guilty parties but as the victims of war and of a dictatorship which had spread over Germany as if it were an enemy country. 'The German people', declared Cardinal Joseph Frings, Archbishop of Cologne, 'were the victim rather than the instrument of these atrocities.' And their sacrifices were not yet at an end. The Germans had been persecuted and deprived of their rights, first by the Nazis and then by the victorious Allies: they were victims in a twofold sense.[31]

Hermann Hesse, who won the Nobel Prize for Literature in 1946, was an acute observer of these developments from his Swiss exile. As he wrote bitterly in a letter to Luise Rinser, he had recently been asked by a German industrialist, a family man, 'what he thought a well-intentioned and decent German ought to have done in the Hitler years? He had been unable to prevent anything, or do anything against Hitler, because that would have been madness, it would have cost him bread and freedom and ultimately even life.' Other Germans, Hesse went on, who had been Nazi Party members for years, now told him 'that throughout all those years they had always had one foot in the concentration camp, and I had to reply to them that I could only take opponents of Hitler seriously if they had had both feet in the camp, not one foot in the camp and the other foot in the party.' Previous acquaintances, who had long been enthusiastic Nazis,

> went into detail about their daily lives, their air-raid damage, their domestic worries, and their children and grandchildren, as if nothing had happened, as

> if there was nothing to separate us, as if they hadn't helped to kill the relatives and friends of my wife, who is Jewish, and to discredit and finally to destroy my life's work.

And then there were others, he went on,

> who invite me to raise my voice in the world outside and to protest as a neutral person and a representative of humanity against the excesses or the negligence of the occupying armies. This is all so naive, it displays such ignorance of the world and the present situation, it is all so pathetic and shamefully childish.[32]

While the increasingly vociferous complaints of the West Germans were initially restricted to de-Nazification, which was described in the Bundestag in 1950 as 'a modern witch-hunt', 'the deformed offspring of totalitarian thinking and the class struggle', or simply 'a crime', the focus of criticism soon moved on to cover the prosecution of Nazi crimes by German and Allied courts. 'Victors' justice' was the central slogan employed here, and there lay behind this a view of history according to which the Second World War and thus also the mass crimes committed by the Germans fell under the category of normal military conflict. According to what was starting to be the dominant conviction, the basis for the criminal proceedings was not the Germans' exceptionally criminal acts but their military defeat.

In 1946, over 70 per cent of West Germans still approved of the trials of the war criminals, but by 1950 the same proportion had come to reject them. At the same time, the West German public viewed de-Nazification, internment camps, tribunals and war crimes trials as proof that punishment and atonement had already taken place. Moreover, the obvious inequities of the de-Nazification procedure were regarded as evidence of the inappropriateness of the whole endeavour, and the resulting 'injustices' were to some extent equated with the crimes of National Socialism.

The political upshot of this broad campaign, which was also partly assisted by the big democratic parties, was the passing during the first few years of the new republic of a series of far-reaching legislative measures for the reintegration of former National Socialists into society. By the amnesty laws of 1949 and 1954, the majority of National Socialist perpetrators who had been punished by the German courts, especially lower-ranking Nazis, were pardoned, and their convictions, and also the verdicts of the de-Nazification tribunals, were expunged from the criminal record.[33]

In this context, the reinstatement of officials was of particular significance. It had originally been intended to allow only the reinstatement of officials who had come to West Germany (or had been 'driven out') from the eastern territories and the GDR. Under pressure from various Civil Service Associations, however, individuals who had lost their posts because their Nazi involvement had been revealed in the course of the de-Nazification process, and who were described in the political jargon of the time as 'people deprived of their rights', were included in this group of officials 'driven out' of the East. At least 100,000 people were favoured in this way. That was more than a third of all those classified as tainted with Nazism in the de-Nazification process. Under this provision, former Nazi officials—who were soon called '131ers' after the relevant article of the Basic Law—obtained not just the chance but the right to resume their official posts. Only a thousand out of almost 345,000 former officials were excluded from this concession because they had been classified by the de-Nazification process as belonging to Categories I and II (main culprits). By now, however, even Nazi Gauleiters and leaders of the SD were being classified in appeal proceedings as 'fellow-travellers' or 'not complicit'. In less than five years, therefore, the overwhelming majority of the cleansing measures of the Western Allies had been reversed, and the bulk of the National Socialist functionaries had been amnestied and largely reintegrated into West German society.[34]

It was an obvious consequence of these far-reaching amnesties that the Nazi war criminals who had been condemned by the Allied tribunals and were now sitting in the prisons of Landsberg, Wittlich and Werl also put themselves forward for rehabilitation. The federal government planned to obtain sentence reductions and early releases as quickly as possible through quiet negotiations, but it hoped to prevent the Western public from becoming aware of what was happening. As against this approach, the small coalition parties, especially the FDP and the DP, started to raise the demand for a 'general amnesty' for all Nazi offenders without regard to the severity of the sentence or the nature of the charge. It could be foreseen that a solution of this kind would lead to conflict with the Western Allies. However, since the Americans were constantly in retreat on the war crimes question, the advocates of a general amnesty estimated that they had a relatively good chance of winning this battle. Moreover, many of them would have welcomed a confrontation with the Americans over the issue as a step towards distancing the Federal Republic politically from the West.[35]

Between 1951 and 1953, a campaign developed for the release of all Nazi criminals, which was sometimes conducted under the slogan 'First general amnesty, then general treaty.' This proved to be on the whole very successful, particularly after the FDP Bundestag deputy and former Wehrmacht officer Erich Mende had declared that his agreement to the Germany Treaty depended on the early release 'of former soldiers still held in captivity inside and outside Germany'. For a short time, indeed, it was even possible to remove the expression 'war criminal' from public use in West Germany, as it was beset with problems in any case, and replace it with the neologism 'war condemned', which was intended to cover both prisoners of war and Nazi criminals, and thus to place them on an equal footing.

In July 1952, the American High Commissioner John McCloy was finally forced to make clear that a general amnesty was absolutely out of the question. The Allies would not purchase the ratification of the Germany Treaty by the Bundestag by making concessions in the amnesty question. This authoritative statement provoked violent indignation among the German public, but there could now be no more thought of a general amnesty. Even so, within less than four years, German institutions managed to force through the release from Allied jails of the overwhelming majority of convicted Nazi criminals, though this was done quietly. Some of those released had been condemned a few years earlier to life imprisonment, or even given the death penalty.[36] One additional reason for the retreat of the Americans on the question of war criminals was that they had secured the services of a considerable number of very useful ex-Nazis. Examples of this were the so-called 'Eastern specialists' of the SS and the Wehrmacht, who had experience in dealing with the Red Army and the Soviet secret services and possessed information about these institutions. There were also engineers like Wernher von Braun, the man who developed the V-2 rockets. Tens of thousands of prisoners had died while building them in the underground facilities of the KZ Mittelbau-Dora in the Harz mountains. But now experts in rocketry were needed to build up similar industries in the USA. As the Cold War intensified, the Americans' threshold of inhibition became lower, so that finally even notorious Nazi criminals such as the former head of the Gestapo in Lyons, Klaus Barbie, could enter the service of the USA as a specialist on communism. These trends naturally worked against McCloy's tougher stance, so that West German demands for the release of Nazi war criminals soon met with little opposition.

Most of the liberated or rehabilitated Nazi officials devoted themselves in subsequent years to restoring their professional positions and gaining legal rehabilitation, an aim in which they were generally very successful. Some of them also found a political home in the emerging milieu of neo-Nazi groups and parties which concentrated around the Socialist Reich Party (SRP) and the German Reich Party (DRP), but persons from the former leadership of the Nazi regime were seldom seen in this environment. They preferred to gather together between 1949 and 1953 in looser associations, 'circles', pub groups and clubs, on the model of the form of organisation adopted by the radical right-wing intellectuals of the 'conservative revolution' of the 1920s, a milieu from which many of them in fact originated. The most well-known of these groups were the 'Naumann Circle' in Düsseldorf, around Werner Naumann, former state secretary under Goebbels and his designated successor, and a partially overlapping circle around the former Gauleiters Florian, Grohé and Kaufmann.

These groups openly attempted to regain political influence by infiltrating into the FDP in North-Rhine Westphalia, and they had some success. The fact that this occurred in close coordination with the foreign policy spokesman of the FDP Ernst Achenbach and Heydrich's former deputy Dr. Werner Best, who had worked in Achenbach's office since 1952, increased the politically explosive character of the whole endeavour. Moreover, unlike other similar circles, this group aimed to go beyond simply attempting to rehabilitate the participants in Nazi crimes individually and historically. Its objective was to develop a collective movement of right-wing nationalists at the heart of the FDP, so as to change the balance of political power in the Federal Republic.[37]

It was the prevailing view at that time that a right-wing nationalist party had great electoral potential, particularly if economic stabilisation took a long time coming. The Socialist Reich Party (SRP) had some 40,000 members and it clearly possessed a certain attraction for younger people, especially former soldiers. There was a pronounced tendency among all political parties to seek out the potential reservoir of support provided by former soldiers. Thus the SPD leader Kurt Schumacher met former high officers of the Waffen-SS in October 1951. He justified this action by saying that, during the war, the Waffen-SS was 'a sort of fourth section of the Wehrmacht' and that it had taken absolutely no part in the mass crimes of the Nazis. On the contrary, he said, most of the 900,000 members of the Waffen-SS had been recruited by force and they ought not to be ostracised. It was necessary 'to provide the great mass of former members of the Waffen-SS with a route to citizenship and future prospects. . . . These people bear no responsibility for any crimes and should be given the chance to come to terms with a world which is new for them.'[38]

Konrad Adenauer also supported the integration into society of people who were complicit in Nazism, and he ostentatiously received former Wehrmacht generals in the Federal Chancellery. In summer 1953, he even visited the imprisoned SS General Kurt Meyer ('Panzer-Meyer' as he was known). Meyer was one of the most highly decorated generals of the Waffen-SS and one of the most popular war heroes of the Nazi period. An Allied military court had condemned him to death for killing prisoners of war, but this was commuted to lifelong imprisonment after numerous interventions from the German side. Adenauer's visit to Werl Prison was a high point of the campaign against the Allied trials of war criminals and it acted like a collective declaration of German innocence. A year later, Meyer was released, and following this he became active in the SS veterans' organisation HIAG, quickly rising to be its leader. His book of memoirs made him one of the stars of the nationalist scene in the Federal Republic.[39]

Nevertheless, the year 1953 marks something of a turning point in the process of rehabilitation and reintegration. For one thing, the neo-Nazi SRP was prohibited in October 1952. In this way, the Federal Republic started to draw a boundary around its readiness to tolerate the neo-Nazi Right. Explicit assent, especially public assent, to the politics and ideology of the Nazi regime was unacceptable.[40] The occupying powers drew a second boundary line in January 1953 when the British simply arrested the members of the Naumann Group and the former Gauleiter Group and kept them behind bars for several months by virtue of their legal powers under the occupation statute. No trial took place, and the participants were all soon released, but the message sent by this step was unmistakable: the threat of Western intervention, which had always been present, but had almost faded from view in the meantime, was now again brought to the fore, and a further limit to the readiness to integrate the Right was now established: political activities of an explicitly National Socialist character by former top Nazis would not be tolerated.

The third decisive factor in this context was the outcome of the autumn 1953 elections to the Bundestag. Parties of the radical Right obtained less than one per cent of the vote and were thereby forced into political insignificance. The nationalist-infiltrated FDP also lost support, as did the DP. Adenauer considered that he had been proved right in his policy towards the former National Socialist officials, which involved their social and economic reintegration provided that they accepted the democratic republic, at least publicly, and refrained from neo-Nazi activities.[41]

By the early 1950s, therefore, the fate of the former National Socialists had taken a direction entirely contrary to the objectives pursued by the Allies and also the democratic parties after 1945. They were almost completely reintegrated into German society, including their leading personnel, with few exceptions. They had successfully re-entered the administration, the judiciary and the ministerial bureaucracy at all levels below the position of State Secretary. The Foreign Office in particular was regarded as a stronghold of these former National Socialists. Even so, they were always under an appreciable degree of pressure to adapt to the rules of the democratic game. This gradually became easier for them, both because the Bonn republic behaved with the utmost generosity towards the old Nazi elites and because it proved to be an extremely successful system of government. Moreover, the legal prosecution of Nazi crimes had now in practice come to a standstill, particularly after the Paris Treaties, which brought the pursuit of these crimes within the jurisdiction of the German authorities.[42]

This reintegration of the Nazis also extended to people right at the core of the policy of terror and annihilation, namely the leading elements of the Gestapo, the SD and the *Einsatzgruppen*. These men were now around fifty years old, they had usually had a university education, often in the law, and they had very good connections. Those who had survived the post-war era were able to settle in again to their professions in the Federal Republic after being released from imprisonment or internment. They did not, of course, resemble in the least the picture people had in Germany, and still more outside Germany, of the typical Nazi criminal. Konrad Adenauer himself had told German journalists in 1952 that very few of the people sitting in the Allied jails who had been 'condemned because of the war' were 'real criminals'. The real criminals were predominantly 'asocials and people with a previous criminal record'.[43] The picture offered here of the Nazi offender was not the Gestapo chief or the commander of an *Einsatzgruppe* but the SA thug and the concentration camp guard, and the concrete crimes people had in mind were the anti-Jewish riots of *Kristallnacht* rather than the murder of millions of Jews four years later, of which the ordinary person could hardly form a concrete conception. A lawyer, on the other hand, who probably had a doctorate, lacked all the characteristics associated with the prevailing picture of a 'criminal', although he was the one accused of participating in mass shootings 'in the East'.

This state of affairs proved to be very useful. Even people who had unquestionably rejected and detested the Nazi regime were unable to make the connection between the crimes of National Socialism, perceived as abnormal and remote from all everyday experience, and the colleague or neighbour who had been exposed as a former Gestapo Area Commander, because it was impossible to make a mental association between the heinous character of the crimes and the respectability of the neighbour or colleague.[44]

But the longer this situation lasted and the better their own social position became, the more problematic did their own past become for the former Nazi functionaries, because it created a potential threat to their newly acquired middle-class respectability. To camouflage one's own past, indeed, if possible to cause it to sink completely into oblivion, so as not to endanger the new future, became of urgent interest. The logical response to this was to lead an unobtrusive, well-adjusted, normal life, to avoid contact with former colleagues (and accessories) as far as possible, and to abstain from any politically suspicious statements.

This psychological mechanism had the effect that many former Nazi officials appeared to blend very effectively into the new West German state and society. This was accompanied by a process of abstraction and desensitisation of the Nazi past, which made the victims of the National Socialists as well as the perpetrators anonymous, and robbed history of their personal details and the location of their deeds, so that it would be possible to speak in public with a certain amount of emotion about the rule of violence in the past without having to deal with concrete places or real human beings. This attitude, for which the term 'repression' is appropriate, was virtually a hallmark of the social evolution of the Federal Republic right up to the 1980s.

But the fact that, despite the millions of victims of National Socialist policy, members of the Nazi elite and even the mass murderers of the Security Police and the SD were able to escape almost scot-free and even to occupy high-level positions as respectable citizens, was a scandal which contradicted all ideas of political morality in such a fundamental way that it could not take place without producing serious and long-lasting consequences for this society, its internal structure and its reputation abroad. For decades, and indeed right into the twenty-first century, the Federal Republic continued to carry this stigma, despite all the successes of democratic stabilisation.

Yet, if we take a sober look at the issue, and bear in mind the actual extent of the crimes committed and the number of those who were responsible or participated directly or indirectly, what is surprising about post-war developments is not the degree to which the Federal Republic was contaminated by the Nazi perpetrators but the fact that despite this weighty burden it became over the course of time a stable democracy. The cringing opportunism with which the former adherents and functionaries of Nazism integrated themselves into the Federal Republic expressed this group's political neutralisation and was a prerequisite for it. Indeed, not a few of those who seized this opportunity and found that it worked in their favour really did turn into good and convinced democrats. Society's acceptance of their opportunistic stance often laid the foundation for an actual change in their attitude.

Thus, the democratic republic started to take root thanks to a change in perceptions of the Nazi regime. This change involved a divorce between the individual's own experience, which was characterised by normality and continuity, and the mass crimes of National Socialism. The existence of those crimes was not publicly questioned, but they continued to be referred to as events which were foreign to the individual's own experience. They were regarded as the product of the memory of the Other, the memory of the victors.

The British Ambassador in Bonn, Sir Christopher Steel, was asked in spring 1959 whether it was true, as rumoured in Britain, that the old Nazis were again in office in West Germany and whether it was impossible to rule out a recurrence of National Socialism. He replied with a thorough analysis of the situation. The traditional German elites, he said, had in fact almost entirely returned to their former position in politics, the economy, the civil service and the world of science, though less so in the army. Moreover, former Nazi bigwigs lived in some comfort and had good positions, predominantly in the free professions and in industry, though seldom in politics. Even so, it would be wrong, he added, to speak of a danger to West German democracy, which was on the contrary completely stable, and the return of National Socialism was extremely unlikely.[45]

But it was not the former National Socialists and their successful resurgence that occupied centre stage in the political and legal disputes of those years. It was true that the right to punish Nazi crimes had lain within the competence of the German authorities since the mid-1950s. But they took no action at first, and hence the criminal prosecution of the biggest Nazi crimes was not undertaken until the end of the decade, with some individual exceptions. The efforts of prosecutors were rather focused on the communists, because in parallel with the international confrontation of the Cold War and the rivalry between the two German states the struggle of the West German authorities against the KPD was conducted with extraordinary harshness and assumed staggering dimensions. During the first few post-war years, the West German KPD was a large party, with 300,000 members. There were communist mayors and ministers, and until 1948 the party was represented in almost all state parliaments and governments. It obtained fifteen seats in the first elections to the Bundestag, though by then it had already gone past its peak. By 1956, the number of members had fallen to roughly 70,000. The workers' rising in the GDR on 17 June 1953 sealed the political fate of the KPD in West Germany, and the party failed to reach the 5 per cent threshold when elections were held to the Bundestag on 8 July 1953. There was a stable anti-communist consensus in the Federal Republic: 80 per cent of West Germans supported a tough attitude towards the KPD, which was regarded by the West German authorities not as an independent party but as the SED's fifth column. Looking back, one can see that they were not wrong to take this view, as the party was led from East Berlin and was first and foremost an instrument of the SED's struggle against the 'Adenauer republic'.

Thus, in West Germany, the pursuit of communists continued to increase in severity. When the Criminal Code Amendment Act was passed in August 1951, the provisions struck out by the Allies after the war covering high treason, endangering the state and sedition were reinserted and they formed the basis for the extensive prosecutions of KPD members which now began. In August 1956, the party was finally prohibited by the Federal Constitutional Court as being anti-constitutional. Political contacts with the GDR were now also subject to criminal prosecution.

The fight against communism in West Germany was part of the Cold War. It was not just a German affair. The 'Reds' were certainly pursued with no less zeal in the USA by Senator Joseph McCarthy than they were in the Federal Republic. But the fight against the communists showed how fragile the constitutional principles of West German democracy still were when the fight was one against a common enemy. Between 1951 and 1968, roughly 125,000 proceedings were conducted against communists for crimes against the state, and between 6,000 and 7,000 persons were convicted. These large numbers themselves sent a political signal, because the number of proceedings for Nazi-era crimes was slightly less, 106,000, and the number of convictions was exactly the same: 6,000. Surveillance of an immense number of telephone conversations and letters was conducted, and the importation of 'subversive publications' was monitored. Between 1955 and 1968, more than 100 million items of mail from the GDR were stopped and redirected to the prosecuting authorities. The anti-communist furore also had an impact on Social Democrats, trade unionists and members of the anti-nuclear movement, all of whom were suspected of being communists in disguise or Moscow's Fifth Column. This climate of illiberalism and mistrust was inflamed still further by the worsening conflict over Berlin at the end of the 1950s.[46]

## Compensation for the Victims of National Socialism

The Allies had announced in 1945 that Nazi perpetrators would be punished. But that was not all. Compensation for the victims of Nazi crimes by the Germans was also one of their core demands, and it was among the first of the measures taken by the occupying powers after the end of the war. But there were striking differences of implementation between East and West. The Soviet Union regarded victim compensation as mainly a matter of welfare provision. In this context, different groups of victims were evaluated differently. Resistance fighters, particularly communists, were right at the top, and they received not just higher monetary payments but also social and political privileges. In contrast to this, the restoration of property stolen from the victims of Nazism, particularly the return of Jewish property 'aryanised' by the authorities and by private individuals, was not permitted. This was the system applied in compensating the victims of National Socialism both in the SBZ and after the establishment of the GDR.[47]

It was entirely different in the West. Here, the victims of Nazism were to be compensated individually according to the degree to which they had suffered physical or material loss, and the three Western occupying powers made it emphatically clear from the outset that high priority would be granted to this question: persons who had been persecuted under the Nazi dictatorship for racial, political or ideological reasons would receive financial compensation. In addition, the victims of Nazism would be given favourable treatment in the allocation of housing, appointments to public office and entry into the professions.

The Germans complied with these instructions by the Allies, but the amount of money at their disposal was far too small to compensate even approximately for the devastations of the Nazi epoch. Moreover, public criticism of the compensation payments to victims of Nazism increased in the Western occupation zones after 1947. Germans who had purchased, or at least received, Jewish property after 1933, resisted its enforced return to the original owners or their descendants.

When the replacement of the Occupation Statute was being discussed, therefore, the Allies were keen to ensure that in taking over the tasks of compensation and restitution on its own account the German side did not derogate in any way from the compensation principles they had laid down before 1949. In the 'Transition Agreement' ('*Überleitungsvertrag*'), which was one of the components of the 'General Treaty', those principles were itemised in detail, and the German side thus accepted a treaty obligation to undertake '*Wiedergutmachung*', or 'restitution', whereby this word, which suggested a gesture of friendship, was preferred by the West Germans to the word '*Entschädigung*', or 'reparation' in English, which was associated with a legal claim.[48]

But now strong resistance emerged from the German side to the role of the Allies in drawing up the rules about payments to victims of Nazism. There was even criticism from within the federal government of the way 'the Transitional Treaty has now forced us to take over the compensation legislation passed by the *Länder* under Allied influence'.[49] The privileges afforded to the victims of Nazism were now often criticised as well. Indeed, the whole justification of restitution was now questioned. 'Today' wrote the representative of an aid organisation for victims of racial persecution at the beginning of 1949, 'we have already arrived at the point where dyed in the wool Nazis, courted for favours, distribute them with a broad smile from the secure vantage point of the best official positions, while the victim of persecution has to leave his place of work to make room for a returning Nazi.'[50]

It also became increasingly clear that there was competition between the claims of the victims of Nazism and those of Germans who had suffered wartime injury or damage. In autumn 1951, 96 per cent of West Germans declared that they supported aid to German war widows and orphans, 93 per cent to those who had been bombed out of their homes, and 90 per cent to refugees and expellees. Even relatives of the 20 July plotters had the support of 73 per cent—but only 63 per cent supported aid to the Jews.[51] At the same time, there was an increasing tendency to place German victims on the same level as victims of the Germans. The abstract category of 'victims of tyranny' now included refugees from East Prussia, or German soldiers who had returned from captivity in the Soviet Union, on the same level as Jews who had survived the Holocaust. This removal of the individual's fate from its historical context not only made it possible to equate perpetrators and victims, it also led in the course of parliamentary discussions over the restitution legislation to repeated attempts to establish a financial linkage between the two groups of claimants: payments to victims of Nazism could only be implemented politically if payments to German war victims were also approved. Thus, agreement to pay restitution to civil servants removed from office for political or racial reasons under the Nazi state was linked with the passing of regulations which favoured the '131ers'.

The question of whether, and in what manner, the Federal Republic should pay compensation to Jews, who after all lived mainly outside the Federal Republic, was only indirectly connected with these debates over the West German restitution legislation. It was the extremely precarious economic situation of Israel which finally induced its government to demand material compensation from the Germans, despite considerable resistance within the country itself. The reaction in the Federal Republic to this demand was overwhelmingly negative. It was therefore highly surprising that Adenauer accepted the Israeli demand for a billion US dollars as a basis for negotiation, and thus made possible the opening of discussions which were politically of great significance.[52]

But the federal government was faced at the same time by demands from foreign creditors, particularly American firms, for the payment of commercial debts which had accumulated from before and after the war. This was important for the German economy because of its connection with the restoration of Germany's creditworthiness. It is one of the most remarkable developments under the early Federal Republic, not easy to disentangle, that the negotiations over restitution payments to Israel (held in Wassenaar) and over the settlement of Germany's debts (held in London) took place at the same time and were also coordinated by the leading German negotiator in London, the banker Hermann Josef Abs. This enabled German negotiators in London to point to the burdens arising from the expected obligations towards Israel, while their colleagues in Wassenaar could tell the Jewish representatives about the demands being negotiated in London. The 'restoration of our credit in the world', Adenauer told his cabinet, 'depends on the success of both negotiations. But that is the purpose of the whole thing.'[53]

At the end of the negotiations, the Federal Republic promised Israel and the Jewish Claims Conference (JCC), which represented non-Israeli Jews, that it would pay a total of 3.45 billion DM, spread out over fourteen years, a third of it in deliveries of German goods. At the London Debt Conference Germany's debts were adjudged to be 15 billion DM. But, owing to the highly successful development of the West German economy, the Federal Republic was able to clear most of these debts by the end of the 1950s.

Both agreements considerably improved the position of the Federal Republic in the world. The London Agreement paved the way for the West German economy to return to the international credit markets. It was also a prerequisite for the free convertibility of the D-Mark. The agreement with Israel and the JCC can be regarded as the foundation stone of West Germany's policy of recognising the country's guilt, although Adenauer was only able to push it through the Bundestag with great difficulty, using the votes of the SPD. He was also flying in the face of German public opinion (only 24 per cent of West Germans were in favour of the agreement).

In London, however, a grave and fundamental decision had been made which went almost unnoticed by the West German public. The representatives of the US government, with the agreement of the German federal government, insisted on the principle that the Federal Republic would initially only have to pay back the debts Germany had incurred before and after the war. These were predominantly owed to Western banks. As against this, more far-reaching claims from the wartime period, particularly those from countries occupied by Germany during the conflict, would be settled in a peace treaty to be negotiated later. This was intended to prevent American support payments to the Federal Republic from flowing out as reparations to third parties or as compensation payments to the countries of the communist eastern bloc. But most of the people who had been harmed by Germany during the war lived in those places. This decision, arrived at despite the protests of the smaller Western European states, meant that the Germans could not be presented with any more demands stemming from the war years until a peace treaty had been signed. And, since a peace treaty could not be expected to happen for a long time, in view of the division of Germany and the global Cold War confrontation, this agreement postponed for an indefinite period all the claims against the Federal Republic made by foreign KZ inmates, forced labourers and people persecuted in other ways—and this covered more than 90 per cent of all the surviving victims of Nazi rule.[54]

The Federal German Compensation Law which was passed a year later was revised and extended after a further four years. It could only get through the Bundestag after the government had accepted a demand from its own supporters that it be combined with a law compensating German prisoners of war. The regulations covering compensation for victims of Nazism were not as generous as the assistance provided by the Equalisation of Burdens Act (*Lastenausgleichs-Gesetz*), but they did provide substantial support to the parties concerned, particularly if they were unwell and incapable of earning a living. The West German compensation payments were also subject to a basic reservation, agreed in London, which drastically restricted the numbers of those entitled to receive them. Under the London Debt Agreement, compensation could only be given to Germans. The effects of this were described by the SPD deputy Hermann Brill, himself a former KZ inmate, using the example of KZ Buchenwald. This camp, he said, had a total of 42,000 registered inmates at the end of the war, 35,000 of whom were within its boundaries at that point. As many as 95 per cent of them were foreigners, of whom no less than 22,000 were Russians. Only 1,800 prisoners were German, and of these 1,100 had been locked up as homosexuals or asocials, so they were not entitled to compensation. Seven hundred of the Germans were political prisoners. Only these 700, 1.6 per cent of the total, were covered by the Compensation Law; the other 41,200 were excluded.[55]

The fact that foreign KZ prisoners and forced labourers, particularly those from Eastern Europe, had been excluded from receiving compensation was only admitted publicly in the Federal Republic forty years later, in connection with Germany's decision finally to begin payments to the former forced labourers. But, even among the Germans themselves, only relatively small groups of victims of Nazi injustice were entitled to compensation. Thus, the so-called 'gypsies' did not qualify, nor did people who had suffered compulsory sterilisation, nor did those who had been imprisoned as 'asocial', nor did the victims of medical experiments and many others. In the public discourse of that time, they were regarded not as the victims of specifically National Socialist injustice but to some extent as people who were justifiably punished. Many years went by before the Germans began to take a broader view of this definition and gradually to recognise these groups too as victims of Nazism.

The rules for the return of stolen property to the mainly Jewish victims of Nazism met with even stronger resistance in the Federal Republic than the Compensation Law. The new German owners usually denied that they had acquired the house, the firm, the home furnishings or the works of art illegally. The result was a series of legal proceedings which in some cases lasted many years. The new German owners also formed organisations, which protested against the 'outrageous and unjustified enrichment and appalling profiteering' involved in being 'forced to pay again a purchase price already paid once'. Some people even justified the 'aryanisation' that took place under Nazi rule. This, it was said, was ultimately nothing but 'compensation' for the 'gigantic property gains made by Jewish speculators' during the inflation period.[56] The federal government therefore tried to bring forward a law to compensate 'people who had suffered from restitution'. Under this law, the state would be obliged to compensate the beneficiaries of aryanisation for the property they were forced to return to its former Jewish owners. But this was stubbornly opposed by American High Commissioner John McCloy.

The monetary value of the restitution that was finally made was roughly 3.5 billion DM. Many of the court cases were only settled years later, and often enough the Jews expropriated in the 1930s had to fight for a long time to recover their houses, land or businesses. Even so, the restitution process was a largely successful attempt to obtain justice for the victims and at the same time to restore property rights as the cornerstone of a capitalist economy and a democratic legal system.

West German restitution to Nazi victims thus presents a mixed overall picture. On the one hand, it is clear that the Germans were reacting essentially to Allied pressure, and were positively compelled by the Americans to take over the compensation regulations which had been introduced during the occupation years. Without this pressure, the small group of advocates of restitution in the Bundestag parties would not have been in a position to put these provisions into effect. On the other hand, it was certainly a remarkable development, eight years after the end of the war, that the West German state took on such extensive financial obligations, at a time when the federal budget was less than 30 billion DM a year. The fact that political and economic considerations were also involved does not diminish this achievement.

## Society in the Fifties

Concentration on the dynamism of the economic miracle and the profound long-term changes in the social structure tends to distort one's picture of the original situation. In the early 1950s, life in West Germany was if anything bleak, and this is how it long continued to be for most citizens of the Federal Republic. The standard of living had, admittedly, recovered by 1950 to the level of the years 1913, 1928 and 1938, but a third of the population, and more than half of the refugees and expellees, still lived in temporary, inadequate or overcrowded accommodation.[57] Half of the employees in West Germany were workers who led lives of heavy physical labour, working an average of almost fifty hours a week, spread over six days, and receiving low wages. In the first half of the 1950s, the average West German family spent two-thirds of its budget on 'basic needs', such as food, housing and clothes, while skilled workers' families spent three-quarters and unskilled workers' families more than 80 per cent.[58]

In their daily lives, industrial workers continued to be strongly embedded in the proletarian milieu and divorced from the rest of society. It is true that the institutions of the socialist and Catholic workers' movements were no longer as effective in the post-war years as they had been in the decades before they were shattered by the Nazis, but social contacts outside the proletarian world, not to mention marriage, continued to be rare. Only a small section of the working class still thought in terms of the class struggle, but the sense of a sharp division of society into upper and lower ranks continued to be dominant. Social mobility continued to be hardly an option. Eighty per cent of children attended the eight-grade elementary school ('*Volksschule*') in 1951, but the high school (*Gymnasium*) continued to be the domain of the middle classes. Only 3 per cent of high school graduates were of working-class origin.

Roughly a quarter of the employed population was engaged in agriculture; more than a million of these people were agricultural workers. Almost half the West German population lived in villages or small towns with fewer than 5,000 inhabitants. Rural life had admittedly been changed to some extent, first by foreign forced labourers during the war, then by refugees after it. Even so, in many regions, rural life in 1950 differed little from the way it had been in 1900: peasant farms were overwhelmingly cultivated by the owners' families themselves, landholdings were small and there was little mechanisation. There had been few changes in the way society was stratified, in ways of working or living or in the economic infrastructure. Culturally, too, traditional attitudes continued to be dominant, above all in religion. Over 50 per cent of the Catholics went to church regularly, and in rural communes this reached 80 per cent. Modernity had still made few inroads into the rural milieu.[59]

The fate of the refugees was regarded as the greatest social problem of the epoch. It contained plenty of political dynamite. The social status of most of the refugees from the eastern regions had declined steeply: before the war less than half of the economically active adults had been employed as workers, but now three-quarters of them fell into that category. These incomers were often fiercely resented by the local population, particularly in confessionally and socially homogeneous rural areas. Many old-established inhabitants perceived the transition from Polish forced labourers to expellees from East Prussia as merely a change from one foreign group to another. Most of the refugees considered their future prospects to be uncertain and bleak. This is easily overlooked when the situation of the refugees is viewed from the perspective of the 1960s alone and the success of the processes of integration and social advancement is taken as a standard of measurement.[60]

At the beginning of the 1950s, West Germans were still a long way from enjoying the 'consumer society'; in many spheres, the pre-war level was not attained until much later. For example, the consumption of beef and pork in German households in 1950 was not yet half as great as in 1937; until the middle of the decade, real coffee was generally replaced by 'Muckefuck', a coffee substitute. Owing to the long working hours there was not much 'leisure time' for relaxation or cultural interests. This affected young people in particular. In 1953, 85 per cent of the eighteen- to twenty-year-old age group, male and female, was in employment; a specific youth culture only emerged later, when working hours were shorter and there was more financial leeway. The tram and the bicycle were the typical modes of transport of the epoch, although the number of motorbikes and mopeds was already increasing. Very few people possessed a motor car, and the ability of most people to move from place to place was very limited. Accommodation was therefore usually located close to the job.[61]

Most people's urgent goal was first of all to recover what they had had before, and in this context the pre-war years were the usual yardstick. We can hardly be surprised, therefore, that the pursuit of peace and security had top priority in the West Germans' scale of values from the early 1950s onwards, in view of the experiences of previous decades and the uncertainty of the present, especially in the shadow of the Korean War.

The economic miracle therefore began to run its dynamic course in a society whose social structure was very similar to that of the 1920s and 1930s. It was a society characterised by deprivation and low social mobility as well as traditional gender roles and a high degree of inequality. On the other hand, wartime and post-war experiences had altered people's sense of their own situation. Social milieux did not appear as firmly fixed as previously, and there was a looser connection between the fate of the individual and that of the social collective.

The continuing resurgence of the economy now began to affect German society, and it transformed it to its very foundations. The rise of fixed employment, offering long-term job security, was the most important change. A statistically average man who reached the age of forty in 1950 would only have spent a few years in continuous paid employment: first from 1924 to 1929, after leaving school, then from 1934 to 1939 after the economic crisis and the period of mass unemployment. Military service, wartime service and prisoner of war camp were then followed until 1950 by another phase of irregular employment. He had therefore only possessed a fixed job for roughly ten of the twenty-five years since leaving school, and this only lasted uninterruptedly for three or four years. This situation now changed fundamentally. From 1950 until his retirement in 1975, this statistically average employee was continuously employed for twenty-five years.

The number of people in employment increased considerably during the 1950s. It rose by almost 20 per cent, from 23.5 million in 1950 to 26.8 million in 1961. This was due partly to the coming of age of the large birth cohorts of earlier years and partly to the influx of refugees from the eastern region and the GDR. Most of the new jobs were in industry: the number of industrial workers doubled between 1950 and 1970, while the number of clerical employees in industrial firms almost tripled. In those two decades, the Federal Republic was more strongly imprinted by industrial labour than any other Western European country. The factory siren and the packed lunch, not the milk bar and the dance band, were the symbols of everyday culture in the first half of the 1950s.

The tremendous labour supply requirements of the booming industries of the 1950s helped to resolve the most urgent social problems. The presence of millions of refugees in the Federal Republic was at first regarded as a severe economic burden, but soon it turned out to be a fortunate circumstance, which contributed considerably to the boom in the economy. It was not just that refugees provided the reservoir of skilled workers needed urgently by expanding industries. They were also imbued with a desire to succeed and a readiness to work hard, and by a determination to 'make it by themselves'.

The countryside also began to change once the refugees had spent a considerable amount of time there, as very few of them were involved in agriculture. Industry was now systematically established in regions previously purely agrarian, particularly in South Germany. This also led to a gradual reduction in cultural and religious homogeneity. Before the war, there had been 1,400 exclusively Catholic villages in Bavaria; after the refugees arrived there were only nine. Moreover, the 3.5 million refugees who had arrived from the GDR by 1961 rapidly became assimilated into the acquisitive society of West Germany. The number of young and professionally qualified individuals among this group was disproportionately high. This was an enormous economic and political gain for the Federal Republic, and a corresponding loss to the GDR. By around 1960, the process of integrating the refugees was already complete. In 1964, three-quarters of the refugees from the east declared that they no longer wished to return to their homeland, even if this were to be possible.[62]

Continuity of employment brought another lasting change: there was a continuous increase in wages and income. The real wages of industrial workers had doubled by 1962, and by 1976 they had quadrupled. In the early 1960s, '*Wohlstand*' (prosperity) started to reach the working class. At the same time, average working hours gradually began to fall. They had reached their highest level in 1955, at 48.6 hours a week. In 1962, they fell below forty-five hours for the first time, and in 1975 they stood at less than forty-one. Campaigns by the trade unions for shorter working hours proved successful, and the slogan 'On Saturdays Daddy belongs to me' was one of the most popular in the history of the DGB (German Trade Union Confederation), though in practice as late as 1960 only a third of the labour force were able to enjoy free Saturdays. In addition, the reduction in working hours was associated with a corresponding push towards rationalisation, which led productivity per head to increase by 157 per cent between 1950 and 1960. Even so, any stronger pressure in the direction of rationalisation was prevented by a constant influx of additional workers, first refugees from the east and the GDR, then after 1961 the '*Gastarbeiter*' (guest workers) from Southern Europe.[63]

Changes in rural life were particularly drastic. The agricultural sector had declined continuously since the turn of the century, but this process was now abruptly accelerated. Between 1950 and 1960, hence within only ten years, the proportion of the workforce employed in agriculture fell from 25 per cent to

14 per cent; over this period some 2 million people left the sector. The number of agricultural workers fell particularly quickly. Maidservants and farmhands were no longer prepared to put up with their badly paid work, and they went into the factories instead. In 1949, there were still 1.9 million agricultural enterprises; twenty-five years later, there were only 900,000. The remaining farms were larger and more intensely rationalised. Improved communications links also tied the rural areas more closely to the towns, and a growing number of country-dwellers commuted back and forth. Village society changed quickly and permanently within less than twenty years. The only reason why it is not entirely accurate to describe this process as 'revolutionary' is that the word is usually associated with explosive social disturbances, and here exactly the opposite was the case.[64]

There were structural changes in the secondary sector of the economy as well. The number of mineworkers started to decline in the mid-1950s. On the other hand, the proportion of people employed in the modern growth areas of chemicals, petroleum products, motor manufacturing and mechanical engineering increased dramatically. The classical handicrafts of baking, painting and tailoring became less significant while the number of building workers and motor mechanics grew rapidly. The proportion of workers to office employees also changed. In 1950, there were three workers to one office employee; in 1960, there were two; and in 1980, one. The distinction between a worker and an office employee had been an integral characteristic of industrial class society for eighty years; it now lost its significance. In the service sector, there was a rapid decline in the domestic professions. The number of 'maidservants' fell particularly steeply. New sectors such as banking, insurance and public services gained in importance.

The number of women in paid employment rose between 1950 and 1960 from 4.3 to 6.8 million, but the female proportion of the total workforce hardly changed at all. It continued to be roughly a third, as it had been almost continuously since the 1920s. Even in 1980, it still stood at 32 per cent. But considerable structural shifts lay behind these figures. The proportion of women aged between fifteen and twenty in employment fell sharply because girls attended school for many more years. Among married women under thirty years of age, on the other hand, the proportion rose from 27 to 43 per cent. Another significant feature was that women increasingly became office employees, usually taking over the worst-paid positions in that sector: in 1961, 73 per cent of female office employees belonged to the two lowest wage groups, but only 22 per cent of the males. The gradual social advancement of the men was accomplished through the insertion below them of a lower social stratum of female employees.[65]

## The Texture of Daily Life

These far-reaching changes in employment inevitably brought about a tremendous process of social and cultural transformation. From the mid-1950s, the proportion of the family budget allocated to the satisfaction of 'basic needs' began to decline significantly. Now the average family household was able for the first time to acquire durable consumer goods. This development was initially reflected in a constant rise in the savings ratio, which tripled in the 1950s, having risen faster than average incomes. Building savings schemes were particularly popular and after the late 1950s the practice of saving up for 'one's own home' began to spread to the working class. The increase in the number of savings schemes with a duration of ten or twenty years also showed that the citizens of the Federal Republic were increasingly confident about the future.[66]

Furniture and other household items, particularly electrical appliances, were at first the main focus of people's aspirations. Mass production now made them affordable, and they were snapped up in large quantities. The number of electric ovens and irons in private households doubled between 1953 and 1958. Washing machines tripled in number, refrigerators quadrupled, and spin dryers registered a tenfold increase. Radios were also in demand: the outdated 'people's radio receivers' were replaced by new sets. These were often music centres finished in oak or varnished wood, with built-in record players. There were also enthusiastic buyers for built-in drinks cabinets. The usual practice was to save up for larger purchases, as 'payment by instalments' was regarded as a risky and ill-judged adventure. In 1964, no more than 11 per cent of households owed instalment payments. The rapid rise in building construction meant that there was an increased need for items of furniture, not least among refugees and victims of Allied bombing, who had lived for many years in temporary accommodation. There was a particular liking for sofas, armchairs, massive living room cabinets and bedroom suites, reflecting a yearning for stable and thoroughly traditional domesticity, which had been absent from people's lives for so long. 'Modern' items of furniture, in contrast, such as kidney-shaped tables, standard lamps and cocktail stools, which are now regarded as emblematic of the fifties, played only a marginal role at that time. The same was true of eating habits. People did not consume fancy novelties like 'toast Hawaii' or 'cheese hedgehogs' but bread, sausage, potatoes and meat. What was new was rather the rapid rise in the consumption of green vegetables and salad. Tomatoes were now especially in demand, as were chicken, milk, ground coffee and 'good', in other words additive-free, butter.

'Leisure time' now began to grow in importance, owing to the gradual reduction in working hours, particularly the introduction of free Saturdays, which began to take effect from the end of the 1950s onwards. Here too, though, traditional activities continued to be the most popular: the focus was on reading, listening to the radio and visiting the cinema, alongside sport, gardening and home improvements. People almost always spent their free time with the family circle. During and immediately after the war, the family had served as an emergency association, because in a desperate situation kinship alone could be relied on with certainty. Now, during the years of the 'economic miracle', the family became a quiet place of retreat in an extremely dynamic environment. Surveys consistently confirmed the existence of this 'need to turn inwards': in 1955, a survey of major leisure activities in a town in the Ruhr found that four-fifths of those questioned named activities in the house, flat or garden. The only important activities outside the home were sport and cinema-going.

But the main use of leisure time was to recover from the strain of work. One typical reply of a worker's wife to questions about leisure ran like this:

> My husband prefers to be at home. He can sit still for hours, in the living room or under a tree in the garden. Work wears him out too much, he has no social life, no leisure activities apart from livestock and the garden. He always goes to bed at 8 o'clock. The work is so heavy that my husband sometimes falls asleep while eating.[67]

Well into the 1960s, the radio was the main focus of the evening. In this respect, there had not been much of a change since the 1930s and 1940s. Variety shows and panel games, often still presented by the entertainers of the wartime years, enjoyed great popularity, as did dance music, and, increasingly, pop songs. Apart from this, there was reading: above all newspapers and magazines. The latter soon acquired tremendous circulation figures. *Quick* and *Stern* were particularly successful, but also the woman's magazine *Constanze.* Not the least of its attractions was the advice given on clothing, personal appearance, health and housekeeping: 'If an issue of *Constanze* contained advice on how to repair a damaged shirt collar, the method was tried out by a million readers.' But the periodical with the largest circulation in West Germany, and soon in the whole of Europe, was the magazine which contained the radio programmes, *Hörzu.* By 1962 this had a circulation of 4.2 million. The popularity of *Hörzu* mirrored the great increase in the importance of the radio, and then, after the end of the 1950s, television. The style of life imparted by this magazine was described accurately by contemporaries as 'stuffy' and 'complacent', but also as 'smart, present-oriented; honest, sincere, non-political and always humorous'.[68]

Finally, there was the cinema. For a long time, the film scene was dominated by the actors of past decades: stars like Heinz Rühmann, Hans Albers or Maria Schell. Repeat showings of previous box office hits were much in demand. Love films, dance films and detective films were all viewed with pleasure, just as they had been ten or twenty years earlier. But the products of American film studios had a much larger audience: between 1949 and 1963, almost half of the films shown in German cinemas were Hollywood productions, mainly Westerns and detective films. The Americanisation of German entertainment culture continued. This was by no means a phenomenon which first arose during the 1950s, and even the war had not entirely interrupted it.

One new development was the 'homeland film' (*Heimatfilm*). These appeared in large numbers, with titles such as *The Heath is Green, Black Forest Girl, The Forester of Silberwald*, or *The Forests Sing Forever*. Almost a fifth of the films produced in Germany during this decade involved a homeland lost and regained. This was not particularly surprising, given the presence of 10 million refugees. What was presented on the screen of course bore little resemblance to real life. These films conjured up a fictitious rural past peopled with modern characters, no different from the version presented by cheap literature for many years. They also proclaimed a timeless morality of loyalty, love, decency and modesty, which could be poured like a sweet sauce over the experiences of the past fifteen years, which had obviously been considerably harsher. The yearning for the homeland was also reflected in pop songs. Freddy Quinn's 1956 song '*Heimweh*' (Homesickness) was the first record of the post-war years to sell more than a million copies, and the text served to arouse numerous recollections: 'Burning hot desert sand, so far from the homeland. Many years of heavy toil, hard work, meagre wages. Day in, day out, no luck, no home. There where the flowers bloom, there where the valleys are green, that is where my home once was. Everything lies so far away, so far away.' It was not difficult to make the connection with the fate of the German prisoners of war not so long ago.[69]

At the end of the 1950s, however, television started its triumphant advance, and nothing had a greater or a more immediate influence on the leisure habits of the citizen than this medium. In 1957, there were a million households with television, and in 1961 4 million. By 1970, the figure was 15 million, which meant that coverage was almost comprehensive. As in all industrial countries, and soon all over the world, the television became the most important modern medium of communication, and without it the cultural ambiance of individual societies could no longer be understood. The coming of television tended to diminish the importance of all other domestic leisure activities, including visits to the cinema. The radio was increasingly listened to only in passing. The average West German citizen started to spend two, and later three, hours a day in front of the television set, usually along with the rest of the family. With its news broadcasts, the television came to define more and more strongly what was important and what could be ignored. Only the tabloid newspaper *Bild-Zeitung* was able to hold its ground alongside television as a mass medium.

Television programmes did, it is true, mainly adapt styles of presentation taken from the radio at first, but the medium rapidly developed its own visual and stylistic vocabulary. It brought distant lands as close to the viewer as national politics, it lessened people's cultural separation from the rest of the world, and it created norms of behaviour and moral attitudes. West German attitudes and perceptions were homogenised by the standardisation of fictional worlds of experience. As a result, distinctive regional and social environments became less significant. The victory of television also meant that political life was increasingly dependent on exposure to this medium. What was on display there had a much greater impact than words could convey by themselves. Thus, television also quickly became an instrument in the Cold War, since the television transmissions from the GDR could reach the West, and those from the West could reach the East. This competition was rapidly won by Western television.[70]

The motor car also became a mass commodity at this time. As late as the mid-1950s, private motor transport was not very widespread in Germany, unlike France, not to mention the USA. But, by 1960, there were already 5 million private motor cars in the Federal Republic, ten times as many as in 1950, and it was apparent early on that there would soon be many more vehicles on the road. The impact of mass motorisation was soon reflected in the shape of the country's urban and rural landscape: the most striking of these changes was the extension of the network of motorways (in 1950 this covered some 2,000 kilometres, while in 1970 it already covered 4,110). Other striking changes were the building of federal highways and country roads and the reconstruction of town centres to make them 'car-friendly'. Town and country moved closer together, the physical proximity of the workplace to the home became less important, and the idea of the 'commuter' became familiar to everyone. But the rise of the motor car had its biggest impact on individuals: the car brought such an increase in mobility that it became the embodiment of individual freedom, because it made it possible to go anywhere the individual wanted and at a time of the individual's choosing.[71]

The motor car was also closely connected with holiday travel, which began to spread on a mass scale at the end of the fifties. Until then, making a holiday trip had been a bourgeois privilege, and the introduction of minimum leave entitlement under the Nazis had not made much difference in practice. In 1950, an average of twelve days' holiday were granted. This amount then rose continuously, reaching twenty days in the mid-1960s and almost thirty days from the 1980s onwards. The West Germans became a people of holiday travellers. By 1960, a quarter of them (and already more than half the office employees) went on a holiday trip each year. Ten years later, the numbers had almost doubled. Holidays were at first taken mainly within West Germany, but from the 1960s onwards, trips were increasingly made abroad, primarily to Italy, Spain and

Austria. Most Germans had never been abroad before, with the exception of men who had been stationed in neighbouring European countries during the war. A considerable number of them returned in the 1960s as tourists to places they had come to know twenty years before as members of the occupying forces.

Unlike television or motor cars, the thirst for travel was a phenomenon specific to West Germany, and it did not emerge on such a mass scale in other countries. The wave of films and hit songs of the 1950s, in which a melancholy yearning for faraway places was described, paradoxically mirrored the contemporary longing for the homeland. It demonstrated that older traditions of German longing for Italy had become mingled with a feeling of weariness with the limited and pressurised nature of post-war German life.[72]

A leisure-oriented society in the narrow sense did not yet exist in the Federal Republic in 1960, because new opportunities only emerged slowly for large parts of the population even though their budgets improved and they enjoyed increasing amounts of free time. But the expectation that things would get better, not just for the children, but perhaps for adults too, who would also see improvements during their lifetime, imbued many people with an optimistic attitude to life which can almost be regarded as a hallmark of the epoch.

These changes in working hours, consumer habits and leisure time were very much bound up with some remarkable transformations in the function of the family and the role of women. 'Withdrawal into the narrowest possible circle', namely the family, in reaction to wartime and post-war turmoil, was already a familiar topos of 1950s discussions. In 1953, the sociologist Helmut Schelsky described the family as 'the ultimate foundation of social refuge and security' and the 'last stable structure of the whole society'. This was, he said, accompanied by a 'restoration of the old and familiar state of affairs and mode of life' according to which men went to work and women took care of the household and brought up the children. There are in fact many indications that such a restoration of traditional family structures was very much desired by the parties concerned, because it seemed to fulfil the requirements of normality whose absence had been lamented for decades. On the other hand, the male partner's salary alone was not sufficient to allow couples to take advantage of the opportunities for consumption which existed after the mid-1950s, which were promoted with the help of increasingly ubiquitous advertising. In 1957, some 50 per cent of working women already stated that they 'went to work' to make it possible to buy things for the household, to become homeowners or to acquire a higher standard of living. Churches, politicians and conservative intellectuals castigated the 'materialistic' attitude of working mothers, who neglected their children and endangered their families. Their efforts were of course in vain: the promise of prosperity clearly contradicted the guiding principles of approved family policy. Only a quarter of married women were in employment in 1950, but this proportion rose continuously during the period. It reached 43 per cent in 1961. At roughly the same time (1960), half the population still supported a ban on female employment.[73]

The Adenauer government's policy towards women was marked by similar contradictions. A number of legislative measures focused on promoting large families and raising the status of housewife, but the government was unable to prevent the standard of living of a family with three children from being over a third lower than the level reached by a childless married couple. The principle of male and female equality asserted in the Basic Law, which was one of the most remarkable innovations of the constitution-makers, came up against a social reality which was far removed from such a norm. The Federal Constitutional Court rejected the most discriminatory of the existing regulations, such as the right of the husband to decide on whether his wife should go to work, and his control of the finances, on the ground that they were unconstitutional. Other male privileges were removed by the Equal Rights Act of 1957, but the notion of a 'natural division of functions' between husband and wife continued to exist, and the entry of a married woman into paid employment continued to be conditional on its being compatible with her marital and familial obligations.[74]

But very fundamental shifts were now becoming apparent, and these began to put in question the guiding principles of married life which had solidified since the industrial revolution, namely the exclusive employment of the husband, the nuclear family and the bringing up of children mainly by the wife. The working environment had begun to change; there was a decline in the proportion of heavy manual labour and an increase in office work; and, at the same time, some of the housewife's traditional activities were made much easier by the introduction of machines. As these developments proceeded, gender roles and conceptions of the family were also transformed.

The 1950s leap into prosperity occurred in other Western European countries in a similar manner, though starting points and rates of change varied. In 1950 (according to a calculation which divided the countries of Europe into four groups according to GDP per capita) there were only three rich states: Denmark, Sweden and Switzerland. West Germany followed in the third group, at roughly the same level as Finland, France and Austria. Fifteen years later, West Germany, like most large Western European countries, belonged to the second group. It did not enter the top group until 1985. The growth of opportunities for consumption followed a similar structural pattern, though the elements of a consumer society developed in Great Britain considerably earlier than in France or West Germany. But, all over Western Europe, the leap into prosperity was perceived as specific to the country in question, and also as being primarily its own achievement.[75]

The impact of the Western European economic boom on particular social strata varied very greatly. Despite considerable gains in real income, differences in income and wealth changed very little. If the West German population is divided into five equally large groups (from the wealthiest to the poorest), in 1950 the members of the wealthiest group received 45 per cent of the total income, while the poorest received 5 per cent. By 1985 there had been little change in this picture of unequal distribution: the wealthiest now received 42 per cent, the poorest 7 per cent. This was not a specifically German phenomenon. West Germany occupied an intermediate position in Western Europe in this regard. Differences in wealth, as opposed to income, were more serious: at the beginning of the 1960s the wealthiest 2 per cent of the West German population possessed over 70 per cent of the country's productive capacity, in the form of businesses, factories etc., and 20 per cent of the total wealth. Only in income did these differences start to diminish slightly after the 1970s; the difference between the working and middle classes became somewhat smaller, though the gap separating them from incomes at the top did not diminish.

Despite these trends, the thesis put forward by Schelsky at the beginning of the economic boom on the 'social levelling of the middle class' was broadly accepted. According to Schelsky's thesis, the differences between classes in West Germany were starting to level out, with the result that the same or similar modes of life could increasingly be observed over the greater part of the society. But this could not be established with statistically demonstrable data. Rather the reverse. The data revealed the continuing existence of social differences; indeed, they showed a continued increase. The comparison with the Weimar years, however, indicates that this issue had an extra dimension. Under Weimar, anger over unequal conditions of life was fed by the plainly visible divergence between the poverty and hopelessness of the lower half of the population and the ostentatious display of opulence by the upper classes. In 1960, the difference between the top of society and the bottom continued to be striking, and on some criteria it was even greater than in the 1920s, but the lowest income levels were considerably higher in 1960. The lower 50 per cent no longer lived below or on the poverty line. They had enjoyed considerable improvements and they had good reason to hope for further increases in their standard of living. This made the perceived social inequality more bearable.[76]

## The Occident and the Moral Law

The overwhelming majority of West German intellectuals adopted a sceptical or negative attitude towards the rapid and immense social changes of the

1950s. In this context 'Americanisation' was one of the more frequently used slogans. Since the turn of the century, the topos of Americanism's cultural emptiness, the way it reduced everything to technology and consumption, linked up with earlier patterns of perception and hostility, had played a constitutive role in forming the attitudes of the educated German bourgeoisie, but it had also been widely accepted in other countries such as France and Switzerland. To take this view was also a way of compensating for the actual powerlessness of the Europeans in the face of American military, political and economic superiority: the contrast between the weight of European tradition and the New World's lack of a historical background was stressed, and an antithesis between American cultural superficiality and occidental profundity was insinuated. Even before the end of the war, considerable sections of the population had found mass culture highly appealing, and this trend strengthened still further in the 1950s and 1960s, causing many conservatives to feel increasing anxiety about an alleged loss of cultural identity. The critique of mass society, consumerism and the media was a coded way of criticising cultural modernity, and it was voiced ever more loudly as the 1950s continued.[77]

The category of 'the Occident' was used as the antonym of cultural modernity. In the first few years after the war, the 'return to the occidental cultural community' was frequently invoked as the only way of redeeming the nation from the loss of spiritual values during the Nazi epoch. This tendency was combined with a return to religion, a veritable re-Christianisation movement, which reflected the enormous contemporary need for long-term guidance and eternal values.[78] The concept of the 'Occident' also stood for one of the fundamental ideologies of the Cold War. The historian Hermann Aubin had until 1945 been a passionate partisan of Nazism. After the end of the war, he began to emphasise in his writings the role Germany had played for a thousand years as the 'sentinel of the Occident' against the Slav onslaught from the East. The defeat of Germany in the Second World War meant that this task was no longer being fulfilled, and the danger that Europe would be overpowered by the East was greater than ever. A renewed focus on the idea of the Occident was therefore indispensable, because this concept

> also involves the commemoration of those components of an age-old community which have been alienated from it today by Sovietisation behind the iron curtain. It also makes us aware how intimately they are linked, by virtue of their historical development, with the forces now joining together to make a new Europe, which includes Germany.[79]

In this vision of the past, three ideas were combined together: Germany's war against the Soviet Union was part of the eternal struggle of the Occident against the eternal Russian; the Germans were the people at the core of the occidental idea; and Europe was a bloc of fighters against Bolshevism. The picture of history presented here, which was widely shared, allowed the mass crimes of National Socialism to be hidden from view, and the war and the rule of the German occupiers in the West to be interpreted as forming part of a quarrel which was to some extent internal, and secondary to the struggle against the Russians.

Even so, the continuing refusal to recognise what had happened during the Nazi dictatorship had weak foundations and could not be sustained intellectually for a lengthy period. The post-1918 situation was not repeated. The attempt by radical nationalists to use the history of ideas as a means of self-maintenance could not be combined this time with a narrative of treason, fraud and injustice which would have lent it emotional power and made radical nationalist views plausible to later generations.

The return to a rejection of cultural modernity combined this time with an acceptance of technological progress was a more profound approach than interpretations of history by such National Socialist apologists. In the leading conservative thinkers of the post-war era, the concept of technology did not stand for machines, motor cars or aeroplanes, but for the rationalisation of the world of life, for the 'apparatus' in course of construction, for the 'secondary system'. The subjection of the outstanding individual to the mass, and to the dictates of bureaucracy, rationalisation and civilisation, was deplored repeatedly: in this interpretation, individuals were being domesticated by urbanisation, the levelling of social distinctions, and the constant increase in population. They were 'like caged tigers and eagles', wrote Hans Freyer in 1955. They must rise in revolt against 'business', against civilisation, against 'these houses with standardised measurements and these journeys with standardised itineraries, canned food, canned music and the female uniform of the nylon stocking'. And he continued:

> One can only reply to alienation of such magnitude by looking back, by bringing up from the deepest strata of our heritage in a broad stream the forces which will replenish the diminished humanity of the present. For these forces, every element of rootedness which can be preserved between the concrete blocks of the secondary system, even if only as a foreign body, every law and right which has been handed down from the past, is a beneficial counterweight to progress and an island of humanity, which must be protected by building a protective dyke.[80]

The 'containment' of modern civilisation and the building of dykes against it were frequently used metaphors. They reflected the alarm felt by the conservative spokesmen of the 1950s over the threats they thought the Germans faced. After the victory of the West, which was practically defined by this 'apparatus' of the bourgeois individual's alienation, the conservatives considered that cultural modernity was threatening to win a definitive victory. This could only be resisted by drawing on tradition and rootedness, form and order.

For Freyer, as for Gehlen and Schelsky, though in different ways, the positive point of reference was no longer the Third Reich (all three were former partisans of National Socialism). The Nazi state was now interpreted rather as a failed attempt to take a stand against modernity by making use of its instrument, mass society. The new point of reference was rather the epoch *before* the rise of the 'secondary system'. This was an imaginary past, from which strength and material could be drawn for the restoration of the 'outstanding individual'. There is an obvious connection here with Friedrich Meinecke's appeal to return to the 'comfortable bourgeois order' to counteract the incursion of modernity which was converting German culture into Western civilisation. Even some of the recommended antidotes to this poison were similar. With Meinecke it was Goethe, while Freyer recommended 'the Humanities as education and a source of decency, as the replenishment of conviviality, as a domestic bookcase and a cult of the great masters', and as a refuge for a spirituality which would immunise the individual against the insipid boorishness of industrial society.[81]

It was easy to draw a political conclusion from this: a dam must be constructed against 'business' and the brutalising effects of civilisation by a consistent orientation towards the values and structures of the age that preceded Weimar. And precisely because technological industrialisation, which was seen as irresistible, was advancing at such a tremendous pace, it was all the more necessary to fight against the brutally and massively 'civilisational' phenomena associated with it.

These invocations of traditional middle-class values went hand in hand with authoritarian conceptions of the state and visions of taming and organising the 'masses'. They bore an unmistakable affinity to the 'concrete ideas of order' put forward in earlier decades, they retained their virulence into the 1960s and the early 1970s, and they formed the starting point of conservative social criticism. They interpreted National Socialism and Communism as variants of mass society and thereby as a confirmation of the fears of the German cultural pessimists who wrote in the period before and after 1914. Politically, they provided the arguments which were relied on by the advocates of an authoritarian model of state and society, who opposed attempts to extend democratic institutions in the direction of broader social participation. Culturally, this mode of thought was directed principally against the spread of liberal conceptions in the family sphere, and in education and private life.

Attempts at containment were particularly evident in these areas. The main focus was placed on concepts such as 'the moral law' and 'morality'. These concepts were intended to denote 'a timelessly valid ethics, a stable and constant entity unaffected by any kind of social change', which would be 'an anchor of mental stability', as the historian Sibylle Steinbacher has written. In this context, it was suggested that society could be healed by the 'internalisation of a decent sexual morality'. 'What is really necessary, in view of the fate we have suffered in the last few decades', said the Freiburg Professor of Criminal Law Hans-Heinrich Jeschek in a lecture given in 1956, 'is a strong criminal code which understands and recognises moral values, presupposes the existence and the binding force of moral obligations and shows the people, as in a mirror, the image of its better self.' The fear revealed by these remarks is that the dangers of modernity have already penetrated so deeply into the daily lives of the German population that it is necessary to counter them with forcible methods.[82]

Proclamations of this nature were issued against all phenomena regarded as deviant and unnatural or as expressions of modern mass society. Juvenile delinquency, 'teenage rowdyism', working mothers, illegitimate children, homosexuality and sexual libertinism were included, but also comic books, jazz, illustrated magazines and mass consumption. In short: 'the irredeemable imprisonment of human beings in the apparatus of civilisation.'[83]

These former National Socialist thinkers, who had now turned themselves into conservatives, also adopted a critical and dismissive attitude towards the newly founded West German state. Carl Schmitt derided the Basic Law as the 'tyranny of values' and Ernst Forsthoff considered that a state like the Federal Republic was no longer capable of 'expressing itself spiritually' because it did not comprehend itself 'as a symbolic spiritual entity', nor was it capable of doing this. As an 'unserious state' it hardly took part in world events any more, and it would 'have to make do with being no longer a subject of events, but merely their object'. A state whose sole purpose was to produce economic progress and social and political security had no real objective. 'Our country is economically sound. That has been proved in recent years with a clarity which is seductive but by now somewhat disturbing', wrote the influential literary critic Friedrich Sieburg. 'But we cannot take pride in this, indeed even gratitude is out of place' because it is clear 'that the present provisional arrangement lacks a soul, and inevitably so. We attempt to talk ourselves into thinking that the Federal Republic has a national reality; but this is mere self-presentation.'[84] The conservative Right could not conceive the state as anything other than an instrument of power. They were bound to despise a state which had the sole purpose of securing the well-being of its citizens.

But there were also critics of the West German state to be found on the Left. The Left shared the Right's critique of the state's primary focus on economic growth and social security. But its attitude of scepticism and rejection towards Bonn was founded in addition on the lack of any open confrontation with the Nazi past and the absence of any revolutionary act of foundation. This complaint rested essentially on a false estimation of the German population's political role and its stance during the Nazi period. According to the Left, the German people—or the working class—had only been waiting for the downfall of National Socialism and had been eager to sweep away the old elites so as to establish a democratic and socially just society with its own strength and by exercising its own rights. It had then been prevented from doing this by the Western powers and the West German politicians. In view of the demonstrable measure of popular support for Hitler and the Nazi state, this picture of history was an example of wishful thinking. But it was a persistently held view.

On the other hand, the widespread feeling in 1945 that after the most frightful of all catastrophes, a new and genuine democracy would, indeed must, arise, cleansed of the dross of the past, was just as understandable as the disappointment over the contrast between this vision and the grey and unspectacular aspect of the actual Federal Republic. But it was also apparent that in the light of the political inexperience of the Germans, a predominantly institutional concept of democracy and an authoritarian understanding of the role of the state, which were characteristic of Adenauer's approach, could also be regarded as part of a learning process. Acclimatisation to a functioning party democracy, and the gradual inculcation of the rules of the game and the mode of functioning of parliamentarism and pluralism turned out to be prerequisites for the gradual modification, and finally the extension and critical reconstruction, of the model of democracy established in 1949.

At the end of the 1950s, however, this lay far in the future. West Germans had made tremendous political, economic and social progress after the American-orchestrated foundation of their state. Forsthoff was right to assert that the stability of the West German state had been 'borrowed from industrial society'. After all, what would have happened to it without the economic boom? It was not yet clear at the end of the 1950s whether the state and the society could successfully be stabilised on a new foundation irrespective of economic prosperity, and whether it would be possible to establish a new social consensus, confirmed by experience and tradition.

The country thus found its cultural focus in the fictitious model of a bourgeois past, which allowed it to compensate at least temporarily for the dynamic changes which had transformed politics, society and the economy. This was the reason for the peculiar rigidity which was later seen as the essential characteristic of those years. West German society simultaneously drew a protective veil over its own participation in the mass crimes of the Third Reich, thereby giving the impression that all was normal and there was no historical baggage in the background. But it was not at all certain that this strategy of suppression and concealment could be kept up in the long run. Finally, the question of the Germans' future as a nation remained open. Here too, it could be predicted that they would not get very far along the route they had chosen. A permanent Cold War was hardly acceptable, considering the risks attached to it, and it was obviously no longer politically possible to secure majority recognition of the existence of two states.

On the one hand, therefore, the situation at the beginning of the 1960s was not firmly grounded enough, whether in foreign policy terms or socially and culturally, to provide long-term stability. On the other hand, the new state had been institutionally consolidated and it had enabled West Germans to gain a degree of security and economic well-being they had not known since 1914. In the light of the political alternatives they had lived through in the past, or indeed the one they could now contemplate in the form of the GDR, the most obvious option was to keep hold of what they had. Adenauer's campaign slogan for the 1957 elections, 'No Experiments', constituted a lapidary encapsulation of this dilemma. With hard work and much good fortune, the West Germans, against all expectations, had achieved more than they could have imagined. The conclusion that it was better not to disturb anything therefore looked highly plausible.

# 13
# The Socialist Experiment

## The Communist Project

The building of socialism in the GDR was more than just an element in the Soviet Union's Cold War policy of expansion and stabilisation. From the point of view of the German communists, it fulfilled the hopes of humanity and the laws of history, and the development of the GDR can only be understood against this background. Their Marxist view of history rested on three assumptions.[1]

The first assumption was that the history of humanity moved forward through class struggles. Since industrialisation, these had taken the form of a struggle between the bourgeoisie and the proletariat. That was the starting point. In this conflict between the working class, which constituted the overwhelming majority of the people, and the owners of the means of production and their political and intellectual accomplices, the workers' movement had developed socialism as a radical alternative to bourgeois society. In Germany, as in other industrially advanced countries, the crisis of bourgeois society around the turn of the century had led to the growth of a conviction on the Left that socialism might soon be achieved, and that this would be done by taking the road of revolution. During the First World War, the struggle between the revolutionary working class and the ruling class had come to a head, and the revolutionary party, the communists, had emerged out of German Social Democracy, which had agreed to the imperialist war by voting for war credits. Meanwhile, the Tsarist regime had been overthrown in Russia by the Bolsheviks and the first workers' state set up. With that, according to the Marxist view of history, the class struggle had taken on a worldwide dimension, because now revolutionary communist and socialist parties arose in all industrially advanced states to challenge the capitalist social order.

The first attempt to establish socialism, which was made in 1918–19, had ended in failure in Germany, as elsewhere. After 1929, however, the coming of the world economic crisis had again brought the situation to a head. In order to suppress the growing revolutionary working-class movement, the economic and political elites in Italy, Germany and other countries had abandoned their previous parliamentary form of government and reached for the instrument of open dictatorship, which they established with the help of mass Fascist parties.

The dictatorship in Italy had taken the form of Mussolini's Fascism, while the form taken in Germany was 'Hitler-Fascism', under the rule of which the workers' movement had been crushed and the Second World War begun. But, at this point, it had turned out that Soviet power was already strong enough to defend itself against Nazi Germany's attack and win the contest.

The second assumption was that, after its victory over Nazi Germany, the Soviet Union could build socialism in the countries freed by the Red Army, with the support of communist movements and against the resistance of the Western powers. In Germany, that was at first only possible in the Soviet occupation zone, owing to the foundation by the USA of the state of West Germany. But, since the victory of socialism was not a matter of historical accident but the expression of a historically inevitable process, it would not take long, the communists were firmly convinced, before socialism was victorious in the whole of Germany and Europe. For the communists, therefore, whether they obtained an electoral majority was not the decisive issue. They called their rule 'democratic' even when they were opposed by an overwhelming majority of the people. Anyone who did not follow them had not yet grasped that the real interests of the majority of humanity could only be served under socialism. The horror of National Socialist domination had finally proved, they were convinced, that the systems of capitalism and imperialism had terrible consequences and must be removed. And, after all, were not the communists the only people who had recognised the true character of Nazi Fascism and paid the heaviest price for this in the blood of their resistance fighters? Anyone who opposed fascism must therefore necessarily be in favour of socialism. There could be no good arguments against socialism because it stood not only for the fight against fascism but for the liberation of humanity from dependence and poverty, and for justice, equality and peace. Anyone who opposed the idea of socialism was working directly against all good and noble principles and should be prevented from doing this.

The third assumption, finally, was that in order to establish socialism in Germany, three things were necessary: firstly, the rule of the working class, embodied in the party of the working class, must be placed on a firm footing. It was, accordingly, a primary objective to deprive the class enemy of power. At the time of the GDR's foundation, the German communists considered that many of their goals had already been achieved with the aid of the Soviet Military Administration. De-Nazification had removed not only the functionaries of National Socialism but also the people regarded by the communists as their supporters and beneficiaries. It had also driven the bourgeoisie to the wall. The communists occupied the decisive positions in all the local administrations of the Soviet zone; in addition, their merger with the SPD gave them a solid mass basis. Secondly, the construction of socialism required the complete abolition of private property in the means of production, particularly in industry and agriculture. By 1949, the most important prerequisites for this were already in existence: the banks and a large part of private industry had been nationalised, and the big landowners had been expropriated; further steps would soon need to follow. Thirdly, however, people's consciousness would have to be altered: the way to do this would be through enlightenment, cultural education and combating harmful external influences. The fight at these three policy levels had not yet been won, however. On the contrary, the class struggle would need to continue until the enemy had been defeated completely and socialism achieved.

The perspective we have just outlined was adopted by convinced communists in 1949, and it must be kept in mind if we are to comprehend not only the numerous inconsistencies and disappointments, but also the enthusiasm, the faith in the future and the fanaticism of the adherents and cadres of the communist movement in the GDR. The certainty they took from history that in building socialism they were striving to achieve the historically necessary and inevitable goal of a society of social equality and justice was combined with an awareness that they had been the first to see through National Socialism and the only group to have fought consistently against it. For them, this combination of socialism and anti-fascism provided a particular source of legitimacy for the GDR and it was also the reason why the cadres of the SED were ready despite continuous setbacks and repeated failures to stick to their conviction that they were working towards the true goal and that they knew how to get there. Johannes R. Becher summarised these convictions in that combination of resolute determination and emotional pathos which was so typical of communist poetry:

You all know what it meant
To take the hardest route
All around the highways
The dead lay close to hand
But we were well aware
We *had to* rise again
And the focus of our yearning
Was a free and German land
But see the greatness we've achieved!
The people's life is made anew
And though the road is hard, so hard
A shout of joy lets rip

Do not forget you have the power
The power that you've received
Make sure it never never more
Escapes your firm and solid grip.[2]

Nevertheless, Marxist certainties were repeatedly intermingled with short-term calculations and tactical considerations. The communists unswervingly held onto their objectives of socialising private property in the means of production, disempowering the class enemy and re-educating the people. But they were prepared to live with a slower pace of transformation if that was what the situation demanded. The history of the GDR is accordingly marked by alternate phases of ideological and political severity and retreat in the face of opposition.

In this context, the policy of the CPSU had special significance, because the German communists followed the Soviet lead with a strictness which practically amounted to self-abnegation. If one bears in mind the excrescences of the Stalinist cult of personality and the economic and political absurdities which were associated with the SED's state of vassalage, the heavy imprint of party loyalty on the German communists is clearly apparent. The SED leadership regarded the systematic economic exploitation of first the SBZ and then the GDR by the Soviet Union as historically legitimate, in view of the damage inflicted by the Germans themselves on that country, but it found it very difficult to explain this to its own citizens. Moreover, it was the Soviet Union itself which stood in the way of a stable GDR in the first few years of the latter's existence, because it was more important to Soviet foreign policy to prevent the establishment of an American-dominated West Germany than to consolidate a socialist state in the eastern part of the country. This induced a certain degree of schizophrenia in the SED leadership. On the one hand, it continued to push forward the socialist reconstruction of East German society, with the help of the Soviet Control Commission (SCC), the body which replaced the SMAD after the GDR was established. But, on the other hand, until 1955, and perhaps even until 1961, the GDR could only continue to exist as a state on the proviso that the Soviet Union no longer regarded the creation of a neutral Germany as a promising or feasible option. Up to that point, the programme, and the propaganda, of the SED was perforce directed towards the reunification of Germany, constantly changing variants of which were put forward in the party's national campaigns. This contradiction was, however, by no means the privilege of the East German state alone. The Federal Republic also accompanied its policy of unconditional orientation towards the West, which ruled out any reunification other than under Western auspices, with passionate rhetoric about national unity.[3]

## Sovietisation

In the construction of socialism in the GDR, economic transformation had priority, and the intention was to follow the Soviet model to the letter in implementing this. That meant firstly a centrally planned economy, directed by the state; secondly the reduction, and later the abolition, of private economic activity, particularly in industry, but in the future in handicraft production and trade as well; thirdly a concentration on building up heavy industry while placing limits on the consumer goods industries; and fourthly the collectivisation of agriculture and the construction of big agro-industrial complexes. The SED pushed ahead with these aims at great speed, and after roughly ten years almost all of them had been achieved. The process was marked by considerable oscillations, however. In most cases these accelerations and reductions in the tempo of transformation were politically motivated, and they depended on two things; the strength of East German society's resistance to the process, and the Soviet government's attitude to the individual measures involved.

When the GDR was established, the economic conditions were extremely unpropitious for such a transformation. Not only had the Soviet-occupied part of Germany been separated from its predominantly agricultural eastern hinterland, it also possessed neither big industrial centres nor the raw materials necessary for industry such as coal and iron ore. In addition, traditional trading relations with the West had been interrupted, and, unlike the Federal Republic, the GDR was not linked to a highly capitalised, wealthy country like the USA, but to the Soviet Union, a country which had been completely exhausted by the war and therefore had an almost insatiable need for reparations. At 1,349 Marks a head, the burden of reparations on the GDR was almost sixty times higher than in the West. As noted earlier, large parts of the industries located at the end of the war in the SBZ had been dismantled, including three-quarters of its motor vehicle, tool-making and locomotive factories and ironworks. Unlike the Federal Republic, which could export to Western Europe, the GDR had no market capable of absorbing the goods it produced, because the countries of the 'Eastern bloc' which were associated together in the Council for Mutual Economic Aid (CMEA), an organisation the GDR joined in September 1950, had little purchasing power and they all suffered from even greater economic problems than it did itself.[4]

Even so, there were some positive aspects to the situation. During the war, a number of new armaments factories had been built in Central Germany because it was beyond the range of Allied air attacks. There were also highly developed industrial enterprises in such branches as chemicals, precision engineering and optics. Given this starting point, the decision of the SED leadership to follow the Soviet model and concentrate all its efforts on building up large-scale heavy industry had particularly serious consequences. Scarce resources were directed into the construction of blast furnaces and steelworks, while the necessary investment in the modern and competitive chemical and optical branches failed to occur. Moreover, the basic materials for the centres of heavy industry which were planned had to be imported from other socialist countries, so that it proved extremely costly to build them.

One of the central aspects of the communist critique of capitalism, apart from its social inequality and injustice, was the unplanned character of the market economy. The communists claimed that the anarchic irrationality of modern capitalism was the reason for the regular crises of overproduction which pushed millions of human beings into adversity, as had been demonstrated dramatically by the world economic crisis of the 1930s. This conviction was shared by far more people than just the supporters of communism. The conclusion that the economy, and all other spheres of social life, ought henceforth to be subject to uniform planning and calculation was also reflected in the programmes of the Social Democratic and Christian Democratic parties of the West. After all, it was said, had not socialist planning of the economy converted backward Russia within a generation into one of the most powerful countries in the world, the Soviet Union, whose arms economy had proved superior even to that of Nazi Germany?

For these reasons, the introduction of a planned economy into the GDR, which had in fact already started in the immediate post-war years, did not meet with much resistance, even from the bloc parties, whose political influence was limited, and in any case tended increasingly to melt away over time. The first Five Year Plan provided for a doubling of industrial output by 1955.

Despite this optimism, several clear problems and inconsistencies in the planned economy showed up very early on. Firstly, there were no historical models for the socialist reconstruction of an advanced industrial country. This was the first time the operation had been performed on a living patient, as it were; its outcome was therefore very uncertain, especially as the experiment was conducted by politicians who had little knowledge or experience of economic matters. Secondly, the SED's claim to lead and dominate in all areas, particularly the economy, led quickly to the growth of an immense bureaucracy of planners, which regulated even subordinate matters of detail centrally and allowed individual enterprises no opportunity for flexible decision-making. Thirdly, the target figures for plan fulfilment led to a concentration on purely quantitative growth, especially as the interests of buyers and consumers were seen in this system as subordinate matters, hence there was little incentive to improve the quality of products and make technical innovations. And fourthly, the primacy of heavy industry meant that the consumer goods industry was neglected, and as a result the population received entirely inadequate provisions for many years to come.

In the GDR too, the hunger of the post-war years was eventually overcome, but shortages, ration cards and the black market continued to dominate everyday life. The basic foodstuffs available as rations in the shops of the state-run Trading Organisation (HO) were very cheap, but in compensation for this the prices of all other goods were very high. Supply problems remained a characteristic of the GDR economy and a source of dissatisfaction among the population right up to the end. Admittedly, this was also a question of the yardstick used for comparison. In relation to the other states of the Eastern bloc, and particularly the Soviet Union, living conditions in the GDR were rather favourable, even in the early 1950s. But the eastern half of divided Germany was always measured against the western half, which prospered immensely after 1953; and the GDR leadership itself used this comparison. This was a contest the GDR economy was never able to win.

The objectives set for economic growth soon proved to be too optimistic. It was possible to explain this by referring to a lack of adequate experience with the mechanisms of centralised economic planning. The excessively low productivity levels, on the other hand, could be ascribed in part to antiquated factories, inadequate mechanisation and a lack of basic materials, but inefficiency at work played an equally large part. The original idea was that the workers would be prepared to improve their performance out of a conviction that they were working for socialism as well as their own interests. But the first piecework systems were introduced as early as 1947, and big propaganda campaigns to increase the productivity of labour accompanied the introduction of payment by results. In imitation of the Soviet 'Stakhanov movement', the mineworker Adolf Hennecke was promoted as an example of the new, socialist attitude to work, after he had exceeded the existing labour norm by 387 per cent, on 13 October 1948. That date was henceforth celebrated as the 'Day of the Activists', a day on which workers who had greatly overfulfilled the plan received decorations. In practice, however, the labour norms imposed by the central planners were a frequent bone of contention, especially as the newly founded Federation of Free German Trade Unions (FDGB) functioned not as a representative of workers' interests but as a transmission belt for the party within the workforce, and the workers therefore hardly had any opportunity to influence the setting of the norms.[5]

By 1952, some 75 per cent of firms, covering roughly 85 per cent of total industrial production, had been converted into '*Volkseigentum*' (People's Property).The process of transformation from private into public ownership had thus already advanced a long way at a very early date. This increased the pressure on the surviving private industrial enterprises to convert themselves into cooperatives or to hand themselves over entirely to the state. But private handicraft businesses and trading companies were still spared. The same was true of agriculture: the drive to join individual peasant farms together to make agricultural producer cooperatives (LPGs) came up against resistance from the farmers, not a few of whom had first received their holdings from the land confiscated from the 'Junkers' and the well-off farmers after 1945. The collectivisation of agriculture was therefore temporarily postponed.[6]

In the first three years after the foundation of the state, the regime largely followed the Soviet model in securing and extending the power of the SED, as it had done in regard to economic policy. By establishing the *Kasernierte Volkspolizei* (People's Police in Barracks) the party created its own instrument of power. It also set up the *Staatssicherheitsdienst* (State Security Service, or Stasi) which employed a network of agents, who at first concentrated mainly on 'enemies' in the West, particularly the Federal Republic. Only at a later stage was the Stasi directed primarily against the citizens of the GDR itself. Meanwhile, domestic political opponents were pursued with the greatest severity, though the number of political prisoners was kept secret. There were probably tens of thousands of them in 1952.[7]

The SED leadership also began to take a stronger line within their own party. In the first big party purge, which took place in 1948, the hunt was on for supporters of 'Social Democratism', 'Schumacherites', who were expelled and in part also subjected to legal harassment. In addition, the structure of the party was altered once again. The Party Executive was subordinated to the Politburo, a power centre consisting of a small number of people. A plurality of voices, and differences of opinion, not to mention 'factions', were no longer tolerated. Ulbricht, as the General Secretary of the SED, was the uncontested leader: here too the East German party followed the example of the Stalinist Soviet Union. The actual government, on the other hand, played a subordinate role in this system. Ministries and administrative authorities were merely executive organs of the party leadership's decisions. The elections of October 1950, with their 'single list' of candidates and 'open voting', resulted in a 99.7 per cent vote in favour of the single list presented by the National Front. Voter turnout was 98 per cent. The 'bloc parties' served merely as pseudo-pluralist decoration, and they had no influence; the parliament was simply used as a rubber stamp and the judicial system was completely under the control of the SED. Within a year after the foundation of the GDR the new state had been stripped of all its democratic embellishment. It was now a dictatorship on the Soviet model.

In the summer of 1950, the SED began a fresh purge of its own ranks, which, as in other Eastern bloc states, was directed against oppositional tendencies, real or imagined. After the quarrel between the Soviet Union and Yugoslavia, the main victims in all the countries within the Soviet sphere of influence were 'Titoists', but there were also attacks, and increasingly so, on communist functionaries of Jewish origin, the so-called 'Cosmopolitans', who in the Stalinist picture of the world were fighting against Soviet rule as agents of worldwide Zionism. Show trials were prepared, in the Soviet Union as well as in Czechoslovakia, Bulgaria, Hungary and Poland, but also in the GDR. There the Jewish communist Paul Merker, who had returned from exile in the West, was the main target. By calling for the return of items stolen from Jewish property owners by the Nazis, he had put himself in opposition to the primary communist objective of the expropriation of private property in the means of production. This campaign contained clearly perceptible anti-Jewish undertones, like the campaigns in the Soviet Union and Czechoslovakia. The latter country held a trial of 'conspirators' led allegedly by the Jewish communist Rudolf Slánský. By autumn 1951, 175,000 members had been expelled from the SED.[8]

These incessant suspicions and the repeated exposure of foreign agents were a clear sign of how paranoid and out of touch with reality the regime was. But the atmosphere was not completely different either in the contemporary United States, shaken as it was by Senator McCarthy's allegations of communist subversion, or in the Federal Republic, where communists were being pursued in a positively hysterical fashion at this time. It is clear, however, that spy hysteria within the communist system was not just a reflection of the worsening of the Cold War during the Korea crisis. It also had structural causes. If something failed to function, if the planned targets were not achieved, if resistance was detected, these problems could not be attributed to the party line of constructing socialism, which was regarded as correct a priori, but must rather be a result either of the errors of individuals or hostile activity by forces from outside, or even working within the ranks of the party. In that sense, the unending search for 'enemies' and spies served time and again as confirmation, in the Soviet Union and now in the GDR as well, that the line was correct in principle, and that all that was needed to remove any defects that still existed was to track down and eliminate 'enemies'. 'Errors' and 'enemies' were therefore the most important ways of explaining setbacks and failures while preserving party legitimacy.

The third decisive step towards the creation of socialism was the transformation of consciousness through enlightenment, cultural education and the fight against harmful influences from outside. In this context, the principal focus was at first educational policy. The aim was to create a new, socialist intelligentsia through education. This would be recruited predominantly from the working class and the peasantry. 'Workers' and Peasants' Faculties' were set up, where students obtained university entrance qualifications through crash courses. It was expected that after their studies they would take over the leading positions which had become vacant through de-Nazification and the removal or flight of the old elites. By 1954, 53 percent of all students were the children of workers or peasants. There was a policy of discrimination against children from middle-class families. Subject studies and political training were given equal weight in educational courses, because the political re-education and ideological formation of the younger generation stood at the forefront of all these educational endeavours. New curricula were introduced, aligning course content towards scientific socialism, teachers were obliged to propagate the 'leading role of the party' in their classes, and the study of the fundamentals of Marxism-Leninism was made obligatory at the universities.[9]

Cultural policy followed the same objectives. The main focus here was on anti-fascism, an obligatory guiding principle which also permeated the way the democratic cultural inheritance was treated. Hostility was primarily focused on reactionary and fascist culture, but the culture of 'American decadence' increasingly came under attack as well. This was said to include jazz, chewing gum and pop music, but also abstract painting and 'formalism', a word which could be stretched to cover stylistic experiments of all kinds. A progressive cultural policy, as defined by the SED in summer 1950, involved a struggle 'against anti-popular theories of cosmopolitanism, against bourgeois objectivism, and against American cultural barbarism'. These various forms of inherited cultural tradition were set against socialist realism, which entirely renounced formal experiments and abstractions and had the task of depicting the reality of socialist construction.[10] It would be wrong to overlook the parallel between the SED's rejection of abstract art and American everyday and youth culture and the very similar criticism of the Americanisation of German national culture and its increasing trivialisation which was voiced by conservative thinkers in West Germany during the same period. Both groups directed their wrath against tendencies towards pluralism and individualism, cultural experiment and commercialisation, and ultimately against cultural modernity, which was countered in both cases by referring to values such as obligation, subordination and a correct upbringing.

What the SED could do to build socialism continued to be limited by Soviet foreign policy priorities. In March 1952, the Soviet Union initiated a further dramatic attempt both to prevent the incorporation of West Germany into the Western economic and military structure and to create a united, neutral Germany by presenting what is known as the 'Stalin Note'. While the SED surpassed itself in its use of nationalist phraseology at this time, it was only too clear that the implementation of the Soviet proposals would mean sacrificing the GDR. But when the Soviet reunification offer was rejected by the West, the SED's nightmare quickly came to an end, and the leadership seized the opportunity to go on the offensive. In July 1952, the party announced the beginning of the 'planned construction of socialism in the GDR', which signified both an ostentatious confirmation of the independent position of the East German state and an acceleration of the transformation process. This leap forward should also be understood as a reaction to the state of the East German economy, which continued to be abysmal, because the SED leaders were convinced that the origin of their economic difficulties lay above all in the excessive compromises they had had to make during the cautious 'people's democratic' approach of the first few years. The SED decided that an intensified struggle against the 'resistance of hostile forces' was now unavoidable, leaning for support on a statement by Stalin, in which he recommended the German comrades to 'intensify the class struggle'.[11]

The SED followed this up by announcing the formation of national armed forces, establishing 'workers' militia groups' (*Betriebskampfgruppen*) as a military reserve and making the country more centralised by abolishing the states (*Länder*) and replacing them with fifteen administrative districts. Those private industrial firms which still existed, as well as craft enterprises and private trading firms, were put under pressure with tax increases and even threatened with the withdrawal of ration cards. The SED was engaged in a 'fight on all fronts'.

In its struggle to collectivise agriculture, the party leadership now cracked down on farmers who refused to join agricultural producer cooperatives by confiscating their land and instituting criminal proceedings against them. A new law prescribed severe penalties for offences against 'people's property'. Within a few months, more than 10,000 people had been punished for this crime, which was almost impossible to define. At the same time, a campaign was started against the Protestant Church. The Christian youth group known as the '*Junge Gemeinde*', which was popular in many places, particularly among secondary school pupils and students, had competed vigorously with the state-run FDJ (Free German Youth). It was now designated an 'illegal organisation of agents and spies'. Some 3,000 young people were expelled from school, and many student chaplains and youth group leaders were arrested and indicted on a charge of 'boycott agitation' (*Boykotthetze*).[12]

The results of the new tough line were disastrous. Flight from the GDR assumed dramatic proportions, but also, even more seriously, a growing rejection of SED policies now became apparent in the towns, in the countryside, in the schools and even within party branches. Moreover, economic difficulties continued to increase: the economic potential of the country was overstretched by the decision simultaneously to invest massively in heavy industry, campaign for the collectivisation of agriculture and expand the army. Military and occupation costs alone amounted to roughly 10 per cent of the state budget. The main problem continued to be inadequate labour productivity, which had reached only half the West German level (although it is difficult to find a proper basis for calculation). In spring 1953, the party leadership felt that the crisis in the economy was so threatening that it had to take drastic measures. It tried to secure a lasting improvement in the country's economic situation by making severe cuts in expenditure, increasing the prices of rationed foodstuffs and, above all, considerably increasing work norms.[13]

## From 17 June to 13 August

In this difficult situation, the death of Stalin was a completely unexpected blow to the SED. Power in the Soviet Union passed to a collective leadership. The first steps towards de-Stalinisation were introduced by none other than the head of the secret police, Beria, who had been responsible, as Stalin's hangman, for the enslavement and death of millions of people. More than a million prisoners were released from the GULAG labour camps, and the state security apparatus, or KGB, was incorporated into the Ministry of Internal Affairs. At the same time, the new leadership decided to deal with the glaring shortages in the Soviet Union by intensifying the production of consumer goods and introducing other economic reforms. But Beria himself was arrested in June 1953 and executed in December of the same year. It took more than three years of obscure power struggles before a new strongman, Nikita Khrushchev, won the upper hand within the party leadership. Even so, the post-Stalinist 'Thaw' in Soviet policy continued throughout this period.[14]

These far-reaching changes had an immediate impact on the GDR. Just a few days after Stalin's death, the new leadership of the Soviet Communist Party bluntly made clear to the German comrades that the policy of intensified class struggle supported by Stalin had led to the destabilisation of the GDR and that the 'New Course' policy applied to it as well. The Soviet leaders demanded measures 'to restore the situation in the German Democratic Republic'. They called for a reversal of the policy of driving out private entrepreneurs, an extension of the consumer goods industries, a slackening of the push towards collectivisation, an end to the conflict with the churches, improvements in 'legality', and 'guarantees for citizens' rights'.[15] This heightened the confusion in East Berlin. Calls were soon made for Ulbricht to be held responsible for the 'errors' of the past. After a few weeks, the SED leadership announced certain concessions on the lines of Moscow's instructions. The tempo of collectivisation would be reduced, and the tax increases on private producers, the expropriations and the arrests would all be reversed. Members of the '*Junge Gemeinde*' were released from prison and pupils expelled from school were readmitted to classes.

The phase of 'intensified class struggle' was thus followed by a phase of 'retreat'. But the 'New Course' proclaimed by the SED by no means fulfilled the expectations aroused in the population by the announcements about changes in the Soviet Union; most importantly, the increase in work norms was not reversed. The SED leadership had hardly paid any attention to the indications which had been emerging for weeks that the workers were seething with discontent. When criticism of the introduction of the increased work norms into the Berlin construction industry appeared even in *Neues Deutschland,* the party's own paper, this served as a signal for revolt.

The people's uprising of 17 June 1953 broke over the SED like a tidal wave. The public hardly noticed that the party leadership had hurriedly cancelled the increase in norms the previous day. The strikes and demonstrations of 17 June started with the workers who were building the Stalinallee, the great boulevard planned for East Berlin. But what was remarkable above all was the rapidity with which they spread throughout the country. The aims of the protesters also expanded quickly. They moved on from attacking the increase in work norms to demanding free elections and the resignation of the government. Protests took place in 242 towns and villages, and half a million people participated in strikes and demonstrations. In many rural areas, the LPGs disintegrated, and in many towns the party's offices were stormed. Within a few hours, the SED had lost control of the country. The People's Police (*Volkspolizei*) proved powerless, and the attempts of the GDR Radio to placate the population had no effect. The citizens of the GDR preferred to get their information on the events from the West Berlin radio station, RIAS.[16]

The Halle–Leuna–Merseburg industrial triangle was one of the centres of the uprising. On 17 June, 3,000 employees of the Leuna Works went on strike. Their numbers quickly swelled to over 20,000. It is true that the SED leadership had in the meantime rescinded the increase in norms, but the demands of the striking chemical workers had long passed beyond that stage. A large group of protesters marched to the town of Halle, where they stormed the prisons and the local SED headquarters. On the afternoon of 17 June 60,000 people gathered in the town centre. They demanded the resignation of the government, free elections, the release of political prisoners and the reunification of Germany. Early in the evening, the first Soviet tanks appeared, the crowd dispersed, and the Soviet secret police and the German state security forces immediately began to hunt for the ringleaders. The chemical works of Leuna and Buna were occupied by Soviet troops. On 20 June, work was resumed there. Nevertheless, a further strike started in Leuna four weeks later, with the participation of 5,000 workers. This too was crushed. The GDR press did not reveal a word about the events in the industrial districts of Central Germany. But even in the West the full extent of the uprising was not known until 1990.[17]

The Soviet Control Commission had already declared a state of emergency and begun to suppress the revolt with military force on the morning of 17 June. The demonstrators quickly dispersed when Soviet tanks appeared in the town centres. By 18 June, the rising had been largely suppressed, although there were repeated protest actions on the following days. Extensive arrests were made: 3,000 people were seized by Soviet troops, and more than 10,000 by the GDR authorities during the next few weeks. Some fifty demonstrators lost their lives. Twenty were shot after being court martialled. It is probable that twenty Soviet soldiers were also shot for refusing to proceed against the demonstrators.

The rising of 17 June embraced all sections of the population, but it was above all one of the greatest workers' revolts in recent German history. Two-thirds of those arrested were workers. There can be no doubt that the main motivations behind the uprising were both dissatisfaction with economic conditions and rejection of the dictatorship of the SED. A convincing demonstration of this was the fact that the rising occurred at precisely this point. People were emboldened to take to the streets against a visibly weakened regime by a range of factors: the death of Stalin, the hopes awakened by the New Course in the Soviet Union, the attempts at reform by the SED leadership, which were regarded as inadequate, and especially the obvious uncertainty of the regime in its approach to developments in Moscow. The calculation that the rulers of the country had been weakened proved to be correct as far as the GDR leadership was concerned: the party leaders and the authorities gave the impression of being paralysed in face of the sheer weight of the uprising. The SED dictatorship was only saved by the deployment of Soviet tanks.

It was a long time before the situation in the GDR reverted to its previous stability, and in some respects the SED never completely recovered from the shock of the 17 June revolt. It had revealed very clearly that among the people, and particularly the working class, the rule of the SED was largely rejected. The rapid increase in the numbers fleeing the country pointed in itself to the population's loss of trust: between 1953 and 1956 more than a million people left for the West. That figure was a reliable indication of the mood in East Germany.[18]

The day of 17 June 1953 had therefore made several things clear. Firstly, no one could have any more doubt that the SED regime was the dictatorship of a minority and not the rule of the people, in whatever possible sense. Secondly, the Soviet Union had demonstrated that it was ready to intervene directly to prop up the power of the SED by military means if its rule over the GDR was endangered. This gave security to the party leadership and it stifled any thought of open revolt for decades to come. Thirdly, the USA had not intervened in the conflict, and had thereby confirmed that it accepted the division of spheres of interest even in conflict situations, and that it continued to adhere to the Four

Power Agreements of 1945. Notwithstanding all propaganda to the contrary, the USSR never had to reckon with the prospect of Western military intervention in the GDR.

Even while the rising was still in progress, the SED leadership had issued the watchword that this was nothing but a 'fascist putsch', and this remained the official version until 1990. But this way of categorising the events only served to conceal the SED's consternation and disappointment over the behaviour of its own base, the working class, because it was only too well known internally who were the people who had demonstrated, and who was the target. Until the end, the SED leadership never entirely lost the distrust for their own working-class base which arose out of, or was confirmed by, these events. The conformist GDR writer Hermann Kant put these words into the mouth of the proletarian hero of his novel after 17 June: 'It was difficult to stay hopeful after the experience of June'. What had to be done in the future, he adds, was this:

> Watch out, take care, remain vigilant, don't be taken in, no rotten liberalism, no Romanticism, the struggle has not ended, and don't worry about the reproach of narrowness if that means not giving an inch of ground to the enemy and never giving an opportunity for a repetition of that June day.[19]

But many reports from lower-level party branches and from the Stasi, for internal distribution only, confirmed that the population had rebelled against the poor supply situation, the shortages and the party's misuse of power. A leading female comrade in the SED Politburo lamented that they had 'defended things which could not be defended, and glossed over situations when it was a crime to do so'. Even so, no one ever expressed any doubts about the party's course: 'The general line of the party' (in other words the "building of socialism") was and remains correct' it was said. It was admitted that it had been a 'mistake' to accelerate the process of transformation. This had made the tempo of change in the economy too great. It had also been wrong to attempt to 'force out and liquidate the middle and lower ranks of the urban bourgeoisie and the well-off peasantry'.[20]

Most of the internal criticism was directed against the authoritarian leadership style of Walter Ulbricht, and at first it appeared that his opponents might win a majority in the party's leading bodies. But, after a few weeks, with the arrest of Beria, the situation in Moscow again became unclear. Ulbricht's critics now recoiled from taking any further steps, and his downfall, which had appeared almost certain, was prevented. He then set to work to deprive his internal opponents of power, and to have many of them arrested and imprisoned, in the usual manner of Communist Party leaderships. Extensive 'purges' of the party followed, particularly in the lower ranks, combined with a strengthening of the security organs, above all the Stasi, which thenceforth concentrated more intensively on dealing with the internal political situation and less on spreading 'enlightenment' among the West Germans.

The party leadership now also started to remove the most important bones of contention, which it was able to do speedily and discreetly. Most of the measures from the time of 'intensified class struggle' were rescinded, and the attempt was made to regain the trust of the population by making improvements in social policy. Wages were raised, prices were reduced and pensions were improved. This meant, however, that it was impossible to stick to the central economic plans made previously, because labour productivity failed to keep pace with wages. The Soviet Union too was concerned to stabilise the situation in the GDR as quickly as possible. It therefore renounced any claim to further reparations, reduced the amount the GDR had to pay to cover the cost of stationing the Red Army in the country and handed back some of the enterprises that had been converted into Soviet Stock Corporations (SAGs) after 1945.

Future developments, however, would be determined by whether the SED leadership succeeded in achieving lasting improvements in economic growth, productivity and the availability of supplies by making more far-reaching reforms. In the Soviet Union, the new party chief Nikita Khrushchev continued the 'New Course'. There, the consumer goods industries were given greater resources, factories and collective farms received more autonomy and the willingness to reform was increased both among the population and within the power apparatus by a reduction in repressive measures.

Khrushchev's reforming course found expression in spectacular fashion at the Twentieth Party Congress of the CPSU. There he settled accounts with Stalin and his crimes in a previously unheard-of manner. His criticisms, however, were directed primarily against the dictator himself, the 'cult of personality' that surrounded him and the political line he had laid down. The party and the power system it had built up remained as untouched as the principles of Marxism-Leninism and the participation of the members of the current Communist Party leadership in the crimes of Stalinism was not mentioned. Even so, Khrushchev's speech was a sensation, because he had said what would previously have cost the speaker his life: that millions of innocent people had been persecuted and murdered under Stalin's dictatorship. He was particularly concerned to stress that the Communist Party itself had also fallen victim to Stalin's terror: 98 out of 139 members of the Central Committee, and 2,210 out of 2,750 District Secretaries of the party had been executed or disappeared into the GULAG system during the Stalin era, he said. Only three out of 200 members of the Ukrainian Party Central Committee survived.[21]

If the 17 June rising was the first shock, Khrushchev's speech was the second shock to the SED leadership, which had fostered the cult around the great leader, Stalin, as unhesitatingly and enthusiastically as all the other Communist Party leaderships. But, in the GDR, it was unconditionally necessary to avoid any 'discussion of errors', and Stalin's crimes were neither made public nor discussed there. It was not until years afterwards that 'Stalinallee' in East Berlin was renamed 'Karl-Marx-Allee', that 'Stalinstadt' became 'Eisenhüttenstadt', and that the gigantic bronze statue of Stalin in the Berlin district of Friedrichshain was removed and melted down. The kind of 'de-Stalinisation' that took place in the GDR did not result in personnel changes. The existing members of the leadership retained their positions, although they were all imbued with Stalinist ideas and had long looked towards Stalin for guidance.

In his Twentieth Party Congress speech, apart from dealing with internal party matters, Khrushchev had also announced changes of course in foreign and economic policy. The principle of 'coexistence' would shift the terrain of competition between the communist world and the states of the West from the military sphere to economics and technology. Different roads to socialism could be accepted in the future, he said, though within limits. The party's main objective should be to match the level of economic and technological development of the West as quickly as possible, perhaps within a decade. Bearing in mind real economic conditions in the Soviet Union, the GDR and the other Eastern bloc countries, this approach seemed like whistling in the dark. But it was intended to impart a new confidence and optimism to party leaderships and populations after the shock of hearing about Stalin's crimes, and to a certain extent it succeeded.

The SED leadership responded more favourably to the economic impulse given by the CPSU's Twentieth Party Congress than to the revelations about Stalin, and it started to set in motion serious economic reforms in conjunction with the new Five Year Plan for the 1956 to 1960 period. The main focus lay on a modernisation offensive, which comprised elements such as automation, mechanisation and the use of nuclear energy. The leadership intended to raise labour productivity within five years by the unbelievable figure of 50 per cent. In addition, the role of private enterprise in industry and handicrafts was to be strengthened, the collectivisation of agriculture was to be taken more slowly, and the consumer goods sector was to be expanded. The workers were promised wage increases of 30 per cent and a forty-hour working week.[22]

Reforms in the political sphere were more tentative. Even so, many party leaders who had been removed from office in previous years and in some cases imprisoned were rehabilitated, and more than 20,000 prison inmates were released. Moreover, many intellectuals responded positively to the slogans issued by the party calling on people to overcome 'dogmatism' and encouraging scientific differences of opinion. There were intensive discussions of the right to free scientific debate and the need for science to be independent of political instructions, particularly in the universities. The most important protagonists of this movement were the philosophers Wolfgang Harich and Ernst Bloch and the literary scholar Hans Mayer. Once again, they started to hope for a reformed socialism in which there could be democracy and freedom of opinion.

The reform impetus was stronger in other Eastern bloc countries than in the GDR. Throughout the region, the suppression of the private economy and the pressure to concentrate on heavy industry had led to appalling supply problems, and the building of a power structure on the Stalin model had aggravated the confrontation between the population and the party apparatus. After the death of Stalin, attempts at reform and signs of unrest increased all over the bloc. In Czechoslovakia, strikes and demonstrations occurred as early as summer 1953. In Poland, attempts to collectivise agriculture had come up against particular resistance, and also the accelerated industrialisation of the country had created far more problems than it solved. Here too, rising prices for consumer goods and marked increases in work norms contributed to a worsening of the mood, especially as the Polish press reported openly on the difficult economic situation.

Khrushchev's February 1956 attack on Stalin created a new situation in that country. The people became bolder and protest became louder. In the industrial city of Poznań in western Poland, a demonstration by local workers in June 1956 against the increased work norms developed within a few days into a popular revolt, during which tens of thousands of people demonstrated against the government, demanded religious freedom and free elections, stormed the city's main prison and sought to defend themselves with firearms against the intervention of the army. Fifty-three protesters were killed and hundreds wounded in the ensuing battle. The crisis seemed at first to have been settled by the appointment of Władysław Gomułka, who had been dismissed the year before, and had the reputation of being inclined towards reform, as First Secretary of the party. The new government pledged that it would end the collectivisation of agriculture, set up independent workers' councils in the factories and allow more freedom for the Catholic Church. When, despite this, the disturbances continued, Khrushchev came to Warsaw and threatened that the Red Army would intervene militarily. Gomułka was only able to avoid this outcome by declaring his unconditional loyalty to the Soviet Union, which thereupon cancelled its military intervention, for which preparations had already been made.[23]

Almost at the same time, events in Hungary reached crisis point. Here too, protest was sparked off by economic distress, but in this case political demands were paramount from the outset, in particular calls for the reappointment of the deposed prime minister Imre Nagy, the holding of free elections and the withdrawal of Soviet troops from the country. When, on the second day of the demonstrations in Budapest, the secret police shot into the crowd, killing thirty people, the movement became an uprising and finally an armed revolution. The Red Army intervened, and soon the whole country was shaken by fierce conflict. After the reappointment of Nagy as head of the government, the situation appeared to become calmer. However,, when he announced the withdrawal of Hungary from the Warsaw Pact and called on the United Nations for assistance, the question of power was posed for the Soviet Union. The Red Army intervened again, with fifteen divisions and 4,000 tanks, and within a week it had inflicted a bloody defeat on the Hungarian uprising; between 3,000 and 4,000 dead were counted on the Hungarian side, and 670 on the Soviet side.

The reassertion of Soviet control was followed by weeks of terror in Hungary. Nagy and other leaders of the revolution were executed along with an estimated several hundred people who had taken part in the uprising. Some 15,000 young Hungarians were deported to the Soviet Union and placed in the GULAG system; and more than 200,000 people fled to the West. The Soviet Union had made an example of Hungary. Over the next twelve years, there were no further revolts in the Eastern bloc.[24]

The uprisings of 1953 and 1956 had a far-reaching political impact. On the one hand, the events in Berlin, Poznań and Budapest made everyone aware that the Soviet Union could only keep hold of the area it controlled by force. All three uprisings largely emerged from the action of the industrial workers. No one in their right mind could still regard as credible the claim of the communist regimes in East Central Europe that they represented the interests of the workers. On the other hand, what had already come to light on 17 June 1953 was confirmed in 1956: the Western world followed the events in Poland and particularly in Hungary with great sympathy, but the USA did not intervene. There could, after all, be no doubt that a Western intervention in Hungary would have led to a war between the two nuclear powers, the USA and the Soviet Union. The status quo was thus again confirmed, and to that extent Moscow's position had been strengthened.

For the population of the GDR, finally, what was clear after 17 June 1953 was reconfirmed by the events of autumn 1956: the SED dictatorship would not allow itself to be removed by way of demonstrations. As in Poland, Czechoslovakia or Hungary, it was necessary to come to terms with the regime for a long time to come. But, unlike the other countries of the Eastern bloc, anyone who was dissatisfied with the situation could simply leave the GDR, and this is what almost a quarter of a million people did every year. That process weakened the political opposition within the country, but at the same time it demonstrated the vulnerability of the SED regime: people were simply running away.

In all the countries of the Eastern bloc, the risings marked the end of the 'thaw'. In the Soviet Union, Khrushchev called for a struggle against 'revisionism', and domestic restrictions were made more severe. In the GDR, Ulbricht considered that his rejection of all forms of 'retreat' in domestic politics had been confirmed, and he again started to take a harsh line against all those who had pushed for more democracy and freedom of opinion since 1953. Wolfgang Harich was arrested and condemned to ten years in prison, Ernst Bloch was forced to retire from his professorship, and the universities were again placed under rigorous supervision. The party leadership disciplined Ulbricht's internal critics and rivals, and it undertook yet another 'party purge', the fourth one within less than ten years. In order to guard against what had happened in Hungary, the list of political crimes was extended. The state security force was expanded and instructed to concentrate more closely on the GDR population. Hopes for a reformed socialism combined with democracy and freedom of opinion had quickly evaporated.[25]

At the same time, however,economic prospects appeared to be improving. The economic reforms were beginning to make an impact: industrial production rose by 8 per cent in 1957, by 11 per cent in 1958, and by 12 per cent in 1959. The chemical industry now started to enjoy particular government support. A massive increase in the production of synthetic materials was planned, on the basis of supplies of oil from the Soviet Union (under the impressive slogan 'Chemicals offer bread, prosperity and beauty'). Substantial growth was also achieved in the consumer goods industry. In 1958, the rationing of fat, meat and sugar was lifted, and food stamps ceased to be a feature of daily life. The rulers of the GDR thought that the mechanisms of state economic planning had finally enabled them to take charge of the situation, and that the 'inevitable' superiority of socialism over capitalism would soon assert itself in a practical way. Moreover, fewer people now fled the country. In 1958, 204,000 left, but in 1959 the figure fell to 143,000. This appeared to signal a certain degree of stabilisation.[26]

The economic situation was also improving in the Soviet Union. But there it was the spectacular successes in natural science and technology which brought the regime worldwide glamour and prestige. The explosion of the first Soviet hydrogen bomb in 1953 had already given Western politicians and military leaders a terrible scare. In 1957, the Soviets made their first foray into space by firing off the 'Sputnik'. This was greeted with enormous interest as well as anxiety in the West, as it seemed to indicate a Soviet lead in science and technology. In the GDR, the Sputnik gave rise to great hopes. 'Desertion from the republic is not only treason; it is also stupidity', wrote the *Berliner Zeitung* in December 1957. 'What kind of intelligent person abandons the stronger battalions!' It was now clear, the paper added, 'that the forces of the socialist camp have overtaken the capitalist remainder of the world for the first time. The Soviet Union's space probes are the symbol and the proof of this shift of power, which from now on will come into effect more and more rapidly.'[27] At one stroke, Khrushchev's announcement that the Soviets would overtake the USA economically by 1970 no longer seemed such a fantasy as the West had initially assumed. Admittedly, the data we now have at our disposal show that the strength of the Soviet economy was immensely overestimated in the West. But, in the minds of contemporaries, it appeared that the outcome of a competition between East and West might still be an open question.

The SED leadership therefore felt it was able to renew the offensive. At the Fifth Party Congress, in 1958, Ulbricht proclaimed that the 'main task' was now to prove 'the superiority of the socialist social system of the GDR over the rule of imperialist forces in the Bonn state'. This was expected to apply even in the consumer goods sector: the GDR was supposed to overtake the Federal Republic within a few years in the areas of food supply and consumer goods.[28]

The GDR economy was shifted onto a Seven Year Plan in October 1959, following the Soviet example. This new plan envisaged raising industrial growth and labour productivity to the Federal Republic's level by 1965. It seemed possible to achieve these goals because it was expected that the West German economy would soon suffer a slump. The GDR economy did in fact experience a phase of economic growth in the early 1960s, which put it in an outstanding position within the community of CMEA states. But the expected slump did not occur in West Germany. As a result, the GDR continued to lag behind the Federal Republic in industrial production, income per head and labour productivity, and this deficit continued to increase, instead of lessening.

Even so, the rising production figures increased the confidence of the SED leadership, and at the 1958 Party Congress it launched a new campaign of intensified class struggle. The first offensive of this kind had led to the uprising of 17 June 1953, which forced it to reverse its policy. Now, a second attempt was expected to achieve the objectives which had been temporarily deferred. The cultural sector was the first to bear the brunt of the onslaught. Teaching in the secondary schools was now expected to be directed more consistently towards education for socialism. Art and literature were to be more thoroughly aligned with socialist realism, and the struggle with the churches was also reinvigorated. The 'dedication of youth' (*Jugendweihe*) was made obligatory, with great success, as it turned out. This was a non-religious ceremony marking entry into adulthood which was intended to be an alternative to the Protestant ceremony of confirmation, and it had been widely used in the workers' movement since the turn of the century. The move to reduce the Church's role in society soon had a significant impact, and it ran parallel to processes of secularisation taking place in the West.[29]

The time had now come, according to the calculations of the SED leadership, to make use of its position of strength and start again with the collectivisation of agriculture, which had been postponed up to that point. Since 17 June 1953, the party had proceeded very cautiously with the operation to rid the country of private landownership. At the beginning of 1960, however, it began a furious campaign against private farming, which outdid everything so far experienced in the GDR. Groups of party agitators went from village to village, and party officials and judges acted against recalcitrant farmers with threats, promises and arrests. In this way, the party achieved the collectivisation of almost 40 per cent of the agricultural area within the first three months of the campaign. By the end of 1961, only 10 per cent of the land was still in the hands of 'individual farmers'.[30]

The consequences were felt immediately. Since open rebellion was impossible, the people had a choice between conforming and fleeing. Thousands of country-dwellers left the GDR for the Federal Republic, whose economic strength offered prospects which appeared to many to compensate for the loss of their homeland. The agitation in the countryside also spilled over into the towns. In 1960, the number of people who fled to the West again rose to 200,000. These numbers included, apart from the farmers, a disproportionate number of young, well-educated people. Economically and politically, this was liable to endanger the very existence of the GDR in the long term. If the SED wanted to avoid suspending its socialist offensive once again, which at the time seemed to be completely out of the question, it would have to react to the emigration crisis.

The problem was West Berlin. Joint four-power responsibility for the German capital had led to the peculiar situation that in the middle of the GDR there existed a piece of the West, in which Western troops were stationed, and in which the laws of the Federal Republic took effect, if in a somewhat convoluted manner. As long as the Soviet Union had maintained the option of a reunited, neutral Germany, the status of West Berlin had not been touched. But in 1955, after both German states had obtained a considerable degree of sovereignty and become fully integrated into their respective power blocs, the role of West Berlin was regarded at least in the East as an open question. The SED leadership now seized on this point. Ulbricht claimed in October 1958 that the whole of Berlin belonged to the GDR's 'area of jurisdiction'. Some weeks later, Khrushchev issued an ultimatum to the Western powers. West Berlin, he said, must be converted into a demilitarised free city within six months, otherwise the GDR, with the support of the Soviet Union, would declare sovereignty over its area of jurisdiction, including the whole of Berlin.[31]

In both the USA and Great Britain, there were certainly suggestions that a compromise ought to be reached with the Soviet Union on the issue, because the position of West Berlin, the open borders and the mass flight from the GDR were dangerously destabilising factors. Federal Chancellor Adenauer, on the other hand, pointed out that if the West disregarded even a single aspect of the legal foundations created after the war in relation to Germany and Berlin, the whole Western legal position would come crashing to the ground. The new US administration which came into office at the beginning of 1961 under President Kennedy stated its position on Berlin in the form of the so-called 'Three Essentials', which guaranteed

> firstly the freedom of the people of West Berlin to choose their own political system, secondly the presence of Western troops in the Western sectors of the city as long as the people wished it and needed them to be there, and thirdly freedom of transit between Berlin and the Federal Republic.[32]

With this, the West Berlin status quo was confirmed, although the joint responsibility of the Four Powers for the whole of Berlin was not specifically mentioned. As in 1953 and 1956, the USA accepted that the Soviet Union had the power to decide what happened in its own sphere of interest, and this also included regulating travel between the Eastern and Western halves of the city.

Risks remained, however. The confrontation between the two superpowers had worsened since Khrushchev's ultimatum. Military threats by the Soviet party boss, the shooting down of an American military aircraft over USSR territory and the abortive American invasion of Cuba had led the conflict to increase in seriousness over the years. In this situation, it was dangerous for the SED leadership to press ahead further on the Berlin issue, and this may explain both its hesitancy and the restrained reaction of the Western powers. On the other hand, the GDR's economic situation became more difficult after 1960. The reforming impulse had quickly run out of steam, and growth rates were lower than expected. The SED therefore urged Khrushchev and the governments of the other countries of the Eastern bloc to provide quick assistance to the GDR. In addition to the inadequate supply of raw materials, the burden of debt and the shortage of labour, the main reason for the economy's dramatic difficulties seemed to be the existence of an 'open border'. In order to keep the population within the country the SED had needed to make considerable concessions. As Ulbricht told Khrushchev, 'the open borders forced us to raise the standard of living more rapidly than corresponded with the strength of our economy.' A way of closing the borders had to be found.[33]

It was true that, if the flight from the GDR were to continue at the level of the previous ten years, during which almost three million people—a sixth of the population—left the country, this would have endangered the country's existence. Other Warsaw Pact countries would, in turn, have suffered the effects of a collapse, not least because they were dependent on imports of machinery and industrial equipment from the GDR. The existence of the GDR was indispensable to the Soviet Union, and not just on economic and strategic grounds. Politically too, the socialist GDR constituted proof 'that communism is a superior and more highly developed social system for industrialised countries as well', as Soviet First Deputy Prime Minister Anastas Mikoyan stated in June 1961. 'If socialism is not victorious in the GDR, if communism does not turn out to be viable and superior there, we too have failed.'[34]

As late as March 1961, however, the leaders of the Eastern bloc states still ruled out closing the Berlin border, as they feared a sharp reaction from the Western side. But then, rumours that the border was to be sealed off spread rapidly, causing the flood of refugees to swell still further, with the result that, by the end of July, almost 150,000 additional refugees had left for the West. This caused the other party leaders to change their minds. At the beginning of August, they agreed to the GDR's proposal to prevent movement between East and West Berlin by building a barrier. During the night of 12 to 13 August 1961, accordingly, GDR military detachments closed the sector boundary which ran through Berlin with barbed wire, and teams of building workers then began to construct a wall. In the weeks and months that followed, this wall was extended right across the city.

## Bringing Socialism through Science and Technology

Anyone who had not left the GDR by 13 August was now imprisoned inside the country, and had willy-nilly to come to terms with the situation. Some found this easy, others did not. 'One was absolved from having to decide whether to flee or to stay', as the writer Günter de Bruyn wrote in his memoirs. 'What had been provisional now took on firm contours; the temporary suddenly looked permanent. One therefore had to settle in for the long haul; because it is hard to live in a state of political schizophrenia.'[35] But this had consequences. 'The building of the wall on 13 August 1961', recalled Joachim Gauck,

> would leave a particularly lasting imprint on people's attitude and mentality. The objective impotence imposed on the population by the all-powerful state apparatus now also became subjective powerlessness. And because people had been deprived of institutional opportunities to participate in exercising power, they gradually lost the ability to act on their own responsibility.[36]

For the SED leaders, on the other hand, the building of the wall was a triumph. 'We were intoxicated with success and flushed with victory', wrote the

Central Committee member Hermann Axen in his autobiography.[37] Now they could finally do as they wanted in their own country, without having to take account of the mood of the population, because the door to the West had been locked and bolted.

In retrospect, the building of the wall did indeed represent a kind of second founding of the GDR. The country achieved economic and political stability, and it increased its importance as a member of the group of Eastern bloc states. It was gradually recognised by the Western powers, even, eventually, by the Federal Republic. The West German government's strategy of simply ignoring the GDR and waiting for its apparently irresistible downfall had ended in failure. The Federal Republic needed to reorient itself, and for this it needed a complete change in its attitude to the German question, but many years were to elapse before a new approach came to the fore in West German politics. The Western powers, for their part, kept a low profile. Since the Soviet Union had not breached the Four Power Agreement and had restricted its activities to its own sphere of interest, the West had no occasion to intervene. This principle had already been demonstrated on 17 June 1953 and in connection with the Hungarian rising of 1956. Western diplomats had already been aware for months that the GDR would close the escape routes, and many of them expected that this would stabilise the situation at one of the flashpoints of the Cold War.

At the same time, however, the Berlin Wall was an obvious symbol, which could be inspected at any time, of the failure of a communism that had to imprison its population and shoot potential escapees in order to maintain its rule. The East German regime could only be stabilised by force, and the leaders of the SED were entirely aware of this. The official description of the Berlin Wall as an 'anti-fascist defence wall' was a laborious attempt to conceal the regime's reliance on force. It also delegitimated its anti-fascism. The SED's propaganda had always asserted that the Federal Republic was a refuge for fascism and militarism, and although this was a distorted picture, it was not entirely without foundation. But no one seriously believed that the wall had been built to resist the onslaught of battalions of West German Nazis. In essence, in cordoning off West Berlin the SED was only acting in accordance with its long-term conviction that socialism derived its legitimacy not from the agreement of the majority of the people but from the historical correctness of the idea itself.

The first measures of the regime after the building of the wall were therefore an intensification of the ideological battle and a wave of violent repression. Between summer 1961 and the end of the year, the number of people imprisoned in the GDR rose by more than 50 per cent. In the second half of 1961, almost 20,000 people were detained for political offences. A new form of punishment was introduced, in the shape of 'labour camps' to which 'workshy' individuals could be committed for 'education through labour'. The 'enemies of socialism' were openly threatened with violence: 'One does not hold discussions with provocateurs. They are first given a thrashing and then handed over to the organs of the state.' Those were the orders issued by the FDJ leadership on the evening of 13 August 1961. Border guards were ordered to use firearms against 'border violators'. Much attention was devoted to combating the influence of the Western media: anyone who watched Western television was subject to criminal prosecution. The FDJ organised a 'Blitz Action Against NATO Transmitters', in the course of which FDJ activists destroyed television antennae which pointed to the West or twisted them round.[38]

Acts of intimidation and force were an everyday occurrence in East Germany in the months after August 1961. Not until December did the SED bring this policy of intensified terror to an end. By then, the power of the state had been consolidated. The building of the wall and the fight against the 'enemy within' appeared to have finally provided the necessary conditions for the implementation of real socialism.

The impulse to restart extensive reforms with fresh enthusiasm and greater effort, so as to overcome the economic problems of the past decade, had two sources, the GDR itself and the Soviet Union. The Soviet Communist Party now repeated its criticisms of Stalin and Stalinism more strongly and put forward as the most important policy aims the modernisation of the economy, coexistence with the West and competition between the rival state systems of socialism and capitalism. Moscow also passed a resolution that the phase of intensified class struggle was at an end, that the Soviet Union was now a 'state of the whole people', not of a single class, and that the transition to communism would be experienced by the present generation. The reforming impulse from the Soviet Union was now accepted by the SED more readily than in the 'thaw' period after the death of Stalin. The newspapers of the GDR reported on the crimes of Stalinism for the first time, and the proposals for thoroughgoing economic reform which were being discussed in the Soviet Union were greeted with attentive interest.[39]

The other reforming impulse came from within the GDR itself. After 1960, the country's economic situation had again worsened. The objectives of the Seven Year Plan had not been fully achieved, and the figures for growth were declining. The rulers of the GDR could now raise work norms and prices without any fear of a rise in the number of emigrants, but the reductions in real wages which were already noticeable in 1962, and the glaring shortages of consumer goods, generated considerable resentment among the workers. The state security organs reported that leaflets were appearing containing the words 'Communists, give us more to eat, or have you already forgotten the Seventeenth of June?' and 'The better the food the faster we work!'[40] There could no longer be any question of catching up with the Federal Republic in the immediate future. The failure of the existing economic policy was clearly visible.

In all essential points, the economic system established by the SED in the GDR after 1949 was an imitation of the Soviet economy. . But large parts of the country whose system it copied continued to have a predominantly agricultural structure, and, for the last thirty years, its industries had endeavoured to catch up with the West by means of the campaigning spurts characteristic of the Stalinist command economy. If the GDR wanted to overtake the Federal Republic in productivity and standard of living, which was its declared goal, it patently needed to apply different methods, tailored specifically to a country that was already highly industrialised.

These two reforming impulses, originating from both countries, gave rise to the 'New Economic System' (NES), which dominated the economic policy debate in the GDR for almost ten years. The NES was intended to bring about extensive modernisation of the system of economic management and a considerable increase in productivity. It was based on the realisation that centralised and detailed economic planning, intervening right down to the level of the individual enterprise, had proved to be ineffective and inflexible. There should therefore be less centralisation, and the central planning authorities should only prescribe a 'plan for the medium term perspective'. Under the new system, enterprises were given much more individual responsibility. This applied above all to the Associations of Nationally Owned Enterprises (VVBs), which now functioned as branch associations or holding companies. The central criterion of success was no longer plan fulfilment but profit. This was a previously unheard-of idea in the GDR. It required prices to be reset, so as to relate them more closely to demand. Policy towards the labour force was also altered. The regime ceased to rely purely on piece rates and political consciousness to encourage the workers to raise their productivity. Instead, they were given material incentives to improve the enterprise's performance, such as bonus payments, differential wage rates and various special allowances.[41]

The chief economists of the GDR believed that by introducing the NES they had found a way to put into practice the theoretically deduced superiority of socialism over the historically outmoded system of capitalism, and thereby to establish for the first time in history a socialist economic system which was adjusted to the conditions of a developed industrial country. This historical perspective was always present to the minds of both the economic planners and the politicians of the SED, especially Walter Ulbricht, who now put himself at the head of the reformers and thereby caused the sceptics to abandon their objections for the time being.

The enterprises and the economic planners were happy with the economic reforms of the NES; indeed, they greeted them with enthusiasm. Many members of the party apparatus, in contrast, remained sceptical, asking how the dominant role of economic rationality and the drive for efficiency could be harmonised with the primacy of politics and the leading role of the party. The answer the reformers gave was this: by applying scientific knowledge. Socialism, after all, was not created voluntaristically by an act of will but was based on economic categories, consequently it had an 'objective' character. The socialist economy must also be conducted on scientific principles. Fundamental research, cybernetics, systems theory, new technologies and organisation studies were the new and frequently used bywords, suggesting that the economic success of socialism in the GDR was the result of a policy based consistently on scientific principles, and was therefore inevitable. 'The economic anarchy of capitalism', proclaimed the SED in its January 1963 Party Programme, 'is replaced by the planned management and development of the socialist economy in accordance with the latest scientific advances . . . This necessitates the application of advanced science and technology, a mastery of the most up-to-date production methods and the skilled management and organisation of the national economy.'[42]

In line with this, the change of course in economic policy was backed up with a substantial and rapid expansion of the educational system. The SED Central Committee stressed that

> the full construction of socialism in the GDR requires mastery of the technological revolution and the development of the socialist community. . . . The technological revolution, the new economic system of planning and managing the national economy and the unified socialist educational system form an indivisible unity. in completing the construction of socialism.[43]

Preschool education, the ten-class polytechnic secondary school, the extension of adult training and technical colleges and the expansion of the universities were the essential elements of this policy, and it enjoyed considerable success: in 1951, only 16 per cent of pupils attended school for more than eight years, whereas in 1970, 85 per cent did. This was a very high proportion in international terms as well.[44]

Yet more changes were associated with the reforms in the economy and the educational system. Young people, from whom the party leadership expected so much, should not be intimidated but encouraged, it was now said. 'Awkward questions from young people' should be taken seriously and not dismissed as provocations, according to a 'Youth Communiqué' issued by the SED in 1963. The GDR does not need 'fainthearts, crawlers and careerists' but 'independent and self-confident citizens of firm character, with a socialist view of the world based on progressive scientific knowledge and acquired through individual reflection and confrontation with backward opinions and reactionary ideologies.'[45]

In order to achieve this, it was necessary to mobilise not just the workers but all strata and classes of the society. The strict social selection criteria for admission to universities were loosened, so that whereas in 1960 less than 15 per cent of the students had parents who were 'intellectuals', this had risen to almost a third by 1966. The reforms finally reached the political and cultural spheres as well. Statues of Stalin disappeared from the towns and cities, and the amnesties of 1962 and 1964 freed more than 16,000 political prisoners. The works of critical authors were published, and they attracted tremendous attention. Christa Wolf's novel *Der geteilte Himmel* (Divided Heaven) was a critical treatment of the themes of flight to the West and the building of the wall. Erik Neutsch's *Spur der Steine* (Trace of Stones) examined conflicts between the workers and the economic bureaucracy. There was a palpable change of atmosphere in the GDR in 1963–4, and it was particularly appreciated by intellectuals.

For the workers, on the other hand, material improvements were the decisive aspect, and indeed the economic data again showed an upward trend: national income rose by 5 per cent in 1964 and 1965, and labour productivity by 7 per cent. The standard of living rose, more slowly than had been hoped and calculated, and it was still far behind that of the Federal Republic, but the improvement was noticeable. Even high-value consumer goods, the symbols of a modest prosperity, were now available to many people: fifty-four out of one hundred GDR households had a television set in 1966, thirty-two a washing machine, and thirty-one a refrigerator. Ten years earlier, these had been exceptional items possessed by few people.[46]

Notwithstanding these figures, it soon became apparent that the fundamental problems of the GDR economy had not been removed by the introduction of the New Economic System. It was true that operational results were no longer calculated simply on the basis of output, so that prices also played a part, but since no market prices were available as a basis for comparison, the success of an enterprise continued to be linked to plan fulfilment. Wages continued to be determined independently of gains in productivity. Incentives for innovation remained weak. It was clear that economic activities directed towards efficiency clashed in many places with the need to retain the political primacy of the party. The SED wanted to implement an economic reform on the basis of a revolution in science and technology. But it could not allow the economic sphere to become independent because this contradicted the party's claim to direct the whole of society, and in particular to control the economy.[47]

In addition, it turned out that the feat of outdoing West Germany exceeded the potentialities of the GDR economy. Khrushchev himself thought that the GDR would only be able to win the competition with the Federal Republic if it received cheap raw materials from the Soviet Union. In the long term, however, this proved to be problematic, because by delivering raw materials at less than world market prices the USSR was subsidising the GDR, and during its own periods of economic crisis it had to reduce its deliveries. When the GDR, under

Ulbricht, responded to this situation by trying to strengthen its trade relations with the West, some Soviet leaders suspected that the GDR's longer term aim was to use its economic reforms to get out of the CMEA.[48]

In December 1965, a revision took place in the NES planning system. The power of the planners was reduced, as was the ability of the enterprises to make their own decisions. Planning was again made more centralised. The primacy of politics over economics, which meant the primacy of the party leadership over the economic specialists, was confirmed once again. A new slogan was devised: the 'Economic System of Socialism' (ESS). This essentially involved concentrating money and resources on areas where technological change was estimated to be particularly pronounced and future prospects particularly good. Examples of this were electronics, especially the field of electronic data processing (EDP), which was just beginning to emerge, the automation of manufacturing processes, chemicals, especially the petrochemical industry, and machine-building and plant construction. In this context, the task of central planning was to set in motion and accelerate processes of innovation and structural change. Enterprises and Enterprise Associations were to receive more autonomy in their own fields, so that labour productivity, product quality and work efficiency could be increased. The GDR economy was expected as a result to make both a quantitative and a qualitative leap, which would enable it to achieve the main goal of overtaking the Federal Republic economically by 1980 at the latest. All efforts were directed towards this aim, which also imparted a strangely nationalist flavour to the GDR's economic efforts.[49]

It was in this context that Ulbricht produced his renowned but also much ridiculed formula, that they would 'overtake' the West 'without having to catch up with it'. Actually, this idea was not entirely far-fetched. It originally came from a Soviet cyberneticist, who stated, in reference to the emerging EDP technology, that the superiority of the socialist system could not be proved by competing with the West with its own means and remaining within the same sphere of activity. What was needed instead was to leap over the current stage of scientific-technical development and demonstrate the superiority of socialism with the technology of the next generation. With the beginning of the digital revolution a few years later, this vision became a reality in a certain sense, although under completely different conditions: not in the context of socialist economic planning and state-backed innovation but through the activities of students with an enthusiasm for technology in the extremely liberal and hippie-like climate of the universities of California.

Inconsistencies and shortcomings rapidly appeared in this variant of socialist economic policy too. The views of specialists, technicians and engineers continued to be consulted. Modernity, efficiency and innovation continued to be the key slogans. Innovative and future-oriented economic projects continued to be pursued. But, since they were of such dimensions that they exceeded the capacity of the GDR economy, priority areas had to be established, mainly large-scale research centres, which received an average of three times as much investment as other branches of industry. This approach inevitably led to the neglect of other areas, not least in the consumer goods sector. In addition, there was a constant rise in the financial requirements of the expanding military and security apparatus, so that the shortage of funds became even greater. To achieve the goal of drawing level with the Federal Republic by 1980, it was necessary to increase productivity by at least 9 per cent a year. Annual increases of roughly 5 per cent were achieved. This was outstanding in comparison with the other CMEA countries, but it did not lessen the Federal Republic's lead.

At the end of the 1960s, therefore, the net result of the policy of reform again fell short of expectations. The standard of living of the GDR population had admittedly improved a great deal, and it was noticeably higher than that enjoyed by the other members of the CMEA. The GDR had overtaken all other CMEA countries in branches of the economy which had received special support, such as chemicals and plant construction, although in technical standard and product quality it was still far below the 'world-class level' so frequently apostrophised by SED representatives. Moreover, the service sector lagged behind chronically, and the areas of infrastructure, consumer goods and energy had been equally neglected. The postponement of investment in these areas was intended to be temporary, until the modernisation of the key sectors had instilled dynamism into the economy as a whole. But shortages and bottlenecks in the supply system were impossible to ignore, and they led to constant popular discontent.

It turned out, therefore, that economic creativity and efficiency could not simply be decreed by a ruling party. The SED found that, in practice, it was unable to prove the superiority of rational socialist management over the anarchic, irrational character of capitalism. The party's constant interference in the work of dedicated technocrats was not the main reason for this. It was central planning itself which was the chief obstacle to economic progress. The lack of any diversity in perspectives and approaches, and the absence of open discussion, performance incentives and competition proved to be a crucial obstacle on the road to a dynamic national economy capable of competing on a global scale.

The implementation of the New Economic System in the early 1960s was also accompanied by distinctive changes in ideology. Like the Soviet Union, which called itself a 'state of the whole people', the SED now described the GDR as a 'society in socialism', 'characterised by comradely cooperation and mutual aid. With socialism, the community of free human beings, connected by free, creative and collective work, begins to be a reality.'[50] Here, the concept of the 'community' once again expressed the idea of a yearning for wholeness and a rejection of the contradictory reality of industrial modernity, with its domination by divergences of interest, conflict and pluralism. According to Ulbricht, the 'heroism of peaceful labour' must also be conveyed by art. It must portray 'the people in the community who build the industrial colossi' or who work as welders 'on the dizzy heights of steel structures'. The GDR, with its staggering 57 per cent of gross added value derived from industry, was one of the most industrialised countries in the world, and industry, technology and science were regarded as the expression of a true humanism, whereas attacks on technology and progress were condemned as expressions of bourgeois decadence and 'capitalist cultural decay'.[51]

This was the starting point for fresh contradictions. The more liberal climate introduced by the activation of economic reforms in 1962, which was also noticeable in the cultural and scientific spheres, gave rise to franker discussions and new forms of art. Natural scientists complained that they were expected to attain an international scientific level, but not allowed to enter into communication with more advanced Western scientists. Lawyers pointed out the deficiencies in the GDR's legal system. Writers portrayed individual deformities in socialism. Cabaret clubs like the Leipzig '*Pfeffermühle*' poked fun at the mania for planning and the worries of everyday life, and it was no surprise that the SED soon reacted by strongly denouncing these new trends. The occasion for a renewed crackdown was provided by Robert Havemann's criticisms of the atmosphere in the GDR. The renowned physical chemist had been condemned to death in 1943 by a Nazi 'People's Court' as a communist, but the execution of the sentence was postponed because he was 'important to the war effort'. He was imprisoned in Brandenburg Prison until 1945. This made him an almost sacrosanct figure in the early years of the GDR. After the Twentieth Party Congress of the CPSU, however, Havemann became a critic of Stalinism, and since then he had called for socialism and democracy to be combined together. He continued to regard the GDR as a 'decisively progressive step in German history', he said, but there were numerous practices which aroused the impression

> that Fascist ways of behaving and thinking lived on in the country, indeed had resurfaced in a new form. There was again 'one' party, a boring, co-ordinated press, an all-too-powerful secret police, a parliament without an opposition, an official cultural policy that interferes in all matters of art and literature, a government-ordained world outlook and government suppression of all deviations from the ruling 'ideology'.[52]

Other less prominent critics would have paid for these outrageous remarks with years of incarceration. Havemann, however, was at first simply expelled from the SED and removed from his chair at Humboldt University. Later on, in

1966, he was placed under house arrest. Havemann's criticisms, which he also publicised in the Western media, confirmed the party leadership in its conviction that the 'wave of leniency' in GDR cultural policy had now gone too far.

In December 1965, therefore, the liberal cultural line was abruptly halted. The SED decided to impose stricter controls over science and culture. The party line should be maintained. 'Some creative artists', said Ulbricht, 'have interpreted the tremendous creative freedom that exists in our social system for writers and artists to mean that the organs of society should avoid giving any direction and grant freedom for nihilism, semi-Anarchism, pornography and other aspects of the American way of life.'[53] The party's reaction was make a 'clean cut' (*Kahlschlag*) in cultural policy. This snuffed out any hope there had been for more open debate, cultural vibrancy and artistic freedom in the GDR.

## Prague and Bonn

The timid beginnings of social and cultural reform were replaced in the GDR by a tougher policy line after December 1965; but developments in other CMEA countries were now moving in a different direction. There too, economic problems were serious, but in Poland, Hungary and Czechoslovakia the impulse towards thoroughgoing reform of the economic system was associated more strongly with cultural openness and freedom of discussion than in the GDR. These trends were sharply criticised by the SED, because, according to the GDR Minister of Culture, Klaus Gysi, it was known from experience that 'any intellectual discussion' could turn political.[54]

The economic reforms also went further in Czechoslovakia than in the GDR. There, the reformers in the Communist Party endeavoured to incorporate elements of the market into the socialist economy while simultaneously permitting pluralism in political discussion. This quickly met with resistance from the conservative wing of the party, which won the upper hand in 1967 and started to crack down on political critics and writers. But, in January 1968, with the election of Alexander Dubček, the reformers again came to the fore, and they pushed forward a process of democratisation which was soon dubbed the 'Prague Spring' in the West. The most important aspects of this movement were the abolition of censorship, fundamental economic reforms and a redefinition of the role of the communist party. Socialism would stay, but it would now have a 'human face'. However, the impetus provided by the Communist Party of Czechoslovakia (CPC) triggered a dynamic process in the course of which more radical expectations were quickly aroused in the population. These more far-reaching objectives were partly influenced by the example of Yugoslavia, but they also contained distinctly Social Democratic elements. The 'Manifesto of Two Thousand Words' which was published at the end of June 1968 and was signed by many writers and intellectuals summed up the movement's more radical goal, which was the creation of a pluralist democracy.[55]

In the Soviet Union, the new party chief Leonid Brezhnev at first expressed approval of the CPC's path to reform, describing it as an internal matter for the Czechoslovak Socialist Republic. But when demands for democracy began to spread in the country and there were also student demonstrations in Warsaw, the Soviet Union saw parallels with 1956 and sharpened its tone towards Prague. In March 1968, the leaders of the Warsaw Pact met in Dresden and called on Dubček to reverse his reforms. The party chiefs of the GDR and Bulgaria in particular were early advocates of forcible intervention. One of their chief arguments was that West Germany was seeking to gain influence in Czechoslovakia. Finally, on 20 August 1968, troops from the Soviet Union, Poland, Hungary and Bulgaria marched into the country, thereby ending the reform experiment. But the troops of the National People's Army of the GDR, which had also helped to prepare the intervention, did not move from the border. Their job was to guard the supply chain. Memories of the German march into Prague twenty-nine years before were still fresh, and to march in now would invite direct comparisons with that earlier invasion.

The interventionists had sent a letter to Dubček before they marched in, justifying their action. They could not, they said, allow 'hostile forces to push your country from the path of socialism and create the danger of a separation of Czechoslovakia from the socialist community. This is no longer your own affair.'[56] This formula was soon to be called the 'Brezhnev doctrine'. It was therefore evident that any reforming movement in a CMEA country would be under threat of intervention by its fraternal allies. The parallel with the course of events in 1956 was extraordinary: a phase of economic and political softening quickly developed a political dynamic, with the result that the Soviet Union saw a threat to its rule and intervened militarily. Afterwards, in both cases, the local Communist Party ceased its attempt at a more liberal approach and returned to relying purely on force.

The SED leadership saw the 'Prague Spring' as a confirmation of its fear that social and cultural reform would quickly lead to political destabilisation, and it considered that it had acted correctly in December 1965 in breaking off its policy of cultural relaxation. It also recognised that there was a direct link between Prague's course towards reform and the intensified efforts of the Federal Republic to improve relations with the states of the Eastern bloc. The accusation of 'Social Democratism' therefore always implied the direct involvement of the West German SPD, which held government responsibility in the Federal Republic for the first time when the Grand Coalition came into office in 1966.

For the SED, therefore, support for the intervention of Warsaw Pact troops in Prague also had a bearing on its relations with the other German state.

The 'national question' was from the beginning one of the biggest and most complex problems facing the GDR leadership. The GDR had until 1955–6 followed in the wake of Soviet policy towards Germany, at least tactically, by supporting national unity and reunification. Later on, it came out in favour of a 'confederation' of the two German states, which would of course be conditional on a 'change in the relation of political forces in West Germany'. After the mid-1960s, however, the foreign policy of the SED was concentrated exclusively on securing international recognition for the GDR, and the recognition of West Berlin as a separate political entity. The retrospective creation of GDR citizenship in 1967 underlined this approach, which was consistently supported by the Soviet Union.[57]

West Germany's policy of claiming to be the sole German state naturally stood in the way of the GDR's aspirations. In accordance with the 'Hallstein Doctrine', named after Walter Hallstein, the long-standing State Secretary in the Foreign Office, the Federal Republic threatened to break off diplomatic relations with any state which recognised the GDR under international law. In view of West Germany's economic strength, this was for a long time an effective policy instrument. In 1963, admittedly, an agreement was made between the GDR and the West Berlin Senate for the first time to facilitate Christmas visits by citizens of West Berlin to their relatives in the East, and from 1964 onwards GDR pensioners were allowed to travel to the West. On the whole, however, relations between the two states in the 1960s were marked by sharp competition and reciprocal attempts at ideological subversion. The Federal Republic rejected a proposal by the GDR to offer Western newspapers for sale there in return for allowing *Neues Deutschland* to be sold in West Germany, because this would have tended to raise the status of the East German state. Its counter-proposal, to exchange speakers between the SED and the SPD, who would speak in public in Hanover and Chemnitz respectively, was rejected in turn by the SED leadership, though it hesitated over this for a long time.

Even so, time seemed to be working in favour of the East rather than the West. In the mid-1960s, the GDR enjoyed its first successes in the struggle for recognition: Ulbricht was received by President Nasser of Egypt as a head of state at the beginning of 1965, and in the same year the GDR was allowed to compete in the 1968 Olympic Games with a team of its own. But, when the Federal Republic's Grand Coalition government relaxed its rigid stance on relations between the two Germanies, tacitly abandoning the policy of claiming the exclusive right to represent Germany, this actually complicated matters for the GDR leadership. Most of the CMEA states were very interested in establishing closer relations with the Federal Republic, owing to their difficult economic position. But the GDR wanted to prevent this as long as it itself remained unrecognised by the Federal Republic under international law. The SED therefore rejected the first offer made by the Kiesinger–Brandt government to take up negotiations. German–German relations accordingly returned to a state of deadlock.

Yet, in the context of the emerging policy of détente between the superpowers, quarrels between the two Germanies gradually became somewhat irksome. The Soviet side wanted to improve relations with the West and step up its economic contacts, in order finally to make some economic progress. The East German leadership's continued adherence to its maximum demands on the German question clashed with this aspiration, while the Federal Republic was in a similar situation in the Western context.

The situation of the GDR government was made still more difficult by the fact that the SPD–FDP coalition which had now come to power in West Germany chose to advance its *Ostpolitik* by negotiating with Moscow. Brandt had admittedly referred for the first time to two German states in his government declaration of autumn 1969, thereby confirming the existence of the GDR, but he had also said that the two states were not foreign countries for each other: 'Their relations to each other can only be of a special kind.'[58] This made the East Germans mistrustful. Erich Honecker, the second most important person in the GDR after Ulbricht, asserted that the Brandt–Scheel government was aiming to 'gain hegemony in Europe step by step, by utilising the economic power of West German imperialism and the ideology of Social Democracy'. To achieve this, it wanted to '"open a door to the East" in the sense of a long-term penetration into the socialist countries'. Ulbricht, for his part, protested against any kind of future national unity in these words: 'There can be no unity between the Krupps and the Krauses, between the billionaires and multimillionaires and the working people.'[59] A common German nation no longer exists, he said, because a separate, socialist nation has formed in the GDR. Even a 'cultural nation' no longer exists, said Ulbricht, because 'one cannot describe West Germany's Americanised cultural swamp as German culture.'[60]

It was only pressure from its Soviet comrades that compelled the SED leadership to change course and enter into discussions with the West German government. The GDR ought to regulate its relations with the Federal Republic with a treaty, the Soviets said, but it should at the same time adopt a course that would clearly separate it from its West German rival, so as to counter West Germany's policy of 'change through *rapprochement*'.[61] The treaties of Moscow and Warsaw and the Basic Treaty of 1972 at last brought the GDR the recognition it had long hoped for, although relations between the two German states continued to be described as 'special', which kept open the idea that a single German nation existed. The SED responded by repeatedly distancing itself from this suggestion and from the Federal Republic. Nevertheless, the signing of the Basic Treaty with West Germany was something in the nature of a third foundation of the GDR, after the first one in 1949 and the second one in 1961. It was now quickly recognised by almost all the states of the globe, it developed worldwide trading relations and it became famous for its sporting excellence. At the Munich Olympics of 1972, its team did better than West Germany's. In terms of foreign policy, it could be said, the GDR's story between 1949 and 1972 was one of success.

## The End of the Ulbricht Era

It was ultimately economic difficulties that brought about the end of the Ulbricht era. Relations between the Soviet and GDR leaderships had long been tense, not least because Ulbricht never tired of praising the successes of the GDR in coming to terms with the scientific-technical revolution and exhibiting the East German state as a model and an example to the other CMEA states. When for instance the SED leader emphasised that the GDR would achieve great economic successes in cooperation with the USSR 'as a genuine German state' because 'after all we are not Belorussia' this piece of arrogance did not make him any friends among the Moscow comrades.[62] In addition, the Soviet leadership grew increasingly wary of the possibility that economic cooperation between the GDR and West Germany might lead to a *rapprochement* between the two German states. 'The future of the GDR lies in the socialist community', warned Brezhnev on many occasions. 'There is not, there cannot be, and there will not be a process of *rapprochement* between the GDR and the FRG.'[63]

By now, the party leadership in East Berlin also regarded Ulbricht as arrogant and incorrigible. Imbued as he was with the conviction that only the GDR could provide the historical proof for the superiority of socialism in developed industrial countries, and that it could only do this under his leadership, Ulbricht saw himself in historical terms as being on a level with the great pioneers of socialism. This attitude increasingly got on the nerves of his Politburo comrades.

Of greater significance, though, was the fact that Ulbricht's passionate interest in the scientific-technical revolution and the preferential treatment he gave to the technologies of the future had led to serious imbalances in the economy. All other branches of the economy suffered from a shortage of resources. Interruptions of supply, a decaying infrastructure, a shadow economy and excessive wastage were the dark sides of an economic balance sheet which only presented record numbers to the outside world. The recent attempt to beat the West on its own favoured ground, by increasing productivity and raising the standard of living, was as much a failure as previous attempts had been. That decided the issue. At the end of 1970, a majority of the SED leadership resolved to make serious amendments to the economic programme. Ulbricht's objections were no longer accepted. Shortly afterwards, thirteen out of the twenty candidates and members of the Politburo, led by Erich Honecker, sent a letter to the Soviet party chief Brezhnev asking him to call on Ulbricht to resign. Ulbricht, said the letter, had 'become estranged from the real life of the party, the working class and all working people' and as a result 'illusory notions and subjectivism' had increasingly taken hold of his mind. 'He is often rude and offensive and he argues from a position of infallibility.' Brezhnev complied with the request, and on 3 May 1971 Ulbricht announced his resignation.[64]

The first twenty years of the GDR were a period of deep-seated and highly revolutionary change. Relying on the power of the Red Army, and following the Soviet model, the SED had set up a socialist dictatorship which was characterised by a constant, tactically motivated alternation between phases of political 'offensive' and periods during which the tempo of transformation was slower, repression was less severe, and there was a greater flexibility in cultural matters. The SED had a monopoly of power. It ruled and regulated the state, the economy and society and finally by building the Berlin Wall it prevented its own citizens from being able to leave the GDR towards the West.

The political objective, and the 'historic task', of the GDR was to establish a socialist society for the first time in a developed industrial country, and thereby confront capitalism and the bourgeois societies of the West with a superior alternative. Its repeated attempts to relaunch the socialist experiment were dominated by the futurological vision of Marxism-Leninism. As was shown on 17 June 1953, in the political, social and cultural spheres, the SED could only assert itself by force, supported if necessary by the tanks of the Red Army, since the vast majority of the population were unwilling to follow it voluntarily. But the economy, which was the core area of transformation, did not respond to orders from above, and neither force nor ideological rigour could alter this. This created difficulties for the SED's claim to legitimacy. Supplies were obviously inadequate, the standard of living was low in comparison with the West, freedom and self-determination no longer existed, and the borders had been closed. If all these evils, which were proclaimed to be temporary, could not be justified by the final attainment of socialism, which promised prosperity, liberty and happiness, what then could legitimate the SED's dictatorship? The fall of Ulbricht also meant that the conviction that it would soon be possible, perhaps even in this generation, to have a better life than in the West, was finally laid to rest. After that, only three ways of justifying the dictatorship remained. First, anti-fascism. Twenty-five years after the war, however, this argument sounded less convincing. Second, peace policy. But this had largely lost its credibility through the military interventions of the Red Army in Hungary and Czechoslovakia. Finally, there was equality, which for many GDR citizens was the most important achievement of socialism, along with security of employment. But since the citizens of the GDR, like the country's leaders, always measured their own situation against the standard of living in West Germany, this was equality at an inferior level, and it did not outweigh the country's economic backwardness and political repression.

The SED leaders naturally interpreted their most recent failures merely as 'mistakes'. They were convinced that by removing Ulbricht and proclaiming new initiatives in economic policy they could eradicate the 'mistakes' and make a renewed attempt to advance, which would undoubtedly be successful this time. Now, however, after two decades of fruitless experiment, the view that in the near future the contradictions of industrial society could be resolved, and the West overtaken, through developed socialism, was held with less verve and enthusiasm. Paradoxically, this decline in self-belief occurred at the very moment when the SED finally expected its recognition by the West to provide its state with security.

# 14
# Harbingers of Change

## *Deutschlandpolitik* during the Cold War

The Soviet Union detonated a hydrogen bomb for the first time in summer 1953. In autumn 1957, it demonstrated the high standard it had reached in rocket technology by launching the Sputnik, and from 1957 onwards it possessed intercontinental missiles which could carry nuclear weapons as far as US territory. This meant a change in the global relationship of forces. The American strategic advantage came to an end, to be replaced by a 'balance of terror' which would characterise world politics for over thirty years. This change in the framework of international relations lent an additional volatility to the major trouble spots of the Cold War. Any intensification of the confrontation between the two rival blocs in Asia, the Middle East or Berlin did not just entail a risk of military conflict: it could bring about a nuclear catastrophe in which the territories of the two Great Powers would also be devastated.

Fewer than twenty years separate this situation, which prevailed at the end of the 1950s, and the culmination of the 'policy of détente' at Helsinki in 1975. During this period, the axioms of global policy, and also policy towards the two German states, underwent a fundamental change. In what follows, we shall give a somewhat schematic ten-point outline of the individual steps in this process, in order to make clear the underlying driving forces, which to some extent operated simultaneously.[1]

1. The numerous summit meetings and conferences of foreign ministers held to discuss the division of Germany between 1955 and 1959 had repeatedly confirmed that it was not possible to secure agreement between the two blocs on this question. This also applied to the suggested solutions of the German question put forward from various sides, such as the proposal devised by the Polish Foreign Minister Adam Rapacki in 1957 to create a nuclear-free zone in Europe, consisting of the Federal Republic, the GDR and Poland. The unification of the two parts of Germany under neutral auspices was advocated by the American diplomat George F. Kennan. This too proved impossible to realise, as did the SPD's March 1959 'Plan for Germany', based on Kennan's proposal, by which a reunited Germany would be removed from the Western military alliance. There was no question of the West German government's being prepared

to change its policy of Western integration. But it also objected to all proposals for the creation of a European security zone or territorial arms limitation, for two reasons: firstly, because the government feared that any change of this kind could lead to a reduction in American protection for the Federal Republic, and secondly because it suspected such a step would recognise the status quo in Europe and thereby also implicitly admit the GDR's right to exist. West Germany insisted that reunification could not be achieved through schemes of this kind but only through a 'policy of strength'. But this assumption was now no longer valid, given the Soviet Union's demonstration of its military capacity.

2. The East–West confrontation came to a head with Khrushchev's ultimatum of 27 November 1958 and the second Berlin crisis triggered by it. In view of the continuous weakening of the GDR by the massive flight of its inhabitants via West Berlin, there were three options for the Soviet Union, as Khrushchev later explained. One was to abandon the GDR. This would be equivalent to renouncing the results of the Second World War and the Soviet Union's territorial gains without any compensation, and was therefore out of the question. Secondly, as demanded in the ultimatum, West Berlin could be incorporated into the GDR. This would have changed the status quo at the expense of the West. US President Kennedy reacted to this by stating the 'Three Essentials', which the USA intended to adhere to unalterably in regard to Berlin. These covered the right of the Western powers to remain in their sectors of West Berlin; their right of access to West Berlin, and the maintenance of the security and the rights of the citizens of West Berlin by the Western powers. In view of the resistance of the USA, the integration of the whole of Berlin into the GDR was therefore impossible to achieve peacefully. Only the third option therefore remained: to seal off West Berlin from the GDR. This route was chosen, because it violated neither the post-war agreements between the Allies nor Kennedy's 'Three Essentials'.[2]

Despite all their protests against the dreadful barriers built by the East Germans through the centre of Berlin, the Western powers were well aware that the building of the wall had contributed towards stabilising the European situation. It cemented the status quo: the West accepted the division of Germany, and the Soviet Union no longer raised any claim to West Berlin. That removed the uncertainty and danger from the Berlin situation. But it also signified the failure of the strategy of the Federal Republic, which had been to maintain the division of Germany as an extremely urgent and unsolved problem of world politics. Neither the Adenauer government, nor the opposition, had an alternative to the line of policy so far followed on the question of Germany's division. The government did try to modify its behaviour towards the states of Eastern Europe in the light of the change in the overall situation, but the substance of its policy remained the same as before. According to the credo of the

CDU politicians, the GDR was a state based on injustice ('*Unrechtsstaat*'): to recognise it was not just to recognise a state but to recognise injustice.

3. With the coming of the Cuba crisis, the Cold War reached a dramatic climax, which was also a historical watershed. US President Eisenhower had already made preparations for an attempt to overthrow the revolutionary government of Fidel Castro in Cuba, but when the attempt was actually made, in April 1961, under his successor, it failed miserably, driving the island nation into the arms of the Soviet Union. A year later Cuba made an agreement with the USSR for the stationing of Soviet nuclear missiles on the island as a protection against any further American military intervention. These missiles were targeted directly against US territory. Khrushchev's motives for this extremely risky action, which brought the world to the edge of a nuclear war, are still somewhat unclear even now. In the Soviet view, the missiles in Cuba were supposed to serve as a counterweight to those stationed by the Americans in Turkey, which were just as much of a threat to Soviet territory as missiles in Cuba would have been to the USA. The West, however, saw this action by the Soviet Union as an attempt to export the revolution and directly challenge the USA. The Soviet Union did in fact support anti-colonial national liberation movements all over the world and repeatedly came into conflict with the Western powers as a result. Ultimately, however, the Soviet Union's action was above all a part of Khrushchev's foreign policy offensive, which was intended in Cuba as in Berlin to demonstrate the military strength and self-confidence of the USSR, not just towards the West but also towards communist China, which was increasingly developing into a rival power. The solution of the crisis which was found at the last minute after dramatic days of anxiety over the prospect of a worldwide nuclear catastrophe involved the immediate withdrawal of the Soviet missiles from Cuba and the withdrawal of American missiles from Turkey, although in the latter case this was done with some delay and the public was not aware that it had happened.[3]

4. The horror of those October days of 1962 had lasting effects. It was obvious to the governments in Moscow and Washington that a continuation of the policy of confrontation would bring a nuclear war ever closer. In January 1963, President Kennedy therefore spoke publicly for the first time of the need to relax the tensions of the Cold War. The result was the signature by both sides of the August 1963 agreement to limit nuclear testing. This was a big contrast to the previous year, when an atomic bomb was exploded for testing purposes every two days, on average. The partial test ban treaty of August 1963 was finally signed by more than one hundred states, and it can be seen in retrospect as the first step towards the emerging policy of 'détente'.

At the same time, the strategic principles of the NATO alliance also underwent re-examination in the USA. According to the doctrine then current, the immediate response to an attack by the Soviet Union with conventional weapons would be a nuclear strike. The threat of a nuclear response was intended to counterbalance the presumed conventional superiority of the Warsaw Pact forces. But it signified that nuclear war was the US government's only defence option. The Kennedy administration therefore replaced this doctrine of 'massive retaliation' with the concept of 'flexible response', which made it possible for the USA to use conventional weapons instead of having to reply to a conventional attack with nuclear weapons. It would only use nuclear weapons in response to a nuclear first strike by the opponent. This change of strategy had a calming effect.[4]

5. The primary goal of the USA was gradually to create a certain basis of trust between itself and the Soviet Union by cooperating on specific questions, so as to prevent a repetition of the crisis of 1961–2 over Berlin and Cuba. The foundation of this cooperation could, however, only be the status quo, in other words, the acceptance of their respective spheres of influence and domination, hence recognition of the division of Europe and Germany between the two power blocs. The West German government, in direct opposition to this, insisted that the status quo should not be recognised: it accepted neither the division of Germany nor the separation of the Eastern territories. This contradiction was inherent in the Federal Republic's policy. The failure of its previous policy on the division of Germany was made apparent by the building of the wall, and the Test Ban Treaty made it clear that the USA and the Soviet Union would in future simply ignore the German question when their own interests were at stake. This was already demonstrated by the fact that the GDR was allowed to sign the Test Ban Treaty with or without the Federal Republic's agreement.

6. The reorientation of American foreign policy after the crisis of 1961–2 cast a perceptible cloud over relations between the USA and the Federal Republic. The West German government considered that these first few steps towards an understanding between the two superpowers posed a threat that they might arrive at a solution of the German question without German participation and without taking the country's vital interests into account. In this situation, increased Franco-German cooperation offered a possible alternative. The French President, Charles de Gaulle, who had returned to power in 1958, after the collapse of the Fourth Republic, had established a presidential system of government tailored to his own personal requirements. He was chiefly concerned to maintain French national sovereignty and to restore France's position in the world. The General rejected both the development of the European Economic Community into a political union and the admission of Great Britain, which had been discussed for some time. But, above all, he resisted America's predominance in Europe, not least by building up his own nuclear arsenal, and he regarded close cooperation between France and the Federal Republic as an

appropriate way of reaching his goal. Adenauer saw an alliance of this nature, combining French leadership and West German economic power, as a promising option, which would prevent him from having to rely exclusively on the Kennedy government, which he viewed with increasing suspicion.

7. The new Franco-German alliance, which was confirmed in 1962 in reciprocal and ostentatiously staged state visits, was therefore above all an expression of strategic calculations and considerations of power politics, on both sides. It did in addition contain a historically significant element of reconciliation between former 'hereditary enemies', who had fought three wars in the previous ninety years. It was also perceived in this way by the West German population, which cheered the French President on his September 1962 visit to Aachen. De Gaulle repeatedly interpreted the Franco-German 'Élysée Treaty', signed shortly afterwards, as being directed primarily against the USA, Great Britain and the continuation of European integration. In order to counter this, but against Adenauer's wishes, the Bundestag added a preamble to the treaty confirming both close ties with the USA and NATO and Germany's determination to move towards deeper European integration, as well as the admission of Britain to the European Economic Community.[5]

The question of whether West Germany should be associated primarily with France or the USA caused serious division within the CDU for several years. At the beginning of the 1960s, politicians in the Federal Republic whose aim was to develop Germany as a great power did not regard a close association with the USA as an acceptable objective, since it involved the exclusion of Germany from access to nuclear weapons. With de Gaulle, on the other hand, access to nuclear weapons appeared at least indirectly attainable, given his conception of a more independent Europe organised around a Paris–Bonn axis. In that case, a more independent power policy was possible, especially as the General's authoritarian style of government offered an alternative model to the consensual liberalism of American mass democracy, which many Christian Democratic politicians continued to view with extreme scepticism. The 'Atlanticists', on the other hand, regarded an attempt by West Germany to pursue an independent great power policy without leaning closely on the USA as both dangerous and futile. They enjoyed a clear majority in the party, and in any case the controversy quickly became unimportant as the policy of détente progressed.[6]

8. After the building of the Berlin Wall, the predominant feeling in Bonn was one of helplessness. This applied to the opposition as much as it did to the government. As late as 1959, the SPD's 'Plan for Germany' had envisaged pulling out of the Western military alliance, and it was not until the great Bundestag speech of the parliamentary party's deputy leader, Herbert Wehner, on 30 June 1960, that the Social Democrats gave their full agreement to Western integration and the establishment of the Bundeswehr.[7] The SPD was sharply opposed

to the SED and the GDR. The Communist Party coup of April 1946 which led to the creation of the SED had not been forgotten, nor had the persecution and imprisonment of Social Democrats who opposed unification under the SED in the early 1950s. Nevertheless, it was the SPD which developed new plans for relations between the two Germanies, at first gradually and then much more quickly, under its leader Willy Brandt. One reason for the SPD's change of line was Brandt's position as mayor of Berlin. As a holder of that office, he had directly witnessed the unhappy consequences of the division of the city and the building of the wall and every day he could see the effect of previous policies on the population of the GDR. But Brandt's views were also closer than those of other German politicians to the views of President Kennedy, who had received a hero's welcome from the people of West Berlin when he made a state visit in summer 1963. Just as Kennedy considered that as long as the Soviet Union and its empire existed it was necessary to mitigate the tense confrontation between the two power blocs, which threatened the very existence of the world, so also Brandt and his trusted associate Egon Bahr became convinced that as the division of Germany could neither be prevented nor removed, its consequences could at least be minimised and alleviated.

Bahr's ideas went much further than this, however. He thought that changes and improvements for the population of the GDR could only be achieved if that state were placed on a more stable footing. The building of the wall was not a sign of strength, but of weakness, he thought. And as long as the SED regime's existence was in danger, the harshness of its dictatorship would not diminish. 'The question to be answered', he concluded,

> is whether there is a way of gradually freeing the regime from these admittedly justified concerns to such an extent that it is able to take a more relaxed approach to the border and the wall, because the risk is bearable. That is a policy one could summarise in the formula: 'change through rapprochement'.[8]

Bahr's underlying idea was that an improvement of the situation for the GDR population could only be achieved if the SED regime was no longer under pressure to secure recognition. Only then would it be in a position to pursue a more liberal and open policy.

9. That idea was of course based on the assumption that the SED system would then be efficient enough in the economic sense to allow it to open up, without being faced with another mass exodus of the pre-1961 type. There was also a widespread view among Western social scientists in the early 1960s that, as modern industrial societies developed further, politico-ideological differences between the two systems would become less significant. This was opposed by others who held that the socialist system was no more capable of

raising its economic performance than it was of domestic liberalisation. At the time, this was an open question.[9]

In the mid-sixties, the vast majority of the West German population still opposed the recognition of the GDR. The attitude of the newspapers was beginning to change, however, and it was now possible to hear the views of people who favoured the recognition of the Oder–Neisse boundary and regarded the dream of eventually reunifying the country as unrealistic. The philosopher Karl Jaspers, who was based in Basel, Switzerland, went furthest in this direction. Priority should be given to the freedom of the inhabitants of the GDR, not to reunification, he stressed. The Germans no longer possessed a right to national unity. They had forfeited that in the years before 1945. Jaspers questioned whether

> there is any sense today in what had some sense in the nineteenth century and once signified a great opportunity, which was then gambled away by Hitler's Reich. That now lies in the past. There is no more sense in pushing for German unity. The only thing that has sense now is to desire freedom for our fellow Germans!

Jaspers' theses had a tremendous impact, though most reactions were critical. People strongly objected to the link he made between the Nazi past and the nation-state. From that time onwards, however, the argument about the underlying principles of Bonn's policy towards the German question never died down.[10]

10. Brandt and Bahr followed up their ideas by negotiating with the GDR over humane measures to improve life for its citizens. A series of so-called *Passierscheinabkommen* (travel permit agreements), the first of which was made in 1963, allowed citizens of West Berlin to visit their relatives in the East over Christmas. 1.2 million applications were made: this alone shows the importance of the measure. But it had its price, because every round of negotiation, however many steps were taken to avoid giving the impression that SED rule over the East was accepted, did after all signify a degree of recognition. 'The wall will not be taken down with travel permits', said the new West German Chancellor, Ludwig Erhard. He saw the agreement between West Berlin and the GDR as a kind of 'Trojan horse': 'This is a cunning and deceitful way of smuggling in the theory of three states.'[11] Erhard placed much more faith in improving relations with the Eastern bloc countries while avoiding recognition of the GDR. The new CDU Foreign Minister Gerhard Schröder did in fact succeed in setting up trade missions in several Eastern bloc states without mentioning the GDR. But the Hallstein Doctrine, under which diplomatic relations would be broken off with any state which recognised the GDR, was still upheld, and it was for a

certain period an effective lever for enforcing the Federal Republic's claim to sole representation, thanks to its economic strength.

In the longer term, however, the West German government was susceptible to blackmail over the recognition issue. This was made evident in May 1965, when most of the Arab states reacted to the military support given to Israel by the Federal Republic by threatening to recognise the GDR, and after the Federal Republic had recognised Israel they did in fact break off diplomatic relations. It became increasingly clear that the Federal Republic could not keep up its policy of isolating the Eastern bloc states and the GDR, because this went against the international trend towards détente and the recognition of post-war realities. The Federal Republic's policy towards the East and the German question had become paralysed. Since 1961, it had been unable to make progress in any direction. It could neither secure an opening to the East, nor gain any improvement in the situation of the GDR population. It was unable to halt the trend towards international recognition of the GDR, which was clearly apparent not just in the diplomatic field but in culture and above all in sport. It had nothing to set against the momentum of the policy of détente on the basis of the status quo. But the CDU and the CSU neither wished to make a new beginning, nor were they capable of doing so.

## The Growth of Criticism and the Crisis of the Adenauer Era

In domestic politics too, the Adenauer government's power to convince and its sense of purpose began visibly to decline soon after the electoral victory of 1957. What became obvious for West Germany's foreign policy after the building of the wall applied also within the country: neither the government nor the parties which composed it had any plausible plan for the future of the Federal Republic after the end of the phase of economic reconstruction. The CDU and the CSU were highly fixated on holding onto power, keeping the chancellorship and winning elections. More far-reaching programmatic debates were absent, as was a party structure of a more professional type. The expression 'the chancellor's election machine' was not coined without reason. The Federal Chancellor who during the first ten years had led the republic so decisively and purposefully over the big questions of economic recovery and the choice of partnership with the West was now subject to frequent attacks of uncertainty, and to inconsistencies and mishaps which gradually tarnished his image. He had turned eighty on 5 January 1956, but in April 1959, to general astonishment, he declared his intention to stand for the office of president, no doubt believing that in this way he could establish a presidential regime, similar to de Gaulle's in France, and rely on his close friend the veteran Finance Minister Franz Etzel to conduct day-to-day business as Federal Chancellor. He only withdrew his candidature when it was made clear to him that this would cause considerable constitutional problems and, moreover, that the Union parties in the Bundestag would elect Economics Minister Erhard (whom he regarded as entirely unsuitable) as Federal Chancellor in his place.[12] The old Chancellor's behaviour not only damaged the office of president but caused people to question his understanding of the constitution. From that time forward, calls for his resignation did not cease.

A year later, the Chancellor put forward the proposal to establish a second television broadcasting service in addition to the existing one, founded in 1954 under the title 'Consortium of German Public Broadcasting Stations', whose increasingly critical attitude towards the government had long infuriated him. The new channel was intended to be under state supervision, but Adenauer's initiative met with sharp criticism and was finally rejected by the Federal Constitutional Court. The 'Second German Television' was then set up as a public broadcasting organisation by the federal states, thereby withdrawing it from the direct control of the federal government.

In both cases, the head of government had acted in a legally questionable manner; but these cases also demonstrated that the institutions guaranteeing the separation of powers in the Federal Republic were able to function in disputed cases. The Federal Constitutional Court in particular proved to be a stroke of good fortune for West German democracy. But Adenauer continued his blunders. The public found it incomprehensible that he did not travel to Berlin immediately after the building of the wall but continued his election campaign in the western part of the country, apparently unmoved by the event. He also slandered his challenger, Willy Brandt, by calling him 'Brandt alias Frahm', which was an allusion to the latter's activity as a member of the Norwegian resistance during the Nazi occupation, as well as a sneering reference to his illegitimacy. All this strengthened the impression that the age of Adenauer was coming to an end.

Nevertheless, the CDU–CSU Union won the September 1961 federal elections, though with some loss of votes. Its 45.5 per cent of the vote was almost five per cent down on the 1957 result, while the FDP had made considerable gains, securing a total of 12.8 per cent. The Union had ruled alone for four years. The FDP, having profited from the decline in Adenauer's reputation, was now able to rejoin the government. The SPD raised its share of the vote by 4.4 per cent to 36.2 per cent, but it remained far removed from achieving a majority. The explanation of these results given by contemporary observers was that the Cold War and the Berlin Wall had inclined many people to play safe and not risk a change of government during such a tense period. In addition, the SPD's decision to change its image from that of a 'workers' party' to a 'people's party' at its Bad Godesberg Congress of November 1959 was too recent a development to persuade many Union voters to change sides.

The mixture of a lack of political clarity and an authoritarian understanding of democracy which could already be observed in the Adenauer of earlier years finally culminated in the 'Spiegel affair'. This happened at the height of the Cuba crisis, which explains the nervous and overheated atmosphere of the time. Moreover, the 'Spiegel affair' can only be understood if one bears in mind the persistent criticism of the government's policy over nuclear armaments made by sections of the public since the start of 1958. In this connection, the journal *Der Spiegel*, which was published by Rudolf Augstein, had taken particular aim at Defence Minister Franz-Josef Strauß, because he had tried hard to persuade NATO to give West Germany access to its nuclear weapons arsenal, thereby arousing the impression that he was in favour of a preventive nuclear attack on the Soviet Union. Early in October 1962 *Der Spiegel* reported on deficiencies in the Bundeswehr's conventional defence capacity, which were allegedly a result of the reliance of the Bundeswehr command and Strauß himself on nuclear weapons for purposes of defence. After the publication of this article, which offered detailed information, the Ministry of Defence instigated the arrest of the chief editors of the journal and a search of its editorial offices. For several weeks only skeleton issues of *Der Spiegel* appeared. Adenauer justified these proceedings, telling the Bundestag that there was a 'bottomless pit of treason'. But this did not stop the wave of criticism, and the court proceedings were later discontinued. It soon turned out that Defence Minister Strauß had gone over the head of the Justice Minister (who was a member of the FDP) and had also lied to the Bundestag about his own involvement in the affair. The FDP responded by withdrawing its ministers from the government and ending the coalition. The FDP chair, Erich Mende, said that there could be no new coalition if Strauß were included. Adenauer was by now eighty-seven years old. He formed a fifth government, with the FDP and without Strauß, but a year later, on 15 October 1963, he was obliged to resign from office, in accordance with the coalition agreement, and make way for his successor Erhard, something he had always tried to prevent.[13]

More significant than the coalition crisis, which was soon overcome, was the reaction of the public to the 'Spiegel affair'. The main concern here was not the alleged treason of Augstein and his colleagues but the attack on press freedom. There were demonstrations and rallies by professors and students in many university towns, everywhere there were panel debates on the role of the state and the freedom of the press, and also, amazingly enough, almost all newspaper editors declared their solidarity with *Der Spiegel*.

It was difficult for Adenauer and his circle to understand this development, because it clashed with their traditional view of the relations between the state, the government and society. The Freiburg historian Gerhard Ritter, a conservative nationalist of the old school, leapt to the defence of the Chancellor, and insisted on the primacy of the state over society:

> Has our constant fixation on the horrors of Hitler's dictatorship almost made us so blind to the reality that surrounds us that we would rather tolerate even the crudest misuse of the civil liberties guaranteed in a constitutionally-governed state than some act of clumsiness (or even incorrectness) by our organs of law enforcement?

He was answered by the Bonn political scientist Karl-Dietrich Bracher, who was thirty years younger. Bracher criticised Ritter's arguments as an attempt to justify 'the pernicious German tradition of the authoritarian state at the expense of our democracy' and as 'the hallmark of a state ideology in which the only valid politics proceeds from the top downwards, and in which matters of state security, understood in foreign policy terms, are assigned almost unconditional priority over domestic liberty and the rule of law.'[14] Bracher's position met with broad support in the organs of public opinion, even in conservative newspapers. This was a sign of the change in the relationship between state and society, and the government and the public which had taken place in the preceding years, largely unnoticed by the government or at least left out of account by it.

As so often, it was the writers who were first to record this change. Two years earlier, a small paperback edited by Wolfgang Weyrauch had appeared, entitled 'I live in the Federal Republic', which put it into words. The programme of the book was stated in the preface: 'Prosperity has swept down upon us and almost gobbled us up . . . For the moment, we are eating instead of thinking.' It was the job of writers to 'express criticism, passionate, self-forgetful criticism . . . . It benefits neither the writer nor the state if the writer's view coincides with that of the state, as in the GDR and Spain for example. Without freedom of expression, states petrify, rot, decay and perish.'[15]

The book attracted much attention, for one thing because it critically examined the situation within the Federal Republic without following the well-trodden paths of the Cold War, and for another because what was at stake here was the Federal Republic's understanding of itself as not just a transitory phenomenon but a state and a society which would last for a long time. There was something of a parallel here with the passionate debate over German–German relations. The widespread disdain felt on both the Left and the Right for the Federal Republic as an interim solution installed by the Allies, lacking in national vitality, was now vigorously challenged. 'The German Federal Republic', asserted Kasimir Edschmid,

> has aroused much displeasure in the ten years of its existence and reaped little praise. But it has been hard-working and efficient, if not exactly rich in ideas. On the whole, however, people have done it an injustice. It is not Germany. But for everyone who lives there it is a decent incarnation of Germany. . . . If in 1948 someone had said to one of the million wretches who now ride around in motor cars that he would one day be prosperous and well-established, go on foreign trips with hard German currency in his pocket, be highly esteemed, and altogether a respectable human being (shortly after he had been collecting the cigarette butts of occupation soldiers from the street) he would have gaped in astonishment and treated the author of the prophecy as an imbecile. Now he regards the change as self-explanatory, and thinks it is his own achievement rather than that of the people who run the country.[16]

Weyrauch's collection also contained an article by Hans Werner Richter, the organiser of the writers' association Group 47, in which he compared the advantages and disadvantages of the Federal Republic as presented to him by students interviewed in East Berlin. On the positive side there were 'legal security, freedom of opinion, freedom of employment, prosperity, unhindered travel'. The negatives, on the other hand, were: 'the return of the National Socialists, a tendency towards dictatorship, excessive militarisation and nuclear armaments'.[17]

The notion that the Federal Republic was simply a kind of extended occupation zone, an interim republic waiting for the arrival of national unity, was obviously becoming less plausible. This was also demonstrated by opinion surveys: in 1951, only 2 per cent of the citizens of the Federal Republic thought they were doing better now than at any other time in the century. Ten years later, almost two-thirds were of that opinion. This change of attitude, which originally took place among intellectuals and then spread to broader circles, meant that the West German state was no longer regarded as something introduced and put into operation by external forces but as the affair of the people themselves.[18]

Up to that point, the big domestic debates had centred on decisions about the republic's basic institutions: Western integration, the division of Germany, representative democracy as a form of state, rearmament, the social market economy and the fundamentals of social policy. Now, however, after its citizens had increasingly begun to see the Federal Republic as an independent entity, which would at least last long enough to outlive Adenauer's chancellor-run democracy, matters other than these basic strategic decisions were subjected to critical examination, such as the concept of a democracy fixated on the state, reliance on an outdated code of morality, and the authoritarian tutelage exercised over West German citizens. Moreover, these debates no longer took place on the familiar lines of the founding years but chiefly took the form of a dispute between the state and the intellectuals.

The relationship between the government and the press was a particularly clear example of this. In the 1950s, the Adenauer government had set up what amounted to a system of media direction, in which restrictions were placed on independent reporting. For the journalists, as the media historian Christina von Hodenberg tells us, this tacit contract with the government meant 'approving government policy in its broad lines, directing political reporting to the educated public, tolerating expressions of nationalism and anti-communism, and avoiding the delicate theme of the Nazi past if at all possible.'[19]

The two fundamental aspects of this concept of a journalism without any controlling function were the primacy of the state over society and public opinion and the way access to information provided by the ruling power was conditional on the journalist's good behaviour. After the late 1950s, however, these limitations were increasingly ignored. One of the main reasons for this was a generational change: the journalists who now came onto the editorial boards had not gained their experience by writing for the newspapers of the Nazi state, but had begun their professional lives in the post-war epoch. Moreover, they tended to look towards the Western, and particularly the Anglo-Saxon, media, which acted very successfully as a 'fourth estate' in checking up on their own governments, and this also played a role in the change of atmosphere. During the first decade of the Federal Republic, criticism and conflict were regarded primarily as elements of division and signs of social collapse, and they were rejected because they appeared to signify a return to conditions in the later years of the Weimar Republic. Towards the end of the 1950s, however, a critical approach to the current epoch, or '*Zeitkritik*', became one of the guiding principles of the new journalism. Critical reports on politics and society were broadcast on television in current affairs programmes such as 'Panorama', 'Report' and 'Weltspiegel'. No subject was taboo, and the government was not consulted in advance.

In the social sciences too, interesting changes began to appear at the end of the 1950s. It is true that the universities had remained largely unchanged in structure and personnel after 1945, but in many disciplines scientists had now gained greater access to the state of international research, particularly in the Anglo-Saxon world. Here too, a generational change began to make its appearance. The number of scientists who returned from exile to West Germany after the war was not great, and universities had not taken much interest in them. But, in the years after 1960, the returning emigrants, sometimes dubbed 'remigrants', played an important role in some specialisms and at certain locations and made a considerable impression on intellectual life. Ernst Fraenkel and Richard Löwenthal at the newly founded Free University in West Berlin, or the sociologists Theodor W. Adorno and Max Horkheimer, who returned from exile to re-establish the Institute for Social Research in Frankfurt, were examples of this phenomenon. The social scientists who were gathered together at the Frankfurt Institute examined such themes as the connection between capitalism and fascism and the threat to liberal democracy posed by the rule of the old elites. They distanced themselves equally from the state socialist dictatorships of the East and the new, consumption-oriented saturation of the West Germans, combining the classic lamentations about the mass culture of Western modernity with a Marxist critique of society. In addition to the publications of the two founders of the Frankfurt School, it was the works of Ludwig von Friedeburg and Jürgen Habermas which were of most significance for the emerging neo-leftist intelligentsia. Unlike Fraenkel and Löwenthal, the Frankfurt group were for a long time ambivalent towards the Federal Republic. They were critical or indifferent towards institutionalised democracy as it had developed since 1949, demanding a more far-reaching democratisation which would affect not just the state, but society. Liberal-conservative intellectuals of the younger generation, on the other hand, such as the Münster School around the philosopher Joachim Ritter and political scientists such as Karl-Dietrich Bracher and Wilhelm Hennis, were able to overcome the scornful detachment from democracy and pluralism inherited from their teachers and to develop theories of institutionalised conflict and interest-group influence.[20]

A circle of literary figures had already formed in the immediate post-war years, under the name of 'Group 47'. This increasingly devoted its critical attention to conditions in the Federal Republic. Three important novels appeared in 1959 in which the division of Germany, the Nazi period and its after-effects were examined, and they had a huge impact: Uwe Johnson's *Mutmassungen über Jakob* (Speculations about Jacob), Günter Grass's *Die Blechtrommel* (The Tin Drum), and Heinrich Böll's *Billard um halb zehn* (Billiards at Half-past Nine). 'Group 47', to which almost all German-language writers of distinction belonged, gained more and more attention and importance over the years. For a number of years after 1960, it formed something in the nature of a politico-literary opposition movement in the Federal Republic and it had a tremendous echo.[21]

Two years after Weyrauch's publication, another book appeared which undertook a critical 'stocktaking' of the situation in the Federal Republic. This book represented a broad spectrum of intellectuals of all schools of thought and disciplines, who would come to dominate the critical debate over social questions in West Germany in the years and decades that followed.[22] There were a few members of the older generation, such as Wolfgang Abendroth, Robert Jungk and Alexander Mitscherlich, but the majority of the writers who appeared in this book were in their thirties: Ralf Dahrendorf, Hans Magnus Enzensberger, Hartmut von Hentig, Walter Jens, Joachim Kaiser, Fritz J. Raddatz and Peter Rühmkorf. This again indicated the emergence of a new generation.

The tendency to focus on the nation, or the *Volk*, and to support the strong state, authority and a patriarchal social structure, had been particularly marked among the age group born between the turn of the century and the First World War. This was not just the generation which provided the strongest backing for the Nazi regime, it was also the founding generation of the Federal Republic. It was now confronted with the generation of those born around 1930, who had direct experience of National Socialism but were still young enough when the war ended to be able to choose a new political orientation. Since the early 1960s, they had often become involved at an early age in leadership functions which the prosperous Federal Republic offered in large numbers, and they retained these for decades, sometimes until the end of the twentieth century. It was from their ranks that attacks first emerged around 1960 on the inadequacies of the Federal Republic's democracy and on the continuing prevalence of inherited norms and values. They were also emphatically sober and practical in their approach. They rejected both the political and intellectual inheritance of the Nazi regime and the battle lines of the Cold War conflict, and they had a fundamentally positive but by no means uncritical attitude towards West German democracy.[23]

The West German social model, explained the sociologist Ralf Dahrendorf in his influential books *Gesellschaft und Freiheit* (1961) [Society and Freedom] and *Gesellschaft und Demokratie in Deutschland* (1965) [Society and Democracy in Germany], was characterised by its inability to tolerate conflicts in a pluralist society:

> Anyone who opposes conflict is thereby announcing a crucial objection to representative institutions. But that objection has an effect in all spheres of German society. Many people would rather see the supposed harmony of a grand coalition than the spectacle of contending political parties; there is also a widespread desire (at least among non-participants) to end industrial disputes between employers and employees; similar reactions can be observed in the educational and legal systems, but also in many private organisations. The tradition of deciding all problems in an authoritarian way is perhaps nowhere so clearly marked as in attitudes towards social conflict; here, too, only the first tentative steps towards change are apparent.[24]

The call to extend democracy beyond institutions and into the way human beings live together in society was also a part of this critique. As Jürgen Habermas formulated the point in 1959, 'Democracy can only be fully realised in a society of mature individuals. For this reason, it is not possible under all social circumstances, but it is not associated with any specific ones either. Democracy is rather this free society itself.'[25] The central German issue of the present day, as Dahrendorf formulated it, was not the question of reunification, but the obstacles facing liberal democracy: 'What has to happen to make liberal democracy possible in Germany?', he asked. It had admittedly been possible, unlike after 1918, to create a state with stable and widely accepted democratic institutions, but the society itself continued to be characterised by an aversion to conflict, authoritarian structures and restrictions on individual freedom. Dahrendorf demonstrated this with numerous examples, including the role of justice, family upbringing, school and university education, power relations between men and women and the treatment of minorities.[26]

Educational policy quickly became a central focus of this discussion. Failings in the educational sphere had been denounced since the late 1950s, when the successful launching of the Soviet 'Sputnik' had provoked an agitated debate both in the USA and the Federal Republic over the way they were 'lagging behind' the communist world. This debate now intensified: 'Today we have fallen far behind both the American and the Russian educational systems, in which the proportion of teachers to schoolchildren is twice as large as with us', wrote Hans Werner Richter in 1962. 'This is a greater danger than any direct military or political threat', he added.[27]

This complaint was given extra force by a series of articles by the Heidelberg philosopher Georg Picht, who depicted the educational backwardness of the Federal Republic and its effect on its citizens' prosperity in dramatic words:

> According to comparative educational statistics, the Federal Republic is right at the bottom of the list of European countries, alongside Yugoslavia, Ireland and Portugal. Its young scientists are emigrating in their thousands because they no longer find the job opportunities they need in their fatherland. An even worse scenario is being prepared in the schools: if nothing happens, in a few years school-age children will have to be sent home again because they have neither teachers nor classrooms. We are facing an almost unimaginable educational emergency.

A sharp increase in the number of secondary school graduates was urgently necessary, he said, because this number indicated 'the intellectual potential of a nation, and in the modern world the competitiveness of the economy, the size of the social product and the international standing of a nation are dependent on its intellectual potential.' His conclusion: the economic progress of the Federal Republic will soon come to an end 'if we lack a skilled pool of younger talent, without which no system of production can achieve anything in this technological age. If the educational system lets us down, the survival of the whole society is threatened.'[28]

Educational policy had admittedly been neglected during the first decade of the republic. The German school system traditionally consisted of the eight-year 'Volksschule' ('people's school'), which was attended mainly by working-class children and was later renamed 'Hauptschule' ('main school'). The 'Gymnasium' was the school of the middle-classes and the elites, and only there was it possible to become qualified to attend university. The 'Realschule' stood between the 'Hauptschule' and the 'Gymnasium' and was intended primarily for the children of the lower middle class. In the immediate post-war years, the Western allies attempted without success to reform this three-class system. After their failure, many years elapsed before the traditional German system was re-established and teachers who had been dismissed in 1945 because of their Nazi past were reintegrated into the educational system. Since the hundreds of thousands of refugees from the GDR included a disproportionate number of well-educated young people, educational reform did not seem to be at all urgent.

Not until the beginning of the 1960s did the accumulated deficiencies in the educational sector, as compared with neighbouring countries, become apparent to a wider public. Educational structures had changed as little since the 1920s as had the social disparities they involved. In 1925, expenditure on the educational sector had amounted to 13.9 per cent of the budget, whereas in 1962 it was 9.2 per cent. Between 1956 and 1962, the share of education in the budget remained almost unchanged. In 1952, 79 per cent of thirteen-year-olds attended a *Hauptschule*, 6 per cent a *Realschule* and 13 per cent a *Gymnasium*. Only 5 per cent obtained a School Leaving Certificate (*Abitur*), and at a time when workers constituted almost 50 per cent of employees, only 5 per cent of students came from working-class families. Slightly less than 7 per cent of employees were salaried officials, but a third of the students came from their families. Girls were particularly disadvantaged, as were children who lived in the countryside or attended religious schools. It was often noted at the time that 'the way of life of the conservative peasantry' was 'an obstacle to education'. In 1965, 45 per cent of West German elementary school pupils attended state religious schools. The proportion in Bavaria was 90 per cent, and in North Rhine-Westphalia, roughly 80 per cent.[29]

Whereas the main focus of attention for Picht was the economic impact of the 'educational catastrophe' and West Germany's disturbing backwardness in comparison with other countries, West and East, Dahrendorf's view of educational policy was determined above all by his 'concern for the survival of the structural core of modern liberalism'. Educational policy ought not to serve 'either the needs of the economy or popular demand'. Instead, it should 'lay the groundwork for the freedom of the individual and the society'. Dahrendorf's stipulation that 'education is a civil right' was frequently quoted, and quickly became a contemporary watchword, and as a result, the reform and expansion of the educational system became one of the paramount reform projects of the Sixties.[30]

The speed with which the atmosphere changed indicates that, in this case, long cherished expectations were being fulfilled. As long as social relations were as firmly fixed as they had been in the first ten years of the republic, educational policy aroused little public interest. But when society began to experience dynamic change, and social mobility became possible, or at least imaginable, the educational system became the focus of greater attention because it was capable of either promoting this process or hampering it. In previous decades, the Germans had frequently seen how quickly they could lose their material possessions. Education and training, however, were permanent values and had proved themselves to be reliable guarantees of Germany's recovery. Hence the boom in educational provision which now started was also a response to a great popular need.

At this point, however, both the method and the content of traditional education started to come under fire, whether in relation to school punishments and militaristic sports lessons or the patriotic pomposity of the conventional literary canon or the furious hostility towards modern mass culture of journalists and protectors of youth. One could now read in educational journals that the fear that films or dance music might corrupt young people arose from 'the ideas of the previous century', and that these ideas, far from protecting youth, served the need of the adults for protection.[31] 'Now it really is time to finish with blond and blue-eyed idols of the type of Horst Wessel or Hitler Youth boy Quex. . . . Hiking ideologies, nationalist attitudes and other highly dubious offerings can only meet with a pitying smile from the young people in the street.'[32] The practice of listing 'immoral acts' was also called into question, especially in the area of sexual morality. 'Views of sexuality and birth control have changed fundamentally during this century', wrote the well-known Frankfurt prosecutor, Fritz Bauer.

> Modern industrial society pulls people towards new norms of behaviour, which are very different from the middle-class conception of morality held at the turn of the century. For large sections of the population, there are divergences between the new foundations of sexual morality, which are in dynamic development, and a static legal system, which continues to uphold

> tradition, and this has led to emphatic and repeated demands for a reform of penal legislation in this area.

The areas of sexual morality covered by the criminal law must therefore be radically reduced. 'It is not the job of the criminal law to punish sins; the secular court is not meant to anticipate the Last Judgment. The state's laws must be limited to the protection of basic legal rights.'[33]

The traditional conceptions of the state and society, education, good behaviour and morality had indeed already met with doubts and objections in the early 1950s; but at the end of the decade these were combined together into a global onslaught, because now the shrill warnings issued earlier about the cultural accompaniments of rampant modernity came into contradiction with people's actual experience in West German society, especially as the frequently cited phenomena of degeneration and neglect had failed to appear. Moreover, since the early fifties, political stability, economic prosperity and opportunities for social mobility had heightened acceptance of the political system of the Federal Republic. There was also less anxiety about modern mass society, and people's ability to find their feet in it had in the meantime become so well-developed that individuals had much less need to put on the protective armour of the moral critique of modernity.

This was not a purely German phenomenon, but a development which took place in all the countries of the capitalist West, though with important variations.[34] In the USA, it was already possible to observe in the late 1940s that after some forty years the social and cultural eruptions which followed the industrial transformations of the turn of the century were less in evidence, and that the mode of life corresponding to the new conditions had gradually become firmer and more stable, and this also created new norms of behaviour.[35] In Western Europe, however, and particularly in Germany, this process of stabilisation had been delayed and postponed by the war and the post-war reconstruction period. Only when the political configuration of the Federal Republic had been confirmed by the Paris Treaties and the third Bundestag election, when the phase of economic reconstruction had been largely completed and when it had become clear that mass poverty had been successfully removed by far-reaching improvements in social benefits, did the guiding principles of the turn of the century lose their significance as factors of compensation and stabilisation.

Needless to say, by no means everyone agreed with the intellectual critics whose voices could now be heard everywhere. There was also vagueness for a long time about what other conceptions could replace the ones hallowed by tradition. People lacked experience of social participation, and democratic procedures, and they had not experienced liberal methods of education or liberal sexual morality. For years, traditional notions and their opposite confronted each other in constant conflict. Thus, the 1960s can be seen as a transitional phase. New elements of social order and cultural practice which were capable of achieving consensus only came into existence after lengthy controversies.

## Coming to Terms with the Past

The Nazi past was the central issue in the *Zeitkritik* of the first half of the 1960s. After ten years of relative quiescence, this emerged as the main challenge to the state and society and it was regarded both within the country and abroad as the most important criterion of the seriousness and credibility of West Germany's democratic development.

This process was set in motion by a case in which it was revealed that a veil had previously been drawn over the past. Since the mid-1950s, a number of former Gestapo officials, who had avoided the death penalty or long terms of imprisonment in the immediate post-war years, had demanded their reinstatement in the state bureaucracy under the provisions of Article 131 of the Basic Law. Their self-confidence was demonstrated by the fact that they made no secret of their activities during the war. The former Police Chief of Memel was among this number. He attempted to gain his reinstatement by starting a lawsuit against the government and in the course of these proceedings he gave information on oath about his activities in the Tilsit *Einsatzkommando* (Task Force Command) of *Einsatzgruppe A*, which had shot hundreds, and later thousands, of Jews in Lithuania immediately after the start of the war against the Soviet Union. This was the starting point for the first big trial of members of the *Einsatzgruppen* in front of a West German court, which was run by an energetic and committed prosecutor in the city of Ulm. It ended with the conviction of the former police chief, who was condemned to serve twelve years in jail.[36]

This trial was thoroughly reported in the press, but the tone of the reports had altered perceptibly. Five years earlier, the implementation of the last of the Nuremberg death sentences on *Einsatzgruppe* commanders had still aroused tremendous indignation in West German public opinion. Now, in contrast, reports of the mass murders committed by police and SS units gave rise to astonishment and disgust. The same illustrated magazines which in the early fifties had criticised the Allied trials of Nazis as an unjustified persecution of innocent German soldiers now printed in large format indignant articles about the mass murderers of Tilsit. Evidently, a certain change of attitude towards the Nazi past had occurred in the meantime. The National Socialist historical background of this West-facing society which already saw itself as fairly stable now looked scandalous, especially when it was embodied in individuals such as the SS and police officers put on trial in Ulm. West German society, which imagined that it was already far removed from the Nazi past, now found it to be an essential part of its identity to distance itself from it.

The first reaction to the scandal was the establishment in Ludwigsburg of the 'Central Office of Judicial Administration' (ZStL), where systematic investigations of Nazi crimes were conducted by experienced state prosecutors. On the other hand, however, the debate over the Ulm trial was also accompanied by a wave of anti-Semitic actions, in which Jewish cemeteries were desecrated and synagogues were daubed with anti-Jewish slogans. This trend reached a climax at the turn of the year 1959–60 in Cologne, where the city's synagogue was defaced. It turned out that these acts of vandalism had been committed by young supporters of the radical right-wing German Reich Party. In the next few weeks almost 500 copy-cat incidents were reported. Evidently, National Socialism did not lie so far in the past as the reactions to the Ulm trial suggested.[37]

This combination of phenomena—public condemnation of Nazi crimes in the context of the trials of National Socialists on the one hand, and the activities of neo-Nazis on the other—led in subsequent months and years to an intense and momentous public debate over 'coming to terms with the past' (*Bewältigung der Vergangenheit*) as it was often described. One element which was involved in this debate was the judicial system. What had been described in the fifties as the patriotic duty of German judges and prosecutors, namely to bring to an end the prosecution of German war criminals imposed on them by the Allies, now turned into a reproach. At the end of 1959, an exhibition was shown in Karlsruhe by students under the title 'Un-atoned Nazi justice'. It met with a big response, and set off a debate on the question of social continuity in the bureaucracy and the judicial system. Wolfgang Staudte's film 'Roses for the Prosecutor' was also being shown in cinemas at this time. The film dramatised the same theme as the Karlsruhe exhibition in a spectacular fashion and it had a big public impact. Simultaneously, the GDR authorities published lists of judges and prosecutors who had been active during the Nazi period and were able to continue their careers undisturbed in the Federal Republic, although these lists, like the 'Brown Books' published later, were quickly dismissed in the Federal Republic as East German propaganda and therefore had a counter-productive effect. Even so, the Nazi past of top West German politicians was now also the subject of increasing criticism, above all the past history of the State Secretary in the Chancellor's Office, Hans Globke and of federal ministers Schröder and Oberländer.

The debate received a further boost from the spectacular arrest of Adolf Eichmann in Argentina and his trial in Jerusalem in 1961, which added an extra dimension to the subject of the Nazi past. Until then, it was the military events and Germany's occupation policy which were best remembered in the rest of the world and particularly among Germany's former military opponents. Now the mass crimes of the Germans against the Jews became the centre of attention. They soon had a more powerful impact than the Blitzkrieg or Stalingrad in determining the way the world pictured the Germans. From that point onwards, how the West Germans confronted the murder of the Jews was more important to their reputation in the world than their past military prowess or their present economic efficiency. (How the East Germans dealt with the past was hardly relevant here, as they lived in a state where there was no freedom of expression.)

The Eichmann trial also attracted considerable attention in the Federal Republic: by 1962 90 per cent of West Germans had heard of it, and two-thirds of them considered it right for Eichmann to be punished. A fourteen-part documentary series on 'The Third Reich' was shown on television between October 1960 and May 1961. It was seen by 60 per cent of the adult population and it was repeated two years later. The West Germans seemed to be catching up with what for years had been neglected, or 'repressed' (to use a word which now came into common use).[38]

The schools played an important part here. Opinion surveys confirmed that young people's knowledge of the Nazi epoch was extremely sketchy, and the spate of swastika-daubing that was being committed overwhelmingly by young people reinforced the concern that there was potential here for a new right-wing radicalism. The 'German Committee for the Training and Education System' declared immediately after the anti-Semitic actions in Cologne that these incidents were connected

> with other symptoms of a certain discontent with democracy and politics in general, with indications of a revived anti-democratic attitude, or a new form of this, but also with the fact that democracy, however self-evident it appears to be today, does not for broad sections of the population possess the strength and certainty of a well-tried conviction founded on experience.[39]

These comments expressed a widespread feeling that rapid action was necessary. One reaction to this was the establishment of the 'Federal Centre for Political Education' in 1963. This was the successor to the 'Federal Centre for Homeland Service' which had been founded in 1952. Its object was to spread knowledge about the Third Reich and the functioning of democracy in both an academic and an extra-academic context. The appropriate instructional guidelines had already been decided by the Conference of Education Ministers held the previous year. There was to be a more intensive treatment of National Socialism in the schools, but under the rubric of 'Totalitarianism', to enable the themes of National Socialism and Stalinism to be treated side by side, with the main focus on the current problem of communist rule in the 'Eastern zone' and Eastern Europe. But this shift of concentration from the Nazi state to the GDR proved less effective than expected. The pupils were mainly interested in the Nazi period, as it was the historical background to their own life, and this interest grew progressively. The teachers on the other hand were often hostile to this approach, so that for many years the educational treatment of the Nazi period was a subject of fierce debate.

The Frankfurt Auschwitz trial, which was prepared by Fritz Bauer, began in December 1963. Since the foundation of the Ludwigsburg Central Office of Judicial Administration the prosecution had opened hundreds, which later became thousands, of preliminary investigations into Nazi perpetrators. Relatively few cases actually came to trial, however. The Frankfurt trial was the first time the systematic murder of millions of Jews had been put before a German court. As a result, the German and international public gradually obtained a more detailed and above all a more accurate picture of the mass crimes than they had been given in the previous fifteen years. Most of the Nazi trials that took place were concerned predominantly with the concentration camp personnel. It proved much more difficult to bring to trial those who were responsible for the policy of extermination, in other words, members of the top leadership of the RSHA, the Gestapo and the German occupation authorities.[40]

At the same period, and in part in connection with the big Nazi trials, important historical studies now appeared on the Nazi regime and the mass crimes committed during the war. The expert reports made by historians to the Auschwitz trial about the persecution and murder of the European Jews, the concentration camp system, the SS and the police were printed in large editions and for decades they defined the state of knowledge about Nazi extermination policy. Whereas previously it had been isolated individuals, most of them former victims of persecution such as Léon Poliakov, Joseph Wulf and Hans-Günther Adler, who had made the scholarly study of Nazi crimes their mission, now academic historians began to conduct more intensive research into the Nazi period, particularly in the institutes for contemporary history located in Munich and Hamburg.[41]

The debate over the Nazi epoch also sparked off discussions over the conditions from which Nazism emerged. The debate over the theses of the Hamburg historian Fritz Fischer was particularly significant. In the book he published in 1961 under the title *Der Griff nach der Weltmacht* (The Grab for World Power) he emphasised the guilt of the German Empire for the outbreak of the First World War. This was a very different view from the one held at that time by the majority of West German historians. Germany, he said, had planned and desired the war, with the aim of annexing vast amounts of territory. Fischer's views soon met with opposition, and a lengthy controversy developed out of the issue. Here too, it was Gerhard Ritter who voiced the most emphatic disagreement. He stressed the defensive posture of the German side, highlighted the isolation and encirclement of the Reich and sharply rejected Fischer's thesis that Germany had provoked the war. Some politicians, including the Chancellor, Ludwig Erhard and the president of the Bundestag, Eugen Gerstenmaier, also stated that they disagreed with Fischer.

Fischer's line of argument was especially shocking for many older historians because his thesis that Germany was mainly responsible for the First World War put in doubt a central element of the national self-image, according to which the Germans had been driven into the hands of Hitler by the war imposed upon them in 1914 and by the subsequent Treaty of Versailles. But now the war of 1914–18 looked like the first German attempt to achieve domination over Europe, followed in 1939 by a second one. Since the publication of Fischer's book also coincided with the trial of Eichmann in Jerusalem, the debate over swastika daubings and the first West German trials of Nazis, the Fischer controversy momentarily took on the character of a settlement of accounts with German history as a whole, especially as GDR historiography also portrayed the German Empire as an imperialist power and a dictatorship.

It is clear, in retrospect, that the Fischer controversy contributed to extricate the German picture of history from its narrow nationalist perspective. The research which followed into the question of war guilt confirmed many of Fischer's theses, though the picture he had drawn was generally criticised as being too one-sided. But, as Konrad Jarausch has commented, the significance of the debate lay less in the concrete theme of the revelation of German war guilt than in 'the universal establishment of national self-criticism as the central task of contemporary history in general'.[42]

The argument over how to 'come to terms with the past' reached a climax with the debate on the length of the statutory limitation period for Nazi crimes. The crime of manslaughter became statute-barred after fifteen years. According to current legal opinion, the majority of Nazi crimes fell under this category. Thus, from 8 May 1960, fifteen years after the end of the war, these crimes could no longer be prosecuted. But, after the wave of anti-Semitism at the beginning of 1960 and the revelation of other scandals affecting individuals, the SPD parliamentary group in the Bundestag altered its previously highly defensive line on dealing with the past and put forward a motion to extend the limitation period by four years, so as to allow the recently founded Ludwigsburg Central Office to continue, and as was thought, conclude, its investigations. This motion was rejected by the Bundestag, above all because the Ministry of Justice opposed it, thereby determining the line the government would take on this question. The man in charge of dealing with the issue was the director of the Criminal Law Division of the Federal Ministry of Justice, Undersecretary Dr. Eduard Dreher, who was of course also acting in his own interest, as the death sentences he had sought during the war as a state prosecutor in the Special Court at Innsbruck themselves fell under the statute of limitations.[43]

At the time, the wider public was largely unaware of this issue. Three years later, in 1965, when the limitation period for murder was about to expire in its turn, things were very different. Numerous Jewish organisations and many politicians in other Western countries had already warned against ending prosecutions for Nazi murders, which had after all only just started. The West German government insisted rigidly on the retention of the statutory period of limitation and wanted to exclude the issue from any parliamentary discussions. They were prevented from doing this, however, by the SPD but also in particular by the Berlin CDU representative Ernst Benda, who came out against the majority opinion of his party and became the most important advocate of extending the limitation period for the crime of murder. The government's plan to prevent an extension of this period with the argument that it was against the constitution now met with increasing opposition. There were vehement protests in a number of Western countries against the government's attitude, and there was a danger that West Germany's relations with Israel and the USA would be seriously damaged as a result. A campaign developed in the Federal Republic and in Austria against the statutory limitation period, and it was supported by numerous well-known personalities, stretching from the writers Uwe Johnson and Hans Werner Richter, to the publishers Ernst Klett and Heinz Ullstein, the professors Iring Fetscher and Walter Jens and the theologians Martin Niemöller and Joseph Ratzinger. Most newspapers also supported the abolition of a statutory limitation period for murder.

The majority of the West German population, on the other hand, opposed any extension of the limitation period, and also any further criminal prosecution of Nazi perpetrators, and many politicians from the governing parties relied on this when they spoke out strongly against the abolition of statutory limitation. 'We cannot allow ourselves to be put under pressure by Israel on a question which is for us a matter of law', declared the FDP Minister of Justice Ewald Bucher categorically. 'We must shoulder the burden of living alongside a few murderers if necessary.' The CSU chair Franz-Josef Strauß went further, declaring that to extend the period of limitation would mean 'to undermine humanity's sense of right and wrong and to falsify history, because it would appear to demonstrate that the Germans alone had committed war crimes'.[44]

It was however Ernst Benda's speech which left the greatest impression in the Bundestag debate. The point about the extension of the period of limitation, he said, was that 'a people's sense of justice would be corrupted in an intolerable fashion if murders have to remain un-atoned, even though atonement is possible.' In a state 'in which someone can get into jail for a childish prank and people who have committed murders can walk around unpunished one has to ask what sense of justice is operating here?' A compromise was finally reached on the issue. An extension for four years was voted, on the assumption that by the end of that time most of the trials would have been completed. This was wrong, as could easily have been predicted.[45]

Nevertheless, the responsible authorities in the Ministry of Justice were able to protect the officials who served in the ministries of Hitler's Reich and in the RSHA from further prosecution by means of a legal trick orchestrated by Dreher. It was laid down in one unnoticed paragraph of the legislation that if a person was an accessory to murder, but could not be proved to have acted 'out of base motives', they should not be punished under the murder regulations but under the attempted murder regulations. With this, the expiry period for prosecution as an accessory to murder automatically changed to fifteen years, hence almost all proceedings against leading personnel of the Gestapo, the SD and the RSHA were brought to an end. Dreher was therefore able to achieve his objective, not by political campaigns for a general amnesty or for the acknowledgement of the statute of limitations, but by a procedural trick.[46]

## The Erhard Government Comes to a Quick End

The government's attempts to rule the Federal Republic in the manner of previous years were not very impressive when faced with the dynamic growth of social criticism and political engagement. The new Chancellor, Ludwig Erhard, did admittedly attempt in his government declaration to respond to demands for a new departure, when he said that they were now on the point of 'leaving behind the post-war epoch'. But his views about the organisation of the future had a rather dated look: 'We run the risk that the productive vigour of our society will increasingly be replaced by the enjoyment of what has been achieved. The fundamental attitude of wide swathes of the population is often determined exclusively by materialism. That is what characterises the present situation.' The main requirement now, he said, was 'to dissuade young people from taking the false path of just earning money and wanting to be provided for.' Anti-consumerist admonitions of this kind sounded surprising, coming from the author of the book *Prosperity through Competition*. Chancellor Erhard's ire was directed particularly towards industrial associations and special interest organisations. He complained that 'the conflict of interests cannot give rise to an organic whole as long as the participants consciously or unconsciously pay homage to the maxim that only what is of advantage to them is right.' What was required instead was that 'the organisations should feel a sense of responsibility towards the whole of society.'[47] There was nothing wrong with that statement, certainly, but it did not indicate either a self-confident faith in pluralist social mechanisms, or, as the aged Adenauer promptly commented, a commitment to deep-rooted Christian principles.

The same could be said of the slogan of the 'joined-up society' which was used in the election campaign of 1965. West German society, said Erhard, had ceased to be a 'class society' and become an 'achievement society'. This society too was 'certainly not free of conflicts of interest. But these are no longer factors in the disintegration of social unity. They act rather as driving forces towards a permanent compromise of interests from the point of view of the general welfare.'[48] If Erhard wanted to tame the social dynamic of capitalism and was unable to offer the alternative either of Christian and Western principles or, like the SPD, of solidarity, all that remained was this appeal to a vague idea of the community and the hope that disagreements between interest groups would not lead to the collapse of society but to a compromise in the interests of the whole. The vision of society offered by Erhard and his advisers was entirely lacking in creativity because it did not go beyond the usual appeal to people to protect themselves from the dangers of modern society.

The degree to which the criticisms of the intellectuals had jarred the nerves of the political rulers of the country was shown by Erhard's spontaneous reaction to a newspaper article in which the playwright Rolf Hochhuth had assailed the West German capitalist system. If the writers are now lining up in support of the social politicians and social critics, he said, we must call them by their proper names: 'namely philistines and bunglers, who utter judgments about things of which they understand nothing'. He went on to add: 'In that case we are no longer dealing with a writer, but a little pipsqueak.' Later on, he even complained about 'a certain intellectualism which flips over into stupidity', concluding with a comment on 'phenomena of degeneration' in modern art.[49]

This was the low point of the relationship between the government and the intellectuals, who were of course highly indignant over Erhard's sallies. The head of government, it seemed, did not have a sustainable plan to deal with the multiplicity of new tasks which had arisen after the end of the reconstruction period and he reacted in a thin-skinned way to criticism. He was also confronted with increasing opposition within his own party. Conflicts within the Union parties between 'Atlanticists' and 'Gaullists' were combined here with long-lasting personal quarrels, and all this was viewed as demonstrating the Chancellor's inadequate capacity for leadership, although Erhard did live up to his reputation as an electoral steamroller in the 1965 Bundestag elections. The CDU–CSU Union had a tremendous victory on this occasion: with 47.6 per cent of the vote, it achieved its second best result, only exceeded in 1957, and it had improved by 2 percentage points since 1961. The FDP, with 9.6 per cent, had returned to its average level during the 1950s, while the SPD again failed to get into government, despite winning 39.3 per cent, the best election result in its history (although opinion surveys had previously rated it at 47 per cent). The SPD did not seem able to win an election by itself, not even with Willy Brandt as its candidate for Chancellor.

The main reason for the Union's clear victory was doubtless the economic situation, which continued to be extraordinarily good, with growth rates of 6.6 and 5.2 per cent in 1964 and 1965 and only 147,000 unemployed (0.7 per cent) as against 700,000 unfilled vacancies. But the incessant economic growth did now seem to be gradually coming to an end. The first signs of an economic downturn had already made their appearance in 1963. Some of the problems were structural: the influx of skilled young workers from the GDR had been abruptly interrupted by the building of the wall, the birth rate had declined and training periods had become longer. In addition, the mining industry had entered into a severe crisis because of the move to replace coal with oil as the economy's main energy source. Many collieries were closed, and protesting mineworkers carried 'black flags on the Ruhr' in a movement which enjoyed a powerful upsurge when an economic recession started in 1966. The first big metalworkers' strike, in 1963, demonstrated the increasing intensity of wage conflicts. Conjunctural developments now intervened to reinforce the structural factors in the crisis: the high export surpluses were not effectively counterbalanced by the revaluation of the Deutschmark, and this inevitably had the result of raising prices. In addition, economic activity in the USA began to weaken, and this quickly had an impact on the Federal Republic as well. West German rates of growth in 1962 and 1963 were only 2.6 per cent and 2.3 per cent respectively. In view of the level of unemployment, which was almost too low to be measured, trends of this kind could essentially be ignored. But, in the Federal Republic, where it was economic development that had first led the new state to gain political acceptance among the population, and where the memory of the role of the world economic crisis in destroying the Weimar Republic was still very fresh, even minor indications of an economic downturn were sufficient to cause concern and uneasiness.

In 1963, the federal government set up an Economic Policy Council, which had the task of investigating how the four paramount economic goals—price stability, a high level of employment, external economic equilibrium and economic growth—could be achieved at the same time. Erhard regarded price stability as the most important objective, and he viewed excessive tariff increases as the main reason for price rises. The experts on the Economic Policy Council, on the other hand, pointed to the big increases in public expenditure. Between 1961 and 1965 the federal government's expenditure rose by 55 per cent, but its income only rose by 49 per cent, and expenditure on consumption by private households rose by 47 per cent. This rise in expenditure was mainly a result of lavish 'election gifts', including tax cuts just before parliamentary elections. A reduction in government expenditure was now necessary, and the Erhard government did undertake to do this, but only by shifting the burden to future generations through increasing the deficit from 1.3 billion DM in 1966 to a proposed 8 billion DM in 1969. Now two different positions emerged in the federal government as to how the approaching crisis should be confronted. Some Union politicians, in particular Franz-Josef Strauß, who now put himself forward as an economic expert, agreed with the SPD in considering inadequate economic growth as the main problem, and he demanded an active financial policy, which would be integrated into a package of measures covering the whole economy. Erhard was opposed to moves of this kind towards economic planning. For him, the great danger was inflation, and he pressed the Federal Bank not to take any counter-cyclical measures. If 'the Federal Bank were to relax the credit squeeze, thereby supposedly lightening the burden on the economy' this would accelerate the inflation and throw Germany 'into almost incalculable chaos'. These fears were mainly rooted in the traumatic experiences Germans had suffered in 1923 and 1948, when their monetary assets were taken from them twice in the course of twenty-five years by the destruction of their value.[50]

There was also a foreign policy problem involved here. The US government, which was under severe economic pressure as a result of the Vietnam War, had called on West Germany to pay a sum of 3 billion US dollars in compensation for the foreign currency losses caused by the presence of American troops. The West Germans were determined to avoid the withdrawal of American troops from Germany and Europe which would have resulted from a failure to pay. The USA stuck to its position that the Europeans, and especially the Germans, must pay for their own security. Erhard did not succeed either in postponing or extending the terms of these payments, and this was interpreted in the Union as a further proof of the Chancellor's lack of leadership. He accordingly came under even greater pressure. In autumn 1966, when the budget for the next year was under discussion, the government proposed to fill the gap between income and expenditure with tax increases. The FDP reacted by withdrawing from the coalition. With that, Erhard's fate was sealed.

On the whole, Erhard's period of office was transitional between the era of Adenauer and the era of reform. Under him, the Union had repeatedly won elections, and won them well, but it did not have a convincing answer in any of the important fields of policy to the questions posed increasingly urgently since the end of the fifties. On the German question, there seemed to be no way out of the impasse created by West Germany's insistence on exclusive representation and future reunification. In foreign policy, there was no dispute about integration into the West, but the Union was paralysed by dissension over whether the Federal Republic's primary focus should be the USA or France. In domestic policy, the Union was unable to offer a perspective for the dynamically changing society of the 1950s and the 1960s, and in economic policy the first crisis since 1949 appeared to be on the horizon. The economic problems did not in fact turn out to be a real threat. They amounted to a cyclical fluctuation rather than a depression. But this was not known in advance, and the anxieties felt by the population and the politicians about the economy were much more deep-seated than the problems themselves. Would the political system of the Federal Republic survive such a strain? Would radically anti-democratic movements again come to the surface? And were the political institutions of the republic stable enough to bear these burdens? A more decisive intervention by the state in the economy and in society seemed to be necessary, as well as a scientifically based policy plan and a governmental alliance which would be strong enough to cope with the challenges. The result was the emergence of the Grand Coalition.

# 15
# Germany around 1965

## Between Two Eras

### Two Societies

1965 was a year of transition. While it marked the zenith of industrial society in West Germany, there were also indications of its impending decline. In the period between 1965 and 1970, roughly 48 per cent of employees in the Federal Republic worked in industry and handicrafts; more than ever before or after those dates. Over the same period, however, there was a significant increase in the proportion who worked in the service sector. This rose from 41 per cent in 1965 to 47 per cent ten years later. By that time, the highly dominant role of industry in West Germany was already an unusual feature internationally, because in other industrialised countries the trend towards services set in earlier. In Great Britain, 47 per cent of GNP was generated by the producer industries in 1960, and only 44 per cent in 1970. The corresponding figures for the USA were still lower, at 38 per cent and 34 per cent, whereas in West Germany they were 54.4 per cent and 53.5 per cent respectively. The particularly large share of industry in the Federal Republic's economy was a result, on the one hand, of the great need to recover from the damage inflicted by war, and on the other hand of the tremendous export successes of West German firms, particularly in the chemical and mechanical engineering sectors but also in electronics and motor manufacturing.

This bias towards industry was reflected in 1965 in the large part played by unskilled and physically strenuous labour, the relatively small number of female employees and the important role of the trade unions, which reached their highest membership figures in the classical industrial sectors. On the other hand, the expansion of the service sector was already beginning, and this involved a rapid increase in office staff and in the number of female employees. More training was required in this sector, and physical labour was of less importance. In the mid-sixties, social and political conditions in West Germany were characterised by this combination of contradictory elements.[1]

The Federal Republic was also a particularly youthful society in 1965. The number of births always exceeded a million a year between 1961 and 1967. It declined after that. In 1978, only half a million babies were born. Between 1960 and 1975, almost a third of the population was less than twenty years old, but after 1975, the proportion fell continuously, so that by 2011 it was one fifth. At the same time, however, opportunities for social mobility improved. Whereas, in 1955, 70 per cent of sons remained in the same social stratum as their father, by 1969, this only applied to 56 per cent, and the proportion continued to fall. Over the same period, the number of jobs available for office staff increased by 2.5 million.

In the mid-sixties, the traditional model of the family held sway almost exclusively. It faced almost no competition. Between 1960 and 1965, an annual average of 514,000 marriages took place, and the divorce rate was only one per cent. Ten years later, the stability of family structure had already undergone some loosening: between 1970 and 1975, the number of marriages fell to an average of 400,000 a year, and ten years after that to 360,000, while the number of divorces more than doubled.

Less than half of all women were in gainful employment in the mid-sixties, and less than a third of married women had jobs. But, by then, it was already noticeable that things were moving in a different direction, a trend which began to dominate in later years and decades. This only happened slowly, however: by 1970, the number of married women in employment had only risen from 30 to 35 per cent. But the number of female office staff increased markedly: in 1960 roughly 30 per cent of officials and office workers were female, while ten years later the proportion was almost 40 per cent. Women's incomes also started to rise, although in 1965 women in industry doing the same job as a man still earned a third less than their male counterparts. This ratio gradually began to improve in subsequent years. But, even forty years later, full equality had still not been achieved.

More than two-thirds of married women remained at home and were responsible for running the household and bringing up children. This fitted in well with the emphatic recommendations of the conservative parties and the churches, bodies which occasionally even called for the imposition of a legal ban on the employment of married women with children. Despite this, the number of married women who went to work rose continuously, particularly among office employees and officials.

The beginnings of a change in people's relationship with religion and church institutions were also becoming apparent. In the mid-sixties, church membership reached its highest level among West Germans since the post-war era, but after that it declined dramatically. In 1965, more than half of Catholics regularly attended Sunday services; by 1973, this proportion had declined to a third, and by 1979 to a quarter. Among Protestants, the number of churchgoers fell from 15 per cent in 1963 to 7.5 per cent in 1973. The number of people ceasing to be members of their churches also increased from the late 1960s onwards: among Protestants, slightly under 40,000 people left the Church in 1965, but five years later this number was five times as high, while among Catholics it grew from 22,000 to 70,000.

Here too, therefore, the situation in the mid-sixties was characterised by the simultaneous operation of two tendencies: the traditional mode of life, involving marriage, children, mothers remaining at home, and church attendance, continued to be dominant. During and just after the war, many of these fixed points of reference had been undermined, but after the mid-fifties they recovered their stability and even became somewhat more prevalent. But a trend in the opposite direction was already perceptible and, after the mid-sixties, it quickly asserted itself: religious ties were cut, fewer, and later, marriages were contracted, women had fewer children, and an increasing number of mothers went to work.

Similar trends could be observed in the educational sphere. In 1960, almost two-thirds of young people, or 59.3 per cent, attended a *Volksschule*. A third continued their education: 12.5 per cent went on to a *Realschule* and 23.9 per cent to a *Gymnasium*. Only 6.1 per cent of the annual intake took an examination for the School Leaving Certificate (*Abitur*). Ten years later, the proportion of pupils attending a *Volksschule* (which was now called a *Hauptschule*) had fallen to 47.6 per cent, but the proportion of *Realschule* pupils had risen to 17.7 per cent and of *Gymnasium* attendees to 27.7 per cent. People's school careers therefore also presented a picture of a traditionally oriented society in which there were already signs of far-reaching change. The number of students in *Realschule* and *Gymnasium* was clearly increasing. After the 1970s, this process became still more rapid and, as early as 1985, the majority of thirteen-year-olds attended a *Gymnasium*.[2]

This had a dramatic impact on the relative levels of education reached by each generation. In 1965, roughly seven or eight times as many adults, in other words, the generations born between 1900 and 1940, had attended a *Volksschule* as had attended a *Gymnasium*. Among young people, those born between 1948 and 1953, the proportion was roughly two to one, while in the age groups born between 1953 and 1974 the balance was already even. Never before had differences in the level of education between the older and the younger generation been so great as in the 1960s and 1970s.

In 1965, therefore, one can, with some exaggeration, draw a general picture in which West German society is analysed in terms of two ideal types, two groups with very different social and cultural orientations. One is an older, working-class group mainly active in the industrial sector, with a low level of education and traditional attitudes as regards the family, marriage, the role of women, and the importance of religion and the Church. Alongside this group there is another one, numerically smaller but constantly growing: younger, better educated, tending more towards office employment in the service sector, and much less traditional in attitudes towards the family, marriage, the role of women and religion. Needless to say, there were also many intermediate cases. Indeed, workers without any church affiliation or officials with extremely conservative characteristics could frequently be encountered. But both orientations, the old and the new, were clearly distinguishable as models of lifestyle and social position and they permeated the social structure as well as cultural attitudes and political alignments.

These two modes of life collided with each other in the mid-1960s in West Germany: one had not yet lost its hold, but the other had already made considerable inroads. In view of the differences between them, tensions and conflicts were to be expected. Indeed, this was well-nigh unavoidable, especially given the way social, generational and cultural differences were intertwined.

## Social Mobility and the Formation of an Underclass

We have already seen that because of the high rate of growth which continued to distinguish the West German economy in the 1960s, the above-mentioned processes of social transformation were accompanied by excellent opportunities for social advancement and a continuing rise in incomes. The monthly net household income of workers and office employees rose by 31 per cent between 1960 and 1965 and by 47 per cent between 1965 and 1970. The real hourly wages of industrial workers rose by 37 per cent and 28 per cent respectively during the two periods.[3]

The trend of apparently everlasting economic growth had now continued for fifteen years and it had produced a far-reaching change in the self-perception of the Federal Republic's wage earners. In a survey made in 1961, 58 per cent of West Germans had described themselves as 'lower class', but by 1972 this had fallen to 38 per cent. The old working-class movement's picture of a divided society, in which the situation of the workers had been seen as immutable, began to disintegrate and was gradually replaced—again, this happened more among the young than among the old—by an optimistic confidence which drew strength from their own personal abilities, and a conviction that they had their fate in their own hands. But the real distribution of income told a different story, and increasingly so: the share of the total national income received by people employed by others fell from 64 per cent in 1950 to 58 per cent in 1960 and 1970. This was a clear indication of rising social inequality. But, since the real income of each individual household continued to rise, the issue did not become socially explosive.

The processes described here did, however, reveal a problem which soon played a significant part in contemporary debates: because the number of people who made the social ascent from worker to office employee was constantly increasing, and the number of jobs for unskilled industrial workers did not decline, owing to the enormous requirements of the industrial sector, there was already a shortage of labour by the end of the 1950s, particularly unskilled labour. The flow of refugees from the GDR ceased after the building of the Berlin Wall, and the labour shortage began to assume alarming dimensions, because it was worsened by a number of additional factors: the much smaller birth cohorts from the wartime years now entered the labour market; improved pensions resulted in earlier retirement; the average working week fell from 44.4 hours (in 1960) to 41.4 (in 1967); and training periods increased in length.[4] The federal government had already decided in principle by the mid-fifties to fill these gaps in the labour force by bringing in foreign workers. Erhard, as Minister of Economics at the time, said that in the light of economic and technological developments, the German workers must be given more intensive training so as to become the specialists so urgently needed, but, 'in order to provide this training, and if this economic boom continues, we must of course allow the more basic kinds of work in Germany to be done by a foreign labour force.'[5]

Large-scale recruitment of foreign workers therefore began after 1961, above all from countries of Southern Europe, where there was a big labour surplus (Italy, Spain, Portugal, Greece, and Yugoslavia), followed later by Turkey. As far as Europe as a whole was concerned, this was nothing new: by 1970, 2.6 million foreigners lived in France, and 2 million in Britain, the majority of whom had come from the former colonies. The highest proportion was registered in Switzerland, where the employment of foreign workers had already begun in the 1950s.[6]

In West Germany, as in the other industrialised countries of Europe, the recruitment of a foreign labour force was seen in an entirely positive light. For the federal government, the high growth rate and the price-reducing effect of the employment of foreigners were paramount objectives, while for the employers it now became much easier to obtain a labour force for unskilled work. In addition, this was also a way of preventing upward wage pressure from being exerted by the shortage of workers in the lower wage groups. The trade unions were ambivalent about the influx of foreign labour. On the one hand, they feared that the recruitment of foreigners would lead wages to fall; but, on the other hand, they thought that this would improve prospects for the reduction in working hours which was one of their main objectives

It was also considered that the export of workers offered nothing but benefits to their countries of origin. It would reduce local unemployment, it would improve the balance of payments owing to wage transfers and it would raise the skill levels of the locals owing to their employment in German factories. It would be 'a bit of development aid for the countries of Southern Europe', as West German politicians frequently pointed out. According to Minister of Labour Theodor Blank, writing in 1964, 'the consolidation of Europe and the coming together in friendship of people of the most varied origins and customs' had become 'a reality' owing to the employment of foreigners in Germany. The number of foreign employees in the Federal Republic rose from 279,000 in 1960 to 1.3 million in 1966, in other words, 6.1 per cent of the total employed population.[7]

The common conviction of all those involved was that the employment of the *Gastarbeiter* (guest workers)—a word which was now universally used, because the previous expression, *Fremdarbeiter* (alien workers) stirred up uncomfortable historical memories—was a temporary phenomenon, a transitional episode. The key figures in political and economic life did not reflect at the time on the eventual consequences of the increasing number of *Gastarbeiter*, as seen from a more long-term perspective. Moreover, the *Gastarbeiter* themselves regarded their presence in the Federal Republic as temporary. They wanted to stay for a few years and then use the money they earned in Germany to build a new and better life in their own country. As a result, social and economic conditions in their homeland were the yardstick of comparison they used to judge the quality of their life in their new place of employment. This meant that they were more ready than the Germans themselves to accept work which was dirty and especially onerous, to do more overtime, and to live as cheaply as possible, forgoing the living standards and levels of consumption their wages entitled them to. As a rule, they showed no interest in political and trade union activities in the Federal Republic.

By 1966, 90 per cent of foreign males present in the country were employed as workers, compared with 49 per cent of adult German males. Almost three-quarters of them worked in industry, as semi-skilled or unskilled workers. They received lower wages because they were less skilled than German workers, or at least that is how they were classified. They suffered industrial accidents rather more often than Germans did, and they also changed their place of work more frequently. In addition, they were mainly employed in sectors where heavy and dirty work, piecework wage rates, the shift system and assembly-line production were particularly prevalent. This offered substantial advantages to businesses at a time when there was a strong demand for labour, because German workers either could not be obtained for work of that nature, or only in return for large wage increases, the payment of which would have made the unskilled jobs in question unprofitable.

At first, the West German population paid little attention to the presence of these foreigners. The feeling was rather that their presence was an unavoidable accompaniment of the economic miracle. Problems only developed with the beginning of the recession in autumn 1965, when the employment of foreign workers coincided with an increase, albeit a slight one, in unemployment among native Germans. This situation led some people to call for German workers to be given unconditional priority over foreign workers, a view which found expression in polemical attacks on the preferential treatment allegedly given to the latter.

A number of economists had in fact already identified possible problems that might arise from the employment of foreigners. Carl Föhl, Professor of Economic Theory in Berlin, calculated that the introduction of unskilled foreign workers would lead to the preservation of uneconomic workplaces with low productivity, and prevent their removal through rationalisation. In the longer term, however, there was another problem connected with this, which had also not been anticipated. The *Gastarbeiter* would only produce a positive economic effect if their stay in Germany was purely temporary and no large public investments needed to be made on their behalf. If they remained for a longer period, additional nurseries, schools, hospitals etc. would be required, and this would wipe out the economic gains. But, equally, they could not be sent back home, because 'the [German] workers who have risen into higher and better paid positions will not want to return to their previous employment. This in itself will make a cut in numbers difficult.'[8]

In making this comment, Föhl drew attention to the secondary effects of the employment of foreigners. They had facilitated an acceleration of social mobility and a rapid increase in the number of places for more highly qualified people. It was the German workers who primarily profited from both developments. Greater rationalisation, which he proposed as an alternative to the utilisation of foreign workers, was in contrast cost-intensive and would have needed more time to implement.

## The Euphoria of Modernity: Innovations in Building

The effects of the end of the reconstruction phase began to be felt in the housing market at the beginning of the sixties. But, contrary to the expectations of most experts in the field, the need for new houses continued to increase, rather than declining. One reason for this was that more people were getting married and having children. But there were also more long-term trends in operation, involving new requirements and aspirations: the elderly increasingly began to move into separate dwellings, so as to bring to an end the conflicts that arose from living in uncomfortable proximity to other people in their children's houses. This accelerated the process of spatial separation between the generations. In addition, now that the most basic needs for accommodation had been satisfied by the mass building programmes of the post-war years, people began to demand larger and better homes. The average size of a dwelling occupied by a family of four was less than 50 square metres in 1950. By 1960 it had risen to 70 and by 1970 to 86 square metres.[9]

There had been broad agreement between specialists and politicians in the 1950s over the principles according to which a large-scale building programme should be organised: the 'garden city' of the 1920s offered the ideal picture. This had been supplemented in the Nazi period with specifically *völkisch* elements, but essentially retained, and it now served as a model. To counter the behemoth of the big city, with its tenement houses and high-rise buildings, the new housing quarters were to be planned according to the principle of urban 'subdivision and dispersal'. They must be located in the suburbs, have large grassy areas, be close to nature, and get plenty of light and sunshine. Much of the planning of the 1950s continued the development projects proposed during the war, in which the destruction of cities by Allied air attacks had been seen as an opportunity for their 'organic' reconstruction. Disencumbered from Nazi ideological ballast, but largely planned by the same architects, many big new housing estates of the fifties were therefore built outside the town centres according to principles of 'decentralisation' and 'greening'.

This was entirely in conformity with the views of the federal government. Chancellor Adenauer never tired of emphasising the way high-rise buildings had 'contributed to the depersonalisation of the human being, particularly because they made impossible the vitally necessary connection of the family, of the husband, the wife and the children, with nature and with the cultivation of a garden.' High-rise dwellings also increased the danger that 'the big city' would become 'a source of corruption to true humanity'. The private home, on the other hand, was best, because it was the most family-friendly form of accommodation. Rented accommodation, said the long-standing Minister of Housing, Paul Lücke, made it difficult for families to have children, thereby contributing to 'contraception, abortion and depravity and thereby to the biological death of the *Volk*.'[10]

Critical attitudes towards the big city were also widespread in the SPD. This applied even more to the trade unions, which had found an important field of policy activity in the development of social housing. The 'Neue Heimat' complex, which was owned by the trade unions, soon grew into one of the biggest housing development companies in the Federal Republic. The building activities around 'Neue Heimat' were a particularly striking expression of the way housing development policy and trade union ideals and conceptions of the future society were combined together.

One of the first big new housing estates produced by 'Neue Heimat' was the garden suburb of Hohnerkamp in Hamburg, completed by the architect Hans Bernhard Reichow. During the war, Reichow had been on the staff of 'General Plan East' for German colonisation. After the war, he began to put forward the principle of 'organic urban architecture', which soon became very influential. In Hohnerkamp, 1,500 dwellings were built on a large vacant area outside the city centre. More than half of the site was laid down to grass, and houses for one or two families and buildings of from three storeys up to a maximum of six storeys were constructed. This was a 'thoroughly green estate' and a 'calm oasis' far from the dangers of the city and industry. A similar housing estate, which was advertised for a long time as a 'masterpiece of urban planning' and a model of modern house building, was erected in Sennestadt, near Bielefeld. A development of this kind, the management board of 'Neue Heimat' affirmed in 1958, did not just satisfy housing needs but in addition 'brought human beings out of the mass and back to themselves, thereby serving social order and giving the family a genuine home'. In 1961, finally, the housing development called Neue Vahr was inaugurated in Bremen. This was acclaimed as the 'most systematic realisation of the programme to "subdivide and disperse the city" in Germany, indeed in the whole of Europe'. It had 10,000 houses for 25,000 people, low building density, generous green spaces and a street plan which kept the traffic away from residential areas.[11]

These showplace estates were simply the vanguard projects of a movement which enticed families, usually young ones, out of severely damaged and provisionally and cheaply restored town centres and into the green suburbs. The result was that the town centres became increasingly desolate, and fewer and fewer people, mainly the elderly, continued to live there. The new garden cities were no doubt very popular among house-seekers. But the disadvantages of these suburban settlements soon appeared as well as their advantages. They were planned as clean, quiet residential areas far away from the hectic tempo of professional life, and as a result they lacked not only infrastructure and shops but in most cases transport links as well. In addition, land values in the surrounding area soon increased substantially, so that builders and local authorities, as well as residents, lost the financial advantages of the garden city estates.

From the beginning of the 1960s, when demand for houses increased again, but was now largely a search for quality, criticism increased of the suburban estates and the social and family ideals associated with them. This reached a climax with the polemical pamphlet issued in 1965 by the Frankfurt social psychologist Alexander Mitscherlich in which he attacked the 'inhospitable nature of our towns'. He criticised the 'urge to get into nature', the expansion of suburban housing estates, the isolation and loneliness of the inhabitants and the functional split between work and home. He called for this to be replaced by a return to urbanism, which would be achieved by reintegrating living and working spaces: 'The old towns, which used to be highly integrated, have suffered functional disaggregation. The inhospitable nature of these new urban districts is oppressive.'[12] This view was shared by many of the younger town planners and building contractors, who sometimes referred back explicitly to the first phase of functionalism in the 1920s. The 'garden cities' in the suburbs, they said, had deprived the towns of their identity. This had included features such as interconnection, integration and communication. To regain these lost functions of communal urban life, 'deconcentration' must be brought to an end, and consolidation and 'intensive settlement' boosted. What was needed, therefore, were 'living arrangements within the framework of high-rise estates' with the aim of 'compressing' the town 'into the smallest possible space' so as to give 'the vast majority of those who live there the opportunity to improve communications within the town centre'.[13] The new ideals of 'socialisation through density' and 'winning back the urban space' were considered as milestones of progress. In the mid-1960s they became the dominant doctrines of urban development. 'Modern building' came to mean high-rise building and production in series, lifts, glass façades, built-in kitchens, refuse chutes and district heating: in short, the 'international style' of functionalist architecture.

From the early 1960s onwards, this trend began to sweep all before it with astonishing rapidity. It was also associated with political commitment, because architects and town planners as well as housing policy chiefs used it as a way of distancing themselves from the town planning ideals of the 1950s and previous years. The new urban planning was thus also conceived as 'an aspect of "de-Nazification" and "de-provincialisation"', a rejection of the conservatives' critique of modernity and civilisation, of the disdain for city life inherent in that critique, and of the exclusive concentration on the family with children as the model of collective life. Suburban housing estates 'in the countryside' were now seen as marking an individualist and anti-urban, indeed practically an anti-social way of living, while the private house was seen as the 'incarnation of urban irresponsibility', and a 'manifestation of private egoism', and the owner of a private house as a 'garden gnome capitalist'.[14]

The new direction of town planning, which was aimed at 're-urbanisation' and greater compactness, was rapidly and persistently reflected in building practices. The many large housing projects built after the mid-1960s were in most cases located close to the town centres. They were planned as multi-storey building complexes so as to make possible 'integration and communication', but also to allow them to be constructed cheaply and quickly without any lowering of standards. Examples were the big housing complex of Mümmelmannsberg in Hamburg, the Emmertsgrund estate in Heidelberg and in Munich the 'overflow city of Neu-Perlach', which with its 25,000 dwellings was one of the biggest estates ever built. Altogether, the sixties saw the creation of some 600,000 dwellings in more than one hundred towns, located in tall and extremely compact high-rise complexes.

This commitment to progressive urban development and functionalism also applied to non-residential buildings. The new style dominated the building of schools, hospitals and town halls, and in particular universities. In order to make up for the country's self-proclaimed deficiencies in higher education as quickly as possible and to include regions and social strata previously deprived of this benefit, a large number of new university buildings were constructed. These were often gigantic high-rise money-saving concrete structures on the outskirts of towns and cities, intended to stand out demonstratively from the traditional elite universities located in the town centres, such as Heidelberg and Göttingen. They were also intended to radiate modernity, social openness and progressive optimism through their form of architecture.

The University of Bochum was a particularly striking example of this new way of building. It had been commissioned by a CDU-run state government, and it entered into operation between 1965 and 1969 as the first university to be located in the working-class region of the Ruhr. The arrangement and architecture of the new university expressed the conceptions of the time in a well-nigh archetypical fashion. Thirteen identical high-rise buildings were erected, using standardised pre-cast concrete components. The buildings were of uniform dimensions, measuring 200 metres in length and 70 metres in width, and they were all twelve storeys high. They were surrounded by parking spaces, with access to the autobahn, and there was a residential area built in the same style. The whole thing gave the impression of an industrial installation, a kind of knowledge machine. But the university's builders did not see this concept as troubling in the slightest degree. On the contrary, they regarded the Ruhr University as an expression of functional, indeed democratic, architecture. Research and teaching should not, they thought, be conducted in the prestige buildings of the imperial epoch or the mansions of the feudal past but in light, modern structures, in which the external identity of all the buildings reflected the aspiration to make all the faculties of equal rank. Even the purpose-built motorway access was intended to symbolise that the university was physically and socially attainable for everyone. 'Equivalence, maximum proximity and human and academic interchange were concepts built into the university, in an architectural style without symbols of domination, which became known as the international style.'[15]

Within less than ten years, this euphoria over extreme modernism in urban building had started to evaporate, after it turned out that the planners' ideas of intensive urban life, communication and integration had not come to fruition, and that, on the contrary, many of the new housing estates presented a picture of neglect, isolation and decay. Nevertheless, the intensity of building development during a period of roughly fifteen years was such that it left behind almost ineradicable traces in the cities of West Germany. The spread of the new housing estates was by no means purely, or mainly, to be traced back to the financial interests of the developers. It was, rather, a reflection of the contemporary trend in town planning towards concentration and urbanism and the sociopolitical conceptions and objectives associated with this. But there was nothing specifically West German about the phenomenon. The 'international style' of functionalist, concentrated housing development was a feature of building activity all over Western Europe, and it was practised in a similar fashion, often still more exaggeratedly, in the countries of the Eastern bloc, not least the GDR.

Another focus of building policy after the mid-1960s was the renovation of the town centres. What was involved here was no longer the restoration of the building stock destroyed during the war, because by the mid-1960s this had already been largely completed, although often with quickly erected low-cost structures. The planners were now more interested in the old residential and commercial buildings which still remained intact in the town centres, and mainly dated from the decades that preceded the First World War. It was above all the 'tenement blocks of the *Kaiserzeit*' which now became the target of fierce criticism. These were parts of the cities where people at the bottom of the social scale lived in old houses which were often completely unmodernised. But the town planners also targeted the middle-class dwellings erected during the *Gründerzeit* and at the turn of the century, especially where they hindered city-centre modernisation. The city centres which had been built at the turn of the century combined together everything that was regarded, irrespective of party, as obsolete and outdated, indeed reactionary. For the Social Democrats and the trade unions in particular, these neighbourhoods symbolised the Germany of oppression and narrowness against which they had begun the fight seventy years previously. The emblem the SPD chose for the 1965 Bundestag elections was a vehicle licence plate with the legend 'SPD 1965', and the party displayed a television advertisement showing an old town in the south of Germany, undamaged by the war, its narrow streets lined with crumbling *Gründerzeit* façades, and with town gates too narrow to allow entry to a lorry loaded with building materials. The next shot was a contrasting vision of a better future: elevated motorways slicing through the city centres of Berlin and Düsseldorf, as examples for the modern, densely concentrated, traffic-friendly cities which the SPD promised to build.[16]

The intention was to bring to an end housing shortages and cramped living conditions, and to clear away the old buildings from the *Kaiserzeit* and previous centuries which had been spared by the war, so as to make way at last for modern life. This was the vision of the future disseminated by the town planners. Urban renovation, declared Albert Vietor, the chair of 'Neue Heimat', in 1967, does not involve

> the restoration and preservation of the town of the Middle Ages, the Renaissance, the Baroque, which was meant for pedestrians, or the appalling degeneracy of the *Gründerzeit,* which would strangle the further development of society, culture, the economy, and life itself, but the creation of new spheres of life in new formations, in such a way that what has been built facilitates continuing development.[17]

The radical character of such ideas was demonstrated in exemplary fashion in Hamburg, where a building project called the 'Alsterzentrum' was presented by 'Neue Heimat' in 1966 as a 'proposal for the transformation of the Hamburg district of St. George'. This involved the complete demolition of the old working-class neighbourhood, which was a dense tangle of old buildings, cheap housing, small shops and red light establishments beside the railway station, and the resettlement of all the inhabitants. It was intended to replace it with a modern Burgring consisting of five interconnected high-rise buildings, 700 metres long and 300 metres wide, with up to sixty-three floors, affording space for 6,000 apartments and 20,000 residents, numerous offices and commercial premises, and 16,000 underground car park places. Such a building, which would have been the largest in the world, bigger than the Pentagon in Washington, was passed by the town planners and local politicians of Hamburg through all the relevant authorities, and it was only for financial reasons that it eventually proved impossible to build it. The trade union newspaper *Welt der Arbeit* was evidently in a state of euphoria when it described its vision of the new centre:

> Right behind the lakeside walk by the Außenalster, where the neighbourhood of St. George (so much in need of regeneration) reaches to the back of the five-star Atlantic Hotel, a modern housing complex spanning the whole of the former neighbourhood will tower up to its white summit like a rejuvenation of the pyramids, but freed from any impression of top-heaviness.[18]

The movement for town centre redevelopment reached its peak in the 1970s. These projects were not put into effect solely, or even primarily, by housing cooperatives. On the contrary, they followed the principles of the free market, which ruled out cheap housing at expensive locations. But the basic idea of town centre redevelopment, which took shape in the mid-1960s, involved a vision of social progress through re-urbanisation, concentration and renewal. 'Modernisation' was the magic word for the victory of progress over the forces of the past, and this expression referred *not* to National Socialism (for neither the estates built in the homeland style of the 1930s nor the grandiose architectural creations of the Nazi state were demolished) but to the period of the German Empire at the end of the nineteenth century, and therefore to the initial social combination of industrialisation and the workers' movement. Conservatives saw the building of modern residential districts for the masses and the demolition of the old city centre working-class neighbourhoods as a way of removing the breeding grounds of social unrest, proletarianisation and immorality. Social Democrats, on the other hand, considered that the new functional city centres, modern university buildings and big housing estates with newly built accommodation for everyone, would overcome the underprivileged social status of the workers and lead to the triumph of progress.

## Nuclear Energy: The Great Hope of the Epoch

There was another large-scale industrial project even more closely associated with an optimistic vision of economic and social progress which made the transition from the planning stage to practical implementation in the mid-1960s: the provision of energy from electricity supplied by nuclear power stations. The construction of the first nuclear reactor to be located outside a research establishment was begun in 1962 at Grundremmingen. It came on stream in 1966. Over the next fifteen years, a total of twenty-one nuclear power stations were built in the Federal Republic, and by 1980 they produced roughly 5.7 per cent of the country's total energy supply.[19]

In the early 1950s, almost fanciful expectations were linked with the idea of the 'peaceful use of atomic energy'. After the first international atomic energy conference in Geneva in 1955, scientists, engineers, politicians and journalists in almost all the industrial countries were equally enthusiastic about the new possibilities it offered. The physicist Edgar Salin wrote a book predicting 'the approach of a new stage in the Industrial Revolution' in which he advised that 'every firm, large or small, involved in the utility sector, in coal and steel production, in chemicals, and so on, should adjust their long-term plans and investments to cover this new situation.' Another physicist, Pascual Jordan, asserted that 'there is absolutely no branch of industry, no factory and no workshop of at least medium size, which could not achieve a considerable saving in labour by obtaining the advice of a practising nuclear physicist.' The new form of energy, the journal *Atomwirtschaft* enthused in 1960, opens up 'an inexhaustible cornucopia of new discoveries, new tasks and new opportunities'[20] for the whole economy.

Later in the decade, during this period of 'nuclear euphoria', no project was seen as too big, or too visionary to be undertaken. All these projects were regarded as realistic possibilities capable of being achieved within a few years. Nuclear energy would desalinate the oceans, warm the polar regions, irrigate the deserts, open up the Arctic, power ships, aeroplanes, trains and motor vehicles, heat houses, produce new synthetic materials and even make possible 'gigantic corrections in the earth's orbit'. There were also people like the Munich physicist Walther Gerlach, who justified the use of nuclear power in simpler terms, saying that in view of the impending shortage of energy it would soon be indispensable, and the above-mentioned journal *Atomwirtschaft* predicted as early as 1956 that nuclear power could soon supply 80 per cent of the country's total energy requirements.

In view of the energy supply situation at that time, such a prediction was hard to believe, since local West German coal production, at 156 million tonnes, had reached its maximum level in 1956. The industry then began to suffer from over-capacity, owing to the import of cheaper coal from abroad and the rapidly growing importance of inexpensive oil supplies. A process of shrinkage and a move towards monopoly began in the coalmining industry of the Ruhr, which eventually led to the establishment of the coalmining corporation Ruhrkohle AG in 1968 and to continuous reductions in workforces and productive capacity. Admittedly, many people, even within the federal government, regarded dependence on imported oil or coal as problematic, particularly after the Suez War of 1956, and advocated maintaining energy autarchy, at least in part. But arguments of this kind were not decisive factors in the large-scale promotion of nuclear energy by the West German state.[21]

Nuclear energy was seen rather as embodying optimism and hopeful anticipation after half a century of political catastrophe, economic collapse and social impoverishment. It was widely believed that many of the problems of past decades, if not all of them, could be solved, or at least made easier to solve, by nuclear energy. In the not too distant future, nuclear energy signified an 'industrial, economic and social revolution greater than all the revolutions of the past', comparable only with the discovery of America. That is how the situation was described in 1957 in a US handbook dealing with the impact of nuclear technology.[22]

The use of nuclear energy for civilian purposes was also seen as a peaceful response to the fear inspired by nuclear weapons. It was also promoted in these terms by the German physicists Heisenberg and Gerlach, who had worked on the development of a German atomic bomb during the war. The previously widespread view that German physicists deliberately refused to develop the atomic bomb for the Nazi state can by now be regarded as without any foundation. But the Göttingen Declaration made in 1957 by leading West German physicists against nuclear weapons also unmistakably emphasised their firm conviction that the German discovery of nuclear fission was a pioneering achievement for the benefit of humanity, which must now be defended against military misuse.[23]

The trend towards nuclear energy was given added political impetus by its close connection with European unification. The European Atomic Energy Agency ('Euratom') and the EEC were founded jointly in 1957. But whereas the European Economic Community soon proved successful, the new atomic energy agency never got beyond a statement of aims. The national egoism of the participating countries, who all wanted to profit in their own way from these miraculous new machines, was too strongly rooted to allow a collective approach. But when the International Exhibition was held in 1958 in Brussels, one of the exhibits was a gigantic structure schematically representing the atoms in an iron crystal. It was called the 'Atomium'. It served as a symbol of European unification and it also illustrated the promise for the future which nuclear energy and European unity bore within themselves in equal measure.[24]

The prospect of nuclear energy was also accompanied by a far-reaching social optimism, particularly, though not exclusively, on the Left. The Marxist philosopher Ernst Bloch regarded nuclear power as the definitive solution of the energy supply problem, indeed the problem of social wealth in general.[25] Leo Brandt, the pioneer of Social Democratic thinking on the question, predicted that nuclear energy, which he described as 'three million times better than coal', could also rid the world of hunger: 'These hungry people will now be provided with power stations which will receive a hundred to two hundred kilos [of uranium] every year by aeroplane.'[26]

The SPD even held a party congress in 1956 devoted almost exclusively to nuclear energy and its possibilities. Leo Brandt gave the main speech, in which he gave a basic outline of the relation between economic and social progress, He claimed that a 'second industrial revolution' was taking place. Automation and rationalisation, just like nuclear energy, had been developed during the war years, he said. Now, in time of peace, what was important was to make use of their tremendous potential to advance human progress. The first industrial revolution, according to Brandt, had worked out to the disadvantage rather than the advantage of the majority of the population: it had been characterised by impoverishment, the sixteen-hour working day, child labour and high death rates. Now, during the second industrial revolution, it was Social Democracy's task to make sure that these evils were not repeated. If, however, they succeeded in introducing nuclear energy in a planned and sensible way, the wealth of a nation could be increased, social tensions could be defused, and even wars could be prevented, because they were, after all, fought over natural resources and energy supplies.[27]

The ideas formulated by Brandt became the basis of Social Democracy's policies in the next few years. They were even included in the preamble of the 1959 Godesberg Programme, which reads as follows:

> These are the contradictions of our era: the elemental power of the atom has been unleashed but the consequences of this are a source of terror; the forces of production have been developed to a tremendous extent and immense wealth has been accumulated, but a fair share in this common achievement has not been provided to all . . . But it is also the *hope* of our time that in the atomic age people can make their lives easier, free themselves from worry and create prosperity for everyone, if they apply their constantly growing power over natural forces exclusively for peaceful purposes.

But only a new and a better way of ordering society could achieve this, namely democratic socialism.[28]

The middle-class parties too were convinced of the epochal significance of the atom. A tangible expression of this feeling was the creation of a government ministry specifically devoted to nuclear energy, under the young and extremely ambitious Franz Josef Strauß, who invited German scientists and entrepreneurs 'to make a genuine contribution, in line with our traditions, to stripping the word "atom" of its horrors.'[29] That was a dig at the Americans, who had employed nuclear power as a weapon against Japan, unlike the Germans, who had invented it. In practice, however, it turned out that the technical and financial problems were much greater than had been imagined. The first 'nuclear programme' was begun in 1957, but only two of the five proposed nuclear power stations came to fruition, because in view of the sales crisis for coal, the extreme cheapness of oil and the already very definite prospects for natural gas, the energy firms saw no commercial need to produce electricity by means of expensive nuclear power stations, which were only at an initial stage of technical development. It was only thanks to massive investment assistance by the state, and guarantees against financial loss, which virtually exempted the firms involved from the risk of failure, that it was possible to construct the first test reactors outside the research centres in Karlsruhe, Jülich and Munich.

The 'nuclear euphoria' therefore soon abated, but the conviction that the future lay with nuclear energy continued to prevail. It was first and foremost the government itself which promoted interest in the development of nuclear reactors. The second nuclear programme, passed in 1963, earmarked 3.8 billion DM for nuclear research and development and the construction and operation of nuclear reactors. Four years later, the amount was raised to 6.1 billion DM for the third nuclear programme. The number of commercial reactors, which continued to be financed largely by the state, increased gradually after the mid-1960s, though at the same time there was a noticeable decline in public interest in the nuclear programme and nuclear energy, and the crisis in coalmining brought about by over-capacity began to occupy the centre of attention.

In addition, a new type of nuclear reactor was developed during this period whose technical possibilities seemed even more breathtaking than those of the older heavy water or light water reactors. This was the 'fast breeder' reactor, in which more fissile material—plutonium—is precipitated by the process of splitting the atom than is consumed through the operation of the reactor. Scientific and political circles rapidly became convinced that with this type of reactor more energy could be produced from the very limited German uranium deposits than from the whole of the country's coal reserves.[30] But none of the big firms was prepared to finance these installations, whether they were builders of power stations or suppliers of energy, because there was absolutely no market for new forms of energy. At the time, the energy company RWE was busy clearing vast areas of the country for the opencast mining of lignite, while other companies were entering the promising business of gas supply. In addition, private business continued to be sceptical about the technical development of power stations of this nature, because they were tremendously expensive to build, especially as it proved to be very difficult to obtain appropriate insurance, because the big insurers refused to enter into any contracts for installations of this kind in view of the highly unpredictable risks involved. According to the historian Joachim Radkau, the insurance experts

> proceeded from the beginning on the assumption that the nuclear risk could not be calculated by a private firm, and they therefore called on the state: and since the state was usually quick to intervene in nuclear matters, the insurers did not need to ponder very long over the quantifiability of this new risk area.[31]

The energy supply firms therefore only became involved in the work on fast breeder projects on condition that the state would completely take over the job of financing them. This applied both to the 'Fast Breeder' built near Kalkar, and the high temperature nuclear reactor constructed at Hamm-Uentrop. Undertakings of this magnitude, the head of the Karlsruhe Fast Breeder Project Wolf Häfele asserted in 1963, could not be measured using the traditional yardstick of economic viability. Nuclear energy, and also space travel, were important 'for the self-assertion of an industry-dependent nation' and this also included 'the continuous development of technological and scientific achievements, even if the price is unimaginable and other things have to be neglected to pay it'. But this was, in principle, nothing new, he added, because throughout history there had been

> actions taken to give material expression to an epoch which could not be justified rationally . . . The advanced Egyptian civilisation built pyramids, the Middle Ages built magnificent cathedrals and the modern period produced big castles. Today it is nuclear cities and missile bases which display the aspirations and abilities of a modern industrial state at their most compelling.[32]

Large-scale technological developments of this kind, added Häfele two years later, guaranteed 'the survival of the nation in a technologically advanced world' and, politically speaking, almost belong to the sphere of defence, 'to which they are also equivalent in financial terms'.[33]

At the same time, issues of the safety of nuclear reactors, and Fast Breeders in particular, hardly played any role in public opinion or political discussion. Nuclear energy was regarded as controllable, and references to possible dangers were seen as unjustifiably transferring anxieties arising from the use of nuclear weapons to the sphere of peaceful applications. There was therefore very little audible criticism in West Germany of the risks associated with the 'peaceful use of nuclear energy'. The optimistic expectation that this form of energy would bring to an end a large part of humanity's material difficulties almost at a stroke was until the mid-1970s one of the fundamental convictions underpinning this short era of progressive euphoria.

## The Hopes of the Planners

Enthusiasm for progress and a passion for modernisation were not the only factors promoting the inordinate construction of giant housing estates, the redevelopment of town centres and the spread of nuclear energy in the mid-1960s; a belief in the primacy of planning and state intervention over the driving forces deriving from the market and society itself also played a large part in the process. 'Planning is the main characteristic of our era. Planning is a key concept of our future which everyone has now become aware of', wrote the legal theorist Joseph H. Kaiser in 1965. 'Planning', he said, 'is the systematic adumbration of a rational system on the basis of all available knowledge' and it is the 'most appropriate instrument for the construction of a better and a more just social order' in the contemporary world.[34] This conviction, which spread during the

1960s, was based on two prevailing beliefs. One was the notion of 'industrial society', which had by now become a dominant topos, replacing the critique of civilisation expressed in the phrase 'mass society'. The other was the realisation that industrial society's social and economic complexity had in the meantime become so immense that it was impossible to handle it either with the means provided by the market—relying on the interests of private business—or with the aid of political ideologies. Only a strictly rational mode of administration, on a scientific basis, was capable of exploiting the multiple possibilities that had emerged in developed industrial society. Moreover, the question of nuclear energy appeared to show that private businesses were either overstretched by such projects or, if they were nuclear monopolies, they would gain so much power that the state should be given preference for that very reason, as Carlo Schmid noted at the SPD's 'nuclear congress' of 1956. If they proceeded in a planned and scientific way they would now be in a position to control, and indeed to direct, the march of progress.[35]

One of the roots of this way of thinking was the theory developed in the later 1950s by Walt Rostow and others in the USA, according to which industrial societies followed a predictable model of modernisation. Rostow's theory arose in the context of the Cold War, decolonisation and the competition between the two superpowers for control over the new nations of what was soon to be called the 'Third World'. It attracted great interest in West Germany, as elsewhere. The initial starting point of Rostow's ideas was this: the Soviet Union was more successful than the USA in attracting the 'Third World' because communist ideology offered the people of the developing countries a vision to aim at, a formula, which promised to lead the poorer countries of the South and the East towards prosperity and social improvement with almost scientific certitude. This vision of the future, which promised that after a period of incredible efforts socialist societies would be able to attain the stage of development of the developed industrial societies within one, or at most two, generations, had already nourished hopes for the construction of socialism in the Soviet Union, and would not fail to operate in the developing countries as well.

Rostow's response was to put forward a parallel theory of modernisation according to which the history of the USA also demonstrated a kind of historical inevitability. If the appropriate conditions were created at an early stage of industrial development, namely a free capital market, a functioning state bureaucracy, a social structure under democratic control, education and an active middle class, the next stage, namely thoroughgoing industrialisation, the expansion of prosperity, and social security for increasing sections of the population, would follow almost inevitably.[36]

This conception rested on the assumption that the development of modern societies pursued a predictable course. The belief in progress also fed on this, because it meant that anyone who knew the laws of history could perceive the future development of societies and plan accordingly. These ideas were closely related to Marxism, to which Rostow's model was also directly indebted, though its conclusions contrasted strongly with those advanced by Marx.[37]

Rostow's theory also implied that the development he outlined could not be artificially accelerated or retarded for political or ideological reasons but was inherent in the dynamic of an industrial society. Supporters of the theory therefore predicted that, after the phase of revolution, the Soviet-dominated countries would in the medium term no longer be ruled by ideological principles but by rational calculation, and that ultimately meant a scientific approach. According to contemporary convergence theorists, industrial societies would increasingly resemble each other as time went by, and the more they applied planning and a scientific approach the more successful they would be. A system of pure market liberalism, on the other hand, would not be in a position to do this, because the short-term interests of the market participants would always have priority, as was shown just as much by the uncontrolled growth of private housing in the suburbs of cities, bemoaned by Mitscherlich, as by the unreadiness of the energy companies to rate the long-term advantages of nuclear energy higher than their short-term interest in making a profit.

Planning was therefore needed to implement the long-term goals which the state had established on scientific foundations. This conviction characterised the long decade of planning euphoria which lasted roughly between 1963 and 1975 in the Federal Republic as it did all over Western Europe. In fact this symbiosis between the state and science had already started to spread in the late 1950s, as was demonstrated by the rapid multiplication of bodies offering scientific advice—Scientific Councils, Education Councils and finally Councils of Experts—and by the growing number of plans—all the way from the Green Plan and the Plan for Long-Distance Federal Highways to the Nuclear Programme and the Plan to Coordinate Regional Planning. The influence of committees of experts had never been greater than in those years. It was not for politicians, deputies or the elected government to decide the future and shape it in line with their own interests and ideologies. That was rather the job of scientific specialists, for whom scientific, computable considerations, not opinions, interests and ideologies were decisive.

The euphoria of the planners was associated not only with the conviction that science offered clear and value-free prescriptions for dealing with the present but also with the confident belief that the future could be investigated scientifically and shaped accordingly. 'Futurology', which flourished in the mid-1960s, gave the impression of being a serious scientific specialism, and it claimed to offer two advantages. On the one hand, it offered the prospect that present-day social problems such as hunger and poverty could solved by the use of technology. On the other hand, it concentrated on predicting economic developments, concerning itself with the ways in which national and international economic systems could be guided, and it offered prognoses about the development of consumption and the maintenance of economic growth. One example was the French economist Jean Fourastié, whose books on *The Great Metamorphosis of the Twentieth Century* and *The Laws of the Future Economy* enjoyed great attention in the Federal Republic. What most of the futurologists had in common was the conviction that scientifically based social planning would be able to deal with the existing social, political and economic defects and problems in a more rational way than had so far been the case. Planning, said one of the most well-known German futurologists, Robert Jungk, would determine the political discussions of the coming decades; indeed, the '"homo novus" who had announced his existence in the form of the planner' would become 'the prototype of a new humanity'.[38]

Critics of this model came overwhelmingly from the conservative side. Thus, the Catholic thinker and Professor of Constitutional Law Ernst-Wolfgang Böckenförde pointed out the problems involved in 'shifting the actual task of political decision-making away from the political authorities to independent, politically neutralised committees of experts' in matters of state planning, and expressed doubts as to whether 'this sort of political de-politicisation produced by giving politics a scientific air is of any benefit'. And the sociologist Helmut Schelsky remarked that futurology was mostly predicated on an overdramatised decision: either you start to plan rationally—or the world will be faced with ruin.

> The alternative 'World Planning or World Destruction' is no alternative at all, for who would 'choose' destruction? . . . Here plan-type thinking openly becomes a doctrine of salvation with chiliastic features, which is set against an apocalyptic catastrophe, the self-destruction of the world. Like all utopias, the planning utopia draws on the most efficacious instruments of religious incantation.[39]

These objections could make no headway, however, in the face of a model of progress based on the linear extrapolation of present-day trends of development, whose central but unexpressed assumption was that economic growth would continue, or perhaps even accelerate. Fifteen uninterrupted years of economic upsurge appeared to refute all sceptical objections to this optimistic prognosis, even the objections of conservative critics of modernity. Few people now listened to the warnings the conservatives had repeated for decades against mass society, material prosperity, moral decline and the levelling of social differences. Warnings like this were regarded as an attempt to preserve social distinction and the privileges of an estate-based society. In contrast, technological and social progress appeared not only as socially and economically rational, but also as almost unavoidable consequences of history itself. That is what gave the belief in progress its extraordinary force of conviction and ability to overcome obstacles. The contradictions of the 'age of ideology', as it was now dubbed, seemed to have been overcome.

## Consumption and Popular Culture

The net incomes of West German workers doubled between 1960 and 1970. Therefore the proportion of income they needed to spend for 'fixed' and 'essential' needs grew smaller, and there was a sharp increase in the amount of 'freely available' income. The working day also grew shorter, the five day week became the rule, and holidays grew longer. West Germans had considerably more money at their disposal and more time in which to spend it. What soon came to be called, always with a critical undertone, 'the consumer society', now began to take root in the Federal Republic. More was meant by this expression than a society with a rising standard of living. The increase in 'excess' income, in other words, income over and above what was needed for food, accommodation and clothing, offered the possibility of free choice. This, in turn, presupposed that commodities of all kinds were available in sufficient quantities, and that people could choose between them, thus compelling the manufacturers to attract customers to their products through advertising. Previously, most people had been wage-dependent employees, who had to earn money to acquire the basic essentials for their families. Now, a new social type appeared, the consumer, who was wooed by the manufacturers into buying one product rather than another. The employer–employee dualism was not abolished by this new configuration of producer and consumer, but it ceased to hold a unique position in society.

The consumer society began to develop in Western Europe in the mid-1950s, first in Great Britain, then from the early 1960s in the Continental countries. Not until the late 1970s did its range extend to cover whole populations, and even then the immense degree of social inequality that continued to exist prevented participation in the benefits of the mass market from being spread evenly. But as a general picture, by the mid-1960s the consumer society was already an effective presence in all the countries of Western Europe.[40]

The domestic needs of the family, the means of transport, and communications received most attention. In the Federal Republic the task of equipping the family dwelling with the most important electrical appliances—the refrigerator, the washing machine, the vacuum cleaner and the electric oven—had almost been completed by the second half of the 1960s. New appliances like the dishwasher, the deep freeze and the dryer appeared a little later. People now began to need larger living areas, smart sitting rooms and new furniture, private houses with oil-fired central heating, and a spacious bathroom. What was previously the vegetable garden became the ornamental garden, and the coal cellar became the party room. In 1965, two-thirds of households already had a telephone, and by the end of the decade almost all households possessed one. In 1971, for the first time, the number of telephone calls made in the Federal Republic (11.7 billion) outstripped the number of letters that were sent (11.5 billion). Experiences open only to the middle classes both before and immediately after the war now gradually became accessible to ever broader strata of the population. The middle-class mode of life remained the model, but it was adopted bit by bit and in a rather naive manner, so that for a long time it was easy to see how recently acquired it was. German entertainment films of the period give a good picture of this, even today.

Apart from the house, the car was the other symbol of progress and individual identity. In 1970, roughly 14 million private motor cars were registered, almost three times as many as in 1960. In the latter year, the prevalence of motor cars in West Germany, with 69 per 1,000 inhabitants, was only slightly higher than the Western European average (67 per 1,000). Ten years later, at 207 per 1,000, it was already much higher, while in 1989 the Federal Republic had the highest motor car density in Western Europe.[41] This, of course, reflected the country's economic growth and the rise in individual incomes, but it was not the only factor. A private car, more than any other consumer good, testified to social advancement. Soon, however, the mere fact of owning a car was no longer sufficient. The question was, what kind of car? The car indicated the social status of its owner and hinted at the owner's financial resources and aesthetic preferences. The driver of a Beetle was no longer poor, while someone who drove an Opel Rekord had managed to leap out of the working class into the office milieu, and the possession of a Mercedes indicated membership of the upper layer of society. There were soon further differentiations: the possession of a French car conferred an aura of sophistication, and a Citroën 2CV, the so-called 'duck', stood for youthfulness and nonconformity.

The degree to which the motor car was also regarded as an element of freedom and self-realisation can be inferred from the long and vain endeavours made by the Federal Ministry of Transport to apply traffic restrictions and speed limits. This seemed urgently necessary, in view of the rapid rise in road traffic accidents and deaths. But in 1960, when it was proposed to introduce a speed limit on main roads, there was a storm of indignation. People spoke of a 'hidden dictatorship' which recalled the Nazi era, or, even worse, the 'régime in the Eastern Zone'. The transport lobby, which was spearheaded by the ADAC (General German Automobile Club), ascribed the rising number of accidents on main roads not to excessive speed but to the many dangerous obstacles at the side of the road, particularly the thickly planted trees that lined the avenues. These were the real 'death traps' for the motorist and they had to be removed urgently, which is exactly what happened. By 1970, almost all the trees that lined the main roads had been cut down. Only in 1972, after more than 21,000 people had died and 500,000 had been injured in road accidents was the Ministry of Transport able to push through a speed limit of 100 km/h on main roads, against the fierce protests of the motoring lobby and the popular press. Even then, the motorways remained exempt.

Travel by car stood for progress and individuality. Road building and motor car manufacture succeeded house building as key branches of the West German economy, and after the mid-1960s the West German motor car industry began to occupy the top position in Europe. Faced with the car, the buses, trams and railways looked like the relics of a collectivist past. The SPD was not immune from this trend. It renounced its support for collective travel in 1957 and thenceforth it presented itself as a party of car owners. This was reflected in 1960 in a particularly fateful decision on how to finance the building of roads: it was decided, against the wishes of the government and with the votes of the SPD, FDP and a minority of CDU and CSU deputies, that in future all income from fuel taxation would be used exclusively for road construction. In no other area of government spending, whether on defence, education or health, was there a comparable link with a specific source of revenue. By granting transport this privileged budget position the government 'exempted road building from the need to secure budget approval every year', as a result of which, according to transport historian Dietmar Klenke, 'the dynamic of motorisation was automatically transferred to road-building': the more traffic there was, the more resources flowed into road building, automatically and without the need for any further votes or legal regulations. The Federal Railways, in contrast, were refused this method of finance. They were seen as an old-fashioned, inefficient state enterprise without a future, and the intention was to retain them, but in a severely restricted form, because soon it would be easier to reach the whole Federal Republic more easily on new motorways by car, van or lorry. The Bundestag also refused to exempt public transport services from either fuel tax or vehicle tax. Local public transport seemed no longer to have much of a prospect. In future, people would no longer travelled to work in trams but in their own cars.[42]

The brand system, whereby products of exactly identical quality were offered for sale all over the whole country, and soon all over Europe and the world, began to prevail in all areas of consumption as much as it did in the case of the motor car. This made it easier to produce, distribute and advertise expensive consumer goods on a mass scale. Moreover, this was a better way of both arousing and satisfying consumers' desires for individuality and distinctiveness. Advertising itself became a branded article. It no longer just sold goods, it sold a whole attitude towards life. The year 1965 saw the popularity of the 'Marlboro Man', a cigarette-smoking cowboy mounted on horseback, who promised the 'taste of freedom and adventure'. In this way, the enjoyment of nicotine was associated with a free, unconstrained life. The image of the dinner-jacketed 'Tchibo Coffee Expert' who travelled round Latin America personally testing the quality of the coffee beans he was buying associated this brand of coffee with the exoticism of foreign adventure as well as a touch of colonialism. And the petrol advertisements of the Esso oil company, with their slogan 'Put a tiger in your tank', promised to give the driver the strength of a predatory animal in the battle for survival on the roads.[43]

The other symbol of the 1960s was the television set. By the end of the decade, almost every West German family had a television, and after 1967 the move from black-and-white to colour sets also began to take off. The First Programme was put out by the ARD (Consortium of Public Broadcasters of the Federal Republic of Germany), while the Second Programme was transmitted by the ZDF (Second German Television Channel), founded in 1963. By the end of the decade they were both transmitting for more than ten hours a day. The viewers were drawn in by television films and entertainment shows, and to an increasing degree by German and international feature films and transmissions of sporting events. In the middle of the decade, Third Programmes were established in each region. In contrast to the other two, which were directed towards a mass public, they transmitted items of classical culture and material of educational and regional interest. By 1970, the average West German was watching the screen for almost three hours a day. This meant that the whole of the additional leisure time acquired since the 1960s was devoted to the television. Events unreported on television were hardly noticed. In addition, the television had a levelling effect: cultural attitudes and sporting preferences became increasingly uniform, as did the impressions gained about distant countries and the people who lived in them.

Here is a list of television offerings in 1965 which illustrates the coexistence of an idyllic picture of bygone German times with a window on the modern world, the presence of 'narrow-minded conformity' alongside 'progress', which was so characteristic of this phase of history: 'Durbridge' crime thrillers like 'The Key', in which German actors played the part of English landowners; trivial family shows, like 'The Trout Residence'; quiz shows like 'What Am I?', 'The Golden Shot' and 'Someone Has to Win'; detailed reporting of the visit of the Queen of England to Germany; the nocturnal victories of the 'Negro

Boxer Cassius Clay' otherwise known as Muhammad Ali; American television series such as 'Bonanza' and 'Laramie'; but also more critical television films like '*Die Unverbesserlichen*' (The Incorrigibles), extensive reports on elections to the Bundestag, the Auschwitz trial and the war in Vietnam; the first transmission of the 'Beat Club' and current affairs programmes such as 'Panorama' and 'Monitor'. Television became West German society's centre of communication and instrument of integration. It reflected and formed both that society's preferences and its heterogeneity. Television blurred the boundary between the event and the report of it far more than other media such as radio, the periodical press or the weekly newsreel.[44] As before, though now to an ever greater extent, the most important point of reference was American society, or what the West Germans were told about it on the television and in American cinema films. Hence the imagined style of life of American middle-class families moulded the social and cultural aspirations of a growing number of citizens of the Federal Republic.

Television, motor car, house, furniture, travel: in the mid-1960s the West Germans threw themselves into a veritable shopping frenzy. At least, this was the view of the critics of consumerism, who were still as numerous as before. But in view of the enthusiasm unleashed by the new world of progress and consumption, the traditionalist and conservatively motivated rejection of modern culture, mass society and the Western way of life met with very little response. The critique from the Left was more successful. It castigated consumer society's superficiality and its stultifying impact. For the Left, the consumer society was an instrument of domination because its advertising inflamed desires people did not have originally for things they did not need, and subordinated everything to the rule of commerce. This type of discourse met with little applause from workers or older Germans, since they were now finally able to make up for what they had missed in decades of deprivation, though only to a modest extent. But younger people and the better-educated sections of society tended to agree with the Left's criticisms. Their basic material needs had largely been satisfied, and the character of their needs and values had begun to alter. The thirst to consume was gradually replaced among this group by a desire for qualitative improvements. This could be expressed as much in a desire for superior forms of consumption more tailored towards the individual as in changes in lifestyle and opinions. The need to be different was reflected in an advertising slogan aimed at the middle-class public, promoting a new kind of cigarette, called, significantly, 'Atika': 'A special flavour is always a bit more expensive.'[45]

But this new trend involved more than the replacement of 'material' by 'post-material' values in a society in which the overwhelming majority of the population now enjoyed basic security. The reduction in working hours and the increased employment of married women changed fundamental aspects of the traditional model of the family. In addition, improved education, the reduction in physically strenuous labour and the increase in intellectually more demanding activities also modified the way the male role was viewed. Industrial labour began to lose its significance as the primary point of reference in life. Equally, the social milieux of socialism and Catholicism continued to be undermined by the process of erosion which had started in the 1950s. Attempts by the state to standardise private life increasingly met with criticism and hostility. The process of liberalisation, which had begun earlier in other Western European countries and the USA, where the transition to the service economy and society had already been made many years before, now also started in the Federal Republic.[46]

This development occurred first among young people in the academic milieu, but after the mid-1960s it quickly and suddenly spread beyond these narrow confines. Even so, traditional alignments were by no means overcome or even marginalised by this process. On the contrary, both styles of life and value systems, the traditional and the modern, continued for many years to stand alongside each other in a number of different forms. This formed the basis for a continuous cultural conflict which thenceforth presented itself as a war of generations between young and old, and also as a political conflict between liberalism and conservatism, although in this case the correlation did not always hold true unequivocally.

What was chiefly involved in this conflict was the relation between the state and the individual, both in questions of participation in public affairs and, more particularly, in the areas of the family, education and sexuality, which were subject to numerous state regulations. In school education, more liberal methods directed towards participation and consensus gained the upper hand over traditional methods which relied on authority and obedience. Authority not legitimated by effective performance declined in importance and was increasingly difficult to enforce. Physical punishment, which was first prohibited in the 1950s, now finally disappeared from educational practice, and there was also a decline in popular support for it, which had previously been widespread: in 1959, two-thirds of West German citizens declared that they were in principle in favour of allowing physical punishment, but by 1971 this proportion had fallen to 41 per cent and by 1974 it was only 26 per cent. In contrast, 53 per cent of the population agreed in 1974 that the goal of education was 'independence and free will', a proportion which rose to 91 per cent among holders of the *Abitur*.[47]

In this context, the importance of sexuality was singled out. Traditional conceptions of the 'moral law' had involved strict norms, particularly in the areas of sexual relations and sexuality, which were enforced by punishment. Marital guilt was a factor in matters of divorce, married women's capacity to conduct business was restricted, homosexuality, even among consenting adults, was prohibited. Many people now reacted to such rules by protesting against them, or, still more effectively, by ignoring them. The regulation of sexuality ceased to be seen as the cornerstone of social order. The main emphasis was now laid on private happiness and the enjoyment of life. The leading social value became the free development of the individual rather than the interests of the nation and the state. The pressure of public opinion in this direction increased, and after the mid-1960s fundamental changes were made in the areas of sexuality and sexual relations. In 1969, a large-scale reform of the criminal law made sexuality largely a private matter. Homosexuality was also decriminalised. After 1966, sex education was taught in the schools. The contraceptive pill allowed sexuality to be separated from reproduction, and this offered many women the possibility of experiencing sex without anxiety. At the end of the 1960s, the comparative lawyer Albin Eser, looking back at this process, referred to a '*saeculum sexuale*' ('age of sex') in these words:

> Subjects about which people remained silent for centuries are today written about and discussed frankly and openly . . . What was regarded from time immemorial as a moral transgression of the most serious kind is today a self-evident part of the experience of any adolescent who wants to be seen as sexually normal and healthy.[48]

The new way of dealing with sexuality was largely regarded as 'progressive', and as 'a liberation from traditional values and from the tutelage of the state', according to the historian Sibylle Steinbacher. 'A new sexual order therefore stood for enlightenment, rationality and the liberal principles of self-determination and freedom of decision' and it was linked in people's perceptions with modernity, individuality, social criticism and indeed a scientific attitude. The journalist Oswalt Kolle became the most successful sex educator in the Federal Republic with books such as *Your Wife, That Unknown Creature*, and films such as *Sexual Partnership*. He saw himself as a reformer fighting against hypocritical morality and for the liberation of sexuality. The 'sex boom', says Steinbacher, 'reflected the ethos of emancipation'. Even the semi-pornographic *Schoolgirl Reports*, which reached a large public in the cinemas, started by mimicking the manner of a sociological study.

But by that point, at the latest, it became apparent that the break with long traditions of sexual paternalism was leading the pendulum to swing in the opposite direction. Women were portrayed in films and magazines as objects to be possessed sexually at any time. The contraceptive pill seemed to make the question of preventing pregnancy a matter for the woman alone, and a rampant sexualisation of everyday life took place. The liberation of sexuality from old-established taboos was associated with its commercialisation. A clear expression of this was the opening of the first Beate Uhse shop for erotic products in 1965 in Flensburg. Four years later, this had become a company with seventeen shops and a turnover of 35 million DM.[49]

Despite the rise of tendencies of this kind, the self-image and self-confidence of young women in particular began to change substantially in the late 1960s. Increasing employment levels, better education, and changing family structures offered new possibilities for self-determination, though this met with tremendous resistance. Notions of masculinity also began to change. The declining importance of heavy manual labour and an increasingly critical attitude towards the military and militarism meant that now men with less dominant, more cooperative characteristics became attractive, as can be inferred from new magazines such as *Parents*, which enjoyed much market success after 1965 and portrayed a new and softer image of fatherhood. Differences in the outward appearance of the sexes began to diminish, in the sphere of fashion, for example, where jeans, pullovers and parkas were favoured equally by men and women. Young men wore their hair long. This was the plainest sign of a departure from the traditional male image. Muscular, sporty torsos were frowned on as much as suits, ties and hats, the insignia of the bourgeois male.[50]

All these elements were particularly well-marked and widespread among young people. The generation gap, which after all had objective causes founded on the economic and social dynamics of the age, was sharply expressed in the contrast between the style of life of the older generation and the youth culture of the sixties, which now started to spread rapidly and moulded the popular culture of subsequent decades. In the 1950s, a tendency to look towards the pop music of the USA, often conveyed through the radio stations of the American and British occupation forces, had been an element in West German youth culture. At that time, however, rock and roll, and '*Schlager*' music, belonged to the working-class cultural domain. The youth of the middle classes listened more to classical music or jazz. That all changed at the beginning of the 1960s. A new, wild style of music, beat music, which had developed from rock and roll, arrived from Great Britain and began its victorious advance to cover the whole world. Raucous and incendiary lyrics, accompanied by electrically amplified guitar music, were sung by bands like the Beatles or the Rolling Stones, whose members and fans now came just as much from the middle as from the working class. Their often provocative performances were characterised by unconventionality, sarcasm and high spirits and they unleashed among the young of West Germany as elsewhere in the Western world an uninhibited enthusiasm which had never been seen before. Several thousand 'beat bands' were formed within a short time in the Federal Republic. This was an expression of the sense of freedom, individuality and rebellion specific to that generation. It took hold of young people of both sexes and all social strata, it spread like wildfire and it set a universal trend.

The beat movement was the first youth subculture in the Federal Republic to be endowed with the resources of the consumer society, and the specificity of its impact lay in this mixture of commercialisation and anti-consumerist critique. Colourful, often eccentric clothing, ostentatiously undisciplined behaviour and meeting places such as youth hostels, rock clubs and later on discotheques, which were attended exclusively by young people, created the distinctive characteristics of the youth culture. This set them apart from the way of life of their elders and created a pre-political space in which the conventions of the affluent society could be both criticised and utilised. This was a 'silent opposition' without a programme, but with strong feelings and a need to be different.[51]

The beat movement soon divided into a multiplicity of musical styles and became mingled with other cultural developments. Its initial impact was on folk music. This had originally grown out of earlier youth movement traditions, but it soon became politicised through the influence of the American folk movement. Large folk gatherings were held, such as the one at Waldeck Castle in 1965 and the Essen days of song in 1968, and the movement spread throughout the country. Adaptations of black soul music led to the establishment of a cultural link with the black civil rights movement in the USA, which had aroused particular attention in Europe by its methods of protest. It was almost inevitable that the beat movement and folk and hippie culture would join hands in the late 1960s with the political protest movement. In this context, English-language pop culture functioned both as a catalyst for the burgeoning political protest movement and a symbolic and habitual expression of it.

At the same time, the lifestyle of the beat generation promoted self-realisation and taking it easy instead of conventional behaviour and the forty-hour working week (though this was not necessarily reflected in their social practice). In the minds of the older generation this was both a rejection of the traditional values of the industrial working class such as discipline, ambition and a focus on material advancement, and an expression of contempt for what they had achieved in the post-war years. This was one of the flashpoints of the generation conflict. The well-known *Schlager* singer Freddy Quinn summed up the fury of the previous generation over the 'layabouts' in these lines: 'You hang around in parks and alleyways. Who can't understand your senseless idleness? We can't! Who is brave enough to be ashamed of you? We are! Who doesn't want our future to be taken away? We don't! Who says that work is disgusting, boring and a total deception? You do!'[52] That song got to the heart of the cultural and generational division, if from an unexpected angle.

Deviant behaviour therefore often met with a harsh reaction. The cultural conflict over 'long-haired layabouts' occasionally turned violent, especially in the provinces. Young men with long hair were physically assaulted, and many schools prohibited long hair for boys as well as mini-skirts for girls. Three-quarters of the over fifties opposed long hair, whereas 61 per cent of the under thirties were in favour, and the lower the educational level the fiercer was the rejection. There were actual demonstrations of popular rage against 'layabouts'. Calls for 'Adolf' and 'Labour Camp' could be heard. Fifty-six per cent of the population thought that idlers should be forced to work.[53]

Men with long hair and layabouts were seen both as emissaries of Americanism and a new variant of communist subversion, and by 1967 at the latest the political character of the fashion for long hair had emerged openly. Immediately after a military junta had seized power in Greece, it prohibited men from growing long hair. Nevertheless, the provocations of the young as well as the reactions of the old went some way beyond a simple reflection of reality; there was also a degree of projection involved. In some American films of the late 1960s—such as *Easy Rider* and *Vanishing Point*—the generational conflict was seen from the youth perspective, and 'the oppressive climate of hostility towards "deviants" and "outsiders" in the small towns and suburbs of middle America was expressed in a concentrated form', as the historian Gerd Koenen puts it. 'In these films it was never possible to make a precise distinction between what was reality and what was an imaginary projection—here there was an interplay of continuously escalating reciprocal aggression, at least in the imagination, which went far beyond the usual degree of generational confrontation.'[54]

In actual fact, West German society became accustomed fairly quickly to the changed appearance of its young men and women, and within a few years this symbolic avowal of individualism and independence and rejection of traditional norms of masculinity and femininity became an all-conquering fashion, which was soon to be found in all social groups. The combination between casual, unconventional dress and long hair and a critically detached attitude towards the majority of society continued to exist into the 1980s as a distinguishing mark, and a sign of membership in a youthful counter-culture. But the boundaries between the two started to become blurred when the semiotics of the subculture were absorbed by the majority culture and the drive to be different gained majority acceptance.

## In a Haunted Land

'There are people in Germany who say that God is using the GDR to punish Germans.' That is how the Israeli writer Amos Elon began his reflections on a journey made to the GDR in 1965, four years after the building of the wall. He had visited the Federal Republic previously, and his impressions had been extremely ambivalent. He noted the impact of the West German 'economic miracle' with some astonishment: 'New cities are flourishing everywhere. Streets can scarcely accommodate the flow of traffic, shop-windows are overflowing with goods which just about everyone can afford.' But he also had this to say: 'Bonn's democracy is no pleasant experience to anyone sensitive to the German past, for in this country you can never be sure whose hand you are shaking.' He perceived the GDR, in contrast, as a grey, tired country inhabited by depressed people who felt they had been cheated of their lives after more than thirty years of dictatorship:

> A traveller's first impression of the GDR is one of oppressive, universal shabbiness. It seems as though the war had ended only the day before yesterday. Large fields of rubble covered with garbage and overgrown with weeds peep out behind red, wooden placard-covered Potemkin walls, that proclaim the blessings of socialism in large letters: 'Our power serves socialism. It secures peace and prosperity!'

The atmosphere of depression and lack of liberty, wrote Elon, was almost physically perceptible. 'Isolation and alienation are universal phenomena of our time. But nowhere is their impact so acute as in East Germany, nowhere do so many people appear so drained of life and so crushed as in this joyless country.'[55]

Elon came from a Western country, and this moulded his point of view. Most visitors from the West reacted in a similar way to the defects of the East German republic, while they often failed to notice the progress it had made. After all, in the GDR as well, the 1960s were characterised by economic growth, rising income, improvements in supply and more free time. Between 1960 and 1965, the average wages of industrial employees rose by 15 per cent, from 471 to 539 marks. In December 1965, the five day week was introduced, first every other week, then continuously. The availability of consumer goods also improved: in 1965, some 54 per cent of all households possessed a television set, 26 per cent a refrigerator, and 28 per cent a washing machine. High-value consumer goods of this kind were, of course, very expensive. A television set cost four times, a refrigerator or a washing machine almost three times, the average monthly wage.[56] Like the Federal Republic, the GDR was one of the most industrially concentrated countries of the world, and the share of industry in the economy reached its highest point between 1965 and 1970. In 1960, 46.5 per cent of the workforce were active in the secondary sector, and 37 per cent in the tertiary sector (the respective proportions in the Federal Republic were 48.9 and 42.6). By 1970, this had risen to 48 per cent in the secondary, and 37 per cent in the tertiary sector (Federal Republic: 48.9 and 42.6). Not until 1970 did the service sector start to expand more quickly in West Germany than in the GDR. The number of people with higher educational qualifications also increased considerably in the GDR. In 1960, 100,000 pupils gained their *Abitur*, and in 1970, the figure was 143,000.[57]

This also had an impact on the social structure. Although the focus continued to be on the working class, as the 'ruling class', and even increased in propaganda terms, GDR society was also increasingly marked by the presence of office employees and 'brain workers'. This contradiction was particularly apparent in cultural and educational policy. The children of workers were supposed to have priority access to university education, but to counter this restriction the concept of a 'worker' was constantly extended.

More significantly, though, the immense apparatus of the state, the party and the planning bureaucracy, with its constantly rising number of staff members, gained greater and greater importance. Members of the 'nomenklatura' had special privileges in the provision of accommodation, in holiday leave and in their children's education. Socially too, this group to some extent filled the place of a middle class, which hardly existed any more in the GDR. Nevertheless, the life of the cadres, as the West German journalist Theo Sommer said in 1964, writing about his impressions of the GDR, was

> by no means spent in idleness and luxury. Discipline is strict, and the tasks the party sets are not always to everyone's taste. A good dose of idealism is needed to agree without objection to be sent anywhere the party leadership thinks fit, whether the destination is an agricultural producer cooperative in the Lausitz region or the grey industrial district around Bitterfeld. And I cannot deny that I have met with a great deal of idealism on my journey, among young officials who live in the expectation of a better future.

One thing Sommer found extremely impressive about the GDR, he wrote, was the existence of 'so much integrity, so much dedication, such indubitably moral aspirations. It would be much easier to understand everything if the officials had knives between their teeth.' But this Western observer found that his experience awakened other memories too:

> Nothing since 1945 has reminded me more of the buried epoch of the brownshirts than the GDR. The idealism of the youth leaders, their good will in the midst of all the injustices, the will to practise decency and honesty in the service of a cause which did not allow decency and honesty to prevail—all these things continue in the GDR. It is only a pity that one cannot shake off the suspicion that the misuse of idealism also continues—which is always the case when a 'cause' is placed above everything else.[58]

It cannot be determined with certainty whether and to what degree the considerable equalisation of living standards in the GDR was welcomed by the population as an 'achievement'. Not only were differences of wealth markedly levelled out after 1945, incomes diverged far less in the GDR than they did in capitalist countries. Social benefits also contributed to the feeling of equality. Neither the health system, nor children's nurseries, nor the schools and not even the holidays offered by the state were linked to the individual's performance or the nature of their employment, if the special position of the party elite is left aside.

For that reason, the small distinctions and privileges that could be obtained by becoming involved in mass organisations or other social activities were all the more important. For example, one worker who was forced to retire early on medical grounds because he had worked in the Wismut uranium mines pointed to his long-standing membership in the workers' militia as well as his involvement in the paramilitary 'Society for Sport and Technology' (GST) in order to obtain a monthly pension supplement of 100 Marks. Another worker referred to his many years occupying 'full-time functions in the youth organisation and the party' when applying for permission to take a trip to Yugoslavia, while a third supported her application to buy an allotment by mentioning her years of activity in the factory trade union leadership and in numerous honorary positions.[59] An individual's participation in GDR social activities was a prerequisite for the acquisition of advantages, or at least for the avoidance of disadvantages. In state service, in particular, among teachers for example, promotion prospects were often associated with extracurricular activities—such as in the Free German Youth (FDJ), the National Front, the German–Soviet Friendship Society, the Democratic German Women's League or the FDGB—and a considerable amount of self-confidence was needed to avoid participating in them.

In spite of these constant attempts by people to differentiate themselves, and to obtain something more, something better, than the equal share the state allotted to all its citizens, the conditions and mode of life of the population were considerably more egalitarian in the GDR than in the Federal Republic or other Western states. Equality was also the watchword in relations between the sexes. The extraordinarily high rate of female employment was no doubt to be ascribed first and foremost to the glaring shortage of labour. As we have seen, the Federal Republic also suffered from a labour shortage at this time and it compensated by recruiting foreign *Gastarbeiter*. The GDR, for its part, compensated by mobilising the female reserve of labour. Even so, there was a certain ambivalence towards the strong pressure this policy exerted on women to enter employment. It is true that the state provided the necessary infrastructure, with the extensive creation of children's day-care centres, which ensured that it was possible both to have a job and bring up children. And, according to all surveys, employment gave women in the GDR greater autonomy, greater independence and also more self-confidence. Employed mothers were expected to involve themselves completely in their professional life. According to a 1974 SED publication dealing with 'Women in Socialism':

> What is important is that a woman can organise her life in accordance with the growing expectations and demands of both spheres of responsibility, and that she does not regard serious compromises in one sphere for the benefit of the other sphere as necessary or irrevocable (for example, either by retreating to part-time employment and rejecting positions of greater responsibility, or by abandoning the marriage and refusing to have any more children).'[60]

But, according to a survey made in 1966, roughly half of all married women and 30 per cent of unmarried women stated that they went to work largely for material reasons, and they would give up their job if the family's income could be kept at the same level in other ways.

In this context, the main problem turned out to be that though the role and self-image of women in the GDR had changed considerably, men's views remained the same. In 1965, the average length of time spent on housework in a four-person household by married women who were in full employment was 37.7 hours a week, while married men spent an average of 5.5 hours. While men had to spend an average of 62.2 hours a week on work, the journey to work, housework and childcare, the figure for employed women was 80.3 hours. Women took over activities previously dominated by men, but men did not take over women's traditional duties. The double burden on women remained one of the characteristic features of GDR social policy into the late 1980s. It is evident, however, that the high level of female employment was perceived as a sign that equality between the sexes had been achieved at least in part, and that it was very much welcomed.[61]

A belief in scientific and technological advance was something East and West Germans had in common. The inhabitants of both halves of the country were certain that the future could be planned, that prosperity could be increased without limit and that prospects were bright, although always on condition that the social model of the side in question was able to win the upper hand. The West German move towards planning, which was perceptible after the beginning of the 1970s, appeared to people in the GDR as the best proof of the correctness of their economic and social model, which had done away with the 'anarchic' laws of the market and replaced them with a rational plan. During those years, therefore, the functionaries and scientists of the GDR were inspired by the idea 'that electronic brains have overcome the main weakness of the system: faulty planning by human beings'. The physicist Manfred von Ardenne, one of the most important scientists of the GDR, enthusiastically explained his view that planning lay at the centre of economic and political thought to Western journalists. 'But planning is still imperfect', he added, 'as the mass of necessary information cannot be developed, discovered and transmitted quickly enough by human beings. Once electronic machines take over this task, we shall overcome all difficulties. Time and technological development are therefore working in our favour.'[62]

The most ambitious plans were those for housing construction. Socialist housing development was aimed quite explicitly against the 'bourgeois' *Gründerzeit* town centres, which were replaced with the socialist city. This would have broad streets, gigantic squares and new housing estates for 30–40,000 people, which would consist of identical apartments with modern kitchens and bathrooms. Living space was in very short supply in the GDR. As late as 1970, an average of 1.4 persons lived in a one-person dwelling. The housing stock was on average sixty years old, and 60 per cent of the houses had neither a bath nor an inside toilet, while 20 per cent did not even have mains water. It was therefore not surprising that the new housing estates that were being planned were keenly awaited by the GDR population, however elephantine and monotonous their aspect, especially as the plans for new housing disregarded the older buildings of the cities, with the result that they fell into increasing decay.

This decline into decay was not primarily a consequence of the ideological dream of obliterating the capitalist city, as has often been surmised, but rather resulted from the method of calculation employed by the planners. They worked out that the productivity of a building worker engaged in constructing a new housing estate would be 17,000 Marks a year, but the productivity of someone repairing an old building would only be 9,000 Marks a year. The amount of material used was also calculated, of course, and since this was much higher in a new housing complex with gigantic pre-cast concrete components than when the roof of an old building was repaired, the job of making repairs was postponed so as not to reduce the productivity figures of the sector and thereby endanger plan fulfilment, although everyone knew that by repairing a roof extra housing space could be obtained at much less cost.

From the mid-1960s onwards, 'prefabrication' began to spread. This was a system of rapid building construction from concrete components, and it allowed roughly 700,000 new dwellings to be built in the 1960s, rising to more than a million in the 1970s. The characteristics of socialist urban development were very similar to those that prevailed at the time in the Federal Republic as well: functional separation, concentrated structural development and car-friendly town centres, as well as 'light, air and sunshine', in order to overcome the legacy of the narrow and unhealthy towns and cities of the *Gründerzeit*.[63]

Four years after the building of the Berlin Wall, a kind of enforced normality started to emerge in the GDR. The basic necessities were available, but what was most symptomatic was the high level of social security. Unemployment of the capitalist type did not exist in the GDR. Redundant workers were not dismissed but retained in the factories, even if this led to a sustained fall in productivity. Rents were low, there were enough places in nursery, school and university and they were free of charge, as was medical treatment and hospitalisation. Holiday travel was now also possible. The main destinations were the Baltic coast or the Harz mountains, and trips were usually organised through the individual's workplace or the FDGB. Only in the 1970s did travel abroad, into other socialist countries, become more frequent. As in the West, campsites were favoured. They were an alternative to the state-run holiday centres, and on a campsite there was greater opportunity for individuals to decide the kind of recreation they wanted, and far less state control. Anyone who could do so built a small weekend house in the countryside, described as a 'dacha'. 'A private niche' became the familiar expression denoting the retreat of the citizen from the permanent public display of political allegiance. Sport played an increasing role, particularly after the state had realised what great opportunities for promoting the GDR's image were offered by success in international sporting competitions, which enjoyed ever-increasing prestige.

For visitors from the rest of the Eastern bloc, the GDR was practically a consumer's paradise. It was by far the most attractive foreign posting for soldiers of the Red Army, and it was a privilege to be transferred there.[64] For Westerners, in contrast, to visit the GDR was to take a journey into the past. 'Old-time Germany' was the name given to it by the West German journalist Countess Marion Dönhoff, who visited the country in 1964. Highways paved with cobblestones, towns not surrounded by the owner-occupied housing estates typically found in the West, very little traffic, complete darkness at night without the permanent glow of shop windows and advertisement hoardings, 'and there they still are: the familiar avenues with their wonderful old trees, which with us have mostly fallen victim to the motor car. Everything is much sadder and bleaker and less glamorous, but also less pretentious and more modest.'[65]

Despite all the GDR's efforts, the production of consumer goods remained the Achilles heel of its economy. In the mid-1960s, the Federal Republic had 140 private motor vehicles for every 1,000 inhabitants; the GDR fewer than ten. The waiting time for the GDR's motor car, the Trabant, was more than seven years; in 1966, 67 per cent of the country's population were waiting for a car they had ordered. At late as 1970, there were only sixty-six private telephone lines for every thousand households. Even ordinary consumer goods were often unavailable, or only available for a short time, in quantities that were inadequate and quality that was inferior. Moreover, they were often unevenly distributed: the big towns were better supplied than the country districts, and Berlin, which was favoured for political reasons, had better supplies than Leipzig or Dresden. Specific groups, such as workers in particularly favoured industrial areas, enjoyed supply privileges, as did young families and party officials, while pensioners were often at a disadvantage.[66]

As a result, informal supply networks grew up alongside the official channels of distribution. Without engaging in barter, it was hardly possible to obtain certain products. Goods 'picked up' from the factories often played an important role in this process. Shortages were a constant accompaniment of daily life in the GDR, and this placed those who 'administered shortage' in a privileged position. Saleswomen in the shops, head waiters in restaurants, but also craftsmen and storekeepers in the big industrial plants controlled goods that were in short supply. These people were envied and disliked by the less privileged. The market power of the consumer did not exist in the GDR, and the regime reacted to the growing anger of the population by making this a taboo subject. Supply shortages were not mentioned officially. Thus the 'parcel from the West' containing coffee beans, jeans or tights gained an almost mythical significance. This was the only way much sought-after Western items could be obtained, and people with no relatives in the West came away empty-handed. 'From each according to his abilities, to each according to his accomplishments', which was the old SED slogan of the early 1950s, was replaced now by 'To each according to where his aunt lives', as the singer and poet Wolf Biermann derisively remarked.[67]

Even so, Amos Elon concluded his impressions by saying that it could not just be a result of the communist regime that life in the GDR looked so joyless. For in comparison with Leipzig or East Berlin Prague, Warsaw and Kiev seemed to be 'veritable models of lightheartedness'. And he added:

> The standard of living does not seem to be the decisive factor. The average Pole, Czech, Hungarian or Russian is considerably poorer than his East German counterpart. East Germany has the highest standard of living in the socialist world. But Poland and Hungary have something the East Germans clearly lack: a certain feeling, a degree of self-confidence, which makes it possible to restore their spiritual equilibrium even in unfreedom. Depression hangs over the country like a thick fog. It is almost a physical feeling.[68]

The feeling of being trapped by the building of the wall, the monotony of life, and the lack of any alternative, were the explanations given most frequently for this condition, which struck most observers from the West. 'Until the wall was built', explained a graphic designer from East Berlin to the Israeli journalist, 'one felt one could always leave if one wanted. That is all over now. Many people see themselves stuck here in this rubble. There's no escaping from it, and that is oppressive.'[69]

The most important reason for the difference in atmosphere between the GDR and the older socialist states, which Elon also notes, was the existence of the Federal Republic. No Western state served as a national point of reference for the Poles or the Hungarians. Citizens of the GDR, on the other hand, took note of the fact that the working week was three hours longer for them than in West Germany, that the household income of working-class families was smaller by almost half, and that pensions were smaller by around two-thirds. It was no compensation that the GDR had achieved the highest level of all the East bloc states in all these categories. Hence 'the West' remained synonymous with prosperity and freedom for large sections of the population, especially as after the building of the wall the impact of Western wealth was no longer put into context by personal observation but filtered through Western television and even intensified by the counter-propaganda of the SED. Whatever happened in the GDR was measured against this picture of the West.[70] The relationship of the citizens of the GDR to the West, which the state regarded with suspicion and endeavoured to counter, was therefore much more intense than the relationship of the West Germans to the GDR, although the Federal Republic did its best to promote and encourage it..

The SED projected everything onto West Germany. It was the 'enemy' which was assumed to be everywhere, and thought capable of almost anything:

> The enemy was ever-present. He was often invisible and could only be revealed by eyes sharpened by the experience of class struggle. But he was all around . . . If the enemy was mentioned in party meetings, voices were involuntarily lowered, as if he were lurking somewhere behind the podium draped in its red banners. If criticisms were raised in our own ranks, the reply was 'Objectively speaking, you are helping the enemy' and faces grew hard and implacable.[71]

Thus for the SED too, the Federal Republic remained the yardstick by which its own successes were measured, the benchmark for its efforts at modernisation, and a backdrop against which it projected its hostility to West Germany's Americanised cultural modernity.

The dynamic expansion of Western popular and consumer culture after the early 1960s led to a further increase in GDR citizens' fascination for the West. The SED took energetic steps to counter this. More than 90 per cent of young people, the Leipzig Youth Institute reported, regularly watched Western television or listened to Western radio programmes.[72] The new youthful protest culture in West Germany, which was rebellious and at the same time consumer oriented, gained ever more adherents in East Germany, as did its fashions in music, clothing and hairstyles. The SED leadership saw a direct connection between these phenomena and the criticisms of conditions in the GDR made by many artists and intellectuals, which had emerged more strongly (with permission) since the early 1960s. According to the assumptions the party was quick to make, critical voices such as those of Robert Havemann and Wolf Biermann were nothing other than an expression of the subversive power of cultural Americanism. As mentioned earlier, it was decided at the Eleventh CC Plenum, held in December 1965, to reduce the pace of economic reform and revoke the cultural concessions of the previous years. In his keynote speech at the plenum Erich Honecker made a direct link between Havemann's criticisms of the GDR, Stefan Heym's novels, Wolf Biermann's songs and the decadent and immoral American mass culture which was exerting an ever stronger influence on young people through music and films:

> Our GDR is a clean state. It has unshakeable standards of ethics and morality, decency and good manners. Our party decisively opposes the propaganda for immorality put out by the imperialists, the purpose of which is to harm socialism . . . Biermann's so-called poems indicate his petit-bourgeois, anarchistic attitude, his arrogance, his scepticism and his cynicism.[73]

Biermann was forbidden to appear in public, and the GDR writers' union issued an obedient statement on the subject. The Minister of Culture, Hans Bentzien, was dismissed and replaced by Klaus Gysi, a man who was willing to reimpose the party line.

The SED leaders not only saw criticism of the party as sacrilegious, they were also hostile to any statement which appeared to cast doubt on the belief in industrial progress, science and technology. Ulbricht countered such 'sceptical and pessimistic' positions with the optimistic declaration that the scientifically directed expansion of the economy would create the conflict-free 'socialist community'. 'If we permit the propaganda of scepticism' he said 'this reduces the increase in labour productivity by one per cent.'[74]

The SED thought that the wave of youth culture spilling over from the West into the GDR posed a particular threat to socialism. Beat groups, 'layabouts', wearers of jeans and long-haired youths were clearly opponents of the socialist community, and the state had them in its sights. The SED leadership concluded that there had been a culpable failure to recognise the danger arising from 'the beat music infiltrated by the imperialists' because 'the enemy uses this kind of music to inflame the young into committing excesses with exaggerated rhythms. The harmful influence of such music on the thought and actions of young people has been grossly underestimated.'[75] As a result, the precaution was taken of 'suppressing everything and declaring everything undesirable', noted the writer Hans Noll in his memoirs about this period.

> Long hair, trousers that were too tight or too loose, colourful polythene bags and chewing gum, Anglicisms and, even worse, Americanisms. All the harmless fashions, mini-skirts, maxi-skirts, striped shirts, one or the other way of dancing, had to fight for a long time before the Central Committee was forced to accept them. And some particularly obdurate comrades continued to conduct their own private war against them, with the secret sympathy of the Central Committee and in the happy consciousness that they were demonstrating their 'unshakeable loyalty' to socialism in a world being softened up by the West. It was not at all unusual for the cadre files of young people to include damaging remarks about their undesirable blue jeans or beards. It was not even unusual for them to be expelled from high school or university for these reasons. After all, they would then be forced to 'stand the test of practical activity.'[76]

But the conviction of the SED that what was happening here was simply an imitation of Western models, or the deliberate infiltration of Western cultural material with the aim of destabilising the GDR, was just as unfounded as the assumption by West German conservatives that the new fashions of the young were an instrument of communist subversion. It was rather that the proliferating enthusiasm for rock and roll, beat music and long hair reflected the heightened need of young people in the GDR to separate themselves from the world of their mothers and fathers, whose values of tranquillity, order and security did not differ from those current in the West. The drive towards self-realisation and the establishment of an individual identity may well have been stronger here than in the West, because the political and social structures were more rigid and the constantly extending control of the population by the state made the desire for an outlet almost overwhelming. The reactions of the authorities were correspondingly harsh.

In autumn 1965, the newspaper of the SED party leadership in Leipzig reported that there were already eighty-three musical groups in the city which should be regarded as politically and culturally dangerous: 'There has been an increasing tendency in the past to use the rhythm of guitars to inculcate Western modes of living into the young.' These were the only groups that young people now followed. Traditional dance orchestras like 'Walter Eichenberg', were positively scorned by the young, the article added.[77] At first, the party leadership attempted to put a stop to this development by incorporating it, with measures such as a centrally organised 'competition for guitar groups', but after receiving reports about a concert given by the Rolling Stones at the Waldbühne venue in West Berlin on 15 September 1965 it took a different view of the situation. More than 20,000 spectators came to the performance, and after the concert they fought for hours with the West Berlin police, demolished the Waldbühne, and damaged many carriages of the (East Berlin) S-Bahn. The party leadership saw these events in West Berlin as so dangerous that the Central Committee decided to revise the whole of its previous youth policy. Henceforth, Western influence would not be allowed to affect East German youth culture, and youthful rebels would be put in labour camps. 'All extravagant behaviour, particularly by guitar groups, which tends towards Americanism, demoralisation and decadence, must be brought to an end.'[78]

In response to this, beat groups were prohibited in Leipzig. The local daily newspaper printed a report under the heading 'There is no room for abuses by young people', angrily complaining about

> young people, who worship and ape an extremely dubious American way of life which they regard as an ideal. The long, shaggy hair they grow as an external mark of their state of mind narrows their horizons to such an extent that they do not see how abnormal, unhealthy and brutish their behaviour is.

This is the way in which imperialism 'foments trouble and conducts a hidden war against the GDR'. Beat groups like The Shatters or The Butlers 'behave in an ape-like fashion in their "performances", emit inarticulate sounds, squat on the floor or roll around on it and shake their arms and legs around in an indecent manner.'[79] The prohibition of the Leipzig beat groups led to disturbances, and finally to a demonstration by youthful enthusiasts, which was attended by more than two thousand people. But only between five and eight hundred of these were beat supporters; all the rest were state security members or policemen, and they immediately proceeded to break up the demonstration. Two hundred and sixty-seven young people were arrested, and had their hair cut by the police. Some one hundred were subsequently convicted in summary trials and transported to do forced labour in the opencast lignite mines which were located south of the city.[80]

What was the nature of the threat which the state and the party reacted to with such severity? The party identified the rebelliousness and the incomprehensible behaviour of young people, along with pornography, 'rolling around indecently' and decadence as an 'extremely questionable Americanised mode of life'. It saw this behaviour as an attack on written and unwritten norms of morality and on the foundations of the family and society. In addition, long hair in men opened the possibility of confusing the two sexes and was therefore seen as a violation of the traditional sexual order. This was unmistakably also a conflict between the generations, for the informers who worked for the party and the Stasi reported that it was above all older people who showed an understanding of the need for tough action against 'layabouts'. At the same time, the accusations of uncleanliness and indolence also indicated the connection with 'scepticism', an attitude which rejected the norms of progress and productivity and must therefore be punished with forced labour in the mining industry. But it was not just the principles of the communist regime that the SED leaders thought were under attack here; the threat reached further than this, affecting the values of a society dominated by industrial labour, which they upheld. The change in the value structure which took place with the rise of the service economy and the consumer society in the West, the accelerated liberalisation of social norms, and the individualisation and differentiation of lifestyles, clashed in the sharpest possible way with the collectivism, discipline and state control of public life characteristic of the GDR.

There were clear parallels here with the critique of the US style of life by West German conservatives. While the beat movement in the Federal Republic was regarded as both the expression of a pernicious Americanism and a product of communist infiltration, which should be opposed accordingly, the 'hullabaloo over beat music' was also perceived by the SED through the categories of the Cold War and far-fetched conspiracy theories: beat music, it was claimed, was a particularly devious method used by imperialism, a kind of brainwashing, to dissuade young people from devoting themselves to the building of socialism.

In the East, as in the West, the enthusiasm of young people for a new form of dance music was felt to be a kind of rebellion, liable to shake the foundations of society. 'Layabouts', beat music and long hair were perceived as a refusal by young people not just to conform to the traditional norms of decency and morality, but also to take part in building up the economy and to affirm their support for the importance of industry, productivity, growth and technological progress. There was evidently something new here, which differed from earlier forms of youth rebellion and posed a threat to the foundations of East German as also of West German society from an angle previously unknown. But whereas, in the Federal Republic, the recalcitrant young were at most threatened with sanctions and 'labour camps' by angry citizens, and even then not very seriously, the 'Beat Youths' in the GDR were actually sent to the lignite mines to do forced labour. That is a measure of the difference between the two systems.

# 16
# Reform and Revolt

## Modern Politics

The 'Grand Coalition' government of the Federal Republic was a short-term alliance for a particular purpose: to overcome the economic crisis and to modernise the state, the economy and the society of West Germany, as called for on all sides. This association between the two big parties was also celebrated as a sign that the Germans had become reconciled with each other, and that the alliance between the working class and the bourgeoisie which had never come to pass during the Weimar years had now finally occurred. In addition, the contrast between the political trajectories of Chancellor Kiesinger, who was formerly a member of the NSDAP and a high official in the foreign office during the Nazi period, and Foreign Minister Brandt, who had gone into exile in Norway and fought there against the German occupiers, also indicated the desire for reconciliation between the supporters and opponents of National Socialism.

For the SPD, participation in government as a junior partner seven years after reversing its social policy at Godesberg and deciding to accept Western integration was now probably the only possible way to achieve the power it had been unable to secure in five Bundestag elections. For the CDU–CSU, on the other hand, the coalition offered the opportunity to realign itself politically after the agony of the late Adenauer years and the disaster of the Erhard government. Of course, the political dangers associated with an alliance between the two parties could not be ignored. A coalition with more than two-thirds of the seats in the Bundestag was faced with just one small opposition party, the FDP, which was in any case riven by an internal conflict between the national liberal tradition and its recent reorientation towards social liberalism. It was therefore no surprise that fresh challenges to this new concentration of power arose from outside. On the Right there was the rising National Democratic Party of Germany (NPD), and on the Left the emerging force of the Extra-Parliamentary Opposition.

An association between the two major parties therefore needed to be justified as an emergency measure in an extraordinarily difficult situation, and the government declaration issued by the new Chancellor in December 1966 was indeed shot through with references to 'the long, smouldering crisis . . . which is being observed by our nation with deep concern.' It was true that the economic indices had worsened since summer 1966, and that in 1967, for the first time in the history of the Federal Republic, they indicated a fall in the Gross Domestic Product (GDP)—by 0.3 per cent. An increase in inflation and a rise in unemployment to 2.5 per cent in spring 1967 were seen as alarming signs, especially as unemployment figures were much higher in certain crisis-hit branches of industry such as mining and textiles. Even so, this was not a real economic crisis, but rather a 'conjunctural downturn'. The pronounced sense of crisis at this time cannot be explained by the economic data alone, which continued to be favourable in comparison with the rest of Europe. It resulted rather from the uncertainty that prevailed over whether the Federal Republic was now stable enough to withstand a serious economic crisis, or whether, as many people feared, an economic crisis would also be accompanied by social and political destabilisation.[1]

In face of weak economic growth, rising prices, a budget deficit, a mining crisis in the Ruhr and the backwardness of the educational sphere, almost all political forces in the country were agreed that these challenges could not be mastered with a traditional economic policy of the kind associated with Erhard. Instead, as Chancellor Kiesinger stated in his government declaration, a radical modernisation of the economy and economic policy was necessary, involving forward-looking state planning. This 'new policy of overall direction' would allow all areas of domestic policy 'to be harmonised with each other and oriented towards the long term'. With the help of more long-range financial planning and innovatory advice and coordination committees, the goal of a 'controlled expansion' of the economy and a lasting growth rate of around 4 per cent would be achieved.

It is astonishing, in retrospect, how rapidly the Federal Republic's economic policy change from market liberalism to Keynesianism was accomplished. It is true that this change was part of the trend already mentioned towards optimism about planning, which had prevailed since the early 1960s in most Western industrial countries. But it can also be seen as a reaction to what the outside world perceived as the extraordinary economic and technological successes of the Soviet Union and its satellites. Many people in the West were convinced that the competition between the Eastern and Western systems could not be won through the free play of market forces, especially as some of the most important fields of this competitive struggle, such as agriculture, social policy, research and defence, had been withdrawn from the action of economic forces and were primarily determined by political considerations. It was the introduction into politics of the criterion of conformity with scientific requirements which gave such a strong, though unevenly developed, impulse to the planning idea among the governments of the industrial countries.

This applied particularly to economic policy. An increasingly widespread conviction emerged that the enormous progress made in the natural sciences and medicine might be paralleled in the economic and social spheres by using scientific methods to find successful solutions to the large-scale problems of conjunctural crisis, unemployment and inflation. Scientific expertise seemed capable of 'providing authoritative information about society, giving clear instructions on how to act, and in this way helping to make the correct decisions.' According to an economics textbook printed in 1967, methods now existed by which crises in the economic organism could be treated as reliably as doctors could cure infectious diseases with the aid of penicillin.[2] Here, economic policy, like policy in general, was viewed as the implementation of quasi-natural laws which could be established scientifically. This meant stripping it of its properly political character, which is the endeavour to strike a balance between different interests and cultural values.

The central pillar of the Grand Coalition's new economic policy was the 'Law for the Promotion of Stability and Economic Growth' devised by Karl Schiller, the SPD Minister of Economics. The policy instruments provided by this legislation were intended to allow fluctuations in growth to be prevented by anti-cyclical demand management, so as to ensure an even rate of economic progress, undisturbed by crises. When business conditions were favourable, the state would build up reserves, so that when economic activity began to slacken, it could be revived by public investment and demand could be stimulated by granting additional credits. Central tasks which could not be performed by the individual *Länder* alone would in future be jointly financed from federal funds, and in this way the central government gained access to areas of policy previously reserved to the local state governments. Examples of this were regional economic development, urban redevelopment, protection of the coasts, and the building of universities, motorways and hospitals. The investment programmes intended to stimulate economic activity would be concentrated in those areas.

In addition to this, the movement of wages and salaries would no longer be determined by time-consuming trials of strength between capital and labour, but by agreement between trade unions, entrepreneurs and the state on the basis of objective data and according to rational criteria. Strikes, lockouts and overnight wage negotiations would become relics of a bygone age in face of the 'concerted action' brought into existence by modern policy instruments. Better coordination, expert scientific advice and the enhanced role of the state would make such rituals superfluous in the future, and would not only contribute to rapidly overcoming the contemporary crisis but also, more generally, bring about the attenuation, or even perhaps the complete elimination, of the cyclical crises affecting the capitalist economy.

When economic activity began to pick up again after the end of 1967, and the economy went on in 1968 and 1969 to achieve tremendous rates of growth, with increases of 5.7 per cent and 7.4 per cent respectively, it seemed as if the new policy had passed the test of time: with the help of global economic management, medium-term financial planning, concerted action and other instruments out of Schiller's box of tricks, not only did the recession appear to have been overcome, but it seemed clear that the market economy could be guided and growth could be planned. Social Democratic economic policy over the last three years, wrote Karl Schiller in 1969, had shown 'what a clearly designed and consistent economic policy could achieve: declining unemployment figures, and rising instead of falling income . . . We have demonstrated that economic reality can be altered by political action.'[3]

Modern policies, provided they were scientifically grounded, could therefore not only change society, by breaking through class boundaries and providing a better education for a larger proportion of the population, they could also overcome the capitalist crises which had scourged industrial societies for almost the whole of the previous hundred years, and abolish unemployment and poverty. This conviction strengthened the progress-oriented optimism of those years, and it placed its stamp on the politics of the time among both the Social Democrats and the middle-class parties.

The coalition intended to modernise not just economic and financial policy but the apparatus of government as well. 'Technically speaking, the Federal Republic is still ruled with implements already known to Bismarck. But his mastery of the craft of governance was much greater': this was the critical judgment of the influential journalist Johannes Gross in 1966.[4] With the reform of government and administration and the establishment of planning staffs and project groups 'patterns of thought and speech derived from management theory and administrative science' entered the thinking and action of politicians and changed the political practice of the ministerial bureaucracy by making it more professional—and by increasing staffing levels.[5]

Along with economic policy, the government concentrated on a series of large-scale plans for legal and social policy reform, the most important of which was without doubt the great reform of the criminal law which had been under preparation since 1954. By this reform the previously dominant criteria of guilt and punishment were increasingly replaced by an emphasis on resocialisation and reintegration. The reform of the law relating to sexual activity began the long overdue retreat of the state from the private lives of its citizens. Homosexual activity between adults ceased to be a punishable offence, and the cohabitation of unmarried pairs was decriminalised. In most cases West

Germany was simply falling into line with changes already made by other countries of Western Europe. But where these changes affected matters of morality the reforms met with increasing resistance from the Union. Members of the CDU and CSU were reluctant to accept equality between legitimate and illegitimate children, and the principle had to be forced through by a judgment of the Federal Constitutional Court, after legitimate children continued to be privileged in the legislative proposals of the CSU Minister of Justice Richard Jaeger.[6]

The conservatives were opposed in the media, particularly on questions of family law and morality, by a phalanx of reform advocates, who gave solid support to the demand for a 'modern law' concerning children born outside marriage: 'For the people they are mongrels and bastards, and for the lawyers of Bonn they remain second-class citizens', wrote *Der Spiegel* in October 1966. 'The proposed law, permeated with ideas of morality which belong to previous centuries, denies the illegitimate child full recognition in society . . . They speak of the good of the child, but the reformers have bourgeois notions of family and marriage.' Conservative positions, which a few years before would have received the support of big majorities, now seemed to have a whiff of anachronism.[7]

The Grand Coalition had substantial political reforms to its credit, even if it started many more than it was able to carry through. But many of the domestic reforms made by the Social–Liberal Coalition that followed it were also based on the initiatives of its predecessor. As regards policy towards German unification and foreign policy in general, on the other hand, the two partners in the Grand Coalition had little in common. They did agree that West Germany would not be able for much longer to continue blocking the endeavours of the Western powers to secure détente. At the very least, a compromise with the Eastern bloc countries was urgently necessary, even if that would inevitably lead to a softening of the Hallstein Doctrine. At first, the federal government tried to improve relations with the Eastern bloc without modifying its attitude towards the GDR. It entered into diplomatic relations with Romania and Yugoslavia and also sought to achieve an improvement of political relations with the other Warsaw Pact countries by intensifying economic contacts. At the same time, it offered to conduct discussions with the SED leadership about ways of reducing the effects of the division of the country, though not about recognising the GDR.

TheEast German government resisted this approach. In the eyes of the countries of the Warsaw Pact, the Federal Republic was extremely attractive as a trade partner. For that reason, the GDR leadership feared that it would become politically isolated within the Eastern bloc. In response, Ulbricht succeeded in enforcing the principle that members of the Warsaw Pact would not normalise their relations with the Federal Republic until the GDR took a similar step. But the prerequisite for this would be international recognition by the Federal

Republic. There was no consensus for this step within the Grand Coalition, however. The SPD advocated a policy of barter: step by step recognition of the GDR in return for humanitarian improvements for the GDR population such as easing travel restrictions; but every step in the direction of recognising the GDR was rejected by the Union. When Warsaw Pact troops marched into Czechoslovakia in summer 1968, the Union saw this as a renewed confirmation of its estimate of the aggressive, totalitarian character of the Eastern bloc dictatorships. Moreover, on the question of German–German relations, the Union had a clear majority of the population on its side: at the beginning of 1967, the Federal Republic's claim to sole representation was supported by 61 per cent of the population. Only 14 per cent were against.[8]

## The International Protest Movement

The protest movements of the 1960s were an international phenomenon. They appeared in almost all the developed industrial countries of the West, and they could be identified, in an altered form, in some Eastern bloc states as well. These movements had very diverse causes, with deep roots in the contradictions of national development in each of the countries in question. Their aims and methods were as heterogeneous as the social groups that underlay them. And yet they were regarded as part of a worldwide movement, and that is also how they regarded themselves. Their greatest common feature was their chronological parallelism, which was seen most palpably in spring 1968 after murderous attacks were made successively within a few weeks on Martin Luther King, Rudi Dutschke and Robert Kennedy. The protests and disturbances in the USA, West Germany, France, Italy, Great Britain, the Netherlands, Japan and many other countries appeared to be directly related.[9]

They also had a basic structural feature in common: they were generational conflicts. Members of the older generation had experienced the Second World War as adults and had been marked by the horror of war, and in many cases had also undergone socialisation as soldiers, which made them think in military categories. After the war, this alignment with the authorities and this tendency to think in terms of friend and foe was confirmed and prolonged by the Cold War and the permanent threat of nuclear conflict. An added factor was pride of the older generation in West Germany's economic and social progress since the war. They did not want their achievements to be challenged and they regarded attempts to change the system as a threat. Admittedly, this is too sweeping and imprecise a generalisation to apply to every individual, but it does characterise a generally perceptible divide between the older generation and its successor.

The next generation had not passed through the same experiences and it often regarded the attitudes and modes of behaviour of its elders as gloomy, narrow and repressive. According to Norbert Elias,

> the break between the worlds experienced by those who grew up before and after the war was, in the case of the great war of 1939–1945, especially deep. This holds for large parts of the world. In particular, it holds true for the imperial countries of Europe. But it is for Germany, however, that it holds to the greatest extent.[10]

One final point: between the 1950s and the 1970s, all Western countries experienced a tremendous surge of economic and social change, which made these societies wealthy, thoroughly churned up their social structure, reconfigured cultural alignments, day-to-day existence and relations between the sexes, and altered people's scale of values. Authority, obedience, doing one's duty were replaced as guidelines by participation, transparency, equality and liberalism, and this was also a characteristic generational change. The collision between the values of the old and those of the young is one of the major reasons for the conflicts which shaped the 1960s in the Western countries. The sharper these contradictions, the sharper the clashes between the 'establishment' and the new opposition movements.[11]

From the political angle, the starting point of protest was disappointment over the unmistakable contradiction between the postulates of peace and democracy formulated in the years after the war and the perceived day-to-day practice of the authorities. This applies particularly to the opposition movement in the USA, whose development served as a basic model, and often a direct example, for protest movements in most of the other Western countries. In the USA, the biggest contradiction between democratic standards and the real situation lay undoubtedly in the systematic discrimination practised against the Afro-American minority. An overwhelmingly black civil rights movement had grown up to oppose this, and since the late 1950s it had gained greater and greater support and significance. The American civil rights movement acted as a detonator for the new protest movements that emerged throughout the Western world. It differed from the pre-war and post-war social struggles in the industrial countries, because the issue at stake was discrimination against an ethnic, not a social, minority. It was concerned with human rights, not class struggle. For the post-war epoch, this was a new phenomenon, and it quickly found imitators.

The increasing protests against the war in Vietnam were also a reaction to the contradiction between the ethical norms of US policy and its actual practice. The targets of protest also broadened. Disapproval of America's military engagement in Vietnam became linked with attacks on the exploitation and oppression suffered by the countries of the Third World in general. Meanwhile, protests against obstructions to freedom of opinion expanded into a general criticism of undemocratic practices in US politics and society, and soon extended their reach far beyond the civil rights movement and the university campuses.

In the mid-1960s, the protest movement began to join forces with a lifestyle rebellion among young people, largely dominated by student oppositionists. A subculture took shape, a counter-culture, which symbolised a cultural rupture with traditional ways of living and the conditions currently being experienced. The movement promoted new, less repressive forms of cohabitation and a sceptical and hedonistic lifestyle. This made the youth protest attractive to strata far wider than the core political opposition and it also gave it the power to transcend national boundaries.[12]

After the murders of Martin Luther King, the charismatic orator of the black civil rights movement, and Robert Kennedy, who as candidate for the presidency had embodied the hopes of some of the youthful protesters, the American protest movement divided into several different tendencies. One section returned to the established organisations and parties, another section founded numerous short-lived communist groupings, while the greater part of the movement established new radical liberal and civil rights formations, the most significant of which was undoubtedly the 'Women's Liberation Movement'. As time went by, the radical feminism which developed out of this movement set its stamp on the new women's movements of the whole Western world, and even further afield. There were also organisations of various disadvantaged minorities, which fought to remove the forms of prejudice and discrimination they suffered: homosexuals, the disabled, and immigrants from Latin America and other regions. The black civil rights movement was also in contact with these groups. A final addition to this coalition was the movement for environmental protection, which emerged in the early 1970s. It was obvious that the field of action of these movements no longer covered the problems or the conflict areas of classical industrial society. The white working class played no role in these newly formed movements; on the contrary, in much of the Western world, its social concerns tended to be opposed to the aims of the new 'rainbow movement'.[13]

In France, on the other hand, the new protest movements were more closely associated with the older ones. France too had experienced an enormous social and economic upsurge in the 1950s and 1960s. The existing class structure had not, however, been as quickly or as comprehensively undermined as it had been in the USA or the Federal Republic. The trade unions and the Communist Party continued to stand indisputably at the centre of the workers' protests, which in the 1960s still followed the familiar path of class struggle. Nevertheless, colonial policy lay at the 'dark centre' of French domestic conflict during this period, particularly the war against the movement for Algerian independence, which after four years led to the demise of the Fourth Republic and its replacement by a Fifth Republic under the presidency of Charles De Gaulle.[14]

In the mid-1960s the situation in France, unlike in other Western countries, remained calm at first. Not until spring 1968 did student protests start to flare up, and they were rapidly joined by radical workers' protests, which spread like wildfire in May of that year. There was barricade fighting in Paris, there were workers' protests, strikes and finally a general strike: what were at first purely contingent student protests acted like a spark in a powder keg. May 1968 in Paris also had a long historical aftermath, which, as in other countries, led first to the fragmentation of the protest movement, but then, subsequently, after De Gaulle's resignation, to the establishment of new party formations on the Left.

Similar events took place in Italy. Here too, protests by students against their miserable academic conditions and career prospects were closely associated with the militant strikes and struggles of the industrial workers, who no longer felt represented by their trade unions. The smouldering after-effects of the struggle between the Fascists and the Italian resistance during the war formed the background to this radicalisation. Issues of democratisation and civil rights were less important in Italy than in the USA. Here, revolutionary Left radical groups of workers and students were fighting against the capitalist economy and the bourgeois state. These disturbances of the late 1960s were the beginning of a decade full of strikes, revolts and also terrorist attacks. The latter started bloodily with the December 1969 outrage in Milan, which caused the death of sixteen people. It was committed by Fascist activists, with the support of Italy's military secret service. After this, the Left also turned to acts of terror, which culminated in the kidnapping and murder of the veteran Italian prime minister Aldo Moro in 1978.[15]

## Structural Features of the Revolt

This international context makes it possible to situate the development of the protest movement in the Federal Republic more clearly. In structure and evolution, it was closer to the American model than to the revolts in France and Italy. As we have seen, the social changes of the fifties and sixties had been particularly rapid and far-reaching in West Germany. Since the early 1960s, lines of conflict between traditionally oriented and modern forces, old and young, authoritarian and anti-authoritarian, had become apparent, and they became more intense as time went on. But closer inspection shows that these boundary lines were permeable, and it is not easy to make a sharp distinction between the opposing forces. Contemporaries, however, tended to take an exaggerated view of the differences, in part because they were wrapped up with earlier conflicts which had found no public outlet in the post-Nazi society of the Federal Republic.

In this context, the part of catalyst was played by the milieu of writers and intellectuals who took for granted the political connection of the Federal Republic with the West (the cultural connection even more so) and on that basis made the divergence between the postulated democracy of West Germany and the real situation a starting point for critical analysis. Despite the existence of some points of contact, there was a clear differentiation between this approach and the traditional left-wing critique of Western integration, the market economy and parliamentary democracy: these thinkers were committed to improving Western-oriented democratic capitalism, not to overcoming it. In this respect, they had much in common with groups within the trade union movement and the SPD which wanted to forge an alliance between the working class and the liberal bourgeoisie, on the lines of the USA's 'consensus democracy'. This milieu become consolidated and larger in size, but without taking on the character of a political camp, in a series of actions during the late 1950s and early 1960s, which included the movement of spring 1958 against arming the Bundeswehr with nuclear weapons, the attack on the continuing influence of Nazi elites in West Germany, the rejection of Adenauer's policy on the German question, and finally the protests of autumn 1962 against the state's role in the Spiegel Affair. A group of liberal journalists, which was constantly increasing in size and significance at this time, played an important part in this milieu. They published articles in periodicals such as *Der Spiegel, Stern, Die Zeit,* and the *Frankfurter Rundschau,* as well as editing programmes for the public broadcasting system ARD. With some exaggeration, it could be said that, after the early 1960s, it was not criticism of West German circumstances which increased but its press coverage.[16]

The campaign against the emergency laws marked a qualitative leap for the opposition movement. The reserved rights in regard to domestic or external emergencies which the Western allies had secured in the Germany Treaty of 1952 formed the jumping-off point. In concrete terms, the issues were privacy of correspondence and telephone communications, the relationship of the executive and the legislative branches at times of tension, the domestic use of military force, restrictions on freedom of movement and job changes, and, last but not least, the right to strike and demonstrate. These reserved rights demonstrated the incomplete sovereignty of the Federal Republic so explicitly that even under Adenauer the federal government had started to consider how they could be dismantled and replaced by a German emergency law. It was only decades later that it became known that the West German and American secret services had circumvented the privacy of correspondence and telecommunications on a large scale, entirely ignoring the legal position, so that the debate on the emergency laws subsequently appeared in a somewhat ambiguous light.[17]

Without doubt, the constitutional regulation of a state of emergency was a political minefield, and not just because German constitutional theory was strongly influenced by Carl Schmitt's definition of sovereignty: 'Sovereign is he who decides on the exception.'[18] The first legislative proposal, presented in 1960 by the Minister of the Interior Gerhard Schröder (CDU), described the state of emergency entirely in Schmitt's sense as 'the hour of the executive' and prescribed for such a case a far-reaching reduction in the powers of parliament, the intervention of the Bundeswehr in domestic affairs on the instructions of the government and the prohibition of strikes. The ideas developed here clearly derived from the concept of authoritarian democracy and still contained perceptible traces of Article 48 of the Weimar Constitution. That quickly awakened memories of the Enabling Act of 1933, especially as the Spiegel Affair had undermined confidence in the steadfastness of the government's commitment to democracy. Although the second draft, presented in 1962, did not dispel this feeling of mistrust, the SPD indicated that it was not opposed to it in principle. Despite this, the discussion on the emergency legislation developed into one of the central fields of political conflict of the 1960s, an area in which, as Hans Günter Hockerts emphasises, 'a great public constitutional debate took place', lasting until spring 1968, 'which made up for the fact that there had been no debate when the Basic Law was promulgated under the guardianship of the Western powers.'[19]

The attack on the emergency laws brought together critics from various different directions. For the intellectuals and writers, who were now able greatly to increase their influence over the Left liberal media, the paramount issue was the divergence between the postulates of democracy and the real situation, and their arguments made use of striking parallels with the later years of the Weimar Republic. The trade unions, too, were early opponents of the emergency laws. The Left-leaning union IG Metall, in particular, was firmly opposed to the planned restrictions on fundamental rights and the suspension of the right to strike envisaged under a state of emergency. When the employers asserted that there was a direct link between industrial disputes and a state of emergency, the DGB openly threatened a general strike: 'It is the task of the DGB to call for a general strike when fundamental democratic rights and the independent trade-union movement are in danger.'[20] It was this threat which first gave the debate over the emergency laws the virulence and existential significance which the proclamations of critical intellectuals could never have engendered by themselves.

Along with the trade unions, groups from the orthodox Left of the SPD as well as the prohibited KPD also became involved in the protest movement. Many of them were veterans of the movement for an Easter march which arose from the campaign against nuclear armaments, and some had close connections with the GDR authorities. Here, as elsewhere, the SED tried to find ways of intervening in the politics of the Federal Republic, by financing individual groups or periodicals, not without a certain amount of success, but ultimately without gaining any substantial influence over the emerging protest movement as a whole.[21]

With the formation of the Grand Coalition, the movement against the emergency laws became the 'Extra-Parliamentary Opposition', in reaction to the practical absence of an opposition within parliament. With this, the movement of public protest had reached a new level, and it moved increasingly into the centre of domestic political controversy, especially as there was now an alliance between three elements: the Left liberal opposition, the trade unions and the more radical student groups.

The emergence of the protest movement at the universities of the Federal Republic was closely connected with the agitation in the American universities, to which many of its members had personal ties. In West Germany, as in the USA, it was the curtailment of the right to free expression of opinion at the universities to which the student movement reacted in the first instance. But, in West Germany, changes in social conditions played a bigger role than they did in the USA. The start of the student movement was, in that sense, linked with the extension of the debate over the failures in university policy which had effectively been brought into the public realm by Georg Picht and Ralf Dahrendorf. Unlike in the 1920s, the demand for wider social access to university education and the influx of students into the universities which soon followed this did not lead young academics to see increased student numbers as a danger to their privileged status as the future elite and therefore to adopt a blockading mentality. On the contrary, there was now a stronger demand for educational reforms to allow a democratic atmosphere to gain entry to the universities as well and to break up the elitist and thoroughly anachronistic structures of the old university system. Democratisation, participation, transparency, wider social access to university education, but also confrontation with the academic legacy of the Nazi dictatorship: these were the most important demands of the students, who were also supported in this by some of the younger professors and by Left liberal public opinion.

The Socialist German Student Federation (SDS) occupied a leading position in these activities. It also supported the movement against the emergency laws, in which it soon had a decisive role . The SDS gathered together Social Democratic students who had not supported the mother party's Godesberg policy shift, and it was therefore regarded as part of the old Left rather than as a new movement. This view changed when the protest movement of students against the emergency laws began to widen its area of activity and the SDS started to recruit new members who had no connection with the Left Social Democratic tradition. The sociology student Rudi Dutschke and his friends were leading examples of this phenomenon. They were strongly influenced by a Munich 'Situationist' group, which made reference to Sartre and Camus in calling for the unity of art and politics and the 'revolutionising of the bourgeois subject'. Political issues, they said, should not be raised by using the forms of protest favoured by classical left-wing movements, but in a new, imaginative manner. And the thrust of the critique should no longer be directed merely at the state and the university, but at the 'establishment' and the 'silent majority', new expressions which were now in frequent use. At the root of these new ideas was the notion that the dividing line between the 'two societies' should no longer be defined primarily in social terms, but in terms of culture, politics and the division between generations. 'Anti-authoritarian' was the comprehensive concept which both unified and mobilised this line of approach, which started to come to the fore in the SDS and elsewhere after 1964–5.[22]

The direction taken by this political movement was highly influenced by the writings of the social scientists who taught at the Frankfurt Institute for Social Research, particularly Theodor W. Adorno and Max Horkheimer. Their 'critical theory', developed in exile in the USA, was much discussed in the Federal Republic after their return to Germany. The point of departure taken by what was soon called the 'Frankfurt School' was a combination of Marx and Freud. For them, Marxism was less illuminating as a scientific interpretation of the capitalist economy than as the basis for an ideological critique of bourgeois society. Freud's theories helped them to analyse the pathologies which arose in that society and the 'false consciousness' which prevented large sections of society from recognising their own situation. The family, and an authoritarian upbringing in general, accordingly became the preferred subjects of 'critical scrutiny', and in their studies on the 'authoritarian character', Adorno and Horkheimer analysed the socio-psychological preconditions for fascism. In the 'administered world', they said, bureaucratisation, the mass media and mass culture also contributed to downgrading the qualities of spontaneity and individuality in favour of conformity and opportunism. These considerations gave rise to the conviction, propagated in particular by Herbert Marcuse, that it would not be the proletariat that overcame bourgeois rule. The instruments of transformation would instead be socially isolated and oppressed marginal groups, a category which included both the liberation movements of the Third World and the critical intellectuals of the metropolitan countries.[23]

This theoretical edifice offered student political activists a plausible interpretation of their own situation and the situation in the Federal Republic and the Western world as a whole. By stressing the connection between capitalism and fascism, it combined an analysis of the present with an explanation for the Nazi dictatorship. It also confirmed the widespread aversion to the dictatorial regimes in Eastern Europe and disputed Soviet Marxism's claim to be a genuinely Marxist theory. Apart from that, it strengthened the anti-authoritarian student movement's focus on the individual and on individual suffering, and it confirmed its aspiration as part of a worldwide movement to challenge authoritarian and undemocratic states of affairs, whether at the university, the national or the international level. The protesting students had an increasing urge to seek theoretical doctrines, concepts and formulas, and in particular to revitalise Marxism. This derived from the need to lay a solid foundation for an attitude towards the world and life which though intensely felt was still imprecise, and to legitimise their craving for radical action. There was a wide sphere of activity for theory in all these respects.

The student protesters of West Germany shared with the protest movements in the USA and most other Western countries a commitment to the peoples of the 'Third World' and the liberation movements in colonial countries. In Great Britain, France and also the Netherlands this was a confrontation both with their own colonial past and with the post-colonial present. The young Europeans of the post-war era, wrote the French philosopher Pascal Bruckner, had grown up suspecting that 'their world contained a fundamental injustice: colonialism.'[24] This increased the vehemence of the criticisms made of the newly arisen dictatorships in the former colonies, which were again enslaving their own population with the help of the Western powers or the Soviet Union. In the Federal Republic, on the other hand, a direct connection of this kind did not exist. Sympathy for the 'developing countries' and protest against their new rulers was based more on a moral attitude founded on human rights, and less on Germany's own historical involvement in the criminal history of colonialism, which of course existed but was very little discussed at the time. But it was not by chance that the protest demonstration against the Congolese dictator Moise Tshombé, who visited the Federal Republic in 1964, was one of the first protest outings of the anti-authoritarian students. Rudi Dutschke later described it as 'the moment when our cultural revolution was born.'[25]

Nevertheless, what really provoked a broad movement of protest was the war in Vietnam. Extensive television coverage of events in Vietnam also played an important part in this development: viewers all over the world could follow the US Army's offensives, the destruction of villages and the bombing of vast areas of the country, while the behaviour of the Vietcong and the North Vietnamese

Army, which was certainly ruthless, did not produce any comparable pictures. The West German population, on the other hand, greeted demonstrations against the US war in Vietnam with very little sympathy, particularly in Berlin. There the immediate post-war period and the Berlin airlift were still matters of recent memory, and the vital importance of American protection was felt every day. In February 1966, when eggs were thrown at the Amerika-Haus in Berlin at a demonstration by 2,500 people, the sense of outrage was consequently enormous. The polemics of the tabloid press against the protesting students became ever fiercer. The majority view was that the Americans deserved to be honoured for liberating the country from National Socialism and protecting it from communism. The students, on the other hand, condemned the Americans for conducting an unjustified and constantly expanding war in South East Asia. These two views of the world could hardly be reconciled.

The West German protest movement had much in common with other movements elsewhere, particularly in the United States. But developments in the Federal Republic were fundamentally set apart from those in all other countries by the need to confront German society's Nazi past. Here too, the student protest movement did not create any new approaches, but rather reinforced and radicalised the critique of the country's 'unsurmounted past' (*unbewältigte Vergangenheit*) which had developed since the early sixties. But there was a big difference. The generation of those born in the 1940s, which now came onto the scene, was the first to have no personal memory of the war or of National Socialism, whereas the 'sceptical generation' of those born around 1930 had at least experienced the terror of the later years of the war, when serving, for instance, as assistants in anti-aircraft artillery batteries. There was thus a break with former experience, and this meant that younger West Germans, the people later called 'sixty-eighters', had little understanding or respect for the situation of their parents' generation. They had been brought up in an atmosphere of embarrassed silence, in which references to past crimes in the garbled life stories of their elders or in reports about the re-emergence of former Nazis in the Federal Republic were rather hinted at than brought out into the open.

While growing up in the early 1960s, however, they had become aware of the first big information campaigns, such as the debate over the Eichmann trial in Jerusalem or the Frankfurt Auschwitz trial, and many of them were deeply affected. The unimaginable extent of the crimes and their own chronological and biographical proximity to them aroused disgust and revulsion. Gerd Koenen, at that time one of the activists of the protest movement, puts it this way: 'Here there remained only a feeling of numbness, horror and shame which made any kind of active sympathy impossible. All this was *our* history, whether we liked it or not. It signified the loss of our childlike confidence in the society from which we originated and in which we grew up' and it left behind an inextricable mixture of feelings of guilt and anger, as well as the 'need for dissociation and reinvention.'[26]

When Hannah Arendt assumed, after speaking with German students in 1961, that they 'could not speak to their fathers because they knew how deeply involved they had been in Nazism' this was only partially true, because they did not at that stage know the depths of this involvement. The little they did know consisted of fragments without geographical locations or personal names, whether of the perpetrators or the victims. Moreover, the public discussions always revolved around figureheads like Globke, Oberländer or Kiesinger. It was not even known in outline how far the mass crimes of the Nazi regime had penetrated into German society, and how many high-ranking National Socialists had actually recovered their positions in West Germany after 1945. If it had already been clear in 1966 that the murder detachments of the Nazi police had been reintegrated in the West German police force almost to a man after 1945 or that the strategists of the RSHA occupied comfortable positions in business, in the Federal Criminal Police, or the BND (Federal Intelligence Service) the protests would probably have taken on quite different dimensions.[27]

One reason why this combination of suspicion and a desire to distance themselves characterised the relation between the generations was that an energetic, self-confident vindication was not to be expected from the paternal side. In January 1966, the rector of the Free University of Berlin replied to the students who had asked about the Nazi past of some of the professors there that they should please refrain from 'treating disciplines and persons in a moralising fashion from the viewpoint of guilt and innocence and attaching labels to them.'[28] Vigorous denials, reinforced by argument, of the imputation of a Nazi past were nowhere to be seen, precisely because the truth went far beyond what the students could even guess.

The actions of the West German protest movement were dominated from the beginning by references to the Nazi past. It was not just students who compared the emergency laws with the Enabling Act of 1933. Journalists and academics also pointed to these parallels, and in 1965, 211 professors, including Karl Dietrich Bracher, the author of a number of path-breaking studies on the Weimar Republic and the Third Reich, signed an appeal which was formulated in this way: 'Laws of exception are the death of democracy, as we have already experienced once. This is also the case when they are agreed and applied in the name of democracy.'[29] Two years later, a proclamation by the 'Board of Trustees "Crisis of Democracy"' was even more explicit:

> Emergency ordinances paved the way to Hitler. Now the government is again demanding emergency laws . . . The power of the executive is becoming too great . . . There is no more control by the people, this is no longer a democracy.

> Whenever the people's rights are restricted, war and dictatorship come closer.
> This time, watch out![30]

The direct parallel some people drew between the Nazi seizure of power and current West German reality was reinforced and given a contemporary flavour by the rise of the neo-Nazi NPD. This party, largely run by former low-level National Socialist functionaries, addressed those parts of the population which had been particularly damaged, or at least rendered insecure, by the recession and the accelerated dynamic of modernisation. Between 1966 and 1968, it was able to win mandates to the parliaments of seven *Länder,* and in Baden-Württemberg it even reached 9.8 per cent of the vote. The NPD should also be understood as a counter-movement against the Extra-Parliamentary Opposition (the APO) and the left-wing trend of politics. The student protesters, conversely, saw the rise of the NPD as a further confirmation of their warnings against a resurgence of National Socialism.[31]

To that extent, constant references to the Nazi past were persuasive and certainly also unavoidable. And yet, in the course of these conflicts, they also became trivialised, and they were used as a shorthand expression for almost all the elements of West German reality which were under criticism: authoritarian structures, undemocratic procedures and repressive methods of education were all lumped together as evidence for the continued existence of traditions of 'fascism' and thereby in a sense irretrievably delegitimised, even if similar phenomena appeared in other countries which had not experienced National Socialist rule. This approach also tended to minimise the distinction between the democratic, law-governed state of the Federal Republic and the dictatorship of National Socialism. In addition, arguments of this kind pushed historical National Socialism into the background and reduced the mass crimes it had committed, particularly the murder of the European Jews, to a subordinate and contingent element.

It is possible, certainly, to refer to this as a 'second repression', or as a variant of the endeavour to distance oneself from one's inherited historical background. But this generation had received from its predecessor a historical burden which would inevitably be too much for it to bear. Notwithstanding all the missed turnings and detours it involved, the relation to the crimes of Nazi history remained the starting point of the West German protest movement, and it was also no doubt the main cause of its tendency to overshoot towards excessive radicalism.

The course of development from the formation of a new opposition movement to the disintegration of the New Left covers the period from the beginning of the 1960s to the end of the 1970s. By roughly 1965, as we have seen, various core groups of liberals and Leftists had coalesced, and they extended into a broader movement during the campaign against the emergency laws and the protests against the Vietnam War. Between the start of 1966 and summer 1967 the various oppositional groups joined together to form the Extra-Parliamentary Opposition, although no unified programme emerged from this. The Grand Coalition was increasingly subjected to criticism from this camp, despite the fact that this was the first time the SPD had taken part in the federal government. The direction and severity of the criticism, however, varied tremendously according to the character of various groups and regions. The most radical critics were members of the SDS in Berlin, Frankfurt and a few other university towns, who had broken with their Left Social Democratic origins and now followed a radically anti-authoritarian line. The Berlin groups became known throughout the country for their imaginative actions, which often resembled 'happenings' rather than political demonstrations. There was the 'pudding attack' on US Vice-President Humphrey, for instance, which some West German newspaper reports blew up into a dangerous assault with unknown chemicals. Ironical and satirical slogans carried on demonstrations and an attitude of total defiance when in court were forms of provocation intended to goad the state authorities and the public into unconsidered and exaggerated reactions, thereby 'unmasking' the repressive core of the society hidden behind the façade of liberalism. In this aim, the radicals often succeeded, because a considerable degree of disgust and hostility towards student protesters had built up in sections of the public, the politicians and the administration. In the popular media, above all in the Springer press, fury over the troublemakers was expressed in a brutal manner, and this gave the students a sense of political importance which had no real foundation.

At the same time, however, sympathy and support for the rebellious students did continue to exist during this phase of development, and indeed it even increased, within the liberal 'establishment' and particularly the Left liberal media, which did occasionally criticise the approach and the methods of the students, but made no bones about the fact that they regarded their fundamental objectives as justified or at least worth discussing. There was a widespread feeling that the students were drawing attention to real political and social abuses and moral aporias in the Federal Republic and the Western world.[32]

The situation changed radically after 2 June 1967, when a policeman shot dead a demonstrator, Benno Ohnesorg, in the course of a demonstration in front of the Deutsche Oper in Berlin against the Shah of Iran's visit. The events of 2 June 1967 brought everything together: a demonstration against a 'Third World' tyrant, funded by the West, who was exploiting his country and bloodily suppressing its population; a West Berlin public, inflamed by the tabloid newspapers, which wanted a final end to the 'terror of the young Reds'; a guard consisting of Iranian secret policemen who were allowed by the Berlin police to beat up the demonstrators; and finally police units whose actions appeared to be impelled by a latent readiness to engage in civil war. The shooting of Ohnesorg became a turning point in the revolt. It was 'an event that formed a generation'. Above all, it marked the moment when the element of violence entered what had until then been a very civilised protest. This violence would accompany domestic political conflicts in West Germany for more than ten years afterwards.

The fatal shots, as well as attempts by the Berlin Senate and many Berlin newspapers to prevent any investigation of the circumstances surrounding Ohnesorg's death, caused an abrupt surge of radicalisation among both the supporters of the student movement and its more detached sympathisers.[33] Political and social conditions in West Germany were now subjected to sharper criticism, and the student movement spread beyond the centres of protest to cover the whole of the Federal Republic. Demonstrations became bigger and noisier, slogans more radical. Wider and wider issues started to be raised. There were protests against bureaucracy and capital, the terror of consumerism and the Vietnam War, alienation and repression, the Soviet Union and the USA, fascism and the Springer press: this was a kaleidoscopic vision of harassment and suffering, joined together by the rather vague feeling that everything was connected with everything else. In this context, for some 'leaders' of the student movement it was often only a small step to take from indignation over the 'prohibition of discussion' by a university to the sense that the world was passing through a revolutionary crisis. The notion that they were living in a period of decisive world-historical events, and perhaps even standing at the centre of them, the idea 'of a time of fulfilment, when everything comes together, sustained by the "dream of freedom from constraint"', imparted a suggestion of urgency and global relevance to the events that took place in the centres of student protest.[34]

This perception was brought to a head on 11 April 1968 by the murderous attack on Rudi Dutschke. Almost no one among the protesters believed that the perpetrator, a young unskilled worker with ties to the NPD, had acted alone. The attack was seen as part of a series running from the murder of Martin Luther King on 4 April in Memphis to the murder of Robert Kennedy on 6 June in Los Angeles. This international configuration both occasioned and confirmed the sense of outrage that flared up in West Germany as much as it did in America. The particular anger of the students in the Federal Republic was directed initially against the Springer publishing house, whose newspaper, *Bild-Zeitung*, had called a few days before the attack on Dutschke for the 'ringleaders' of the revolt to be seized ('We should not leave all the dirty work to the police and their water-cannons.') In the days that followed 11 April 1968 there was rioting in many places; buildings belonging to the Springer publishing house were attacked and newspaper delivery vans were set on fire.[35]

There was now an intense debate in many circles of the student movement over violence and counter-violence. One thing that fed the debate was a feeling of powerlessness in the face of the measures taken by the state, but solidarity with revolutionary movements in the countries of the 'Third World' played a still more important part. It was now proclaimed at SDS congresses that left-wing student protests were a part of the global movement of the oppressed against their oppressors, most sharply expressed in the liberation movements and guerrilla groups of those countries. Rudi Dutschke had already made this point in February 1968, in line with Herbert Marcuse's theories:

> Complete identification with the need for revolutionary terrorism and revolutionary struggle in the Third World is an indispensable condition for the liberation struggle of the nations engaged in this fight and for the development of forms of resistance among ourselves, which bear an essentially violent character, without having the special aspect, the nastiness, of hatred and revolutionary terror.[36]

Despite the hesitation which is apparent from this formulation, the call for violent action bore fruit. In April 1968 a group associated with the Berlin SDS set fire to a Frankfurt department store. This was intended to serve as a symbolic protest against American incendiary bombing in Vietnam, and it was the starting point for the terrorist activities of the later 'Red Army Faction'. Another group willing to engage in violence named itself after the symbolic date which began the escalation: the Movement of the Second of June. It became known later, though it was already suspected at the time, that this and other groups had received their dynamite and their weapons from a liaison officer of the Berlin Constitutional Protection Force (*Verfassungsschutz*), whose task was to turn the verbal violence of the left-wing groups into actual violence, so as to be able to arrest them. The expectation of force and the readiness to use force fed upon each other; an escalatory spiral was deliberately being created.[37]

Those spring weeks of 1968 marked the zenith of the protest movement. On 30 May 1968, a few weeks after the attack on Dutschke and the Easter disturbances, the Bundestag passed the emergency laws, against massive resistance from the opponents of the legislation, who called for a giant demonstration to be held in Bonn. Certain specific provisions of the law had in the meantime been softened, and the demands of the anti-emergency movement had largely been taken into account. In addition, the trade unions distanced themselves from the attempt to put the Bonn parliamentarians under direct pressure, and they did not take part in the Bonn demonstration. Instead, they mounted a rally of their own in Dortmund. Now there was no longer an alliance between the trade unions and the left-wing protest movement. The emergency laws went through the Bundestag, and no general strike took place. The revolution, which had never actually begun, now belonged to history.

There is much disagreement both in the memoir literature and among historians as to whether the year 1969 marks the end of 'sixty-eight' or the revolt continued in an altered form. It seemed obvious that, in its existing form, the protest movement had now come to an end. There were diametrically opposed views among the chief actors in the movement, and their supporters, as to how to proceed in the future. When the social–liberal coalition took power under Chancellor Willy Brandt, many of the concerns of the APO and the student movement, though not of its radical ringleaders, were taken on board both politically and symbolically. In addition, there appeared to be a greater chance than ever before of exerting direct influence over the actions of the government. Hence, a section of the supporters of the protest movement, perhaps the biggest group in numerical terms, flocked towards the established parties, the SPD first and foremost, where, as 'Young Socialists', they soon formed an influential 'neo-Left'.

Another part of the movement, however, changed its line of approach entirely, becoming much more radical. Since the spontaneous anti-authoritarian movement seemed to have failed, many people began to search for a theoretical basis for continuing and extending their Left radical activism, and they found it in the orthodox scenarios of the communist movement. That was paradoxical in the sense that one of the conceptual innovations of the student movement had been precisely to say goodbye to the political projects of the traditional Left, which were oriented towards the class struggle and proletarian revolution, and were clearly contradicted by social, economic and cultural developments in the countries of Western Europe and particularly the Federal Republic. On the other hand, an orientation towards communism of the Soviet or Chinese stamp also expressed the need to establish maximum distance from the political actuality of the Federal Republic. Many left-wing students now joined together in the Maoist parties which had rapidly sprung up, or in the newly founded pro-Moscow DKP (German Communist Party), which soon became influential in the student milieu. They were prepared to live with the fact that, by doing this, they were renouncing their own political starting point, namely the creation of democratic conditions in the Federal Republic and all over the world.

This did not happen just in West Germany. It was exactly paralleled by trends in most other Western countries, above all in France and Italy. The Bolshevik tone of command which these groups quickly adopted, their neglect of, indeed their contempt for, democratic principles, their readiness to accept subordination as soldiers of the party in centralised cadre organisations and their acceptance of political theories like Marxism-Leninism or Maoism, which had entailed the imprisonment in labour camps of millions of people in the Soviet

Union and China and the death of millions more—all these things make this indubitably one of the most bizarre developments in West German and Western European post-war history. As a result, perhaps more than 50,000 mainly young and academic supporters and members experienced many years, and often more than a decade, of continuous political socialisation in these neo-communist cadre groups. Guesses have been made about the long-term effects of this experience, but there are no firmly grounded findings.[38]

It is a striking fact that these orthodox Leftists now returned completely to a schematic view of the working class and industrialism, and like the regimes in the Soviet sphere confirmed the ruling consensus about progress and modernisation. Industrial labour on a mass scale moulded their conception of the future, and the problems of the present were explained in the traditional Marxist manner by referring to the main contradiction between capital and labour. Everything else counted as a 'subordinate contradiction'. These views were also to be found, though with a reformist perspective, among the Young Socialists who were streaming into the SPD. To that extent, it is not entirely accurate to assert, as has sometimes been done, that the sixty-eighters planned to 'break through into an open future, different from the one the planners of global management wanted to place on a permanent footing and identified with progress.'[39]

The comment just quoted applies far more to the conceptions of the third element in the student movement, which came out in opposition to 'the terror of consumerism' and in favour of 'sexual liberation' and followed Marcuse in putting forward marginal social groups and intellectuals as the motive forces of protest. After 1969, this tendency dominated the numerous independent Leftist groupings, which could often be described as a 'scene' rather than a camp describable in political terms. The 'alternative milieu' arose from this seedbed, and it expanded steadily during the 1970s. It had a wide impact with political campaigns against property speculation, and later against nuclear power stations, and it produced an alternative subcultural space which was made up of housing communes, craft workshops and bars, and was largely isolated from the bourgeois world. The roots of many of what were later called 'new social movements', citizens' initiatives and self-help groups emerged from this environment. The most important of these was without doubt the feminist movement.[40]

The citizens' initiatives were at first entirely autonomous, existing independently of the New Left. By the early 1970s, they had already moved towards concentrating on specific, mainly local, problems, such as inadequate nursery provision, road-building projects and industrial zones. In origin and character, they were usually middle-class oriented and Left liberal, and apart from their intensified desire to become involved there was nothing to link them with the actions of the left-wing students. The first generation of the student movement was by no means hostile to technology. The utopias of the Left usually had a strong orientation towards technological progress. In that sense, the new Left was exactly the same as the old Left. Since modern capitalism would soon make it possible for the working day to be reduced to a few hours, and since modern office devices would make the work of secretaries superfluous, the realm of necessity would soon be overcome, and people would be able to devote their efforts entirely to the transformation of society. The link with environmental protection and citizens' initiatives did not arise until the late 1970s, by which time the imaginary figure of the revolutionary proletariat had completely dissolved.

The movement we have described above was very wide-ranging: it stretched from the APO through the student milieu to the alternative milieu, the communist groups and terrorism. To integrate it into the general picture is not easy, owing to its oscillating and contradictory character. It is evident that, in the late 1950s and early 1960s, more came to an end than just the phase of economic reconstruction. There were clearly more deep-rooted reasons why protest movements formed in such different countries as France, West Germany, Italy, Denmark, Japan, the USA, Mexico and Great Britain and despite clear national differences displayed numerous similarities and had many common features. One reason is that the economic consequences of the Second World War had been overcome, another is that the confrontation between the two power blocs had lost its rigidity, and a third is the replacement of one generation by the next. They all indicate the end of a phase of cultural orientation towards security, obedience, family, morality, authority and the state, which had itself been a reaction to the extreme changes of the Second World War and the immediate post-war years. But the political and cultural overhang proved to be so firmly entrenched, the various illiberal structures specific to each nation proved to be so fossilised, that the movement against them assumed a ferocious and sharp-edged character, and the more rigid the structures the more radical it turned out to be. This is the reason for the radicalisation of the protest movements, and it also explains the contradiction between the authoritarian rhetoric of the revolutionaries and the liberalising intentions of the protest movement.

The protest movement in the Federal Republic contributed to accelerating and broadening the trends that were already moving towards a less authoritarian, more liberal society. To that extent, it was the expression of a fundamental wave of social development which can be traced from the late fifties to the early eighties. Because the conditions being attacked were highly authoritarian and illiberal, ever more radical steps seemed to be required and justified to change them. As in almost all the revolts of modern times, this created a tendency towards overreach, towards a degree of radicalisation which eventually made the end result unrecognisable. This radicalisation must be seen as a reaction to the existing inadequacies of liberalism and modernity, which overshot the mark, moving over into the opposite extreme. That this led in West Germany, France and Italy to particularly sharp eruptions, and to the emergence of Left radical terrorist groups, is not surprising in view of the highly conspicuous anti-democratic survivals from the time of Hitler, Pétain and Mussolini.

But distinctions need to be made here. In Italy and France, class antagonisms and accordingly political dividing-lines between Left and Right were so firmly rooted that the demands of the students could be linked with those of the revolutionary working class. In the Federal Republic, on the other hand, with its inherited corporatism and its lack of sharp social dividing lines, there was no trace of this. There were also two other factors involved: the Communist Party was prohibited for a long time and the existence of the GDR offered a stronger obstacle than existed elsewhere to all notions of a humanitarian socialism.

The struggle between the state and the protest movements in West Germany should also be seen as a process of reciprocal radicalisation. References to the violence expected from the protesters produced an atmosphere of excessive reactions on the part of the state, as events in Berlin demonstrated in particular. The so-called 'Anti-Radical Decree' (*Radikalenerlass*) of 1972 should also be seen within this context. To prevent supporters of the new Left from getting jobs in the civil service, the Constitutional Protection Authority (*Verfassungsschutz*) was instructed to check each individual applicant's loyalty to the constitution. More than a million people had passed through this process by the beginning of the 1980s, and roughly 1,000 of them were in fact excluded from public employment. The Anti-Radical Decree was specific to Germany. In no other Western country was there a similar procedure, and it accordingly met with sharp criticism from abroad. In 1976, the central authorities ceased to operate the practice, although many of the *Länder* continued it until the end of the 1970s.[41]

It is nevertheless true that processes of Westernisation and democratisation were accelerated and expanded in the course of these conflicts in the Federal Republic, as also in most other Western European countries. To quote Axel Schildt, the protest movement 'both drove forward and exaggerated the dynamic modernisation process of West German society and its political culture,' it contributed to 'the delegitimation of pre-democratic concepts of authority and hierarchy' and it hastened the transformation of social values which had long been apparent. In that sense, the revolt contributed to 'the progress of reform under the label of revolution'.

But it can also be said that '1968' was possible because the Federal Republic had become 'more Western and more liberal' since the early 1960s.[42] For a considerable section of young academics, the revolt contributed in the 1970s to a far-reaching estrangement from, indeed a contempt for, democracy and the constitutional state, combined with approval, or even admiration, for monstrous dictatorships, along with an enthusiasm for liberation movements which soon turned out to be neither libertarian nor democratic. To say that the anti-liberal and anti-democratic manifestations of '1968', even the most radical of them, had the net effect of promoting the progressive liberalisation of West German society, is to make an unfounded equation between two different processes, which leaves behind many contradictions and open questions.

Despite the Anti-Radical Decree and the 'bans on employment' (*Berufsverbote*), the democracy of the Federal Republic, berated by left-wing students as 'merely institutional', was distinguished from the dictatorship in the GDR, which was immovable and incapable of passing through a learning process, by the fact that it was able to withstand even situations of extreme social tension such as occurred in the late 1960s and the early 1970s and was in a position to incorporate the impulses arising out of them. This capacity for change ensured that it remained dynamic and preserved its legitimacy and after the 1980s it made possible a gradual reintegration of the sixty-eighters into West German society, which had itself in the meantime become different from what it was in the early 1960s.

This was also evident from the 1970s onwards at the other end of the political spectrum: in view of the way that parts of the critical youth movement had drifted towards Leftist radicalism, a considerable number of bourgeois conservatives and German nationalists abandoned their line of cultural criticism and contempt for mass democracy and went over to defending the republic and the connection with the West against the neo-communist challenge. This process was certainly no less significant historically than the evolution of the left-wing protest movement.

## A Vigorous New Start

The change of government after the Bundestag elections of autumn 1969 was widely perceived as both a sensation and a confirmation of the stability of West German democracy. This demonstrates that it was by no means a natural and inevitable development. Forty-one years after the resignation of Hermann Müller, a Social Democrat was again elected Chancellor, in the shape of Willy Brandt, a man who also embodied 'the other Germany' in his person and his biography as an exile and an opponent of Hitler. The symbolic force of this event was great, much greater than when he was appointed Foreign Minister three years earlier.

The start of his chancellorship therefore aroused much higher expectations than was normally the case with changes of government. For some years, this emphasis on a fresh start strengthened the new government's ability to assert itself and made it easier for it to implement in a very short time an enormous programme of domestic reforms and a reorientation of foreign policy. But it is also very clear that this mood of enthusiasm drowned out moderate voices and critical objections and thus laid the basis for the disappointments that set in when the intoxication began to evaporate and the dull routine of pragmatic government activity again occupied centre stage.

With 46.1 per cent of the vote, the Union actually did better in 1969 than it had in 1961, and it regarded itself as the true winner of the election. For a long time afterwards, it presented the impression that the formation of the social–liberal coalition had done it an injustice. Indeed, after twenty years in government, it took a long time for the Union to be comfortable in its role as an opposition. The NPD, meanwhile, the rise of which had caused great concern in previous years within the country and all over the world, failed to pass the 5 per cent hurdle and thus fell back into the lunatic fringe of far Right politics. The vote for the FDP, a party which was now largely social–liberal in orientation, fell from 9.5 per cent to 5.8 per cent. But its election slogan had been 'Let's make a clean break with the past', and in line with this it decided, under its new leader, Walter Scheel, to make the riskier choice of a coalition with the Social Democrats, because this corresponded better to its endeavour to establish an independent, reform-oriented profile than a renewed coalition with the Christian Democrats. With 42.7 per cent, the SPD had achieved its best result of the post-war era. Indeed, it was the best result in the party's history. But it had failed to achieve the goal of becoming the majority party in the Bundestag.

The new coalition had a very slim majority. In one sense this had a stabilising effect, particularly in relation to the FDP's German nationalist wing, which was an unwilling participant in the coalition and later left it. In general, though, the area of agreement between the two parties was reasonably wide. This related to two issues above all: policy towards the Eastern bloc and the GDR, and 'domestic reform', especially law reform. The main differences of opinion between the two coalition parties were over economic and social policy, although both sides shared the conviction that central economic planning, on the lines indicated by Karl Schiller, was the most effective approach.

The most important features of Brandt's government declaration, issued on 28 October 1969, were a will to reform, an insistence on democratisation, a spirit of optimism and an enthusiasm for planning. In retrospect, there was a striking contradiction between the announcement that the country's citizens would enjoy an extensive degree of joint responsibility and participation and the equally extensive growth in the state's role in planning and directing the economy, but contemporary observers rarely saw this as an issue. What remained in people's minds far more were the phrases which, oscillating between magniloquence and modesty, served as emblems of the new start, and highlighted the intended break with authoritarian and anti-democratic traditions: 'We want to risk more democracy', 'Lasting security can only come through change', 'We want a society which offers more freedom and calls for more joint responsibility', 'The school of the nation is the school', 'We are not looking for devotees; we need people who think critically', 'We are not the elect; we are the elected', and finally: 'We are not standing at the end of our democracy, we are just getting started.'[43]

It was this final phrase which aroused a storm of indignation among the Christian Democrats, because they saw it as vilifying the Union-led republic of the last twenty years for a lack of genuine democracy. And, in fact, there was a deep-rooted conviction in the coalition, shared by Brandt himself, that the Union saw democracy as a way of regulating the business of the state rather than a principle dominating the whole society. In subsequent years, this question would often be a source of disagreement. In the context of the government's declaration, however, Brandt's proclamation that 'we are just getting started' was intended as a reply to critical objections from the Left, for example from Hans Magnus Enzensberger, the poet of the radical Left, who had written in an English newspaper that: 'the end of the second German democracy may be in sight.'[44] Brandt wanted to counter this by making clear, both at home and to the world outside, that he wanted to incorporate and pursue the democratic impulse of the student revolt, but categorically rejected the disaffection with democracy which was rife in that milieu.

## *Ostpolitik*

In the first three years of the Brandt–Scheel government, however, the centre of attention for both West German and international public opinion was not domestic policy but the 'New Eastern Policy' (*Neue Ostpolitik*). Until that time, Bonn had always insisted that progress on détente was dependent on progress in the German question. The guiding principle was: the German question comes first. But the intensification of Cold War conflict in the 1960s, culminating in the clashes over Cuba and Vietnam, had freed the agenda of the Great Powers from its preoccupation with Germany. Their main aim now was to avoid an open conflict. The Nuclear Non-Proliferation Treaty was the first important step in this direction. In the 1950s, when the Soviets were engaged in a policy of force, West Germany's refusal to recognise the division of Germany had possessed a certain moral legitimacy. In the course of the 1960s, however, it had become a disruptive anachronism. If the Bonn republic wanted to regain its flexibility in foreign policy and take part in the consensus of its Western allies in favour of détente, it would have to invert its order of priorities: first progress in détente and then, through that, the possibility of improvements in the German question. Such was the starting point for the new eastern policy.[45]

The aim of the federal government in the conversations which began in December 1969 was accordingly to strike a bargain: in return for a guarantee of the western borders of Poland and Czechoslovakia and a de facto recognition of the GDR, the Federal Republic wanted to achieve a secure status for West Berlin and appreciable improvements in the lives of the GDR's inhabitants. At the same time, however, it wanted to safeguard, indeed it had to safeguard, the option of an eventual reunification of the two German states.

These objectives could only be achieved through negotiations with the Soviet leadership. Discussions with the GDR, Poland and Czechoslovakia could only be useful and productive after an agreement with Moscow. The situation was favourable at that point because the Soviet Union was keen to settle problems with the West owing to its escalating conflict with China, and therefore appeared to be ready to make certain concessions. In addition, the Soviet Union and the other Eastern bloc states had lost so much ground during the sixties in their economic competition with the West that closer economic relations with the latter, particularly with the Federal Republic, had a high priority. That improved the negotiating position of the Brandt–Scheel government, which did not have much to throw into the scales otherwise.

At the initial discussions in Moscow, which were conducted first by Brandt's emissary Egon Bahr and then by Foreign Minister Walter Scheel, the Soviet side presented maximum demands: full international recognition of the GDR, abandonment of reunification in the long term, and the immutability of all the borders, both the border within Germany and the Oder–Neisse line. The Federal Republic was expected to conclude treaties with Poland, the GDR and Czechoslovakia on this basis, and then as a third step a European security conference, which had long been demanded by the Soviet Union, would definitively confirm the existing power structures and the territorial arrangements arrived at after the end of the war.

The West German side managed to achieve some important modifications to these proposals. Firstly, the treaties with Moscow, Warsaw and Prague would be combined with an agreement over Berlin, to be negotiated by the four victors of 1945. This agreement would formalise the continuing responsibility of the four Powers for Berlin and confirm that West Berlin would continue to be excluded from the Federal Republic by international law. But, at the same time, it would be made easier to travel within the city, there would be more generous rules for visiting the GDR and the continued presence of the Federal Republic in West Berlin would be guaranteed. In comparison with the escalating tensions of the past, when Berlin had always stood at the centre of the Cold War, these were important marks of progress, which also perceptibly reduced the GDR's opportunities for intervention. Secondly, during the Moscow negotiation the status of the borders was altered from 'immutable' to 'inviolable'. That left open the perspective of an agreed change, and thus at least offered the possibility that the internal German border might be removed after a rapprochement between the two German states or their unification.

The most difficult point turned out to be whether recognition of the GDR by the Federal Republic, however it was formulated, would be compatible with the postulate of reunification stipulated in the Basic Law. Brandt had taken up a clear position on this in his government declaration. He did, it is true, refer frankly to the existence of 'two states in Germany', but he also emphasised that 'recognition of the GDR under international law by the federal government cannot come into consideration. Even if two states exist in Germany, they are still not foreign countries to each other. Their mutual relations can only be of a special type.'[46] Here too, the Soviet leadership was prepared to accommodate the West German side. The federal government issued a 'Letter on German Unity' in which it stated that the provisions of the treaty did not stand in contradiction with the Federal Republic's endeavour 'to work towards a European peace in which the German nation would recover its unity through free self-determination.'[47] By consenting to this letter, the Soviet side did at least accept that on this question the two contracting parties held differing views. 'Recognition of the inviolability of the borders without a definitive abandonment of reunification': that was the core of the Moscow Treaty, and to that extent it predetermined decisive aspects of subsequent agreements.[48] It was therefore logical that the Bundestag only agreed to the German–Soviet Treaty after the conclusion of the agreements with Poland and the GDR and the negotiations over Berlin.

These prior determinations proved to have momentous consequences for the negotiations with Poland. The recognition of the Oder–Neisse boundary was the Polish side's most important objective. For the federal government, this was not controversial, despite all the protests of the expellees' associations and the right wing of the Union against 'Abandonment' and 'Treachery'. The Polish side, however, also wanted a guarantee that this recognition would be binding on a future reunited Germany. The federal government refused. It could not give such a guarantee, it said, firstly because of the reserved rights of the Four Powers over Germany as a whole, and secondly because it could not speak in the name of a united Germany. Even so, the treaty was signed, although the disagreement could not be ironed out entirely. Twenty years later, in the Two Plus

Four negotiations of spring 1990, this once again became a burning issue. West German Chancellor Kohl had to be forced by Western pressure to agree that the Oder–Neisse border would be recognised by a united Germany.

The sensational highpoint of Willy Brandt's journey to Warsaw to sign the treaty on 7 December 1970 was when he fell to his knees before the memorial to the Jews killed in the Warsaw Ghetto uprising of 1943. This was a silent gesture of humility which was perceived all over the world like no other as an admission of German guilt and a plea for forgiveness. In Poland too, Brandt's genuflection received great attention. But here the reverberations were not entirely positive. Brandt had fallen to his knees before the memorial to Polish Jews, not the memorial to the Warsaw Uprising of 1944. On this reading, Brandt's admission of guilt covered the murder of the Jews but not the killing of more than 2 million non-Jewish Poles who had died during the German occupation. There was some criticism of him for this.[49] Relations between the Federal Republic and Poland continued to be difficult even after the German–Polish Treaty. Poland had been expected to reciprocate for the recognition of the Oder–Neisse boundary by allowing Germans living in Poland to emigrate to the Federal Republic, but the Polish government was not at first prepared to take this step. The Poles' distrust of the Germans had not entirely evaporated, and it even outlasted the collapse of the communist regime in 1990.

In the negotiations over the Prague Treaty of December 1973, which marked the conclusion of the series of Eastern treaties, the recognition of the post-war border was not the actual problem. The disputed issue here was rather the interpretation of the Munich Agreement of 1938, which the Czechoslovak government regarded as 'invalid from the outset', whereas the West German government only conceded that it was invalid at the present time. At stake, above all, were the property rights of 3 million Germans from what was previously called the 'Sudetenland', who had been expropriated and expelled from Czechoslovakia after 1945. If the Munich Agreement was regarded as 'invalid from the outset', the 'Sudeten Germans' were Czechoslovak citizens in 1945, and their expropriation was accordingly an internal matter for the Czechoslovak Republic. If not, what had happened was an expropriation of foreign citizens, and claims for the restitution of expropriated 'Sudeten German' property could be derived from this. The two sides finally agreed to regard the Munich Agreement as 'null and void', and the disputed questions were left to one side. In the Prague Treaty, which was signed on 11 December 1973, both states renounced all territorial claims and accepted the inviolability of their common borders. But the legality of the expulsion and expropriation of the 'Sudeten Germans' remained a contentious issue between the two countries.[50]

The negotiations between the Federal Republic and the GDR were still more difficult. Two meetings had already taken place between Willy Brandt and Willi

Stoph, the prime minister of the GDR, in spring 1970. Germans on both sides of the border followed these meetings on television with breathless excitement. The fact that a cheering crowd of people gathered outside the hotel where Brandt was staying in Erfurt was nothing less than a public humiliation for the GDR leadership. Both this meeting and a follow-up meeting a few weeks later in Kassel proceeded in a frosty atmosphere and produced no concrete results. Both sides therefore agreed to await the results of the Moscow discussions and the Berlin negotiations, before engaging in further conversations. But, since the Soviet Union had compromised with the views of the Federal Republic over the Berlin question and the possibility of reunification, the GDR government was unable to retreat from these agreements. It had to give up its negotiating objective, which had been to make concessions to the Federal Republic conditional on complete recognition of the GDR under international law. On the contrary, after long negotiations, the 'Basic Treaty' between the two Germanies enshrined the compromise solution previously agreed in Moscow: the Federal Republic accepted the existence of the GDR and guaranteed the inviolability of its borders, but it did not grant complete recognition under international law. A separate GDR nationality was never recognised. Thus, official representatives of both states resided in each other's capitals, but no embassies were set up, only 'Offices of the Permanent Representative'.[51]

The negotiations had thus produced mixed results for both sides. The GDR had only received second-class recognition from the Federal Republic, but, in the international context, the new status of the GDR as a second German state with equal rights alongside the Federal Republic was undisputed, and this was confirmed by the fact that both the GDR and the Federal Republic now entered the United Nations. The federal government had thus given up its claim to be the sole representative of Germany and had granted the GDR de facto recognition, but it had successfully retained the option of reunification and the reservation that relations between the two states were 'of a special kind'.

The federal government now expected the GDR to reciprocate by 'normalising' relations and in particular easing some of the restrictions on the population. A number of small steps were in fact taken. Even before the Basic Treaty had been signed, a number of agreements were concluded concerning postal communications, and improved regulations on travel to West Berlin and transit through the GDR. The GDR leadership also issued an amnesty for numerous prisoners, who were released into the Federal Republic. But it did not make any concessions over either family reunification, the movement of private goods, or permission to travel. On the contrary, it sharpened its tone and attitude towards the federal government after the treaties had been signed, partly to dispel Soviet apprehensions about excessively close relations between the two German states, but much more in order to counter the hopes that had emerged within the GDR that the living conditions of its citizens would now quickly improve owing to the treaty with the Federal Republic. This 'escalation' in the 'fencing off' of the GDR from West Germany disappointed any hope of a more permanent relaxation in the relationship between the two German states.[52]

The domestic aspect of social–liberal *Ostpolitik,* meanwhile, was no less sensational than the treaty negotiations themselves. The Union's criticisms of the treaties with the East were extremely vehement, and between 1969 and 1973 the government was repeatedly exposed to fierce accusations that it had abandoned German legal rights too easily or even that it was engaged in 'selling out the nation'. It was in vain that Brandt repeatedly and correctly pointed out that the treaties had given away nothing that had not been lost long ago. But the attitude of the Union on this question was not entirely uniform. The liberal wing approved the fundamental direction of social–liberal *Ostpolitik,* but had reservations about a number of omissions and objectionable formulations. The conservative nationalist group, particularly the CSU, led by Franz Josef Strauß, completely rejected the treaties. The majority of the Union vacillated. They saw no alternative to a compromise with the East, but they thought the price to be paid—namely the recognition of the GDR and the Oder–Neisse border—was too high.

The confrontation between the government and the opposition became still fiercer when the Nobel Peace Prize was awarded to the Chancellor in 1971 for his policy of reconciliation with the East, and the international isolation of the German opponents of *Ostpolitik* became evident. After the content of the Moscow agreements became known, the German nationalist wing of the FDP left the coalition, and the government lost its tiny parliamentary majority. On 27 April 1972 the Union attempted to overthrow the Chancellor with a constructive vote of no confidence. This did not succeed, for somewhat unclear reasons. There were apparently considerable sums of money involved on both sides, in order to induce unreliable representatives to vote with the government or to persuade them to change sides. After the failure of the opposition to overthrow the Chancellor, the government called early elections. These took place in November 1972.

Disagreements over *Ostpolitik* were not fought out purely within parliament. They led to a level of public polarisation and politicisation which had never yet been seen in the Federal Republic. The trend towards public declarations of commitment to political parties had already become apparent in the 1960s with the electoral initiatives mounted by the Social Democrats, and it was strengthened by the student disturbances. Now it reached a climax. It was not surprising that disagreements over *Ostpolitik* reached such a level of intensity, since what was at stake here was not just a correction of the foreign policy course but one of the core questions of twentieth-century German politics and identity, namely the relationship of the Germans to the nation.[53]

The radical nationalism which emerged in the late nineteenth century had been primarily a compensation for the lack of a strong tradition of national unity in Germany. After the First World War, it had assumed exaggerated and obsessive forms as a reaction to the weakness, rather than the strength of the German nation-state, and it culminated in the Nazi period, resulting finally in the destruction of the nation-state itself. Even so, attachment to the German nation as an undeniable and unquestioned entity remained firmly embedded in the consciousness of considerable sections of the population even after the Second World War. It was by no means limited to the adherents of the Nazi regime. This was shown after 1945, not least in the rigid orientation of the SPD towards national unity and reunification, and the point naturally applied even more to the conservative nationalist bourgeoisie. Adenauer, however, had altered the hierarchy of values with his policy of Western integration. National unity no longer took precedence over everything else. First freedom, then unity, was Adenauer's credo. And since this was a matter of asserting the freedom of West Germans against communism, the conservative nationalists of West Germany followed his lead, apart from some small groups.

The West Germans compensated for the abandonment of national unity as an immediate political goal by calling even more vociferously for reunification, and this sense of unity was probably never felt more strongly than when it was forcibly eliminated by the building of the Berlin Wall in summer 1961. Even at the end of the 1960s, people continued to have personal connections, including family connections, with the former 'Eastern zone' of Germany, and for many citizens of West Germany the unity of the German nation had great significance. In the meantime, however, these ties had weakened. People had accustomed themselves to the fact of division. Westernisation, particularly in the cultural field, had spread far and wide, and a new generation had grown up which was no longer imbued with a commitment to the nation. In addition, the realities of power in the international context had turned the West German 'policy of strength' into a policy of weakness, and it therefore lost support in the conservative camp as well.

The conflict over the new government's *Ostpolitik* also raised the question of whether the notion of the nation as a value in itself, possibly the highest of all values, would now cease to be accepted. This explains in part the acrimonious character of the disagreements and also the decision of the right wing of the FDP to break away from the coalition.[54]

The Union ultimately allowed the treaties of Moscow and Warsaw to pass the Bundestag, which they did on 17 May 1972. There was a certain contradiction between this decision and the energy with which the party had campaigned against *Ostpolitik*. On the other hand, it was clear that its constant insistence on the reunification option had contributed to stiffening the Brandt government's own negotiating position, and therefore had led to some successes, such as the Letter on German Unity. The Brandt government's position on German unity was confirmed in July 1973 by the Federal Constitutional Court when it resolved that the Basic Treaty was in line with the constitution, but also emphasised the objective of reunification as laid down in the Basic Law, which excluded any recognition of the GDR under international law, and also meant that there could be no GDR nationality.

That the conflict over the treaties with the East did not grow more severe after they had been passed, and that the Union finally adopted the compromise with the East as the basis of its own policy was largely a result of the Social Democrats' success in the Bundestag elections of 19 November 1972. Both sides had turned these elections into a plebiscite on *Ostpolitik*, and the people had decided. The turnout of voters, at 91.1 per cent, was the highest in German history. The SPD obtained 45.8 per cent, the FDP 8.4 and the Union 44.9. This was a clear victory for the government coalition, which could now rule with a secure majority.

In the international context, the treaties with the East had removed an important obstacle, perhaps the most important one, to a normalisation of relations between the two Cold War camps. In spite of the proxy wars which continued to rage at the periphery—the Vietnam War above all, but there were soon conflicts in Africa and Latin America as well—it now seemed possible to convert Europe at least into a zone of peaceful cooperation, after the tensions over Berlin, the two German states and the western parts of Poland had been defused. Of course, this also meant that the division of Germany was not only confirmed but declared to be in effect the essential condition for détente, because a firm and unambiguous boundary had now been drawn between the zones of influence of the Great Powers, and also because there was no prospect that a permanently divided Germany would attempt to dominate Europe.

## Domestic Reforms

Most of Willy Brandt's government declaration had been about domestic reforms. It presented an immense catalogue of individual measures, which bore witness to the all-embracing desire for change and reconstruction felt within the new government, in particular its Social Democratic element. Many of these reforms went back to initiatives and preparatory work already done by the Grand Coalition, but unlike the Union, as Brandt emphasised in a programmatic statement he made in 1969, the SPD possessed

> a democratic and social conception of how democratic society could be changed and improved in the interests of the whole people while giving the best possible attention to the interests of the individual and specific groups, how it could be adapted to reflect structural changes and how a high degree of technological modernisation and intellectual renewal could be achieved.[55]

This vision of a society which could be improved fundamentally within a few years undoubtedly possessed much power to attract and motivate, especially as the inhibiting pressures of a crisis-prone market economy appeared to have vanished thanks to the proven effectiveness of Schiller's system of 'overall demand management'. According to Schiller, the growth framework which would shape economic policy for the coming decade lay between a lower variant of 3.5 to 4 per cent, and an upper one of 4.5 to 5 per cent. In both cases, one could proceed on the assumption that over the next ten years 'annual national income per head would increase by between 50 and 60 per cent.'[56] With a prognosis like this, there would clearly be no difficulty in financing even costly reforms.

The clearest elements of continuity with the preceding government were to be observed in the area of law reform. Criminal law, including the law relating to sexual offences, was further liberalised; and in family and marriage law the principle of equality between the sexes was further extended. In divorce law the principle of marital breakdown replaced traditional conceptions of the guilt of one or the other partner.[57] Changes in social policy, on the other hand, did not involve the introduction of new concepts so much as the extension of benefits. In autumn 1972, during the Bundestag election campaign, a pension reform was passed. This envisaged comprehensive benefit increases and the introduction of a flexible retirement age, on the basis of calculations that predicted a surplus of almost 200 billion DM in the pension fund on the assumption of uninterrupted economic growth for the next fifteen years. 'The increase in pensions and the flexible retirement age', remarked Helmut Schmidt at the SPD Party Congress in 1972, 'are based on the assumption that in the next 10, or next 20 years, a Social Democratic policy of full employment will be pursued, and that all active employees will pay social insurance contributions, as will the employers too. But, after all, this is what will actually come about.' In view of this confidence, it is not surprising that the period of the Brandt–Scheel government turned out to be a time when 'the expansion of the social state was tremendously accelerated.'[58] Between 1961 and 1969 the social budget increased by an average of 9.5 per cent a year, but between 1970 and 1973 it increased by an average of 14 per cent. Social expenditure rose during this period from 174.7 billion to 334.1 billion DM, and the share of social expenditure in GDP rose from 25.5 to 33.4 per cent.[59]

Moreover, completely new areas of life now became subject to state direction and political remodelling. A programme of regional development was adopted. This was intended to help in creating uniform living conditions throughout the country, and it led in particular to permanent alterations in the external appearance of the countryside. The Urban Development Law made it easier for local municipalities to rehabilitate run-down urban areas (and it invited the cooperation of the people affected, for the first time); but it also offered a basis for the increasing tendency to destroy older city centres. The environment also became an object of systematic government policy for the first time. The first environmental laws, and an 'emergency programme for environmental protection', outlined a field of policy whose importance was hardly recognised then by public opinion. The pioneer in this area was actually the FDP, which in its 'Freiburg Theses' of 1971 had already called for the introduction of a fundamental right 'to a decent human existence' and the protection by the state of the natural basis of life. But these environmental policies did not at first have a widespread impact.[60]

Most of these reforms were supported by the opposition apart from some disagreements over detail. The big confrontations between the parties over reform happened in other areas, above all education, abortion and co-determination. On educational policy there had been a broad consensus until the late 1960s about the need to improve the level of education, to iron out social, gender-related and confessional disparities and to build more universities and high schools. Spending on education by the federal government, the *Länder* and the municipalities, taken together, almost tripled between 1965 and 1973, rising from 15.7 to almost 45 billion DM. A uniform reorganisation of the top classes of the high schools was agreed by the Education Ministers of all the *Länder*. It prescribed that grades 11 to 13 in high schools would no longer be taught in formal classes but on a seminar basis. When the social–liberal coalition came into office, however, the consensus on educational policy began to dissolve. In view of the considerable increase in the number of school leavers and students many middle-class parents in particular became worried about both the quality of education in high schools and universities and the declining exclusiveness of the status of graduate. The reorganisation of teaching methods in the top classes also meant the abandonment of the compulsory neo-humanist canon, which dated from the 1900s, and thus the end of a symbol of middle-class distinctiveness. Throughout a century of political rupture and dynamic modernisation an understanding of the ablative absolute had always retained its role as the distinguishing mark of an educated person. Now it disappeared, because for Social Democrats educational policy was first and foremost an instrument for improving equality of opportunity. 'Equality' versus 'achievement': those words marked out the front line in the acrimonious controversies over educational policy.

These controversies first came to a head in the debate on the 'General Guidelines for Social Studies' issued for schools in Hesse. These guidelines proclaimed 'Self-determination and co-determination' as the supreme educational objective, but stressed that genuine participation in social decision-making processes could only be achieved by the removal of unequal life chances. Political education must therefore be an instrument of social change. These proposals sparked off a storm of indignation, and the whole of the Social Democrats' educational policy was placed under suspicion of being ideologically driven. Their endeavour to get rid of the tripartite school system and make the comprehensive school the norm met with protests not only from *Länder* governed by the Union but also from parents' associations with no political affiliation. The final result was that the comprehensive school did not become the norm and one-third parity was not achieved in university committees. The social liberals in government in Bonn attempted to make educational policy more strongly centralised and reduce the educational autonomy of the *Länder.* But they failed, and so each individual *Land* pursued a different educational policy according to the colour of its governing majority. The resultant fragmentation of the German school and university environment has often been lamented. But it did also lead to a multiplicity of systems and an atmosphere of competition the consequences of which were not entirely deleterious. In any case, educational policy remained for decades one of the most strongly contested and polarised areas of domestic politics.[61]

The planned revision of the law on abortion was another area of conflict. Two mutually incompatible standpoints confronted each other: the women's movement, which had in large part grown up around this issue, based its arguments on a woman's right to decide for herself, whereas the Catholic Church insisted that 'to commit abortion is to destroy a human life, and it is therefore morally objectionable.'[62] The political and also the parliamentary debate revolved around these two polar opposites. There was essentially no disagreement that the regulations on abortion needed to be reformed, if only because of the large number of abortions, estimated at somewhere between half a million and a million a year. The coalition majority was able to push through a regulation establishing a deadline, under which abortion was not punishable for the first twelve weeks of pregnancy, but the Federal Constitutional Court rejected this as unconstitutional. Finally, an 'indications' model prevailed, which permitted abortion under certain conditions. Unlike in the USA, however, the conflict over Paragraph 218 became less acute after a few years, because the compromise that had been found could be interpreted flexibly and met with widespread acceptance.

The other contested reform objective was co-determination in the workplace. This was a subject of particularly fierce debate. For decades, the 'democratisation of the economy' had been one of the main goals of the trade unions. Parity of representation on management boards had already been introduced in 1951 for the coal and steel industry, and the trade unions now did their utmost to make it compulsory for all large enterprises. The employers exerted an equal amount of energy in resisting this proposal, and they were supported within the coalition by the FDP. The upshot was that the law finally adopted in 1976 after a long tug of war was once again a compromise: representatives of the employers and the employees sat across the table from each other in equal numbers, but senior managers were also counted as employees though in status they were far closer to the employers. Moreover, where the board was equally divided, the chair's casting vote counted double, so that in conflict situations the employers had a majority. Neither side was satisfied with this solution. The employers instituted a legal challenge to the new rules, but in 1979 this was rejected by the Federal Constitutional Court, which was increasingly taking on the role of an extra-parliamentary mediator.[63]

Co-determination, so fiercely disputed in the early 1970s, now disappeared from the newspaper headlines. Right from the beginning of the Weimar Republic, corporatism and co-determination had been more characteristic of the German economy than the economies of other countries, and this had not led to any great disadvantages, a point also emphasised by the Federal Constitutional Court. On the contrary, says the economic historian Werner Abelshauser, co-determination lessened wage conflicts and their associated costs for the German economy, and contributed to ensuring 'that the basic features of the German system of production were preserved during every political catastrophe that occurred.'[64]

The balance sheet of the social–liberal reforms had both positive and negative aspects. On the one hand, many of the government's ideas for changing the country by liberalising, democratising and modernising it were carried through successfully, though they conformed with the 'general line of development of other European societies', as the sociologist Rainer M. Lepsius noted in 1979, and in international terms they represented rather a 'catching up process than an innovation'.[65]

On the other hand, the reforms resulted in a considerable increase in the amount of state regulation. In this case, changing and improving society always meant intervening and shaping it through the action of state institutions, whether the issue was educational policy, land consolidation or industrial relations. Such an extension of the state's jurisdiction could hardly be reversed in the future, and it also clearly contradicted the government's objective of increasing individual involvement. In particular, the social–liberal reforms led within a few years to a historically unparalleled extension of claims to social benefit. This was based on projections which tended to exclude the possibility of further economic crises and made the welfare budget independent of the level of economic growth. Both these aspects turned out to be extremely burdensome in the longer term.

## The German Model

In many respects, the year 1972 marked both the climax and the turning point for social liberalism and the optimistic progressivism associated with it. The implementation of the Eastern treaties ran parallel with the signing of the first SALT agreement between the two superpowers for the limitation of the nuclear arms race. Both developments gave encouragement to the conviction that the Cold War and the scramble to obtain nuclear weapons would soon come to an end, along with the hostility between the two German states. Since 1968, the West German economy had continued to grow enormously at an annual rate of over 4 per cent. Many of the domestic reforms, including the reform of pensions, had already been completed. The Nobel Peace Prize awarded to Willy Brandt in 1971 was a sign of the Federal Republic's increased international reputation, and the Nobel Prize for Literature awarded a year later to the decidedly Left-leaning Catholic writer Heinrich Böll strengthened this impression. The clear victory of the coalition in the 1972 Bundestag elections confirmed that it was going in the right direction. There was an increasingly strong feeling that the Federal Republic had become a particularly successful and modern society, and that through its uninterrupted economic growth and its extensive network of social benefits it had produced an exceptional combination of dynamism and security. This society had also freed itself from the inheritance of the Nazi state and accepted the democratic culture of the West, and it now projected the image of a new and liberal Germany across the globe.

This new self-image was strongly expressed when the Olympic Games were held in Munich in summer 1972. The games were intended to present a modern, westward-looking Germany to the world. They would be the exact opposite of the games of 1936: cheerful, easygoing, young, cosmopolitan, unpretentious and unmilitary. Swing music would replace military bands; there would be no perfect physiques on display in the Riefenstahl manner as PR symbols. Instead, there would be a pastel-coloured dachshund and a hypermodern Olympic stadium with a delicately curved canopy, which became the architectural icon of the era of social liberalism. This shining festival of progress was suddenly disrupted when the Palestinian group 'Black September' mounted a terror attack, during which nine Israeli athletes lost their lives. This assault has often been seen as a kind of portent of the crises and challenges that were to follow.

Even so, the Munich games still hold their place in memory as the symbol of a modern, purer Germany, something Germans could again be proud of.[66]

It was also with this slogan, namely 'Germans, we can again be proud of our country', that the SPD went into the Bundestag election contest in autumn 1972. Not everyone considered this choice of words appropriate, because of its tinge of nationalism. But traditional nationalism was replaced here by the offer of a post-nationalist identification with the Federal Republic as a 'modern' society, and that meant a society which was economically successful, socially just, and emphatically democratic, a society which had taken to heart the lessons of the past.

Four years later, however, the SPD went into the electoral battle under the slogan 'The German Model'. This was intended to make it clear that the critical point of reference was not the Nazi inheritance but the whole of the twentieth century. It was suggested rather that the ensemble of economic growth, social policy, liberal law reform, cultural openness, compromise with the East and European integration which had developed in the Federal Republic was a conclusive solution to the problems that had shaken Germany and the industrial world since the turn of the century. This was the perspective presented by the slogan 'The German Model' and the vision it contained, and as Helmut Schmidt emphasised, it did not just apply to the Federal Republic: 'Much of what we have built up together is of exemplary quality. Perhaps it is even a model for others.'[67] From this point of view, everything appeared to have been solved: the national question and the social question, the disagreements over political and economic structures and cultural orientation, and external conflicts in Europe. After decades of struggle, the proper way of organising the industrial world seemed to have been found.

# PART FIVE

# 1973–2000

# 17
# Crisis and Structural Change

## The End of Bretton Woods and the First Oil Price Crisis

Scarcely a year passed before the euphoria and progressive certainty of 1972 turned into a sense of crisis and unease. After twenty years of rising growth and prosperity, a long-lasting economic crisis began for the first time since the end of the war in the Federal Republic, as it did in all the other Western European states. It had the effect of transforming not just the economic and social situation of the country but also its culture and lifestyle, and even its foreign policy. The notion that politicians could direct the economy in its entirety also turned out to be an illusion. There could no longer be any question of an active, 'scientifically led' management of the national economy. Instead, politicians were obliged to engage in short-term crisis management in reacting to unexpected developments to which all the experience accumulated in the previous eighty years provided no answer.

In the popular memory, the crisis is largely associated with two turning points: the oil price crises of 1973–5 and 1980–2. But what was in fact involved here was a critical transformation process with manifold causes and consequences which ran its course jerkily and unevenly over roughly a decade. It has been described as a tension-filled 'series of developments running in parallel at different speeds and in various directions', developments which were 'by no means dependent on each other or causally intertwined in every case'.[1] This process was moulded in part by internal political and economic factors, but much more by the ever growing economic interdependence of the industrial countries, particularly the European community, by the collapse of the international monetary system, by the crisis over energy prices, and by the emergence of new participants in the world market as well as long-term and far-reaching structural changes in the national economies of Western Europe and North America.

The basis on which West Germany's economic development had been planned for the next few years was Karl Schiller's growth forecast of roughly 4 per cent a year. This was an extrapolation from the trends of the previous twenty years. After recovering from the short period of recession in 1966 and 1967 the West German economy in fact underwent a boom unprecedented since the late 1950s: between 1968 and 1973, GDP grew by an average of 5.1 per cent a year. In quantitative terms, it amounted to 918.8 billion DM in 1973, almost four times the 1959 figure. Unemployment stood at less than one per cent. The economic upsurge had admittedly brought some problems. The rate of inflation increased from 3.7 to 6.9 per cent between 1970 and 1973. In a country like Germany, traumatised by memories of past hyperinflation, this was a politically explosive figure. The shortage of labour was also a serious problem. But it seemed that all these matters could be handled, in view of the excellent economic data.[2]

According to Keynesian doctrine, as well as Schiller's system of 'global demand management', curbs on economic activity were now the order of the day. But, in practice, it turned out to be almost impossible for the government's financial and economic specialists to induce the responsible authorities in the *Länder* and the municipalities and even in individual federal ministries to exercise fiscal discipline in the interests of a counter-cyclical economic policy. They flung back a question to their interlocutors: when could the promised improvements in pensions and medical insurance and the building of schools and swimming baths be undertaken, if not now? As early as May 1971, the Minister of Finance, the Social Democrat Alexander Möller, was forced to resign because he was unable to restrain high government spending; this was an initial warning sign which was rapidly forgotten because the highly respected Karl Schiller now rose to become a 'super minister' covering both economic affairs and finance. Just over a year later, however, in July 1972, Schiller also handed in his resignation, because like Möller he no longer saw any possibility of harmonising the measures needed to combat the overheating of the economy with the spending policy of government ministries. In addition to this, the attempts that were made to fight against rising prices proved to have little impact. Neither an 'economic supplement' nor the formation of a 'cyclical fiscal reserve' (*Konjunkturausgleichsrücklage*) led to any lasting dampening of inflation.[3]

After 1968, employers had again reverted to the tried and tested means of making up for a shortage of labour: the large-scale recruitment of foreign workers. The industrialists, who urgently needed more workers, pointed out that, with the help of additional *Gastarbeiter*, it would be possible to fill the growing gaps in the workforce and, at the same time, counter the wage-push impact of labour scarcity. The newspaper *Die Zeit* came out in support of the proposal, saying that it was also in the public interest, because

> a single *Gastarbeiter* would raise the annual GDP of the Federal Republic by roughly 20,000 Marks. The average wage he received would be in the region of 10,000 Marks, while an amount of 10,000 Marks would accrue from

> the product of his labour in the shape of taxes, social contributions and the gross profit received by the employer. It would not be excessive to increase the number of *Gastarbeiter* from one million to 1.5 or even 2 million.[4]

This pointed the way to the policy operated over the next few years. Between 1968 and 1973, more than 1.5 million foreign workers were brought to the Federal Republic, with the result that the proportion of foreigners among the employed population rose from 4.7 to 11.9 per cent. Most of the new recruits came from Turkey. The number of Turks in West Germany rose from 85,000 in 1964 to more than 600,000 in 1973. By February 1972, Turks were the largest national group among the *Gastarbeiter.* They were predominantly employed as unskilled workers, above all in heavy industry, car manufacturing and construction, and thus their presence had the further effect of allowing German workers to rise into better paid positions.[5]

But the employment of foreigners did not result in lower wage increases. On the contrary, after 1969, wage disputes between the employers and the trade unions started to sharpen. Since 1968, the extraordinarily good economic environment after the end of the recession had allowed entrepreneurial profits to enjoy almost explosive growth. But the trade unions had accepted very moderate and long-dated wage agreements under the 'Concerted Action' programme launched under the impact of the 1967 crisis, and therefore wages had only risen very slightly in the interim. Now the economic situation improved more rapidly than expected, so that the blades of the scissors between wages and profits opened wider. This disequilibrium led to some unrest in the labour force, and eventually, in September 1969, there were spontaneous work stoppages, which were not organised by the trade unions. This was a new development for the Federal Republic, where strikes were a rarity. In response to this challenge, the trade unions, first and foremost the left-inclined union IG Metall, began a wage offensive, which led to considerable wage increases in the next few years. In 1973, there was a recrudescence of wildcat strike activity, and the pressure on the trade unions increased. They now attempted to achieve a genuine redistribution of income by calling for wage increases which would go further than simply compensating for the increase in profits. This campaign was very successful: between 1969 and 1974, wages and salaries rose by an average of 11.8 per cent, whereas labour productivity only rose by 2.7 per cent over the same period. As a result, the wage ratio (the share of gross income from employed labour in the total national income) rose between 1968 and 1974 from 61.2 to 66.4 per cent.

One of the consequences of this trend was a perceptible decline in investment expenditure. If this continued, there would be slower economic growth in the foreseeable future. The 'Concerted Action' programme launched by the employers, the workers and the government in 1967 had shown that all sides were aware of these alarm signals. Much had been hoped for from the advisory body set up under this programme. But, in view of the worsening social climate, it proved to be an inappropriate mechanism for solving the current problems. The federal government's efforts to combat inflation were also ineffective, because the cause of these difficulties lay only to a small extent in domestic economic developments. Thus, despite the continuing economic boom, fears for the future began to be voiced, especially as extra-economic data, in particular relating to financial policy, augured further setbacks.[6]

Since the 1950s, the growth of the German economy had been derived in ever-increasing measure from exports, in particular exports by industries that produced capital goods and consumer products. The share of foreign trade in GNP was 27.7 per cent in 1955, 29.9 per cent in 1960 and 34.3 per cent in 1970. The Federal Republic achieved enormous export surpluses. The figures for the three years 1955, 1960 and 1970 were 1.2, 5.2 and 15.7 billion DM. Between 1967 and 1973 almost half of West Germany's exports went to the six EEC countries. But the strong international involvement of the West German economy also went hand in hand with an increase in its importance in the world economic context. This was particularly evident in its relationship with the USA, whose trade surpluses now began to decline. In 1971, for the first time, the USA even recorded a trade deficit, while the Federal Republic continued to achieve big surpluses. This trend only became problematic because, as was equally the case with other European currencies, the exchange rates between the dollar and the DM were not determined by the market, which would have enabled them to adjust to changed economic data, but were instead set by the government. This meant that the divergent development of the two national economies produced a mismatch between monetary systems and economic performance. This led to a crisis in the international monetary system.[7]

This had been set up shortly before the end of the war, in 1944, at the resort of Bretton Woods, in the USA, and its main aim was to avoid a repetition of the mistakes of the post-1918 period. In particular, the intention of the Bretton Woods system was to prevent the exclusive pursuit of national interests by binding the different national economies more closely together and by introducing a system of fixed exchange rates. The individual national currencies were to be tied firmly to the US dollar as the reserve currency, and only very slight fluctuations in the rate of exchange were permitted. The US dollar was in turn directly linked to the price of gold, and the USA guaranteed that its currency would be convertible into gold. Changes in exchange rates would only occur in exceptional cases, such as where there were large balance of payments deficits or surpluses. International capital movements and international trade were thus stabilised, and this was one of the foundations of the tremendous economic upsurge which began in the West in the 1950s.

The system only functioned smoothly as long as the American economy remained stable. In the 1960s, however, the cost of President Johnson's social policies and above all of the Vietnam War, led to enormous and rapidly growing budget deficits and rises in inflation, which produced a greater and greater disequilibrium between the USA and those states which generated big foreign trade surpluses, namely Japan and West Germany. This differential could have been removed by the revaluation of the D-Mark. But this would have made West German exports more expensive, and the politicians of the Grand Coalition, and in particular Finance Minister Strauß, were not ready to take such a step so soon, given that the 1967 recession had only just ended.

But since the D-Mark was now highly undervalued, an increasing quantity of speculative capital flowed into the Federal Republic in expectation of the ultimately unavoidable revaluation and the abundant profits which would result from this. This increased inflationary pressure within the country still further. In autumn 1969, immediately after the change of government, the social–liberal coalition raised the exchange value of the D-Mark by 9.3 per cent. This was too little and too late to have any more than a short-term impact. US dollars continued to flow in large quantities to West Germany, and inflation increased yet again. The federal government reacted by deciding in May 1971 to allow the temporary relaxation of controls on the DM exchange rate. The US dollar did then begin to rise against the D-Mark, but the influx of speculative capital into the Federal Republic did not decline. By then, the USA's foreign debts were four times as large as its gold reserves. In this situation, President Nixon decided on a spectacular, though consistent, step, and on 15 August 1971 he ordered the suspension of the dollar's convertibility into gold. That solved the problem of the dollar exodus for the moment. But confidence in the Bretton Woods system was shaken by the measure, and it could not be restored even by the return to fixed exchange rates in December 1971.

Between 11 and 14 March 1973, the heads of government of the European Community decided to abandon the system of fixed exchange rates definitively, and to let their currencies 'float', in other words to allow the market to determine the rate of exchange between them. The attempt to limit the fluctuation in European currencies to an agreed band (the 'currency snake') was a failure, because the economies of the individual European countries varied too much in strength. For the Federal Republic, the renewed appreciation of the D-Mark resulting from the floating exchange rate meant that the influx of dollars dried up and inflation was reduced. But, at the same time, the prices of the products Germany exported rose steeply. Until then, although the under-valuation of the D-Mark had worked to promote inflation, it had brought considerable advantages to West Germany's export industries. Now they were exposed to stronger competition on the world market, and this put some branches into lasting difficulty.

Looked at from a broader perspective, the end of the Bretton Woods system marked the beginning of a change in the way the capitalist world economy was governed. This was a change from management by the state to a more autonomous role for market conditions. International financial markets were increasingly liberated from state intervention and they soon developed a tremendous momentum. This was accompanied in economic and financial policy by the abandonment of Keynesianism. Theorists like Milton Friedman and Friedrich August von Hayek had long criticised state direction of economic activity. They maintained that economic dynamism required the creation of the best conditions for business enterprises, and not demand-side measures such as higher wages. Similarly, the value of money ought not to be stabilised by state instructions but by using independent central banks to control its quantity. These banks would be responsible only to the market, and not to governments.

There were considerable variations in the speed and the extent to which the countries of Western Europe changed the direction of their economic policy from Keynesianism to monetarism. But central banks now became increasingly important in all industrialised countries. With the new regime of floating exchange rates, the West German Federal Bank (*Bundesbank*) had much more room for manoeuvre and it increasingly started to play a vital role in financial policy side by side with, rather than in subordination to, the federal government. It now began to combat imported inflation and at the same time to limit the generous spending policies of the state sector by means of a restrictive policy of tight money.[8]

One extra reason for the expansion of the Western economies since the 1960s had been the almost limitless availability of crude oil at low prices. In 1974, the Federal Republic derived 58.6 per cent of its energy supplies from oil, France 72.5 per cent and Italy as much as 78.6 per cent. In the twenty boom years, prices for crude oil—like those of almost all raw materials—had remained well-nigh static. In 1953, a barrel of crude had cost $1.93, while at the beginning of February 1971 it still only cost $2.18. The permanently low level of oil prices clearly reflected the economic and political supremacy of the West. The fall in the value of the dollar after the abandonment of the gold standard now substantially lessened profit margins for raw materials (which were always valued in dollars). The raw material producers endeavoured to compensate for this by raising prices. In the case of crude oil, the price had already risen to roughly $3 by the end of September 1973. The next month, when a war between Israel and a coalition of Arab states took place, the oil producers, associated together in the Organisation of Petroleum Exporting Countries (OPEC), used the price of oil as a political weapon for the first time. They initially employed it against the Netherlands and the USA, then against all the Western countries which had supported Israel. By the end of the year, the price had almost quadrupled, reaching $11.65 a barrel. As a result, in 1974 the Federal Republic had to pay 17 billion DM more than the previous year for its oil imports, although the imports themselves had fallen in quantity by 6 per cent.[9]

This oil price rise had far-reaching and multifaceted effects. Firstly, relations between the industrialised countries and the raw-material producing countries were reset. By deliberately raising prices, the Arab states emerged from a relation of postcolonial dependence on the West and began to apply the economic power created by their oil wealth in the political sphere as well. Conversely, the industrialised countries were now brought face to face with the fact of their dependence on oil. The obvious reply was to search for other sources of energy. In particular, nuclear power rapidly became more important. At the same time, the Middle East became the central focus of international interest, both politically and militarily.

Secondly, the autumn 1973 crisis over the rising price of oil administered a profound shock to the populations of the industrialised Western countries because, unlike the currency problems, which were difficult to grasp, the oil price crisis dramatically demonstrated the vulnerability of the industrialised lands of the West and the fragility of their personal prosperity. This shock was heightened in the Federal Republic by the Sunday driving ban imposed in four successive weeks at the end of autumn, because for the citizens of West Germany, motoring was a veritable symbol of their own economic progress, and their country's too.

Currency problems, inflation and the crisis over oil prices overlapped and reinforced each other at a time when the economic data for the countries of Western Europe were indicating that above-average rates of growth were in any case coming to an end. The boom of the 1950s and 1960s, and in particular the expansion of the West German economy, had been based on a series of special factors, which were now starting to lose their impact. In the labour market, the potential supply of skilled workers had been exhausted, the country had caught up technologically with the USA, the post-war reconstruction of the infrastructure had been completed, and the productivity of the economies of Western Europe and in particular West Germany was now as high as that of the USA. All these signs indicated that in the future the West Germans could only count on growth rates close to those reached in the pre-war decades, in other words, barely 2 per cent a year.

From the end of 1973, these different influences came together to create the first really noticeable crisis in the West German economy since the immediate post-war era. The figures for 1973 still gave grounds for optimism: the growth rate was 4.7 per cent and there were only 582,000 unemployed workers (1.2 per cent). All this was entirely in line with expectations. But a steep decline was to follow: in 1974 the rate of growth was nil, and in 1975 it was minus 1.1 per cent. The number of people unemployed doubled to 1,074,000. In addition, the baby-boom generation now appeared on the labour market, hence considerably greater growth than in previous years was required to reach a situation of full employment. The indebtedness of central and local government rose rapidly, from 125.9 billion DM in 1970 to 328.5 billion DM in 1977. Lastly, despite negative economic growth, the rate of inflation did not fall, but remained at a level of 6 to 7 per cent. Stagnation and inflation at the same time ('stagflation') was something new for economic policymakers; none of the recipes provided by 'global economic management' fitted this situation.[10]

## Structural Change

The crisis of 1974–5 was felt throughout the world. The annual rise in the world's production of goods, which had been 6 per cent in the previous ten years, fell to 2 per cent between 1973 and 1982. The growth of world trade in industrial goods, which had been 11 per cent a year up to 1973, now declined to 4.5 per cent. Both developing countries and industrialised countries with low export earnings were put into difficulties by the higher energy prices. In most of the countries of Western Europe, however, the rise in the price of oil was only one of several factors in the crisis.

The extent and character of the difficulties which now came to the surface are clearly apparent if we take a look at the situation in neighbouring European countries. In Great Britain, where the effects of the energy crisis were felt particularly strongly, the economy had already suffered from low productivity, a reluctance to invest and a negative balance of trade during the first two post-war decades. In addition, its ability to compete had steadily declined owing to the ageing of its manufacturing facilities and infrastructure. A process of de-industrialisation had thus already begun by the mid-1960s. This particularly affected the mining regions of Wales and central and northern England. Pits were closed, the shipbuilding industry declined, and the textile industry almost vanished. In addition, extremely high tax rates (up to 80 per cent on income and up to 98 per cent on capital gains) led to a continuous flight of capital. The state sector was extremely large, at roughly 50 per cent, and since most of the state enterprises were run uneconomically, a growing proportion of tax receipts had to be used to prop up these ailing firms. The oil price explosion worsened this already difficult situation, and the 1970s thus became a decade of permanent crisis and tough battles between the trade unions and successive governments over wages and reforms. While governments, whether Labour or Conservative, attempted to restore the stability of the currency and balance the budget, and to reduce state benefits, the trade unions fought against dismissals and rationalisation and for higher wages to compensate for the constantly rising prices. Between 1975 and 1980, wages rose by an incredible 100 per cent, but since prices also rose in these years by the same amount, the wage increases were completely wiped out. The crisis culminated in the winter of 1978–9, when almost all trade unions called strikes to obtain wage increases of up to 80 per cent. The country lay idle. Schools were closed, rubbish piled up in the streets and the number of unemployed rose to 1.6 million. The government was paralysed, and the end of the industrial system seemed to have arrived.[11]

In France, too, the oil price crisis made itself felt in a severe decline in investment, a weakening of growth and a rise in the unemployment figures. For the population, though, it was the price increases which were most painful, reaching 14 per cent, and leading in 1973 to the first general strike since 1968, although the social conflicts were not as devastating as they were in Great Britain. In any case, a process of modernisation began after Valéry Giscard d'Estaing became president of the republic. Industry was made more competitive, and productivity rose owing to the promotion of technological innovations. Nevertheless, the rate of inflation remained high, and unemployment continued to increase.[12]

The situation in the Federal Republic was more stable by comparison. From 1976 to 1979, the economy grew by an annual average of almost 4 per cent. In fact, in 1976, the exceptionally good result of 5.5 per cent was achieved. It seemed, therefore, that the crisis over oil prices had only temporarily retarded the growth of the West German economy and that the upswing was now continuing as it had done between 1968 and 1972. The unemployment figures, however, were over 4 per cent, which indicated that the crisis had not been a cyclical economic downturn but an expression of deeper problems. Industry had been affected most of all, particularly heavy industry. Between 1973 and 1976, the number of workers employed in industry declined by 1.4 million, whereas the number working in the tertiary sector, in particular the banks, insurance companies and public services, rose by 570,000. These changes were expressed particularly clearly in the figures for the gross value added in different branches of the economy. While GDP rose between 1970 and 1983 by a total of 34 per cent, gross value added in mining fell over the same period by 42 per cent, in shipbuilding by 13 per cent and in the iron and steel producing industry by 10 per cent. In chemicals, in contrast, gross value added almost doubled, while in information technology it more than tripled.[13] It was not only branches which had long been in crisis such as mining and textiles, but also iron and steel, engineering, shipbuilding and car manufacturing, traditionally strong sectors of the German economy, which now began to falter.[14]

It was not difficult to see the reasons for this. Firstly, the revaluation of the D-Mark had considerably increased pricing pressures on export-oriented

West German industries. Secondly, new competitors, such as Japan and the emerging economies of East Asia, particularly South Korea and Taiwan, had now appeared on the world market. They were able to manufacture mass-produced industrial goods more cheaply than German suppliers owing to their wage structure. The conditions of industrial mass production in the Federal Republic, with its unskilled labour force and its relatively high level of wages and social security contributions, were much less favourable. Thirdly, it was very clear that the West German economy, which had in international terms a very high proportion of people employed in industry (in 1980 the secondary sector still accounted for 44 per cent of all employees), was particularly sensitive to crises of this kind, while the service sector, which continued to grow, could only absorb a small proportion of the redundant industrial workforce. Fourthly, it had to be noted on the basis of international comparisons that the West German economy had clearly fallen behind in certain particularly promising branches such as data processing, microelectronics and biotechnology.[15]

West German firms reacted to these developments in several ways. They altered their product mix and their marketing outlets but they also made savings, cut costs, rationalised production and laid off workers. These measures had drastic implications for their employees. The number of workers in the Federal Republic fell between 1973 and 1982 by roughly 2 million. The steel industry is a particularly vivid example of this trend. Techniques of production and the organisation of labour there had hardly changed since the turn of the century. More than two-thirds of the labour force were semi-skilled workers; in 1960, the proportion expected to receive further training, in other words the future specialists, was less than 4 per cent. Changes only took place here with the coming of the technological innovations of the 1960s. The most important of these was the replacement of the Siemens-Martin process, which required a great deal of heavy physical labour, by more modern methods of steel production with a high degree of automation, in which semi-skilled workers were needed to a far lesser degree. The scene was no longer dominated by the 'hard grafter' but by the skilled foundry worker or the process technician, who had to go through a three-year apprenticeship and acquire a large amount of technical knowledge. Manufacturers preferred to lay off semi-skilled workers and compensate them by means of 'severance schemes' and 'early retirement'. The proportion of unskilled and semi-skilled workers in the total workforce fell between 1970 and 1989 from 41 to 23 per cent. In 1981, more than half the unemployed were unskilled workers, but only 26 per cent of the available jobs were suitable for them.[16]

In addition, firms now started to move away from cheap mass production to a concentration on specialised items of higher value, even in the classical branches of industry. At the end of the 1960s, the characteristic hallmark of the West German motor industry was still the 'Beetle'. This was Volkswagen's most successful export item. There were millions of them, they were cheap, and they used old-fashioned technology. In the 1970s this situation began to change. What was now typical of West German car production was the technically intricate and costly vehicle in the medium and luxury categories such as the BMW or the Mercedes, and soon the Volkswagen as well. There was a similar change of direction in the fields of electrical equipment, aircraft construction, chemicals and, particularly successfully, mechanical engineering. The spread of modern technology increased the demands on the workforce. In this context, it was an asset to have in place a dual education system and a three-year apprenticeship for skilled workers.

These changes were, of course, accomplished over a lengthy period, from the early 1970s to the mid-1980s, and they gave rise to many industrial conflicts. The number of strikes increased, and massive demonstrations were held in protest against the closure of factories, both in the big industrial locations of the Ruhr, the Rhineland and Baden-Württemberg and in the coastal cities. Unlike in Great Britain, however, these social confrontations did not lead to temporary social paralysis. In West Germany, the structures and traditions of corporatism turned out to be helpful in organising structural change in such a way that it appeared to be 'socially tolerable', in other words, it was cushioned by fiscal means. The trade unions focused, on the one hand, on helping younger employees to acquire new professional skills and moving them into other branches of industry, while the future of older employees—and that often meant employees of forty-five and upwards—would be assured by severance schemes providing a slightly lower income in the short term, followed later by early retirement. On the other hand, they called for radical reductions in working hours, so as to spread out 'the available work' over more employees. In the long run, this accelerated rationalisation, but it also helped to spread the structural changes over a longer time period.

During these years, the trade unions not only enjoyed a considerable increase in membership (from 6.3 million in 1966 to 7.8 million in 1978) but they also reached the zenith of their political influence. They were represented by several cabinet ministers, and their big campaigns for the humanisation of the world of work and above all for shorter working hours were very successful. Some three-quarters of trade unionists continued to be industrial workers. But, in the economy as a whole, the number of office employees and civil servants exceeded the number of workers for the first time in 1975. The importance of the trade unions declined in proportion to this shift away from classical industrial labour to the areas of administration, banking, insurance and technical and scientific knowledge.[17]

Structural change brought about far-reaching social and topographical transformations in all the big industrial regions of Europe. Everywhere, whether it was the English Midlands, the north of France, the south of Belgium, the Ruhr or the Saar, one could see abandoned factories, industrial wastelands and decayed town centres. Municipalities got into acute financial difficulties, working-class districts close to abandoned installations were soon inhabited mainly by the unemployed and people who had had to take early retirement. Some towns lost more than a third of their inhabitants in less than fifteen years. Even so, other towns were able after a long time to establish new industrial branches and develop a new dynamism, dominated largely by employment in administration, finance and the sciences. But most of the former mining districts, in Western Europe and Great Britain as much as in the USA, were left behind for decades in a state of decline and deterioration.

Dortmund, for example, which was the seventh largest city in the Federal Republic in the mid-1960s, with more than 650,000 inhabitants, had been one of the centres of heavy industry since the beginning of industrialisation. In 1958 170,000 of the 275,000 people employed there had industrial jobs. Of these, 120,000 were employed in the mining industry, particularly in the numerous local collieries, and in iron and steel firms such as Hoesch, Phoenix or Dortmunder Union. After the early 1960s, however, the effects of the crisis in coalmining began to be felt: in 1961 more than 50,000 people were employed in the city's fifteen coalmines, but by 1973 the number had shrunk to 18,000, and in 1987 the last colliery ceased operations. The iron and steel firms also fell into crisis in the early 1970s, and one after another they closed down, even Hoesch AG, which had dominated the city, as it possessed the largest number of sites. The outdated Siemens-Martin installations were decommissioned first, then the number of workers was reduced through various closures and mergers from over 30,000 in 1970 to 13,000 in 1987. Finally, in 2001, steel production in Dortmund ended completely. The steel plants themselves, which had been modernised at great expense, were sold to a Chinese firm, which dismantled the whole installation and re-erected it in Shanghai.

These developments had a tremendous impact on the city itself. In the early 1980s the proportion of people unemployed reached almost 20 per cent, and in the working-class districts to the north it was twice as much. Tax receipts collapsed and the population fell by almost 100,000. Large areas in the centre of the city and in its northern districts became industrial wastelands, on which new commercial undertakings could only be established in a few cases. The majority of the new employment opportunities arose in banking and insurance, but also in and around the university, which had been founded in 1968. By 1995 the proportion of employees who worked in industrial production had fallen below 20 per cent. What happened to Dortmund's traffic plans was a striking example of the rapid change from the euphoria of modernisation to the collapse of the iron and coal industry: in the late 1960s, the city decided in view of the continuing expansion of the steel industry to build a separate motorway link for each entrance to the Hoesch factory complex. Work on these roads was finally completed in 2001. This was exactly the year when Hoesch closed the last of its factories.[18]

The politicians and the people of West Germany reacted to this crisis with surprise and bewilderment. After all, economic development had started in the mid-1950s by arousing expectations that prosperity would grow in line with the growth of industry, then it had confirmed these expectations during the 'economic miracle', and finally, after the recession of 1966–7 had rapidly been surmounted, the results had been consolidated. It took a long time before the realisation dawned on people that this was not just a cyclical economic downturn, which would soon be replaced by a return to expansion, but a fundamental structural transformation, the start of an 'erosion of the existing economic structure of the classical society of industrial labour which had given Germany its economic and social contours for over a hundred years'.[19]

Thus the beginning of the end of industrial mass production also shook the political, social and cultural foundations of the type of industrial society created before the turn of the century, the order and arrangement of which had been the focal point of political controversy for eight decades. The Social Democratic and trade union option, which was directed towards growth, progress and the management of the economy on Keynesian lines, and had enjoyed great success in previous years, had now evidently reached the end of the line. A conservative alternative, leading back into the regulatory model of the fifties, was not realistic, given the social and political changes and the cultural dynamic of the intervening decades. In the mid-1970s, the American variant of the Western social system was undergoing one of the biggest crises of its history, with the defeat in Vietnam, which was followed by the shameful resignation of President Nixon and the social upheavals connected with the decline of the classical industrial economy. The latter affected Great Britain too, to an even greater extent. And, as will be shown later, the state socialist system of the Eastern bloc countries was still more strongly affected than the capitalist world and was barely able to keep afloat economically.

At that point in time, none of these social systems could offer a road map, a model of how to cope with the tasks that lay ahead. The decline of heavy industry and of the industrial worker as the dominant social figure of the epoch deprived these systems of both foundations and future prospects. The new problems were more diverse and more ambiguous than the old, and they could not be solved with the old remedies. Placing ailing enterprises under state control did not make them more competitive. Nationalism was no defence against the continuing internationalisation of the world economy. Early retirement did not create any fresh jobs. And state planning of the economy proved to be a failure both in the East and the West. It was clear that henceforth politics could no longer concentrate just on increasing, improving and streamlining what already existed. Many of the problems now on the agenda were no longer an expression of the challenges which arose around the turn of the century side by side with the spread of industrial society but rather the results or side effects of the way those challenges had already been dealt with. If 'high modernity' is understood to mean the phase which began thirty years before the First World War, in which the dominant issue was the challenge faced by classical industrial society in the search for the political and social system appropriate to it, it was now clearly approaching its demise.

## Social Change and Contemporary Interpretations

How were these developments reflected in the structure of West German society? If one looks at the long-term data on social structure, three aspects catch the eye: firstly, there was a clear increase in the average age of the population. In the mid-1970s more deaths than births were registered in West Germany, for the first time. In the early 1960s, almost 40 per cent of the population were below the age of twenty, but by 1990 the proportion of young people had fallen below 20 per cent, while the number of over-sixty-fives had risen from 8.4 million in 1960 to 12.3 million in 1985. The number of newborn babies fell continuously, from 1.04 million in 1965 to 586,155 in 1985. That in turn was connected with changes in marital behaviour: in 1960, there were 521,445 marriages, while in 1980 there were only 362,408; in 1965, the average number of children a woman brought into the world was 2.5, while in 1985 it was only 1.28. Average lifetimes continued to increase, but the average length of time spent in work declined because longer periods were spent in education and training and people retired earlier: in 1980, fewer than 20 per cent of all employed people continued to work until the age of sixty-five.[20]

Secondly, more people were employed in the service sector than in the producing industries for the first time during these years. Like the demographic ageing process, this was a trend apparent over the whole of Europe. In Europe taken as a whole, there were in 1970 83 million people employed in industry and 80 million in the service sector. In 1980, there were 85 million people employed in industry and 102 million in services. The Federal Republic continued to be the country with the highest proportion of industrial employees, but here too the service sector overtook the industrial sector after the middle of the

1970s, although statistical differentiation between the two sectors became increasingly problematic because of the considerable increase in industry-related services, as for example in microelectronics and business consultancy.[21]

Thirdly, however, the unequal social structure underwent very little change. In the largest segment of society, the intermediate segment, wealth continued to increase, though more slowly. Disposable income per head rose once again between 1970 and 1990 by 50 per cent (from 16,169 DM to 25,121 DM).[22] Owing to the expanded social policy measures of the social–liberal coalition the share of wages in total income as compared with the income of people who were not dependent on wages increased temporarily. In 1970, the proportion had been 68:32, while in 1980 it was 76:24. Ten years later, however, the previous ratio had almost been restored (it was 70:30 in 1990). There was also little change in the distribution of income and wealth. Both in 1960 and in 1990, the upper 20 per cent of West German society received somewhat more than 40 per cent of total income, the intermediate 60 per cent received slightly under 50 per cent, and the lower 20 per cent received less than 8 per cent. The unequal distribution of wealth was particularly striking: in 1986 the upper 12 per cent of all households continued to possess 60 per cent of the total wealth. German inheritance law played a vital part in cementing in place this distribution of wealth. Differences in income did not remain static, however, but increased dramatically: between 1970 and 1990 average income from self-employment rose from 140 per cent to 250 per cent of average incomes.

These inequalities were heightened by the sharp rise in unemployment after 1974. After a temporary improvement in the years 1979 and 1980, the proportion of people unemployed rose again, reaching 9.1 per cent in 1983. Right through to the end of the 1980s, some 2 million people were reported as unemployed, and after a year without a job a third of them counted as long-term unemployed, and were almost impossible to place in a job. With the return of unemployment, which had often seemed to be a thing of the past after twenty years of prosperity, poverty was again recognised as a current problem. In statistical terms, a person who received less than half the average income counted as poor. That category included 6.5 per cent of the population in 1973, but in 1990 it already covered 10 per cent, and over the same period the number of people receiving social welfare payments rose from 1.5 million to 3.6 million.[23]

By far the hardest hit were the unskilled and semi-skilled workers and their families. In this group, the proportion of foreigners was particularly high. The number of foreign workers who had jobs fell between 1973 and 1978 by almost a third, to 1.8 million. Part of this decline could be ascribed to the rise in unemployment. Until 1975, the number of unemployed foreigners had always been far smaller than the number of unemployed Germans, but now foreign unemployment rose disproportionately higher. By 1981, 8.2 per cent of foreign workers were unemployed, as opposed to 5.5 per cent of German workers. On the other hand, the federal government had reacted in November 1973 to the oil price crisis by prohibiting the recruitment of foreign workers from abroad. It was calculated that in this way the number of foreigners in West Germany would be reduced by roughly 250,000 a year, which meant that in ten years the number would have fallen by at least a half. Between 1973 and 1980, roughly 500,000 *Gastarbeiter* did in fact return to their homeland. At the same time, however, many foreign workers, particularly from crisis-ridden Turkey, brought their families over to join them, so that the number of foreigners living in the Federal Republic was actually one million higher in 1980 than it had been in 1972.

In particular, the proportion of women among the foreign-born population increased. In 1961 there had been 451 women for every thousand men, while twenty years later the ratio between men and women in the younger age group was almost equal. At the same time, the number of children born to foreign parents increased sharply: by 1974, the proportion of newborn babies with foreign parents had already reached 17 per cent, while the overall proportion of foreigners in the country was 6.7 per cent.

Thus the ban on foreign recruitment did not work out as predicted. On the contrary, all the indications were that an increasing number of foreigners wished to remain in the Federal Republic for a considerable length of time, perhaps even permanently. They established families, they had children, and they moved out of temporary accommodation and into rented housing. Their savings ratio also fell, they started to consume more, and their links with the homeland become more tenuous: the *Gastarbeiter* had become immigrants. But, with the onset of the economic crisis, it became more and more difficult for them to find employment, because these were unskilled workers the German recruiters had concentrated on bringing into the country during the boom years so as to fill in the gaps that had opened up in the lower pay grades. Moreover, for Turks in particular, a return to the homeland did not present an attractive alternative because it was plagued by internal disturbances and its economy was languishing. Hence the proportion of unskilled foreign workers who were unemployed and reliant on social security benefits in the decades that followed was far greater than was the case for the native-born population.[24]

What was said at the time about the 'two-thirds society' therefore did not apply precisely to the social structure of West Germany at the end of the 1970s. It was rather that a small group of wealthy people, between 5 and 10 per cent of the population according to various definitions, continued to increase their wealth, while at the other end of the scale there was a group of socially deprived and poor people covering roughly 10 to 15 per cent of the population, who hardly entertained any hope at all of social advancement. Three-quarters of the population stood between these two groups. They had a secure and slowly rising income. This larger central group had numerous social layers and differentiations, and there were striking differences of income within it. But the extension of the education sector and greater access to high schools and universities had made the prospects of social advancement for the next generation more realistic than ever before, even if the economic and structural crisis had increased their uncertainty about their own future.

The parallel presence of two ideal-typical social models was a characteristic feature of the mid-1960s. One was oriented towards industry and tended towards cultural traditionalism. The other was a service-oriented model, 'modern' in cultural terms. By the 1970s, the balance had clearly shifted in favour of the latter model. Both orientations continued to exist, but in the meantime the older model had largely lost its power to shape society, and the characteristics of the service-oriented consumer society had made further inroads. The classical models of working life and family structure had lost their monopoly position. But they were not simply replaced by other models. There were instead a growing number of options on offer: repeated changes in the place of work, in the employer or even in the kind of work became a common practice for more and more people, as also did changes in working hours, to allow time for child-rearing, for instance.

The 'third age', following youth and working life, now also became more significant. As the time span between retirement and death continued to increase, existence as a pensioner ceased to be a dreaded prospect and became a period of life with positive connotations, which could often be shaped actively by the individual owing to the improved health enjoyed by the elderly. In essence, what was involved here was a shift in the period of employment. Traditionally, unskilled and semi-skilled workers had begun their working life after finishing the eighth class of elementary school, hence at the age of fourteen or fifteen, and they had ended it at sixty-five, so that the average male drew a pension for five years before he died around the age of seventy. Now, however, working life began at nineteen or twenty after a long period of school and apprenticeship, or, among academics, at twenty-five, and it ended as early as sixty, so that statistically there were then sixteen years in which to draw a pension, and in most cases to enjoy much better health than previous generations.

The demographic ageing process was associated with grave sociopolitical problems, firstly because the cost of paying pensions increased tremendously, and this had to be borne by those who were still actively working, a group which was becoming smaller and smaller. Secondly, health costs also rose, because the benefits offered by health insurance funds increased and greater use was made of them owing to the higher average age of those insured. From that time onwards, pensions and health were permanent sociopolitical problems for the Federal Republic, which were not solved even by endlessly repeated attempts at reform.[25]

During these years, the traditional organisation of the family, by which the man was the sole bread-winner, and the woman was the guardian of the household and the children, also lost its monopoly position. Just as the rise of industrial society had once caused fundamental changes in family structure and relations between the sexes, so now the growing service-based society started to alter gender roles and the way families lived together. The number of families with two working parents increased, as did the number of childless marriages and families with only one parent. The number of one-person households also increased. The idea of 'singledom' began to spread, and after the early 1980s almost half the households in the cities of West Germany consisted of one person.[26]

It was women in particular who were affected by the changes outlined above. By 1980, the proportion of women in employment had risen to 53 per cent, while the figure for married women was 48 per cent. In 1960, three-quarters of all women and girls aged between fifteen and twenty were in employment, but by 1990 this had fallen to one-third. Among those aged between forty and forty-five, on the other hand, the proportion in employment rose from 45 to 70 per cent. For women, continuous employment was now increasingly a matter of course; the age of marriage rose and the educational level improved rapidly. The proportion of female holders of the School Leaving Certificate rose from less than 40 per cent in the mid-1960s to over 50 per cent in the mid-1980s. At the beginning of the 1990s, there were as many female university students as male ones. But this did not result in equality in professional life. In the mid-1970s, women doing the same job as men continued to receive a 25 per cent lower wage, and they were also considerably over-represented in the more badly paid branches of the economy (being employed as teachers, salespersons, carers and office secretaries). Moreover, when steps were taken to create the infrastructure needed for the employment of mothers, such as nursery places and whole-day schools, they met with ideological objections from the churches and the conservatives, so that it was often impossible for women to remain at work for the whole day. This constituted a pronounced disadvantage, particularly for women with university degrees.

Marriage, the family and the bringing up of children began to lose their position as the inevitable course of a woman's life. Many functions which had previously been performed by the family were now taken over by the state, such as the care of the elderly and also some aspects of child-rearing in the case of families where the mother had a job. The liberalisation of divorce law increased individuals' ability to decide on how to lead their life, and the number of divorces rose by 60 per cent between 1970 and 1985, reaching over 120,000.

At the same time, the number of childless and unmarried partnerships for life started to increase considerably. Moreover, after the 1960s, the spread of methods of contraception uncoupled sexual activity from reproduction, while the number of legal abortions rose from 13,044 in 1976 to 91,064 in 1982.

There was also strong pressure on men to live their lives in a different way. Longer periods of unemployment, increased skill requirements, frequent changes of profession, the increase in female employment and, not least, the rise of highly skilled female competitors began to undermine the man's role as sole provider and the assignment of social roles associated with this. The overall picture is of a change in the manner in which people lived their lives, something which had previously remained fixed for almost one hundred years. This occurred with relative rapidity, although it required two decades before it was fully completed. Its central feature was the replacement of conformist and standardised ways of living by the choices of individuals, who might well change direction several times during their life.[27]

As a result of these transformations, industrial society now became what was soon to be described as 'post-industrial society'. This process was attentively followed and interpreted by contemporary observers. But the analyses of sociologists and political journalists were not just reactions to perceived changes; many of the theories and concepts they advanced moulded and influenced perceptions of the present and thus contributed to shaping them. This was particularly true of modernisation theory, various versions of which had given rise to different interpretations of the post-1945 world. Walt Rostow's theory, according to which industrialised societies almost inevitably became wealthy, as long as democracy and a free capital market as well as a functioning state apparatus and an active middle class were present, was as influential in many countries of the 'Third World' as it was in Western Europe.[28] The American sociologist Daniel Bell, in his book 'The End of Ideology', published in 1960, stated that there was by now substantial unanimity over the fundamental elements required to shape the modern world, which were 'acceptance of the welfare state and the desirability of decentralised power; a mixed economy and political pluralism'. The alternatives to liberal society had failed everywhere. This applied both to the big totalitarian ideologies and to liberalism of the 'classical' type. Almost none of liberalism's supporters was still convinced that the state ought to play absolutely no role in the economy, just as almost no serious conservative maintained that the welfare state was 'the road to serfdom'. According to the conviction widely shared at the end of the 1960s, progress could be made perpetual if the following conditions were present: predictable economic growth, the containment of capitalism's social contradictions by means of compensatory social policies, and the integration and stabilisation of society through liberal democracy.[29]

But the changes already evident in the 1960s but much accelerated in the next decade cast doubt on the validity of these predictions, because the rise of the service professions, the approaching disappearance of the army of unskilled industrial workers and the use of modern technologies in the interests of rationalisation increasingly cast doubt on the central significance of traditional industries in modern times. Industrial society, Daniel Bell pointed out in 1973, was in the process of being transformed into 'post-industrial' society. Physical labour and industrial production no longer occupied centre stage. They had been replaced by knowledge and technology. An information society was emerging, in which the prosperity of a country was no longer determined by its industrial but by its scientific potential.[30] These ideas were picked up by politicians who now frequently used the phrase 'the second industrial revolution', partly in order to justify the enormous efforts that were being made to improve educational opportunities in the Western countries.

The notion of 'post-industrial society' also contained the elements of an explanation for the unmistakable changes that had occurred during the 1960s in the values and moral horizons of Western societies. According to the American sociologist Ronald Inglehart, writing at the end of the decade, the central aspect of these changes was the conflict between the generations and the resulting transformation of values. The values of the older generation had been moulded by the structures of traditional industrial society, and for them the most important objective was to rise out of poverty and build a secure and stable existence. Their actions were led by particular conceptions of value and morality, such as security, order, achievement, discipline, obedience and punctuality. The younger generation, in contrast, had grown up in a period of relative stability, they were better educated and they were much more frequently involved in the service sector. In their case, accordingly, a shift was perceptible towards post-material values such as freedom for individual development, participation, self-determination and autonomy.[31]

Analyses of this kind were initially derived from the experience of the Anglo-Saxon countries, but, after a certain amount of time had elapsed, observations made in the Federal Republic confirmed and indeed extended this picture. The considerable increase in disposable income over and above what was needed for the maintenance of life, the extension of free time owing to the reduction in working hours, improvements in education and the expansion of the service sector offered a basis for paying greater attention to questions which went beyond simple reproduction. This context was also used to explain the processes of liberalisation and pluralisation which were regarded as characteristic of most Western European societies in the 1960s. The same was true of shifts in sexual morality and in ideas about the family and the nature of education, as well as the dissolution of milieux connected by socio-moral ties, particularly the Catholic movement and the working-class movement, and the decline of church attendance and religious affiliation.[32]

In essence, however, these theories of post-industrial society and shifting values continued to be based on the principles of progress and growth and on confidence in the future. The diagnosis offered was that the system had changed, but it would not break down. In contrast to this, some French philosophers, such as Jean-François Lyotard, Michel Foucault and Jacques Derrida, developed much more radical analyses of contemporary change. Most of these thinkers were former radical Leftists in search of alternatives after their view of the world had collapsed in ruins. For them it was not only Marxism that had become less convincing but also modernisation theory, whether in its liberal or its Social Democratic variant. Faced with a world which was becoming more diverse and pluralistic, they drew the following two conclusions: that the Marxist or Keynesian view that it was possible to control events could no longer be maintained, and that large-scale political programmes, and 'grand narratives' in general, no longer had any effectiveness or legitimacy. Functional logic, prediction and systematic thought had lost their influence and meaning, said Lyotard. 'Post-modern science' was interested more in 'undecidables, the limits of precise control, conflicts characterised by incomplete information, "*fracta*", catastrophes and pragmatic paradoxes'.[33]

Increasing attention was paid to these arguments, and they sparked off a veritable revolution in thinking in the field of the humanities. Their significance in the political context consisted above all in the fact that they contested not only the necessity but also the possibility of developing new overall plans and standardising concepts, which interpreted social development in terms of one single source and chose uniform objectives for the future. These ideas were of assistance in understanding the European scene during the 1970s because they neither sought to judge the confusing multiplicity of novel processes and challenges according to a single yardstick nor to distinguish between main and subordinate contradictions but rather to characterise the new processes as multiform, plural and contradictory. That was progress indeed.

## The Aporias of Industrial Society

West Germany was now ceasing to be dominated by classical industrial society. As a result, its aporias and defects tended to become more clearly visible and to come under greater public scrutiny. A critique of the harmful side effects of an industrial development which was aimed purely at quantitative expansion emerged quite independently of the oil price crisis, though this did play a part in accelerating the change in atmosphere.

Here too, the chief impulse came from the USA, where an environmentalist movement had already taken shape by the end of the 1960s. In 1970, more than 100,000 people demonstrated at an 'Earth Day' held in the USA for the protection of nature and the environment. A commitment to nature as such had already been widespread in Germany since the turn of the century, but mainly as an expression of hostility to urbanism and a rejection of modernity, and therefore as late as the beginning of the 1970s it still tended to be located on the Right of the political spectrum. The first beginnings of a policy directed explicitly towards the environment came in fact from above rather than from below. The new policy was instituted by the Federal Ministry of the Interior in the late 1960s, but it did not meet with much response at the time: in an opinion survey made in 1970, 60 per cent of those questioned did not understand what was meant by the phrase 'protection of the environment'.[34]

This situation changed rapidly in the years that followed, when reports began to accumulate about the contamination of rivers and oceans, air pollution and the effects of poisonous substances like DDT and asbestos. On 5 October 1970 *Der Spiegel* made the subject of the 'poisoned environment' its lead story, under the heading 'Mankind is Destroying the Earth', while the *Süddeutsche Zeitung* wrote at roughly the same time that 'People have been shocked by strontium in the milk, oil in the Baltic Sea, palls of smog over the towns and the way traffic crawls through overcrowded streets.'[35] Situations which had been accepted for decades, or even welcomed, as the unavoidable accompaniments of a prosperous industrial society, appeared in a different light once the inevitability of industrial progress was no longer regarded as a matter of course.

There was one study of this situation which attracted great attention. This was a report commissioned by an as yet largely unknown private organisation called the 'Club of Rome'. It was presented in 1972 under the title 'The Limits of Growth'. Its authors, led by two US social scientists, Donella and Dennis L Meadows, used computer analysis to develop a number of different scenarios, in which they predicted the future worldwide course of industrialisation, population increase, food shortages, the exploitation of raw material reserves and the destruction of natural habitat. This was the conclusion they reached: 'If the present growth trends in world population, industrialisation, pollution, food production and resource depletion continue unchanged, the limits to growth on this planet will be reached sometime within the next one hundred years.'[36]

The report confirmed the calculations of previous investigations, according to which social, economic and ecological equilibrium would be endangered and industrial progress would destroy its own foundations if existing developments were to continue into the future in the same manner. Many scientific objections were made, however, to what was called the 'Meadows Report', particularly as regards its warnings against further increases in world population. There was also criticism of the prediction that supplies of important raw materials would soon run short and become unattainably expensive. But one reason for the enormous impact of the book was that the raw material crisis brought about by the oil price crisis of 1973 provided a dramatic indication of the limited character of the world's resources, and in that sense appeared directly to confirm the predictions of the 'Club of Rome'. Hence the book met with an extraordinary response, was sold in millions of copies and can be regarded as the starting point of the European environmental movement.

The warnings and prophecies of the report received particularly strong support in the Federal Republic. Many people were surprised that the environmental idea had such a powerful resonance in the most industrialised country of Europe. But there were reasons for this. Firstly, the harmful environmental side effects of growth were particularly perceptible in the heavily industrialised conurbations of West Germany, and secondly the Federal Republic possessed the financial resources needed to take action. Pundits in the media, who had previously seized on Willy Brandt's earlier call for 'blue sky over the Ruhr' as an opportunity for biting sarcasm, now executed a complete about-turn. What had hitherto been regarded as a natural accompaniment of industrial modernity quickly came to be seen as a scandal.

But the implications of the Club of Rome's report went far beyond a critique of environmental pollution and a call for thermal insulation. If the industrial system was in danger of destroying its own foundations, as appeared from the scenarios predicted in the report, the foundations of the industrial system themselves needed to be questioned. In 1974, the Social Democratic politician Erhard Eppler made these connections in a particularly forceful and effective manner: he asserted that the first half of the 1970s represented a far-reaching historical watershed. Since the start of industrialisation, the driving force of European history had been 'the repeated demonstration that limits could be overcome. Limits of knowledge and perception, limits of achievement, limits of velocity, limits of productivity and production, limits of space.' But now, he said, referring explicitly to the Meadows Report, the limits of growth and progress had become plain. 'How much can our earth tolerate? How many people, supplied with enough raw materials, energy, water, food and space for development, can it support?' Eppler also stressed the need to limit increases in population. But his main line of argument was directed more to the need to limit the consumption of raw materials, and to limit private consumption in the industrialised countries. In view of the standard of living that had now been achieved there, what was on the agenda was not a further quantitative increase in prosperity but a fairer distribution of the available wealth and a qualitative improvement in living conditions, in the 'quality of life'.

This phrase, which Willy Brandt had already employed in his government declaration of autumn 1972, marked the emergence of a new category, which persuasively and effectively encapsulated the sea change that was occurring in the political mindset. 'Quality of life' was unmistakably a subjective category, related rather to the individual than to large groups. It indicated that a situation had now been reached which made it possible to go beyond bread-and-butter concerns and seek an improvement in life itself. In a country where the material situation of four-fifths of the population was at least satisfactory, the objective was no longer merely an increase in affluence but a qualitative improvement of the conditions of life. This referred to matters such as health, nature and a clean environment, but also to education, job opportunities, free time and, finally, the possibility of 'self-realisation', a notion which soon became one of the leading ideas of the time.[37]

Criticism of the devastating side effects of industrial society spread quickly and was to be observed in all political camps. A prominent example was the book by the CDU politician Herbert Gruhl, *A Planet is Being Plundered*, which soon became a bestseller.[38] It became clear that questions of environmental protection and quality of life transcended the Left–Right schema, which had largely been related to the antagonism between capital and labour that had determined the course of the industrial age. This is the explanation for the innovative character and explosive political thrust of the new development. Exaggerations and irrational fears also resonated in these warnings against the destruction of the environment and nature; apocalyptic scenarios and a recrudescence of anti-modern resentments were present as well as typical media hyperbole. On the whole, however, the analyses and warnings of Meadows, Eppler, Gruhl and others about the extent of environmental destruction and its associated dangers were too convincing to be ignored in the longer term, and this is the main reason for their astounding success, not the 'psychological instability' of West German society or 'industrial society's boredom with itself', as has often been speculated.[39]

The new political content demanded new forms of action. Protest was no longer expressed in trade unions or political parties, but rather in 'Citizens' Initiatives', at first directed mainly against local and regional vexations, such as the building of motorways or airports, the demolition of historical town centres, the emission of harmful substances by factories and the poisoning of lakes and rivers. These action groups, most of which were originally loose and temporary, soon joined together to form inter-regional associations, thereby becoming a prominent political force. This also indicated that the purely representative model of participation offered by official democracy was under challenge.

In these new groups, the ideal of democracy at the basis was combined with notions of a better, post-industrial life, and also a large dose of Romanticism. Similar trends were evident in other industrialised countries, such as Canada, where in 1971 a group of pacifist activists protested against the resumption of atmospheric nuclear tests by the USA and a year later by France by taking a boat into the prescribed testing area, thereby accepting self-endangerment. This was the beginning of 'Greenpeace', an organisation which used daring and spectacular actions to draw attention to environmental dangers all over the world. By 2009 it had some 3 million members.

But it was the debate over nuclear energy which began to occupy the central position in the conflict between industrial society and the environmental movement. In view of the growing uncertainty about the supply of cheap oil, it was tempting to engage in a large-scale expansion of nuclear energy production, especially as energy prices had quadrupled since the end of 1973. There was a growing conviction in all industrialised countries that nuclear energy alone could close the 'energy gap' and guarantee 'reliability of supply'. Unlike in the 1960s, the energy industry was now also interested in an extensive development of nuclear power in the Federal Republic, and the Fourth Nuclear Programme, issued on 5 December 1973, envisaged a threefold increase in the share of nuclear power stations in total energy production. Eleven nuclear power stations were already operating by 1974, and a further seventeen were scheduled for construction. Within fifteen years, according to the plans, almost 50 per cent of the country's energy needs would be met by nuclear power.[40]

Criticism of the nuclear power stations was centred mainly on the risks associated with the production process and the final disposal of used fuel rods. The opponents of nuclear energy argued that the 'Maximum Credible Accident' (MCA), a meltdown of the core in a nuclear plant, might lead to a massive release of radioactivity and to the death of everyone who lived within a radius of some 50 kilometres from the accident as well as the radioactive contamination of many more people. The advocates of nuclear power regarded such a turn of events as entirely unlikely. What this dispute essentially involved was the degree to which the advantages of an inexhaustible and inexpensive source of energy could be balanced off against the disadvantages of an unforeseeable future danger whose extent could not be calculated with any certainty.

It took a long time, however, before a realistic understanding developed of the dangers presented by nuclear energy production. For decades, the 'peaceful use of nuclear energy' had had exclusively positive associations. Prophecies that this inexhaustible source of energy could be used to desalinate oceans, irrigate deserts and solve both the conflict between North and South and the social question still echoed in many people's ears. The first protests against the building of nuclear power stations could therefore hardly be distinguished from protests against other large industrial installations in agricultural regions. In February 1975, farmers and vintners from the wine-producing village of Wyhl am Kaiserstuhl, in southern Baden, who feared the harmful effects of a planned nuclear power station on their fields and vines (which might for example include blocking out sunlight or heating the ground by the discharge of waste water from the cooling rods), joined forces with left-wing students from the neighbouring town of Freiburg, who were interested in opposing capitalism and protesting against Hans Filbinger, the prime minister of Baden-Württemberg. The latter's defiant attitude towards his Nazi past made him an appropriate opponent for the students, as much as his threat that 'the lights would go out' in Baden without this nuclear power station. He refused to negotiate with the demonstrators, and instead he ordered the police forcibly to clear the Wyhl building site occupied by the demonstrators. It was therefore the aggressive response of the state which first made the nuclear programme into the battleground of the debate over the future of industry.[41]

In the course of the next few years, almost every time a new nuclear power plant was constructed there were fierce protests, which mobilised hundreds of thousands of people, and entailed a degree of violent conflict not previously known in the history of the Federal Republic. Brokdorf, Grohnde, Kalkar, Wackersdorf and above all Gorleben, where West Germany's 'temporary storage facility' for burned-out fuel rods was to be erected, became flashpoints for the conflict between radical opponents of nuclear power and the police, who had to use thousands of officers and a large quantity of equipment to protect the sites where building was taking place. In March 1979, a serious accident occurred at the Three Mile Island nuclear power plant near Harrisburg, USA. An event of this kind had long been feared by opponents of nuclear power, though its advocates regarded it as out of the question. The Three Mile Island incident strengthened support for the movement against nuclear power. Nevertheless, the nuclear programme set forth in 1973 was by and large successfully implemented, notwithstanding all the protests, and by 1988, nuclear power plants provided a third of West Germany's energy production. The protest movement did however succeed in preventing the further expansion of nuclear power, whereas in France this expansion continued, so that by 2010, nuclear power plants supplied 74 per cent of the country's energy needs.

In West Germany, the disputes over nuclear energy continued into the late 1990s with undiminished intensity, and it was only after the Federal Republic's complete withdrawal from the field after the 2011 nuclear disaster in Fukushima, Japan, that they reached something of a conclusion. The confrontation between the two sides could almost be described as Manichaean. It was a war of rival faiths, in which more was obviously at stake than problems of energy supply. The writer Hans Christoph Buch noted in his 'Gorleben Diary' on 12 January 1977 that he like many other demonstrators did not know exactly what a reprocessing plant was, 'only that it is something terrible, a thousand times worse than any nuclear power plant'. He was prepared to ascribe all kinds of unpleasantness to the supporters of nuclear energy, including links with Nazism: 'The terminology—final storage, final disposal—reminds you of the final solution to the Jewish question.' On the other side of the fence, young police officers recalled that before going into action at Gorleben they were shown a film about Grohnde, 'so as to psych them up for the coming clashes'.[42]

The supporters of nuclear energy, among them the energy industry, the trade unions and, last but not least, Chancellor Helmut Schmidt, regarded the protests as an attack by the radical Left on the foundations of industrial progress and accordingly on the established principles underpinning West German prosperity. The chair of IG-Metall, Eugen Loderer, accused the critics of nuclear energy of 'blocking essential developments in an almost fanatical manner, thereby endangering our jobs and the material conditions of our life'.[43] The opponents of nuclear energy, for their part, regarded the building of nuclear power plants as an attempt to establish a 'nuclear state' in which the population would be exposed to deadly risks with the aim of maximising profits. This view was based on the fear, expressed in a book by Robert Jungk, that the state would have to go over to a nationwide surveillance system in order to control the dangers of nuclear power. This view seemed to have been substantiated by the illegal bugging measures against Klaus Traube, one of the leading managers of the nuclear industry, who had also taken part in developing the 'fast breeder reactor' at Kalkar. Traube's contacts with a number of left-wing intellectuals led to the (absurd) accusation that he was in contact with the Red Army Faction (RAF). The resulting scandal led to the resignation of the Minister of the Interior, Werner Maihofer, but it also showed the amount of suspicion and hysteria that marked the domestic situation in the Federal Republic during those years.[44]

Towards the end of the decade, however, the line-up of the two sides became less rigid. In the government, and particularly in sections of the SPD, clear doubts started to be expressed about the future of nuclear energy. Ideas about reducing energy consumption or using 'alternative' sources of energy now became more prevalent, though it took some time before these attitudes predominated. In addition, the anti-capitalism of the movement against nuclear energy began to lose its appeal, because nuclear power stations were being built in the socialist countries as well. Criticism of the harmful impact of industrial societies—whether in the West or the East—on nature and the environment was not compatible with classical left-wing ideology. This set in train a process by which the political Left was transformed into an environmental movement spanning both camps, graphically demonstrated, and accelerated, by the formation of the party of the 'Greens' at the beginning of 1980.

The signs of transformation were even clearer in the case of the 'alternative milieu', which was in part identical with the movement against nuclear energy. Like most of the developments described here, this too followed the example of its predecessors and exemplars in the USA. There the end of the American protest movement had seen the emergence of a multiplicity of self-organised, decentralised groups which saw the future in terms of a change in lifestyles rather than an attempt to exert direct influence on politics in the wider sense. In this environment of radical feminists, associations of ethnic minorities, gay groups, early environmentalists, and hedonistic 'dropouts' concerned with their own self-realisation, a counter-milieu emerged, which played a pioneering role above all in the university towns in testing out different, 'alternative' lifestyles. It was very clear that the areas of activity of these groups no longer corresponded with the problems and battle lines of classical industrial society. In these newly formed movements, the white working class played almost no role, and the workers' social concerns often tended to conflict with those of the new movement, which was predominantly derived from the academic middle class, and associated industry not with jobs and a prosperous life but with the destruction of the natural environment and risks to health. From this angle, the true social dichotomy was not the contradiction between capital and labour but between the majority of society and a heterogeneous group of minorities, and ultimately between society and the individual.[45]

Similar movements now developed in the cities of Western Europe, in Paris, Rome and London as well as in Copenhagen, Stockholm and Zürich. They had a strong presence in Berlin, Frankfurt and other university towns and cities of the Federal Republic. The 'alternative milieu' was initially based on the attempt to live outside bourgeois society, financed by 'self-determined labour' in community cafés, repair workshops, bookshops and other 'projects' which in fact sometimes received state subsidies by indirect routes. The guiding principles of these groups were decentralisation, collective property and an all-embracing and permanent requirement to participate. A characteristic feature was: 'the aspiration towards self-realisation in a community of like-minded people according to ideals such as individual freedom, solidarity, authenticity and sustainability and with the objective of transforming society as a whole.' To live 'alternatively' meant, in the words of contemporaries, 'to live and work together in a self-determined, equal, decentralised way, which is understood to be anti-capitalist, and which seeks to achieve a human and natural existence'.[46] In this milieu, new, anti-authoritarian ways of bringing up children were discussed, alternative types of living arrangement in communes were tried, and new forms of association between the sexes and attitudes towards minorities were propagated. This was the starting point for the gay movement as also for self-help groups of disabled people. Many of these experiments and discussions led nowhere, or ended in fiasco, but it can be seen that an experimental space was emerging here for new forms of social communication which would follow the prospective end of classical industrial society. The new movements absorbed impulses from processes of social individualisation, but they also simultaneously radiated them out over the whole of society.

The feminist movement was particularly important in this respect. It arose relatively late in the Federal Republic, and it was significant that it first emerged within the SDS as a rebellion by female members of that organisation against male leaders who set the tone and behaved in an authoritarian manner. Very quickly, however, the new women's movement gained considerable support and agreement far beyond student and left-wing circles. Here too the example was set by the USA and France. Authors such as Betty Friedan (*The Feminine Mystique*), Kate Millett (*Sexual Politics*) and Simone de Beauvoir (*The Second Sex*) became leading figures of a radical feminism whose core concern was to politicise the many forms of social inequality between men and women and bring gender-related disparities to an end. A feminist counter-culture emerged, which created a tight network through women's bookshops, self-help groups and women's journals. Soon this network separated out from the alternative milieu, stamping a lasting imprint on a younger generation of West German women. The feminist impulse was the motive force behind an initially hesitant, but later systematic, political drive to oppose discrimination against women and win an equal position for them in work and public life. However, unlike the rapid changes in overall social and family structures which characterised the 1970s, real change in the areas affecting women took place slowly, haltingly and against constantly renewed resistance.[47]

The alternative milieu, which probably included more than 400,000 predominantly young people of above average education, was a hybrid. It was on the one hand one of the 'New Social Movements', and as such it was directed towards political change, organisation and demonstrations. On the other hand, however, it was distinguished by its extreme informality. It was fluid and without fixed outlines, it was anti-hierarchical and it was marked by random actions and a creative lack of professionalism. On the one hand, it celebrated a culture of attentiveness, warmth and directness, but on the other hand it was closely interwoven with the 'militant' scene of the 'spontaneists' and 'autonomists' who sought violence by engaging in 'urban warfare', as in Frankfurt, or in demonstrations against nuclear power stations, as in Brokdorf, and whose existential radicalism led them close to terrorism. Indeed, at its margins, the movement merged with terrorism. On the one hand, the alternative milieu was a product of the New Left and a direct successor of the sixty-eighter movement, and more than 95 per cent of the people who counted themselves as part of the alternative 'scene' said they were on the Left or the extreme Left. On the other hand, their stress on subjectivity, 'first-person politics', 'authenticity' and self-realisation prepared the ground for the spread of individualism which was also to characterise the majority society in the years that followed.

## Terrorism

It was these parts of the extreme Left which were most closely linked with the terrorism which kept West German politicians and the population itself on tenterhooks for almost a decade. More than fifty deaths, many injuries, a tremendous growth in the police and the security services and an intensely emotional and polarised public mood resulted from, and accompanied, the development of terrorism. As stated earlier, this was not a purely West German phenomenon. There were similar movements in France, the USA, Japan and above all Italy, and they were politically and organisationally linked. Even so, in many respects, it is the configuration of domestic forces that explains the West German Left terrorism of the 1970s rather than developments of an international character.

The movement emerged in the context of the escalating violence of the confrontation between the power of the state and the rebellious students in the late 1960s. Since June 1967, there had been discussions in many places and in many circles of the left-wing student movement about the possibility of 'taking up armed struggle'. The main motivating forces which led to the radicalisation of part of the New Left in many Western European countries were as follows: the feeling of powerlessness vis-à-vis the organs of the state after the killing of Benno Ohnesorg by a Berlin policeman, perceptions of America's conduct in the war in Vietnam (and also the possible victory of the Vietnamese guerrilla movement, the 'Vietcong'), the rise of left-wing liberation movements in Africa and South America, and sympathy with the Palestinians after the occupation of the West Bank by the Israeli army.

In the Federal Republic, however, the confrontation with the Nazi past, which caused a paralysing sense of horror among some people, but among others triggered an urge to make up for previous failures to resist, conferred an element of unconditionality which tended to legitimate even the most extreme measures. The intensity of this feeling was unmatched in other countries, with the possible exception of Italy.[48] 'We have learned that to speak without taking action is to do wrong.' This was how Gudrun Ensslin justified the attempt to burn down two Frankfurt department stores in April 1968. 'It was right for something to be done. We have said clearly enough that we did the wrong thing' but 'this must be discussed with people who think as we do.'[49] The perceived injustice was so great that what was needed now was action, the 'liberating deed'. In comparison with this, more far-reaching justifications and objectives were of secondary importance. This action-oriented existentialism was as closely bound up with West German terrorism as was their narcissistic self-dramatisation as outlaws and romantic revolutionaries who committed their outrages in full public view, and by adopting a heroic pose directly challenged the whole state. In terms of ideology, however, the Left terrorism of the RAF was nothing more than an armed Marxism-Leninism whose proclamations only differed from the pamphlets of the student communist parties in that the latter thought the time for armed struggle had not yet come, whereas the RAF said it had already arrived. The group around Baader, Meinhof, Ensslin and Mahler presented itself as the Marxist-Leninist faction which no longer wanted to agitate among the workers but to create a 'Red Army' and begin the armed struggle. In one of its first proclamations it stated that the question now at issue was '*how* will the dictatorship of the proletariat be established'. Its slogans were 'Develop the class struggle! Organise the proletariat! Construct the Red Army!'[50] In this connection, it borrowed theoretical legitimacy from the writings of South American guerrilla groups, which had called for the fight of 'Third World' liberation movements to be conducted in the Western countries as well, for instance, by means of attacks on the public agencies of their main enemy, the USA. This approach was followed by the RAF in May 1972 when it directed its first actions and assaults against the headquarters of the US Army in Heidelberg and Frankfurt, as well as against the Springer Press and numerous police stations. The leading figures of the group were arrested shortly afterwards.

In the next five years, up to the bloody climax of autumn 1977, the 'struggle of the international proletariat against imperialism' was only a secondary focus of the political activity of the 'second generation' of the RAF and similar groups like the 'Second of June' or the 'Revolutionary Cells'. Their main concern was rather to liberate their imprisoned comrades and to continue the struggle against the organs of the state. The kidnapping of the leader of the Berlin CDU Peter Lorenz in spring 1975 was aimed—successfully—at forcing the release of their political associates. Some weeks later, a unit of the RAF seized the West German embassy in Stockholm. When the federal government refused to release the imprisoned group of RAF leaders around Andreas Baader, who were held in Stuttgart, the terrorists shot two members of the embassy, then set the building on fire. When the trial of the ringleaders of the RAF began in Stammheim in 1975, the cult around these 'political prisoners' extended still further, sometimes taking on bizarre forms. A not inconsiderable section of the New Left expressed their solidarity with the terrorists sitting in jail, agitating against the 'torture by isolation' and the 'destructive detention' they were being subjected to. These allegations were unfounded. No other prisoners received privileges as extensive as those enjoyed by the RAF. But, at the same time the latter styled themselves as potential victims of the fascist German police state, and the analogy between their own imprisonment and the murderous policies of the National Socialists was often used, and frequently believed. 'The political meaning of Toter Trakt, Cologne, I say this loudly and clearly, is gas', wrote Ulrike Meinhof. And Gudrun Ensslin declared that, 'we who are in here, to speak quite bluntly, can only be surprised that we have not received fatal injections. Otherwise nothing surprises us.'[51] This was pushing her imaginary identity as a victim of the Nazi 'final solution' to its ultimate limit.

RAF activities, which escalated to a climactic point in 1977, continued to be marked by a struggle against the West German security organs and an attempt to free the group's leading members. In April, the RAF shot the chief federal prosecutor, Siegfried Buback, and two of his escorts; in July, the head of the board of directors of the Dresdner Bank, Jürgen Ponto, was killed in the course of an attempt to kidnap him. Finally, in September, Hanns Martin Schleyer, the head of the Union of German Employers' Associations, was successfully kidnapped. Four people with him at the time were murdered in the course of the attack. As an early member of the NSDAP and the SS, Schleyer seemed an ideal symbol of the continuity of elites between the Third Reich and the Federal Republic. During the war, as an official of the German occupation in Prague, he had been involved in 'Aryanising' Jewish firms, while after 1949 he had risen rapidly to a high position in the Daimler-Benz company. The RAF believed that their kidnapping of the top representative of the German employers' associations would exert maximum pressure on the federal government and thus make it possible to force the release of the Baader group. But, after its previous experiences, the federal government was not prepared to give way to these demands.

In autumn 1977, there was an undeclared state of emergency in the Federal Republic. After the attack on Israeli athletes at the Munich Olympic Games in 1972 and the miserable failure of the attempt by the German police to free the hostages, the security apparatus had been greatly extended and modernised. In particular, the Federal Criminal Police Office (*Bundeskriminalamt*) had become a centre for new techniques of investigation. The collection of masses of data, which were collated with the help of electronic data processing (EDP), was intended to achieve success in tracing criminals, but at the same time involved accepting the systematic surveillance of many of the country's citizens. The West German public paid more and more attention to the hunt for the terrorists, and the degree of political polarisation, which was already very pronounced, increased yet further. On the one hand, the tabloid newspapers proclaimed that the terrorists were the greatest danger since the war, who should be dealt with in short order and that considerations of legality should be set aside in fighting them. On the other hand, a quarter of the country's citizens under the age of thirty expressed 'a certain amount of sympathy' for the RAF. The motives of the terrorists were often met with understanding in the Left liberal milieu, even if their actions were criticised. Within the Leftist 'scene', finally, some people expressed a 'surreptitious delight' at the murder of Buback, as a Göttingen University student put it.[52]

The federal government reacted relatively calmly to these challenges. After the kidnapping of Schleyer, Chancellor Brandt set up a crisis committee including representatives of all the political parties. A consensus was arrived at that Baader and his fellow prisoners would not be released. At the same time, the government increased the intensity of its investigations. The radical escalation that followed bore witness to the international connections of the RAF. The organisation had long been in close contact with militant Palestinian groups, particularly the Popular Front for the Liberation of Palestine (PFLP), which had also organised a raid on the meeting of the OPEC states in Vienna in December 1975. On 13 October a PFLP unit hijacked the 'Landshut', a Lufthansa aircraft with eighty-two passengers and five crew members on board, and demanded that the federal government release eleven German terrorists, including those imprisoned in Stammheim. When the government continued in its refusal to concede this demand, the kidnappers shot the captain and threatened to dynamite the aircraft with all its passengers still inside. The federal government reacted by sending an elite unit to Mogadishu Airport, where the plane had finally landed after its wanderings. The hostages were freed and three of the four kidnappers were killed. Baader, Ensslin and Raspe the prisoners held in Stammheim, reacted to this news by committing suicide. A few days later, Hanns Martin Schleyer was shot. His body was discovered shortly afterwards.

People began to regard the events of the 'German autumn' of 1977 as a watershed and a turning point almost immediately after this dramatic ending. In retrospect, however, this evaluation is only correct to the extent that German post-war Left radicalism had passed its zenith with the events of October 1977 and was now on a downward path. Scattered groups continued to exist. For many more years, they continued to engage in attacks in the name of the RAF, and they did not disband until the end of the 1990s. But, by murdering Schleyer and his companions and kidnapping the 'Landshut', the terrorists had so manifestly departed from all existing political goals and moral principles that sympathies for them quickly evaporated. At the same time, questions began to be raised about a left-wing radicalism whose slogans were largely taken from the arsenal of interwar communism and whose answers to the actual problems of the present, from the world economic crisis to the Iranian revolution, appeared even more anachronistic than they had been ten years earlier.

As a result, in subsequent years the overwhelming majority of radical left-wingers in West Germany cut their links with communism and gradually started to form a left bourgeois camp, which was largely absorbed by the Greens. Joschka Fischer, who was one of the ringleaders of Frankfurt Left radicalism in the 1970s, and had many contacts with the different variants of terrorism at that time, is an eloquent example of this trend. He was a co-founder of the Greens in 1980, and finally in 1998 he became German Vice-Chancellor and Foreign Minister. Once again, this turn of events was not a specifically German phenomenon, but has its parallels both in France and Italy.

The dramatic and tragic story of West German terrorism can thus be regarded as the last, exaggerated tremor of extreme Left radicalism, which had finally lost touch with its own political objectives, concentrating on its own liberation instead of the emancipation of the working class and the developing world, and which was ready to employ all conceivable means to achieve this goal. Here the influence of both international and specifically German factors was clearly apparent. Thus, the Soviet Union's support for Palestinian terrorists and the readiness of the GDR to provide asylum to former RAF members made it clear that the fight of the terrorists against the Federal Republic was much more strongly rooted in the context and the logic of the Cold War than the protagonists and supporters of the terrorist scene themselves imagined. At the same time, the dark aura of German Left terrorism as the returning ghost of German history was clear by 1976 at the latest, when three German members of the 'Revolutionary Cells' joined a Palestinian commando group in hijacking a French aircraft and taking it to Entebbe, where they performed a 'selection', dividing the passengers into Jews and non-Jews.

As far as the state was concerned, the years of terror were marked by extreme reactions, which made the country occasionally appear as if it were in a state of siege. Nationwide checkpoints and vehicle examinations, police with submachine guns and bulletproof waistcoats, house searches sparked off by vague suspicions, and above all a new, modern way of tracing suspects instituted by the Federal Criminal Police Office with the help of large-scale data collection, raised concerns, even among people who were fiercely opposed to the terrorists, about the increasing ability of the state to gain access to its citizens' details. Laws passed specifically to prevent RAF prisoners from communicating freely with their defence lawyers led to questions about proportionality and constitutionality, even if some of them abused their legal privileges as much as they could and finally even slid into terrorism themselves. The promotion of public hysteria also belongs in this context: a year-long barrage by the tabloid press against 'terror sympathisers' created an image of the enemy which did not fail to have an effect.

Despite this, and in contrast to the perception held commonly on the Left at least, the democratic rules that governed the state largely remained intact. Individual members of the Bonn crisis committee did, it is true, briefly consider after the hijacking of the 'Landshut' whether the Stammheim prisoners ought perhaps to be shot under martial law, but fantasies of this kind were quickly rejected. The tough actions of the federal government, which in most cases had constitutional backing, were accepted by large sections of the population. It had of course taken into account the possible death of Schleyer in its deliberations.[53]

One may perhaps be permitted to doubt whether, as has sometimes been suggested, West German society achieved a sense of identity by mastering the terrorist challenge. Even so, the democracy of the Federal Republic did indubitably gain a degree of 'emotional acceptance' which it had often not possessed, at least at the conservative nationalist end of the spectrum, thanks to its confrontation with terror.[54] To that extent, the West German state had proved itself, by seeking to assert its sovereignty not through a state of emergency but through respect for democratic principles, even in difficult situations.

## Politics as Crisis Management

The political shift which occurred during the 1970s was appropriately symbolised by the replacement of Brandt as Federal Chancellor by Schmidt. Willy Brandt had achieved much with his *Ostpolitik,* and his modernising and democratising reforms. The electoral triumph of autumn 1972 and the Nobel Peace Prize, but also the extraordinary influx of members, particularly young people, into his party, bore witness to the support and enthusiasm he enjoyed at home as well as all over the world. As a resistance fighter against Nazi dictatorship and as the mayor of Berlin, who became a symbol of resistance against the communist threat during the building of the Berlin Wall, his struggle against the two big totalitarian dictatorships of the twentieth century made him an almost unique figure in German politics. He managed to attach large sections of the rebellious youth of the 1960s to his party and to democracy, he set in motion the compromise settlement with the East, and he was jointly responsible for the reforming initiatives of both the Grand Coalition and the Social–Liberal Coalition, which were aimed at enhancing social justice and extending the rule of law.

But when faced with new challenges, such as the currency crisis, the oil price crisis, and the general structural crisis of the economy, he was at a loss. Moreover, after the SPD election victory of 1972 it proved difficult to form a new government. Discord within the party increased, and no one could find a way of financing the domestic reforms. The previous economic policy appeared to be obsolete, but there was no sign of a new direction. The fact that Brandt's fall was finally brought about by the discovery of a GDR spy in the Chancellor's office was not without a certain historical irony in view of his efforts to secure an agreement between the two Germanies, although it is not completely clear which East German spy service was involved and what its aims were, even now.

Helmut Schmidt, his successor, was cut from different cloth. Four years younger than Brandt, he had served as a First Lieutenant in the Wehrmacht during the war. Immediately after his return from prisoner-of-war camp, he joined the SPD, finished his education, and obtained a degree in economics. He was one of the first post-war leaders of the Young Socialists, he was elected to the Bundestag in 1953 and in 1967 he became head of the SPD parliamentary group. He had occupied key positions in the social–liberal coalition, first as Minister of Defence then as Minister of Finance and Economics, and after Brandt's resignation he was his unquestioned successor. The election of Schmidt in May 1974 meant that there was now a Chancellor in office who represented the 'Right' of the party, namely the workers and the trade unionists, and whose attitude towards the new Left of the SPD, which had emerged from the student movement and stood for a return to Marxist politics, was as reserved as it was towards the increasingly vocal criticisms being made of industrial society and the call to make the 'quality of life' the first priority.

The language of Schmidt's first government declaration was already an indication that the Brandt era had come to an end: the new guiding principles were now realism, sobriety, stability and security. Schmidt stressed his commitment to the market economy and the promotion of investment in opposition to all attempts by the SPD Left to 'test the limits of the capitalist economy's load-bearing capacity' by a policy of 'structural change'. He did, it is true, announce that the policy of reform would continue, but only if it could be financed. Schmidt therefore met with early and sustained opposition within his own party. In the population at large, on the other hand, he achieved very high popularity scores, even among conservatives, who liked his dashing style, which was somewhat authoritarian but, in any case, promised leadership and assertiveness.[55] A section of his party, on the other hand, especially the representatives of the new middle strata which had flocked towards the SPD since the late 1960s, retained the perspectives of the old and the new Left. Neo-Marxist politicians of the younger generation, such as Gerhard Schröder and Heidemarie Wieczorek-Zeul, occupied leading positions in the Young Socialists, and the impression occasionally arose that the '*Jusos*', with their calls to pursue socialist policies and 'overcome the system', were closer to the DKP than to Helmut Schmidt's SPD.[56]

The Christian Democrats changed their leadership after the electoral disaster of 1972. Helmut Kohl, the prime minister of Rhineland-Palatinate, was the new party leader. He was a young man, having been born in 1930, and he was regarded as a reformer. His first task was to make the CDU a modern party with a mass membership. He succeeded in doing this, and he also brought the party programme up to date. With his associates Heiner Geissler and Kurt Biedenkopf, he was able to attack the SPD on its very own terrain, social policy, by stressing the fate suffered by those social groups which were not represented by trade unions or protected by collective wage agreements. In this way, he raised a 'new social question' which affected the old, the unemployed, women, and large families. Like the SPD, which in 1977 achieved a membership of over one million for the first time, the Union also experienced a tremendous increase in numbers, counting more than 875,000 members in 1981, as against the 370,000 registered in 1969. These statistics demonstrate the high degree of politicisation during the 1970s, which led to record figures for election turnout and a record number of votes cast for three or sometimes four parties, in a situation of extreme polarisation.[57]

This atmosphere was reflected for example in the political declarations of the CSU chair Franz-Josef Strauß, who gave a speech at an internal party meeting in the town of Sonthofen, in Bavaria, in November 1974 in which he called on the Union to intensify its confrontation with the government. The state and the economy would need to sink to as low a level as possible, he said, before the Union again had the prospect of coming to power. 'Just attack and warn, but don't mention any concrete remedies', he urged his party friends. 'We must push them so far that they will have to propose a law to safeguard the budget or declare state bankruptcy.' The party must

> always identify the Social Democrats as representatives of socialism and unfreedom, as representatives of collectivism and bureaucratic rule, whose policy will lead to the hegemony of the Soviet Union over Western Europe. The fact that there is a whole bunch of people among them who do not want that to happen should not hinder us from saying it, because of an excess of objectivity.[58]

Strauß did not find majority support in the Union for his ideas, and the more reserved Helmut Kohl was chosen instead as the party's candidate for the chancellorship in the Bundestag elections of 1976. Even so, the Union did enter these elections under the slogan 'Freedom, not Socialism'. In Bavaria, indeed, the slogan was 'Freedom *or* Socialism', which further raised the temperature of an already highly charged political atmosphere.

There was something artificial and anachronistic about this attempt by the Union to clarify a politically and economically confusing situation by returning to the old front line battle cries of 'freedom' and 'socialism', so as to make it easy to distinguish friend from foe, especially as Schmidt could hardly be called a 'socialist'. It also gave the impression that the categories of 'Left' and 'Right' had greatly increased in significance in the political debate, at the precise moment when they had ceased to be real marks of differentiation. They did, it is true, offer familiarity and distinctiveness in a situation fraught with many uncertainties and unforeseen developments. This was a general feeling, in the Union as much as in the SPD, as well as among the radical Left and the new social movements of the period.

The 1976 elections gave the Union its best result since 1957. With 48.6 per cent, it only just failed to reach an absolute majority. Despite this, the elections were actually won by the government parties, partly because economic conditions in West Germany had improved rapidly and a growth rate of 5 per cent in the year 1976 led people to forget their economic worries for the moment. The SPD fell back to 42.5 per cent, the FDP to 7.9 per cent. In spite of its losses, therefore, the social–liberal coalition could form a government for a third time.

Schmidt's second government declaration did not propose any kind of master plan. In fact, there was not even any evidence of a clear policy. The themes that dominated his second period of office—the crisis in the currency system and the world economy, and the changes in the international scene—were rather imposed on him from outside. The art of politics, it seemed, now no longer consisted in developing the vision and impetus to achieve goals already pursued for many decades, but in reacting appropriately and on a short-term basis to new and unforeseen challenges.

## Old and New Fronts

The fundamental conditions of security policy had also changed. The point of departure here was the Conference on Security and Cooperation in Europe (CSCE), a project the Soviet Union had been trying to get off the ground for a considerable period of time. Once the Eastern treaties had been concluded, the Americans agreed to the Soviet suggestion of a large-scale conference, which accordingly took place in the Finnish capital Helsinki in summer 1975. All the European states participated, and the USA and Canada as well. For the Soviet side what was important was to ensure the territorial integrity of the area it had dominated since 1945. This involved guaranteeing the inviolability of the borders, non-intervention and sovereignty. In essence, the Soviet leadership's 'craving for acceptance' mirrored its uncertainty about the stability of the association of states it controlled.[59] A statement of Western commitment to the territorial integrity of the Soviet sphere was so important to the Soviets that they were prepared in return to go a long way towards meeting Western demands for guarantees of 'human rights and fundamental freedoms, including freedom of thought, conscience, religion and opinion'. In addition to the guarantee of economic and scientific cooperation, far-reaching concessions were made on freedom of travel and information and increased opportunities for personal contact were promised.[60] Admittedly, these were merely statements of intent, but the leaders of the Eastern bloc states had to reckon with the possibility that the Helsinki agreements, which would also be published in Eastern bloc newspapers, might be taken seriously by the citizens of those countries. And, in fact, in the next few years, the human rights activists of Charter 77 in Czechoslovakia as well as oppositional groups in Poland and dissidents in the Soviet Union repeatedly appealed to the rights of freedom of expression and respect for human rights guaranteed by their own governments.

These results of the Helsinki Conference therefore constituted an important advance in the direction of greater human rights. They also clearly contradicted the principle of 'non-intervention' insisted on by the Soviet Union. This principle was aimed at strengthening the autonomy of individual states in dealings with the Great Powers (and particularly the dealings of decolonised countries with their former colonial masters), but it could also be used as a protective shield against external criticism of internal conditions within particular countries. In contrast to this, the assertion at Helsinki of the primacy of human rights made it legitimate to raise these questions. US President Carter based his foreign policy programme entirely on this foundation, with varying success, but this did mean that breaches of human rights, wherever they took place, increasingly became the subject of worldwide public criticism. In some Soviet-dominated states the momentum this produced had explosive consequences.[61]

Military and defence matters had been excluded from the CSCE negotiations, to make it possible to achieve any results at all. In 1973, after the USA and the Soviet Union had completed the first round of their negotiations over disarmament in the area of strategic nuclear weapons (SALT I), they began discussions over the second round (SALT II), which ended in 1979 with an amicable agreement, the results of which were not confirmed by the US Senate owing to an increase in international tension. In both negotiations, the main issue was a reduction or at least a limitation of the number of nuclear missiles which were aimed by each superpower directly at the territory of the other, in other words, missiles which had a very long range. Shorter range nuclear missiles, such as those which affected Europe alone, were not discussed in these talks, because they were not relevant to the direct threats made by the two superpowers towards each other. The Soviet Union considerably updated its arsenal of medium-range missiles after 1977 by replacing some 600 outdated rockets with new intermediate-range ballistic missiles of the 'SS 20' type, which had a much greater destructive power. This endangered the fundamental principle of the Cold War in Europe, the 'balance of terror', the doctrine according to which peace was ensured when a nuclear aggressor ran too great a risk of being destroyed by a counter-strike. The superiority acquired by the Soviet Union in Europe as regards both conventional armed forces and medium-range missiles now altered this balance. At least, that is how the situation was seen by West European politicians, who feared that the security of Europe would become a secondary issue for the two superpowers if they came to an agreement limiting or reducing their strategic long-range weapons. This scenario was particularly dangerous for the Federal Republic, because all Cold War plans assumed that a conventional war, and also a war with medium-range nuclear weapons, would initially take place largely on German territory, while the Federal Republic neither possessed nuclear weapons nor had any direct influence on political decisions over nuclear armament or disarmament.[62]

Helmut Schmidt, the former Defence Minister and present Chancellor, was well aware of strategic considerations of this kind. In October 1977 he made a speech in London, which attracted much attention. In it he pointed to the danger that Europe might become disconnected from the security structure of the superpowers:

> A strategic arms limitation restricted to the two world powers, the USA and the Soviet Union, would inevitably compromise the security requirements of the West European alliance partners vis-à-vis the Soviet Union, which is militarily superior in Europe, if it does not prove possible to reduce the disparities existing in Europe in parallel with the SALT negotiations.[63]

Schmidt therefore called on the USA to station medium-range missiles in Europe in order to balance the expanded Soviet weapons arsenal.

This demand was not uncontroversial, because although France and Great Britain had also modernised and extended their medium-range missiles, these had not been included in calculations of the 'balance' between the Great Powers. The Soviet Union therefore disagreed with Schmidt's analysis. The USA too initially hesitated to agree to Schmidt's demand for the stationing of American medium-range missiles in Europe to re-establish the balance with the Soviet Union. In the course of the next year, however, relations between the USA and the Soviet Union began to worsen, above all because of the USSR's increasing engagement in Africa, which was perceived by the Americans as an act of aggression. They therefore became increasingly determined to take a hard line with the Soviet Union, and as a result they declared that they were ready to accede to Europe's wishes, and to station intermediate-range missiles on that continent.

Meanwhile, however, Schmidt's initiative had been heavily criticised in the countries of Western Europe, and particularly in the Federal Republic. Large sections of the population regarded the results of the policy of détente as irreversible, and since an increase in the stock of nuclear missiles clearly endangered the agreement between East and West, it was widely rejected. Large parts of the SPD also shared this attitude, and Schmidt could only win the upper hand within the party for his line of policy by proposing a twin-track approach: the West would refrain from stationing the missiles if the Soviet Union made a corresponding reduction in its intermediate-range nuclear capacity. If it did not do this, the new missiles would be put in place. NATO also adopted this approach, and on 12 December 1979 it finally made the so-called 'Double-Track Decision': if the Soviet Union did not reduce its number of intermediate-range missiles, the alliance would itself station intermediate-range nuclear missiles in Europe. It would 'upgrade' its armaments, according to the official form of words.

This decision reflected the worsening confrontation between the two world power blocs at the end of the 1970s, which soon began to be called the 'Second Cold War'. A number of different developments came together to create this new situation. The potentiality of some communist policies for extreme violence was dramatically displayed before the whole world by the news that the Khmer Rouge had murdered millions of their compatriots in Cambodia. Then the invasion of Afghanistan by Soviet troops at the end of December 1979 and the subsequent boycott of the Moscow Olympic Games by the West marked the definitive end of détente. As a result, the USA did not ratify the agreement on the limitation of intercontinental nuclear missiles which had already been negotiated. A proxy conflict between the two superpowers was already proceeding in several parts of the world. This was intensified in Latin America by the victory of the revolutionary left in Nicaragua and the deployment of counter-revolutionary forces there by the USA.[64]

These events all fell within the customary categories of the Cold War. In 1978, however, the Islamic revolution in Iran brought a new factor into international relations which did not fit in with the existing global lines of conflict. This new challenge to the West reached a critical point when members of the American embassy in Teheran were seized and held hostage for a period which lasted from November 1979 to January 1981. There was also an economic context to these events: the tensions between the oil producers and the industrialised countries which could be observed since the start of the decade, and which served to trigger the second world economic crisis. In terms of politics, they were a part of the conflict between the West and the postcolonial countries of the South, because the pro-Western regime of the Shah of Iran, Reza Pahlavi, had been strongly supported by the USA for decades and had now been removed by a popular uprising. There were parallels here with other anti-colonial and anti-Western liberation movements in the developing countries of the 'Third World'. But the Iranian revolutionary movement differed from other anti-Western liberation movements. Its members were not Marxists: it was led by Islamic clerics, and its aim was not socialism but an Islamic theocracy. What happened in Iran had a considerable impact on other countries with a predominantly Muslim population, particularly in the Arab world. The hopes of Muslims for a better future and for economic progress, but also for greater self-confidence and dignity in relations with the all-powerful industrialised countries, were now no longer attached to corrupt nationalist military dictatorships, like those in Libya, Egypt and Syria, which placed their faith in industrialisation and modernisation, whether of the state socialist kind or otherwise. Rising Islamism preached a very different path: progress would be achieved, the Islamists said, on the basis of indigenous traditions, above all religious ones, and an aggressively anti-Western approach.[65]

The lines of global conflict therefore began to shift. Tensions between East and West were now accompanied by a confrontation between North and South, conducted in political, economic, cultural and religious terms, which took the form in the Middle East of antagonism between political Islam and the industrialised states. But this also affected the Soviet Union, as soon became evident. The West regarded the march of the Red Army into Afghanistan as an expansion of the Soviet Union beyond the area it had dominated up until then. But, in reality, the invasion was motivated by the Soviet leaders' fear of the spread of Islamism into Afghanistan and from there into the predominantly Muslim areas in the south of the Soviet Union. The support of the West for the Islamic rebels, who included the Taliban and Arab fighters under the command of the Saudi businessman Osama Bin Laden, is just one of the many irregular crosscurrents and contradictions of this period which indicated how the configuration of international forces had changed. In 1980, it was still impossible to foresee the extent of the antagonism between Islamism and the West. In hindsight, however, one can see that in international relations the bipolarity between East and West was being replaced by a multipolarity which could no longer be reduced to dichotomous categories. This multiplied the sources of international conflict.

## The World Economic Crisis and World Economic Policy

The economic crises of the 1970s indicated a decline in Western power which extended beyond the economic sphere. The defeat of the Americans in South

East Asia, the rise of largely Marxist-oriented liberation movements in Asia, Africa and Latin America and the protest movements against industrial society in the countries of Western Europe and in the USA led to increasing doubts about the ability of Western systems of organisation to withstand, or even survive, these crises. Western governments, warned US President Gerald Ford in November 1975, would have to make sure that 'the present economic situation is not seen as a crisis of the democratic or the capitalist system.'[66]

The collapse of the Bretton Woods currency system had made it clear that only close coordination would allow the economies of the European countries to weather the problems in financial markets. As Chancellor Helmut Schmidt in particular never tired of emphasising, no industrialised country was any longer in a position to exert a directing influence on the gigantic forces of the world economy with an economic policy limited to the national framework. To cope with these challenges, the governments of the West would have to consult and cooperate together more intensively, both within the European framework and at the global level.[67]

But the European Community had lost a considerable amount of its impetus in the course of the 1960s. The main reason for this was the attitude of the French President Charles de Gaulle, whose policy had always been strongly oriented toward France's own national interests. He had also, right to the end of his period in office, prevented Great Britain from joining the Community. After his resignation in 1969, the European project recovered its momentum. The international economic and financial crisis greatly increased the project's importance. But the process of European integration was also considerably accelerated by the Brandt–Scheel government's policy on the German question, and its *Ostpolitik*. This gave rise to uneasiness among the governments of the other Western European states, particularly France, because it was felt there was a danger that the Federal Republic would start to pursue a separate course and move away from the Western consensus. In this context, it again became clear that one purpose of European unification, and not the least important one, was to bind West Germany firmly to the Western camp. Of course, stronger European cooperation was also in the interests of the Federal Republic, which had most to gain from the European common market because of its strongly export-oriented economy. As at the time of the Marshall Plan, so now too the intentional political containment of Germany was combined with its unintentional economic reinforcement.

In 1973, the EC was enlarged by the inclusion of Great Britain, Ireland and Denmark. This marked a successful northern and western extension of the community, bringing to an end a decade of deadlock. The increased political importance and attractiveness of the EC was demonstrated even more strongly in the mid-1970s, after the collapse of the long-established right-wing dictatorships in Portugal and Spain and also the military dictatorship established in 1967 in Greece. With the active assistance of the EC countries and the Socialist International under Willy Brandt and the Swedish Prime Minister Olof Palme, the basic requirements were put in place for the creation and rapid stabilisation of democratic institutions in all three countries. By supporting democratic parties which were just being built up, by giving financial assistance, by offering favourable trade agreements and by holding out the prospect of membership in the Community, the EC was able within a few years to achieve the political stabilisation of these three Mediterranean countries and integrate them into the circle of Western democracies. It was clear from these events that the Europe of the EC had become immensely attractive to the countries on the continent's periphery.

The word 'Europe' continued to have positive connotations in the public opinion of most of the EC countries, even if individual decisions by Brussels were hardly noticed or even severely criticised. If the governments could only agree, great steps towards integration would be possible without the need for votes to be taken or for inhibiting public debates to be held. In the long term, however, this produced a deficit of democracy and legitimacy.[68]

An important step towards strengthening the integration of the EC states was the decision to improve coordination between the foreign policies of the different countries of Western Europe. This was given institutional form in 1970 under the title European Political Cooperation (EPC). A year later, it was agreed to hold regular meetings of the heads of state and government. These developed into a cross between a series of coordinating meetings and a government of Europe, under the name 'European Council'. In 1979, direct elections were held for the first time to the European Parliament. This body admittedly possessed almost no real powers, but it served as evidence that the democratisation of the European project was one of the ultimate objectives. The crisis of the Western economies and the agony of the Americans after Vietnam thus gave fresh impetus to European cooperation, though this applied first and foremost to cooperation between governments, not to the extension of the supranational structures and institutions of integration.

The EC's economic interdependence also continued to increase. The agricultural market was already largely pan-European, though this worked overwhelmingly to the disadvantage of the consumer, because the countries with a strong farming sector, above all France, were able to use the financial means of the EC to retard structural changes in that area. They made sure that prices for agricultural products were kept at an artificially high level, even when far more was produced than the market required. As a result, EC expenditure on agriculture increased tremendously; almost 90 per cent of the EC's budget was devoted to subsidising the agricultural sector, and Germany, Italy and Great Britain had to take responsibility for these payments as net contributors. This had nothing to do with market economics, but was tolerated because the political and social problems that would result from an accelerated decline in agriculture were regarded as a greater evil.[69]

A European industrial policy, on the other hand, hardly yet existed, and if it did, it consisted rather in a Europeanisation of losses, while profits remained within the national framework. A number of joint European undertakings did develop, however, including the Airbus consortium and the European Space Agency. Initial rather timid attempts were also made to cooperate over technology, energy and transport. In addition to this, a more unified social policy began to emerge after 1972, as well as a regional development policy which involved giving support to the economically weaker regions of the Community. These were not the big steps forward repeatedly demanded by journalists and public opinion; measured against those demands, the progress actually achieved looked rather hesitant and unadventurous. But powerful European structures did gradually arise as a result, and they developed a momentum of their own which had an ever greater impact on the life of the member states and the way they were governed. In particular, a European legal framework emerged, administered by an influential European Court of Justice, the decisions of which were binding. The connections between the European nations therefore grew gradually closer in an unspectacular but effective manner.

It continued to be felt, however, that what would really advance political integration would be an intensification of economic interdependence. But moves in this direction soon came up against obstacles. For one thing, it was usually separate national interests which came to the fore in cases of conflict. Moreover, different countries held very different views about the long-term objectives of the European project. Some countries, particularly Great Britain, saw the Community as an extended free trade zone, while others, particularly the Federal Republic, wanted integrated economic policies and also closer political ties. And while the British, after Margaret Thatcher had come to power, set their sights on a strict orientation towards the free market and a reduction in state involvement, the French, under François Mitterrand, wanted their national policy of state intervention in the economy to prevail at the European level as well.

Despite these disagreements, Europe became increasingly integrated. This was a result more of the pressure exerted by world economic forces than the enthusiasm of the member countries. The intensification of European cooperation and the establishment of a European currency system were above all a reaction to the weakening of the USA's economic and political position. The decline of the dollar continued, and this led to a further strengthening of inflationary tendencies in the countries of Western Europe. A controversy arose at this time as to whether it was more sensible to create a new internationally agreed currency system or further to liberalise the financial sector. The obstacle to choosing the first alternative was that the basis of a future internationally agreed system was unclear, if the dollar was no longer the reserve currency. The second alternative certainly offered the prospect of a more dynamic financial market, but this would mean an increased danger of financial crisis, leading to economic destabilisation. In both cases the prospects were uncertain, because experience could not be used as a guide.

The first meeting of the heads of state and government of the six leading industrialised countries, as suggested by Giscard d'Estaing and Schmidt, took place at Rambouillet, near Paris, in November 1975. Its aim was to improve the coordination of international economic and currency policy. The currency problem formed the most important point on the agenda. Here, a compromise was finally found, but this merely identified the problem rather than solving it. The French had called initially for the return of a fixed currency system, but the majority of the heads of government decided on free-floating exchange rates, combined with an appeal to individual countries to conduct a more disciplined fiscal and financial policy. In the judgement of an American observer, this also signified a long-term commitment 'to the free market and the free economy rather than to government intervention', and the danger of establishing separate national markets was thereby averted for the time being.[70] This did not solve the problem of the weak dollar and the slow pace of economic growth in most industrial countries (except Japan and the Federal Republic). In 1978, when storm clouds again gathered over the world economy, the USA and Great Britain started to call on the states with a positive balance of trade—Japan and the Federal Republic—to stimulate their domestic economies more strongly with the help of state counter-cyclical programmes, thereby acting as 'locomotives of the world economy' by pulling other countries back into economic activity. A limited increase in inflation, Britain and America were convinced, was entirely acceptable.

The federal government, however, refused to adopt measures of this kind, not least on account of Germany's experiences with inflation in earlier decades. 'Inflation is not a way of combating unemployment but one of its chief causes', stressed the president of the German Federal Bank, Karl Otto Pöhl. German public opinion entirely agreed with Chancellor Schmidt's rejection of the Anglo-American proposals. For example, according to the *Süddeutsche Zeitung*, Schmidt was right to resist 'the notion, which seems ineradicable despite its absurdity, that the Federal Republic only needs to press the monetary accelerator, in other words make more inflation, to set the world economy back on its feet again.'[71] But the pressure on the federal government soon turned out to be too strong, and at the Bonn summit meeting in summer 1978 Schmidt was compelled to announce a big stimulus programme. This measure plainly contradicted the anti-inflationary austerity policy of his government, although it certainly accorded well with the wishes of the German trade unions and the SPD for policies aimed at stimulating the economy and creating more jobs. In practice, however, Schmidt's measures had little effect on the economy.

In return for this concession, the federal government called on the other industrial countries to make a serious effort to confront world economic instability. Its chief demands were that they fight inflation, balance their budgets and end their trade deficits. This was mainly aimed at the USA, whose balance of payments deficit had risen within five years from $5 billion to $45 billion. The main reason for this was the enormous increase in the amount of oil imported by America from the OPEC countries. But since the USA refused to introduce incentives towards reducing energy consumption and did not take any serious measures against either the budget deficit or the trend towards inflation, the situation remained precarious, despite the agreement made at the July 1978 Bonn summit. The fall in the value of the dollar accelerated, the rate of inflation remained high, and the high US trade deficit meant there was little hope of any early improvement.

In this situation, a rapid move towards a European currency union was a logical, but also a courageous, step. The EC started to work out a far-reaching plan for an economic and currency union as early as 1970. This proposal, called the 'Werner Plan', was a reaction to the looming currency problem, and it involved recommendations which already largely anticipated decisions that were made ten years later to harmonise economic and currency policy. But most EC countries were not yet ready to give up their sovereign rights over their own currency, and so the plan did not come to fruition. Not until the oil price crisis of 1973 did things start to move again. The first attempts at a coordinated currency policy (involving the floating of currencies and the 'currency snake') came to grief owing to the pull of divergent national interests, but in 1978 a 'European Monetary System' (EMS) was put into operation on the initiative of the leaders of France and Germany. Under this system, fixed exchange rates were established between the European currencies with variation permitted within a narrow band on either side of the central rate. This proved to be generally effective in overcoming monetary turbulence, although Great Britain at first remained outside the arrangement. At the same time, the Community introduced a notional currency, the European Currency Unit, or ECU, which was based on a basket of EMS currencies weighted according to the economic strength of each member. At first, this was nothing more than an accounting tool, but the possibility of a single currency was implied from the outset. Hence the decline in the effectiveness of their individual national policies led the countries of Western Europe to respond to the crisis in the world economy by intensifying inter-European cooperation. From the perspective of the late 1960s, this was a surprising step, but there was no doubt that it was a promising avenue of policy.

There were therefore very clear changes in the starting conditions for national economic policy. More intensive trading relations, turbulent conditions in the energy sector, the spread of free capital markets with growing international interdependence and the increasing proportion of companies with shares quoted on stock exchanges: all these features marked the end of sovereign national economic policies, but they also placed limits on any attempt by politicians to manage the world economy.

There were two ways in which these developments were of significance for the Federal Republic. On the one hand, as the third strongest country in the world in economic terms it was increasingly drawn into becoming responsible for the world economy as a whole, and during these years Helmut Schmidt enjoyed the reputation of 'economist to the world'. On the other hand, the influence of the federal government on the national economy turned out to be severely limited, as was true for all industrialised countries, in view of the way they were interconnected within the global economy. Despite this, the federal government was regarded as politically responsible for economic conditions. This placed it in a dilemma.

At the end of 1978, after the Iranian revolution, oil prices again began to rise rapidly. It then became apparent that the measures the Western industrialised countries had so far taken to protect themselves were inadequate. The disequilibria in the current account balances of the industrialised countries and the absence of any effective international coordination of financial and economic policy prevented them from devising a strategy to counter the crisis. Oil production in Iran, the second biggest oil producer in the world, temporarily came to a standstill. Panic buying increased the shortages and the price of oil rose from $13 to $34 a barrel. The crisis was worsened when Iraq seized the opportunity to make war on its weakened neighbour and attack the country's oil installations. Iran's counter-measures led to a fall in Iraq's oil production as well, thus driving prices still higher.

In the industrialised countries, most of which were still suffering from the after-effects of the first oil shock of 1973, these developments resulted in the worst economic crisis since 1929. From summer 1980, they were faced with a fall in growth figures, a rise in unemployment, high rates of inflation, budget deficits, rising state debt, declining social benefits and a worsening structural crisis. In addition to this, the world economic crisis meant that many developing countries were no longer in a position to cover their increased energy costs or pay the interest on their loans. This, in turn, produced a banking crisis which destabilised a number of European and American banks and further exacerbated the recession in the industrial countries. It was clear that the economic policy pursued until then by the industrialised countries of the West, both nationally and internationally, had run out of options.

## The End of the Social–Liberal Era

At the end of the decade, almost nothing remained the same as it had been at the beginning. The world economy, which had appeared so strong and healthy in 1970, had passed through one recession, followed in 1980 by another much harsher one. The international monetary system had collapsed, the structures of the Western economies, oriented towards industrial mass production, were crumbling away, governments had no plan to deal with growing unemployment, and the economic system and way of life of Western societies were being challenged by protest movements. The effectiveness and reach of national policies had also clearly come up against limits. A settlement of East–West differences, which the policy of détente had seemed to promise in 1970, had again receded into the far distance, and the Iranian revolution had introduced a new kind of global confrontation.

Nevertheless, most of the industrialised countries of Europe had experienced a further increase in their prosperity in the 1970s, though the crisis had reduced the tempo of growth. The rituals of consumer society and popular culture had spread far and wide, educational opportunities had grown considerably and concepts such as individualisation, liberalisation and pluralisation were used everywhere to describe the processes permeating these societies

West Germany was no exception to the above trends. But, in other respects, it differed greatly: the Federal Republic had withstood the economic crisis of the mid-1970s better than most other industrial countries. It had been able to reintegrate much of the protest movement of the late 1960s into party structures and the parliamentary system. Its well-developed social policies did indeed threaten to overburden public resources, but they cushioned the massive structural changes sufficiently to prevent the outbreak of severe disturbances among the dispossessed workers of the kind experienced in the United Kingdom, for example. At the same time, however, a left-wing terrorism emerged of a kind paralleled only in Italy. This dominated the domestic political climate for several years, and the mass protests against nuclear power stations and the 'weapons upgrade' met with much greater support in West Germany than in other countries. In addition, the renewed intensification of the East–West confrontation was more clearly apparent here than anywhere else in the Western world. The hopes aroused by the process of 'change through rapprochement' in relations between the two German states had also not been fulfilled.

This was the situation in autumn 1980, when elections were held to the Bundestag. After a highly confrontational and polemical election campaign, the government coalition was victorious, because the person nominated by the Union as candidate for the chancellorship, Bavarian Prime Minister Strauß, was unacceptable not just to Social Democrats but to many middle-class voters as well. The economic situation at the time still seemed relatively good. If the elections had been held a mere six months later, the coalition would probably have been defeated, because the economic data would have been worse. As it was, the Union lost more than 4 percentage points, falling to 44.5 per cent. The SPD vote did not change much, increasing slightly to 42.9 per cent. Middle-class voters scared off by Strauß turned mainly to the FDP, which made significant gains, rising to 10.6 per cent. The Greens, who were standing in the Bundestag elections for the first time, remained insignificant with 1.5 per cent. With a turnout of over 90 per cent, 90 per cent of the voters had again given their support to one of the three traditional parties. This could be interpreted either as a proof of broad support for the West German party system or as an expression of intense polarisation between the rival political camps, although real policy differences were much less profound than the polemical confrontations during the campaign had made them appear.[72]

This electoral outcome was a clear defeat for the right wing of Christian Democracy, and now a man of the centre, in the shape of Helmut Kohl, became the unquestioned leader of the opposition. He offered a more serious alternative, for liberals as well, than the unpredictable Franz-Josef Strauß. The victory of the social–liberal coalition allowed Helmut Schmidt, who was far better liked among the population at large than in his own party, to form his third government. By now, however, the members of this new coalition had very little in common politically. Their core concerns, *Ostpolitik* and domestic reform, had been achieved, and extensive programmes of social policy could no longer be financed. The joint approach on the two most important questions of the era, nuclear upgrading and economic policy, was beginning to disintegrate, because parts of the SPD were opposed to the Chancellor's course.

After NATO's 'double-track' decision of December 1979, the peace movement quickly gained strength in the Federal Republic. Gigantic demonstrations, with many hundreds of thousands of participants, brought national, and, more importantly, international attention. It is true that there were demonstrations in other countries as well—in particular Italy, the Netherlands and Great Britain—but nowhere else were they on such a scale. Like all movements of this kind, the West German peace movement was highly heterogeneous. There was a Left social democratic wing and a middle-class Protestant wing, but the peace movement was also strongly influenced both by the Greens, who first became established as a political party through the fight against nuclear power stations and new nuclear weapons, and by people who were close to the DKP. The latter group imbued the movement with a strongly anti-American tendency, whereas the rearmament policies of the Soviet Union did not provoke any outrage or criticism on their part.[73]

By 1983, more than 5 million citizens of the Federal Republic had signed the 'Krefeld Appeal', which called for the decision to station US intermediate-range missiles on West German territory to be rescinded. There is no doubt that this was not primarily because they were under communist influence. It expressed instead the anxieties of what was clearly a substantial section of the population. Their concerns were further heightened by indications that the USA wanted to use the tremendous growth in its military arsenal under President Reagan to force the USSR to its knees, and that it seemed to be ready to accept the risk of fighting a nuclear war on German soil to achieve this aim. The US President's rhetoric also tended to confirm this impression, as when he referred to a nuclear war as 'manageable' or spoke of the Soviet Union as the 'evil empire'.[74]

The support the peace movement enjoyed was also a result of the fact that, by now, large sections of the population valued détente and compromise with the East so much that they feared a return of the Cold War more than the risk of alienating the USA from West Germany. There was also the point that the intermediate-range missiles which would be stationed in Europe would be targeted largely at German territory, whether East or West. The victims of a European nuclear war, the peace movement emphasised, would be first and foremost Germans. That argument gave the protests a Left nationalist slant. This was a previously unfamiliar phenomenon, and it was greeted with anxious concern by Western governments. The Soviet Union, on the other hand, placed great hopes on the Western, and in particular the West German, peace movement, in the expectation that in this way it would still be able to prevent NATO from deploying its new weapons.

The political basis for Schmidt's position on the rearmament question was increasingly undermined when the SPD Left moved closer to the peace movement, and it was entirely unclear whether the Chancellor would be in a position to push through his policy if the negotiations with the Soviet Union failed and NATO missiles began to be emplaced on West German territory.

The emphasis placed on national interests in the protests over nuclear armaments also coloured German–German relations. These had steadily worsened since the CSCE Treaty, but the threatened stationing of intermediate-range missiles seemed to offer a basis on which the Federal Republic and the GDR could jointly defend their common interests. Schmidt told Honecker that the importance of the two German states should not be underestimated:

> In reality, we both play a weighty part in our economic and military systems, and we both have a right to throw this weight into the scales, because this is the heart of Europe, in which a third world war would take place, and it would suffer the greatest amount of damage if a third world war actually started. We are obliged to throw our weight into the scales in the name of humanity.[75]

This stress on common German interests was naturally greeted with suspicion in Moscow, as it was in the West, because both sides feared the tendency towards a creeping neutralisation of the two German states. The idea of 'Finlandisation' was already being put forward in the Federal Republic. And, in fact, there were forces both in the SPD and in the peace movement which advocated a rapprochement between the two German states and a loosening of the ties that kept them bound to their respective power blocs. These people regarded the character of the GDR as a dictatorship as a secondary issue, or they even denied that it was a dictatorship. Attitudes of this kind were not very influential politically, but in view of the increasing tensions of the 'Second Cold War' there was a widespread conviction within the SPD, and beyond its ranks too, that maintaining peace was more important than criticising the violent dictatorships that ruled the socialist states of East Central Europe.

The federal government's attempt to avoid breaking off political and economic cooperation with the GDR, despite the acute tensions between East and West, did not meet with much reciprocity from East Berlin. It was admittedly possible to maintain economic relations, in which the GDR had a burning interest owing to its severe economic problems. But the GDR leadership rebuffed all steps taken by the Federal Republic to improve political relations. On the contrary, it drastically increased the minimum level of currency exchange obligations, which were a kind of entry fee for West Germans who wanted to visit the GDR, and this made personal and family contacts more difficult. This policy of maintaining separateness reached new heights with Schmidt's visit to the GDR at the end of 1981, which did not lead to any improvement in relations, but was depressingly symbolic in the way it was handled. When Schmidt and Honecker visited Güstrow at the end of Schmidt's stay in the country, the GDR authorities remembered what had happened when Willy Brandt visited Erfurt ten years earlier, and they placed the town under a state of emergency. The inhabitants were forbidden to leave their houses, or even to look out of their windows. The route of the two politicians through the town was guarded by a thick line of police and state security officials, to prevent the population from having any spontaneous contact with the West German Chancellor. The whole spectacle was shown on television and it thus communicated to the world an impressively grim picture of the real character of the East German state.[76]

Schmidt's visit to the GDR was made even more dramatic, however, by the fact that it coincided with the proclamation of martial law in Poland, which took place in December 1981. Tension had been increasing there since the summer of the previous year. There were two major reasons for this. One was a drastic worsening in the local economic situation, as also in the Eastern bloc as a whole. The increase in the price of energy which followed the second oil price crisis hit the industrialised countries of the Eastern bloc particularly hard, since the Soviet Union now also raised the heavily discounted prices it had previously charged the fraternal socialist countries for oil, and the latter did not have sufficient foreign currency at their disposal to cover the shortfall with supplies of expensive oil bought on the world market. The consequences were particularly dramatic in Poland, and they finally led to a crisis in food supply, something the country had not experienced for twenty years. Moreover, this happened in an economy which still had a predominantly agricultural structure. In this situation a movement of protest rapidly developed considerable momentum.[77]

The second reason for the increase in tension was the election to the papacy of the Archbishop of Kraków, Cardinal Karol Wojtyła, in October 1978. This gave great impetus to the movement of Catholic nationalism in Poland, which was traditionally strong in any case. When Pope John Paul II (as he now was) visited his homeland in summer 1979, the millions of cheering supporters who lined the streets bore witness to the growing strength and self-confidence of Polish Catholicism. A year afterwards, fresh increases in the price of food led to an explosion of popular anger. The workers of the Lenin Shipyard in Gdańsk went on strike and this was soon followed by strikes in other places. Within a few weeks, the free trade union 'Solidarity' was founded, and it quickly gained support all over the country.

The communist regime, which had now been completely forced onto the defensive, was obliged to accept the demands of 'Solidarity' for free trade unions, the right to strike, freedom of opinion and press freedom. Within a year, 'Solidarity' had almost 10 million members, among them numerous members of the Polish Communist Party. The Polish freedom movement was the biggest challenge to communist rule in Soviet-dominated Europe since the Prague Spring of 1968, and it was evident that the principles of 'Solidarity' were not compatible with the communist dictatorship. Two mutually antagonistic rivals could not share power for long, and it was only logical that the leaders of the fraternal communist countries, particularly the GDR and Czechoslovakia, were quick to call for this situation to be forcibly brought to an end by a Warsaw Pact invasion. That would indubitably have meant a further dangerous sharpening of the tensions between East and West. The Soviet leadership urgently wanted to avoid this, because in its difficult economic situation it could not do without Western material support. It therefore threatened to invade, but did not actually do so. Instead of this, on 13 December 1981 the Polish government proclaimed martial law, arrested many thousands of activists and supporters of 'Solidarity', took back the concessions made in autumn 1980 and restored sole communist rule, though this was now exercised in the form of a military dictatorship under General Jaruzelski, who became prime minister.

In the West, and in the Federal Republic above all, the Polish events were considered largely in the context of the new East–West confrontation. This had already become alarmingly acute thanks to the 'double-track decision', the invasion of Afghanistan and the boycott of the Moscow Olympics, which had all stirred up fears of military escalation. Many people were convinced that a destabilisation of communist rule in Poland would heighten these tensions and increase the danger of war. The Polish freedom movement met with scepticism and rejection from the Left, because its Catholic nationalist character led it to be perceived as standing on the Right politically. Until 1981, Günter Gaus headed the Permanent Representation of the Federal Republic in the GDR. At the beginning of 1982, with reference to Poland, he called for a clear 'rejection of the verbal radicalism which calls for a fatally dangerous tempo of change and approves the sort of transformation which is aimed at defeating the other side'. And Egon Bahr, the strategist of détente, declared in spring 1982 that 'the self-determination of the nation must in principle be subordinate to the maintenance of peace. This also applies to the Poles. The national ambitions of the Poles must come second to the interest of maintaining peace.'[78] It was not just events in Poland but *all* changes in the relationship of forces in the Eastern bloc that were regarded here as disruptive factors, because they might lead to an increased prospect of war.

The West German and Western European Left also largely ignored the opposition movements in the countries of the Eastern bloc, which were becoming increasingly important. It was not perceived that there had long been deep cracks in the supposedly monolithic bloc of the Soviet-dominated dictatorships. The stability of the Eastern dictatorships was overestimated, and gestures of solidarity with the movement in Poland were criticised as excessively risky. The conservatives, for their part, despite their sharp condemnation of the actions of the Polish military, were also unable to find any alternative to the consolidation of the status quo.[79]

International relations and the world economy therefore both underwent radical destabilisation processes between 1979 and 1982, which overlapped chronologically and influenced each other. Hence the application of the much-misused word 'crisis' to this period is justified in two senses. Problems in the world economy had already come to the surface in 1979, and after the winter of 1980–1 they left their mark on the Federal Republic as well. The increase in the price of crude oil resulting from the Iranian revolution, the declining demand for West Germany's exports, the continuing economic crisis in the USA and unsolved currency problems were important external factors leading to a deterioration in economic conditions. But there were also problems in the domestic economy. The impact of the crisis was worsened by a decline in the competitiveness of German enterprises, which had fallen behind their Japanese rivals and only reluctantly implemented technological innovations in the areas of data processing and the automation of production. In addition, structural changes continued at an accelerated pace. Classical heavy industry continued to decline, and the steel industry in particular suffered a tremendous drop in sales.[80]

The trade unions, backed by the working-class wing of the SPD, called for an increase in state subsidies for steel production so as to protect jobs, and a reduction in working hours so as to combat unemployment, on the ground that this would be a way of distributing the available work over more individuals. They thought that these measures would be an effective way of combating the structural crisis. But this was not the way to solve the main problem of the iron, steel and coal industries, which was their lack of international competitiveness, resulting from low productivity. After all, a reduction in the hours of work would not produce any gains in productivity.

The federal government attempted to react to the structural changes by encouraging reductions of capacity in branches of industry that were no longer competitive, while at the same time guaranteeing continued employment in branches that were no longer productive. This was a self-contradictory policy, but the alternative, which was a rise in unemployment of at least 30 per cent in areas of heavy industry, was politically impossible. In those branches of the economy, therefore, the subsidies mainly served to extend the structural changes over a longer time period, so as to attenuate their social impact and gain time for restructuring and the creation of new employment opportunities in the affected areas, such as the Saar and the Ruhr.

But now the structural crisis and the world economic crisis began to reinforce each other, and the government came under heavy pressure to take action. The economy, which had continued to grow by 1.9 per cent in 1980, shrank in 1981 by 0.2 per cent, and the year after by 1.1 per cent. The unemployment rate, which had not declined in the previous years, despite the growth of the economy, now reached record levels: in 1981, it rose to 5.3 per cent, in 1982 to 7.6 per cent and in 1983 to 9.3 per cent. Two million workers were registered as unemployed in 1983. In spite of this, the rate of inflation remained high (it was 6.1 per cent in 1981) and most employees had to accept a considerable decline in real wages during this period. Tax receipts fell dramatically, so that public sector expenditure, which increased between 1970 and 1982 from 196 billion to 548 billion DM, had to be financed by ever greater borrowing. The national debt rose during the same period from 125 billion to 614 billion DM. Social benefits made up a large proportion of the state's expenditure. Their level had been raised considerably under the Grand Coalition, and this was even more the case under the Brandt–Scheel government. The social expenditure ratio—the proportion of total social benefits to the Gross National Product—rose between 1965 and 1975 from 25 per cent to 33.7 per cent, and it only fell slightly in subsequent years (in 1980 it was still 32.1 per cent).[81]

In view of these alarming developments, the question which was now posed was whether a demand-oriented or a supply-oriented economic policy was a better way out of the crisis. Would higher wages and social benefits and state counter-cyclical programmes to stimulate demand restore impetus to the economy, as had happened in the USA thanks to its enormously swollen defence budget? But this approach would have pushed state indebtedness still higher and increased the danger of inflation. Moreover, the effectiveness of such programmes had been put in doubt since the stimulus programme introduced under American pressure after the 1978 Bonn summit of the G8 countries had proved largely ineffective. Or would it be better to reduce taxes on business and income, cut state indebtedness, reduce interest rates and dismantle social benefits, so as to promote investment and generate growth? This debate had been running since the first oil price crisis, and most West German economists had moved since then into the camp of supply-side economics, although they tended more to advise a balanced mixture of measures than to advocate radical restructuring.[82]

The further expansion of social benefits had been halted already in 1974, when Schmidt came into office. But it was impossible to do anything about the long-term costs of the social policy measures introduced after 1966 and to a still greater extent after 1969. Since the system of financing social policy in the Federal Republic was tied to the contributions of the employed population, the structural problem of this model now became apparent: in times of crisis the outgoings increased, while the contributions fell. This situation clearly paralleled developments in Germany during the world economic crisis of 1929–32.

After the 1980 elections to the Bundestag, the federal government implemented considerable budget reductions. In view of the fall in tax receipts, this was unavoidable, but at the same time it inevitably weakened demand and worsened the conjunctural downturn. The intensification of the crisis meant that further savings now had to be made. But a reduction in the defence budget was unthinkable in view of the tense international situation, as the views of the

NATO partners had to be considered. The question was therefore posed as to whether the time had come to undertake reductions in the social budget as well.

In the FDP, there had been clear majority support since the Bundestag election for a change of course, including a reduction in social benefits. This was a challenge to the trade unions and the working-class wing of the SPD. The FDP leader, Genscher, said that the 'claimant mentality' had to come to an end. Reductions in unemployment benefit, housing subsidies, health insurance and housing policy should be undertaken in order to achieve fiscal consolidation.[83]

For the SPD, this was a vital political issue. If the government gave way to pressure from the trade unions, Schmidt and his Finance Minister Matthöfer were convinced that they would be unable to master the combination of a structural crisis with the crisis in the world economy. If the government followed the proposals of the FDP and pushed through fiscal consolidation, there was a risk of losing the support of its most important group of voters, the working class. The dilemma was clearly apparent at the SPD's party congress, held in spring 1982. As far as defence policy was concerned, the majority of the party gave its backing to Schmidt's 'double-track' strategy. In economic and social policy, however, the majority reaffirmed the party's traditional line of state intervention and demanded a state job-creation and investment programme, subsidies for crisis-hit industries and no reduction in social benefits. But this approach was not compatible with the government programme of the social–liberal coalition.[84]

The coalition parties lost several Diet elections in the course of 1982, and the collapse of the government was simply a matter of time. It was sealed by a memorandum, which was published immediately, in which the liberal Economics Minister, Count Lambsdorff, summarised his views on economic policy, at Schmidt's request. Lambsdorff conceded in his analysis that there were also international causes for the continuing weakness of the economy, but he asserted that the main domestic economic causes of the crisis were the decline in investment and the rise in the ratio of state expenditure to GNP. The remedies he advocated were: fiscal consolidation, a state economic policy more oriented towards the market, a redistribution of public expenditure from consumption to investment, and 'an adjustment of social security systems to the altered growth prospects'. In specific terms, this meant a whole catalogue of reductions in benefits, including unemployment benefit, holiday allowances, pensions, health insurance and social welfare, as well as less generous wage rises to reduce the cost of the labour factor of production, the liberalisation of tenancy law, the withdrawal of taxes unrelated to income, an increase in Value Added Tax, the removal of business taxes, a reduction in wealth tax, and a lessening in the progressive character of income tax.[85]

The memorandum caused a tremendous stir, and was immediately regarded as the social–liberal coalition's divorce certificate. But, on closer examination, Lambsdorff's plan was not fundamentally different from ideas which had long been discussed within the Ministry of Finance, which was actually headed by a Social Democrat. 'The Minister of Economics is right', wrote the new Minister of Finance, Manfred Lahnstein (SPD), in a confidential paper,

> to press for greater attention to be paid to the economic principles of competition, the role of the market in price-formation (including the formation of the price of labour) and the allocation of resources, more adaptive flexibility, sustained incentives for entrepreneurial actions and investments, and a reduction in social security burdens.

Proposals for more flexible wages and working hours, adjustments in the system of social insurance, more individual responsibility in matters of health and changes in unemployment insurance also found a place in this paper by Lahnstein.[86]

The Ministries of Finance and Economics agreed that it was indispensable to intervene to change social benefits, to increase incentives for investment and to make a sharp reduction in federal government expenditure. The government and its ministries were therefore still united over economic policy. In contrast to this, the differences between the two political parties were more acute than ever. The FDP's inclination towards a supply-side economic policy and the focus of the trade union wing of the SPD on state direction of investment and state control of the economy were mutually incompatible. Thus, the economic and social policy objectives set out in Lambsdorff's memorandum indicated that the coalition partners no longer shared any common ground.

An episode of political posturing now followed. Genscher started to negotiate with the Union to form an alternative coalition, and Schmidt gave an effective reply by accusing the FDP of 'treachery'. After he left office, he took up the role of statesman and world leader which he was to play with extraordinary skill over the next thirty years. The FDP now decided to form a coalition with the Union. This led to the loss of its left wing, which continued to regard the perspective of a social–liberal alliance as more promising than a middle-class government. The political survival of the liberals, following their alliance with the Union, was therefore not at all certain. But the change of government itself took place without a hitch. On 1 October 1982, the Bundestag passed a constructive vote of no confidence in the Schmidt government, and Helmut Kohl was elected Chancellor by the combined vote of the Union and the FDP.

The end of the social–liberal coalition was a turning point in the political history of the Federal Republic. Even so, the key features of social–liberal policy—the social reforms, the expanded social policies, the treaties with the East and the attempt to improve relations with the GDR—were not altered by the new government. It was already clear from this that there was a broad foundation of support in West German society for the changes of the 1970s, which no coalition could readily ignore, given the Federal Republic's political and governmental system, geared as it was towards compromise and conciliation. The self-image and self-perception of society in the Federal Republic had altered unmistakably in the years that followed the Grand Coalition. It had become more Western, more European, more liberal and also more inclined to the Left. Even in the years of crisis, the Federal Republic's economic strength had continued to increase, and its importance in world politics had grown. By now, the old conflicts over the correct form of organisation for an industrial society lay largely in the past, although the Cold War had again become more acute and the question of social justice continued to constitute one of the points of rupture in the social fabric. But parliamentary democracy, the tie with the West, the social market economy and European integration were accepted across the political spectrum and supported by the overwhelming majority of the population. Even the New Left, which had so strongly shaped the contours of the 1970s, was unquestionably on its way back to bourgeois society.

In the cultural sphere, the traditional rejection of modern society and mass culture by the conservatives had largely dissipated. The cultural critics did not cease to lament the disintegration of the family, hedonism and selfish individualism, but since these phenomena had penetrated a long way into the lives even of conservative social strata, such complaints had lost their power to persuade. By now, the universal appeal of Western popular culture had completely prevailed in the Federal Republic. Even young CDU politicians now wore their hair fashionably long, rock concerts were attended by tens of thousands of people, and it was no longer a political statement to go to one. The habit of rebellion and unconventionality had been lost. Bourgeois high culture was highly subsidised and continued to maintain a very high standard, but it too had an altered significance. It was no longer an expression of national narcissism but an integral part of the culture of modernity, and in this capacity it was a unique characteristic, valued all over the world.

In this context, a remarkable reversal of roles had taken place between Left and Right. Previously, the Left had supported technological advance, mass culture and the modernisation of everyday life, whereas the conservatives had placed their faith in the preservation of existing values and taken a reserved attitude to mass culture and utopias of progress. Now, however, criticisms of industrial growth were associated more with the Left, side by side with a pronounced cultural and political anti-Americanism. Variants of cultural pessimism were also frequently to be found on the Left as well. The conservatives, for their part, were now the strongest advocates of growth and modern technology, though not entirely consistently. But, like their American and British exemplars, they succumbed to a very materialistic concept of progress, which threatened in some respects to undermine the foundations of their own ideology.

New problems, such as deindustrialisation and structural change, the globalisation of the world economy, the destabilisation of the world monetary system, the destruction of the environment, nuclear energy, the North–South conflict and Islamism, were of a different kind and they could not be related to the situation at the turn of the century, or at least not without difficulty. The optimism about the future which still motivated West German society at the beginning of the 1970s had now evaporated. It was almost as if West Germany had lost its confidence and optimism along with its coal, iron and steel industries. After the second world economic crisis within seven years, the intensification of the Cold War and the threat of a new arms race, the decade which had begun with such optimism and vigour ended in doubt and anxiety.

# 18

# The World Economy and National Politics

## Globalisation and National Economic Policy

The recessions of the 1970s compelled businesses as well as governments to change course. For large firms the analysis was almost the same everywhere: the era of cheap, mass-produced commodities was clearly over, at least for the industrialised countries of the West. Labour costs in Western Europe, Japan and the USA were also much too high for them to keep pace with low-wage exporters such as Korea or Singapore. There was a great need for high-value products—machines, medicaments, motor cars, aeroplanes and electrical goods—but the absorption capacity of national markets was too small to recoup the enormous development costs involved. New products, reduced costs, improved sales strategies and fresh markets were therefore needed to restore economic viability. As a result, many enterprises increased their expenditure on research and development, focusing more intensively on the global market. They set up production facilities in low-wage countries, so as to reduce labour costs, and they endeavoured to improve their foreign sales potential.

There was nothing new about any of this. In previous decades, the expansion and integration of world trade had already led to repeated growth spurts, such as in the twenty years before the First World War, and then in the 1950s and 1960s under the aegis of American economic hegemony. From the late 1970s onwards, these developments were accelerated by the saturation of national markets after the end of post-war reconstruction, the structural changes associated with the decline of the coal, iron and steel industries, and the emergence of new competitors in low-wage countries. But it was only in the 1990s that the process was given a name: globalisation.[1]

If we are to describe the mechanics of globalisation, the involvement of a multiplicity of reciprocally interacting factors has to be borne in mind. Thus, the increase in world trade was the result of the liberalisation of trade regulations, the dismantling of customs barriers and the harmonisation of legal requirements. Conversely, the expansion of world trade also pushed governments towards further liberalisation, and technological innovations and improvements in transport were both the engine of globalisation and its manifestation. The cumulative effect of several such processes was therefore characteristic of the phase that succeeded the late 1970s. In this context, one can pick out six factors which worked to bring about or accelerate the globalisation process:

1) The increase in foreign direct investment. This indicates the degree of international economic interdependence. It rose between 1986 and 1993 from $96 billion to $242 billion, reaching the remarkable figure of $1,231 billion in the year 2000. In other words, it increased 2.5 times over within seven years, and twelve times over within fifteen years.
2) The growth in world trade. Between 1980 and 2007 the volume of world trade rose from $2.4 trillion to $18.0 trillion. This meant that *trade* had expanded three times as much as *production* over the period. The export of manufactured goods increased (by 85 per cent between 1970 and 1990) as did the export of services (by 114 per cent between 1980 and 1990), whereas the export of raw materials only rose by 15 per cent between 1970 and 1990.
3) The spread of multinational enterprises, which are the most important agents of globalisation. They increased in number from 1970 to 1990 from roughly 10,000 to 35,000, and by 2002 there were 63,000 of them. They distributed their sites of production and development all over the globe, and they established their headquarters in localities where they enjoyed the most favourable conditions. States and governments vied with each other to persuade as many of these companies as possible to settle within their jurisdiction, so as to generate tax receipts and jobs. The result was that individual states competed to create the most favourable local environment for these companies.
4) The rise of global financial markets. The growth of direct investment also caused a considerable increase in share dealing. While the worldwide value of *the shares themselves* tripled within ten years, from $2.9 trillion in 1980 to $8.9 trillion in 1990, the total value of *shares traded* increased twenty-fold, from $0.3 trillion in 1980 to $5.7 trillion in 1990. Share-dealing activity thus increased much more than the volume of trading in goods. This reflected the increase in speculative activity. The acceleration of international communication also played a considerable part in stimulating the financial markets. Within a short time, there was a tremendous increase in the volume of financial resources which were rapidly transferred to various points on the globe so as to realise short-term gains by using time-related advantages, such as different interest rates in different currency areas. This was particularly apparent in the foreign exchange market: the worldwide value of a single day's currency dealing rose from $120 billion in 1980 to $820 billion in 1992. The latter

figure was only slightly less than the total value of the world's currency reserves.

5) Technological innovations. Between 1980 and 2008, there was a fivefold increase in the research and development expenditure of the thousand largest companies: it grew from $96 billion a year to almost $500 billion. By far the largest part of this input was directed to five areas: the pharmaceutical industry and biotechnology, the motor industry, technical equipment and installations, electronics and software, and computer services. All these fields were characterised by a high export ratio and involved a particularly large number of multinational companies.
6) The revolution in data processing and communications. In the 1960s, the creation of integrated circuits by connecting together a large number of semi-conductors (transistors) placed data processing on a new basis, and from that time onwards it expanded massively. Photocopiers, fax machines and finally personal computers were introduced across the board in the USA from the 1970s and in Western Europe from the early 1980s. The capacity of computers increased phenomenally and their use became as widespread in the economy and the administration as in science. At the same time, data transfer by means of satellites and high-performance cables multiplied international connections and laid the basis for a revolution in communications which linked the world together in a completely new way, with the spread of electronic postal communication (email) in the 1980s and the development of the World Wide Web in the 1990s.

The processes outlined above started off in the early 1970s. They began to spread in the 1980s, and they dominated the scene after the 1990s. The increase in international economic linkages exerted pressure on national governments to conduct social and economic policies which would improve the ability of their own economies to compete effectively on the world market. In almost all cases this meant a greater role for the market, less state involvement and less regulation. After almost ten years of short-term and largely unsuccessful crisis containment on Keynesian lines, politicians and economists finally thought they saw in these prescriptions a new strategic approach which would allow them to escape permanently from the economic cycle. The withdrawal of the state from the economy, the liberalisation of rules on trade and taxation, fiscal stabilisation, more flexible wages, the privatisation of public services, the reduction of social expenditure, deregulation and a reduction in bureaucracy: these were the seductive watchwords of the change in economic policy paradigms which now started to be referred to as 'neo-liberalism' but was not particularly new in reality, because it was largely derived from the classical models of economic liberalism put forward in the 1920s and the 1950s. What was new about 'neo-liberalism' was rather that, in almost all countries, it had to be forced through against the resistance of a solid structure of public welfare and state intervention and social rights acquired by large sections of the population, which had been in place for decades. As a result, 'neo-liberalism' often came to signify aggressive confrontation and class conflict.[2]

It was above all in the USA, under Ronald Reagan, and in Great Britain, under Margaret Thatcher, that new governments undertook far-reaching changes in economic policy, beginning in the period 1979–81. They changed direction towards a supply-oriented treatment of the economy, which was aimed at overcoming the crisis by increasing company profits, heightening entrepreneurial inclinations towards investment, and concentrating more on the world market. In the USA, significant reductions in taxes on business and income were the main focus of the policy. The top income tax rate was reduced from 70 per cent to 33 per cent. Reagan's economic advisers prophesied that this would produce such a strong incentive towards investment that, after a while, the government's tax receipts would not fall. They would even rise. Expenditure on social policy, on the other hand, was brought down under Reagan, and the range of public tasks performed by the state was reduced. At the same time, economic growth was fuelled by a degree of expansion in the country's defence budget which was completely unparalleled in peacetime. The US government also brought increasing pressure to bear in the direction of a worldwide removal of obstacles to trade, and in particular towards freeing financial transactions from any restriction.

This economic policy, which came to be called 'Reaganomics', had extremely mixed results. The US rate of inflation, which had been 12 per cent in 1979, only fell slowly, and there was a considerable increase in unemployment. After the mid-1980s, however, the economy began to recover. The rate of investment rose, as did the figures for employment, leading people in the Federal Republic to talk enviously of the American 'job miracle'. In particular, the successes of the USA in the new sectors of biotechnology and communication science were exceedingly impressive. But this boom in the economy was accompanied by a ballooning of the national debt. It rose by 180 per cent during Reagan's term of office, reaching a stunning $2.6 trillion. This, remarked Helmut Schmidt accurately, was a policy of 'state demand expansion through rapidly growing budget deficits of a magnitude which had not been seen in the whole of the industrial world since the 1930s.' One consequence was a dramatic rise in the degree of social inequality: the income of top earners increased immensely, while the bottom sixth of the population fell below the poverty line.[3]

The new Prime Minister of Great Britain, Margaret Thatcher, had been following a similar course since May 1979. Her aim, after the economic débâcle the country had suffered in the preceding years, was to curtail state influence on the economy, lessen the tax burden, reduce public expenditure and break the power of the trade unions. The liberalisation of financial markets, which was one of the central elements in 'Thatcherism', gave a tremendous impetus to the financial sector, and resulted in an economic revival, which created many new and largely well-paid jobs in the service sector. Most of the countries in the EC followed the United Kingdom in removing controls on the movement of capital. The risks associated with this move were not unknown: unrestricted mobility of capital meant that governments became highly dependent on the vagaries of the international currency trade. On the other hand, the liberalisation of capital markets gave such an impetus to economic growth that no government was inclined to resist this trend.[4]

Mrs Thatcher also engaged in an extensive deregulation of trade and investment. She began with a large-scale privatisation of previously public enterprises: steelworks, coalmines, airlines and finally the railways and North Sea oil. This was a wave of privatisation on a previously unimagined scale. Immense profits were made in sectors where there was strong market demand, while less profitable areas were soon shut down. The removal of subsidies led to a further shrinkage of the industrial sector, which was already in decline, so that the deindustrialisation of Great Britain progressed much more quickly than in France or West Germany. Social expenditure was also reduced in Britain, so that the gap between rich and poor grew wider. The drastic reduction in the level of income tax did, it is true, lead in the medium term to a rise in investment, but it also led to a significant reduction in tax receipts. To compensate for this, the government raised the rate of Value Added Tax, thereby redistributing the tax burden from the wealthier to the less wealthy. The Conservative government did finally win its extraordinarily hard-fought and long-lasting struggle with the trade unions, but it succeeded neither in curbing inflation, which reached 21.9 per cent the year after it was elected, nor in reducing unemployment, which rose to 12.4 per cent in the course of the 1980–82 recession.[5]

These radically pro-market measures strengthened the position of businesses and favoured the recipients of high incomes. They went hand in hand with opposition to the welfare state and a tendency to reduce the state's role in the economy. In the USA and Great Britain, this led in the medium term to a return to strong economic growth, but also a worsening of social inequality, and in the USA to a breakdown in the nation's finances. On the other hand, the reforms, particularly the tax cuts and the increase in wage flexibility, improved the position of both economies on the world market. That, in turn, affected the attitude of the big companies to investment, as they were constantly looking all over the globe for the places which offered the best conditions for production and development.

It was therefore not surprising that almost all Western European governments reacted in a similar way to the crisis of 1980–2. They attempted to stabilise their budgets, improve competition conditions and reduce expenditure on social policy, or at least limit its increase. The pronouncements of the Kohl–Genscher government were no exception. The most characteristic catchwords of Kohl's first government declaration were 'freedom, dynamism and personal responsibility'. It proposed to reduce the public debt, improve the fiscal position, offer greater incentives to investment, lessen the tax burden on businesses, and introduce a 'breathing space' in social policy. These measures were all intended to bring about a rapid and lasting improvement in the economy.[6] The new government thus adopted a position which separated it both from the demands of the trade unions and the Left of the SPD and the programmes being implemented by Thatcher and Reagan. The new West German coalition did not envisage dismantling social policy or curtailing co-determination and the power of the trade unions. Instead, its announcements followed the line taken by the Ministry of Finance towards the end of the Schmidt government, and they mainly related to six areas: the federal budget and tax policy, the labour market, deregulation, privatisation, social policy, and cuts in subsidies.

The recovery of the world economy after 1982 offered the new government a favourable jumping-off point. Its main success was in stabilising the budget. Federal expenditure had risen between 1973 and 1982 by an annual average of 8.6 per cent, but this fell to 3.3 per cent in the next six years, up to 1988, and the rise in new borrowing by the Federal Republic fell from 17.8 per cent to 6.8 per cent. The rate of inflation fell almost to zero, while the rate of growth in national income was an average 2.1 per cent until 1987, increasing to an average 4 per cent between 1988 and 1990. Exports again increased strongly, partly because of the rise in the dollar exchange rate, and by 1989 there was a gigantic foreign trade surplus of more than 130 billion DM. The top rate of tax was reduced from 56 to 53 and then to 50 per cent in order to improve business profitability. The ratio of taxes to GDP also fell from 43 to 41 per cent between 1982 and 1990. Business rates of return in fact improved considerably during these years, but even so the investment ratio failed to rise. In addition, investments were not primarily directed towards the extension of manufacturing capacity or the introduction of new products. They were mainly used for rationalisation. This was logical, given the strength of international competition, but it did not contribute to reducing unemployment.[7]

In spite of the improved economic situation, the unemployment figures continued to be over 2 million throughout the period 1981–9. The link between rising rates of growth and declining levels of unemployment, which had been reliably confirmed since the 1950s, had now clearly been broken. It continued to be the unskilled who lost their jobs, and they came disproportionately from the crisis-hit branches of steel, mining and shipbuilding. The number of new employment opportunities in the service sector certainly rose, but not sufficiently to fill the gaps in the classical industrial branches. As a result, the government placed its faith in a plan to make the labour market 'more flexible'. The phrase itself was a euphemism, because in practice it meant allowing working conditions and remuneration, especially among the lower income jobs, to be adjusted more closely to the possibilities and needs of the employers. The Employment Promotion Act passed in 1985 made it possible to employ people on fixed-term contracts or as part-time or underemployed workers and step up the use of temporary labour. The rise in the number of part-time positions helped many women to gain employment, but it also strengthened the tendency to undermine the normal employment relationship, precisely among the lower wage groups. Fixed-term contracts became more frequent and in some sectors they were practically the rule. Temporary employment agencies loaned individual employees or whole groups of workers to third parties for short periods, and these temporary workers earned distinctly less than the permanent staff.[8]

The practical effects of the structural changes were now clearly apparent. In previous decades most of the lowest segment of the labour market had consisted of jobs done by unskilled workers in the big factories. These jobs were now transferred abroad or simply ceased to exist. They were increasingly replaced by 'precarious' employment relationships, which only lasted for a short time and entailed lower than normal wage rates and an inferior level of social security. This did not necessarily mean a real social deterioration; after all, in the 1950s and 1960s unskilled female factory workers and semi-skilled agricultural labourers had not earned more than the minimum existence level. But, in the past, most workers had felt that they suffered not as individuals but as part of a social class. For an individualised labour force employed on a temporary or part-time basis this was no longer true. The 'proletariat' had turned into a 'precariat', and the causes of impoverishment and social deprivation were no longer seen as an expression of the class structure of society but as a consequence of the individual's bad luck or inadequacy.[9]

It was hard for the trade unions to fight against this trend. Their membership and their political influence had declined significantly since the structural transformation had begun to accelerate. Because of the high level of unemployment, they were also increasingly exposed to the accusation that their campaigns for higher wages and better working conditions were exclusively in the interests of those who already had jobs. The trade unions, particularly IG Metall and IG Druck und Papier, therefore now concentrated increasingly on the demand for the introduction of the thirty-five-hour week, already raised in the later 1970s. The aim of the reduction in working hours was to share work between more than one person and thereby increase the number of people in employment. This could be offset by smaller wage rises. The ultimate outcome of the plan would thus be more employees receiving lower wages. To some extent, the trade unions succeeded in putting these demands into effect. After a long and hard industrial dispute, the working week was reduced to 38.5 hours.

But it turned out to be difficult to gauge the combined effect of these two measures, the increase in labour flexibility and the reduction in working hours. At any rate, the unemployment figures failed to fall. Other measures were more effective, even if they served less to raise the number of people in employment than to reduce the number of people registered as unemployed. 'Job Creation Schemes' (ABMs) were one example. These schemes created state-financed temporary employment opportunities in private and public enterprises. In positive cases, the temporary employees would be taken on after a certain period as ordinary long-term workers. But this only happened occasionally. The Job Creation Schemes had no more than a slight impact on the labour market. The instrument of early retirement was more extensively applied: older workers who became unemployed received a supplement to their unemployment benefit until they reached retirement age, after which the payments were taken over by pension funds. From the fiscal point of view, this was purely a shift from one social benefit department to another, but the people withdrawn from the system no longer counted as unemployed, and many of those affected were happy to accept the new regulations. The 'early retiree', in his early fifties and usually in excellent physical shape, became as widespread a social type in the former mining regions as the 'ABMers' who wandered for years from one temporary job to the next.[10]

The call to reduce the number of state regulations covering private business and in general to lessen the influence of the state on the economy also proved difficult to put into effect. Attempts at 'deregulation' often failed in purely everyday matters. Thus, the government was unable to make it possible for firms to determine the opening hours of businesses and shops at their own discretion, and it took almost twenty-five years before fixed closing times for shops were abolished. The government was more successful in deregulating the radio system and authorising private companies to offer radio and television programmes. Nevertheless, even here the health of the labour market was not the sole, or even the dominant, consideration. Three other factors were far more important. Firstly, the Union parties had objected ever since the 1960s to what they considered was the one-sidedly left-wing orientation of public service broadcasting, and had long sought ways of breaking up this 'monopoly of public opinion'. Secondly, new cable systems had created greater technological capacities for the transmission of sound and pictures, and these promised excellent profit opportunities for private business. And thirdly, experience in the USA and some Western European countries, in which there were already private radio and television stations, showed that these enjoyed great popularity among the public. The acceptance of the 'private providers' and the authorisation in 1986 by the Federal Constitutional Court of the 'dual model' involving a combination of public and private provision in the field of communications marked a clear break with the previous history of German radio, which right from its beginnings in the 1920s had consisted of nothing other than public service broadcasting. There was fierce debate over the cultural effects of this move to open up the media landscape. But, in economic terms, it was a success. The media market expanded in subsequent years, creating a considerable number of new jobs and professions.[11]

On the whole, however, the opportunities for deregulation turned out to be very limited. This was not just because of the so-called 'veto-wielders', in other words, the numerous interest groups, long fiercely criticised by the champions of the market, which hindered the dismantling of state regulations covering private enterprise. More important was the fact that the high regulatory density of West Germany also offered legal protection against abuses, and was a way of balancing out conflicting interests. Where legal provisions ceased to operate, there was freedom for economic activity, but also for fraud and corruption. Anyone who wanted to deregulate labour protection, with its plethora of rules, would have to take into account the likelihood of an increase in industrial accidents and corresponding demands for compensation. Anyone who wanted to simplify building regulations would have to accept lower standards of environmental protection, building safety and liability law. The situation was analogous with regard to factory inspection, the protection of tenants and the establishment of 'free schools'.

The federal government was more successful in its endeavours to privatise partially or completely state-owned enterprises. There were no problems attached to this where the enterprise had not taken over any 'sovereign' functions involving the provision of public services or the preservation of security, as for example in the cases of the fire service, the police or the courts. It was therefore not difficult to privatise large enterprises such as the VEBA (United Electricity and Mining AG) or the VIAG (United Industrial Enterprise AG). The same applied to the parts of the Salzgitter AG or the Volkswagen AG which belonged to the Federal Republic. Both firms were state enterprises founded in the Nazi era, and they could now be largely privatised. There was more disagreement over the privatisation of partly or wholly state-run transport undertakings such as Lufthansa and, above all, the German railway system (*Deutsche Bundesbahn*). Experiences in other countries, particularly the USA, showed that the exclusion of the state from such areas led the enterprise to adopt a strictly profit-oriented approach and as a result to neglect the provision of services for structurally weaker regions, because it was cost-intensive. This caveat applied even more to areas such as health and education. Private hospitals no longer treated all patients independently of their financial resources with the best (and the most expensive) methods and medicaments. Private health and pension insurance companies neglected the poor and the permanently sick. Private schools and universities were extremely costly for the parents of schoolchildren and students.

In dealing with these matters the federal government steered a middle course, despite intensive efforts by the FDP, which struggled to achieve a greater degree of privatisation. Lufthansa was privatised, and after 1990 it faced competition from many new airlines. The *Deutsche Bundesbahn*, on the other hand, remained in state ownership, although its corporate structure was modified to make it more like a private company. Here too, there were line closures, while the extensive investments that were made mainly affected the profitable long-distance routes. Even so the social and infrastructural functions of the railway were preserved. The schools, universities, hospitals and administrative services remained largely under state control, but they were put under pressure to increase efficiency at some points by the introduction of additional private providers. In general, the view prevailed that the state ought not to privatise its core roles, if it was to continue meeting its obligations.

The postal service was a special case. This was often regarded as the prime example of a state enterprise which was overstaffed, incapable of innovating and not very efficient. After long discussions, the federal postal service was privatised after 1989 in two stages. Three separate businesses emerged from this: the so-called 'yellow post', which developed in the course of the following years into the biggest logistics enterprise in the world; *Deutsche Telekom,* which served the booming field of telecommunications and became one of the most lucrative German companies; and, finally, the *Postbank,* which developed into a stable and independent credit institution. Here, then, privatisation proved to be a success both economically and in labour market terms. In other fields, such as the municipal services of water, energy, waste disposal and local transport, this was not always so, and in many towns and cities the privatisations undertaken in the 1980s were later reversed.[12]

Kohl's announcement that the government would take a 'pause for breath' in social policy had provoked protest and unease among the social organisations and the political opposition. In practice, however, there were no noteworthy cutbacks in social benefits until 1989. Immediately after it came into office, the government adopted an austerity package which also envisaged cuts and deferments in social benefits. The Federal Training Assistance Act (BAföG) was no longer applied to secondary schoolchildren, pension adjustment was postponed for six months, housing benefit and child support payments were reduced. These were all notable reductions, but similar measures had also been taken under Schmidt. In any case, the government's declared goal of reducing the proportion of social benefits to GDP was attained: it fell from 32.6 to 29.2 per cent between 1980 and 1990.[13]

Criticism of the constant expansion of social benefits since the 1950s came from more than one direction. There were warning voices from supporters of market liberalism against the creation of a new class of recipients of social benefit, who would fall into long-term dependence on the state and no longer return to the sphere of gainful employment. This would destroy the individual's readiness to take personal responsibility. Moreover, this trend of development would tend to create an unchanging society lacking in dynamism. Other critics, in contrast, concentrated more on the new forms of injustice created by social policy. Young families with a large number of children suffered disadvantages. At the same time, insufficient account was being taken of the demographic changes through which the number of pension recipients would increase rapidly, while the number of contributors would fall. Both lines of thought found a hearing within the government, although all proposals for radical changes in the structure of social policy were strongly rejected by the popular Minister of Social Affairs, Norbert Blüm.

If the intention was to strengthen the principle of individual responsibility, or 'subsidiarity', and at the same time take demographic developments into account, it was necessary, in the coalition's view, to start with the family. This is where the government placed the main emphasis of its commitment to social policy. The newly established child benefit and parental leave arrangements placed considerable resources at the disposal of young families. Mothers who left their jobs to have children had them guaranteed for one year, child-raising periods were counted towards pension entitlement and child allowances and child support payments were increased. The total amount of benefit paid to families between 1985 and 1989 was over 30 billion DM. This was a clear and perceptible change of emphasis in social policy.

But these reforms were based on a model of the family clearly at odds with the reality that was emerging. The government's measures were aimed at making it easier financially for mothers to concentrate on childbirth and child-raising and to avoid or at least mitigate subsequent disadvantages in their professional lives. They were not aimed at making it possible to combine motherhood and gainful employment at the same time. That would have required a tremendous investment in nurseries and day-care facilities, and in any case it was incompatible with the Union's views about the family. The proposal by the Family Minister, Ursula Lehr (CDU), to provide nursery places for two-year-olds provoked a storm of indignation from within her own party, as did the FDP's call for tax credits for childcare assistants. The cry was: we will not pay for employed dentists' wives to have housemaids, nor will we encourage mothers 'to drop off their two year olds in the morning'. The upbringing of small children and a professional career should happen in sequence, not simultaneously, it was thought. Hence the family-oriented social policy of the Union reinforced the model of the traditional family, with the man as breadwinner and the woman as mother.[14]

The second innovation in social policy during these years was the introduction of an independent system of statutory nursing care insurance. This too was a response to demographic change. But, in all other areas, it proved to be almost impossible to make a genuine change of course in social policy in view of the multiplicity of mutually contradictory interests. On the one hand, this was regrettable, because important reforming initiatives, in the health system for instance, where there was a dramatic increase in costs, could only be implemented against great resistance. A pension reform too, which was announced with a great fanfare, came down to a few changes and cost reductions. On the other hand, a look at comparable social welfare systems in other countries showed that the price to be paid for the privatisation of the system of old-age pensions, for example, whether partial or complete, was not only a cut in benefits but also to some extent a worsening of social inequality. The other alternative, the tax-financed pension, as in Great Britain, was not graduated according to the amount of contributions (and hence the individual's accumulated lifetime income) but was a uniform and basic amount, which also needed to be topped up with private insurance. The decision to stay with the existing system in principle, and where necessary to introduce piecemeal adjustments, was to that extent an expression of path dependency in social policy, in other words the impossibility of diverging in essential matters, once a given path had been adopted. On the other hand, the West German system of social benefits subsequently proved to be more effective and considerably more robust than its critics had predicted.[15]

Let us look finally at the proposal to dismantle subsidies. The concept of 'subsidies' was itself not entirely unambiguous, because it could be understood to include both tax relief for large families and financial aid for crumbling state enterprises. In essence, though, the issue was the degree to which the impact of structural change should be softened by government measures. The prime example of this was the so-called 'coal penny', a 10 per cent addition to electricity prices imposed after 1974 to subsidise coal production in the Ruhr and the Saar, which had long been unprofitable. It was argued that the country needed a 'national energy reserve', and on this basis coal mining in West Germany was not discontinued, as had long been clearly necessary on economic grounds, but artificially kept alive. The main objective of the subsidy, however, was to slow down the decline in the size of the workforce. Similar methods had been applied since the early 1960s in European agriculture; the retention of agricultural employment was seen as politically desirable, and large grants from the European Community had made it possible.[16] The European steel industry, the shipyards and many companies which supplied the iron and coal industries were in a similar situation. The world economic crisis had resulted in a clear decline in the worldwide production of steel (it was 746.4 million tonnes in 1979, and 645 million tonnes in 1982), but at the same time the new steel-producing countries of Japan and China entered the market, and now even former 'developing countries' such as Brazil and India were producing steel for sale on the world market. European steel firms were faced with heavy price competition from all over the world, and this compelled them to reduce overcapacity and engage in severe rationalisation. The crisis came as a complete surprise in the Federal Republic, because as late as 1974 almost 500,000 people were still employed in the country's steel industry, which was producing 53 million tonnes of crude steel and generating its highest ever profits since the end of the war.[17]

By 1990 annual steel production had fallen to 43 million tonnes, a decline of almost 20 per cent. According to the teachings of economic liberalism, factories should have been closed down and there should have been large-scale dismissals. The federal government's Council of Economic Experts advised against using state funds to preserve workplaces in branches where there was overcapacity:

> It doesn't make sense for every country to build a steel industry which is both highly modern and highly subsidised. The maintenance of overcapacity at the expense of the taxpayer, and the preservation of workplaces where they cannot be retained in the medium term, should also be rejected in the short term. It costs time and money which are required for necessary reorganisation.[18]

For the politicians, in contrast, the problem was different, because the crisis affected whole regions of the country, in which there would be no other adequate sources of employment available for years and even for decades. References to the market were of no assistance here, because they presupposed the unlimited mobility of the 'human capital', in other words of the people who were affected. This conundrum was not unique to the Federal Republic. It applied to all the industrialised countries of Europe. In Great Britain, however, the Thatcher government did not shy away from massive pit closures. The prime minister's struggle against the British coalminers' trade union, which lasted for many years and was conducted with almost unprecedented harshness, was a powerful demonstration of the social costs such an approach could incur. The case of steel was different: here the British government devoted immense resources to subsidising its domestic industry, as did governments in Italy, Belgium and France.

The steel firms of West Germany reacted to the crisis with large-scale rationalisation and a thoroughgoing process of concentration. However, the workers who had lost their jobs replied with a tremendous protest movement, which culminated in 1987 in mass demonstrations and roadblocks on the Ruhr against the threatened closure of the Krupp Smelting Plant in Duisburg-Rheinhausen. This situation led the federal government to decide in many cases to prevent or at least delay plant closures by granting state subsidies to ailing companies, so as to ease the necessary adjustment processes and gain time. In terms of market economics, this was pointless and expensive, because it used taxpayers' money to prop up industries which were no longer capable of competing on the world market. It also reinforced the conviction among the people affected that factory closures were absolutely unnecessary if the politicians did not want them to happen.[19]

In social policy terms, by contrast, there was hardly any alternative to transitional subsidies, because the urban decay of the big industrial regions could not be tolerated politically, and it also contradicted the principle, confirmed time and again in the Federal Republic, of a social market economy not exclusively dominated by economic considerations. 'Do you simply want to cut off a whole region in the Saar, or in North Rhine-Westphalia?', asked Chancellor Kohl in 1988, speaking to the Union's parliamentary group in the Bundestag. Thus, between 1980 and 1990, the total amount of subsidies rose by almost 30 per cent, from 25 billion DM to 32 billion DM. The number of people employed in the steel industry continued to fall, although more slowly than before: it was 400,000 in 1982 and 320,000 in 1990.[20]

Meanwhile, the development of world steel production followed a different course after 1990 from that expected by specialists. World demand for steel again rose thanks to the rapid process of industrialisation in China and other places, soon to be described as 'emerging countries'. By 2007, world output had reached 1,346 million tonnes, more than twice the figure for 1982. But the Federal Republic only accounted for 3 per cent of this.

An examination of the way West Germany's national economic policy evolved in the 1980s in its relation to global economic development thus reveals that there was a clear mismatch between the federal government's grandiloquent proclamations of 'freedom, dynamism and personal responsibility' and the practical continuity of its approach to social benefits and subsidies. The Kohl–Genscher government did, however, succeed in softening the obvious rigidities of a system which combined growing indebtedness, an increasing share of the state in GDP and an expansion in social policy expenditure, and in promoting individual commitment. To that extent, the government had responded favourably to the views expressed by market liberals, although they criticised its reforms as being inadequate. During this period, big companies shifted parts of their basic industrial mass production processes abroad and undertook extensive measures of rationalisation, but at the same time the government of the Federal Republic, like the governments of all other Western European countries affected by the crisis, endeavoured to cushion the social impact of the structural changes with heavy transitional subsidies, and also to promote technological modernisation and investment in future-oriented industries such as telecommunications. This approach was far removed from the market radicalism of the changes seen in the USA and Great Britain. But far-reaching changes of that type, amounting to a complete reconstruction of the West German economic and social order, would have been hard to justify, and almost impossible to implement politically, given the positive development of economic conditions and the significant export successes of the West German economy in the 1980s.

## Transformations in Domestic Politics

At the elections to the Bundestag, which had been brought forward to 1983, the Union obtained its second most successful result since 1957, receiving 48.8 per cent of the vote. A clearer rejection of the previous government could hardly be imagined. The FDP did, it is true, suffer some losses in comparison with 1980, when fear of Strauß's influence had led many voters to move over to the liberals. Its share of the vote fell from 10.6 to 7.0 per cent. But the new government still had a sizeable majority. The SPD, in contrast, with 38.2 per cent, fell below 40 per cent for the first time since 1965; it would never again attain that level, except in 1998. The Greens were a new presence in the Bundestag, with 5.6 per cent; for the first time since 1957 the Federal Republic's characteristic three-party system had been disrupted.

Without doubt,the main emphases of the new federal government's programme lay on economic policy and security, and it enjoyed success in both fields. In other areas, Kohl announced a vague programme calling for a 'spiritual and moral turnaround'. This was an attempt to accommodate the expectations of his conservative voters. For this purpose, he again took up the old formulae of cultural pessimism, in particular its rejection of individualism, secularisation and hedonism, phenomena he considered to be linked with the 'deep uncertainty, fed by anxiety and helplessness' about structural change, economic crisis and unemployment, which was indeed widespread at the beginning of the 1980s.[21] The antidotes he prescribed had a familiar ring: the Christian view of human beings, a focus on the family, and 'subsidiarity' instead of state intervention. But proclamations of this kind, though they led to agitated reactions from the political Left, did not result in practical political action. The social reforms of the 1960s and 1970s were not reversed, and the liberalising measures in education and sexual policy were not withdrawn. The new government was not even able to revise the rules allowing abortion to be partially exempted from punishment, although many conservative voters were firmly convinced it would be able to do this. There was simply no majority for the measure within the CDU parliamentary group.

The nature of the government's political ideals was better displayed by its emphasis on increasing the role of the market and individual initiative and its conspicuous highlighting of technological and economic progress. Nevertheless, there was a certain tension between Kohl's 'economic turnaround' and his postulated 'spiritual and moral turnaround', because the promotion of advancement for the individual and the dismantling of state regulation themselves helped to create and accelerate the process of individualisation and the decline in social solidarity which Kohl so vehemently lamented. The privatisation of television, a project dear to the Chancellor's heart, was a case in point. For unlike the public service broadcasters, the new private television stations were financed exclusively through advertising, and they were therefore primarily interested in getting the best possible viewing figures, hence cultural and educational programmes hardly came into question. The programmes produced by the private broadcasters therefore competed with each other in triviality and shallowness, and the population's average daily television consumption also increased rapidly. One could hardly imagine a greater difference between the jeremiads of the cultural pessimists and the government's practical policy towards the media. The Union's old problem, that on the one hand it sought to pursue a policy of accelerated modernisation and, on the other hand, it was critical of its cultural and social effects, surfaced once again, even more strongly than before.[22]

But programmatic consistency was not Kohl's chief concern. He was above all a power politician, whose strength lay in his control of the apparatus. This applied particularly to the party, which was his actual power base. The 'Kohl system' consisted of a network of personal connections to fellow party members, extending right down to the local level. These people were loyal and devoted, and they often owed him favours. The same system was also effective within the government. Kohl did not make decisions in cabinet, but in a very close circle of associates in the office of the federal chancellor, or in coordination with leading members of the party with which he was in coalition, the FDP. Kohl did not possess Willy Brandt's gift of far-reaching political vision, nor did he step forth as a brilliant, intellectually superior world statesman in the manner of Helmut Schmidt. But he did possess an unerring instinct for moods and majorities, as well as the ability to recognise counter-currents early and to neutralise them. This was particularly apparent after his second victory, in the 1987 Bundestag elections, when disappointment over the government's failure to make domestic political reforms came to the fore in the CDU. An opposition group around the prime minister of Baden-Württemberg, Späth and the party's general secretary, Geissler, which was prepared to overthrow Kohl, was rebuffed and frozen out. At that time, Kohl's position as chancellor was very much under dispute, and the pollsters predicted that at the next federal election, in 1991, the government was more likely to be voted out than confirmed in office.[23]

It was not just in the CDU, however, that there were tensions between the changed social conditions and the party's programme and traditions. The dichotomy between the Bavarian CSU's traditional milieu of Catholic peasant society and the dynamic economic development of the region was particularly noticeable. As the site of modern high technology firms such as Siemens, BMW and Audi, or the arms manufacturer MTU, Bavaria, like Baden-Württemberg and Hesse, was a particularly successful federal state in economic terms, much less affected by the crisis in the classical industrial sectors than for example the Saar or North Rhine-Westphalia. The interests pursued by the well-educated and well-paid employees of these firms in Munich or Augsburg, with their emphatically urban and individually oriented style of life, were completely different from those of the farmers of the Bavarian Forest or the Chiemgau, who were heavily dependent on state subsidies. The CSU, as the permanent governing party, dealt with this divergence by conducting an industrial policy strongly oriented towards technology and science and friendly to entrepreneurship, combined with a classical social policy directed to helping its core clientèle.

It glossed over the contradiction between the two approaches by stressing its links to the Bavarian homeland, its countryside traditions and its conservative values, giving these an increasingly folkloric flavour. Franz Josef Strauß, who was Bavaria's prime minister from 1978 to 1988, was himself a living expression of this link between the old and the new. He was notorious as a conservative nationalist hardliner, who blustered vociferously against socialism, individualism and the corruption of morals, but he was also a diligent networker, who brought an increasing number of promising firms to Bavaria, maintained close connections between politics and the economy, and helped to make the state the most important place in Germany for scientific research. This combination of roles was graphically expressed when Prime Minister Strauß, dressed in huntsman's garb, opened a genetic research laboratory to the accompaniment of a traditional Bavarian band.[24]

It was more difficult for the SPD to gloss over contradictions. Its previous model of success, the combination of heavy industry, expanding social policy and state direction of economic policy, had reached its limits in the 1970s. 'Progress', the central category of Social Democratic thought, had been challenged in numerous directions. By the end of the twentieth century, large sections of the party had become critical of growth-oriented industrial capitalism. But at the same time the Social Democrats could do little to counter the almost irresistible advance of globalisation and neo-liberalism. Their traditional social base, the industrial working class, was melting away. In 1980, only 28 per cent of party members were workers, while 36 per cent were civil servants and office employees. The new groups which supported the party had almost no contact with the old structures of the Social Democratic milieu, whether they were works councils, miners' association hospitals or social housing projects. The party was, to some extent, a victim of its own success. The educational improvement and professional advancement of the workers' children had been one of the party's most important causes. It was pursued for decades with great energy, and it turned out to be one of its greatest successes. But, after gaining their school leaving certificates and studying at university, these same children not only left their native social milieu, they also often moved away from the SPD's ideological world.

The reorientation of the SPD programme, which had already started before the party left government, therefore proved very difficult. It had to adapt itself to changes in the economic and social situation; but it also had to avoid losing its political identity. Identical, or similar, problems were faced by all the socialist and Social Democratic parties of Western Europe. 'Modernisers' and 'traditionalists' confronted each other everywhere, although the issues no longer had much to do with the traditional Left–Right antagonism. One group called for the modernisation of the economy, the strengthening of market forces and a turn towards ecological issues, while others insisted on the central role of the state in the economy and continued to be convinced that the market was incapable of ensuring a just distribution of opportunities, income or wealth. While one side ran the risk of adopting a programme indistinguishable from that of the Greens, the other side's prescriptions were identical with those that had already proved inadequate in the 1970s. The SPD therefore failed to find a unified, programmatically coherent strategy, and that was the essential reason why they found themselves in opposition for sixteen long years.

Here too, though, contrary developments could be observed. The Prime Minister of North Rhine-Westphalia Johannes Rau was able to combine a regional, local identity with a political option for the SPD in the same way as Strauß had done in Bavaria for the CSU. 'We in North Rhine-Westphalia' was one of the slogans with which he won an absolute majority in his home region in 1985. Here, as in Bavaria, and also in Baden-Württemberg under its CDU Prime Minister Lothar Späth, new, post-ideological trends were apparent, whose significance was destined to grow still greater in the future. Regional connections and the personality of the leading candidate were now decisive everywhere, while the programmatic profiles of the parties became increasingly blurred.[25]

One might have imagined that the FDP would be the beneficiary of the withdrawal of the state from the economy and the policy of debt reduction. The liberalisation of the economy and society, the reduction in the excessive role of the state, the accentuation of the freedom of the individual: all these were traditional liberal demands. But in actual fact the party now entered a period of crisis. Firstly, the change of coalition partners in 1982 led to a shift in its electoral base and a decline in membership. An influential group of FDP Bundestag deputies, who were strongly in favour of social liberalism, changed sides and joined the SPD, and as a result the political profile of the FDP in the Bundestag took on a more conservative aspect. Secondly, the party was unable to explain how the withdrawal of the state from the economy, and the increased stress on market forces, were connected with the rights of citizens and human beings, and so it was unable to take advantage of the obvious increase in the importance of these areas of politics. Ecology was also a problem for the party. The liberals, who had succeeded in 1970 in bringing environmental protection within the purview of the state, now adopted a defensive position on the issue, partly because of the fear that environmental regulations would lead to economic losses. As a result, the FDP retained its image of being a somewhat old-fashioned party of the middle classes and the artisanate, associated by the public above all with demands for tax reductions and the repeal of the law regulating shop opening hours. The FDP was as disconnected from the new stratum of 'young urban professionals' as it was from the new enterprises specialising in computers or biotechnology. It was most effective as a liberal counterweight to a conservative or indeed a reactionary Union, just as before 1982 people had voted for it as a restraint on a socialist and state-fixated SPD. But this corrective function of the FDP started to lose its significance as the Union progressively abandoned its conservative and anti-modern orientation and its right wing began to wither away following the exit of Franz-Josef Strauß from federal politics.[26]

For a long time, it remained unclear how far the Greens would be able to establish themselves as a political party. It is true that in the course of the 1980s the new party entered the parliaments of almost all the *Länder*, and its status was clearly confirmed at the 1987 Bundestag elections, where it secured 8.1 per cent of the vote, but it did not succeed until the end of the century in unambiguously determining its position within the West German political framework. The main reason for this was that the Greens saw themselves as the parliamentary extension of the alternative milieu and the new social movements. They thought their own electoral success endangered their detachment from the traditional business of politics, which they regarded as corrupt, cynical and out of touch with ordinary human beings. For the Greens, therefore, entry into parliament as an opposition group fundamentally critical of parliamentarism resulted in the same kind of conflict as Social Democracy had experienced at the beginning of the twentieth century during the dispute over revisionism.

The attempt of the Greens to combine parliamentary politics with a commitment to grassroots democracy led to a series of compromise decisions which were new to the German parliamentary system, such as the separation of party leadership and parliamentary mandates, the replacement of elected deputies after two years by designated 'successors', and also the introduction for the first time of a gender quota in drawing up lists of party election candidates. The quota idea soon proved effective, and it was later adopted by other parties in a similar manner, but the rules intended to preserve grass-roots democracy soon led to permanent conflict within the Greens. For one thing, they were an obstacle to the political professionalisation of the party, and for another thing the party's political stars, like Joschka Fischer, Otto Schily and Petra Kelly, who were rapidly making their mark, were no longer prepared to go along with them. The party's feuds, which were conducted in harsh and sometimes wounding language, were as much a feature of its public image during the first ten years as was their political programme.

It was, on the other hand, impossible to overlook that with their core issues of ecology, disarmament and feminist politics the Greens had occupied or redefined substantial fields of politics which the classical parties had neglected or grossly underestimated. Despite initial mockery from numerous established politicians, who made fun of campaigns to protect toad migration or grasshoppers, the ecological issue proved to be of millennial significance, and as global in its scope as the social question itself. The same thing could be said of the demand for equality between the sexes: a considerable amount of the political dynamism of the women's movement of the 1970s flowed into the Green Party. The Greens were also distinguished from all other parties by their unanimous opposition to the 'two-track decision' and the 'weapons upgrade', questions which dominated the early 1980s. Other parties either supported the stationing of missiles or, as in the case of the Social Democrats, were split over the issue.

Not least, however, the Greens were also the party of a particular generation. They expressed the attitude towards life and the social culture of those born in the 1940s and 1950s, insofar as they were socialised in the broad environment of the 'sixty-eighters' and the 'alternative milieu'. Young, predominantly of middle-class origin, academically educated and working in the service sector: that was the characteristic social profile of Green Party members and voters. The focal points of their activity were located in the metropolitan cities and the traditional university towns; in other words, the same places where the alternative milieu had been most strongly developed. The many political currents which found their way to the Greens soon condensed into two broad tendencies. On one side there was a 'fundamentalist' wing, which was strongly anti-capitalist and rejected participation in government as well as the establishment of groups of professional politicians of the Green variety in the parliaments. On the other side there were the *Realpolitiker*, or 'Realos', who did support government participation and who regarded the idea of an eco-socialist 'revolution' as completely absurd. The parliamentary groups at federal and state level were dominated largely by 'Realos', while the 'fundamentalists' had their strongest bastion of support in the party apparatus. After 1990–1, however, when most of the civil rights campaigners of the former GDR joined the Greens, the anti-socialist forces gained the upper hand, and many left-wingers resigned from the party.

The political influence of the Greens extended far further than their election results and the small number of seats they occupied in the parliaments. The ecological question moved ever closer to the centre of public concern, particularly after the warnings of the opponents of nuclear power were confirmed in an almost unimaginable way by the Chernobyl accident of April 1986. The growth of ecological legislation after the 1980s, the formation of the Federal Ministry of the Environment, and also the federal government's international endeavours, in the context of the United Nations Environment Programme (UNEP) for instance, all demonstrated the Federal Republic's growing readiness to take up and put into effect the stimuli coming from the Greens. This also applied to women's equality, which became a central item in the programmes, first of the SPD and then also of parties to the Right of it, as well as being reflected in internal party organisation.

The Greens' style of politics, their grass-roots democracy and association with citizens' initiatives, and the unconventional demeanour of their leading figures, naturally attracted much attention and had a strong impact on the hitherto traditional conduct of politics. But the emergence of this new and explicitly 'young' party also had its problematic side. The Greens received enormous attention and approval in the media when they went against the rules of parliamentarism, described political compromises as a betrayal of principles and poked fun at professional politicians of the traditional type. Their actions promoted the emergence of a populist form of politics all over Western Europe, which was characterised by a growing detachment from the political division of labour, a contempt for political parties, and an idealisation of direct democracy. This new populism could swing to the Left, as in the case of the Greens, but also to the Right, as was shown by the new political groups which formed in Scandinavia, the Netherlands and France.[27]

The Kohl–Genscher government was confirmed in office by the 1987 Bundestag elections, though it did lose some support. In comparison with 1983, the Union lost 4.5 per cent of its previous vote (it fell to 44.3 per cent), while the FDP gained 2.2 per cent (it rose to 9.1 per cent). The SPD lost 1.2 per cent, ending with 37.0 per cent, while the Greens added 2.7 per cent, which brought them up to 8.3 per cent. But, in contrast to 1983, when the waves of domestic politics were very choppy and the polarisation within society was at its height over the stationing of nuclear missiles, the Bundestag elections of 1987, at which Johannes Rau was Kohl's challenger for the SPD, were somewhat unexciting. The political climate in the Federal Republic had become distinctly calmer since the Bundestag had made its decision and American intermediate-range missiles had actually been installed in the country. The political system of the Federal Republic had survived this crucial test as well as the change in government, and the new party in the Bundestag, whose emergence was initially treated as a sensation, soon became a normal feature of the political scene.

This process of stabilisation and normalisation also went hand in hand with a certain complacency and self-satisfaction among the political elite. This found expression in a series of scandals, which dominated the headlines of the 1980s. By far the most significant of these were the Flick Affair and the scandal over party donations. The affair had its origins in the way political parties were financed indirectly by anonymous donors, which was illegal but had long been common practice. According to a provision of the law on contributions to political parties, the origin of amounts exceeding 20,000 DM should be disclosed. But for years the CDU and CSU, as well as the SPD and the FDP, had evaded this regulation by allowing large companies to pay donations into the accounts of charitable organisations or dummy firms at home or abroad, which then reached party treasuries through an indirect route. The origins of these contributions to the parties were thus concealed, but the companies in question could still deduct their donations for tax purposes. It seemed obvious that this procedure was illegal (some of the money was brought over the border into the Federal Republic in suitcases) but it was clearly very effective.

After 1976, however, this form of finance came to public attention in connection with another scandal which soon had far-reaching repercussions. This originated with the Flick group, which had sold its Daimler-Benz shares to Deutsche Bank for 1.9 billion DM. It now appeared to owe 980 million DM in taxes as a result. To avoid payment, Flick asked the competent federal Economics Ministry to recognise the transaction as a reinvestment of particular value in promoting the development of the economy and therefore to exempt the proceeds from taxation. This proposal was accepted in respect of three-quarters of the profit made on the sale, so Flick received a tax reduction of roughly 700 million DM. When it became known that the firm had previously repeatedly distributed large amounts of money as party donations to leading government politicians (including 750,000 DM to the CSU chair Franz Josef Strauß, 100,000 DM to Count Otto Lambsdorff and 200,000 DM to his predecessor as Minister of Economics, Hans Friderichs) the issue suddenly became more than a breach of the law on party donations. Bribery and corruption were now suspected. These suspicions were corroborated when the tax investigator discovered the account book of a leading staff member of the Flick group, which detailed all these transactions, mostly conducted by the discreet transmission of bulging envelopes. Between 1974 and 1980, Flick distributed 25 million DM in party donations, 15 million DM to the Union, 6.5 million to the FDP and 4.3 million to the SPD.[28]

Between 1983 and 1987, these overlapping scandals concerning the Flick group and its party donations were one of the dominant themes of West German domestic politics, since numerous leading politicians and all political parties apart from the Greens were affected in one way or another. Repeated attempts by the government parties and by the SPD to end the affair with a quick amnesty provoked such a storm of public indignation that they had to be abandoned hastily; indeed, the law on contributions to political parties was now made more severe. In the criminal trials that followed the Flick affair, a manager at Flick, Eberhard von Brauchitsch, was condemned to a term of imprisonment for tax evasion, and Friderichs and Count Lambsdorff, who had resigned from his post after the proceedings were instituted, were fined for assisting in tax evasion. The prosecution was unable to prove corruption, however.

The political impact of the Flick affair was considerable. The politicians involved displayed furious indignation, aggressively proclaiming their innocence. Chancellor Kohl complained that it was an 'intolerable situation' that 'entirely respectable citizens' who had placed financial means at the disposal of democratic parties 'were now being criminalised'. And Franz Josef Strauß responded to the embarrassing revelations of the committee investigating the affair by fulminating against the 'ultra-moral super-rigorism of people who were "as pure as the driven snow"'. Everyone had known, he said, that indirect party financing existed, and that had not worried anyone for years.

> This whole complex was only rolled out in the second half of the 1970s, when the general class struggle principle gradually began to enjoy a comeback with a corresponding persecution of the 'capitalists' in this country, and when the 'march through the institutions' had brought former APOs or protesters or levellers on principle into office. Until then this had been a 'quiet zone' for many, many years.[29]

Kohl, meanwhile, only survived as Chancellor by the skin of his teeth. The Green Bundestag deputy Otto Schily, who had distinguished himself by his unrelenting pursuit of the Flick affair and the scandal over political donations, now filed a criminal complaint against the Chancellor for allegedly committing perjury in answering the questions of the investigation committee of the Rhineland-Palatinate Diet. Kohl was only able to escape a formal prosecution by exerting considerable political pressure and with the help of a very lenient examining magistrate. For public opinion, though, the affair strengthened the impression that the leaders of the political parties acted above all in their own self-interest, that the bosses of big companies were clearly able to buy favourable decisions from the ministries, and that the politicians did not keep to the laws they themselves had made. This feeling was reflected in a widespread 'disenchantment with politics'.

## From the Debate on Foreigners to the Asylum Campaign

Despite the recruitment ban imposed in autumn 1973 the number of foreigners living in the Federal Republic continued to increase and by 1980 it had reached 4.4 million, a million more than in 1972. The number of foreigners in employment had fallen by half a million. The reason for this was the increasing trend towards permanent residence among the former Gastarbeiter, who had now started to bring in their families, and had changed their future perspective from a temporary to a long-lasting stay in the country. But this trend towards assimilation into the native population was not reflected in the working environment. In 1984, 70 per cent of the foreigners were still employed in unskilled or semi-skilled occupations and only 19 per cent were specialist workers or foremen. Seventy-five per cent of male and 60 per cent of female foreigners earned less than the average wage of the overall workforce. In 1982, when the overall proportion of unemployed workers in West Germany was 7.5 per cent, the figure was 11.9 per cent for foreigners. More than a quarter of the children of foreigners left school in 1985 without completing their education, and only 6 per cent went on to attend a *Gymnasium*.[30]

One of the reasons for this unsatisfactory turn of events was the concept of 'temporary integration' which was proposed after the recruitment ban of 1973 and which all governments, state and federal, held onto until the late 1980s. Permanent residence in the country, immigration in other words, was only envisaged in exceptional cases. Children born in Germany or brought into the country at a later time would be integrated into the German school system, but they were also expected to keep in contact with the culture of their parents' homeland, so as to keep open the 'option of a return'. The result was that many foreign children fell by the wayside and developed into 'bilingual illiterates', proficient neither in their parents' language nor in that of their classmates. In view of this situation, their chances of achieving a professional qualification were dramatically reduced, and these young people, who were in any case socially isolated, increasingly fell victim to social exclusion.

These unintended consequences of the process of immigration gave rise to feelings of anxiety, and rendered many Germans hostile to the idea,, especially if they had been particularly affected during the economic crisis by unemployment and uncertainty about the future. In 1978, 39 per cent of West Germans declared that 'the Gastarbeiter should go back to their own country.' In 1980, this figure was 48 per cent, and by March 1983, it had risen to 80 per cent. Such a tremendous shift of opinion within such a short time was almost unprecedented in the history of the Federal Republic, especially as it took place largely unnoticed by politicians and the media.[31] But those who criticised the results of immigration rapidly found that they were accused of xenophobia. The guilt was thus transferred from the responsible political leaders to the population, and an objective problem which was the result of decades of policy towards foreigners was now turned into subjective misbehaviour: the incorrect attitude of the people who had most to do with the foreigners, namely the socially deprived strata of the German population. The reason for the accumulating difficulties lay rather in the political conception underlying the organisation of foreign employment. Until the early 1970s, the customary approach was to recruit foreign labourers, insert them flexibly and cheaply at the lower end of the labour market and then send them back home when economic growth slowed down, so that the economy and the state did not incur any follow-up costs. After 1976–7 this plan was no longer effective. On the contrary, a completely changed situation arose in regard to migration. The politicians and the population at large reacted to this new situation defensively but also helplessly.[32]

In his government declaration of October 1982, Chancellor Kohl had picked out policy towards foreigners as one of his government's priority areas, along with the creation of new employment opportunities, social policy and foreign and security policy. To place the issue in the forefront in this way was itself an indication of its increasing public and political significance. The results of a public opinion survey on the subject could be read in the press: 'Every Bonn party risks coming into conflict with many of its supporters if it plays down the foreigner problem and while resisting any further influx steers a course towards the necessary integration of a considerable section of the present Gastarbeiter.'[33] Majorities were clearly to be won and lost over this issue. In order to take advantage of this mood, the Union in particular endeavoured to react to the population's hostility to foreigners and to take political control of this issue, which until then had been rather secondary. But the Social Democrats were also confronted with increasing pressure from some of their supporters on the same issue.

The federal government laid down three priority objectives, under the heading 'Germany is not a land of immigration': 'integration' of the foreigners living in Germany, encouragement to return home and prevention of any further influx.[34] But there was no effective plan for 'integration', nor any precise conception of what the goal might be. It was not even clear what the word implied. Should naturalisation be made easier? Should foreign children be sent to mainstream German schools? The latter course contradicted the option of returning home, while if foreign children were educated in separate classes in their mother tongue, this contradicted the objective of integration.

Even a drastic reduction in the number of foreigners living in the country was difficult to implement, as soon became apparent. To reduce the influx of foreigners by limiting the entry of family members into the country contradicted the special protection of the family which was enshrined in the Basic Law. Moreover, restrictions on foreigners from EC countries, such as Italy, and after 1986 Spain and Portugal as well, were no longer possible under agreed EC regulations. In addition, the residency of non-EC foreigners had by now been established on a firmer legal foundation, and the rights they had acquired could not simply be ignored. Despite this, the discussions concentrated increasingly on the Turks, who were by far the largest group of non-EC foreigners.

In order to reduce the number of foreigners living in Germany, every family which left the country early was offered a 'returners' grant' of 10,000–15,000 DM. The intention was to reduce the number of foreigners from 4.6 million to between 2 and 3 million within six years. In actual fact, however, only 300,000 foreigners returned home on the basis of this 'law of return', which was only a slight increase on the figure for previous years. Hence, the inducement had a statistically insignificant effect. This attempt to induce resident foreigners to return home in large numbers therefore ended in failure. The underlying assumption was that foreigners, and Turks in particular, regarded their stay in Germany as temporary and would return in large numbers if they received appropriate incentives. It turned out that this was erroneous. As early as 1984, 83 per cent of the Turks in Berlin no longer knew when they would return to Turkey, and whether they would do so at all.[35]

After 1980, the growing economic crisis led to an intensification in political agitation against the Turks, who were seen as particularly alien and neither willing nor able to integrate. These were exactly the same accusations as had been made fifteen years before against the Italians and the Yugoslavs. The debate over the Turks, however, was distinguished by a heightened aggressiveness, above all in the social flashpoints of the big cities, where migrants and locals came into direct contact. Agitation against foreigners increasingly became the main political focus of organised right-wing radicalism, and it met with greater approval from some sections of the population than the empty glorification of the Nazi regime relied on by the extreme Right in previous decades.

The religion of Islam also played an increasing part in these debates after the Iranian revolution of 1979. Although it was well known that more than 80 per cent of the Turks living in the Federal Republic rejected Islamic fundamentalism as strongly as they did political radicalism of the Left or Right, a fear of Islamisation and rule by 'Hodzhas' was stimulated by news about Koranic schools which attacked Western civilisation, and this gave added sustenance to the fear that Iranian conditions would soon be dominant in Turkey and indirectly in the Federal Republic as well. It is true that a regime of the mullahs did not emerge in Turkey, nor did the anti-democratic Muslim Brotherhood attain perceptible influence among the Turkish colony in the Federal Republic. But it became more and more difficult for moderate forces to prevail against this ideological complex, which was made up of xenophobia, fears for the future and essentialist cultural criticism.[36]

The atmosphere created by a combination of economic calculation and cultural anxiety was now reflected in increasingly contradictory policies. It was obvious that the great majority of the foreign population would remain in Germany permanently. But the government did not change the basic lines of its policy towards foreigners, so as not to lose support among its own electorate. It continued instead to maintain that Germany was not a land of immigration, that the foreigners were only here to work temporarily, and that the majority of them would sooner or later return to their countries of origin. This contradiction between reality and political proclamations was the most important reason for the intensifying dispute in the Federal Republic over the question of foreigners.

Two overlapping developments which had a bearing on this question could be observed during and after the 1980s. The first was the ending of the phase of labour transfer within Europe, which had been symbolised in the Federal Republic by the Gastarbeiter. The transfer of labour came to an end because the countries of Western and Southern Europe had now converged economically. The second was the beginning of mass migration from the 'Third World', a process driven by poverty and civil war. This had traditionally been directed towards other countries in the same region, but starting with the early 1980s, the migration process increasingly became supra-regional and transnational.[37] There was therefore an increase in immigration from distant regions to all the countries of Western Europe. In the Federal Republic this found expression above all in an increase in the number of asylum seekers. Until the mid-1970s there had never been more than 10,000 asylum seekers a year, and they were primarily political refugees from the communist-ruled Eastern bloc. But in 1980 more than 100,000 people sought asylum in West Germany, including many Turks, on account of the military coup that had just taken place there. The number of asylum seekers again started to rise substantially from the mid-1980s onwards. Now the overwhelming majority of them no longer came from Turkey or sub-Saharan Africa and Asia, as was often supposed, but from East Central Europe: in 1988, out of roughly 100,000 asylum seekers, more than half came from Poland and from Yugoslavia, a country which was now under the threat of civil war.[38]

In order of magnitude, this movement of immigration was no greater than the influx of family members which followed the 1973 ban on the recruitment of foreign workers. But once again it was the socially deprived strata of the population who experienced its impact. Their reaction to the entry of foreigners and asylum seekers into the Federal Republic was made more aggressive by competition for jobs, accommodation and social benefits and also by irritation at the increasingly alien appearance of their familiar environment. As a result, the second half of the 1980s saw a confrontational debate about asylum policy, which broadened out into one of the fiercest domestic policy arguments ever seen in the history of the Federal Republic. It had far-reaching political and social repercussions.

To reduce the number of asylum seekers, the authorities had accelerated the procedures for admission, tightened the criteria determining the right to asylum, made it more difficult to enter the Federal Republic and, as a deterrent, worsened the living conditions of applicants. None of these measures proved successful. Asylum seekers were finally assigned to refugee camps. They were also forbidden to obtain employment, so as to prevent 'silent integration'. They were therefore forced into idleness, often over a period of several years, and thus appeared to the German public as loungers and parasites, while the high proportion of claims rejected, particularly in the case of civil war refugees, was soon regarded as a proof of the view that these people were 'economic migrants' who were in reality not political refugees but had come to Germany for purely material reasons. There was probably a kernel of truth in this, because the political disintegration of the home country, whether it was Lebanon, Yugoslavia or Poland under martial law, was usually also accompanied by a severe worsening of material conditions. The arrival of the asylum seekers set off a powerful wave of irritation and anger in the Federal Republic. 'Asylum policy' became a symbol for the exasperation many Germans felt but had refrained from expressing until then over several issues: immigration, the supposedly privileged position of the Other, and the social imbalances resulting from the economic crisis and globalisation in general.

Even so, the right to asylum was embedded in the Basic Law; this was a direct consequence of the experience of Nazism. For this reason, the Social Democrats and the Greens rejected any attempt to weaken it. But since it was not possible to restrict the entry of asylum seekers without altering the Basic Law, the leaders of the Union began to increase their pressure on the SPD, in order to reach the two-thirds majority needed to do this. The rapidly accelerating debate over 'asylum cheats' had already begun to have an adverse impact during the 1987 election campaign. The first attacks on refugee centres were reported, and soon the radicals of the Right made the subject of asylum the central issue of their propaganda. During the next year, the number of asylum seekers again rose, and there was a further escalation in the protests, during which little distinction was made between asylum seekers, 'Gastarbeiter' and ethnic Germans from Poland and the Soviet Union who were being resettled in the Federal Republic.

On the other hand, the Greens, and some of the Social Democrats, made the uncompromising maintenance of the right to asylum into an acid test of the status of democracy and human rights in the Federal Republic. They regarded references to 'abuses of the right to asylum' and to the conversion of a worldwide migration movement into an asylum procedure as mere pretexts, and they saw the concerns of large parts of the population and their increasing fear of strangers as nothing more than a product of the propaganda of the federal government and the Union against foreigners. The Greens and their periphery finally went so far as to demand a 'general right to remain' for all immigrants, in order 'to make partial reparation for the damage done by the colonial conquests of the last hundred years', as the left-wing newspaper *die tageszeitung* put it.[39] This was the beginning of a political stalemate which made it difficult to arrive at a pragmatic solution.

## The Political Culture of the Eighties

It was almost impossible in the year 1984 to avoid alluding to George Orwell's novel of the same name, because the gloomy predictions of this book, which foretold the coming of the surveillance state, were so much in tune with the feelings of the time. The stationing of American intermediate-range missiles in the Federal Republic, the effects of the world economic crisis and the ecological catastrophes of the period produced a basic attitude of pessimism, which found expression in the watchword of the punk movement: 'No future'.

The government's attempt to hold a population census in the Federal Republic appeared to bear a very close relation to Orwell's book. There had already been a number of post-war censuses (in 1950, 1956, 1961 and 1970), but a broad groundswell of protest developed against the one now proposed. On the one hand, this was certainly an expression of the mistrust of the New Left for the Bonn Republic and its political leaders, particularly after the liberal–conservative government of Kohl and Genscher came into office. But it was also an expression of uneasiness over the new digital data processing systems which were gradually becoming widespread in the country. The new systems gave rise to the fear that the state would gain uncontrollable access to its citizens' personal data. Opinion surveys conducted in 1987 showed that after the danger of war, unemployment and environmental catastrophe, the misuse of people's data was seen as the next greatest threat. The connection was quickly made with the census of May 1939, in which, among other things, the National Socialist state had collected data about the German Jews, which then served as a basis for their deportation and murder. But was it really possible to see the enumeration and murder of the Jews as a warning for the future of the census in the democratic Federal Republic of Germany? This line of argument, based on the continuing repercussions of the Nazi period, which had not been adequately processed in the Federal Republic, was however a routine and long-established feature of West German politics.[40]

The protests against the census were partially successful. The Federal Constitutional Court declared that while the census conformed in principle to the requirements of the constitution, its legal foundation needed to be altered, by adding that it was subject to 'the right of the individual to control the information provided'. This was a new conception, which soon began to spread into the judicial system. 'Data protection' now quickly became a widely accepted and universally used concept. But when the census was actually conducted in 1987, having received a new legal foundation, calls for a boycott met with little response.

The mood of the time, as manifested in these events, was pessimistic, and imbued with fears and doubts about the future. There was a certain amount of political calculation involved. But the new mood did have a concrete basis, and the ever more frequent announcements about environmental catastrophes contributed to this, as did the continuous series of economic crises. Large-scale devastation of coastal areas after accidents with oil tankers, dramatic increases in the amount of waste in the industrialised countries, water contamination, pollution of the air by harmful substances, and damage to forests: these issues were all much discussed at the time, and they caused great anxiety. In 1984, almost 60 per cent of the population as a whole, and 80 per cent of people under thirty who had a School Leaving Certificate were dissatisfied with the level of environmental protection.[41] Environmental damage did not simply start in the 1970s, and even tanker accidents and emissions of poisonous gases had occurred repeatedly before then. But the spread of ecological awareness meant that the amount of attention paid to such events was now much greater, and whereas in the 1960s, bubbles of foam a metre high on the river barrages were accepted as the unavoidable accompaniments of industrial society, such things now aroused indignation and protest. In the early 1980s, people often had a feeling that they were facing an ecological catastrophe. Some of the reports and discussions about damage to the environment unmistakably bore signs of hysteria and exaggeration. There was a boom in apocalyptic films describing life after an environmental or nuclear catastrophe. On the other hand, the proportion of harmful substances in the atmosphere had actually declined since 1970, despite all reports to the contrary (although it continued to be too high). Moreover, the prediction that much of the forest would die in the next few years, because it had already been severely affected by emissions from motor vehicles and coal-fired power stations, turned out to be highly exaggerated; on the contrary, in the years that followed there was an increase in the area covered by trees.[42]

It was not easy to make a realistic estimate of the risks humanity actually incurred through environmental pollution, since in many cases there were neither sufficient empirical data nor clear scientific conclusions. In December 1984, in the Indian state of Bhopal, there was a big leak of poisonous gas from a factory owned by the US chemical company Union Carbide, as a result of carelessness and inadequate safety precautions. Roughly 5,000 people lost their lives, and there was a natural apprehension that this sort of incident could be repeated elsewhere at any time.[43]

These fears were felt still more strongly in the case of the accident which happened in the nuclear power station of Chernobyl, in Ukraine, on 26 April 1986. Everything the opponents of nuclear power had predicted in previous years, which had been dismissed by its supporters as irresponsible scaremongering, had now come true: an explosion in a reactor, a meltdown of the core, the Maximum Credible Accident (MCA), the leakage of large amounts of radioactivity from the plant, the contamination of a whole region and the windborne spread of radioactive matter to far distant areas. It had previously been regarded as unimaginable that the Federal Republic could be affected, but this is exactly what happened, when a weak radioactive 'fallout' spread from Ukraine to Scandinavia and Western Europe. The authorities in West Germany were not prepared for this. There was neither clear guidance nor an explicit allocation of responsibilities. Reports in the press fluctuated between underestimation, ignorance and exaggeration, the experts contradicted one other, and as a result rumour and speculation were rife. The number of victims of the accident was unknown, though it was estimated that there were over 100,000 dead. In actual fact, the direct consequences of the accident in Ukraine proved to be less dramatic than this. It was later established that the number of people killed directly by the accident was in the region of fifty. The longer-term effects were difficult to estimate. In the medium term there was a clear increase in the number of cases of thyroid cancer among children. By 1995, roughly 800 cases had been registered. A region as large as the Saar had been irradiated, and a zone of 4,300 square kilometres around the devastated power station was contaminated to an extent that no one was (or is) permitted to enter the area. The catastrophe had an almost incalculable impact on the local economy.[44]

The reaction in West Germany to reports of the Chernobyl nuclear accident was marked by uncertainty and outrage, but above all fear, because people saw themselves confronted with an unpredictable and imperceptible danger against which there was no protection. The catastrophe therefore had an impact on West German attitudes to life and it created a sense of danger that went far beyond the individual's own direct involvement. Some journalists and scientific observers placed Chernobyl on a level with Auschwitz and Nagasaki. The Munich sociologist Ulrich Beck thought that Chernobyl marked the end of the existing form of civilisation:

> All the pain, all the misery, all the violence human beings have inflicted on other human beings, was suffered until now by people categorised as 'the other': Jews, Blacks, Women, Asylum-seekers, Dissidents, Communists etc. There were fences, camps, urban districts, military blocks on one side, and on the other side there were the individual's four walls – real and symbolic boundaries, behind which people who were apparently unaffected could withdraw. All this no longer exists since Chernobyl. The experience of nuclear contamination means the end of 'the Other', the end of all our highly cultivated distancing techniques. Wretchedness can be kept at a distance; the dangers of the nuclear age cannot. Therein lies the novelty of its cultural and political impact. Its power is the power of danger, which abolishes all the protective zones and differentiations of modernity.[45]

For the sociologist Beck, Chernobyl was a symbol of the end of the 'first' modern age, classical modernity with its consciousness of progress, its industrial mass production, its class conflicts and its imperialist wars. According to this interpretation, the by-products and repercussions of industrialism had now become more influential than the process itself. Ecological catastrophes affected the northern as much as they did the southern hemisphere, and the globalisation of markets and dangers deprived national and ideological boundaries of their meaning. This was an epochal watershed, separating the present from the history of the past two hundred years. Many people found Beck's thesis convincing, but there were also many criticisms. It was objected that the possibility of global self-destruction had existed since the invention of the atom bomb. But this development was a product of the technological progress and the ideological conflicts of the twentieth century, and thus, in Beck's terminology, of the 'first' and not the 'second' modernity. Despite this objection, many people thought and felt that the events in Chernobyl constituted a turning point in the history of science and technology, and beyond that, human civilisation.

The government reacted to the Chernobyl disaster by establishing the Federal Ministry of the Environment and considerably strengthening its commitment to environmental policies. The extensive plans made to build reprocessing plants and new, more modern but also more dangerous types of nuclear power station now became so much waste paper. The 'fast breeder' in Kalkar, which had cost roughly 7 billion DM, was not put into operation, nor was the planned high temperature reactor in Hamm-Uentrop. The projected reprocessing plant in Wackersdorf, in the Upper Palatinate, which had been protected with thousands of police against tens of thousands of demonstrators by the Bavarian state government, was also finally abandoned, not in this case because of a government resolution but rather because the developer, the energy company VEBA, changed its mind. The company no longer regarded the project as economically viable, and with this it brought the federal government's whole conception of energy policy crashing down.[46]

Thanks to environmental catastrophes, the stationing of intermediate-range missiles, structural change and the misuse of data, the anxieties and threats of these years were much more varied than those of the 1960s and 1970s had been. Above all, they were not tied together by the unifying thread of a politico-ideological analysis, as had often been the case in the two previous decades with Neo-Marxism. Thus, the protest milieu in the 1980s was more variegated and contradictory than that of the sixty-eighters or the alternative Left milieux of the 1970s. Its characteristic form of expression was the Citizens' Initiative. There were many places where these now emerged. They were directed against land consolidation, restructuring plans and road-building projects as much as against nuclear power stations. Self-determination, grass-roots democracy and freedom from ideology determined their self-perception, though not necessarily their practice. The fundamental politicisation which had been brought about in the previous decade by the fierceness of the argument between the political parties now changed its course, and gave strength to these manifold initiatives.

There was no doubt that the Citizens' Initiatives reflected an increased aspiration on the part of the citizens towards participation in the state and in politics, although it should not be overlooked that there were often attempts to force through particular interests against the interests of the country as a whole.

But, in general, these grass-roots movements led to a considerable increase in the democratic legitimacy of the Federal Republic's political system, which quickly and wholeheartedly incorporated them, although the attempts of the political parties to join forces with the Citizens' Initiative movement in various places were not usually successful.[47]

These protest movements were characterised by a peculiar mixture of political 'progressivism' and cultural pessimism which is sometimes difficult to come to terms with from a distance. For these protesters, everything was connected with everything else: capitalism and the destruction of nature, imperialism and grass roots democracy, communism and nuclear power, the protection of water and the divine order. Among the activists of the 'Hüttendörfer' in Gorleben or those who protested against the 'Western Aircraft Runway' in the Frankfurter Wald, radical democratic motives played as great a part as support for the community idyll, Left radical jargon and agrarian romanticism. The new scene also had obvious connections with the post-religious supporters of the 'New Age' movement, who highlighted the growing yearning for spirituality and transcendence, while the Christian churches continued to lose members and influence.[48]

That was one side of the citizens' protest. The other side could be observed in the almost military appearance of the confrontation between demonstrators and police on the building sites of the nuclear installations in Brokdorf, Kalkar, Gorleben and Wackersdorf or in the violent conflicts over the expansion of Frankfurt Airport. Here, one could recognise the deep alienation from, indeed the hostility towards, the West German state of the section of German youth which was within the ambit of the New Left. This alienation also found expression in the riots by young people in Hamburg and Berlin, who were protesting against the redevelopment of old urban neighbourhoods and whose spectacular house occupations occasionally met with a sympathetic response from sections of the population. At its margins, the left-wing protest movement of these years also had points of contact with the third generation of RAF terrorists. This group carried out a number of attacks between 1985 and 1991, killing two US soldiers, the industrial managers Ernst Zimmermann and Heinz Beckurts, along with their driver, Ministerial Director Gerold von Braunmühl, Alfred Herrhausen, the Chair of the Board of Managing Directors of the Deutsche Bank, and Detlev Rohwedder, head of the Treuhandanstalt, the agency set up to privatise the state enterprises of the former GDR.[49]

It would be wrong to underestimate the effectiveness of the protest milieu of the 1980s. It was characterised by a contradictory mixture of idealism and militancy, and an environmental awareness which stressed its opposition to modernity, and it was reacting to a number of developments which were themselves in part contradictory: the decline of traditional sociocultural milieux, intensified individualisation and the increasing demand for participation in the activities of the state and the administration. But it was also a reaction to the progressive modernisation of the cities, it expressed a fear of ecological catastrophe, a rejection of the new 'post-Fordist' world of work and a protest against the exclusion of a growing number of migrants from majority society. Citizens' Initiatives and alternative protest movements were therefore by no means structured in a collective or homogeneous fashion. On the contrary, in their political inconsistency and cultural profusion they were exactly the appropriate experimental space in which to observe the interactions of pluralism and individualism.

The same phenomenon was also reflected in the field of culture, where these developments were taken up and reinforced. In the visual arts, as in the theatre and in film, traditional forms were often mixed up, reissued as quotations and combined together. Functionalism and the Bauhaus tradition in architecture and urban development had long been under attack in theory, but now new concepts also began to prevail in practice. The new State Gallery in Stuttgart or the new museums in Frankfurt combined classical stylistic elements with formal features drawn from Pop Art and a multiplicity of historical borrowings. Instead of the demolition of long-established urban structures and the segregation of functional areas for life, work and leisure, the new thinking advocated pluralism and the blending of urban use-modes, as well as the inclusion of historical structures and above all the retention of value. 'The fundamental historical structure of the city must be a constant foundation of urban development.' As early as 1978, a path-breaking statement by the West Berlin Senate asserted this, continuing as follows: 'In developing the city the traces of history must be included, and the existing buildings must be retained.'[50] Henceforth, the old buildings in the centre of the city should no longer be torn up but restored. Houses from the *Gründerzeit,* the favourite victims of the town planning frenzy of the 1960s, were rediscovered by the new middle class in the 1980s as favourite places to live, and in many cases the old urban neighbourhoods which had been saved from demolition by the squatters' movement became new middle-class residential areas. What had been observed in the USA for twenty years or more now took place in West Germany: slum-ridden urban centres with decayed but cheap housing were taken over by students, foreigners, dropouts and artists. The colourful and creative life which arose here soon drew in the wealthier strata, and within a few years formerly disreputable urban areas such as Ottensen, Kreuzberg, Lehel and Ostertor became favoured parts of town with rapidly rising house prices, until the foreigners, students and artists came together in a different area and the cycle of 'gentrification' began all over again. Nowhere was the interplay between social minorities, the cultural avant-garde and the market as clearly apparent as here.

The International Building Exhibition held in Berlin even included the protest against itself as an item. Here, new forms of citizen-friendly urban development were planned in collaboration with self-help groups. Radical pluralism replaced unity of form and function. The postmodernism which found expression here in a playful, collage-like treatment of traditions and functions was opposed not just by conservative cultural critics, who saw it as a sign of cultural collapse and decadence, but also by left-wingers, who were inclined to regard it as the cultural expression of Helmut Kohl's 'spiritual and moral turnaround'. Both views turned out to be wrong. The new cultural trends which asserted themselves in the course of the 1980s were not in the least distinguished by uniformity and political functionality. They were marked rather by a cycle of innovation, integration, commercialisation, new approaches from outsiders, the integration of the latter, renewed commercialisation, and so on.[51]

It was apparent here that unlike in the 1960s, when the youth rebellion came up against the determined opposition of earlier generations who were guided by a conventional way of life and conventional morality, this protest movement was no longer faced with such solid defences. On the contrary, a process of integration took place, and the protest movement became part of a politically and culturally diverse majority culture, which seemed to be ready to revitalise itself by incorporating every critical position and every radical counter-project. Thus, the critical gesture itself became a feature of mainstream culture and the desire to be different became the predominant attitude. The real meaning of the political culture of the 1980s lies in this process of transformation, which involved both the assimilation and appropriation of the dissidents and a far-reaching pluralisation of majority culture itself.

Pop music was the most colourful expression of this new diversity.[52] Punk, a loud, crude and provocative form of rock music which emerged from the devastated industrial regions of Great Britain in the seventies, propagated a cult of simplicity, ferocity and ugliness, and soon became a trend copied all over the world. It reinvigorated mainstream pop, thereby becoming part of it. The music of Afro-Americans in the USA, which was originally an expression of their revolt against discrimination, had already enjoyed great success in the seventies with the commercialisation of soul music, and in the shape of Michael Jackson it produced the first worldwide Afro-American musical star. He dominated the global pop music scene for six or seven years with an ingenious mixture of 'black music' and commercial pop, in which revolt and rebellion now only appeared as aestheticised quotations. His female counterpart was the Italian-American singer Madonna, who presented herself as a self-aware *femme fatale*, reinventing herself ironically in constantly renewed metamorphoses and identities. She was an idol of post-feminism who had an extraordinary influence on the image of the new woman in Tokyo and São Paulo as much as in

Boston and Berlin. There were similar trends in the German scene: musicians like Udo Lindenberg or Nina Hagen, who were originally obstinate and provocative manifestations on the margins of mass taste, now became stars. With their emergence, the language of German pop music became brasher and more allusive—and more effective. The use of quotation and irony were also features of the short-lived New German Wave at the beginning of the 1980s. This mixed elements of German popular hits with the new pop music, and criticised the commonplace with a light touch, often combined with Dadaist *motifs* ('Da-Da-Da') or ironic references to the obsession with growth ('Now we shall roll up our sleeves again—we're raising the GDP!') or with progress ('Don't pause for breath—history is being made—things are getting moving!'). The protest singers and the political rock bands, with their completely un-ironic and often emotional lyrics, found it increasingly difficult to compete with this approach. Their songs were heard only on demonstrations, and they were soon forgotten.

The fears over the new data processing systems, which had aroused such surges of revolt as the census boycott, now gave way to a more relaxed attitude. The new storage media, such as video cassettes and CDs, which now made their way into living rooms and children's bedrooms, were at first greeted with as much scepticism by both conservative and progressive pedagogues on account of their superabundance of colourful pictures and their trivial content as the gaming console and the 'Walkman', which also spread like wildfire. But the objections of people like this had less and less impact on the public. On the contrary, electronic devices were some of the most successful consumer articles of the eighties, and that was particularly true for the 'computer', which did arouse apprehensions because of the wave of office rationalisation it was expected to produce, but also became the symbol and motivating force behind a new optimism, evoking a fresh enthusiasm for technology. By 1990, there were already almost 4 million computers in West Germany, though they were not able to communicate with one another at that stage, since it was only after 1995 that the World Wide Web began to spread, and in fact in the Federal Republic it only caught on after the millennium. It had been imagined and feared in the 1980s that computerisation would function as a process directed and supervised from above, by the state, for instance. Instead, a process of playful appropriation and conversion to other uses took place from below. Many schools set up computer courses, it is true, but the acquisition of the new storage media by the predominantly youthful users happened at a much faster rate, which can only be compared with the adoption of radio by listeners in the 1930s and of television by viewers in the 1960s.[53]

From the late 1980s onwards, the world of the computer expanded tremendously, and its rise was soon almost unaffected by anti-consumerist and anti-technological criticisms. Rock music, which was formerly at the heart of the rebellious counter-culture, now lost its extra-musical significance and was reduced to functioning as a branch of an entertainment industry which was becoming more and more diverse and commercialised. One expression of this change was the 'video clip', a visual illustration of the music and a symbol of the entertainment culture of the 1980s. The music video, which soon developed its own stylistic idiom, did not convey youthful rebellion, as the former 'Beat Clubs' had done. It conveyed above all an invitation to buy the corresponding long-playing record or CD—the latter also an innovation of the 1980s. In the 1960s, advertisers had adopted the *motifs* and the aesthetic of revolt. Now rock music and its video clips took over the evocative forms of presentation of the advertising industry, whose importance increased by leaps and bounds in those years, and whose stylised aesthetic also exerted a strong influence on the cinema and on visual art. The advertisers' message was not focused on the use-value of the product but linked to promises of adventure and sophistication. Since everyday products differed very little in their use-value, the packaging made all the difference. The design of the product, the aesthetics of the surface appearance, linked the image of the product with the image of the buyer. The brand name signalled this connection. As if in an act of defiance, a culture of superficiality which was ironically, but above all pleasurably enjoyed replaced the decade of commitment, anti-consumerism and protest.[54]

Nowhere was this more apparent than in fashion. As in advertising and pop music, the fashion trends of those years were characterised by 'the desire to represent "life styles", the conversion of things into objects of worship, and the colourful diversity of "anything goes"'.[55] Two paradoxical developments came together here: on the one hand the trend towards individualisation, or the self-determined organisation of one's own life irrespective of social or cultural predispositions. On the other hand, there was the simultaneous removal of social differentiation in the middling social strata, people who became increasingly similar in income level and way of life, leaving aside the 5 per cent who were above them and the 15 per cent who were below them. This increased the importance of the 'fine distinctions' which signified individuality but also the desired membership of a cultural milieu, though this cultural milieu was more an imagined than a real community. It was no longer clothing that indicated a person's place in the social hierarchy or political attitude. It was lifestyle orientation, and now for the first time the brand names of firms such as 'Benetton', 'Nike' or 'Boss' were worn externally on a person's clothes so as to convey to the outside world the desired affiliation along with the lifestyle associated with it.

These manifold processes were bound up with the cultural globalisation or universalisation which was shown not only in the tendency towards the standardisation of musical tastes, dress styles and eating habits, but also in the mode of life people sought to adopt. Certainly, this expressed first and foremost the ability of the big American and European companies which dominated international markets to penetrate into people's minds. But this success was not just a reflection of the power of the market and of psychological manipulation. The consumer had to want, indeed to yearn for, the products which promised to associate their possessors with the Western style of life. Western consumer goods and the attitude to life associated with them were adapted and transformed by consumers all over the world in their own individual way. At the same time, however, these objects fed a worldwide tendency for styles of life and conceptions of morality to converge towards the example set by the Western metropolis. This applied to the way consumption was styled as the meaning of life, but also to the focus on particular images of beauty and youth, gender roles, individualism and dynamic activity.[56]

There is some dispute as to the degree to which the products of the global consumption industry also mediated the cultural values of the West. But it is noticeable that the period when the worldwide protest movement lost its impetus and Western popular culture extended its global reach was also the period when a new conception of morality and custom, of right and wrong, began to spread. This new conception had grown up in the metropolitan centres of the West, above all in the universities, and it was only loosely connected with the left-wing watchwords of the 1970s. The convention of universal morality which was now established no longer related primarily to the traditional social inequality between rich and poor but to a prohibition against discrimination because of sexual, physical, racial or religious deviations from the norm. The demand for the egalitarian levelling out of social differences came into conflict with the rule that a plurality of individual orientations should be accepted. The latter postulate proved so successful that it was given the epithet of 'political correctness' by conservatives in the USA and later on in Western Europe, who accused its supporters of reverting to a new 'terrorism of virtue'. While social inequality greatly increased in Western societies, an anti-discrimination policy prevailed, which interpreted the requirement of equality in a cultural rather than a social sense.[57]

In general, therefore, in the Federal Republic of the 1980s 'political culture'—a concept which is itself a product of the culturalisation of the political during that period—did not become more restrictive, as the Left had feared after Kohl came to power, but more self-confident, more relaxed and more cosmopolitan. It also became more superficial, more frivolous and more consumerist. The mood of pessimism referred to earlier also became less pronounced during the 1980s: on New Year's Eve 1981 only 32 per cent of those surveyed were broadly hopeful about the coming year, but by 1985 the figure had risen to 61 per cent, and by 1989 to 68 per cent.[58] This was because, apart from the improved economic situation, there was a prospect of an end to the Cold War, owing to the change in the international atmosphere after the coming to power of Gorbachev in the Soviet Union. In addition, the apocalyptic vision of the future, so popular in the early 1980s, had now faded away. Neither a repetition of Chernobyl nor the death of the forest had come to pass. No one sang 'No future' in summer 1989: the hit of that year was entitled 'Don't worry, be happy'.

The warnings of disaster and the anxieties over the dangers of modern life, which had been increasing since the mid-1970s, therefore now gave way gradually to a more relaxed attitude. The modern world, it was thought, was no longer prescribed from above but appropriated by the individual from below. Politics also became less sharply polarised, and the ideological bonds of the political camps lost their effectiveness. The effect of the multifarious processes of liberalisation and pluralisation had been to increase social integration, so that by the end of the decade there was no longer much trace of a radical rejection of the state by the Left. The conservatives, for their part, regarded the present state as their own—particularly as the Left had opposed it for so long—and they were therefore themselves liberalised along with it.

At the same time, the importance of national differences continued to decline in Western Europe. This applied to consumption, lifestyles, and the appearance and infrastructure of town and country, as well as the dominant position of the motor car, state-provided social benefits, transformed gender relations and evening television programmes. These features of the Western way of life were combined in the Federal Republic with a particularly well-marked endeavour to become the same as everyone else, in other words, to have a normal society and a normal state with the usual problems and successes. The Federal Republic had finally acknowledged its own existence as a political and cultural entity—a process already completed long before as far as the economy was concerned. In that sense, West Germany's present had become normalised. But not its past, as was soon to become apparent.

## The Return of History

Until the late 1970s, the big questions of recent German history were still felt to be part of the present. This was as true of the unsolved national question as it was of the National Socialist dictatorship and the development of industrial society, for three reasons. Firstly, the division of Germany had not until then been accepted as a part of normal existence. The de facto recognition of the GDR was still too fresh, the after-effects of the bitter debates over the Eastern treaties were still too strongly felt, for people to regard the parallel existence of the Federal Republic and the GDR as anchored in history. Secondly, half of all

West Germans living in the 1970s had themselves experienced the Nazi regime as adults or children, and the overwhelming majority of the Nazi perpetrators, big and small, were still alive, so that the National Socialist antecedents of the present possessed an actuality which was often repressed but always perceptible. This indicates how youthful the Nazi movement once was, but it also explains why the history of the Nazi regime was taught for so long with the names of places and individuals omitted. Thirdly, classical industrial society, with its focus on coal and steel production and the creation of a mass army of unskilled workers was still such a familiar and routine feature of the present that even the mass redundancies and factory closures of those years were not seen as a sign of the impending end of this economic and social formation but as the simple expression of an economic downturn, of the kind that took place in 1967 and 1974.

Between 1979 and 1985, this state of mind began to change. As usual, the transformation of a period previously regarded as belonging to the present into a historical epoch was not a sudden occurrence. But it did take place relatively quickly, and this is probably the most important reason why the 1980s and also the 1990s were dominated so strongly by public debate on history, above all contemporary history.[59]

Changes in the perception of classical industrial society had already appeared on the horizon in the 1970s. The debates over the architectural heritage of industrialism, in particular the big factory complexes and mining installations, but also over the many workers' housing estates, were advance indications of the change that was setting in. One can see this by looking at the dispute over the 'Eisenheim' housing estate in Oberhausen. This was built in the mid-nineteenth century for the workers of the neighbouring engineering company, Gutehoffnungshütte (GHH), and until the turn of the century it underwent a gradual expansion. Like most of the housing estates in the Ruhr it came to be regarded as a slum. The inhabitants were usually dependent on a single employer, who was also their landlord. The houses were small, they often had neither a kitchen nor a bath, and for a long time dirty water flowed directly into a gutter in front of the house. After the 1950s, these conditions, and the stigma of having to live in the 'colony', caused the inhabitants to regard these estates, which existed in large numbers wherever industry was located, as old-fashioned, indeed as anachronistic. For that reason, many old houses in the Eisenheim estate, and in many other places too, had already been demolished during the post-war era. In the late 1960s there was a plan to flatten the estate completely and replace it with more modern apartment blocks equipped with kitchens and bathrooms, very much to the satisfaction of the inhabitants. As the local press wrote enthusiastically: 'Here the oldest "colony" of the GHH will be charmed away at a stroke. The old Eisenheim will be unrecognisable, so to speak, when the job is finished.'[60]

In the mid-1970s, however, resistance to this process began to grow. It was characteristic that this emerged out of a University of Bielefeld study group, which had originally only wanted to document the estate before it was torn up. The arguments in favour of the demolition of the ill-famed quarter were countered by references to the close social bond between the residents, and their deep roots in the local area. Things previously regarded as burdensome and disadvantageous, such as living in close proximity and being subjected to the supervision of your neighbours, were now classified as an expression of mature social relationships. A Citizens' Initiative was set up, and it campaigned to prevent the housing estate from being torn down. This brought Eisenheim to the attention of the whole country, and eventually it became the first housing estate to be placed under a preservation order. It was preserved and modernised, and the Eisenheim Citizens' Initiative soon became a model for many other similar associations for the preservation of old working-class colonies.

The Eisenheim case echoed the growing change of direction in architecture and housing development towards the retention of historic architectural structures. This was also accompanied by symptomatic changes in the perception of working-class life. Historians became more interested in the old industrial structures once they were in decline. What had long been regarded as shabby and antiquated was now increasingly felt to be an expression of proletarian community spirit which was worthy of preservation. The working class, perceived by the Left for decades as the revolutionary subject of future transformation, was now an object of historical investigation. Workers' houses, workers' pubs, working conditions above ground or below ground, in short the everyday life of the industrial workers and their families now occupied the centre of interest, and this interest was by no means limited to historians alone.[61]

The turn to 'the history of the everyday' (*Alltagsgeschichte*) was also associated with a changed understanding of the nature of the subject. It was now considered that the history of the workers and their families should not be written *about* them but *with* them, as a process of joint recollection, but also strengthened self-awareness and pride in their 'own history'. The 'Hochlarmark Reader' was a particularly striking example. This was a book about a workers' housing estate in Recklinghausen, written during 1980 and 1981 by the inhabitants together with a group of historians and social scientists, and it contained their recollections and photographs, and descriptions of the modes of life and work of their parents and grandparents, covering the whole period up to the present day. There were initiatives of this kind in many places, and a genuine historical movement gradually arose out of this. A number of history workshops were founded, and soon local history publications appeared everywhere about the history of industry and working-class life 'on the ground'.[62]

When they examined the way of life of the 'little people', the historians of the everyday were often surprised to discover contradictions and inconsistencies which could not be brought into harmony with classical working-class history, and these helped them to escape both from the social historian's arithmetical approach to class and social stratification and from the concentration on heroic figures often met with in socialist working-class history.[63]

It can well be understood that this development did not proceed without disagreement and controversy. Criticism was directed above all at the romanticised and idyllic picture of the industrial past that emerged from this historicising look at what had shortly before been familiar and customary. This criticism was not without validity. The trend towards a 'history of the everyday' was linked to the rediscovery of the concept of the '*Heimat*' (homeland), which was now no longer understood in terms of the peasantry and its native soil or the vast lands in the East but as a private place of retreat, providing protection from progress and alienation. This approach was also inherent in the fight conducted by many regional Citizens' Initiatives against industrial projects.

There was nothing specifically German about this shift in perspective. The call to 'dig where you are standing' was a Swedish initiative aimed at the international integration of research in local and everyday history. There were similar movements in Italy and Great Britain, as also in the USA. In all these places, the focus on the region, the neighbourhood, daily life and the individual could be regarded as a cultural reaction to the rationalising and modernising impulses of previous decades as well as to the evident breakdown of the 'grand narratives' of the past, particularly Marxism.

Nevertheless, the results of the history of daily life as practised in the Federal Republic differed somewhat from those experienced in other countries. What the West German historians of daily life uncovered in their interview projects and neighbourhood investigations was not the life of a people united in class struggle, nor the idyll of an unalienated proletarian community, but stories of war and nightly bombing raids, experiences on the front line, service in the Hitler Youth and post-war hunger. No idylls were on display here, and no clear victim–perpetrator relations emerged. People discovered that their own part of town, their own next-door neighbour, father or great uncle had a Nazi past which until then had usually been carefully kept secret, but could also not be fitted into the dichotomy of 'persecution and resistance', which was the way most of the exhibitions of the 1970s about the Nazi era continued to be presented.

Other topics and questions now came up in the course of these studies, and they soon became the subject of ever wider public discussion. There were questions about the present whereabouts of Jews from one's own town, about the way 'alien workers' (*Fremdarbeiter*) were treated on the farms and in the collieries, about men's wartime experiences in Eastern and Western Europe, and about women's experiences on the 'home front'. Evidently, enough time had now elapsed for difficult questions to be posed about 'one's own history'. What was new, above all, was that a younger generation was prepared to grapple seriously with the experiences of older people during the Nazi era and not just to treat them as a political foil for the argument over the impact of the Third Reich. In schools, universities and archives, and in editorial boards and courts of law, former Nazi activists had often prevented a personalised confrontation with the Nazi era. Now their direct influence had been broken, and it therefore became possible to focus on individual attitudes and actions below the level of the top Nazi leadership.[64]

Hence the endeavour to create a history of industrial society in the Federal Republic was combined in a curious way with the historical analysis of National Socialism, and this also involved a return to the concrete. There was, admittedly, a risk that an approach which started from the day-to-day experiences of the participants might have led to the adoption of a sham neutrality and a position halfway between the perpetrators and the victims. In fact, however, it meant the beginning of a long and sustained phase of research and public analysis of the Nazi period, in the course of which West German society attained a more concrete awareness and an expanded and deepened knowledge of the subject. In the wake of these endeavours, a number of memorial sites were freshly erected and demands started to be raised for the payment of compensation to the 'forgotten victims' of National Socialism, while many popular works as well as scholarly writings about the Nazi era were published, some of them in large print-runs. But this was above all a journey of historical self-discovery from below, which initially arose from the protest initiatives of democrats at the grass-roots level, and had no connection with the activities of professional researchers in the universities. Soon, however, this movement also made its way into the universities and the research institutes. The discovery of what was in any case self-evident, namely, that the personal lives of 'the people' stretched back beyond the year 1945, thus became the starting point for a process of critical self-reflection by West German society on its past history.

The newly elected federal government was itself also concerned to strengthen the historical consciousness of its citizens, though its reasons and objectives were very different. The point of departure here was the realisation, not least by Chancellor Kohl himself, that a growing section of the West German population, particularly younger people, had largely come to terms with the division of Germany, accepted the GDR as a separate state, and was beginning to move away from the sense of belonging to a common nation with the East Germans. German history should not be reduced to the Nazi era, it was now said, and the history of the Federal Republic should not be left to its critics, 'because this history is being systematically altered in seminars on contemporary history held in German universities'.[65] Kohl himself had a doctorate in history, and right from the start of his chancellorship he mounted a whole series of historical initiatives against these tendencies. The aim was to establish a new historical identity for the Germans, reaching back before the Nazi period, which would offer a perspective of German unity. This was intended to combine self-confidence and pride in what had been achieved with the memory of the German past. Only in this way, calculated the head of the government, could a consciousness of the continued existence of the German nation and a desire for its reunification be kept alive despite the existing division into two states.

Unsurprisingly, the memory of the Nazi regime and the crimes committed by the Germans on a mass scale during the Second World War proved to be an obstacle to this attempt to establish a new national and historical awareness. Even the initiative to establish a central memorial in Bonn demonstrated the problems involved in such an approach. It was intended that this memorial would not distinguish between perpetrators and victims but rather refer to all the people of the time as victims of 'war and dictatorship'—soldiers and civilians, Germans and Jews, as well as the inhabitants of countries occupied by Germany. There were protests against this assumed parallelism, which were further fuelled by the Chancellor's other initiatives and by his frequently questionable choice of words in commemorative speeches. Thus, when he visited Israel in 1984 he spoke of being in 'the fortunate position of having been born late', which was understood to mean that Kohl's generation of wartime 'flak helpers', not to mention all those Germans who were born even later, no longer felt responsible for the legacy of the Third Reich. Then, in summer 1985, Kohl agreed to participate in a meeting of Silesian exiles in Germany, which was organised under the watchword 'Forty Years of Expulsion—Silesia Remains Ours' and was perceived as a hostile refusal to compromise with Poland.[66]

People were therefore quick to interpret Chancellor Kohl's historical endeavours as an attempt to escape from the burden of the Nazi past. The history of the Nazi regime had played little significant role in the public discussions of the 1970s. Now it entered the centre of cultural and political debate, entirely against Kohl's own wishes, but thanks to his actions. As early as 1979, when the television series 'Holocaust' was transmitted, it gained unexpectedly high viewing figures, which showed that more attention was being paid to the Nazi past. In addition, the sensational publication in *Stern* of the alleged diaries of Hitler (which soon turned out to be a crude forgery) indicated that after the 'generation of contemporary witnesses' had left professional life, a new interest in the Nazi era had grown up which was no longer a result of direct experience.

Preparations for the fortieth anniversary of the end of the war, which fell on 8 May 1985, began under these auspices. Unlike ten years earlier, the commemorative events received much media attention. A discussion had already arisen beforehand as to whether Germany had been 'defeated' or 'liberated' on that day in 1945. In this context the very different perspectives associated with this choice of alternatives quickly became commingled. If the perceptions of the Germans themselves in 1945 were examined, it could not be ignored that they had been defeated, and that most of them felt they had been defeated. Only later on did they realise that this defeat also meant personal liberation. In 1985, however, various different historical meanings were attached to the event, and they coincided with the division between Left and Right. When the Left maintained that 1945 was a liberation, it was emphasising the perspective of the victims of National Socialism. It placed itself in their tradition, and it forced the entire German people into that tradition, after the event. When the conservatives asserted that 1945 had been a defeat, this was a way of stressing national continuity and at the same time assigning absolute value to the perceptions of contemporaries.[67]

The anniversary speech by the President of the Federal Republic Richard von Weizsäcker on 8 May 1985, had an exceptional significance for this discussion. It was greeted with extraordinary attention and approval, above all because he commemorated all the victims of the war and the policy of extermination, including those who until then had not been listed in the canon of the official commemoration policy—for example, the forced labourers, the communists, the Sinti and Roma, and the victims of compulsory sterilisation. One section of the West German public, which was now diminishing in number, saw this as a provocation. The majority, however, and all foreign observers, celebrated von Weizsäcker's speech as an act which liberated history from politics. Admittedly, he only spoke of the perpetrators in very general terms. An unprejudiced treatment of the various groups of victims was now possible, but it was evidently too early to treat the Nazi perpetrators and the issue of the mass support of the German people for the regime in the same manner.[68]

The 8 May 1985 day of commemoration was organised by the Chancellor's Office as a symbolic gesture of reconciliation between former wartime opponents. In the late summer of 1984, on the seventieth anniversary of the start of the First World War, Kohl and Mitterrand had symbolically redefined the conquest of the past by shaking hands over the graves of the fallen soldiers of both sides at the cemetery of Verdun, though this ceremony was also a kind of compensation for the failure to invite the Germans to the D-Day commemorations of July 1984 in Normandy.[69] Referring to this, Kohl now told the Americans that he would like a similar symbolic gesture, this time in relation to the *Second* World War, with the justification that by now two-thirds of Germans had either not experienced the war at all, or only as children. As a parallel to Verdun, a military cemetery which seemed appropriate as a symbolic location for the German and American soldiers who fell in the Second World War was selected as the setting for the ceremony. This was Bitburg in the Eifel region, the burial place of the Germans who fell in the 'Ardennes Offensive' of December 1944. It was soon discovered that members of the Waffen-SS were also buried at Bitburg. Until then, there had not been much interest among the US public in Ronald Reagan's planned visit to Germany. Now, however, the journey very quickly became a political event, under the heading 'Waffen-SS'. The idea that the American President was visiting a German cemetery to honour soldiers of the Waffen-SS (possibly including members of the units which on 17 December 1944 had committed the 'Malmédy Massacre' of eighty-seven American prisoners of war) aroused fierce protests, not least from young American Jews. Elie Wiesel, who had survived the Nazi extermination camps as a child, now came forward to speak on their behalf. By visiting Bitburg, he said, President Reagan was 'honouring the SS'. Many American newspapers and members of the American Congress came out in support of Wiesel. The government responded by combining Reagan's Bitburg visit with a prior trip to the former concentration camp of Bergen-Belsen, though this did not cause any of the criticisms to die down.[70]

The American President's travels were of great interest to the West German public, particularly after Kohl had described the possible cancellation of the Bitburg visit as an 'insult' which would be 'deeply wounding to the feelings of our nation'. The Freiburg historian Heinrich August Winkler, on the other hand, feared that the meeting between Reagan and Kohl in the Eifel would give the impression that 'the Federal Republic of Germany and the United States of America had agreed henceforth to look upon the Second World War as a normal European war.' Never since the establishment of the Federal Republic had German–American relations been as strongly affected by the Nazi past as during this state visit.[71]

Thus, Kohl's attempt to put the Nazi era firmly in the past by an act of symbolic reconciliation did not lead to the national unity he desired. On the contrary, the repression and reinterpretation of the past now gave place to a greater degree of interest, a new sensibility, which led the National Socialist background of the Federal Republic and in particular the continuity of personnel, to be regarded as a burden and a scandal. Right-wing critics continued to oppose this view. Friedrich Karl Fromme, one of the editors of the *Frankfurter Allgemeine Zeitung*, complained that 'in the case of the Jews' the 'otherwise freely permitted division of one's fellow humans into people one likes and people one doesn't like so much' is forbidden to the Germans. Young Germans, he added, have really gone to great pains to help the Jews. But it has to be granted 'that their patience has its limits'.[72]

It was against this political background that there developed in 1986–7 what is known as the 'historians' quarrel' (*Historikerstreit*). This was ignited by two polemical theses put forward by the Berlin historian Ernst Nolte. He postulated that there was a causal connection between the mass crimes committed in the Soviet penal system, the 'Gulag archipelago' and the launching of the mass murder of the Jews by the Germans during the Nazi era: 'Wasn't the "Gulag Archipelago" primary to Auschwitz? Wasn't the "class murder" of the Bolsheviks logically and factually prior to the "racial murder" of the National Socialists?' Since the Gulag was 'primary to' Auschwitz, he said, there was a 'causal nexus' between them. Nolte interpreted the Holocaust as a presumed act of self-defence by the European bourgeoisie against the predicted desire of the Bolsheviks to annihilate it. In saying this, he confirmed the National Socialists' identification of the Jews with Bolshevism and reduced National Socialism to a variant of radical anti-Bolshevism. In addition, he described the 'declaration of war' on National Socialist Germany by the Jewish World Congress in 1939 as the beginning of a formal state of war between Jews and Germans, and another factor to be taken into account in assessing the murder of the Jews.[73]

These statements provoked a storm of indignation in Germany and elsewhere. The controversy soon gave rise to a multitude of public declarations and diversified into several separate debates. The first attack was launched by Jürgen Habermas. He related Nolte's theses directly to Kohl's policy towards history:

> The planners of ideology want to create a consensus about the revivification of a national consciousness, and at the same time they must banish the negative images of the German nation-state from the domain of NATO. Nolte's theory offers a great advantage for this manipulation. He hits two flies with one swat. The Nazi crimes lose their singularity in that they are at least made comprehensible as an answer to the (still extant) Bolshevist threats of annihilation. The magnitude of Auschwitz shrinks to the format of technical innovation and is explained on the basis of the 'Asiatic' threat from an enemy that still stands at our door.[74]

In the debate that subsequently erupted, however, there was no public discussion of evidence-based positions. Instead, political conclusions from the Nazi era were transported from there into the debate and treated as if they applied to the present day. Thus, the *Historikerstreit* took on the role of a proxy war between the rival political camps of the Federal Republic. What was primarily at stake here was whether the Nazi past, and in particular the murder of the Jews, would lose its significance for West German society in the course of time, or whether it would become a kind of reverse state rationale of the Federal Republic.

But, at the same time, many of the public declarations made during the *Historikerstreit* were also deeply marked by personal memories and past suffering: the death of a brother, the horror of war, the experience of being driven out of your home. Here it became apparent that when the history and politics of the Nazi regime were being examined, individual experiences, traumas and injuries had remained in the private realm, and had not been publicly discussed or processed. This intersection between political attitudes towards the Nazi era and the memories and experiences of individuals left behind distortions which now became visible and also had an impact on the verdict of historical scholarship.[75]

An additional discovery, which was surprising at first, was that the debate lacked an adequate scientific basis. In the long run, neither of the main approaches to the interpretation of the Nazi regime which had usually been adopted in the Federal Republic had proved to be either plausible or authoritative. This applied both to the interpretation of the events as a 'German catastrophe', which explained National Socialism and its crimes as part of a false route towards modernity, and to the view that reduced the Nazi regime to 'Hitler's dictatorship', alongside which all other factors were secondary. Until then, the murder of the Jews had not been at the centre of historical research, and there was little awareness of the origin and course of this mass murder either among the historical profession or the wider public.

From the late 1960s onwards, however, a new approach emerged towards the interpretation of the Holocaust. Previously, the view was widely held that the initiation, radicalisation and implementation of the genocide could be reduced to a simple progression from 'ideological motivation' to 'political implementation', and that Hitler alone was ultimately responsible. The new view was that the genocide had taken shape gradually over the years between 1940 and 1942 in the course of a dynamic process. This thesis, developed most notably by Martin Broszat and Hans Mommsen, led to fierce controversy, particularly because the regime's (and Hitler's) self-presentation clashed with the results of an analysis of the mechanism by which it ruled. Even so, this approach, like the previous ones, increased the visibility of structures and modes of operation rather than concrete places and actions. In addition, the analysis was so strongly concentrated on proceedings within the German leadership that no clear outline of the victims emerged and they appeared as mere objects of the extermination policy, interchangeable at will. Despite all the differences, therefore, this line of interpretation, path-breaking as it was in many respects, stood in the post-1945 German tradition of avoiding concrete details.[76]

West German historical scholarship had not until then been able to establish a firm foundation of knowledge about the initiation, implementation and extent of the mass murder of the Jews, or about its participants, and on that basis to draw up a serious interpretative framework. Hence discussions about the murder of the Jews had the character of purely symbolic value statements. The events themselves were condemned for their barbarous and criminal character, but no one felt the need to obtain more precise knowledge about them.

At that point, however, the *Historikerstreit* entered a second episode, which was of greater scientific significance. This was reflected in an exchange of letters between the Israeli historian Saul Friedländer and the director of the Munich-based Institute of Contemporary History, Martin Broszat.[77] Friedländer criticised Broszat, and German historians in general, for failing to take the murder of the Jews as a starting point when examining National Socialism, and consequently for failing to make it the focus of their interpretation. As a result, he said, they reduced the murder of the Jews to an event in *German* national history, and did not make the perspective of the victims a constituent part of their historical observations. But his most important point was that German historians regarded a presentation of the Holocaust from the perspective of the victims as 'subjective' and 'unscientific', while treating analyses of the motives and actions of the perpetrators as genuine examples of historical science.

This discussion had definite implications for the German view of history, and it led to a paradigm shift in the academic debate over the history of the Nazi regime, which was soon followed by a change in the terms of public discussion. The initiation and implementation of the murder of the Jews now started to replace the Nazi seizure of power in 1933 and the beginning of the Second World War as central events that needed explanation. As well as this, the perception of the genocide by its victims started to be examined side by side with the motives of the responsible figures and the direct perpetrators on the German side, not simply for moral reasons but to promote an overall understanding of what had occurred, not just an understanding of the logic that determined the perpetrators' action. It is this change of perspective that constitutes the more long-term significance of the *Historikerstreit*. It allowed the Germans, as Germans, not only to examine the National Socialists' policy of mass murder in the context of subsequent developments, but also to distance themselves from the events and to join in mourning for the victims.

During the next twenty or so years the confrontation with the Nazi past was a constant theme of domestic debate in the Federal Republic. Thus, movements from both above and below which aimed at transforming history had a completely different effect from that originally intended on either side of the debate.

## Germany, the Soviet Union and the End of the Cold War

On 22 November 1983, the German Bundestag voted by a majority, made up of the coalition parties, to station American intermediate-range nuclear missiles on the territory of the Federal Republic, after the disarmament negotiations between the USA and the Soviet Union had turned out to be unsuccessful.[78] In the months preceding this decision, the conflict over the 'weapons upgrade' (*Nachrüstung*) had come to a head once again. By deciding to deploy nuclear weapons the new government wanted not only to demonstrate its own political effectiveness but also to confirm that the Federal Republic was anchored in the Western alliance. The SPD was deeply divided. The left wing, around Oskar Lafontaine, demanded Germany's exit from NATO and a political general strike against the deployment of nuclear weapons. The right wing insisted that it was after all Helmut Schmidt who was the first to criticise the USSR for increasing its intermediate-range missile stocks and to say that either the Soviets should disarm or the weapons of the Americans should be upgraded. The majority of the SPD, however, were inclined to oppose the measure. They regarded themselves as a part of the peace movement, which included sections of the Protestant and Catholic Churches and of course the Greens, whose programme was entirely concentrated during those years on opposing nuclear weapons deployment and calling for nuclear power stations to be decommissioned.

In the weeks and months before the Bundestag made its decision on the issue, there were again immense demonstrations. In fact, they were the biggest in West Germany's history. The Easter Marches of April 1983 attracted more than half a million people. Demonstrations, protest marches and 'peace actions' took place all over the country that summer. On 22 October, more than a million people took part in the action against nuclear weapons deployment. In Baden-Württemberg, approximately 200,000 formed a human chain between Stuttgart and Neu-Ulm.

But the protest movement fell apart relatively quickly after the parliament had made its decision. In this respect, there was a clear parallel with what had happened to the campaign against the emergency laws after the Bundestag had voted for them on 30 May 1968. The actual stationing of the missiles, which began in December 1983, was accompanied, it is true, by numerous actions on the part of the peace movement, in the Swabian town of Mutlangen for example. But the movement was deprived of its momentum after 1985 by the new and sensational disarmament proposals of the Soviet leader Mikhail Gorbachev and the negotiations that followed between the USA and the Soviet Union. It was obvious that the movement had failed to achieve its objective, which was to prevent the stationing of the missiles. There is no doubt, however, that it radically changed perceptions of the strategy of nuclear deterrence in the Federal

Republic and beyond, and that it contributed to delegitimising the concept of the balance of terror. In addition, and this was not the least of its contributions, the existence of the West German peace movement and the political climate it generated played a decisive part in the formation of the peace movement in the GDR, and this developed into one of the core elements of the emerging opposition movement against the SED dictatorship.

The government's decision to station nuclear missiles improved the German–American relationship and strengthened the role of the Federal Republic in the Western alliance. This was also urgently necessary, because under Schmidt and Carter, German–American relations had entered a period of crisis. Even so, divergences between the two allies had not been removed completely. The harshly anti-American tone of the West German debate over the nuclear missiles and the aspiration to leave NATO and adopt a position 'equidistant' from both Great Powers, which extended as far as leading circles in the SPD, marked one side of this problem; the divergence of economic interests, especially the rapidly growing budget deficit of the USA, and American criticisms of European subsidy policy, marked the other. In this situation, the Bundestag's vote in favour of stationing the missiles was understood in the USA as a pledge of West Germany's continued membership of the Western alliance. This gave the Federal Republic a certain room for manoeuvre in its foreign and German policy, which it certainly needed in view of the deterioration in the international situation.

This was because the most important consequence of the decision to upgrade the nuclear arsenal was a manifest worsening of relations between East and West. It set off an ice age in international politics, the effects of which were serious and in November 1983 absolutely unforeseeable. This applied in particular to the relationship between the Soviet Union and the Federal Republic. The nuclear weapons decision was interpreted in Moscow as a hostile act by West Germany against the USSR, and the country's attitude was seen as part of the Reagan administration's policy of arms expansion and international intimidation. Another factor was the Moscow leaders' disappointment over the failure of the West German peace movement, which they had supported as much as they could, having placed great hopes on its success. From a distance of over thirty years, it is now clear how important the peace movement was for Moscow, because by the end of the 1970s it was only with great difficulty that the Soviet Union could keep up with America's armaments programme. If the stationing of nuclear missiles in West Germany could be prevented with the help of the Western peace movement, this would perhaps provide a further reprieve and allow some scope for urgently needed measures of domestic modernisation to be carried out. As this did not happen, the Moscow leadership continued to be subjected to extreme pressure by the arms race, and it had very few means of combating this.[79]

The extent of the deterioration in relations between Moscow and Bonn was something the world public learned a year later, when a long-planned visit by Honecker to the West German capital had to be cancelled under Soviet pressure. Until then, relations between the two Germanies had developed in an entirely positive manner, despite the icy conditions prevailing in world politics. The Kohl–Genscher government had adopted the previous government's policy towards the German question, and in view of the current situation, which was evidently unalterable even in the long term, it continued to cultivate a pragmatic policy of coexistence, with the primary objective of securing an improvement in the living conditions of people in the GDR. At the same time, however, Kohl emphasised more strongly than his two predecessors the political and moral distance that separated him from the East German state. The federal government firmly rejected the four demands for a change of policy made by Honecker in 1980, which were the closure of the Central Registry of State Judicial Administrations set up in Salzgitter to monitor GDR human rights violations, the recognition of GDR citizenship, the conversion of the 'permanent representation' of the Federal Republic in the GDR into a normal embassy and finally an adjustment of the state boundary which ran along the river Elbe. On all other matters, though, the federal government was prepared to hold discussions.[80]

In view of the worsening economic problems suffered by the GDR after 1980, a basic model of relations between the two Germanies developed, which passed through a number of different variants. The federal government feared that any further deterioration of the economic situation in the GDR would produce a situation similar to that experienced in Poland, and a political crisis with unpredictable consequences might grow out of this. In comparison with this prospect, the stabilisation of the SED regime with the help of financial credits seemed the lesser evil. The West German side was also reacting against the effective boycott of the Eastern bloc countries by Western credit institutions, after Poland had declared itself bankrupt in 1981 and Romania too had ceased to be able to cover its foreign debts. The federal government did however expect substantial concessions from the GDR leadership in relation to the living conditions, and particularly the travel restrictions, suffered by GDR citizens, as well as improved border arrangements.

It was the prime minister of Bavaria who set off this process of rapprochement. Strauß's urge to play a role in foreign policy, for personal rather than political reasons, was a recurrent feature of the Bonn political scene during those years. He was capable of criticising the policies of the SED with inimitable ferocity, but he used personal connections to engineer the granting of a credit of a billion DM to the GDR, and he insisted that the Federal Republic itself stand as a guarantor. A few months later, in return, the GDR began to clear away the automatic firing devices installed at its borders, and in 1984 it permitted 34,000 people to emigrate legally to the Federal Republic, more than three times as many as in all the previous years taken together. This was followed by a credit of another billion DM from the West.[81]

What was remarkable about this was not only the lack of embarrassment with which money was exchanged for human rights, but also the fact that the federal government made advance payments without securing a contractual obligation in return. It was therefore placing its faith in East German trustworthiness, a faith the GDR did its best to avoid disappointing. In the context of the worsening confrontation between the Cold War blocs, this strengthening of trust between the two German states was internationally unique, and it led to renewed speculation about the future of the German question. The motives of both sides, however, were simpler than this: they thought that if they were drawn along in the wake of the escalating East–West confrontation, this would inevitably result in both a further worsening of the economic situation in the GDR and a withdrawal of the human rights concessions made earlier. It was in the interest of both sides to avoid these consequences.

They also had a certain degree of success in this aim. The GDR was, it is true, affected by the Western embargo on the export of advanced technology, but trade between the two Germanies continued to increase. The number of GDR citizens who visited the Federal Republic also increased, as did the number of West Germans who made journeys in the opposite direction. In political terms, the formula of 'a community of responsibility' was coined, though this did not express anything more than the will to achieve peace, in a situation where the two German states had no influence over the armament or disarmament policies of the two superpowers with which they were respectively allied. In this phase of broadening pragmatic cooperation between the two German states, the cancellation of Honecker's visit to Bonn in September 1984, owing to Soviet objections, was a setback which made clear that a separate development of German–German relations was impossible within the context of the confrontation between the blocs. On the contrary, by forcing Honecker to abandon his visit, the Soviet Union showed its absolute opposition to any further rapprochement between the two German states, which it suspected might lead the GDR to become dependent on the Federal Republic.

Two years after the government coalition of liberals and conservatives came to power in West Germany, therefore, it was faced with markedly unfavourable conditions in foreign policy in general and policy towards the German question in particular. The discord between West Germany and the United States had been reduced somewhat by the stationing of nuclear missiles in the country, but there continued to be conflicts of interest in economic and financial matters. Relations with the Soviet Union were worse than they had been at any point since the 1960s, and the pragmatic cooperation between Bonn and East Berlin had been seriously damaged by the cancellation of the Honecker visit.

In addition, the process of European unification was also in crisis. It was paralysed by far-reaching differences over financial and agricultural matters, and for years there had not been a single step forward. It is true that Helmut Kohl, unlike Helmut Schmidt, who had always been critical of Brussels, was an enthusiastic pro-European, repeatedly emphasising the ideological and historical aspects of European unification. But in fact the scope for political initiatives in this direction had narrowed considerably, owing to the economic crisis which had lasted almost continuously since 1973–4 in most parts of the European Community. National interests were dominant. This was true in the case of the continuing dispute over the financial contribution of Britain to the EC, which the Thatcher government regarded as far too high, not entirely without reason. It was also true with regard to the continuing currency problems and the EC's eternal apple of discord, agricultural policy, which in 1984 comprised an immense 71 per cent of the EC budget, and had led to an almost irresistible increase in subsidies for excess agricultural production. In European public opinion the EC was practically identified with butter mountains and milk lakes.[82]

Moreover, clear reservations were also being expressed within the EC about the growing closeness of relations between the two Germanies, by people who had always had these views, but seldom previously uttered them in public. Thus the Italian Foreign Minister Andreotti warned of the danger of a renewal of 'Pan-Germanism', in the context of Honecker's planned visit to Bonn. The status quo, he said, must be maintained, so as not to endanger Europe's borders: 'There are two German states, and that is how it should remain.' In the Federal Republic this was felt to be a scandalous remark, and it put a cloud over German–Italian relations. But Andreotti had no doubt merely expressed what many people in Europe thought, notwithstanding all the trite declarations made about the Germans' right to self-determination.

At the end of 1984, therefore, whether one looked at the USA, the Soviet Union, the GDR or Europe, West Germany's foreign policy faced difficulties everywhere, and there seemed to be no way out.

Quite unexpectedly, however, an Eastern escape route suddenly opened up. . Ultimately, the reason for this change in political fortunes was to be sought in the epochal transformations of the period 1973 to 1983, which had already had a lasting impact on domestic conditions in the Western European countries, but had affected conditions in the USSR still more strongly. In the final decade of the Brezhnev Era, it became impossible to ignore the tremendous economic problems of the Soviet Union. The living standard of the population was stagnating, but a reduction in the resources allocated to industry and a long-term increase in expenditure on consumption was not possible owing to the high level of military spending. The government was therefore unable to remove the bottlenecks in the supply system. As a result, there was an increase in discontent, and the country's stability could only be guaranteed by repression and isolation from the outside world.[83]

The Soviet Union had, it is true, been able to earn more from the export of raw materials since the explosion of oil prices which followed the first oil price crisis of 1973–4, so that it now appeared to have a better starting point. On this basis, the Soviet government intended to modernise the infrastructure and the production facilities of the country. Urgently needed technological innovations now appeared possible. But, in practice, the cumbersome apparatus of the planning administration proved unable to carry through this sort of restructuring, and the technological gap with the West continued to grow in areas such as mechanical engineering, electronics and chemistry. The Soviets therefore had to rely on the purchase of Western technology. But this cost foreign currency, which put the country's finances under excessive strain. In this situation, it was even forced to stop delivering cheap oil to its Eastern bloc allies, and this substantially worsened their economic situation and political stability. Every fresh round of the arms race, which culminated in the stationing of intermediate-range missiles in West Germany, reduced the Soviet Union's room for manoeuvre in relation to economic reform and modernisation. The Western economies reacted dynamically to the crisis of 1973–82, engaging in a thorough transformation process, marked by the victorious advance of micro-electronics and communications technology, the globalisation of world trade and the integration of financial markets. The Soviet economy, on the other hand, which was built on heavy industry and the production of raw materials, had nothing of similar effectiveness to set against this.

The balance sheet of the five year plan which ended in 1984 was devastating: in almost all areas, the planned targets were not attained. Underfulfilment of the plan plumbed depths not seen since the year 1941. In his history of the Soviet Union, Manfred Hildermeier summarises the situation in the early 1980s as follows: 'It was neither a weakening of state authority nor a suppression of the desire for political freedom nor the push for national independence but a declaration of economic insolvency which lay at the root of the great crisis which would bring about the fall of the Soviet Union.'[84]

The Soviet population was accustomed to suffering, and there had been periods in which the economic situation of the country and the supply of essential commodities to the population had been much worse than in the 1980s, without causing the stability of the regime to be impaired. But since at least the time of Khrushchev the Soviet leadership had proclaimed that the Soviet Union would one day outpace the West in prosperity, and thus 'the legitimacy of the regime had become attached to the guarantee of prosperity', as the historian of Eastern Europe Dietmar Neutatz has stressed. 'By making this claim, they made themselves and their successors dependent on the fulfilment of their promises, and the less the Soviet economy was able to satisfy the population's increasing demands, the more questionable was the justification for the communist party's monopoly of power.'[85]

The conception of the state and the economy embedded in Soviet communist ideology had arisen as an alternative to capitalism and a response to the challenges of the age of heavy industry and mass production. It had achieved results in those areas, particularly in the field of industrialisation, though at the cost of terrible efforts and millions of victims. But while Western capitalism was constantly passing through metamorphoses and was always able to respond flexibly to new developments, the communist system remained in the grip of traditional industrialism. It lacked all the essential requirements for reacting to the new challenges of the modern world, characterised by globalisation, the service economy and cutting-edge technology. This was the reason for its ultimate collapse.

In March 1985, the Communist Party leadership reacted to these threatening developments by deciding that the young reformer Mikhail Gorbachev should be its new chief. Without a doubt, he was faced from the outset with a well-nigh Herculean task. The economic situation of the country had to be substantially improved, productivity had to be raised, the direction of planning had to be reversed, industry had to be modernised and the infrastructure had to be renewed. These were objectives which in hindsight would have been unachievable even under much more favourable circumstances. But both the will and the prerequisites were absent in the Soviet Union for a Chinese-style alternative, which was being put into effect at exactly this time. A dictatorship of capitalist modernisation was established in China under the control of the Communist Party. The Soviet *nomenklatura* was not ready for this. Gorbachev, its chosen leader, was therefore given the task of implementing a reform programme on the basis of the socialist planned economy in order to save it.[86]

To create sufficient financial leeway for these reforms to take place, a reduction in arms expenditure was absolutely unavoidable. This was the only way of setting free adequate resources within a short space of time. In that sense, Gorbachev's radical disarmament initiative, which came as a complete surprise to the West, was not a compensation for the lack of domestic reforms, or for their limited success, but rather a prerequisite for them. At the same time, the decision to end cheap oil exports showed that the Soviet Union, owing to its own plight, was unable to look after its interests in the allied states of the Eastern bloc in the way that it had done in previous decades. In particular, a military intervention in a rebellious satellite state, or even a credible threat of such an intervention, would have contradicted the current requirements of Soviet policy. Both developments, the disarmament initiative and the relaxation of pressure on the Warsaw Pact allies, lay in the logic, if not the intention, of the reform programme decided in 1985–6, which from that time onwards came to be synonymous throughout the world with the name of Gorbachev.

The events that followed took place at a speed which was as breathtaking for contemporaries as it continues to be for the retrospective observer. The starting-point of the process was Gorbachev's stated readiness to negotiate with the USA over particularly far-reaching steps towards disarmament. Large-scale measures of disarmament were already under discussion at the first summit meetings between Gorbachev and Reagan in November 1985 in Geneva and in 1986 in Reykjavik. Negotiations first took place over arms limitation, then over the complete elimination of nuclear weapons. In July 1986, it was agreed that all intermediate-range missiles should be included in the negotiations.

On 8 December 1987, the Intermediate-Range Nuclear Forces Treaty (INF Treaty) was signed by Reagan and Gorbachev. Both sides agreed to destroy all land-based nuclear missiles with a range of between 500 and 5,500 kilometres. This corresponded closely to the 'double zero solution' which had been described in NATO's 'double-track decision' of 1979 as a way to avoid the stationing of nuclear missiles in West Germany. By 1991, 846 American missiles and 1,846 Soviet missiles had been destroyed. This was a historically unprecedented development, which ended the Cold War and many decades of nuclear confrontation between the two superpowers.[87]

Unlike its tremendously rapid steps towards disarmament, the Soviet Union's attempts at domestic reform, which were publicised very energetically but greeted in the West with astonished disbelief, were entirely unsuccessful. In view of the entrenched structures of the planned economy, radical changes in the economic system could hardly be implemented, and certainly not in the short term. On the contrary, the economic situation in the Soviet Union began to deteriorate still further, productivity fell, shortages of goods became more noticeable, and discontent increased. But the loosening of censorship restrictions, which had hitherto been very harsh, and the toleration of a limited amount of critical public discussion led to the rapid growth of a public opinion, which had a dynamic effect on development within the country. What the Soviet Union now needed, however, was above all economic assistance from the West, and here the Federal Republic also became involved.

Relations between West Germany and the Soviet Union had remained tense even after Gorbachev had come to power. The Bonn government was sceptical about the political initiatives coming from the new boss of the Kremlin, and, in the words of the leader of the Union in the Bundestag, Alfred Dregger, it regarded them as nothing more than 'attempts to gain influence over the Western public by clever concealment of the truth, reinterpretation of the facts and propaganda'.[88] In October 1986, Chancellor Kohl gave an interview with the American news magazine *Newsweek* in which he compared Gorbachev with Goebbels. On the Soviet side there was uproar. Ministerial visits were cancelled, and sharp attacks were made on the federal government in the Soviet press. In view of the progress taking place in Soviet–American disarmament negotiations and the great sympathy with which Gorbachev's reform endeavours were greeted in the West, the Federal Republic was now almost isolated in its policy towards the East.

This did not change until the federal government specified its attitude to the disarmament question. The result of the negotiations in Geneva was a 'double zero solution' involving the destruction of all missiles of a range of over 500 kilometres. This again brought up the question of the particular threat posed to the Federal Republic by so-called tactical nuclear weapons of a range of less than 500 kilometres. The right wing of the Union was strongly opposed to the Geneva decision. But in view of the opportunity to obtain a degree of international disarmament which had never been achieved before, this specifically German concern was likely to put the Federal Republic in the position of a troublemaker, and an opponent of international reconciliation. Kohl and Genscher therefore finally declared their agreement with the Geneva disarmament proposals, against considerable opposition from within their own parties, although the question of the specific threat to Germany had not been resolved. In response, the Soviet side now said it was ready to re-enter discussions with the Federal Republic.[89]

The modernisation of the Soviet Union's economy and society continued to be the main focus of Gorbachev's interest. This made economic and technological cooperation with West Germany extremely important. When Kohl made his first state visit to Moscow, in October 1988, three years after Gorbachev had come to power, questions of economic, scientific and technological cooperation were intensively discussed, and the numerous treaties of cooperation which were concluded were largely related to those areas. This laid the foundation for a further improvement in relations, as the events of the next year would demonstrate.[90]

The question of the two Germanies played a subordinate role in these discussions. Even so, certain statements emanating from the General Secretary's circle of advisers led Germans to prick up their ears. Thus, a representative of the Soviet embassy to the United Nations said that the wall 'would soon no longer exist', and that 'it had reached the end of its days'.[91] But isolated remarks of this kind only became really significant in the context of Gorbachev's statement that each socialist country was free to go its own way. In April 1987, on a visit to Prague, he declared:

> We are also far from wanting to call on anyone to copy us. Every socialist country has its own specific character. The fraternal parties take account of national conditions in determining their political course . . . The independence of every party, its responsibility to its own people and its right to solve its own country's problems of development are for us self-evident principles.[92]

This was a clear departure from the Brezhnev Doctrine, and it was not the only one. The way thus seemed to lie open for the Eastern bloc states to pursue their own development independently of the Soviet Union. How far this independence would extend was something that would have to be tested in practice.

As far as the German question was concerned, it was obvious that the Soviet leadership had no clear strategy. Domestic reforms had the priority, because these ultimately involved the economic salvation of the country, or more precisely the regime. As the situation became more difficult, so the readiness of the Moscow leadership to make even far-reaching concessions increased, and since tremendous military, political and financial exertions were required to keep Soviet hegemony over the states of Eastern Europe, whose economies were also failing, it was not out of the question that the connection with the GDR might be loosened. But the time-scale of this development, and how far it would go, were as yet entirely unclear.

By signing the INF Treaty, the USA and the Soviet Union had made possible a wave of disarmament that had never been thought possible, and in practice they had brought the Cold War to an end. Gorbachev's abandonment of the Brezhnev Doctrine indicated that the countries of the Eastern bloc now had more room for manoeuvre. On the other hand, his policy of domestic reform had so far brought little success. The economic data in particular showed an alarmingly downward trend. At that time, however, it was impossible to foresee how these developments would unfold for the Soviet Union and what this would mean for the area it controlled.

## The Acceleration of European Integration

The deep-seated shock of the world economic crisis between 1973 and 1982 was also the reason why the process of European unification became imbued with fresh dynamism after the mid-1980s. The movement towards unification ran parallel with the opening up of the Soviet Union, and it brought about results of similar historical magnitude, although it gained far less public attention than Gorbachev's policies. In 1982, at the end of the crisis, both inflation and unemployment in the countries of the EC averaged around 10 per cent, national budgets were chronically overstretched and the effects of structural change would continue to be felt for many years to come. In addition, the European economy continued to be grossly out of balance. During the 1980s, GDP per person in the Federal Republic was roughly 30 per cent above the EC average. In France the figure was 15 per cent above, in Britain one per cent.[93] Moreover, Europe was by now a long way behind the USA and Japan in technological development, above all in the fields of information and communication. The Japanese challenge was seen in the European states as particularly dangerous, because the Japanese not only sold large numbers of motor vehicles in Europe but were even ousting European firms from the European market in the field of electronics. These challenges could not be overcome unless the Europeans joined together, not least because individual national markets were far too small for modern, and costly, production lines.

A second motive for strengthening European integration lay, as so often, in the anxieties of the other Europeans about West German economic domination. In France in particular there was a widespread fear of the ever-growing economic power of the West Germans. The new French president, the socialist François Mitterrand, therefore focused on achieving a closer economic association with the Federal Republic, which would both promote the modernisation of his own country's economy and prevent the conversion of West Germany's economic hegemony in Europe into political hegemony. But he was critical of any attempt to extend European integration into the political sphere, as advocated by the Germans, not least because he considered that this would endanger French national sovereignty.

The conditions for a renewed acceleration of the European project were not present until spring 1983, when Mitterrand changed his approach to economic policy. The replacement of a demand-oriented Keynesian policy by monetarist and supply-oriented conceptions had long been completed in most of the industrialised countries of the EC. In France, in contrast, the Mitterrand government, which was a coalition of socialists and communists, had at first continued to place its confidence in the old instruments of state intervention and deficit spending, although without success. Now, under the new French Finance Minister Jacques Delors, French economic policy also went over to the line of tax cuts and budget discipline, which meant that a common European economic policy would in future be much easier to put into effect. A year later, Mitterrand also changed his position on European political unity. Europe's closer economic integration would now be accompanied by political integration and a strengthening of European institutions. Since the federal government completely concurred with these ideas, a powerful engine for the acceleration of the European movement was now present in the shape of cooperation between the EC's two economically strongest states. This turned out to be the decisive factor.[94]

Developments now proceeded with astonishing rapidity. Between summer 1984 and February 1986, the Europeans were able to remove several of their more long-lasting problems from the agenda. After a long struggle, a compromise was found on the question of Britain's budget contribution. In addition, Greece was admitted into the EC, followed by Spain and Portugal. The process of European integration thus began to move forward again, and it now had a much broader territorial basis.

The first step was to deal with agriculture.But agricultural policy again turned out to be a major stumbling-block. The Community's budget was burdened to a completely unacceptable extent by the agricultural over-production stimulated by the EC subsidy policy. There were two possible ways of ending this situation. One was to leave things to the market, which would lead to a fall in the prices of agricultural products. The majority of members advocated this course. However, such a policy would have favoured large-scale agricultural enterprises, because they could produce their goods much more cheaply than family-owned farms. These would be ruined by the downward pressure on prices. The federal government wanted to prevent this outcome at all costs. Its slogan was: 'Preserve the family farm!' Social and ecological (and electoral) considerations played a role here, over and above economic ones. The other way of solving the problem was by applying *dirigisme*. The federal government argued in favour of this course. It supported restrictions on production and the setting aside of agricultural land, and it vetoed any other decision. Controversy over the question was so intense that it threatened the much-desired further development of the EC. The federal government then responded by softening its position. It accepted the suggested price reductions and expressed its readiness in turn to use the federal budget to subsidise family-owned farms in the Federal Republic. This involved annual payments of around 5 billion DM. It was the only way to resolve the impasse that had arisen in the EC and to speed up the work of integration. Here was a method which was repeatedly applied in the politics of European integration: the economically powerful Federal Republic would get around a deadlock by taking a disproportionately high share of the financial burdens. At the same time, the West German side could also be certain, on this occasion as well, that a deepening of economic cooperation would be of particular benefit to the strongest economic power in Europe, namely itself, and that it would soon recoup the financial contribution it had invested in order to achieve the compromise.[95]

The second step was taken in February 1986, after the agricultural obstacle had been overcome. By the 'Single European Act' (SEA) the member countries agreed to work towards establishing a single market within Europe. This was a great leap forward. It was proposed that by the end of 1992, goods, services and capital would be able to circulate within the EC area without tariff barriers, or any other barriers, and that restrictions on travel within the EC would also be abolished. In many respects preparations to meet this deadline were not yet well advanced, but the act of commitment was itself a breakthrough, because the separate governments thereby put themselves under pressure to dismantle all obstacles to trade and travel by a fixed date. It also appeared that the 'European Union' which they were now aiming to achieve would be above all an economic union, because coordination in foreign and security policy was referred to here in much less mandatory language. Once again, the main source of disagreement within the European Community became visible: the majority of member countries were interested first and foremost in economic integration and were essentially hesitant about strengthening political integration, whereas the Federal Republic insisted that you could not Europeanise the economy without Europeanising the political sphere, including economic policy. This conflict would henceforth occupy a central position in all the debates over deepening European integration.

The third step, finally, related to the sensitive issue of currency policy. As stated earlier, the EC countries (Great Britain excepted) had introduced the European Monetary System (EMS) at the beginning of 1979, so as to stabilise the European currencies and reduce the risk of currency fluctuations by establishing exchange rates which would be fixed but flexible within certain limits. The new system performed its function to some extent successfully, but it also had the result that the strongest currency in the EMS, the Deutschmark, rose to occupy the position of a European reserve currency. If there was inflation in a European country, this led either to its depreciation vis-à-vis the Deutschmark or to a loss of competitiveness. The influence of the Bundesbank as the guardian of the most stable currency in Europe grew considerably, and its decisions on interest rates were followed by most European countries. But the dominant position of the Bundesbank not only emphasised the economic disequilibrium of the EC, it also endangered its political balance.

The economic predominance of the Federal Republic began to increase still further after the West German economy, despite all its problems, emerged from the economic crisis of 1973–82 in a stronger position than most of the other European economies. West Germany's export surplus in relation to the other EC countries, which was 18.3 billion DM in 1983, had risen by 1980 to 80 billion DM. It became apparent that to achieve an economic union, which would be implied by the planned single market, it would not be sufficient merely to coordinate the European currencies. The idea of a European currency union, which had repeatedly been discussed since the Werner Plan of 1970 and the establishment of the EMS in 1979, now came under discussion once again.[96]

The advocates of a rapid move towards currency union believed that a common currency would exert enormous pressure on the individual countries to adapt themselves to a common policy: A European central bank would make it possible for national economic and financial policies to be both unified and coordinated. That was a process which would otherwise take a lot of time. French politicians were never shy about asserting that the all-powerful position of the German Bundesbank stood in the way of any further deepening of European integration. Most of the EC countries clearly hoped that a currency union would allow the whole Community to profit to a greater extent than before from German economic and financial strength and make it possible to remove economic disequilibria.

On the other hand, the opponents of a quick transition towards a currency union, above all the West German government, pointed to the risks that would be incurred by a unification of the currencies of national economies of widely differing characteristics. Economic policies in the individual countries continued to be extremely diverse, in relation to inflation and levels of taxation, for example. Currently, these differences, between higher and lower inflation, and stronger or weaker economic growth, for example, had an impact on individual national currencies which could if necessary be balanced out by revaluation or devaluation. A unified currency, on the other hand, would be split apart by these inconsistencies. The West German position was that a currency union could only arise after a long transitional phase, after the economic and financial policies of the individual countries had already become adjusted to each other and their economic performance had become approximately the same.

In the late 1980s, the idea of a currency union was also unpopular among the West German population, because its experience of the economic upsurge after 1948–9 was so closely bound up with the history of the Deutschmark. There was also the fear that in a currency union the German Bundesbank would lose its strong position, and it would therefore no longer be able to bar the way to inflationary tendencies in Europe, which met with far less opposition in the other EC countries than in the Federal Republic.

It was difficult to find a path that both sides of the argument, and in particular the French and the West Germans, regarded as practicable. A possible solution emerged when the French side agreed that the currency union would be organised in line with the principles put forward by West Germany as a binding framework for national economic and financial policy: central bank independence, uniform economic growth, price stability, balanced budgets, low unemployment, and the ultimate goal of achieving a uniform living standard throughout Europe. In Bonn, therefore, the view now prevailed that under such conditions there was no longer any objection in principle to a currency union. In June 1988 the European heads of government, meeting in Hanover, agreed to make a start with the concrete preparations. It was, however, still an open question whether it would be possible to find a viable basis, shared by all EC members, for this project. There was also uncertainty about the amount of time it would take to establish a common currency.

The extraordinary acceleration of the process of European integration between 1984 and 1988 was a political miracle in a class of its own. In view of the stagnation and the numerous setbacks the Community had experienced in the previous ten years, no one writing in the early 1980s would have dared to predict such a development. It was predominantly economic factors which contributed to the tremendous increase in the desire to achieve European union, and pushed traditional nationally oriented reservations into the background for a number of years. The dynamics of globalisation had made it clear that the individual nation-states by themselves were no longer able to guarantee that the Western European standard of living would be maintained, let alone increased to any perceptible extent. The long-lasting economic crisis and the structural changes associated with it had given rise to a new economic structure built on services, high-level technology and digitisation. This imposed development costs of a magnitude only a few individual nations could afford. Striking examples of this were aircraft construction, space travel, genetic research and the communications industry. It was understandable that the European countries would want both to limit West Germany's superiority in these areas and make use of it, and it was equally legitimate for the West Germans to wish to combine economic with political integration so as to ensure political coherence and responsibility.

Neither the economic nor the power-political motive was decisive by itself. This was emphatically demonstrated by the entry of the economically weak countries of Southern Europe into the EC, because from the economic point of view this expansion made little sense: in Portugal and Greece, GDP per head was 40 per cent below the European average, and in Spain it was 30 per cent below the average.[97] These countries were included primarily for political reasons. Until the mid-1970s, they had all been ruled by right-wing authoritarian dictatorships, which in Spain and Portugal had been in power for decades. These dictatorships had been a severe burden for democratic Europe. The prospect of early admission to the EC once democracy and the rule of law were firmly established was without doubt, along with direct financial aid, one of the strongest factors working to stabilise the young democratic institutions in those countries. The European idea, however permeated it was with calculations of an economic nature, undoubtedly had a core of idealism, without which the many antagonisms and differences of national interest could not have been overcome. This European idealism was powerfully moulded by the experience of the Second World War and the first half of the twentieth century in general, and in that sense it was also clearly supported by the people of Europe.

But the accomplishment of European integration was an elite project, greeted by the wider public with friendly but cautious interest. This was probably the reason why it had been possible to bring the process forward for so long without strong domestic opposition. There had, with a few exceptions, been no elections or referenda over European integration, although entry into the EC had affected the national sovereignty and the interests of the member states to an extraordinary degree. As long as the economic consequences of membership were felt to be overwhelmingly positive, no problem arose. But if this were ever to change, there were considerable dangers inherent in the democratic deficit of the European project, because it did not possess any legitimacy independently of its economic success.

After the Soviet Union had vetoed Honecker's 1984 visit, relations between the two Germanies did not at first progress as steadily as they had in the previous years. Nevertheless, the GDR government did respond to West German financial aid with a considerable expansion of travel opportunities. In 1982, only 45,000 GDR citizens below the age of retirement had been able to visit the Federal Republic. This figure increased to 573,000 in 1986 and to 1.2 million in 1987. In this way, the long-cherished desires of many GDR citizens were fulfilled, although the impact of the visits to the West on the mood of the population was highly ambivalent, because the standard of living the visitors experienced was so different from what they were used to in the GDR.[98]

The federal government justified the financial support it had given to East Germany by pointing out that any further economic decline would have worsened the social and political situation for the inhabitants of that country. There was of course a thin line between giving humanitarian aid and collaborating with the regime. As long as it was a question of transit permits, for which the federal government finally paid the GDR authorities almost one billion DM a year, assistance of this kind was still acceptable. But it was different with what was described as 'buying prisoners free'—ransoming them in other words. The federal government paid roughly 95,000 DM to the East German authorities for the liberation of each political prisoner. Between 1977 and 1988, a total 1.2 billion DM was spent to free 13,000 people. Hence the SED regime could increase the flow of foreign currency simply by increasing the number of political prisoners. This was a dirty business. From the West German point of view, however, there did not seem to be a feasible alternative.[99]

While the federal government was steering a middle course between hostile rhetoric and pragmatic cooperation in its relations with the GDR, the SPD took up much more direct contact with the SED at the party level. When the Solidarity movement emerged in Poland, followed later by General Jaruzelski's declaration of martial law, the more pacifically inclined wing of the SPD, led by Egon Bahr and Oskar Lafontaine, decided to follow the principle of 'peace before human rights'. They now applied this approach to the GDR as well. According to Bahr's thesis, the common threat posed to the two German states by the nuclear weapons of the superpowers was such a strong bond that their ideological antagonism was a secondary matter.[100] The 'security partnership' of the two German states therefore meant that political disagreements should stay in the background. This strategy, confirmed at SPD party congresses held in the mid-1980s, led to intense discussions with the SED, which culminated in August 1987 in the publication of a document adopted by both parties, entitled 'Conflicting Ideologies and Mutual Security'. The SPD saw this document as a direct continuation of the *Ostpolitik* it had pursued in Willy Brandt's time, but the Bonn government was very critical of it. 'Both social systems', according to the text, 'must admit each other's capacity to develop and reform.' Political competition between the two systems would strengthen the will to reform on both sides. In view of the initiatives taken by Gorbachev, this was doubtless understandable. But it could rightly be asked whether this also applied to the GDR, given that its leadership had explicitly distanced itself from Gorbachev's reforms. The decisive passage of the document was as follows: 'Common security requires the abandonment of attempts to interfere directly in the practical policies of other states.'[101] Those who hoped for reform in the GDR in 1987 continued to believe that the spark from the Soviet Union would leap over into East Berlin, but to call for the abandonment of 'interference' was to go much further than this, and the statement was regarded as a promise to refrain from criticising human rights abuses in the GDR. It was therefore not surprising that the SPD spoke almost exclusively to the SED leadership and showed no interest in contacting the GDR opposition, as the Greens did, although their representatives were quickly prevented from entering the country.

The August 1987 document made it clear that parts of the SPD and journalists associated with the party regarded the division of the country as permanent, and had also ceased to regard the GDR as a dictatorial and illegitimate state. This was a much more serious matter. One explanation was ignorance and a lack of interest in the state of affairs within the GDR, but there was also the widespread notion that the right to freedom enjoyed in the Federal Republic was to some extent balanced by the GDR's protection of social rights.[102]

In this situation, Honecker's state visit to the Federal Republic, which the Soviet leadership now finally permitted, tended to confirm the idea that conditions in the GDR were 'normal'. At the beginning of September 1987, he was received with all the honours of a foreign statesman, and his travels around the country were followed with great attention by the West German public. It was clear that the visit signified the Federal Republic's official recognition of the GDR, which had been awaited for decades, and Honecker could imagine that he had reached the pinnacle of political success. The fact that it was a conservative Chancellor who had made Honecker's triumph possible was the more remarkable in that it appeared to show that there was no longer any opposition to the recognition of Germany's division which the Honecker state visit plainly indicated.

This impression was however corrected by Kohl on 7 September in a speech made at the official reception ceremony for the East German leader, which was also transmitted live on GDR television. He stressed that it was both sensible and necessary to regulate practical questions affecting the two German states, and that a great deal of progress had been achieved in this regard. But he also emphasised that in both states 'the awareness of the unity of the nation' was 'as alive as ever' and that 'the will to preserve it' remained 'unbroken'. The German question remained open, even if it was not the appropriate time to solve it. The Germans were suffering from partition, and from the Wall: 'They want to be able to meet each other because they belong together.' Kohl then added, clearly alluding to the SPD–SED document that had just been published:

> Peace begins with respect for the unconditional and absolute dignity of the individual human being in all spheres of life. All human beings must be able to make their own decisions about themselves. That is why it was explicitly recognised in the Final Act of the CSCE agreement that 'respect for human rights and fundamental freedoms is an essential factor in the establishment of peace, justice and well-being'.[103]

Kohl's speech was understood—not least by viewers in the GDR—as a clear correction of the impression left by Honecker's state visit that the division of Germany had been accepted, and an emphatic reminder of the differences between Western democracy and socialist dictatorship. But the speech also contained an unambiguous rejection of the views of some members of the Union, who imagined that in view of Gorbachev's reforms the option of German reunification was again under discussion. Kohl stressed that reunification was 'not on the agenda of world history at this point' and that 'we would also need the consent of our neighbours to do this.'

Kohl's statement was in fact a precise summary of the situation that prevailed in relations between the two Germanies at that date. Cooperation in settling pragmatic questions had been stepped up, including the provision of continuous financial aid to the GDR so as to prevent its collapse; a clear line of moral separation from the SED dictatorship had been drawn; and West Germany continued to insist on the desirability of unification, though this was described as a distant dream rather than a present-day perspective.

When the Federal Republic took stock of the situation at the end of 1988, it could look back with some satisfaction. 'It could well be said that everything's going splendidly for us in the Federal Republic', was the way ARD TV summed up the year at the end of December. 'The economy is flourishing, and the Minister of Finance says that 1988 has been the best year for two decades. In foreign travel we hold the world championship, and we buy enough cars and luxury items to make the cash tills ring non-stop.'[104] Most West Germans had a highly optimistic view of their own and their country's future. The disarmament agreements between the two superpowers were not the least of the reasons for this, and the policies of Gorbachev, who enjoyed a high degree of sympathy in West Germany, strengthened hopes of further improvement in relations between East and West. Unemployment, the environment and the rising number of asylum seekers were regarded as the country's biggest problems, though discussions over the failure to make structural reforms and the future of the Kohl government also aroused much interest. Apart from this, the number of holiday trips by West Germans reached a new record, at almost 40 million, and the number of cars produced, at 4.6 million, was almost a million higher than in 1980. Moreover, a record number of people watched the German tennis stars Graf and Becker on television. People were happy that the confrontation between the world powers seemed to be coming to an end, and that there was some progress in relations between the two German states. And they noted with relief that the deep crisis of the early 1980s had been overcome, and the economy was humming again. West Germany appeared to have no major problems at present. It had a highly developed, and also highly polarising, interest in its recent past, but it lacked any precise idea of the shape of its future.

# 19

# Recovery, Crisis and Collapse in the GDR

## 'The Main Task'

At the turn of the year 1969–70, no one in the GDR could remain unaware of its economic problems. A cold winter placed an excessive strain on the country's crumbling supply system; fuel was scarce; schools and houses remained cold; the street lights were turned off. There was a severe housing shortage, sometimes there were even insufficient supplies of milk or potatoes, and it was no consolation that things were just as bad elsewhere in the Eastern bloc. In the Soviet Union, the reforming impulse of the mid-1960s had quickly melted away, and despite considerable economic growth, supply shortages in the towns and poverty in the countryside had hardly been alleviated. Conditions in Poland were particularly difficult. In December 1970, when the Polish party leadership announced a big increase in consumer prices, the workers replied with strikes which spread out rapidly from their original centre in Gdańsk (Danzig). The regime reacted with troops, tanks and orders to shoot. Forty-five people were killed and over a thousand injured.[1]

The Soviet leadership took careful note of the events in Poland and it forced the immediate resignation of the local Communist Party chief, Stanisław Gomułka. Memories of the events in Czechoslovakia two years previously were still fresh; and further protests and uprisings in the other socialist countries on account of bad living conditions, price rises and shortages of accommodation appeared to be by no means impossible. In April 1971, therefore, the CPSU altered its economic course and announced that the most important objective of the next Five Year Plan would be 'the improvement of the material and cultural standard of living of the people'.[2] In contrast to previous policies, economic plans would in future pay greater attention to the consumer goods industry and the provision of supplies, so as to counteract the discontent of the population.

The other Eastern bloc states, including the GDR, immediately adopted the same approach. But Ulbricht's 'structural policy', with its long-term orientation, obviously contradicted the new course. With its scientific predictions and its 'cybernetic' planning methods, it concentrated investment resources on modernising the industries of the future, and neglected the supply question. Immediately after his appointment as SED General Secretary, therefore, Honecker initiated a thorough reorganisation of economic policy. It was emphasised that 'the main task' was now 'to raise the material and cultural living standards of the people'.[3] This general line, later described as the 'unity of economic and social policy', was henceforth to take priority over everything else. The most important criteria by which individual policy measures were now to be evaluated were improved availability of consumption goods, greater social benefits, and rising wages, accompanied by stable prices and continued full employment. The situation of the weaker members of society was to be improved, inequality was to be overcome and the material interests of the workers were to be made the party's central preoccupation. The experts and engineers who had played such an important role in earlier years were now again made subordinate to the requirements of politics. The direction of state and society was to be set by political goals, not scientific formulae or economic calculations.

Previously, Ulbricht's policies had incurred displeasure in Moscow because they were felt to be high-handed and arbitrary. Now, with this policy adjustment, the GDR had again clearly rejoined the ranks of the Soviet-dominated countries of the Eastern bloc. But the main purpose of the new line was to placate the GDR's own citizens, particularly the workers, because the rise of discontent in the country and the disturbances in Poland had brought back memories of 17 June 1953. When the frondeurs around Honecker wrote to Brezhnev, calling for the removal of Ulbricht from office, they added: 'We are also bearing in mind certain lessons of the events in People's Poland and the Czechoslovak Socialist Republic.'[4] This consideration continued to the very end to be a leitmotif of GDR policy.

As was invariably the case, developments in the Federal Republic also had a role in inducing the SED to change course. The reforming policies of the social–liberal government under Willy Brandt and its push to expand state provision of social benefits put the East German party under pressure to undertake similar efforts. But it had to work within narrow limits, because the GDR's economic productivity was roughly 40 per cent lower than West Germany's, and it would probably take years, if not decades, before the country could catch up using traditional methods. According to the principles which had operated until then, productive efficiency would first have to increase, and only after that the standard of living. 'We shall live tomorrow as we work today': this was the ubiquitous GDR motto. But now the working class in particular did not seem ready any longer to accept a one-sided concentration on the investment goods industries at the expense of its standard of living. Rapid improvements therefore had to be made, and the recommended sequence was accordingly inverted. The new watchword was: first raise the standard of living, then raise productivity. Underlying this approach was the leadership's conviction that if the state paid up front, the workers would be motivated to increase their productivity, and this would generate the resources needed to cover the expenditure on social benefits. As Honecker put it in July 1971, the improvement in the population's standard of living would 'develop consciousness' and thus make it possible 'to attain higher productivity'.[5]

This change of direction towards a new consumer socialism, decided on by the SED in 1971, was not without risk. In previous decades the utopian vision of a socialism of equality, liberty and abundance, which would one day be achieved, had masked the sad reality of inadequate supplies and low living standards, at least for believers. But a decision to focus on a rapid improvement in living conditions here and now would expose the promises of the state and the party to concrete verification. The indicator of success and the barometer of loyalty towards the SED and its state would no longer be the prospect of a glorious future but the present-day standard of living.

In the post-Ulbricht decade, therefore, the GDR government made great efforts to improve the living standards of the population in all areas. It succeeded in part. Up to 1980, average incomes rose each year by approximately 3.5 per cent. Minimum wage and pension levels were raised as early as 1971. They were increased again in 1976. In 1975, shift workers were given longer holiday entitlement. Mothers received shorter working hours, their holidays were lengthened, child benefit was increased, and there was a big expansion in childcare places. By 1980, 90 per cent of the country's children had a place available in a crèche or a nursery school. The budgets of individual households were improved by these social benefits but also by subsidies on basic foodstuffs, children's clothing, energy, transport and rent. Bread, vegetables and fuel were made so cheap that their prices did not even cover the cost of transport and storage.[6]

The house-building programme was the most ambitious attempt the party made to achieve a rapid and long-lasting improvement in living conditions. Between 1971 and 1976, 577,000 new homes were built. By 1980, this figure had increased to over a million, and by 1989 to roughly 2 million. With 430 dwellings for every thousand inhabitants, and an average living space of 28 square metres per head, the GDR was internationally in a leading position in terms of accommodation. The new flats, located as a rule in vast residential complexes on the outskirts of the cities, had modern equipment, including baths and central heating, and were much sought after, despite their prefabricated and standardised construction, especially as the rents of roughly one Mark per square metre did not amount to more than 3 per cent of a family's average income. They were also so low that they did not cover the state's costs.[7]

The rapid improvement in many aspects of the standard of living in the GDR was a remarkable achievement. How it was viewed, however, depended very much on the perspective adopted by the observer. Living conditions in the

GDR in the 1970s were without doubt on a much higher level than in any other CMEA state. Moreover, the GDR also did well on another yardstick of comparison adopted by the older communists who dominated the SED leadership. Their political socialisation had occurred largely during the 1920s, and their first political experience had been gained in the struggle to overcome the poverty and deprivation suffered by the working-class population. A new dwelling with heating and a bath, cheap basic foodstuffs and a secure job were for them the categories that defined a successful social policy. 'The people need cheap bread, a dry apartment, and work', said Erich Honecker. 'If these three things are all right, nothing can happen to socialism.'[8] But for the population of the GDR, above all the younger generation, the yardstick was rather the standard of consumption in the Federal Republic, or, as the case might be, what they learned about this from the Western media. In those years, the GDR's successes in social policy were always qualified by this tendency to look towards the West.

But the main problem associated with this tremendous increase in welfare provision was financial. The extension of social benefits and subsidies cost 65 billion Marks between 1971 and 1975, and this did not include increases in wages. At first, however, financial considerations played a subordinate role in the decisions of the political leadership. It was assumed in the GDR, almost in the same way as in the Federal Republic, that the future would bring continuous economic growth. This view was boosted by the certainty that under socialism there were no crises of the kind experienced in the capitalist countries of the West. Words of warning coming from State Planning Commission circles that too much was being expected of the GDR economy therefore had little chance of being heard. The economy was the handmaiden of politics, and the party leaders continued to be firmly convinced that under socialist economic planning, economic growth, price formation and increases in productivity would not be determined by the market as they were under capitalism but could be set politically. In spite of all setbacks and notwithstanding all critical objections the Politburo of the SED insisted that 'the guidelines for a socialist treatment of the economy' were 'not set by the balance of payments but by the decisions of the Eighth Party Congress, and the unity of economic and social policy.'[9]

According to the SED's conception, there were three ways of obtaining the money needed to finance this policy: an increase in productivity, a greater centralisation of economic planning, and an expansion of trading relations with the 'non-socialist Economic Area' (*Nichtsozialistisches Wirtschaftsgebiet* or NSW), in particular the Federal Republic.

A noticeable increase in productivity did in fact take place during those years. It rose as much as 6 per cent during the year 1973–4. But this level was never reached again, and the figures for productivity growth declined continuously in later years.[10] It was not difficult to understand why. One reason was that it was a mistake to expect that the expansion of social benefits by the state would make people more motivated to work. As the chair of the FDGB, Harry Tisch, complained:

> We have carried out over 100 measures of social policy, but the sickness rate keeps on rising. It now stands at over 6 per cent. There are some people among us who think that everyone should take the six weeks of sick leave which are paid for at 90 per cent.[11]

Absenteeism increased, partly because more and more employees were queueing for articles in short supply, visiting the doctor or waiting in government offices during working hours. Another reason was that the equalisation of wages acted as a disincentive to performance. It was just not worth exerting oneself to produce more. Appeals to morality or working-class honour did not lead to any improvement in job motivation. The GDR leadership was faced with the fact that a rising standard of living, far from reducing social demands on the state, actually increased them.

But the decisive factor in the inadequate rise in productivity was a lack of rationalisation. To change this situation, modern plants and machines were needed, and that required investment. The regime had initially profited from the structural policies of the Ulbricht era, which had been directed specifically towards the industries of the future. Now, however, investments were diverted into the consumption sector, above all into housing, and this meant that resources were no longer available for the modern industrial sector. Even expenditure on research and development declined, and the expansion of major research facilities was delayed. It now became difficult for many physicists, chemists and information specialists to obtain work. The limits of the short-term economic policy of this period, which was directed exclusively towards quick success, were more apparent in those branches of activity than in any others.[12]

The increasing centralisation of economic policy under the State Planning Commission was intended to avoid wastage and duplication of effort, and to prevent individual enterprises from pursuing their own narrow aims. In the previous period, under the 'New Economic System', there had been an increasing tendency to measure the success of an enterprise according to its profits. Now the primary focus was again placed on the number of goods produced, in other words on a purely quantitative indicator. The result was that the relationship between cost and yield was ignored, and the success of an enterprise was primarily measured according to its total output, however that figure was reached. The most important GDR economic entity was now the 'combine'. There were roughly 130 of these organisations. They were horizontal combinations of enterprises, monopolistic in character. They answered directly to the central planning authorities in Berlin. Their functions included research and development as well as production and distribution. They were responsible for the whole of commodity production in their sector, and in some cases they were almost autarchic. Since the process of exchange and the division of labour did not function reliably in the GDR economy, the combines also produced their own input materials and sometimes even their own working equipment. They hoarded goods and raw materials so as to be able to exchange them if necessary for urgently needed material or machinery. They also employed far more workers than they needed, so as to be prepared for all eventualities and sudden surges in demand. Since only the total amount produced was important, and not the expenditure on labour and materials, their extravagance was entirely consistent with the system under which they operated.[13]

At this point there were still 14,000 private and 7,000 semi-private firms surviving in industry and handicrafts. They were now nationalised, along with the 4,000 handicraft cooperatives, and subordinated to the central planning system. The aim of this measure, it was said, was to put an end to the high incomes enjoyed by private entrepreneurs and place the whole economy under unified direction. The effect, however, was that serious gaps developed in the supply and production of consumer goods, particularly in areas of niche handicrafts.

The biggest problem, however, turned out to be foreign trade. According to the ideas put forward by the SED planners, the GDR economy could achieve the urgently necessary boost in productivity by importing modern investment goods from the West. These imports would be financed by credits. Using the new production facilities created as a result, the GDR would produce high-value industrial commodities and export them to the West, so as to pay back the loans with the foreign currency acquired in this way. The strategy was not entirely new. It had been employed in a similar way in other CMEA states, particularly Poland. It presupposed, however, that the credits from the West would actually be used to produce modern industrial facilities, that these new installations could produce items capable of competing in the West, and that enough Western customers could be found prepared to pay good prices. The plan also assumed that growth would pursue a linear path, that interest rates would stay the same, and that prices would only fluctuate moderately. None of this came to pass.

It soon became clear that the idea of making up the productivity deficit by intensifying foreign trade with the West was in contradiction with the 'main task' as formulated by the party leadership, which was to increase the supply of consumer goods and improve the population's living standard. In the 1970s, the GDR imported mainly consumer goods and food for both animals and humans from the West, whereas investment goods constituted only a quarter of its imports from that source. This was a direct result of the policy of the 'main task', entirely focused as it was on short-term improvements in the standard of living and the supply of consumer goods. At the same time, the GDR economy was unable to produce sufficient quantities of the technologically sophisticated commodities which were in demand on the world market.

As a result, the GDR's indebtedness to Western banks grew rapidly and alarmingly, but the country was unable to export enough to obtain the financial means needed to repay what it owed. Its debt to the West rose from 2 billion 'Foreign Exchange Marks' in 1971 to 22 billion in 1980. (The 'Foreign Exchange Mark', or VM, was the GDR's foreign exchange unit, which corresponded essentially to the West German Deutschmark.) The GDR's balance of trade with Western countries, which was already slightly negative between 1966 and 1970, amounted to minus 12.8 billion VM for the period 1971 to 1975 and minus 25.2 billion VM for the period 1976 to 1980.[14]

This situation also reflected the impact of the increase in the prices of raw materials after the first oil crisis. The GDR acquired its raw materials, particularly oil, almost exclusively from the Soviet Union. The USSR had opened up immense deposits of oil and natural gas in the 1960s and in the next few years it rose to the position of the world's greatest exporter of those commodities. In the 1970s some 80 per cent of its foreign exchange earnings were derived from the export of raw materials, which turned out to be an excellent business operation, thanks to the rapid increase in world market prices. The Soviet Union also used these revenues to subsidise the national economies of the other CMEA countries, which were suffering under the rise in oil prices, by calculating the cost of the oil it exported to them according to the average world market price during the previous five years. Under this method of calculation, price increases were only passed on with a considerable delay. The other CMEA countries did well out of this. The GDR in particular did not itself use most of the crude oil it imported from the Soviet Union. Instead it refined it in its chemical plants to make petroleum products and then sold those to the West at world market prices. This was one of the country's most important sources of foreign currency. After 1975, however, the Soviet Union gradually started to bring the prices it charged the CMEA countries up to the world market level. In 1976 the GDR paid some 50 per cent of the world market price for Soviet crude oil, but by 1978 this was 80 per cent.

In order to counter this threatening development, the GDR leadership decided in 1978 to use the imported oil exclusively for export, after refinement, and to cover its home energy needs as much as possible by using its own domestic lignite supplies. It succeeded in doing this, but only at the cost of heavy investment expenditure and appalling environmental damage. At all events, this approach allowed the GDR to keep back 6 million tonnes of oil from domestic consumption and allocate it for export to the West.[15]

Barely a decade after they had been started, the new economic measures introduced so optimistically in 1971 turned out to be disastrously mistaken. The decision to raise living standards had led to a tremendous rise in state expenditure, but the corresponding increase in productivity expected by the GDR leadership had not materialised. Imports from the West had led to a dramatic increase in foreign currency debts, but an expansion in exports to the West was not to be expected, in view of the way the GDR economy continued to lag behind in the sphere of technology. In addition, the rise in the price of Soviet crude oil had reduced the previously reliable flow of foreign currency drawn from the export of petroleum products.

It was not easy to find a solution to this dilemma. If they wanted to boost exports to the West in order to pay back the country's increasing debts, the exporting industries would need to receive more investment. But this was only possible if the resources allocated to social policy and subsidies were diverted away from there and towards investment. Both the State Planning Commission and the SED's economic experts warned against continuing the policy of concentrating on the 'main task', because they said it overloaded the country's economic capacity. Subsidies and social benefits should be reduced, they said, and the payment of wages should be determined to a greater extent by the level of work performance. The political leadership completely rejected these ideas. Reductions in the social sphere might lead to an unpredictable reaction from the population. Honecker made the point crystal clear: 'If we do this, the Politburo may as well resign straight away, and the government too.'[16]

Since the protection of the consumer, and social policy, were sacrosanct, and payment obligations to the West had to be fulfilled to maintain the country's creditworthiness, there had to be more investment in the export-oriented sectors, so as to obtain foreign currency, whatever the cost. This policy only succeeded to a limited extent, however, because so much investment had already been sunk into housing development and into changing the source of energy from oil to lignite. In order to raise the most important future-oriented industrial sector, microelectronics, to an international level, the GDR launched a gigantic development programme, the cost of which merely between 1977 and 1980 was more than 2 billion Marks. The first step was to build replicas of devices and systems which were protected by Western embargoes, and therefore acquired illegally in Western Europe, and on this basis to build a GDR microelectronics industry. But the decision to concentrate on microelectronics led to the neglect of other areas, not least the maintenance of existing installations and infrastructure. The cake was simply too small, however they cut it. If they concentrated on one side, they had to neglect another. The GDR was living beyond its means; from the economic point of view a definite reduction in social benefits and subsidies was necessary. But after the experiences of Prague and Gdańsk this was regarded as too risky in political terms.

## Integration and Opposition

The GDR leadership consistently and successfully avoided confronting these looming economic problems. Its self-confidence was never greater than in the 1970s. It had achieved international recognition as a separate state, good economic growth rates, improvements in the living standards of the population and, in addition, recognition as one of the most successful sporting nations in the world. On the thirtieth anniversary of its establishment, the GDR felt itself to be in a situation of strength and was optimistic about the future.

It was true that life had improved. The population could feel this in all areas. The housing shortage had been mitigated, if not removed, by the building programme. At the end of the decade, almost every household possessed a refrigerator, a washing machine and a television set, savings accounts held 90 per cent more money than ten years earlier, and almost half the country's inhabitants were able to take an annual holiday, usually organised by the FDGB.[17] The silent rejection that the regime had encountered from the population under Ulbricht was now replaced by a friendly indifference, which wavered between public acceptance and private aloofness. This is how Günter de Bruyn described this development in his memoirs:

> Compared with Ulbricht's time, material living conditions were better, and methods of surveillance were more efficient, but less obtrusive. The ruled had learned to content themselves with little things, and the rulers had begun to resign themselves to the people. They continued to proclaim the inviolable doctrines, because their legitimacy was based on these alone, but they largely refrained from pursuing their bold political objectives. They spoke more of order and tranquillity than of making advances and achieving victories. Enthusiasm was only demanded of those who wanted to get promoted, for the rest submission was sufficient. The most effective agitational slogan was 'security' (*Geborgenheit*). There was a kind of standstill agreement between the rulers and the ruled. Anyone who accepted the existing distribution of power and followed its rules was largely left in peace.[18]

The plant lay at the centre of people's lives. The employees did not just earn their keep there; they received accommodation and children's nursery places from it as well. The big enterprises had their own medical sections, some even had their own outpatients' clinics. It was almost impossible to lose one's job. Workers were in demand, and no one had to consider the possibility of being dismissed for substandard performance or absenteeism. Enterprise hierarchies were flat, income differences were small, and often unskilled workers earned as much as, or more than, specialists with a university degree. It was generally not worth making an effort, and the frequency with which slogans about over-fulfilling the plan or the socialist work ethic were heard is an indication of how necessary it was to repeat them. State security agencies reported again and again that lengthy downtimes, low productivity and a large number of rejected items were common practice. The factories, the Ministry for State Security reported, were constantly complaining about 'the laziness, irresponsibility, and low working morale' of many employees. 'Some factories', the report continued,

> are a complete shambles: materials are wasted, working hours are not fully utilised and valuable raw material is uselessly squandered, in part because of a lack of planning. Often production is not carried on at a steady rhythm, and this leads to an increase in the number of hours of overtime worked (despite reductions in the length of the working day).[19]

Since productivity did not rise sufficiently, more and more workers were needed. This led the proportion of women in the workforce to increase to record levels. At the end of the 1980s, more than 90 per cent of women of working age were professionally active, and even among women with children, the proportion was over 80 per cent, many of them working part-time. Childcare was guaranteed by the nationwide construction of a network of crèches and nurseries. The proportion of women studying at university also rose sharply: in 1976, 48 per cent of university students and 65 per cent of technical college students were female. Women placed a high value on the independence achieved by exercising a profession. In a survey conducted by the Leipzig Institute for Youth Research, 84.6 per cent of young women questioned stated that their primary goal in life was to have a career.[20]

The high level of female employment and education was not reflected in the proportion of women occupying leading positions. With one or two exceptions, it was impossible to find a woman exercising a high-level function in the factories, the state or the party. It was admittedly true that, unlike in West Germany, men and women received equal pay for equal work, but their distribution around the different wage groups revealed a different picture. Fifty-six per cent of the women, but only 21 per cent of the men, were in the two lowest wage groups. Conversely, the proportion of men in the two highest wage groups was five times as high as that of women. Thus, in 1980, women in full-time employment earned an average of 580 Marks, while men in a similar position earned 819 Marks. The distribution of housework also conformed to the traditional pattern. More than 60 per cent of women did two hours or more of housework every day, but only 14 per cent of men.[21]

Workers, women and families were the most important target groups for GDR social policy. They were a particular concern of the state, and their care was a priority. It was easier for the children of workers to gain access to secondary schools and universities, though the concept of a 'worker' gradually underwent considerable extension. Families were favoured in the allocation of the much sought-after holiday resorts run by the FDGB. The GDR was proud that in the 1970s, unlike West Germany, it was able to register a rise, though a slight one, in its population. This was correctly ascribed to the tremendous efforts made by the regime to promote larger families.

Pensioners on the other hand stood on the lowest rung of the social scale. In 1980, the average pension was 340 Marks, roughly a third of the average income of an employed person, and while the incomes of those in work rose between 1980 and 1988 by 24 per cent, pensions only rose by 11 per cent. Pensioners were no longer productively active and had to be financed by the state. Unlike employed people, therefore, they were also allowed to travel to the Federal Republic, and the GDR government was not unhappy for them to stay there and draw their pensions from West German sources. Many pensioners, particularly women, lived at the minimum existence level in the GDR, and in almost no other area was the difference between East and West so striking as in provision for the elderly.[22]

In spite of the improvements that had been made, day-to-day life in the GDR continued to be marked by shortages. This applied not just to the coveted Western items which occasionally surfaced in the shops. It also affected certain types of vegetable, clothing, shoes, cleaning materials, household goods and furniture. A large number of items of everyday use, leaving aside basic foodstuffs, were unavailable, either occasionally, or frequently, or continuously. Like services, distribution and trade were the poor relations of the planned economy, and waiting and queueing were characteristic features of daily life. This was felt particularly acutely when the attempt was made to buy a motor car. As in the West, a car was one of the most sought-after items of consumption. Some 3 million private vehicles were allowed onto the roads in the early 1980s. More than a third of all GDR households possessed a car. These vehicles were almost all produced within the country. Most of them were 'Trabants' or 'Wartburgs', which were not only very expensive but still at the level of the late 1950s in their technology, layout and design. They were very much inferior to the average car in the West. Moreover, the waiting time for the delivery of a Trabant was between twelve and fourteen years. As a result, there were flourishing black and grey markets, where used cars could be acquired immediately, though at very high prices. In fact, they sometimes cost more than a new car.[23]

The fact that the basic requirements of life were subsidised resulted in a great deal of waste. Bread, sugar and meat were squandered. Energy too: a heating system turned up all the way, with the windows left open, was practically the hallmark of public institutions, though the phenomenon was also widespread in private households. A bread roll cost 5 pfennigs, a pound of pork 5 Marks, 10 kilowatt-hours of electricity 80 pfennigs. On the other hand, unsubsidised goods, such as clothing, household appliances and furniture, but also certain foodstuffs, were offered at excessive prices. In the early 1980s, salad cucumbers cost roughly 5 Marks each, a kilo of tomatoes 7 Marks, a bar of chocolate 3 Marks, a bottle of Algerian red wine 11 Marks and a pair of tights 20 Marks.[24]

In order to absorb the considerable amount of excess purchasing power which resulted from the combination of high wages and a narrow range of available products, the so-called 'Delikat' and 'Exquisit' shops were established, starting in 1977. These were stocked with products catering to more sophisticated requirements. Here GDR citizens could buy goods from the West as well as GDR products that were in short supply, at extremely inflated prices of course. Purchases in these shops covered some 5–10 per cent of the total retail turnover. In Berlin, almost a fifth of all clothing purchases were made from 'Exquisit' shops. These were an enclave of the market economy within socialism: scarce goods produced in the GDR were extremely expensive in them, and imported Western products bought there in Eastern Marks cost five to ten times the price asked in West Germany in Deutschmarks. Employees who received good wages could afford to buy these items. For pensioners, on the other hand, they were prohibitively expensive. This too was a constant cause of complaint.[25]

There were also 'Intershops', which had been established much earlier. These contradicted the principles of socialist policy towards consumption and society in an even more blatant fashion. They were originally set up in railway stations and airports to serve the needs of Western tourists, but there were many more of them after 1974, when GDR citizens were permitted to possess foreign currency, which above all meant Deutschmarks. In the Intershops everything which was not otherwise available in the GDR could be bought with Western currency. By 1980, there were almost 500 of them, and in some cities they were expanded into veritable department stores, in which it was possible to buy not only Western cigarettes, chocolate, washing powder and tinned food, but household appliances, electrical goods and do-it-yourself supplies. In the mid-1980s, the turnover of the Intershops amounted to over a billion DM. This indicated that the purchase of Western goods had become a constant accompaniment of

GDR life, but it also showed how much Western money was circulating in the country by then.

The Intershop trade was extremely profitable for the GDR economy, particularly after it was placed under the jurisdiction of the 'Coordination of Commerce' organisation (*Kommerzielle Koordinierung* or KoKo) headed by Alexander Schalck-Golodkowski. The task of this remarkable institution, which occupied a position midway between the Ministry of Economics and the Ministry of State Security, was to acquire hard currency in any possible way, whether by speculating on Western stock exchanges, by receiving payments by the Federal Republic for travel to Berlin and the issuing of visas and payments by Western tourists of the minimum obligatory amount of exchange money, or, finally, by pocketing the money spent in the Intershops. The KoKo was also a route for gifts of all kinds of Western goods made to GDR citizens by Western relatives, from freezers to motor cars to prefabricated houses. The foreign currency obtained in this way flowed into the state budget. The amount for 1980 was estimated at between 2 and 3 billion VM.[26]

The Deutschmark thus increasingly became the unofficial means of payment in the GDR, and the possession of Western currency became the most important aspect of East German social inequality. The extension of the network of Intershops and 'the differing ability of some GDR citizens to enjoy certain advantages in the GDR through the possession of Deutschmarks' were at the forefront of popular complaints. According to the Ministry of State Security, citizens mainly objected to the fact that the Intershops 'were only accessible to a particular section of the GDR population and to privileged persons'. This, it was said, had split society into four groups:

> 1. Workers, pensioners and other citizens with lower incomes without Western currency, who also have to restrict their consumption because they are affected by the austerity measures (and cannot buy coffee in an Intershop); 2. Citizens with a higher income which allows them to make purchases in 'Exquisit' shops; 3. Persons who have obtained possession of Deutschmarks and can satisfy their needs in Intershops; and 4. Privileged persons and high-level functionaries, who buy in 'special shops', drive expensive Western cars and are in no way affected by any kind of austerity measures.[27]

The Intershops were probably more damaging politically to the GDR than they were useful economically. The mere possession of Deutschmarks offered GDR citizens the chance to escape the dreariness and shortcomings of the products of the GDR economy. Moreover, the variegated abundance of the world of the Western consumer as displayed in the Intershops outshone all the anti-Western propaganda of the GDR media. Hard currency had become the most valuable possession in the GDR, thanks to the promotion of the socialist consumer society and the intensification of trade with the West. People in the GDR were therefore made aware almost every day of the difference between Western and socialist economic performance. This was a competition the socialist planned economy could never win, and it accelerated its downfall.

The SED had now given up its fight with the Western media. Originally, like the other CMEA states, the GDR government had decided to adopt the French SECAM colour television system rather than the West German PAL system. But, after 1977, GDR televisions were equipped with both SECAM and PAL. They were expensive, costing 4,000–6,000 Marks, but they were sold in large numbers. Thus, ARD and ZDF could be received almost all over the GDR, and people probably watched them more frequently after the 1970s than they did the programmes of GDR television. This constant consumption of Western television meant that GDR citizens were informed about political events in the world, and in the GDR itself, mainly from the perspective of the more reliable reports on Western channels, while the reports from the GDR media were perceived as SED propaganda, which is after all what they were. But, in addition to the news programmes, the Western channels transmitted entertainment programmes, feature films and television series which allowed people to immerse themselves every evening in the gaudy consumer aesthetics of the Western media and contemplate the glittering world of Hollywood. For the SED this was politically undesirable, because the Western media were after all transmitting 'the voice of our political antagonist', as a member of the Politburo emphasised in 1977.[28] Despite this, after 1975 the GDR authorities made no effort to combat the spread of the Western media, because they knew all too well that to disconnect the country from Western television by technical means would lead to discontent and anger among the population. On the other hand, continuous consumption of the Western media also had an indirectly stabilising effect, because the virtual journey they made every day to the Federal Republic meant that many GDR citizens no longer felt the need to travel to the West in person.

The change of government in 1971 also produced changes in cultural policy. Honecker's remarks about art in December 1971 received great attention: 'If one proceeds from the firmly established socialist position, there can in my view be no taboos in the sphere of art and literature. This applies both to the shaping of the content and to the style.'[29] This was said by the same Honecker who had introduced the 'clean cut' in cultural policy in 1965, thereby opening a long phase of censorship and repression. Once again, then, there was a change of direction. Artists and writers, theatre directors and film-makers had the feeling that this offered a fresh start, and this impression was strengthened by the easing of censorship and of the rules governing publication.

This applied particularly to literature, which had always drawn the greatest attention from the political leaders and the authorities. The GDR was proud of its reputation as a 'land of readers'. Novels by GDR authors had a high circulation, and new books by literary stars such as Stefan Heym, Hermann Kant, Erich Loest, Volker Braun, Günther de Bruyn, Stephan Hermlin and Christa Wolf were sensations, which were intensively discussed and interpreted. Since the GDR media were completely true to the party line (and correspondingly tedious), only literature offered the possibility of publicly drawing attention to things which were otherwise not mentioned. Whether it was a matter of political or social abuses, individual experiences and problems, or hidden criticism of the censorship and the network of informers, the readers of GDR books sought out 'passages' in them, read between the lines, and admired the courage or the cunning of the author. Thus, literature took on the role of an alternative discourse about their own society, and gained enhanced significance from the absence in the GDR of a public opinion in the narrower sense.

'Breadth and variety' was the new formula the regime now adopted to describe its policy towards art and culture, and the release of books such as Heym's *König David Bericht* (King David Report) and Hermann Kant's *Das Impressum* (The Imprint), whose publication had long been prevented, indicated that authors now had more room for manoeuvre. Even such a defiant text as Ulrich Plenzdorf's *Die neuen Leiden des jungen W.* (The New Sorrows of Young W.) was allowed to appear, and it was the subject of extensive and controversial debate in the literary journals. This pointed the way to new freedoms, although by 1973, Honecker was already warning the writers not to put the problems and defects of GDR society too much in the foreground. Some texts, like Heym's *Fünf Tage im Juni* (Five Days in June) or Erich Loest's *Es geht seinen Gang oder Mühen in unseren Ebenen* (Things are Taking their Course, or Troubles in Our Plains) remained under wraps, and the poet Reiner Kunze was expelled from the Writers' Union in October 1976 for his poems and prose pieces about the oppressive paternalism suffered by young people in the GDR, although, or perhaps because, his collection *Die wunderbaren Jahre* (The Wonderful Years) only appeared in the Federal Republic.[30]

On the other hand, it was absolutely clear that most of the well-known GDR writers were in agreement with the fundamental ideas of socialism, and had in principle a positive attitude towards the regime, despite their criticism of individual details. If that had not been the case, they would not have been able to achieve the popularity they actually possessed. In any case, the relaxation of cultural policy in the early 1970s, which was reminiscent of the 'thaw' of the 1950s and the new departure after the 'youth communiqué' of 1963, awakened hopes among the literary community that this change would last longer, and that the methods of the past would be completely abandoned.

Certain modifications could also be observed in GDR youth policy after 1971. Ever since 1965, the regime had expressed its hostility to young people's partiality for the music and behaviour of the rebellious teenagers of the Western world, on the ground that it was decadent and imperialist, and it had reacted by attempting to suppress these phenomena. Now its attitude began to change. The government gave way to the wishes of the young on some points, but it also tried to make use of the forces that had emerged from below for its own purposes. Long hair, blue jeans and Western music were tolerated—within limits—but gestures of disobedience and protest were directed into safe channels. The 'Festival of Political Song', which took place every year from 1970 onwards in East Berlin, played an important part in this process of incorporating the Western protest movement and removing its essential core of revolt. These festivals were attended by music groups from the Third World and left-wing songwriters from the West. They protested against neo-colonialism, the American war in Vietnam, the putsch in Chile and the military junta in Greece. Large audiences came to listen to musicians like Mikis Theodorakis, Dieter Süverkrüp and Franz-Josef Degenhardt. These events were organised by the FDJ, but in form and manner they were staged to look like left-wing rock festivals of the Western type. Unlike the 'singing movement' of the 1960s, which was supposed to make the 'fighting songs of the German and international working class' accessible to young people, the GDR's festivals of political song were greeted with much interest and broad acceptance.[31]

This development reached a height with the Tenth World Festival of Youth, held in summer 1973. The SED leadership, headed by Erich Honecker, had put in a year of preparation for this gigantic event. It offered the opportunity to demonstrate to the whole world the self-confidence of the GDR and the attachment of the population to their state. The political character of the festival was obvious. Its overall motto was 'For Anti-Imperialist Solidarity, Peace and Friendship' and its official song had the rousing title 'The youth of the world are Berlin's guests, they couldn't care less about bourgeois pests.' But the festivals were also thought of as a reply to the Munich Olympic Games, and the emphasis on an informal, easy and tolerant atmosphere during the events was intended to transmit a completely new picture of the GDR to the world public. More than 300,000 young people from the GDR met in East Berlin with some 25,000 visitors from more than a hundred countries, to listen to bands in a cosmopolitan atmosphere manifestly without state regimentation, to engage in political discussions and to applaud theatre groups. For many young East Germans, the festival offered the chance to meet school pupils and students from the West for the first time. This was an important experience, twelve years after the building of the Berlin Wall.

In reality, however, the whole festival was planned down to the smallest detail by the regime, organised by the FDJ and monitored by the Ministry of State Security. All the GDR participants belonged to the FDJ. They had been obliged to undergo months of training beforehand, during which their political reliability was checked and in particular they were instructed on how to argue against 'Social Democratism'. Before the festival started, 2,700 'negative and hostile' persons were arrested. The Ministry of State Security uncovered 'inadequate political reliability', 'a decadent appearance' and 'immoral and hooligan-like behaviour' affecting more than 20,000 people, and they were informed that they would not be allowed to attend. During the preparations for the festival, the authorities initiated proceedings against several thousand people for 'anti-social behaviour'. Many of them were committed to psychiatric clinics and other places of confinement.

The West German participants, who consisted of representatives of youth organisations with links to the DKP, as well as a delegation of Social Democratic youth organisations, were monitored particularly carefully. The GDR authorities had also invited 400 experienced West German DKP functionaries to the festival as unofficial tourists, to step in against the expected attempts at 'Social Democratic diversion'. Together with more than 4,000 Stasi operatives, they mingled with the participants, so as to keep control of the events.[32]

The efforts that were made to keep control of the World Youth Festival provide a good insight into the political strategy of the SED leadership under Honecker. On the one hand, it deeply distrusted its own population, and it only allowed it to come into contact with foreign visitors after rigorous selection and intensive training and under total supervision. On the other hand, it wanted to arouse the impression that the GDR was a tolerant and sovereign socialist republic, which was treated by its citizens with respect and enthusiasm. Since open repression would have contradicted that picture, the state's apparatus of repression and surveillance was arranged with greater subtlety and the methods of the Ministry of State Security were made more refined. Its main approach was no longer repression, arrest and terror but prevention. The head of the Stasi, Erich Mielke, wrote that the primary way of combating the enemy was to take 'measures to recognise and destroy negative and hostile forces in good time, and prevent them from becoming active in an oppositional way'. But 'our measures against forces of this kind ought not to provide the enemy with any pretext for political discrimination against the GDR'.[33]

To achieve this aim, the web of informants covering the whole of East Germany was drawn ever tighter. Between 1971 and 1980, the number of full-time Stasi officials increased from 45,600 to 75,100. By 1989, there were 191,000. Meanwhile, the number of unofficial collaborators (*Inoffizielle Mitarbeiter*, IMs) also increased, from roughly 100,000 in 1971 to 170,000 in 1989. By the end of the regime, 4 per cent of all adult citizens of the GDR were working for the Stasi.[34] Potential 'enemies' were detected, put under surveillance and combatted with increasingly sophisticated methods of 'disruption' thanks to this tightly controlled network of informers. The first steps were to stir up conflicts with friends, to organise professional failures and marital problems, and to circulate rumours, suspicions and denunciations. Only right at the end of the chain of repression did the state apparatus have recourse to arrests and convictions. The feeling of constant surveillance, and the impression that the Stasi was present everywhere, were intended to restrain deviant behaviour and words or actions critical of the state long before they happened. Even people who were entirely in agreement with the regime, or were active in the SED and other official organisations, were under constant observation. As a result, the Stasi acquired a considerable degree of independent importance. It became a significant force within the state, although it continued to be subject to the party. It was the party's 'sword and shield', and its self-image was moulded by this function.[35]

But the notion of a ubiquitous and constantly active opponent had something absurd about it. From the 1950s onwards, anyone who openly rejected the GDR, or even simply opposed it, was either in the West or in prison. Criticisms or protests against specific measures by the regime—such as those that followed the intervention against the Prague Spring—were noted by the Stasi as soon as they happened and immediately suppressed. The government was thoroughly informed by the Ministry of State Security about complaints from the population over inadequate food supplies, defects in social provision or excessive prices. If the criticism came from the working class or circles close to the party, the authorities paid attention to it, right up to Politburo level, though this did not mean that the critics themselves were not called to account.

The state apparatus was particularly concerned with criticism and opposition from the Left, because this could not simply be brushed off by referring to fascism and imperialism. Robert Havemann continued to be at the centre of a 'democratic communist' opposition. Invoking the legacy of Rosa Luxemburg, he advocated a free socialist society

> with press freedom even for those who think differently, freedom of assembly, the right to strike, ideological and religious freedom, freedom of artistic creation, i.e. the abolition of any kind of state interference or tutelage in the cultural and scientific fields . . . Socialism is free pluralism in all spheres of social life.[36]

People who adopted attitudes of this kind were dangerous to the SED leadership because conditions in the GDR, when measured against the communist ideal, looked uninviting and mediocre.

The line taken by *The Alternative*, a book by Rudolf Bahro, a member of the SED, was similar to Havemann's. It was published in the West in 1977, and it criticised the rigidity of life under the bureaucratic dictatorship of the SED:

> The party is headed by an institution which, in the shape of the Politburo, is practically self-perpetuating. It is those already in this leading body who decide who is to be newly co-opted onto it, and not even all of them. . . . The dictatorship of the Politburo is a grotesque exaggeration of the bureaucratic principle, in as much as the party apparatus subordinate to it is at the same time both church hierarchy and super-state. The whole structure is quasi-theocratic . . . For the core of its political power . . . is power over minds, with the constant tendency towards inquisition, so that the party is already in itself the real political police.

Bahro combined his harsh and acute criticism of the rule of the SED with a proposal to establish a new social order governed by socialist idealism. He called for 'an association of communes into a national society' and 'an association of nations in a contentedly cooperating world'. The book ended with the words: 'Communism is not only necessary; it is also possible.'[37]

Bahro's book drew its strength from the revolt of utopian socialism against what Honecker described as 'real socialism'. It was thus in part a courageous testimony of protest against the dictatorship of the bureaucratic state apparatus. Politically, however, it was entirely caught up in the internal debates of socialist theoreticians who had been polishing their doctrines for almost a hundred years. Bahro was arrested immediately after his book was published. He was condemned to eight years in prison, but a year later he was 'bought free' by the Federal Republic, and allowed to leave for West Germany. Once in the West, he joined the Green Party, but later on he disappeared into the cloudy realm of spiritualism.

Another left-wing critic was Wolf Biermann, who had been the GDR's *enfant terrible* since the early 1960s. He regularly upset the GDR leadership with his songs, and he had been forced to make his way against greater and greater obstacles and acts of repression. But his great popularity and the fame he enjoyed on both sides of the border prevented the regime from simply locking him up. As a result, he was forbidden to perform in public or to publish, but the regime allowed his Berlin apartment to become both a studio for making recordings which would then be issued in the West, and a meeting point for explicitly left-wing oppositionists. Biermann continued to regard himself as a communist. His songs against the putsch in Chile or the Vietnam War and his criticisms of conditions in West Germany soon made him as popular among Western Leftists as he was in the GDR, where his disrespectful rhymes about the SED met with a big response among intellectuals and were also supported by sections of the

GDR cultural elite. As early as 1965, in one of his most well-known poems, he had combined his criticism of the false socialism of the SED bosses with a call for the building of true socialism: 'Many will ensure/That socialism wins/Today! Today! Don't wait till tomorrow!/Freedom never comes too early/And the best means against/Socialism (I say this aloud)/Is that you build socialism/BUILD! Build. Build.' A year later he added this: 'Just tell me this: what is the use/of the whole brood of bureaucrats?/They tread upon the people's necks/With fervour and dexterity/History's giant wheel/I've had enough of that!'[38]

In November 1976, Biermann received permission to undertake a concert tour of the Federal Republic, and immediately after his first concert, which took place in Cologne, the GDR government deprived him of East German citizenship and forbade him to return to the country. This spectacular move by the GDR leadership was extremely surprising, in view of its careful moves towards liberalising cultural policy and its laborious attempts to present a more friendly image to the outside world. Still more astounding, however, was the reaction within the GDR. A number of prominent authors, including Christa Wolf, Volker Braun, Stephan Hermlin, Stefan Heym, Heiner Müller, Rolf Schneider and Jurek Becker, published a declaration, in which they stated: 'Biermann himself has never left any doubt, not even when performing in Cologne, as to which of the two German states he supports, notwithstanding all his criticisms. We protest against the removal of his citizenship and we ask for a reconsideration of the measures that have been decided.'[39]

This declaration itself was entirely written in the typical style of principled loyalty to the socialist state, but it was still sensational, because until then there had never been such a public protest in the GDR against measures carried out by the SED leadership. It provoked a tremendous response. Many more writers and artists associated themselves with it, and the party leadership was inundated with a flood of statements of solidarity. The Politburo had not reckoned with such a wave of protest, and was at first uncertain how to respond. No action was taken against the most prominent signatories, but the lesser known were arrested and tried. With this, the real or supposed phase of cultural liberalisation was clearly at an end. The artists and writers who had believed that in future the areas of freedom in the GDR would extend, if slowly, saw now that they had been mistaken, and thenceforth turned their backs on the country. The 'alliance between the intellect and politics' was occasionally invoked in emotional tones in the GDR. If it had ever even existed, it had now certainly disappeared. Shortly afterwards, writers and artists started to leave the GDR, and in the next few years, more than a hundred took this route. They were even assisted in doing so by the authorities, because the SED leadership believed that this would be a way of getting rid of rebellious spirits and restoring tranquillity to the country.

Biermann meanwhile was greeted rapturously by most of the Western media, although not by all. After his performance in Cologne, which was broadcast on television, *Bild-Zeitung* offered this comment:

> Wolf Biermann—locked out of his paradise in the zone. Poor old Biermann? *Westdeutscher Rundfunk* paid him 10,000 DM to appear on television. To get this you have to be called Biermann. You have to be a communist. And you have to spit on the Federal Republic's democracy. Poor old Biermann? Poor old Germany![40]

Critical writers and artists were therefore *expected* to leave the GDR. But citizens who absolutely *wanted* to leave were prevented from doing so. This policy was of course in obvious contradiction to the provisions of the CSCE Final Act also signed by the GDR in 1975 as well as the United Nations International Covenant on Civil and Political Rights, which entered into force in spring 1976. The CSCE Final Act had been published in the newspapers of the Eastern bloc countries, and while in Czechoslovakia this was the starting point for the activities of oppositional political groups such as Charter 77, in the GDR it was reflected in the rising number of applications to leave the country. Once again, this demonstrated the difference between the GDR and the other CMEA states. In the latter, rising discontent and resentment found expression in an aggravation of domestic tensions, whereas in the GDR it led to an increase in attempts to emigrate to the other Germany. Between 1977 and 1982, some 70,000 people applied to be released from GDR citizenship. Every year 3,000–4,000 of these applications were approved.

The 'leavers', as they were soon called, were a particular problem for the GDR authorities, firstly because they relied on the international agreements the GDR leadership was proud to display as a proof of its worldwide recognition. Secondly these 'leavers', unlike the departing writers and artists, rejected the GDR unconditionally and irrevocably. They were not interested either in a better kind of socialism or in reforms, and as a rule they had no contact with the opposition groups which were slowly being formed in the country. The 'leavers' wanted only one thing: to leave the GDR as quickly as possible, whether for personal, economic or political reasons. In the GDR, moreover, an application to leave signified a kind of social death. The 'leaver' was isolated and avoided, he or she had to reckon with tough sanctions, which stretched all the way from discrimination against the leaver's children at school to loss of employment and the threat of imprisonment. If the application became public knowledge or its existence became known in the West, the leaver would be arrested and convicted. For this reason, those who had made an application to emigrate had nothing more to lose from that time onwards. Their behaviour was usually more provocative than that of the political opposition, and they were also ready to take greater risks. They established contact with correspondents from the Western media and on occasions such as visits from foreign politicians they mounted sudden and vociferous demonstrations in front of Western cameras against the rejection of their applications. This repeatedly caused tremendous embarrassment to the Stasi.[41]

The rising number of emigration applications, and the expulsion of Biermann, were the two clearest signs that since 1976 there had been an increase not only in economic but also in political problems within the country. The change of course undertaken by the SED in 1971 in the direction of consumer socialism had it is true had a stabilising effect, but its generous distribution policies had also aroused great expectations. Never sure of support from its own people, the SED leadership reacted nervously to any indication of discontent, particularly among the workers. Its reaction took two forms: it expanded its surveillance apparatus and it increased social security benefits. But when the first serious economic difficulties started to surface, the timid reform proposals of the economic planners met with resistance from the Politburo, which was convinced, probably rightly, that cuts in social benefit and price rises would put an end to the already fragile loyalty of the GDR population. At the same time, however, the insidious penetration of Western money and Western commodities into the country led the population's expectations of living standards to rise to the Western level. Whether a person was rich or poor was measured by how many Deutschmarks he or she possessed, while supply shortages, waiting in queues and the decay of the infrastructure repeatedly reinforced the population's dissatisfaction with conditions in the GDR despite all the leadership's efforts to improve the situation of the consumer.

The attempts of the early 1970s to liberalise cultural policy led to a similar shift in expectations. After the softer line signalled in 1971, the intellectuals had hoped for gradual emancipation from the shackles of censorship and an end to bans on publication. They had hoped for free discussion and an international exchange of ideas. When these expectations were ostentatiously repudiated by the expulsion of Biermann, this snapped the always tenuous and shaky tie between the writers and politics.

## The Debt Crisis

The GDR's financial balance sheet at the end of the 1970s was not positive, because its considerably increased expenditure, above all for social benefits, was not matched by any comparable increase in revenue. Productivity had risen much less than income and consumption, productive investment had fallen, the capital stock of industry had deteriorated, more consumer goods than investment goods were being imported from the West, exports were stagnating and foreign currency indebtedness to the West was rising rapidly.[42]

The GDR was already in this situation when it was struck by the effects of the second crisis over oil prices. Some initial immunity from the rapid rise of prices on the international market for raw materials could admittedly be achieved by relying on the prices set by the CMEA, but this did not last. In 1980 the Soviet Union informed the GDR that it would deliver 17 million tonnes of crude oil over the next five years, up to 1985, instead of the 19 million tonnes previously agreed. The GDR would be aware, the message continued, 'that over the last five years the fraternal countries had enjoyed a direct gain of 15 billion rubles on their imports of energy and raw material supplies from the USSR, and that in the next five years this would amount to almost 30 billion.' This news put the GDR leadership in a veritable panic. Honecker replied that 'this undermines the cornerstone of the German Democratic Republic's existence' and he sent an urgent letter to the head of the Soviet Party in which he asked 'whether it is really worth destabilising the GDR and shaking people's confidence in the party and state leadership for 2 million tonnes of crude oil?' But the Soviet Union was in an equally difficult economic situation, and Brezhnev replied as follows: 'The USSR has suffered a great misfortune. If you are not ready to share with us the consequences of this misfortune, there is a danger that the Soviet Union will be unable to retain its present position in the world, and that has consequences for the whole socialist community.' The disputed 2 million tonnes were finally granted to the GDR, but only in return for hard currency, so that the country had to pay roughly $640 million for the oil. There was a thirteen-fold increase in the overall price of Soviet oil between 1970 and 1985, and this reduced the price difference between the cheap Soviet oil and the expensive petroleum products sold to the West, which were so important for the GDR's balance of trade.[43]

Thus, the foreign currency debts of the GDR continued to increase. In 1982 they reached their highest level ever, at 25.1 billion VM: this figure was four times the total amount the GDR received from its exports to the West. Moreover, the interest demanded by Western banks had risen rapidly since 1979–80; at times it exceeded 20 per cent. 'Owing to the present level of indebtedness', warned the State Planning Commission in June 1980,

> the GDR is no longer able to pay all its interest and repayment obligations from its own currency receipts, even with immensely increased exports, because the annual interest and repayment obligations are higher than the annual export receipts. The interest payments alone amount to two-thirds of the export receipts of one year in convertible currency. If the capitalist banks refuse to grant the GDR any more credit

concluded the planners, 'within a few months we should be in a situation where the GDR ceased to be solvent and could no longer continue importing.'[44]

This precarious state of affairs was placed under additional strain by the worsening of the confrontation between East and West and above all by the events in Poland. The revolt of the Gdańsk shipworkers and the rise of the Solidarity movement were essentially a result of the dramatic worsening of the Polish economic crisis. The fall in real wages, the price increases and the supply shortages, which finally affected even basic foodstuffs, were the main reasons for the fury of the Polish population. The inhabitants of the GDR did not have much sympathy for the strikes and demonstrations of the Solidarity movement. On the contrary, they confirmed widespread anti-Polish prejudices, and the Stasi reported that the GDR population had reacted to the proclamation of martial law in Poland with approval and a sense of relief.[45] The reaction of the SED leadership to Solidarity was naturally much more negative. Honecker called for the harshest measures to be taken against the strikers and in a conversation with Kania, the head of the Polish party, in February 1981, he referred back to his own experiences with the rebels of 17 June 1953: 'At that time, we were helped by the fact that for example in Halle well-known Nazis, who had been brought out of the prisons, placed themselves at the head of the demonstrations. A whole group of them were court-martialled and shot. That gave many people cause to reflect.'[46]

To the GDR leadership the Polish events looked like a warning of impending catastrophe. Poland too had placed its faith in a policy of modernisation on the basis of Western credits, and had hoped to use the hard currency it acquired through exports to pay off the credits and improve social welfare provision. In Poland, as in the GDR, this plan did not prove successful. In 1980 debt repayment swallowed up 82 per cent of Poland's export earnings, and the Polish People's Republic was finally compelled to negotiate more foreign credits to allow its debts to be repaid. At the end of 1981, when martial law was already in force, the government ordered a 240 per cent increase in the price of provisions, so as to reduce the burden of subsidies. This increased the embitterment of the population, but it did not improve the economic situation. Poland's mountain of debt rose yet higher. By the end of 1982, the country was essentially bankrupt, and it ceased to receive credits from Western banks. Romania too was obliged to concede at this time that it was insolvent. As a result, Western banks became increasingly cautious about granting credit to CMEA states. Until then, Western lenders had regarded the rule of the Soviet Union over the countries of East Central Europe as a kind of guarantee against financial loss. But an awareness of Soviet economic conditions now began to shake this confidence as well.[47]

The events in Poland showed the political leaders of the SED the possible consequences of a rise in food prices and a drastic deterioration in the population's standard of living. This strengthened their conviction that subsidies and social benefits should be kept at a high level to maintain a stable situation in the country. To improve the GDR's economic situation, therefore, they fell back on tried and tested methods: the next party congress of the SED simply issued instructions to increase economic growth and raise exports.

To do this, they decided to concentrate investment on a small number of important export industries, though they also wanted to pay greater attention to scientific research. This amounted to an attempt to combine Ulbricht's policy of structural improvement with Honecker's 'main task'. But a redirection of investment of this kind could only be effective in the long term. As far as the present was concerned, the GDR's payment problems had become even greater since the end of 1982, and now the State Planning Commission openly articulated what it had previously only warned about:

> Given the course taken so far by exports to the NSW, the GDR's ability to pay its debts in convertible currency is not guaranteed for certain months of the years 1982 and 1983. Payment difficulties have already arisen for the months of August and September. Whereas a credit reserve to cover a cash deficit of 2 billion DM was available in 1982, there is no possibility of this in 1983.[48]

By mentioning the threat of insolvency, the State Planning Commission had uttered the word that would thenceforth hang like a sword of Damocles over all the economic activities of the GDR. There was only one way out: to seek help from the Federal Republic. But there was resistance to this, not least in Moscow. After the Basic Treaty of 1972 and the international recognition of the GDR in the 1970s, the Soviet leadership had emphatically opposed any further rapprochement between the two German states, because it regarded this as posing the threat that they would enter a special relationship. From a political point of view, the SED leaders would have preferred a more distant relationship with the Federal Republic, because there was nothing they feared more than the creeping conversion of the GDR into a social democracy, which they suspected was the real intention behind Bahr's concept of 'change through rapprochement'. This politically motivated rejection of closer contact with the Federal Republic was reinforced by the worsening confrontation between East and West which had followed NATO's 'double-track decision' and the Soviet invasion of Afghanistan.

Even so, despite the GDR's conspicuous display of separateness from the Federal Republic, the thread of discussions between the two governments was never entirely broken off, not least because the conflict between the superpowers over missiles powerfully highlighted one interest the two German states did actually have in common. But it was above all economic motives that led the SED leadership to keep in close touch with the Federal Republic. The federal government, for its part, was very ready to support the GDR financially because it feared that if a crisis situation developed there it might lead to disturbances and possibly to military rule as in Poland. In comparison with this, the financial stabilisation of the GDR appeared to be the lesser evil, even if it was liable to strengthen the SED dictatorship politically. That is why the federal government was ready to guarantee a total of 2 billion DM of credits over the years 1983 and 1984, thereby helping the GDR out of its acute payment problems. The federal government's credit injections provided the GDR government with a basis for taking on further debt, because it did not make use of this money but left it in the account, which was a way of implying the creditworthiness of its economy. So, for the time being, it had been saved from bankruptcy.[49]

With its readiness to address the demands of the federal government over humanitarian matters in return for financial assistance, the SED leadership finally converted into hard currency the only exchangeable item it still possessed: the repression of its own citizens. The granting of credits by the federal government was followed by several GDR concessions. The automatic firing devices on the border between the two Germanies were dismantled, travel restrictions were eased, the obligatory exchange requirement was reduced, and finally 34,000 people were given permission to emigrate, in the year 1984 alone. The release of political prisoners and their deportation to the Federal Republic was also part of this approach.

Relations with West Germany undoubtedly gave the GDR a privileged status among the CMEA countries. It profited not just from the successive credits it received but also from other payments made by the Federal Republic as a result of the travel treaty, the obligatory exchange of currency by visitors from the West, the overdraft facility granted to it and finally the increase in inter-German trade. By 1984, at the latest, the GDR possessed no economic alternative to this special relationship with the Federal Republic. The Soviet leadership recognised the threat this posed that the GDR would become estranged from the USSR and the other CMEA states, and increasingly dependent on the Bonn republic economically. The attempt the Soviets made in 1984 to torpedo the special relationship by forbidding Honecker's planned visit to Bonn temporarily postponed this development, but it could not stop it.

The SED Politburo, for its part, felt that the two credits it had received from West Germany were a confirmation that it was unnecessary to make any fundamental changes in economic and social policy. They had restored the GDR's creditworthiness, so that now further credits would pour in, and the 'unity of economic and social policy' could be maintained. In the next three years the country managed the remarkable accomplishment of reducing its debts to the West, though this occurred at the expense of investment. Right up to the collapse, the GDR economy remained stuck in a vicious circle from which it was unable to escape: debts needed to be serviced and social costs remained high, hence the resources available for investment shrank progressively. This in turn reduced the ability of GDR products to compete in the world market, so less hard currency could be obtained. But this meant that there was less hard currency available to reduce the level of debt, and as a result, investment had to fall yet further.

At the same time, the gap between the GDR and the leading economies of the world continued to increase. The reason for this was GDR economy's ever-increasing technological inferiority, its primary orientation towards heavy industry and its grievous shortcomings in the research and service sectors. Concentration on the classical industries led to overcapacity in sectors producing goods for which there was progressively less demand on the world market, and which could also be produced more cheaply in other parts of the globe. In the expanding industrial branches, such as microelectronics, communications, aircraft production and biochemicals, the GDR was so far behind that it would not be able to develop any competitive products for years to come. If it concentrated on markets in the CMEA countries, the Soviet Union above all, it could certainly sell its products, but this did not produce any hard currency. It also meant continuing to stick to old-fashioned production standards, which meant in turn that its products would finally become completely unsaleable on the world market.

In the late 1970s, the regime started to construct its own microelectronics industry without taking account of the global division of scientific and technological labour. This attempt bore witness to the tremendous inventiveness of East German engineers, but it probably cost 14 billion Marks (plus a further 4 billion of hard currency for the necessary Western imports). The final result was the production of a 256 kilobyte memory chip, which could be bought in the West for between 4 and 5 Marks, but cost 534 Marks to produce in the East. As long as the CMEA market remained sealed off from the Western world, products of this kind were in demand in the Eastern bloc. But, by the time the GDR had launched its chip production, most of the CMEA countries were already buying more modern products from the West, and the quickly outdated products of the GDR microelectronics industry had no chance of competing against them.[50]

How could the GDR leadership get out of this downward economic spiral? There were not many options, but the people at the top of the SED behaved for a long time as if this alarming trend were not actually happening. One reason for this was the party's system of organised self-deception over the real state of the GDR economy. The legend that the GDR's industry was the eleventh largest in the world, indeed that it was larger than Great Britain's, was spread in the West, and even believed, despite its absurdity. The statistics were vague and in part crudely falsified, and the value of a 'Foreign Exchange Mark' was not clearly defined. Accordingly, the level of foreign indebtedness was not a fixed magnitude but could be interpreted in different ways. But anyone who travelled around the country could not fail to perceive what a dreadful state it was in. Its industrial installations were completely obsolete, its infrastructure was in a state of collapse. The roads, the railway network and local transport were only partially capable of functioning. Old buildings were not being renovated, and the telephone network was crumbling.

The story of the GDR's economic development is accurately summarised as follows by the economic historian André Steiner: 'For years the GDR had lived above its means, as reflected in its domestic and foreign indebtedness and in the decay of its capital stock. Indeed, the economic break-up should have been foreseeable if there were no thorough-going change to the system's economic conditions.' A new economic environment had emerged in the late 1970s, characterised by the declining importance of classical industry, the globalisation of markets and the spread of new, EDP-based forms of production. The socialist economic regime proved unable to react to these changes. In Steiner's view, therefore, the decisive reason for the decline of the GDR economy was 'the socialist economic system's immanent incapacity to produce structural and technological or innovatory change.'[51]

Could the GDR leadership have confronted these issues with greater determination? The SED leaders were of the opinion that if they took the road of a rigorous austerity policy, with price increases and cuts in social policy and subsidies, the country would become ungovernable within a short time. A policy of consistent economic reform, on the other hand, would lead to the victory of the principle of supply and demand, performance-related pay and an orientation towards productivity and ultimately to a quasi-capitalist economic system. Either choice would have called both socialism and the rule of the SED into question.

## A Society with Limited Prospects

Against this background, it is hardly surprising that the SED leadership adopted not just a critical but an entirely negative attitude towards Gorbachev's initiatives. There were certainly members of the party who were sympathetic to Gorbachev's course, but the leadership quickly slapped down all attempts to emulate the Soviet Union's reforming endeavours. In April 1987, Kurt Hager commented on Gorbachev's policies in words which soon became proverbial: 'By the way, if your neighbour decided to redecorate, would you feel you ought to redecorate as well?'[52] 'Glasnost' and 'Perestroika', in other words, public discussion and the restructuring of the state and the economy, were exact descriptions of what the SED leadership feared most. 'Glasnost' threatened the party's monopoly of opinion and its claim to leadership, because in a pluralistic society there would soon be calls for the authorisation of opposition parties, and eventually for free elections, as indeed happened in the Soviet Union. A 'Perestroika', or restructuring of the economy, by which private initiative was encouraged and market forces were strengthened, would sooner or later push aside the state economy of socialism. But this would mean the end of the GDR as a socialist state, as Günter Mittag, the SED's chief economic planner, unequivocally asserted: 'If the economic base is formed in a capitalist way, the socialist superstructure cannot maintain itself.'[53] The fears of the SED leadership were probably more realistic and also more far-sighted than Moscow's reforming enthusiasm, especially as the SED had few illusions about the outcome of free elections.

There was another factor, too. The SED leaders felt that Honecker's state visit to the Federal Republic had confirmed their view of the world. According to a report to the Politburo, the visit, and Honecker's respectful treatment in Bonn, 'documented the independence and equal rights of both German states, and underlined their sovereignty and the international character of their relationship'.[54] The GDR stood at the zenith of its worldwide reputation. It was greatly valued as a stable and reliable force in the framework of international relations. In face of this recognition, which the SED leaders had long yearned for, the internal problems of the GDR and the irritation caused by developments in Moscow seemed to fade into the background. It seemed easier to cooperate with the Federal Republic and get a grip on the country's economic problems by that method.

The SED leaders therefore did not mince their words in criticising Gorbachev's reforming course, and they tried to curtail his influence on the GDR as much as possible. 'Previously we only had to meet a frontal attack conducted in the German language; now it is happening behind our backs in every nook and cranny', the FDGB chair Harry Tisch told the Politburo.[55] Criticisms of this type referred very specifically to the historical debate which was now emerging in the Soviet Union, a debate which for the first time ever involved not just a denunciation of the mass crimes of Stalinism and a demand for the rehabilitation of the victims, but also a critical examination of the role of the Soviet Union in the Second World War. A German-language version of the Soviet journal *Sputnik* had always been widely distributed in the GDR. But, on November 1988, it published an article about the Hitler–Stalin Pact of summer 1939 and its secret appendix. The GDR authorities reacted by refusing to distribute the periodical. This was an action unprecedented in the whole history of relations between the GDR and the Soviet Union, and it made clear the depth of the alienation that now existed between the two ruling socialist parties.[56]

Gorbachev's international initiatives were even more dangerous for the GDR than his domestic reforms. His vision of a 'common European home', in which different systems and ideologies would live alongside one other and enter into competition, could be seen as a way of excluding the USA from the 'common home' because it was a non-European power. But it was also understood, particularly in the Eastern bloc countries, as a denial of the class struggle and the political antagonism between East and West. The GDR evidently no longer played a prominent role in the thinking of the Soviet Party leadership, and in this context Gorbachev's abandonment of the Brezhnev Doctrine, at first expressed unclearly but then ever more explicitly, was seen as an alarm signal. It was regarded as both an expression of the Soviet Union's lessening involvement in the 'fraternal countries' and an invitation to them to pursue their own path to socialism.

In September 1986 the Soviet and GDR positions came into direct confrontation. The Soviet writer Yevgeny Yevtushenko stated in an interview on West German television that in his view separate 'West German' and 'East German' literatures did not exist, and he added: 'I think that this great German nation, which has produced such great philosophy, music and literature, must in future be reunited.' The Soviet government did not react to this, but Honecker, who regarded these remarks as a 'counter-revolutionary provocation' directed against the GDR, angrily told the head of the Soviet Party 'you should arrange for these people to appear in Siberia, not in West Berlin.'[57]

Within East German society, in contrast, Gorbachev's ideas and his reforms met with wholehearted agreement. More than that, they gave rise to the hope that things would perhaps improve in the near future, although the blight of declining socialism had almost choked off enthusiasm and creativity even within the party. The preferred way of life in the GDR of the 1980s was to perform the absolutely necessary duties during the week and then retreat at the weekend into real life, in other words, private life. The authorities and the party no longer insisted on citizens' active commitment. Unless a person made trouble, the party did not intervene.

Counter-cultural 'scenes' had now emerged in the cities. Those who took part treated the normal way of life in the GDR as completely unreal, as an artificial stage presentation. Beginning in the early 1980s, political opposition groups also emerged in this milieu. Such groups were fluid and without any clear affiliations, and they were also small and hard to distinguish from simple friendship networks. They did not number more than perhaps 5,000 people in the whole of the country. Like Biermann, Havemann, Bahro and their supporters, most members of these groups were idealistic left-wingers, and their preferred goal was not to join the Federal Republic or the West but to create a reformed and democratic, but also somehow socialist, GDR. Almost all of them had developed in the environment of the Protestant Church, the function of which in the GDR was both unique and ambivalent. On the one hand, it was 'the church in socialism'. It had made its peace with the regime, and had been rewarded by the grant of relative autonomy. On the other hand, many of its congregations offered a refuge for those who were unable to adjust, the non-conformists, the conscientious objectors or simply the discontented. Most, if not all, were young people whose attitudes and political ideas were aligned with the alternative Left of the Western world, and above all West Germany.

They also shared their most pressing political objectives with this alternative Left. In the first phase, which began in 1980, the ideas of the peace movement were dominant. However, the demands of the opposition differed from the constant peace proclamations by East German state and party leaders in their stress on the need for disarmament by both West *and* East. The SED always praised the West German peace movement when it protested against NATO's plans to extend nuclear armaments to Germany, but the supporters of the peace movement in East Germany were persecuted as enemy agents, and pacifism was 'unmasked' there as a bourgeois ideology. Even the wearing of the 'Swords into Ploughshares' emblem was forcibly repressed by the state. Policemen tore off the emblem when it was sewn onto jackets or coats, and schoolchildren who wore it received a school reprimand, although the emblem itself was a copy of a bronze artefact by a Soviet artist which the Soviet Union had presented to the United Nations Organisation in 1959.[58]

The first major event in the GDR peace movement took place in February 1982. Shortly before that date, Robert Havemann and the East Berlin pastor Rainer Eppelmann had reinforced the demand for worldwide disarmament by issuing their 'Berlin Appeal', which was also distributed to the Western media. After Eppelmann's temporary arrest, some 5,000 people demonstrated in front of the ruins of the Frauenkirche in Dresden for peace, on the anniversary of the city's destruction at the end of the Second World War.

It was also remarkable that the Berlin Appeal called for the withdrawal of the troops of the Great Powers from both parts of Germany, and even addressed the possibility of reunification. The recovery of German nationhood was occasionally raised as an issue in this movement, as also happened in West Germany. The Open Letter to Leonid Brezhnev composed by Robert Havemann in 1981 was a prime example of this. Havemann demanded the withdrawal of 'all occupation troops from both parts of Germany', adding: 'How we Germans will then solve our national question must be left to us, and no one ought to find that a more frightening prospect than nuclear war.' Havemann's Berlin Appeal was signed by Rainer Eppelmann and the physicist Gerd Poppe, both of whom were leading protagonists of the early opposition movement in the GDR, but it was also signed by West German supporters, such as the Protestant theologians Heinrich Albertz, Helmut Scharf and Helmut Gollwitzer, the writers Martin Walser and Walter Jens and the politicians Hans Ulrich Klose (SPD) and Otto Schily (Green Party).[59] Havemann explained his ideas later in an interview with West German television journalists. He said that in view of the acute danger of annihilation, the confrontation between East and West was the greatest evil of all, and, in comparison with it, the class struggle between socialism and capitalism was a secondary matter. He was therefore ready to accept reunification, even if 'it did not occur quite in accordance with my wishes . . . Issues of vital importance to the German people must not be decided by the police but by the will of the population.'[60]

On the whole, though, these were isolated voices. The national question was not an important issue for the GDR peace movement. Ecological matters had begun to assume greater significance. Pollution of the environment, which had been regarded until then, as it was in the West in the 1960s and 1970s, as an unavoidable concomitant of progress and industrial growth, was now criticised by newly emerging groups of environmentalists on the ground that it was destroying the natural foundations of life. The nuclear accident at Chernobyl in spring 1986 had a climactic impact on this movement, although the GDR population learned very little about it from the state media, and nothing that was accurate. No warnings about radioactive fallout were given, and all references to safety problems in the GDR's two nuclear reactors were suppressed. The population was therefore once again dependent on the Western media. Soon a number of action groups drew attention to the hazardous character of the GDR's nuclear power stations, which had been constructed in the Soviet Union, under the slogan 'Chernobyl is Everywhere'. Their efforts were supported by groups from West Germany, above all the Greens, who also helped to establish the Berlin 'Environmental Library'.

Anarchist ideas also emerged in the GDR, as they did elsewhere. The anarchists were vague and confused in their politics, but they did express the search for something as far away as possible from the model of society called GDR socialism. There was also a punk movement. This had been spreading in the GDR since the early 1980s. It was repeatedly subjected to repression by the authorities, and it too found a refuge in some church communities. The opposition spread through all the cities, and numerous different groups were formed.

Books and texts rejected by the censor were distributed, 'blues masses' were held, combining religious services with blues music, support was given to gays and lesbians, and peace forums were organised, at which songs critical of the regime were sung. Most of these activities, however, remained closely tied to the Church institutions and did not win any influence on the majority of East Germans. But, despite their small numbers, the authorities and the Stasi saw the opposition groups as dangerous, especially as their criticism of nuclear weapons and environmental pollution as well as their stress on the threat from nuclear accidents could not readily be stigmatised as subversive and anti-socialist.[61]

From 1987 onwards, these dissident currents were increasingly inspired by Gorbachev's policies. His reforms addressed questions of democracy, human rights, transparency and economic reform, and since the opposition groups appealed to the example set by the leader of the Soviet Communist Party, it was difficult for the Stasi to know how to proceed. It reported with irritation that prayers were said in church services for the success of the Soviet leader's reform policy. The authorities attempted to get a grip on these movements with infiltration, surveillance and subtle pressure rather than by arrests and the use of force. This was the method used in November 1987, for instance, when the oppositional songwriters Freya Klier and Stephan Krawczyk were scheduled to appear at a church service in the small Lusatian town of Groß Bademeusel. Coachloads of security personnel arrived there a few days in advance. The place looked as if it had been put under martial law, checkpoints were established on all access routes, local traffic was interrupted, the church was occupied by members of the Stasi, and the meeting was finally called off.[62] This completely disproportionate expenditure of effort testified to the nervousness and apprehension felt by the state and party authorities. In June 1988, according to the Ministry of State Security, there were only 160 oppositional groups in the country, comprising some 2,500 individuals altogether, 600 of them in 'leading positions'. Of these groups, 150 were connected with the churches, including thirty-five 'peace circles', thirty-nine of an ecological orientation, twenty-three groups in favour of 'peace and the environment', seven women's rights groups, three doctors' groups and some further groups of conscientious objectors and 'third world activists'.[63]

These groups had no political support, or almost none, from the population at large. 'We were an insignificant minority, without the kind of backing from the people enjoyed for instance by Solidarity in Poland' is how Reinhard Schult, one of the most prominent opposition leaders, describes the situation in retrospect.[64] Most people in the GDR had never heard of the dissidents, or were only aware of them through Western television. It was often insinuated that these activists for peace and the environment were mainly trying to get expelled to the West. These rumours were eagerly confirmed by the Stasi's unofficial collaborators (IMs). The widespread hostility to the Church which was felt within the SED also played a role in the way the activists for peace and the environment were perceived, as they were always associated with church communities. Moreover, in the GDR, as indeed in the West, people were dismissive and contemptuous of long-haired daydreamers who were uninterested in making a career or improving their social position. After 1990 it turned out that half the members of some of these groups were Stasi spies; even so, the authorities did not succeed in entirely disabling or destroying them. It became apparent at the end of the 1980s that an energetic and very self-confident core of activists had now emerged, and the events of 1989 brought them increasingly into the heart of political developments in the GDR.

Since the late 1970s, the socialist world had tested various ways of escaping its predicament. The first way, represented by North Korea, was to continue the Stalinist military dictatorship of Kim Il-Sung. This involved breaking off all economic contacts with the West and reducing the standard of living of the population so much that devastating food shortages developed. The second option was the Chinese road. Since the early 1980s, a unique combination of communist dictatorship and capitalist economics had arisen under Deng Xiaoping. Since then, China had registered more than two decades of tremendous growth and soon it started to operate in the world market with extraordinary success. The cost of this, however, was the emergence of an impoverished army of millions of migratory workers, who barely had enough to live on, while the new middle and upper classes became wealthy and adopted a thoroughly Western way of life. The third road was taken by Gorbachev, with his reforms, which aimed to restructure the Soviet Union both economically and politically, in order to maintain both communist rule and the socialist planned economy. For the GDR leaders, neither a military dictatorship nor a combination of communist rule with a market economy as in China was a conceivable choice. But they also regarded Gorbachev's reforms as a path to their own certain downfall, not without good reason.

In 1987, the average age of the twenty-one members of the SED Politburo was sixty-five. The formative experiences of most of them dated back to the pre-war years. Their picture of the world was dominated economically by handicrafts and heavy industry, and politically by the antagonism between the working class and the bourgeoisie, and between capitalism and communism. They clung onto this picture of the world, even when it had turned out that the 1971 change of direction towards consumer socialism was a failure. In their eyes, the correctness and necessity of socialism, which they regarded as the historically inevitable and scientifically correct reply to capitalism, was unaffected by what the economic situation had to offer, because the rules of historical inevitability could not be called into question by a mere economic crisis. According to the observations of the sociologist M. Rainer Lepsius, the 'fragmented perceptions of reality' that were rife among the top functionaries of the SED were 'bridged over by their common belief in the superior quality of socialism as a principle, by the charisma of the idea, as it were'.[65] The course that commended itself, therefore, was to continue to muddle through, to increase exports, to intensify trade with the CMEA countries, where GDR goods were in demand, and to hope for the continued support of the Federal Republic and the continued availability of Western credits. At some point in the future, the superiority of socialism would become evident. 'It could already be foreseen that the whole thing would topple over'. That is how the General Director of a cosmetics combine described the situation between 1986 and 1989 in retrospect. 'I always thought', she continued,

> Who knows? Maybe someone will manage to find a way out. I actually thought, because at that time the outcome was a bit in the balance, perhaps we shall cooperate with the Federal Republic on an economic basis, or something like that. But I didn't think things would come out as they actually did.[66]

The ordinary inhabitants of the GDR, on the other hand, reacted to the increasingly evident defects in the functioning of the system and the constant barrage of propaganda by losing interest in politics and withdrawing into their own restricted private sphere. Most GDR citizens were forced to adapt themselves to standardised living conditions which left little room for individual decisions. Nevertheless, the mode of life was not so intolerable as to force people into open revolt, as had happened in Poland. They therefore attempted to make the best of an apparently immutable situation by enjoying as much private life as possible and offering as much official conformity as was necessary. The chief features of life in the GDR were the lack of any prospect of change, and a sense of hopelessness, which the individual faced with opportunism, sarcasm or apathy. These reactions varied according to the temperament of the person in question. But the socialist virtues demanded by the SED were closely connected with the traditional values of the authoritarian state, and the social processes of individualisation and liberalisation which had gained the upper hand since the 1960s in the West were suppressed in the GDR.

Despite this suppression, developments which had taken place in the West, particularly in the cultural field, were tremendously attractive to young people in the GDR, because the 1970s had seen the widespread replacement of the East German mentality of obedience by ideas of self-realisation and individuality. This change did not take on a political character because the East Germans did not possess any public spaces where they could bring these attitudes to bear. The opposition groups were small and isolated and they were hardly even noticed by the population. They nevertheless formed a kind of intellectual and cultural power centre which at the moment of upheaval brought forth a counter-elite, which for several months exerted a strong influence on the process of transformation. Only when the regime had actually collapsed did the magnitude of the psychological and political distance which already separated the population of East Germany from the SED system finally became clear.

# 20
# Germany in 1990

## A Twofold Unification

The period 1989–90 was one of the most eventful in modern German and European history. It can be compared with 1789, 1812, 1848–9, 1914 and 1945. Like those dates, 1989–90 witnessed the culmination of a series of long-term tendencies, medium-term developments and short-term events, which finally brought about an explosion, setting off profound tremors and long-lasting transformations. When accumulated tensions are unloaded in this way it is also noticeable that even contemporaries are able to perceive the changes as significant and historic, the more so when they come as a complete surprise, like the events of the night of 9 to 10 November 1989. 'Madness!' was the word used most often by those citizens of the GDR who were suddenly permitted by the border guards to pass through the Wall unimpeded and thus to get into West Berlin, only a few months after twenty-year-old Chris Gueffroy had been shot dead by the border guards when he attempted to climb over the Wall. 'Madness!' meant that something entirely unbelievable and unforeseen but at the same time utterly delightful had occurred, something no one had previously thought possible, in spite of the political earthquakes of the preceding weeks and months in the GDR and the whole of the Eastern bloc.

But here the difference between the views of contemporaries and the perspective of the historian comes into play. In retrospect, why such an event was regarded as so unexpected and sensational requires just as much explanation as the contemporary expectations and convictions which suddenly turned out to be misperceptions, engendering a false sense of security. Many things which seemed inexplicable to contemporaries appear logical and comprehensible in hindsight. But the perceptions of contemporaries are themselves a factor which influenced the course of events: if everyone had expected the Wall to be opened, the whole episode would have taken place differently—or indeed it might not have occurred at all.

The First World War can be understood from a historical perspective not only as the 'original catastrophe' of the twentieth century, but also as the product of a far-reaching series of earlier upheavals in all spheres of society; in the same way, a historical view of the years before 1989 needs to identify the developments which preceded, made possible and conditioned the opening of the Wall and the collapse of the Soviet empire. Globalisation, changes in the structure of industry, the digital revolution and the cultural upheavals of the 1970s and 1980s can then be recognised as factors which contributed to the downfall of Soviet domination in Europe. At the same time, however, these factors far transcend that single event both chronologically and in depth of impact.

It should be added that the symbolic character of the date '1989' is not limited to Germany and Europe. It marks a decisive turning point in the modern history of South Africa and Afghanistan, and not all of these events can be traced back to common roots. Even so, they interacted with one another. A dominant sense of upheaval arose, which itself acquired worldwide historical potency, promoting a global thrust towards democratisation of a kind otherwise present only in 1919 and 1945. In this case the limitations of a purely national approach to history appear still more clearly than in other epochs. Thanks to the way Germany lay right at the heart of the Cold War division, a fact that was once again made abundantly clear in 1989, it looks more plausible to write a 'German' history for the period before that date than afterwards. After 1989–90, the world becomes more polycentric and German history less self-referential, and indeed less important from a global perspective, though it is admittedly hard to find a proper standard of measurement for evaluations of this nature.

The list of protagonists who had an impact on German history in this long year which lasted from spring 1989 to autumn 1990 is long, and by no means all of them were German. If one proceeds from the reunification of Germany as the core event which needs to be described here, several concentric circles comprising ten or more groups of active participants need to be specified: first the government of the GDR, the opposition groups and the GDR population itself; then the forces in West Germany: the government, and particularly the West German Chancellor, and the West German public, while the parliamentary opposition is less in evidence as an independent factor. Then the Soviet government, in which Mikhail Gorbachev in many respects played the decisive role, alongside the complex field of political forces and counter-forces in the CPSU during the later phases of perestroika. Finally, the diverse aggregates composed of communist governments, reforming forces, opposition groups and popular masses in the countries of a deliquescent Central and Eastern Europe, particularly Poland, Hungary and Czechoslovakia. The decisive role on the Western side was undoubtedly played by the US government under George Bush, though developments were also influenced to various degrees by the heads of government in France and Great Britain, as well as the European Community and NATO.

Finally, however, it was also significant, and indeed towards the end of pivotal importance, that at this time the Western states, and particularly the Federal Republic, were in the middle of an economic boom, which considerably increased their financial room for manoeuvre in negotiations. Personal factors, the sympathies and antipathies of individuals, also played a part in these events, and not least sheer chance. The large number of protagonists, and the extraordinary dynamism of the development in which these groups were simultaneously active in varying configurations, would suggest an approach which does not proceed subject by subject but is structured in chronological phases, each phase lasting roughly a quarter of a year, beginning in spring 1989 and ending late in the autumn 1990.

## The Erosion of the Eastern Bloc

The Federal Republic celebrated its fortieth birthday in May 1989 with a mixture of guarded pride and studied scepticism. 'Our picture is made up of light and shade, as is the case everywhere', declared President von Weizsäcker on the fortieth anniversary of the proclamation of the Basic Law. On the one hand, he said, the Federal Republic is one of the richest countries in the world. On the other hand, however, many people 'do not have a high standard of living, and they suffer rather under great difficulties'. The state must step in energetically to assist them. But the extension of social policy has the drawback that in the society of the Federal Republic a 'safety-first mentality' has developed. 'The individual's interests are safeguarded and given priority at the expense of society as a whole. The threshold of tolerance has become lower.' Life in the Federal Republic is therefore characterised by contradictions:

> More specialisation, less breadth of vision; more technological connections, less human contact; more restlessness, less time; more goods on offer, less concentration; more prosperity, less clarity over the task in hand; greater openness to the world, fewer roots. We are moulded by the age of technology. But the constitution and the legal system can hardly inform us about the essential character of technology. Our way of life, and thus the whole of our culture, is characterised by tensions of this kind.

We therefore have to learn 'to live with the contradictions of progress.'[1]

Similarly restrained analyses came from the other side of the political spectrum, from the Left liberal newspapers, and also from magazines like *Stern*, which devoted a special issue to the anniversary. According to its leading article, the Federal Republic's fortieth birthday should not be marked simply by 'congratulations'. The country's Nazi past, the resurgence of the former Nazi elites, the emergency laws and the reduction of life to economic growth did not permit that. The Federal Republic had made production and consumption 'the first duty of the citizen'. There were no 'intellectual giants' in its top leadership bodies, only 'chief accountants adding up export figures'. Mediocrity ruled—'but is there anywhere in the world where the best and the wisest are in charge?' It was true that people had never had it so good, and that the Federal Republic was without doubt 'the freest and most socially focused community' in German history. But this was not a big achievement, given the nature of that history. In general, then, it was enough to say that this state was 'by and large O.K.' A 'strongly critical commitment' and a 'combative political culture' were 'ultimately more supportive of the state than any sort of pompous affirmation of faith in the nation and the fatherland.'[2]

This cool reaction still clearly bore the echoes of the conflicts of the 1970s and 1980s, though there is also an unmistakable element of coquettish posing here. But mixed verdicts of this kind also reflected the negative experiences Germans had previously had with expressions of national self-satisfaction and obdurate affirmations of progress. Hence the articles and speeches commemorating the fortieth anniversary were dominated by a rather artificial endeavour to display a self-critical attitude and a certain mistrust of both the past and the future, which was intended to demonstrate that democratic and liberal maturity had finally been acquired.

The intended audience was the outside world as well as the people at home. The affirmation that the Federal Republic was a reliable and loyal partner of the West also served as a counterweight to the increasingly widespread perception of West Germany as the dominant economic power in Europe, which provoked anxiety and suspicion in many countries, not least France.

In domestic politics, it had become apparent that by now the Left, including the Greens, regarded this state as their own. Their response, though, was to raise the volume of their criticisms. Even among the politicians of the Union, no anniversary text was without its reference to the great importance of ecology and critical initiatives by the country's citizens. On the other hand, there was no longer any trace of the conservatives' traditional anti-Western reservations or their cultural critique of the Federal Republic as a state imposed by the West. When Federal Chancellor Kohl gave a historical retrospect a few months earlier, he was clearly concerned to convince the supporters of his party once again that the involvement of the Federal Republic in the movement for European unification did not contradict the perspective of an eventual reunification of Germany. 'If we are pushing forward with European unification, this is not because we have written off our compatriots in the GDR or our other European neighbours in Central, East and South East Europe. On the contrary: we have faith that the European unity project will prove greatly attractive.' Apart from that, Kohl, like the others, qualified his satisfaction with what the country had achieved with grave warnings against 'smugness, satiety and complacency'.[3]

People who warn against the danger of satiety haven't usually suffered much from hunger, and indeed things were in general going very well for the Federal Republic at the end of the 1980s. In the GDR, on the other hand, the crisis of the regime, which had been clearly apparent since the start of the decade, began to come to a head at the end of 1988. The Soviet Union's perestroika policy had considerably worsened the situation. The banning of the Soviet journal *Sputnik*, which had published documents on the Hitler–Stalin Pact, showed the panic the new course had provoked in the SED leadership, and the decision was even questioned by party members. The death of Chris Gueffroy on 6 February 1989 aroused so much concern both domestically and internationally that shortly afterwards the GDR government suspended the order to shoot at people attempting to cross the border, though it kept the decision secret. The SED leadership reacted to the increasing unrest in the country in its accustomed manner, by mounting a purge of the party. The purge started in Dresden, for several reasons. Firstly because the local population had been particularly critical of the bad supply situation and other deficiencies, and secondly because a particularly large number of emigration applications had been made from there. In addition to that, the head of the Dresden SED, Hans Modrow, was regarded, rightly or wrongly, as a supporter of Gorbachev, hence the intention behind the choice of Dresden was to send a clear signal that the party was opposed to 'reformers' in its ranks. In actual fact, however, this measure led to further unrest within the party, which contained a fair number of supporters of Gorbachev, and it confirmed the impression that the SED was in the throes of severe disagreements and factional struggles.[4]

But the beginning of the end of the GDR should actually be dated from 7 May 1989, when local elections were held. Until then, no one had paid much attention to GDR elections. The candidates of the SED and the bloc parties had always obtained more than 95 per cent of the vote, and everyone had always known that the results were manipulated. After these elections too, it was announced that 99 per cent of the electorate had turned out to vote, and only one per cent had cast their votes against the United List. But this time critics of the regime in many towns and cities had set out to observe the voting procedure and witness the counting of the votes, following the example of the opposition movement in Poland. The SED tried to put a stop to this, but it was no longer strong enough in every case to prevent an action which was in fact nominally guaranteed by the constitution. The result was an immense increase in the significance of the dissident citizens' opposition. Nothing like this had ever been known before in the GDR.

At first only small groups of people were openly involved. There were a few hundred dissidents in Leipzig, for example. Most of them came from the milieu of the Protestant Church, which since the early 1980s had been the focal point of discontent over the lack of democracy in the country. The encouraging example of the Polish opposition, as well as developments in the Soviet Union, played a great role in the growth of the GDR protest movement. The fact that the SED no longer seemed able to confront the democratic election observers energetically and by force if necessary was also a contributory factor to the opposition's success.

According to the election observers, the actual voter turnout was only 70 per cent, and the number of votes against the United List lay between 3 per cent and 30 per cent. News of the SED's obvious, and in most cases clumsy, manipulation of the results spread quickly, and the elections immediately became a symbol for the untrustworthiness of the ruling party. In many places, a local citizens' movement emerged from this campaign to observe the elections. It was also the starting point for the regular Monday demonstrations held in Leipzig, which were originally directed against the electoral fraud but later broadened their target to the rule of the SED as such.[5]

In the Soviet Union, on the other hand, the first partially free elections for seventy-five years had just been held, with a completely different result. A semi-parliamentary body was elected there on 26 March 1989, under the title 'Congress of People's Deputies', and it rapidly laid claim to an extensive range of prerogatives. Parts of the election campaign were transmitted on television, and a large number of political tendencies, wings and groups formed within and alongside the Communist Party. An increasingly pugnacious public debate began to be conducted about the political future of the country. Soviet citizens denounced corruption and repression, and even the KGB was openly criticised. Individuals and groups calling for pluralism and a market economy stepped forward with increasing self-confidence. Nationalist movements also began to criticise Russian rule more aggressively, demanding partial autonomy, or even the separation of their territories from the Soviet Union. They received strong support from the local population, above all in the Baltic region and the Caucasus.

As late as 1988 the Soviet Union was still able to register positive economic growth figures, but in 1989 the situation began to worsen dramatically. A supply crisis started in the spring of that year, and it spread rapidly, soon becoming the central issue faced by the whole country. Because of these internal developments, the Soviet leadership, and the Soviet population, paid less and less attention to matters of foreign policy. But it became increasingly clear that if the country wanted to deal with the critical domestic situation it would have to reduce its international obligations. Gorbachev met this requirement by withdrawing his troops from Afghanistan, as well as by making disarmament agreements with the USA. In view of the worsening internal crisis, however, the relationship of the Soviet Union with its European satellites and the burdens that imposed also needed critical examination. Gorbachev had repeatedly said that in future the Soviet Union's allies would have to go their own way. In December 1988, speaking to the United Nations, he reaffirmed his renunciation of force and the threat of force, and proclaimed the right of every country to choose its own social system freely. In July 1989, at a meeting of Warsaw Pact heads of government, this principle was publicly reinforced, and a declaration was adopted 'that every nation determines its own fate and has the right to choose the social, political and economic system and the state constitution which it deems appropriate to its situation'.[6]

The Kremlin leadership had of course often spoken in previous years about the renunciation of force and respect for national sovereignty—and practised the opposite. To that extent, these and similar comments by the General Secretary of the CPSU were initially greeted with mistrust in the Eastern bloc countries. Both the governments and the opposition movements ventured forward only cautiously and slowly in the direction of pluralism and reform, because they always feared that if they proceeded too assertively the Red Army would intervene, even now. The historian Andreas Rödder sums up the situation in this way: 'The Brezhnev Doctrine only really ceased to operate when the Soviet leadership ceased to apply it *and* the people no longer feared it.'[7]

It was in Poland and Hungary that the process of emancipation from Moscow first became evident. In Poland, the government of General Jaruzelski had ruled since 1981 under martial law. It was now in terminal decline. By September 1988, economic distress had finally attained such dimensions that the Polish United Workers' Party (the Communist Party) appointed the reforming communist Mieczyław Rakowski as prime minister. Rakowski immediately began to institute reforms aimed at establishing a market economy, but he soon came to grief with these, and eventually decided that the only way out was to conduct 'roundtable discussions' with representatives of the opposition. These began in February 1989. They led first to the re-legalisation of Solidarity and then to the calling of fresh elections on a genuinely free and secret basis. They resulted in a landslide victory for the opposition, which obtained an incredible 160 out of 161 possible seats in the Polish parliament, the Sejm, and ninety-two out of one hundred seats in the Senate. On 24 August 1989 Tadeusz Mazowiecki, a leading member of Solidarity, was elected as prime minister. This was 'the first government in the whole of the Eastern bloc that was not dominated by the communists', notes the Polish historian Włodzimierz Borodziej: 'Poland had demonstrated to its neighbours how actually existing socialism could be peacefully dismantled. This was an event of epoch-making significance.'[8]

In Hungary, the socialist government had also begun to dismantle itself in February 1989. The regime in Budapest counted as more liberal, and its economic policy as more consumer-friendly than that of its allies in Prague or East Berlin. But the rule of János Kádár, who had been in power for more than thirty years, was overshadowed right to the end by the bloody suppression of the rising of 1956. The rehabilitation of the Hungarian uprising and its leaders, particularly Imre Nagy, who had been executed in 1958, therefore became a symbol of liberation from the dictatorship. In February 1989 roundtable discussions with the opposition began over the introduction of a multi-party system, and in mid-June the group started to discuss a new constitution. But it was not fully apparent that communism in Hungary was about to collapse until 16 June 1989, when the mortal remains of Imre Nagy were reburied in a place of honour, at a ceremony attended by more than 200,000 people. This event was a signal that communist rule was about to come to an end. Hungarian border troops had already removed the barbed wire fences from the boundary with Austria on 2 May, and at the end of June the border between the two countries was officially opened. This was the first step towards dismantling the Iron Curtain that ran across Europe.[9]

The oppositional forces faced greater difficulties in the other countries of the dissolving Eastern bloc, namely Czechoslovakia, Bulgaria and Romania. But here too, clear signs of an upheaval could be distinguished, particularly in Prague, where the opposition centred around the writer Václav Havel, which had been suppressed for decades, now began to re-emerge. Despite developments in Poland and Hungary, however, the situation in East Central Europe continued to be completely open. The oppositionists were still not able entirely to trust Moscow's assurances of non-intervention, especially as no one knew how long Gorbachev and his foreign minister Shevardnadze would be able to maintain themselves against the opposition of the military and the hardliners in the CPSU. Simultaneous events in China were a clear demonstration of the possible risks. A democratic opposition movement had grown up in China since the mid-1980s. It had many supporters, particularly among university students. The opposition had been holding mass demonstrations in Tiananmen Square since the beginning of April 1989, and these came to the attention of the world in the middle of May 1989 during Gorbachev's visit to Beijing. On 4 June, however, the Chinese Communist Party ordered armed detachments of the People's Liberation Army to suppress them by force. The number of deaths that resulted probably exceeded 2,000, including more than one hundred soldiers.[10]

Developments in East Central Europe were followed particularly attentively in the GDR. The SED leaders continued to oppose reform movements there as fiercely as they opposed what was happening in the Soviet Union. When Gorbachev expostulated with Honecker that the problems of socialism would not be solved by 'the old system of command and administration', the latter replied defiantly that in the GDR the unity of economic and social policy had proved its value as the foundation of socialism. The SED leadership's line continued to be the promotion of social policy rather than concessions to democracy. The GDR differed from the other Eastern bloc states in that its existence was inextricably connected with socialism. Hungary and Poland, said the rector of the Berlin Academy of Social Sciences, Otto Reinhold, in August 1989, already existed before their socialist transformation, and their state existence was therefore independent of their social system. The GDR on the other hand was 'only imaginable as an anti-Fascist, socialist alternative to the Federal Republic. What right to exist would a capitalist GDR have, alongside a capitalist Federal Republic? None at all, of course.'[11]

Even so, many observers were surprised by the SED leadership's explicit support for the Tiananmen Square massacre. 'People's Liberation Army of China Crushes a Counter-Revolutionary Revolt' announced *Neues Deutschland* on 5 June, and the GDR People's Chamber explicitly welcomed the action of the Chinese leadership, which had succeeded, it said, in 're-establishing order and security by deploying the armed forces' after the 'violent and bloody excesses committed by elements hostile to the constitution'.[12] These were clear warning signs to the opposition movement in the GDR, because the way the GDR media commented on the events in Beijing led to the fear 'that the GDR leadership might also use armed force against demonstrations'.[13]

But the destabilisation of the SED regime during the summer of 1989 was not propelled by mass rallies and demonstrations but rather by the growth of a movement of flight and emigration. Events in Hungary lay at the source of this movement. Having dismantled the country's frontier barriers in May 1989, the Hungarian government no longer carried out border controls as carefully as before. When word began to spread of this, GDR citizens started to pour into the country as tourists, with the aim of eventually reaching the West. On 19 August 1989, 661 GDR citizens fled across the border into Austria, and more followed as time went on. News of these events spread rapidly to the GDR through media reports, and as a result, the influx into Hungary increased still further, and the Hungarian government had to set up refugee camps for several thousand people. But Hungarian border guards now began to prevent any further attempts to cross into Austria. Many GDR citizens reacted to this development by taking refuge in the Federal Republic's embassies in Budapest and Prague, as well as in the Office of the Federal Republic's Permanent Representative in East Berlin.

Up to that point, the federal government in Bonn had reacted to developments in East Central Europe and the GDR in a sympathetic but also a reserved manner. Now, however, it seized the initiative and at a secret meeting with the Hungarian government held on 25 August near Bonn it was agreed that the Hungarians would open the border between Austria and Hungary to refugees from the GDR. In return, Hungary was guaranteed a credit of a billion DM, which the country urgently needed in view of its own economic problems. The border with Austria was opened for GDR citizens on 11 September, and during the next three weeks almost 30,000 of them fled through Hungary to the West. Western television stations reported on these events every evening, and this underlined the impotence of the GDR government, which was powerless to stop the exodus, and received no support in doing so from the Soviet Union. The GDR foreign minister sarcastically asked Moscow what the actual purpose of the alliance was if it failed to operate in such a situation.[14]

An even more difficult question for the SED leadership was how to deal with those GDR citizens who had taken refuge in the embassies of the Federal Republic. In Prague almost 4,000 people had ensconced themselves in the grounds of the West German embassy, filling them to capacity, and days went by before Foreign Minister Genscher was able after protracted negotiations to announce to the thunderous applause of those who had chosen to remain that they could now emigrate to the Federal Republic. These events did not take place as in previous decades amid obscurity and disinformation but in full view of the cameras of Western television companies, which transmitted their pictures over the globe.

By the end of the summer, the SED leadership was in a difficult, almost hopeless situation. Owing to the collapse of socialist regimes elsewhere, the GDR authorities had been forced to close the country's borders with its neighbours in order to stem the flow of refugees, and this increased the level of domestic discontent still further. The GDR authorities were convinced that reforms on the Polish or Hungarian model would call into question not only the SED regime's right to exist but also the right of the GDR itself to continue as a separate state. But if the GDR leadership opted for a solution by violence as in China the only stable backing it would then have for its rule over the country would be a military government, supported by the Red Army. This would of course have led to the loss of financial aid from the Federal Republic, the existence of which was the only reason for the GDR's economic survival. When confronted with this choice, the SED leadership could not decide either way. It therefore began to look paralysed and disoriented.

## A German Autumn

The demonstrations held every Monday in Leipzig now took on special significance. Some 2,000 people took part in a demonstration held on 11 September; the police and the Stasi intervened and arrested many of them. But this no longer had an intimidatory effect; it led instead to an increase in popular mobilisation. The Monday demonstration two weeks later was attended by more than 5,000 people, and the 2 October demonstration had 20,000 participants. The slogans also changed. 'We are the people', they chanted. This was directed against the SED, which always presented itself as the champion of the 'mass of the people'. 'We are staying here!' was another slogan, in opposition to the movement of emigration. The leading idea of the citizens' movement was to change conditions in the GDR, not take flight to the West. Finally, the slogans 'No violence!' and 'Not another China!' expressed the demonstrators' greatest anxiety. The state had in fact made preparations for the forcible suppression of the movement. Internment camps with places for over 80,000 people had already been set up. But on 2 October the authorities did not go further than the use of truncheons and the arrest of a few demonstrators.

While the SED leadership observed these events almost without taking action, and the party newspaper cursed the refugees as 'provocateurs' and 'rowdies' whom 'we could well do without', the opposition began to organise. New groups like 'New Forum', 'Democracy Now' and 'Democratic Awakening', and also a Social Democratic Party in the GDR (the 'SDP') founded by the Protestant pastors Martin Gutzeit and Markus Meckel, made their appearance in public although their political objectives did not go much beyond calling for freedom of travel, democracy and the end of SED rule. On 4 October these groups issued a joint declaration calling on the citizens of the GDR to engage in 'a democratic transformation of state and society'. To achieve this, elections should be held under the supervision of the United Nations. The opposition groups would form an alliance and stand jointly for election.[15]

This declaration was well timed, as the regime planned to hold ceremonies between 5 and 7 October to celebrate the fortieth anniversary of the establishment of the GDR. It had been making elaborate preparations for these ceremonies for more than a year. Inside the Palace of the Republic in Berlin the party and state leaders of East Germany met the leaders of the socialist world, to hear Gorbachev warn the GDR leadership of the need to join in the policy of perestroika, so as 'not to leave it too late'.[16] Outside, meanwhile, on Alexanderplatz, a few hundred individuals were chanting 'Help us, Gorby!' They were driven off by the police and beaten up, in front of Western television cameras, which transmitted the events live.

But the really critical point of these developments was expected to be reached in Leipzig the following Monday. There were rumours that the party leadership was planning the violent suppression of the Leipzig protests. But now a number of leading figures in Leipzig society, among them Kurt Masur, the director of the Leipzig Gewandhaus Orchestra, spoke to the three regional party secretaries of the SED, and they were able to convince them of the dangers of the situation. They composed a joint appeal for peaceful dialogue, which was also read out over the radio. A still more important factor was that the Soviet ambassador in East Berlin called on the GDR authorities to avoid bloodshed. The Western Group of the Soviet Army also received orders not to intervene in Leipzig whatever happened. As a result, the confrontation feared by the opposition and certainly prepared for by the authorities did not take place. More than 50,000 people demonstrated, but the police and the workers' militias backed down from using force to suppress the demonstration.

This was the turning point. Without Moscow's agreement, the SED was neither able nor willing to put down the public protests by force. The opposition movement had won. This victory accelerated the dynamic of destabilisation.[17] The following days and weeks witnessed demonstrations against the SED regime all over the country. They took place in more than 200 places. In Leipzig, 120,000 people demonstrated on 16 October, 250,000 on 23 October and 300,000 on 30 October. Now the SED leadership began a self-dismantling process. On 17 October Honecker was forced to resign. He was succeeded by Egon Krenz, who had long been regarded as the next in line. Krenz was not a reformer. As the man responsible for the fraudulent conduct of the local elections, who had also publicly shown his sympathy for the suppression of the opposition movement in China, he certainly did not stand for a new beginning. But Honecker's departure showed that the SED leadership had now begun to perceive the extent of the crisis. Still more shocking was the stark disclosure of the real economic situation of the GDR, which the leadership had apparently only partially been aware of until then. The head of the planning commission, Gerhard Schürer, reported as follows to the Politburo on 30 October: 'Merely to stop the rise of indebtedness would require a fall of 25 to 30 per cent in living standards in the year 1990, and this would make the GDR ungovernable.'[18] Various other members of the old leadership were now dismissed, others simply resigned. The SED had reached the end of the road.

Despite this, Krenz was still trying to regain the political initiative at this point. The authorities authorised a big demonstration in Berlin on 4 November. This was organised by writers and actors and it was addressed not only by representatives of the opposition but by celebrities who had until then been close to the regime, and even by members of the SED, including Markus Wolf, the long-standing head of the GDR's foreign espionage organisation, and Günter

Schabowski, who was a member of the Politburo. It is true that their speeches were drowned out by the whistles of the 500,000 people there, but this demonstration, which was transmitted live by GDR television, signified a change in SED strategy: after the removal of the old leadership the party sought to join forces with sections of the opposition, so as to preserve the existence of a socialist GDR in a reformed constitutional system.

To achieve this, the first task was to solve the emigration problem. Visa-free travel to Czechoslovakia was again permitted at the beginning of November, and again tens of thousands of GDR citizens streamed across into the West through that country. Krenz then proposed to restore restrictions on travel, but this met with furious resistance and made the situation still tenser. At a session held on 9 November, which mainly discussed the country's economic predicament, the SED Central Committee reacted to this opposition by giving its blessing to a modified travel law. Early that evening, Günter Schabowski, acting as party spokesperson, though without any preparation and without knowing the circumstances in detail, presented this new law to the world's press, which was waiting to hear the news from the Central Committee meeting. According to the new law, private travel abroad could thenceforth be applied for without presenting special reasons and also permanent emigration would in future be possible without further requirements and visas would be granted within a short period. In both cases, however, application had to be made in writing. Schabowski's somewhat confused presentation of this document allowed room for the interpretation that it would be possible to leave the country immediately and without formality, and that is how the Western press interpreted his words. 'The GDR has opened its borders' proclaimed the ARD channel, which was watched by many people in the GDR. Thereupon more and more people descended on the border crossings in East Berlin, demanding the immediate opening of the barriers. By ten o'clock in the evening the pressure of the masses was so great that the border guards issued the famous order 'We are opening the floodgates!' and actually opened the crossings to West Berlin.

What followed was that ecstatic night of reunification, characterised by surprise, disbelief, enthusiasm and happiness, which was certainly one of the highpoints of German history in the twentieth century. It was not just the Germans who rejoiced at the fall of the Wall. Almost all over the world the opening of the Berlin border was acclaimed as a symbol of freedom and the peaceful overthrow of a dictatorship. But, at the same time, a discussion began over what should follow. Was this only the end of the SED dictatorship, or was it the prelude to the unification of the two German states? And what did that mean for the international framework, for Europe and for relations between the Great Powers?

The very next day after the opening of the Berlin Wall, Gorbachev sent Chancellor Kohl a personal message in which he indirectly made a sharp criticism of the federal government: 'Slogans expressing irreconcilability and intolerance of the reality that two sovereign German states exist have only one purpose, which is to destabilise the situation in the GDR.' No one should 'stir up emotions and passions' because otherwise 'a chaotic situation would arise with unforeseeable consequences.'[19] American President Bush also asked Kohl to 'abstain from big rhetorical gestures. He should also avoid speaking about reunification or a timetable for tearing down the Wall' so as to 'avoid unforeseeable reactions on the part of the GDR or the Soviet Union.'[20] The heads of government of the EC, invited by French President Mitterrand on 18 November to a special summit in Paris, had still greater misgivings. The reservations of the EC governments were formulated most clearly by the British Prime Minister Margaret Thatcher. She emphatically called for the maintenance of the status quo. The question of borders, including the border between the two Germanies, was not on the agenda at the Paris summit. But, as Kohl remarked later, 'it was impossible to ignore that there was once again a feeling of mistrust towards us Germans' not just among the British but also among other European government representatives, such as the Dutch and the Italians. '"Now the Germans are talking about unity again, they are no longer interested in Europe" was the cry . . . The old fear that Germany was becoming too strong surfaced once again.'[21]

After 9 November, nothing could ever be the same again in the GDR. Krenz resigned, along with many other SED office-holders. The SED now offered to appoint Hans Modrow, who was regarded as a reformer, as the head of the government instead of Krenz. But the party's authority was now steadily dwindling away. Reports about the machinations of the Stasi and the GDR's level of indebtedness were spreading fast. The wave of emigration also continued: between November 1989 and the end of January 1990 more than 300,000 citizens left the GDR.

On 28 November, West German Chancellor Kohl presented a 'Ten Point Plan' to the Bundestag. This was intended to offer a clear perspective for the future, but also to dispel foreign misgivings and curb the exaggerated expectations held in both German states. In his address, Kohl made the provision of the extensive assistance requested by the GDR government conditional on the introduction of fundamental changes in the political and economic system. At the same time, he outlined the path to a 'contractual community' which would have the objective of developing 'confederative structures between both German states', which he interpreted as 'a federal system for Germany'.[22] But the process of German unification adumbrated in this way would also be embedded within a process of international integration, in Europe and beyond. 'Self-determination' was the key concept here: the Germans, like other peoples, should have the right to decide their own fate. Kohl made use of this international legal concept so as to avoid uttering the provocative word 'reunification'. No one could seriously deny the Germans the right of self-determination, in public, especially as Kohl emphasised that the primary objective of the federal government was first to create conditions in which the citizens of the GDR would be free to decide their own fate.

With this speech, Kohl had placed the question of German unification on the political agenda once again, and he had also put himself in control of the process. The American President alone received an advance copy of the Chancellor's text. Neither the Soviet Union, nor West Germany's European allies, nor even Foreign Minister Genscher, had been let into the secret. Initially, the international community reacted to Kohl's speech with considerable alarm. The US government supported his proposals in principle, but it answered his ten points by formulating four requirements, which had to be fulfilled before the USA supported the unification of the two German states: firstly, the principle of self-determination was valid, but the outcome must not be prejudged; secondly, a reunited Germany must belong to the European Community and NATO; thirdly, the process of unification must take place peacefully and step by step; and fourthly, the inviolability of borders must be respected.[23] With this, the USA endorsed the perspective of German unity, but by advancing these basic requirements it appeared to be postponing unification, of whatever kind, to a far distant future. The GDR was the most visible symbol of Soviet victory in the Second World War, and there were more than 300,000 Soviet soldiers on its territory. How could the Soviet Union ever agree to hand the country over to NATO?

Moscow's reaction to Kohl's Ten Points was brusquely negative. Kohl had issued an ultimatum, a diktat. This was the reproach levelled by a furious Gorbachev at Foreign Minister Genscher, who had hurried to Moscow to see him. 'The Germans should remember', he said, 'what a policy without rhyme or reason had led to in the past.' The independence of the GDR was inviolable, but Kohl was treating the citizens of the GDR as his own subjects. 'If you treat the GDR in this manner today, you will probably do the same tomorrow with Poland and Czechoslovakia and then with Austria.' Soviet Foreign Minister Shevardnadze underlined Gorbachev's implied historical parallel by commenting: 'Even Hitler wouldn't have taken such a liberty.'[24] The Soviet leadership feared that German reunification would seal the decline of their country as a Great Power, and undermine Gorbachev's position at home. The latter told Mitterrand that the day German unity was proclaimed, 'a Soviet marshal will be sitting in my chair.'[25]

In reality, however, the Soviet leadership had no clear policy towards the German issue. On the one hand, its rejection of German reunification was to some extent contradictory with Gorbachev's repeated assertion that his allies should be free to determine their own fate. On the other hand, the abandonment of the GDR could not be brought into harmony with the Soviet Union's view of its own Great Power status. Even so, between acceptance and rejection of German unity there was a broad spectrum of options available which took into account the Soviet Union's economic and security interests. But in the following weeks the Soviet government was unable to work out a clear agenda on this point. It hesitated and wavered. One reason for this was a division of opinion within the leadership, another was that problems with the Soviet economy, with the distribution of supplies to the population, and with the separatist movements, absorbed almost all of the Kremlin's energy, and left very little time to pay attention to what was happening within the borders of the Warsaw Pact allies.

The reactions of most of the Western European governments to Kohl's Ten Point Plan were almost as negative as Gorbachev's. For Margaret Thatcher, German reunification opened a Pandora's box: the problems with a strong and powerful Germany were all too well known from history. Now they threatened to return. Mitterrand too was very worried by Kohl's speech. On 20 December, as if to verify his concerns, he set out for a visit to the GDR. This was the first time a French president had ever visited the country. What he saw there merely confirmed the extent of the SED government's political decline.

Another reason for the critical reaction of Western European heads of government to Kohl's Ten Points was that they did not clarify the issue of Poland's western border. The position of the federal government was that a final renunciation of the claim to Germany's former eastern territories could only be made by a parliament representing the whole of Germany. That was correct in law, but the legal position did not prevent the Chancellor from making a clear statement of intent. Concern over the reaction of the associations of expellees, which were very powerful within the Union, also played a role in Kohl's decision. Another reason, not less important, was the calculation that in a negotiation with Poland this assurance could be given in return for concessions on other matters, for instance the payment of reparations. In the preceding months some people in the Union and associated groups had started to talk about the '1937 borders'. The result was that the federal government encountered a considerable degree of mistrust on the issue at European summit meetings and elsewhere.

In the Federal Republic, the events of 9 November 1989 and Kohl's Ten Points had suddenly brought the national question back onto the agenda. Without a doubt, the idea of a German nation encompassing both the Germans of the Federal Republic and those of the GDR continued to enjoy widespread popularity among older and more conservative people. In the younger generation and on the Left, the sense of the nation's unity had gradually started to decline after the building of the Berlin Wall and the policy of détente which emerged in the late 1960s. The day of 17 June, established as a German national holiday in 1963, with its solemn declarations of faith in the unity of the nation, had soon become a compulsory event without any binding emotional force, and as West Germany developed into one of the wealthiest European states and was converted into a Western society by the processes of democratisation and liberalisation, a specifically West German consciousness gradually took shape. Traditional notions of what should be regarded as typically German, and also awareness of historical and cultural commonalities shared with the GDR, had ceased to mould people's opinions. According to a view first expressed in the early 1970s by the Heidelberg political scientist Dolf Sternberger, and subsequently repeated by many other people, identification with the Federal Republic ought to be based rather on an acceptance of the principles of a liberal and democratic system. It ought to be a constitutional patriotism.[26] The Bochum historian Hans Mommsen went further. In the Federal Republic, he wrote in 1981, a consciousness of national identity had arisen step by step since the 1960s, whereas in the GDR people felt more strongly that they belonged to the German nation as a whole. But, to the extent that the modernisation process which had already been completed in the Federal Republic also took hold in the GDR, that country too would see the growth of a nationally coloured awareness of belonging to a separate state. The German nation-state, said Mommsen, was only a short episode in the history of Germany, and not a happy one. In that sense, the existence of more than one German state in the present was not a historical exception. It was therefore to be expected that, as previously in the case of Austria, a separate national consciousness would develop in both German states, though at the same time 'national cultural solidarities' would arise irrespective of the division into separate nation-states.[27]

Mommsen's position was by no means an isolated view among West German Left liberals. It was in keeping with the much-discussed idea of a German 'cultural nation' which no longer needed state unity. It was true that in 1973 the Federal Constitutional Court had again reminded all federal governments that according to the preamble of the Basic Law national unity had necessarily to be understood as state unity.[28] Despite that, West Germans continued during the 1980s to turn away from the notion of a united German nation. Three-quarters of those questioned supported German unification in principle, but only 9 per cent assumed that they would live long enough to experience it. In 1986–7, a third of all those surveyed, but half the under-thirties, regarded the GDR as a foreign country.[29]

The GDR, on the other hand, had followed an anti-Western, nationally oriented course from the beginning, at the behest of the Soviet Union. Even so, by the end of the 1960s at the latest, the SED had given up the idea of a single

Germany, and started to promote the GDR as a separate socialist nation. The capitalist nation of the Federal Republic, and the socialist nation of the GDR did it was true possess a common past, but the social, cultural and political alignments of the two societies were so different that it was no longer possible to speak of a nation. In practice, however, it had never been possible to secure general acceptance for this theory of a socialist nation-state.

After coming to power in Bonn, Helmut Kohl accepted his predecessors' *Ostpolitik*. He sought a pragmatic compromise with the GDR, but he never abandoned the demand for German unification, thus maintaining the traditional approach of his party. When Honecker visited the Federal Republic in 1987, Kohl gave a publicly effective reminder of this fundamental position in his response to the GDR leader, and this also had a deep impact on the population of the GDR. But, if one looked more closely, definite fissures could be discerned in the apparent firmness of the Union's position. The right of the party, and particularly the expellee associations, insisted on reunification within the borders of 1937, and this involved a claim to eastern areas of Germany which had been occupied by Poland or the Soviet Union since 1945. The majority of the Union's members, however, proceeded on the basis of a 'small' reunification of the two existing German states, and even that was regarded by many Union politicians as a distant utopia. But in any case, the German question had now been reopened, and Kohl's Ten Points offered the party a clear line which distinguished the Union clearly from other West German parties.

The SPD was split over the matter. Willy Brandt had, it is true, described the demand for 'reunification' as the 'lifelong delusion of the Federal Republic', but the former Chancellor, who continued to be highly respected, had very clearly and publicly committed himself to the unity of the nation after the events of 1989.[30] The SPD's representatives in the Bundestag reacted similarly to Kohl's Ten Points, openly applauding the Chancellor. On the other hand, Oskar Lafontaine, who was the prime minister of the Saar, and entered the Bundestag election campaign of 1990 as SPD candidate for Chancellor, regarded German reunification as an anachronism. He considered nation-states in general, and particularly the German one, as historically outdated. 'For us, the question of reunification has already been answered', he declared two weeks after 9 November 1989. 'The SPD is in favour of European unification . . . The old style nation-state is increasingly losing significance.' Lafontaine also refused to accept the counter-argument that the movement of emigration from the East signified a reunification from below. In order to curb the wave of emigration, he said, the current law regarding citizenship should be changed where appropriate, so as to prevent GDR citizens who entered the Federal Republic from gaining access to West German social benefits. The overriding objective was not national unification but the creation of equivalent living conditions in East and West. This position was, however, strongly disputed within the SPD, and in the weeks that followed the advocates of unity won the upper hand over Lafontaine. In any case, though, the divisions within the SPD were a true reflection of the state of opinion among the West German public.[31]

The Greens were still more emphatic in their rejection of unification. For many years, they had been in close contact with the citizens' movements in the GDR, Poland and Czechoslovakia, and they now opposed the attempts being made to reinterpret the movement for democracy as a movement for unification. 'What is emerging in the GDR', declared deputy Antje Vollmer in the Bundestag, 'is the first independently achieved democracy on German soil, which has not been bestowed on us by war or by the fiat of the victors.' The attitude of the federal government, she added, when it speaks of the 'victory of Western values' reflects 'a new, federal German nationalism, a federal chauvinism derived from our prosperity. It assumes that the main motive for the East's struggle for freedom is the wish to gain access to Western television channels and travel freely on West German autobahns.' Talk about reunification, said Vollmer, was now 'more historically outdated than it had ever been'. The GDR regime was no longer a totalitarian regime to which recognition had to be denied because it withheld elementary basic rights from its inhabitants. Now the GDR had an independent 'reform movement, which insists vigorously on its distinctive views, its autonomy and its own history . . . To talk about reunification now, in this specific situation, is to postulate and presuppose the failure of the reform movement.'[32]

The position taken by the Greens corresponded with that taken by most opposition groups in the GDR. Until spring 1990, they explicitly rejected reunification. New Forum declared: 'Reunification is not an issue for us, since our starting point is the existence of two German states and we are not aiming at a capitalist social system. We want to make changes in the GDR.'[33] When the Social Democratic Party of the GDR was founded in October 1989, Markus Meckel, one of its founders, gave a speech in which he said that in view of the way the European diplomatic constellation had evolved since 1945, 'talk about reunification is completely unproductive and in essence backward-looking.' If the reform movement succeeded, said Antje Vollmer in the Bundestag, the GDR would remain independent and seek its own path. That was the perspective outlined by both the Greens and the GDR opposition groups. The interjection of a CDU Bundestag deputy, however, drew attention to the underlying difficulty facing such a position: 'Let the people decide for themselves!' he said.[34]

## Demos and Ethnos

A change of mood on this question was already apparent at the Monday demonstration held in Leipzig on 13 November. For the first time, the word 'Reunification' appeared on the banners. German flags without the hammer and sickle could be seen, and groups chanted the words 'Germany, united fatherland'. This was a reference to the GDR national anthem, which could no longer be sung in public because of this verse. As the weeks went by, the protests became directed less to a reform of the GDR and more towards German unity. Helmut Kohl's visit of 19 December to Dresden converted these tendencies into a movement. Kohl spoke in front of tens of thousands of cheering GDR citizens, who brandished a sea of German flags. He spoke about the services of the citizens' movement in the GDR and the future of the Germans, warning, however, that they had to proceed sensibly and with sound judgement, and not awaken excessive expectations. But he added: 'My goal remains the unity of our nation, if the historical moment permits it.'[35] The enthusiasm of the masses in front of the Dresden Frauenkirche after these words was so extraordinary that no one could any longer have any doubt about what was really at stake. 'Self-determination' meant reunification. It was impossible to ignore this.

Meanwhile, the 1989 revolution continued to spread in the countries of East Central Europe. The communist regime in Czechoslovakia was overthrown. Václav Havel was elected president of Czechoslovakia on 29 December. In Bulgaria Todor Zhivkov, the head of the Communist Party and of the state, was removed from office. In Romania there were bloody conflicts during the Christmas period, in the course of which the head of the state, Nicolae Ceauşescu and his wife were shot by soldiers. Within a few months, the communist dictatorships in East Central Europe had been swept away and replaced by democratic governments of varying origin. This European dimension gave the events in the GDR greater legitimacy and driving force. The endeavour to secure German unity was part of an overall European mass movement for freedom and democracy, which imbued what happened in Germany with a significance which reached beyond the events themselves. A separate movement purely aimed at German unification would probably not have met with the same European acceptance.[36]

The SED, which was now disintegrating rapidly, attempted to maintain some of its power by holding roundtable discussions with the opposition. But the bulwarks protecting its position continued to fall to the ground. The clearest indication of this was the storming of the State Security headquarters on 15 January 1990 by demonstrators from the citizens' movement, who ransacked the building. This action was the culmination of decades of powerless fury towards a much-feared institution of surveillance and terror, staffed by over 100,000 people.

The roundtable discussions were above all transitional phenomena, expressing the shift from the old system to the new one. And since the situation was changing at this time at almost breakneck speed, they were soon felt to be an anachronism. It is true that representatives of the citizens' movement were included in the Modrow government at the beginning of January. But the government lacked power, resources, legitimacy, and also time to undertake far-reaching reforms and in particular to work out a new constitution for the GDR. The dominant view in the roundtable was that the process of democratising the country and harmonising the conditions of life between East and West would be a long process, and it would probably stretch out for many years.

Three factors worked against this conception of the future. The first was that the mass movement in the GDR was now directed explicitly and ever more vociferously towards the quickest possible reunification of the country. The former dissident groups, on the other hand, with their conception of a reformed GDR, in which a new and democratic version of socialism might possibly be tried, rapidly lost support. The slogan 'We are the people' no longer dominated the demonstrations. The new slogan was 'We are *one* people', and this change in the content of the word 'people' (*Volk*) from republican to national, from *demos* to *ethnos*, represented the transformation that was taking place in the popular mood.

Secondly, the full extent of the economic crisis in the GDR became much clearer after Christmas. In no time at all, the Deutschmark became the preferred means of payment, the East European markets for GDR goods collapsed, and when compared with West German businesses the GDR's firms started to look like the relics of a bygone era. The GDR urgently needed extensive financial assistance, but the Bonn government was not prepared to make far-reaching offers of credit without a reliable prospect of fundamental political change. In addition to this, the number of people moving to the Federal Republic increased every day, and these emigrants were overwhelmingly young people as well as highly educated specialists such as engineers and doctors, who had no problem in finding employment in the Federal Republic.

The third factor that propelled events forward in the GDR was the uncertain situation in the Soviet Union. There were increasing signs that Gorbachev might not be able to retain power for very long. But a government of hardliners or a military dictatorship would destroy all hope of German unity, of whatever kind. That was unquestionably an argument in favour of accelerating the move towards reunification. But, at the same time, reunification would endanger Gorbachev's position at home, and might accelerate his fall. The Bonn government had to steer a course between these two dangers. Meanwhile, everyone was aware that the much discussed 'window of opportunity' would probably not remain open for very long.

Time pressure thus became a dominant factor, although it is often hard to establish whether this is what forced governments in Bonn and Washington to take action, or, conversely, those governments themselves created the time pressure in order to accelerate developments.

Two groundbreaking decisions now set their stamp on the progress of events in the two German states: the calling of elections in the GDR for 18 March and the announcement of an economic and currency union. The need to prepare for the elections led to very rapid changes in the party structure. The old bloc parties—the CDU and the Liberals—quickly merged with their West German mother parties, after the removal of a few leading figures, and the newly founded Social Democratic Party (SDP) united with the West German Social Democrats (SPD). It was generally thought that the Social Democrats would win the elections, because they were not burdened by connections with the old GDR bloc parties and their strongholds had always been the former centres of the workers' movement in Sachsen-Anhalt, Saxony and Berlin. That was of course a long time ago: the last free elections there had taken place in 1932. The situation of the citizens' rights groups was more difficult. They joined together to form the 'Alliance 90'. The Greens, for their part, also had no noteworthy support in the GDR. The SED was in utter dissolution, until a group of people around the young lawyer Gregor Gysi, who had previously belonged to the opposition within the party, refounded it under the new name: 'Party of Democratic Socialism' (PDS). Most of the communist parties in the collapsing Eastern bloc were taking similar action. They thereby obtained not just a large membership but also control over the former Communist Party's finances. This latter prospect played an important part in the decision to transform the SED into the PDS.

The federal government's decision to aim at the quickest possible unification of the economy and the currency was a risky move, and it met with sharp criticism from most West German economists. They pointed out that in the European context the federal government had always opposed calls for the EC countries to join together quickly in a currency union on the ground that a change of this nature could only be done step by step and the political prerequisites had first to be present. This also applied to a German currency union, they said. The political requirements had to be in place to allow the East German economy to be converted step by step from being subject to the instructions of a planning authority to responding to the signals of the free market. A common currency could only emerge at the end of that development, in order to 'crown' the process of transformation, so to speak. The Council of Economic Experts emphasised in its report to the federal government that 'a currency union which did not take place in parallel with a fundamental reconstruction of the GDR economic system would simply incur costs, without placing the population's economic prospects on a better, more viable basis.' A rapid, or possibly abrupt, transition to the market economy and the Deutschmark would create the false impression that equal living standards had already been achieved by the currency conversion. But, as was well known, living standards depended on economic productivity, and the current statistics showed that the productivity of the GDR economy, far from being 40 per cent of that of West Germany, as had been assumed, was actually at the 20 per cent level. The only way to make wages in East Germany even approximately equal to those in the West was to engage in massive financial transfers. Moreover, currency conversion would expose the GDR economy at a single stroke to Western competition, and this would quickly lead to its ruin.[37]

These arguments were not purely speculative. In fact, almost all of the predictions made by the economists turned out to be correct. But the policy approach they advocated also involved considerable risks. Years would no doubt be needed before the East German economy reached the West German level. But, in a country divided into two economic zones at such different levels, the possibility had to be considered that the more ambitious citizens would move from the poorer East to the richer West, where they could earn five times the amount of money. This could be stopped by restricting their freedom of movement and making it impossible for them to travel to the West. But that would be a breach of the Basic Law, and the political costs of such a decision would be impossible to predict. Even if the economic and currency unions were accomplished in stages, the East German economy would need tremendous financial contributions from the Federal Republic during this period, which would certainly be no whit smaller than the transfer payments required in the case of an immediate currency conversion.

In the light of these options, the federal government decided on an immediate changeover of the GDR economy to a free market system and the immediate introduction of the Deutschmark, accepting the associated economic risks. In the last resort, therefore, the primacy of politics prevailed. Economic considerations took second place to the primary political objective of reunification.

In addition to this, in offering an economic and currency union the CDU played a trump card which turned out to have a decisive influence on the March elections. Anyone who wanted the Deutschmark and German unity voted for Helmut Kohl. The result therefore confounded all previous expectations. The conservative coalition formed around the CDU, which called itself the 'Alliance for Germany', was the victor, with 48 per cent of the vote. The SPD only received 21.9 per cent, the PDS secured 16.4 per cent, and the Free

Democrats, led by Foreign Minister Genscher, who had a high reputation in the GDR, obtained 5.3 per cent. These elections thus represented a very clear decision in favour of German reunification and Western democracy, and that is how they were interpreted both nationally and internationally. The advocates of unity had received some 75 per cent of the vote, its opponents roughly 20 per cent. The groups of the citizens' opposition, who had combined together in 'Alliance 90', received only 2.9 per cent of the vote, while the Greens obtained 2 per cent. Hence the former SED had been able to bring its core electorate to the ballot box, but for the citizens' movement the results had been devastating. It had admittedly been enormously important in spearheading opposition to SED domination, but its conception of a future independent, democratic and perhaps neo-socialist GDR had been clearly rejected by the population. The same applied to the post-materialist political conceptions of the Greens, who were unlikely to receive support in a society which was short of everything.

Otto Schily, a prominent Green member of the Bundestag, who later changed his allegiance to the SPD, was interviewed on television at this time. When asked why the East Germans had voted for unity in the elections, he replied by placing a banana on the table. The East German writer Monika Maron criticised the attitude that underlay this gesture, saying it showed the 'arrogance of a well-fed person who is disgusted by the table-manners of a famine victim'.[38] No doubt the East Germans did desire unity because it promised to give them more in a material sense, and do this more quickly than a reformed GDR. How could it be otherwise? The GDR was at the end of its tether economically. Its industries had been run into the ground, and its infrastructure had collapsed. Why should someone in such a situation decide for a reform of the GDR when the alternative course of joining the Federal Republic existed? In addition to that, Schily's attitude failed to take into account the desire for liberty, the rule of law and freedom of movement which had built up in the course of forty years and was expressed as strongly in the elections as the will to unity. Moreover, the yearning for a better life, for future opportunities and for prosperity is no less legitimate as a motive for unity than the desire for political freedom, especially as it was precisely the West Germans of the 1950s and 1960s who had accepted Western democracy as a bonus in addition to the 'economic miracle' rather than actually struggling to achieve it.

Even so, there were widespread doubts in West Germany about reunification, above all among the younger generation. These doubts were expressed with particular accuracy and forcefulness by the writer Patrick Süskind, born in 1949, who wrote as follows in summer 1990 in *Der Spiegel*:

> Forty years of a European post-war system which was entrenched, solid and seemingly unshakeable suddenly slid away from beneath our feet. We grew

> up under this system. We knew no other . . . Our attitude to the state in which we lived—namely the Federal Republic—was at first marked by reserve and scepticism, later rebelliousness, then pragmatism, and finally perhaps even by a detached sympathy. This state had proved that it was not just provisional, it was liberal, democratic, governed by laws, and practical.

But now the reply given to someone who asks 'Why German unity? To what end?' is that there is no longer any alternative: 'The train has left.' The rapidity of this development made him uneasy, he said, 'with the uneasiness of someone who is sitting in a fast-moving train travelling on a precarious track towards an unknown destination.'[39]

Süskind's essay attracted much attention, both positive and negative. Without doubt, it reflected the astonishment of many West Germans over the speed of the events and the abruptness of the decisions, especially as they were not asked whether they wanted unity and a common currency and whether they were ready to bear the costs that would fall predominantly upon their shoulders. Opinion surveys did, it is true, indicate a growing acceptance of the unification process, but there was no referendum, nor was there any announcement of the burdens that were to be expected. Süskind's objections also corresponded with the fears of many that reunification would lead to return of nationalist attitudes in Germany. The citizens of the GDR, it was pointed out, had been subjected to authoritarian political socialisation, and in a united state what had already been achieved in West Germany in previous years in the democratic and cultural fields would also be politically endangered, perhaps even reversed. 'The citizens of the Federal Republic', wrote Jürgen Habermas after the announcement of an economic and currency union, 'had developed a non-nationalist sense of themselves and a sober view of what emerges from the political process for each individual in terms of cash and use values.' But with reunification, this post-nationalist state of mind would be at stake, he wrote, as would the multicultural society, the road to Europe and the fundamental liberalisation of West German society that had been achieved in the previous twenty years.[40]

But did the West Germans have the right to ignore the will to unity of the citizens of the GDR, after the latter had had to bear a much larger share of the consequences of the Second World War than the West Germans? The standard of living in West Germany was roughly four times as high as in the GDR in 1989, and no one could maintain that this was the fault of the GDR's population. The West Germans were the winners of the post-war era, the East Germans the losers. In addition, as the historian Heinrich August Winkler had pointed out long before, the Germans in the Federal Republic do not have 'the moral right to revoke their national solidarity with the Germans in the GDR' because the withdrawal of the West Germans from the common nation would also mean that they did not want to share joint responsibility for the consequences of the war. That was a strong argument in a society like West Germany, which regarded a critical confrontation with the Nazi past as one of the most important elements of its identity and a proof of its purification through democracy.[41]

## Summit Diplomacy

The elections of March 1990 marked the breakthrough to unity as far as domestic policy was concerned. In the GDR a 'Grand Coalition' government was established under the East German CDU politician Lothar de Maizière. Its most important, and ultimately its sole task, was to put in place the legal prerequisites for unity.

The foreign policy framework, however, continued to be unclear. By mid-January at the latest, the West European states had accustomed themselves in principle to the idea of German reunification. But they also continued, sometimes loudly, sometimes more quietly, to point out that the Soviet Union might veto reunification, and above all it might veto united Germany's entry into NATO, the measure the USA had made a condition of its agreement to unification. The Soviet turnaround from rejection of German reunification to acceptance even of Germany's NATO accession took place between January and July 1990 in the course of many discussions, conferences and agreements. This was not a linear process, however. It was a negotiating marathon, characterised by numerous contradictions, concessions and revocations, and it can be divided into three phases.

1) The beginning of the process was marked by the change in the Soviet leadership's attitude from rejection to acceptance of German unity. A decisive role in this was played by the strengthening impression in Gorbachev's entourage, especially after Kohl's speech in Dresden, that German unity was inevitable, and that it was important to make sure that the Soviet Union could help to direct the process and profit from it. Gorbachev was convinced that it was advantageous for the Soviet Union, particularly from the economic point of view, to cultivate good relations with the Federal Republic. This was meant quite literally, because at the same time as it gave way on the question of unity, Moscow asked the Federal Republic for extensive food deliveries. Kohl was delighted to agree to the proposal immediately.[42] The connection between economic support and political concessions was completely obvious here, and the federal government was aware that this linkage could be utilised in other areas as well.

At a meeting with Kohl in Moscow on 10 February 1990, Gorbachev conceded

> that there are no differences of opinion between the Soviet Union, the Federal Republic and the GDR over the question of unity and over people's right to seek this unity and to decide on further developments . . . The Germans in the Federal Republic and the GDR can be assumed to know themselves the path they wish to take.[43]

Gorbachev also said that he agreed with the USA's proposal to conduct the necessary discussions on the road to German unity in a conference of the four victorious Powers with the two German states, for which the shorthand expression 'Two Plus Four' quickly came into use. But the Kremlin categorically opposed the entry of a united Germany into NATO.

2) Then, on 24 and 25 February 1990, during a visit by Kohl to the USA, the American and West German governments coordinated their next steps. A form of division of labour was worked out: the US agreed to influence the Two Plus Four process with the aim of preventing delays and making sure German interests were protected. In return, the federal government adopted the American position that a united Germany must become a member of NATO. This already demonstrated the clear shift in world power-relations. It was true that where possible the Western partners were prepared to take account of the interests of the Soviet Union and ensure the continued existence of the Gorbachev government. But the intention was to concede very little influence to the Soviet side. 'To hell with that', said Bush, during these informal and unusually frank discussions with Kohl. 'We prevailed and they didn't. We can't let the Soviets clutch victory from the jaws of defeat.' Kohl for his part saw a further aspect of the situation. It was perfectly possible, he told Bush, that 'the agreement of the Soviets . . . might just be a matter of money.' The Soviets should be urged to 'name their price'.[44]

At this meeting, apart from the question of NATO, the US government also clarified its position on the problem of Poland's western border. Kohl's resolute refusal to make a definitive statement on this had given rise to growing anger on the part of his Western allies and had led the Bonn government to become increasingly isolated over the issue. After long and very contentious negotiations a final agreement was achieved, by which Poland's borders would be determined in advance by the Two Plus Four conference as an international commitment for a united Germany. At the same time, once the election of 18 March had taken place in the GDR, both German parliaments would make identically worded declarations, stating that the right of the Poles to live within secure borders would not be called into question by the Germans either at present or in the future. After reunification, the question would be conclusively regulated by an appropriate border treaty with Poland.

Kohl agreed to this, knowing very well that it would not be easy to get his party to accept this agreement, because the border question was complicated by the issue of reparations. The London Debt Agreement of 1953 had postponed the settlement of the question of reparations until the conclusion of a peace treaty. But since the Two Plus Four negotiations would undoubtedly have the character of a peace treaty, the federal government tried as hard as it could to keep the reparations problem off the agenda because it feared that it might be faced with unforeseeable demands in that regard. The Polish side was particularly concerned to secure individual compensation for civilian forced labourers and concentration camp inmates. Kohl and his officials always countered these demands by pointing out that the Federal Republic had already made compensation payments of more than 100 billion DM. What Kohl failed to mention, however, was the fact that the vast majority of these payments had been made according to the provisions of the Federal Compensation Law, which related only to Germans. Foreign victims of Nazism were not entitled to compensation. It had been agreed in 1953 that their claims would one day be settled in a peace treaty. Therefore, if the Two Plus Four discussions were adjudged to be negotiations over a peace treaty, the federal government would be threatened with compensation claims of an incalculable magnitude. Kohl and his colleagues finally managed to get the reparations question left out of the discussions by making recognition of the Polish border conditional on the renunciation of reparations claims. The question of compensation for forced labourers, it was agreed in advance, would be regulated separately.[45] With these agreements between West Germany and the US, the most important markers had been laid down, and they formed the basis for the Two Plus Four negotiations which began in Bonn on 5 May 1990.

3) The change in Gorbachev's position on the question of a united Germany's membership of NATO took place between March and June 1990. The Soviet leadership initially regarded its agreement to German reunification and to the Two Plus Four negotiations as its furthest possible concession. It categorically rejected the extension of NATO as far as the Polish border, partly for military and political reasons, but also out of concern for the reaction of the Soviet population, which would perceive an expansion of NATO to cover the territory of the GDR as an admission that the Soviet Union had been defeated in the Cold War.

But, in the spring of 1990, the crisis within the Soviet Union escalated to such an extent that this attitude could not be maintained. All the economic data had turned negative: this applied to industrial production and investment as well as productivity and foreign trade. In many regions, even milk and meat were affected by supply problems. According to the official consumption statistics,

1,000 out of 1,200 articles of everyday need were not available. The collapse of the state supply system led to the spread of a black market. Poverty, which was in any case widespread, became still more evident, and more publicly visible. In the Ukrainian coalfield of the Donets basin more than half a million miners went on strike. By now, Gorbachev's policy of perestroika was being described in many places as 'katastroika'.[46]

The Soviet leadership was split, however, over economic policy. The programme proposed by radical reformers was the immediate transformation of the state-run economy into a market economy. Other plans envisaged a more gradual transition. One particularly disputed question was whether to allow the ownership of land by individuals. At the same time, campaigns for regional and national autonomy won increasing support. In March 1990, Lithuania declared its independence, followed a little later by Estonia, and then Latvia. 'The old society is crumbling, but . . . there are no traces of a new one emerging', noted one of Gorbachev's advisers at this time. 'Judging from my recent observations', he added, 'Gorbachev is losing a sense of being in control of developments.'[47] The danger that the Soviet Union would collapse brought the military and conservative forces back into play. They were admittedly a minority within the party, but they were still strong enough to cause repeated rumours of an impending military putsch to emerge. This explains the harsh reaction of the Moscow government to events in Lithuania. It held manoeuvres, it sent in KGB units and it imposed economic sanctions. But this demonstration of toughness at home caused problems abroad: counter-measures were immediately discussed in the USA, and the United States Senate voted not to extend economic aid to the Soviet Union for the moment.

In this situation of great confusion, the Soviet government now had to decide on united Germany's membership of NATO. A neutralisation of the country, as repeatedly, but not very emphatically, proposed by the Soviet Union, was out of the question for the Western powers. The US government considered that a neutral Germany would be a disturbing element in Europe, owing to the country's size and economic strength. German membership of NATO, on the other hand, would contribute both to stabilising that country and reassuring its European neighbours. Despite this, the Soviet side persisted in its categorical rejection of the idea.

The deadlock was eventually broken by the Soviet Union, which urgently needed financial assistance in spring 1990 in order to overcome its acute economic crisis. At the beginning of May, Soviet Foreign Minister Shevardnadze asked the West German Chancellor for a provisional increase in credits. The Soviet Union, he said, had a liquidity shortfall of 20 billion DM. Moreover, by far the greater part of the country's foreign debt, amounting to roughly 23 billion DM, was owed to West Germany, a fact which added further weight to Bonn's central role in these financial questions. As in January, Kohl saw Shevardnadze's request as an opportunity to achieve political concessions by financial means, because, he said, the Soviets were 'hardly likely to pursue a confrontational course' over the NATO issue 'while they were simultaneously hoping for financial support'. The German side responded by offering a short-term credit of 5 billion DM, knowing very well that this money would probably be lost for ever. The Soviets were informed that 'this support must be understood as part of an overall package, which ought to contribute to the solution of the German question.'[48]

The actual breakthrough was achieved on 31 May during Gorbachev's visit to the USA. After the Soviet side had initially maintained its inflexibility on the question of NATO, a completely unexpected and dramatic turn of events took place at the end of the day, when President Bush once again inquired: 'According to the CSCE principles in the Helsinki Final Act, all nations have the right to choose their own alliances freely. Germany should therefore be entitled to decide which alliance it wishes to belong to. Is this correct?' To the astonishment of the Americans and the dismay of the Soviet delegation, Gorbachev replied in the affirmative. It was then agreed that 'it is for united Germany itself to decide which alliance it wishes to join.'

Gorbachev's reply to Bush contradicted all previous statements by the Soviet leadership, and several minutes elapsed before the participants realised what had happened here: the Soviet Union had agreed that a united Germany could belong to NATO. People have long speculated about what induced Gorbachev to make such a concession, to diverge on his own authority from the line previously laid down in Moscow. Several factors played a role here. Firstly, it may be that when the American President referred to the right of self-determination, which Gorbachev himself had repeatedly put forward, he 'may have caught him off guard'.[49] Secondly, a tough line over this question would have led to a worsening of relations between the Soviet Union and the West. This would have applied not just to the USA but also to the Federal Republic, and the Soviet side absolutely wished to avoid this in view of the economic situation at home. Thirdly, however, Gorbachev's concession also made clear the weak negotiating position of the USSR during these months, when the failure of reform, the economic distress, the internal unrest and the secessionist movements at the periphery of the empire were making it almost ungovernable.

Gorbachev never retreated from the position he had taken up on 31 May. At the CPSU Party Congress held at the beginning of July, he was able to point not just to the economic assistance from the West but also to the far-reaching reconstruction of the NATO alliance, which was now, he said, aiming to take the Soviet Union into partnership. Moreover, NATO troops would not be stationed on the territory of the former GDR. This allowed him to defeat his opponents at the Party Congress, and to reconstruct his top leadership team.

During the famous meetings between Kohl and Gorbachev in Moscow and the Caucasus on 15 July 1990, the decisions previously agreed with the Americans were given concrete shape and enshrined in a series of draft treaties. In return, the federal government promised extensive economic assistance to the Soviet Union. Twelve billion DM were to be paid to cover the cost of withdrawing Soviet troops, and an interest-free credit of 3 billion DM was to be given.[50] With this, the road to German unity lay open.

## Unity and Its Costs

During the spring of 1990, while discussions were taking place between the Great Powers on Germany's reunification and NATO membership, negotiations within the country on the terms of that reunification were advancing rapidly. The economic, legal and administrative arrangements for unification were worked out. In the legal sense, unification did not create anything new: what happened was the accession of the GDR to the Federal Republic under Article 23 of the Basic Law. This distinction was of importance, because it made the administrative processes much simpler. The other method, the re-foundation of an enlarged Federal Republic, had met with strong resistance from Kohl's party. The Union was very keen to avoid a lengthy debate on a new constitution, both because it did not think the Basic Law was in need of any fundamental improvement, and because after several Diet elections the relationship of forces in the Bundesrat had changed considerably in favour of the SPD and the outcome of a constitutional debate therefore appeared uncertain.

The regulatory principles of the Federal Republic were applied to the GDR from 1 July 1990 onwards by the promulgation of what was called the 'Economic, Social and Currency Union'.[51] This was largely undisputed, as was the decision to apply the main features of the West German system of social policy to the GDR. The problem lay in the extreme divergence in their respective levels of economic efficiency, particularly the big difference in productivity between the two economies. To replace the East German Mark with the West German Mark in East Germany the relative values of the two currencies had to be defined. Officially, the ratio was 1:4, but on the black market the ratio was 1:8. If productivity was taken as a basis, the exchange ratio would have had to be around 1:5. The lower the valuation of the East Mark, the lower the accounting value of East German commercial debt. But, if the rate of exchange was fixed at 1:1, the old East Mark debts would have to be covered at their full Deutschmark value, and this would place an impossible burden on most firms. Conversion at 1:2, on the other hand, would mean halving the wages paid previously in East

Marks. In view of the differences in productivity, this would still be a favourable rate for wage earners. But since average wages in the GDR were around 850 East Marks, they would have amounted to roughly 425 DM after conversion, whereas in the Federal Republic average income was 1,800 DM, thus over four times as high. A difference as great as this was hardly sustainable politically. In addition, in such a case the number of people who emigrated to the Federal Republic would probably have increased still further. Apart from that, prior to the March elections the propaganda of the 'Alliance for Germany' had aroused expectations that East Marks would be changed into Deutschmarks at a 1:1 ratio. Therefore, even the rumour that the conversion rate might be 1:2 gave rise to furious protests.

The federal government's decision to convert wages and salaries, and small savings accounts, at a ratio of 1:1, but to convert higher incomes and company debts at a ratio of 1:2, was therefore politically motivated, and most economic specialists protested vigorously against it. Taken together, these conversion rates amounted to an average rate of 1:1.8. This provided the citizens of the GDR with the high wages they expected to receive, but for the GDR economy it was an intolerable burden.

The result was the collapse of East German industry, which already started a few days after 1 July 1990. Many firms went bankrupt, and within a few weeks there was a fourfold increase in unemployment. This was not unexpected. The decision to exchange the currencies at a rate of 1:1, like the decision for a quick economic and currency union, was taken in full knowledge of its economic consequences. What did surprise those responsible was that these were not short-term conversion difficulties, but long-lasting problems which would burden the public finances for years, indeed for decades. The potential performance of the GDR economy had been judged far too optimistically. In addition, the markets in Eastern Europe now broke away from their erstwhile supplier, which meant that within a short time the East German economy lost its most important customers.

Was there a possible alternative? Even with a more realistic forecast of the potential performance of the East German economy, the political arguments in favour of rapid reunification would have remained valid. It is true that in that case the federal government would have had to make clear unreservedly to the West Germans how high the expected burdens of unity would be, and also to tell the East Germans that it would take a much longer time before their wages reached the level enjoyed in the West. But to make public a realistic estimation of the risks might have considerably reduced the enthusiasm for reunification (and also for the parties in government). Hence the economic optimism spread by the government was above all aimed at improving the political mood. Many Germans in East and West were in fact waiting during these months for the much-discussed 'blood, sweat and tears' speech which the Chancellor was expected to make to the citizens, calling for national solidarity, saving, sharing and the acceptance of a reduced standard of living, in response to the burdens of unity. But the first elections to the Bundestag of a united Germany had been set for December 1990, and there was no sign of such a speech.

How should the cost of unity be financed? Tax increases and capital levies would have been an obvious choice, but to the federal government this seemed too awkward politically. Instead of this, in May 1990 it set up a 'Fund for German Unity'. This was essentially a financial trick, because it was a special credit-financed fund not included in the federal budget. One hundred and ten billion DM were deposited in it, 47.5 billion of which was to be raised by the West German *Länder* and local authorities. If further funds were needed, which was not at first considered likely, they would be raised by the central government. In short: unification was financed with debts which did not appear in the normal accounts of the federal budget.[52]

The real extent of the burden was therefore very much underestimated. German unification, the end of the Cold War and the boom conditions which had persisted since the mid-1980s had led to a feeling of exhilaration and a sense of unlimited possibilities. It was therefore confidently anticipated that the expected economic boom would quickly balance out the costs of unification, which were now about to fall due. The Ministry of Finance initially proposed in June 1990 to lay in a reserve of a mere 8 billion DM to cover the GDR economy for the year 1991. By the beginning of August, however, the sum required had already been increased to 50 billion.

One of the most delicate problems in relation to the transformation of the GDR economy was the question of previously expropriated wealth. Since the early 1950s the implementation of a socialist planned economy in the GDR had led to the large-scale expropriation of private possessions, factories, landed property and houses. It was not disputed that the wealth of former property-owners should be returned to them. What was in dispute was whether this should take place through financial compensation or restitution. Restitution was without doubt a more appropriate legal procedure. But many of these property matters were complex, and it was likely that it would take many years before the claims of individuals could be settled in court. This affected not just money and houses but also economic undertakings, plots of land and factories, so that to stipulate restitution would delay or even prevent the restarting of firms and the introduction of new investments. Despite this, the government decided to adopt the principle of 'restitution before compensation'. This was a serious error in the eyes of many economists, because it increased the difficulty of restoring the health of the East German economy.[53]

Complete administrative unity was finally given the force of law by the Unification Treaty, which was signed on 31 August 1990. This essentially adapted the GDR's legal and administrative structures to those of the Federal Republic. The Bonn government postponed a constitutional discussion, which had been demanded by the GDR government and the Bonn opposition, until after the completion of unification. On 23 August the East German People's Chamber (*Volkskammer*) voted for the GDR's 'entry into the area of jurisdiction of the Basic Law of the Federal Republic of Germany'. On 3 October 1990, the 'Day of German Unity', the division of the country into two states was brought to an end—exactly a year after the opposition groups in the citizens' movement had made their joint declaration calling on the citizens of the GDR 'to make a democratic transformation of the state and the society'. For the first time in German history, as Federal President von Weizsäcker emphasised in his speech on this occasion, it had been possible firmly to establish over the whole of German territory the foundations of Western democracy, as they had taken shape in the French Revolution and during the development of the states of the Western world. Moreover, for the first time for a long period, Germany was no longer a contentious issue on Europe's agenda. The identity and integrity of united Germany had been confirmed by its neighbours, and its borders had been recognised on all sides. United Germany had now found a firm place in Europe and the circle of Western democracies.[54]

## German Unity and the European Union

While the attention of the German and international public had been directed towards the drama of the collapse of the GDR and the negotiations over German unity, the ground was being laid, simultaneously, for a second, parallel process of unification: the creation of a European economic and currency union. This was conducted in part by the same political actors, and its historical significance was as great as German reunification, but it was received with far less public interest. Even so, the two unification processes were combined together and related to each other in many ways.

The dominant position of the West German economy had increased the fear of German hegemony in Europe, which was felt particularly in France. French President Mitterrand did not hesitate to affirm that he regarded the economic and currency union agreed in principle in Hanover in summer 1988 as a decisive step towards containing Germany's economic strength. In summer 1989, the heads of government of the EC states, meeting in Madrid, took a further step towards union. They agreed a three-stage timetable for the achievement of the currency union, proposed by Jacques Delors, the president of the European Commission. During the first stage, all the EC states would coordinate their economic policies more closely and take part in the exchange rate mechanism known as the European Monetary System (EMS). A treaty would then be negotiated for the creation of a European economic and currency union, and this would lay the foundation for the second stage of the process, the creation of a European Central Bank. During the third and final stage, important responsibilities of the individual governments in economic and monetary policy would be transferred to the European Community, fixed exchange rates would be agreed, and at the end of the process a single European currency would be introduced.

Certain rules would have to be observed. All the participating states wanted to establish obligatory rules of economic and budgetary policy so as to achieve price stability and a roughly equal rate of economic growth for each national economy and keep the balance of trade in equilibrium. These rules largely corresponded with the federal government's desiderata. Unlike in previous negotiations, an exact date was set for the completion of the first stage. It was to come into effect on 1 July 1990. Moreover, most of the restrictions on the movement of capital within Europe would be lifted on that date. This was expected to provide a tremendous stimulus, which would lead to dynamic economic growth.[55]

No fixed deadlines were set for the second and third stages, however, and on the German side there was very little interest in accelerating the unification process. One reason for this was that Federal Chancellor Kohl had no intention of publicly discussing the politically sensitive topic of the abandonment of the Deutschmark in favour of a single European currency before the Bundestag elections of December 1990. Another was that the federal government urgently wanted progress in European economic and currency integration to be linked with corresponding progress in the establishment of a political union. This applied in particular to the handing over of national governments' responsibilities to the institutions of the EC, to the common foreign and security policy, and to the extension of the jurisdiction of the European Parliament. The French and British governments took a very reserved attitude over all three of these points. France's endeavours were aimed above all at the integration of the German economy and the creation of a common currency, through which the European partners would profit from the strong German economy and currency, while the threat of German hegemony over Europe would be averted.

The fears of Germany's European partners were not limited to that country's expected economic predominance. The Federal Republic, said Mitterrand, had attained a certain degree of economic predominance in Europe and it would also want to make use of this politically in the future. Moreover, the Germans were jealous of France's nuclear armaments, he stated on another occasion, and they wanted to compensate for this with the help of their currency: 'The Deutschmark is in a sense a nuclear weapon.'[56]

Whether analogies of this sort were appropriate or not, from summer 1989 onwards France and most of the other EC states pressed strongly for a conference of governments to be called, so as to prepare the move to the second stage of the unification process. The process of European unification now became increasingly interwoven with the question of German unity, which had suddenly appeared on the table. The attention of the federal government was now entirely concentrated on developments in the GDR, but the prospect of German unity increased the insistence of the French side on the earliest possible start to preparations for stage two of the European unification process and the irreversible initiation of the European currency union. Chancellor Kohl was equally keen to avoid any advance commitments of this kind.

The news of the events in East Central Europe in autumn 1989 increased the suspicion felt in France and other EC countries—Italy, the Netherlands and Great Britain in particular—over the dynamic character of developments in the two German states, particularly after November, when Chancellor Kohl issued his Ten Points without discussing them with his European partners. When he spoke to Foreign Minister Genscher on 30 November, Mitterrand made no secret of his dismay over Kohl's headlong advance towards German reunification, as well as his reserved attitude towards the call for an immediate initiation of preparations for a European currency union:

> If German unity is realised before European unity, you will have the Triple Alliance of France, Great Britain and the USSR against you, just as in 1913 and 1939. . . . You will be encircled, and that will end in a war in which all Europeans will again be allied against the Germans. Is that what you want? If, on the other hand, German unity is created after European unity has made progress, we shall help you.[57]

That was forceful language indeed, and it illuminates the degree of anxiety, indeed hysteria, which emerged among Germany's European allies in face of the impending reunification of the country. But it also clearly implied a linkage between the two processes, which meant that the Western Europeans would accept German unity if the Germans agreed in advance to the economic and currency union of Europe.[58]

The summit meeting in Strasbourg, on 8 and 9 December 1989, was the scene of a severe clash of opinions. It could be read beforehand in the newspapers that Kohl would refuse to set a definite date for the start of a conference of heads of government to deal with a European currency union. In reaction to this, it was claimed, France would oppose German reunification. But, in actual fact, after heated discussions, the heads of government assembled in Strasbourg finally came to an agreement. It was repeatedly denied that there had been any 'horse-trading', but in fact the Strasbourg meeting did appear to have ended with reciprocal concessions of that nature: the German side agreed to the establishment of a conference of heads of government as early as the year 1990. This would allow concrete preparations for the single European currency to be started. In return the European Council issued a declaration confirming the right of the Germans to restore their unity by free self-determination. Nevertheless, existing treaties must be safeguarded—this was a reference to the need to confirm Poland's western border—and the process of German reunification must be 'embedded within the perspective of European integration'.[59]

In this way, therefore, the agreement of the Europeans to the imminent reunification of Germany was associated with the accelerated implementation of the second stage of European economic and monetary union. The abandonment of the Deutschmark and the inclusion of Germany in the European monetary union were intended to make the economic power of a reunited, stronger Germany a communal European possession, as it were. This approach was in line with the policy the Western Powers had followed ever since the immediate post-war years of counteracting the danger of German predominance by Europeanising that country's economic potential. This policy had been very successful over several decades, and it had secured the integration of the Federal Republic into the West and worked to the economic advantage of the European states. Equally, the Germans had also continuously gained in strength.

Thus, 1 July 1990 was not just the date when the economic and monetary union between the two German states entered into force, but also the beginning of the first stage of European economic and monetary union; the latter development took place in the shadow of the former. The conference of European governments, for so long a subject of contention, finally began its work in December 1990, and in the months that followed the preparations for European economic union and the single European currency went ahead rapidly. A short time afterwards, a working group was established to prepare for *political* union, but it met with greater difficulties, which it turned out were ultimately insuperable. As far as economic and financial matters were concerned, European unity had primacy. In the political field, in contrast, the primacy of national sovereignty was untouchable. In later years too, this dichotomy would be a feature of the contradictory dynamics of the European Union.

But the problems which might arise from this did not occupy the centre of attention at the end of this unique year of history. Without a doubt, the result of the reunification of Germany and the now firmly agreed European economic and monetary union was that the kind of fundamental changes in the territorial, political and economic structure of the European continent that took place in 1945 would no longer be repeated. The impact of these upheavals was still not completely clear, and many citizens of a newly reunited Germany, those in the East in particular, contemplated the future with trepidation. But the general feeling was one of confidence, and people felt that they were observers or even participants in a historically unique and fortunate series of events. In those two years, 1989 and 1990, far-reaching transformations took place in other regions of the world as well—in Eastern Europe, South Africa and somewhat earlier in Latin America—and these events combined together to constitute a triumphal march towards democracy and human rights. This meant that the Germans were now included in a global dynamic of liberation. Germany as the world-wide symbol of freedom, what a turn of events!

# 21
# A New Unity

## The End of History?

In spring 1989, even before the stirring events in Berlin, Prague and Budapest, the American political scientist Francis Fukuyama had published an article under the title 'The End of History', which met with a lively response all over the world. In it the author developed the thesis that liberalism, by which he meant a combination of democracy, capitalism and the welfare state, had won a definitive and final victory. At the beginning of the twentieth century, it had been challenged first by survivals of absolutism, then by Bolshevism and various varieties of fascism. These conflicts had been waged with a hitherto unknown violence, which threatened to lead to a nuclear apocalypse. After the downfall of fascism, and now also of socialism, history seemed to have returned at the end of the century to its original starting point. It had returned 'not to an "end of ideology" or a convergence between capitalism and socialism, as earlier predicted, but to an unabashed victory of economic and political liberalism'. What could be observed at present, he wrote, was 'not just the end of the Cold War, or the passing of a particular period of postwar history, but the end of history as such: that is, the end point of mankind's ideological evolution, and the universalisation of Western liberal democracy as the final form of human government.'[1]

The striking title of the article appeared in those months of 1989 to offer the appropriate catchword for the crisis of the socialist state system and the victory of democratic capitalism. It therefore came as no surprise that the thesis of the final victory of liberalism was immediately and weightily contradicted. Some critics pointed out that self-evidently 'history' as such would always exist, and so the idea of an 'end of history' was therefore senseless. Other critics were convinced that socialism had only been weakened temporarily and would return in a more democratic and more effective form. A third group in turn objected that Western liberalism had ultimately brought about wars and magnified social inequality to a previously unknown extent and was therefore absolutely unsuitable to serve as the zenith and endpoint of history. These somewhat shallow criticisms failed to address Fukuyama's basic thesis, however. His argument, which he elaborated two years later in a comprehensive study, was interesting. After the downfall of fascism and National Socialism at the end of the Second World War, and after the impending failure of the current Soviet and Chinese variants of communism, he said, there was no longer any universal ideology which could offer a better solution to the fundamental challenges of the modern world than liberalism, even as a tentative outline. Neither nationalism nor Islamic fundamentalism were in a position to do this. Fukuyama did not deny that there would be gigantic, and probably increasingly serious, problems in the future, which urgently awaited a solution. He instanced poverty, social injustice, racism and ecological catastrophe. And he naturally did not deny the continued existence of history in the sense of crises, wars and dynamic transformation processes. In Fukuyama's view, however, there no longer existed any form of social organisation which was capable of solving (or which could lay claim to solving) these global human problems better than capitalist democracy, whether in the short or the long term.

If one leaves aside the triumphalist tone which is inherent in this thesis, despite all the author's attempts to differentiate himself from such a position, it is evident that the victory of the West also posed a dilemma. If Fukuyama was correct in his claim that the radical alternatives to the liberal system that had developed in the twentieth century had definitively collapsed, and there was little reason to doubt this, the great problems of humanity could no longer be approached with the stimulating hope of finding a total alternative, an overthrow of the existing system, the construction of a completely different and a better society, but only within the parameters of the existing social and political system. After a century of unrestrained political violence this was an occasion for celebration rather than grief, especially in Germany. But Fukuyama's insight also signified that in future the limited range of possible political change would have to be accepted. Indeed, in recent decades the notion of the 'final assault' which will introduce the definitive victory of Good over Evil has been unmasked as an illusory and romantic dream of ultimate salvation.

The new post-1989 situation had a further aspect. The main reason for the collapse of Soviet communism had undoubtedly been its rigidity and inflexibility. It was a product of the age of heavy industry, of the focus on progress through industrial growth, and an answer to that immense need for security and equality which had spread after the victory of modern industrial society in the last third of the nineteenth century. But it had no answer to offer to the need for freedom, individualisation and consumption, and it no longer had a place in a world that had moved beyond heavy industry and the working class.

Capitalist democracy, on the other hand, which few people in Europe in the decade immediately preceding the First World War had thought likely to survive, had turned out to be extraordinarily dynamic and adaptable. And, in fact, the liberal societies of the 1980s had very little in common with their 1920s counterparts. Changes in state socialism since 1917, in contrast, had been essentially limited to variations in the amount of violence it employed. This strengthened the argument that open societies like the liberal West were best placed to react flexibly to new challenges.

It was, however, already apparent soon after 1989 that certain problems, not mentioned by Fukuyama in his observations, were inscribed in the victory of capitalist democracy. The animating principle of the capitalist economy is growth, and since the problems of the poorer regions of the world have to be solved by increasing their growth and prosperity rather than redistributing what is already there, this sets a limit to the ability of the Western model to solve these problems. 'If all the peoples of the earth possessed the same number of refrigerators and automobiles as those of North America and Western Europe, the planet would become uninhabitable', wrote one of Fukuyama's critics. 'The ozone layer is being rapidly depleted, temperatures are rising sharply and nuclear waste is accumulating.'[2] The more successful world capitalism becomes, the more threatening the associated ecological risks. On the other hand, it was also true that there was no other political principle on the horizon which was in a better position than liberal democracy to react to this problem without destroying democratic freedoms.

Twentieth-century liberalism's extraordinary adaptability can convincingly be traced back to the way it reacted to the challenge of alternative totalitarian concepts. Western societies strengthened their democratic profile in the conflict with fascism and National Socialism. To achieve this, they were compelled to reject dictatorship and racism explicitly and to emphasise the importance of the individual and the value of personal freedom as against the compulsion exercised by the community and the state. But they also competed with the authoritarian and fascist regimes in guaranteeing social security and national integration. Competition with communism led Western countries to extend social benefits, legislate against monopolies, acknowledge that property had social obligations and promote the growth of a consumer society. Capitalist democracy achieved dynamism and flexibility by demonstratively setting itself apart from the radical political alternatives that challenged it.

It could be argued against Fukuyama that, once the challenge from totalitarian competitors, above all communism, had come to an end, capitalist democracy no longer had to face any opposition, and a new, purer form of capitalism began to spread, which was no longer held back by the need to compete with rival systems. The liberalisation of financial markets and the worldwide removal of barriers to the free flow of capital promised new and unlimited possibilities. This also involved the inordinate development of profit-maximising strategies to an extent never seen before, unrestrained by anti-capitalist or at least anti-universalising counter-movements. Tendencies of this kind had, it is true, existed even before 1989, but after the downfall of the Soviet system they prevailed to a much greater degree. It seemed that, once capitalism was liberated from political considerations and competing views of the world, it had a tendency to take more and more risks in seeking to maximise profits, and thus eventually to jeopardise its own existence.

It is useful to keep these international and diachronic perspectives in mind when considering the reunification of Germany and the developments which took hold subsequently, because the reunification process did not proceed from Germany, nor was it decided in Germany. On the contrary, the downfall of the GDR and the triumph of the Federal Republic reflected the global confrontation between ways of ordering society which originated in the decades that preceded the First World War and received reinforcement both after 1914 and after 1945. Since this confrontation was now indubitably at an end, further developments in Germany as also in Europe were moulded by new criteria and new correlations of forces.

United Germany approached this new age, often described as 'post-totalitarian', with enthusiasm and great expectations. It soon turned out, however, that this attitude of self-assurance was far too optimistic. The triumph of the old Federal Republic rested on conditions which it was not certain the new united Germany would be able to guarantee in the future. This applied above all to the cost of unity, the magnitude of which had not yet even been surmised at the end of 1990. To raise a country of the size of the GDR, whose economic basis was largely in ruins, to the level of the second or third strongest economy in the world, politically as well as administratively, and in terms of economic strength, productivity, growth, social benefits and living standards, and all this within a short time, was an experiment which had never previously been undertaken. The economic absorption of the southern United States after the American Civil War, which was frequently adduced as a comparison, took almost a century and was more likely to serve as a portent of future disaster than an example to be followed.

The Federal Republic had, it is true, weathered the decade of economic crisis between 1973 and 1982 better than most other Western countries. In the late 1980s, the West German economy had again achieved a considerable rate of growth. But one could not fail to see that the country had still found no adequate answers to the profound economic and social changes that had resulted from structural change and globalisation. Structural unemployment among unskilled workers, the growing need for a highly qualified labour force, which necessitated a longer period of training, the ageing of the society, the tendency for gainful employment to be shared equally between men and women, and the changes in the family environment and children's upbringing associated with this, were all problems which could not be handled by the traditional social model inherited from industrial society in its classical phase. West German society was on the one hand highly individualised, but on the other hand it rested on a broad-based collectivist model of the social state. The liberal–conservative government of the 1980s had failed to adapt this model to changed conditions and requirements. This was partly because its priority objective was to balance the budget, and partly because a restructuring of this kind would have evoked concern and anxiety among the population, and was not a way of winning elections. As Andreas Wirsching has commented, the Federal Republic therefore transferred 'an essentially unreformed West German fiscal and social system to the new *Länder* . . . as a dominant culture permeated with prosperity, individualisation and "subtle distinctions" '.[3]

Unity also changed Germany's international significance. The *old* Federal Republic, as it was soon described, had benefited from either keeping out of most international entanglements, or only involving itself under the protection of the USA, and never militarily. The coming of the *new* Federal Republic, however, led paradoxically to an increase both in the fear of its European neighbours that Germany would now act with greater vigour and self-confidence and in the hope and expectation that the Germans would do exactly that. The Federal Republic was not equipped for such a change of role, and it needed some time to find its proper position and to fulfil it with any degree of adequacy. But since the downfall of the Soviet Union meant that international power relations in general had to find a new balance, this was not a problem for the Germans alone, a fact which made it easier to readjust.

In this context, the security systems established in the course of the unification process by the USA and Germany's European partners proved to be very helpful. After all, what would have happened to a neutral Germany without the NATO anchor during the crises in the Middle East, Yugoslavia, and the Gulf region or indeed after a military putsch in the Soviet Union? The accelerated process of European integration and the prospect of European monetary union, despite all the risks they entailed, also contributed to stabilising the new role of a united Germany in the international context. But the hope that a united Europe would soon act as a single force in foreign and security policy, and that Germany, now enlarged, would appear as an actor on the stage of world politics, but only in cooperation with its European partners, turned out to be vain. Here, more than in any other sphere of activity, the persistent strength of the national idea and the nation-state was confirmed.

## Unification Crisis

German jubilation over the fall of the Berlin Wall and the approaching reunification of the country was further heightened in summer 1990 by the World Cup victory of the country's football team. This feeling had still not faded away when other events started to pour in upon the country. There was the catastrophic and unexpected collapse of the East German economy; the war in the Gulf, which raised the question of a new world order and the place of Germany in it; the long civil war in Yugoslavia, which produced more than a hundred thousand deaths and eventually led to the Bundeswehr's first ever military intervention; the attempted putsch in Moscow by conservative communists, which brought in its train the dissolution of the Soviet Union; and a series of arson attacks and pogroms against asylum seekers and foreigners in Germany, which for a short period forced all other issues into the background. There was finally the decision to introduce a common European currency. All these events resulted in one way or another from the 1989–90 upheaval in world politics and the economic changes that had preceded this. They necessarily have to be described in succession, but it must always be borne in mind that all of them—the Gulf War, the conflict in Yugoslavia, the economic collapse in East Germany, the dissolution of the USSR, the debate over asylum and the preparations for the euro—took place at the same time, around the turn of the year 1991. Thus the 1990s were, in many respects, a decade overloaded with events.

The Bundestag elections of December 1990 confirmed the Kohl–Genscher government in office. At 43.8 per cent, the Union's result was slightly below the 1987 figure, and the FDP did slightly better, while the critics of reunification who formed the opposition were penalised. The SPD, headed by its candidate for the chancellorship, Lafontaine, received only 33.5 per cent of the vote, its worst result since 1957, and the Greens remained below the 5 per cent hurdle. A year earlier, the Social Democrats had looked like certain winners. On the other hand, the electoral victory of the government parties, after the triumph of reunification, which was entirely attributed to Kohl, the 'unity Chancellor', was not exactly outstanding. What the election result did show was the remarkable political stability of the country. Even in the lands of the former GDR (described thenceforth as 'the new federal states') the government parties obtained more than 54 per cent of the vote, while the Social Democrats secured only 24.3 per cent. In contrast to this, the former SED, now relabelled the 'Party of Democratic Socialism' (PDS), obtained a respectable result, with 11.1 per cent of the vote. This coincided with the estimate commonly made of the SED's core support. But soon the PDS developed into the voice of those who had done badly out of the change of regime, and in federal state elections in the East it obtained 15 per cent, and later over 20 per cent of the vote. The civil rights campaigners of Alliance 90, who were joined by the Greens, received 6.2 per cent of the vote in the East, and were able to enter the Bundestag on the basis of special provisions made for these first pan-German elections.[4]

Lafontaine had concentrated his election campaign entirely on the financial burdens to be expected from reunification. His calculations were not unrealistic, but they sounded like a rejection of German unification in general. The government parties, on the other hand, relied on optimism about the economic situation in East Germany, and Kohl's announcement that 'thriving vistas' would soon be seen in the East was further reinforced by his promise that an economic 'upsurge in the East' would be achieved without any tax increases.[5]

In practice, however, signs of economic difficulty in East Germany had already begun to multiply after the economic and currency union of summer 1990. The effect of Kohl's election promises was to preclude the option of increasing the tax burden on the West Germans to compensate for the considerably higher cost of unification which was now expected. In any case, according to the federal government, German unification would pay for itself, after a short transitional phase. It was planned to transfer around 25 billion DM to the East German *Länder* in 1990 and a further 40 billion DM in 1991. The most important economic institutes foresaw that payments of this order of magnitude would continue for a lengthy period of time, roughly eight to ten years, during which 40 to 50 billion DM would need to be raised every year.[6]

The optimism displayed by these estimates rested on three assumptions. The first was that economic growth in West Germany, which was already very good, would receive an additional impulse from unification, especially as costs related to the division of the country, such as government aid to border regions, would no longer be incurred. Secondly, the privatisation of the state-owned enterprises in the GDR by the *Treuhandanstalt* (Trust Agency) set up for that purpose would bring in enough profits to finance a large part of the necessary restructuring measures. The federal government's third assumption was that the expected dynamic economic growth in the East would be set in motion by a tremendous influx of private investment capital. The necessary means for stimulating economic dynamism in the East were to be raised by a 'German Unity Fund', which would be financed largely from the centre but to a lesser extent also by the *Länder*. But the government did not want to raise taxes, so the necessary financial resources were procured mainly by borrowing. In addition, they were placed in a special fund, outside the normal budget, so as make it appear that the budget deficit had not increased.

Manipulations of this kind were unable to cover up the fact that the economic situation in the East German *Länder* had worsened catastrophically since the economic and currency union. 'At present there are no indications at all of a turnaround in the East', wrote *Der Spiegel* in April 1991.

> So far, all that is certain is that the decline of the economy is proceeding at ever greater speed. What is happening in eastern Germany at present is something that has never yet occurred in time of peace: an entire industrial region is being run into the ground. Whether you look at shipyards or textile factories, at steelworks or computer firms, their products and their prices are all utterly outdone by Western competition. Hardly a single enterprise will survive in its old form. Most of them are overdue for bankruptcy. The old comes crashing down, but there is no sign of the new. For a long time to come, sums amounting to billions and billions of marks will flow from West to East every year. The cost of reconstructing the economy of eastern Germany is calculated in trillions.[7]

This was not an exaggeration. The GDP of the new *Länder* fell in 1991 to barely 60 per cent of its 1989 level. In 1991 the amount of value added by industry was only 40 per cent of the 1989 figure, and still less was added by agriculture. Not one of the optimistic predictions made earlier turned out to be correct: the privatisation of industry brought losses instead of gains, private investment was largely absent and after two years the 'unification boom' turned out to be a flash in the pan.

It was easy to see the reasons for this catastrophic collapse. The East German economy, which had been protected from the world market until 1989, was exposed to Western competition at a single stroke by the currency union of 1 July 1990. Its products turned out to be unmarketable: they were too expensive, of inadequate quality and their technology was obsolete. On 1 January 1991, trade with the former CMEA countries was also placed on a hard currency basis, and within a few weeks this led to the almost complete obliteration of eastern Germany's exports to the East, which until 1989 had formed in a sense the backbone of the GDR economy. Hard currency was in short supply in the Soviet Union, as it was in Poland and Czechoslovakia, and the small supply available was used rather to purchase Japanese computers and West German motor cars than 'Trabis' and Leica cameras. By the end of 1991, exports from the eastern part of Germany to the former CMEA countries had fallen by roughly 75 per cent. Hence the firms of eastern Germany were unable either to sell their products domestically or export them, but after the currency conversion they had to pay wages in Deutschmarks, converted from Eastern Marks at a rate of 1:1. In 1994, the effective wage in the East was 70 per cent of the West

German level, but comparative productivity was only 39 per cent. Hence, it was impossible for firms in eastern Germany to produce at a profit.[8]

Within a few months, this situation led to mass dismissals on a historically unprecedented scale. By 1993, the number of gainfully employed people in the eastern *Länder* had fallen by a third, from 9.7 to 6.2 million, and 1.7 million had emigrated to the West, with half a million more commuting there to work. Official figures showed 1.2 million unemployed; some 800,000 were being sheltered by government programmes such as job creation, further training and retraining; and 850,000 had taken early retirement. Thus, while there were 6.2 million people in employment, there were almost 3 million people suffering from either open or hidden unemployment. Moreover, in 1993, less than 30 per cent of employed East Germans were in the same job as before reunification.

Older workers of both sexes and women in general were much harder hit by unemployment than younger men. Eighty per cent of the over-fifties lost their jobs. Two-thirds of the unemployed were female. Moreover, once a person was unemployed, new jobs were hard to come by: in 1993, almost half of the unemployed had spent a year or more without work. In 1995, 76 per cent of women were in this category.[9]

The federal government had originally thought that this tidal wave of economic and social disaster would be a transitional phenomenon, lasting two years, or three at most. After that, the firms of eastern Germany, by then largely privatised, would function effectively and competitively, and they would bring the economy of eastern Germany up to the western level within a foreseeable period of time. To achieve this, the de Maizière government had created the *Treuhandanstalt* (Trust Agency), and by July 1990 this organisation had already privatised or closed a large proportion of the smaller firms. After the economic and currency union, the Treuhand (as it came to be called) began to operate on a larger scale. The former head of the Hoesch Works in Dortmund, Detlev Rohwedder, an experienced restructuring specialist, was appointed to head it.[10]

On 1 July 1990, the Treuhand took over more than 7,800 firms, which employed 4 million people. In addition, an area of land which amounted to half the territory of the GDR was transferred to it. The Treuhand was mainly expected to privatise the assets it administered, but also where appropriate to help with the necessary restructuring, and if necessary, when individual firms turned out to be non-competitive, to close them down.[11]

The Treuhand originally assumed that the profits of privatisation would be enormous. Rohwedder's estimate in autumn 1990 had been that 'the whole shebang comes to about 600 billion.'[12] But it soon became apparent that such notions were unrealistic. Only a small number of assets were of interest to Western buyers: the electricity company, for instance, which promised crisis-free long-term profits after restructuring, or well-situated plots of land. In addition, in many cases the principle of 'restitution before compensation' prevented a rapid sale owing to the legal disputes which were to be expected, though in retrospect it is hard to say how significant the economic impact of this regulation actually was.[13] The main problem was rather that it was very difficult, and sometimes impossible, to find buyers for the enterprises on offer, because the factories were dilapidated, the equipment was inadequate, and the workforces were much too large. In addition, buyers had to reckon with considerable pollution, the removal of which often cost more than the factory itself was worth.

The greatest difficulty was experienced in selling enterprises which belonged to the classical branches of industry, such as steelmaking, shipbuilding and textiles, but also chemicals and machine building, because those branches were in crisis in the West as well, owing to globalisation and structural change. Moreover, the GDR policy of establishing industrial combines had created regional mono-structures, and the collapse of these gigantic enterprises now sealed the economic fate of whole towns and districts.

Not until spring 1991, when the extent of the economic collapse of the East German *Länder* could no longer be ignored, did the federal government react to these disastrous developments. Its individual measures can be summarised under four headings. Firstly, it did finally increase taxes, though hesitantly and with the somewhat embarrassed explanation that it wanted to pay for the cost of the war in Iraq by increasing receipts from taxes on tobacco, spirits and energy. A more important addition was the 'Solidarity Contribution', a supplement to income tax, which was only supposed to apply for one year and even perhaps to be reimbursed later. But when there seemed to be no end to the crisis, it was made permanent.

The second measure, however, was much more drastic: a massive 50 per cent increase in the rate of unemployment insurance contributions, from 1 April 1991 onwards. The enormous additional cost of pensions, unemployment benefit and active labour market policies in eastern Germany was financed in this way through social insurance. The government was therefore able to avoid unpopular tax increases. But the effect of the measure was that labour costs rose still further and the labour market, which was already in difficulties, was placed under an extra burden both in the East and in West Germany. It was therefore labour, as a factor of production, that carried the load of the unification crisis.[14]

Thirdly, private investment was encouraged through allowances, special tax write-offs and credits. These inducements were sometimes very substantial. Someone who invested a million DM in the East received an allowance of 230,000 DM. The investor was also exempted from paying taxes on the profits of half the sum invested, as well as not having to pay wealth tax and business capital tax on the profits of the firm in eastern Germany. In this manner, the state paid back almost half the 50 per cent tax burden on a large firm in the East, and up to 42 per cent of the tax burden on a smaller firm.[15] This generosity naturally led to numerous incorrect investment decisions and to the misuse of funds on a grand scale. It is true that, in the first months and years after reunification, petty criminals and swindlers of all kinds took advantage of the unregulated transition zone between socialism and capitalism, but the privatisation efforts of the Treuhand led to profiteering and fraud of a much larger order of magnitude. Occurrences of this kind attracted much attention and were liable to bring the whole process of economic restructuring into disrepute. From a wider perspective, however, these were just individual cases and phenomena incidental to much larger problems.

These big problems were most clearly evident in the industrial policy of the Treuhand, which is the fourth point we need to consider. Because of the slow pace of industrial privatisation in East Germany, the Treuhand was compelled, under pressure from the federal government, to conduct the necessary enterprise restructuring itself, and at its own expense, in order to interest any investors at all in these assets. This applied particularly to regions with industrial mono-structures. Big enterprises like the Buna Works in Halle, the steel firm EKO-Stahl in Brandenburg and the shipyards on the Baltic coast were not competitive according to the criteria of business economics, because the necessary costs of restructuring far exceeded the expected profit, even in the longer term. The policy pursued by the Treuhand was a repetition of what had already been tried out in the Federal Republic in the 1960s in coalmining and in the 1970s and 1980s in the steel sector and other industrial branches: the temporary preservation of non-competitive enterprises by means of state subsidies, in order to prevent the economic collapse of whole regions and cities. In the Saar or the Ruhr these measures had served to gain the time needed for the gradual dismantling of workplaces and the construction of other factories which had better future prospects.

What was now involved in the former GDR was the use of tax receipts to restructure 'industrial heartlands' dominated largely by ailing firms so as to allow these firms to be turned into viable workplaces as quickly as possible. Carl Zeiss in Jena, for instance, was supported with a promise of 3.6 billion DM, with the aim of preserving roughly 10,000 jobs. To enable the privatisation of the North East German shipyards, the Treuhand paid out between 6 and 7 billion DM. This preserved a further 10,000 jobs. In the case of the Buna Works and other chemical firms, the purchaser, the Dow Chemical Company, received some 10 billion DM in state subsidies for 5,600 jobs, though this worked out in the long run at a mere 1,800. Thus, the state paid roughly 600,000 DM to secure a single workplace in the shipyards, while Dow received 5 million DM for each workplace it preserved in the chemical industry. These were spectacular sums, but they look less singular when one bears in mind that between 1958 and 2005 €129 billion were allocated to the West German coalmining industry, a figure which does not include 'eternity costs', in other words, the long-term ecological cost of mining operations.[16]

The Treuhand ceased its activities at the end of 1994. Since its establishment, 12,370 enterprises had been transferred to it. By 1994, it had privatised 6,000, returned roughly 1,000 to their previous owners and handed a smaller number to municipal authorities, while 3,712 enterprises had been liquidated. Some 1.5 million jobs had been kept in existence, and new ones had been added. The Treuhand had received 68 billion DM from the sale of enterprises and plots of land, but it had paid out 343 billion DM to cover the cost of restructuring, decommissioning, taking over old debts and cleaning up polluted environments. It therefore made an overall loss of 275 billion DM, which was taken over by the Treasury.[17]

It is impossible to establish the exact total of the transfer payments made to the East German *Länder.* There are several estimates to the effect that between 1991 and 1995 the total cost came to 620 billion DM. This is a net figure, taking into account the taxes and fees that flowed back to the state. It works out at an annual payment of roughly 120 billion DM. For the period between 1991 and 1999, a figure of 1.2 trillion DM has been estimated, an annual average of almost 140 billion DM, which is roughly a third of Germany's annual budget. If the period between 1991 and 2003 is taken as a whole, the estimate is a trillion DM in total and an average annual cost of 75 billion DM, because the years between 1991 and 1995 were much more costly than the later period owing to the losses suffered by the Treuhand.[18]

This massive state intervention had a serious impact on the economy as a whole. The percentage of GDP spent by the government rose from 43.6 in 1990 to 54.8 in 1995. The national debt doubled, from 929 billion DM in 1989 to 1,996 billion DM in 1995. Interest payments on the debt increased during the same period from 60.6 billion to 128.3 billion DM. But a considerable proportion of this debt had been shifted to special accounts. The 'Inherited Liabilities Redemption Fund' (*Erblastentilgungsfonds*) included the Treuhand's losses (205 billion) the cost of currency conversion in East Germany (30 billion), the GDR state debt (28 billion) and the debts of GDR housing development companies (29 billion). The credits with which the transfer payments to the East German *Länder* had been paid until 1994 (84 billion DM) were collected together in the 'German Unity Fund', while the costs of subsidising East German firms (34 billion DM) were pooled together in the 'European Recovery Programme Special Asset Fund'.[19] The overwhelming majority of these transfer payments were not investments but subsidies and social security benefits, and roughly a quarter of the payments were in fact financed through the social insurance system. As a result of this, the Federal Republic's social expenditure ratio began to rise again: it had fallen from 33 to 29 per cent between 1982 and 1989, but by 1996 it had reached 34.9 per cent.[20]

Until 1992, owing to the 'unification boom', the West German economy experienced an exceptional upsurge, with growth figures of more than 5 per cent a year. This set the country apart from the other economies of the West, which had been in crisis since 1988. At the end of 1992 this began to change. The tremendous financial cost of unification worsened the situation of the West German economy, and from 1993 it experienced a downward trend, while in the other OECD countries the economic climate started to improve. The GDP of Germany as a whole shrank by one per cent in 1993, and indeed GDP in West Germany alone shrank by 2 per cent, which was its worst result since the immediate post-war period.[21] Unemployment now increased in the old *Bundesländer* as well as the new ones. It rose from 6.3 per cent in 1991 to 9.2 per cent in 1994. But above all, hardly any new jobs were being created. Incidental wage costs increased considerably during the unification crisis, and this made it more expensive to take on workers. As a result, West German firms also reduced their staffing levels, so as to make productivity gains.

In East Germany, economic growth only proceeded very slowly, despite the enormous transfer payments. Until 1995, growth rates of up to 10 per cent were achieved, but this was because of the extremely low starting level in 1990. After that, however, the upsurge flattened out, falling to a rate of 2 per cent. Economic output per person in East Germany was still only 55.1 per cent of the West German figure in 1997, and labour productivity was 60 per cent of West Germany's. Even so, by the last third of the 1990s it had proved possible to bring the rapid deindustrialisation of the region to an end, and its striking weaknesses in the field of exports were diminishing. In the first few years after reunification the construction sector had served as the driving force of economic growth thanks to gigantic infrastructure projects. Later on, though, this function was taken over by the service sector, which had been strongly underrepresented in the former GDR.

The destruction of many of the industrial and agricultural workplaces in the former GDR, the massive unemployment there and the removal of many women from gainful employment had a devastating impact on people's attempts to plan their lives, on social cohesion and on trust in the economic and social system of the new state. The rift which arose as a result between Germans in the East and those in the West became one of the major problems of the unification process in the years that followed. Positive effects did, it is true, also emerge from the drastic economic measures put in place after reunification, such as the renovation of the town centres, the building of a new transport infrastructure, and the establishment of an efficient administration. The economic data also gradually improved in the East German *Länder* after the turn of the century. But even in 2003–4 the ratio between West and East was 19:11 for annual income per head, and 15:6 for wealth. The unemployment ratio was 9:20, and the productivity ratio 10:7, though there were considerable regional differences. In urban areas like Dresden and Leipzig, living conditions were comparable after the turn of the century with those enjoyed in West German cities, but in other parts of eastern Germany, particularly Mecklenburg-West Pomerania, Brandenburg and Saxony-Anhalt, there were areas which continued to be in crisis, with far higher than average unemployment figures, continuous youth emigration and meagre future prospects.

Was there any alternative to the way the federal government conducted its reunification policy? Left-wing critics accused it of trusting blindly to the market. Faith in the market's ability to correct itself had never been so clearly refuted as in this case, said the critics. Instead of relying on this, they said, the federal government should have continued to run the existing firms as state enterprises, restructured them, and only then privatised them where this was appropriate.[22] To this, the reply can be made that even state-owned enterprises could only have continued to operate if they were commercially viable. This could not be achieved with productivity rates of less than half those of the worldwide competition, especially in branches of industry which operated in other parts of the world at a fraction of the cost. For the state to subsidise such businesses permanently would have been like throwing money into a bottomless pit, a point to which the collapse of the GDR economy itself delivered eloquent testimony.

The criticism of the advocates of a pure market economy, on the other hand, was that instead of concentrating on establishing promising new businesses, the state was spending billions of Deutschmarks on subsidising uncompetitive industrial enterprises, so as to preserve places of employment which had no future.[23] An approach of the kind these critics recommended would of course have led to the closure of most of the industrial enterprises of East Germany immediately after the currency conversion. This would have meant that whole regions were abandoned, and left to decay probably for years, until efficient new firms eventually settled down there—or perhaps not. Leaving aside the fact that this approach, modelled on the actions of the British government of Margaret Thatcher during the early 1980s, would have been politically impossible to achieve in East Germany, the reason for subsidising its industrial areas was similar to the reason for earlier subsidies given to West German industrial districts, namely to gain time during the transitional period until these districts could be economically restructured with state assistance. The idea behind this was that without such measures the cost of paying unemployment benefit to tens of thousands of people would not be less than the cost of subsidies, but would leave no future options open.

Moreover, the privatisation or closure of almost the whole of an economy within a few years was something that had never happened before. There was therefore no experience to go by. The number of mistakes and failed investments was therefore high. To that extent, it was not surprising that the Treuhand, which had the job of winding up, restructuring and privatising the East German economy, became an object of hatred and despair and a symbol of East Germany's economic plight. It was, however, not responsible for the desolate condition of most East German enterprises. On the contrary, its actions simply laid bare what the GDR authorities had hidden from the public for many years: the disastrous condition of the East German economy.

The mistakes in economic policy in connection with the unification process had been made right at the beginning. The refusal to raise taxes for reasons of political opportunism, and the general failure to inform people in Germany about the true state of the East German economy, to ask them to make sacrifices and to justify these, were probably the worst mistakes. The burden of debt was much increased, and the additional costs were hidden away inside the system of unemployment and social insurance. Relations between East and West Germans were also put under strain because there was no public discussion or agreement over the amount of the burden each side had to bear.

As the economic and social crisis in East Germany intensified, relations between East and West Germans assumed greater and greater prominence. It was not a surprise that a certain degree of alienation became apparent early on. Most West Germans knew almost nothing of the experiences and attitudes of the East Germans before 1989, and most East Germans knew the West Germans and their habits only from West German television. People continued to rejoice over the reunification of the country, but the mood in the new *Bundesländer* was increasingly marked by disappointment and anxiety over the future. In 1994, only 17 per cent of East Germans considered that the economic situation in Germany was good or very good. By 1998, this proportion had fallen to 12 per cent. More than half of the East Germans were of the opinion that the situation in the GDR in regard to the distribution of income had been fairer than it was in reunited Germany, and roughly 80 per cent considered that they had previously enjoyed more social security and social solidarity. Almost three-quarters of them were of the opinion that socialism was in itself a good idea, but had not been carried out properly. There was a particularly widespread feeling that they had been short-changed by cunning West German profiteers, and abandoned to the mercy of arrogant West Germans who behaved like colonial officials.[24]

Not the least of the reasons for this was that the elites of the GDR, in politics, administration, business, science and the security forces, had been almost completely deprived of authority and replaced by West Germans. The new system meant a tremendous degree of promotion for West German managers and executives, and their behaviour in the East was often felt to be high-handed and overbearing. On the other hand, it would probably not have been possible, or at least not possible so quickly, for the West German model in economics, politics and administration to be transferred to the East German *Länder* without West German specialists. Observers like the historian Jürgen Kocka soon drew attention to the successes of restructuring in Eastern Germany. An example of this was the rapid and almost unnoticed construction of an efficient administration in the municipalities, the health service, the courts, the job centres, the social organisations and the *Land* authorities. The same applied to the integration of the GDR National People's Army into the Bundeswehr, which was completed within a few years without any disturbances, or at least none that came to the notice of the outside world.[25]

Even so, the introduction of the new West German elite into the East was associated with numerous injustices. Not everything was determined by performance, and discontent was loudly expressed by many people, not just by officials of the SED and the Stasi who had been dismissed from their posts. In fact, most members of the old GDR elite were able, after some time, to find their footing in the new republic, and even former party functionaries found good positions, sometimes leading positions, in the private sector, in areas such as real estate, insurance and finance.[26]

But the gap in attitudes between East and West was unmistakable. More than 80 per cent of the East Germans felt that they were second-class citizens when asked in summer 1991. The proportion was the same in summer 1997. On the other hand, 70 per cent of West Germans criticised the East Germans for 'wanting to live like westerners and work like they used to do in the East'. While the East Germans viewed the citizens of the old Federal Republic as arrogant, self-confident and business-like, the West Germans viewed their compatriots in the new *Länder* as insecure and parochial.[27]

The media reported these findings extensively, often with an undercurrent of alarmism, and the debate was conducted in shrill tones on both sides of the divide. East and West Germans long continued to differ markedly in cultural character and mental attitudes. But most of the stereotypes soon faded away. With time, a more differentiated overall picture emerged. In 1998, two-thirds of East Germans stated that they were better off than they had been in 1990. Only 18 per cent said they were worse off, though more than half the unemployed were of that opinion. In fact, average East German net household income rose considerably during this period. It had been 75 per cent of the West German level in 1991, but by 1998 it had risen to almost 90 per cent. By 1996, the average East German male pension had risen to the West German level, and for women it was almost 1,200 DM, a third higher than in West Germany, owing to the higher level of female employment in the East.[28]

In spite of these positive tendencies the situation in East Germany remained difficult. 'Fragmented development' was the expression used by social scientists in this connection. According to an interim verdict delivered in 2005:

> The much-quoted successes, the flourishing businesses, the redeveloped town centres and the extended infrastructure are offset by the closed firms, the ruined coalmines, the abandoned housing districts and the disappearing villages . . . Alongside high earners under time pressure one finds many people who are on low pay or have to live continuously on social assistance and whose lives have been blighted by unemployment. Well-qualified young people are leaving the area, birth rates are at rock bottom and the population is ageing. The budgets of the East German *Länder* and municipalities are under-financed and in addition they cannot be balanced out of their own resources. The same is true of social benefits. East Germany is highly dependent on transfer payments, and there is no end in sight.[29]

By 2012, however, unemployment in East Germany had fallen to 12 per cent. It was still twice as high as the overall level in the old Federal Republic, but it approximated to the level in the regions of West Germany that had previously suffered economic crisis.

Ten years after reunification, and even fifteen years afterwards, therefore, the balance sheet was mixed. The new state structures had been established relatively quickly and successfully. But economic unification had led to a veritable catastrophe, from which the country took not years but decades to extract itself. At the same time, social and psychological differences proved to be persistent and difficult to offset. Certainly, if one cast a glance at the former GDR's partner countries in East Central Europe, what had happened in Germany could not be characterised as anything other than successful. But that was not the yardstick by which people measured success and failure. In that sense, how the situation in East Germany was judged was a matter of perspective.

## In the New World Order

On 21 November 1990, the end of the Cold War and the triumph of the West was solemnly attested by the 'Charter of Paris'. In this document, all the European countries, including the Soviet Union, committed themselves to constitutionalism and democracy, the protection of human rights, social justice and economic freedom at home, and the renunciation of force and the peaceful settlement of conflicts abroad. This was no doubt a remarkable moment, but it could better be described as a snapshot of a unique occasion, because the end of the East–West confrontation was simultaneously the starting point for the formation of a new global power structure.[30]

The future direction of the Federal Republic's foreign policy after the end of the confrontation between rival political and social systems appeared to have been predefined by the inclusion of the former GDR into NATO and the European Community. The main policy focus was now on the unification of Europe as a whole. This included both the impending European economic and currency union and the speediest possible integration of the formerly communist states of East Central Europe into the general European framework, in the short term through economic support and in the medium and long term through integration into the European Union, and if possible into NATO as well. It was also important to pursue a policy of cooperation and self-restraint, so as to dispel the doubts felt by many European states about German unification. In January 1991, in his first government declaration, Kohl stated that it would be inappropriate for the nation to act 'unilaterally' or to display a 'hunger for power' in giving effect to German's new sovereignty. There was 'only one place in the world' for the Germans, which was as part of 'the community of free peoples'.[31]

In order to achieve this, the worldwide political earthquakes of 1989–90 needed to be followed by a phase of tranquillity and consolidation in foreign policy. But it turned out that no breathing space was available. On the contrary, within a few years, indeed a few months, a profusion of world-shaking events completely transformed the political agenda of the Federal Republic. The war against Iraq, the collapse of the Soviet Union and the civil war in Yugoslavia reset the basic parameters of international politics, and the Federal Republic suddenly saw itself confronted with challenges of an entirely new kind, which it had not had to meet in previous decades because of its protected position in the shadow of the Cold War.

On 2 August 1990, some 100,000 Iraqi soldiers invaded and occupied Kuwait. There had long been disputes between the two states over their territorial borders (which had been set somewhat arbitrarily at the end of the British mandate), but the invasion happened for a different reason: Iraq had been weakened economically by its nine-year war with Iran, and was heavily in debt to its Arab neighbours. It owed $80 billion to Kuwait alone. The attempt by the Iraqi dictator Saddam Hussein to improve the country's financial situation by sharply increasing the price of oil had been defeated, not least because of Kuwaiti resistance. By marching into that country, Iraq wanted both to get rid of its debts and also gain control of its neighbour's rich oil reserves.

Saddam Hussein headed a Left nationalist military government and enjoyed close relations with both the Soviet Union and the USA. With this surprise attack he wanted to create a fait accompli while the attention of the world was elsewhere, concentrated as it was on the collapse of the Soviet empire and the events in Germany and East Central Europe. This turned out to be a miscalculation, for the attack on Kuwait was condemned not only by the West but also, almost unanimously, by the other Arab states. Under a UN mandate, the USA started to build a coalition which eventually comprised more than twenty countries. This coalition then opened hostilities against Iraq, starting on 17 January 1991 with massive air attacks, followed on 24 February by a ground invasion. By 28 February, the Iraqi Army had been defeated. The number of coalition dead was around 200, and on the Iraqi side the number killed was estimated to be between 50,000 and 100,000. When they withdrew from Kuwait, Saddam Hussein's troops set fire to Kuwait's oil wells. They also altered the course of the pipelines so that oil poured into the Persian Gulf. These actions created a tremendous environmental catastrophe.[32]

The political result of the first Gulf War was the establishment of a new global power structure even before the collapse of the Soviet Union was complete. The USA, the country which provided three-quarters of the coalition's troops, was able to inflict a devastating defeat within a few days on Iraq, despite its considerable military potential. This made it clear that the USA alone, as the sole surviving superpower, was capable of establishing a unilaterally structured world order after the end of the bilateral one, and in a position to do so.

The dictatorship of Saddam Hussein was not more brutal that the regimes of US allies in the Middle East such as Saudi Arabia, Syria and Egypt, even if the tremendous propaganda campaign which accompanied the war gave the impression that he was 'the new Hitler'. The fact that the Americans did not occupy the country completely, and that they defeated Saddam but did not overthrow him, demonstrated that in addition to protecting their own political and economic influence in the Middle East they were concerned above all to establish a balance of forces there and prevent further wars, without being obliged to engage in a long-term troop commitment.

The Germans were not part of the anti-Iraq coalition. There were several reasons for this. One was that the Basic Law as currently interpreted forbade the engagement of the Bundeswehr outside the area of NATO—'out of area' engagement was the expression used at the time. Another was that the preparations for the Iraq War began in summer 1990. These were the weeks of Germany's reunification, when the country was more inward-looking than ever before. There were also 300,000 Red Army soldiers on German soil when the war started. But the most important reason was this: nowhere else were protests against the Gulf War so continuous and so massive as in Germany.

The federal government had pushed for a negotiated peace right up to the outbreak of war, but it had also made clear from the beginning that Germany would not participate in military action, chiefly for constitutional reasons. This reluctance to go to war was sharply criticised by the Western powers, especially as the continuous mass demonstrations against the Gulf War in German cities were thoroughly reported in the media. Germany, remarked US Senator John McCain, was in the process of rising to become one of the leading world powers, alongside Japan and the USA, but it was not ready to undertake the greater responsibilities that followed from this: 'If the German federal government and the German people do not change their attitude, this could seriously damage relations between Germany and the USA.' The former US State Secretary for Foreign Affairs, Henry Kissinger, also emphasised America's disappointment that Germany, a country whose reunification had been continuously supported by the USA, and which had been protected for decades from the Eastern danger, was now demonstrating against US involvement in the Middle East. It is true that statements of this kind contradicted the position of the US government, which by no means expected the Federal Republic to become involved militarily, wanting instead substantial financial participation, something it also required of Japan. Even so, when it became known that German firms had not only delivered weapons to Iraq but also chemical installations which could be used to produce poison gas, this strengthened the image of a nation of unscrupulous traders, who were ready to make money out of the war but too cowardly to fight alongside their allies.[33]

The extent of the peace movement's demonstrations and protest actions against the Gulf War (a rally in the Hofgarten in Bonn was attended by more than 100,000 people) had also surprised German politicians. Those who protested against the war that threatened to break out were predominantly university and school students, members of the generation born in the 1970s, who were still too young at the time of the 'double-track decision' to take part in the demonstrations against rearmament. People protested out of a mixture of motives: they wanted to outbid each other in pacifism, and there was a definite anti-American emphasis, which found expression in slogans like 'No blood for oil' and 'Americans out of Saudi Arabia', while the fact that Iraq had attacked Kuwait was largely ignored. In addition, there was the fear of a worldwide environmental catastrophe, which was then particularly widespread in the Federal Republic. It was reflected in apocalyptic scenarios of a global ice age, which was expected to arrive if the oil wells of Kuwait were set on fire. But the continued debate over the mass crimes of National Socialism also played an important part in these protests. One of the impulses that distinguished the anti-war protests in Germany from those in other countries was the desire 'never again to be the perpetrator'.[34]

The peace demonstrations of 1990–1 were far less political than their predecessors. A certain hysteria was also evident. This was reflected in the widespread feeling, mixed in some cases with a kind of disaster obsession that this might be the beginning of World War Three. But, above all, the Gulf War and the state of moral emergency which accompanied it in Germany (in 1991 even the carnival processions on the Monday before Lent were cancelled!) effaced the dividing line between Left and Right which had previously applied. Until then, almost every movement or revolt in the 'Third World' against the West and the Americans in particular had been able to count on sympathy and support from the Left all over the world, and particularly in Germany. Now this clear front began to waver. Saddam Hussein had attacked his small neighbour Kuwait like a criminal robbing a bank, he had then spread terror over the country and finally even bombarded Israel with missiles, although that country was not involved in the conflict. Even people who distrusted Western propaganda, which soon became all-pervasive, could not approve of such actions. Moreover, military intervention in Iraq had been legitimated by decisions of the United Nations Organisation and the Security Council, and in view of the fact that twenty nations were participating in the war, it could not be said that the Americans were acting unilaterally.

An instructive debate followed among German intellectuals on this subject. Writers who had been regarded until then as on the Left, such as Hans Magnus Enzensberger and Wolf Biermann, advocated going to war against Iraq, not only referring to Saddam's breach of international law in attacking Kuwait and threatening Israel, but even comparing American action in Iraq with the liberation of Germany by the Allies at the end of the Second World War. The cultural critic Jan Philipp Reemtsma wrote an eye-catching article shortly before the war started in which he declared that he was 'uncomfortable' with the slogan 'Americans out of Saudi Arabia!' because 'we do not really know—leaving aside the possibility that there might not actually be a war—what we would want to happen to the inhabitants of the region in question: to be dominated by the USA or by Saddam Hussein. Personally, I would prefer the former.'[35] Objections of this kind were vehemently contradicted by supporters of the peace movement, but their arguments no longer had much force.

The dispute between the 'warmongers' and the peace movement suddenly brought back to the surface the question of how to define a just war, for the Left as well, and the justification for Germany's special role in foreign policy, and particularly in military affairs, was thrown into doubt. The intimate connection between the debate over the Gulf War and Germany's past was clearly apparent from the composition of a group of German historians who discussed the war on the First German TV Channel the evening after it had started. It contained several specialists on the Nazi era, and not one expert on the Middle East.

According to public opinion surveys, two-thirds of Germans were convinced that this war against Iraq was necessary, and that the USA and its allies were right not to wait any longer. The biggest German concerns about the war were first that Israel might be drawn into it, and second that the burning of the oilfields might result in a worldwide ecological catastrophe. But, at the same time, three-quarters of those surveyed were of the opinion that Germany should not participate actively in the war. The same proportion were opposed to changing the Basic Law to make it possible for Germany to intervene militarily outside the NATO area. The Germans thus approved the coalition's intervention in Iraq but did not want to abandon the country's traditional line of restraint in foreign policy, particularly in regard to military involvement in other countries.[36]

In the first few months of 1991, therefore, the federal government found itself in a difficult situation. On the one hand, it was absolutely determined to avoid becoming involved in the military proceedings in Iraq. On the other hand, it had become clear that a reunited Germany would have to redefine its political role in the world more quickly than had been expected. Kohl and his colleagues remembered of course that some of the Western politicians who were now loudly calling for Germany to send troops to the Gulf had been warning only a few weeks earlier against the political and military threat that a united and strengthened Germany would pose. But there was no doubt that, in future years, it would become more difficult for the country to continue its avoidance of participation in military actions by the UN. It was therefore necessary for it to define its own foreign policy interests. But what were they?

This became an important subject of debate during the next few years. The new role the Federal Republic was expected to play provided an opportunity to shed the historical burden of the Nazi past and take part with its own troops in UN military interventions. But vehement protests were raised against this approach. Moreover, there was no sign that the European Community might adopt a common line in foreign policy, which would have freed the federal government from its dilemma. On the contrary, Great Britain had clearly demonstrated its remoteness from any attempt to establish a common European policy in foreign and military affairs by emphatically supporting the war and sending almost 50,000 soldiers to fight in Iraq.

Hence the federal government continued to reject any active participation in the Gulf War, but it supported the coalition's operations in the Gulf to a hitherto unprecedented extent, with logistical, technical and above all financial aid. Generous support was given not only to the USA and Great Britain but also to Egypt, Saudi Arabia, Syria, Turkey, Jordan and above all Israel. The total amount of extra money spent by Germany on the Gulf War was 18 billion DM. This served two purposes. On the one hand, it seemed to be enough to placate Germany's allies; on the other hand, as stated earlier, a reference to these costs provided an opportunity to raise the taxes and thus cover the financial needs produced by the distress of the East German economy without drawing too much public attention to the issue.[37]

On 19 August 1991 the opponents of reform in the Soviet leadership mounted a coup, with the object of depriving Gorbachev and his supporters of power, reversing his domestic reforms and preventing the secession of any more Soviet republics from the USSR. What had long been feared in the West and particularly in Germany thus finally came to pass. For almost a week, between 19 and 24 August, the prospect of a takeover in Moscow by communist hardliners, who would use the Red Army to restore Soviet domination in Eastern Europe and again consolidate the frontlines of the Cold War, struck fear into the hearts of people in the West and in the former Soviet satellites. However, since neither the army nor the bureaucracy supported the putschists, the rising failed and Gorbachev returned to office as Soviet president.

In reality, the coup attempt marked the beginning of the end for the USSR. The constituent republics declared independence from the Soviet Union in rapid succession, plans for a new confederation failed, and a new and self-confident leadership, Russian rather than Soviet, established itself in Moscow under Boris Yeltsin. On 31 December 1991 the Soviet Union ceased to exist. Several years of chaotic transformation now followed, during which the old power structures collapsed or were reorganised, the socialist economy was privatised in an act of arbitrary economic Darwinism, food shortages occurred intermittently, and a new upper layer of super-rich oligarchs established itself. Moreover, the Red Army's nuclear arsenal was now divided up among at least four of the former Soviet republics. In addition to Russia, nuclear weapons were now held by Ukraine, Belarus and Kazakhstan, and the extreme instability of these countries thereby became a matter of great foreign policy sensitivity.[38]

The collapse of the Soviet Union imposed considerable responsibilities on reunited Germany. For one thing, the federal government supported Russia and Ukraine with large sums of money so as to help to stabilise economic conditions there sufficiently to provide at least a certain degree of predictability to the situation. How large these payments were is not entirely clear. In September 1991, Kohl said that 60 billion DM had been paid to the Soviet Union since 1989, most of the money being paid as compensation for Soviet acceptance of German reunification and to cover Soviet withdrawal costs. In addition, a further 30 billion DM had been paid to the countries of East Central Europe.[39] It was, of course, in the overriding interest of Germany and the West to prevent Russia and the other ex-Soviet states from falling into complete chaos. It was also important to develop close and stable relations with them. The endeavour to accept the countries of Eastern Europe as quickly as possible into NATO and the European Community, or at least to bring them closer to those institutions, was also part of this policy. Once again, it was above all thanks to the financial strength of the Federal Republic that the uncertain situation in the post-Soviet states did not escalate into a dangerous crisis.

The collapse of the Soviet bloc in Europe sparked off awkward and in part violent conflicts in places where national antagonisms had not been resolved during the decades of communist rule but rather suppressed. This applied particularly to the periphery of the former USSR, as exemplified by the conflict between Azerbaijan and Armenia over Nagorno-Karabagh, and wars in the rebellious Muslim province of Chechnya and also in Georgia. From the Western European point of view, these regions lay far away at the eastern edge of the continent and therefore attracted comparatively little attention. It was very different in the case of Yugoslavia, which was of great significance to the European political balance because of its situation in South Central Europe. For many years, the country had been a favourite holiday destination for other Europeans, and indeed in 1984 it had hosted the Winter Olympic Games. It came as a complete shock for most people that it now became the scene of the bloodiest conflict in Europe since the Second World War, a conflict which cost the lives of more than 100,000 people. The Yugoslav catastrophe also indicated the kind of explosions that might have occurred, but did not, in other regions during the post-1989 disintegration of the Soviet bloc.

Tito's state had been set up during the Second World War during the struggle of the Yugoslav partisans against the German occupiers of the country. It was characterised by the exclusive domination of the Communist Party, but it was not a part of the Soviet bloc. During the Cold War, it had made its mark as one of the leading members of the group of so-called non-aligned countries. Tito's Yugoslavia was composed of various different ethnic and religious groups, and for a long time the relatively stable political and economic situation there and the memory of the common inheritance of anti-fascism held it together. But the economic crisis of 1979–82 and the associated decline of heavy industry, which had been vigorously developed there, as in other parts of East Central Europe, intensified the already well-marked economic differences between the constituent republics of the country. Divergences were particularly great between the wealthier north-western republics of Croatia and Slovenia, on the one hand, and the more populous and politically most powerful republic of Serbia, on the other. Yugoslavia was formally structured as a federal state, it is true, but in practice the country was ruled from the centre, which was located in the capital city of Belgrade, in Serbia. With the economic decline of the country as a whole, Croatia and Slovenia intensified their endeavours to achieve greater independence, which were accompanied by increasingly nationalist tendencies. At the same time, nationalist forces gained the upper hand in Serbia, not least in the

Communist Party, in which the Greater Serbian nationalists around Milošević came to power.[40]

The ethnic groups of Yugoslavia were increasingly separating on national and religious lines, but they did not live in ethnically homogeneous regions. On the contrary, most of the republics contained large minority groups. This applied particularly strongly to Bosnia-Herzegovina, in the centre of the country, where there was a mixture of predominantly Serbian, Croatian and Muslim districts.

In June 1991, after plebiscites in Croatia and Slovenia had decided in favour of independence by overwhelming majorities, both republics declared their exit from federal Yugoslavia. The Serb-dominated Yugoslav Federal Army replied to this by sending troops against the two rebel republics, so that the conflict over secession turned into a civil war between Serbia on one side and Croatia and Slovenia on the other. The aim of each side in this war was to obtain the largest possible homogeneous settlement area for its own nation. In the case of the conflict between Serbia and Croatia this soon led to the mass expulsion of each other's ethnic minority populations, a process known as 'ethnic cleansing', and an explosion of violence.

The governments of the European Community were unable to end this conflict, or even to reduce its intensity. There were two reasons for this: their lack of unity and their unreadiness to intervene by military means should it prove necessary. Germany's position was particularly embarrassing and riddled with contradictions. Firstly, the federal government was under pressure to demonstrate a greater degree of commitment in foreign policy matters, after the damage done to Germany's reputation by its reluctance to intervene in the Gulf conflict. Secondly, however, the lines of conflict inherited from the Second World War continued to affect the Yugoslav situation. There were fears in France and Great Britain that a united Germany would seek to restore its traditional hegemony over the Balkans, possibly in cooperation with Austria. Thirdly, while it was true that the Federal Republic was prepared to take a more active role in the Balkans than in Iraq, military action by the Bundeswehr in Yugoslavia, a country which had suffered terribly under four years of German occupation during the Second World War, was out of the question for reasons both political and historical.

The federal government's decision of December 1991 to recognise the independence of Croatia and Slovenia in international law, unilaterally and against the objections of the other EC states, was therefore extremely surprising. The aim was to put a stop to Serbian aggression against Croatia and internationalise the conflict. It was a step which had long been under discussion within the EC, but a decision had been postponed, not least on account of the fear that the recognition of the two Yugoslav republics would also encourage secessionist movements in other regions of Europe, such as Northern Ireland, Corsica and the Basque region. But now, by pressing ahead, the Federal Republic had produced a fait accompli. It was sharply criticised for this by its European neighbours. It is true that the other EC states also subsequently agreed to recognise the two republics that had seceded. It was clearly apparent, however, that Germany's unilateral action had reinforced the anxieties of the Europeans over its strength, and led them to draw historical analogies. As on many previous occasions, President Mitterrand was reminded of the situation in 1914: Germany on the side of Croatia, France and Great Britain on the side of Serbia. According to Mitterrand, the Federal Republic was pursuing a nationalist policy in Yugoslavia 'in order to create a sphere of influence for itself in Central and Eastern Europe and in the Balkans'.[41] But the federal government was under public pressure in its own country too: the conservative press in particular was conducting a fiercely anti-Serbian campaign, in which historical analogies and, not least, personal reminiscences, played an important role.[42]

But the most problematic effect of the decision to recognise Croatia and Slovenia was the encouragement it gave to Bosnia-Herzegovina to hold a referendum, which resulted in a clear majority in favour of independence. But the referendum was boycotted by the local Serbs, who constituted a third of the population. They then set up their own 'Serbian Republic of Bosnia-Herzegovina', organised their own army, and with the support of the central government in Belgrade, began to use force to extend the area they controlled, so as to establish a direct connection through the north of the republic with the Serbian motherland. The Croatian, and more particularly the Muslim, inhabitants, of the Serb-controlled area were driven out. This escalating civil war was marked by forced evictions, mass rapes and finally mass shootings. The Serbs were not the only people to use these methods, but they were the main culprits. The policy of eviction and murder reached a climax in summer 1995 in the town of Srebrenica, which was a place of refuge for thousands of Bosnian Muslims who had fled from the advancing troops of the Bosnian Serbs. In July 1995, the Serbs conquered the town, led some 8,000 male Bosnian Muslims into the surrounding forest and shot them.[43]

The massacre of Srebrenica was the worst war crime committed in Europe since the end of the Second World War. This was the continent where, after the Charter of Paris had been signed, people had dreamed of an end to conflict and the start of a long epoch of peace and prosperity. But Srebrenica was also a turning point in the Bosnian war. It had not been possible to end the war, either by sending blue-helmeted UN soldiers, or by establishing 'safe zones', or by the various attempts at negotiation undertaken by the European Community. Now the USA took a hand. NATO warplanes bombarded Serbian positions, thereby compelling the Serbs to sign an armistice which ultimately led to a fragile, but stable peace.

The Srebrenica massacre became a symbol for the Yugoslav civil war. It marked the nadir of post-war European history, and it changed the political debate in Europe and in Germany. It was clear to everyone that the European states had been unable to devise and put into effect a common position on this conflict which was happening right on their doorstep. The USA, not the Europeans, brought the civil war in Yugoslavia to an end. If the Europeans wanted to be able to take action on their own continent, changes were clearly necessary, because it was too much to expect the two dominant post-war European powers, France and Great Britain, to enforce peace by themselves, and the states of the EC as a whole were too disunited to take on this task. As far as Germany was concerned, it had pressed ahead with the recognition of Croatia and Slovenia, but it had not been in a position to offer protection to either of those states or to Bosnia-Herzegovina, and certainly not in a military sense. In addition, the Yugoslav conflict had once again emphatically illustrated the reserved attitude of the other European states towards united Germany. Anyone who had believed that after reunification Germany would be a 'normal nation' was bound to be disappointed.

But what conclusions could be drawn from this? German foreign policy was not aimed at increasing the country's influence by intervening militarily abroad. There could be no doubt about that. Germany's objective was rather to arrive at a coordinated, or perhaps even a joint, foreign and security policy, within the framework of the EC. Constitutional objections to military intervention ceased to have any legal effect after July 1994, when the Federal Constitutional Court permitted the deployment of German troops outside the NATO area under a United Nations mandate. Deployments of this kind did, however, have to be approved by parliament; the Bundeswehr had now become a 'Bundestag Army', as many commentators pointed out.[44]

The federal government's first attempts at providing semi-military assistance abroad were undertaken after the Iraq War and in response to the widespread criticism made at the time of Germany's reluctance to intervene. Germany provided assistance in Cambodia, Somalia and in monitoring the airspace over Bosnia. A number of German reconnaissance aircraft also took part in NATO's activities against the Bosnian Serbs in Sarajevo. But these were only symbolic contributions, of a rather experimental character, intended to demonstrate Germany's readiness to stand by its allies. The government obtained majority support in the Bundestag for foreign interventions of this kind, but not among the population at large. There was no mandate for a new, 'forceful' foreign policy.

## Asylum Policy and the Multicultural Society

Flows of migration driven by poverty had been increasing ever since the 1980s, as a result of globalisation. The trend was further intensified by the collapse of communist rule in Europe and the civil war in Yugoslavia.

The pressure of migration took different forms in different European countries. The number of illegal immigrants was particularly high in countries adjoining the Mediterranean. A large proportion of the migrants who entered Britain and France came from their former colonies. Refugees who fled towards Germany, the Netherlands, Sweden and Switzerland, on the other hand, gained access through relatively liberal asylum laws. After the opening of the borders of Eastern Europe the number of asylum seekers increased sharply. There were 120,000 in the Federal Republic in 1989, and 190,000 in 1990. By 1992 the number had risen to 438,000, but after the amendment of Article 16 of the Basic Law in December 1992 this figure fell back to its starting point of 120,000 a year. Two-thirds of the asylum seekers came from Eastern Europe. Switzerland and Sweden had the highest number in proportion to total population between 1990 and 1998, with twenty-five asylum seekers for every 1,000 inhabitants. The proportion in Germany was lower, at roughly twenty per 1,000. But, in any case, it was clear that the countries of Western Europe did not have a common policy in this regard.[45]

After the opening of the border with the East, the West found that its victory over the communist world had produced some alarming results. Calculation, fear and panic soon raised the number of refugees expected to arrive from Eastern Europe to almost inconceivable levels. In West Germany, the debate over policy towards foreigners and asylum seekers had already reached such an intensity in the course of the late 1980s that observers at the time described this issue as 'the biggest domestic political controversy of the coming decade.' It was reported in several newspapers at the end of 1990 that 'experts are predicting a wave of immigration of up to 10 million people.' These were unfounded exaggerations, but people's ideas of how many asylum seekers had arrived in Germany so far had already lost all relation to reality. School-leavers at one Munich *Gymnasium*, when asked the percentage of asylum seekers in the total German population, replied '30 to 40'.[46] The proportion of asylum seekers in the overall number of immigrants was also overestimated. Between 1990 and 1994, just under 1.5 million asylum seekers came to Germany, but there were also 2.1 million foreigners who entered Germany for other reasons. Most of these people were members of existing migrant families or foreigners from other EU countries with rights of entry and residence in Germany.[47]

The parties of the Union had already insisted since 1988 that the great increase in immigration to Germany must be brought to an end by altering

Article 16 of the Basic Law on the provision of political asylum. There were disputes on the question within the SPD. These also reflected the opposed positions represented in society as a whole: on one side there were those who were confronted in the towns and rural communities with the effects of immigration and the rising irritation of the indigenous population, while on the other side there were those who did not want to abandon the fundamental right to asylum which had played such a significant part in the political tradition of the Federal Republic.

The Union started a campaign for the modification of the right to asylum in the run-up to the first Bundestag elections covering the whole of Germany, held in December 1990. The objective of this was chiefly to attack the SPD for its indecisiveness. The Union's central contention was that asylum seekers were largely swindlers and cheats who were attracted by the high social benefits available in the Federal Republic. According to *Die Welt,* 'as more than 90 per cent of them are swindlers this situation could become a threat to the existence of our social services.' The Berlin historian Arnulf Baring, writing in *Bild-Zeitung,* called for the immediate abolition of the right to asylum, because the 'fundamental problem' was 'that our good-natured social legislation has become a magnet which draws in the poor of the whole planet'. Accordingly, 'even the granting of asylum should not include the right to social assistance which Germans are entitled to.' The Bavarian Minister of the Interior, Stoiber, declared that: 'the Basic Law is unlikely to be altered until the old men in Bonn, who are completely without practical experience, are given a good kicking by their own people.'[48]

The opening of the Berlin Wall and the reunification of the country converted the influx of foreigners and asylum seekers from a West German problem into a problem for the whole of Germany. The conditions and experiences of the two societies were extraordinarily different in precisely this area. There had never been many foreigners in the GDR. At the beginning of 1989 the country contained roughly 190,000 people, less than one per cent of the population, who were classified as foreigners. The largest group came from friendly socialist countries such as Vietnam and Mozambique. They had been brought into the country as 'contract workers' to help reduce the labour shortage. They were, as a rule, young, single men, who had come to the GDR without any family. They lived there under legally insecure and socially difficult conditions, and almost without exception in isolated hostels. The foreigners were strictly separated from the local inhabitants, who were obliged to report any contact with them to the authorities. Since there was no public discussion about the presence of foreigners in the country apart from the compulsory references to friendship between the peoples of the world, and since a good part of the xenophobic tradition of Stalinism still lived on in the SED, it was no surprise that sentiments of hostility to foreigners were widespread in the East German population. Until 1990, of course, these views were generally repressed.[49]

After the opening of the border, and reunification, people in East Germany were confronted with the foreign world of the West, in which the 8 million foreigners must have seemed doubly alien. Hence nationalist and xenophobic attitudes quickly gained ground. It was noted as early as April 1990 that 'racism and hostility to foreigners are now uninhibitedly expressed in the GDR. These sentiments were inadequately repressed by the SED regime. Hatred towards Vietnamese, Poles and other minorities is stirred up by nationalist sentiments and economic shortages. There is an increase in violent attacks.'[50]

In April 1991, when the border between Germany and Poland was formally opened at Frankfurt an der Oder, hundreds of youths bombarded the Poles who entered the country with showers of stones. In Dresden, hostility to foreigners reached a climax on Easter Sunday 1991, when youths attacked a former GDR contract worker of Mozambican origin and pushed him out of a moving tram; the man died of his injuries.[51] The tone of the anti-asylum campaign grew sharper with every month, as rising numbers of asylum seekers were reported. Berlin CDU politician Klaus-Rüdiger Landowsky complained about foreigners who 'wander the streets begging, defrauding people and even stabbing them, and when they are arrested burden the taxpayer with seven years of criminal proceedings simply by uttering the word "asylum" '.[52]

Hence the first political experience the East Germans had in reunited Germany was the highly emotional debate over asylum, in which violence against foreigners was described as a danger but also understood as a threat. As a result, a political climate gradually arose in which, in volatile situations, the young in particular could gain the impression that attacks on foreigners were legitimate and would be tolerated, possibly even with a nod and a wink.

By now, the anti-asylum campaign had taken on a life of its own. Politics was dominated by the tabloids and the street. Opinion surveys indicated that no other issue moved Germans as much as asylum policy during those years. In the two years between June 1991 and July 1993, the issue of 'asylum/foreigners' was for Germans the most important problem of the age. When questioned in summer 1991 and summer 1992 almost 80 per cent of Germans held the opinion that the asylum issue took priority over both the unification crisis and the Yugoslav wars.[53] *Der Spiegel* reported on 9 September 1991 that 'attacks on asylum seekers are already on the agenda, especially in the East. Many Germans are secretly delighted about these deeds of violence. Around 40 per cent of young East Germans regard foreigners as at least "a nuisance" . . . Every fourth person regards "actions against foreigners" as correct.'[54]

A few days later there was a particularly spectacular outburst of xenophobic violence in the Saxon town of Hoyerswerda. For several days, starting on 17 September, hundreds of young people besieged a hostel for foreigners, which housed asylum seekers and former contract workers, threw stones and incendiary devices, and attempted to storm the building. When the police arrived to protect it, they too were pelted with Molotov cocktails and steel balls. The forces of law and order finally capitulated to the mob, sending buses to the hostel to evacuate the residents. What was remarkable about the Hoyerswerda events was that they were enthusiastically applauded by spectators of all age groups.

The events in Hoyerswerda were followed by further xenophobic attacks and outrages in more than twenty-one places in East and West Germany. In October 1991, four Lebanese refugee children were taken to hospital with severe burns after an arson attack in the Lower Rhine municipality of Hünxe. In Gotha, a group of youths overpowered four Soviet soldiers and threw them out of a window. In Greifswald, some 200 hooligans attacked a home for asylum seekers after a football game, inflicting injuries on thirty-five people, some of them severe.

Such largely unexpected eruptions of violence against foreigners and asylum seekers in the East had a stimulating effect on the Right Radical scene which had always existed in isolated pockets in the West. Moreover, these groups already felt that they were on a rising trend thanks to the re-establishment of nationalist symbolism and phraseology after November 1989. Although right-wing radicalism continued to be rejected by the overwhelming majority of the German population in East and West, the question of asylum seekers provided it with an agitational target, and it endeavoured to break out of its isolation by using this issue. In some regions of East Germany, it was successful.

Since the number of asylum seekers continued to rise, and there was no prospect of an amicable settlement of the conflict, the asylum debate, which had died down for some time after the shock of the Hoyerswerda outrage, restarted at full volume in spring 1992. The municipalities again anxiously called for a curb on immigration, and again the tabloid press whipped up the atmosphere. As a consequence, attacks on foreigners again increased in summer 1992. The number of fatalities also started to rise. These brutal attacks culminated in a kind of pogrom, which started on 22 August in the Lichtenhagen district of the city of Rostock, and lasted for several days. More than 2,000 young people attempted to storm a hostel for foreigners and asylum seekers which had only received inadequate protection from the police. The hostel, which was largely inhabited by Vietnamese, was set on fire, while the crowd outside bellowed 'String them up!' The mob, supported by jeering bystanders, were even able to drive away the police for a short time, and finally to force them to evacuate the foreigners who lived in the hostel, to the accompaniment of applause from supporters and onlookers.[55]

There were various reactions to the Rostock events. On the one hand, increasing resistance developed in German society against the excesses of xenophobia. This found expression in big demonstrations and rallies, and it had a lasting impact on the political climate of the republic. On the other hand, however, the campaign against asylum seekers did not slacken. What had been expressed in Rostock, said one Union politician, was not racism, 'but a completely justified resentment over the mass misuse of the right of asylum'.[56]

On 23 November 1992 two youths set fire to a house inhabited by Turks in the town of Mölln, in Schleswig-Holstein. Three people, a woman and two girls, burned to death as a result. This was the most frightful and the most serious attack on foreigners in Germany since the war, and it evoked bewilderment and horror.[57] Increasing concern was now also expressed outside Germany, and the hesitant attitude of the government came in for criticism. As the Israeli newspaper *Ha'aretz* wrote:

> It will be difficult for the German government and Helmut Kohl to clear themselves of the suspicion that there is a particular reason for their failure to stop the wave of violence against foreigners: they hope to mobilise a reluctant Social Democratic opposition in the Bundestag to help them remove article 16. . . . Each day that goes by strengthens the impression that the federal government has failed in two elementary tasks: to maintain public order and to protect the lives and possessions of foreigners.[58]

Under the pressure of these events and the continued escalation of the campaign against Article 16, it began to emerge that the Social Democrats would not be able to persist in their refusal to alter this article of the Basic Law. In December 1992, the governing coalition and the SPD finally agreed a so-called 'asylum compromise', whereby anyone who entered Germany from a state which recognised the validity of the principles of the Geneva Refugee Convention and the European Convention on Human Rights no longer had a right to claim asylum in Germany. But, since Germany was surrounded on all sides by states which guaranteed these principles, no one who arrived in Germany by land could apply for asylum any more. This meant that Germany was in practice sealed off from the entry of asylum seekers. From then onwards, political asylum could only be obtained by someone who entered Germany by air.[59]

A day after the new asylum law had passed the Bundestag, it was made clear in devastating fashion that the alteration of the Basic Law had not brought an end either to the debate or to outrages committed against foreigners. In Solingen, an arson attack on a house with Turkish residents cost the lives of five people, three children and two adults. Between 1990 and 1993, at least forty-nine people were murdered by right-wing extremists.

Almost all were foreigners. By the year 2000, the number of deaths had risen to more than one hundred.[60]

The escalation of the campaign against asylum seekers was a clear indication of the enormous political dynamite this question contained. On one side of the fence there were socially deprived people, often subject to political persecution, who had run tremendous risks to get to the rich countries of the West, in search of a better future. On the other side were the indigenous inhabitants of West Germany and the other countries of the European Union, who felt threatened in their social existence by the poverty-stricken incomers, because it was exactly the poorer sections of the native population who were in competition with the foreigners for the available resources of social benefit, accommodation and public sympathy. In that sense, a reduction in the opportunities for immigration afforded by the right of asylum was probably unavoidable, although until 1989 the actual migration figures were not at all dramatic. But, at the same time, the anti-asylum campaign stimulated and radicalised the fears already present in the more socially deprived sections of society. It offered a manifest means of compensating for the fears of social decline that had grown up in East Germany during the reunification process, because the asylum seekers bore a triple stigma, which left them with no scope for action of any kind: they were poor, alien and illegal.

Even so, the xenophobic agitation of the early 1990s did not originate independently. It required a push from outside. That is the significance of the campaign against asylum, which in an extremely critical situation of social upheaval provided the public with a clearly identifiable enemy. This was a competition in hysteria, and it set in motion a shedding of inhibitions. This was a process which increasingly fed upon itself. The campaign of the early 1990s against the right of asylum led to the formation in both East and West Germany of a new form of organised right-wing radicalism, particularly among young people, which was much more violent in approach than all the previous incarnations of this milieu. Numerous Right radical groupings emerged. They created a threatening climate for foreigners and left-wingers, announcing that some parts of the country were 'nationally liberated zones'. The 'National Socialist Underground', which emerged from the Jena milieu of right-wing radicalism, began to engage in its first actions against Jews and foreigners in the 1990s, and between 2000 and 2006 it murdered nine men from Greece and Turkey as well as a German policewoman.[61]

But it soon turned out that the debate over the right of asylum had only obscured the real question, which was how Germany should approach the issue of immigration in the future. The asylum compromise of 1993 was therefore followed by a discussion over the future of immigration, which rapidly broadened in scope. One of the core concepts whose meaning was disputed was the idea of the 'multicultural society'. In the USA, where the term had long been in use, it was defined as the coexistence on equal terms of different immigrant cultures, involving a rejection of the predominantly white model of society and culture, which was characteristically Anglo-Saxon and European in orientation. In Germany, on the other hand, the concept rather implied a general acceptance of foreign cultures, almost 90 per cent of which were European in character in view of the current composition of the wave of immigration. The fear that the European cultural tradition might be called into question by other cultural influences therefore related predominantly to Muslim immigrants from Turkey.

Large parts of German society had considerable objections to the idea of multiculturalism. These objections were of various kinds. They stretched from criticisms of the practicality and accuracy of the concept to an emphasis on the identity of the nation-state, and, more radically, the racially motivated postulate of a culturally homogeneous *Volk*. The Federal Ministry of the Interior defined the cultural identity of the Germans as 'an overarching fundamental pattern of common memories, values and conceptions which creates German identity and connects (most) Germans together as members of a nation.' To put forward the idea of a multicultural society of immigrants, on the other hand, would be 'to awaken fears of foreign penetration which would push the indigenous inhabitants into a defensive attitude. . . . If all patterns of national cultural identification were thrown overboard, the result would soon be a dry and matter-of-fact state formation which no longer offered any sense of cohesion.'[62] These comments left open the question of the actual content of the identity-forming elements of German culture and history, and did not specify what should be required of foreigners apart from a mastery of the language and obedience to the law. Such attempts to respond to disturbing developments by falling back on traditional cultural models and symbols led immediately to an inflated use of the concept of 'identity', which was the more strongly invoked as a way of virtually homogenising political and social groups the more it appeared that the people, the nation and the culture were becoming increasingly heterogeneous.[63]

On the other hand, many liberals and left-wingers criticised the concept of 'multiculturalism' because it strengthened the idea of the nation-state rather than transcending it. In the USA, indeed, it had led to self-segregation and a demand for non-interference from various ethnic groups, while processes of integration and ethnic mixing were denounced as 'cultural genocide'.[64]

'Multiculturalism' was a concept which welcomed the new multiplicity of modes of life and cultural practices that Germany had gained through the presence of foreigners, without indicating the problems which had manifestly arisen as a result. By and large, the long and contentious debate on the subject was not particularly revelatory. On the Right it was interpreted in a normative sense, and rejected with different degrees of emphasis as an attack on German history, identity and 'national substance'. The arguments on both sides had little to do with the complex reality of immigration into Germany, which was now producing such a high degree of disharmony. It was the red–green government which first took some of the sting out of this problem with a new immigration law, passed in 2004. Nevertheless, questions of immigration, integration and the establishment of equal rights for foreigners remained controversial and were regularly propelled into the limelight of public and acrimonious debate every four or five years or so, by either a new law, a new book or, especially after 2001, the actions of Islamic fundamentalists. In this new environment, the pogroms and murders of the 1990s were quickly forgotten.

## Maastricht

Europe itself was the goal of European political aspirationsafter 1990. European unity seemed to be the inevitable outcome of history, desired by almost everyone, now that the division of the continent had been brought to an end by the collapse of the communist Eastern bloc. In concrete terms, this found expression in two dynamic processes, which were described by European politicians as 'expansion' and 'deepening'.[65] 'Expansion' signified above all the extension eastwards of the European Community, which until then had been a club for Western Europeans only. For the new democracies of East Central Europe the EC had decisive importance as a model and a vision of the future: it promised a secure path towards economic prosperity, and it would also have a stabilising effect on the democratisation process in the region. The criteria for a country's admission to the EC were a stable democratic system, the maintenance of human rights, the protection of minorities and a competitive market economy. Since there were numerous internal conflicts in the former Eastern bloc and democratic institutions were still weak, these criteria offered a clear direction of travel, and, as previously in the former dictatorships of the south, Spain, Portugal and Greece, they were of considerable assistance in legitimating the democratic forces.

Only three years after the fall of the communist regime in the East, therefore, the Council of Europe decided to start negotiations with the countries of East Central Europe as soon as these had fulfilled the necessary membership requirements. In 1995, three economically powerful Western countries also joined the EC. These were Austria, Finland and Sweden, whose neutral status had prevented their admission before 1990. As early as 1997, the EC started accession negotiations with Hungary, Poland, the Czech Republic, Slovakia and Estonia, thereby stressing the political character of European integration. There was little alternative to this process, although there were different views as to how quickly it should happen. These countries had spent decades under dictatorship. Hence in the absence of any prospect of entry into the EC, internal conflicts would have escalated there even more strongly than they in fact did, In addition, without the EC's eastward expansion, the persistence of economic differences between East and West would have produced a new division of the European continent, with an uncertain outcome.

On the other hand, the planned expansion of the EC considerably increased the divergence between the richest and the poorest countries of the Community, and it could be foreseen that a lasting improvement in the circumstances of life in the former communist countries could only come about with long-term economic and financial assistance from the richer members of the EC. But this would lead to a fall in living standards in the rich countries, and it was unclear whether majority support could be found in the longer term for these measures.

It was also of importance that the structure of the EC had been created to organise a community of six countries only. An increase in size to ten, fifteen or even twenty states required completely different institutions and decision-making processes. Moreover, how could such an expansion of the community be reconciled with the ever louder call for increased democracy and transparency?

In the 1990s, when these questions began to take on a more concrete shape, doubts started to arise over the constant increase in European integration, which had until then been regarded almost as a self-evident ultimate objective, though as yet there was hardly anything that could be called a European public sphere. On the contrary, debates on the process of European unification took place largely within a national framework, while overall European perspectives were represented by the European Commission in Brussels. This antinomy became progressively sharper, and it signalled the end of Europe as a project of the elite.

The lack of a European public sphere started to make itself felt particularly strongly in relation to the other important aspect of the European unification process, namely 'deepening', a term which denoted the intensification of both economic and political integration. On 12 December 1991, a full year after the reunification of Germany, the countries of the European Community, which had now been renamed the European Union, entered into the Maastricht Treaty, which was the most important and momentous agreement since its foundation in March 1957. It went far beyond anything so far achieved in terms of European commonalities, and it also included the decision to create a currency union. The member states of the European Union, declared Chancellor Kohl in the Bundestag after the Maastricht Conference, were now 'bound to one another for the future in a manner which makes impossible a re-emergence of previous conceptions of the nation-state, or a regression to them, with all the dire consequences that would entail.'[66]

The federal government had already indicated its agreement in principle to a common currency in 1988. But it had said then that such a thing would only be possible and worthwhile if the relevant political prerequisites were in place, in particular the harmonisation of budgetary and fiscal policy. As explained earlier, at the end of 1989, West Germany's European partners had made their acceptance of German reunification conditional on the rapid implementation of an economic and currency union, and the federal government had initially shelved its reservations in response. In the negotiations over preparations for the Maastricht Conference, however, the German view appeared to have prevailed. The European partners agreed to establish an independent European Central Bank on the German model, which was intended to guarantee that European monetary policy would be determined by economic considerations and not the political preferences of the various governments. Moreover, the heads of government meeting in Maastricht voted for a Stability Pact, by which the introduction of the common currency would be dependent on 'convergence criteria', namely, that the annual budget deficit of a participating state should not exceed 3 per cent of its annual GDP, and that the country's total indebtedness should not exceed 60 per cent of its annual GDP. Kohl told the Bundestag that they had agreed 'internationally binding rules, which would prevent a monetary policy aimed at price stability from being undermined by incorrect national budgetary policies'. With this, the road to European economic and currency unification had been 'marked out clearly and established irrevocably'.

To reach this point, however, the German Chancellor had been obliged to make considerable concessions. The desired progress towards political unity had not been achieved. It was not surprising that there were difficulties in the way of a common foreign and security policy in view of the discord which was evident precisely at this time between the European partners over the Yugoslav question. Moreover, resistance emerged wherever European regulations had the potentiality to interfere with the rights of national governments and parliaments. German endeavours to extend the competence of the European Parliament were also unsuccessful. The view urged strongly by the German government that the economic unification of the continent could only succeed through the strengthening of political unity, which would also produce unity in economic policy, was unable to prevail against the reservations of its European partners. Kohl himself finally had to admit that the hoped-for state unity of Europe on the American model was unachievable. 'Events have overtaken us', he remarked on the prospects for a federal European state. 'It will not come about in this way.'[67]

Thus, the sequence originally envisaged was now reversed. The starting point was no longer the gradual deepening of political integration, followed by an increasing coordination of national policies, which would finally lead to a common currency. The single currency was now itself the starting point. The single currency, according to the arguments of its supporters, would hold the individual member countries together with such a strong bond that their policies at home and abroad would inevitably become one. For the Germans, however, there was no doubt that in the long run a currency union could only survive 'within a political union of a state-like character', as the president of the Bundesbank, Hans Tietmeyer, stated emphatically. That was the dilemma.[68]

Thus the new 'European Union' had an asymmetrical structure. A euphemism was pressed into service immediately to describe it: the image of the 'three pillars'. The first pillar was economic and monetary policy. This would henceforth be regulated in common, hence supranationally. Foreign policy, the second pillar, and domestic and legal affairs, the third pillar, would continue to be 'inter-governmental', hence they would be decided by the heads of government of the member states. In addition to this, Great Britain negotiated substantial exemptions from the treaty. According to these provisions, the country reserved the right not to join the common currency (which was later named the 'euro'). It also reserved the right not to accept agreements in relation to social policy and not to be obliged to include decisions of the European Union within British law.[69]

One important factor in the German side's readiness to compromise over its original demands was the feeling that the collapse of the Soviet Empire provided a possibly unique chance to advance the process of European unification in a decisive fashion or perhaps even to 'complete' it. It was Chancellor Kohl who repeatedly referred to the historical opportunity which was now being offered, and who pushed for the process of European unification, including economic and monetary union, to be made 'irreversible' as quickly as possible. There were clear parallels here with the way German reunification had developed: Kohl had always stressed that this must be accelerated, because the 'window of unity' might quickly close again, if for instance Gorbachev fell from power in the Soviet Union. The objections of German economic specialists should therefore be ignored, he had said, and the financial burdens expected to result from an economic and currency union of East and West Germany should simply be accepted as inevitable. Now he took up the same basic line of argument in the European context. An opportunity of this kind, he said, would not soon return. It had to be exploited, even if some of Germany's aims were not achieved thereby. 'If Maastricht is a failure', Kohl had warned before the beginning of the conference, 'it will take more than a generation before we again have a similar opportunity.'[70]

This attitude was also reflected in the timetable now proposed. The third stage of monetary union, in other words, the actual introduction of the common currency, was originally scheduled to begin when a majority of member states had actually fulfilled the convergence criteria. When, and indeed whether, a single currency was actually to be introduced had thus remained an open question. It was then agreed, under pressure from France and Italy, that a decision would be made by 31 December 1996 at the latest, irrespective of whether the conditions for moving on to the third stage had been fulfilled or not. Moreover, if by the end of 1997, no alternative deadline had been set, the third stage would automatically begin on 1 January 1999, irrespective of how many states had fulfilled the convergence criteria and were thereby entitled to participate in the monetary union. This stipulation considerably increased the concreteness and binding force of the project, and almost achieved its hoped-for 'irreversibility'. On the other hand, it also created an automatic mechanism which made it almost impossible to avoid proceeding with the monetary union, even if all the requirements had not been met.

All the parties represented in the Bundestag, except the PDS, voted to confirm the Maastricht Treaty. In the debate, repeated reference was made to the economic advantages that monetary union would produce, particularly for Germany's exports, which amounted to almost a third of the country's GNP, and almost 60 per cent of which were sold to other European countries. The increased convenience, for the economy and for consumers alike, of having a single European currency was also often emphasised. Consumers' associations had calculated that a tourist who made a round trip through the capital cities of all the states in the European Community with 50,000 Belgian francs would only have 25,241 francs left at the end without spending any money for personal use. The rest would be lost through currency conversion and the associated transaction charges.[71]

In Germany, however, the European Union was regarded first and foremost as a political project aimed at guaranteeing a lasting and stable peace in Europe, overcoming nationalism and attenuating the anxiety Germany's neighbours felt that the country was becoming too powerful. The spokeswoman of the SPD parliamentary party in the Bundestag, Ingrid Matthäus-Meier, began her reply to Kohl's government announcement of the Maastricht Treaty on 13 December 1991 with these words:

> On this day 75 years ago the First World War battle of the Somme, in Northern France, was brought to an end. More than a million soldiers had lost their lives there since 24 June, over 614,000 on the British and French side and over 420,000 on the German side. The most important result of European unification is that such a catastrophic conflict between the British, the French

> and the Germans is now inconceivable. We are all thankful that these bygone divisions between our peoples have been buried. The fact that we have now agreed a common European currency in Maastricht demonstrates what a distance we in Europe have now travelled together.[72]

Apart from these historical references, the experiences of the period of German reunification also played a great part in the reaction to Maastricht. The Social Democrats had been accused in 1989 and 1990 of failing to address the question of national unity. They did not want to repeat this mistake in dealing with European unity. The Greens also supported European unity, as a peace project first and foremost. It was hardly possible to dismiss this as excessive idealism, in the light of the Gulf War that had just come to an end and the current escalation of conflict in the Yugoslav civil war. For the Greens, monetary union was a neo-liberal, but also an anti-nationalist project, and on those grounds they were ready to cooperate even with Helmut Kohl. In view of the 'atrocious violence of European history', as Joschka Fischer put it, there was 'no alternative' to European unification.[73] Only the PDS opposed the treaty, because it regarded the European Union as a Europe of the banks and the business conglomerates, but its view did not receive much support either in the Bundestag or among the wider public.

The dominant conviction was that without a united Europe it would be impossible to meet the challenges of the globalised world that had emerged since the end of the Cold War. 'Europe must become the decisive cornerstone, the point of orientation, of our continent', stated Theodor Waigel, the chair of the CSU. 'We are giving the nations an example of how to live together peacefully.'[74]

Compared with perspectives like this, criticisms of the treaty almost had an air of timidity. Within the parliament, it was above all the previous Minister of Economics, Count Lambsdorff, who pointed to the hidden dangers of the Maastricht Agreement. He was particularly critical of the 'automatism' created by the decision to set a deadline. It meant that the train could no longer be halted, even if the European states found that they were unable to meet the stability criteria and rein in their budget deficits: 'Then even the deadlines and automatic mechanisms of Maastricht will be overrun. No government, and certainly not the federal government, would then be able to take this risk.' Moreover, he also regretted the absence of any way of excluding states which had not reached economic stability from the currency union if necessary. Finally he warned against allowing over-indebtedness and budget deficits to arise through subsidiary budgets, a practice just demonstrated by the Federal Republic in regard to the Treuhand for example: 'If we can do it, so can others.'[75]

Lambsdorff stood largely alone in parliament in making these objections. The strongest resistance to the Maastricht project came from outside it, though with some delay: disputes over reunification, the Gulf War, Yugoslavia and asylum seekers had largely absorbed the attention of the public, not Maastricht. Europe seemed like a rather boring issue favoured by bureaucrats and politicians, and it was only little by little that it attracted increased interest. In the media, *Der Spiegel*, the *Süddeutsche Zeitung* and the papers of the Springer Group were critical of the Maastricht Treaty, while the *Frankfurter Allgemeine Zeitung* and *Die Zeit* supported it.

Many arguments were put forward, though some of them were in contradiction with each other. The first objection concerned the anticipated costs. These were so high, the critics said, that the Federal Republic, which already had to bear the burden of German reunification, payments to the Soviet Union, and payments to the countries of East Central Europe, would be completely overextended financially. In addition, the absence of a European political union meant that sectors which were central to the stability of the currency, such as budgetary, fiscal and wage policy, remained within the jurisdiction of the individual states, and the EU as a whole had no influence on them.

Secondly, the European Monetary Union was exclusively an elite project, it was said. The population had not been asked about it, and the area of competence of the European Parliament had not been extended, so that the chasm between the will of the ruling elite and the desires of the mass of the population grew ever wider. Thirdly, the former Minister of Economics, the Social Democrat Karl Schiller, warned that now the example of German transfer payments from West to East had been set, the poorer countries of Southern Europe would make demands of a similar magnitude upon the richer countries of the North, pointing to 'their general backwardness in development, their lack of competitiveness, which would weigh particularly heavily now that they were all in a single currency area, and the considerable wage increases which would be required in the single currency, and would have somehow to be financed.'[76]

Fourthly, they had to bear in mind, it was said, that some countries operating the single currency would come under pressure from the financial markets because of over-indebtedness and budget deficits, but they would no longer be able to compensate for this by devaluation. Admittedly, the stability criteria had been developed to prevent this from happening, but there was no scenario envisaged for either a voluntary or an enforced abandonment of the single currency.

Fifthly, there were looming tensions between the European Commission and a number of individual countries over social policy. One reason for this was that in the course of the 1990s, a clearly neo-liberal line of approach had gradually gained the upper hand in the Commission. In opposition to this, it was above all the trade unions of each country which had fought to prevent the dismantling of labour regulations, retain subsidies and avoid reductions in social welfare budgets. They only succeeded to a limited extent, with the result that an increasing gap opened up between the social policy concerns of the individual states and the market-oriented line of the Commission.

Sixthly, the treaty led to an increase in the drive towards the standardisation of national laws and regulations, and this applied in almost all spheres of activity—all the way from industrial, energy and environmental policy to food supply and consumer affairs. This was reflected in a plethora of ordinances and directives, thereby strengthening the already widespread criticism of Brussels bureaucracy.

Seventhly, and finally, objections of a clearly nationalist character were also voiced in Germany by some conservative critics. They argued that the German government's first task was to represent German interests, but that Chancellor Kohl set a higher value on European and above all French interests than he did on German ones.

Kohl replied to complaints of this kind by stating his conviction that Germany's interest lay precisely in making Europe as a whole as strong as possible, both politically and economically. But the single currency was the essential condition for this. 'Nationalism means war. We want to take precautions against this. That is why we need Europe, and that is why we need the single currency.' This was one of the standard arguments he used when addressing election meetings.[77]

Despite Kohl's efforts, the German population began to have increasing doubts about the European project. Up to this point, European unification had always met with great approval. This now began to change. At the beginning of 1992, 49 per cent of those surveyed opposed a European currency, and only 26 per cent were in favour. This tendency continued to grow. The consensus on policy towards Europe, which had characterised the previous decades, had persisted while the concrete effects of European unification were essentially restricted to commercial and economic affairs and only had an indirect impact on people's lives. But now irritation started to mount, although journalists and politicians not infrequently poked fun at this attitude, calling it an irrational 'German worry over the Deutschmark'. There is no reason, wrote *Der Spiegel* in December 1991, 'for people to panic that the Greeks, the Spaniards, the Italians and the Irish will rob the rich Germans once they get their hands on the ECU'.[78] A few years later, however, the journalists were already more sceptical: as Rudolf Augstein warned in spring 1998, there was no doubt that 'the little man and the little woman have an objective justification for fearing that they and their children will have to pay the debts of more undisciplined countries. They will find it hard to understand that theirs is the only country which has to remain disciplined.'[79] The clash between a European perspective and a more nationalist public mood emerges clearly from these remarks.

These increasing differences of opinion were also reflected in the debate over the ratification of the Maastricht Treaty. In most member countries a public debate now flared up over whether European unification was likely to further the national interest or not. In Germany, as so often, the Federal Constitutional Court turned out to be the only real obstacle. It finally allowed the treaty to go through, though it qualified its verdict with a number of critical comments to the effect that the process of European unification lacked democratic legitimacy. In other countries, however, it proved much more difficult to ratify the treaty. In Denmark the voters rejected it in an initial referendum. A second referendum was then held, and after considerable concessions had been made (such as exemption from the single currency and from European citizenship) the Danes narrowly voted in favour. In France, the treaty was accepted on 19 September 1992 by a wafer-thin majority. The treaty was ratified in all other countries, but only after long and acrimonious debate. But this wearisome procedure was the only way of achieving democratic legitimation of the unification process. The time when the European elite could act unilaterally had come to an end.[80]

Just before the French referendum a fresh danger emerged. When rumours began to spread that voters might reject the treaty, there was a dramatic fall in the exchange rate of the French franc, the British pound and the Italian lira. This was the first large-scale public demonstration of the power the financial markets had obtained since the liberalisation measures of the mid-1980s. The market revealed disparities between a country's economic strength and the value of its currency, and it could thereby exert considerable pressure on national governments, while their room for manoeuvre in carrying out their economic and financial policies grew narrower and narrower. It was hoped, however, that a single currency would make it easier to confront these dangers.[81]

As a matter of fact, it turned out to be extraordinarily challenging for many countries to comply with the Maastricht criteria. The 3 per cent maximum limit on budget deficits was a serious obstacle. Belgium, Italy, Spain and even France found it hard to achieve this, and they pleaded for the criterion to be applied more flexibly. The federal government was against this, although Germany itself had great difficulty in fulfilling the entry conditions for the euro, owing to the economic crisis endemic in the country since 1993 and the tremendous increase in the national debt resulting from the cost of German reunification. But without the Federal Republic, a common European currency was clearly pointless, and so after 1996 the federal government was forced to introduce severe austerity measures, which intensified the already existing downward trend of the crisis-ridden German economy. But the government was prepared to accept this, even running the risk that it might lose the next Bundestag elections, which were set for 1998. This was because all observers were agreed that a failure of the euro would have devastating consequences and lead to 'competitive devaluation, trade wars and protectionism', as predicted by the President of Germany, Roman Herzog. The result would be deflation, and perhaps even economic depression, in other words a return to the 1930s. If the introduction of the euro were to be postponed, as various people proposed, it was quite likely that most European countries would abandon their unpopular austerity measures. The conditions for a common currency would then no longer exist. The result of this, said the French Prime Minister Alain Juppé, would be 'complete paralysis. The disappointment would be so great, the feeling of failure so strong, that Europe would come apart at the seams.'[82]

In December 1995, the heads of government of the EU confirmed the agreed timetable for monetary union. Eleven countries, including Belgium and Italy, did in fact succeed over the next two years in complying with the rule that budget deficits should be no more than 3 per cent of GDP, though some of them had to engage in a considerable amount of creative accounting to achieve this. Compliance with the second criterion, a total public debt ratio of not more than 60 per cent of GDP, was not examined so closely. Several countries exceeded this margin; Italy and Belgium had ratios of over 100 per cent.

On 23 April 1998, the Bundestag voted to accept the list of member countries entitled to participate in the third stage of the EMU, and to accept the introduction of the euro into legislation and public administration. On 2 May 1998 the EU heads of government decided to introduce the euro on 1 January 1999, first as an accounting unit based on irrevocably fixed exchange rates between the existing currencies. Then, at the start of the year 2002, euro banknotes and coins were to be issued to replace the currencies of the member states as well as the European Currency Unit (ECU), which was the European accounting unit that already existed.

The decision to introduce a single currency had developed a remarkable momentum of its own. The politicians involved in this process assumed, or at least they gave this impression in public, that a postponement, or, even worse, an abandonment, of the euro would inflict damage on the movement for European unity, or even bring it to an end altogether. There were good reasons to question this view, but the EU heads of government considered that the opportunity to secure a single currency must be taken now, or it would not recur for some time. There was therefore no going back, despite the various weighty objections to the project. Different countries had very different reasons for pursuing the course they did. While the German side did see the economic advantages of the single currency, this was not the main factor behind its decision to support the introduction of the euro. What was of paramount importance for the Germans was the endeavour to secure European political unity, end European divisions and move beyond the country's particular historical role in the shadow of the

Nazi past. The French, on the other hand, were interested above all in hindering German economic hegemony, which would inevitably be followed by political domination. The euro would help them to do this by making Germany's economic strength a common European possession. Political unification, in contrast, was only supported by the French to the extent that it seemed unavoidable in view of German priorities. The economically weaker countries of Southern Europe, finally, considered that the euro offered them the possibility of having a strong, hard currency which would provide significantly more favourable financial conditions in the capital markets, as well as connecting them with the economically stronger countries of the North. The success of the single currency now depended on whether it would be possible to persuade all these heterogeneous national economies to steer a common course in economic and financial policy.

There is no doubt that Europe had been a success story since the late 1950s, and even more so since the 1990s. The vision of an undivided continent, exclusively democratic, and closely bound together both politically and economically, became a reality even before the twentieth century came to an end. This seemed like a political miracle when one considered the starting conditions of 1945. But younger people were far less aware of this contrast. Unlike the generation of Kohl and Mitterrand, they did not regard the memory of war and destruction as the chief yardstick for evaluating the new developments. Henceforth, the political option in favour of European unification would have to stand the test of sober calculation, as a means to an end, and it was by no means certain whether Kohl's utopia of a politically united Europe would ultimately prevail, or the more sceptical approach of a treaty-based association of independent nation-states, as favoured for example by the British, would come to the fore.

## Two Pasts

After autumn 1989, some sections of the German public expected, indeed even hoped, that reunification would push the Nazi past into the background, and that Germany would finally become a 'normal' nation, to use the phrase so often heard at the time. After all, was not the 'peaceful revolution' a proof of the democratic maturity of the Germans, and did it not constitute something in the nature of a moral historical compensation for the burdens that stemmed from the Nazi period? And was it not time to make the misdeeds of the SED regime and other communist dictatorships the centre of attention and to expose them in detail? But the reactions of Germany's European neighbours to reunification pointed in a different direction. Their dominant fear was that after achieving unity as a single state, the Germans would not only fail to assume their responsibility for the crimes of the Nazi regime; they would also rediscover their appetite for continental hegemony.

In point of fact, the fifteen years after 1990 were the most intensive phase of public debate about the Nazi past in the whole post-war period. Moreover, unlike in previous decades, the mass crimes and the extent to which Germans participated in them were at the forefront of these discussions. This was a continuing discussion of the political past, which often dominated the headlines for weeks, and even for months, and occasionally veered into obsessiveness. In 1972 a total of sixteen books appeared in the German language about the history of the Nazi state, and in 1981 there were sixty. In 1997, however, there were 174, and between 1990 and 2009 the annual average was 142. In 2012 the figure fell back to seventy-four.

There are three major controversies which require more detailed consideration at this point: the 'Goldhagen debate', the argument over compensation for forced labour, and the discussion around the 'Crimes of the Wehrmacht' exhibition.

The American historian Daniel Goldhagen's book appeared in 1995, and the debate it unleashed exceeded at least in quantitative terms all previous public controversies over National Socialism in Germany. Goldhagen's subject was the attitude of 'ordinary Germans' to the murder of the European Jews, and the forcefulness and simplicity of his thesis certainly contributed to the sensational reaction it provoked. That was not the decisive factor, however. There had already been numerous fully documented studies of the mass crimes of the Nazis and the attitude of the German population, and they did not receive a fraction of the attention garnered by this book, which was largely based on those earlier studies, and which sold almost a quarter of a million copies in Germany alone.[83]

Goldhagen's book was criticised for its inadequate scholarship and simplistic approach by almost all the specialist historians who commented on it, in Israel and the USA as much as in Germany and Great Britain. Even so, Goldhagen depicted the killings themselves with such detail and precision that in face of the devastating impact of the horrors described by him any criticism of his conclusions appeared to be carping and pedantic. After all, in Goldhagen's thesis the magnitude and monumentality of the crime was matched by an equally monumental and simple explanation: the Holocaust was a national German project, the point at which a German obsession which had been centuries in the making reached its culmination and final outcome.

In contrast to the increasingly complex explanatory approaches of most historians, who had provided thorough and nuanced analyses of the events in question, but had been unable to give an answer which permitted any identification with the victims, Goldhagen's explanation offered this possibility even to Germans who strove to avoid or reject the implication that these crimes were part of their social inheritance. Goldhagen suggested to Germans of the younger generation that they could fulfil an understandable desire: by accepting his thesis they could stand with the righteous, not with those who had been covered in infamy.

In some parts of German society, the book was perceived in the traditional manner: it was viewed as a repetition of the collective guilt thesis. This book, one could read in *Die Welt,* was 'the resurrection of a scientific cadaver, which was thought to have crumbled into dust long ago: namely the thesis of the collective guilt of all Germans for the annihilation of the European Jews during the Second World War'.[84] This long-familiar defence reaction seemed to make it unnecessary to examine the subject more closely. But it no longer had the power to convince.

Goldhagen made a large number of polemical and speculative assertions in his book, but he had in fact touched on a central point, namely, how much significance should we ascribe to the attitude of the German population to the genocidal murder of the Jews? This question now came strongly into the forefront of attention, both in the German public and among historians, and it increased people's readiness to perceive the murder of the Jews not as a metaphor but as an actual series of events. Shortly afterwards, the diaries of the Jewish Professor of Romance Philology Victor Klemperer dealing with his sufferings under the Nazi regime became a bestseller which was as frequently read and discussed as the autobiography of the well-known literary critic Marcel Reich-Ranicki.[85]

The momentum provided by this debate led to the success of an initiative which had already been begun in 1988 by the Stuttgart historian Eberhard Jäckel and the journalist Lea Rosh. They called for a memorial to the murdered European Jews to be erected in the centre of the new government quarter in Berlin. Only at this point was it realised that the absence of such a memorial was remarkably odd. But it took a long time before the idea of a memorial was finally accepted, after a very contentious debate, and before agreement could be reached on the plan proposed by the American architect Peter Eisenman: a large 'field of stelae' with 2,700 sloping concrete slabs, which would be combined with a permanent information centre about the history of the murder of the European Jews.[86]

The memorial, and the statement of commitment it implied, also met with protest and uneasiness in some quarters. It was the writer Martin Walser who gave the clearest expression to this feeling, during the speech he made in the Frankfurt Paulskirche in autumn 1998 when accepting the Peace Prize awarded by the German Book Trade. He complained about the way the Nazi past was being approached, and he confessed 'that something within me rebels against this permanent display of our shame'. He described the Berlin Holocaust Memorial as 'a nightmare the size of a football pitch' which 'turned shame into a monument'. This, and the continued debate over National Socialism had turned Auschwitz into 'a constantly available means of intimidation', a 'moral cudgel' wielded by the 'guardians of the nation's conscience', the 'soldiers of opinion' who 'at the point of a moral pistol' force the public into the 'service of an opinion'. 'But is it really a cause for suspicion', he continued, 'when one says that the Germans are now a completely normal nation, an entirely ordinary society?'

Walser's speech was greeted with a standing ovation in the Paulskirche. His choice of expressions—'moral cudgel', 'means of intimidation', 'service of an opinion'—associated him with a much more radical refusal to examine the Nazi past than he had perhaps intended. His remarks were therefore sharply contradicted, not least by the president of the Central Council of Jews in Germany, Ignaz Bubis. Walser's speech, said Bubis, was 'a fresh attempt, not, it is true, to relativise Auschwitz, but to begin a new calendar, in line with the motto: Everything that happened is terrible, but after 50 years it is time to go over to "normality"'.[87] This debate, which continued for several weeks, clearly indicated the problems raised by the continuing confrontation with the Nazi era, because a sustained involvement in the subject was necessary precisely because the next generation, unlike Walser's age group, had no memory of the events themselves and therefore had to seek information on the subject from books or exhibitions. Understandably, therefore, it was impossible to avoid a 'permanent display'.

When Walser described his feeling that the motive for this 'display of our shame' was not 'remembrance and the avoidance of forgetting' but 'the exploitation of our shame for present-day purposes' these remarks were unavoidably also directed at another issue in the politics of the past which re-emerged during those months, the matter of compensation for foreign slave-labourers. This was not a new problem. In 1953, as part of the London Debt Agreement, all reparations demands against Germany were postponed until the making of a peace treaty. Moreover, only states could claim, not individuals. With the signing of the Two Plus Four Treaty, however, one requirement had been fulfilled, in the sense that this agreement was generally considered to be a peace treaty. In addition to this, the Federal Constitutional Court had declared in 1996—changing its previous ruling—that individual claims for compensation were also admissible.

This decision alone, however, would not have given the issue the impetus it now took on without the class action mounted in the USA by former forced labourers against German firms they had been compelled to work for during the war, including such top-ranking companies as Daimler-Benz, Deutsche Bank and Allianz-Versicherung. Moreover, a number of Swiss banks, which had taken care of Jewish assets during the Nazi period, but kept hold of them after the war, also came under criticism in the USA. Their swift decision to pay a considerable amount of compensation to the former owners placed German industry under such tremendous political and legal pressure that it turned to the federal government for assistance. After long negotiations with the representatives of the former forced labourers—for Jewish victims the Claims Conference, and for civilian workers of Eastern European origin the representatives of the relevant Eastern European states—the German side finally agreed to furnish an endowment fund with a total of 10 billion DM, financed in equal portions by industry and government, as a 'financially conclusive indication of their moral responsibility for the events of that time'. This money was then used in the years that followed to make single payments of between 5,000 DM and 25,000 DM to the survivors. The amount paid was graduated according to the presumed severity of the fate of each group of forced labourers.[88]

These compensation payments were also controversial, although the protests were far more restrained than in previous decades. It was repeatedly pointed out that Germany had already paid more than 100 billion DM in compensation to victims of Nazism. The critics omitted to mention, however, that most of this money had been paid under the Federal Compensation Law (*Bundes entschädigungsgesetz*). These payments were made exclusively to Germans or former Germans, who constituted fewer than 10 per cent of the victims of National Socialist violence.[89] Notwithstanding protests by some people, therefore, a widespread conviction developed within Germany in the course of the argument over compensation payments that by transferring millions of foreign citizens to Germany to do forced labour the Nazis had committed an injustice, and that German industry had been significantly involved in this.

Discussions around the third issue in the debates of those years about the Nazi period took an entirely different course. This issue was the role of the Wehrmacht during the Second World War, particularly during the war against the Soviet Union. It was a highly controversial matter, and it led to sharp confrontations. In the preceding fifteen years, a whole series of fresh investigations had confirmed that the Wehrmacht as a whole was involved in the mass crimes of the Nazis. In addition, numerous cases had come to light in which individual Wehrmacht units directly committed mass murder. As in the case of the Goldhagen debate, these studies, and the first exhibitions mounted on the topic, were not generally noticed by the wider public. On the contrary, the conception of a 'clean' Wehrmacht, which was only involved in the crimes of the Nazis in isolated cases, remained intact, particularly among the generation which had participated in the war.[90]

In spring 1995, the Hamburg Institute for Social Research, directed by Jan Philipp Reemtsma, opened an exhibition on the 'Crimes of the Wehrmacht', which essentially brought together the results of the historical research of the preceding years, and documented the participation of units of the Wehrmacht in the murder of the European Jews and the civilian population of the Soviet Union as well as the responsibility of the Wehrmacht for the death of almost 3 million Soviet prisoners of war. The exhibition, which was on show for four years in numerous towns and cities, was seen by a very large number of visitors, and after a while it provoked a storm of criticism.[91] The critics were mainly former soldiers, who accused the exhibition organisers of 'misusing the history of German soldiers for political ends'. The *Bayernkurier* commented that the exhibition was aimed at 'taking away the honour of millions of Germans' and conducting a 'campaign of moral annihilation against the German people'. This was followed by marches in several towns by traditional soldiers' clubs and expellee associations, protesting against the exhibition's 'defamation of the German soldier'.[92]

But because the core message of the exhibition about the crimes of the Wehrmacht had a strong evidential basis and was hardly open to serious challenge, the main thrust of criticism was directed against the form of presentation, which was criticised as being prejudicial and insufficiently nuanced. The treatment of the photographs on display was described as unprofessional, since many of the pictures exhibited were of uncertain origin and did not match what was asserted in the captions that accompanied them.[93] In November 1999, after the criticisms had started to accumulate, Reemstma closed the exhibition and had it examined by a committee of historians. The committee rebuked the exhibition organisers for a 'careless use of photographic sources' and a mode of presentation that was 'in part too sweeping and made impermissible generalisations'. But it entirely confirmed the factual assertions in the exhibition.[94]

The debate on this subject culminated in the Bundestag on 13 March 1998, when the Wehrmacht exhibition and questions arising from it were examined. The discussion began with a contribution from the former chair of the CDU/CSU in parliament, Alfred Dregger, who had this to say on behalf of those who fought in the war:

> The soldiers of the Second World War and their families are not a small group that can be marked off from the rest of the nation, but the whole of the population at that time. Almost all men were called up. This is a matter of our relationship with a whole generation of our people. Anyone who attempts—and these attempts are being made—to stamp the whole war generation as members and accomplices of a band of criminals wants to strike at the heart of Germany. We must defend ourselves against this. We cannot tolerate it.[95]

Otto Schily, a former Green and now a member of the SPD, replied to Dregger in a noteworthy and well-received speech. He sharply criticised Dregger's remarks, and he also included some personal reminiscences in his contribution:

> My uncle Fritz Schily, a man of honourable character, was a colonel in the Luftwaffe . . . At the end of the war he commanded an air base in the vicinity of Ulm. In despair over the crimes of the Hitler regime, he sought death by exposing himself to the bullets of a low-flying aircraft. My eldest brother Peter Schily refused to join the Hitler Youth and tried to flee abroad. When this failed he volunteered to be sent to the front. After a short period of training he was sent to the Russian campaign with the engineers. He suffered severe injuries, losing an eye and the use of one of his arms. My father, who had an outstandingly entrepreneurial character, and to whom I owe an immense debt of gratitude, was a declared opponent of the Nazi regime, but having been a reserve officer in the First World War he felt it was a deep humiliation that he was not called up to do military service because of his membership in the Society of Anthroposophists, which was prohibited by the Nazis. Only later did he recognise the insanity—I use his own expression here—of his former attitude. The father of my wife, Jindrich Chajmovic, an unusually courageous and self-sacrificing man, fought against the German Wehrmacht in Russia as a Jewish partisan. Now I shall utter a phrase which in its severity and clarity must be accepted by myself and by all others: the only one out of the four people I have named here—the only one!—who gave his life for a just cause was Jindrich Chajmovic. He fought against an army in the rear of which stood the gas chambers in which his parents and his whole family were murdered. He fought against an army which was conducting a war of extermination and annihilation, which supported the mass murders of the infamous *Einsatzgruppen* or at least allowed them to take place. He fought to prevent thousands more women, children and old men from being slaughtered in the most brutal manner. He fought against a German Wehrmacht which had sunk to the level of being the agent of the fanatical racism and inhumanity of the Hitler regime and had thereby lost its honour.[96]

This debate was a watershed. It signified the establishment of a consensus which went beyond party boundaries, a consensus which was not universal, certainly, but was even so very extensive. The style of the exhibition, and its one-sidedness, continued to be criticised in many quarters, but henceforth the large-scale participation of the Wehrmacht in the mass crimes of the Nazis was only disputed in public by people on the extreme Right of the political spectrum.[97]

With these great debates of the late 1990s, Germany's confrontation with National Socialism reached a climax, but also to a certain extent a conclusion. It is true that there was still public disagreement over this period of history, and an increasing number of personal scandals came to light. The degree of continuity in personnel between the 'Third Reich' and the Federal Republic, and to a lesser extent also the GDR, was now widely known. The presence of hundreds of heavily compromised former functionaries of the SD and the SS in the West German secret services, which had been kept secret for many years, also became known somewhat later. But even when it leaked out that the post-war German authorities had protected mass murderers such as Eichmann and Mengele from prosecution, the news no longer led to large-scale social eruptions. Such revelations were now regarded as possible and even likely, and whoever expressed doubts was under pressure to provide proof. Since there were no more taboos to break, no more previously concealed secrets to ventilate, the debate on the Nazi past retreated to the libraries and lecture halls. It continued to be an important, indeed a central issue—but purely a historical one.

The debates of the 1990s over history were strongly marked by politics because the intensified examination of National Socialism and the earliest attempts to appraise the history of the SED dictatorship collided and interlocked with each other. This was nowhere clearer than in the case of Buchenwald. This concentration camp, established by the SS in 1937 on the Ettersberg, near Weimar, was by the end of the war the largest KZ on German soil, with its 136 satellite camps.[98] More than 250,000 people were incarcerated there. Of those, some 56,000 died in the camp, among them more than 11,000 Jews. In July 1945 the camp was handed over by the Americans to the Red Army, which set up what was called Special Camp No. 2 on the same spot. It was mainly used to intern NSDAP functionaries and officers of the Wehrmacht, but it also contained many young persons and 'undesirables', who had been brought into the camp as a result of denunciations or purely arbitrary acts by the authorities. Twenty-eight thousand people were interned in Buchenwald between 1945 and1950. More than 7,000 died, most of them during the hard winter of 1946–7. In February 1950, the camp was disbanded. Some 1,400 of the inmates were condemned by GDR justice in the notorious 'Waldheim Trials', the remainder were released.[99]

In the 1950s, the GDR authorities erected a place of remembrance there, in the centre of which stood the statues of German communist resistance fighters. This was intended to emphasise the anti-fascist tradition of the SED and legitimate its claim to power. After reunification, it was decided, as in all KZ places of remembrance in the former GDR, to introduce a new form of exhibition and to change the character of the whole camp area. The intention was to memorialise both the Nazi concentration camp and the Soviet special camp. But the plans the committee worked out soon ran up against tremendous protests. Under the new conception of a memorial, the fate of all groups of prisoners would be displayed. The main objections came from the associations of communist prisoners, whose prominent role in GDR memorial policy would be lost under this new system. But the prisoners of the former Soviet camp also protested against the decision of the committee that the memorial to the Nazi concentration camp victims would receive more space than the memorial to the Soviet special camp victims. Finally, the associations of KZ prisoners were up in arms against the exhibition on the Soviet special camp, because the former Nazi functionaries who had been interned there would be styled as victims as a result. Thus, it came about, that on 11 April 1995, the 50th anniversary of the liberation of the concentration camp by US troops, two demonstrations protested simultaneously against the proposals of the committee of historians: one group was protesting against the conversion into heroes of former National Socialists, the other group against the conversion into heroes of communists, many of whom were later functionaries of the SED.[100]

The example of Buchenwald illustrates the way the twofold history of German dictatorship produces complex historical superimpositions and interconnections. The first impulse of many West German politicians, not just the conservatives, after reunification and the collapse of SED dictatorship was to try not to repeat the errors made after 1945 in dealing with Nazi office-holders. After reunification, therefore, all important positions in the new East Germany were occupied either by people untainted by an SED past or by West Germans. In addition, a start was made with the investigation of almost a million GDR citizens to establish what they had done during the SED dictatorship. Four hundred and fifty border guards were indicted for fatal shootings at the Berlin Wall, and roughly 300 of these were given custodial sentences. Seven of them received prison terms without the possibility of parole. Proceedings were taken against legal officials for perversion of justice, and 150 judges and state prosecutors were found guilty of this offence. Several thousand criminal proceedings were opened against employees of the Ministry of State Security, and some sixty people were convicted. In addition, several leading members of the SED were charged, including Erich Honecker, Willi Stoph, Günter Mittag, Egon Krenz and Erich Mielke, and some received long prison terms.[101]

The investigation of former informal collaborators with the Stasi (IMs) who had state employment, was much more time-consuming. Altogether roughly 800,000 employees were investigated. Six per cent of them were found to be tainted, above all because of their work with the Stasi. By the end of the 1990s, roughly 22,000 people had been dismissed from the public service for this reason. Was that too many or too few? Everything depended on how the GDR was evaluated historically. For someone like Günter Grass, who regarded the GDR as a 'comfortable dictatorship', or for someone who saw it as an ultimately unsuccessful but originally entirely legitimate attempt to create a new, just society after 1945 on an anti-fascist and democratic basis, trials and investigations of this kind were nothing more than the justice of the victors. On the other hand, for someone who concentrated on the fate of the thousands of political prisoners, who were often locked up for years for attempting to leave the GDR ('*Republikflucht*') or making critical observations about SED rule, and who regarded the Stasi's comprehensive system of spying on citizens as a crime, the treatment of the former functionaries of the SED state was far too mild.

The collapse of the SED regime was a part of the collapse of all the regimes of the Soviet Empire in Central and Eastern Europe, and neither the causes nor the forms of the collapse of the GDR differed in essence from those that operated to destroy communist dictatorships in Poland, Czechoslovakia or Hungary. But the case of the GDR was distinguished by two extra factors. Firstly, unlike in Poland or Hungary, there was a competing nation-state, West Germany, which had a decisive impact on developments in the East after 9 November 1989, and also determined the manner in which the defeated socialist regime was treated. And secondly—whether one approved of this or not—the process of 'coming to terms' with the GDR past was immediately related to, and compared with, the effort to 'come to terms' with Germany's Nazi past.[102]

The West German republic had proved its superiority over the GDR not just economically but also politically. This meant that the demand for a political, individual and legal reckoning with the GDR regime was also a way of asserting political domination, and it was soon perceived by parts of the East German population, including people who had kept their distance from the SED, as something imposed by the victorious West on the defeated East. This made it easier to discredit the investigation of the history of the GDR as an unjust imposition by the Western victors rather than to view it as an act of critical self-examination conducted by the former GDR population itself. In 1998, more than 70 per cent of the citizens of the former GDR were opposed to the idea of investigating whether someone had worked for the Stasi or not.

A comparison with the other former Eastern bloc countries is instructive in this respect. Nowhere else was the exchange of elites as complete as in the former GDR. Nowhere else were such extensive legal proceedings conducted against former political leaders. Nowhere else were the archives of the secret services so thoroughly seized and made public as here, and what is more, this was done by an independent institution established for the purpose, with several thousand employees, called the 'Gauck Commission' after its first president. At the same time as the SED leaders were on trial, the federal government was negotiating with the former top functionaries of the East European ruling parties, who had quickly turned themselves into Social Democrats, as representatives of the new democracies of Eastern Europe. Was that fair? It was exactly this difference in approach that was strongly criticised by former opponents of the regime in Poland, Czechoslovakia, the Soviet Union, Romania and Hungary: in those places no exchange of elites took place, or only a half-hearted one, the henchmen of the former regime suffered very little punishment and the machinations of the secret services were not brought out into the open.

It was clear in these cases that without external assistance or pressure, societies emerging from dictatorship could not liberate themselves from the leading groups of the former dictatorship, at least not in the form of a peaceful transition, and not quickly. State and society were too closely connected together, and politics, society and the economy were too dependent on the old elites for this transition to happen. If one leaves aside small counter-elites, members of which entered government straight from prison or from working as unskilled labourers and firemen, as in Czechoslovakia for example, there were, as a rule, no alternative elites available. This was not a specific feature of post-communist societies, however. Similar observations can be made about Spain after Franco, and about Argentina or Chile after the end of military dictatorships there.

Political screening was often criticised in Germany as the justice of the West German victors. This attitude led to a partial rehabilitation of the SED dictatorship, which went beyond the need of the inhabitants of the former GDR to find a way of identifying with their own history. It gave rise to the danger that nostalgic memories would acquire a patina of historical legitimacy, and that oppression and crimes would be downgraded into marginal phenomena. In 1999, 72.9 per cent of East Germans assessed the GDR as an 'attempt to achieve a more just society, which failed', and in 1997, 48 per cent were still of the opinion that, taken as a whole, the good aspects of the GDR outweighed the bad ones.[103]

The conservative camp, on the other hand, saw these events as a way to seek compensation for past political disasters. For years, the Left had used the Nazi past as a weapon against the conservatives; now the conservatives wanted to use the GDR past as a weapon against the Left. The problem that arose, however, was that this was implicitly to equate the Nazi dictatorship with the SED regime, in particular to equate the misdeeds of both regimes. But the GDR had neither unleashed a world war nor committed genocide. To equate the two regimes undoubtedly constituted a bizarre trivialisation of the mass crimes of the National Socialists. There was no lack of attempts to draw parallels of this kind, but in the last resort they never caught on, partly because they proved to be counter-productive for the conservative critics of the GDR. The specific forms of repression in the GDR as in the other CMEA states found expression in the all-embracing surveillance and paternalism endured by the population, which was of positively Orwellian dimensions, the punishments handed out for contacts with the outside world which seemed dangerous, and the border regime which led hundreds of people to meet their death at the Berlin Wall. But in comparison with the mountains of corpses left by the Nazis, the state crimes of the GDR inevitably appeared to be of almost secondary importance. If, on the other hand, the GDR was seen as a 'normal' dictatorship, so to speak, without any historical back-projection for political purposes, the breaches of human rights which characterised the SED regime were more clearly illuminated.

Thus the first fifteen years after reunification were marked by an unprecedented debate over the reappraisal of German history, which branched out into many different issues and controversies. On the one hand, this was part of the political and cultural self-affirmation of a newly constituted nation, which in many respects felt strange to itself, and which was endeavouring to emerge from the so often apostrophised 'shadow of the past' by thoroughly investigating it. On the other hand, people's everyday experience of the dictatorial excesses that had taken place in German history melted into the past as time went by and radical changes occurred in the economic, political and cultural structure of the country. For the emerging generations, Hitler and Stalin were figures from a distant epoch, with which they no longer had any direct connection. Despite all the tearful sentimentality of the 'Ostalgics', by the end of the decade even Honecker and Mielke appeared as figures from a different epoch. Discussions about the history of the GDR continued as long as there were controversies over the 'Stasi past' of individual politicians or officials. But they were no longer conducted with the bitterness and acrimony that distinguished the 1990s.

# 22
# Millennium

## A New Economy?

'Breakthrough into the Twenty-First Century' was the title of the keynote speech delivered in Berlin on 26 April 1997 by the president of Germany, Roman Herzog. In this address, which was unusually hard-hitting in form and content for a president of the Federal Republic, Herzog reaffirmed the criticisms of Germany's economic and social system which had long been voiced by people from several points of the political spectrum, and he called for extensive reforms. The country, he said, was faced with 'the biggest challenges for fifty years' and would have to go through some very difficult times:

> 4.3 million unemployed, the erosion of social insurance owing to the inversion of the age-pyramid, the economic, technological and political challenge of globalisation . . . the loss of economic dynamism, the increasing rigidity of society, and an incredible amount of mental depression: these are the key phrases which sum up the crisis.

A mania for regulation, pessimism and a fixation on the state had produced an enormous modernisation bottleneck, which was made even more serious by group egoism and an ideological hostility to technology. 'Germany must snap out of it' was Herzog's answer to the problem. It soon became a familiar catchphrase.

What was needed, he said, was for each individual to take on more personal responsibility, there should be a more flexible labour market, wage-related costs should fall, subsidies should be reduced, there should be fewer state regulations and instructions, the wages of the lowest-paid should be increased, health benefits should be reduced and taxes should also be lower. In addition, the length of courses in schools and universities should be reduced. What was necessary in the educational sphere was to increase competition and promote cutting-edge technology.[1]

In this speech, which met with much public approval, though it was criticised by the trade unions, Herzog included many key ideas already discussed intensively since the late 1970s. As early as September 1982, as we have seen,

Count Otto Lambsdorff, in the memorandum which led to the dissolution of the Schmidt–Genscher government, had demanded an economic policy more rigorously oriented towards the market and an adjustment of the social security system which would reflect the reduced prospects for economic growth. And in his internal reply to Lambsdorff's memorandum, the Social Democratic Minister of Finance, Manfred Lahnstein, had himself advocated greater flexibility over wages and working hours, modifications of the social security system, more individual responsibility in health matters and changes in unemployment insurance.[2] Since then, there had been continuous calls for a reform of German economic and social arrangements to take account of the changed starting conditions, namely, the decline of the classical industries, the ageing of the society and the effects of globalisation.

In its first few years in office, the Kohl–Genscher government had restructured the budget, but it had not introduced a package of thoroughgoing reforms, and critics of Kohl such as Geissler, Biedenkopf and Späth, who called for a more radical approach, had been sidelined within the party. After 1990, expenditure on social policy and the level of state indebtedness had again risen rapidly as a result of reunification, and by 1995, government spending as a proportion of GDP had risen above 50 per cent for the first time ever. Moreover, since many of the transfer payments to East Germany were financed through social insurance, wage-related costs had now reached a record level.

But the main problem continued to be high unemployment. In 1997, for the first time, more than 4 million people were out of work, over 1.5 million of them for longer than a year. Moreover, the number of people receiving welfare payments had risen to over 2 million by 1995, and the proportion of people who had a permanent full-time job had fallen to 67 per cent. These developments had a tremendous impact on the social security budget: ever fewer full-time workers were financing ever more unemployed people, and fewer and fewer young employees were protecting the old-age pensions of more and more retired people. The 'reform bottleneck'—that was the buzzword of 1997—was unmistakable.

A look at job centre statistics shows where the difficulties lay: the most overrepresented groups among the unemployed were workers (61 per cent) and persons who had not completed their professional training (47 per cent). The big employers in the traditional industries now started to reduce their workforces in West Germany as well, either shifting their production sites to low-wage countries or ceasing production completely because of the shrinkage of the market. The number of new workplaces for low-skilled employees in the service sector or the expanding industries—for example synthetic materials, electrical technology, and business machines—was too small to compensate for the loss of jobs elsewhere.[3]

Without a doubt, many of the problems referred to by federal President Herzog had emerged as a consequence of reunification, but by no means all of them. It was very clear that in new branches of technology, especially information technology and biotechnology, German firms had been outpaced by their competitors in Japan and the USA. This was an indication of the diminishing willingness of German businesses to innovate, and the responsibility for this was increasingly laid at the door of the close interrelationship between the big firms and the banks, which in effect created a kind of 'Germany Ltd.' ('*Deutschland AG*'), which had sealed itself off from the international capital market and become sluggish and inert. German firms like Siemens and Daimler-Benz had lost out to young and dynamic newcomers such as Apple, Microsoft or Intel, and one reason for this was that in Germany it was almost impossible to obtain financial support for new and potentially risky ideas.[4]

Developments in the USA and Great Britain were increasingly seen as offering a solution to these problems. It was often emphasised that the reorganisation of the social system undertaken by Thatcher and Reagan had resulted in far-reaching changes, which had proved extremely successful by the late 1990s. While unemployment in Germany was over 10 per cent, in Great Britain it had fallen to 3.4 per cent by 1996, and in the USA to 5.6 per cent. In the USA, wage-related costs were half as high as in Germany, while in Great Britain they were only a third as high. In the Federal Republic, the people who were soon to be described as 'neo-liberals' pointed to these developments in making their demands, which found increasing support from the German public after 1995, particularly in the run-up to the Bundestag elections of 1998. According to the 'neo-liberals', the state should intervene as little as possible in the economy, and the self-regulating forces of the market were a far more appropriate way of directing the economic policy of a country than the intervention of politicians, which was influenced by numerous extra-economic interests and considerations. To end the economic woes of the Federal Republic, primacy in economic affairs should again pass back from politics to economics. A rapid reduction in social benefits was needed to reduce government debt and increase the incentive to work. Periods of education in schools and universities should be made shorter to as to increase the working lifetime of employees. The system of health and social insurance should be privatised so as to encourage citizens to take responsibility for themselves. Restrictions on the right to dismiss workers should be removed so as to make dismissals easier, but also to make it easier to employ people. Low wages should be supplemented by the state, so as to encourage the employment of unskilled workers, and above all there should be large-scale reductions in taxation so as to strengthen investment, and the banking system should be further liberalised so as to promote the global financial sector.[5]

Numerous articles now appeared, portraying the advantages of Anglo-American capitalism. During this period, the journal *Der Spiegel* was one of the main champions of neo-liberalism. It printed a series of articles highlighting the defects of the German economic and social system and advocating a different route to success:

> In places where new job opportunities have arisen on a mass scale in recent years, there has been not more, but less assistance from the state: less unemployment money, less protection from dismissal, fewer subsidies for farmers, fewer obstructions to investment and fewer regulations such as building rules and early closing times for shops. And above all, lower wages.

Great Britain had been particularly successful in this regard, added *Der Spiegel*: 'The law no longer obliges firms to pay a minimum wage, periods of notice have been reduced to a few days . . . whole branches of industry are union-free zones, and employers negotiate wage contracts on an individual basis.' As a result, Britain had become a favourite destination for foreign investors. Between 1990 and 1996, the amount of foreign investment in Britain was six times as high as it was in Germany. 'Liberalisation and deregulation have created new, competitive enterprises, London has built up a position as the centre of the European money market, and in young industrial branches like biotechnology a veritable start-up fever prevails.'[6]

But the drawbacks of the neo-liberal model adopted in Britain and America were also very evident. Two-thirds of the newly created positions of employment in the United Kingdom were part-time jobs. Companies dismissed a large number of permanent employees, replacing them with temporary workers on lower wages. In the USA, the incomes of more than a third of the newly employed workforce were below the lowest union wage rates in Germany, and more than a fifth of them were below the poverty line, receiving less than $10,000 a year. In the USA the industrial working class had been replaced by an army of cheap workers, who were employed mainly in the service sector, as shoe-shiners, doorkeepers, waiters, shelf-fillers or cooks, and many of them were 'stand-ins', only employed during peak hours. The expression 'McJobs' was coined for these occupations. They were jobs from which people could be dismissed without notice, and they had neither insurance against sickness nor a right to paid holidays.[7]

Despite such disturbing trends, the neo-liberal or market fundamentalist model was regarded as an example to be followed both in Germany and in East Central Europe. It promised to bring results more quickly than the ponderous German system, which admittedly guaranteed large benefits to the employees but was extremely expensive and now appeared to have fallen behind economically as well. In Poland, the Czech Republic and Hungary growth rates were high during the first few years, after the change of system and the introduction of the 'shock therapy' principles of market economics, and unemployment was relatively low. Under pressure from the European Union and the IMF, institutions which were committed to budgetary stability, low taxes, deregulation and privatisation, governments offered extremely favourable investment conditions for foreign investors by reducing wages and the overall wage bill, reducing the tax burden and introducing greater job flexibility. The downside of these developments was experienced by the employees themselves, who had neither secure jobs nor an adequate level of social security.[8]

Since 1990, the German federal government under Helmut Kohl had pursued an economic and social policy marked by contradictions. Its decision to abstain from radical tax increases, and to shift the cost of unification onto the social insurance system, which was motivated by considerations of electoral tactics, did not sit well with its attempt to reduce labour costs and promote investment by a more supply-oriented economic policy. It intended to achieve the latter goal by reducing taxes on individual items, by introducing a series of measures to restrict various social benefits, such as the continued payment of wages in cases of ill-health, unemployment assistance, and protection against dismissal without notice, and by raising the age of retirement.

This line of approach was in turn contradicted by the introduction of long-term care insurance. With the increase in the elderly population, the proportion of people in need of long-term care also increased, and experts on social issues had long agreed that it was indispensable to introduce a fourth social security system—for long-term care—alongside the three that already existed—for sickness, unemployment and old age. But because the overall national wage bill was already far too high, long-term care insurance could not be financed through this route. One alternative was private insurance. But this would have imposed an almost unbearable additional burden on the poorer sections of the population. The government therefore decided on an unusual solution: in order to finance the new kind of social insurance it abolished one of Germany's official holidays, the Day of Prayer and Repentance.[9]

But this stopgap solution did not address the fundamental question of how the German system of social welfare would be financed in the future, and how it might be restructured where appropriate. The government could not make up its mind to undertake a thorough reform of the social welfare system, firstly because these measures were a subject of dispute within the coalition, secondly because it feared an electoral backlash, and thirdly because since 1997 the SPD had possessed a majority in the Bundesrat and was certain to obstruct any further reduction in social benefits.

In 1994, the black–yellow coalition had again won the Bundestag elections, though this time very narrowly. The Union (on 41.1 per cent, down 2.4 per cent) and the FDP (on 6.9 per cent, down 4.1 per cent) had both suffered considerable losses, particularly the FDP, while the SPD (on 36.4 per cent) and the Greens (on 7.3 per cent) had each increased their share of the vote by roughly 2 per cent. The PDS, which obtained 4.4 per cent, an improvement of 2.0 per cent, remained below the 5 per cent hurdle, but re-entered the Bundestag thanks to the four direct mandates it had secured. This election showed that a five-party system had taken shape, and this would continue to characterise the political landscape of the Federal Republic for some time to come. The two big parties, which until the early 1980s had together accounted for over 90 per cent of the vote, were now reduced to 77 per cent. This was a further indication that support for the two political camps, which had previously been firmly fixed, had begun to erode. The 'floating voter' was becoming a decisive element in Germany's day-to-day politics.

The pivotal role in the coalition's unexpected victory was played by discord within the SPD. Its chair, Björn Engholm, had resigned shortly before the election. In the contest to succeed him, the Prime Minister of the Rhineland-Palatinate Rudolf Scharping had gained a surprising victory over his rivals Oskar Lafontaine and Gerhard Schröder. He was unable to develop a clear political profile, however, because the SPD, like almost all the Social Democratic parties of Europe, was having difficulties with its programme. It could not abandon its key electorate in the industrial centres and forgo the cooperation of the trade unions, and therefore, just like the French socialists, it advocated a policy directed towards maintaining jobs in industry and preserving the party's achievements in the social field. But many Social Democrats thought they should follow the example of the British Labour Party. Under Tony Blair, who had been party leader since 1994, 'New Labour' explicitly abandoned previous policies of nationalisation and increased social welfare, and broke away from its close connection with the trade unions and its traditional role as the party of the working class. Mrs Thatcher's rigidly neo-liberal reforms were no longer rejected by the Labour Party. Blair's opening to the middle classes and his support for pushing ahead with a market economy in reliance on services and the financial sector brought the party new voters. By 1997 this had resulted in victory in parliamentary elections.[10]

The German Social Democrats were still not ready to face this crucial test. They continued to vacillate between the two policy alternatives. In autumn 1995, at a dramatic party congress, Oskar Lafontaine succeeded in dislodging Scharping from his position as SPD leader. After that, the SPD pursued a moderately left-wing course, opposing any kind of reduction in social benefits when reform proposals were being debated. In 1997, the party also vetoed a thoroughgoing pension reform laid before the Bundesrat by the federal government.

But the CDU–CSU Union was itself not of one mind on this issue. The employee-oriented wing of the party, around Minister of Labour Blüm, wanted to modify but essentially to maintain the existing system of social policy. The business wing, on the other hand, joined with the FDP in opposing the 'immobility' of the German social model and unfolding dismal scenarios of economic collapse. Despite these differences, all sides agreed on the need for extensive social reform. What was not certain, however, was what this ought to look like. No side wanted to make a clear commitment ahead of the 1998 elections to the Bundestag, hence the sense of stagnation and planlessness intensified, and the unemployment figures continued to rise. This situation was also reflected in the election manifestoes of the two big parties. The Union stepped forward with the colourless slogan 'Safely Towards the World of Tomorrow' and underlined its focus on Helmut Kohl, who to the exasperation of large parts of the party again presented himself for election, under the curious watchword 'World Class for Germany'. The SPD's election motto, which was 'Innovation and Fairness', again showed the party's ambivalence, since it implied both reform and the preservation of the way things were. The two leading personalities in the party symbolised this ambivalence. The party chair, Lafontaine, stood for the traditional, Keynesian line, oriented towards demand economics and social policy, while the party's candidate for German Chancellor, Schröder, supported a supply-side policy on the lines adopted by Blair in Britain. Taken together, they represented an attempt to square the circle.[11]

But, while the state's indebtedness and the figures for unemployment were both rising to record levels, and the president of Germany was lamenting German society's pessimism and refusal to reform, a completely different mood was coming to the fore on the national and international stock exchanges, where there was no trace of the 'increasing rigidity and mental depression' referred to by Herzog. On the contrary, share prices were reaching extraordinary heights and shareholders were making tremendous profits. The USA set the trend in this respect. In 1998 alone, American investors bought equity funds worth $159 billion—twenty-seven times as much as in 1984. Between 1984 and 1998, the value of share capital in the USA increased by more than $10 trillion.[12]

This boom was started by President Reagan's economic policies, which had been very favourable to investors and businesses. The deregulation of financial markets in the USA and then in Britain had largely freed the banks and investment institutions from supervision by politicians and parliaments. At the same time, control over the supply of money, a key function of economic policy, was placed in the hands of autonomous central banks, whose actions were guided by market conditions, not political considerations. Lastly, the worldwide competition to create the most favourable investment locations resulted in a reduction in taxes and social spending in almost all industrial countries, especially since in most places strong institutionalised counterweights, in the form of trade unions for example, no longer existed.

The immense quantities of available capital now sought out new investment opportunities. In this context, traditional industries which were predicted to have very little future were avoided, and new, more lucrative investment sectors were favoured. Interest was concentrated on areas of activity such as telecommunications, information technology, multimedia and biotechnology, which appeared to have particularly promising future prospects because they were based on new technology. The traditional forms of business, which now received the sobriquet of 'the old economy', had engaged in industrial mass production. The new branches, in contrast, produced non-material goods such as data-processing systems, film rights and techniques of DNA analysis. They were based on creativity, research and marketing rather than on raw materials, mass production and large workforces. Since very large profits were expected from these new branches, the share values of enterprises involved in them often rose very quickly even when they were just starting out and consisted of little more than an idea and an office.

Among German savers, however, shares in the stock market were traditionally of marginal importance. The Germans placed their faith in secure and non-speculative investment products such as building loan contracts or life insurance policies. But in view of the sad state of the German economy after reunification and reports of the boom in US share prices, a change began to take place here too after the mid-1990s, which was also promoted by the constant criticisms directed by the neo-liberals at the current social and economic system of the Federal Republic. The impression began to spread that it was better to trust to business than to the state. Pensions and social policy seemed to be not only at risk, but also incapable of offering more than security at a low income level. To invest in shares and investment funds, on the other hand, clearly promised a far more profitable future.

In 1995, the internet started to spread rapidly, and thanks to the popularity of the Telekom share offer, which was accompanied by a big advertising campaign, the number of shareholders in Germany grew by leaps and bounds during the second half of the decade. It was soon evident that most of the new investors were not betting on the traditional industries but on the shares of the young, innovative firms which promised greater profits in a shorter time, but were often avoided by traditional investors who generally took a more cautious approach owing to the unpredictable risks involved. At the end of 1999, the German share index reached the previously unimaginable level of 6,958, which was 39 per cent higher than in the previous year. This was in line with international trends: the London Stock Exchange ended the year 17.8 per cent higher than in 1998, the increase in Paris was 50 per cent, in Milan 22 per cent, in Seoul 82 per cent and in Singapore 78 per cent.

The unbelievable increases in the share prices of some of the 'start-ups', as the new publicly quoted companies were called, acted like an intoxicant, and led many people to abandon their habitual caution. In Germany, the shares of certain firms which were regarded as particularly promising, were already many times oversubscribed shortly after flotation. The firm EM-TV, which specialised in buying and selling TV rights, increased its share price by 200 per cent in eight weeks, and within the first eighteen months, its price had risen by a miraculous 16,600 per cent. A new share index was created for 'New Economy' firms. This was called the 'Nemax'. It was already at 2,738 points by 1998 and had increased by 174 per cent in a single year. In March 2000, it reached 8,546 points and included 229 companies with a total market value of almost 500 billion DM. Even enterprises which lacked a convincing business model enjoyed rapid increases in their stock market value.

The 'old economy', in the meantime, almost started to appear as the anachronistic survival of a bygone era. The software firm Microsoft, which had a turnover of roughly $14.5 billion and fewer than 30,000 employees, had a stock market value of $435 billion at this time, which was more than Telekom, Daimler-Chrysler, Mannesmann, SAP, Bayer, Metro, Siemens and Hoechst put together, though these firms had a total turnover of $387 billion and 1.3 million employees. At the beginning of the year 2000, the dodgy TV rights company EM-TV was valued at nearly $14 billion, which was almost as much as the German steel giant Thyssen-Krupp.

The new 'start-ups' had a distinctive and original style, which the *Financial Times Deutschland* perceptively described as follows:

> The stock market segment for young firms has become the scene of an unprecedented bull market. Alongside skilled investors, many phoneys and fraudsters are profiting from this—until the bubble bursts. 'Money Madness', runs a headline in the *Bild-Zeitung*, and it asks the question which interests millions of readers: 'Can I too get rich?'. At last we are faced with American conditions! Meetings between risk investors and aspiring entrepreneurs no longer take place only in Palo Alto but on the Chausseestraße in Berlin as well. Many young entrepreneurs maintain a student life-style, they live in lodgings and travel to work in second-hand cars. But when they arrive they burn millions and hope to gain billions. 'Cash burn' is an important yardstick in the dotcom economy. It measures the speed at which the start-up entrepreneur burns through the money of investors, usually before earning a single cent. Much of the money is blown out on marketing. Risk investors who manage

> to get their protégées onto the Neuer Markt can count on increasing their investments many times over. If things go well, a profit of 500 or 600 per cent is on the cards. Aspiring internet firms such as Pixelpark or SinnerSchrader, which hardly make a profit and have a turnover of a few millions, reach the billion mark within a few months on the Neuer Markt.[13]

Share values reached their highest level in the spring of 2000, first in the USA and then in Germany. The fall that followed was rapid and precipitous. Many of the new enterprises, it turned out, had no business model, or at least not one that functioned. In some cases, the turnover statistics presented were completely fraudulent, and soon the first insolvency proceedings were initiated. Critical voices had previously been ignored, but now they could be held back no longer. Between March 2000 and April 2001, the Nemax 50 Index fell from 9,665 to 1,300 points. By September 2002 it was at 662 points, and on 5 June 2003 it was shut down completely. Several hundred firms went bankrupt and were liquidated. Experienced investors had already sold their holdings, but many new investors lost all their assets. For most of them the brief delirium and the dream of making a quick buck was over. Some had borrowed money so as not to miss out on this apparently lucrative stock exchange business. Now, after the euphoria over the 'New Economy' had ended, they were deeply in debt and had to apply for private bankruptcy. In the USA, the fall in share prices was exacerbated by the terrorist attack of 11 September 2001. The Federal Reserve sharply reduced its interest rate in order to revive the US economy. Immense quantities of investment capital had now been set free, and in the search for new and lucrative opportunities investors seized on the US real estate market, unleashing a tremendous boom in this sector. This ended in 2007 in an even more serious stock exchange crash, which preceded the worldwide financial and banking crisis of 2008.

Thus, within a few years, the hothouse growth of the international financial markets, and the idea of a post-industrial 'New Economy', which was supposed to replace the outmoded model of classical commodity production, had led to critical situations of extreme instability and danger. In the Federal Republic, which had been ridiculed around the turn of the century as the 'sick man on the Rhine' on account of its economic difficulties (by analogy with the Ottoman Empire a hundred years earlier), most people were now very pleased that they still possessed a solid core of traditional industries which, contrary to expectations, had not only proved to be capable of dynamic change and modernisation but also offered a more reliable foundation during the storms of the financial crisis than an economy based on hedge funds and risky investments.

What was crystal clear, however, was that the decline of traditional industrial mass production, the victory of the neo-liberal economic model and the simultaneous boom in share prices had in one respect brought about a result common to all industrial countries: a clear increase in social inequality. This tendency, which had previously been most pronounced in the Anglo-Saxon countries, could now be observed in the Federal Republic as well. Between 1980 and 1995, the number of millionaires in Germany roughly doubled (it rose from 67,000 to 131,000) as did the number of people in receipt of social welfare payments (it rose from 922,000 to almost 2.3 million). Between 1980 and 1995, the average real income of individuals employed by others fell by 10 per cent, while the income of the self-employed rose during the same period by 54 per cent. Between 1990 and 1997, net wages and salaries rose by 8.4 per cent; but the value of shares traded on the German stock market rose by 288 per cent. Taxes on the wages and social security contributions of an average wage-earner increased during this period by 35 per cent; but taxes on business profits, which in 1980 had constituted 16 per cent of total tax receipts, made up only 5 per cent by 1995.

At the end of the century, the industrialised countries of Europe were faced with an economic policy dilemma. If they pushed ahead with neo-liberal economic reforms, cut taxes and social benefits and improved investors' chances of making a profit, they could count on higher economic growth. At the same time, they would also have to acquiesce in a perceptible worsening of social inequality and accept a situation in which the lower social strata, making up between 10 per cent and 30 per cent of the population, lived close to the subsistence level and had jobs which did not offer them a secure existence, while the rich rapidly increased their wealth. If, on the other hand, they held fast to the traditional economic structures, and made sure that the lower social strata received wage increases and a high level of social security, this would lead to slow economic growth, high unemployment and increasing budget deficits.

This is how the former American Secretary of Labor Robert B. Reich described the current alternatives in economic and social policy in summer 1998: there are essentially two parties, he said, and they cut across traditional party lines. On one side there are the representatives of the 'save the jobs party', 'who will do anything to preserve the old jobs and the existing economic structures. They are anxious, because their voters are anxious about the changes.' On the other side there is the 'sink or swim party'. 'Here one meets mainly representatives of industry, well provided people, who say: let the free market do as it wants, drive the government out of the economy, let everyone swim. They will drown? Too bad. If they know how to swim, they will be stronger than before.'[14]

## The Red–Green Coalition and the War in Kosovo

The Bundestag elections of 27 September 1998 ended with a victory for the SPD and Alliance 90/the Greens. For the first time, a government was replaced by two parties which had previously stood in opposition. Even so, the change of government, unlike in 1969 or 1982, took place almost noiselessly. 'For the first time since the creation of the republic', wrote the journalist Heribert Prantl, 'what was actually a matter of course was regarded as such. It was a beginning which differed from all previous beginnings in the history of the Federal Republic—a beginning without agitation, triumph or euphoria, but also without any parliamentary lamentations.'[15]

Even in 1994, the Union and the FDP had only just won the elections. In view of the steady deterioration in the economic situation and the constant rise in the number of people unemployed, the climate of opinion had been changing to the disadvantage of the Kohl government since 1996. Unemployment was by far the most important issue in the election campaign, but the government's planned social policy reforms, particularly the plan to cut the level of continuing wage payments during sickness, had also given rise to sharp protests.

The opposition's victory was therefore expected. Nevertheless, it was not simply a case of changing the guard. In the shape of the Greens, the government now contained a party which had emerged neither from the social conflicts of the late nineteenth century, like the SPD, nor from the debris of the Christian and middle-class parties after the collapse of the Nazi regime, like the CDU, CSU and FDP, but from the contradictions and dynamic developments of the post-industrial phase that followed the 1970s. It is true that the leading Social Democrats of the current generation, such as Schröder, Lafontaine, Scharping and Wieczorek-Zeul, also looked back to the inheritance of 1968, which they had experienced as Young Socialists and helped to shape. But their understanding of politics continued to be moulded by the traditions of the workers' movement and the social conflicts of industrial society. The Greens, on the other hand, had emerged by distancing themselves from these alignments. For them, the journey they had undertaken from participating in the West and East German protest milieux of the 1980s to entering the federal government in 1998 was much longer than the SPD's journey, especially as the Left radical wing of the West German Greens had split off in the 1990s, to join up in part with the PDS. With 6.7 per cent of the vote, the electoral performance of the Greens was not exactly impressive, but they had at least become the third strongest party, ahead of the FDP, which with 6.2 per cent had its worst result since1949, and the PDS, which achieved 5.1 per cent. The Union had incurred considerable losses, falling to 35.1 per cent, so that it was below the 40 per cent figure for the first time since 1949, while the SPD, which was under the dual leadership of

Schröder and Lafontaine, had increased its vote by almost 5 per cent, making it with 40.9 per cent the largest party in the Bundestag, for the first time since the 'Willy Brandt election' of 1972.[16]

The policies of the coalition partners coincided in many respects, despite their different starting points, and the commitments in the coalition agreement and the government declaration envisaged very ambitious goals, which they planned to achieve as quickly as possible, namely, a reduction in unemployment, an energy revolution, an ecological transformation of fiscal and energy policy, a withdrawal from the nuclear industry, a reform of citizenship law, and an expansion of social policy. Even a more experienced government could only have implemented such a list of policies with great difficulty. The fledgling red–green coalition, however, made so many mistakes right at the outset that the expression 'days of chaos' made the rounds, and both parties lost the first Diet elections that were held by enormous margins.

The biggest challenges facing the new government, however, were not related to their projects of domestic reform but, quite unexpectedly, to foreign policy, in which a crisis occurred even before they had taken the oath of office.

The Dayton Agreement had brought a temporary end to the conflict over the legacy of the defunct federal republic of Yugoslavia. The evolution of the situation up to 1995 had produced two results: firstly, five independent states had emerged from the former Yugoslavia. They had achieved their independence largely in the course of violent conflict, and within a short time they had been recognised by the Western states, then by the whole world. In this case, then, the wish of ethnic minorities to secede had gained a victory over the principle of the sovereignty of the central power. Secondly, the outcome of the civil wars in Yugoslavia had been decided by intervention from outside, first and foremost by the armed involvement of the USA. After the Europeans had failed in their numerous attempts to settle the conflicts in the Balkans, the Americans had forcibly slashed through the Gordian knot. Unlike the Europeans, who were aware of the complicated mixture of ethnic and political conflict involved here, the Americans took sides without further ado against the Serbs, whom they identified as the guilty party. They helped the Croats to achieve a military victory over the Serbs in the Krajina and they forced the end of the conflict in Bosnia-Herzegovina by making massive air attacks on Serb positions. At the end of the conflict, the Europeans stood there as incompetent ditherers, while by engaging in war in the Gulf and taking action in Yugoslavia the USA had impressively demonstrated its position as the hegemonic world power, ready to intervene at any time.

America's intervention provided NATO with a new purpose. When the Cold War ended, there had been doubts as to whether such a military alliance was needed any longer, given the completely altered world situation, which left it without a clear enemy. But the USA's military intervention in Yugoslavia, which had been coordinated with NATO, was an indication of the kind of ideas about the alliance's future that were circulating, in Washington at least, namely that NATO would no longer be a military alliance to wage large-scale conflicts of an international kind but rather a force capable of intervening in the world's trouble spots. This meant a change in the notion of war, but it also raised the question of the legitimacy of such a strategy. The idea that NATO could become a kind of armed agency of the United Nations was regarded in large parts of the world, particularly in Asia, Africa and Latin America, as completely unacceptable. But military interventions without a UN mandate had absolutely no foundation in international law.[17]

Unlike most of the other ethnic minorities in Yugoslavia, the inhabitants of Kosovo had so far tried to achieve independence by peaceful means. Some 80 per cent of the inhabitants of the province, which was one of the poorest regions in Europe, were Muslim Albanians. The other 20 per cent were Serbs. Under Tito, Kosovo was legally a part of the federal Yugoslav state of Serbia, but it had received a considerable degree of autonomy. The first calls for Kosovan independence began to be heard in the early 1980s; in response to this the force of emergent Great Serbian nationalism became stronger. The Great Serbs regarded a mythically transfigured Kosovo as the historic homeland of the Serbian people. In 1988, the Kosovars began to hold protest meetings and anti-Yugoslav demonstrations. The central government in Belgrade responded by abolishing the province's autonomy. The Serbian nationalists held mass demonstrations demanding that their government take a hard line in Kosovo. Finally, the Serbian leader Slobodan Milošević declared a state of emergency, ordered the closure of the Kosovan parliament, and forcibly suppressed further demonstrations by the local Kosovar Albanian majority. In September 1991, the Kosovars countered this by setting up the 'Independent Republic of Kosova', and in secret elections they chose the writer Ibrahim Rugova as their president. Unlike the leaders of the secessionist movements in Croatia and Slovenia, however, Rugova called on his compatriots to engage in peaceful protests, rather than to rise up in revolt.[18]

It was perhaps for this reason that Western governments were largely uninterested in the province at that time. The Kosovo issue also played no role in the negotiations over the Dayton Agreement. Things only began to change after 1997, when the situation in Kosovo started to become critical. After violent uprisings in other parts of Yugoslavia had led to American intervention and to independence, Rugova's non-violent approach came under pressure, and an increasing number of Kosovars placed their hopes on a forcible separation from Serbia on the model of Croatia and Bosnia. At the end of 1997 an armed organisation entered the field, known as the UÇK (Kosovo Liberation Army). It had an extremely dubious reputation, even among Western observers, owing to its close links with criminal gangs. It began its activities by attacking Serbian police units. The Serbs reacted as expected with sanguinary measures of retribution. Reciprocal violence led to rapid escalation, and when the Serbian side began to reply to the UÇK's attacks with executions and the destruction of whole villages, the international community finally woke up to the seriousness of the conflict. There were soon an increasing number of reports of expulsions and massacres committed against the civilian population of the province, and these reinforced calls for the bloodshed to end, and also for the West to intervene.

Particular concern was aroused by the increasing number of refugees who had been driven out of Kosovo by the Serbs or who simply wanted to escape from the armed conflict. By spring 1998, there were already more than 200,000 of them. On 23 September 1998 the United Nations Security Council condemned the actions of Serbian units in Kosovo, characterising them as 'a threat to peace', but it also criticised the violent methods of the UÇK. The Security Council resolution did not call for the conflict to be brought to an end by external intervention, by UN-mandated troops, and both the Chinese and the Russian representatives made it clear that they would not agree to any such decision.

NATO defence ministers had, however, already begun to discuss military options in summer 1998. They were in favour of air attacks on the Serbian units in Kosovo, following the example of Bosnia three years earlier, when a bombing campaign lasting only a few days had been sufficient to compel the Serbs to back down and withdraw their troops. To prepare for this, NATO issued an Activation Order (ACTORD), which could provide the basis for rapid military intervention if need be, but in this case was meant above all to serve as a means of pressure on the Serbian government. But because there was no prospect of securing the agreement of the Security Council, owing to the attitude of Russia, NATO's military intervention in Kosovo could, it was thought, also take place without a UN mandate. In view of the plight of the refugees, it could be justified as a 'humanitarian intervention'.

At the same time, the US Special Envoy David Holbrooke was negotiating with Milošević to secure a ceasefire and the return of the refugees to their homes during the approaching winter months. To strengthen his position vis-à-vis the Serbian leader, Holbrooke urgently needed to involve Germany, a country which had previously refused to take part in any military action either in Bosnia or the Gulf. It was now thought essential to include the Germans in the team in order to make it impossible for the Serbian side to exploit divisions within NATO.

It is likely that the US government also had another objective in mind: the outcome of the elections to the Bundestag had aroused the fear that the new

German government would turn aside from the Western alliance and, at the very least, refuse to go along with NATO's new interventionist strategy. American mistrust was particularly directed against the Greens, who had pacifist inclinations, and whose party programme had long called for the dissolution of NATO. Thus, compliance with ACTORD was seen as a kind of acid test of the red–green coalition's reliability, and the American government increased its pressure on this issue during the period of political transition between 27 September, the date of the election, and 16 October, when the new government took office.

Gerhard Schröder and Joschka Fischer flew to the USA immediately after the German elections to explain to the US president why Germany would also refuse to participate in military action in Kosovo. They gained the impression that Clinton understood their point of view. In subsequent days, however, the American attitude hardened, a change which can probably be traced back to Holbrooke, who had told Milošević that all NATO countries, including Germany, supported the threat of military intervention. On 11 October, therefore, the US government demanded a quick decision from the Germans.

Schröder and Fischer responded by abandoning their previous position and indicating their compliance with America's demands. They justified their change of line as follows in an internal memorandum:

> The question of German participation is absolutely decisive for the Red–Green coalition's chances of entering government. Faced with the conflict of priorities between the veto of the UN Security Council resolution, loyalty to the alliance and international law, the new coalition must decide against the interpretation of international law which has prevailed until now.[19]

Just one day later, on 12 October, members of the previous government of the Federal Republic met with Schröder and Fischer, and all parties agreed to empower NATO to take military action against the Serbs when the time was appropriate. Four days after that, a special sitting of the old Bundestag was held to give the necessary parliamentary consent.

If the new German government had refused its consent, Schröder told the Bundestag on 16 October, it would not only have been regarded by the US as an unreliable ally, but it would also have been held responsible for any further worsening of the humanitarian situation in Yugoslavia:

> Since it could no longer be excluded that Germany's attitude might have a vital influence on Belgrade's reactions, we could not maintain our position. It would have been seen as a German refusal, and would have caused severe . . . damage to the alliance and probably also to the European Union. We

> could have been blamed for a failure of the negotiations. The Federal Republic of Germany would have suffered a devastating loss of reputation and influence as a result.[20]

Almost all the political parties in the Bundestag agreed to the decision on Germany's military involvement. The only party to vote against it unanimously was the PDS. The wider German public did, it is true, greet the news with surprise, but there was no large-scale debate on the issue, although what had been decided was nothing less than the participation of German troops in a military intervention without a United Nations mandate.

The coalition's decision was greeted with relief and approval by the USA, the CDU, the CSU, and the FDP and also by the German diplomats and soldiers involved in the affair. Many of them were tired of sitting on the sidelines of world politics and they remembered all too well, as one of them commented, 'the malicious remarks they were obliged to put up with in 1991–1992 owing to Germany's absence from the Gulf War. That increased their readiness to take responsibility this time.'[21]

But the Germans also assumed—or hoped—that the decision to participate would be rendered superfluous by the further course of events in Kosovo. As it turned out, they were wrong. The ceasefire negotiated by Holbrooke did allow the refugees to return to their homes during the winter. But at the same time UÇK units rapidly advanced into districts from which Serbian units had withdrawn, occupying almost half of the province. The Serbian side again reacted to this with severe acts of repression, images of which led to worldwide outrage when distributed through the media. This meant that the peace talks which began in February 1999 in the Château de Rambouillet near Paris took place under unfavourable auspices.

The peace proposals laid before the Serbs at Rambouillet resembled a dictate. Admittedly, Kosovo would continue to be a part of Serbia, and the UÇK would be disarmed. But 30,000 NATO troops would be stationed both in Kosovo and in Serbia. These were conditions, Rudolf Augstein wrote in *Der Spiegel*, that 'no educated Serb could subscribe to.'[22] When Milošević refused to sign, military action automatically followed.

On 24 March, NATO began to bomb Serbian positions in Kosovo. This was not a small-scale action, as had been hoped, but a war that continued for more than three months. It was one of the most massive aerial warfare operations in recent military history. By the time it had ended, more than 1,000 fighter aircraft had taken part, flying more than five hundred missions a day. The attacks were soon extended to cover strategic points in Serbia itself, and eventually the city of Belgrade was also a target. The expression 'collateral damage' gained unexpected celebrity.

The German air force participated in the military operations from the start, though it only flew a tiny proportion of the missions. It was the political meaning of this action that was decisive, however, because this was Germany's first military deployment since 1945, and it was directed against a country which had not attacked the Federal Republic. It meant that Germany's foreign policy had entered a new age. In October 1998, as we saw, there had been little public debate during the preparatory decision-making process. Now, however, an intense public dispute began over Germany's military intervention.

The sharpest of the criticisms related to the failure to secure a mandate from the Security Council of the United Nations. This was a clear breach of the principles of German foreign policy, which had also been confirmed by the coalition agreement. The representatives of the German government therefore no longer emphasised the need to secure the unity of the NATO alliance and avoid putting Germany in an isolated position as the main motive for joining the war. Instead, they justified the military action as a humanitarian intervention, a kind of supra-legal emergency, which legitimated a military strike without a UN mandate, because the 'blocking tactics' of Russia and China had rendered the UN Security Council incapable of acting. Now the actions of the Serbs started to be described and condemned in increasingly sharp terms. Expulsion became annihilation, executions became impending genocide. Foreign Minister Fischer, in a remarkable escalation of rhetoric, equated the misery of the refugees and the behaviour of Serbian units in Kosovo with the mass crimes of the National Socialists. 'No comparison can ever be made with *Auschwitz*', he said. 'But I have two fundamental principles: War never again, and Auschwitz never again. Genocide never again and Fascism never again. For me these things belong together.'[23] NATO's action, he said, was not a war but a defensive fight against the 'fascist' troops of the Serbs:

> We are not conducting a war, we are engaging in resistance, we are defending human rights, freedom and democracy. I am reminded of what the Spanish resistance fighter 'La Pasionaria' used to say. 'No pasaran'—the Fascists shall not pass—this was the slogan under which the republicans fought against the Franco regime.[24]

Defence Minister Scharping also repeatedly had recourse to Nazi-era historical parallels: 'Selections are being made there. I am using that word deliberately: selections.'[25]

No doubt these arguments also reflected the trauma of Srebrenica, where UN troops had passively stood by during the mass execution of thousands of Bosnian men. But historical exaggerations of this kind were problematic, because they made it impossible to raise the stakes any further. If civil war and expulsions in Kosovo were compared with the Holocaust, what level of military force should be used to react to atrocities like those in Rwanda or the Congo? As the journalist Frank Schirrmacher wrote,

> Auschwitz, and everything it stands for, was for decades the basis for Germany's absolute commitment to peace. But now Auschwitz has come to stand for the ethical necessity to go to war. The Germany of the previous century is now to be purified by taking part in a just war, a delayed war of revenge against Adolf Hitler. I should feel more at ease if Germany took part in an attack for ethical reasons without needing to repeat the defeat of Hitler at the same time. Milošević is not Hitler. And Kosovo is not Auschwitz.[26]

But the dilemma existed, even if it was an exaggeration to call Serbian policy the work of the devil, and even if the share of guilt had been distributed more evenly between the UÇK and Serbian military units than was usually the case during the Kosovo War. Even if one regarded the increasingly gruesome details of massacres and tortures reported by Defence Minister Scharping, or the news of the immense deployment plans of the Serbs ('the horseshoe plan') as exaggerated or invented, and there were numerous indications that this was the case, it remained indisputable that Milošević's policy was aimed at suppressing the Kosovar struggle for autonomy, and that he was ready to trigger the flight of hundreds of thousands of people and to accept the death of hundreds of them, in order to achieve this goal. The question of principle was therefore inescapable: if a government commits severe human rights violations against its own citizens, does this create a kind of supra-legal emergency situation, which justifies humanitarian interventions? Or does it not? 'The misappropriation of state power for terrorist ends', wrote Jürgen Habermas in *Die Zeit,* 'converts a classical civil war into a mass crime. If there is no other alternative, democratic neighbours must hasten to provide emergency aid, which is legitimate under international law.'[27]

Even if this view was adopted, as it was by a clear majority of the Bundestag and in the meantime by the population as well, problematic consequences still emerged. Almost every military aggression has been preceded by a legitimating reference to the oppression of sections of the population by a country's government. Deputy Ludger Volmer, speaking in the Bundestag for the left wing of the Greens, was quick to point to the effect of circumventing the UN Security Council:

> The lack of a Security Council resolution cannot be counterbalanced by other legal constructs. . . . Any regional power at all, which in future wants to establish order in its neighbourhood, and can invoke a UN resolution, be it

> only partially appropriate, will be able to point to this example. It opens the floodgates for military alliances to mandate themselves to act. If the Security Council is always circumvented when there is the threat of a veto this abolishes its power to guarantee the UN's monopoly of the use of force.[28]

In evaluating the consequences of the war over Kosovo, three aspects of the outcome need to be grasped. Firstly, the hegemony of Serbia over Kosovo was broken, the Kosovar refugees returned to their homes, and the province recovered its autonomous status, without becoming independent in terms of international law. The social and economic situation of the inhabitants of Kosovo did, it is true, continue to be extremely precarious, and armed incidents occurred repeatedly. But the expulsions and massacres, and the situation of open civil war, had come to an end. Secondly, America's claim to world hegemony was confirmed by the military intervention in Kosovo, although no consensus had been achieved which went beyond that particular concrete case. The Kosovo War did not become a precedent, and it did not set an example. One reason for this was that it took place at a time when post-Soviet Russia was passing through its worst crisis and was therefore hardly in a position to react effectively. A strong Russia would certainly not have accepted this approach to international affairs, and it would not do so in the future. Another reason was that the war lasted for many months, against all predictions, and inflicted much more devastation than had been either planned or expected. Thirdly, the intervention seriously undermined the UN Security Council's monopoly of power. In view of the continuing increase in the number and significance of the regional conflicts and civil wars raging over many parts of the globe, this damage was possibly not less momentous than the successes achieved by the war over Kosovo.

For Germany, the Kosovo War was unmistakably an important turning point. The 'culture of restraint' in foreign policy had been abandoned in order to prevent the country, and in particular the new government, from being marginalised in world politics. The humanitarian justifications given were not without plausibility, it is true, but they still gave the impression of having been added after the event. Loyalty to the alliance was the overriding motive, and there were, after all, already more than 300,000 refugees in Kosovo when Schröder and Fischer initially refused Clinton's request for military participation. Here too, the diminishing power of historical references to the Nazi regime and its crimes was apparent. Comparisons with the Second World War and the Holocaust became overstrained and ineffective, once Fischer had made his disastrous attempt to instrumentalise them. It was clear that henceforth, Germany would have to derive its foreign policy goals and its mode of action from its own interests and political principles, without trying to secure legitimation by referring to historical events. Two years later, the Schröder government justified its refusal to take part in the Iraq War prepared by the USA after the terrorist attacks of 11 September 2001 not by referring to history but by using political and pragmatic arguments, and its approach met with the approval of the majority of the parliament and the population.

The German population showed far less interest in the Kosovo War, a war in which German soldiers participated, than in the Gulf War of 1991, in which Germany had not participated at all. This remarkable circumstance strengthened the impression that most Germans had in fact been convinced by Fischer's assertion that this was not a war but a humanitarian intervention to save the refugees. Of course, the anxiety aroused by the Gulf War was related to the fear that it could escalate into world war, whereas the Kosovo intervention, for all its drama, was always perceived as a purely regional conflict. Not the least of the reasons for the public's lack of interest, however, was that the forces most likely to protest were now involved in the new government. A conservative government would probably have experienced great political difficulty in pushing through such a decision.

For the new government, therefore, the Kosovo War signified a kind of initiation. It raised its international profile and influence and it also led to an increase in its domestic self-confidence. In comparison with the challenge of war, the tasks it faced in domestic policy did not seem so tremendous, especially now that its idealism was no longer so exuberant. For the Greens and their supporters, the time for pure and immaculate criticism had now passed. That made it easier to govern.

## Third Options and New Roads

With the appointment of Schröder as Chancellor and Lafontaine as party leader and Minister of Finance, a conflict over the direction of policy was built into the new coalition, and it did not take many weeks before it came to the surface. As usual, personal factors also played a part, but they were certainly no more strongly embedded than the personal disputes that had dogged previous government coalitions, although contemporaries thought they were. It was ideological differences that were decisive here, and they had deep roots in basic issues of social democratic policy. These differences were made plain even by the party's successful election slogan 'Innovation and Justice'. Lafontaine stood for 'justice', which meant that in harmony with the party's social policy experts and the trade unions, his main concern was to defend the welfare state's protection of workers against the attempts of the neo-liberals to move towards greater flexibility, and at the same time to intensify the state's endeavours to reinvigorate the country's sluggish economy. Hence the new government's first measures bore the stamp of the Lafontaine approach. The Kohl government's cuts in social benefit were reversed, the size of the red–green coalition's first budget increased by 6 per cent, and expenditure on social services rose by 12 per cent. These were essentially classical demand-side measures. Outside the SPD Left, however, Lafontaine's plans found hardly any support, because they merely continued the policy that had been pursued without success since the late 1970s, a policy which had led at that time to a continuous increase in unemployment, and there were few signs that things would be different this time.[29]

Schröder, in contrast, stood for 'innovation', although at first nothing more was associated with this than an image, or at least an expectation. He was, however, strongly influenced by the successful policies of the British Prime Minister Tony Blair, with whom he presented a joint paper in June 1999 on the future direction of social democratic policy. It was called 'The Policy of the New Centre and the Third Way'. This 'Third Way', however, did not mean a path halfway between capitalism and socialism but rather a compromise between neo-liberalism and the traditional policy of state intervention. According to the 'Third Way' programme 'the last two decades of neo-liberal laissez faire' were over. But they ought not to be replaced 'by a renaissance of deficit spending and heavy-handed state intervention in the style of the 1970s'. Social Democratic governments, the authors continued, had made fatal mistakes in previous decades: they had burdened labour with higher and higher costs, purchased increased social justice with growing budget deficits, and increased the amount of red tape and bureaucracy. They had 'overestimated the weaknesses of the market and underestimated its strengths'. To achieve economic growth, reduce unemployment and bring about social justice, state expenditure must in future be reduced, social security systems must be adapted to the changed conditions of life and the responsibility of individuals for their and their family's lives must be strengthened. The tax burden on enterprises and the less well-off must be reduced, the 'product, capital and labour markets' must in all cases be flexible and social policy must be designed in such a way as to make it 'in people's interest to go to work'. The change from an industrial society to one based on services was irresistible. In fact, the longer one attempted to oppose this change, the worse the undesirable consequences would be, but in any case 'it would be wishful thinking to deny it.'[30]

This paper was in essence a social democratic variation on familiar neo-liberal themes, namely, the need to increase the strength and flexibility of market forces, reduce taxes, rein in the social involvement of the state, and lessen the tax burden imposed on business by politicians. It listed all the measures repeatedly called for by the critics of a 'blocked society' during the previous twenty years. Schröder's 'Third Way' naturally met with tremendous opposition from the Left of the SPD, and the party's trade-union wing. The Greens, in contrast, entirely agreed with its arguments. It must be added, however, that the Greens had not yet developed their own economic and financial programme, and they essentially followed the guidelines laid down by the Social Democrats, as also in the sphere of education.

The debate within the SPD on this issue continued to fester for years, until in 2003 Schröder executed a complete about-turn in the light of the continuation of depressingly high unemployment figures, issuing a new programme, under the title 'Agenda 2010'. Lafontaine had already resigned from the government in spring 1999. He also gave up his seat in the Bundestag and ceased to chair the SPD, a decision which was interpreted first and foremost as a reaction to the defeat by the 'modernisers' of the forces within the party which favoured an active social policy and state intervention in the economy.

To view matters in this way, however, is to overlook the fact that the differences between Schröder and Lafontaine were not related exclusively to social and budgetary policy. Financial and monetary issues also entered the picture. This aspect was largely ignored in the speculations over Lafontaine's reason for resigning. In the paper produced by Schröder and Blair there was one somewhat cryptically formulated, but significant remark on the subject: 'The product, capital and labour markets must all be flexible: we must not combine rigidity in one part of the economic system with openness and dynamism in the rest.' If one takes into account that the economic successes of Great Britain in the preceding years were due to a considerable extent to the increased flexibility of capital markets, the meaning of the statement becomes clear. The far-reaching reductions in banking supervision, the almost complete removal of all obstacles to international financial transfers and the enormous profits opened to currency speculation by the abandonment of fixed exchange rates had made possible the resurgence of the City of London as the leading international financial market. These measures were also responsible in large part for the boom in the United Kingdom economy. This comment in the Schröder–Blair paper was therefore directed above all against any attempt to do no more than dismantle or simply reduce state regulation of trading activity and the labour market, while at the same time retaining existing regulations in the financial sphere, especially in the currency markets. But economic and budgetary crises were already occurring in Asia, Mexico and Brazil, as a result of currency speculation, and it is striking to observe in retrospect how the signs of a global financial crisis began to mount up after the turn of the century in the absence of any attempt by politicians to act against them On the contrary, financial markets were deregulated in almost all the economically powerful countries, because the experts were of the opinion that the indications of an impending crisis in the financial sphere were to be ascribed precisely to a lack of financial deregulation.

As against this, Oskar Lafontaine and the French Minister of Finance Dominique Strauss-Kahn were convinced that stricter rules and closer supervision of the banks were needed to prevent the financial markets from dragging down entire economies in times of crisis. Lafontaine therefore proposed the establishment of 'exchange rate target ranges' for the most important currencies, so as to dampen down currency speculation, because, as he later emphasised,

> currency transactions, amounting to one trillion dollars per day, take place every day, and only 5 per cent of them involve trade. The remaining 95 per cent . . . are speculative dealings and arbitrage transactions, because dealers who are used to investing huge sums are looking to make quick profits from exchange rate and interest rate fluctuations.[31]

The proposal to establish 'exchange rate target ranges' would have meant that currencies could only fluctuate within fixed margins, and this would curb currency speculation.

If one views these proposals with hindsight, bearing in mind the financial crises which broke out after 2001, and particularly after 2008, it cannot be denied that Lafontaine's arguments have a certain plausibility. But, at the beginning of the year 1999, they stood in complete contradiction to the views of most economic specialists, who regarded uninhibited financial and stock market speculation as an expression of the dynamism of a market that had been finally freed from state supervision. The German Federal Bank and the European Central Bank therefore rejected the proposal, as did the Bank of England, and the attacks of the British press on the German Finance Minister became sharper than ever.[32]

Lafontaine's idea of harmonising taxes throughout Europe met a similar fate. This too was an obvious step to take, in the light of the divergences in economic policy right across the European Union. At this time, a number of European countries, including Britain, wanted to increase their attractiveness to investors by offering low business taxes. As a result, there was a race between EU countries, and other countries outside the EU, to reduce taxes as far as possible. Lafontaine's proposal was therefore firmly rejected by almost all European finance ministers. Lafontaine had a third proposal, which was also rejected. He wanted the Federal Bank and the European Central Bank to reduce their interest rates, so as to stimulate the economy and reduce unemployment. But in order to ease the introduction of the euro and attract foreign investors it was important to maintain a high interest rate. Moreover, currency stability was the key hallmark of the German Federal Bank's policy.

Even if it is conceded that Lafontaine's ideas about budgetary and social policy appeared to have little future, as they essentially signified the return of well-known policies which had repeatedly failed, the same cannot be said about his proposed alterations in financial and monetary policy. Ten years later, his ideas could be seen as pointing the way towards a financial policy aimed at avoiding a repetition of the catastrophic outcome of the post-2008 financial crisis, in which the profits of the banks were privatised but their losses, which had risen to an order of magnitude previously regarded as impossible, were included in state budgets. But Lafontaine had become German Minister of Finance at a point when the boom in share prices and the excesses of the 'New Economy' were reaching their zenith, so his attack on the financial markets seemed rather like Don Quixote's battle with the windmills he imagined to be giants. In this case, though, the windmills really were giants.

The red–green coalition's truly path-breaking projects, however, were in entirely different areas. It is noticeable that although the reforms begun between 1998 and 2001 were hotly contested, after a few years they made their appearance in the government programmes of all the differently constituted coalitions that succeeded this one. This applies particularly to the ecological tax reform. The basic idea of this reform derived from the experience of previous decades during which energy was too cheap and labour was too expensive. If high taxes were imposed on energy consumption, and the proceeds of this were used to reduce non-wage labour costs, this would not only reduce energy consumption but also stimulate employment. That was the theory. In practice, however, powerful interest groups were opposed to a restructuring of this kind, which represented a break with the existing principles of economic policy. These included the oil and energy companies, the motor car manufacturers, the ADAC, and not least motorists and the publishers of tabloid newspapers. There was such fierce hostility in spring 1998 to the proposal by the Greens to allow petrol prices to rise in the long term to 5 DM per litre that the party's chance of entering the Bundestag was seriously under threat. In actual fact, the energy tax increases turned out to be so moderate, owing to pressure from the SPD, that their impact was far smaller than had been planned. Nevertheless, this reform represented a breakthrough, and ten years later the need for energy consumption to be regulated by taxation was no longer contested by anyone. By then, taxes on energy were the government's third largest source of income. A similar story could be told of the increased promotion of renewable energy. Wind turbines, solar panels and increased energy efficiency were encouraged with state subsidies and then taken over by private firms, although the appropriate level of subsidy payments continued to be disputed.[33]

The most significant measure taken by the red–green government was to phase out nuclear energy. This had long been one of the central political objectives of the Greens, but there had also been some rethinking in the SPD over the issue. After lengthy negotiations, it proved possible to reach an agreement with the four largest energy companies for a gradual abandonment of nuclear energy, a process which was expected to take more than thirty years. In view of the high costs associated with the expansion of renewable energy sources, compared with the extreme cheapness of nuclear energy (for the simple reason that the follow-up costs of the latter were borne by society as a whole), this course of action was not without its risks, especially as Chernobyl had already been forgotten and most neighbouring European states, above all France, continued to place their faith in nuclear power. Among the Greens too, the compromise with the energy companies was controversial because it provided for such a long transitional period that the expression 'phasing out nuclear energy' no longer seemed entirely appropriate. Nevertheless, Germany was the first industrialised country in the world to decide to abandon nuclear energy on the ground of its excessive riskiness, and in subsequent years it established a position in the commercially attractive markets for renewable energy. Ten years later, however, the nuclear compromise was cancelled by the liberal–conservative government owing to pressure from the energy companies, and the winding-down period for nuclear energy was in effect extended by half as long again. Then, in spring 2011, the nuclear accident at Fukushima in Japan provoked a further rethink. Now it was finally decided to phase out nuclear energy more rapidly, and indeed the deadline was brought forward to 2022.[34]

These reform projects by the red–green government were a reaction to processes of economic and social change that had been under way since the late 1970s. They appeared to be 'post-materialist' in the sense that they had not been devised in accordance with the existing principles of industrial and technological progress. But this was a superficial view. From a more long-term perspective, the phasing out of nuclear energy and the changeover to renewable energy were entirely rational economic steps, even without taking into account the damage triggered by accidents such as the one at Fukushima. But even leaving this aside, the years between 1998 and 2001 saw the completion of a paradigm shift which, however jerkily and clumsily it was set in motion by the Schröder–Fischer government, did at least offer a new approach in economic and social policy, which proved irreversible in later years. In that sense, the balance sheet of the red–green government's domestic policy was quite respectable. It must be admitted, however, that in the first four years of its existence it did not respond effectively to the big economic and social policy challenges that confronted it.

## The End of the Twentieth Century

When did the twentieth century come to an end? If one sets the calendar aside, this question is connected with the problem of dividing historical time into phases or epochs. Historical periodisations are interpretations. They highlight particular events and developments for their significance in shaping a phase of history, a phase which they then analyse and classify from this perspective. But an interpretation of this kind presupposes a certain amount of temporal separation from the events in question. Important long-term historical processes can only be recognised and separated out from those of lesser historical significance from a distance. What, then, should be the end date of a history of Germany in the twentieth century? In endeavouring to answer this question, we lack the clarity which can only be acquired through chronological distance, and we cannot measure how certain problems which appear highly contentious today will look in thirty or a hundred years' time, nor can we reliably determine which current developments will turn out to have a decisive historical impact in the longer term.

And yet the choice of the final date of an epoch is of some significance for the evaluation of earlier decades. For the British historian Eric Hobsbawm, who sees the twentieth century as 'one of the darkest epochs in history', it began in 1914 with the First World War and ended in 1990 with a double crisis: 'on the one hand the collapse of the experiment called socialism, on the other hand the failure of the attempt made after the Second World War to make capitalism more humane and socially responsible.' For Hobsbawm, therefore, the twentieth century is essentially characterised by the struggle between two social systems, both of which can be seen in retrospect as pernicious.[35] Francis Fukuyama also chose 1990 to mark the end of the twentieth century, although unlike Hobsbawm, he connected the downfall of the Soviet system with the victory of liberal democratic capitalism as the only system of social organisation that was appropriate to industrial modernity. 1990 is the clearest and therefore the most plausible caesura, historically speaking. It is a date which is associated with both the collapse of the Soviet Empire and the end of the primacy of classical industrial society. It should not, however, be overlooked that to adopt such a date is to make the antagonism between East and West the central element in the interpretation of the epoch, rather than the antagonism between North and South, for 1990 was not a decisive date in colonial and post-colonial history.

In recent years it has become a familiar topos to refer to the end of the twentieth and the beginning of the twenty-first century as a historical turning point, but the expression has been applied to a whole range of historical fissures and developments. We shall therefore conclude our reflections by examining and placing in context the alternatives that have been proposed, all of which have implications for the evaluation of earlier decades.

1) Alongside the epochal year of 1990, the significance of which as a turning point in world history is no longer in doubt, the year 1995 has also been considered as a historic point of transition, though of a more symbolic character. The date 1995 can be seen as the starting-point of the worldwide spread of the internet, which became established in Western Europe at that time, and thus it marks the end of the analogue era and the beginning of the digital age. To contemporaries, this seemed a provocative and ironic mode of classification, but the two subsequent decades have shown that it is perhaps not completely off the wall. The digital revolution has changed economic life more powerfully than almost any other innovation since the time of advanced industrialisation, it has also expanded communications, relativised distances and speeds, and not least moulded the professional and private lives of large parts of the human race. But it has also brought with it new dangers, unrecognised until now. The new means of communication make it possible to shift tremendous financial resources from one stock exchange (or financial platform) to another, thereby unleashing unforeseen economic cataclysms affecting whole industries, whole nations or even the whole world. At the same time, anyone who owns a mobile phone or a computer can now be put under investigation. This could already be done in earlier times through tapping telephones, but it has now become possible to establish profiles of people's lives, with all their preferences and peculiarities, to trace their movements, to investigate their financial situation and their state of health, and to spy on their political inclinations and their behaviour as consumers, and all of these actions can be carried on as long as necessary and to whatever extent is necessary. As had happened so often before, the new possibilities offered by technological innovation have thrown open the doors to misuse, either by the state or by international companies, in a manner and to an extent that could not have even been imagined previously. However one evaluates the effects of the digital revolution, the issue at stake in locating it historically is whether it has the magnitude of a third or fourth industrial revolution and whether the beginning of the digital age should be viewed as the start of a new historical epoch. No definite judgement can be made on this from our present standpoint. But it cannot be ruled out.[36]

2) The 1998 change of government has also been judged to be a turning point of historical significance, in Germany at least, because it marked the replacement of the 'Kohl generation' by people born in the 1940s, in other words, the replacement of the 'forty-fivers' by the 'sixty-eighters'. With this, the first post-war generation came to power, after a delay of ten years caused by reunification. This was the first generation which had not consciously experienced National Socialism, and also the first, at least in the West, whose economic experience

has been limited to growth and nothing else. In addition, the new generation represented a political current which maintained a critical distance from German society's emphasis on reconstruction and industrial progress. The year 1998 could therefore be seen both as a symbol of the reconciliation of the protest generation with liberal democracy and the social capitalism of the Federal Republic and as a starting point for the transformation of those characteristics. Some of the reforms of the red–green government were important milestones; but did they really have epoch-making significance? The political system of the Federal Republic continued to be marked by continuity, especially as the many links that existed between the federal republic and its constituent states, and between the opposition and the government, generally worked against abrupt changes in policy.

Perhaps it was rather Germany's participation in the Kosovo War which was of long-term significance, even though this episode faded from memory astonishingly quickly. It was Germany's first military engagement since 1945, it was carried out without a Security Council mandate and the country was not defending itself against hostile attack. This was an indication of how much Germany's position in the world had changed since 1990, and it also showed that Germany's politicians possessed neither a plan nor a clear objective in foreign policy. On the other hand, Germany's reserved attitude to subsequent military conflicts—particularly over Iraq in 2002–3, but also over Afghanistan and later over the question of intervention in Libya—made it clear that participation in the war against Serbia in 1999 was viewed by German politicians, whether in government or in opposition, as a special case which should not be allowed to prejudice any decisions about later, more extensive military operations. This makes it less plausible to maintain that intervention in the Kosovo conflict marked a watershed of great significance. Whether that will continue to be the case in ten or twenty years' time is an open question.

3) The abrupt fall from grace of the veteran German Chancellor Helmut Kohl has also been described as 'historic'. In autumn 1999, it became known that in spite of the Flick scandal, which continued from 1981 to 1987, the practice of accepting illegal party donations had not come to an end, at least not in the Union. For years the CDU and in particular its leader had accepted undeclared donations of millions of Deutschmarks from industry, using the money to finance the party's election campaigns. The Union had not only received numerous illegal donations; it had also deposited them in secret bank accounts, some of them set up in Switzerland and cynically camouflaged as 'Jewish Bequests'. These cases were particularly controversial because Kohl refused to reveal the names of the donors, thus placing his duty to protect their confidentiality above his legal obligations. This turned the scandal into a political firestorm. Kohl lost his position as 'honorary president' of the CDU, and his

successor as party leader, Wolfgang Schäuble, also finally had to resign, while the previous party treasurer Leisler Kiep and the former Minister of the Interior Manfred Kanther were both convicted and given suspended sentences. The party itself had to forfeit €21 million which had been earmarked for the reimbursement of electoral expenses.

This scandal was interpreted by contemporary observers as a farewell to the old CDU, because the 'Kohl system', which had functioned for more than twenty years thanks to its network of personal connections and dependencies, had now led to the biggest crisis in the history of the party, and could not be continued any longer. Some people saw in this a parallel with the fate of the Christian Democratic Party in Italy, which had disintegrated in 1994 after a corruption affair involving many top party representatives, thereby plunging the Italian system of government into a severe crisis.[37] But it is clear, in retrospect, that it was probably less the fall of Kohl that marked a break in continuity than the assumption of the party leadership in 2000 by Angela Merkel (and her election as Chancellor five years later). For a divorced Protestant female physicist from the GDR, a politician who had not emerged from the power groups and patronage networks of the old Union, to become Federal Chancellor, half a century after Adenauer had taken office, was a real watershed. It symbolised three things: the advancing integration of the East Germans into the Federal Republic, which had until then been very much dominated by Westerners, a profound change in the role of women in state and society, and the end of the sharp ideological division between the two political camps of the Union and the SPD. In the Grand Coalition which lasted until 2009, and then in her subsequent coalition with the FDP, Chancellor Merkel practised a policy which was increasingly seen as social democratic, and she won four successive Bundestag elections by adopting the attitude of a matter-of-fact politician who dealt with matters 'as they came up' and without political preconceptions. There was a tremendous difference between this and the ideological confrontation seen twenty-five years earlier in the election contest of 1980 between Schmidt and Strauß, which was fought out under the slogan 'freedom or socialism'. The change from Kohl to Merkel will perhaps eventually be seen as the end of the phase of ideologically determined politics and the beginning of 'post-democracy', in which, as some sociologists have predicted, a politics which is guided by practical needs and is oriented towards the good of the community will only assign to the democratic process the purely instrumental function of guaranteeing legitimacy.[38]

4) On 11 September 2001 approximately 3,000 people were killed in the USA by the biggest terrorist attack that had yet been committed. Nineteen terrorists hijacked four passenger aircraft and forced two to crash into the World Trade Center in New York. The third was forced to hit the Pentagon in Washington. The fourth was also sent towards Washington but came down in Pennsylvania

as a result of passenger action. The perpetrators were affiliated to a radical Islamist network built up by the Saudi businessman Osama bin Laden, who was living at the time in Afghanistan. The group justified its action by referring to the American war on Iraq in 1991, America's support for Israel and the continuing exploitation and colonisation of the Muslim world. The USA initially reacted with an attack on Afghanistan, which was accepted as legitimate by the United Nations, because Afghanistan had given refuge to bin Laden and his supporters. It then took a further step by attacking Iraq, although the charges brought against the Iraqi dictator, Saddam Hussein, namely that he was cooperating with Al Qaida and that he possessed weapons of mass destruction, were extremely debatable (and were later proved to be false). In February 2003, the UN Security Council refused to support a US resolution calling for war against Iraq. Germany, France, Russia and China were all opposed to the war. Despite this, the USA then attacked Iraq, with the support of a small number of countries, including Italy and the United Kingdom. Saddam Hussein was overthrown, and Iraq was occupied by the USA. Prisoners who were suspected of being connected with the terrorists were tortured and imprisoned without trial for many years in the US naval base of Guantanamo Bay, in Cuba.

Contemporaries were strongly of the opinion that the 11 September 2001 attacks marked a turning-point in world history. It is true that there had already been serious attacks by Islamist terrorists on American installations, but the sheer scale of the 9/11 attacks gave them a much greater significance. The terrorist attacks and the reaction of the Americans can be seen as a historical watershed in the sense that they confirmed the existence of a new line of global conflict, indications of which had already been present since the Islamic revolution of 1979 in Iran. In view of this, contemporaries sometimes reached the conclusion that the end of the Cold War conflict had been followed by the emergence of a new worldwide political antagonism.[39]

There are, however, some objections to be made against this interpretation of the events. The 9/11 attacks and the assertion that Saddam Hussein possessed weapons of mass destruction (a claim which was not supported by any evidence) provided only a makeshift justification for the American attack on Iraq. What this attack indicated was that the USA had decided to use the situation as an opportunity to carry out long-prepared military and diplomatic plans, in particular the plan to overthrow hostile regimes in the Middle East and Central Asia. This was nothing new, but marked rather a hardening of the endeavour pursued by the USA since the 1980s, and more strongly apparent since 1990, to extend and stabilise its position as the sole global superpower.

Al Qaida's attacks were also not a new historical development, but rather an expression of the worsening antagonism between the rich world of the North and the poor world of the South, which was a delayed effect of colonialism and the economic dominance of the industrialised countries. The USA and the Western countries were not the only targets of Islamist terrorists. Russia was also exposed to attacks from fighters who hailed from the Muslim lands of the Caucasus colonised by the Tsarist Empire in the nineteenth century. Another reason to doubt whether the conflict of the industrialised countries with Islamist terrorists should be understood as a new kind of worldwide political antagonism was that a fight pitting large and powerful states against small terrorist groups which were prepared to stop at nothing did not have the significance of a global confrontation. However, if one views these conflicts from a more long-term perspective as the inheritance of colonialism and imperialism, such an interpretation is entirely plausible.

5) On 1 January 2002 a single currency, called the euro, was introduced in twelve European states, after it had already functioned behind the scenes since 1999 as an accounting unit. It replaced the existing national currencies at a fixed rate of exchange. The Deutschmark was one of them. Many Germans welcomed the measure, but just as many deplored the loss of economic independence it entailed. The resulting rise in prices met with criticism, and although this was not confirmed by the statistics and was more a feeling than a true reflection of reality, the expression '*Teuro*', a combination of the term *euro* with the German word for 'expensive', *teuer*, took root: it was the buzzword of 2002. The choice of 2002 as the end of the history of Germany in the twentieth century is associated with the grand European narrative of the past and the optimistic prognosis of the future which Helmut Kohl never tired of emphasising: after centuries of war, which reached their terrible culmination between 1914 and 1945, and pushed humanity to the verge of extinction, the introduction of a common European currency forty-five years after the Rome treaties marked an irrevocable step towards European unification. By having a common currency, the European states had become so strongly associated together and so interwoven that a return to the war-ravaged past was out of the question. Thus a century of nationalist disruption and war would be followed after 1 January 2002 by an era of European cooperation and peace.

This narrative is certainly persuasive, in spite of the contradictions and obstacles which bedevilled the euro's origins, and it may well be that this date of 2002 will come to be regarded as more epoch-making than the others. Even so, the years that followed the currency's introduction also revealed financial and economic dangers which had already been tested out in theory, but whose full extent only became apparent when the euro and possibly the whole European unification project were pushed to the brink of collapse in the post-2008 crisis. A failure of the euro continues to be a possibility, and without doubt such an event would mark just as epochal a turning point as its opposite, the continuing success of the currency.

This applies particularly to Germany, whose increasing economic strength after the crises of the 1990s has confirmed and extended the country's dominant role in Europe in a manner which is emphatic, but also dangerous. Anxieties about a 'new German question' have surfaced. The fear is that Germany's economic supremacy over the continent may bring all other European states into a position of dependency, which might spill over into the political sphere. But most European governments consider that this is likely to be counteracted by the structures of the European Union, which are directed towards securing compromise and power sharing. In this case, even more than in others, it is clear that the historical significance of an event can only be recognised from a distance.

6) In his government declaration of 14 March 2003, Chancellor Schröder presented a reform programme, under the title 'Agenda 2010', which envisaged the most radical social and labour market reforms in the history of the Federal Republic. This programme was Schröder's reaction to the changes in the economic and social structure of Germany which had become increasingly apparent since the 1970s. The impact of these changes had already been discussed for decades, but no substantial reforms had ever emerged. Now, however, the 'New Economy' had collapsed and the consequences of the terror attack of 11 September 2001 had had a severe impact on the German economy. The economic data were dire: 4 million people were unemployed (more than 5 million in actual fact), economic growth was less than 0.5 per cent over the year and share values were falling rapidly. All these things indicated a need for immediate action. Schröder's 'Agenda 2010' programme laid out a wealth of measures which involved massive benefit cuts and far-reaching interventions into the existing structures of the social welfare system: entitlement to unemployment money was to be cut down from thirty-two months to twelve, unemployment assistance and social security benefits were to be combined together, the rules protecting workers against dismissal were to be made less stringent, the pensionable age was to be raised, cutbacks were to be made in health provision, and temporary employment and part-time work were to be increased—taken together these measures amounted to a 'paradigm shift in the German welfare state'.[40] With this, the red–green government proposed to bring about what had been regarded as unavoidable by many people since, at the latest, the crisis of 1980–2: the end of the social welfare policy of classical industrial society. The 'Agenda 2010' reforms did in fact contribute markedly to the improvement of the German economy in the ten years that followed. The number of new jobs increased dramatically, and there was a marked fall in unemployment. On the other hand, the policy also led to a further increase in social inequality and created a mass army of the 'insecure', in other words, people who were either not employed permanently or had to accept very bad employment conditions.[41]

Politically, too, 'Agenda 2010' had considerable consequences. The trade unions and the left wing of the SPD opposed the Chancellor's policies, the SPD lost one Diet election after another, and it finally also lost the Bundestag elections, which had been brought forward to 2005. It suffered considerable losses in its former working-class strongholds. The PDS reacted to the new policies by uniting with the West German socialist milieu to form the party called 'The Left', under the former SPD chair Oskar Lafontaine, which became a stable force to the Left of the SPD, in both the east and the west of the country. Just as in the cases of New Labour in Great Britain and the Social Democratic parties of the Scandinavian countries, the SPD lost its traditional function as a workers' party, without appearing to have any demonstrably new role.

To bring the twentieth century to a close with 'Agenda 2010' is to imply that the chief phenomena of the epoch were the long-term changes in industrial society. These can be summed up as the spread of modern industrial society in the twenty-five years before the First World War, followed by the search for new systems of social organisation, which led after the war to the creation of radical alternatives to the liberal model. Then, after the catastrophic events of the Second World War, a model of capitalism mitigated by social policy and managed by the state, which was explicitly differentiated from both National Socialism and communism, emerged in most of the countries of Western Europe. It reached its zenith with the reforms of the 1960s and 1970s along with the delusions of that time about the ability of the planning system to solve all problems, but after that, it entered on a long-lasting crisis which was associated with the decline of heavy industry. 'Agenda 2010' marked the culmination of the crisis, because by then the traditional social model had become unaffordable, and it presented an obstacle to the dynamic further development of the globalised economy. Of course, the injustices bound up with the 'Agenda 2010' reforms soon created a fresh need for corrective measures. But to point this out tends to militate against the ostentatiously asserted historical significance of Agenda 2010, because if we take a broader perspective, the policy simply appears as another version of the repeated attempts that have been made to find a compromise between economic dynamism and social justice. It does have historical significance in another sense, however, because it cost the SPD the chancellorship and reduced it to a party stuck at the 25 per cent level without any prospect of achieving majority support. This leads to a worrying, though not entirely new, conclusion: anyone who pushes through necessary, but unpopular and drastic social reforms in a democracy must count on being voted out of office.

7) In summer 2007, a crisis started in the US real estate market. Within a few months this had turned into the biggest financial crisis of the post-war decades. Only the Great Depression of 1929–32 had comparable worldwide

consequences. It was set off by a number of factors, both short-term and long-term. From the time of President Reagan onwards, US economic policy had led to the accumulation of an immense amount of capital in the hands of the upper income groups. These funds were now in search of profitable investment opportunities. At the same time, in America as in Europe, the financial markets had been deregulated and credit transactions had largely been liberalised. Many banks responded to this by creating new financial products, allowing them to circumvent the rules governing banking activities, and to engage, for instance, in equity dealing and risk diversification.

During the same period, the income of Americans who were less well-off was stagnating or falling. Many of them reacted by taking out loans to bolster their living standards. After the crisis of the 'New Economy' in 2000, the US Federal Reserve attempted to stimulate business activity by holding down interest rates. In addition, the acquisition of private residential property was encouraged by the politicians, to help stimulate the sluggish economic environment. The banks now offered increased mortgages to people in the lower and middle income groups, under favourable conditions, but at flexible interest rates, so that the risks were borne entirely by borrowers. These borrowers were confident that constantly rising property prices would in a sense take the burden of debt off their shoulders. The banks in turn packaged these risky credits together in opaque financial instruments which they claimed would yield high returns, and they then sold them to investors in the USA and Europe, not least to European banks, which wanted to turn a quick profit.

From the end of 2005 onwards, however, the business climate began to weaken in the USA, and in addition the Federal Reserve raised its key rate of interest. As a result, many low-income US citizens were no longer able to meet their mortgage obligations. This soon led to heavy selling and a rapid fall in house prices. This in turn caused a fall in the amount of money held in deposit in banks and investment funds, leading to the insolvency of at first one or two banks, and then more and more of them. In order to put a stop to the downward trend of the economy, the US government decided to prevent many banks from going bankrupt by injecting large amounts of taxpayers' money, thereby in effect nationalising them. But in September 2008, after the government had refused to do the same in the case of the investment bank Lehman Brothers, the avalanche was set in motion. Banks stopped giving each other credit, the number of bankruptcies rose sharply and the crisis spread from the financial sector to what was now called 'the real economy'. The US financial crisis quickly spread out to the rest of the world. Many European banks, German banks included, were directly pulled into the downward spiral by their involvement in the American mortgage market. In addition to this there was the bursting of the Spanish housing bubble, which had come into existence in a similar manner to the American one. The governments of Europe now also found themselves compelled to support their banks with enormous state subsidies, because the consequences of a collapse of those institutions for the real economy would have been incalculable. After autumn 2008, the European economy entered into a severe recession. By autumn 2009, industrial production in the eurozone had fallen by some 20 per cent; this was the same fall as the one registered in 1930 during the world economic crisis. The proportion of people unemployed in the European Union reached almost 10 per cent in 2009, and in the summer of that year the IMF estimated the level of worldwide losses as a result of the financial crisis at $12 trillion.[42]

By 2010, state assistance to the value of €1.6 trillion had been spent in the countries of the EU to rescue the banks, and in addition to this, considerable extra amounts of money were spent by governments to stimulate their economies. This meant an immense increase in government debt. In the Federal Republic alone, public budget deficits rose between 2008 and 2010 by almost 10 per cent. The increase in debt put the economically weaker members of the EU into considerable difficulty. This was particularly true for countries such as Greece, Spain, Portugal, Ireland and Italy, which had all entered the eurozone. They could no longer solve their payment problems by devaluing their national currency, they were rated as 'risk countries' because of their indebtedness, and they could therefore only obtain credit at high rates of interest. Accordingly, many of them teetered on the edge of bankruptcy. To prevent the economic collapse of these states, above all Greece, the wealthier members of the eurozone organised a guarantee scheme, which provided countries in difficulty with credit at generous rates of interest, on condition that they modernised their economies and restored their creditworthiness partly by reforming their economic and social institutions, but more particularly by drastically reducing government expenditure.

The post-2007 financial crisis thus developed seamlessly into a world economic crisis and a debt crisis for the eurozone countries. It confirmed all the pessimistic predictions made at the time about the effects of financial deregulation, an unequal distribution of income and an economic strategy directed predominantly or exclusively towards increasing the profits of investors. What the bursting of the 'dotcom bubble' in 2001 had suggested was now repeated on a much larger scale. But now the issues at stake were no longer just the collapse of dubious internet firms and the losses suffered by private investors. The crisis impoverished whole countries, made governments insolvent and dramatically increased the number of people suffering from starvation throughout the world. This rose by 100 million during the crisis, to a total of one billion human beings. In November 2008, *Der Spiegel* summarised the reasons for the crisis as follows:

> The unregulated international flow of money and the increase in the quantity of money produced by spiralling credit over the past decade have established a form of capitalism which is driven by the financial market and no longer founded on goods, commodities and trade. This constantly creates, and has to create, new speculative bubbles. The financial market has replaced the classical economy as the actual market: the value of financial investments has now become three times as great as the value of all the goods and services sold throughout the world. And it is this excess of capital which again and again sets off new booms and bubbles.[43]

The momentum of a financial capitalism largely emancipated from political shackles and ties had reached a point at which a crisis entailed catastrophic consequences not just for individual firms and national economies but for the world as a whole. At the moment of catastrophe the losses of private enterprise were shifted onto the shoulders of the state because the banks were 'of systemic importance', hence too big for governments to accept the consequences of their collapse. This policy not only contradicted all the criteria of fairness, but also prepared the ground for a repetition of the unrestrained high-risk transactions that had caused the crisis. These could now happen at any time, because the state had shown its readiness to step into the breach if the need arose.

Hence, if one considers the opening scene of the twenty-first century to be a financial crisis, stretching from the dotcom crisis of 2001 to the banking crisis of 2008 and then to the post-2010 euro crisis, this gives rise to a depressing prognosis. On this view, the society which is based on a liberal capitalism cushioned by social policy, and which appeared to have emerged victorious from the history of the twentieth century, after the collapse of radical alternatives on the Left and the Right, is not capable of reining in its own dynamism. The forecast which emerges is entirely pessimistic, especially as it has been seen that economists, politicians and theorists were unprepared to meet the crisis because experience had provided no way of analysing the possible effects of the rise of a deregulated financial capitalism with a global sphere of action.

Thus the hazards confronting Germany in the future will not emerge from the internal tensions and contradictions of the country itself, as was the case a hundred years ago, although the pogroms against foreigners of the 1990s have given rise to the perturbed inquiry as to whether the liberal and democratic basis of German society is firm enough to ward off long-run tendencies towards xenophobia. Even so, the biggest challenges seem rather to be presented by the international constellations of which Germany is an integral part: unrestrained financial capitalism, which after the exhaustion of all alternatives has revealed self-destructive aspects; the continuing vigour of the North–South conflict, the dimensions of which it is impossible to foresee; the contradictions of a Europe in economic disequilibrium, dangerously dominated by Germany; and the problems arising from the likelihood that the USA as the sole world power will be unable to cope with the strain of trying to strike a balance between the divergent interests of old and new Great Powers by itself and without a well-balanced security system.

Notwithstanding these threats, most Germans have a positive attitude towards life in the second decade of the new century. There is a feeling of security and optimism about the future. Experience since 1945, and also since 1990, has given some justification for this positive view of the future. After the catastrophes of the first half of the twentieth century, who could have predicted such an outcome? Nevertheless, the way the Germans are viewed will long continue to be linked with the violent excesses of the Second World War and the policy of mass annihilation, because, as has been shown earlier, this story refuses to fade away. But Germany's recovery to the position of a rich and respected democratic country is to be ascribed in no less a degree to its readiness to confront these crimes than it is to its economic success. In addition, its success in creating stable democratic institutions, reshaping capitalism after 1945 into a social market economy, reaching a settlement with the countries of the east, liberalising people's way of life and mode of behaviour and accepting the culture of modernity all form part of the experiences which have justified optimism about the future. The same can be said of the way the difficult economic, social and cultural consequences of reunification have been handled, although this process is still not entirely complete.

It would be wrong, when drawing a balance of the twentieth century for Germany, to conclude that all periods have experienced an equal amount of fortune and misfortune. That would be to misjudge the developments that have occurred since 1945 and 1990, and also to ignore the experience of the people who have lived and continue to live in this country. But the possibility cannot be excluded, even so, that ultimately the dangers that emerge from this fortunate trend of development will prove to be just as threatening as the ones that have been overcome.

# List of Abbreviations

AA *Auswärtiges Amt* (Foreign Office)
ABM *Arbeitsbeschaffungsmaßnahmen* (Job Creation Schemes)
ACDP *Archiv für Christlich-Demokratische Politik* (Archive for Christian Democratic Politics)
ACTORD Activation Order
ADAC *Allgemeiner Deutscher Automobil-Club* (General German Automobile Club)
*ADAP* *Akten zur deutschen auswärtigen Politik* (Documents on German Foreign Policy)
*AdR* *Akten der Reichskanzlei* (Documents of the Reich Chancellery)
AEG *Allgemeine Elektrizitätsgesellschaft* (General Electricity Company)
*AfS* *Archiv für Sozialgeschichte* (Archives of Social History)
*AHR* American Historical Review
AOK *Armee-Oberkommando* (Supreme Command of the Army)
APO *Außerparlamentarische Opposition* (Extra-Parliamentary Opposition)
*APuZ* *Aus Politik und Zeitgeschichte* (On Politics and Contemporary History)
ARD *Arbeitsgemeinschaft der öffentlich-rechtlichen Rundfunkanstalten der Bundesrepublik Deutschland* (Consortium of Public Broadcasters of the Federal Republic of Germany
AstA *Allgemeiner Studentenausschuß* (General Students' Committee)
BA *Bundesarchiv* (Federal Archives)
BAföG *Bundesausbildungsförderungsgesetz* (Federal Training Assistance Act)
BA-MA *Bundesarchiv-Militärarchiv* (Federal Archives, Military Department)
*Bd.* *Band* (Volume)
*BGBl* *Bundesgesetzblatt* (Federal Law Gazette)
BHE *Bund der Heimatvertriebenen und Entrechteten* (League of Expellees andPeople Deprived of their Rights)
BMWF *Bundesministerium fur Wissenschaft und Forschung* (Federal Ministry of Science and Research)
BND *Bundesnachrichtendienst* (Federal Intelligence Service)
BverfG *Bundesverfassungsgericht* (Federal Constitutional Court)
BVP *Bayerische Volkspartei* (Bavarian People's Party)

| | |
|---|---|
| CARE | 'Cooperative for American Remittances to Europe' (name of private US relief organisation between 1945 and 1953) |
| CDU | *Christlich Demokratische Union* (Christian Democratic Union) |
| CMEA | Council of Mutual Economic Aid |
| CPC | Communist Party of Czechoslovakia |
| CSCE | Conference on Security and Cooperation in Europe |
| CSSD | *Chef der Sicherheitspolizei und des SD* (Head of the Security Police and the Security Service) |
| CSU | *Christlich Soziale Union* (Christian Social Union) |
| *DA* | *Deutschland Archiv* (Germany Archive) |
| *DBFP* | *Documents on British Foreign Policy 1919–1939* |
| DDP | *Deutsche Demokratische Partei* (German Democratic Party) |
| DDR | *Deutsche Demokratische Republik* (German Democratic Republic) |
| DGB | *Deutscher Gewerkschaftsbund* (German Trade Union Confederation) |
| *DGFP* | *Documents on German Foreign Policy 1918–1945* |
| DINTA | *Deutsches Institut für technische Arbeitsschulung* (German Institute for Technical Work Training) |
| DKP | *Deutsche Kommunistische Partei* (German Communist Party) |
| DM | *Deutschmark* (German Mark) |
| DNVP | *Deutschnationale Volkspartei* (German National People's Party) |
| Doc. | Document |
| DP | *Deutsche Partei* (German Party) |
| DRP | *Deutsche Reichspartei* (German Reich Party) |
| *DRZW* | *Das Deutsche Reich und der Zweite Weltkrieg* (The German Reich and the Second World War) |
| DVP | *Deutsche Volkspartei* (German People's Party) |
| EC | European Community |
| ECSC | European Coal and Steel Community |
| ECU | European Currency Unit |
| EDC | European Defence Community |
| EDP | Electronic Data Processing |
| EEC | European Economic Community |
| *EHR* | English Historical Review |
| EMNID | *Erforschung der öffentlichen Meinung, Marktforschung und Meinungsforschung, Nachrichten, Informationen, Dienstleistungen* (Investigation of Public Opinion, Market and Opinion Research, Information, Services) |
| EMS | European Monetary System |
| EPC | European Political Cooperation |
| ERP | European Recovery Programme |

ESS Economic System of Socialism
EWG *Europäische Wirtschaftsgemeinschaft* (European Economic Community)
EU European Union
*FAZ* *Frankfurter Allgemeine Zeitung*
FDGB *Freier Deutsche Gewerkschaftsbund* (Federation of Free German Trade Unions)
FDJ *Freie Deutsche Jugend* (Free German Youth)
FDP *Freie Demokratische Partei Deutschlands* (Free Democratic Party of Germany)
*FR* *Frankfurter Rundschau*
FRG Federal Republic of Germany
*FRUS* Foreign Relations of the United States
GATT General Agreement on Tariffs and Trade
GDP Gross Domestic Product
GDR German Democratic Republic
*Gestapo* *Geheime Staatspolizei* (Secret State Police)
*GG* *Geschichte und Gesellschaft* (History and Society)
GG *Grundgesetz* (Basic Law)
GHH *Gutehoffnungshütte* (large mining, smelting and engineering company)
GNP Gross National Product
GPU *Gosudarstvennoe Politicheskoe Upravlenie* (State Political Administration)
*GSD* *Geschichte der Sozialpolitik in Deutschland seit 1945* (History of Social Policy in Germany since 1945)
GST *Gesellschaft für Sport und Technik* (Society for Sport and Technology)
*GSWW* Germany and the Second World War
GULAG *Glavnoe Upravlenie Lagereï* (Main Administration of Labour Camps)
*GWU* *Geschichte in Wissenschaft und Unterricht* (History in Scholarship and Education)
HIAG *Hilfsgemeinschaft auf Gegenseitigkeit der ehemaligen Angehörigen der Waffen- SS* (Mutual Aid Association of Former Members of the Waffen-SS)
HJ *Hitlerjugend* (Hitler Youth)
HO *Handelsorganisation* (Trading Organisation)
HstAD *Hessisches Staatsarchiv Düsseldorf* (Hessian State Archive, Düsseldorf)
*HZ* *Historische Zeitschrift* (Historical Journal)

IAR International Authority for the Ruhr
IfZ *Institut für Zeitgeschichte* (Institute of Contemporary History)
IM *Inoffizieller Mitarbeiter* (Unofficial Collaborator)
IMF International Monetary Fund
IMT International Military Tribunal (Nuremberg)
INF Intermediate-Range Nuclear Forces
IT Information Technology
*JbWG* *Jahrbuch für Wirtschaftsgeschichte* (Economic History Yearbook)
JCC Jewish Claims Conference
*JMEH* Journal of Modern European History
KGB *Komitet Gosudarstvennoi Bezopasnosti* (State Security Committee)
KPD *Kommunistische Partei Deutschlands* (Communist Party of Germany)
KSZE *Konferenz fur Sicherheit und Zusammenarbeit in Europa* (Conference on Security and Cooperation in Europe)
KZ *Konzentrationslager* (Concentration Camp)
LDP *Liberal-Demokratische Partei* (Liberal Democratic Party)
LDPD *Liberal-Demokratische Partei Deutschlands* (Liberal Democratic Party of Germany)
LPG *Landwirtschaftliche Produktionsgenossenschaft* (Agricultural Producer Cooperative)
MBF *Militärbefehlshaber Frankreich* (Military Commander, France)
MCA Maximum Credible Accident
MfS *Ministerium für Staatssicherheit* (Ministry for State Security)
*MGM* *Militärgeschichtliche Mitteilungen* (Communications about Military History)
MSPD *Mehrheitssozialdemokratische Partei Deutschlands* (Majority Social Democratic Party of Germany)
MTU *Motoren- und Turbinen-Union* (Engine and Turbine Union)
NATO North Atlantic Treaty Organisation
NES New Economic System
NKVD *Narodnyi Komissariat Vnutrennikh Del* (People's Commissariat for Internal Affairs)
NPD *Nationaldemokratische Partei Deutschlands* National Democratic Party of Germany)
NS *Nationalsozialistisch* (National Socialist)
NSDAP *Nationalsozialistische Deutsche Arbeiterpartei* (National Socialist German Workers' Party)
NSV *Nationalsozialistische Volkswohlfahrt* (National Socialist Public Welfare)

| | |
|---|---|
| NSW | *Nichtsozialistisches Wirtschaftsgebiet* (Non-Socialist Economic Area) |
| OC | Organisation Consul |
| ÖDP | *Ökologisch-Demokratische Partei* (Ecological Democratic Party) |
| OECD | Organisation for Economic Co-operation and Development |
| OEEC | Organisation for European Economic Co-operation |
| OHL | *Oberste Heeresleitung* (Army High Command) |
| OKW | *Oberkommando der Wehrmacht* (High Command of the Armed Forces) |
| OLG | *Oberlandesgericht* (Higher Regional Court) |
| OMGUS | Office of Military Government, United States |
| OPEC | Organisation of Petroleum Exporting Countries |
| OSS | Office of Strategic Services (US secret service) |
| PAA | *Politisches Archiv des Auswärtigen Amts* (Policy Archives of the Foreign Office) |
| PDS | *Partei des Demokratischen Sozialismus* (Party of Democratic Socialism) |
| PFLP | Popular Front for the Liberation of Palestine |
| RAD | *Reichsarbeitsdienst* (Reich Labour Service) |
| RAF | *Rote Armee Fraktion* (Red Army Faction) |
| RFSS | *Reichsführer SS* (Reich Leader of the SS) |
| *RGBl* | *Reichsgesetzblatt* (Reich Law Gazette) |
| RIAS | *Rundfunk im amerikanischen Sektor* (Radio in the American Sector) |
| RKF | *Reichskommissar für die Festigung deutschen Volkstums* (Reich Commissioner for Strengthening the German Race) |
| RKPA | *Reichskriminalpolizeiamt* (Reich Criminal Police Office) |
| RM | *Reichsmark* (Reich Mark, 1924–48) |
| RSHA | *Reichssicherheitshauptamt* (Reich Security Main Office) |
| RuSHA | *Rasse- und Siedlungshauptamt* (Main Office for Race and Settlement) |
| RWE | *Rheinisch-Westfälisches Elektrizitätswerk AG* (Rhineland-Westphalia Electric Power Company) |
| RWI | *Rheinisch-Westfälisches Institut für Wirtschaftsforschung* (Rhineland- Westphalia Institute for Economic Research) |
| SA | *Sturmabteilung* (Storm Division) |
| SAG | *Sowjetische Aktiengesellschaft* (Soviet Joint-Stock Company) |
| SALT | Strategic Arms Limitation Talks |
| SAPD | *Sozialistische Arbeiterpartei Deutschlands* (Socialist Workers' Party of Germany) |
| SBZ | *Sowjetische Besetzte Zone* (Soviet-Occupied Zone) |

| | |
|---|---|
| SCC | Soviet Control Commission |
| SD | *Sicherheitsdienst* (Security Service) |
| SDP | *Sozialdemokratische Partei* (Social Democratic Party) |
| SDS | *Sozialistischer Deutscher Studentenbund* (Socialist German Student Federation) |
| SEA | Single European Act |
| SED | *Sozialistische Einheitspartei Deutschlands* (Socialist Unity Party of Germany) |
| SHAEF | Supreme Headquarters, Allied Expeditionary Force |
| SMAD | *Sowjetische Militäradministration in Deutschland* (Soviet Military Administration in Germany) |
| Sopade | *Sozialdemokratische Partei Deutschland, Exil Vorstand der SPD* (Social Democratic Party, Germany, Leadership of the SPD in Exile) |
| SPD | *Sozialdemokratische Partei Deutschlands* (Social Democratic Party of Germany) |
| SPK | *Staatliche Plankommission* (State Planning Commission) |
| SRP | *Sozialistische Reichspartei* (Socialist Reich Party) |
| SS | *Schutzstaffel* (Protection Squad) |
| Stasi | *Staatssicherheitsdienst* (State Security Service of the GDR) |
| *SZ* | *Süddeutsche Zeitung* |
| *taz.* | *Die Tageszeitung* (The Daily Newspaper, Berlin) |
| UÇK | *Ushtria Çlirimtare e Kosovës* (Kosovo Liberation Army) |
| UfA | *Universum Film A.G.* (Universe Film Company) |
| UNCTAD | United Nations Conference on Trade and Development |
| UNEP | United Nations Environment Programme |
| UNO | United Nations Organisation |
| USA | United States of America |
| USPD | *Unabhängige Sozialdemokratische Partei Deutschlands* (Independent Social Democratic Party of Germany) |
| USSR | Union of Soviet Socialist Republics |
| VDA | *Verein für das Deutschtum im Ausland* (Association for Germanism Abroad) |
| VEBA | *Vereinigte Elekrizitäts- und Bergwerks AG* (United Electricity and Mining Company Limited) |
| VEJ | *Die Verfolgung und Ermordung der europäischen Juden durch dasnationalsozialistische Deutschland, 1933–1945* (National Socialist Germany's Persecution and Murder of the European Jews, 1933–1945) |
| *VfZ* | *Vierteljahrshefte für Zeitgeschichte* (Quarterly Journal of Contemporary History) |

VIAG *Vereinigte Industrieunternehmens AG* (United Industrial Enterprise Company Limited)
*VM* *Valutamark* (Foreign Exchange Mark)
*VSWG* *Vierteljahresschrift für Wirtschafts- und Sozialgeschichte* (Quarterly Journal of Economic and Social History)
VVB *Vereinigung Volkseigener Betriebe* (Association of Nationally Owned Enterprises)
WAV *Wirtschaftliche Aufbauvereinigung* (Economic Reconstruction Union)
WFE World Federation of Exchanges
WiRüAmt *Wehrwirtschafts- und Rüstungsamt im OKW* (Wehrmacht Office for Military Economics and Armaments)
WP *Wahlperiode* (Electoral Term)
WTO World Trade Organization
WVHA *Wirtschafts- und Verwaltungsamt* (Head Office for Business and Administration)
*ZAA* *Zeitschrift für Agrargeschichte und Agrarsoziologie* (Journal of Agricultural History and Sociology)
ZAG *Zentralarbeitsgemeinschaft* (Central Association for Cooperation between Industrial and Commercial Employers and Employees)
ZDF *Zweites Deutsches Fernsehen* (Second German Television Channel)
*ZfG* *Zeitschrift für Geschichtswissenschaft* (Journal of Historical Studies)
ZStL *Zentrale Stelle der Landesjustizverwaltungen zur Aufklärung nationalsozialistischer Verbrechen, Ludwigsburg* (Central Office of Judicial Administration for the Investigation of National Socialist Crimes)

# Notes

## Chapter 1

1. Helfferich, *Deutschlands Volkswohlstand 1888–1913*, pp. 6 and 123–5. In 1915 Helfferich was appointed State Secretary of the Imperial Treasury (*Reichsschatzamt*) and thereby became responsible for managing Germany's wartime finances. A year later he became Secretary of State of the Interior and Vice Chancellor, taking over the whole of the economic direction of the war. After the defeat he turned away from liberalism and joined the German National People's Party (DNVP), becoming a radical opponent of the Weimar Republic. See Williamson, *Karl Helfferich*.
2. Conrad, *Globalisation*, pp. 24–51; David Blackbourn, 'Das Kaiserreich transnational. Eine Skizze', in Conrad and Osterhammel, eds., *Das Kaiserreich Transnational*, pp. 302–24; Torp, *Die Herausforderung der Globalisierung*, pp. 27–50.
3. For the following paragraphs, see Fisch, *Europa*, pp. 237ff.; Wehler, *Gesellschaftsgeschichte*, vol. 3, pp. 547–699; Wolfram Fischer, 'Wirtschaft und Gesellschaft Europas 1850–1914', in Wolfram Fischer, ed., *Europäische Wirtschafts- und Sozialgeschichte*, pp. 1–207.
4. Hohorst, Kocka and Ritter, eds., *Materialien*, pp. 66–8.
5. Max Rolfes, 'Landwirtschaft 1850–1914', in Aubin and Zorn, eds., *Handbuch*, vol. 2, pp. 495–526; Hohorst, Kocka and Ritter, eds., *Materialien*, pp. 42–4; Henning, *Landwirtschaft*, vol. 2, pp. 113–74.
6. Wolfram Fischer, 'Bergbau, Industrie und Handwerk 1850–1914', in Aubin and Zorn, eds., *Handbuch*, vol. 2, pp. 527–62, here pp. 543–50.
7. Hobsbawm, *The Age of Empire*, pp. 317–40; Tannenbaum, *1900: The Generation Before the Great War*, pp. 7–39; Romein, *The Watershed of Two Eras*, pp. 324–39; Wilhelm Treue, 'Die Technik in Wirtschaft und Gesellschaft 1800–1970', in Aubin and Zorn, eds., *Handbuch*, vol. 2, pp. 51–121, here pp. 51–105; Wetzel, *Naturwissenschaften und chemische Industrie*; König and Weber, *Netzwerke, Stahl und Strom*, pp. 314–92; Sandgruber, *Strom der Zeit*.
8. Mann, ed., *Medizin, Naturwissenschaft, Technik*, pp. 52–68; Woller, *Aufbruch ins Heute*, pp. 118–59.
9. Ben-David, *The Scientist's Role in Society*, pp. 188–9.
10. McClelland, *State, Society and University*, pp. 233–340; Konrad Jarausch, 'Universität und Hochschule', in Berg, ed., *Handbuch der deutschen Bildungsgeschichte*, vol. 4, pp. 313–45.
11. Siegrist, Kaelble and Kocka, eds., *Europäische Konsumgeschichte*, pp. 245–66; Möser, *Geschichte des Autos*, pp. 67–86; Thomas, *Telefonieren in Deutschland*, pp. 55–138; Elsaesser, *Filmgeschichte*, pp. 94–124.
12. Marschalck, *Bevölkerungsgeschichte*, pp. 27–52; Brüggemeier, *Leben vor Ort*; Bade, *Vom Auswanderungsland zum Einwanderungsland?*, pp.17–28; Mommsen, *Bürgerstolz und Weltmachtstreben*, pp. 62–7.

13. Krabbe, *Die deutsche Stadt*, pp. 68–98; Reulecke, *Geschichte der Urbanisierung*, pp. 68–146; Hohorst, Kocka and Ritter, eds., *Materialien*, pp. 15–56.
14. Kocka, ed., *Bourgeois Society in Nineteenth-Century Europe*, in particular the article 'Businessmen and the Bourgeoisie in Western Europe', pp. 103–26; Kocka, ed., *Bürger und Bürgerlichkeit*, pp. 101–20; Blackbourn and Evans, eds., *The German Bourgeoisie*, pp. 1–45.
15. Ritter and Tenfelde, *Arbeiter im Deutschen Kaiserreich*, pp. 467–536; Langewiesche and Schönhoven, eds., *Arbeiter in Deutschland*, pp. 7–36.
16. Ritter and Tenfelde, *Arbeiter im Deutschen Kaiserreich*, pp. 113–54; Hentschel, *Wirtschaft und Wirtschaftspolitik*, pp. 62–81; Rothenbacher, *Soziale Ungleichheit*, pp. 180–207.
17. Reif, *Adel im 19. und 20. Jahrhundert*, pp. 96–9; Jürgen Laubner 'Zwischen Industrie und Landwirtschaft. Die oberschlesischen Magnaten–aristokratische Anpassungsfähigkeit und Krisenbewältigung', in Reif, ed., *Ostelbische Agrargesellschaft*, pp. 251–66; Wagner, *Bauern, Junker und Beamte*, pp. 499–526; Heß, *Junker und bürgerliche Großgrundbesitzer*, pp. 27–42.
18. Max Rolfes, 'Landwirtschaft 1830–1914', in Aubin and Zorn, eds., *Handbuch*, vol. 2, pp. 495–526; Wolfgang Kaschuba, 'Peasants and Others. The Historical Contours of Village Class Society', in Evans and Lee, eds., *The German Peasantry*, pp. 235–64; Hans-Jürgen Puhle, 'Lords and Peasants in the Kaiserreich', in Moeller, ed., *Peasants and Lords*, pp. 81–109; Henning, *Landwirtschaft und ländliche Gesellschaft*, vol. 2, pp. 113–74.
19. Weber, *Die Lage der Landarbeiter*, pp. 68–108; Kocka, *Arbeitsverhältnisse und Arbeiterexistenzen*, pp. 147–219; Plaul, *Landarbeiterleben*, pp. 147–278; Jacobeit, Mooser and Sträth, eds., *Idylle oder Aufbruch?*, pp. 263–76.
20. Fisch, *Europa*, pp. 236–71.
21. Mark Twain, 'The German Chicago', in *The £1,000,000 Bank-Note and Other New Stories*, 1996 [1893], p. 210.
22. Rehbein, *Leben eines Landarbeiters*, p. 65.
23. Alexander Granach (Jessaia Gronach), *Da geht ein Mensch. Roman eines Lebens*, quoted in Glatzer, *Das Wilhelminische Berlin*, p. 128.
24. Siemens, *Zeitalter*, pp. 95–6.
25. Krafft-Ebing, *Nervosität und neurasthenische Zustände*, p. 10; Lamprecht, *Deutsche Geschichte*, pp. 170–2; Radkau, *Das Zeitalter der Nervosität*, pp. 19–73; Nolte, *Ordnung der deutschen Gesellschaft*, pp. 61–77; Borscheid, *Der Tempo-Virus*, pp. 215–38.
26. Bollenbeck, *Tradition, Avantgarde, Reaktion*, pp. 99–193; Hepp, *Avantgarde*; Bergmann, *Agrarromantik und Großstadtfeindschaft*, pp. 33–173; Beßlich, *Wege in den 'Kulturkrieg'*, pp. 1–44.
27. Rohkramer, *Eine andere Moderne*, pp. 217–342.
28. Nipperdey, *Deutsche Geschichte 1866–1918*, vol. 1, pp. 428–530; Marbach, *Säkularisierung und sozialer Wandel*, pp. 41–90.
29. Sieder, *Sozialgeschichte der Familie*, pp. 125–45; Borsched and Teuteberg, eds., *Ehe, Liebe, Tod*, pp. 66–79; Klaus Saul et al., eds., *Arbeiterfamilien im Kaiserreich*, pp. 5–68;

Eric Hobsbawm, 'Kultur und Geschlecht im europäischen Bürgertum', in Frevert, ed., *Bürgerinnen und Bürger,* pp. 175–89; Mitterauer, *Sozialgeschichte der Jugend,* pp. 96–161; Buske, *Fräulein Mutter und ihr Bastard,* pp. 31–88.

30. Stümke, *Homosexuelle in Deutschland,* pp. 21–52; Michael Kandora, 'Homosexualität und Sittengesetz', in Herbert, ed., *Wandlungsprozesse,* pp. 379–401; Hommen, *Sittlichkeitsverbrechen,* pp. 23–34; Blasius, *Ehescheidungen in Deutschland,* pp. 127–54; Mosse, *Nationalismus und Sexualität,* pp. 63–83.
31. Huret, *Berlin um Neunzehnhundert,* p. 76.
32. Clark, *Kaiser Wilhelm II,* pp. 80–224; Straub, *Kaiser Wilhelm II,* pp. 131–84.
33. John, *Reserveoffizierskorps,* pp. 279–340; Rohkrämer, *Militarismus,* pp. 83–174; Frevert, *Die kasernierte Nation,* pp. 139–301.
34. Ritter and Tenfelde, *Arbeiter im Deutschen Kaiserreich,* pp. 86–94; Tenfelde, *Arbeiter und Arbeiterbewegung,* pp. 13–62.
35. Granach, *Da geht ein Mensch,* pp. 185–98.
36. Kleßmann, *Polnische Bergarbeiter;* Herbert, *Foreign Labor,* pp. 72–85; Hoerder, *Cultures in Contact,* pp. 436–42; Hoerder and Nagler, eds., *People in Transit,* pp. 127–226.
37. Knud Ahlborn, 'Das Meißnerfest der Freideutschen Jugend [1913]', in Kindt, ed., *Grundschriften,* pp. 105–15, quoted on p. 109; Herrmann, ed., '*Mit uns zieht die neue Zeit . . .*'; Laqueur, *Young Germany;* Koebner, Janz and Trommler, eds., *Mythos Jugend;* Detlev Peukert, '"Mit uns zieht die neue Zeit"; Jugend zwischen Disziplinierung und Revolte', in Nitschke et al., eds., *Jahrhundertwende,* vol. 1, pp. 176–202.
38. Zweig, *The World of Yesterday,* p. 37.
39. Anz and Stark, eds., *Expressionismus;* Helmut Kreuzer, 'Eine Epoche des Übergangs', in Kreuzer, ed., *Jahrhundertende-Jahrhundertwende,* pp. 1–32; Bollenbeck, *Tradition, Avantgarde, Reaktion,* pp. 99–193.
40. Nipperdey, *Deutsche Geschichte 1866–1918,* vol. 1, p. 782; Breuer, *Ästhetischer Fundamentalismus,* pp. 21–94; Karlauf, *Stefan George,* pp. 253–462; Raulff, *Kreis ohne Meister,* pp. 9–29.
41. Thomas Mann, 'Leiden und Größe Richard Wagners' [1933] in Thomas Mann, *Gesammelte Werke,* vol. 10, pp. 346–409. The quotation is from p. 402.
42. Hepp, *Avantgarde;* Rohkrämer, *Eine andere Moderne,* pp. 37–116; Beßlich, *Wege in den 'Kulturkrieg',* pp. 119–91; Stern, *Politics of Cultural Despair,* pp. 183–298; Bollenbeck, *Tradition, Avantgarde, Reaktion,* pp. 11–43.
43. Kuhn, *Die deutsche Arbeiterbewegung,* pp. 90–106; Ritter and Tenfelde, *Arbeiter im Deutschen Kaiserreich,* pp. 679–780.
44. Hildermeier, *Geschichte der Sowjetunion,* pp. 44–7 and 178–82.
45. Hobsbawm, *Nations and Nationalism,* pp. 101–30; Wehler, *Nationalismus,* pp. 62–89; Anderson, *Imagined Communities,* pp. 50–66.
46. Stern, *Politics of Cultural Despair,* pp. 3–298; Mosse, *The Crisis of German Ideology;* Hein, *Die Brücke ins Geisterreich,* pp. 132–95.
47. *Verhandlungen des Reichstags, Stenographische Berichte,* 290 (1913), p. 5, 282; Gosewinkel, *Einbürgern und Ausschließen,* pp. 278–94; Herbert, *Foreign Labor,* pp. 66–72.

48. Karády, *Juden in der europäischen Moderne,* pp. 174–202; Volkov, *Deutsche Juden,* pp. 1–8; Lowenstein et al., *Umstrittene Integration,* pp. 193–277; Herbert, *Foreign Labor,* pp. 66–72.
49. Ludwig Klages, 'Mensch und Erde' [1913], in Klages, *Sämtliche Werke, Philosophie III,* vol. 3, pp. 614–36, here pp. 616, 621 and 623; Lieber, *Kulturkritik und Lebensphilosophie*; Schröder, *Ludwig Klages,* as well as Brinkmann, *Ludwig Klages,* and Leo, *Wille zum Wesen,* whose comments I follow here.
50. Ludwig Klages, 'Heidnische Feuerzeichen. Aufruf zu Wahrung und Förderung heidnischer Lebenselemente' [1900], quoted in Brinkmann, *Ludwig Klages,* p. 79.
51. Ludwig Klages, 'Typische Ausdrucksstörungen und der hysterische Charakter' [1904], in Klages, *Sämtliche Werke, Graphologie I,* vol. 7, pp. 83–118, here pp. 87–9, 92–3 and 94.
52. Darwin, *On the Origin of Species*; Haeckel, *Anthropogenie oder Entwicklungsgeschichte*; Haeckel, *Die Welträtsel.*
53. Schallmeyer, *Vererbung.*
54. Grotjahn, *Krankenhauswesen und Heilstättenbewegung,* p. 4; Nadav, *Die Politik der Sozialhygiene*; Schwartz, *'Proletarier' und 'Lumpen'.*
55. Fisch, *Europa,* pp. 297–301.
56. Wehler, *Gesellschaftsgeschichte,* vol. 4, p. 203.

## Chapter 2

1. Theodor Fontane to Georg Friedländer, 1 May 1890, in Fontane, *Briefe an Georg Friedländer,* pp. 170–3, here pp. 171–2.
2. The German Conservative deputy Elard von Oldenburg-Januschau, speaking on 9 January 1910 in the Reichstag (*Verhandlungen des Reichstags. Stenographische Berichte* 259 (1910), p. 898. For the next few paragraphs, see Wehler, *Gesellschaftsgeschichte,* vol. 3, pp. 848–1168; Nipperdey, *Machtstaat vor der Demokratie,* pp. 85–109; Mommsen, *Bürgerstolz*; Winkler, *Germany: the Long Road West,* vol. 1, pp. 192–238; Fisch, *Europa,* pp. 75–98; Müller and Torp, eds., *Imperial Germany Revisited*; Retallack, ed., *Imperial Germany, 1871-1918*; Conrad and Osterhammel, eds., *Das Kaiserreich Transnational*; Frie, *Das Deutsche Kaiserreich*; Ullmann, *Politik im deutschen Kaiserreich.*
3. Nipperdey, *Machtstaat vor der Demokratie,* pp. 109–200; Jeserich et al., eds., *Deutsche Verwaltungsgeschichte,* vol. 3, pp. 109–27.
4. Henning, *Landwirtschaft und ländliche Gesellschaft,* vol. 2, pp. 113–74; Prass, ed., *Ländliche Gesellschaften.*
5. Loth, ed., *Deutscher Katholizismus*; Loth, *Katholiken im Kaiserreich*; Clark and Kaiser, eds., *Kulturkampf.*
6. Ritter and Tenfelde, *Arbeiter im Deutschen Kaiserreich,* pp. 679–780; Welskopp, *Banner der Brüderlichkeit,* pp. 419–61; Tenfelde, ed., *Arbeiter und Arbeiterbewegung.*
7. Haupt and Hausen, *Die Pariser Kommune.*

8. Welskopp, *Banner der Brüderlichkeit*, pp. 668–711.
9. Ritter, *Der Sozialstaat,* pp. 61–87; Hentschel, *Geschichte der deutschen Sozialpolitik,* pp. 11–54; Hennock, *The Origin of the Welfare State,* pp. 182–211; Christoph Conrad, 'Wohlfahrtsstaaten im Vergleich', in Haupt and Kocka, eds., *Geschichte und Vergleich,* pp. 155–80.
10. Fisch, *Europa,* pp. 272–301.
11. Hildebrand, *Deutsche Außenpolitik 1871–1918,* pp. 27–52; Frie, *Kaiserreich,* pp. 56–68; Schneider, *Die deutsche Rußlandpolitik.*
12. Conrad, *Globalisation*, pp. 23–51.
13. Hobsbawm, *Nations and Nationalism,* pp. 14–45; Breuilly, *Nationalismus und moderner Staat,* pp. 235–316; Walkenhorst, *Nation, Volk, Rasse,* pp. 38–79.
14. Van Laak, *Über alles,* pp. 22–47 and 70–103; Eckert, *Kolonialismus,* pp. 100–4; Kundrus, *Moderne Imperialisten,* pp. 27–42; Geulen, *Wahlverwandte,* pp. 309–67; Conrad, *German Colonialism,* pp. 36–65; Kundrus, ed., *Phantasiereiche.* This book is also relevant to the next section.
15. Walkenhorst, *Nation, Volk, Rasse,* pp. 226–49; Hering, *Konstruierte Nation,* pp. 109–219; Oldenburg, *Der Deutsche Ostmarkenverein,* pp. 70–183; Breuer, *Die Völkischen in Deutschland,* pp. 147–264; Rohkrämer, *Militarismus,* pp. 27–82.
16. For the revised programme of the German Conservative Party (the 'Tivoli Programme') see Treue, *Parteiprogramme,* pp. 87–90, here pp. 88–9.
17. Puhle, *Agrarische Interressenpolitik,* pp. 143–212.
18. Epkenhans, *Die wilhelminische Flottenrüstung,* pp. 15–30; Hobson, *Imperialism at Sea*; Eley, *German Right.*
19. Memorandum by the Imperial Naval Secretary, Rear Admiral Tirpitz, July 1897, in Berghahn and Deist, eds., *Rüstung,* pp. 122–7, here p. 122.
20. Tirpitz, *Erinnerungen*, p. 52.
21. Helfferich, *Deutschlands Volkswohlstand*, p. 126.
22. Hull, *Absolute Destruction,* pp. 5–90; Zimmerer and Zeller, eds., *Genocide.*
23. Theodor Mommsen, 'Was uns noch retten kann', in *Die Nation* 20 (1902), pp. 163–4, here p. 163.
24. Ritter and Tenfelde, *Arbeiter im Deutschen Kaiserreich,* pp. 691–716; Tenfelde, ed., *Arbeiter und Arbeiterbewegung,* pp. 507–659; Lösche, *Bolschewismus.*
25. Public statement opposing the Prussian three-class electoral law: 'Für die Preußische Wahlreform', *Berliner Tageblatt,* no. 260, 7 December 1909.
26. Dick Geary, 'Protest and Strike. Recent Research on "Collective Action" in England, Germany and France', in Tenfelde, ed., *Arbeiter und Arbeiterbewegung,* pp. 363–87; Lösche, *Bolschewismus,* pp. 34–47.
27. Gustav Noske, speaking in the Reichstag on 10 June 1913 (*Verhandlungen des Reichstags. Stenographische Berichte* 290 (1913)), p. 5,434.
28. Frymann, Daniel [Heinrich Claß], *Wenn ich der Kaiser wär'*; Walkenhorst, *Nation, Volk, Rasse,* pp. 82–101, here pp. 89–91.
29. Aly, *Why the Germans?,* pp. 62–75.
30. Jochmann, *Gesellschaftskrise*; Mosse, *Crisis of German Ideology*; Bergmann, *Geschichte des Antisemitismus,* pp. 41–51; Aly, *Why the Germans?,* pp. 77–98.

31. Stevenson, *Armaments,* pp. 64–111.
32. Compare Rudoerffer [Kurt Riezler], *Grundzüge der Weltpolitik*; see also Hillgruber, *Riezlers Theorie.*
33. Boeckh, *Von den Balkankriegen zum Ersten Weltkrieg*; Mombauer, *The Origins*; Joll, *The Origins.*
34. Letter from Bassermann to Kiderlen-Waechter, 24 July 1911, quoted in Werneke, *Wille,* p. 33.
35. Von Bernhardi, *Deutschland und der nächste Krieg,* pp. 18 and 111–12; *Die Post* editorial quoted by Winkler, *Long Road West,* vol. 1, p. 283; August Bebel, speaking on 9 November 1911 in the Reichstag (*Verhandlungen des Reichstags. Stenographische Berichte,* 268 (1911)), p. 7,730.
36. Record of discussion of 8 December 1912, quoted from Müller, *Der Kaiser,* p. 125.
37. Theobald von Bethmann-Hollweg, document 3, confidential message from the Reichskanzler to the Ambassador in London, 16 June 1914, in Kautsky, Montgelas and Stücking, eds., *Dokumente zum Kriegsausbruch,* vol. 1, pp. 3–4, here p. 4. In general, on the July Crisis, see Clark, *Sleepwalkers,* pp. 367–562; Winkler, *Geschichte des Westens,* vol. 1, pp. 1148–88; Mommsen, *Bürgerstolz,* pp. 450–564; Keegan, *The First World War,* pp. 27–77.
38. Clark, *Sleepwalkers,* pp. 471–562; Mombauer, *The Origins,* pp. 21–77.
39. Storz, *Kriegsbild und Rüstung,* pp. 369–73.
40. Moltke, *Erinnerungen, Briefe, Dokumente,* p. 308; Förster, *Der deutsche Generalstab,* pp. 61–95; Afflerbach, *Dreibund,* p. 824; Wolfgang J. Mommsen, 'Der Topos vom unvermeidlichen Krieg. Außenpolitik und öffentliche Meinung im Deutschen Reich im letzten Jahrzehnt vor 1914', in Mommsen, ed., *Der autoritäre Nationalstaat,* pp. 380–406.

## Chapter 3

1. On this section, see Hirschfeld, Krumeich and Renz, eds., *Brill's Encyclopedia of the First World War*; Horne, ed., *Companion*; Winkler, *Germany: the Long Road West,* vol. 1, pp. 296–338; Winkler, *Age of Catastrophe,* pp. 1–91; Mommsen, *Bürgerstolz,* pp. 564–827; Chickering, *Imperial Germany*; Herwig, *The First World War*; Strachan, *The First World War,* vol. 1; Mommsen, *Urkatastrophe*; Berghahn, *Der Erste Weltkrieg*; Salewski, *Der Erste Weltkrieg.*
2. Gerald D. Feldman, 'Die sozialen und politischen Grundlagen der wirtschaftlichen Mobilmachung in Deutschland 1914–1916', in Feldman and Rosenberg, eds., *Vom Weltkrieg zur Weltwirtschaftskrise,* pp. 13–35.
3. Hew Strachan, 'The War Experienced: Command, Strategy and Tactics, 1914–1918', in Horne, ed., *Companion,* pp. 35–49; Mombauer, *Helmut von Moltke*; Snyder, *The Ideology of the Offensive*; Linnenkohl, *Vom Einzelschuß zur Feuerwalze.*
4. Horne and Kramer, *German Atrocities, 1914*; Laurence van Ypersele, 'Belgium', in Hirschfeld, Krumeich and Renz, eds., *Brill's Encyclopedia of the First World War,* pp. 28–32.

5. Showalter, *Tannenberg*; Stone, *The Eastern Front*, pp. 44–69; Mommsen, *Bürgerstolz*, pp. 581–606; Pyta, *Hindenburg*, pp. 285–93.
6. Materna, *Berichte des Berliner Polizeipräsidenten*; Ullrich, *Die Hamburger Arbeiterbewegung*. On this section, see Verhey, *The Spirit of 1914*; Raithel, *Das 'Wunder' der inneren Einheit*; Wolfgang Kruse, 'Die Kriegsbegeisterung im Deutschen Reich 1914. Entstehungszusammenhänge, Grenzen und ideologische Strukturen', in van der Linden and Mergner, eds., *Kriegsbegeisterung*, pp. 73–87; Marcel van der Linden, 'Kriegsbegeisterung? Zur Massenstimmung bei Kriegsbeginn', in Cornelißen, ed., *Eine Welt von Feinden*, pp. 159–95.
7. For William II's speech of 31 July 1914, see Bihl, *Deutsche Quellen*, no. 1, p. 45; the school essay is in Cartarius, ed., *Deutschland im Ersten Weltkrieg*, p. 22.
8. German text of these lines:

   'Wir wußten nicht, wozu wir blühten,/Und Jugend schien uns Fluch und Last,/Ein Fest, an dem wir nicht erglühten,—/Man trank—man ging—ein satter Gast./Und unser Blut ging dick und träge,/Wir hatten allzu blanke Wehr,/Wir hatten allzu glatte Wege,/Wir hatten keine Lieder mehr./Drum jauchzen wir in diesen Tagen,/Drum sind wir trunken ohne Wein,/Drum dröhnt's uns aus der Trommeln Schlagen:/O heil'ges Glück, heut jung zu sein!'

   Ina Seidel's poem 'Deutsche Jugend 1914' is quoted in Hamann, *Der Erste Weltkrieg*, p. 27; for Zuckmayer's description of the war as an adventure see Jeffrey Verhey, 'August Experience', in Hirschfeld, Krumeich and Renz, eds., *Brill's Encylopedia of the First World War*, pp. 340–2, here p. 340. By 1915, 235 books of war poetry had been published in Germany alone. See Philippi, *Volk des Zorns*, Bridgwater, *The German Poets*, and Anz and Vogl, eds., *Die Dichter und der Krieg*.
9. For William II's speech of 1 August 1914, see Bihl, *Deutsche Quellen*, no. 5, p. 49.
10. Otto von Gierke, 'Krieg und Kultur', in Zentralstelle für Volkswohlfahrt, ed., *Deutsche Reden*, pp. 75–101. On the charges brought by British academics against Germany's conduct of the war, see Barker, *Why We are at War*; for the German reaction to this, see the Proclamation to the Civilised World (*Aufruf an die Kulturwelt*), issued on 4 October 1914, and signed by 56 university professors. (Kellermann, ed., *Der Krieg der Geister*, pp. 64–8.)
11. Plenge, *1789 und 1914*, pp. 15 and 20.
12. Bethmann Hollweg's 'September Programme', dated 9 September 1914, quoted from Fischer, *Germany's Aims*, pp. 98–106, here p. 105. War Aims Memorandum by Heinrich Claß, agreed on 20 August 1914, printed at the beginning of September 1914, Fischer, *Germany's Aims*, pp. 106–108; Memorandum by August Thyssen, 9 September 1914, in Fischer, *Germany's Aims*, pp. 109–10. All the war aims memoranda are printed in Opitz, ed., *Europastrategien*, pp. 221–66; cf. Naumann, *Central Europe*.
13. Petition from six industrial associations to the Reich Chancellor, 20 May 1915, in *Ursachen und Folgen*, vol. 1, no. 188, pp. 351–5; confidential memorandum by German university professors and officials to Reich Chancellor von Bethmann Hollweg, 20 June 1915, in *Ursachen und Folgen*, vol. 1, no. 188a, pp. 355–62; Schwabe, 'Ursprung und Verbreitung'; Christophe Prochasson, 'Intellectuals and Writers', in Horne, ed., *Companion*, pp. 323–37.

14. Mommsen, *Bürgerstolz,* pp. 618–35; Soutou, *L'or et le sang*; Neitzel, *Weltmacht oder Untergang.*
15. Kruse, *Krieg und nationale Integration*; Hans-Christoph Schröder, 'Die deutsche Arbeiterbewegung und der Erste Weltkrieg', in Böhme and Kallenberg, eds., *Deutschland und der Erste Weltkrieg,* pp. 253–74; Miller, *Burgfrieden*; Raithel, *Wunder,* pp. 203–8; Wehler, *Gesellschaftsgeschichte,* vol. 4, pp. 39–47; Mommsen, *Bürgerstolz,* pp. 564–81; Winkler, *Germany: the Long Road West,* vol. 1, pp. 299–305.
16. *Verhandlungen des Reichstags, Stenographische Berichte* 306 (1914), pp. 7 and 9.
17. Haenisch, *Sozialdemokratie,* p. 33.
18. Haupt, *Socialism and the Great War,* pp. 183–249.
19. Walter Mühlhausen, 'Die Sozialdemokratie am Scheideweg—Burgfrieden, Parteikrise und Spaltung im Ersten Weltkrieg', in Michalka, ed., *Der Erste Weltkrieg,* pp. 649–671; Kruse, *Krieg und nationale Integration,* pp. 90–151; Miller, *Burgfrieden,* pp. 31–74.
20. Stone, *The Eastern Front.*
21. Langemarck, 'Bernd Hüppauf, Schlachtenmythen und die Konstruktion des "Neuen Menschen"', in Hirschfeld and Krumeich, eds., *Keiner fühlt sich hier mehr als Mensch,* pp. 43–84.
22. Richert, *The Kaiser's Reluctant Conscript,* p. 9.
23. Letter from the front, 2 July 1916, quoted in Ulrich and Ziemann, *Frontalltag,* p. 92.
24. Benjamin Ziemann, 'Soldiers', in Hirschfeld, Krumeich and Renz, eds., *Brill's Encyclopedia of the First World War,* pp. 118–28; Ziemann, *War Experiences in Rural Germany,* pp. 29–41; Groehler, *Der lautlose Tod,* pp. 16–69; Gudmundsson, *Stormtroop Tactics*; Spilker and Ulrich, *Der Tod als Maschinist*; Mommsen, *Bürgerstolz,* pp. 599–606; Jünger, *Storm of Steel*; Jünger, *Der Kampf als inneres Erlebnis.*
25. MacDonald, *Somme,* pp. 55–127; Hirschfeld et al., eds., *Scorched Earth: the Germans on the Somme, 1914–1918*; Keegan, *The First World War,* pp. 300–58.
26. Werth, *Verdun*; Afflerbach, *Falkenhayn*; Stone, *The Eastern Front,* pp. 262–81; Chickering, *Imperial Germany,* pp. 71–6.
27. Wehler, *Gesellschaftsgeschichte,* vol. 4, p. 53; Salewski, *Weltkrieg,* pp. 172–86; Theo Balderstone, 'Industrial Mobilization and War Economies', in Horne, ed., *Companion,* pp. 217–53.
28. Dieter Krüger, 'Ein "Morgenrot wirklicher Sozialreform"', in Mai, ed., *Arbeiterschaft,* pp. 29–75; Feldman, *Army,* pp. 64–73.
29. Daniel, *The War from Within,* pp. 38–49; Kundrus, *Kriegerfrauen,* pp. 45–70; Wall and Winter, eds., *The Upheaval of War,* pp. 249–326; Susan R. Grayzel, 'Women and Men', in Horne, ed., *Companion,* pp. 263–78.
30. Herbert, *Foreign Labor,* pp. 87–119; Jochen Oltmer, 'Unentbehrliche Arbeitskräfte. Kriegsgefangene in Deutschland', in Oltmer, ed., *Kriegsgefangene,* pp. 67–96; Hinz, *Gefangen,* pp. 248–318; Westerhoff, *Zwangsarbeit*; Thiel, *'Menschenbassin Belgien'.*
31. Walther Rathenau to Leopold Ziegler, 22 July 1918, in Rathenau, *Briefe,* vol. 2, pp. 53–5, here p. 54.
32. Helfferich's Reichstag speech of 20 August 1915, in *Verhandlungen des Reichstags, 13. Legislaturperiode,* vol. 306 (1915), p. 224.

33. Manfred Zeidler, 'Die deutsche Kriegsfinanzierung 1914 bis 1918 und ihre Folgen', in Michalka, ed., *Der Erste Weltkrieg,* pp. 416–33; Mommsen, *Bürgerstolz,* pp. 672–82; Feldman, *The Great Disorder*; Holtfrerich, *The German Inflation.*
34. Chickering, *Imperial Germany,* pp. 42–3.
35. Public Opinion Report no. 83 by the Berlin Police Chief's office, 18 April 1917, in Cartarius, ed., *Deutschland im Ersten Weltkrieg,* pp. 277–9, here p. 278.
36. Chickering, *Imperial Germany*, p. 146.
37. Roerkohl, *Hungerblockade,* pp. 317–23; Winter and Robert, eds., *Capital Cities at War*; Offner, *The First World War*; Vincent, *The Politics of Hunger*; Mommsen, *Bürgerstolz,* pp. 682–95; Chickering, *Imperial Germany,* pp. 150–5.
38. Feldman, *Army,* pp. 253–73; Mai, *Das Ende des Kaiserreichs.*
39. Keegan, *The First World War,* pp. 279–300 and 376–97.
40. Hildermeier, *Geschichte,* pp. 64–86; Neutatz, *Träume,* pp. 152–70; Winkler, *Age of Catastrophe*, pp. 19–27.
41. Winkler, *Germany: the Long Road West,* vol. 1, pp. 310–19; Salewski, *Weltkrieg,* pp. 227–41.
42. Hagenlücke, *Deutsche Vaterlandspartei,* pp. 143–5.
43. Rosenthal, *Die Ehre des jüdischen Soldaten,* pp. 54–78.
44. Prussian Minister of the Interior, 23 April 1918, HStAD RP Düss. 9084; Rosenthal, *Die Ehre des jüdischen Soldaten,* pp. 54–78; Peter Pulzer, 'The First World War', in Lowenstein et al., *Integration in Dispute,* pp. 360–84; Helmut Berding, 'Der Aufstieg des Antisemitismus im Ersten Weltkrieg', in Benz and Bergmann, eds., *Vorurteil und Völkermord,* pp. 304–40; Wertheimer, *Unwelcome Strangers*; Maurer, *Ostjuden.*
45. Hildermeier, *Geschichte,* pp. 105–33; Neutatz, *Träume,* pp. 152–70; Winkler, *Age of Catastrophe*, pp. 39–49.
46. Wilson's Fourteen Points, in *Ursachen und Folgen,* vol. 2, no. 199a, pp. 374–6: Knock, *To End all Wars,* pp. 194–245; Winkler, *Age of Catastrophe,* pp. 52–60
47. Baumgart, *Ostpolitik 1918,* pp. 258–367; Liulevicius, *War Land,* pp. 203–26.
48. Liulevicius, *War Land,* pp. 247–77; Strazhas, *Deutsche Ostpolitik,* pp. 221–3.
49. Boebel and Wentzel, eds., *Streiken gegen den Krieg*; Miller, *Burgfrieden,* pp. 351–95; Ullrich, 'Januarstreik 1918'.
50. Keegan, *The First World War,* pp. 401–56; Stedman, *German Spring Offensive*; Markus Pohlmann, 'Return to the Somme 1918', in Hirschfeld, Krumeich and Renz, eds., *Scorched Earth,* pp. 179–201.
51. Nicolai's report of 24 August 1918, in *Ursachen und Folgen,* vol. 2, document 351, pp. 290–1.
52. Letter from the front, quoted in Ulrich and Ziemann, *Frontalltag,* p. 202; compilation of monthly reports on the popular mood sent in August 1918 by the representative of the General Command to the Prussian War Ministry, 3 September 1918, in Otto and Schmiedel, eds., *Der erste Weltkrieg,* no.131, pp. 320–322, here p. 321. Riezler's diary entry for 13 September 1918, in Riezler, *Tagebücher*, p.475.
53. Former State Secretary Paul von Hintze's evidence on 14 August 1922 to the Parliamentary Investigation Committee examining the events at General Staff

Headquarters on 29 September 1918, in *Ursachen und Folgen,* vol. 2, document no. 365b, pp. 319–20, here p. 320.

54. Diary Entries by General Staff Colonel von Thaer, 30 September and 1 October 1918, in *Ursachen und Folgen,* vol. 2, no. 368, pp. 322–4, here p. 323.
55. Report of the Bavarian Military Representative to the OHL, 7 October 1918, quoted in Feldman, *Army,* p. 516.
56. Hindenburg, *Aus meinem Leben,* p. 403.
57. Notes from US President Wilson to the Reich Chancellor, 8 and 14 October 1918, in *Ursachen und Folgen,* vol. 2, nos. 405 and 413, pp. 384–5 and 393–4; Schwabe, *Deutsche Revolution,* pp. 88–226.
58. Wilson's note of 23 October 1918, *Ursachen und Folgen,* vol. 2, no. 425, pp. 429–31; Hindenburg's Army Order of 24 October 1918, in Ludendorff, ed., *Urkunden,* pp. 577–8, here p. 578.
59. Deist, 'Politik der Seekriegsleitung'; Afflerbach, 'Mit wehender Fahne'.
60. Dähnhardt, *Revolution in Kiel,* pp. 48–50.
61. For William II's comments, made on 8 November 1918, see Ilsemann, *Der Kaiser in Holland,* vol. 1, p. 35.
62. Kennan, *Decline,* p. 3.
63. See Nolte, *Der Europäische Bürgerkrieg,* p. 524.

## Chapter 4

1. Hildermeier, *Geschichte der Sowjetunion,* pp. 105–56; Neutatz, *Träume,* pp. 152–70.
2. On the German Revolution of 1918–19, see Winkler, *Arbeiter,* vol. 1, pp. 19–152; Winkler, *Weimar,* pp. 33–86; Winkler, *Germany: the Long Road West,* vol. 1, pp. 329–50; Peukert, *The Weimar Republic*; Büttner, *Weimar,* pp. 33–64; Mommsen, *Rise and Fall*; Longerich, *Deutschland*; Kluge, *Weimarer Republik,* pp. 17–58. On the European context, see Mai, *Europa,* pp. 7–17; Raphael, *Imperiale Gewalt,* pp. 38–81; Winkler, *Age of Catastrophe,* pp. 70–86.
3. Ebert's proclamation of 9 November 1918: Ritter and Miller, eds. *Deutsche Revolution,* p. 80.
4. Winkler, *Arbeiter,* vol. 1, pp. 75–80; Mommsen, *Rise and Fall,* pp. 51–88; Feldman and Steinisch, eds., *Industrie und Gewerkschaften.*
5. Kluge, *Soldatenräte,* pp. 136–43; Büttner, *Weimar,* pp. 43–53.
6. Winkler, *Arbeiter,* vol. 1, pp. 100–9; Kolb, *Arbeiterräte.*
7. *Allgemeiner Kongreß der Arbeiter—und Soldatenräte Deutschlands. Stenographische Berichte,* I (1919), columns 209–224, here columns 217, 219 and 224.
8. Weber, *Kommunismus in Deutschland,* pp. 31–45.
9. Winkler, *Arbeiter,* vol. 1, pp. 135–52; Büttner, *Weimar,* pp. 105–11.
10. Gusy, *Weimarer Reichsverfassung*; Rödder, ed., *Weimar*; Winkler, *Arbeiter,* vol. 1, pp. 227–42.
11. Kluge, *Weimarer Republik,* pp. 59–68; Weisbrod, 'Gewalt'.
12. Schulze, *Freikorps*; Hannover-Drück, ed., *Mord.*

13. Lucas, *Märzrevolution*, vol. 1, pp. 21–50; Mommsen, 'Deutsche Revolution'.
14. Karl, *Münchener Räterepublik*; Winkler, *Arbeiter*, vol. 1, pp. 184–91; Martin H. Geyer, 'Formen der Radikalisierung in der Münchener Revolution', in Konrad and Schmidlechner, eds., *Revolutionäres Potential*, pp. 63–87.
15. Naimark, *Fires of Hatred*, pp. 17–56; Mazower, *Balkans*, pp. 185–224; Hirschon, *Crossing the Aegean.*
16. Kolb, *Frieden*; Schulz, *Revolutions*; Winkler, *Weimar*, pp. 87–98; Ulrich Herbert, 'Eine neue Weltordnung. Die Friedenverträge 1919 und ihre Auswirkungen', in Brüll, ed., *ZOOM*, pp. 23–52; Krumeich, ed., *Versailles 1919*, pp. 237–58; Eric D. Weitz, 'From the Vienna to the Paris System'.
17. Both quotations come from the evening edition of the *Frankfurter Zeitung*, 9 May 1919.
18. Quoted from Winkler, *Arbeiter*, vol. 1, p. 217.
19. Hermann Oncken, 'Gedächtnisrede auf die Gefallenen des Großen Krieges, 16. Juni 1919', in Oncken, *Nation*, p. 8.
20. Best, *Unter französischer Herrschaft*, p. 94; *Mainzer Anzeiger*, 28 November 1918; cf. Herbert, *Best*, p. 30.
21. Broszat, *Hitler and the Collapse*, p. 47.
22. In German: 'Seid eingedenk, ihr Feinde, aus den Gebeinen [der Gefallenen] wird ein Rächer entstehen'. (*Deutsche Nationalversammlung im Jahr 1919*, vol. 4, Berlin, 1919, p. 2,716.)
23. *Deutsche Nationalversammlung im Jahre 1919*, vol. 4, p. 2,646.
24. Hindenburg's words were: 'This period saw the start of a planned and secret subversion of the fleet and the army, which continued similar attempts already made in time of peace; as an English general rightly said: "The German army was stabbed in the back."' (*Deutsche Nationalversammlung, 15 Ausschuss, Stenographischer Bericht über die öffentlichen Verhandlungen des Untersuchungsausschusses, 14. Sitzung*, 18.11.1919, p. 731.)
25. Ernst Troeltsch, 'Der Putsch der Prätorianer und Junker' [23.3.1920], in Troeltsch, *Spektator-Briefe. Aufsätze über die deutsche Revolution und die Weltpolitik 1918/1922*, Tübingen, 1924 [reprinted Aalen 1966], pp. 117–25, here pp. 117–18.
26. Könnemann and Schulze, eds., *Kapp-Lüttwitz-Ludendorff-Putsch*; Hürten, *Kapp-Putsch*; Winkler, *Arbeiter*, vol. 1, pp. 295–324.
27. Winkler, *Arbeiter*, vol. 1, pp. 324–42; Lucas, *Märzrevolution*; Ludewig, *Arbeiterbewegung.*
28. Schulze, *Otto Braun*; Hennig, *Johannes Hoffmann*, pp. 430–49.
29. Holtfrerich, *The German Inflation*, p. 202; see also Feldman, *The Great Disorder*, and Feldman et al., eds., *The German Inflation.*
30. Mommsen, *Rise and Fall*, pp. 89–128; Kent, *Spoils of War*; Trachtenberg, *Reparation.*
31. Sabrow, *Rathenaumord*; Sauer, *Schwarze Reichswehr.*
32. Holtfrerich, *The German Inflation*; Feldman, *The Great Disorder.*
33. Kroner, 'Überreizte Nerven', in *Berliner Illustrirte Zeitung*, no. 34, 26 August 1923, pp. 673–4, quoted in Jürgen Frh. von Kruedener, 'Die Entstehung des Inflationstraumas. Zur Sozialpsychologie der deutschen Hyperinflation 1922/23', in Feldman et al., eds., *Konsequenzen der Inflation*, pp. 213–86, here p. 278.

34. Canetti, *Crowds and Power*, p. 218. On the psychological impact of the inflation, see Geyer, *Verkehrte Welt* and Kruedener 'Die Entstehung des Inflationstraumas'.
35. Kurt Tucholsky, 'Das Gesicht der Stadt' [1920] in Tucholsky, *Gesammelte Werke*, vol. 1, p. 758.
36. Anonymous letter, dated 12 October 1923, to the economic department of the General State Commissioner, quoted in Geyer, *Verkehrte Welt*, pp. 245–6.
37. Mann, *Tagebücher 1918–1921*, p. 143.
38. Report from the Bavarian State Recruitment Centre of Group Command 4, 5 March 1920, quoted in Geyer, *Verkehrte Welt*, p. 283.
39. Linse, *Propheten*.
40. Report from the Bavarian State Recruitment Centre of Group Command 4, 5 March 1920, quoted in Geyer, *Verkehrte Welt*, pp. 309–10.
41. Ruck, *Gewerkschaften*; Winkler, *Arbeiter*, vol. 1, pp. 553–669; Wulf, *Hugo Stinnes*, pp. 344–425; Schwabe, ed., *Die Ruhrkrise 1923*; Zimmermann, *Frankreichs Ruhrpolitik*.
42. Winkler, *Arbeiter*, vol. 1, pp. 585–600 and 649–64; Winkler, *Weimar*, pp. 186–243; Angress, *Stillborn Revolution*.
43. Mommsen, *Rise and Fall*, pp. 89–128; Winkler, *Germany: the Long Road West*, vol. 1, pp. 388–403; Thoss, *Ludendorff-Kreis*, pp. 307–49.
44. Friedrich Meinecke, 'Zweites Referat', in Kahl, Meinecke and Radbruch, *Deutsche Universitäten*, pp. 17–31, here p. 26.
45. Kluge, *Die Weimarer Republik*, pp. 95–104; Ritschl, *Deutschlands Krise*, pp. 107–91.
46. Büttner, *Weimar*, pp. 350–63; Mommsen, *Rise and Fall*, pp. 172–216; Hildebrand, *Vergangenes Reich*, pp. 475–508; Krüger, *Außenpolitik*, pp. 372–428.
47. Stresemann to the German Embassy in London, 19 April 1926, *ADAP* B, II.1, pp. 363–5; Krüger, *Außenpolitik*, pp. 269–301.
48. Winkler, *Arbeiter*, vol. 2, p. 13–176; Mommsen, *Rise and Fall*, pp. 217–68; Preller, *Sozialpolitik in der Weimarer Republik*; Timm, *Deutsche Sozialpolitik*; Sachße and Tennstedt, eds., *Geschichte der Armenfürsorge in Deutschland*, vol. 2.
49. Weisbrod, *Schwerindustrie*, pp. 415–56; Schneider, *Unternehmer*, pp. 76–84; Winkler, *Arbeiter*, vol. 2, pp. 557–72; Mommsen, *Rise and Fall*, pp. 217–68.
50. Rainer M. Lepsius, 'Parteiensystem und Sozialstruktur: Zum Problem der Demokratisierung der deutschen Gesellschaft', in Ritter, ed., *Deutsche Parteien*, pp. 56–80; Lehnert and Megerle, eds., *Politische Teilkulturen*.
51. Büttner, *Weimar*, pp. 344–50; Pyta, *Hindenburg*, pp. 441–78; Mommsen, *Rise and Fall*, pp. 172–216.

## Chapter 5

1. For this section, see Wolfram Fischer, 'Wirtschaft, Gesellschaft und Staat in Europe 1914–1980', in Fischer, ed., *Europäische Wirtschafts- und Sozialgeschichte*, pp. 1–221, here pp. 84–171; Hoffmann, ed., *Untersuchungen zum Wachstum*; Ritschl and Spoerer, *Bruttosozialprodukt*; Balderston, *Origins and Course*; James, *The German Slump*; Petzina, *Die deutsche Wirtschaft*; Feinstein, *The European Economy*; Wehler,

*Gesellschaftsgeschichte,* vol. 4, pp. 239–83; and Munting and Holderness, *Crisis, Recovery and War.*

2. Petzina, Abelshauser and Faust, *Materialien,* p. 98; Winkler, *Arbeiter,* vol. 2, pp. 46–75.
3. Peukert, 'Erwerbslosigkeit'; Peukert, *Jugend zwischen Krieg und Krise;* Frevert, *Women,* pp. 333–4; Wellner, 'Industriearbeiterinnen'.
4. Kluge, *Agrarwirtschaft und ländliche Gesellschaft,* pp. 19–21; Max Rolfes, 'Landwirtschaft 1914–1970', in Aubin and Zorn, eds., *Handbuch,* vol. 2, pp. 741–75; Fischer, 'Wirtschaft, Gesellschaft und Staat', in Fischer, ed., *Europäische Wirtschafts- und Sozialgeschichte,* vol. 6, pp. 103–16; Friedrich-Wilhelm Henning, 'Deutschland von 1914 bis zur Gegenwart', in Fischer, ed., *Europäische Wirtschafts—und Sozialgeschichte,* vol. 6, pp. 416–81, here pp. 430–2; Löffler, *Agrarwirtschaft;* Gessner, *Agrarverbände.*
5. Pyta, *Dorfgemeinschaft,* pp. 195–233; Stoltenberg, *Politische Strömungen,* pp. 107–55; Bernd Weisbrod, 'Die Krise der Mitte oder "Der Bauer stund auf im Lande"', in Niethammer et al., *Bürgerliche Gesellschaft,* pp. 396–410.
6. Priemel, *Flick,* pp. 87–149; Wilfried Feldenkirchen, 'Concentration in German Industry 1870–1939', in Pohl, ed., *Concentration Process,* pp. 113–36; Reckendrees, *Das 'Stahltrust' Projekt.*
7. Saldern and Hachtmann, 'Das fordistische Jahrhundert'; Saldern and Hachtmann, '"Gesellschaft am Fließband"'; Freyberg, *Industrielle Rationalisierung;* Brady, *Rationalization Movement,* pp. 3–64.
8. Wilhlem Röpke, 'Staatsinterventionismus', in Elster, ed., *Handwörterbuch der Staatswissenschaften,* pp. 861–82.
9. Petzina, Abelshauser and Faust, *Materialien,* p. 150; Priemel, *Flick,* pp. 111–20.
10. Metzler, *Der deutsche Sozialstaat,* pp. 54–86; Hentschel, *Geschichte der deutschen Sozialpolitik,* pp. 63–135; Preller, *Sozialpolitik;* Abelshauser, ed., *Weimarer Republik;* Führer, *Mieter;* Führer, *Arbeitslosigkeit.*
11. Jürgen Kocka, 'Soziale Entwicklung und politische Orientierung der Angestellten im Ersten Weltkrieg und in der Weimarer Republik', in Kocka, *Die Angestellten,* pp. 141–70; Schulz, *Die Angestellten.*
12. Winkler, *Arbeiter,* vol. 2, pp. 46–75 and 168.
13. Frevert, *Women,* pp. 149–204; Rouette, *Sozialpolitik als Geschlechterpolitik;* Büttner, *Weimar,* pp. 253–67.
14. Quoted in Bock, *Women in European History,* pp. 179–81; Kessemeier, *Sportlich.*
15. Frevert, *Women,* pp.149–204; Frevert, '"Wo du hingehst ..." Aufbrüche im Verhältnis der Geschlechter', in Nitschke, Ritter and Peukert, eds., *Jahrhundertwende,* vol. 2, pp. 89–118.
16. Grossman, *Reforming Sex.*
17. Zweig, *The World of Yesterday,* p. 61.
18. Peukert, *Weimar Republic,* p. 135.
19. Peukert, *Jugend zwischen Krieg und Krise;* Peukert, *Weimar Republic,* pp. 89–95; Peukert, '"Mit uns zieht die neue Zeit ..." Jugend zwischen Disziplinierung und Revolte', in Nitschke, Ritter and Peukert, eds., *Jahrhundertwende,* vol. 1, pp. 176–202; Büttner, *Weimar,* pp. 258–67.

20. Gründel, *Die Sendung der jungen Generation,* pp. 32–59; Suhrkamp, 'Söhne ohne Väter'; cf. Lethen, *Cool Conduct,* pp. 17–20; Ulrich Herbert, '"Generation der Sachlichkeit". Die völkische Studentenbewegung der frühen 20er Jahre in Deutschland', in Bajohr et al., eds., *Zivilisation und Barbarei,* pp. 115–44; Karl Prümm, 'Jugend ohne Väter. Zu den autobiographischen Jugendromanen der späten zwanziger Jahre', in Koebner, Janz and Trommler, eds. *Mythos Jugend,* pp. 563–89.
21. Stambolis, *Mythos Jugend,* p. 162.
22. Reichardt, *Faschistische Kampfbünde,* p. 373; Peukert, 'Erwerbslosigkeit', pp. 325–6.
23. Peukert, *Jugend zwischen Krieg und Krise,* p. 199.
24. Joachim, 'Romane aus Amerika', p. 398.
25. Räuscher, 'Berlin', p. 25.
26. Brunn and Reulecke, eds., *Metropolis Berlin*; Lange, *Berlin.*
27. Hans Stimmann, 'Weltstadtplätze und Massenverkehr', in Boberg, Fichter and Gillen, eds., *Die Metropole,* pp. 134–43, here p. 140; cf. Bienert, *Eingebildete Metropole,* pp. 105–18.
28. Kurt Tucholsky, 'Berliner Verkehr' [1926], in Tucholsky, *Gesammelte Werke, Ergänzungsband,* pp. 539–42, here p. 541.
29. Bollenbeck, *Tradition, Avantgarde, Reaktion,* p. 254; see also Gassert, 'Amerikanisierung', Lüdtke et al., eds., *Amerikanisierung,* and Becker, ed., *Mythos USA.*
30. Pollack, *Revolution des Gesellschaftstanzes,* pp. 72–3; my discussion here follows Maase, *Grenzenloses Vergnügen,* and Kosok and Jamin, eds., *Viel Vergnügen.*
31. These figures are from Maase, *Grenzenloses Vergnügen,* p. 300.
32. Deutscher Textilarbeiterverband, ed., *Mein Arbeitstag,* p. 21.
33. Zweig, *The World of Yesterday,* pp. 152–3; Erich Beyer, 'Sport in der Weimarer Republik', in Ueberhorst, ed., *Geschichte der Leibesübungen,* vol. 3, part 2, pp. 657–700; Eisenberg, 'Massensport'; Becker, *Amerikanismus.*
34. M. Rainer Lepsius, 'Parteiensystem und Sozialstruktur. Zum Problem der Demokratisierung der deutschen Gesellschaft', in Ritter, ed., *Deutsche Parteien,* pp. 56–80; Rohe, *Wahlen und Wählertraditionen*; Weichlein, *Sozialmilieus und politische Kultur*; Dieter Langewiesche, 'Politik–Gesellschaft–Kultur'.
35. Ulrich Herbert, '"Generation der Sachlichkeit"'; Lethen, *Cool Conduct.*
36. On the remainder of this section, see Büttner, *Weimar,* pp. 296–334; Kniesche et al., eds., *Dancing on the Volcano*; Gay, *Weimar Culture;* Hoffmann et al., eds., *Kultur unseres Jahrhunderts,* vol. 2; Willett, *New Sobriety*; Hermand and Trommler, *Kultur der Weimarer Republik*; Schrader and Schebera, *The 'Golden' Twenties*; Stölzl, ed., *Die Zwanziger Jahre in München.*
37. Kurt Tucholsky, 'In der Provinz' [1920], in Tucholsky, *Gesammelte Werke,* vol. 1, pp. 647–50, here p. 647.
38. Ludwig Finckh, 'Der Geist von Berlin' [1919], quoted in Kaes, ed., *Weimarer Republik,* pp. 14–16, here p. 15; Stapel, 'Geistige'.
39. Spengler, *The Decline of the West,* vol. 2, p. 103; Jung, *Die Herrschaft der Minderwertigen,* p. 207; Fritz von Haniel, quoted in Adelheid von Saldern, 'Überfremdungsängste. Gegen die Amerikanisierung der deutschen Kultur in den zwanziger Jahren', in Lüdtke, Marßolek and von Saldern, eds., *Amerikanisierung,*

pp. 213–44, here p. 226; Joseph Roth, 'Die Vereinigten Staaten von Amerika. Eindrücke und Gedanken beim 28. Eucharistischen Weltkongreß in Chicago', in *Gelbe Hefte*, 3.1 (1927), pp. 337–61, here p. 350.

40. Bollenbeck, *Tradition, Avantgarde, Reaktion*, pp. 221–4; Huizinga, *Im Schatten von Morgen*, p. 18; Bollenbeck, *Geschichte der Kulturkritik.*
41. Mai, *Europa*, pp. 18–51; Bolz, *Auszug aus der entzauberten Welt*, pp. 7–11; Herf, *Reactionary Modernism*, pp. 1–48; Rohkrämer, *Eine andere Moderne*, pp. 343–62.

## Chapter 6

1. Stresemann, at a meeting of the central executive of the DVP, 26 February 1929, as quoted in Bernhard, ed., *Gustav Stresemann*, pp. 428–33, here p. 433; Ludwig Kaas, 'Von der kulturellen Sendung der Katholiken im Volksganzen', in Sekretariat des Lokalkomitees, ed., *Generalversammlung*, pp. 246–56, here p. 257.
2. Pyta, *Hindenburg*, pp. 555–76; Neebe, *Großindustrie, Staat und NSDAP*, pp. 50–60.
3. James, *The German Slump*, pp. 283–323; Meister, *Die große Depression*, pp. 209–34; Kindleberger, *The World in Depression*, pp. 95–116; Treue, ed., *Deutschland in der Weltwirtschaftskrise*; Aldcroft, *From Versailles to Wall Street*; Blaich, *Der Schwarze Freitag*; Raphael, *Imperiale Gewalt*; pp. 166–85; Ritschl, *Deutschlands Krise.*
4. Clavin, *Great Depression*; John Pinder, 'Europa in der Weltwirtschaft 1920-1970', in Fohlen, ed., *Die europäischen Volkswirtschaften*, pp. 377–411; Ziebura, *World Economy*, pp. 154–87; Rees, *The Great Slump.*
5. Bauer, 'Jugend'; Weiland, *Kinder der Arbeitslosen*, p. 54; Herrnstadt, *Die Lage der arbeitslosen Jugendlichen.*
6. Winkler, *Arbeiter*, vol. 3, pp. 19–122; Büttner, *Weimar*, pp. 826–7, Tables 23 and 24; Lewek, *Arbeitslosigkeit und Arbeitslosenversicherung*; Stachura, ed., *Unemployment and the Great Depression*; Führer, *Arbeitslosigkeit*; Evans and Geary, eds., *The German Unemployed.*
7. Winkler, *Age of Catastrophe*, pp. 245–301, Raphael, *Imperiale Gewalt*, pp. 186–205.
8. Peukert, *Weimar Republic*, p. 255.
9. Mallmann, *Kommunisten in der Weimarer Republik*; Mallmann, 'Gehorsame Parteisoldaten'; Andreas Wirsching, '"Stalinisierung"'; Winkler, *Arbeiter*, vol. 2, pp. 416–65.
10. Bavaj, *Von links gegen Weimar*, pp. 137–82; Müller, *Intellektueller Linksradikalismus.*
11. Undated report (probably July 1925) to the Reich Minister of the Interior, *Zentrales Staatsarchiv, Potsdam*, 15.07/325, pp. 66–74.
12. Mommsen, *Rise and Fall*,, pp. 231–2, 255–6 and 306–12; Schulz, *Aufstieg des Nationalsozialismus*, pp. 274–90; Breuer, *Grundpositionen der deutschen Rechten*; Breuer, *Anatomie der konservativen Revolution*; Herbert, *Best*, pp. 51–99.
13. Diehl, *Paramilitary Politics*; Schumann, *Political Violence*; Weisbrod, 'Gewalt'.
14. Hitler's retrospective comments, 9 August 1941, printed in Hitler, *Hitler's Table Talk*, pp. 24–8, here p. 24.

15. Weinberg, ed., *Hitler's Second Book*; Hitler, *Mein Kampf*, p. 598.
16. Schmitz et al., eds., *Völkische Bewegung*; Mosse, *Crisis of German Ideology*; Breuer, *Grundpositionen*; Herbert, *Best*, pp. 57–64 and 92–4.
17. Binding and Hoche, *Freigabe der Vernichtung lebensunwerten Lebens*, pp. 31–2 and 62.
18. Weingart, Kroll and Bayertz, *Rasse, Blut und Gene*, pp. 274–320; Schmuhl, *Rassenhygiene, Nationalsozialismus, Euthanasie*, p. 119; Nowak, *'Euthanasie' und Sterilisierung im 'Dritten Reich'*, p. 28; Lösch, *Rasse als Konstrukt*, pp. 161–230; Becker, *Sozialdarwinismus, Rassismus, Antisemitismus und völkischer Gedanke*.
19. Barkai and Mendes-Flohr, *Renewal and Destruction*, pp. 21–9; Werner T. Angress, 'Juden im politischen Leben der Revolutionszeit', in Mosse, ed., *Deutsches Judentum*, pp. 137–316; Aly, *Why the Germans?*, pp. 99–126
20. Lohalm, *Völkischer Radikalismus*, pp. 176–237.
21. Zweig, 'Die antisemitische Welle', p. 385.
22. Hecht, *Deutsche Juden und Antisemitismus*, pp. 206–24; Walter, *Antisemitische Kriminalität und Gewalt*, pp. 222–43; Werner Jochmann, 'Die Ausbreitung des Antisemitismus in Deutschland 1914–1923', in Jochmann, *Gesellschaftskrise*, pp. 99–170; Werner Jochmann, 'Der Antisemitismus und seine Bedeutung für den Untergang der Weimarer Republik', in Jochmann, *Gesellschaftskrise*, pp. 171–94; Niewyk, *The Jews in Weimar Germany*, pp. 45–81.
23. On the rise of Hitler, see Kershaw, *Hitler*, vol.1, pp. 173–98; Winkler, *Weimar*, pp. 334–74; Broszat, *Hitler and the Collapse*, pp. 50–91; Evans, *The Coming of the Third Reich*, pp. 195–230; Schulz, *Aufstieg*, pp. 355–478; Büttner, *Weimar*, pp. 406–18.
24. Jung, 'Neubelebung'.
25. Raphael, *Imperiale Gewalt*, pp. 186–230; Winkler, *Age of Catastrophe*, pp. 245–337.
26. For the quotations from Goebbels and Heß, see Kershaw, *The 'Hitler-Myth'*, pp. 26–7; Wehler, *Gesellschaftsgeschichte*, vol. 4, pp. 542–80; Herbst, *Hitlers Charisma*.
27. Jürgen W. Falter, 'Die Wähler der NSDAP 1928–1933. Sozialstruktur und parteipolitische Herkunft', in Michalka, ed., *Machtergreifung*, pp. 47–59; Falter and Kater, *Wähler und Mitglieder der NSDAP*; Falter, *Hitlers Wähler*, pp. 155–203.
28. Büttner, *Weimar*, pp. 423–35; Meister, *Depression*.
29. Winkler, *Age of Catastrophe*, pp. 484–502; Schivelbusch, *Three New Deals*, pp. 17–48.
30. Winkler, *Weimar*, pp. 444–76.
31. Reusch to Kastl, 11 September 1931, quoted in Neebe, *Großindustrie*, p. 99; see Marx, *Paul Reusch*, pp. 308–26.
32. Count von Westarp, 'Weshalb ich für Brüning stimmte', in *Volkskonservative Führerbriefe*, no.11, 20 October 1931.
33. Neebe, *Großindustrie*, pp. 127–74; see also Ulrich Herbert, 'Die Dynamik der Gewalt. Der gescheiterte Versuch der nationalsozialistischen Krisenlösung', in Niethammer et al., eds., *Bürgerliche Gesellschaft*, pp. 413–524.
34. For these developments, see Büttner, *Weimar*, pp. 464–85; Winkler, *Weimar*, pp. 477–520; Winkler, *Germany: the Long Road West*, vol. 1, pp.435–488; Peukert, *Weimar Republic*, pp. 258–272; Mommsen, *Rise and Fall*, pp. 451–544.
35. Reusch to Dörge, 4 August 1932, quoted in Neebe, *Großindustrie*, p. 131.

36. Cf. Mommsen, *Rise and Fall*, pp. 487–88. ('Ott Simulation Exercise').
37. Schildt, *Militärdiktatur*.
38. Reusch, 22 December 1932, quoted in Neebe, *Großindustrie*, p. 144.
39. Winkler, *Revolution, Staat, Faschismus*, p. 81.

## Chapter 7

1. Report by the French Ambassador in Berlin on the attitude of the German population to National Socialism, 1933, printed in Michalka, ed., *Deutsche Geschichte*, pp. 36–7, here p. 36; Jean-Marc Dreyfus, '"Und dann wählen sie Männer wie Hitler zum Werkzeug ihrer Katastrophe aus". Die Berichterstattung Botschafter André François-Poncets und der französischen Konsuln aus dem Deutschen Reich bis 1939', in Bajohr and Strupp, eds., *Fremde Blicke*, pp. 138–62.
2. Proclamation by the Reich government to the German people, 1 February 1933, in Michalka, ed., *Deutsche Geschichte*, no. 1, pp. 13–16. On this section, see Frei, *National Socialist Rule*, pp. 31–69; Herbst, *Das nationalsozialistische Deutschland*, pp. 59–89; Broszat, *The Hitler State*, pp. 57–240; Bracher, *The German Dictatorship*, pp. 252–311; Evans, *The Coming of the Third Reich*, pp. 309–90; Thamer, *Verführung*, pp. 231–336; Wendt, *Deutschland*, pp. 67–200.
3. For Hitler's address of 3 February 1933 to army and navy commanders about his political objectives (the 'Liebmann record'), see Michalka, ed., *Deutsche Geschichte*, no. 3, pp. 17–18, here p. 17.
4. Reich minister Goering's speech at an NSDAP rally in Essen, 10 March 1933, in Michaelis and Schraepler, eds., *Ursachen und Folgen*, vol. 9, no. 2002, pp. 82–4, here p. 83.
5. This formulation probably originated from Hitler himself, rather than von Papen. See Edinger, *German Exile Politics*, p. 268, note 22.
6. Emergency Decree of 4 February 1933, *RGBl 1933, I*, pp. 35–40.
7. Winkler, *Arbeiter*, vol. 3, pp. 867–950.
8. *Miesbacher Anzeiger*, 2 March 1933, quoted in Kershaw, *Popular Opinion*, pp. 117–18. For government support for the Nazi movement see the circular by the Prussian Minister of the Interior, 17 February 1933, in *Ministerial-Blatt für die Preußische innere Verwaltung, Teil I*, Berlin, 1933, I, p. 169. Decree of 28 February 1933, *RGBl 1933, I*, no. 17, p.83. For the debate on the Reichstag fire, see Backes et al., eds., *Reichstagsbrand*. The various attempts to throw doubt on the view that van der Lubbe acted alone have not as yet produced any convincing evidence. See for example Schmädecke, Bahar and Kugel, 'Reichstagsbrand'.
9. Sackett to Secretary of State Cordell Hull, 3 March 1933, in Becker and Becker, eds., *Hitlers Machtergreifung*, document 77, pp. 116–17.
10. Broszat, *The Hitler State*, p. 101; Herbert, *Best*, pp. 119–30.
11. Schneider, *Unterm Hakenkreuz*, pp. 107–17; Winkler, *Arbeiter*, vol. 3, pp. 884–6.
12. Rudolf Diels 'Die Nacht der langen Messer', *Der Spiegel*, 9 June 1949, pp. 17–20; Peukert, *KPD im Widerstand*, pp. 83–9.

13. Sermon delivered by the General Superintendant of the Kurmark Brandenburg, Otto Dibelius, in the Nikolaikirche, Potsdam, 21 March 1933, in Becker and Becker, eds., *Hitlers Machtergreifung,* doc. 114, pp. 156–7, here p. 157.
14. Quoted in Thamer, *Verführung und Gewalt,* pp. 278–9, who took it from Fest, *Hitler,* pp. 410–11.
15. Schneider, *Unterm Hakenkreuz,* pp. 31–120; Winkler, *Arbeiter,* vol. 3, pp. 907–50.
16. Klönne, *Jugend,* pp. 15–41; Kater, *Hitler Youth,* pp. 115–47.
17. Ernst-Wolfgang Böckenförde, 'Der deutsche Katholizismus im Jahre 1933', in Jasper, ed., *Von Weimar zu Hitler,* pp. 317–43; Scholder, *The Churches,* vol. 1, pp. 237–53.
18. Broszat, *The Hitler State,* pp. 17–56; Kershaw, *Hitler 1889–1936,* vol. 1, pp. 429–95.
19. Röhm's Order of 30 May 1933, as quoted in Broszat, *The Hitler State,* p. 199.
20. On Röhm and the SA in 1933 and 1934, see Longerich, *Die braunen Bataillone,* pp. 165–205; Frei, *National Socialist Rule,* pp. 3–27; and Herbst, *Das nationalsozialistische Deutschland,* pp. 111–18.
21. Müller, *The Army, Politics and Society in Germany,* pp. 16–53; Geyer, *Aufrüstung und Sicherheit,* pp. 326–412.
22. Forschbach, *Edgar J. Jung*; Longerich, *Die brauen Bataillone,* p. 215; Frei, *National Socialist Rule,* pp. 16–22.
23. Law on State Emergency Defence Measures, 3 July 1934, *RGBl. 1934, I,* p. 529; Ministerial Meeting of 3 July 1934, in *Regierung Hitler,* vol. 1.2, no. 375, pp. 1,354–8, here p. 1,358; Schmitt, "Führer schützt das Recht'; Hitler's speech of 21 July 1934 to the Reichstag, in Michaelis and Schraepler, eds., *Ursachen und Folgen,* vol. 10, pp. 221–2.
24. Jung, *Plebiszit und Diktatur.*
25. *Nationalsozialistische Monatshefte,* 4 (1933), H.34, pp. 1–3, in VEJ, vol. 1, doc. 2, pp. 67–9, here pp. 68–9.
26. *Jüdische Rundschau,* no. 9, 31 January 1933, p. 1, in VEJ, vol. 1, doc.1, pp. 65–7, here p. 65. For the next section, see Longerich, *Holocaust,* pp. 29–69; Hilberg, *The Destruction of the European Jews,* pp. 79–153; Friedländer, *Nazi Germany,* vol. 1, pp. 15–210; Reinhard Rürup, 'Das Ende der Emanzipation. Die antijüdische Politik in Deutschland von der Machtergreifung bis zum Zweiten Weltkrieg', in Paucker, ed., *Juden im nationalsozialistischen Deutschland,* pp. 97–114; Adam, *Judenpolitik im Dritten Reich,* pp. 19–71.
27. Walter Gyssling, 'Mein Leben in Deutschland vor und nach Hitler', in VEJ, vol. 1, doc. 6, pp. 76–8, here p. 78.
28. Exilvorstand der Sozialdemokratischen Partei, ed., *Deutschland-Berichte,* Juli 1937, pp. 931–2, here p. 931. This report is a retrospective view of the regime's policy towards the Jews since 1933.
29. *The Times,* no. 46409, 4 March 1933, p. 14, quoted in VEJ, vol. 1, doc. 22, pp.110–12, here p. 112; Friedländer, *Nazi Germany,* vol. 1, pp. 19–24; Wildt, *Hitler's Volksgemeinschaft,* pp. 89–93.
30. Adam, *Judenpolitik,* pp. 72–84.
31. Walk, ed., *Kurzbiographien*; Friedländer, *Nazi Germany,*, vol. 1, pp 36–9.
32. *Nationalsozialistische Monatshefte,* 4 (1933), *Heft.*38, pp. 195–7, in VEJ, vol. 1, doc. 48, pp. 167–8.

33. Cf. Rosenstock, *Exodus*; Strauss, *Jewish Emigration*, p. 326.
34. Wildt, ed., *Judenpolitik*, p. 21; Friedländer, *Nazi Germany*, vol. 1, pp. 138–40.
35. The Gestapo to the Reich Ministry of Justice, 9 September 1935, in *Bericht d.Abt.*II.112 d. SD (at the end of 1936), IfZ, MA 557; Otto von Bolschwing, 'Momorandum "Zum Judenproblem", Januar 1937', Wildt, ed., *Judenpolitik*, doc. 9, pp. 95–105, here p. 99.
36. On the Nuremberg Laws, see in particular Essner, '*Nürnberger Gesetze*'; Longerich, *Holocaust*, pp. 57–61; Gruchmann, *Justiz*, pp. 864–86. On provisions for their implementation, and on their impact, see Lothar Gruchmann, '"Blutschutzgesetz"'; Gruchmann, *Justiz*, pp. 874–86; Meyer, '*Jüdische Mischlinge*', pp. 24–94; and Przyrembel, '*Rassenschande*', pp.127–82
37. SD-Oberabschnitt Nord-West II 112, Hamburg, 14 January 1937, in Jäckel and Kulka, eds., *Juden in den geheimen Stimmungsberichten*, no. 294, pp. 250–2, here p. 251; *Sopade-Berichte*, July 1937, pp. 941–2, here p. 942.
38. Kuller, *Bürokratie und Verbrechen*, pp. 185–306.
39. Bajohr, '*Aryanization' in Hamburg*; Bajohr, 'Verfolgung'; Barkai, *From Boycott to Annihilation*; Barkai, 'Die deutschen Unternehmer und die Judenpolitik im "Dritten Reich"', in Büttner, ed., *Die Deutschen und die Judenverfolgung*, pp. 207–29.
40. Treue, 'Hitlers Denkschrift'; Ralf Banken, 'Das nationalsozialistische Devisenrecht als Steuerungs- und Diskriminierungsinstrument 1933–1945', in Bähr and Banken, eds., *Wirtschaftssteuerung*, pp. 121–236.
41. *Sopade-Berichte*, January 1936, pp. 24–6; Cardinal Faulhaber to Alois Wurm, 8 April 1933, in VEJ, vol. 1, doc. 30, pp. 135–6, here p. 135.
42. Report from the British Ambassador in Berlin, Horace Rumbold, to the British Foreign Secretary, Sir John Simon, 21 March 1933, in *DBFP*, Second Series, Volume IV, no. 268, p. 470.
43. On the Gestapo and the SS, see Dams and Stolle, *Gestapo*, Paul and Mallmann., eds., *Die Gestapo im Zweiten Weltkrieg*; Paul and Mallmann, eds., *Die Gestapo: Mythos und Realität*; Rürup, ed., *Topography of Terror*; Browder, *Hitler's Enforcers*; Hein, *Elite*; Rohrkamp, '*Weltanschaulich gefestigte Kämpfer*'; Schulte, ed., *Die SS*; Herbert, *Best*, pp. 133–249; Orth, *Die Konzentrationslager-SS*.
44. Ulrich Herbert, 'Das "Jahrhundert der Lager": Ursachen, Erscheinungformen, Auswirkungen', in Reif-Spirek and Ritscher, eds., *Speziallager*, pp. 11–27; Kotek and Rigoulot, *Jahrhundert der Lager*.
45. Herbert, Orth and Dieckmann, eds., *Konzentrationslager*, pp. 43–166; Benz and Distel, eds., *Herrschaft und Gewalt*; Benz et al., eds., *Instrumentarium der Macht*; Orth, *System*.
46. Hans-Walter Schmuhl, 'Rassismus unter den Bedingungen charismatischer Herrschaft', in Bracher, Funke and Jacobsen, eds., *Deutschland 1933–1945*, pp. 182–97; Bock, *Zwangssterilisation*.
47. Groß, *Rassenpolitische Erziehung*, p. 13.
48. Bock, *Zwangssterilisation*, pp. 88 and 101; Bock, 'Rassenpolitik'; *Gesetz zur Verhütung erbkranken Nachwuchses (GzVeN), RGBl. I, 1933*, pp. 529–31; cf. Gütt, Rüdin and Ruttke, *Gesetz zur Verhütung*; Schmuhl, *Rassenhygiene, Nationalsozialismus, Euthanasie*; Ulrich Herbert, 'Traditionen des Rassismus', in Niethammer et al. *Bürgerliche Gesellschaft*, pp. 472–88; Raphael, 'Ordnungsdenken'.

49. *Gesetz gegen gefährliche Gewohnheitsverbrecher und über Maßregeln der Sicherung and Besserung* (Law against dangerous habitual criminals and concerning measures for their safeguarding and cure), *RGBl. I 1933*, p. 995; Gütt, Rüdin and Ruttke, *Gesetz zur Verhütung*, p. 215.
50. Robert Ritter, 'Primitivität und Kriminalität', in *Monatsschrift für Kriminalbiologie und Strafrechtsreform*, 31 (1940), pp. 198–210, here pp. 200–2.
51. Werner Best, 'Die Geheime Staatspolizei', p. 126.
52. Orth, *System*, p. 51; Martin Broszat, *Konzentrationslager*, p. 81, gives the total number of inmates as 25,000. Cf. Tuchel, *Konzentrationslager*, p. 313. The so-called 'asocials' were distributed unevenly over the various concentration camps.
53. Tooze, *Wages*, pp. 23–4; James, *The German Slump*, pp. 119–25; Kindleberger, *The World in Depression*, pp. 123–34.
54. Rudolf Heberle, 'Soziologie', p. 442
55. Herbst, *Das nationalsozialistische Deutschland*, pp. 92 and 97. On these issues, see Tooze, *Wages*, pp. 37–134 and Overy, *Nazi Economic Recovery*.
56. 8 February 1933, AdR, *Regierung Hitler*, I/1, pp. 50–1.
57. Hitler's address to army and navy commanders, 3 February 1933, in Becker and Becker, eds., *Hitlers Machtergreifung*, no. 13, pp. 40–1.
58. Tooze, *Wages*, p. 65.
59. Tooze, *Wages*, p. 63, Table 2; pp. 682–5, Tables A3 and A4.
60. Tooze, *Wages*, pp. 203–43.
61. Hans-Erich Volkmann, 'The National Socialist Economy in Preparation for War', in GSWW, vol. 1, pp. 157–372; Volkmann, 'Aufrüstung'.
62. Hitler's address to army and navy commanders, 3 February 1933, in Becker and Becker, eds., *Hitlers Machtergreifung*, no. 13, p. 41.
63. Hitler's 'Peace Speech' of 17 May 1933, in Becker and Becker, eds., *Hitlers Machtergreifung*, no. 259, pp. 307–8, here p. 308.
64. On the next section, see Hildebrand, *The Foreign Policy of the Third Reich*; Recker, *Außenpolitik*; Herbst, *Das nationalsozialistische Deutschland*, pp. 99–100.
65. Joseph Goebbels, diary entry for 3 May 1936, in Goebbels, *Tagebücher*, Part 1, vol. 2, p. 607. On Italy's action in Ethiopia, see Mattioli, *Experimentierfeld* and Woller, *Geschichte Italiens*, pp. 142–52.
66. Alfred Jodl on 4 June 1946 at the Nuremberg trials, IMT, vol. 15, pp. 386–7; Schmidt, *Statist*, p. 320.
67. *Sopade-Berichte*, March 1936, p. 310; April 1936, pp. 465 and 468.
68. Rougemont, *Journal*, pp. 64–6.
69. Domarus, *Hitler*, vol. 2, pp. 787–90, here p.790; Kershaw, *The 'Hitler Myth'*, p. 82; cf. Wehler, *Gesellschaftsgeschichte*, vol. 4, pp. 676–8; Armin Nolzen, 'Der "Führer" und seine Partei', in Süß and Süß, eds., *Das 'Dritte Reich'*, pp. 55–78.
70. Thamer, *Verführung und Gewalt*, p. 546; Ribbentrop, *Memoirs*, p. 59; Baumeister and Schüler-Springorum, eds., *'If you tolerate this'*; Bernecker, *Geschichte Spaniens*, pp. 135–76; Winkler, *Age of Catastrophe*, pp. 602–21.
71. For the next section, see Hachtmann, *Industriearbeit*; Hachtmann, 'Arbeitsmarkt', Zollitsch, *Arbeiter*, pp. 72–107; Frese, *Betriebspolitik*; Herbert, 'Arbeiterschaft im "Dritten Reich"'.

72. Aly, *Hitler's Beneficiaries,* pp. 36–72; Sachße and Tennstedt, *Geschichte der Armenfürsorge*; Baranowski, *Strength through Joy.*
73. Ayaß, '*Asoziale*'; Wagner, *Volksgemeinschaft.*
74. Timothy W. Mason, 'Die Bändigung der Arbeiterklasse im nationalsozialistischen Deutschland', in Sachse, Siegel and Spode, et al., eds., *Angst, Belohnung, Zucht und Ordnung,* pp. 11–53; Kershaw, *The 'Hitler Myth',* pp. 121–32.
75. Corni and Gies, *Brot, Butter, Kanonen*; Münkel, *Bäuerliche Interessen*; Mai, *Rasse und Raum*; Oberkrome, *Ordnung und Autarkie*; Wehler, *Gesellschaftsgeschichte,* vol. 4, pp. 699–707.
76. Wehler, *Gesellschaftsgeschichte,* vol. 4, pp. 715–30; Erker, *Industrieeliten*; Ziegler, ed, *Großbürger.*
77. Jansen, *Professoren und Politik*; Michael Grüttner, 'Die deutschen Universitäten unter dem Hakenkreuz', in Connelly and Grüttner, eds., *Zwischen Autonomie und Anpassung,* pp. 67–100; Oexle, '"Zusammenarbeit mit Baal"'; Hartmut Titze, 'Hochschulen', in Langewiesche, ed., *Weimarer Republik,* pp. 209–40; Lehmann and Oexle, eds., *Nationalsozialismus*; Langewiesche, ed., *Universitäten*; for the next few paragraphs see Ulrich Herbert, 'Der deutsche Professor im Dritten Reich. Vier biografische Skizzen', in Orth and Oberkrome, eds., *Deutsche Forschungsgemeinschaft,* pp. 483–503.
78. Quoted in Hartmut Titze, 'Hochschulen', in Langewiesche and Tenorth, eds., *Handbuch der deutschen Bildungsgeschichte,* pp. 209–39.
79. Grüttner and Kinas, 'Vertreibung'.
80. Hahn, *Mein Leben,* p. 145.
81. Gottfried Benn, 'Antwort an die literarischen Emigranten (1933)' in Benn, *Gesammelte Werke,* ed. by Dieter Wellershof, vol. 7, p. 1701, quoted in Thamer, *Verführung und Gewalt,* p. 300.
82. Hitler's speech at the official opening of the 'House of German Art' in Munich, 19 July 1937, in Michaelis and Schraepler, eds., *Ursachen und Folgen,* vol. 11, pp. 79–80.
83. Evans, *The Coming of the Third Reich,* ch. 6, 'Hitler's Cultural Revolution', pp. 391–461; Reichel, *Schöner Schein*; Merker, *Bildende Künste*; Schäfer, *Gespaltenes Bewusstsein*; Friedländer, *Kitsch und Tod.*
84. Shirer, *Berlin Diary,* p. 59.
85. François-Poncet, *The Fateful Years,* p. 204.
86. Shirer, *Berlin Diary,* p. 74.
87. Hjalmar Schacht, 'Protokoll über die Sitzung des Ministerrates am 12. Mai 1936', in Michaelis and Schraepler, eds. *Ursachen und Folgen,* vol. 10, pp. 525–30; Tooze, *Wages,* p. 216.
88. Memorandum by Hitler, August 1936, in Michaelis and Schraepler, eds., *Ursachen und Folgen,* vol. 10, pp. 534–42.
89. Göring, speaking on 4 September 1936, quoted in Wendt, *Deutschland,* p. 422; Herbst, *Das nationalsozialistische Deutschland,* pp. 160–76; Tooze, *Wages,* pp. 203–43.
90. The Hoßbach Memorandum, 5 November 1937, in *DGFP,* Series D (1937–1945), vol. 1, no. 19, p. 34.
91. *Time Magazine,* 2 May 1938, 'Genius Hitler'.

92. Schapira, 'Leben in Deutschland', pp. 1–2, Harvard Prize Competition no. 199, in VEJ, vol. 2, doc. 17, p. 113–16, here p. 114 (italicised in the original).
93. Instruction by Hitler, 30 May 1938, in IMT, vol. XXV, pp. 434–5.
94. Hill, ed., *Weizsäcker Papiere,* vol. 2, p. 128.
95. Memorandum by Ludwig Beck, 29 May 1938, in Müller, *General Ludwig Beck,* doc. 43.
96. Hoffmann, *German Resistance,* pp. 49–96; Hans Mommsen, 'The position of the military opposition to Hitler in the German resistance movement', in Mommsen, *Germans Against Hitler,* pp. 238–52.
97. Herbst, *Das nationalsozialistische Deutschland,* pp. 192–200; Wendt, *Deutschland,* pp. 423–45; Smelser, *Sudetenproblem.*
98. Confidential Report by the World Jewish Congress, 14 October 1938, in VEJ, vol. 2,doc. 106, pp. 308–19, here p. 309.
99. October–December 1938 report by the *Kreisleiter* of Erding, quoted in Kershaw, *The 'Hitler Myth',* p. 135.
100. Report no. 196 from the US Ambassador in Berlin, Hugh R. Wilson, to the State Secretary in Washington, dated 22 June 1938, in VEJ, vol. 2, doc. 47, pp. 176–9, here p. 179.
101. Barkai, *From Boycott to Annihilation,* p. 118; SD Report, September 1938, quoted in Uwe Dietrich Adam, 'How spontaneous was the pogrom?', in Pehle, ed., *November 1938,* pp. 73–94, here p. 86.
102. Brechtken, *Madagascar,* p. 217.
103. Friedländer, *Nazi Germany,* vol. 1, pp. 241–304; Longerich, *Holocaust,* pp. 95–117; Herbst, *Das nationalsozialistische Deutschland,* pp. 200–17; Tomaszewski, *Auftakt zur Vernichtung,* pp. 113–44.
104. Report by Odilo Globocnik, undated, in VEJ, vol. 2, doc. 133, pp. 383–7.
105. Josef Goebbels, diary entry for 10 November 1938, in VEJ, vol. 2, doc. 124, pp. 363–6.
106. Report from the French Chargé d'Affaires in Berlin to the French Foreign Minister, 15 November 1938, in VEJ, vol. 2, doc. 156, pp. 457–61, here p. 460.
107. Replies to the administrative circular from the Bielefeld Gestapo station, 14 November 1938, in Kulka and Jäckel, eds., *Jews in the Secret Nazi Reports,* nos. 357–79, pp. 343–68.
108. Conference chaired by Göring, 12 November 1938, VEJ, vol. 2, doc. 146, pp. 408–37, here p. 436.
109. Monthly Report from the District President of Lower Bavaria and the Upper Palatinate, 8 December 1938, quoted in Broszat, Fröhlich and Wiesemann, eds., *Bayern in der NS-Zeit,* vol. 1, pp. 473–4, here p. 473.
110. Conference chaired by Göring, 12 November 1938.
111. Göring's speech to the National Defence Council, 18 November 1938, in Mason, ed., *Arbeiterklasse und Volksgemeinschaft,* pp. 908–33, here pp. 925–6.
112. Decree on Atonement Payments by Jews of German Nationality, 12 November 1938, in VEJ, vol. 2, doc. 143, p. 403; Decree for the Exclusion of the Jews from German Economic Life, 12 November 1938, in VEJ, vol. 2, doc. 144, pp. 403–4.
113. 'Law on Jewish Rental Arrangements', 30 April 1939, *RGBl. I,* pp. 864–5; Tenth Ordinance arising from the Reich Citizenship Law, 4 July 1939, *RGBl. I,* pp. 1097–9;

Göring quotation: Conference of 12 November 1938, VEJ, vol. 2, doc. 146, pp. 408–37, here p. 435.

114. *Das Schwarze Korps*, 24 November 1938; cf. Bernward Dörner, 'Der Holocaust. Die "Endlösung der Judenfrage"', in Benz, ed., *Vorurteil*, p. 96; Wolf Gruner, 'Terra incognita?—Die Lager für den "jüdischen Arbeitseinsatz" (1938–1945) und die deutsche Bevölkerung', in Büttner, *Die Deutschen und die Judenverfolgung*, pp. 131–59.
115. Göring, speaking on 12 November 1938 at the conference held in the Reich Ministry of Aviation on the economic consequences of the pogrom, VEJ, vol. 2, doc. 146, pp. 408–37, here p. 436.
116. Hitler, speaking to the Great German Reichstag, IV. Electoral Period, 1st Sitting, 30 January 1939, in VEJ, vol. 2, doc. 248, pp. 678–80, here p. 680.
117. Schmitt, *Völkerrechtliche Großraumordnung*; Schmitt, 'Großraum gegen Universalismus', in Schmitt, *Positionen und Begriffe*, pp. 295–302.
118. Hitler, '*Der Führer antwortet Roosevelt*': *Reichstagsrede vom 28.4.1939*, p. 34.
119. Hitler's speech of 10 February 1939 to army group commanders, printed in Müller, *Armee und Drittes Reich*, pp. 365–75.
120. Best, 'Rechtsbegriff und "Völkerrecht"', in *Deutsches Recht*, 9 (1939), pp. 1,345–8, here p. 1,348; Best, 'Nochmals: Völkische Großraumordnung statt "völkerrechtliche" Großraumordnung', in *Deutsches Recht*, 11 (1941), pp. 1,533–4.
121. Hitler's speech of 23 May 1939 to the commanders of the Wehrmacht, as recorded in the Schmundt Minute (*Ursachen und Folgen*, vol. 13, p. 292.)
122. *DGFP*, Series D, vol. 7, nos. 228–9, pp. 245–7. For the Soviet perspective, see Hildermeier, *Geschichte der Sowjetunion*, pp. 585–600, and Bonwetsch, 'Hitler-Stalin Pakt'.

## Chapter 8

1. For occupation policy in Poland, see the following: Böhler, *Auftakt*; Madajczyk, *Okkupationspolitik Nazideutschlands*; Gross, *Polish Society*; Rossino, *Hitler Strikes Poland*; Borodziej, *Geschichte Polens*, pp. 189–216; Broszat, *Nationalsozialistische Polenpolitik*; Seidel, *Deutsche Besatzungspolitik*; Horst Röhde, 'Hitler's first Blitzkrieg and its Consequences for North-eastern Europe', in GSWW, vol. 2, pp. 67–150; Tomasz Szarota, 'Poland under German Occupation, 1939–1941', in Wegner, ed., *From Peace to War*, pp. 47–61.
2. Hitler's directive of 23 May 1939 to the Wehrmacht, in IMT, vol. 37, doc. 079-L, p. 548.
3. Roth and Ebbinghaus, 'Vorläufer des "Generalplans Ost"', pp. 84–91.
4. Markus Krzoska, '"Bromberger Blutsonntag"', pp. 237–48; Jansen and Weckbecker, '*Volksdeutscher Selbstschutz*'; Jastrzebski, *Bromberger Blutsonntag*.
5. Heydrich, on 7 September 1939, according to the minutes of a meeting of department heads of the RSHA, dated 8 September 1939, BA, R 58/825; Hitler's speech of 17 October 1939, in IMT, vol. 26, doc. PS-864, pp. 378–80; Krausnick, *Hitlers Einsatzgruppen*, pp. 26–88.

6. Situation report from SS-Sturmbannführer Franz Röder, commander of SD *Einsatzkommando* 16 to the head office of the SD, 20 October 1939, quoted in Lutz Hachmeister, 'Pressforschung und Vernichtungskrieg', in Duchkowitsch, Hausjell and Semrad, eds., *Spirale des Schweigens,* p. 77. ('Congressers' refers to Congress Poles, inhabitants of the area established as the Kingdom of Poland by the Congress of Vienna in 1815. Many Poles continued to invoke the memory of Congress Poland even after the restoration of an independent Polish state in 1918.) See also Jansen and Weckbecker, *'Volksdeutscher Selbstschutz',* p. 171.
7. Speaker's notes by the Supreme Commander in the East, von Blaskowitz, 6 February 1940, BA-MA RH 53-25/23, quoted in Röhr, *Faschistische Okkupationspolitik,* p. 134; Helmuth Stieff to his wife, 21 November 1939, in Mühleisen, ed., *Helmuth Stieff,* p. 109.
8. Jochen Böhler, '"Tragische Verstrickung" oder Auftakt zum Vernichtungskrieg?', in Mallmann and Musial, eds., *Genesis des Genozids,* pp. 36–56; Wildt, *Uncompromising Generation,* pp. 217–41.
9. Seraphim, ed., *Politisches Tagebuch Alfred Rosenbergs,* pp. 98–9.
10. Hitler's speech to the German Reichstag, 6 October 1939, in VEJ, vol. 4, dok. 17, pp. 99–102.
11. Piotrowski, ed., *Hans Frank's Diary,* p. 211.
12. Heinemann, *'Rasse, Siedlung, deutsches Blut'*; Koehl, *RKFDV.*
13. Seraphim, *Judentum*; on Conze, see Aly and Heim, *Architects of Annihilation,* pp. 58–72; cf. Mühle, *Für Volk und deutschen Osten*; Haar, *Historiker im Nationalsozialismus,* pp. 307–11; Fahlbusch, *Wissenschaft*; Burleigh, *Germany Turns Eastwards.*
14. On this, see Mallmann and Musial, eds., *Genesis des Genozids*; Musiał, *Deutsche Zivilverwaltung,* pp. 101–92; Browning, *Origins,* pp. 12–54; Aly, *Final Solution,* pp. 14–32; Młynarczyk, *Judenmord in Zentralpolen.*
15. Seifert, *Jude,* pp. 68 and 83; Gruner, *Jewish Forced Labor,* pp. 3–102; Browning, *Nazi Policy,* pp. 84–116.
16. Note on the meeting of department chiefs and commanders of *Einsatzgruppen,* 21 September 1939, dated 27 September 1939, BA R 58/825; Heydrich to commanders of *Einsatzgruppen* of the security police in Poland, 21 September 1939, in VEJ, vol. 2, doc. 12, pp. 88–92.
17. Heydrich's letter of 21 December 1939, in VEJ, vol. 4, doc. 66, pp. 190–3.
18. Mlynarczyk, *Judenmord in Zentralpolen,* pp. 67–110; Seidel, *Deutsche Besatzungspolitik,* pp. 87–169.
19. Minutes of Hans Frank's meeting with the District Commissioners and Town Governors of the Radom region, 25 November 1939, in Berenstein et al., *Faschismus, Getto, Massenmord,* p. 46; Groscurth, *Tagebücher,* pp. 361–3; minutes of meeting of department heads on 29 September 1939, BA, R 58/825, sheets 36 and 37.
20. Himmler's letter of 20 May 1940, in Pätzold, ed., *Verfolgung, Vertreibung, Vernichtung,* doc. 235, p. 264.
21. *Das Schwarze Korps,* 24 November 1938.
22. Löw, *Juden im Ghetto Litzmannstadt*; Trunk, *Łódź Ghetto*; Młynarczyk, *Judenmord,* pp. 110–72; Ulrich Herbert, 'Arbeit und Vernichtung. Ökonomisches Interesse

und Primat der Weltanschauung', in Herbert, ed., *Europa und der 'Reichseinsatz'*, pp. 384–426.

23. Letter from Hitler to Mussolini, 8 March 1940, GDFP, Series D, vol. 8, No. 663, pp. 871–80, here p. 872; Overy, *Why the Allies Won*, p. 314; Buchheim, ed., *German Industry*.
24. Hitler on 24 March 1940, quoted in Tooze, *Wages*, p. 337.
25. *Sopade-Berichte*, August–October 1939, pp. 975–83; *Sopade-Berichte*, January 1940, pp. 29–30.
26. Corni and Gies, *Brot, Butter, Kanonen*, pp. 397–584; Buchheim, 'Mythos'.
27. Heß to Göring, 18 September 1939, quoted in Recker, *Nationalsozialistische Sozialpolitik*, p. 44.
28. Recker, *Nationalsozialistische Sozialpolitik*, pp. 37–58; Aly, *Hitler's Beneficiaries*, pp. 60–90.
29. Werner, *'Bleib übrig!'*; Aly, *Hitler's Beneficiaries*, pp. 299–304. On the development of social policy during the war, see Recker, *Nationalsozialistische Sozialpolitik*; Tooze, *Wages*, pp. 285–395; Eichholtz, *Kriegswirtschaft*, vol. 1, pp. 384–91; Overy, *Why the Allies Won*; Overy, '"Blitzkriegswirtschaft"?'; Overy, *War and Economy*; Mason, ed., *Arbeiterklasse und Volksgemeinschaft*; Herbert, 'Arbeiterschaft'.
30. Franz Seldte, 14 July 1938, quoted in Herbert, *Hitler's Foreign Workers*, p. 41.
31. Willeke, 'Arbeitseinsatz'.
32. Heinrich Himmler, 29 February 1940, in Himmler, *Geheimreden*, p. 134; Decree of 8 March 1940, BA R 58/1030. Cf. Herbert, *Hitler's Foreign Workers*, pp. 71 ff.; Spoerer, *Zwangsarbeit*; and Naasner, *Neue Machtzentren*.
33. On the euthanasia programme, see in particular Schmuhl, *Rassenhygiene, Nationalsozialismus, Euthanasie*, p. 180; Friedlander, *Origins of Nazi Genocide*; Aly, ed., *Aktion T 4*; Süß, '*"Volkskörper"*'; Faulstich, *Hungersterben*; Aly, *Die Belasteten*.
34. Testimony of Dr. Karl Brandt before the US military court at Nuremberg, Case 1, quoted in Kogon, ed., *Nazi Mass Murder*, p. 14.
35. Statement made during a meeting of Prussian provincial asylum directors in October 1936, quoted in Schmuhl, *Rassenhygiene, Nationalsozialismus, Euthanasie*, p. 180.
36. Nuremberg Document NO-824, quoted in Klee, ed., *Dokumente zur 'Euthanasie'*, p. 85.
37. Letter of 13 August 1941 from Dr Antonius Hilfrich, Bishop of Limburg, to the Reich Minister of Justice, Franz Gürtner, quoted in Klee, ed., *Dokumente zur 'Euthanasie'*, p. 231.
38. Orth, *System*, p. 115; Grode, *'Sonderbehandlung 14f.13'*.
39. Groß, *Rassenpolitische Erziehung*, p. 13.
40. See on this section Hillgruber, *Hitlers Strategie*, pp. 144–397; Kershaw, *Fateful Choices*, pp. 11–90; Kershaw, *Hitler 1936–45*, pp. 231–79; Herbst, *Nationalsozialistisches Deutschland*, pp. 312–50; Jürgen Förster, 'Germany's Acquisition of Allies in South-east Europe', in GSWW, vol. 4, pp. 386–428; Hans Umbreit, 'The Battle for Hegemony in Western Europe', in GSWW, vol. 2, pp. 227–326; Detlef Vogel, 'Germany's Intervention in the Balkans', in GSWW, vol. 3, pp. 449–556; Detlef Vogel, 'Deutsche und alliierte Kriegführung im Westen', in Boog, ed., *Deutsches Reich*, pp. 419–639.

41. Joseph Goebbels, diary entry for 9 April 1940, in Goebbels, *Tagebücher,* part 1, vol. 8, p. 41.
42. Joseph Goebbels, diary entry for 21 June 1940, in Goebbels, *Tagebücher,* part 1, vol. 8, p. 186; Petrow, *Bitter Years*; Ottmer, *'Weserübung'*; Frieser, *Blitzkrieg-Legende*; Jackson, *Fall of France*; May, *Strange Victory.*
43. 'Power Politics: Germany Over All', *Time Magazine,* 24 June 1940.
44. Reports from the District Leader of Augsburg, 9 July 1940, and the District President of Swabia, 9 July 1940, quoted in Kershaw, *Hitler 1936–45*, p. 300.
45. Alexander von Müller, 'Vorwort', in *HZ* 162 (1940), pp. 229–30.
46. Meinecke to Kaehler, 4 July 1940, in Meinecke, *Werke,* vol. 6, pp. 363–4, here p. 364.
47. Franz Halder, diary entries for 13 July, 22 July and 31 July 1940, in Halder, *The Halder War Diary*, pp. 226–7, 230–3, and 244–5.
48. Order No.21, Operation Barbarossa, 18 December 1940, BA–MA, RW 4/v.522.
49. Adolf Hitler, on 17 October 1941, in Hitler, *Hitler's Table Talk*, p. 69.
50. Madajczyk, ed., *Generalplan Ost*; Rössler and Schleiermacher, eds., *'Generalplan Ost'*; Heinemann, *Wissenschaft und Homogenisierungsplanungen*; Konrad Meyer, 'Der "Generalplan Ost" und die Deutsche Forschungsgemeinschaft', in Heinemann and Wagner, eds., *Wissenschaft—Planung—Vertreibung,* pp. 45–72; Oberkrome, *Ordnung und Autarkie.*
51. Adolf Hitler, on 30 March 1941, in Halder, *The Halder War Diary,* p. 346.
52. OKW Instructions, 13 March 1941, BA-MA RW 4/v.522.
53. Führer Decree on Military Jurisdiction in the War against the Soviet Union, 13 May 1941, BA-MA RH 22/155.
54. OKW Order, 6 June 1941, concerning the treatment of political commissars, BA-MA RH 2/2082; Römer, *Kommissarbefehl,* p. 367.
55. Memorandum, 2 May 1941, IMT, vol. 31, doc. 2718—PS, p. 84.
56. Economic policy guidelines for the Eastern Economic Organisation, Agricultural Group, 23 May 1941, IMT, vol. 36, doc. 126-EC, pp. 135–57.
57. Gerlach, *Kalkulierte Morde,* pp. 45–78; Rolf-Dieter Müller, 'From Economic Alliance to a War of Colonial Exploitation', in GSWW, vol. 4, pp. 118–224; the same author, 'Das "Unternehmen Barbarossa" als wirtschaftlicher Raubkrieg', in Ueberschär and Wette, eds., *'Unternehmen Barbarossa',* pp. 125–57. On the Barbarossa operation, see Hartmann, *Operation Barbarossa*; Hartmann, *Wehrmacht,* Overy, *Russia's War*, Herbst, *Nationalsozialistisches Deutschland,* pp. 65–73 and Tooze, *Wages,* pp. 461–85.
58. Diary of Dr. Willi Lindenbach, entry for 22 June 1941, in Kempowski, *Das Echolot,* p. 46; Maschmann, *Account Rendered,* p. 91. For the next section, see in particular Förster, 'Germany's Acquisition', GSWW, vol. 4, pp. 386–428.
59. Franz Halder, diary entry for 11 August 1941, in Halder, *The Halder War Diary,* p. 506.
60. Adolf Hitler, on 8 November 1941, quoted in Domarus, *Hitler's Speeches and Proclamations,* vol. 4, p. 2,509.
61. Rolf-Dieter Müller, 'The Failure of the Economic "Blitzkrieg Strategy"', GSWW, vol. 4, pp. 1,081–188, here pp. 1,185–6; Herbst, *Nationalsozialistisches Deutschland,* pp. 356–67.

62. Army Order by the Supreme Commander of the 17th Army, Colonel-General Hoth, 17 January 1941, concerning the principles of military conduct, BA-MA RH 20 17/44.
63. Quotations from the letters of German soldiers from the Front, between 3 July and 29 October 1941, in Buchbender and Sterz, *Das andere Gesicht,* pp. 73–85; Latzel, *Deutsche Soldaten*; Raß, *'Menschenmaterial'*.
64. Private Josef L., 10 February 1942, quoted from Sven Oliver Müller, 'Nationalism in German War Society 1939–1945', GSWW, vol. 9, part 2, pp. 11–93, here p. 81.
65. Gotthard Heinrici, on 23 June 1941, in Heinrici, *Deutscher General,* p. 63; on the next section see Pohl, *Herrschaft der Wehrmacht*; Förster, 'Germany's Acquisition', GSWW, vol. 4, pp. 386–428; Müller, 'From Economic Alliance', GSWW, vol. 4, pp. 118–224; Bartov, *Hitler's Army*; Gerlach, *Kalkulierte Morde*; Hartmann, Hürter and Jureit, eds., *Verbrechen der Wehrmacht*; and Dieckmann, Quinkert and Tönsmeyer, eds., *Kooperation und Verbrechen.*
66. Gerlach, *Kalkulierte Morde*, pp. 503ff.; Hill, *War Behind the Eastern Front,* pp. 69ff.; Pohl, *Herrschaft der Wehrmacht,* pp. 158ff.; Mazower, *Hitler's Empire,* pp. 167–73; Hartmann, 'Verbrecherischer Krieg'.
67. Army group South, 21 October 1941, BA-MA RH 20-6/131; Hitler, on 8 July 1941, in Halder, *The Halder War Diary,* p. 458.
68. Incident Report USSR no. 170 by the CSSD, 18 February 1942, BA R 58/220; see Hürter, 'Wehrmacht vor Leningrad', and Ganzenmüller, *Das belagerte Leningrad.*
69. Göring, on 16.9.1941, IMT, vol. 36, doc. 003-EC., p. 107.
70. Pohl, *Herrschaft der Wehrmacht,* pp. 192 ff.; Tanja Penter, 'Zwischen Hunger, Terror und einer "glücklichen Zukunft". Der Arbeitseinsatz im Steinkohlenbergbau des Donezbeckens unter deutscher Besatzung', in Tenfelde and Seidel, eds., *Zwangsarbeit im Bergwerk,* pp. 433–66; Norbert Kunz, 'Das Beispiel Charkow: Eine Stadtbevölkerung als Opfer der deutschen Hungerstrategie 1941/42', in Hartmann, Hürter and Jureit, eds., *Verbrechen der Wehrmacht,* pp. 136–44. For the next section, see Gerlach, *Kalkulierte Morde,* pp. 231–318.
71. Wagner, on 13.11.1941, quoted in Pohl, *Herrschaft der Wehrmacht,* pp. 218–19; Economic Staff East, 29.9.1941, in ibid.
72. Corporal Emil E., 29.10.1941, quoted in Müller, 'Nationalism', GSWW, 9.2, p. 86.
73. Pohl, *Herrschaft der Wehrmacht,* pp. 201–41, here p. 221; Gerlach, *Kalkulierte Morde,* pp. 774–858; Mazower, *Hitler's Empire,* pp. 159–66; Hartmann, 'Massensterben'; now also Keller, *Sowjetische Kriegsgefangene.*
74. Führer Order concerning armaments in 1942, 10.1.1942, in Thomas, *Geschichte,* pp. 483–7; on the December 1941 turning point, see Tooze, *Wages,* pp. 486–512; Eichholtz, *Geschichte,* vol. 1, pp. 1–117; and four articles by Rolf-Dieter Müller: 'From Economic Alliance to a War of Colonial Exploitation', GSWW, vol. 4, pp. 118–224; 'The Failure of the Economic "Blitzkrieg Strategy"', GSWW, vol. 4, pp. 1,081–188; 'The Mobilization of the German Economy for Hitler's War Aims', GSWW, vol. 5, part 1, pp. 405–786; and 'Albert Speer and Armaments Policy in Total War', GSWW, vol. 5, part 2, pp. 293–832.
75. Tooze, *Wages,* pp. 396–407.

76. Boelcke, *Kosten,* pp. 83–159; Tooze, *Wages,* pp. 354–6; Aly, *Hitler's Beneficiaries,* pp. 330–2; Evans, *Third Reich in Power,* pp. 485–8; Evans, *Third Reich at War,* pp. 429–31.
77. Memorandum on War Finance, 30 May 1939, quoted in Boelcke, *Kosten,* p. 99; cf. Aly, *Hitler's Beneficiaries,* pp. 286–93.
78. Miry, *Black Market,* p. 76; Buchheim, 'Mythos', pp. 314–16
79. Tooze, *Wages,* pp. 388–91; Boelcke, *Kosten,* pp. 110ff.; Mazower, *Hitler's Empire,* pp. 259–93; Aly, *Hitler's Beneficiaries,* pp. 145–55; Overy et al., *'Neuordnung' Europas*; Buchheim, 'Die besetzten Länder'; Freymond, *Le IIIe Reich.*
80. Cf. Gross, *Polish Society,* pp. 92–116; Böhler, *Auftakt,* pp. 181–5; Rosenkötter, *Treuhandpolitik.*
81. Müller, 'The Failure of the Economic "Blitzkrieg Strategy"', GSWW, vol. 4, pp. 1,081–188, here p. 1,185; Herbst, *Nationalsozialistisches Deutschland,* pp. 356–67.
82. Göring, on 6 August 1942, IMT, vol.39, doc. 170—USSR, pp. 384–425, here p. 386.
83. Baron de Launoit's words are quoted in Gillingham, *Industry and Politics,* pp. 147 and 159.

## Chapter 9

1. Holzman, *Dies Kind*; on Lithuania, see in detail Dieckmann, *Besatzungspolitik.*
2. Holzman, *Dies Kind,* pp. 80–81; see Dieckmann, *Besatzungspolitik,* vol. 2, pp. 929–66.
3. Holzman, *Dies Kind,* pp. 262–3; see Dieckmann, *Besatzungspolitik,* vol. 2, pp. 1,296–8.
4. Hitler's instructions of October 1942 to the newly appointed commander of German troops in Denmark, Hermann von Hanneken, as noted by Werner von Grundherr, 3.10.1942, *ADAP,* Series E, vol. 4, no. 5.
5. Meyer, *Deutsche Besatzung,* pp. 34–53; Meyer, *Täter im Verhör,* pp. 67–137; Meyer, *Wissen um Auschwitz,* pp. 15–33; Seibel, *Persecution and Rescue,* pp. 29–56; Ulrich Herbert, 'The German Military Command in Paris and the Deportation of the French Jews', in Herbert, ed., *National Socialist Extermination Policies,* pp. 128–62.
6. OKH (Wagner) to MBF, 7.9.1941, BA-MA, RW 35/543, 18; Head of the OKW, 16.9.1941, BA-MA, RW 35/543, pp. 19ff.; *Das Geiselverfahren im Bereich des Militärbefehlshabers in Frankreich von August 1941 bis Mai 1942,* in BA-MA, RW 35/524; and *Vorbeugungs- und Sühnemaßnahmen des Militärbefehlshabers in Frankreich zur Bekämpfung der Sabotage in Frankreich,* n.d., BA-MA, RW 35/308, p. 41; Luther, *Französischer Widerstand.*
7. Herbert, 'The German Military Command'; Meyer, *Deutsche Besatzung,* pp. 20ff.; Klarsfeld, *Vichy-Auschwitz,* pp. 20 ff.; Kasten, *'Gute Franzosen',* pp. 95ff.
8. MBF to OKH, 1.11.1941, in *Das Geiselverfahren im Bereich des Militärbefehlshabers in Frankreich von August 1941 bis Mai 1942,* in BA-MA, RW 35/542, p.77, quoted in Herbert, *Best,* p. 304; Delacor, *Attentate,* pp. 17–45; Meyer, *Deutsche Besatzung,* pp. 55–72; Neumaier, 'Escalation'.
9. Instructions from the AOK 6, 10.8.1941, BA-MA RH 24-17/255, quoted in Bernd Boll and Hans Safrian, 'On the Way to Stalingrad: The 6th.Army in 1941–42', in

Heer and Naumann, eds., *War of Extermination,* pp. 237–71, here p. 249; on this, see Pohl, *Herrschaft der Wehrmacht,* pp. 243–82, Dieter Pohl, 'Die Einsatzgruppe C 1941/42' in Klein, ed., *Einsatzgruppen,* pp. 71–87, Jürgen Förster, 'Wehrmacht, Krieg und Holocaust', in Müller and Volkmann, eds., *Wehrmacht,* pp. 948–63 and Arnold, 'Eroberung', pp. 23–66.

10. Incident Report no. 97, 29.9.1941, Nuremberg Document NO-3145. Cf. Krausnick, *Hitlers Einsatzgruppen,* p. 324; Rüß, *Massaker*; Wiehn, ed., *Schoah von Babij Jar,* pp. 448ff.; Boll and Safrian, 'On the Way', in Heer and Naumann, eds., *War of Extermination,* pp. 253–5.
11. Quoted from Ehrenburg and Grossman, eds., *The Black Book,* pp. 6–7. Omissions not indicated.
12. Bargatzky, *Hotel Majestic,* p. 103; Victor Klemperer, diary entry for 19.4.1942, in Klemperer, *To the Bitter End*, p. 39.
13. On the overall history of the holocaust, see Aly, *Final Solution*; Longerich, *Holocaust*; Friedländer, *Years of Extermination*; Yahil, *The Holocaust*; Evans, *The Third Reich at War*, pp. 217–318; and the introductions to volumes 1 to 7 of *VEJ*.
14. Heydrich to Ribbentrop, 24.5.1940, PAA Inl. II g 177; on the next section see Aly, *Final Solution*, pp. 113–19; Longerich, *Holocaust,* pp. 259–304; Christopher R. Browning, 'The Decision Concerning the Final Solution', in Browning, *Fateful Months,* pp. 8–38; Friedländer, *Years of Extermination*; and Longerich, *Unwritten Order.*
15. Helmut Krausnick, 'Denkschrift Himmlers'.
16. Note by Legation Secretary Rademacher (Germany Department), 'The Jewish Question in the Peace Treaty', 3 July 1940, in GDFP, Series D, vol. 10, no. 101, pp. 111–13. See also Brechtken, *'Madagascar für die Juden'.*
17. Order from the RSHA, IV B 4, to all police stations and to the SD, 20.5.1941, in *VEJ*, vol. 3, doc. 182, pp. 161–2, here p. 162.
18. Operations Order by Heydrich, 2.7.1941, in *VEJ*, vol. 7, doc. 15, pp. 145–8.
19. Memorandum for Eichmann, by Rolf Höppner, the head of the Central Migration Office in Poznań, RSHA, 16.7.1941, in *VEJ*, vol. 4, doc. 314, pp. 680–1.
20. Göring to Heydrich, 31.7.1941, in *VEJ*, vol. 3, doc. 196, pp. 496–7.
21. Manoschek, *'Serbien ist judenfrei'.*
22. Radio Message from SS Cavalry Regiment 2, 1.8.1941, quoted in Hürter, *Hitlers Heerführer,* p. 558.
23. Letter from Karl Kaufmann to Hermann Göring, 4.9.1942, quoted in Frank Bajohr, 'Hamburgs "Führer". Zur Person und Tätigkeit des Hamburger NSDAP-Gauleiters Karl Kaufmann (1900–1969)', in Bajohr and Szodrzynski, eds. *Hamburg,* pp. 59–91, here p. 81.
24. Pohl, *Nationalsozialistische Judenverfolgung,* pp. 139–210; Sandkühler, *'Endlösung',* pp. 137–41, here p. 138.
25. Arad, *Belzec, Sobibór, Treblinka*; Rückerl, ed. *NS-Vernichtungslager.*
26. Report of Hitler's remarks on 22 July 1941, dated 25.10.1941, in *ADAP*, Series D, vol. 13, part 2, Appendix 3, pp. 835–8. [This report is not included in the English edition, GDFP, Series D, vol. 13.]
27. Joseph Goebbels, diary entry for 13.12.1941, in Goebbels, *Tagebücher,* section 2, vol. 2, pp. 498–9.

28. Speech by Frank, 16.12.1941, in Frank, *Hans Frank's Diary*, pp. 259–60. Omissions not indicated.
29. Gerlach, 'Wannsee-Konferenz'; Roseman, *The Villa, the Lake, the Meeting.*
30. Minutes of the Wannsee Conference, printed, among other places, in Roseman, *The Villa, the Lake, the Meeting*, pp. 108–18.
31. Meyer, *Täter im Verhör*, pp. 44ff.
32. Himmler, 19.7.1942, *VEJ*, vol. 9, doc. 19, 7.1942. On this see Berger, *Experten der Vernichtung*; Musial, *Origins*; Grabitz and Scheffler, *Letzte Spuren.*
33. RFSS Decree of 8.12.1938, quoted in Zimmermann, *Rassenutopie*, p. 25; for the next section, see this book, and also Lewy, *The Nazi Persecution*, and Wagner, *Volksgemeinschaft.*
34. Memorandum by Tobias Portschy, 'Die Zigeunerfrage', Eisenstadt, 1938, quoted in Zimmermann, *Rassenutopie*, pp. 104–5.
35. RFSS Order of 16.12.1942. quoted in Zimmermann, *Rassenutopie*, p. 301; the number of Sinti and Roma murdered during the Nazi period continues to be a subject of dispute. Estimates vary between 100,000 (Zimmermann and Lewy) and 600,000, as put forward by the Central Council of German Sinti and Roma.
36. Braham, *Politics*; Gerlach and Aly, *Kapitel.*
37. Pohl, *Verfolgung und Massenmord*; Benz, ed., *Dimension.*
38. As quoted in Bajohr and Pohl, *Holocaust*, p. 56. For the next section, see also Bankier, *Final Solution*, and Longerich, *'Davon haben wir nichts gewusst!'.*
39. As quoted in Monica Kingreen, 'Gewaltsam verschleppt aus Frankfurt. Die Deportationen der Juden in den Jahren 1941–1945', in Kingreen, ed., *'Nach der Kristallnacht'*, pp. 357–402, here p. 378.
40. Report from the SD Branch Office in Minden, 6.12.1941, in Kulka and Jäckel, eds., *The Jews*, pp. 563–4, no. 3387.
41. Joseph Goebbels, 'Die Juden sind schuld!', *Das Reich*, 16.11.1941.
42. Obenaus and Obenaus, eds., *'Schreiben, wie es wirklich war'*, pp. 106–27.
43. This section follows Harbou, *Wege und Abwege*, Munich, 2013.
44. Harbou, *Wege und Abwege*, p. 127.
45. These figures are taken from *Kräftebilanz der deutschen Industrie*, BA Berlin R 12 I/79. For the next section, see Herbert, *Hitler's Foreign Workers*; Spoerer, *Zwangsarbeit*; Seidel and Tenfelde, eds., *Zwangsarbeit*; Tenfelde, ed., *Arbeitseinsatz*; Ziegler et al., eds., *Zwangsarbeit*; and GSWW, vol. 9, part 2.
46. Comments by Mansfeld, 19.2.1942, memorandum to the WiRüAmt, in Nuremberg Document PS-1201.
47. Figures from: IMT, vol.27, doc. 1,166–PS, pp. 46–52, a list drawn up by the WVHA, dated 15.8.1944, on the number of prisoners.
48. Cf. Broszat, *Konzentrationslager*, pp. 131–2. On the next section, see Orth, *System*; Herbert, Orth and Dieckmann, eds., *Konzentrationslager*, pp. 533–754; Frei, Steinbacher and Wagner, eds., *Ausbeutung, Vernichtung, Öffentlichkeit.*
49. Schulte, *Zwangsarbeit*; Allen, *Business.*
50. Gruner, *Jewish Forced Labor*; Browning, *Nazi Policy, Jewish Workers.*
51. On the next section, see Bajohr and Wildt, eds., *Volksgemeinschaft*; Jörg Echternkamp, 'The Essential Features of German Society in the Second World War', in GSWW, vol. 9

part 1, pp. 1–83; Hans-Ulrich Thamer, '"Everything will be totally changed". German Society and the War. A Summing Up', in GSWW, vol. 9, part 2, pp. 991–1,006; Norbert Frei, '"Volksgemeinschaft". Erfahrungsgeschichte und Lebenswirklichkeit in der Hitler-Zeit', in Frei, *1945 und wir,* pp. 107–28.

52. Kundrus, *Kriegerfrauen,* p. 434; Aly, *Hitler's Beneficiaries,* pp. 68–72.
53. *Meldungen aus dem Reich,* vol. 12, 19.2.1942, p. 3,337.
54. *Meldungen aus dem Reich,* vol. 9, 23.3.1942, p. 3,505. Omissions not indicated.
55. Speech by Göring, 4.10.1942, printed in Aly, ed., *Volkes Stimme,* pp. 149–94. Omissions not indicated.
56. Konrad Warner, quoted in Schäfer, ed., *Berlin im Zweiten Weltkrieg,* pp. 112–13. Omissions not indicated. Konrad Warner was the pseudonym of the Swiss Helmuth Grossmann, who recounted his experiences in Berlin in 1943 under the title *'Schicksalswende Europas?'. Ich sprach mit dem deutschen Volk ... Ein Tatsachenbericht,* Rheinfelden, 1944.
57. Stargardt, *Witnesses of War,* pp. 21–55, 262–316, and 319–52; Benz, *Sozialisation und Traumatisierung*; Lorenz, *Kriegskinder*; Klönne, *Jugend im Dritten Reich*; Klönne, *Gegen den Strom*; Kock, *'Der Führer sorgt für unsere Kinder ...'*; Jahnke and Buddrus, *Deutsche Jugend 1933–1945*; Schörken, *Luftwaffenhelfer und Drittes Reich.*
58. René Schindler, 'Ein Schweizer erlebt das geheime Deutschland. Tatsachenbericht [1945]', in Schäfer, ed., *Berlin im Zweiten Weltkrieg,* p. 117. On the 'black market', see Zierenberg, *Stadt der Schieber,* pp. 85–176; Wildt, *Der Traum vom Sattwerden,* pp. 101–13; Steege, *Black Market,* pp. 18–33; Stargardt, *Witnesses of War,* pp. 319–52; Werner, *Bleib übrig!,* pp. 217ff.; Herbert, *Hitler's Foreign Workers,* pp. 326–9.
59. *Meldungen aus dem Reich,* vol. 9, 12.3.1942, p. 3,450, and 23.3.1942, p. 3,505. Omissions not indicated.
60. Armin Nolzen, 'The NSDAP, the War, and German Society', in GSWW, vol. 9 part 1, pp. 111–206; Bajohr, *Parvenüs und Profiteure.*
61. On the air war, see Süß, *Death*; Müller, *Bombenkrieg 1939–1945*; Horst Boog, 'The Strategic Air War in Europe and Air Defence of the Reich, 1943–1944', in GSWW, vol. 7, pp. 7–458 and Boog, 'The Anglo-American Strategic Air War over Europe and German Air Defence', in GSWW, vol. 6, pp. 469–628; Murray, *War in the Air*; Overy, *The Air War, 1939–1945*; Ursula Büttner, '"Gomorrha" und die Folgen. Der Bombenkrieg', in Forschungsstelle für Zeitgeschichte in Hamburg, ed., *Hamburg,* pp. 613–31; Krause, *Flucht vor dem Bombenkrieg.*
62. John H. Morrow, 'Die deutsche Flugzeugindustrie im Ersten und Zweiten Weltkrieg. Ein Vergleich', in Militärgeschichtliches Forschungsamt, ed., *Luftkriegsführung,* p. 71.
63. Arvid Fredborg, 'Hinter dem Stahlwall [1943]', in Lubrich, ed., *Berichte aus dem Abwurfzone,* pp. 167–82, here p. 180.
64. The quotations are from Herbst, *Nationalsozialistisches Deutschland,* p. 442, and Fredborg, 'Hinter dem Stahlwall', p. 179.
65. Joseph Goebbels, diary entry for 26.2.1942, in Goebbels, *Tagebücher,* Part 2, vol. 3, p. 377; cf. Goebbels, 'Die Moral als kriegsentscheidender Faktor' in Goebbels, *Der steile Aufstieg,* pp. 406–13. On the cultural efforts of the Nazis, see especially Birthe Kundrus, 'Total Entertainment? Cultural Warfare 1939–1945 in Film, Radio,

and Theater', in GSWW, vol. 9, part 2, pp. 95–162; Evans, *The Third Reich at War,* pp. 563–92; Maase, *Grenzenloses Vergnügen,* pp. 196–234; Reichel, *Der schöne Schein,* pp. 157–207; Drewniak, *Theater im NS-Staat,* pp. 344–55; Rentschler, *The Ministry of Illusion,* pp. 1–24; Stahr, *Volksgemeinschaft vor der Leinwand?,* pp. 168–267; Marßolek and von Saldern, eds., *Zuhören und Gehörtwerden,* vol. 1; and Klingler, *Nationalsozialistische Rundfunkpolitik, 1942–1945,* pp. 201–37.

66. *Meldungen aus dem Reich,* vol. 5, 26.8.1940, p. 1,508.
67. Birthe Kundrus, 'Total Entertainment?', GSWW, vol. 9, part 2, pp. 95–162, here p. 117.
68. *Meldungen aus dem Reich,* vol. 11, 10.8.1942, p. 4054; cf. Schäfer, ed., *Berlin,* pp. 9–80; Steinert, *Hitler's War,* pp. 55–65 and 147–83; Kater, *Different Drummers.*
69. Schumann and Haverstein, *Deutsche Bildung?,* pp. 233–4. Omissions not indicated. See also Bollenbeck, *Tradition,* pp. 340ff.
70. *Meldungen aus dem Reich,* vol.11, 3.9.1942, p. 4,164. Omissions not indicated.
71. Reports from the NSDAP District Education Office, Rothenburg ob der Tauber, 22.10.1943, and the SD Regional Office, Schweinfurt, n.d., 1944, in Kulka and Jäckel, *The Jews,* nos. 709 and 726, pp. 636 and 643.

## Chapter 10

1. Surveys: Keegan, *Second World War;* Müller, *Zweiter Weltkrieg;* Schreiber, *Zweiter Weltkrieg;* Weinberg, *A World at Arms;* GSWW, vols. 6–8.
2. Hitler's Directive no. 41, 5.4.1942, in Trevor-Roper, *Hitler's War Directives,* pp. 178–83, here p. 178.
3. Tooze, *Wages,* p. 597.
4. Himmler's speech to SS leaders in Kharkov, 24.4.1943, quoted in Himmler, *Geheimreden,* pp. 186–7, here p. 186. Cf. Armin Nolzen, '"Verbrannte Erde". Der Rückzug der Wehrmacht in den besetzten sowjetischen Gebieten, 1941/42–1944/45', in Kronenbitter, Pöhlmann and Walter, eds., *Besatzung,* pp. 161–75; Bernd Wegner, 'The Perplexities of War: the Soviet Theatre in German Policy and Strategy from the summer of 1943', GSWW, vol. 8, pp. 209–70, here p. 266.
5. Borodziej, *Warsaw Uprising,* pp. 74–139.
6. On the next section, see Herbst, *Totaler Krieg,* pp. 198–231. Tooze, *Wages,* pp. 517–19 and Eichholtz, *Kriegswirtschaft,* vol. 2, p. 41–103.
7. Sauckel's report to Hitler, 18.11.1943, quoted in Eichholtz, *Kriegswirtschaft,* vol. 2, p. 234; for the role of women in the economy, see Kundrus, *Kriegerfrauen,* pp. 245–394 and Winkler, *Frauenarbeit,* pp. 102–21.
8. Goebbels, diary entry for 21.3.1941, in Goebbels, *Tagebücher,* Section II, vol. 11, p. 520. Hitler, speaking on Sauckel's report at the 54th meeting of the Central Planning Office, 1.3.1944, p. 10, quoted in Müller and Ueberschar, *Kriegsende 1945,* p. 26; Göring's remarks were recorded in a letter from SS-Gruppenführer Berger to Himmler, 2.4.1942, quoted in Heiber, *Reichsführer!,* doc. 104, pp. 113–14.

9. News Service of the Reich Women's Leadership, special edition, August 1940, quoted in Sachse, *Angst, Belohnung,* p. 260.
10. Quoted in Herbert, *Hitler's Foreign Workers,* p. 257.
11. Joseph Goebbels, 'Die Optik des Krieges', *Das Reich,* 24.1.1943, quoted in Herbst, *Totaler Krieg,* p. 201; Herbert, *Hitler's Foreign Workers,* p. 257.
12. Both quotations are from *Meldungen aus dem Reich,* vol. 13, 8.3.1943, p. 4903.
13. Wachsmann, *Hitler's Prisons,* pp. 112–64 and 402–3.
14. Conference of Ministers, 21.1.1943, in Boelcke, *Wollt ihr den Totalen Krieg,* pp. 322–4, here p. 324.
15. The text of Goebbels' speech is printed in *Goebbels-Reden,* ed. Heiber, vol. 2, pp. 172–208.
16. Hitler's proclamation of 30.1.1943, quoted in Domarus, *Hitler's Speeches and Proclamations,* vol. 4, pp. 2747.
17. Ministerial proposal by Taubert, 31.1.1943, quoted in Herbert, *Hitler's Foreign Workers,* p. 260.
18. Goering, at his meeting with the Reich Commissioners and the representatives of the Military Commanders of the occupied territories, 6.8.1942, in IMT, vol. 39, doc. 170-USSR, p. 391. On the next section, see Mazower, *Hitler's Empire,* pp. 259–93 and pp.416–521; Conze, *Europa,* pp. 56–110; and Herbert and Schildt, eds. *Kriegsende in Europa.* On Nazi 'European policy' see Michael Salewski, 'Ideas of the National Socialist Government and Party', in Lipgens, ed., *Documents on the History of European Integration,* vol. 1, pp. 37–178, and Herbert, *Best,* pp. 251–322.
19. Mazower, *Hitler's Empire,* pp. 416–45. Röhr, ed., *Okkupation und Kollaboration*; Benz, Houwink ten Cato and Otto, eds., *Anpassung, Kollaboration, Widerstand*; Moore, ed., *Resistance in Western Europe*; Smith, *Occupation, Collaboration and Resistance.*
20. Beltran, Frank and Rousso, eds., *La vie des entreprises sous l'Occupation*; Hirschfeld and Marsh, eds., *Collaboration in France*; Gordon, *Collaborationism in France*; Paxton, *Vichy France.*
21. Mazower, *Hitler's Empire*; Nolte, *Faschistische Bewegungen*; Paxton, *Anatomy of Fascism.*
22. Head of the OKW, 16.9.1941, BA-MA, RW 35/543, pp. 19ff.
23. Mazower, *Hitler's Empire,* pp. 471–521; Gerlach, *Kalkulierte Morde,* pp. 946–74; Moore, ed., *Resistance in Western Europe*; Foot, *Resistance*; van Roon, ed., *Europäischer Widerstand im Vergleich.*
24. Borodziej, *Warsaw Uprising.*
25. Hobsbawm, *Age of Extremes,* p. 164.
26. See, on the resistance to Hitler, the analyses in Mommsen, *Germans Against Hitler*; Ulrich Heinemann, 'Military Resistance Activities and the War', in GSWW, vol. 9.1, pp. 771–925; Fest, *Staatsstreich*; Hoffmann, *History of the German Resistance*; Steinbach and Tuchel, eds., *Widerstand*; and Christian Gerlach, 'The Men of 20 July and the War in the Soviet Union', in Heer and Naumann, eds., *War of Extermination,* pp. 127–45.
27. The quotations are from Hans Mommsen, 'The position of the military opposition to Hitler in the German resistance movement', in Mommsen, *Germans Against Hitler,* pp. 238–52, here p. 245.

28. Erler, *'Nach Hitler kommen wir'*; Koebner et al., eds., *Deutschland nach Hitler*; Hirschfeld, *Exil in Großbritannien*; Langkau-Alex, *Was soll aus Deutschland werden*; Radkau, *Die deutsche Emigration*; Später, *Vansittart.*
29. Herbert, *Hitler's Foreign Workers*, pp. 345–6.
30. First quotation: *Meldungen aus dem Reich,* vol. 17, 28.7.1944, p. 6684; second quotation: President of the OLG, Nuremberg, as quoted in Kershaw, *The 'Hitler Myth'*, p. 217.
31. For the next section, see Kershaw, *The End* and DRZW, vol. 10.1.
32. Süß, *Death from the Skies*, pp. 105–8, and 451–4; Taylor, *Dresden*; Widera, *Dresden*; Müller et al., eds., *Zerstörung Dresdens.*
33. Einsiedel, *Shadow of Stalingrad,* pp. 167 and 168; Manfred Zeidler, 'Die Rote Armee auf deutschem Boden', in DRZW, vol. 10.1, pp. 681–776; Atina Grossmann, 'A Question of Silence', in Moeller, ed., *West Germany Under Construction,* pp. 33–52; Regina Mühlhauser, 'Vergewaltigungen in Deutschland 1945. Nationaler Opferkurs und individuelles Erinnern betroffener Frauen', in Naumann, ed., *Nachkrieg in Deutschland,* pp. 384–408.
34. Quoted in Longerich, *'Davon haben wir nichts gewusst'*, p. 310; on the expulsion of Germans from Eastern Europe, see Michael Schwarz, 'Ethnische Säuberungen als Kriegsfolge. Ursachen und Verlauf der Vertreibung der deutschen Zivilbevölkerung aus Ostdeutschland und Osteuropa 1941 bis 1950', in DRZW, vol. 10.2, pp. 509–655; Kossert, *Kalte Heimat*; Borodziej and Lemberg, eds., *Unsere Heimat*; Naimark, *Fires of Hatred*; Aust and Burgdorff, *Die Flucht*; Nitschke, *Vertreibung*; Robert G. Moeller, 'Deutsche Opfer, Opfer der Deutschen. Kriegsgefangene, Vertriebene, NS-Verfolgte: Opferaugleich als Identitätspolitik', in Naumann, ed., *Nachkrieg in Deutschland,* pp. 29–58.
35. Extract from article XIII of the Potsdam Agreement., printed in Rhode and Wagner, eds., *The Genesis,* pp. 257–8; Zayas, *Nemesis at Potsdam,* p. 166.
36. Quoted in Franck, *Jahre unseres Lebens,* p. 52.
37. First quotation: Naimark, *Fires of Hatred,* p. 110; second quotation: 'Differences of opinion arise in the House of Commons concerning the Polish frontiers', in Rhode and Wagner, eds., *The Genesis,* no. 130, pp. 206–13, here p. 212.
38. For the next section, see Kershaw, *The End*; GSWW, Vol. 9, Part 1; Arendes, ed., *Terror nach innen*; Henke, *Amerikanische Besatzung*; Herbert and Schildt, eds., *Kriegsende in Europa*; Rusinek, *Gesellschaft in der Katastrophe*; Hillmann and Zimmermann, *Kriegsende 1945*; Ueberschar and Müller, *1945*; and Münkler, *Machtzerfall.*
39. According to the calculations of Manfred Messerschmidt and Fritz Wüllner a total of 35,000 German soldiers were convicted of desertion during the war. Of these, 22,750 were condemned to death, and some 15,000 sentences were carried out. See Messerschmidt and Wüllner, *Wehrmachtjustiz,* pp. 66ff. and 90ff.
40. Himmler, on 3.4.1945, quoted in Elisabeth Kohlhaas, '"Aus einem Haus, aus dem eine weiße Fahne erscheint, sind all männlichen Personen zu erschießen." Durchhalteterror und Gewalt gegen Zivilisten am Kriegsende 1945', in Arendes, ed., *Terror nach innen*, pp. 51–79, here p. 65; Henke, *Die amerikanische Besetzung,* p. 846.

41. Frank Bajohr, 'Hamburg—Der Verfall der "Volksgemeinschaft"', in Herbert and Schildt, eds., *Kriegsende in Europa*, pp. 318–36, here p. 325.
42. Kohlhaas 'Aus einem Haus', in Arendes, ed., *Terror nach innen*, pp. 55ff.
43. Rusinek, *Gesellschaft in der Katastrophe*; Herbert, *Hitler's Foreign Workers*, pp. 359–81.
44. Himmler's order of 17.6.1944; Commander of the Security Police in Radom, 21.7.1944, Nuremberg Document L–053, from Daniel Blatman, 'Die Todesmärsche—Entscheidungsträger, Mörder und Opfer', in Herbert, Orth and Dieckmann, eds., *Die nationalsozialistischen Konzentrationslager*, pp. 1,063–92.
45. Levi, *If This is a Man*, pp. 174–5; Wagner, *Produktion*, pp. 278–88; Blatman, *The Death Marches*; Greiser, *Die Todesmärsche von Buchenwald*; Gring, *Die Todesmärsche und das Massaker von Gardelegen*.

## Chapter 11

1. There is an early use of the term in Morin, *L'an zéro de l'Allemagne*, and in the title of a neo-realist film made by Roberto Rossellini in 1947–8 ('Germania anno Zero'). See in general for this section Henke, *Amerikanische Besetzung*; Bessel, *Germany 1945*; Bessel and Schumann, eds., *Life after Death*; Biess and Moeller, eds., *Histories of the Aftermath*; Müller, ed., *Der Zusammenbruch*; Naumann, ed., *Nachkrieg*.
2. Erika S., on 2 May 1945, in Breloer, *Geheime Welten*, pp. 103–32, here p. 123.
3. Menzel, *Stadt ohne Tod*, p. 223.
4. Kardorff, *Berliner*, p. 305.
5. Report by Lt. Daniel Lerner, SHAEF, 18.4.1945, in Borsdorf and Niethammer, eds., *Zwischen Befreiung und Besatzung*, p. 34; report by a SHAEF Press Officer, Robert T. Pell, April 1945, about a journey to Frankfurt am Main, in the same source, pp. 145–55.
6. Smith, *Heimkehr aus dem Zweiten Weltkrieg*; Overmans, *Deutsche militärische Verluste*; Sorge, *The Price of Hitler's War*; Robert G. Moeller, 'Deutsche Opfer, Opfer der Deutschen. Kriegsgefangene, Vertriebene, NS-Verfolgte: Opferausgleich als Identitätspolitik', in Naumann, ed., *Nachkrieg*, pp. 29–59.
7. Ulrich Herbert and Karin Hunn, 'Beschäftigung, soziale Sicherung und soziale Integration von Ausländern' in GSD, vol. 2.1, pp. 813–28; Wyman, *DPs*; Jacobmeyer, *Vom Zwangsarbeiter*; Goeken, *Weg zurück*; Pavel M. Poljan, 'Die Deportation der Ostarbeiter im Zweiten Weltkrieg', in Gestrich and Hirschfeld, eds., *Ausweisung und Deportation*, pp. 115–40.
8. Königseder and Wetzel, *Lebensmut im Wartesaal*, pp. 14, 47 and 247ff.; Jacobmeyer, *Jüdische Überlebende*; Fritz-Bauer-Institut, ed., *Überlebt und unterwegs*; Grossmann, *Jews, Germans and Allies*.
9. Bremer Ausschuss für Wirtschaftsforschung, *Am Abend der Demontage*, pp. 141–3; Harmssen, ed., *Reparationen, Sozialprodukt, Lebensstandard*, vol. 3 B, part 2, pp. 11ff.

10. Report to SHAEF, 14.5.1945, in Borsdorf and Niethammer, eds., *Zwischen Befreiung und Besatzung*, pp. 47–57, here p. 48.
11. Erker, *Ernährungskrise*; Trittel, *Hunger und Politik*; Gries, *Die Rationen-Gesellschaft*; Udo Wengst, 'Rahmenbedingungen', in *GSD*, Vol. 2, Part 1, pp. 1–77.
12. Lutz Niethammer, 'Privat-Wirtschaft', in Niethammer, ed., *Hinterher merkt man*, pp. 17–196; Zierenberg, *Stadt der Schieber*, pp. 317ff.; Boelcke, *Der Schwarzmarkt*; Steege, *Black Market*.
13. OSS Field Intelligence Report no. 33, 19.10.1945, in Borsdorf and Niethammer, eds., *Zwischen Befreiung und Besatzung*, pp. 199ff., here p. 202.
14. Diary entry by Eva Richter-Fritsche, Berlin-Pankow, 4.5.1945, quoted in Stefan-Ludwig Hoffmann, 'Besiegte, Besatzer, Beobachter: Das Kriegsende im Tagebuch', in Fulda, Herzog and Hoffmann, eds., *Demokratie im Schatten der Gewalt*, pp. 25–55; Herbert and Schildt, eds., *Kriegsende*; Gildea, Wieviorka and Warring, *Surviving Hitler*.
15. Lt.Nunn, *Memoirs*, 1946, quoted in Hoffmann, 'Besiegte', p. 49.
16. For the next section, see Düllfer, *Jalta*, pp. 122–52 and 178–200; Benz, *Potsdam 1945*; Benz, ed., *Deutschland unter allierte Besatzung*; Mai, *Allierter Kontrollrat*; Kleßmann, *Doppelte Staatsgründung*; Wehler, *Gesellschaftsgeschichte*, vol. 4, pp. 941–84; Winkler, *Long Road*, vol. 2, pp. 108–89; Kielmannsegg, *Nach der Katastrophe*, pp. 15–130.
17. Volger, *Geschichte*, pp. 18–28.
18. Mausbach, *Zwischen Morgenthau und Marshall*, pp. 41–80; Greiner, *Morgenthau-Legende*; for the next section see also Stöver, *Der Kalte Krieg*, pp. 40–84; Vanden Berghe, *Der Kalte Krieg*, pp. 97–121; Loth, *The Division of the World*, pp. 125–39; and Yergin, *Shattered Peace*, pp. 109–37 and 152–92.
19. Kielmannsegg, *Nach der Katastrophe*, p. 12.
20. Smith, *Die vermißte Million*, pp. 35–49; for the next section, see Wettig, *Entmilitarisierung*, pp. 23–207; Jarausch, *After Hitler*, pp. 19–45; Goltermann, *Gesellschaft der Überlebenden*, pp. 47–162; Smith, *Heimkehr aus dem Zweiten Weltkrieg*; Engelbert and Benz, eds., *Kriegsgefangenschaft*; Held, *Kriegsgefangenschaft in Großbritannien*; Krammer, *Nazi Prisoners of War in America*; and Overmans, *Soldaten hinter Stacheldraht*.
21. On this point, see Klaus-Dietmar Henke, 'Die Trennung vom Nationalsozialismus. Selbstzerstörung, politische Säuberung, "Entnazifizierung," Strafverfolgung', in Henke and Woller, eds., *Politische Säuberung*, pp. 21–83; Helga A. Welsh, '"Antifaschistisch-demokratische Unwälzung" und politische Säuberung in der sowjetischen Besatzungszone Deutschlands', in Henke and Woller, eds., *Politische Säuberung*, pp. 84–106; and Wember, *Umerziehung*.
22. Wember, *Umerziehung*, p. 190; the 'idea' of National Socialism, on the other hand, continued to be regarded positively, as 'German socialism'. See also Lutz Niethammer, 'Zum Wandel der Kontinuitätsdiskussion', in Herbst, ed., *Westdeutschland*, pp. 65–84.
23. Neumann, *Behemoth*, pp. 425–63.
24. Buscher, *US War Crimes Trial*; Heydecker, *Nürnberger Prozess*; Ueberschär, ed., *Nationalsozialismus vor Gericht*; Weinke, *Nürnberger Prozesse*. On the reporting of the trials, see Radlmaier, ed., *Nürnberger Lernprozess*, and Brandt, *Verbrecher und andere Deutsche*.

25. Earl, *The Nuremberg SS-Einsatzgruppen Trial*; Weindling, *Nazi Medicine*; Peschel-Gutzeit, ed., *Nürnberger Juristen-Urteil*; Priemel and Stiller, eds. *Reassessing*.
26. On the process of denazification in West Germany, see Henke and Woller, eds., *Politische Säuberung*; Vollnhals, ed., *Politische Säuberung*; Vollnhals and Schlemmer, eds., *Entnazifizierung*; Norbert Frei, 'Nach der Tat. Die Ahndung deutscher Kriegs- und NS-Verbrechen in Europa—eine Bilanz', in Frei, ed., *Transnationale Vergangenheitspolitik*; Frei, *1945 und wir*; Niethammer, *Mitläuferfabrik*; Schuster, *Entnazifizierung in Hessen*.
27. Frei, *Adenauer's Germany*, pp. 5–39; Brochhagen, *Nach Nürnberg*, pp. 17–172.
28. Van Melis, *Entnazifizierung*; Welsh, *Revolutionärer Wandel auf Befehl*; Klonovsky and von Flocken, *Stalins Lager*; Reif-Sperek and Ritscher, eds., *Speziallager in der SBZ*; Greiner, *Suppressed Terror*.
29. Werkentin, *Politische Strafjustiz in der Ära Ulbricht*, pp. 174ff.; Fricke, 'Justizielles Unrecht'; Schroeder, *SED-Staat*, pp. 109ff.
30. Fisch, *Reparationen nach dem Zweiten Weltkrieg*; Buchheim, ed., *Wirtschaftliche Folgelasten*; Buchheim, *Wiedereingliederung*, pp. 1–49; Kramer, *Britische Demontagepolitik*; Köchling, *Demontagepolitik und Wiederaufbau*.
31. Kleßmann, *Die doppelte Staatsgründung*, pp. 110–20; Abelshauser, *Deutsche Wirtschaftsgeschichte*, pp. 100–6; Dietmar Petzina and Walter Euchner, 'Wirtschaftspolitik in der Besatzungszeit', in Petzina and Euchner, eds., *Wirtschaftspolitik im britischen Besatzungsgebiet*, pp. 7–23.
32. Karlsch, *Allein bezahlt?*; Karlsch and Laufer, eds., *Sowjetische Demontagen in Deutschland*; Buchheim, ed., *Wirtschaftliche Folgelasten*.
33. Matschke, *Industrielle Entwicklung*, pp. 293ff.
34. Arndt Bauernkämper, 'Von der Bodenreform zur Kollektivierung. Zum Wandel der ländlichen Gesellschaft in der Sowjetischen Besatzungszone und der DDR', in Kaelble, et al., eds., *Sozialgeschichte der DDR*, pp. 119–43; Schöne, *Frühling*, pp. 73–153.
35. Oskar Anweiler, 'Bildungspolitik', in *GSD*, Vol. 2, Part 1, pp. 699–733; Füssl, *Die Umerziehung der Deutschen*; Rosenzweig, *Erziehung zur Demokratie?*.
36. For the quotation from Schmidt, see Anweiler, 'Bildungspolitik', p. 721.
37. Niethammer, *Verhältnis*; Reusch, *Deutsches Berufsbeamtentum*.
38. Friedrich, *Rundfunk und Besatzungsmacht*; Frei, *Amerikanische Lizenzpolitik*.
39. Proclamation by the KPD Central Committee, 11.6.1945, in Flechtheim, ed., *Dokumente zur parteipolitischen Entwicklung*, vol. 3, pp. 313–19.
40. Weber, *Geschichte der DDR*, pp. 47–185; Staritz, *Die Gründung der DDR*; Kleßmann, *Die doppelte Staatsgründung*, pp. 261–95; Naimark, *Russians in Germany*, pp. 251–317.
41. Clay, *Decision in Germany*. In Bavaria and Hamburg, the Diet elections had already taken place in autumn 1946.
42. Rogers, *Politics after Hitler*, pp. 20–48.
43. Klotzbach, *Der Weg zur Staatspartei*, pp. 37–129.
44. Suckut, *Parteien in der SBZ/DDR*; Keiderling, ed., *'Gruppe Ulbricht'*; Faulenbach, *Sozialdemokraten und Kommunisten*; Lux, ed., *Das politische System der SBZ/DDR*.

45. Schwarz, *Adenauer,* vol. 1, pp. 291–381; Buchstab, ed., *Die Gründung der Union*; Kleinmann, *Geschichte der CDU.*
46. *L'Ordre,* 21.9.1946, quoted by Kleßmann, *Die doppelte Staatsgründung,* p. 143; Gurland, *CDU/CSU,* pp. 171–207.
47. Letter from Adenauer to Heinrich Weitz, the mayor of Duisburg, 31.10.1945, quoted in Adenauer, *Memoirs, 1945–1953,* pp. 35–6.
48. Kaack, *Zur Geschichte,* pp. 7–16; Herbert, *Best,* pp. 461–5; Frei, *Adenauer's Germany,* pp. 27–39; Buchna, *Nationale Sammlung*; Papke, *Liberale Ordnungskraft.*
49. For Truman's speech of 12.3.1947, setting forth the Truman Doctrine, see Schlesinger, *Dynamics,* vol. 1, pp. 111–15.
50. For Marshall's speech of 5.6.1947, see Schlesinger, *Dynamics,* vol. 1, pp. 52–4. Kennan's 'long telegram' is printed in FRUS, vol. 6, pp. 696–709. On the Marshall Plan in general see Gimbel, *The Origins,* pp. 179–280, Abelshauser, *Deutsche Wirtschaftsgeschichte,* pp. 120–53; Mausbach, *Zwischen Morgenthau,* pp. 368ff.; Maier, ed., *The Marshall Plan and Germany*; Holzamer, ed., *Der Marshallplan*; Herbst, ed., *Vom Marshallplan zur EWG*; Dülffer, *Jalta,* pp. 201–24; and Herbst, *Option,* pp. 35–59.
51. Herbst, *Option,* p. 47 (omission unindicated); Berger and Ritschl, 'Rekonstruktion der Arbeitsteilung'.
52. *Die Welt,* 1.4.1948; *Frankfurter Rundschau,* 16.3.1948; Merritt and Merritt, eds., *Public Opinion,* pp. 116–17 and 269–70; Lehmann, *Marshall-Plan,* pp. 166–95.
53. Buchheim, *Währungsreform 1948*; Zschaler, 'Vergessene Währungsreform'.
54. 'Deutsche Sachverständigen-Kommission für die Geldreform 8.6.1948', in Wandel, *Entstehung,* pp. 188–91, here p. 191. See Hughes, *Shouldering the Burdens,* pp. 43–6; Abelshauser, *Deutsche Wirtschaftsgeschichte,* pp. 154–75; Brackmann, *Vom totalen Krieg zum Wirtschaftswunder.*
55. Abelshauser, *Deutsche Wirtschaftsgeschichte,* pp. 89–105, here p. 100; Müller-Armack, *Wirtschaftslenkung und Marktwirtschaft.*
56. Abelshauser, *Deutsche Wirtschaftsgeschichte,* pp. 275–314; Löffler, *Soziale Marktwirtschaft,* pp. 95–6.
57. As quoted in Haenschke, *Modell Deutschland?,* p. 11.
58. Kielmannsegg, *Nach der Katastrophe,* p. 42.
59. Merritt and Merritt, eds., *Public Opinion,* pp. 261, 263, 267 and 271–2.
60. Wolf, 'Auch wir können nicht schweigen', p. 204.
61. Klemperer, *The Lesser Evil,* diary entries for 23.11.1945, p. 72; and 16.12.1949, p. 305. Cf. Steven E. Aschheim, '"Genosse Klemperer"—Kommunismus, Liberalismus und Judesein in der DDR, 1945–1959', in Zuckermann, ed., *Zwischen Politik und Kultur,* pp. 184–209; Wolfrum, *Geschichte als Waffe,* pp. 66–9; Ullrich, *Weimar-Complex,* pp. 93–108.
62. Schumacher, on 11.5.1946, quoted in Albrecht, ed., *Die SPD unter Kurt Schumacher,* vol. 1, p. 4. Cf. Klotzbach, *Weg,* pp. 66–77 and Merseburger, *Der schwierige Deutsche.*
63. Theodor Heuss, on 6.1.1946; Reinhold Maier, on 6.1.1946, both quoted in Ullrich, *Weimar-Complex,* p. 100.
64. Meinecke, *The German Catastrophe,* pp. 1–2, 30, 107. Gerhard Ritter, lecture manuscripts 'Der moderne Staat der Gegenwart' [1937], and 'Die historischen

Voraussetzungen für den Aufstieg des Nationalsozialismus' [10.5.1951], both quoted in Cornelißen, *Ritter*, pp. 526 and 530. See also Axel Schildt, 'Deutschlands Platz in einem "christlichen Abendland"', in Koebner, Sautermeister and Schneider, eds., *Deutschland nach Hitler*, pp. 344–69; Schildt, *Zwischen Abendland und Amerika*; and Weisbrod, *Akademische Vergangenheitspolitik*.

65. Müller-Armack, *Das Jahrhundert ohne Gott*; Wiechert, *Rede an die deutsche Jugend*.
66. The Frankfurt Recommendations of the American, British and French Military Governors to the Prime Ministers of the Western Zones of Occupation, 1 July 1948, printed in Michaelis and Schraepler, eds., *Ursachen und Folgen*, vol. 26, doc. 3782 A, pp. 148–51.
67. For the first two figures see Noelle-Neumann, *Jahrbuch der öffentlichen Meinung, 1956*, p. 157. For the third figure see Kielmannsegg, *Nach der Katastrophe*, p. 62.
68. Schmitt, *Hüter der Verfassung*; Ullrich, *Weimar-Komplex*, pp. 175ff.; Winkler, *Germany: the Long Road West*, vol. 2, pp. 123–4; Laak, *Gespräche*, pp. 160–1.
69. Feldkamp, *Der Parlamentarische Rat*; Bommarius, *Das Grundgesetz*.
70. Lüders, *Das Ruhrkontrollsystem*.
71. Loth, *Division of the World*, pp 98–100; Stöver, *Der Kalte Krieg*, pp. 89–144.
72. For details, see Weber, *Geschichte der DDR*, pp. 47–185, and Staritz, *Gründung der DDR*, pp. 147–88.
73. Frank, *Walter Ulbricht*.

## Chapter 12

1. On this section, see Abelshauser, *Deutsche Wirtschaftsgeschichte*, pp. 214–15 and 275–314; Abelshauser, *Wirtschaftsgeschichte der Bundesrepublik Deutschland*; Eichengreen, *The European Economy*, pp. 15–51 and 93; Karl Hardach, 'Deutschland 1914–1970', in Fohlen, ed., *Die europäischen Volkswirtschaften im zwanzigsten Jahrhundert*, pp. 47–99, here pp. 71–95; Gerold Ambrosius and Hartmut Kaelble, 'Einleitung: Gesellschaftliche und wirtschaftliche Folgen des Booms der 1950er und 1960er Jahre', in Kaelble, ed., *Der Boom*, pp. 7–34; Prollius, *Wirtschaftsgeschichte*, pp. 50–124; Erker, *Dampflok, Daimler, DAX*, pp. 218–44; Kielmansegg, *Nach der Katastrophe*, pp. 432–88; and Wehler, *Deutsche Gesellschaftsgeschichte*, vol. 5, pp. 48–87.
2. Slightly different figures are given by Wolfram Fischer, 'Wirtschaft, Gesellschaft und Staat in Europa 1914–1980', in Fischer, ed., *Handbuch*, pp. 1–221, here p. 96, and Kaelble, *Social History*, pp. 38ff.
3. Therborn, *European Modernity*, pp. 133–63; Crafts, *Golden Age*; Killick, *United States*.
4. Schulz, *Wiederaufbau in Deutschland*, pp. 239–314; Schulz, 'Eigenheimpolitik und Eigenheimförderung im ersten Jahrzehnt nach dem Zweiten Weltkrieg', in Schildt and Sywottek, eds., *Massenwohnung und Eigenheim*, pp. 409–39; Michael Krummacher, 'Soziale Wohnungsbau in der Bundesrepublik in den fünfziger und sechziger Jahren', in pp. 440–60 of the same publication.

5. Henrik Bispinck, '"Republikflucht". Flucht und Ausreise als Problem für die DDR-Führung', in Hoffmann, Schwartz and Wentzler, eds., *Vor dem Mauerbau*, pp. 285–310, here p. 309.
6. Buchheim, *Wiedereingliederung*; Rombeck-Jaschinski, *Das Londoner Schuldenabkommen*; on this point see below in this chapter, in the section 'Compensation for the Victims of National Socialism'.
7. Abelshauser, *Deutsche Wirtschaftsgeschichte*, pp. 175–214. Gerd Hardach, 'Die Rückkehr zum Weltmarkt 1948–1958', in Schildt and Sywottek, eds., *Modernisierung*, pp. 80–104; Neebe, *Weichenstellung für die Globalisierung*; Buchheim, *Wiedereingliederung*, pp. 109–70.
8. Werner Abelshauser, 'Der Rheinische Kapitalismus im Kampf der Wirtschaftskulturen', in Berghahn and Vitols, eds., *Gibt es einen deutschen Kapitalismus?*, pp. 186–99; Abelshauser, *Deutsche Wirtschaftsgeschichte*, pp. 51–9 and 166–74.
9. Kniep, *Wiederaufbau*, p. 136.
10. Josef Mooser, 'Das Verschwinden der Bauern. Überlegungen zur Sozialgeschichte der "Entagrarisierung" und Modernisierung der Landwirtschaft im 20. Jahrhundert', in Münkel, ed., *Der lange Abschied vom Agrarland*, pp. 39–68; Kluge, *Agrarwirtschaft*, pp. 36–61; Kluge, 'Wandel ohne Entschädigung', pp. 39–68; Mai, 'Agrarische Transition'. The sources vary slightly in their figures for agricultural employment and agriculture's contribution to GNP.
11. In 1951, 42 per cent of those surveyed indicated that life had been best for them between 1933 and 1939, while 45 per cent preferred life in pre-1918 Germany (Noelle and Neumann, eds., *Jahrbuch der Öffentlichen Meinung 1968–1973*, p. 209).
12. For the next section, see Herbst, *Option für den Westen*; Hildebrand, *Integration und Souveränität*; Stöver, *Der Kalte Krieg*; Felken, *Dulles und Deutschland*; Rupieper, *Besetzter Verbündeter*; Loth, *Ost–West Konflikt*; Loth, *Division of the World*; and Loth, *Helsinki*.
13. Comment allegedly made by Lord Hastings Ismay, and quoted by Hennessy, *Whitehall*, p. 412. According to Hennessy, a rumour circulating in the British Ministry of Defence had it that 'Ismay produced this unforgettable job description while explaining NATO's functions to a private meeting of conservative backbenchers in 1949'.
14. Bührer, *Westdeutschland in der OEEC*; Gillingham, *Coal, Steel*; Lüders, *Das Ruhrkontrollsystem*.
15. Ulbricht's remarks of 3 August 1950, transmitted by the East German radio station, Berliner Rundfunk, as quoted in Steininger, *Deutsche Geschichte seit 1945*, p. 149; Noelle and Neumann, *Jahrbuch der öffentlichen Meinung, 1947–1951*, p. 354. By May 1954 the respondents had reverted to their previous view, with 84 per cent giving the answer 'No'.
16. Militärgeschichtliches Forschungsamt, ed., *Anfänge westdeutscher Sicherheitspolitik*, vol. 2; Bald, *Die Bundeswehr*, pp. 18–69.
17. 'Memorandum zur Frage der Neuordnung der Beziehungen der Bundestrepublik zu den Besatzungsmächten vom 29.8.1950', in von Schubert, ed., *Sicherheitspolitik der Bundesrepublik Deutschland*, part 1, pp. 79–83, here p. 83.

18. Schwarz, *Die Legende von der verpassten Gelegenheit*; Schwarz, 'Die USA und das Scheitern der EVG' in Steininger, ed., *Die doppelte Eindämmung*, pp. 75–89; Steininger, *Eine Chance zur Wiedervereinigung?*, pp. 73–6.
19. On the next section, see Loth, *Weg nach Europa*, pp. 113–33; Brunn, *Die europäische Einigung*, pp. 100–23; Herbst, *Option für den Westen*, pp. 159–93; Herbst, Bührer and Sowade, eds., *Vom Marshallplan zur EWG*; Küsters, *Die Gründung der Europäischen Wirtschaftsgemeinschaft*.
20. Adenauer's 19 January 1956 Directive on European Policy, printed in Adenauer, *Erinnerungen, 1955–1959*, pp. 253ff.
21. For West German political developments in this period see Conze, *Suche nach Sicherheit*, pp. 45–184; Kielmannsegg, *Nach der Katastrophe*, pp. 256–85; Herbst, ed., *Westdeutschland 1945–1955*; Kleßmann, *Die doppelte Staatsgründung*, pp. 223–35; Kleßmann, *Zwei Staaten—eine Nation*, pp. 108–57; Schmidt, *Das politische System der Bundesrepublik Deutschland*; Wolfrum, *Die geglückte Demokratie*, pp. 46–143; Görtemaker, *Geschichte*, pp. 83–118 and 271–377.
22. Lösche and Walter, *Die SPD*, pp. 77–227; Klotzbach, *Weg zur Staatspartei*, pp. 131–355.
23. Schwarz, *Konrad Adenauer*, vol. 1, pp. 435–585; Schwarz, ed., *Konrad Adenauers Regierungsstil*; Bösch, *Die Adenauer-CDU*, pp. 236–82.
24. Bald, *Atombewaffnung*; Nägler, ed., *Die Bundeswehr*; Adenauer, speaking at a press conference on 5 April 1957, quoted in Adenauer, *Erinnerungen, 1955–1959*, p. 296.
25. Werner, *'Ohne mich' Bewegung*; Holl, *Pazifismus in Deutschland*, pp. 220–37.
26. For social policy, see Günther Schulz, 'Sozialpolitische Denk- und Handlungsfelder', in GSD, vol. 3, pp. 73–176; Schmidt, *Sozialpolitik in Deutschland*, pp. 75–111; Hockerts, *Sozialpolitische Entscheidungen in Nachkriegsdeutschland*; Hockerts and Süß, eds., *Soziale Ungleichheit im Sozialstaat*; Hockerts, ed., *Drei Wege deutscher Sozialstaatlichkeit*.
27. Wolfgang Rüfner, 'Ausgleich von Kriegs- und Diktaturfolgen', in GSD, vol. 3, pp. 690–757, here pp. 724–53; Wenzel, *Die große Verschiebung?*, pp. 71–173; Wiegand, *Der Lastenausgleich*; Hughes, *Shouldering the Burdens*.
28. Reinhard Richardi, 'Arbeitsverfassung und Arbeitsrecht', in GSD, vol. 3, pp. 179–226; Buchhaas, *Gesetzgebung*.
29. Kaelble, *Social History*, pp. 312–22.
30. On the next section, see Frei, *Adenauer's Germany*, pp. 41–67; Frei, *Karrieren im Zwielicht*; Herbert, *Best*, pp. 444–61; Herbert, 'Zweierlei Bewältigung', in Herbert and Groehler, eds., *Zweierlei Bewältigung*, pp. 7–29; Brochhagen, *Nach Nürnberg*, pp. 32ff.
31. For the reference to 'murderous associates' see the pastoral letter of 9 April 1946 from the Bavarian bishops entitled 'The Life of Faith and the Problems of the Present', in *Dokumente deutscher Bischöfe*, vol. 1, pp. 99–103, here p. 103; for the concentration camps see the pastoral letter of 28 June 1945 from the Bavarian episcopate, in *Akten Faulhabers*, vol. 2, pp. 1,080–4, here p. 1,083. The quotation from Frings is in 'Denkschrift v. Josef Frings, 2.8.1945', *Akten deutscher Bischöfe*, vol. 6, pp. 625–8, here p. 625.

32. Hermann Hesse 'Brief an eine junge Deutsche, Frühjahr 1946', in Wagenbach, ed., *Vaterland, Muttersprache*, pp. 51ff.
33. *Deutscher Bundestag. I. Wahlperiode*, 13.3.1950, pp. 1,329ff.; Noelle and Neumann, eds., *Jahrbuch der öffentlichen Meinung 1947–1955*, p. 140; Merritt and Merritt, eds., *Public Opinion*; Frei, *Adenauer's Germany*, pp. 97–250.
34. Curt Garner, 'Der öffentlicher Dienst in den 50er Jahren: Politische Weichenstellungen und ihre sozialgeschichtlichen Folgen', in Schildt and Sywottek, eds., *Modernisierung*, pp. 759–90.
35. Schwartz, 'Begnädigung'; Buscher, *U.S. War Crimes Trial*.
36. Mende's declaration of 19.6.1952 and McCloy's statement of 16.7.1952 are quoted in Herbert, *Best*, pp. 444ff.
37. Herbert, *Best*, pp. 461–76; Frei, *Adenauer's Germany*, pp. 27–39; Ullrich, *'Ich fühl' mich nicht als Mörder'*.
38. Merseburger, *Der schwierige Deutsche*, pp. 501ff.; Horst W.Schmollinger, 'Die Sozialistische Reichspartei', in Stöß, ed., *Parteien-Handbuch*, pp. 2,274–336.
39. Meyer, *Grenadiere*; Meyer (Jr.), *Geweint wird, wenn der Kopf ab ist*.
40. Federal Constitutional Court Judgement, 2 October 1952. Cf. Jenke, *Verschwörung von rechts?*, pp. 103ff.
41. Adenauer's address of 26 January 1953 to the CDU Federal Executive Board, printed in Adenauer, *'Es musste alles neu gemacht werden'*, pp. 308–9.
42. Conze et al., *Das Amt*, pp. 319–620; Döscher, *Verschworene Gesellschaft*; Döscher, *Seilschaften*; Müller, *Relaunching*.
43. Adenauer, *Teegespräche 1950–1954*, p. 219.
44. Cf. Frei, *Adenauer's Germany*, pp. 226–9 (the Sandberger case); Wildt, *Uncompromising Generation*, pp. 419–24 and 439–48; Frei, ed., *Karrieren im Zwielicht*; Ullrich, *Mörder*; Hachmeister, *Der Gegnerforscher*; Mallmann, ed., *Karrieren der Gewalt*; Roth, *Herrenmenschen*.
45. Steel to the Foreign Office, 9.3.1959, quoted in Brochhagen, *Nach Nürnberg*, p. 266.
46. Noelle and Neumann, eds., *Jahrbuch der öffentlichen Meinung 1947–1955*, pp. 272–3. On subsequent developments, see Kössler, *Abschied von der Revolution*; Kössler, 'Kaderpartei oder Milieupartei?'; Foschepoth, *Überwachtes Deutschland*; Foschepoth, 'Rolle und Bedeutung'; Schildt and Siegfried, *Deutsche Kulturgeschichte*, pp. 140ff.
47. See in detail on this section Spannuth, *Rückerstattung Ost*; Goschler, *Schuld*, pp. 61–124; Olaf Groehler, 'Verfolgten- und Opfergruppen im Spannungsfeld der politischen Auseinandersetzungen in der Sowjetischen Besatzungszone und in der Deutschen Demokratischen Republik', in Danyel, ed., *Vergangenheit*, pp. 17–30.
48. On the question of restitution, see Goschler, *Schuld*; Goschler, *Wiedergutmachung*; Herbst and Goschler, eds. *Wiedergutmachung*; Hockerts and Kuller, eds., *Nach der Verfolgung*; Hockerts, *Wiedergutmachung in Deutschland*; Frei, ed., *Die Praxis der Wiedergutmachung*; Pawlita, *'Wiedergutmachung' als Rechtsfrage*.
49. Ernst Féaux de la Croix, 9 March 1964, quoted in Goschler, *Schuld*, p. 151.
50. M.Mayer, 2 January 1949, quoted in Goschler, *Schuld*, p. 128.
51. Merritt and Merritt, eds., *Public Opinion*, p. 146.

52. Jena, 'Versöhnung mit Israel?'; Wolffsohn, *Deutsch-israelisches Wiedergutmachungsabkommen.*
53. Adenauer, on 16 May 1952, quoted in Goschler, *Schuld,* p. 166; cf. Buchheim, *Wiedereingliederung,* and Romback-Jaschinski, *Das Londoner Schuldenabkommen.*
54. Goschler, *Schuld,* pp. 152ff.; Ulrich Herbert, 'Nicht entschädigungsfähig? Die Wiedergutmchungsansprüche der Ausländer', in Herbst and Goschler, eds., *Wiedergutmachung,* pp. 273–302.
55. Hermann Brill, addressing the Bundestag Committee on the Legal System and Constitutional Law on 4 May 1953, quoted in Goschler, *Schuld,* p. 193.
56. 'Offener Brief an die Bundesregierung, 7.2.1951, Der Grundbesitz Mai 1948', quoted in Goschler, *Schuld,* p. 207. Cf.Lillteicher, *Raub, Recht und Restitution*; Goschler and Lillteicher, eds., *'Arisierung' und Restitution*; and Goschler and Ther, eds., *Raub und Restitution.*
57. Schildt, *Sozialgeschichte der Bundesrepublik,* pp. 14–15; Oltmer, *Migration,* p. 50.
58. On the next section, see Mooser, *Arbeiterleben*; Geißler, *Sozialstruktur,* pp. 230ff.; Tenfelde, ed., *Arbeiter im 20. Jahrhundert*; Süß, *Kumpel und Genossen,* pp. 127–76.
59. Exner, *Ländliche Gesellschaft*; Balcar, *Politik auf dem Land*; Kluge, *Agrarwirschaft,* pp. 36–61.
60. Ackermann, *Der 'echte' Flüchtling*; Erker, *Vom Heimatvertriebenen.*
61. Andersen, *Der Traum vom guten Leben*; König, *Geschichte der Konsumgesellschaft*; Wildt, *Am Beginn der Konsumgesellschaft.*
62. Kielmannsegg, *Nach der Katastrophe,* p. 395.
63. Geißler, *Sozialstruktur,* pp. 184–304; Hradil and Bolte, *Soziale Ungleichheit,* pp. 111–278.
64. Geißler, *Sozialstruktur,* pp. 152–5.
65. Geißler, *Sozialstruktur,* pp. 365–400; Frevert, *Women in German History,* pp. 253–327; Budde, ed., *Frauen arbeiten.*
66. For the next section, see Schildt, *Moderne Zeiten,* pp. 73–109, and Wildt, *Am Beginn der 'Konsumgesellschaft',* pp. 76–108 and 143–53.
67. Quoted in Schildt, *Moderne Zeiten,* p. 112. See also Schildt, '"Mach mal Pause"' On the family, see Bertram, ed., *Familie in Westdeutschland*; and Niehuss, *Familie,* pp. 128–72.
68. Rolf Becker, 'Die neue Gartenlaube. Über die deutsche Rundfunk-Illustrierte "Hör Zu"', in *Der Monat* 12 (1959), Issue 133, pp. 52–8, quoted in Schildt, *Moderne Zeiten,* p. 133.
69. Schildt and Siegfried, *Deutsche Kulturgeschichte,* pp. 108–20; Walter Uka, 'Modernisierung im Wiederaufbau oder Restauration? Der bundesdeutsche Film der fünfziger Jahre', in Faulstich, ed., *Kultur der fünfziger Jahre,* pp. 71–89; Kaschuba, *Der deutsche Heimatfilm.*
70. Hickethier, *Geschichte des deutschen Fernsehens,* pp. 68–94; Schildt, *Moderne Zeiten,* pp. 262–305.
71. Kielmannsegg, *Nach der Katastrophe,* p. 425; Edelmann, *Vom Luxusgut zum Verbrauchsgegenstand*; Südbeck, *Motorisierung,* p. 94.
72. Schildt, *Moderne Zeiten,* pp. 180–208.

73. Schelsky, *Wandlungen*, pp. 63 and 87; Pfeil, *Berufstätigkeit*, p. 79. On the next section, see Frevert, *Women in German History*, pp. 278–302, and Schildt, *Sozialgeschichte*, p. 37.
74. Moeller, *Protecting Motherhood*, pp. 79ff.; Reich-Hilweg, *Männer und Frauen*, pp. 13–37; Niehuss, *Familie*, pp. 214–26.
75. Therborn, *European Modernity*, p. 138.
76. Geißler, *Sozialstruktur*, pp. 69–120; Hradil and Bolte, *Soziale Ungleichheit*, pp. 279–343. Cf. Wehler, *Gesellschaftsgeschichte*, vol. 5, pp. 119–24 and 207ff.; Schelsky, *Wandlungen*.
77. Lüdtke, Marssolek and von Saldern, eds., *Amerikanisierung*; Jarausch and Siegrist, eds., *Amerikanisierung*; Schildt, *Abendland*; Middendorf, *Massenkultur*.
78. Cf. Köhler and van Melis, eds., *Siegerin in Trümmern*; Wilhelm Damberg, 'Milieu und Konzil. Zum Paradigmenwechsel konfessionellen Bewusstseins im Katholizismus der frühen Bundesrepublik', in Blaschke, ed., *Konfessionen im Konflikt*, pp. 335–50; Gauly, *Kirche und Politik*, pp. 149–217.
79. Hermann Aubin, 'Abendland, Reich, Deutschland und Europa', in Bundesministerium für Verteidigung, ed., *Schicksalsfragen der Gegenwart*, vol. 1, pp. 27–63, here p. 63.
80. Freyer, *Theorie*, pp. 219–41.
81. Freyer, *Theorie*, p. 230.
82. Steinbacher, *Wie der Sex nach Deutschland kam*, p. 351; Jeschek, *Das Menschenbild unserer Zeit*, pp. 7–8. See Michael Kandora, 'Homosexualität und Sittengesetz', in Herbert, ed., *Wandlungsprozesse*, pp. 379–401.
83. Freyer, *Theorie*, p. 230.
84. Schmitt, *Tyranny of Values*; Forsthoff, *Der Staat der Industriegesellschaft*, pp. 56–60. Cf. Hacke, *Die Bundesrepublik als Idee*, pp. 25ff. Sieburg, *Die Lust am Untergang*, p. 126.

## Chapter 13

1. For a discussion of these issues, see for example Furet, *Passing of an Illusion*, and Koenen, *Was war der Kommunismus?*
2. In German: 'Ihr wißt, was es hieß,/Den Weg, den schweren, gehen./Es lagen an dem Rand/Des Wegs der Toten viel,/Wir aber wußten dies:/Wir *müssen* auferstehen./Ein freies deutsches Land/War unsrer Sehnsucht Ziel./Seht, Großes wird vollbracht,/Das Volk schafft sich sein Leben./Und war der Weg auch schwer,/Ein Jubel sich erhebt./Seid euch bewußt der Macht!/Die Macht ist euch gegeben,/Daß ihr sie nie, nie mehr/Aus euren Händen gebt!' Source: Johannes R. Becher, 'Partei, du bist Friede auf Erden! ['Kantate des Jahres 1950'], Part II, in Becher, *Gesammelte Werke*, vol. 6, pp. 462–4, here p. 463.
3. On the history of the GDR, see Staritz, *Geschichte der DDR*; Weber, *Die DDR 1945–1990*; Weber, *Geschichte der DDR*; Schroeder, *Der SED-Staat*; Dierk Hoffmann and Michael Schwarz, 'Politische Rahmenbedingungen', in GSD, vol. 8, pp. 1–72; Schwarz,

'Gesellschaftliche Strukturen und Sozialpolitische Handlungsfelder', in GSD, vol. 8, pp. 73–157; Hoffmann, *Die DDR unter Ulbricht*; Christoph Kleßmann, 'Politische Rahmenbedingungen', in GSD, vol. 9, pp. 1–76; Peter Hübner, 'Gesellschaftliche Strukturen und Sozialpolitische Handlungsfelder', in GSD, vol. 9, pp. 77–146; Kleßmann, *Die doppelte Staatsgründung*; Kleßmann, *Zwei Staaten, eine Nation*; Kleßmann, *Arbeiter im 'Arbeiterstaat' DDR*; Fulbrook, *Anatomy of a Dictatorship*; Mitter and Wolle, *Untergang auf Raten*; Meuschel, *Legitimation und Parteiherrschaft*; Ihme-Tuchel, *Die DDR*; Halder, *Von Ulbricht bis Honecker.*

4. Karlsch et al., eds., *Sowjetische Demontagen in Deutschland*; Karlsch, 'Umfang und Struktur der Reparationsentnahmen aus der SBZ/DDR 1945–1953. Stand und Probleme der Forschung', in Buchheim, ed., *Wirtschaftliche Folgelasten*, pp. 45–78; Buchheim, 'Kriegsfolgen'. On the economic aspects, see also Steiner, *The Plans that Failed*; Steiner, ed., *Überholen ohne einholen*, pp. 218–47; Küchler, *Die Wirtschaft der DDR*; Staritz, *Geschichte der DDR*, pp. 50–60; and Weber, *Geschichte der DDR*, pp. 213ff.
5. Kleßmann, *Arbeiter*, pp. 215–26.
6. Schöne, *Frühling*, pp. 73–153.
7. Werkentin, *Politische Strafjustiz in der Ära Ulbricht*, pp. 362–83; Weber, *Justiz und Diktatur*, pp. 163–252; Fricke, ed., *Opposition und Widerstand in der DDR*, pp. 15–16.
8. Herf, *East German Communists*; Spannuth, *Rückerstattung Ost*, pp. 71–269.
9. Oskar Anweiler, 'Bildungspolitik', in GSD, vol. 8, p. 553–88; Staritz, *Geschichte*, pp. 66–75.
10. Resolution of the Third Party Congress of the SED, 24.7.1950, in Weber, ed., *DDR. Dokumente zur Geschichte*, no. 91, pp. 176–7; cf. Sabrow, *Diktat des Konsenses*, pp. 342–464, here pp. 442ff.
11. Decision of the Second Party Conference of the SED, in *Protokoll der Verhandlungen der II. Parteikonferenz der SED*, pp. 489–97, here p. 492.
12. Pollack, *Kirche*, pp. 114ff.; Ewald Frie, 'Autonomiespielräume der Kirchen in der DDR', in Kaiser and Frie, eds., *Christen, Staat und Gesellschaft*, pp. 121–42; Clemens Vollnhals, 'Die kirchenpolitische Abteilung des Ministeriums für Staatssicherheit', in Vollnhals, ed., *Die Kirchenpolitik von SED und Staatssicherheit*, pp. 79–119.
13. On labour productivity, see Ritschl, 'Aufstieg und Niedergang', p. 16. Various estimates have been given for GDR labour productivity. The highest is 78 per cent of the West German level, the lowest 44 per cent.
14. Neutatz, *Träume*, pp. 358ff.; Hildermeier, *Geschichte der Sowjetunion*, pp. 757–87; Stephan Merl, 'Entstalinisierung, Reformen und Wettlauf der Systeme 1953–1964', in Hellmann, ed. *Handbuch der Geschichte Russlands*, vol. 5.2, pp. 175–203. (This volume was edited by Stefan Plaggenborg.) For ease of comprehension, the more customary method of transliteration is used here rather than the international scholarly system.
15. Minutes of the emergency sitting of the Politburo of the Central Committee on 5.6.1953, quoted in Staritz, *Geschichte*, pp. 108ff.
16. Armin Mitter, 'Der "Tag X" und die "Innere Staatsgründung" der DDR', in Kowalczuk, Mitter and Wolle, eds., *Der Tag X*, pp. 9–30; Mitter and Wolle, *Untergang*

*auf Raten,* pp. 27–162; Diedrich, *Der 17. Juni,* pp. 55–141; Staritz, *Geschichte,* pp. 117ff.; Schroeder, *SED-Staat,* pp. 119–30.
17. Rupieper, ed., *Einheit*; Löhn, *Spitzbart.*
18. Figures given in a report by the Federal Ministry for All-German Affairs, 1961, quoted in Weber, *Geschichte der DDR,* p. 325.
19. Kant, *Impressum*, pp. 208–9, with unindicated omissions.
20. Decision of the CC of the SED, 21.6.1953, and communiqué from the 15th. Session of the SED Central Committee, 24–26.7.1953, in *Dokumente der SED,* vol. 4, pp. 451ff., here p. 473. Contribution by E. Schmidt to the discussion of 7.7.1953 in the Politburo of the CC of the SED, quoted in Schroeder, *SED-Staat,* p. 126; Resolution of the CC of the SED, 26.7.1953, quoted in Weber, ed., *DDR. Dokumente zur Geschichte,* no. 110, pp. 200–1.
21. Hildermeier, *Geschichte der Sowjetunion,* pp. 762ff.; Neutatz, *Träume*, pp. 363–75.
22. See, on this and on later developments, Weber, *Geschichte*, pp. 280ff. and Staritz, *Geschichte,* pp. 149ff.
23. Borodzeij, *Geschichte Polens,* pp. 257–300.
24. Dalos, *1956*; Walentin A. Pronko, 'Ungarn—UdSSR: Herbst 1956', in Heinemann, ed., *Das internationale Krisenjahr 1956,* pp. 75–94.
25. Staritz, *Geschichte,* pp. 164ff.; Schroeder, *SED-Staat,* pp. 135ff.
26. Steiner, *Plans,* pp. 69–104.
27. *Berliner Zeitung,* 11.12.1957, quoted in Weber, *DDR. Dokumente zur Geschichte,* no. 132, pp. 232ff.
28. Ulbricht's report to the Fifth Party Congress of the SED, 10.7.1958, in Schroeder, *SED-Staat,* doc. 11, pp. 670–1.
29. Chowanski and Dreier, *Jugendweihe.*
30. Schöne, *Frühling auf dem Lande?,* pp. 154–234; Kluge, ed., *Bodenreform,* pp. 157–74.
31. On the Berlin crisis, see Uhl, *Krieg um Berlin?*; Hoffmann, ed., *Vor dem Mauerbau*; Lemke, *Berlin-Krise*; Wettig, *Chruschtschows Berlin-Krise 1958 bis 1963*; Felken, *Dulles und Deutschland*; Bremen, *Die Eisenhower-Administration.*
32. Kennedy's 'Three Essentials', as quoted in Schroeder, *SED-Staat,* p. 163; Loth, *Helsinki,* pp. 81–4; Stöver, *Der Kalte Krieg,* pp. 135–6.
33. Ulbricht's letters to Khrushchev of 19.1.1961 and 4.8.1961, quoted in Schroeder, *SED-Staat,* pp. 164–5.
34. Anastas Mikoyan, speaking in June 1961, according to Lemke, *Berlin-Krise,* p. 161.
35. Bruyn, *Vierzig Jahre*, p. 110.
36. Gauck, *Winter im Sommer—Frühling im Herbst,* p. 73.
37. Axen, *Ich war ein Diener der Partei*, p. 228.
38. Werkentin, *Politische Strafjustiz,* pp. 250–2. and 267; Staritz, *Geschichte*, pp. 199–200; Schroeder, *SED-Staat,* pp. 168–9.
39. Hildermeier, *Geschichte*, p. 788ff.
40. Steiner, *Plans*, p. 108.
41. Steiner, *Plans,* pp. 109ff. André Steiner, 'Von "Haupfaufgabe" zu "Hauptaufgabe". Zur Wirtschaftsentwicklung der langen sechziger Jahre in der DDR', in Schildt, et al., eds., *Dynamische Zeiten,* pp. 218–47; Meuschel, *Legitimation und Parteiherrschaft,* pp. 181ff.

42. Party Programme of the SED, 18.1.1963, quoted in Weber, *DDR*, no. 153.
43. *Neues Deutschland*, 14.2.1965, quoted in Kleßmann, *Zwei Staaten*, p. 349.
44. Weber, *DDR*, p. 65; Oskar Anweiler, 'Bildungspolitik', in GSD, vol. 9, pp. 582ff.
45. SED Youth Communiqué, 17.9.1963, quoted in Weber, *DDR*, no. 156; Ohse, *Jugend nach dem Mauerbau*, pp. 64–82.
46. Steiner, *Plans*, pp. 126–32.
47. Meuschel, *Legitimation*, p. 191; Steiner, *Plans*, pp. 111–13.
48. Przybylski, *Tatort Politbüro*, vol. 2, pp. 149–50.
49. Steiner, *Plans*, pp. 119–39; Staritz, *Geschichte*, pp. 218–29; Meuschel, *Legitimation*, pp. 181–220.
50. Party Programme of the SED, 18.1.1963, quoted in Weber, *DDR*, no. 153.
51. Ulbricht, at the Second Bitterfeld Conference, 24–25.4.1964, quoted in Meuschel, *Legitimation*, p. 226.
52. Havemann, *Questions Answers Questions*, pp. 254–5.
53. 'Probleme des Perspektivplans bis 1970' [Ulbricht's report to the Eleventh Plenum of the CC of the SED, 16–18.12.1965], in Schubbe, *Dokumente*, vol. 1, pp. 1,081–8, here p. 1,087.
54. Jäger, *Kultur und Politik*, p. 115.
55. Veser, *Der Prager Frühling 1968*; Pauer, *Prag 1968*.
56. Prieß et al., *SED*, p. 193.
57. On the GDR's search for recognition, see Bender, *Episode oder Epoche?*, pp. 82–99; Kleßmann, *Zwei Staaten*, pp. 447–68; Schroeder, *SED-Staat*, pp. 189ff.; Kielmannsegg, *Nach der Katastrophe*, pp. 513–23; Winkler, *Germany: The Long Road West*, vol. 2, pp. 256–75.
58. Brandt's government declaration, 28.10.1969, in *Verhandlungen des Deutschen Bundestages. Stenographische Berichte, 6. Wahlperiode*, vol. 71, pp. 20–34, here p. 21.
59. Honecker, speaking on 16.2.1970, reported in *Neues Deutschland*, 22.2.1970; Ulbricht, speaking on 19.1.1970, in *Dokumente zur Außenpolitik der DDR*, vol. 8.2, pp. 723–37, here p. 727.
60. Ulbricht, speaking on 21.11.1970, quoted in Schwarz, *Bundesrepublik Deutschland*, p. 159. '*Ostpolitik*' is examined in more detail in Chapter 18 of this volume.
61. Siebs, *Außenpolitik*, pp. 114–15.
62. Meeting between the CC of the CPSU and the CC of the SED, 21.8.1970, quoted in Przybylski, *Tatort Politbüro*, vol. 1, p. 289–96, here p. 296.
63. Brezhnev, speaking on 20.8.1970, quoted in Przybylski, *Tatort Politbüro*, vol. 2, pp. 230–345, here p. 342.
64. Letter of 21.1.1971, quoted in Przybylski, *Tatort Politbüro*, vol. 1, p. 111.

## Chapter 14

1. For the development of the process of détente, see in particular Leffler and Westad, eds., *Crises and Détente*, pp. 1–21; Loth, *Helsinki*, pp. 49–132; Stöver, *Der Kalte Krieg*, pp. 381–409; Bender, *Neue Ostpolitik*, pp. 87–115; Lemke, *Die Berlinkrise*, pp. 228–73;

Bierling, *Außenpolitik,* pp. 111–69; Hacke, *Außenpolitik,* pp. 63–123; Haftendorn, *Coming of Age,* pp. 83–119; Dülffer, *Europa in der Ost-West-Konflikt,* pp. 18–37.

2. Uhl, *Krieg um Berlin*; Wettig, *Chruschtschows Berlin-Krise*; Khrushchev, *Khrushchev Remembers,* pp. 452–60.
3. Greiner, *Kuba-Krise: 13 Tage in Oktober*; Greiner, *Die Kuba-Krise*; Münger, *Kennedy.*
4. Stöver, *Der Kalte Krieg,* pp. 81–91; Leffler and Westad, eds., *Crises and Détente,* pp. 198–218.
5. Lappenküper, *Beziehungen,* pp. 1,707–855; Defrance and Pfeil, *Nachkriegsgeschichte,* pp. 98–115; Ziebura, *Beziehungen,* pp. 157–71.
6. Geiger, *Atlantiker gegen Gaullisten,* pp. 197ff.; Conze, *Suche nach Sicherheit,* pp. 309–21.
7. *Deutscher Bundestag, 3. WP, Plenarprotokoll,* 30.6.1960, pp. 7,052–61.
8. *Dokumente zur Deutschlandpolitik,* vol. 5 part 9, p. 573; Bender, *Neue Ostpolitik,* pp. 103–29; Bender, *Episode oder Epoche?,* pp. 160–8.
9. Cf. for example Ludz, *Changing Party Elite.*
10. Karl Jaspers, 'Deutsches Nationalbewußtsein und Wiedervereinigung', in Jaspers, *Freiheit und Wiedervereinigung,* pp. 39–56; Thilo Koch, 'Der Streit um Jaspers. Was die Kritiker des Philosophen übersehen haben', *Die Zeit,* 19.8.1960.
11. Erhard, speaking in the Bundestag on 15.10.1964: *Deutscher Bundestag, 4. WP, Plenarprotokoll,* pp. 6,778–88, here p. 6,779; and on 9.1.1964, in the same source, pp. 4,840–9, here p. 4,847.
12. On this episode, see Schwarz, *Ära Adenauer, Epochenwechsel 1957–1963,* pp. 177–92; Schwarz, *Ära Adenauer,Gründerjahre 1949–1957,* pp. 365–626; Bösch, *Adenauer-CDU,* pp. 335–68; Bösch, *Macht und Machtverlust,* pp. 19–28; Görtemaker, *Geschichte,* pp. 328–90; Conze, *Suche nach Sicherheit,* pp. 265ff.; Kielmannsegg, *Nach der Katastrophe,* pp. 283ff.
13. 'Bedingt abwehrbereit', in *Der Spiegel,* 10.10.1962; Adenauer, speaking in the Bundestag, in *Deutscher Bundestag, 4. WP, Plenarprotokoll,* 7.11.1962, pp. 1,981–4, here p. 1,984. On the Spiegel Affair, see Schoenbaum, *'Ein Abgrund von Landesverrat'* and Seifert, ed., *Die Spiegel-Affäre.*
14. Gerhard Ritter, 'Blind für die Wirklichkeit', letter to the *FAZ,* 10.11.1962; Karl-Dietrich Bracher, 'Demokratie oder Obrigkeitsstaat', letter to the *FAZ,* 13.11.1962. Both letters are reprinted in Ellwein, Liebel and Negt, *Die Reaktion,* pp. 401–3.
15. Wolfgang Weyrauch, 'Bemerkungen des Herausgebers', in Weyrauch, ed., *Ich lebe in der Bundesrepublik,* pp. 7–9, here p. 8.
16. Kasimir Edschmid, 'Aus meinem Notizbuch', in Weyrauch, ed., *Ich lebe in der Bundesrepublik,* pp. 50–9. On the next section, see Anselm Doering-Manteuffel, 'Westernisierung. Politisch-ideeller und gesellschaftlicher Wandel in der Bundesrepublik bis zum Ende der 60er Jahre', in Schildt, Siegfried and Lammers, eds., *Dynamische Zeiten,* pp. 311–41; Ulrich Herbert, 'Liberalisierung also Lernprozeß. Die Bundesrepublik in der deutschen Geschichte—eine Skizze', in Herbert, ed., *Wandlungsprocesse,* pp. 7–49; Matthias Frese and Julia Paulus, 'Geschwindigkeit und Faktoren des Wandels—die 60er Jahre in der Bundesrepublik', in Frese et al., eds., *Demokratisierung,* pp. 1–26; Conze, *Suche nach Sicherheit,* pp. 227–89.

17. Hans Werner Richter, 'Zu spät?', in Weyrauch, ed., *Ich lebe in der Bundesrepublik*, pp. 60–6; Dominik Geppert, 'Von der Staatsskepsis zum parteipolitischen Engagement. Hans Werner Richter, die Gruppe 47 und die deutsche Politik', in Geppert and Hacke, eds., *Streit*, pp. 46–68.
18. *Allensbacher Jahrbuch der Demoskopie*, vol. 8, p. 187.
19. Christina von Hodenberg, 'Die Journalisten und der Aufbruch zur kritischen Öffentlichkeit', in Herbert, ed., *Wandlungsprozesse*, pp. 278–314, here p. 293. See also Hodenberg, *Konsens und Krise*, which also covers the next section.
20. Albrecht, Behrmann and Bock, eds., *Gründung*, pp. 132–69 and 448–529; Hacke, *Bundesrepublik als Idee*, pp. 17–24, 68–74, and 88–93.
21. Peter Øhrgaard, '"Ich bin nicht zu Herrn Willy Brandt gefahren"—Zum politischen Engagement der Schriftsteller in der Bundesrepublik am Beginn der 60er Jahre', in Schildt, Siegfried and Lammers, eds., *Dynamische Zeiten*, pp. 719–33; Müller, *Die literarische Republik*.
22. Richter, ed., *Bestandsaufnahme*.
23. Ulrich Herbert, 'Drei politische Generationen im 20.Jahrhundert', in Reulecke, ed., *Generationalität*, pp. 95–115; Herbert, 'Liberalisierung', pp. 43ff.; Albrecht, Behrmann and Bock, eds., *Gründung*, pp. 497–529; Dirk A.Moses, 'Die 45er. Eine Generation zwischen Faschismus und Demokratie', in *Die Neue Sammlung*, 40 (2000), pp. 211–32; Jureit, *Generationsforschung*, pp. 40–85; Lutz Niethammer, 'Die letzte Gemeinschaft. Über die Konstruierbarkeit von Generationen und ihre Grenzen', in Weisbrod, ed., *Historische Beiträge zur Generationsforschung*, pp. 13–38; Schelsky, *Die skeptische Generation*; Nolte, *Ordnung*.
24. Ralf Dahrendorf, 'Die neue Gesellschaft. Soziale Strukturwandlungen der Nachkriegszeit', in Richter, ed., *Bestandsaufnahme*, pp. 203–20; cf. Moritz Scheibe, 'Auf der Suche nach der demokratischen Gesellschaft', in Herbert, ed., *Wandlungsprozesse*, pp. 245–78.
25. Jürgen Habermas, 'Über den Begriff der politischen Beteiligung', in Habermas et al., eds., *Student und Politik*, pp. 11–55, here pp. 16–17.
26. Dahrendorf, *Society and Democracy in Germany*, p. 15; Dahrendorf, *Gesellschaft und Freiheit*.
27. Hans Werner Richter, 'Bilanz. Ein Nachwort', in Richter, ed., *Bestandsaufnahme*, pp. 561–72.
28. Picht, *Die deutsche Bildungskatastrophe*, pp. 16–17 and 26. On the German system of education, see also Thomas Ellwin, 'Die deutsche Gesellschaft und ihr Bildungswesen. Interessenartikulation und Bildungsdiskussion', in *Handbuch der deutschen Bildungsgeschichte*, vol. 6, pp. 87–108, and Tippelt, *Bildung und sozialer Wandel*.
29. Peisert, *Soziale Lage und Bildungschancen*, pp. 145–6.
30. Dahrendorf, *Bildung ist Bürgerrecht*, p. 151.
31. Kleist, 'Kritische Notizen'.
32. Gerhard Fischer, 'Jugendfunktionäre, Fußwanderer und anonyme Jugendarbeit', in *Deutsche Jugend* 2 (1954), pp. 32–4, quoted in Julia Ubbelohde, 'Der Umgang mit jugendlichen Normenverstößen', in Herbert, ed., *Wandlungsprozesse*, pp. 402–35, here p. 420.

33. Fritz Bauer, 'Sexualtabus und Sexualethik im Spiegel des Strafgesetzes', in Bauer, *Schuld und Sühne*, pp. 1–22; Bauer et al., 'Vorwort der Herausgeber', in Bauer et al. eds., *Sexualität und Verbrechen*, pp. 7–10, here pp. 7–8.
34. Cf. Kaelble, *Social History of Europe*, pp. 62–86.
35. Chafe, *The Unfinished Journey*, pp. 53–139; May and Larry, *Recasting America*; Heideking, *Geschichte der USA*, pp. 342–4; Edward Purcell 'Consensus', in Fox et al., eds., *Companion to American Thought*, pp. 140–2.
36. For the next section, see von Miquel, *Ahnden oder amnestieren*, pp. 23–142 ('Justice and the Nazi past'); and 146–207 (on the Central Office of Social Administration); Brochhagen, *Nach Nürnberg*, pp. 240ff.; and Rückerl, *NS-Verbrechen vor Gericht*, pp. 139–40.
37. Brochhagen, *Nach Nürnberg*, p. 282. Cf. Werner Bergmann, 'Antisemitismus als politisches Ereignis. Die antisemitische Welle im Winter 1959/1960', in Bergmann and Erb, eds., *Antisemitismus in der politischen Kultur*, pp. 253–75.
38. Fritsche, *Vergangenheitsbewältigung*, pp. 100–38. This fourteen-part documentary series by Heinz Huber, Arthur Müller, Gerd Ruge and Waldemar Besson, was shown on ARD between 21.10.1960 and 19.05.1961. It reached 58 per cent of television viewers, on average. See also Reichel, *Vergangenheitsbewältigung*, pp. 209–16; Reichel, Schmid and Steinbach, eds., *Der Nationalsozialismus*; Weinke, *Eine Gesellschaft ermittelt*; and Detlef Siegfried, 'Zwischen Aufarbeitung und Schlussstrich. Der Umgang mit der NS–Vergangenheit in den beiden deutschen Staaten, 1958 bis 1969', in Schildt, Siegfried and Lammers, eds., *Dynamische Zeiten*, pp. 77–114.
39. Deutscher Ausschuß für das Erziehungs- und Bildungswesen, 'Declaration in Response to the Anti-semitic Outrages of 30.1.1960', p. 50, quoted in Albrecht, Behrmann and Bock, eds., *Gründung*, pp. 395–6.
40. Wojak, ed., *Auschwitz-Prozeß*.
41. Buchheim et al., *Anatomie*.
42. Konrad H. Jarausch, 'Der nationale Tabubruch. Wissenschaft, Öffentlichkeit and Politik in der Fischer-Kontroverse', in Sabrow, Jessen, and Große Kracht, eds., *Zeitgeschichte als Streitgeschichte*, pp. 20–40, here p. 36; Fischer, *Germany's Aims*; Große Kracht, *Die zankende Zunft*, pp. 47–67; Bruno Thoß, 'Der Erste Weltkrieg als Ereignis und Erlebnis. Paradigmenwechsel in der westdeutschen Weltkriegsforschung seit der Fischer-Kontroverse', in Michalka, ed., *Der Erste Weltkrieg*, pp. 1,012–44.
43. Von Miquel, *Ahnden*, pp. 193–319. This is also relevant to the next section.
44. On Bucher: 'Notfalls mit einigen Mördern zusammenleben, sagte Bucher', in *SZ*, 18.1.1965, quoted in von Miquel, *Ahnden*, p. 256. Strauß's statement: *FAZ*, 8.2.1965, quoted in von Miquel, *Ahnden*, p. 290.
45. Benda, in *Deutscher Bundestag, 4.WP, Plenarprotokoll*, 10.3.1965, pp. 8,519–26, here p. 8,524; Deutscher Bundestag, ed., *Zur Verjährung nationalsozialistischer Verbrechen*, pp. 158ff.
46. Von Miquel, *Ahnden*, pp. 327–43; Herbert, *Best*, pp. 508–19. This refers to the Introductory Statute to the Law on Violations of Public Order. Most of the 167

articles of this Statute were directed to establishing new regulations for the treatment of public order offences, particularly in the area of transport. Ministerial Director Dr Dreher was the driving force behind these regulations, which were issued in the context of the 'great reform of the criminal law'.

47. Erhard's government declaration: *Deutscher Bundestag, 4.WP, Plenarprotokoll,* 18.10.1965, pp. 4,192–209, here pp. 4,193–4.
48. Erhard's government declaration: *Deutscher Bundestag, 5.WP, Plenarprotokoll,* 10.11.1965, pp. 17–33, here p. 19.
49. Erhard, speaking on 5.7.1965 in Düsseldorf and on 7.7.1965 in Cologne, quoted in Görtemaker, *Geschichte,* p. 417, see also pp. 391–435. Löffler, 'Rahmenbedingungen', in GSD, vol. 4, pp. 3–83; Hentschel, *Erhard,* pp. 622–7; Hildebrand, *Von Erhard zur Großen Koalition,* pp. 202–18.
50. Erhard to Barzel, 12.8.1966 and Erhard to Strauß, 15.8.1966, quoted in Görtemaker, *Geschichte,* p. 433. On the next section, see Lindlar, *Wirtschaftswunder,* pp. 157–62; Abelshauser, *Wirtschaftsgeschichte der Bundesrepublik Deutschland*; Gerd Hardach, 'Krise und Reform der Sozialen Marktwirtschaft. Grundzüge der wirtschaftlichen Entwicklung in der Bundesrepublik der 50er und 60er Jahre', in Schildt, Siegfried and Lammers, eds., *Dynamische Zeiten,* pp. 197–247; Görtemaker, *Geschichte,* pp. 427–37; and Kleßmann, *Zwei Staaten,* pp. 193–200.

## Chapter 15

1. On West German society in the 1960s, see Schildt, *Sozialgeschichte,* pp. 30–54; Schildt, 'Materieller Wohlstand—pragmatische Politik—kulturelle Umbrüche', in Schildt, Siegfried and Lammers, eds., *Dynamische Zeiten,* pp. 21–54; Löffler, 'Rahmenbedingungen', in GSD, vol. 4, pp. 1–83; Abelshauser, *Deutsche Wirtschaftsgeschichte,* pp. 315–60; Mooser, *Arbeiterleben,* pp. 113–25; Mooser, 'Abschied von der Proletarität', in Conze and Lepsius, eds., *Sozialgeschichte,* pp. 169ff.; Conze, *Die Suche nach Sicherheit,* pp. 259–90; Matthias Frese and Julia Paulus, 'Geschwindigkeiten und Faktoren des Wandels—die 1960er Jahre in der Bundesrepublik', in Frese, Paulus and Teppe, eds., *Demokratisierung und gesellschaftlicher Aufbruch,* pp. 1–27; and Wehler, *Gesellschaftsgeschichte,* vol. 5, pp. 108–215.
2. These figures are taken from 'Allgemeinbildende Schulen 1950–1994, Schüler nach Schularten', in *Handbuch der deutschen Bildungsgeschichte,* vol. IV.1, p. 646, and BMBF, ed., *Grund- und Strukturdaten 1998/99,* pp. 80–5.
3. Löffler, 'Rahmenbedingungen', in GSD, vol. 4, pp. 17–19; Geißler, *Sozialstruktur,* pp. 184–304; Bolte and Hradil, *Soziale Ungleichheit,* pp. 111–278.
4. Cf. Statistisches Bundesamt Wiesbaden, *Bevölkerung und Wirtschaft 1872–1972,* pp. 148 and 260; Herbert, *Ausländerpolitik,* pp. 206–16; Ulrich Herbert and Karin Hunn, 'Beschäftigung, soziale Sicherung und soziale Integration von Ausländern', GSD, vol. 4, pp. 685–724; Hunn, *'Nächstes Jahr kehren wir zurück',* pp. 29–70.

5. Erhard, speaking on 6.6.1954, 'Interview des NWDR mit Wirtschaftsminister Erhard, 6.12.1954', 10.12.1954, BArch, B 136/8841. See Herbert and Hunn, 'Beschäftigung', GSD, vol. 4, pp. 685–724, quotation on p. 704.
6. Bade, *Migration*, pp. 227–34.
7. Theodor Blank, 'Eine Million Gastarbeiter', in *Bulletin des Presse- und Informationsamtes der Bundesregierung*, 30.10.1964, no. 160, p. 1,480.
8. Carl Föhl, 'Stabilisierung und Wachstum beim Einsatz von Gastarbeitern', *Kyklos* 20 (1967), pp. 119–46.
9. Schildt, *Sozialgeschichte*, pp. 39ff.; von Beyme and Berger, eds., *Neue Städte aus Ruinen*; Flagge, ed., *Geschichte des Wohnens*, vol. 5; Kramper, *Neue Heimat*.
10. Adenauer, speaking in 1957, quoted in Kramper, *Neue Heimat*, p. 180; Lücke, 22.9.1951, quoted in Kramper, *Neue Heimat*, p. 201.
11. Harro Iden, member of the management board of Neue Heimat, in 1958, quoted in Kramper, *Neue Heimat*, p. 201; Kramper, *Neue Heimat*, p. 176.
12. Mitscherlich, *Unwirtlichkeit*, p. 9.
13. Mitscherlich, *Unwirtlichkeit*, p. 60.
14. The quotations are from Mitscherlich, *Unwirtlichkeit*, p. 13; Wulf Tessin, 'Die Entstehungsbedingungen der Großsiedlungen', in Herlyn, von Saldern and Tessin, eds., *Neubausiedlungen*, pp. 75–101, here p. 88; and Alexander Mitscherlich, addressing the Bundestag Committee for Town Planning, Construction and Urban Development, 19.9.1973, quoted in Kramper, *Neue Heimat*, p. 287.
15. Architecture of the Ruhr University, Bochum, http://www.ruhr-uni-bochem.de/universitaet/campus-und-kultur/campusentwicklung/architektur/ [17.4.2011]; cf. Oliver Schmidtke, 'Die Architektur der Ruhr-Universität Bochum sowie der Universität Bielefeld und ihre Entsprechung im technokratischen Deutungsmuster von Wissenschaft', in Franzmann and Wolbring, eds., *Zwischen Idee und Zweckorientierung*, pp. 137–82.
16. This film is available on the internet via http://www.bild.de/video/clip/spd/1965-8431290.bild.html [14.11.2011].
17. Albert Vietor, 23.2.1967, quoted in Kramper, *Neue Heimat*, p. 349.
18. *Welt der Arbeit, Extradienst*, July 1973, quoted in Kramper, *Neue Heimat*, p. 348.
19. Hans Michaelis, 'Die Energiewirtschaft der Bundesrepublik Deutschland von 1970 bis 1990', in Hohensee and Salewski, eds., *Energie-Politik-Geschichte*, pp. 51–74, here p. 53. On the next section, see Radkau, *Aufstieg und Krise*, pp. 196–258; Brüggemeier, *Tschernobyl*, pp. 205–8; Keck, *Der schnelle Brüter*; Oetzel, *Die geplante Zukunft*; Rusinek, *Das Forschungszentrum*, pp. 89–152.
20. Salin, *Ökonomik der Atomkraft*, p. 4; Jordan, *Atomkraft*, p. 57; *Atomwirtschaft* 5 (1960), p. 155, quoted in Radkau, *Aufstieg*, pp. 78–9.
21. Abelshauser, *Deutsche Wirtschaftsgeschichte seit 1945*, pp. 200–14.
22. Wendt, *The Prospects of Nuclear Power and Technology*, p. 156, quoted in Radkau, *Aufstieg*, p. 93.
23. Cf. Rusinek, *Das Forschungszentrum*, p. 94; Walker, *German Nationàl Socialism*, p. 189.
24. The original intention of the designer of the Atomium, the British engineer André Waterkeyn, was to depict an iron molecule 'in homage to the basic material of the

industrial revolution', but after it had been built it was reinterpreted as the symbol of the atomic age. Cf. Kretschmer, *Geschichte der Weltausstellungen*, p. 221.

25. Bloch, *The Principle of Hope*, vol. 2, p. 664: 'A few hundred pounds of uranium and thorium would be enough to make the Sahara and the Gobi desert disappear, and to transform Siberia and Northern Canada, Greenland and the Antarctic into a riviera.'
26. Leo Brandt, 'Wir werden durch Atome leben (30.5.1956)', in Mittermaier and Rusinek, eds., *Leo Brandt*, pp. 65–111, here pp. 79–80.
27. Brandt, *Die zweite industrielle Revolution*, especially pp. 3–6.
28. 'Grundsatzprogramm der Sozialdemokratischen Partei Deutschlands', in Flechtheim, ed., *Dokumente zur parteipolitischen Entwicklung in Deutschland*, vol. 3, no. 187, pp. 209–26.
29. Strauß, on 19.7.1956, quoted in Rusinek, *Forschungszentrum*, p. 94.
30. Radkau, *Aufstieg*, pp. 161 and 221–2; Keck, *Der schnelle Brüter*; Rusinek, *Forschungszentrum*, pp. 74–8.
31. Radkau, *Aufstieg*, p. 289.
32. Häfele, *Neuartige Wege*, pp. 36–7.
33. Häfele, in 1965, quoted in Radkau, *Aufstieg*, p. 222.
34. Kaiser, ed., *Planung*, vol. 1, p. 7.
35. Metzler, *Konzeptionen*, pp. 74–80 and throughout; Metzler, '"Geborgenheit in gesichertem Fortschritt". Das Jahrzehnt von Planbarkeit und Machbarkeit', in Frese, Paulus and Teppe, eds., *Demokratisierung*, pp. 777–97; Winfried Süß, '"Wer aber denkt für das Ganze". Aufstieg und Fall der ressortübergreifenden Planung im Bundeskanzleramt', in Frese, Paulus and Teppe, eds., *Demokratisierung*, pp. 349–77; see also Hans Günter Hockerts, 'Einführung', in Frese, Paulus and Teppe, eds., *Demokratisierung*, pp. 249–58; Michael Ruck, 'Ein kurzer Sommer der konkreten Utopie—zur westdeutschen Planungsgeschichte der langen 60er Jahre', in Schildt, Siegfried, and Lammers, eds., *Dynamische Zeiten*, pp. 362–401; and Alexander Schmidt-Gernig, 'Die gesellschaftliche Konstruktion der Zukunft', in *Welttrends*, 18 1998), pp. 63–84.
36. Rostow, *Stages of Economic Growth* (1960. Translated into German the same year as *Stadien der wirtschaftlichen Entwicklung*). Cf. Latham, *Modernization as Ideology*, and Metzger, *Konzeptionen*, pp. 225ff.
37. See Schmidt-Gernig, 'Konstruktion' and Joas, 'Demokratisierung'.
38. Fourastié, *Die große Metamorphose des 20.Jahrhunderts*; Fourastié, *Gesetze der Wirtschaft von Morgen*; Robert Jungk, 'Gesucht: ein neuer Mensch. Skizze zu einem Modell des Planers', in Jungk and Mundt, eds., *Der Griff nach der Zukunft*, pp. 505–16, here pp. 515–16.
39. Böckenförde, *Organisationsgewalt*, p. 257; Helmut Schelsky, 'Planung der Zukunft. Die rationale Utopie und die Ideologie der Rationalität', in Schelsky, ed., *Soziologie*, p. 160.
40. On the rise of consumer society, see Jakob Tanner, 'Industrialisierung, Rationalisierung und Wandel des Konsums- und Geschmacksverhaltens im europäisch-amerikanischen Vergleich', in Siegrist, Kaelble and Kocka, eds., *Europäische Konsumgeschichte*, pp. 583–614; Andersen, *Der Traum vom guten*

*Leben*; Michael Prinz, 'Konsum und Konsumgesellschaft', in Prinz, ed., *Der lange Weg in den Überfluss*, pp. 11–34; König, *Geschichte der Konsumgesellschaft*; Schildt, *Sozialgeschichte*, pp. 30–53; Schildt, 'Materieller Wohlstand', in Schildt, Siegfried and Lammers, eds., *Dynamische Zeiten*, pp. 21–53; and Schildt and Siegfried, *Deutsche Kulturgeschichte*, pp. 249–77.

41. Hartmut Kaelble, 'Europäische Besonderheiten des Massenkonsums 1950–1990', in Siegrist, Kaelble and Kocka, eds., *Europäische Konsumgeschichte*, pp. 169–204, here p. 197.
42. Klenke, *Freier Stau*, pp. 52–9; Südbeck, *Motorisierung, Verkehrentwicklung und Verkehrspolitik*.
43. Schröter, 'Amerikanisierung'.
44. Schildt and Siegfried, *Deutsche Kulturgeschichte*, pp. 197–203 and 254–5; Hickethier, *Geschichte des deutschen Fernsehens*; Knut Dussel, 'Vom Radio- zum Fernsehzeitalter. Medienumbrüche in sozialgeschichtlicher Perspektive', in Schildt, Siegfried and Lammers, eds., *Dynamische Zeiten*, pp. 673–92.
45. *Der Spiegel*, 20 (1966), 'Geschichte ohne h', 9.5.1966; Schildt and Siegfried, *Deutsche Kulturgeschichte*, p. 246; König, *Kleine Geschichte der Konsumgesellschaft*, pp. 270ff.; Victoria de Grazia, 'Amerikanisierung und wechselnde Leitbilder der Konsum-Moderne (*consumer-modernity*) in Europa', in Siegrist, Kaelble and Kocka, eds., *Europäische Konsumgeschichte*, pp. 109–39.
46. Ulrich Herbert, 'Liberalisierung als Lernprozeß. Die Bundesrepublik in der deutschen Geschichte—eine Skizze', in Herbert, ed., *Wandlungsprozesse*, pp. 7–52; Conze, *Die Suche nach Sicherheit*, pp. 259–89; Wolfrum, *Die geglückte Demokratie*, pp. 241–82.
47. Torsten Gass-Bolm, 'Das Ende der Schulzucht', in Herbert, ed., *Wandlungsprozesse*, pp. 436–66. The same author treats this subject in more detail in *Das Gymnasium*.
48. Silies, *Liebe, Lust und Last*, p. 431; Eser, 'Sexualität', p. 218; Michael Kandora, 'Homosexualität und Sittengesetz', in Herbert, ed., *Wandlungsprozesse*, pp. 379–401.
49. Steinbacher, *Wie der Sex nach Deutschland kam*, pp. 318 and 329; Heineman, *Before Porn was Legal*.
50. Schildt and Siegfried, *Deutsche Kulturgeschichte*, pp. 264ff.
51. Baacke, *Beat—Die sprachlose Opposition*, pp. 11–30. On the next section, see in particular Siegfried, *Time is on my Side*, pp. 209–79 and Poiger, *Jazz, Rock and Rebels*, pp. 31–70.
52. Freddy Quinn, 'Wir', issued by Polydor in 1966.
53. Siegfried, *Time is on my Side*, pp. 388–95 and 411–13.
54. Koenen, *Jahrzehnt*, p. 80.
55. Elon, *Journey*, pp. 93, 95, 100 and 161.
56. Steiner, *Plans*, p. 130; for later developments see Klessmann, 'Politische Rahmenbedingungen', in GSD, vol. 9, pp. 3–76 and Klessmann, *Arbeiter im 'Arbeiterstaat' DDR*, pp. 647–766.
57. André Steiner, 'Die siebziger Jahre als Kristallationspunkt des wirtschaftlichen Strukturwandels in West und Ost?', in Jarausch, ed., *Ende der Zuversicht*, pp. 29–49; Bundesministerium für Arbeit und Soziales and André Steiner, *Statistische*

*Übersichten zur Sozialpolitik in Deutschland seit 1945 (Band SBZ/DDR),* table 9.4.4, p. 258.

58. Theo Sommer, 'Die Welt der Funktionäre', in Dönhoff, Leonhardt and Sommer, *Reise in ein fremdes Land,* pp. 109–20, here pp. 110–11.
59. Quoted in Fulbrook, *The People's State,* pp. 239–40.
60. Alena Köhler-Wagnerova, 'Die Frau im Sozialismus (1974)', quoted in Gisela Helwig and Barbara Hille, 'Familien-, Jugend- und Altenpolitik', in GSD, vol. 9, pp. 496–558, here p. 513.
61. Helwig and Hille, 'Familien-, Jugend- und Altenpolitik', in GSD, vol. 9, pp. 496–558; Karl Spiegelberg, 'Der Einfluss von materiellen und ideell-moralischen Motiven für die Berufstätigkeit auf das Verhältnis der Frauen zur Berufstätigkeit', in *Wirtschaftswissenschaft* 14 (1966), p. 1,144, quoted in Helwig and Hille, 'Familien-, Jugend- und Altenpolitik', p. 512.
62. Quoted in Theo Sommer, 'Die Welt der Funktionäre', in Dönhoff, Leonhardt and Sommer, *Reise in ein fremdes Land,* p. 116.
63. Jay Rowell, 'Wohnungspolitik', in GSD, vol. 9, pp. 699–719; Frank Betker, 'Die "sozialistische" Stadt in der DDR: zentral geplant, lokal entworfen, plattengerecht gebaut', in Timmermann, ed., *Das war die DDR,* pp. 97–115; Jenkins, *Wohnungswirtschaft;* Hannemann, *Die Platte.*
64. Annette Kaminsky, 'Konsumpolitik in der Mangelwirtschaft', in Vollnhals and Weber, eds., *Schein der Normalität,* pp. 81–112; Merkel, *Utopie und Bedürfnis,* pp. 38–88, 320–2.
65. Marion Gräfin Dönhoff, 'Die Entdeckung der Rentabilität', in Dönhoff, Leonhardt and Sommer, *Reise in ein fremdes Land,* pp. 19–31, here p. 23.
66. Merkel, *Utopie und Bedürfnis,* p. 321.
67. Quoted in Kaminsky, 'Konsumpolitik', p. 104.
68. Elon, *Journey,* pp. 105–6.
69. Elon, *Journey,* p. 108, with unmarked omissions.
70. Wehler, *Gesellschaftsgeschichte,* vol. 5, pp. 232–4; Staritz, *Geschichte,* pp. 230–9.
71. Mitter and Wolle, *Untergang,* p. 378.
72. Zentralinstitut für Jugendforschung, ed., *Jugend und Freizeit,* 1968, p. 25, quoted in Fulbrook, *The People's State,* p. 70.
73. Honecker's speech to the CC of the SED, 15.12.1965, in Weber, *DDR,* doc. no. 160, pp. 282–4.
74. Günter Agde, 'Zur Anatomie eines Tests. Das Gespräch Walter Ulbrichts mit Schriftstellern und Künstlern am 25. November 1965 im Staatsrat der DDR', in Agde, ed., *Kahlschlag,* pp. 128–47, here p. 140.
75. Horst Schumann, 'Für parteilichen Standpunkt der Jugend. Aus der Diskussion auf dem 11. Plenum des Zentralkomitees der SED', in *Junge Welt,* 21.12.1965, p. 4. See also Ohse, *Jugend nach dem Mauerbau,* pp. 83–96.
76. Noll, *Abschied,* pp. 234–5.
77. SED-District Leipzig, 1.11.1965, in Wierling, *Geboren im Jahr Eins,* p. 217; Poiger, *Jazz, Rock and Rebels,* pp. 168–205; Liebing, *'All you need is beat'.*
78. Central Committee Proposal for the Development of Dance Music, 18.10.1965, in Wierling, *Geboren im Jahr Eins,* p. 218.

79. *Leipziger Volkszeitung*, 20.10.1965, quoted in Wierling, *Geboren im Jahr Eins* p. 219.
80. Weirling, *Geboren im Jahr Eins*, pp. 221–2.

## Chapter 16

1. Kiesinger's government declaration, in *Deutscher Bundestag, 5.WP. Plenarprotokoll*, 13.12.1966, pp. 3,656–65; on subsequent developments, see in particular Hans Günter Hockerts, 'Rahmenbedingungen. Das Profil der Reformära', in GSD, vol. 5, pp. 3–155; Conze, *Die Suche nach Sicherheit*, pp. 331–462; Görtermaker, *Geschichte*, pp. 437–74; Winkler, *Germany: the Long Road West*, vol. 2, pp. 234–51; Schönhoven, *Wendejahre*; Schmoeckel and Kaiser, *Die vergessene Regierung*; and Schneider, *Die Kunst des Kompromisses.*
2. Häuser, *Volkswirtschaftslehre*, p. 128, quoted in Hockerts, 'Rahmenbedingungen', in GSD, vol. 5, p. 32; Schanetzky, *Die große Ernüchterung*, p. 269.
3. Karl Schiller, 'Wirtschafts- und Agrarpolitik', in Ehmke, ed., *Perspektiven*, pp. 92–8, here p. 93.
4. Johannes Gross, 'Dem Kanzler ins Stammbuch. Wer werden mit mittelalterlichen Methoden regiert', *Die Zeit*, 2.12.1966, quoted in Metzler, *Konzeptionen*, pp. 288–9.
5. Metzler, *Konzeptionen*, p. 346.
6. Federal Constitutional Court decision of 29 January 1969, BVerfGE 25.167.
7. *Der Spiegel*, 39/1966, p. 82. The expression 'modern law' comes from the FDP politician Wolfgang Mischnick, according to Sibylle Buske, 'Die Debatte über die "Unehelichkeit"', in Herbert, ed., *Wandlungsprozesse*, pp. 315–47, here p. 341. See also Buske, *Fräulein Mutter*, pp. 234–69, and Busch, *Strafrechtsreform*, pp. 40–131.
8. Glaab, *Deutschlandpolitik in der öffentlichen Meinung*, pp. 247ff.
9. On the next section, see Frei, *1968*; Koenen, *Das rote Jahrzehnt*; Gilcher–Holtey, *Die 68er Bewegung in Deutschland*; Gilcher-Holtey, ed., *1968*; Kraushaar, *1968, Das Jahr, das alles verändert hat*; Kraushaar, *1968 als Mythos, Chiffre und Zäsur*; and Schildt and Siegfried, eds., *Between Marx and Coca Cola.*
10. Elias, *The Germans*, p. 413.
11. For international comparisons, see François et al., eds., *1968—ein europäisches Jahr?*; Marwick, *The Sixties*; DeGroot, ed., *Student Protest*; Fink, Gassert and Junker, eds., *1968: The World Transformed.*
12. Anthony, *Summer of Love*; Farber, *Age of Great Dreams*, pp. 167–89.
13. Cf. Farber, *Age of Great Dreams*, pp. 90–116.
14. Gilcher-Holtey, *'Die Phantasie an die Macht'*; Nooteboom, *Paris, Mai 1968*; Rauch and Schirmbeck, *Die Barrikaden von Paris.*
15. Kurz, *Die Universität auf der Piazza*; Lumley, *States of Emergency.*
16. See summaries in Doering-Manteuffel, *Wie westlich sind die Deutschen?* and Hodenberg, *Konsens und Krise*, especially pp. 245ff.
17. On the emergency laws, see Schneider, *Demokratie in Gefahr?*, pp. 39–188; Schönhoven, *Wendejahre*, pp. 267–89; and Nevermann, ed., *Der 2.Juni 1967*. Cf. Foschepoth, *Postzensur*, and the same author, *Überwachtes Deutschland.*
18. Schmitt, *Political Theology*, p. 5.

19. Hockerts, 'Rahmenbedingungen', in GSD, vol. 5, p. 54.
20. Statement by the Federal Committee of the DGB, 25.7.1962, quoted in Schneider, *Demokratie in Gefahr?*, p. 94.
21. Cf. Wolfgang Kraushaar, 'Unsere unterwanderten Jahre. Die barbarische und gar nicht schöne Infiltration der Studentenbewegung durch die Organe der Staatssicherheit', in *FAZ*, 7.4.1998, p. 45.
22. Lönnendonker et al., *Die antiautoritäre Revolte*; Fichter and Lönnendonker, *Kleine Geschichte des SDS.*
23. Kraushaar, ed., *Frankfurter Schule und Studentenbewegung*; Wiggershaus, *The Frankfurt School*; Albrecht, Behrmann and Bock, eds., *Gründung.*
24. Bruckner, *Le sanglot de l'homme blanc*, p. 7.
25. Rudi Dutschke, 'Vom Antisemitismus zum Antikommunismus', in Dutschke et al. *Rebellion der Studenten*, p. 63; Balsen and Rössell, eds., *Hoch die internationale Solidarität.*
26. See Koenen, *Das rote Jahrzehnt*, pp. 95–122. The quotation is from p. 96, with unindicated omissions.
27. Frei, *1968*, pp. 79–88; Thamer, 'NS-Vergangenheit'; Gassert and Steinweis, eds., *Coping with the Nazi Past.*
28. Hans-Joachim Lieber, rector of the Free University of Berlin, speech at the opening of the 1966 university open days, on 'National Socialism and the German university', p. 5, quoted in Frei, *1968*, p. 82.
29. The Appeal of April 1965, in Otto, ed., *APO*, p. 299.
30. 1967 poster, printed in Kielmannsegg, *Nach der Katastrophe*, p. 325. See Wolfgang Kraushaar, 'Die Furcht vor einem "neuen 33." Protest gegen die Notstandsgesetzgebung', in Geppert and Hacke, eds., *Streit um den Staat*, pp. 135–50.
31. Niethammer, *Angepaßter Faschismus*; Staud, *Moderne Nazis.*
32. Cf. Riccardo Bavaj, 'Verunsicherte Demokratisierer. "Liberal-kritische" Hochschullehrer und die Studentenrevolte von 1967/68', in Geppert and Hacke, eds., *Streit um den Staat*, pp. 151–68.
33. Cf. Lönnendonker et al., *Die antiautoritäre Revolte*, pp. 333ff.; 'Der nicht erklärte Notstand. Dokumentation und Analyse eines Berliner Sommers', *Kursbuch* 12 (1968); Nevermann, ed., *Der 2.Juni.* When it was later revealed that the policeman responsible for Ohnesorg's death, Karl-Heinz Kurras, was an informal Stasi collaborator, the shooting of 2 June acquired an even more contradictory aspect. Cf. Fuhrer, *Benno Ohnesorg.*
34. Dutschke, *Wir hatten ein barbarisches, schönes Leben*, p. 55.
35. *Bild-Zeitung*, 7.2.1968.
36. Dutschke, replying to Marcuse, 19.7.1967, quoted in Marcuse, *Das Ende der Utopie*, p. 151.
37. Koenen, *Das rote Jahrzehnt*, pp. 359–414; Koenen, *Vesper, Ensslin, Baader*; Aust, *Der Baader-Meinhof-Komplex*, pp. 58–62; Baumann, *Wie alles anfing.*
38. Koenen, *Das rote Jahrzehnt*, pp. 257–316.
39. As stated by Anselm Doering-Manteuffel in the chapter entitled 'Die Planung des Fortschritts und das Paradigma der Modernisierung', in Doering-Manteuffel and Raphael, *Nach dem Boom*, p. 26.

40. Reichardt and Siegfried, eds., *Das alternative Milieu*; Reichardt, *Authentizität*; Koenen, *Das rote Jahrzehnt*, pp. 317–58.
41. On this subject, see Braunthal and Gerard, *Politische Loyalität*.
42. Schildt, 'Vor der Revolte', p. 13; on this, Frei, *1968*, pp. 137–8, and Conze, *Die Suche nach Sicherheit*, p. 359.
43. Brandt's government declaration, in *Deutscher Bundestag, 6.WP, Plenarprotokoll*, 28.10.1969, pp. 20–34.
44. Hans Magnus Enzensberger, 'The Writer and Politics', in *The Times Literary Supplement*, 28.9.1967. Cf. Hockerts, 'Rahmenbedingungen', in GSD, vol. 5, p. 72.
45. On the new *Ostpolitik*, see Bender, *Neue Ostpolitik*; Niedhart and Bange, '"Relikte der Nachkriegszeit"'; Sarotte, *Dealing with the Devil*; Bierling, *Außenpolitik*, pp. 171–200; Hacke, *Außenpolitik*, pp. 159–68; Haftendorn, *Coming of Age*, pp. 163–70; Dülffer, *Europa im Ost-West-Konflikt*, pp. 82–4; Kielmannsegg, *Nach der Katastrophe*, pp. 205–12; Loth, *Helsinki*, pp. 133–42.
46. Brandt's government declaration, in *Deutscher Bundestag, 6.WP, Plenarprotokoll*, 28.10.1969, pp. 20–34.
47. Letter on German Unity, 12.8.1970, printed in *Texte zur Deutschlandpolitik*, vol. 10, pp. 96–7.
48. Kielmannsegg, *Nach der Katastrophe*, pp. 191–212.
49. Borodziej, *Geschichte Polens*, pp. 316–7; Bierling, *Außenpolitik*, pp. 183–4.
50. On the Munich Agreement of 1938 and the Prague Treaty of 1973, see Bender, *Neue Ostpolitik*, pp. 196–202.
51. Bender, *Episode oder Epoche?*, pp. 179–84.
52. The quotation is from Garton Ash, *In Europe's Name*, p. 189.
53. Niclauß, *Kontroverse Deutschlandpolitik*, pp. 57–70; Grau, *Gegen den Strom*, pp. 248–403; Glaab, *Deutschlandpolitik in der öffentlichen Meinung*, pp. 384ff.
54. Korte, *Der Standort der Deutschen*; Herdegen, *Perspektiven*.
55. The closing words of Brandt's declaration, quoted in Ehmke, ed., *Perspektiven*, p. 166.
56. Karl Schiller, 'Wirtschafts- und Agrarpolitik', in Ehmke, ed., *Perspektiven* , p. 95.
57. The reforms are outlined in Hockerts, 'Rahmenbedingungen', in GSD, vol. 5, pp. 90–107, Hockerts, 'Metamorphosen des Wohlfahrtsstaates', in Broszat, ed., *Zäsuren nach 1945*, pp. 35–45, and Winfried Süß, 'Sozialpolitische Denk- und Handlungsfelder in der Reformära', in GSD, vol. 5, pp. 157–222.
58. Doering-Manteuffel and Raphael, *Nach dem Boom*, p. 47.
59. *Außerordentlicher Parteitag der Sozialdemokratischen Partei Deutschlands in Dortmund, 12.-13.10.1972, Protokoll*, p. 38, quoted in Süß, 'Sozialpolitische Denk- und Handlungsfelder', in GSD, vol. 5, p. 221; Hockerts, 'Rahmenbedingungen', in GSD, vol. 5, p. 101; Winfried Schmähl, 'Sicherung bei Alter, Invalidität und für Hinterbliebene', in GSD, vol. 5, pp. 407–82.
60. Brüggemeier, *Tschernobyl*, pp. 216–19.
61. Oskar Anweiler, 'Bildungspolitik', in GSD, vol. 5, pp. 709–54; Carl-Ludwig Furck, 'Das Schulsystem: Primarbereich—Hauptschule—Realschule—Gymnasium—Gesamtschule', in Führ and Furck, eds., *Handbuch der deutschen Bildungsgeschichte*, vol. 6.1, pp. 282–356, here pp. 328–43.

62. Pastoral Letter issued by the Conference of German Bishops, 6.5.1973, quoted in Ursula Münch, 'Familien, Jugend- und Altenpolitik', in GSD, vol. 5, pp. 633–707, here p. 652; Gante, *§218 in der Diskussion*; Schulz, *Der lange Atem der Provokation*, pp. 143–7; Frevert, *Women in German History*, pp. 294–5.
63. Reinhard Richardi, 'Arbeitsverfassung und Arbeitsrecht', in GSD, vol. 5, pp. 225–76, particularly pp. 229–40.
64. Abelshauser, *Deutsche Wirtschaftsgeschichte*, p. 431.
65. Lepsius, *Demokratie in Deutschland*, p. 179.
66. Schiller and Young, *The 1972 Munich Olympics*, pp. 87–156; Large, *Munich 1972*.
67. Hertfelder and Rödder, eds., *Modell Deutschland*, p. 13. The outside world took a more cautious view. 'West Germany', wrote a British observer on the subject, 'is better seen neither as a special problem nor as a recommended example for others to follow'. (Gordon Smith, 'Does West German democracy have an "Efficient Secret"?', in Paterson and Smith, eds., *The West German Model*, pp. 166–76, here p. 175.)

## Chapter 17

1. Doering-Manteuffel and Raphael, *Nach dem Boom*, p. 13.
2. On this section, see Hockerts, 'Rahmenbedingungen', in GSD, vol. 5, pp. 121–38; Geyer, 'Rahmenbedingungen', in GSD, vol. 6, pp. 47–63; Hohensee, *Ölpreisschock*, pp. 109–228; Abelshauser, *Deutsche Wirtschaftsgeschichte*, pp. 416–35; Schanetzky, *Ernüchterung*, pp. 37–45; Lindlar, *Wirtschaftswunder*, pp. 248–84 and 334–44; James, *Rambouillet*, pp. 131–4; Giersch, Paqué and Schmieding, *Fading Miracle*, pp. 176–84; Doering-Manteuffel and Raphael, *Nach dem Boom*; von Karczewski, *Weltwirtschaft*, pp. 31–70; Mazower, *Dark Continent*, pp. 332–9.
3. Scherf, *Enttäuschte Hoffnungen*, pp. 82–8.
4. 'Aufstocken statt aufwerten', *Die Zeit*, 29.11.1968.
5. Herbert, *Ausländerpolitik*, pp. 223–9; Herbert and Hunn, 'Beschäftigung, soziale Sicherung und soziale Integration von Ausländern', in GSD, vol. 6, pp. 751–77.
6. Schanetzky, *Ernüchterung*, p. 43; Hockerts, 'Rahmenbedingungen', in GSD, vol. 5, p. 136.
7. For the impact of the crisis on the international monetary system, see also James, *Rambouillet*, pp. 131–60; Geirsch, Paqué and Schmieding, *Fading Miracle*, pp. 176–84; Hockerts, 'Rahmenbedingungen', in GSD, vol. 5, pp. 12–127; Schanetzky, *Ernüchterung*, pp. 40ff.; and Nützenadel, *Stunde der Ökonomen*, pp. 344–52.
8. Pies and Leschke, eds., *Milton Friedmanns ökonomischer Liberalismus*; Doering-Manteuffel and Raphael, *Nach dem Boom*, pp. 51–2.
9. Hohensee, *Ölpreisschock*, pp. 59 and 221.
10. Geyer, 'Rahmenbedingungen', in GSD, vol. 6, pp. 47–59; Hohensee, *Ölpreisschock*, pp. 218–28; Gerstenberger, *Strukturwandel*; Yergin, *The Prize*.
11. Brüggemeier, *Geschichte Großbritanniens*, pp. 274–9; Mergel, *Großbritannien*, pp. 60–3 and 179–88; Pollard, *The Development of the British Economy*, pp. 229–300; Hudson, *Wrecking a Region*.

12. Berstein and Sirinelli, eds., *Les années Giscard*; Becker, *Histoire politique de la France*, pp. 145–63.
13. *Statistisches Bundesamt, Fachserie 18, Reihe S 29, 1970–1991*, pp. 17–19. Slightly different figures are given in https://www.destatis.de/DE/Publikationen/Thematisch/VolkswirtschaflicheGesamtrechnungen/Inlandsprodukt/InlandsproduktsberechnungRevidiertJ2189029919004.pdf?_blob=publicationFile [9 12.2013].
14. Giersch, Paqué and Schmieding, *Fading Miracle*, p. 199.
15. Gerstenberger, *Strukturwandel*, pp. 83–9; Donges et al., *Mehr Strukturwandel*; Piore and Sabel, *The Second Industrial Divide*; Abelshauser, *Deutsche Wirtschaftsgeschichte*, pp. 302–14; Geyer, 'Rahmenbedingungen', in GSD, vol. 6, pp. 58–68.
16. Hindrichs et al., *Der lange Abschied vom Malocher*, pp. 13–20; Wirsching, *Preis der Freiheit*, pp. 223–42; Franz and Steiner, eds., *Der westdeutsche Arbeitsmarkt*; Gerstenberger, *Strukturwandel*, p. 214.
17. Abelshauser, *Deutsche Wirtschaftsgeschichte*, pp. 426–35; Schroeder, ed., *Gewerkschaften*.
18. Bömer, ed., *Stadtentwicklung in Dortmund seit 1945*; Goch, ed., *Strukturwandel und Strukturpolitik*.
19. Geyer, 'Rahmenbedingungen', in GSD, vol. 6, p. 62.
20. *Statistisches Jahrbuch* 1992, pp. 45–8; Schildt, *Sozialgeschichte*, pp. 54–5.
21. Kaelble, *Kalter Krieg und Wohlfahrtsstaat*, p. 185. These figures exclude Russia and Turkey.
22. Schildt, *Sozialgeschichte*, p. 59. These are figures for real disposable income in West Germany at 1991 prices. On the next section, see Schildt, *Sozialgeschichte*, pp. 54–62; Geißler, *Sozialstruktur*, pp. 81ff.; and Wehler, *Gesellschaftsgeschichte*, vol. 5, pp. 119–24.
23. *Datenreport* 1992, pp. 102 and 233.
24. Herbert, *Ausländerpolitik*, table 23, p. 238.
25. Winfried Schmähl, 'Sicherung bei Alter', in GSD, vol. 6, pp. 393–514; Aurelio Vincenti and Gerhard Igl, 'Gesundheitswesen und Sicherung bei Krankheit und im Pflegefall', in GSD, vol. 6, pp. 525–65; Martin H. Geyer, 'Sozialpolitische Denk- und Handlungsfelder: Der Umgang mit Sicherheit und Unsicherheit', in GSD, vol. 6, pp. 111–232.
26. Bertram, ed., *Die Familie in Westdeutschland*; Nave–Herz, ed., *Wandel und Kontinuität der Familie*.
27. Frevert, *Women in German History*, pp. 265–86; *Datenreport 1997*, p. 80; Wehler, *Gesellschaftsgeschichte*, vol. 5, pp. 171ff. Aulenbacher and Goldmann, eds., *Transformationen im Geschlechterverhältnis*.
28. See Rostow, *Stages of Economic Growth*.
29. Bell, *The End of Ideology*, pp. 402–3.
30. Bell, *The Coming of Post-Industrial Society*, pp. 33–45. My remarks here are based on Wagner, *Sociology of Modernity;* and Knöbl, *Die Kontingenz der Moderne*. Cf. also Doering-Manteuffel and Raphael, *Nach dem Boom*, pp. 57–90, and Wolfgang Welsch, 'Postmoderne. Genealogie und Bedeutung eines umstrittenen Begriffs', in Kemper, ed., *'Postmoderne'*, pp. 9–36.

31. Inglehart, *The Silent Revolution*, particularly pp. 96ff. For international comparisons see *Culture Shift*, by the same author.
32. These developments are summarised in Klages, *Wertorientierungen im Wandel.*
33. Lyotard, *The Postmodern Condition*, pp. 38 and 60.
34. Brüggemeier, *Tschernobyl*, pp. 202–22; Radkau, *Age of Ecology*, pp. 79–113, 137–61 and 259–338; Radkau, *Aufstieg und Krise*, pp. 434–61; Engels, *Naturpolitik in der Bundesrepublik.*
35. *Der Spiegel*, 5.10.1970, p. 74; *Süddeutsche Zeitung*, quoted in Brüggemeier, *Tschernobyl*, p. 215.
36. Meadows et al., *The Limits to Growth*, p. 23.
37. Eppler, *Ende oder Wende*, p. 11 and throughout; Zapf, *Individualisierung.*
38. Gruhl, *Ein Planet wird geplündert.* Gruhl left the CDU in 1978, joined the Green Party for a short time, and finally became a founder-member of the ÖDP.
39. Cf. Kielmannsegg, *Nach der Katastrophe*, p. 345; Karl-Werner Brand, 'Umweltbewegung', in Roth and Rucht, eds., *Die sozialen Bewegungen*, pp. 219–44; Linse, *Ökopax und Anarchie.*
40. Radkau, *Aufstieg und Krise*, pp. 112–32.
41. Dieter Rucht, 'Anti-Atomkraft-Bewegung', in Roth and Rucht, eds., *Die sozialen Bewegungen*, pp. 245–66; Jens Ivo Engels, 'Umweltschutz in der Bundesrepublik—von der Unwahrscheinlichkeit einer Alternativbewegung', in Reichardt and Siegfried, eds., *Das alternative Milieu*, pp. 405–22; Bernd A.Rusinek, 'Wyhl', in François and Schulze, eds., *Deutsche Erinnerungsorte*, vol. 2, pp. 652–66.
42. As quoted in Radkau, *Age of Ecology*, p. 262.
43. As quoted in Mohr, *Die Gewerkschaften im Atomkonflikt*, pp. 80–1.
44. Jungk, *The Nuclear State*; Klaus Traube 'Lehrstück Abhöraffäre', in Narr, ed., *Bürger*, pp. 61–78.
45. Schulman, *The Seventies*; Farber, *The Age*, pp. 190–262. On the development of these movements in the Federal Republic, see in detail Reichardt and Siegfried, eds., *Das alternative Milieu.*
46. 'Alternative Fair: live differently and survive' (1978), quoted in Dieter Rucht, 'Das alternative Milieu in der Bundesrepublik. Ursprünge, Infrastruktur und Nachwirkungen', in Reichardt and Siegfried, eds., *Das alternative Milieu*, pp. 61–88, here p. 75. The first quotation ('aspiration towards self-realisation') is from Schildt and Siegfried, *Deutsche Kulturgeschichte*, p. 373.
47. Hockerts, 'Rahmenbedingungen', in GSD, vol. 5, quotation on p. 155. See also Nave-Herz, *Die Geschichte der Frauenbewegung*; and Birgit Meyer, 'Frauenbewegung und politische Kultur in den 80er Jahren', in Süß, ed., *Die Bundesrepublik in den 80er Jahren*, pp. 219–34.
48. On the next section, see Aust, *Baader-Meinhof Complex*; Koenen, *Das rote Jahrzehnt*, pp. 359–414; Peters, *Tödlicher Irrtum. Die Geschichte der RAF*; Pflieger, *Rote Armee Fraktion*; and Bundesministerium des Innern, ed., *Analysen zum Terrorismus*, 4 vols.
49. Quoted in Aust, *Baader-Meinhof Complex*, p. 41.
50. Quoted in Koenen, *Das rote Jahrzehnt*, p. 369. Present author's emphasis.
51. Quoted in Koenen, *Das rote Jahrzehnt*, p. 397.

52. 'A Göttingen Apache's obituary for Buback' quoted in Atzert, ed., *Küss den Boden*, pp. 363ff.
53. Scheiper, *Innere Sicherheit*; Weinhauer, ed., *Terrorismus in der Bundesrepublik.*
54. Conze, *Suche nach Sicherheit*, p. 485.
55. Helmut Schmidt's government declaration, in *Deutscher Bundestag, 7.WP, Plenarprotokoll*, 17.5.1974, pp. 6,593–605.
56. Merseburger, *Willy Brandt*; Soell, *Helmut Schmidt*, 2 vols. On subsequent developments, see Wolfgang Jäger, 'Die Innenpolitik der sozial-liberalen Koalition 1974–1982', in Bracher, Jäger and Link, eds., *Republik im Wandel 1974–1982*, pp. 9–272; Werner Link, 'Außen- und Deutschlandpolitik in der Ära Schmidt, 1974–1982', in Bracher, Jäger and Link, eds., *Republik im Wandel 1974–1982*, pp. 273–446; Conze, *Sicherheit*, pp. 473–578; and Görtemaker, *Geschichte*, pp. 578–96.
57. Bösch, *Macht und Machtverlust*, pp. 29–53; Dreher, *Helmut Kohl.*
58. *Der Spiegel*, 10.3.1975, pp. 34–41.
59. Kielmannsegg, *Nach der Katastrophe*, pp. 220–4.
60. Loth, *Helsinki*, pp. 9–19 and 164–170; Schlotter, *Die KSZE im Ost-West-Konflikt.*
61. Eckel, 'Utopie der Moral'; Hoffmann, ed., *Moralpolitik.*
62. Loth, *Helsinki*, pp. 191–9; Werner Link, 'Außen- und Deutschlandpolitik in der Ära Schmidt, 1974–1982', in Bracher, Jäger and Link, eds., *Republik im Wandel*, pp. 275–432, here pp. 310–41.
63. Schmidt on 28.10.1977, speaking in London, quoted in Haftendorn, *Sicherheit und Stabilität*, pp. 196–7.
64. Loth, *Helsinki*, pp. 199–216; Stöver, *Der Kalte Krieg*, pp. 410–36; Layritz, *Der NATO-Doppelbeschluß.*
65. Kurzman, *The Unthinkable Revolution in Iran*; Amirpur and Witzke, *Schauplatz Iran.*
66. Gerald Ford, speaking at the G7 summit at Rambouillet, 15–17.11.1975, quoted in James, *Rambouillet*, p.10. Cf. Charles S. Maier, '"Malaise." The Crisis of Capitalism in the 1970s', in Ferguson et al., eds., *The Shock of the Global*, pp. 25–48.
67. On the next section, see James, *Rambouillet*, pp. 131–207; von Karczewski, *Weltwirtschaft*, pp. 111–210; Abelshauser, *Deutsche Wirtschaftsgeschichte*, pp. 432–46; Geyer, 'Rahmenbedingungen', in GSD, vol. 6, pp. 88–101; Schmidt, *Men and Powers*, pp. 266–79; and Emminger, *D-Mark.*
68. Knipping, *Rom*, pp. 156–217; van der Wee, *Prosperity and Upheaval*, pp. 48–65; Brunn, *Die europäische Einigung*, pp. 179–227.
69. Patel, *Europäisierung wider Willen.*
70. Garrissen de Vries, *The International Monetary Fund*, vol. 2, p. 761, quoted in James, *Rambouillet*, p. 11; Abelshauser, *Nach dem Wirtschaftswunder*, pp. 378–434.
71. Pöhl, quoted in James, *Rambouillet*, p. 169; 'Inflation—kein Welthandelsrezept', in *Süddeutsche Zeitung*, 26.1.1977, quoted in von Karczewski, *Weltwirtschaft*, p. 299.
72. Wolfgang Jäger, 'Die Innenpolitik der sozial-liberalen Koalition 1974–1982', in Bracher, Jäger and Link, eds., *Republik im Wandel 1974–1982*, pp. 166–72.
73. Gassert, ed., *Zweiter Kalter Krieg und Friedensbewegung*; Schregel, *Der Atomkrieg vor der Wohnungstür*; Ziemann, ed., *Peace Movements.*
74. Reagan, speaking on 8 March 1983 to the National Association of Evangelicals. See Dülffer, *Europa im Ost-West-Konflikt*, p. 94.

75. As quoted in Bölling, *Nachbarn*, p. 140.
76. Werner Link, 'Außen- und Deutschlandpolitik in der Ära Schmidt, 1974–1982', in Bracher, Jäger and Link, eds., *Republik im Wandel 1974–1982*, pp. 353–82.
77. On developments in Poland, see Borodziej, *Geschichte*, pp. 340–82, Kühn, *Das Jahrzehnt der Solidarność*, and Holzer, *Solidarität*.
78. Bahr, *Was wird aus den Deutschen?*, p. 23; Günter Gaus, 'Polen und die westliche Allianz oder Ein Plädoyer für die Entspannungspolitik', in Böll et al., eds., *Verantwortlich für Polen?*, pp. 109–18, quotation on p. 116. Cf. Garton Ash, *In Europe's Name*, pp. 250–301; Winkler, *Germany: the Long Road West*, vol. 2, pp. 346–54.
79. Link, 'Außen- und Deutschlandpolitik', pp. 304–9 and 374ff.
80. Wirsching, *Abschied*, pp. 246–50.
81. *Datenreport 1985*, p. 216; *Datenreport 1992*, pp. 221–2; Rödder, *Bundesrepublik*, p. 301.
82. Geyer, 'Sozialpolitische Denk- und Handlungsfelder', in GSD, vol. 6, pp. 121–5; Scherf, *Enttäuschte Hoffnungen*; Giersch, Paqué and Schmieding, *Fading Miracle*; Notermans, *Money, Markets and the State*, pp. 160–221.
83. Circular from Genscher to members of the FDP, August 1981, quoted in Geyer, 'Rahmenbedingungen', in GSD, vol. 6, pp. 97–8.
84. Apel, *Abstieg*, pp. 208–9.
85. Otto Graf Lambsdorff, 'Konzept für eine Politik zur Überwindung der Wachstumsschwäche und zur Bekämpfung der Arbeitslosigkeit, 9.9.1982', *Neue Bonner Depesche*, 9/82: Dokumentation. Online: https://www.freiheit.org/sites/default/files/uploads/2017/09/05/lambsdorff-papier.pdf
86. Undated memorandum by Lahnstein (sent between 1 and 9 September 1982), quoted in Abelshauser, *Deutsche Wirtschaftsgeschichte*, pp. 441ff.; also Abelshauser, *Nach dem Wirtschaftswunder*, pp. 538–44. The subject is covered in detail in Geyer, 'Sozialpolitische Denk- und Handlungsfelder', in GSD, vol. 6, pp. 168–82.

## Chapter 18

1. For the next section, see Fäßler, *Globalisierung*; Osterhammel and Petersson, *Globalization*, pp. 113–52; Ferguson et al., eds., *The Shock of the Global*, pp. 128–58; Wirsching, *Preis der Freiheit*, pp. 226–307; and Zohlnhöfer, *Globalisierung der Wirtschaft*. The figures are from WTO, *International Trade Statistics 2005, 2008, 2010–11*; United Nations Conference on Trade and Development (UNCTAD), *Handbook of Statistics 2008*; 'Zahlen und Fakten Globalisierung' online at http://www.bpb.de/nachschlagen/zahlen-und-fakten/globalisierung [3.4.2012]; World Federation of Exchanges (WFE), *Annual Report*, various years, online at http://www.world-exchanges.org [3.4.2012]; Department for Business, Innovation & Skills (BIS), *The 2009 R & D Scoreboard*; and my own calculations.
2. Cf. Butterwegge, ed., *Neoliberalismus*. The trend of economic thinking at this time is examined in Manfred G. Schmidt, 'Rahmenbedingungen', in GSD, vol. 7, pp. 1–60, here pp. 58–60.

3. Greenspan, *The Age of Turbulence*, p. 82; Schmidt, *Men and Powers*, p. 266; Wilentz, *The Age of Reagan*, pp. 285–322. In the USA 35.3 million people, or 15.2 per cent of the population, lived in poverty in 1983. See the poverty statistics of the USA in http://www.npc.umich.edu/poverty/ [12.5.2012].
4. James, *Europe Reborn*, p. 353.
5. Brüggemeier, *Geschichte Großbritanniens*, pp. 309–33; Mergel, *Großbritannien*, pp. 179–201; Hutchinson, *Reaganism*, pp. 15–37.
6. Helmut Kohl's government declaration, in *Deutscher Bundestag, 9. WP, Plenarprotokoll*, 13.10.1982, pp. 7,213–29, here p. 7,218.
7. *Datenreport 1992*, pp. 248–91; Manfred G. Schmidt, 'Rahmenbedingungen', in GSD, vol. 7, pp. 1–60, here pp. 41–7; Zohlnhöfer, *Wirtschaftspolitik*, pp. 110ff.
8. Reinhard Richardi, 'Arbeitsverfassung und Arbeitsrecht', in GSD, vol. 7, pp. 157–96, especially pp. 168–73; Günther Schmid and Frank Oschmiansky, 'Arbeitsmarktpolitik und Arbeitslosenversicherung', in GSD, vol. 7, pp. 237–88, here pp. 249–68. On the next section see also Manfred G. Schmidt, 'Gesamtbetrachtung', in GSD, vol. 7, pp. 749–812.
9. Wolfgang Voges, 'Lebenslagen im Sozialstaat—Dilemmata beim Fokus auf eine komplexe Bezugsgröße', in Hammerschmidt and Sagebiel, eds., *Soziale Frage*, pp. 21–38.
10. Schmidt and Oschmiansky, 'Arbeitsmarktpolitik und Arbeitslosenversicherung', in GSD, vol. 7, pp. 270–2.
11. Claudia K.Huber, 'Medienkonzerne', in Hachmeister, ed., *Grundlagen der Medienpolitik*, pp. 160–7; Rüdiger Steinmetz, 'Initiativen und Durchsetzung privat-kommerziellen Rundfunks', in Wilke, ed., *Mediengeschichte*, pp. 167–91.
12. Zohlnhöfer, *Wirtschaftspolitik*, pp. 168–70; Wirsching, *Abschied*, pp. 255–8; Ritter, *Deutsche Telekommunikationspolitik*, pp. 27–40.
13. Figures from Schmidt, *Sozialpolitik*, p. 154. Slightly different figures, but tending in the same direction (a fall from 30.3 percent in 1980 to 26.8 percent in 1990) are given in 'Sozialbudget 2006' issued by the Federal Ministry of Labour and Social Affairs.
14. *Bayernkurier*, 28.1.1989, quoted in Wirsching, *Abschied*, p. 347. See Ursula Münch and Walter Horstein, 'Familien-, Jugend- und Altenpolitik', in GSD, vol. 7, pp. 520–62, here pp. 520–35, and also Münch, *Familienpolitik*, pp. 240–58.
15. Winfried Schmähl, 'Sicherung bei Alter, Invalidität und für Hinterbliebene', in GSD, vol. 7, pp. 318–87, here pp. 346–65; Jürgen Wasem et al., 'Gesundheitswesen und Sicherung bei Krankheit und im Pflegefall', in GSD, vol. 7, pp. 392–440, here pp. 428ff.
16. Kluge, *Vierzig Jahre Agrarpolitik*, vol. 2, pp. 36–46.
17. Dieter, *Krise der deutschen Stahlindustrie*, pp. 209–74.
18. 'Jahresgutachten 1982–83 des Sachverständigenrates zur Begutachtung der gesamtwirtschaftlichen Entwicklung', *Deutscher Bundestag, 9.WP, Drucksache 9/2118*, 23.11.1982, p. 158.
19. Cf. Bierwirth, ed., *Schmelzpunkte.*
20. Kohl, at the meeting of the CDU–CSU parliamentary group held on 19.9.1988, quoted in Wirsching, *Abschied*, p. 252.

21. Helmut Kohl's government declaration, in *Deutscher Bundestag, 9.WP, PLenarprotokoll,* 13.10.1982, p. 7,213.
22. Hickethier, *Geschichte des Deutschen Fernsehens,* pp. 422–9; Martin Eifert and Wolfgang Hoffmann-Riem, 'Die Entstehung und Ausgestaltung des dualen Rundfunksystems', in Schwarzkopf, ed., *Rundfunkpolitik in Deutschland,* vol. 1, pp. 50–116.
23. Schwarz, *Helmut Kohl,* pp. 489–504; Dreher, *Helmut Kohl,* pp. 239–431; Bösch, *Macht und Machtverlust,* pp. 73–155.
24. Mintzel, *CSU-Hegemonie,* pp. 92–112.
25. Walter, *SPD,* pp. 201–41; Lösche and Walter, *SPD,* pp. 336–78.
26. Dittberner, *FDP*; Lösche and Walter, *Die FDP,* pp. 115–26.
27. Mende, *Nicht rechts*; Klein and Falter, *Der lange Weg.*
28. On this subject, see Priemel, *Flick,* pp. 744–50; Kilz and Preuss, *Die gekaufte Republik*; Wirsching, *Abschied,* pp. 65–79; Landfried, *Parteifinanzen,* pp. 188–214; and Bösch, *Macht und Machtverlust,* pp. 171–83.
29. Statements by Kohl and Strauß at the meeting of the CDU–CSU parliamentary group on 3.5.1984, quoted in Wirsching, *Abschied,* pp. 69–71.
30. On this section, see Herbert, *Foreign Labor,* pp. 235–45; Ulrich Herbert and Karin Hunn, 'Beschäftigung, soziale Sicherung und soziale Integration von Ausländern', in GSD, vol. 7, p. 619–52; and Klaus J.Bade and Michael Bommes, 'Migration und politische Kultur im "Nicht-Einwanderungsland"', in Bade, Münz and Bommes, eds., *Migrationsreport 2000,* pp. 163–204.
31. Meier-Braun, *Integration und Rückkehr?,* p. 44.
32. Staas, *Migration und Fremdenfeindlichkeit*; Danckwortt and Lepp, eds., *Von Grenzen und Ausgrenzung.*
33. 'Ausländerfeindlichkeit: Exodus erwünscht', *Der Spiegel,* 3.5.1982, pp. 32–44; on subsequent developments see also Bade, *Ausländer—Aussiedler—Asyl*; and the same author's *Migration in European History,* pp. 262–75.
34. Extract from the September 1982 coalition agreement between the CDU–CSU and the FDP, printed in *Handelsblatt,* 29.9.1982.
35. 'Wunsch nach Integration wächst', FAZ, 6.3.1984. See Heiko Körner, 'Das Gesetz zur Förderung der Rückkehrbereitschaft von Ausländern vom 28.November 1983. Eine kritische Bilanz', in Körner and Mehrländer, *Die 'neue' Ausländerpolitik in Europa,* pp. 65–72; and Jan Motte, 'Gedrängte Freiwilligkeit. Arbeitsmigration, Betriebspolitik und Rückkehrbeförderung 1983/84', in Motte, Ohliger and von Oswald, eds., *50 Jahre Bundesrepublik—50 Jahre Einwanderung,* pp. 165–83.
36. Cf. 'Prediger mit drohenden Thesen', *SZ,* 5.9.1987; 'Khomeini von Köln', *Bonner Rundschau,* 4.8.1987.
37. Cf. Moch, *Moving Europeans,* pp. 185–9; Hedwig Rudolph, 'Die Dynamik der Einwanderung im Nichteinwanderungsland Deutschland', in Fassmann and Münz, eds., *European Migration,* pp. 161–81.
38. Münch, *Asylpolitik in der Bundesrepublik Deutschland,* p. 253.
39. 'Der Druck muß sich erst noch erhöhen', article quoted in *Der Spiegel,* 27.8.1986, p. 79.

40. EMNID survey reported in *Die Zeit*, no. 49, 27.11.1987; Bergmann, *Volkszählung*; Scheuch, Gräf and Kühnel, *Volkszählung*; Aly and Roth, *The Nazi Census*.
41. *Datenreport 1985*, p. 378. On contemporary attitudes, see Faulstich, ed., *Kultur der achziger Jahre*; Schildt and Siegfried, *Deutsche Kulturgeschichte*, pp. 405–70; Glaser, *Deutsche Kultur*, pp. 368–422; Conze, *Suche nach Sicherheit*, pp. 654–88; and Görtemaker, *Geschichte*, pp. 597–686.
42. Brüggemeier, *Tschernobyl*, pp. 236–51; Radkau, *Age*, pp. 162–81.
43. Radkau, *Age*, pp. 352–3; 'Indien: Die chemische Apokalypse', *Der Spiegel*, 20.12.1984.
44. Brüggemeier, *Tschernobyl*, pp. 7–33; Radkau, *Age*, pp. 350–77.
45. Beck, *Risikogesellschaft*, p. 7.
46. Cf. Traube, *Plutonium-Wirtschaft?*; Wirsching, *Abschied*, pp. 390–1. Nuclear energy in the Federal Republic received a total of €125.6 billion in subsidies (in 2008 prices) from the public purse between 1950 and 2008. See Meyer, Schmidt and Eidems, *Staatliche Förderungen der Atomenergie*.
47. Guggenberger, *Bürgerinitiativen*; Roth and Rucht, eds., *Neue soziale Bewegungen*.
48. Freia Anders, 'Wohnraum, Freiraum, Widerstand. Die Formierung der Autonomen in den Konflikten um Hausbesetzungen Anfang der achtziger Jahre', in Reichardt and Siegfried, eds., *Das alternative Milieu*, pp. 473–98; Schwarzmeier, *Die Autonomen*.
49. Allerbeck and Hoag, *Jugend ohne Zukunft?*; Lang, *Mythos Kreuzberg*; Scheer and Espertz, *Deutschland*; Peters, *RAF*, pp. 299–383; Straßner, *Die Dritte Generation*.
50. Quoted in Ricarda Strobel, 'Das Jahrzehnt des Designs. Architektur, Alltagsgegenstände und Mode', in Faulstich, ed., *Kultur der achtziger Jahre*, pp. 51–69, here p. 55; cf. Koepf, ed., *Stadtbaukunst*, and Schildt and Siegfried, *Deutsche Kulturgeschichte*, pp. 450ff.
51. Ecker and Schmals, *Stadterneuerungspolitik*; Blasius and Dangschat, eds. *Gentrification*; Friedrichs and Kecskes, eds., *Gentrification*.
52. On this subject, see Hecken, *Pop*, pp. 345–468; Peter Wicke, 'Music, Dissidence, Revolution and Commerce. Youth Culture between Mainstream and Subculture', in Siegfried and Schildt, eds., *Between Marx and Coca-Cola*, pp. 109–26; and Maase, ed., *Die Schönheiten des Populären*.
53. Ralf Stockmann, 'Der Videoboom der achtziger Jahre', in Faulstich, ed., *Kultur der achtziger Jahre*, pp. 123–35; Werner Faulstich, 'Die Anfänge einer neuen Kulturperiode. Der Computer und die digitalen Medien', in Faulstich, ed., *Kultur der achtziger Jahre*, pp. 233–47; Schildt and Siegfried, *Deutsche Kulturgeschichte*, pp. 418–24.
54. Bartels, '"Design Mythos"'.
55. Ricarda Strobel, 'Das Jahrzehnt des Designs, Architektur, Alltagsgegenstände und Mode', in Faulstich, ed., *Kultur der achtziger Jahre*, pp. 51–69, here p. 62.
56. Wagner, ed., *Kulturelle Globalisierung*.
57. Hughes, *Political Correctness*, pp. 1–85; Erdl, *Legende*, pp. 72–132.
58. *Allensbacher Jahrhuch der Demoskopie 1984–1992*, p. 1,102.
59. On these issues, see Conze, *Suche nach Sicherheit*, pp. 654–64; Wirsching, *Abschied*, pp. 466–91; and Wolfrum, *Geschichtspolitik*, pp. 316–45.
60. Quoted in Morsch, *Eisenheim*, pp. 19–20; Günter, *Leben in Eisenheim*.

61. Cf. Fuchs-Heinritz, *Arbeiterleben nach 1945;* Welskopp, 'Klasse als Befindlichkeit?'
62. Niethammer, 'Anmerkungen zur Alltagsgeschichte'; Lüdtke, ed, *The History of Everyday Life*; Lindenberger and Wildt, 'Radikale Pluralität'; and Hochlarmarker Geschichts-Arbeitskreis, ed., *Hochlarmarker Lesebuch.*
63. See for example Niethammer, ed., *Lebensgeschichte und Sozialkultur im Ruhrgebiet.*
64. As exemplified in Galinski et al., eds., *Nazis und Nachbarn*; Focke and Reimer, *Alltag unterm Hakenkreuz*; and Berliner Geschichtswerkstatt, *Projekt Spurensicherung.*
65. Chancellor Kohl, speaking to the CDU–CSU parliamentary group, 23.3.1983; Kohl's address, delivered in the Reichstag building, 30.1.1983, quoted in Wirsching, *Abschied,* pp. 473–5. Cf. Moller, *Entkonkretisierung,* pp. 137–40.
66. Cf. Mommsen, 'Suche'. This view is challenged by Ulrich von Hehl, 'Kampf um die Deutung', p. 426. See also Wolfrum, *Geschichtspolitik,* pp. 316ff.
67. Gunther Hofmann, 'Der sperrige Gedenktag', *Die Zeit,* 18.1.1985; Gordon Craig, 'Eine Selbstverpflichtung für den Frieden', *Die Zeit,* 22.3.1985.
68. For von Weizsäcker's speech, made on 8 May 1985, see Weizsäcker, *Zum vierzigsten Jahrestag.* See also Wirsching, *Abschied,* pp. 481–5, which covers subsequent developments as well.
69. Cf. Reichel, *Politik mit der Erinnerung,* pp. 280–1.
70. Hartman, ed., *Bitburg in Moral and Political Perspective.* For the way this controversy was perceived in the Federal Republic, see Funke, 'Bitburg'; and Wolfrum, *Geschichtspolitik,* pp. 339ff.
71. For the Kohl quotation, see Reichel, *Politik mit der Erinnerung,* p. 284. See also Heinrich August Winkler, 'Aus der Geschichte lernen? Zum Verhältnis von Historie und Politik in Deutschland nach 1945', *Die Zeit,* 20.3. 2004.
72. Friedrich Karl Fromme, 'Feingefühl, allerseits', *FAZ,* 28.2.1986, quoted in Winkler, *Germany: the Long Road West,* vol. 2, p. 401.
73. Ernst Nolte, 'Between Historical Legend and Revisionism? The Third Reich in the Perspective of 1989', in Knowlton and Cates, *Forever in the Shadow,* pp. 1–15. Cf. Nolte, *Das Vergehen der Vergangenheit*; Nolte, *Der europäische Bürgerkrieg, 1917–1945*; and Nolte, *Streitpunkte.*
74. Jürgen Habermas, 'A Kind of Settlement of Damages. The Apologetic Tendencies in German History Writing' in Knowlton and Cates, *Forever in the Shadow,* pp. 34–44, here p. 41. On the *Historikerstreit* as a whole cf. Klaus Große Kracht, 'Der "Historikerstreit". Grabenkampf in der Geschichtskultur', in Große Kracht, ed., *Die zankende Zunft,* pp. 91–114; and Ulrich Herbert, 'Der Historikerstreit. Politische, wissenschaftliche, biographische Aspekte', in Sabrow, ed., *Zeitgeschichte,* pp. 94–114.
75. Cf. Lutz Niethammer, 'Über Kontroversen in der Geschichtswissenschaft', in Niethammer et al., *Deutschland danach,* pp. 414–24.
76. See the summaries in Kershaw, *Nazi Dictatorship,* pp. 1–19 and 93–133. Cf. in particular Hans Mommsen, 'Nationalsozialismus', in Kernig, ed., *Sowjetsystem und demokratische Gesellschaft,* vol. 4, pp. 695–713; and Hans Mommsen., 'Der Nationalsozialismus. Kumulative Radikalisierung und Selbstzerstörung des Regimes', in *Meyers Enzyklopädisches Wörterbuch,* Stuttgart, 1976, pp. 785–90. There

is an overview of the controversy in Jäckel and Rohwer, eds., *Der Mord*; see also Berg, *The Holocaust and the West German historians.*

77. The correspondence was published in: Broszat and Friedländer, 'Um die "Historisierung des Nationalsozialismus"'.
78. On this, see Haftendorn, *Sicherheit und Entspannung*, pp. 234–67; Wirsching, *Abschied*, pp. 79–106; Gassert, ed., *Zweiter Kalter Krieg und Friedensbewegung*; Leif, *Die strategische (Ohn–)Macht*; and Ziemann, ed., *Peace Movements.*
79. Haftendorn, *Sicherheit und Entspannung*, pp. 217–34.
80. On this, see Korte, *Deutschlandpolitik in Helmut Kohls Kanzlerschaft*, pp. 117–437, and Wirsching, *Abschied*, pp. 591–628.
81. See Korte, *Deutschlandpolitik in Helmut Kohls Kanzlerschaft*, pp. 166ff.; Potthoff, *Koalition*, pp. 145–57; and Zeitlin, *The Currency of Socialism*, pp. 220–1.
82. Gaddum, *Europapolitik*, pp. 93–187; Thiemeyer, *Europäische Integration*, pp. 61–70; Knipping, *Rom*, pp. 218–48; Brunn, *Die europäische Einigung*, pp. 230–55.
83. Hildermeier, *Geschichte der Sowjetunion*, pp. 1,014–52; Brown, *The Gorbachev Factor*; Conert, *Die Ökonomie des unmöglichen Sozialismus.*
84. Hildermeier, *Geschichte der Sowjetunion*, p. 899.
85. Neutatz, *Träume*, p. 530. For a somewhat different view, see Jörg Baberowski, 'Criticism as Crisis'.
86. See Hildermeier, *Geschichte der Sowjetunion*, pp. 1,019–52; Neutatz, *Träume*, pp. 498–531.
87. See the summary in Haftendorn, *Sicherheit und Entspannung*, pp. 242–67.
88. Comments made by Alfred Dregger in 1985, quoted in Wirsching, *Abschied*, p. 550.
89. Loth, *Helsinki*, pp. 262–72.
90. Garton Ash, *In Europe's Name*, pp. 110–13.
91. Quoted in Fred Oldenburg, 'Neues Denken in der sowjetischen Deutschlandpolitik?', *Deutschland Archiv* 20/2 (1987), pp. 1,154–60, here p. 1,159.
92. Michail Gorbatschow, 'Rede auf der Kundgebung der tschechoslowakisch-sowjetischen Freundschaft, 10.4.1987', in Gorbatschow, *Ausgewählte Reden und Aufsätze*, vol. 4, pp. 530–1.
93. Europäische Kommission, *Die EU-Wirtschaft. Jahresbilanz 2000*, no. 71, 2000, pp. 254ff. On the next section, see Gaddum, *Europapolitik*, pp. 65–188; Wirsching, *Abschied*, pp. 513–43; Knipping, *Rom*, pp. 218–67; and Schwarz, *Kohl*, pp. 431–9.
94. Lappenküper, *Mitterrand und Deutschland*, pp. 197–258; Miard-Delacroix, *Im Zeichen der europäischen Einigung*, pp. 307–26.
95. Gaddum, *Europapolitik*, pp. 93–187; Kluge, *Vierzig Jahre Agrarpolitik*, vol. 2, pp. 284–350.
96. Gaddum, *Europapolitik*, pp. 283–357; Olaf Hillenbrand, 'Europa als Wirtschafts- und Währungsunion', in Weidenfeld, ed., *Europa-Handbuch*, pp. 498–521; Guido Thiemeyer, 'Helmut Schmidt und die Gründung des Europäischen Währungssystems', in Knipping and Schönwald, eds., *Aufbruch*, pp. 245–68.
97. Europäische Kommission, *Die EU-Wirtschaft. Jahresbilanz 2000*, no. 71, 2000, pp. 254ff.
98. Korte, *Deutschlandpolitik*, pp. 417–37.

99. Karl F.Schumann, 'Flucht und Ausreise aus der DDR insbesondere im Jahrzehnt ihres Unterganges', in *Materialien der Enquête-Kommission*, vol. V.3, pp. 2,359–405.
100. Bahr, *Sicherheit vor und für Deutschland*. On this point, see also Garton Ash, *In Europe's Name*, pp. 312–42.
101. Grundwertekommission der SPD und Akademie fur Gesellschaftswissenschaften beim ZK der SED, 'Der Streit der Ideologien und die gemeinsame Sicherheit', in *Informationsdienst der SPD*, no. 3, 3.8.1987.
102. Glaab, *Deutschland-Politik in der öffentlichen Meinung*, pp. 296–368.
103. Speech by Chancellor Kohl, 7.9.1987: http://helmut-kohl.kas.de/index.php?msg=1941 [1.12.2010]
104. Jahresrückblick ARD-Fernsehen, 30.12.1988: 'Günstige Wirtschaftslage'.

## Chapter 19

1. Hildermeier, *Geschichte der Sowjetunion*, pp. 877ff.; Borodziej, *Geschichte Polens*, pp. 317–19.
2. Staritz, *Geschichte*, p. 279. On the next section, see Staritz, *Geschichte*, pp. 276–88; Peter Skyba and Christoph Boyer, 'Politische Rahmenbedingungen', in GSD, vol. 10, pp. 1–66; Skyba and Boyer, 'Gesellschaftliche Strukturen und sozialpolitische Handlungsfelder', in GSD, vol. 10, pp. 67–143; Weber, *Geschichte der DDR*, pp. 404–59; Steiner, *Plans*, pp. 141–69; Steiner, 'Zwischen Konsumversprechen und Innovationszwang. Zum wirtschaftlichen Niedergang der DDR', in Jarausch and Sabrow, eds., *Weg in den Untergang*, pp. 153–92; Steiner, 'Bundesrepublik und DDR'; Pirker et al., eds., *Plan als Befehl*.
3. *Protokoll der Verhandlungen des VIII. Parteitages der Sozialistischen Einheitspartei Deutschlands, 15. bis 19. Juni 1971 in Berlin*, vol. 1, pp. 61–2.
4. Letter from the Politburo of the SED to Leonid Brezhnev, 21.1.1971, printed in Przybylski, *Tatort Politbüro*, pp. 297–303, here p. 300.
5. Staatliche Plankommission, 'Beratung der Grundlinien im Politbüro, 23.4.1971', quoted in Steiner, *Plans*, p. 145.
6. Steiner, *Plans*, pp. 146–7; Wolle, *Die heile Welt*, pp. 182–8; Gisela Helwig and Barbara Hille, 'Familie-, Jugend- und Altenpolitik', in GSD, vol. 10, pp. 471–540, here p. 490; André Steiner, 'Preisgestaltung', in GSD, vol. 10, pp. 304–24.
7. Jay Rowell, 'Wohnungspolitik', in GSD, vol. 10, pp. 681–701.
8. As related by Gerhard Schürer, who chaired the SPK until 1988, at a conference held in 1999, quoted in Steiner, *Plans*, p. 160.
9. Günter Schabowski, *Der Absturz*, p. 123.
10. Steiner, *Plans*, p. 151.
11. Speaking on 27.11.1979, as quoted in Skyba and Boyer, 'Politische Rahmenbedingungen', in GSD, vol. 10, p. 20.
12. Steiner, *Plans*, pp. 152–3.

13. Wolfgang Biermann, 'Man mußte ein König der Improvisation sein', in Pirker et al., eds., *Plan als Befehl,* pp. 213–35; Roesler, 'Kombinate'.
14. Staritz, *Geschichte,* p. 307; Volze, 'Valutamark'; Ritschl, 'Aufstieg', p. 33.
15. Skyba and Boyer, 'Politische Rahmenbedingungen', in GSD, vol. 10, p. 46.
16. Honecker, speaking to the Politburo on 27.11.1980, quoted in Hans-Hermann Hertle, 'Die Diskussion der ökonomischen Krisen in der Führungsspitze der SED', in Pirker et al., eds., *Plan als Befehl,* p. 318; Staritz, *Geschichte,* p. 311; Steiner, *Plans,* pp. 162–3.
17. Wolle, *Heile Welt,* pp. 213–21; Wolter, '*Ich harre aus im Land und geh, ihm fremd*'.
18. De Bruyn, *Vierzig Jahre,* pp. 185–6.
19. MfS, Zentrale Auswertungs- und Informationsgruppe, 'Hinweise auf Tendenzen der Unzufriedenheit in der Reaktion der Bevölkerung der DDR, 12. September 1977', in GSD, vol. 10, CD, Doc.10/94; Wolle, *Heile Welt,* pp. 227–30.
20. Zentralinstitut für Jugendforschung, *Frauenstudie 1984,* p. 6,138; Winkler, ed., *Frauenreport '90,* p. 43.
21. Helwig and Hille, 'Familien- Jugend- und Altenpolitik', in GSD, vol. 10, pp. 494–500, here p. 498.
22. Dierk Hoffmann, 'Sicherung bei Alter, Invalidität und für Hinterbliebene, Sonderversorgungssysteme', in GSD, vol. 10, pp. 326–62, here p. 361; Winkler, *Sozialreport '90,* p. 226.
23. Wolle, *Heile Welt,* pp. 217ff.
24. These prices are taken from the report by Peter Christ, 'Mächtig stolz auf die eigene Leistung', in Sommer, ed., *Reise ins andere Deutschland,* pp. 78–90, here p. 89.
25. Steiner, 'Preisgestaltung', in GSD, vol. 10, p. 312.
26. Wolle, *Heile Welt,* pp. 74–8 and 204–10.
27. MfS, Zentrale Auswertungs- und Informationsgruppe, 'Hinweise auf Tendenzen der Unzufriedenheit in der Reaktion der Bevölkerung der DDR, 12. September 1977', in GSD, vol. 10, CD Doc. 10/94.
28. Remarks of Werner Lamberz, speaking on 25 or 26 May 1977, quoted in Wolle, *Heile Welt,* p. 69.
29. Honecker, at the CC Plenum held on 17.12.1971, quoted in Jäger, *Kultur und Politik,* p. 140.
30. Jäger, *Kultur und Politik,* pp. 139–62; Walther, *Sicherungsbereich Literatur.*
31. Helwig and Hille, 'Familien- Jugend- und Altenpolitik', in GSD, vol. 10, p. 519.
32. Ohse, *Jugend nach dem Mauerbau,* pp. 339–55; Wolle, *Heile Welt,* pp. 164–6; Breßlein, 'Weltjugend'.
33. Mielke, 6.7.1977, quoted in Skyba and Boyer, 'Politische Rahmenbedingungen', in GSD, vol. 10, p. 28.
34. Skyba and Boyer, 'Politische Rahmenbedingungen', in GSD, vol. 10, p. 64.
35. Schroeder, *SED-Staat,* pp. 311ff. Pingel-Schliemann, *Zersetzen*; Klaus-Dietmar Henke, 'Staatssicherheit', in Weidenfeld and Korte, eds., *Handbuch zur deutschen Einheit,* pp. 721–30.
36. Havemann, *Berliner Schriften,* p. 187. See Vollnhals, *Der Fall Havemann.*
37. Bahro, *The Alternative,* pp. 243–4 and 453; Neubert, *Geschichte der Opposition,* pp. 230–4.

38. The first poem, in German: 'Viele werden dafür sorgen/daß der Sozialismus siegt/Heute! Heute, nicht erst morgen!/Freiheit kommt nie verfrüht/Und das beste Mittel gegen/Sozialismus (sag ich laut)/Ist, daß ihr den Sozialismus/AUFBAUT!!! Aufbaut! (aufbaut)'. ('Warte nicht auf beßre Zeiten', in Biermann, *Drahtharfe*.) The second poem, in German: 'Und sagt mir mal: Wozu ist gut/Die ganze Bürokratenbrut?/Sie wälzt mit Eifer und Geschick/Dem Volke über das Genick/Der Weltgeschichte großes Rad/—die hab ich satt!' ('Die hab ich satt!' [1966] in Biermann, *Chausseestraße*). The Biermann case is discussed in Berbig et al., eds., *In Sachen Biermann*; Jäger, *Kultur und Politik*, pp. 165–86; and Neubert, *Geschichte der Opposition*, pp. 154–5.
39. Letter of Protest, 17.11.1976, in Weber, ed., *DDR*, doc. 209.
40. *Bild-Zeitung*, 20.11.1976 issue.
41. Neubert, *Geschichte der Opposition*, pp. 338ff., 536ff., and 671–2; Schroeder, *SED-Staat*, pp. 276–8.
42. Skyba and Boyer, 'Politische Rahmenbedingungen', in GSD, vol. 10, pp. 21–2; Steiner, *Plans*, pp. 161–2.
43. Transcript of a discussion between Brezhnev and Honecker on 3.8.1981 in the Crimea, quoted in Hans-Hermann Herle, 'Die Diskussion der ökonomischen Krisen in der Führungsspitze der SED', in Pirker et al., eds., *Plan als Befehl*, pp. 320–1; conversation between Konstantin Rusakov and Honecker on 21.10.1981, quoted in Schroeder, *SED-Staat*, p. 270; Skyba and Boyer, 'Politische Rahmenbedingungen', in GSD, vol. 10, p. 48.
44. Staatliche Plankommission, 'Konzeption zum Abbau der Höhe der Verbindlichkeiten der DDR gegenüber dem nichtsozialistischen Wirtschaftsgebiet vom 27.6.1980', in GSD, vol. 10, CD, Doc. 10/200; Statistisches Bundesamt 46–9; cf. Gerhard Schürer and Siegfried Wenzle, 'Wir waren die Rechner, immer verpönt', in Pirker et al., eds., *Plan als Befehl*, pp. 92–3.
45. Staritz, *Geschichte*, p. 313; Wolle, *Heile Welt*, pp. 92–3.
46. Honecker to Kania, 17.2.1981, quoted in Kubina and Wilke, eds., '*Hart und kompromisslos durchgreifen*', doc. 37, pp. 221–7, here p. 223.
47. Borodziej, *Geschichte Polens*, pp. 359 and 372ff.
48. 'Staatliche Plankommission, 27.6.1980', in GSD, vol. 10, CD, doc. 10/200.
49. Steiner, *Plans*, p. 174.
50. Skyba and Boyer, 'Politische Rahmenbedingungen', in GSD, vol. 10, p. 51.
51. Steiner, *Plans*, p. 193.
52. Hager, in an interview with *Stern* magazine, 9.4.1987.
53. Günter Mittag's remarks to the Politburo on 29.8.1989, printed in Stephan and Küchenmeister, eds., '*Vorwärts immer*', doc. 15, p. 105.
54. Report to the Politburo on 15.9.1987, quoted in Schröder, *SED-Staat*, p. 294.
55. Harry Tisch, addressing the Politburo on 29.8.1989, printed in Stephan and Küchenmeister, eds., '*Vorwärts immer*', doc. 15, p. 102.
56. Oliver Werner, 'Die "Sputnik" Krise in der SED 1988/89', in Heydemann, Mai and Müller, eds. *Revolution und Transformation*, pp. 117–36.
57. Honecker's remarks to Gorbachev, in a conversation on 3.10.1986, quoted in Stephan and Küchenmeister, eds., *Honecker-Gorbatschow*, doc. 13, pp. 140–65, here pp. 161–2.
58. Neubert, *Geschichte der Opposition*, pp. 398–404.

59. Open Letter to Leonid Brezhnev, 20.9.1981, in Büscher, Wenierski and Wolscher, eds., *Friedensbewegung*, pp. 181–4, here p. 183.
60. Neubert, *Geschichte der Opposition*, p. 407.
61. Neubert, *Geschichte der Opposition*, pp. 626–35.
62. Neubert, *Geschichte der Opposition*, p. 649.
63. Neubert, *Geschichte der Opposition*, pp. 706ff.
64. Wolle, *Heile Welt*, p. 266.
65. M. Rainer Lepsius, 'Handlungsräume und Rationalitätskriterien der Wirtschaftsfunktionäre in der Ära Honecker', in Pirker et al., eds., *Plan als Befehl*, p. 362.
66. Christa Bertag, 'Ich dachte, wir finden schon eine Lösung', in Pirker et al.,eds. *Plan als Befehl*, pp. 237–54, here p. 254.

## Chapter 20

1. Federal President Richard von Weizsäcker, '40 Jahre Grundgesetz der Bundesrepublik Deutschland, Bonn, 24.Mai 1989', in http://www.bundespraesident.de [1.6.2012].
2. Klaus Liedtke, 'Brief ans Vaterland', in *Stern Extra (40. Jahre Bundesrepublik Deutschland)*, 22.5.1989, p. 6.
3. Helmut Kohl, speech at the opening of the CDU Congress on 'Forty Years of the German Federal Republic', Bonn, 18.1.1989, ACDP, http://www.cdugeschichte.de [1.6.2012].
4. Kowalczuk, *Endspiel*, pp. 311–17.
5. Kloth, *'Zettelfalten'*, pp. 160–9; Kowalczuk, *Endspiel*, pp. 318–33.
6. *Tagung des politischen beratenden Ausschusses*, 8.7.1989, pp. 14–26.
7. Rödder, *Deutschland*, p. 53.
8. Borodziej, *Geschichte Polens*, p. 384.
9. Garton Ash, *Uses of Adversity*, pp. 319–34.
10. Dabringhaus, *Geschichte Chinas*, pp. 190–4.
11. Otto Reinhold, speaking on Radio DDR, 19.8.1989, in *Blätter für deutsche und internationale Politik*, 34 (1989), p. 1,175.
12. *Volkskammer, 9. WP, 9. Tagung, Protokoll*, 8.6.1989, p. 192.
13. Initiative for Peace and Human Rights statement, 5.6.1989, quoted in Kowalczuk, *Endspiel*, p. 340.
14. Conversation between Oskar Fischer and Viacheslav Kochemasov, 5.9.1989, quoted in Hertle, *Fall der Mauer*, p. 105.
15. Joint Declaration, 4.10.1989, quoted in Kowalczuk, *Endspiel*, p. 387.
16. Gorbachev, addressing the SED Politbureau, on 7.10.1989, quoted in Küchenmeister, ed., *Honecker-Gorbatschow*, pp. 252–66.
17. Jankowski, *Tag*; Winkler, *Germany: the Long Road West*, vol. 2, pp. 455–7.
18. Gerhard Schürer, 'Analyse der ökonomischen Lage der DDR vom 30.Oktober 1989', in Hertle, *Fall der Mauer*, doc. 7, p. 458.

19. Message from Gorbachev to Kohl, 19.11.1989, in Küsters, ed., *Deutsche Einheit,* doc. 80, pp. 504–5.
20. Telephone conversation between Kohl and Bush, 17.11.1989, in Küsters, ed., *Deutsche Einheit,* doc. 93, pp. 538–40.
21. Kohl, *Deutschlands Einheit,* p. 150. On the next section, see Rödder, *Deutschland,* pp. 146–225 and Schwarz, *Kohl,* pp. 535–81.
22. Chancellor Kohl's speech to the Bundestag, in *Deutscher Bundestag, 11.WP, Plenarprotokoll, 28.11.1989,* pp. 13,510–14.
23. US Secretary of State James Baker, 'Four Principles', in Kaiser, ed., *Deutschlands Vereinigung,* p. 169.
24. Discussion between Gorbachev, Shevardnadze and Genscher, 5 December 1989, quoted in Zelikow and Rice, *Germany Unified,* p. 136, and in von Plato, *The End of the Cold War?,* pp. 88–92. Both texts refer to the Russian minutes of the discussion.
25. Quoted in Zelikow and Rice, *Germany Unified,* p. 137.
26. Dolf Sternberger, 'Verfassungspatriotismus', in Sternberger, *Verfassungspatriotismus,* pp. 13–16.
27. Hans Mommsen, 'Aus Eins mach Zwei. Die Bi-Nationalisierung Rest-Deutschlands', *Die Zeit,* 6.2.1981.
28. Judgement by the Federal Constitutional Court, 31.7.1973 (2BvF 1/73).
29. Herdegen, 'Perspektiven und Begrenzungen'.
30. Brandt, *My Life in Politics,* pp. 141–2.
31. Oskar Lafontaine,interview with the *Süddeutsche Zeitung,* 25.11.1989.
32. Antje Vollmer, speaking on 8.11.1989, in *Deutscher Bundestag, 11.WP, Plenarprotokoll,* pp. 13,030–4.
33. Neues Forum, quoted by Hans-Jochen Vogel in the Bundestag, in *Deutscher Bundestag, 11.WP, Plenarprotokoll, 8.11.1989,* p. 13,022.
34. Markus Meckel's speech of 7.10.1989, in Meckel and Gutzeit, *Opposition in der DDR,* p. 394.
35. Chancellor Kohl's speech to the rally outside the Frauenkirche in Dresden on 19.12.1989, quoted from https://www.bundesregierung.de/Content/DE/Bulletin/1980-1989/1989/150-89_Kohl.html (30.3.2018)
36. Garton Ash, *In Europe's Name,* pp. 343–56.
37. Letter to Kohl from the chair of the Council of Economic Experts, Schneider, 9.2.1990, in Küsters, ed., *DeutscheEinheit,* no. 167, pp. 778–81; Grosser, *Wagnis,* pp. 149–226.
38. Monika Maron, 'Das neue Elend der Intellektuellen', *tageszeitung,* 6.2.1990; Kowalczuk, *Endspiel,* pp. 540–1.
39. Patrick Süskind, 'Deutschland, eine Midlife-crisis', *Der Spiegel,* 38/1990, 17.9.1990.
40. Jürgen Habermas, 'Der DM-Nationalismus', *Die Zeit,* 30.3.1990.
41. Heinrich August Winkler, 'Nation ja—Nationalstaat nein', *Die Zeit,* 13.2.1981.
42. Teltschik, *329 Tage,* pp. 100 and 114. The federal government provided a subsidy of 220 million DM to cover the delivery of food supplies.
43. Conversation between Gorbachev and Kohl in Moscow, 10.2.1990, in Küsters, ed., *Deutsche Einheit,* no. 174, pp. 795–807. The quotation is on p. 801.

44. Zelikow and Rice, *Germany Unified*, p. 215.
45. Küsters, *Integrationsfriede*, especially pp. 849–63.
46. Hildermeier, *Geschichte*, pp. 1,040ff.
47. As recorded by Anatoly Cherniaev in his diary. See Cherniaev, *My Six Years With Gorbachev*, p. 264.
48. Horst Teltschik at a meeting on 14 May in the Kremlin with Nikolai Ryzhkov and Eduard Shevardnadze. Teltschik promised that if this condition was observed, Kohl would do what he could to help (Zelikow and Rice, *Germany Unified*, pp. 258–9).
49. The quotations are from Zelikow and Rice, *Germany Unified*, pp. 277 and 279.
50. The minutes of these discussions are printed in Küsters, ed., *Deutsche Einheit*, pp. 1,340–66. See Rödder, *Deutschland*, pp. 261–2 on the financial negotiations.
51. On this section, see Grosser, *Wagnis*, pp. 209–329, and Wirsching, *Abschied*, pp. 674–83.
52. Grosser, *Wagnis*, pp. 365–85.
53. On this point, see Grosser, *Wagnis*, pp. 330–45.
54. Speech of 3 October 1990 in Berlin by the German President, von Weizsäcker, http://www.bundespraesident.de [1.10.2012].
55. On this issue, see Knipping, *Rom*, pp. 218–67; Gaddum, *Europapolitik*, pp. 65–188; Wirsching, *Abschied*, pp. 513–43; and Loth, 'Helmut Kohl'.
56. Statement by Mitterrand, according to the reminiscences of his close friend Jacques Attali, as quoted in Schabert, *How World Politics is Made*, pp. 188–9, and in Schwarz, *Kohl*, p. 431. On the reliability of Attali's reminiscences, see Loth, 'Helmut Kohl', p. 460.
57. Attali's reminiscences, as quoted in Loth, 'Helmut Kohl', p. 467.
58. The thesis advanced by Wilfried Loth, that a linkage of this kind never existed, is not justified by his own arguments. See Loth, 'Helmut Kohl'.
59. Declaration of the European Council in Strasbourg, 8–9.12.1989, in Kaiser, ed., *Deutschlands Vereinigung*, pp. 171–3. See Lappenküper, *Mitterrand*, pp. 269–73.

## Chapter 21

1. Francis Fukuyama, 'The End of History?' *The National Interest*, summer 1989, p. 1; the same author, *The End of History and the Last Man*.
2. Perry Anderson, 'The Ends of History', in *A Zone of Engagement*, pp. 352–3.
3. Wirsching, *Abschied*, p. 701.
4. On the process of unification, see Ritter, *Price*, pp. 69–116; Grosser, *Wagnis*, pp. 329–505; Zohlnhöfer, *Wirtschaftspolitik*; Schroeder, *Die veränderte Republik*, pp. 199–301; Schwarz, *Helmut Kohl*, pp. 642–51; Conze, *Sicherheit*, pp. 820–52; Roland Czada, 'Zwischen Stagnation und Umbruch. Die politisch-ökonomische Entwicklung nach 1989', in Süß, ed., *Deutschland*, pp. 203–26; and Kocka, *Vereinigungskrise*, pp. 133–69.
5. Kohl's television address of 1 July 1990, in http://www.helmut-kohl.de [25.2.2013]. On the tax increases, see Schwarz, *Helmut Kohl*, pp. 595–9.

6. Grosser, *Wagnis*, pp. 365–6.
7. 'Eine Industrieregion zerbricht', *Der Spiegel*, 16/1991, 15.4.1991.
8. Grosser, *Wagnis*, p. 464; Conze, *Sicherheit*, p. 791.
9. Ritter, *Price*, p. 84; Grosser, *Wagnis*, pp. 474–80.
10. Rohwedder only exercised his function for a short time. As noted earlier, he was murdered on 1 April 1991 by RAF terrorists.
11. Grosser, *Wagnis*, pp. 355–65.
12. Quoted in 'Abschied eines Buhmanns', *Der Spiegel*, 51/1994, 19.12.1994.
13. Thomas G. Betz, 'Die Eigentumsfrage. Das Prinzip "Rückgabe vor Entschädigung" und seine Folgen', in Bahrmann and Links, eds., *Am Ziel vorbei*, pp. 107–23.
14. Hans F. Zacher, 'Grundlagen der Sozialpolitik in der Bundesrepublik Deutschland', in GSD, vol. 1, pp. 333–684, here p. 593. See Ritter, *Price*, pp. 69–72.
15. Grosser, *Wagnis*, pp. 470–3; Heilemann and Rappen, 'Sieben Jahre'; 'Dann fahr' ich gegen den Baum', *Der Spiegel*, 11/1991, 11.3.1991; 'Eine Industrieregion zerbricht', *Der Spiegel*, 16/1991, 15.4.1991.
16. Karl Lichtblau, 'Industrielle Kerne und neue Wachstumstheorie', in Oppenländer, ed., *Wiedervereinigung*, p. 361; Grosser, *Wagnis*, pp. 362–4. The Treuhand is discussed in Freese, *Privatisierungstätigkeit*; Rohwedder, *Abschlussbericht*; and Seibel, *Verwaltete Illusionen*. On the coalmining industry, see Frondel, Kambeck and Schmidt, 'Kohlesubventionen'.
17. Kerstin Schwenn, 'Privatisierung der volkseigenen Betriebe', in Oppenländer, ed., *Wiedervereinigung*, p. 354. Slightly different figures are given in Schroeder, *Preis*, pp. 143–4.
18. Grosser, *Wagnis*, pp. 365–83. There are divergent calculations in Schroeder, *Die veränderte Republik*, pp. 246–52.
19. Ritter, *Price*, pp. 91–6; Schroeder, *Preis*, p. 139; Roland Czada, 'Zwischen Stagnation und Umbruch. Die politisch-ökonomische Entwicklung nach 1989', in Süß, ed., *Deutschland*, pp. 211–13; 'Avanti Dilettanti', *Der Spiegel*, 24/1997, 9.6.1997; https://www.bundesfinanzministerium.de/Content/DE/Monatsberichte/2013/03/Inhalte/Kapitel-6-Statistiken/6-1-19-staatsquoten-im-internationalen-vergleich.html (30.3.2018)
20. Weidenfeld and Korte, eds., *Handbuch*, p. 369; Ritter, *Price*, pp. 92–3; Schwarz, *Preis*, pp. 143–4; Ragnitz, 'Transferleistungen'.
21. Statistisches Bundesamt: https://www.destatis.de/de/DE/ZahlenFakten/Gesamtwirtschaft/Umwelt/VGR/Inlandsprodukt/Inlandsprodukt.html [28.2.2013].
22. Cf. for example Priewe and Hickel, *Preis*.
23. These views were put forward in the annual reports of the Council of Economic Experts on the course of economic development for the years 1991–4 (*Jahresgutachten des Sachverständigenrates*).
24. Volker Kunz, 'Einstellungen zu Wirtschaft und Gesellschaft in den alten und neuen Bundesländern', in Falter, Gabriel and Rattinger, eds., *Wirklich ein Volk?*, pp. 509–38; Katja Neller, 'DDR-Nostalgie? Analysen zur Identifikation der Ostdeutschen mit ihrer politischen Vergangenheit, zur ostdeutschen Identität und zur Ost-West-Stereotypisierung', in Falter, Gabriel and Rattinger, eds., *Wirklich ein Volk?*, pp. 571–608.

25. Jürgen Kocka, 'Zwischen Befürchtung und Faszination', in Kogel et al., eds., *Neues Deutschland*, pp. 65–8, here p. 67.
26. Ritter, *Price*, pp. 129–30.
27. 'Erst vereint, nun entzweit', *Der Spiegel*, 3/1993, 18.01.1993, p. 59.
28. Volker Kunz, 'Einstellungen zu Wirtschaft und Gesellschaft in den alten und neuen Bundesländern', in Falter, Gabriel and Rattinger, eds., *Wirklich ein Volk?*, pp. 516 and 519; Schroeder, *Preis*, pp. 148 and 169.
29. Rainer Land and Andreas Willisch, 'Ostdeutschland—ein Umbruchszenario', in Bahrmann and Links, eds., *Am Ziel vorbei*, pp. 11–13, here p. 11.
30. The 'Charter of Paris for a New Europe' was the final document of the CSCE Conference held in Paris between 19 and 21 November 1990, and it was signed by thirty-two European countries plus Canada and the USA. See Wolfgang Kubiczek, 'Das Pariser Treffen der KSZE—Beginn einer neuen Ära', in Staack, ed., *Aufbruch*, pp. 335–66.
31. Kohl's government declaration, in *Deutscher Bundestag, 12.WP, Plenarprotokoll, 30.1.1991*, pp. 67–79, here p. 69.
32. On the war against Iraq, see Barzilai, Klieman and Shidlo, eds., *Gulf Crisis*; Hiro, *Desert Shield*; Kaiser and Becher, *Deutschland und der Irak-Konflikt*; and Kirste, *Die USA und Deutschland.*
33. Interview with Senator John McCain, 'Bonn soll seinen Beitrag leisten', *Der Spiegel*, 38/1990, 17.9.1990. Kissinger's views are quoted in 'Das wird ein schwieriges Jahr', *Der Spiegel*, 5/1991, 28.1.1991. On the attitude of the US government, see Michael H. Haltzel, 'Germany, the United States and the Gulf War. Danger Signals for the Future', in Gutzen, ed., *Transatlantische Partnerschaft*, pp. 131–42. On the poison gas installations, see Leyendecker and Rickelmann, *Exporteure.*
34. 'Massendemonstrationen in ganz Deutschland. Größte Friedensaufmärsche seit dem Nachrüstungsjahr 1983', *Neue Zürcher Zeitung*, 15.1.1991. On the peace movement, see Baier, *Ich will reden*; Buro and Roth, eds., *Friedensbewegung*; and Jourdan, *Gegen den Krieg.*
35. Jan Philipp Reemtsma, '... the bad and the ugly', *Konkret*, 12/1990, pp. 26–7. See Klaus Hartung, 'Frieden oder Rettet Israel', *taz.*, 19.1.1991, p.10; Hans Magnus Enzensberger, 'Hitlers Widergänger', *Der Spiegel*, 6/1991, 4.2.1991; Wolf Biermann, 'Kriegshetze, Friedenshetze', *Die Zeit*, 6/1991, pp. 59–60.
36. Seventy-four per cent of those questioned were opposed to a change in the Basic Law which would have made possible a military intervention outside the NATO region; Kaiser and Becher, *Deutschland und der Irak-Konflikt*, pp. 13–36.
37. Kaiser and Becher, *Deutschland und der Irak-Konflikt*, pp. 47–69 and 114–26.
38. Neutatz, *Träume*, pp. 532–57; Hildermeier, *Geschichte der Sowjetunion*, pp. 1,061–78.
39. Kohl's remarks to Esko Aho, the prime minister of Finland, on 26.9.1991, quoted in Schwarz, *Kohl*, p. 676.
40. On the war in Yugoslavia, see Calic, *Geschichte Jugoslawiens*, pp. 297–326; Calic, *Krieg und Frieden*; and Melčić, ed., *Jugoslawien-Krieg.*
41. As recorded by Hubert Védrine, in *Les mondes de François Mitterrand*, p. 625, quoted here from Schwarz, *Helmut Kohl*, p. 683.

42. Cf. Neu, *Jugoslawien-Kriegsberichterstattung.*
43. Calic, *Geschichte Jugoslawiens*, pp. 321–5; Bogoeva and Fetscher, *Srebrenica.*
44. BverfGer 12 July 1994, BverfGer 90, 286; Out-of-area deployments: http://www.servat.uni.be.ch/dfr/bv090286.html [13.11.2012]
45. Herbert, *Foreign Labor*, pp. 248–57; Ulrich Herbert and Karin Hunn, 'Beschäftigung, soziale Sicherung und soziale Integration von Ausländern', in GSD, vol. 9, pp. 781–810.
46. 'Im Jahr 2000 ein türkischer Kanzler', *Der Spiegel*, 7/1989, 13.2.1989; 'Sowjetdiplomaten warnen den Westen vor Millionen Zuwanderern', *FR*, 6.12.1990; 'Stoiber, Massen-Treck verhindern', *FAZ*, 14.12.1990.
47. The balance sheet of net migration was as follows: total foreign immigration 5.5 million; total emigration 3.3 million. See Herbert, *Foreign Labor*, pp. 248–57 and Münz, Seifert and Ulrich, *Zuwanderung*, p. 47.
48. Ulrich Reitz, 'Versagen beim Asylproblem', *Die Welt*, 6.7.1990; 'Die Wochenendasylanten', *Bild am Sonntag*, 21.10.1990; Arnulf Baring, 'Ein offenes Wort zum Thema Asylanten', *Bild-Zeitung*, 13.10.1990; 'Wettrennen in Schäbigkeit. Burkhard Hirsch (FDP) und Edmund Stoiber (CSU) über das Asylrecht', *Der Spiegel*, 45/1990, 5.11.1990.
49. Cf. Müggenburg, *Die ausländischen Vertragsarbeitnehmer*, pp. 139ff.; Bade, *Ausländer—Aussiedler—Asyl*, pp. 178ff.
50. 'Schon nahe am Pogrom', *Der Spiegel*, 14/1990, 2.4.1990.
51. 'Angst unter Dresdens Ausländern', *taz.*, 10.4.1991.
52. As quoted in Heribert Prantl, 'Asylpolitik zwischen Hysterie und Hilflosigkeit', *SZ*, 3.8.1991.
53. Roth, 'Was bewegt die Wähler?'.
54. 'Soldaten an die Grenzen', *Der Spiegel*, 37/1991, 9.9.1991.
55. *Der Stern*, 2.10.1991. See also 'Überfälle und Anschläge auf Ausländer in ganz Deutschland', *SZ*, 7.10.1991; 'Welle der Gewalt gegen Ausländer', *taz.*, 7.10.1991; 'Häßliche Details einer Brandnacht', *SZ*, 25.5.1992; Heribert Prantl, 'Parteitaktisches Lavieren im Rauch der Brandsätze', *SZ*, 10.11.1991; and 'Alle drei Wochen ein Toter', *Der Spiegel*, 36/1992, 31.8.1992.
56. According to Ulrich Beck, 'Biedermänner und Brandstifter', *Der Spiegel*, 46/1992, 9.11.1992.
57. Cf. Cords, ed., *Das Verfahren.*
58. As quoted in 'Pöbel auf den Straßen', *SZ*, 26.11.1992.
59. Bill jointly put forward by the Union, the SPD and the FPD, 19.1.1993 (*Deutscher Bundestag*, Drucksache 12/4152); 'Gesetz zur Änderung asylverfahrens-, ausländer- und staatsangehörigkeitsrechtlicher Vorschriften, 30.6.1993', BGBl.I, p. 1,062. Cf. Barwig, ed., *Entschädigung*; and 'Der neue Überfall auf Polen', *SZ*, 1.3.1993.
60. Röpke and Speit, *Blut und Ehre.*
61. See Gensing, *Terror.*
62. Address by Ministerialdirektor Eckart Schiffer, Hanns-Seidel-Stiftung, July 1991, reproduced in part in 'Ein Modebegriff geht um in Europa, die multikulturelle Gesellschaft', *FR*, 15.8.1991.

63. Niethammer, *Kollektive Identität*, pp. 482ff.
64. Radke, 'Multikulturalismus'.
65. On this subject, see Marsh, *Euro*, pp. 132–261; Schwarz, *Helmut Kohl*, pp. 710–16 and 797–818; Wirsching, *Preis der Freiheit*, pp. 153–91 and 241ff.; Knipping, *Rom*, pp. 256–96; Dyson and Featherstone, *Road to Maastricht*; Loth, *Helmut Kohl*; Gillingham, *European Integration*, pp. 228–58; Paul, *Zwangsumtausch*; Tietmeyer, *Herausforderung Euro*, pp. 142–266; Conze, *Suche*, pp. 860–72.
66. Chancellor Kohl's government declaration, in *Deutscher Bundestag, 12.WP, Plenarprotokoll 13.12.1991*, pp. 5,797–802.
67. Speech to the Federal Executive of the CDU on 20.2.1994, printed in Kohl, *Berichte*, p. 553.
68. Quoted in 'Es gibt kein Zurück', *Der Spiegel*, 50/1991, 9.12.1991.
69. Treaty of European Union ('Maastricht Treaty'), 7.2.1992, in Läufer, ed., *Europäische Gemeinschaft*.
70. Kohl, in an interview with *La Libre Belgique*, 22.11.1991, quoted in Rudolf Augstein, 'Abschied von der Mark?', *Der Spiegel*, 49/1991, 2.12.1991.
71. 'Es gibt kein Zurück', *Der Spiegel*, 50/1991, 9.12.1991.
72. Ingrid Matthäus-Maier (SPD), in *Deutscher Bundestag, 12.WP, Plenarprotokoll, 13.12.1991*, pp. 5,803–6.
73. Joschka Fischer (Alliance 90 -Greens), in *Deutscher Bundestag, 12.WP, Plenarprotokoll, 23.4.1998*, p. 21,077.
74. Federal Finance Minister Theo Waigel (CSU), in *Deutscher Bundestag, 12.WP, Plenarprotokoll, 13.12.1991*, pp. 5,817–19.
75. Count Lambsdorff (FDP), in *Deutscher Bundestag, 12.WP, Plenarprotokoll, 13.12.1991*, pp. 5,804–6.
76. Karl Schiller, 'Deutschland ohne DM? Plädoyer gegen die schnelle Verwirklichung einer europäischen Währung', *Der Spiegel*, 50/1991, 9.12.1991.
77. As quoted in Wolfgang Proissl and Christian Wernicke, 'Der Euro-Fighter', *Die Zeit*, 29.4.1998.
78. 'Es gibt kein Zuruck', *Der Spiegel*, 50/1991, 9.12.1991 (this issue bears the caption 'Fears for the Mark').
79. Rudolf Augstein, 'Neue Menschen, neue Menschen!', *Der Spiegel*, 18/1998, 27.4.1998.
80. *Urteil des BVerfGE 89,155*, 12 October 1993, printed in Hölscheidt and Schotten, *Von Maastricht nach Karlsruhe*, pp. 64–91; Gerhard Brunn, 'Die Ratifikation des Vertrages von Maastricht', in Brunn, ed., *Neoliberalismus*, pp. 57–80.
81. Tietmeyer, *Herausforderung*, pp. 173–212.
82. The remarks of Herzog and Juppé are quoted in 'Euro-Trip ins Ungewisse', *Der Spiegel*, 8/1997, 17.2.1997.
83. On this section, see Goldhagen, *Hitler's Willing Executioners*; Schoeps, ed., *Volk von Mördern?*; Michael Schneider, '"Goldhagen-Debatte"', pp. 67–83; Ulrich Herbert, 'Academic and Public Discourses', pp. 35–54.
84. Frank Ebbinghaus, 'Warum ganz normale Männer zu Tätern wurden', *Die Welt*, 27.4.1996, quoted in Schoeps, ed., *Volk von Mördern?*, pp. 140–6, here p. 140.

85. Klemperer, *Ich will Zeugnis ablegen bis zum letzten* (1995; English translation 1998–99); Reich-Ranicki, *Mein Leben* (1999; English translation 2001).
86. See Heimrod, ed., *Der Denkmalstreit*; Rosh and Jäckel, *Die Juden*; and Stavginski, *Holocaust-Denkmal.*
87. Frank Schirrmacher, ed., *Walser-Bubis-Debatte,* pp. 7–17. The quotation from Bubis is taken from 'SPD-Debatte mit Walser', in Spiegel-online, 8.5.2002, http://www.spiegel.de/politik/deutschland/spd-debatte-mit-walser-spiegels-moralkeule-gegen-den-kanzler-a-195295.html9 [11.4.2013].
88. Goschler, *Schuld und Schulden,* pp. 413–76; Mink, *Zwangsarbeiter*; Adamheit, *Deutsche Wirtschaft*; Borggräfe, *Entschädigung.*
89. See the section 'Compensation for the Victims of National Socialism' in Chapter 12 of this book.
90. For examples of this approach, see *GSWW*, vol. 4; Müller, *Hitlers Ostkrieg*; Wilhelm, *Rassenpolitik und Kriegsführung*; and Friedrich, *Gesetz des Krieges.*
91. See Heer et al., eds., *Verbrechen der Wehrmacht. Ausstellungskatalog*; Hartmann, Hürter and Jureit, *Verbrechen der Wehrmacht*; Hamburger Institut für Sozialforschung, ed., *Eine Ausstellung*; Prantl, *Wehrmachtsverbrechen*; Thiele, ed., *Wehrmachtsausstellung.*
92. Proske, *Wider den Missbrauch*; 'Wie Deutsche diffamiert werden', *Bayernkurier,* 22.2.1997.
93. Cf. Musial, 'Bilder einer Ausstellung'; Ungváry, 'Echte Bilder'.
94. Omer Bartov et al., 'Bericht der Kommission zur Überprüfung der Ausstellung "Vernichtungskrieg. Verbrechen der Wehrmacht 1941 bis 1944", November 2000', in http://www.hisonline.de//fileadmin/user_upload/pdf/veranstaltungen/Ausstellungen/Kommissionsbericht.pdf [25 July 2013].
95. Alfred Dregger (CDU), in *Deutscher Bundestag, 13.WP, Plenarprotokoll, 13.3.1997,* pp. 14,710–11, with unindicated omissions.
96. Otto Schily (SPD), in *Deutscher Bundestag, 13.WP, Plenarprotokoll, 13.3.1997,* pp. 14,714–15.
97. After the committee of historians had reached its conclusions, Reemtsma was commissioned to construct a new version of the exhibition. This opened in 2001, and while it went still further than the original version in its statements about the criminality of the Wehrmacht, it was more restrained in its mode of presentation and it entirely dispensed with the private photographs made by Wehrmacht soldiers during their period of service. This exhibition too met with an unfavourable reaction from the political Right, but there were no more criticisms of its character as history.
98. On this subject, see Stein, *Konzentrationslager Buchenwald.*
99. Ritscher, ed., *Speziallager*; Greiner, *Suppressed Terror.*
100. Härtl, ed., *Neukonzeption*; Niethammer, ed., *Antifaschismus*; Herf, *Divided Memory.*
101. On this, and on the next section, see Schroeder, *Die veränderte Republik,* pp. 352–64.
102. On this point, see Sabrow, ed., *Geschichte als Herrschaftsdiskurs.*
103. Schroeder, *Die veränderte Republik,* pp. 332–5; Sabrow et al., eds., *DDR-Erinnerung.*

## Chapter 22

1. Federal President Roman Herzog: 'Aufbruch ins 21.Jahrhundert', Berlin, 26.4.1997, in http://www.bundespraesident.de/SharedDocs/Reden/DE/Roman-Herzog/Reden/1997/04/19970426_Rede.html [5.12.2013].
2. See the section 'The End of the Social–Liberal Era' in Chapter 17 of this book. For Lambsdorff's Memorandum see Otto Graf Lambsdorff, 'Konzept für eine Politik zur Überwindung der Wachstumsschwäche und zur Bekämpfung der Arbeitslosigkeit, 9.9.1982', *Neue Bonner Depesche,* 9/82: Dokumentation. Online: http://www.freiheit.org/sites/default/files/uploads/2107/09/05/lambsdorff-papier.pdf [5.12.2013]. For Lahnstein's undated memorandum of 1982, see Abelshauser, *Deutsche Wirtschaftsgeschichte,* pp. 441ff., and Abelshauser, *Nach dem Wirtschaftswunder,* pp. 538–44.
3. *Datenreport 1992,* p. 110.
4. On '*Deutschland AG*', see Streeck and Höpner, eds., *Alle Macht dem Markt?*; Freye, *Führungswechsel.*
5. For the controversial concept and project of Neoliberalism, see Schui and Blankenburg, *Neoliberalismus*; Crouch, *Neoliberalism*; and Willgerodt, 'Neoliberalismus'.
6. 'Arbeit, Arbeit, Arbeit', *Der Spiegel,* 17/1997, 21.4.1997. See the summary in Steingart, *Deutschland.* As the editor, Gabor Steingart was the driving force behind *Der Spiegel*'s advocacy of a neoliberal economic policy during the 1990s.
7. See Brüggemeier, *Geschichte Großbritanniens,* pp. 309–46, and Pierson, *Dismantling the Welfare State.*
8. Wirsching, *Preis,* pp. 254ff.
9. Gerhard Igl, 'Die Entstehung der sozialen Pflegeversicherung und ihre Konsequenzen', in GSD, vol. 11, pp. 694–717.
10. Brüggemeier, *Geschichte Großbritanniens,* pp. 346–80; Ludlam and Smith, eds., *New Labour.*
11. Conze, *Suche nach Sicherheit,* pp. 798–807. See also the articles in Süß, ed., *Deutschland in den neunziger Jahren,* pp. 53–124.
12. 'Wie in einer Lotterie', *Der Spiegel,* 12/1999, 22.3.1999. On this subject, see also Arnoldi, *Geld.* and Henwood, *New Economy.*
13. 'Das Gute an der New-Economy-Blase', in *Financial Times Deutschland,* 10.3.2010, with unmarked omissions.
14. 'Die Bedürfnisse sind grenzenlos', *Der Spiegel,* 31/1998, 27.7.1998.
15. Prantl, *Rot-Grün,* p. 9.
16. On this subject, see also Conze, *Sicherheit,* pp. 798–819; Wolfrum, *Rot-Grun,* pp. 26–63; and Egle, Ostheim and Zohlnhöfer, eds., *Rot-grünes Projekt.*
17. See Franke, *Nato,* pp. 307–18.
18. On the Kosovo conflict, see Rathfelder, *Kosovo*; Chiari, ed., *Kosovo*; Friedrich, *Deutsche Außenpolitik*; Reuter and Clewing, *Kosovo-Konflikt*; Loquai, *Kosovo-Konflikt*; and Joetze, *Krieg in Europa.*
19. This follows Antje Vollmer, 'Moralische Nötigung', in *Spiegel Geschichte,* 2/2009, 31.3.2009, pp. 134–7. Cf. Fischer, *Rot-grüne Jahre,* pp. 104–8.

20. Gerhard Schröder, in *Deutscher Bundestag, 13.WP, Plenarprotokoll, 16.10.1998,* pp. 23,135–8.
21. Joetze, *Der letzte Krieg*, pp. 38–9.
22. Rudolf Augstein, 'Arroganz der Macht', *Der Spiegel,* 18/1999, 3.3.1999, p. 24.
23. Joschka Fischer, at the Bielefeld Party Congress of the Greens, quoted in Rathgeb, *Engagierte Nation,* pp. 415–16.
24. 'Milošević wird der Verlierer sein', an interview with Fischer, in *Der Spiegel,* 16/1990, 19.4.1999.
25. As quoted in Frank Schirrmacher, 'Luftkampf. Deutschlands Anteil am Krieg', *FAZ,* 17.4.1999, p. 41.
26. Schirrmacher, 'Luftkampf', p. 41, with unmarked omissions.
27. Jürgen Habermas, 'Bestialität und Humanität. Ein Krieg an der Grenze zwischen Recht und Moral', *Die Zeit,* 29.4.1999.
28. Ludger Volmer, in *Deutscher Bundestag, 13.WP, Plenarprotokoll, 16.10.1998,* pp. 23,151–2.
29. Reimut Zohlnhöfer, 'Rot-grüne Finanzpolitik zwischen traditioneller Sozialdemokratie und neuer Mitte', in Egle, Ostheim and Zohlnhöfer, eds., *Das rot-grüne Projekt,* pp. 193–214; Arne Heise, 'Innovation und Gerechtigkeit? Wirtschafts- und beschäftigungspolitische Modernisierungskonzepte der Schröder-Regierung', in Heyder, Menzel and Rebe, eds., *Das Land verändert,* pp. 29–45; Wolfrum, *Rot-Grün,* pp. 110–68.
30. Gerhard Schröder and Tony Blair, 'Weg nach vorne'.
31. Lafontaine, *Heart,* p. 124. In this context he refers to Anthony Giddens, author of *The Third Way,* the book which was in fact the source of the ideas put forward by Blair and Schröder.
32. Wolfrum, *Rot-Grun,* pp. 117ff. Otte, 'Finanzkrise'; Sinn, *Kasino-Kapitalismus,* pp. 15–43.
33. Lutz Mez, 'Ökologische Modernisierung und Vorreiterrolle in der Energie- und Umweltpolitik. Eine vorläufige Bilanz', in Egel, Ostheim and Zohlnhöfer, eds., *Das rot-grüne Projekt,* pp. 329–50; Reiche and Krebs, *Einstieg.*
34. Raschke, *Zukunft,* pp. 170–205; Wolfrum, *Rot-Grün,* pp. 230–45; Schneehain, *Atomausstieg.*
35. 'Der Traum geht nicht unter', an interview with Eric Hobsbawm, 27.12.1999, in *Der Spiegel,* 52/1999, pp. 144–8.
36. Cf. Hafner and Lyon, *Where Wizards.*
37. Resolution and Report of the Bundestag Investigating Committee on Party Donations, 13.6.2002, *Deutscher Bundestag, Drucksache 14/2139*; Matthias Krupa, 'Permanente Erregung. Helmut Kohl hat geschwiegen, Brigitte Baumeister geweint und Edmund Stoiber gewütet. Nach zweieinhalb Jahren beendet der Untersuchungsausschuss zur Parteispendenaffäre seine Arbeit', *Die Zeit,* 24/2002, 6 June 2002.
38. Crouch, *Post-democracy*; Jörke, 'Auf dem Weg'.
39. On this point, see Aust and Schnibben, eds., *11 September 2001*; Greiner, *9/11*; and Wright, *Looming Tower.*
40. Wolfrum, *Rot-Grün,* p. 544.

41. Wolfrum, *Rot-Grün,* pp. 528–83; Kindler, Regelmann and Tolney, eds., *Die Folgen der Agenda 2010.*
42. Wirsching, *Preis,* pp. 392–409; Beck and Wienert, 'Anatomie'; Sinn, *Kasino-Kapitalismus*; Enderlein, 'Krise'; Otte, 'Finanzkrise'.
43. 'Der Bankraub', *Der Spiegel,* 47/2008, 17.11.2008.

# Bibliography

## Section 1: Sources, Documents and Personal Accounts


Adenauer, Konrad, *Erinnerungen,* 4 vols., Stuttgart, 1965–8.

Adenauer, Konrad, *Teegespräche,* 2 vols., ed. by Hanns Jürgen Küsters, Berlin 1984–6.

Adenauer, Konrad, *'Es mußte alles neu gemacht werden'. Die Protokolle des CDU-Bundesvorstandes 1950–1953,* ed. by Günter Buchstab, Stuttgart, 1986.

Adenauer, Konrad, *'Wir haben wirklich etwas geschaffen.' Die Protokolle des CDU-Bundesvorstandes 1953–1957,* ed. By Günter Buchstab, Stuttgart, 1990.

Akten der Reichskanzlei, Regierung Hitler, *Die Regierung Hitler, Teil I, 1933/34,* ed. by K.H. Minuth, vol. 1, 30.1.-31.8.1933, Boppard, 1983.

Akten der Reichskanzlei, Weimarer Republik, ed. by Karl Dietrich Erdmann et al., *Das Kabinett Cuno,* ed. by K.H.Harbeck, Boppard, 1978; *Die Kabinette Brüning I and II,* ed. by T. Koops, 2 vols., Boppard, 1982; *Das Kabinet Schleicher,* ed. by A.Golekki, Boppard, 1986.

*Akten zur auswärtigen Politik der Bundesrepublik Deutschland,* ed. by Institut für Zeitgeschichte, Munich, 1989ff.

*Akten zur deutschen auswärtigen Politik: 1918–1945. Aus dem Archiv des Auswärtigen Amts,* Göttingen, 1950ff.

*Akten deutscher Bischöfe über die Lage der Kirche 1933–1945, Bd.6: 1943–1945,* ed. by Bernhard Stasiewski., Mainz, 1985.

*Akten Kardinal Michael von Faulhabers, Bd.2: 1935–1945,* ed. by Ludwig Volk, Mainz, 1978.

*Allensbacher Jahrbuch der Demoskopie, Bd.8, Allensbach 1978–1983,* Munich, 1983

*Allensbacher Jahrbuch der Demoskopie, Bd.9, Allensbach 1984–1992,* Munich, 1992.

*Allgemeiner Kongreß der Arbeiter- und Soldatenräte Deutschlands. Stenographische Berichte* Berlin, 1919.

Anweiler, Oskar, ed., *Bildungspolitik in Deutschland 1945–1990. Ein historisch-vergleichender Quellenband,* Bonn, 1992

Apel, Hans, *Der Abstieg 1978–1988. Politisches Tagebuch eines Jahrzehnts,* Stuttgart, 1990.

Baadte, Günter and Rauscher, Anton, eds., *Dokumente deutscher Bischöfe. Bd.1. Hirtenbriefe und Ansprachen zur Gesellschaft und Politik 1945–1949,* ed. by Wolfgang Löhr, 2nd edition, Würzburg, 1986.

Bargatzky, Walter, *Hotel Majestic. Ein Deutscher im besetzten Frankreich,* Freiburg, Basle and Vienna, 1987.

Berbig, Roland et al., eds., *In Sachen Biermann. Protokolle, Berichte und Briefe zu den Folgen einer Ausbürgerung*, Berlin, 1994.

Bihl, Wolfdieter, ed., *Deutsche Quellen zur Geschichte des Ersten Weltkrieges*, Darmstadt, 1991.

Binding, Karl and Hoche, Alfred, *Die Freigabe der Vernichtung lebensunwerten Lebens. Ihr Mass und ihre Form*, Leipzig, 1920.

Boelcke, Willi A., ed., *Wollt ihr den totalen Krieg? Die geheimen Goebbels-Konferenzen 1939–1943*, Stuttgart, 1967.

Bogoeva, Julija and Fetscher, Caroline, eds., *Srebrenica. Dokumente aus dem Verfahren gegen General Radislav Krstić vor dem Internationalen Strafgerichshof für das ehemaligen Jugoslawien in Den Haag*, Frankfurt am Main, 2002.

Borodziej, Włodzimierz and Lemberg, Hans, eds., *Die Deutschen östlich von Oder und Neiße 1945–1950. 'Unsere Heimat ist uns ein fremdes Land geworden.' Dokumente aus polnischen Archiven*, 4 vols., Marburg an der Lahn, 2000–2004.

Brandt, Willy, *My Life in Politics*, London, 1992.

Breloer, Heinrich, ed., *Geheime Welten. Deutsche Tagebücher aus den Jahren 1939 bis 1947*, Frankfurt am Main, 1999.

Broszat, Martin, Fröhlich, Elke, and Wiesemann, Falk, eds., *Bayern in der NS-Zeit. Soziale Lage und politisches Verhalten der Bevölkerung im Spiegel vertraulicher Berichte*, vol. 1, Munich and Vienna, 1977.

Bruyn, Günter de, *Vierzig Jahre. Ein Lebensbericht*, Frankfurt am Main, 1999.

Buchbender, Ortwin and Sterz, Reinhold, eds., *Das andere Gesicht des Krieges. Deutsche Feldpostbriefe 1939–1945*, Munich, 1982.

Bundesministerium für Arbeit und Soziales and André Steiner, *Statistische Übersichten zur Sozialpolitik in Deutschland zeit 1945 (Band SBZ/DDR)*, Bonn, 2006.

Bundesministerium für Innerdeutsche Beziehungen, ed., *Dokumente zur Deutschlandpolitik, begründet von Ernst Deuerlein*, Frankfurt am Main and Munich, 1961ff.

Bundesministerium für Innerdeutsche Beziehungen, ed., *Texte zur Deutschlandpolitik*, vol. 10, Bonn, 1972.

Cherniaev, Anatoly, *My Six Years With Gorbachev*, University Park, Pennsylvania, 2000.

Cords, Lars-Christian, ed., *Das Verfahren vor dem Oberlandesgericht Schleswig über die Anschläge in Mölln im November 1992: Dokumente und Eindrücke*, Kiel, 1994.

Delacor, Regina M., ed., *Attentate und Repressionen. Ausgewählte Dokumente zur zyklischen Eskalation des NS-Terrors im besetzten Frankreich 1941/42*, Stuttgart, 2000.

Department of State, ed., *Papers Relating to the Foreign Relations of the United States. The Paris Peace Conference 1919*, vol. 6, Washington, D.C., 1946.

*Deutsche Einheit. Sonderedition aus den Akten des Bundeskanzleramtes 1989/90*, ed. by Hanns Jürgen Küsters, Munich, 1998.

Deutscher Bundestag, ed., *Materialien der Enquête-Kommission 'Aufarbeitung der Geschichte und Folgen der SED-Diktatur in Deutschland', 12.WP des Deutschen Bundestages,* 9 vols., Baden-Baden, 1995.

Deutscher Bundestag, ed., *Protokolle der Volkskammer der Deutschen Demokratischen Republik, 1990,* Berlin, 2000.

Deutscher Bundestag, ed., *Zur Verjährung nationalsozialistischer Verbrechen. Dokumentation der parlamentarischen Bewältigung des Problems 1960–1979,* Bonn, 1980.

Deutscher Textilarbeiterverband, ed., *Mein Arbeitstag—mein Wochenende*, Berlin, 1931.

*Die Verfolgung und Ermordung der europäischen Juden durch das nationalsozialistische Deutschland,* 16 vols., Munich, 2008ff.

*Documents on British Foreign Policy 1919–1939,* Second Series, Volume IV, London, 1950.

*Documents on German Foreign Policy 1918–1945,* Series D (1937–45), vol. I, London, 1949.

Domarus, Max, *Hitler: Speeches and Proclamations, 1932–1945. The Chronicle of a Dictatorship,* 4 vols., London, 1990–2004.

Einsiedel, Heinrich Graf von, *The Shadow of Stalingrad: Being the Diary of a Temptation*, London, 1953.

Emminger, Otmar, *D-Mark, Dollar, Währungskrisen. Erinnerungen eines ehemaligen Bundesbankpräsidenten*, Stuttgart, 1986.

Erler, Peter, ed., *'Nach Hitler kommen wir.' Dokumente zum Programmatik der Moskauer KPD-Führung 1944–45 für Nachkriegsdeutschland*, Berlin, 1994.

Exilvorstand der Sozialdemokratischen Partei, ed., *Deutschland-Berichte,* Prague 1933–1940.

Fischer, Joschka, *Die rot-grünen Jahre. Deutsche Außenpolitik vom Kosovo bis zum 11.September*, Cologne, 2007.

Flechtheim, Ossip K, ed., *Dokumente zur parteipolitischen Entwicklung in Deutschland seit 1945. Programmatik der Deutschen Parteien*, vol.3, Berlin, 1965.

Fontane, Theodor, *Briefe an Georg Friedländer*, ed. by Kurt Schreinert, Heidelberg, 1954.

Freyer, Hans, *Theorie des gegenwärtigen Zeitalters*, Stuttgart 1955.

Goebbels, Joseph, *Der steile Aufstieg. Reden und Aufsätze aus den Jahren 1942/43,* Munich, 1944.

Goebbels, Joseph, *Die Tagebücher,* 32 vols., ed. by Elke Fröhlich, Munich 1993–2008.

Goebbels, Joseph, *Goebbels-Reden,* 2 vols., ed. by Helmut Heiber, Düsseldorf, 1971–2.

Gorbatschow, Michail, *Ausgewählte Reden und Aufsätze*, vol. 4, Berlin, 1988.

Grabitz, Helge and Scheffler, Wolfgang, *Letzte Spuren. Ghetto Warschau—SS- Arbeitslager Trawniki—Aktion Erntefest. Fotos und Dokumente über Opfer des Endlösungswahns im Spiegel der historischen Ereignisse*, Berlin, 1988.

Groscurth, Helmuth, *Tagebücher eines Abwehroffiziers 1938–1940*, ed. by Helmut Krausnick and Harold C.Deutsch, Stuttgart, 1970.

Gütt, Arthur, Rüdin, Ernst, and Ruttke, Falk, *Gesetz zur Verhütung erbkranken Nachwuchses vom 14.Juli 1933. Mit Auszug aus dem Gesetz gegen gefährliche Gewohnheitsverbrecher und über Maßregeln der Sicherung und Besserung vom 24.November 1933*, Munich, 1934.

Haenisch, Konrad, *Die deutsche Sozialdemokratie in und nach dem Weltkriege*, Berlin, 1916.

Hahn, Otto, *Mein Leben. Autobiographie*, Munich, 1969.

Halder, Franz, *The Halder War Diary, 1939–1942*, ed. by Charles Burdick and Hans-Adolf Jacobsen, Novato, California, 1988.

Hartmann, Christian, 'Massensterben oder Massenvernichtung? Sowjetische Kriegsgefangene im "Unternehmen Barbarossa." Aus dem Tagebuch eines deutschen Lagerkommandanten', *VfZ*, 49(2001), pp. 97–158.

Heiber, Helmut, ed., *Reichsführer! Briefe an und von Himmler*, Stuttgart, 1968.

Heinrici, Gotthard, *Ein deutscher General an der Ostfront. Die Briefe und Tagebücher des Gotthard Heinrici 1941/42*, ed. by Johannes Hürter, Erfurt, 2001.

Himmler, Heinrich, *Geheimreden 1933 bis 1945 und andere Ansprachen*, ed. by Bradley F.Smith, Frankfurt am Main and Berlin, 1974.

Hindenburg, Paul von, *Aus meinem Leben*, Leipzig, 1920.

Hitler, Adolf, *Der Führer antwortet Roosevelt. Reichstagsrede vom 28.April 1939*, Munich, 1939.

Hitler, Adolf, *Hitler's Second Book: the unpublished sequel to Mein Kampf*, ed. Gerhard L. Weinberg, New York, 2003.

Hitler, Adolf, *Mein Kampf*, translated by Ralph Manheim, London, 1969.

Hitler, Adolf, *Hitler's Table Talk 1941–1944*, translated by Norman Cameron and R.H. Stevens, London, 1953.

Holzman, Helene, *Dies Kind soll leben. Die Aufzeichnungen der Helene Holzman, 1941–1944*, ed. by Reinhard Kaiser and Margarete Holzman, Frankfurt am Main, 2000.

Hubatsch, Walther, ed., *Hitlers Weisungen für die Kriegführung 1939–1945. Dokumente des Oberkommandos der Wehrmacht*, Frankfurt am Main, 1962.

Ilsemann, Sigurd von, *Der Kaiser in Holland. Aufzeichnungen des letzten Flügeladjutanten Kaiser Wilhelms II*, vol. 1, Munich, 1967.

IMT (International Military Tribunal), *Trial of the Major War Criminals before the International Military Tribunal, Nuremberg, 14 November1945—1 October 1946*, 42 vols., Nuremberg, 1947–9.

*Jahresgutachten des Sachverständigenrats zur Begutachtung der gesamtwirtschaftlichen Entwicklung*, Wiesbaden, 1991–4.

Jourdan, Hans-Peter, ed., *Gegen den Krieg. Eine Dokumentation der Schülerinnenproteste gegen den Golfkrieg*, Herborn, 1991.

Jüdisches Historisches Institut Warschau, ed., *Faschismus, Getto, Massenmord. Dokumentation über Ausrottung und Widerstand der Juden in Polen während des Zweiten Weltkrieges, ausgewählt, bearbeitet und eingeleitet von Tatiana Berenstein, Artur Eisenbach, Bernard Mark und Adam Rutkowski*, Berlin, 1960.

Kaes, Anton, ed., *Weimarer Republik. Manifeste und Dokumente zur deutschen Literatur 1918–1933*, Stuttgart, 1983.

Kaiser, Jakob, *Wir haben Brücke zu sein. Reden, Äusserungen und Aufsätze zur Deutschlandpolitik*, Cologne, 1988.

Kardorff, Ursula von, *Berliner Aufzeichnungen. Aus den Jahren 1942 bis 1945*, Munich, 1962.

Kautsky, Karl, Montgelas, Max and Schücking, Walter, eds., *Die deutschen Dokumente zum Kriegsausbruch 1914*, Berlin, 1922.

Keller, Rolf, *Sowjetische Kriegsgefangene im Deutschen Reich 1941/42: Behandlung und Arbeitseinsatz zwischen Verrichtungspolitik und kriegswirtschaftlichen Erfordernissen*, Göttingen, 2011.

Kellermann, Hermann, ed., *Der Krieg der Geister. Eine Auslese deutscher und ausländischer Stimmen zum Weltkrieg 1914*, Weimar, 1915.

Kempowski, Walter, *Das Echolot. Barbarossa '41. Ein kollektives Tagebuch*, Munich, 2002.

Kindt, Werner, ed., *Grundschriften der deutschen Jugendbewegung*, Düsseldorf and Cologne, 1963.

Klarsfeld, Serge, *Vichy-Auschwitz. Die Zusammenarbeit der deutschen und französischen Behörden bei der 'Endlösung der Judenfrage' in Frankreich*, Nördlingen, 1989.

Klee, Ernst, ed., *Dokumente zur 'Euthanasie'*, Frankfurt am Main, 1985.

Klein, Peter, ed., *Die Einsatzgruppen in der besetzten Sowjetunion 1941–42. Die Tätigkeits- und Lageberichte des Chefs der Sicherheitspolizei und des SD*, Berlin, 1997.

Klemperer, Victor, *Ich will Zeugnis ablegen bis zum letzten. Tagebücher 1933–1945*, 8 vols., Berlin, 1995.

Klemperer, Victor, *I shall bear witness: the diaries of Victor Klemperer 1933–1941*, London, 1998.

Klemperer, Victor, *The Lesser Evil: the Diaries of Victor Klemperer 1945–1959*, London, 2003.

Klemperer, Victor, *To the Bitter End: the Diaries of Victor Klemperer 1941–1945*, London, 1999.

Klonovsky, Michael and Flocken, Jan von, *Stalins Lager in Deutschland 1945–1950. Dokumentation, Zeugenberichte*, Berlin and Frankfurt am Main, 1991.

Knowlton, James, and G.Truett Cates, *Forever in the Shadow of Hitler?: original documents of the Historikerstreit, the controversy concerning the singularity of the Holocaust*, Atlantic Highlands, NJ, 1993.

Könnemann, Erwin and Schulze, Gerhard, eds., *Der Kapp-Lüttwitz-Ludendorff-Putsch. Dokumente*, Munich, 2002.

Kogon, Eugen, Langbein, Hermann and Rückerl, Adalbert, eds., *Nazi Mass Murder. A Documentary History of the Use of Poison Gas,* New Haven, Conn., 1993.

Kohl, Helmut, *'Ich wollte Deutschlands Einheit'*, ed. by Kai Diekmann, Berlin, 1996.

Kohl, Helmut, *Berichte zur Lage 1989–1998. Der Kanzler und Parteivorsitzende im Bundesvorstand der CDU Deutschlands*, Düsseldorf, 2012.

Kulka, Otto D. and Jäckel, Eberhard, eds., *The Jews in the secret Nazi reports on popular opinion in Germany, 1933–1945,* New Haven, 2011.

Lafontaine, Oskar, *Das Herz schlägt links*, Munich, 1999.

Levi, Primo, *If This is a Man,* translated by Stuart Woolf, London, 1987.

Lipgens, Walter and Loth, Wilfried, eds., *Documents on the History of European Integration,* 4 vols., Berlin and New York, 1985–91.

Longerich, Peter, ed., *Die Ermordung der europäischen Juden. Eine umfassende Dokumentation des Holocaust 1941–1945*, Munich and Zürich, 1989.

Madajczyk, Czesław, ed., *Vom Generalplan Ost zum Generalsiedlungsplan. Dokumente,* Munich, 1994.

Ludendorff, Erich, ed., *Urkunden der Obersten Heeresleitung über ihre Tätigkeit 1916–18,* Berlin, 1920.

Mann, Thomas, *Tagebücher 1918–1921*, ed. by Peter de Mendelssohn, Frankfurt am Main, 1979.

Mason, Timothy W., ed., *Arbeiterklasse und Volksgemeinschaft. Dokumente und Materialien zur deutschen Arbeiterpolitik 1936–1939*, Opladen, 1975.

Materna, Ingo, ed., *Berichte des Berliner Polizeipräsidenten zur Stimmung und Lage der Bevölkerung in Berlin 1914–1918,* Weimar, 1987.

Meckel, Markus and Gutzeit, Martin, *Opposition in der DDR. Zehn Jahre kirchliche Friedensarbeit—kommentierte Quellentexte*, Cologne, 1994.

*Meldungen aus dem Reich. Die geheimen Lageberichte des Sicherheitsdienstes der SS, 1938–1945,* 17 vols., ed. by Heinz Boberach, Herrsching, 1984.

Menzel, Matthias, *Die Stadt ohne Tod. Berliner Tagebuch 1943/45*, Berlin, 1946.

Merritt, Anna J. and Merritt, Richard L., eds., *Public Opinion in Occupied Germany. The OMGUS Surveys 1945–1949,* Urbana, Chicago and London, 1970.

Michaelis, Herbert and Schraepler, Ernst, eds., *Ursachen und Folgen. Vom deutschen Zusammenbruch 1918 und 1945 bis zur staatlichen Neuordnung Deutschlands in der Gegenwart. Eine Urkunden und Dokumentensammlung zur Zeitgeschichte,* 26 vols., Berlin, 1958–79.

Michalka, Wolfgang and Niedhart, Gottfried, eds., *Deutsche Geschichte 1918–1933, Dokumente zur Innen- und Außenpolitik*, Frankfurt am Main, 1992.

Michalka, Wolfgang, ed., *Das Dritte Reich,* 2 vols., Munich, 1985.

Moltke, Helmuth von, *Erinnerungen, Briefe, Dokumente 1877–1916*, Stuttgart, 1922.

Müller, Georg Alexander von, *Der Kaiser . . . Aufzeichnungen des Chefs des Marinekabinetts über die Ära Wilhelms II*, Göttingen, 1965.

Nevermann, Knut, ed., *Der 2. Juni 1967. Studenten zwischen Notstand und Demokratie. Dokumente zu den Ereignissen anläßlich des Schah-Besuchs*, Cologne, 1967.

Noelle, Elisabeth and Neumann, Erich Peter, eds., *Jahrbuch der öffentlichen Meinung, 1947–1955,* Allensbach, 1974.

Obenaus, Herbert and Obenaus, Sybille, eds., *'Schreiben, wie es wirklich war.' Die Aufzeichnungen Karl Dürkefäldens aus der Zeit des Nationalsozialismus*, Hanover, 1985.

Oncken, Hermann, *Nation und Geschichte. Reden und Aufsätze 1919–1935*, Berlin, 1935.

Otto, Karl A., ed., *APO. Außerparlamentarische Opposition in Quellen und Dokumenten (1960–1970)*, Cologne, 1989.

Pätzold, Kurt, ed., *Verfolgung, Vertreibung, Vernichtung. Dokumente des faschistischen Antisemitismus 1933 bis 1942*, Leipzig, 1983.

Piotrowski, Stanisław, ed., *Hans Frank's Diary*, Warsaw, 1961.

Przybylski, Peter, *Tatort Politbüro. Die Akte Honecker*, Berlin, 1991.

Rathenau, Walter, *Briefe*, 2 vols., Dresden, 1926.

Rathgeb, Eberhard, ed., *Die engagierte Nation. Deutsche Debatten 1945–2005*, Munich, 2005.

Reich-Ranicki, Marcel, *The Author of Himself: the life of Marcel Reich-Ranicki*, London, 2001.

Reich-Ranicki, Marcel, *Mein Leben*, Stuttgart, 1999.

Rhode, Gotthold and Wagner, Wolfgang, *The Genesis of the Oder-Neisse Line in the Diplomatic Negotiations during World War II: Sources and Documents*, Stuttgart, 1959.

Ribbentrop, Joachim von and Ribbentrop, Annelies von, *Zwischen London und Moskau. Erinnerungen und letzte Aufzeichnungen. Aus dem Nachlass*, Leoni, 1961.

Richert, Dominik, *The Kaiser's Reluctant Conscript. My Experiences in the War 1914–1918*, Barnsley, 2012.

Riezler, Kurt, *Tagebücher, Aufsätze, Dokumente*, Göttingen, 1972.

Roehm, Ernst, 'SA und deutsche Revolution', *Nationalsozialistische Monaftshefte*, 4 (June 1933).

Röhr, Werner, ed., *Die faschistische Okkupationspolitik in Polen 1939–1945*, Cologne, 1989.

Rosenberg, Alfred, *Das politische Tagebuch Alfred Rosenbergs. Aus den Jahren 1934/35 und 1939/40*, ed. by Hans-Günther Seraphim, Göttingen, 1956.

Roth, Karl Heinz, and Ebbinghaus, Angelika, 'Vorläufer des "Generalplans Ost." Eine Dokumentation über Theodor Schieders Polendenkschrift vom 7.Oktober 1939', *1999. Zeitschrift für Sozialgeschichte des 20. und 21.Jahrhunderts*, 7.1 (1992), pp. 62–94.

Rürup, Reinhard, ed., *Topography of Terror: Gestapo, SS and Reichssicherheitshauptamt on the 'Prinz-Albrecht-Terrain': a Documentation*, Berlin, 1989.

Schabowski, Günter, *Der Absturz*, Berlin, 1991.

Schirrmacher, Frank, ed., *Die Walser-Bubis-Debatte. Eine Dokumentation*, Frankfurt am Main, 1999.

Schlesinger, Arthur M., ed., *The Dynamics of World Power. A Documentary History of United States Foreign Policy 1945–1973, volume 1, Western Europe*, New York, 1973.

Schmidt, Helmut, *Men and Powers: a Political Retrospective* New York, 1989

Schmidt, Helmut, *Menschen und Mächte*, 2 vols., Berlin, 1988–90.

Schmidt, Paul, *Statist auf diplomatischer Bühne*, Bonn, 1949.

Shirer, William L., *Berlin Diary: the journal of a foreign correspondent 1934–1941*, London, 1941.

Statistisches Bundesamt, ed., *Bevölkerung und Wirtschaft 1872–1972*, Stuttgart and Mainz, 1972.

Statistisches Bundesamt, ed., *Datenreport 1985. Zahlen und Fakten uber die Bundesrepublik Deutschland*, Bonn, 1985.

Statistisches Bundesamt, ed., *Datenreport 1992. Zahlen und Fakten uber die Bundesrepublik Deutschland*, Bonn, 1992.

Statistisches Bundesamt, ed., *Datenreport 1997. Zahlen und Fakten uber die Bundesrepublik Deutschland*, Bonn, 1997.

Stephan, Gerd-Rüdiger and Küchenmeister, Daniel, eds., *'Vorwärts immer, rückwärts nimmer!' Interne Dokumente zum Zerfall von SED und DDR 1988/89*, Berlin, 1994.

Stephen, Gerd-Rüdiger and Küchenmeister, Daniel, eds., *Honecker-Gorbatschow. Vieraugengespräche*, Berlin, 1993.

Stresemann, Gustav, *Vermächtnis. Von Thoiry bis zum Ausklang*, vol. 3, Berlin, 1933.

Suckut, Siegfried, ed., *Blockpolitik in der SBZ, DDR 1945–1949. Die Sitzungsprotokolle des Zentralen Einheitsfront-Ausschusses. Quellenedition*, Cologne, 1986.

*Tagung des Politischen Beratenden Ausschusses der Teilnehmerstaaten des Warschauer Vertrages*, Berlin, 1989.

Teltschik, Horst, *329 Tage. Innenansichten der Einigung*, Berlin, 1991.

Tirpitz, Alfred von, *Erinnerungen*, Leipzig, 1919.

Treue, Wilhelm, ed., *Deutschland in der Weltwirtschaftskrise in Augenzeugenberichten*, Düsseldorf, 1967.

Treue, Wilhelm, 'Hitlers Denkschrift zum Vierjahresplan 1936', *VfZ* 3 (1955), pp. 184–210.

Trevor-Roper, Hugh Redwald and Hubatsch, Walter, eds., *Hitler's War Directives 1939–1945*, London, 1964.

Ulrich, Bernd and Ziemann, Benjamin, eds., *Frontalltag im Ersten Weltkrieg. Wahn und Wirklichkeit. Quellen und Dokumenten*, Frankfurt am Main, 1994.

*Verhandlungen des Deutschen Bundestages. Stenographische Berichte*, Berlin, 1950ff.

Vollnhals,Clemens, ed., *Entnazifizierung. Politische Säuberung und Rehabilitierung in den vier Besatzungszonen 1945–1949*, Munich 1991.

Wagenbach, Klaus, ed., *Vaterland, Muttersprache. Deutsche Schriftsteller und ihr Staat seit 1945*, Berlin, 1979.

Weber, Hermann, ed., *DDR. Dokumente zur Geschichte der Deutschen Demokratischen Republik 1945–1985*, Munich, 1987.

Weizsäcker, Ernst von, and Hill, Leonidas E., *Die Weizsäcker-Papiere 1933–1950,* 2 vols., Berlin, Frankfurt am Main and Vienna, 1974–82.

Wildt, Michael, ed., *Die Judenpolitik des SD 1935 bis 1938. Eine Dokumentation*, Munich, 1995.

Zentralstelle für Volkswohlfahrt, ed., *Deutsche Reden in schwerer Zeit*, Berlin, 1914.

Zweig, Stefan, *The World of Yesterday*, London,, 1943.

## Section 2: Literature

Abelshauser, Werner, ed., *Die Weimarer Republik als Wohlfahrtsstaat*, Stuttgart, 1987.

Abelshauser, Werner, *Deutsche Wirtschaftsgeschichte seit 1945*, Munich, 2004.

Abelshauser, Werner, *Nach dem Wirtschaftswunder. Der Gewerkschafter, Politiker und Unternehmer Hans Matthöfer*, Berlin and Bonn, 2009.

Abelshauser, Werner, *Wirtschaftsgeschichte der Bundesrepublik Deutschland 1945–1980*, Frankfurt am Main, 1983.

Ackermann, Volker, *Der 'echte' Flüchtling. Deutsche Vertriebene und Flüchtlinge aus der DDR 1945–1961*, Osnabrück, 1995.

Adam, Uwe Dietrich, *Judenpolitik im Dritten Reich*, Düsseldorf, 1972.

Adamheit, Ulrich, *Jetzt wird die Deutsche Wirtschaft von ihrer Geschichte eingeholt. Die Diskussion um die Entschädigung ehemaliger Zwangsarbeiter am Ende des 20. Jahrhunderts*, Berlin, 2004.

Afflerbach, Holger, *Der Dreibund,* Vienna, Cologne, and Weimar, 2002.

Afflerbach, Holger, *Falkenhayn*, Munich, 1994.

Afflerbach, Holger, 'Mit wehender Fahne untergehen. Kapitulationsverweigerungen in der deutschen Marine', *VfZ* 49.4 (2001), pp. 595–612.

Agde, Günter, *Kahlschlag. Das 11.Plenum des ZK der SED 1965*, Berlin, 1991.

Albrecht, Clemens, Behrmann, Günter C. and Bock, Michael, *Die intellektuelle Gründung der Bundesrepublik. Eine Wirkungsgeschichte des Frankfurter Schule*, Frankfurt am Main and New York, 1999.

Albrecht, Willy, ed., *Die SPD unter Kurt Schumacher und Erich Ollenhauer 1946 bis 1963. Sitzungsprotokolle der Spitzengremien*, vol.1, Berlin and Bonn, 2000.

Aldcroft, Derek H., *From Versailles to Wall Street, 1919–1929*, London: Allen Lane, 1977.

Allen, Michael Thad, *The Business of Genocide. The SS, Slave Labor, and the Concentration Camps,* Chapel Hill, NC and London, 2002.

Allerbeck, Klaus R. and Hoag, Wendy, *Jugend ohne Zukunft? Einstellungen, Umwelt, Lebensperspektiven*, Munich and Zürich, 1986.

Aly, Götz, ed., *Aktion T 4 1939–1945. Die 'Euthanasie'-Zentrale in der Tiergartenstraße 4*, Berlin, 1987.

Aly, Götz, ed., *Volkes Stimme. Skepsis und Führervertrauen im Nationalsozialismus*, Bonn, 2006.

Aly, Götz, *'Final Solution': Nazi Population Policy and the Murder of the European Jews*, London, 1999.

Aly, Götz, *Die Belasteten. 'Euthanasie' 1939–1945. Eine Gesellschaftsgeschichte*, Frankfurt am Main, 2003.

Aly, Götz, *Hitler's Beneficiaries: How the Nazis Bought the German People*, London, 2007.

Aly, Götz, *Why the Germans? Why the Jews?: Envy, Race Hatred, and the Prehistory of the Holocaust*, New York, 2014.

Aly, Götz and Heim, Susanne, *Architects of Annihilation. Auschwitz and the Logic of Destruction*, Princeton N.J., 2002.

Aly, Götz and Roth, Karl Heinz, *The Nazi Census. Identification and Control in the Third Reich,* Philadelphia, Pa., 2004.

Amirpur, Katajun and Witzke, Reinhard, *Schauplatz Iran. Ein Report,* Freiburg im Breisgau, 2004.

Andersen, Arne, *Der Traum vom guten Leben. Alltags- und Konsumgeschichte vom Wirtschaftswunder bis heute*, Frankfurt am Main and New York, 1997.

Anderson, Benedict R., *Imagined Communities. Reflections on the Origin and Spread of Nationalism*, London, 1986.

Anderson, Perry, *A Zone of Engagement*, London, 1992.

Anderson, Terry H., *The Movement and the Sixties*, New York and Oxford, 1995.

Angress, Werner T., *Stillborn Revolution: the communist bid for power in Germany, 1921–1923*, Princeton: Princeton University Press, 1963.

Anthony, Gene, *Summer of Love. Haight-Ashbury at its Highest,* Millbrae, California, 1980.

Anz, Thomas and Stark, Michael, eds., *Expressionismus: Manifeste und Dokumente zur deutschen Literatur 1910–1920*, Stuttgart: Metzler, 1982.

Anz, Thomas and Stark, Michael, eds., *Die Modernität des Expressionismus*, Stuttgart and Weimar, 1994.

Anz, Thomas and Vogl, Joseph, eds., *Die Dichter und der Krieg*, Munich and Vienna, 1987.

Arad, Yitzhak, *Belzec, Sobibor, Treblinka. The Operation Reinhard Death Camps*, Bloomington, Indiana, 1987.

ARD-Fernsehen, *Jahresrückblick 30.12.1988: 'Günstige Wirtschaftslage'.*

Arendes, Cord, ed., *Terror nach Innen. Verbrechen am Ende des Zweiten Weltkrieges*, Göttingen, 2006.

Arnold, Klaus Jochen, 'Die Eroberung und Behandlung der Stadt Kiew durch die Wehrmacht im September 1941. Zur Radikalisierung der Besatzungspolitik', *MGM*, 58 (1999), pp. 23–66.

Arnoldi, Jakob, *Alles Geld verdampft. Finanzkrise in der Weltrisikogesellschaft*, Frankfurt am Main, 2009.

Atzert, Thomas, ed., *Küss den Boden der Freiheit. Texte der Neuen Linken*, Berlin and Amsterdam, 1992.

Aubin, Hermann and Zorn, Wolfgang, eds., *Handbuch der deutschen Wirtschafts- und Sozialgeschichte*, 2 vols., Stuttgart, 1976.

Aulenbacher, Brigitte, ed., *Transformationen im Geschlechterverhältnis. Beiträge zur industriellen und gesellschaftlichen Entwicklung*, Frankfurt am Main and New York, 1993.

Aust, Stefan, *The Baader-Meinhof Complex*, London, 2008.

Aust, Stefan and Burgdorff, Stephan, eds., *Die Flucht. Über die Vertreibung der Deutschen aus den Osten*, Stuttgart and Munich, 2002.

Axen, Hermann, *Ich war ein Diener der Partei. Autobiographische Gespräche mit Harald Neubert*, Berlin, 1996.

Ayaß, Wolfgang, *'Asoziale' im Nationalsozialismus*, Stuttgart, 1995.

Baacke, Dieter, *Beat—die sprachlose Opposition*, Munich, 1970.

Baberowski, Jörg, 'Criticism as Crisis, or Why the Soviet Union Still Collapsed', *JMEH* (2011), pp. 148–66.

Bachmann, Ursula, *Reichskasse und öffentlicher Kredit in der Weimarer Republik 1924–1932*, Frankfurt am Main, 1996.

Backes, Uwe, et al., *Reichstagsbrand. Aufklärung einer historischen Legende*, Munich and Zürich, 1986.

Bade, Klaus J., *Ausländer—Aussiedler—Asyl. Eine Bestandsaufnahme*, Munich, 1994.

Bade, Klaus J., *Migration in European History*, Oxford, 2003.

Bade, Klaus J., *Vom Auswanderungsland zum Einwanderungsland?* Berlin, 1983.

Bade, Klaus J., Münz, Rainer and Bommes, Michael, eds., *Migrationsreport 2000. Fakten, Analysen, Perspektiven*, Bonn, 2000.

Bahr, Egon, *Sicherheit für und vor Deutschland. Vom Wandel durch Annäherung zur Europäischen Sicherheitsgemeinschaft*, Munich and Vienna, 1991.

Bahr, Egon, *Was wird aus den Deutschen? Fragen und Antworten*, Reinbek bei Hamburg, 1982.

Bähr, Johannes and Banken, Ralf, eds., *Wirtschaftssteuerung durch Recht im Nationalsozialismus. Studien zur Entwicklung des Wirtschaftsrechts im Interventionsstaat des 'Dritten Reichs'*, Frankfurt am Main, 2006.

Bahrmann, Hannes and Links, Christoph, eds., *Am Ziel vorbei. Die deutsche Einheit—eine Zwischenbilanz*, Berlin, 2005.

Bahro, Rudolf, *The Alternative in Eastern Europe*, London, 1978.

Baier, Lothar et al., *'Ich will reden von der Angst meines Herzens', Autorinnen und Autoren zum Golfkrieg*, Frankfurt am Main, 1991.

Bajohr, Frank and Pohl, Dieter, *Der Holocaust als offenes Geheimnis. Die Deutschen, die NS-Führung und die Allierten*, Munich, 2006.

Bajohr, Frank, *'Aryanization' in Hamburg: the Economic Exclusion of Jews and the Confiscation of their Property in Nazi Germany*, Oxford, 2002.

Bajohr, Frank, *Parvenüs und Profiteure. Korruption in der NS-Zeit*, Frankfurt am Main, 2001.

Bajohr, Frank, 'Verfolgung aus gesellschaftsgeschichtlicher Perspektive. Die wirtschaftliche Existenzvernichtung der Juden und die deutsche Gesellschaft', *GG* 26 (2000), pp. 629–52.

Bajohr, Frank, Johe, Werner and Lohalm, Uwe, eds., *Zivilisation und Barbarei. Die widersprüchlichen Potenziale der Moderne*, Hamburg, 1991.

Bajohr, Frank and Strupp, Christoph, *Fremde Blicke auf das 'Dritte Reich'. Berichte ausländischer Diplomaten über Herrschaft und Gesellschaft in Deutschland 1933–1945*, Göttingen, 2012.

Bajohr, Frank and Szodrzynski, Joachim, eds., Hamburg *in der NS-Zeit. Ergebnisse neuerer Forschungen*, Hamburg, 1995.

Bajohr, Frank and Wildt, Michael, eds., *Volksgemeinschaft. Neue Forschungen zur Gesellschaft des Nationalsozialismus*, Frankfurt am Main, 2009.

Balcar, Jaromir, *Politik auf dem Land. Studien zur bayerischen Provinz 1945 bis 1972*, Munich, 2004.

Bald, Detlef, *Die Atombewaffnung der Bundeswehr. Militär, Öffentlichkeit und Politik in der Ära Adenauer*, Bremen, 1994.

Bald, Detlef, *Die Bundeswehr. Eine kritische Geschichte 1955–2005*, Munich, 2005.

Balderston, Theo, *The Origins and Course of the German Economic Crisis November 1923 to May 1932*, Berlin, 1993.

Balsen, Werner and Rössel, Karl, *Hoch die internationale Solidarität. Zur Geschichte der Dritte-Welt-Bewegung in der Bundesrepublik*, Cologne, 1986.

Bankier, David, *The Germans and the Final Solution: public opinion under Nazism*, Oxford, 1996.

Baranowski, Shelley, *Strength Through Joy. Consumerism and Mass Tourism in the Third Reich*, Cambridge, 2004.

Barkai, Avraham, *From Boycott to Annihilation: the Economic Struggle of German Jews, 1933–1943*, London, 1989.

Barkai, Avraham, Mendes-Flohr, Paul and Lowenstein, Steven M., *Renewal and Destruction 1918–1945* (German-Jewish History in Modern Times, vol. 4), New York, 1998.

Barker, Ernest, *Why We Are at War*, Oxford, 1914.

Bartels, Daghild, '"Design-Mythos"', *Kursbuch* 106 (December 1991), pp. 1–8.

Bartov, Omer, *Hitler's Army: soldiers, Nazis and war in the Third Reich*, Oxford, 1991.

Barwig, Klaus, ed., *Entschädigung für NS-Zwangsarbeit. Rechtliche, historische und politische Aspekte*, Baden-Baden, 1998.

Barzilai, Gad, Klieman, Aharon and Shidlo, Gil, eds., *The Gulf Crisis and Its Global Aftermath*, London, 1993.

Bauer, Fritz et al., eds., *Sexualität und Verbrechen*, Frankfurt am Main, 1963.

Bauer, Georg, 'Jugend klagt an', *Das Freie Wort*, 3/19 (1913).

Baumann, Michael, *Wie alles anfing*, Munich, 1975.

Baumeister, Martin, and Schüler-Springorum, Stefanie, *'If you tolerate this . . .'. The Spanish Civil War in the Age of Total War*, Frankfurt am Main and New York, 2008.

Baumgart, Winfried, *Deutsche Ostpolitik 1918. Von Brest-Litowsk bis zum Ende des Ersten Weltkrieges*, Munich and Vienna, 1966.

Bavaj, Riccardo, *Von links gegen Weimar. Linkes antiparlamentarisches Denken in der Weimarer Republik*, Berlin and Bonn, 2005.

Becher, Johannes R., *Gesammelte Werke*, ed. by Johannes-R-Becher-Archiv der Deutschen Akademie der Künste in Berlin, 18 vols., Berlin and Weimar, 1966–81.

Beck, Earl R., *Under the Bombs. The German Home Front*, Lexington, 1986.

Beck, Hanno and Wienert, Helmut, 'Anatomie der Weltwirtschaftskrise. Ursachen und Schuldige', *APuZ* 20/2009, pp. 7–12.

Beck, Ulrich, *Risikogesellschaft. Auf dem Weg in eine andere Moderne*, Frankfurt am Main, 2007.

Becker, Frank, ed., *Mythos USA*, Frankfurt am Main and New York, 2006.

Becker, Frank, *Amerikanismus in Weimar. Sportsymbole und politische Kultur 1918–1933*, Wiesbaden, 1993.

Becker, Frank, *Den Sport gestalten. Carl Diems Leben (1882–1962). Weimarer Republik*, vol. 2, Duisburg, 2011.

Becker, Jean-Jacques, *Histoire politique de la France depuis 1945*, Paris, 2008.

Becker, Josef and Becker, Ruth, eds., *Hitlers Machtergreifung 1933. Vom Machtantritt Hitlers 30.Januar 1933 bis zur Besiegelung des Einparteienstaates 14.Juli 1933*, Munich, 1983.

Becker, Peter Emil, *Sozialdarwinismus, Rassismus, Antisemitismus und völkischer Gedanke*, Stuttgart and New York, 1990.

Bell, Daniel, *The Coming of Post-Industrial Society. A Venture in Social Forecasting*, New York, 1973.

Bell, Daniel, *The End of Ideology. (On the exhaustion of political ideas in the Fifties.)*, New York, 1960.

Beltran, Alain, Frank, Robert and Rousso, Henry, eds., *La vie des entreprises sous l'Occupation. Une enquête à l'échelle locale*, Paris, 1994.

Ben-David, Joseph, *The Scientist's Role in Society. A Comparative Study*, Englewood Cliffs, New Jersey, 1971.

Bender, Peter, *Episode oder Epoche? Zur Geschichte des geteilten Deutschland*, Munich, 1996.

Bender, Peter, *Neue Ostpolitik. Vom Mauerbau zum Moskauer Vertrag*, Munich, 1986.

Benn, Gottfried, *Gesammelte Werke in acht Bänden*, ed. by Dieter Wellershoff, Munich, 1975.

Benz, Ute, ed., *Sozialisation und Traumatisierung. Kinder in der Zeit des Nationalsozialismus*, Frankfurt am Main, 1992.

Benz, Wolfgang, ed., *Deutschland unter allierter Besatzung 1945–1949*, Berlin, 1999.

Benz, Wolfgang, ed., *Dimension des Völkermords. Die Zahl der jüdischen Opfer des Nationalsozialismus*, Munich, 1996.

Benz, Wolfgang et al., eds., *Instrumentarium der Macht*, Berlin, 2003.

Benz, Wolfgang, *Potsdam 1945. Besatzungsherrschaft und Neuaufbau im Vier-Zonen-Deutschland*, Munich, 1986.

Benz, Wolfgang and Bergmann, Werner, eds., *Vorurteil und Völkermord*, Freiburg im Breisgau, Basle and Vienna, 1997.

Benz, Wolfgang and Distel, Barbara, eds., *Herrschaft und Gewalt. Frühe Konzentrationslager 1933–1939*, Berlin, 2002.

Benz, Wolfgang, Houwink ten Cate, Johannes and Otto, Gerhard, eds., *Anpassung-Kollaboration-Widerstand. Kollektive Reaktionen auf die Okkupation*, Berlin, 1996.

Berg, Christa, ed., *Handbuch der deutschen Bildungsgeschichte. Von der Reichsgründung bis zum Ende des Ersten Weltkrieges 1870–1918*, vol. 4, Munich, 1991.

Berg, Nicolas, *The Holocaust and the West German historians: historical interpretation and autobiographical memory*, Madison, Wisconsin, 2015.

Berger, Helge and Ritschl, Albrecht, 'Die Rekonstruktion der Arbeitsteilung in Europa. Eine neue Sicht des Marshallplans in Deutschland', *VfZ* 45 (1995), pp. 473–519.

Berger, Sara, *Experten der Vernichtung. Das T4-Reinhardt-Netzwerk in den Lagern Belzec, Sobibor und Treblinka*, Hamburg, 2013.

Berghahn, Volker R., *Der Erste Weltkrieg*, Munich, 2003.

Berghahn, Volker R. and Deist, Wilhelm, *Rüstung im Zeichen der wilhelminischen Weltpolitik*, Düsseldorf, 1988.

Berghahn, Volker R., and Vitols, Sigurt, eds., *Gibt es einen deutschen Kapitalismus? Tradition und globale Perspektiven der sozialen Marktwirtschaft*, Frankfurt am Main and New York, 2006.

Bergmann, Klaus, *Agrarromantik und Großstadtfeindschaft*, Meisenheim am Glan, 1970.

Bergmann, Nicole, *Volkszählung und Datenschutz. Proteste zur Volkszählung 1983 und 1987 in der Bundesrepublik Deutschland*, Hamburg, 2009.

Bergmann, Uwe et al., *Rebellion der Studenten oder Die neue Opposition. Eine Analyse*, Reinbek bei Hamburg, 1968.

Bergmann, Werner, *Geschichte des Antisemitismus*, Munich, 2004.

Bergmann, Werner and Erb, Rainer, eds., *Antisemitismus in der politischen Kultur nach 1945*, Opladen, 1990.

Berliner Geschichtswerkstatt, *Projekt Spurensicherung. Alltag und Widerstand im Berlin der 30er Jahre*, Berlin, 1983.

Bernecker, Walther L., *Geschichte Spaniens im 20. Jahrhundert*, Munich, 2010.

Bernhardi, Friedrich von, *Deutschland und der nächste Krieg*, Stuttgart and Berlin, 1912.

Berstein, Serge, Rémond, Réné and Sirinelli, Jean-François, eds., *Les années Giscard. Institutions et pratiques politiques (1974–1978)*, Paris, 2003.

Bertram, Hans, ed., *Die Familie in Westdeutschland. Stabilität und Wandel familialer Lebensformen*, Opladen, 1991.

Bessel, Richard, *Germany 1945*, London and New York, 2009.

Bessel, Richard and Schumann, Dirk, eds., *Life After Death. Approaches to a Cultural and Social History of Europe During the 1940s and 1950s*, Washington, DC, 2003.

Beßlich, Barbara, *Wege in den 'Kulturkrieg'*, Darmstadt, 2000.

Best, Werner, 'Die Geheime Staatspolizei', *Deutsches Recht* 6 (1936), pp. 125–8.

Best, Werner, 'Nochmals: Völkische Großraumordnung statt: "Völkerrechtliche" Großraumordnung', *Deutsches Recht*, 11 (1941), pp. 1,533–4.

Best, Werner, 'Rechtsbegriff und "Völkerrecht"', *Deutsches Recht* 9 (1939), pp. 1,345–8.

Best, Wilhelm, 'Unter französischer Herrschaft in Mainz', *Volk und Scholle* 9 (1931), pp. 88–94 and 162–7.

Beyme, Klaus von and Berger, Hans, eds., *Neue Städte aus Ruinen. Deutscher Städtebau der Nachkriegszeit*, Munich, 1992.

Bienert, Michael, *Die eingebildete Metropole. Berlin im Feuilleton der Weimarer Republik*, Stuttgart, 1992.

Bierling, Stephan G., *Die Außenpolitik der Bundesrepublik Deutschland. Normen, Akteure, Entscheidungen*, Munich and Vienna, 2005.

Biermann, Wolf, 'Die hab' ich satt!', in Biermann, Wolf, *Chausseestraße 131*, Berlin, 1969.

Biermann, Wolf, *Die Drahtharfe. Balladen, Gedichte, Lieder*, Berlin, 1965.

Bierwirth, Waltraud, ed., *Schmelzpunkte Stahl. Krise und Widerstand im Revier*, Essen, 1988.

Biess, Frank and Moeller, Robert G., eds., *Histories of the Aftermath. The Legacies of the Second World War in Europe*, New York and Oxford, 2010.

Bittner, Thomas, *Das westeuropäische Wirtschaftswachstum nach dem Zweiten Weltkrieg. Eine Analyse unter besonderer Berücksichtigung der Planification und der sozialen Marktwirtschaft*, Münster etc., 2001.

Blackbourn, David and Evans, Richard J., eds., *The German Bourgeoisie. Essays on the Social History of the German Middle Class From the Late Eighteenth to the Early Twentieth Century*, London and New York, 1993.

Blaich, Fritz, *Der Schwarze Freitag. Inflation und Wirtschaftskrise*, Munich, 1990.

Blank, Theodor, 'Eine Million Gastarbeiter', *Bulletin des Presse- und Informationsamtes der Bundesregierung*, 30.10.1964, no. 160, p. 1,480.

Blaschke, Olaf, ed., *Konfessionen im Konflikt. Deutschland zwischen 1800 und 1970: Ein zweites konfessionelles Zeitalter*, Göttingen, 2002.

Blasius, Dirk, *Ehescheidung in Deutschland 1794–1945*, Göttingen, 1987.

Blasius, Dirk, *Ehescheidung in Deutschland im 19. und 20.Jahrbundert*, Frankfurt am Main, 1992.

Blasius, Jörg and Dangschat, Jens S., eds., *Gentrification. Die Aufwertung innenstadtnaher Wohnviertel*, Frankfurt am Main and New York, 1990.

Blatman, Daniel, *The Death Marches. The Final Phase of Nazi Genocide*, London, 2011.

Bloch, Ernst, *The Principle of Hope*, vol. 2, Oxford, 1986.

Boberg, Jochen, Fichter, Tilman and Gillen, Eckhart, eds., *Die Metropole*, Munich, 1986.

Bock, Gisela, *Women in European History*, Oxford, 2002.

Bock, Gisela, 'Rassenpolitik, Medizin und Massenmord im Nationalsozialismus', *AfS* 30 (1990), pp. 423–53.

Bock, Gisela, *Zwangssterilisation im Nationalsozialismus. Studien zur Rassenpolitik und Frauenpolitik*, Opladen, 1986.

Böckenförde, Ernst-Wolfgang, *Die Organisationsgewalt im Bereich der Regierung. Eine Untersuchung zum Staatsrecht der Bundesrepublik Deutschland*, Berlin, 1964.

Boebel, CHaja and Wentzel, Lothar, eds., *Streiken gegen den Krieg. Die Bedeutung der Massenstreiks in der Metallindustrie vom Januar 1918*, Hamburg, 2008.

Boeckh, Katrin, *Von den Balkankriegen zum Ersten Weltkrieg. Kleinstaatenpolitik und ethnischen Selbstbestimmung auf dem Balkan*, Munich, 1996.

Boelcke, Willi A., *Der Schwarzmarkt 1945–1948. Vom Überleben nach dem Kriege*, Brunswick, 1986.

Boelcke, Willi A., *Die Kosten von Hitlers Krieg. Kriegsfinanzierung und finanzielles Kriegserbe in Deutschland 1933–1948*, Paderborn etc., 1985.

Böhler, Jochen, *Auftakt zum Vernichtungskrieg. Die Wehrmacht in Polen 1939*, Frankfurt am Main, 2006.

Böhme, Helmut and Kallenberg, Fritz, eds., *Deutschland und der Erste Weltkrieg. Ringvorlesung an der Technischen Hochschule Darmstadt im Wintersemester 1984/85. Eine Dokumentation*, Darmstadt, 1987.

Böll, Heinrich et al., eds., *Verantwortlich für Polen?*, Reinbek bei Hamburg, 1982.

Bollenbeck, Georg, *Eine Geschichte der Kulturkritik*, Munich, 2007.

Bollenbeck, Georg, *Tradition, Avantgarde, Reaktion*, Frankfurt am Main, 1999.

Bölling, Klaus, *Die fernen Nachbarn. Erfahrungen in der DDR*, Hamburg, 1983.

Bölsche, Jochen, ed., *Waterkantgate. Die Kieler Affäre*, Göttingen, 1987.

Bolz, Norbert, *Auszug aus der entzauberten Welt. Philosophischer Extremismus zwischen den Weltkriegen*, Munich, 1989.

Bömer, Hermann, *Stadtentwicklung in Dortmund seit 1945. Von der Industrie- zur Dienstleistungs- und Wissenschaftsstadt*, Dortmund, 2010.

Bonwetsch, Bernd, 'Vom Hitler-Stalin Pakt zum "Unternehmen Barbarossa." Die deutsch-russischen Beziehungen von 1939–1941 in der Kontroverse', *Osteuropa* 41 (1991), pp. 562–79.

Borggräfe, Henning, *Entschädigung als Selbstaussöhnung. Die deutsche Auseinandersetzung um NS-Zwangsarbeit, 1979–2005*, Göttingen, 2014.

Borodziej, Włodzimierz, *The Warsaw Uprising of 1944*, Madison, Wis., 2006.

Borodziej, Włodzimierz, *Geschichte Polens im 20.Jahrhundert*, Munich, 2010.

Borscheid, Peter, *Der Tempo-Virus. Eine Kulturgeschichte der Beschleunigung*, Frankfurt am Main, 2004.

Borscheid, Peter and Teuteberg, Hans, eds., *Ehe, Liebe, Tod. Zum Wandel der Familie, der Geschlechts- und Generationsbeziehungen in der Neuzeit*, Münster, 1983.

Borsdorf, Ulrich and Niethammer, Lutz, eds., *Zwischen Befreiung und Besatzung. Analysen der US-Geheimdienstes über Positionen und Strukturen deutscher Politik 1945*, Wuppertal, 1976.

Bösch, Frank, *Die Adenauer-CDU. Gründung, Aufstieg und Krise einer Erfolgspartei 1945–1969*, Stuttgart and Munich, 2001.

Bösch, Frank, *Macht und Machtverlust. Die Geschichte der CDU*, Stuttgart and Munich, 2002.

Boskin, Michael J., *Reagan and the Economy. The Successes, Failures and Unfinished Agenda*, San Francisco, 1987.

Bracher, Karl Dietrich, *The German Dictatorship. The Origins, Structure and Consequences of National Socialism*, Penguin Books, 1973.

Bracher, Karl Dietrich, Funke, Manfred and Jacobsen, Hans-Adolf, eds., *Deutschland 1933–1945. Neue Studien zur nationalsozialistischen Herrschaft*, Düsseldorf, 1992.

Bracher, Karl Dietrich, Jäger, Wolfgang and Link, Werner, eds., *Republik im Wandel 1969–1974. Die Ära Brandt*, vol. 1, Stuttgart, 1986.

Brackmann, Michael, *Vom totalen Krieg zum Wirtschaftswunder. Die Vorgeschichte der westdeutschen Währungsreform 1948*, Essen, 1993.

Bradbury, Malcolm (ed.), *Modernism*, Harmondsworth, 1976.

Brady, Robert A., *The Rationalization Movement in German Industry*, Berkeley, California, 1933.

Braham, Randolph L., *The Politics of Genocide. The Holocaust in Hungary*, 2 vols., New York, 1981.

Brandt, Leo, *Die zweite industrielle Revolution*, Bonn, 1956.

Brandt, Willy, *Verbrecher und andere Deutsche. Ein Bericht aus Deutschland 1946*, Bonn, 2007.

Braunthal, Gerard, *Politische Loyalität und Öffentlicher Dienst. Der 'Radikalenerlass' von 1972 und die Folgen*, Marburg, 1992.

Brechtken, Magnus, *'Madagaskar für die Juden.' Antisemitische Idee und politische Praxis 1885–1945*, Munich, 1997.

Bremen, Christian, *Die Eisenhower-Administration und die zweite Berlin-Krise1958–1961*, Berlin and New York, 1998.

Bremer Ausschuss für Wirtschaftsforschung, *Am Abend der Demontage. Sechs Jahre Reparationspolitik*, Bremen, 1951.

Breßlein, Erwin, 'Die Weltjugend und der Dogmatismus: Geschichte und Problematik der Weltjugendfestspiele', *APuZ* 22/1975, pp. 1–31.

Breuer, Stefan, *Anatomie der konservativen Revolution*, Darmstadt, 1995.

Breuer, Stefan, *Ästhetischer Fundamentalismus*, Darmstadt, 1995.

Breuer, Stefan, *Die Völkischen in Deutschland. Kaiserreich und Weimarer Republik*, Darmstadt, 2008.

Breuer, Stefan, *Grundpositionen der deutschen Rechten 1971–1945*, Tübingen, 1999.

Breuilly, John, *Nationalismus und moderner Staat. Deutschland und Europa*, Cologne, 1999.

Bridgwater, Patrick, *The German Poets of the First World War*, London and Sydney, 1985.

Brinkmann, Jens, 'Ludwig Klages Lebensphilosophie seit der Jahrhundertwende', (Master's Degree Dissertation), Freiburg im Breisgau, 2003.

Brochhagen, Ulrich, *Nach Nürnberg. Vergangenheitsbewältigung und Westintegration in der Ära Adenauer*, Hamburg, 1994.

Broszat, Martin, ed., *Zäsuren nach 1945. Essays zur Periodisierung der deutschen Nachkriegsgeschichte*, Munich, 1990.

Broszat, Martin, *The Hitler State: the foundation and development of the internal structure of the Third Reich*, London, 1981.

Broszat, Martin, *Hitler and the Collapse of Weimar Germany*, Leamington Spa and New York, 1987.

Broszat, Martin, *Konzentrationslager, Kommissarbefehl, Judenverfolgung*, Olten, 1965.

Broszat, Martin, *Nationalsozialistische Polenpolitik 1939–1945*, Stuttgart, 1961.

Broszat, Martin and Friedländer, Saul, 'Um die "Historisierung des Nationalsozialismus." Ein Briefwechsel', *VfZ* 36 (1988), pp. 339–72.

Browder, George C., *Hitler's Enforcers: the Gestapo and the SS Security Service in the Nazi Revolution*, Oxford: Oxford University Press, 1996.

Brown, Archie, *The Gorbachev Factor*, Oxford, 1996.

Browning, Christopher R., *Fateful Months. Essays on the Emergence of the Final Solution*, New York, 1992.

Browning, Christopher R., *Nazi Policy, Jewish Workers, German Killers*, Cambridge, 2000.

Browning, Christopher R., *The Origins of the Final Solution: the evolution of Nazi Jewish policy, September 1939–March 1942*, London, 2004.

Bruckner, Pascal, *Le sanglot de l'homme blanc: Tiers-monde, culpabilité, haine de soi*, Paris, 1983.

Brüggemeier, Franz-Josef, *Geschichte Großbritanniens im 20. Jahrhundert*, Munich, 2010.

Brüggemeier, Franz-Josef, *Leben vor Ort. Ruhrbergleute und Ruhrbergbau 1889–1919*, Munich, 1983.

Brüggemeier, Franz-Josef, *Tschernobyl, 26. April 1986, die ökologische Herausforderung*, Munich, 1998.

Brüll, Christoph, ed., *ZOOM 1920–2010. Nachbarschaften neun Jahrzehnte nach Versailles*, Eupen, 2012.

Brunn, Gerhard, ed., *Neoliberalismus. Die Entstehung des Maastrichter Vertrages und die Auswirkungen der Währungsunion auf Nordrhein-Westfalen*, Baden-Baden, 1999.

Brunn, Gerhard, *Die Europäische Einigung. Von 1945 bis heute*, Stuttgart, 2009.

Brunn, Gerhard and Jürgen Reulecke, eds., *Metropolis Berlin. Berlin als deutsche Hauptstadt im Vergleich europäischer Hauptstädte 1871–1939*, Bonn, 1992.

Buchhaas-Buirkholz, Dorothee, *Gesetzgebung im Wiederaufbau. Schulgesetz in Nordrhein-Westfalen und Betriebsverfassungsgesetz. Eine vergleichende Untersuchung zum Einfluß von Parteien, Kirchen und Verbänden in Land und Bund 1945–1952*, Düsseldorf, 1985.

Buchheim, Christoph, ed., *German Industry in the Nazi Period*, Stuttgart, 2008.

Buchheim, Christoph, ed., *Wirtschaftliche Folgelasten des Krieges in der SBZ/DDR*, Baden-Baden, 1995.

Buchheim, Christoph, 'Der Mythos vom Wohlleben. Der Lebensstandard der deutschen Zivilbevölkerung im Zweiten Weltkrieg', *VfZ* 58 (2010), pp. 299–329.

Buchheim, Christoph, 'Die besetzen Länder im Dienste der deutschen Kriegswirtschaft während des Zweiten Weltkrieges', *VfZ* 34 (1986), pp. 117–45.

Buchheim, Christoph, 'Die Währungsreform 1948 in Westdeutschland', *VfZ* 36 (1988), pp. 189–231.

Buchheim, Christoph, *Die Wiedereingliederung Westdeuschlands in die Weltwirtschaft 1945–1958*, Munich, 1990.

Buchheim, Christoph, 'Kriegsfolgen und Wirtschaftswachstum in der SBZ/DDR', *GG* 25 (1999), pp. 515–29.

Buchheim, Hans et al., *Anatomie des SS-Staates*, 2 vols., Olten and Freiburg im Breisgau, 1965.

Buchna, Kristian, *Nationale Sammlung an Rhein und Ruhr. Friedrich Middelhauve und die nordrhein-westfälische FDP 1945–1953*, Munich, 2010.

Buchstab, Günter and Gotto, Klaus, eds., *Die Gründung der Union. Traditionen, Entstehung und Repräsentanten*, Munich, 1981.

Budde, Gunilla, ed., *Frauen arbeiten. Weibliche Erwerbstätigkeit in Ost- und Westdeutschland nach 1945*, Göttingen, 1997.

Bührer, Werner, *Westdeutschland in der OEEC. Eingliederung, Krise, Bewährung*, Munich, 1997.

Bundesministerium des Inneren, ed., *Analysen zum Terrorismus*, 4 vols., Opladen, 1981–4.

Bundesministerium für Verteidigung, ed., *Schicksalsfragen der Gegenwart. Handbuch politisch-historischer Bildung*, vol. 1, Tübingen, 1957.

Burleigh, Michael, *Germany Turns Eastwards. A Study of Ostforschung in the Third Reich*, Cambridge, 1988.

Busch, Tim, *Die deutsche Strafrechtsreform. Ein Rückblick auf die sechs Reformen des deutschen Strafrechts (1969–1998)*, Baden-Baden, 2005.

Buscher, Frank M., *The U.S. War Crimes Trial Program in Germany 1946–1955*, New York, 1989.

Büscher, Wolfgang, Wensierski, Peter and Wolscher, Klaus, eds., *Friedensbewegung in der DDR. Texte 1978–1982*, Hattingen, 1982.

Buske, Sybille, *Fräulein Mutter und ihr Bastard. Eine Geschichte der Unehelichkeit in Deutschland 1900 bis 1970*, Göttingen, 2004.

Butterwegge, Christoph, ed., *Neoliberalismus. Analysen und Alternativen*, Wiesbaden, 2008.

Büttner, Ursula, *Weimar. Die überforderte Republik 1918–1933*, Stuttgart, 2008.

Büttner, Ursula and Jochmann, Werner, eds., *Die Deutschen und die Judenverfolgung im Dritten Reich*, Hamburg, 1992.

Calic, Marie-Janine, *Geschichte Jugoslawiens im 20. Jahrhundert*, Munich, 2010.

Calic, Marie-Janine, *Krieg und Frieden in Bosnien-Hercegovina. Ursachen, Konfliktstrukturen, internationale Lösungsversuche*, Frankfurt am Main, 1996.

Canetti, Elias, *Crowds and Power*, New York, 1984.

Cartarius, Ulrich, ed., *Deutschland im Ersten Weltkrieg*, Munich, 1982.

Chafe, William Henry, *The Unfinished Journey. America since World War II*, New York, 1986.

Chiari, Bernhard, *Kosovo*, Paderborn, 2008.

Chickering, Roger, *Imperial Germany and the Great War, 1914–1918*, 2nd ed., Cambridge: Cambridge University Press, 2004.

Chowanski, Joachim and Dreier, Rolf, *Die Jugendweihe. Eine Kulturgeschichte seit 1852*, Berlin, 2000.

Clark, Christopher M., *Kaiser Wilhelm II: a life in power*, London, 2009.

Clark, Christopher M., *The Sleepwalkers. How Europe Went to War in 1914*, London, 2012.

Clark, Christopher M. and Kaiser, Wolfram, eds., *Kulturkampf in Europa im 19. Jahrhundert*, Leipzig, 2003.

Clavin, Patricia, *The Great Depression in Europe 1929–1939*, Basingstoke and New York, 2000.

Clay, Lucius D., *Decision in Germany*, Garden City, N.Y., 1950.

Cohn, Norman, *Warrant for Genocide: the myth of the Jewish world-conspiracy and the 'Protocols of the Elders of Zion'*, Harmondsworth, 1970.

Conert, Hansgeorg, *Die Ökonomie des unmöglichen Sozialismus. Krise und Reform der sowjetischen Wirtschaft unter Gorbatschow*, Münster, 1990.

Connelly, John and Grüttner, Michael, eds., *Universities under Dictatorship*, University Park, Pennsylvania, 2005.

Conrad, Sebastian and Osterhammel, Jürgen, eds., *Das Kaiserreich transnational. Deutschland in der Welt 1871–1914*, Göttingen, 2004.

Conrad, Sebastian, *German Colonialism: a Short History*, Cambridge, 2012.

Conrad, Sebastian, *Globalisation and the Nation in Imperial Germany*, Cambridge, 2010.

Conze, Eckart, *Das Amt und die Vergangenheit. Deutsche Diplomaten im Dritten Reich und in der Bundesrepublik*, Munich, 2010.

Conze, Eckart, *Die Suche nach Sicherheit. Eine Geschichte der Bundesrepublik Deutschland von 1949 bis in die Gegenwart*, Munich, 2009.

Conze, Vanessa, *Das Europa der Deutschen. Ideen von Europa und Deutschland zwischen Reichstradition und Westorientierung*, Munich, 2005.

Conze, Werner and Lepsius, Mario Rainer, eds., *Sozialgeschichte der Bundesrepublik. Beiträge zum Kontinuitätsproblem*, Stuttgart, 1983.

Cornelißen, Christoph, *Gerhard Ritter. Geschichtswissenschaft und Politik im 20. Jahrhundert*, Düsseldorf, 2001.

Cornelißen, Christoph and Kruse, Wolfgang, eds., *Eine Welt von Feinden. Der Große Krieg 1914–1918*, Frankfurt am Main, 1997.

Corni, Gustavo and Gies, Horst, *Brot, Butter, Kanonen. Die Ernährungswirtschaft in Deutschland unter der Diktatur Hitlers*, Berlin, 1997.

Crafts, Nicholas F.R., 'The Golden Age of Economic Growth in Western Europe 1950–1973', *Economic History Review*, 48 (1995), pp. 429–47.

Crouch, Colin, *Post-democracy*, Cambridge, 2005.

Crouch, Colin, *The Strange Non-Death of Neoliberalism*, Cambridge, 2011.

Dabringhaus, Sabine, *Geschichte Chinas im 20. Jahrhundert*, Munich, 2009.

Dähnhardt, Dirk, *Revolution in Kiel. Der Übergang vom Kaiserreich zur Weimarer Republik 1918/19*, Neumünster, 1978.

Dahrendorf, Ralf, *Bildung ist Bürgerrecht. Plädoyer für eine aktive Bildungspolitik*, Hamburg, 1965.

Dahrendorf, Ralf, *Gesellschaft und Freiheit. Zur soziologischen Analyse der Gegenwart*, Munich, 1961.

Dahrendorf, Ralf, *Society and Democracy in Germany*, Westport, Connecticut, 1979.

Dalos, György, *1956. Der Aufstand in Ungarn*, Munich, 2006.

Dams, Carsten and Stolle, Michael, *The Gestapo: Power and Terror in the Third Reich*, Oxford: Oxford University Press, 2014.

Danckwortt, Barbara and Lepp, Claudia, ed., *Von Grenzen und Ausgrenzung. Interdisciplinäre Beiträge zu den Themen Migration, Minderheiten und Fremdenfeindlichkeit*, Marburg, 1997.

Daniel, Ute, *The War from Within. German Working-Class Women in the First World War*, Oxford, 1997.

Danyel, Jürgen, ed., *Die geteilte Vergangenheit. Zum Umgang mit Nationalsozialismus und Widerstand in beiden deutschen Staaten*, Berlin, 1995.

Darwin, Charles, *On the Origin of Species by Means of Natural Selection, or, The Preservation of Favoured Races in the Struggle for Life*, 1st edn., London, 1859.

Defrance, Corine and Pfeil, Ulrich, *Eine Nachkriegsgeschichte in Europa (1945 bis 1963)*, Darmstadt, 2011 (Deutsch-Französische Geschichte 10).

Deist, Wilhelm, 'Die Politik der Seekriegsleitung und die Rebellion der Flotte Ende Oktober 1918', *VfZ*, 14.4 (1966), pp. 341–68.

Dieckmann, Christoph, *Deutsche Besatzungspolitik in Litauen 1941–1944*, 2 vols., Gottingen, 2011.

Dieckmann, Christoph, Quinkert, Babette and Tönsmeyer, Tatjana, eds., *Kooperation und Verbrechen. Formen der 'Kollaboration' im östlichen Europa 1939–1945*, Göttingen, 2003.

Diedrich, Torsten, *Der 17.Juni 1953 in der DDR. Bewaffnete Gewalt gegen das Volk*, Berlin, 1991.

Diehl, James M., *Paramilitary Politics in Weimar Germany*, Bloomington, Indiana and Indianopolis, Indiana, 1977.

Dieter, Alexander, *Die Krise der deutschen Stahlindustrie. Darstellung, Ursachenanalyse und theoretisch-empirische Überprüfung strategischer Konzepte der Krisenbewältigung*, Würzburg, 1992.

Dittberner, Jürgen, *Die FDP. Geschichte, Personen, Organisation, Perspektiven. Eine Einführung*, Wiesbaden, 2005.

Doering-Manteuffel, Anselm, *Wie westlich sind die Deutschen? Amerikanisierung und Westernisierung im 20. Jahrhundert*, Göttingen, 1999.

Doering-Manteuffel, Anselm and Raphael, Lutz, *Nach dem Boom. Perspektiven auf die Zeitgeschichte seit 1970*, Göttingen, 2008.

Donges, Jürgen B. et al., *Mehr Strukturwandel fur Wachstum und Beschäftigung. Die deutsche Wirtschaft im Anpassungstau*, Tübingen, 1988 (Kieler Studien. Institut für Weltwirtschaft an der Universität Kiel 216).

Dönhoff, Marion Gräfin, Leonhardt, Rudolf Walter and Sommer, Theo, *Reise in ein fremdes Land. Bericht über Kultur, Wirtschaft und Politik in der DDR*, Hamburg, 1964.

Döscher, Hans-Jürgen, *Seilschaften. Die verdrängte Vergangenheit des Auswärtigen Amts*, Berlin, 2005.

Döscher, Hans-Jürgen, *Verschworene Gesellschaft. Das Auswärtige Amt unter Adenauer zwischen Neubeginn und Kontinuität*, Berlin, 1995.

Dreher, Klaus, *Helmut Kohl. Leben mit Macht*, Stuttgart, 1998.

Drewniak, Bogusław, *Das Theater im NS-Staat. Szenarium deutscher Zeitgeschichte 1933–1945*, Düsseldorf, 1983.

Duchkowitsch, Wolfgang, Hausjell, Fritz and Semrad, Bernd, eds., *Die Spirale des Schweigens*, Vienna, 2004.

Dülffer, Jost, *Europa im Ost-West-Konflikt 1945–1991*, Munich, 2004.

Dülffer, Jost, *Jalta, 4. Februar1945. Der Zweite Weltkrieg und die Entstehung der bipolaren Welt*, Munich, 1998.

Dutschke, Gretchen, *Wir hatten ein barbarisches, schönes Leben. Rudi Dutschke. Eine Biographie*, Cologne, 1996.

Dutschke, Rudi et al., *Rebellion der Studenten oder Die neue Opposition. Eine Analyse*, Reinbek bei Hamburg, 1968.

Dyson, Kenneth and Featherstone, Kevin, *The Road to Maastricht. Negotiating Economic and Monetary Union*, Oxford, 1999.

Earl, Hilary Camille, *The Nuremberg SS-Einsatzgruppen Trial 1945–1958. Atrocity, Law and History*, Cambridge, 2009.

Eckel, Jan, *Geist der Zeit. Deutsche Geisteswissenschaften seit 1870*, Göttingen, 2008.

Eckel, Jan, *Hans Rothfels. Eine intellektuelle Biographie im 20. Jahrhundert*, Göttingen, 2005.

Eckel, Jan, 'Utopie der Moral, Kalkül der Macht. Menschenrechte in der globalen Politik seit 1945', *AfS* 29 (2009), pp. 437–84.

Eckel, Jan and Moyn, Sam, eds., *Moral für die Welt? Menschenrechtspolitik in den 1970er Jahren*, Göttingen, 2012.

Eckel, Jan et al., eds., *Universalisierung des Holocaust? Erinnerungskultur und Geschichtspolitik in internationaler Perspektive*, Göttingen, 2008.

Ecker, Ludwig and Schmals, Klaus M., 'Stadterneuerungspolitik. Analysiert an einem Fallbeispiel', *Soziale Welt* 32.2 (1981), pp. 196–218.

Eckert, Andreas, *Kolonialismus*, Frankfurt am Main, 2006.

Edelmann, Heidrun, *Vom Luxusgut zum Gebrauchsgegenstand. Die Geschichte der Verbreitung von Personenkraftwagen in Deutschland*, Frankfurt am Main, 1989.

Edinger, Lewis Joachim, *German Exile Politics: the Social Democratic Executive Committee in the Nazi Era*, Berkeley, Cal., 1956.

Egle, Christoph, Ostheim, Tobias and Zohlnhöfer, Reimut, eds., *Das rot-grüne Projekt. Eine Bilanz der Regierung Schröder 1998–2002*, Wiesbaden, 2003.

Ehmke, Horst, ed., *Perspektiven. Sozialdemokratische Politik im Übergang zu den siebziger Jahren, erläutert von 21 Sozialdemokraten*, Reinbek bei Hamburg, 1969.

Ehrenburg, Ilya and Grossman, Vasily, eds., *The Black Book: the ruthless murder of Jews by German-fascist invaders throughout the temporarily-occupied regions of the Soviet Union and in the death camps of Poland during the war of 1941–1945*, New York, 1981.

Eichengreen, Barry J., *The European Economy since 1945: coordinated capitalism and beyond*, Princeton, NJ, 2007.

Eichholtz, Dietrich, *Geschichte der deutschen Kriegswirtschaft 1939–1945*, 3 vols., Munich 1969–96.

Eisenberg, Christiane, 'Massensport in der Weimarer Republik. Ein statistischer Überblick', *AfS* 33 (1993), pp. 137–77.

Eley, Geoff, *Reshaping the German Right. Radical Nationalism and Political Change after Bismarck*, Ann Arbor, Michigan, 1991.

Elias, Norbert, *The Germans. Power Struggles and the Development of Habitus in the Nineteenth and Twentieth Centuries*, Oxford, 1997

Ellwein, Thomas, Liebel, Manfred and Negt, Inge, *Die Reaktion der Öffentlichkeit*, Olten, 1966.

Elon, Amos, *Journey Through a Haunted Land. The New Germany*, New York, 1967.

Elsaesser, Thomas, *Filmgeschichte und frühes Kino. Archäologie eines Medienwandels*, Munich, 2002.

Elster, Ludwig, *Handwörterbuch der Staatswissenschaften, Ergänzungsband*, Jena, 1929.

Enderlein, Henrik, 'Die Krise im Euro-Raum: Auslöser, Antworten, Ausblick', *APuZ* 43 (2010), pp. 7–12.

Engelbert, Otto, *Kriegsgefangenschaft. Berichte über das Leben in Gefangenenlagern der Allierten*, Munich, 1991.

Engels, Jens Ivo, *Naturpolitik in der Bundesrepublik. Ideenwelt und politische Verhaltensstile in Naturschutz und Umweltbewegung 1950–1980*, Paderborn etc., 2006.

Enzensberger, Hans Magnus, ed., *Kursbuch 12. Der nicht erklärte Notstand. Dokumentation und Analyse eines Berliner Sommers*, Frankfurt am Main, 1968.

Epkenhaus, Michael, *Die wilhelminische Flottenrüstung 1908–1914*, Munich, 1991.

Eppler, Erhard, *Ende oder Wende. Von der Machbarkeit des Notwendigen*, Stuttgart, 1975.

Erdt, Marc Fabian, *Die Legende von der Politischen Korrektheit. Zur Erfolgsgeschichte eines importierten Mythos*, Bielefeld, 2004.

Erker, Paul, *Dampflok, Damiler, DAX. Die deutsche Wirtschaft im 19. und 20. Jahrhundert*, Stuttgart and Munich, 2001.

Erker, Paul, *Ernährungskrise und Nachkriegsgesellschaft. Bauern und Arbeiterschaft in Bayern 1943–1953*, Stuttgart, 1990.

Erker, Paul, *Industrieeliten in der NS-Zeit. Anpassungsbereitschaft und Eigeninteresse von Unternehmern in der Rüstungs- und Kriegswirtschaft 1936–1945*, Passau, 1993.

Erker, Paul, *Vom Heimatvertriebenen zum Neubürger. Sozialgeschichte der Flüchtlinge in einer agrarischen Region Mittelfrankens 1945–1955*, Stuttgart, 1988.

Eser, Albin, 'Die Sexualität in der Strafrechtsreform', *Juristische Analysen* 2 (1970), pp. 218–41.

Essner, Cornelia, *Die 'Nürnberger Gesetze' oder Die Verwaltung des Rassenwahns 1933–1945*, Paderborn etc, 2002.

Evans, Richard J., *The Coming of the Third Reich*, London, 2003.

Evans, Richard J., ed., *The German Working Class 1888–1933. The Politics of Everyday Life*, London, 1982.

Evans, Richard J., *The Third Reich at War, 1939–1945*, London, 2008.

Evans, Richard J., *The Third Reich in Power, 1933–1939*, London, 2005.

Evans, Richard J. and Geary, Dick, eds., *The German Unemployed. Experiences and Consequences of Mass Unemployment from the Weimar Republic to the Third Reich*, London and Sydney, 1987.

Evans, Richard J. and Lee, W.Robert, eds., *The German Peasantry. Conflict and Community in Rural Society from the Eighteenth to the Twentieth Centuries*, London and Sydney, 1986.

Exner, Peter, *Ländliche Gesellschaft und Landwirtschaft in Westfalen 1919–1969*, Paderborn etc., 1997.

Fahlbusch, Michael, *Wissenschaft im Dienst der nationalsozialistischen Politik? Die 'Volksdeutschen Forschungsgemeinschaften' von 1931–1945*, Baden-Baden, 1999.

Falter, Jürgen W., *Hitlers Wähler*, Darmstadt, 1991.

Falter, Jürgen W., Gabriel, Oscar W. and Rattinger, Hans, eds., *Wirklich ein Volk? Die politischen Orientierungen der Ost- und Westdeutschen im Vergleich*, Opladen, 2000.

Farber, David R., *The Age of Great Dreams. America in the 1960s*, New York, 1994.

Fäßler, Peter E., *Globalisierung. Ein historisches Kompendium*, Cologne, Weimar and Vienna, 2007.

Fassmann, Heinz, and Münz, Rainer, eds., *European Migration in the Late Twentieth Century: historical patterns, actual trends, and social implications*, Aldershot, 1994.

Faulenbach, Bernd, ed., *Sozialdemokraten und Kommunisten nach Nationalsozialismus und Krieg. Zur historischen Einordnung der Zwangsvereinigung*, Essen, 1998.

Faulstich, Heinz, *Hungersterben in der Psychiatrie 1914–1949. Mit einer Topographie der NS-Psychiatrie*, Freiburg im Breisgau, 1998.

Faulstich, Werner, ed., *Die Kultur der achtziger Jahre*, Munich, 2005.

Feinstein, Charles H., Temin, Peter and Toniolo, Gianni, *The European Economy Between the Wars*, Oxford, 1997.

Feldman, Gerald D., *Army, Industry and Labor in Germany, 1914–1918*, Princeton N.J., 1966.

Feldman, Gerald D. et al., eds., *The German Inflation Reconsidered: a preliminary balance*, Berlin: De Gruyter, 1982.

Feldman, Gerald D., *The Great Disorder: Politics, Economics and Society in the German Inflation, 1914–1924*, New York and Oxford, 1997.

Feldman, Gerald D. and Steinisch, Irmgard, eds., *Industrie und Gewerkschaften 1918–1924. Die überforderte Zentralarbeitsgemeinschaft*, Stuttgart, 1985.

Feldman, Gerald D. et al., eds., *Konsequenzen der Inflation*, Berlin, 1989.

Feldman, Gerald D., *Vom Weltkrieg zur Weltwirtschaftskrise. Studien zur deutschen Wirtschafts- und Sozialgeschichte 1914–1932*, Göttingen, 1984.

Felken, Detlef, *Dulles und Deutschland. Die amerikanische Deutschlandpolitik 1953–1959*, Bonn, 1993.

Ferguson, Niall, et al., eds., *The Shock of the Global. The 1970s in Perspective*, Cambridge, Massachusetts and London, 2010.

Fest, Joachim, *Staatsstreich. Der lange Weg zum 20. Juli*, Berlin, 1994.

Fichter, Tilman, *Kleine Geschichte des SDS. Der Sozialistische Deutsche Studentenbund von Helmut Schmidt bis Rudi Dutschke*, Essen, 2007.

Fichter, Tilman, and Lönnendonker, Siegward, *Kleine Geschichte des SDS. Der Sozialistische Deutsche Studentenbund von 1946 bis zur Selbstauflösung*, Berlin, 1977.

Fink, Carole, Gassert, Philipp and Junker, Detlef, eds., *1968. The World Transformed*, Cambridge and New York, 1998.

Fisch, Jörg, *Europa zwischen Wachstum und Gleichheit 1850–1914*, Stuttgart, 2002.

Fisch, Jörg, *Reparationen nach dem Zweiten Weltkrieg*, Munich, 1992.

Fischer, Fritz, *Germany's Aims in the First World War*, London, 1967.

Fischer, Gerhard, 'Jugendfunktionäre, Fußwanderer und anonyme Jugendarbeit', *Deutsche Jugend* 2 (1954), pp. 32–4.

Fischer, Wolfram, ed., *Europäische Wirtschafts- und Sozialgeschichte vom Ersten Weltkrieg bis zur Gegenwart*, Stuttgart, 1987.

Flagge, Ingeborg, *Geschichte des Wohnens*, 5 vols., Stuttgart 1996–1999.

Focke, Harald and Reimer, Uwe, *Alltag unterm Hakenkreuz*, 3 vols., Hamburg, 1979–85.

Föhl, Carl, 'Stabilisierung und Wachstum beim Einsatz von Gastarbeitern', *Kyklos* 20 (1967), pp. 119–46.

Fohlen, Claude, *Die europäischen Volkswirtschaften im 20. Jahrhundert*, Stuttgart and New York, 1980 (Europäische Wirtschaftsgeschichte 5).

Forschbach, Edmund, *Edgar J. Jung. Ein Konservativer Revolutionär. 30. Juni 1934*, Pfullingen, 1984.

Forschungsstelle für Zeitgeschichte in Hamburg, ed., *Hamburg im 'Dritten Reich'*, Göttingen, 2005.

Förster, Gerhard, *Der preußisch-deutsche Generalstab 1640–1965*, Berlin, 1966.

Forsthoff, Ernst, *Der Staat der Industriegesellschaft. Dargestellt am Beispiel der Bundesrepublik Deutschland*, Munich, 1971.

Foschepoth, Josef, 'Postzensur und Telefonüberwachung in der Bundesrepublik Deutschland (1949–1968)', *ZfG* 57 (2009), pp. 413–26.

Foschepoth, Josef, *Überwachtes Deutschland. Post- und Telefonüberwachung in der alten Bundesrepublik*, Göttingen, 2012.

Fourastié, Jean, *Die große Metamorphose des 20. Jahrhunderts*, Düsseldorf and Vienna, 1967.

Fourastié, Jean, *Gesetze der Wirtschaft von Morgen. Drei grundlegende Essais*, Düsseldorf and Vienna, 1967.

Fox, Richard W. and Kloppenberg, James T.A., *Companion to American Thought*, Oxford and Cambridge, Massachusetts, 1995.

Franck, Dieter, *Jahre unseres Lebens 1945–1949*, Munich and Zürich, 1980.

François, Etienne, ed., *1968—ein europäisches Jahr?*, Leipzig, 1997.

François, Etienne and Schulze, Hagen, *Deutsche Erinnerungsorte*, 3 vols., Munich, 2003.

François-Poncet, André, *The Fateful Years. Memoirs of a French Ambassador in Berlin, 1931–1938*, London, 1949.

Frank, Mario, *Walter Ulbricht. Eine deutsche Biographie*, Berlin, 2001.

Franke, Ulrich, *Die Nato nach 1989. Das Rätsel ihres Fortbestandes*, Wiesbaden, 2010.

Franz, Wolfgang and Steiner, Viktor, eds., *Der westdeutsche Arbeitsmarkt im strukturellen Anpassungsprozeß*, Baden-Baden, 1995.

Franzmann, Andreas and Wolbring, Barbara, eds., *Zwischen Idee und Zweckorientierung. Vorbilder und Motive von Hochschulreformen seit 1945*, Berlin, 2007.

Freese, Christopher, *Die Privatisierungstätigkeit der Treuhandanstalt. Strategien und Verfahren der Privatisierung in der Systemtransformation*, Frankfurt am Main, 1996.

Frei, Norbert, ed., *Die Praxis der Wiedergutmachung. Geschichte, Erfahrung und Wirkung in Deutschland und Israel*, Göttingen, 2009.

Frei, Norbert, ed., *Karrieren im Zwielicht. Hitlers Eliten nach 1945*, Frankfurt am Main and New York, 2002.

Frei, Norbert, ed., *Transnationale Vergangenheitspolitik. Der Umgang mit deutschen Kriegsverbrechern in Europa nach dem Zweiten Weltkrieg*, Göttingen, 2006.

Frei, Norbert, *1945 und wir. Das Dritte Reich im Bewußtsein der Deutschen*, Munich, 2005.

Frei, Norbert, *1968. Jugendrevolte und globaler Protest*, Munich, 2008.

Frei, Norbert, *Adenauer's Germany and the Nazi Past. The Politics of Amnesty and Integration*, New York, 2002.

Frei, Norbert, *Amerikanische Lizenzpolitik und deutsche Pressetradition. Die Geschichte der Nachkriegszeitung Südost-Kurier*, Munich, 1986.

Frei, Norbert, *National Socialist Rule in Germany: the Führer State 1933–1945*, Oxford, 1993.

Frei, Norbert, Steinbacher, Sybille and Wagner, Bernd, eds., *Ausbeutung, Vernichtung, Öffentlichkeit. Neue Studien zur nationalsozialistischen Lagerpolitik*, Munich, 2000.

Frese, Matthias, *Betriebspolitik im 'Dritten Reich'. Deutsche Arbeitsfront, Unternehmer und Staatsbürokratie in der westdeutschen Großindustrie 1933–1939*, Paderborn, etc. 1991 (Forschungen zur Regionalgeschichte 2).

Frese, Matthias, Paulus, Julia and Teppe, Karl, eds., *Demokratisierung und gesellschaftlicher Aufbruch. Die sechziger Jahre als Wendezeit der Bundesrepublik*, Paderborn etc., 2003.

Frevert, Ute, ed., *Bürgerinnen und Bürger. Geschlechterverhältnisse im 19. Jahrhundert*, Göttingen, 1988.

Frevert, Ute, *Die kasernierte Nation. Militärdienst und Zivilgesellschaft in Deutschland*, Munich, 2001.

Frevert, Ute, *Women in German History: from bourgeois emancipation to sexual liberation*, Oxford, 1989.

Freyberg, Thomas von, *Industrielle Rationalisierung in der Weimarer Republik. Untersucht an Beispielen aus dem Maschinenbau und der Elektroindustrie*, Frankfurt am Main and New York, 1989.

Freye, Saskia, *Führungswechsel. Die Wirtschaftselite und das Ende der Deutschland AG*, Frankfurt am Main, 2009.

Freymond, Jean, *Le IIIe Reich et la réorganisation économique de l'Europe 1940–1953. Origines et projets*, Leiden, 1974.

Fricke, Karl Wilhelm 'Das justizielle Unrecht der Waldheimer Prozesse', *Neue Justiz* 45.5 (1991), pp. 209–10.

Fricke, Karl Wilhelm, ed., *Opposition und Widerstand in der DDR: Politische Lebensbilder*, Munich, 2002.

Frie, Ewald, *Das Deutsche Kaiserreich*, Darmstadt, 2004.

Friedlander, Henry, *The Origins of Nazi Genocide: from euthanasia to the final solution*, Chapel Hill, NC, 1995.

Friedländer, Saul, *Nazi Germany and the Jews. The Years of Persecution, 1933–1939*, New York, 1997.

Friedländer, Saul, *The Years of Extermination: Nazi Germany and the Jews, 1939–1945*, London, 2007.

Friedländer, Saul, *Reflections of Nazism: an essay on Kitsch and Death*, New York, 1984.

Friedrich, Jörg, *Das Gesetz des Krieges. Das deutsche Heer in Rußland 1941 bis 1945. Der Prozeß gegen das Oberkommando der Wehrmacht*, Munich, 1993.

Friedrich, Roland, *Die deutsche Außenpolitik im Kosovo-Konflikt*, Wiesbaden, 2005.

Friedrich, Sabine, *Rundfunk und Besatzungsmàcht. Organsation, Programm und Hörer des Südwestfunks 1945 bis 1949*, Baden-Baden, 1991.

Friedrichs, Jürgen and Kecskes, Robert, eds., *Gentrification. Theorie und Forschungsergebnisse*, Opladen, 1996.

Frieser, Karl-Heinz, *Blitzkrieg-Legende. Der Westfeldzug 1940*, Munich, 1995.

Fritzsche, Christiane, *Vergangenheitsbewältigung im Fernsehen. Westdeutsche Filme über den Nationalsozialismus in den 1950er und 60er Jahren*, Munich, 2003.

Fritz-Bauer-Institut, ed., *Überlebt und unterwegs. Jüdische Displaced Persons in Nachkriegsdeutschland*, Frankfurt am Main and New York, 1997.

Frondel, Manuel, Kambeck, Rainer and Schmidt, Christoph M., 'Kohlesubventionen um jeden Preis? Eine Streitschrift zu den Argumentationslinien des Gesamtverbandes des deutschen Steinkohlenbergbaus', *RWI Materialien, Heft 25*, Essen, 2006.

Frymann (pseudonym of Heinrich Claß), *Wenn ich der Kaiser wär'*, Leipzig, 1912.

Fuchs-Heinritz, Werner, *Arbeiterleben nach 1945. Lebensgeschichten in der Geschichte der Arbeiterschaft in Offenbach am Main seit dem Zweiten Weltkrieg Projektplan*, Marburg an der Lahn, 1979.

Führ, Christoph and Furck, Carl-Ludwig, eds., *Handbuch der deutschen Bildungsgeschichte*, vol.6, part 1, Munich, 1998.

Fuhrer, Armin, *Wer erschoss Benno Ohnesorg? Der Fall Kurras und die Stasi*, Berlin, 2009.

Führer, Karl Christian, *Arbeitslosigkeit und die Entstehung der Arbeitslosenversicherung in Deutschland 1903–1927*, Berlin, 1990.

Führer, Karl Christian, *Mieter, Hausbesitzer, Staat und Wohnungsmarkt*, Stuttgart, 1995.

Fukuyama, Francis, 'The End of History?', *The National Interest* 16 (1989), pp. 3–18.

Fukuyama, Francis, *The End of History and the Last Man*, London, 1992.

Fulbrook, Mary, *Anatomy of a Dictatorship. Inside the GDR 1949–1989*, Oxford, 1995.

Fulbrook, Mary, *The People's State: East German Society from Hitler to Honecker*, New Haven and London, 2005.

Fulda, Daniel, Herzog, Dagmar and Hoffmann, Stefan-Ludwig, eds., *Demokratie im Schatten der Gewalt. Geschichten des Privaten im deutschen Nachkrieg*, Göttingen, 2010.

Funke, Hajo, 'Bitburg, Jews, and Germans. A Case Study of Anti-Jewish Sentiment in Germany during May 1985', *New German Critique* 38 (1986), pp. 57–72.

Furet, François, *The Passing of an Illusion: the Idea of Communism in the Twentieth Century*, Chicago: 1999.

Füssl, Karl-Heinz, *Die Umerziehung der Deutschen. Jugend und Schule unter den Siegermächten des Zweiten Weltkriegs 1945–1955*, Paderborn etc., 1994.

Gaddum, Eckart, *Die deutsche Europapolitik in den 80er Jahren. Interessen, Konflikte und Entscheidungen der Regierung Kohl*, Paderborn etc., 1994.

Galinski, Dieter, ed., *Nazis und Nachbarn. Schüler erforschen den Alltag im Nationalsozialismus*, Reinbek bei Hamburg, 1982.

Gante, Michael, *§18 in der Diskussion. Meinungs- und Willensbildung 1945–1976*, Düsseldorf, 1991.

Ganzenmüller, Jörg, *Das belagerte Leningrad 1941–1944. Die Stadt in den Strategien von Angreifern und Verteidigern*, Paderborn etc., 2005.

Garton Ash, Timothy, *Ein Jahrhundert wird abgewählt. Aus den Zentren Mitteleuropas 1980–1990*, Munich and Vienna, 1990.

Garton Ash, Timothy, *In Europe's Name: Germany and the Divided Continent*, London, 1993.

Garton Ash, Timothy, *The Uses of Adversity: essays on the fate of Central Europe*, New York, 1989.

Gass-Bolm, Torsten, *Das Gymnasium 1945–1980. Bildungsreform und gesellschaftlicher Wandel in Westdeutschland*, Göttingen, 2005.

Gassert, Philipp, 'Was meint Amerikanisierung? Über den Begriff des Jahrhunderts', *Merkur* 54 (2000), pp. 785–96.

Gassert, Philipp, *Zweiter Kalter Krieg und Friedensbewegung. Der NATO-Doppelbeschluss in deutsch-deutscher und internationaler Perspektive*, Munich, 2011.

Gassert, Philipp and Steinweis, Alan E., eds., *Coping with the Nazi Past. West German Debates on Nazism and Generational Conflict 1955–1975*, New York and Oxford, 2006.

Gauly, Thomas M., *Kirche und Politik in der Bundesrepublik Deutschland 1945–1976*, Bonn, 1990.

Gay, Peter, *Weimar Culture. The Outsider as Insider*, Harmondsworth, 1974.

Geiger, Tim, *Atlantiker gegen Gaullisten. Außenpolitischer Konflikt und innerparteilicher Machtkampf in der CDU/CSU 1958–1969*, Munich, 2008.

Geißler, Rainer, *Die Sozialstruktur Deutschlands. Zur gesellschaftlichen Entwicklung mit einer Bilanz zur Vereinigung*, Wiesbaden, 2011.

Gensing, Patrick, *Terror von rechts. Die Nazi-Morde und das Versagen der Politik*, Berlin, 2012.

Geppert, Dominik and Hacke, Jens, eds., *Streit um den Staat. Intellektuelle Debatten in der Bundesrepublik 1960–1980*, Göttingen, 2008.

Gerlach, Christian, 'Die Wannsee-Konferenz, das Schicksal der deutschen Juden und Hitlers politische Grundsatzentscheidung, alle Juden Europas zu ermorden', *Werkstatt Geschichte* 18 (1997), pp. 7–44.

Gerlach, Christian, *Kalkulierte Morde. Die deutsche Wirtschafts- und Vernichtungspolitik in Weißrußland 1941 bis 1944*, Hamburg, 1999.

Gerlach, Christian and Aly, Götz, *Das letzte Kapitel. Realpolitik, Ideologie und Mord an den ungarischen Juden 1944/45*, Munich, 2002.

*Germany and the Second World War*, 9 vols., Oxford, 1990–2017.

Gerstenberger, Wolfgang, *Strukturwandel unter verschlechterten Rahmenbedingungen. Strukturberichterstattung 1983*, Berlin and Munich, 1984.

*Geschichte der Sozialpolitik in Deutschland seit 1945*, ed. Bundesministerium für Arbeit und Sozialordung und Bundesarchiv, 11 vols., Baden-Baden, 2001–8.

Gessner, Dieter, *Agrarverbände in der Weimarer Republik. Wirtschaftliche und soziale Voraussetzungen agrarkonservativer Politiker vor 1933*, Düsseldorf, 1976.

Gestrich, Andreas and Hirschfeld, Gerhard, eds. *Ausweisung und Deportation. Formen der Zwangsmigration in der Geschichte*, Stuttgart, 1995.

Geulen, Christian, *Wahlverwandte. Rassendiskurs und Nationalismus im späten 19. Jahrhundert*, Hamburg, 2004.

Geyer, Martin H., *Verkehrte Welt. Revolution, Inflation und Moderne*, Göttingen, 1998.

Geyer, Michael, *Aufrüstung und Sicherheit. Die Reichswehr in der Krise der Machtpolitik 1924–1936*, Wiesbaden, 1980.

Giddens, Anthony, *The Third Way: the Renewal of Social Democracy*, Cambridge, 1998.

Giersch, Herbert, Paqué, Karl-Heinz and Schmiedling, Holger, *The Fading Miracle. Four Decades of Market Economy in Germany*, Cambridge, 1994.

Gilcher-Holtey, Ingrid, *'Die Phantasie an die Macht'. Mai 68 in Frankreich*, Frankfurt am Main, 1995.

Gilcher-Holtey, Ingrid, ed., *1968. Vom Ereignis zum Gegenstand der Geschichtswissenschaft*, Göttingen, 1998.

Gilcher-Holtey, Ingrid, *Die 68er Bewegung. Deutschland-Westeuropa-USA*, Munich, 2008.

Gildea, Robert, Wieviorka, Oliver and Warring, Anette, eds., *Surviving Hitler and Mussolini. Daily Life in Occupied Europe*, Oxford and New York, 2006.

Gillingham, John, *Coal, Steel, and the Rebirth of Europe 1945–1955. The Germans and the French from Ruhr Conflict to Economic Community*, Cambridge, 1991.

Gillingham, John, *European Integration, 1950–2003. Superstate or New Market Economy?*, Cambridge, 2003.

Gillingham, John, *Industry and Politics in the Third Reich: Ruhr Coal, Hitler and Europe*, London, 1985.

Gimbel, John, *The Origins of the Marshall Plan*, Stanford, California, 1976.

Glaab, Manuela, *Deutschlandpolitik in der öffentlichen Meinung. Einstellungen and Regierungspolitik in der Bundesrepublik Deutschland 1949 bis 1990*, Opladen, 1999.

Glaser, Hermann, *Deutsche Kultur 1945–2000*, Munich, 1997.

Glatzer, Ruth, ed., *Das Wilhelminische Berlin 1980–1918. Panorama einer Metropole*, Berlin, 1997.

Goch, Stefan, ed., *Strukturwandel und Strukturpolitik in Nordrhein-Westfalen*, Münster, 2004.

Goeken-Haidl, Ulrike, *Der Weg zurück. Die Repatriierung sowjetischer Kriegsgefangener und Zwangsarbeiter während und nach dem Zweiten Weltkrieg*, Essen, 2006.

Goldhagen, Daniel, *Hitler's Willing Executioners: ordinary Germans and the Holocaust*, New York, 1996.

Goltermann, Svenja, *Die Gesellschaft der Überlebenden. Deutsche Kriegsheimkehrer und ihre Gewalterfahrungen im Zweiten Weltkrieg*, Munich, 2009.

Gordon, Bertram M., *Collaborationism in France during the Second World War*, Ithaca and New York, 1980.

Görtemaker, Manfred, *Kleine Geschichte der Bundesrepublik Deutschland*, Frankfurt am Main, 2005.

Goschler, Constantin, *Schuld und Schulden. Die Politik der Wiedergutmachung fur NS-Verfolgte seit 1945*, Göttingen, 2005.

Goschler, Constantin, *Wiedergutmachung, Westdeutschland und die Verfolgten des Nationalsozialismus 1945–1954*, Munich, 1992.

Goschler, Constantin and Lillteicher, Jürgen, eds., *'Arisierung' und Restitution. Die Rückerstattung jüdischen Eigentums in Deutschland und Österreich nach 1945 und 1989*, Göttingen, 2002.

Goschler, Constantin and Ther, Philipp, eds., *Raub und Restitution. 'Arisierung' und Rückerstattung des jüdischen Eigentums in Europa*, Frankfurt am Main, 2003.

Gosewinkel, Dieter, *Einbürgern und Ausschließen. Die Nationalisierung der Staatsangehörigkeit vom Deutschen Bund bis zur Bundesrepublik Deutschland*, Göttingen, 2001.

Granach, Alexander, *Da geht ein Mensch*, Weimar, 1949.

Grau, Andreas, *Gegen den Strom. Die Reaktion der CDU/CSU-Opposition auf die Ost- und Deutschlandpolitik der sozial-liberalen Koalition 1969–1973*, Düsseldorf, 2005.

Greenspan, Alan, *The Age of Turbulence. Adventures in a New World*, New Haven, Connecticut, 2005.

Greiner, Bernd, *9/11. Der Tag, die Angst, die Folgen*, Munich, 2011.

Greiner, Bernd, *Die Kuba-Krise. Die Welt an der Schwelle zum Atomkrieg*, Munich, 2010.

Greiner, Bernd, *Die Morgenthau-Legende. Zur Geschichte eines umstrittenen Plans*, Hamburg, 1995.

Greiner, Bernd, *Kuba-Krise: 13 Tage im Oktober. Analysen, Dokumente, Zeitzeugen*, Nördlingen, 1988.

Greiner, Bettina, *Suppressed Terror. History and Perception of Soviet Special Camps in Germany*, Lanham, 2014.

Greiser, Katrin, *Die Todesmärsche von Buchenwald. Räumung, Befreiung und Spuren der Erinnerung*, Göttingen, 2008.

Gries, Rainer, *Die Rationen-Gesellschaft. Versorgungskampf und Vergleichsmentalität: Leipzig, München und Köln nach dem Kriege*, Münster, 1991.

Gring, Diana, *Die Todesmärsche und das Massaker von Gardelegen. NS-Verbrechen in der Endphase des Zweiten Weltkrieges*, Gardelegen, 1993.

Gritschneider, Otto, *Bewährungsfrist für den Terroristen Adolf H.*, Munich, 1990.

Grode, Walter, *Die 'Sonderbehandlung 14 f.13' in den Konzentrationslagern des Dritten Reiches. Ein Beitrag zur Dynamik faschistischer Vernichtungspolitik*, Frankfurt am Main, 1987.

Groehler, Olaf, *Der lautlose Tod. Einsatz und Entwicklung deutscher Giftgase von 1914 bis 1945*, Berlin, 1978.

Groot, Gerard J.de, ed., *Student Protest. The Sixties and After*, London, 1998.

Gross, Jan Tomasz, *Polish Society under German Occupation. The Generalgouvernement 1939–1944*, Princeton, New Jersey, 1979.

Groß, Walther, *Rassenpolitische Erziehung*, Berlin, 1934.

Große Kracht, Klaus, *Die zankende Zunft. Historische Kontroversen in Deutschland nach 1945*, Göttingen, 2005.

Grosser, Dieter, *Das Wagnis der Währungs- Wirtschafts- und Sozialunion. Politische Zwänge im Konflikt mit ökonomischen Regeln*, Stuttgart, 1998.

Grossmann, Atina, *Jews, Germans and Allies. Close Encounters in Occupied Germany*, Princeton, New Jersey, 2007.

Grossmann, Atina, *Reforming Sex. The German Movement for Birth Control and Abortion Reform, 1920 to 1950*, New York, 1995.

Grotjahn, Alfred, *Krankenhauswesen und Heilstättenbewegung im Lichte der sozialen Hygiene*, Leipzig, 1908.

Gruchmann, Lothar, '"Blutschutzgesetz" und Justiz. Zur Entstehung und Auswirkung des Nürnberger Gesetzes vom 15. September 1935', *VfZ* 31 (1983), pp. 418–42.

Gruchmann, Lothar, *Justiz im Dritten Reich 1933–1940. Anpassung und Unterwerfung in der Ära Gürtner*, Munich, 1988.

Gruhl, Herbert, *Ein Planet wird geplündert. Die Schreckensbilanz unserer Politik*, Frankfurt am Main, 1975.

Gründel, Ernst Günther, *Die Sendung der jungen Generation. Versuch einer umfassenden revolutionären Sinndeutung der Krise*, Munich, 1932.

Grundwertekommission der SPD und Akademie für Gesellschaftswissenschaften beim ZK der SED, 'Der Streit der Ideologien und die gemeinsame Sicherheit', *Informationsdienst der SPD*, no. 3, 3.8.1987.

Grüner, Wolf, *Jewish Forced Labor Under the Nazis. Economic Needs and Racial Aims 1938–1944*, Cambridge, Massachusetts and New York, 2006.

Grüttner, Michael, *Studenten im Dritten Reich*, Paderborn, 1995.

Grüttner, Michael and Kinas, Sven, 'Die Vertreibung von Wissenschaftlern aus den deutschen Universitäten 1933–1945', *VfZ* 55.1 (2007), pp. 123–86.

Gudmundson, Bruce L., *Stormtroop Tactics. Innovation in the German Army 1914–1918*, New York, 1989.

Guggenberger, Bernd, ed., *Bürgerinitiativen und repräsentatives System*, Opladen, 1978.

Günter, Janne, *Leben in Eisenheim. Arbeit, Kommunikation und Sozialisation in einer Arbeitersiedlung*, Weinheim and Basle, 1980.

Gurland, Arcadius R.L., *Die CDU/CSU. Ursprünge und Entwicklung bis 1953*, Frankfurt am Main, 1980.

Gusy, Christoph, *Die Weimarer Reichsverfassung*, Tübingen, 1997.

Gutzen, Dieter, ed., *Transatlantische Partnerschaft. Kulturelle Aspekte der deutsch-amerikanischen Beziehungen*, Bonn, 1992.

Haar, Ingo, *Historiker im Nationalsozialismus. Deutsche Geschichtswissenschaft und der 'Volkstumskampf' im Osten*, Göttingen, 2002.

Habermas, Jürgen, *Student und Politik. Eine soziologische Untersuchung zum politischen Bewußtsein Frankfurter Studenten*, Neuwied am Rhein and Berlin, 1961.

Hachmeister, Lutz, ed., *Grundlagen der Medienpolitik. Ein Handbuch*, Munich, 2008.

Hachmeister, Lutz, *Der Gegnerforscher. Die Karriere des SS-Führers Franz Alfred Six*, Munich, 1998.

Hachtmann, Rüdiger, 'Arbeitsmarkt und Arbeitszeit in der deutschen Industrie', *AfS* 27 (1987), pp. 177–229.

Hachtmann, Rüdiger, *Industriearbeit im 'Dritten Reich'. Untersuchungen zu den Lohn- und Arbeitsbedingungen in Deutschland 1933–1945*, Göttingen, 1989.

Hacke, Christian, *Die Außenpolitik der Bundesrepublik Deutschland. Von Konrad Adenauer bis Gerhard Schröder*, Berlin, 2004.

Hacke, Jens, *Die Bundesrepublik als Idee. Zur Legitimationsbedürftigkeit politischer Ordnung*, Hamburg, 2009.

Haeckel, Ernst, *Anthropogenie, oder Entwickelungsgeschichte des Menschen. Gemeinverständliche wissenschaftliche Vorträge über die Grundzüge der menschlichen Keimes- und Stammes-Geschichte*, Leipzig, 1877.

Haeckel, Ernst, *Die Welträthsel. Gemeinverständliche Studien über monistische Philosophie*, Bonn, 1899.

Haenschke, Frank, *Modell Deutschland? Die Bundesrepublik in der technologischen Krise*, Reinbek bei Hamburg, 1977.

Häfele, Wolf, 'Neuartige Wege naturwissenschaftlich-technischer Entwicklung', *Forschung und Bildung. Schriftenreihe des BMWF* 4 (1963), pp. 36–7.

Haffner, Sebastian and Venohr, Wolfgang, *Das Wunder an der Marne. Rekonstruktion der Entscheidungsschlacht des Ersten Weltkriegs*, Bergisch Gladbach, 1984.

Hafner, Katie and Matthew Lyon, *Where Wizards Stay Up Late. The Origins of the Internet*, New York, 1996.

Haftendorn, Helga, *Coming of Age. German Foreign Policy Since 1945*, Lanham, Maryland, 2006.

Haftendorn, Helga, *Sicherheit und Entspannung. Zur Außenpolitik der Bundesrepublik Deutschland 1955–1982*, Baden-Baden, 1983

Haftendorn, Helga, *Sicherheit und Stabilität. Außenbeziehungen der Bundesrepublik zwischen Ölkrise und NATO-Doppelbeschluß*, Munich, 1986.

Hagenlücke, Heinz, *Deutsche Vaterlandspartei. Die nationale Rechte am Ende des Kaiserreiches*, Düsseldorf, 1997.

Halder, Winfried, *Von Ulbricht zu Honecker. Die DDR 1945–1989*, Berlin, 2010 (Deutsche Geschichte im 20. Jahrhundert, 15).

Hamann, Brigitte, *Der Erste Weltkrieg. Wahrheit und Lüge in Bildern und Texten*, Munich and Zürich, 2004.

Hamburger Institut für Sozialforschung, ed., *Eine Ausstellung und ihre Folgen. Zur Rezeption der Ausstellung 'Vernichtungskrieg. Verbrechen der Wehrmacht 1941 bis 1944'*, Hamburg, 1999.

Hammerschmidt, Peter and Sagebiel, Juliane, eds., *Die Soziale Frage zu Beginn des 21. Jahrhunderts*, Neu-Ulm, 2011.

Hannemann, Christine, *Die Platte. Industrialisierter Wohnungsbau in der DDR*, Wiesbaden, 1996.

Hannover-Drück, Elisabeth, ed., *Der Mord an Rosa Luxemburg und Karl Liebknecht. Dokumentation eines politischen Verbrechens*, Frankfurt am Main, 1967.

Harbou, Knud von, *Wege und Abwege: Franz Josef Schöningh, Mitbegründer der Süddeutschen Zeitung: eine Biografie*, Munich, 2013.

Harmssen, Gustav Wilhelm, ed., *Reparationen, Sozialprodukt, Lebensstandard. Versuch einer Wirtschaftsbilanz*, 5 vols., Bremen, 1948–1951.

Härtl, Ursula, ed., *Die Neukonzeption der Gedenkstätte Buchenwald*, Weimar, 2001.

Hartman, Geoffrey H., ed., *Bitburg in Moral and Political Perspective*, Bloomington, 1986.

Hartmann, Christian, *Operation Barbarossa: Nazi Germany's war in the East, 1941–1945*, Oxford, 2013.

Hartmann, Christian, 'Verbrecherischer Krieg—verbrecherische Wehrmacht? Überlegungen zur Struktur des deutschen Ostheeres 1941–1944', *VfZ* 52 (2004), pp. 1–75.

Hartmann, Christian, *Wehrmacht im Ostkrieg: Front und militärisches Hinterland 1941/42*, Berlin, 2012.

Hartmann, Christian, Hürter, Johannes and Jureit, Ulrike, eds., *Verbrechen der Wehrmacht. Bilanz einer Debatte*, Munich, 2005.

Haupt, Georges, *Socialism and the Great War. The Collapse of the Second International*, Oxford: Clarendon Press, 1972.

Haupt, Heinz-Gerhard and Hausen, Karin, *Die Pariser Kommune von 1871. Erfolg und Scheitern einer Revolution*, Frankfurt am Main and New York, 1979.

Haupt, Heinz-Gerhard and Kocka, Jürgen, eds., *Geschichte und Vergleich. Ansätze und Ergebnisse international vergleichender Geschichtssschreibung*, Frankfurt am Main and New York, 1996.

Häuser, Karl, *Volkswirtschaftslehre*, Frankfurt am Main, 1967.

Havemann, Robert, *Berliner Schriften*, ed. by Andreas W. Mytze, Munich, 1977.

Havemann, Robert, *Questions, Answers, Questions: from the biography of a German Marxist*, Garden City, NY, 1972.

Heberle, Rudolf, 'Zur Soziologie der nationalsozialistischen Revolution. Notizen aus dem Jahre 1934', *VfZ* 13 (1965), pp. 438–45.

Hecht, Cornelia, *Deutsche Juden und Antisemitismus in der Weimarer Republik*, Bonn, 2003.

Hecken, Thomas, *Pop. Geschichte eines Konzepts 1955–2009*, Bielefeld, 2009.

Heer, Hannes and Naumann, Klaus, eds., *War of Extermination. The German Military in World War II 1941–1944*, Oxford, 2000.

Heer, Hannes et al., eds., *Verbrechen der Wehrmacht. Dimensionen des Vernichtungskrieges 1941–1944. Ausstellungskatalog. Hamburger Insitut für Sozialforschung*, Hamburg, 1996.

Hehl, Ulrich von, 'Kampf um die Deutung. Der Nationalsozialismus zwischen "Vergangenheitsbewältigung", Historisierungspostulat und "neuer Unbefangenheit"', *Historisches Jahrbuch* 117 (1997), pp. 406–36.

Heid, Ludger, *Maloche—nicht Mildtätigkeit. Ostjüdische Proletarier in Deutschland 1914–1923*, Hildesheim, Zürich and New York, 1995.

Heideking, Jürgen, *Geschichte der USA*, Tübingen and Basle, 2003.

Heilemann, Ullrich, and Rappen, Hermann, 'Sieben Jahre deutsche Einheit: Rückblick und Perspektiven in fiskalischer Sicht', *APuZ*, 40-41 (1997), pp. 38–46.

Heilfron, Eduard, ed., *Die Deutsche Nationalversammlung im Jahre 1919 in ihrer Arbeit für den Aufbau des neuen deutschen Volksstaates*, Berlin, 1919.

Heimrod, Ute, ed., *Der Denkmalstreit—das Denkmal? Die Debatte um das 'Denkmal für die ermordeten Juden Europas'. Eine Dokumentation*, Berlin and Vienna, 1999.

Hein, Bastian, *Elite für Volk und Führer?Die allgemeine SS und ihre Mitglieder 1925–1945*, Munich: Oldenbourg Verlag, 2012.

Hein, Peter Ulrich, *Die Brücke ins Geisterreich. Künstlerische Avantgarde zwischen Kulturkritik und Faschismus*, Reinbek bei Hamburg, 1992.

Heinemann, Elizabeth, *Before Porn was Legal. The Erotica Empire of Beate Uhse*, Chicago, 2011.

Heinemann, Isabel, *'Rasse, Siedlung, deutsches Blut'. Das Rasse- und Siedlungshauptamt der SS und die rassenpolitische Neuordnung Europas*, Göttingen, 2003.

Heinemann, Isabel and Wagner, Patrick, eds., *Wissenschaft—Planung—Vertreibung. Neuordnungskonzepte und Umsiedlungspolitik im 20. Jahrhundert*, Stuttgart, 2006.

Heinemann, Winfried, ed., *Das internationale Krisenjahr 1956. Polen, Ungarn, Suez*, Munich, 1999.

Held, Renate, *Kriegsgefangenschaft in Großbritannien. Deutsche Soldaten des Zweiten Weltkriegs in britischem Gewahrsam*, Munich, 2008.

Helfferich, Karl, *Deutschlands Volkswohlstand 1888–1913*, Berlin, 1914.

Hellmann, Manfred, Zernack, Klaus and Schramm, Gottfried, eds., *Handbuch der Geschichte Russlands,* 5 vols.Stuttgart, 1981–2004.

Henke, Klaus-Dietmar, *Die amerikanische Besetzung Deutschlands*, Munich, 1995.

Henke, Klaus-Dietmar and Woller, Hans, eds., *Politische Säuberung in Europa. Die Abrechnung mit Faschismus und Kollaboration nach dem Zweiten Weltkrieg*, Munich, 1991.

Hennessy, Peter, *Whitehall*, London, 1990.

Hennig, Diethard, *Johannes Hoffmann. Sozialdemokrat und bayerischer Ministerpräsident*, Munich etc., 1990.

Henning, Friedrich-Wilhelm, *Landwirtschaft und ländliche Gesellschaft in Deutschland 1750 bis 1976*, Paderborn etc., 1988.

Hennock, Ernest P., *The Origin of the Welfare State in England and Germany 1850–1914. Social Policies Compared*, Cambridge, 2007.

Hentschel, Volker, *Geschichte der deutschen Sozialpolitik 1880–1980. Soziale Sicherung und kollektives Arbeitsrecht*, Frankfurt am Main, 1983.

Hentschel, Volker, *Ludwig Erhard. Ein Politikerleben*, Munich and Landsberg am Lech, 1996.

Hentschel, Volker, *Wirtschaft und Wirtschaftspolitik im wilhelminischen Deutschland. Organisierter Kapitalismus und Interventionsstaat?*, Stuttgart, 1978.

Henwood, Doug, *After the New Economy*, New York, 2003.

Hepp, Corona, *Avantgarde. Moderne Kunst, Kulturkritik und Reformbewegungen nach der Jahrhundertwende*, Munich, 1987.

Herbert, Ulrich, ed., *Europa und der 'Reichseinsatz'. Ausländische Zivilarbeiter, Kreigsgefangene und KZ-Häftlinge in Deutschland 1938–1945*, Essen, 1991.

Herbert, Ulrich, ed., *Nationalsozialistische Vernichtungspolitik 1939–1945. Neue Forschungen und Kontroversen*, Frankfurt am Main, 1998.

Herbert, Ulrich, ed., *National Socialist Extermination Policies. Contemporary German Perspectives and Controversies*, Oxford, 2000.

Herbert, Ulrich, ed., *Wandlungsprozesse in Westdeutschland. Belastung, Integration, Liberalisierung, 1945 bis 1980*, Göttingen, 2002.

Herbert, Ulrich, 'Academic and Public Discourses on the Holocaust. The Goldhagen Debate in Germany', *German Politics and Society*, 17.3 (1999), pp. 35–54.

Herbert, Ulrich, 'Arbeiterschaft im "Dritten Reich". Zwischenbilanz und offene Fragen', *GG*, 15.3 (1989), pp. 320–60.

Herbert, Ulrich, *Best. Biographische Studien über Radikalismus, Weltanschauung und Vernunft, 1903–1989*, Bonn, 1996.

Herbert, Ulrich, 'Europe in High Modernity. Reflections on a Theory of the 20th. Century', *JMEH* 5 (2007), pp. 5–21.

Herbert, Ulrich, *Fremdarbeiter. Politik und Praxis des 'Ausländer-Einsatzes' in der Kriegswirtschaft des Dritten Reiches*, Bonn, 1986.

Herbert, Ulrich, *Geschichte der Ausländerpolitik in Deutschland. Saisonarbeiter, Zwangsarbeiter, Gastarbeiter, Flüchtlinge*, Munich, 2001.

Herbert, Ulrich, *A History of Foreign Labor in Germany, 1880–1980: seasonal workers, forced laborers, guest workers*, Ann Arbor, Michigan, 1990.

Herbert, Ulrich, *Hitler's Foreign Workers: Enforced Foreign Labor in Germany under the Third Reich*, Cambridge, 1997.

Herbert, Ulrich and Groehler, Olaf, *Zweierlei Bewältigung. Vier Beiträge über den Umgang mit der NS-Vergangenheit in den beiden deutschen Staaten*, Hamburg, 1992.

Herbert, Ulrich, Orth, Karin and Dieckmann, Christoph, eds., *Die nationalsozialistischen Konzentrationslager. Entwicklung und Struktur*, Göttingen, 1998.

Herbert, Ulrich and Schildt, Axel, eds., *Kriegsende in Europa. Vom Beginn des deutschen Machtzerfalls bis zur Stabilisierung der Nachkriegsordnung 1944–1948*, Essen, 1998.

Herbst, Ludolf, ed., *Westdeutschland 1945–1955. Unterwerfung, Kontrolle, Integration*, Munich, 1986.

Herbst, Ludolf, *Das nationalsozialistische Deutschland 1933–1945*, Frankfurt am Main, 1996.

Herbst, Ludolf, *Der totale Krieg und die Ordnung der Wirtschaft. Die Kriegswirtschaft im Spannungsfeld von Politik, Ideologie und Propaganda 1939–1945*, Stuttgart, 1982.

Herbst, Ludolf, *Hitlers Charisma. Die Erfindung eines deutschen Messias*, Frankfurt am Main, 2010.

Herbst, Ludolf, *Option für den Westen. Vom Marshallplan bis zum deutsch-französischen Vertrag*, Munich, 1989.

Herbst, Ludolf and Bührer, Sowade, eds., *Vom Marshallplan zur EWG. Die Eingliederung der Bundesrepublik Deutschland in die westliche Welt*, Munich, 1990.

Herbst, Ludolf and Goschler, Constantin, eds., *Wiedergutmachung in der Bundesrepublik Deutschland*, Munich, 1989.

Herdegen, Gerhard, 'Perspektiven und Begrenzungen. Eine Bestandsaufnahme der öffentlichen Meinung zur deutschen Frage', *Das Freie Wort* 20 (1987), pp. 1259–73.

Herf, Jeffrey, *Divided Memory. The Nazi Past in the Two Germanys*, Cambridge, 1997.

Herf, Jeffrey, *East German Communists and the Jewish Question. The Case of Paul Merker*, Washington, D.C., 1994.

Herf, Jeffrey, *Reactionary Modernism. Technology, Culture and Politics in Weimar and the Third Reich*, Cambridge, 1990.

Hering, Rainer, *Konstruierte Nation. Der Alldeutsche Verband 1890 bis 1939*, Hamburg, 2003.

Herlyn, Ulfert, Saldern, Adelheid von and Tessin, Wulf, eds., *Neubausiedlungen der 20er und 60er Jahre. Ein historisch-soziologischer Vergleich*, Frankfurt am Main and New York, 1987.

Hermand, Jost and Trommler, Frank, *Die Kultur der Weimarer Republik*, Frankfurt am Main, 1989.

Herrmann, David G., *The Arming of Europe and the Making of the First World War*, Princeton, New Jersey, 1996.

Herrmann, Ulrich, ed., *'Mit uns zieht die neue Zeit . . . .' . Der Wandervogel in der deutschen Jugendbewegung*, Munich, 2006.

Herrnstadt, Ernst, *Die Lage der arbeitslosen Jugend in Deutschland*, Berlin, 1931.

Hertfelder, Thoms, ed., *Modell Deutschland. Erfolgsgeschichte oder Illusion?*, Göttingen, 2007.

Hertle, Hans-Hermann, *Der Fall der Mauer. Die unbeabsichtigte Selbstauflösung des SED-Staates*, Opladen and Wiesbaden, 1999.

Hertle, Hans-Hermann and Wolle, Stefan, *Damals in der DDR. Der Alltag im Arbeiter- und Bauernstaat*, Munich, 2004.

Herwig, Holger H., *The First World War. Germany and Austria-Hungary 1914–1918*, London, 1997.

Heß, Klaus, *Junker und bürgerliche Großgrundbesitzer im Kaiserreich. Landwirtschaftlicher Großbetrieb, Großgrundbesitz und Familienfideikommiß in Preußen*, Stuttgart, 1990.

Heydecker, Joe J., and Leeb, Johannes, *Der Nürnberger Prozess*, Cologne, 1995.

Heydemann, Günther, Mai, Günther and Müller, Werner, eds., *Revolution und Transformation in der DDR 1989/90*, Berlin, 1999.

Heyder, Ulrich, Menzel, Ulrich and Rebe, Bernd, eds., *Das Land verändert? Rot-grüne Politik zwischen Interessenbalancen und Modernisierungsdynamik*, Hamburg, 2002.

Hickethier, Knut, *Geschichte des deutschen Fernsehens*, Stuttgart and Weimar, 1998.

Hilberg, Raul, *The Destruction of the European Jews*, 3rd edn., New Haven, Connecticut, 2003.

Hildebrand, Klaus, *Das vergangene Reich. Deutsche Außenpolitik von Bismarck bis Hitler*, Stuttgart, 1999.

Hildebrand, Klaus, *Deutsche Außenpolitik 1871–1918*, Munich, 1989.

Hildebrand, Klaus, *The Foreign Policy of the Third Reich*, Berkeley, Cal., 1973.

Hildebrand, Klaus, *Integration und Souveränität. Die Außenpolitik der Bundesrepublik Deutschland 1949–1982*, Bonn, 1991.

Hildebrand, Klaus, *Von Erhard zur Großen Koalition. 1963–1969*, Stuttgart, 1984.

Hildermeier, Manfred, *Geschichte Russlands. Vom Mittelalter bis zur Oktoberrevolution* Munich, 2013.

Hildermeier, Manfred, *Geschichte der Sowjetunion 1917–1991. Entstehung und Niedergang des ersten sozialistischen Staates*, Munich, 1998.

Hill, Alexander, *The War Behind the Eastern Front. The Soviet Partisan Movement in North-West Russia 1941–1944*, London and New York, 2005.

Hillgruber, Andreas, *Hitlers Strategie. Politik und Kriegsführung 1940–1941*, Frankfurt am Main, 1965.

Hillgruber, Andreas, 'Riezlers Theorie des kalkulierten Risikos und Bethmann-Hollwegs politische Konzeption in der Julikrise 1914', *HZ* (1966), pp. 333–51.

Hillmann, Jörg and Zimmermann, John, eds., *Kriegsende 1945 in Deutschland*, Munich, 2002.

Hindrichs, Wolfgang, *Der lange Abschied vom Malocher. Sozialer Umbruch in der Stahlindustrie und die Rolle der Betriebsräte bis in die neunziger Jahre*, Essen, 2000.

Hinz, Uta, *Gefangen im Großen Krieg. Kriegsgefangenschaft in Deutschland 1914–1921*, Essen, 2004.

Hippler, Jochen, 'Die Folgen des 11. September 2001 für die internationalen Beziehungen', *APuZ* 3–4 (2004), pp. 3–6.

Hiro, Dilip, *Desert Shield to Desert Storm. The Second Gulf War*, New York, 1992.

Hirschfeld, Gerhard, ed., *Exil in Großbritannien. Zur Emigration aus dem nationalsozialistischen Deutschland*, Stuttgart, 1983.

Hirschfeld, Gerhard, and Marsh, Patrick, eds., *Collaboration in France: politics and culture during the Nazi occupation 1940–1944*, Oxford, 1989.

Hirschfeld, Gerhard, Krumeich, Gerd, and Renz, Irina, eds., *Brill's Encyclopedia of the First World War*, Leiden, 2012.

Hirschfeld, Gerhard and Krumeich, Gerd, eds., *Keiner fühlt sich hier mehr als Mensch. Erlebnis und Wirkung des Ersten Weltkriegs*, Essen, 1993.

Hirschfeld, Gerhard, Krumeich, Gerd and Renz, Irina, eds., *Scorched Earth: the Germans on the Somme, 1914–1918*, Barnsley, 2009.

Hirschon, Renée, ed., *Crossing the Aegean. An Appraisal of the 1923 Compulory Population Exchange Between Greece and Turkey*, New York and Oxford, 2003.

Hobsbawm, Eric J., *The Age of Empire 1875–1914*, London, 1987.

Hobsbawm, Eric J., *The Age of Extremes: the Short Twentieth Century, 1914–1991*, London, 1995.

Hobsbawm, Eric J., *Nations and Nationalism since 1780: Programme, Myth, Reality*, Cambridge, 1990.

Hobson, Rolf, *Imperialism at Sea. Naval Strategic Thought, the Ideology of Sea Power, and the Tirpitz Plan, 1875–1914*, Boston, Mass., 2002.

Hochlarmarker Geschichts-Arbeitskreis, ed., *Hochlarmarker Lesebuch. Kohle war nicht alles. 100 Jahre Ruhrgebietsgeschichte*, Oberhausen, 1981.

Hockerts, Hans Günter, ed., *Drei Wege deutscher Sozialstaatlichkeit. NS-Diktatur, Bundesrepublik und DDR im Vergleich*, Munich, 1998.

Hockerts, Hans Günter, *Sozialpolitische Entscheidungen im Nachkriegsdeutschland. Allierte und deutsche Sozialversicherungspolitik 1945–1957*, Stuttgart, 1980.

Hockerts, Hans Günter, 'Wiedergutmachung in Deutschland. Eine historische Bilanz 1945 bis 2000', *VfZ* 49 (2001), pp. 167–214.

Hockerts, Hans Günter and Kuller, Christiane, eds., *Nach der Verfolgung. Wiedergutmachung nationalsozialistischen Unrechts in Deutschland?*, Göttingen, 2003.

Hockerts, Hans Günter and Süß, Winfried, eds., *Soziale Ungleichheit im Sozialstaat. Die Bundesrepublik Deutschland und Großbritannien im Vergleich*, Munich, 2010.

Hodenberg, Christina von, *Konsens und Krise. Eine Geschichte der westdeutschen Medienöffentlichkeit 1945–1973*, Göttingen, 2006.

Hodenberg, Christina von and Siegfried, Detlef, eds., *Wo 1968 liegt. Reform und Revolte in der Geschichte der Bundesrepublik*, Göttingen, 2006.

Hoerder, Dirk, *Cultures in Contact. World Migrations in the Second Millenium*, Durham, North Carolina and London, 2002.

Hoerder, Dirk and Nagler, Jörg, eds., *People in Transit. German Migrations in Comparative Perspective*, Cambridge, 1995.

Hoffmann, Dierk, ed., *Geglückte Integration? Spezifika und Vergleichbarkeiten der Vertriebenen-Eingliederung in der SBZ/DDR*, Munich, 1999.

Hoffmann, Dierk, *Die DDR unter Ulbricht. gewaltsame Neuordnung und gescheiterte Modernisierung*, Zürich, 2003.

Hoffmann, Dierk and Schwartz, Michael, eds., *Deutsche Demokratische Republik 1949–1961: Im Zeichen des Aufbaus des Sozialismus*, Baden-Baden, 2004 (Geschichte der Sozialpolitik in Deutschland nach 1945, vol. 8).

Hoffmann, Dierk, Schwartz, Michael and Wentker, Hermann, eds., *Vor dem Mauerbau. Politik und Gesellschaft in der DDR der fünfziger Jahre*, Munich, 2003.

Hoffmann, Hilmar et al., eds., *Die Kultur unseres Jahrhunderts 1918–1933*, vol. 2, Düsseldorf etc., 1991.

Hoffmann, Peter, *The History of the German Resistance 1933–1945*, London, 1977.

Hoffmann, Stefan-Ludwig, ed., *Moralpolitik. Geschichte der Menschenrechte im 20. Jahrhundert*, Göttingen, 2010.

Hoffmann, Walther, ed., *Untersuchungen zum Wachstum der deutschen Wirtschaft*, Tübingen, 1971.

Hohensee, Jens, *Der erste Ölpreisschock 1973/74. Die politischen und gesellschaftlichen Auswirkungen der arabischen Erdölpolitik auf die Bundesrepublik Deutschland und Westeuropa*, Stuttgart, 1996.

Hohensee, Jens and Salewski, Michael, eds., *Energie-Politik-Geschichte. Nationale und internationale Energiepolitik seit 1945*, Stuttgart, 1993.

Hohorst, Gerd, Kocka, Jürgen and Ritter, Gerhard A., *Sozialgeschichtliches Arbeitsbuch. Materialien zur Statistik des Kaiserreichs 1870–1914*, vol. 2, Munich, 1975.

Holl, Karl, *Pazifismus in Deutschland*, Frankfurt am Main, 1988.

Hölscheidt, Sven and Schotten, Thomas, *Von Maastricht nach Karlsruhe. Der lange Weg des Vertrages über die Europäische Union*, Rheinbreitbach, 1993.

Holtfrerich, Carl-Ludwig, *The German Inflation 1914–1923: causes and effects in international perspective*, Berlin and New York, 1986.

Holzamer, Hans-Herbert, ed., *Der Marshall-Plan. Geschichte und Zukunft*, Landsberg am Lech, 1997.

Hölzenbein, Bernd, *Die strategische Verteidigungsinitiative (SDI) als Problem bundesdeutscher Außen- und Sicherheitspolitik. Analyse des Entscheidungsprozesses der Bundesregierung*, Berlin, 1990.

Holzer, Jerzy, *Solidarität. Die Geschichte einer freien Gewerkschaft in Polen*, Munich, 1985.

Hommen, Tania, *Sittlichkeitsverbrechen. Sexuelle Gewalt im Kaiserreich*, Frankfurt am Main and New York, 1999.

Horne, John N., ed., *A Companion to World War I*, Oxford, 2012.

Horne, John N., and Kramer, Alan, *German Atrocities, 1914. A History of Denial*, London, 2001.

Hradil, Stefan and Bolte, Karl Martin, *Soziale Ungleichheit in Deutschland*, Opladen, 2001.

Huber, Joseph, *Wer soll das alles ändern. Die Alternativen der Alternativbewegung*, Berlin, 1980.

Hudson, Ray, *Wrecking a Region. State Policies, Party Politics and Regional Change in North East England*, London, 1989.

Hughes, Geoffrey, *Political Correctness. A History of Semantics and Culture*, Malden, Massachusetts and Chichester, 2010.

Hughes, Michael L., *Shouldering the Burden of Defeat. West Germany and the Reconstruction of Social Justice*, Chapel Hill, North Carolina, and London, 1999.

Huizinga, Johan, *Im Schatten von Morgen: eine Diagnose des kulturellen Leidens unserer Zeit*, Berne, 1935.

Hull, Isabel, *Absolute Destruction. Military Culture and the Practices of War in Imperial Germany*, Ithaca, New York, 2005.

Hunn, Karin, *'Nächstes Jahr kehren wir zurück . . . ' Die Geschichte der türkischen 'Gastarbeiter' in der Bundesrepublik*, Göttingen, 2005.

Huret, Jules, *Berlin um Neunzehnhundert*, Berlin, 1997.

Hürten, Heinz, *Der Kapp-Putsch als Wende. Über Rahmenbedingungen der Weimarer Republik seit dem Frühjahr 1920*, Opladen, 1989.

Hürter, Johannes, 'Die Wehrmacht vor Leningrad. Krieg und Besatzungspolitik der 18. Armee im Herbst und Winter 1941/42', *VfZ* 49 (2001), pp. 377–440.

Hürter, Johannes, *Hitlers Heerführer. Die deutschen Oberbefehlshaber im Krieg gegen die Sowjetunion 1941/42*, Munich, 2007.

Hutchinson, Colin, *Reaganism, Thatcherism and the Social Novel*, Basingstoke, 2008.

Ihme-Tuchel, Beate, *Die DDR*, Darmstadt, 2007.

Inglehart, Ronald, *Culture Shift in Advanced Industrial Society*, Princeton NJ, 1990.

Inglehart, Ronald, *The Silent Revolution. Changing Values and Political Styles Among Western Publics*, Princeton, New Jersey, 1977.

Isserman, Maurice and Kazin, Michael, *America Divided. The Civil War of the 1960s*, New York, 2008.

Jäckel, Eberhard, ed., *Der Mord an den Juden im Zweiten Weltkrieg. Entschlussbildung und Verwirklichung*, Stuttgart, 1985.

Jackson, Julian, *The Fall of France. The Nazi Invasion of 1940*, New York and Oxford, 2003.

Jacobeit, Wolfgang, Mooser, Josef and Strath, Bo, eds., *Idylle oder Aufbruch? Das Dorf im bürgerlichen 19. Jahrhundert*, Berlin, 1990.

Jacobmeyer, Wolfgang, 'Jüdische Überlebende als "Displaced Persons" 1945–1947. Untersuchungen zur Besatzungspolitik in den deutschen Westzonen and zur Zuwanderung osteuropäischer Juden', *GG* 9 (1983), pp. 421–52.

Jacobmeyer, Wolfgang, *Vom Zwangsarbeiter zum heimatlosen Ausländer. Die Displaced Persons in Westdeutschland 1945–1941*, Göttingen, 1985.

Jäger, Manfred, *Kultur und Politik in der DDR 1945–1990*, Cologne, 1995.

Jahnke, Karl Heinz, ed., *Deutsche Jugend 1933–1945. Eine Dokumentation*, Hamburg, 1989.

James, Harold, *Europe Reborn: a history 1914–2000*, Harlow, 2003.

James, Harold, *The German Slump: Politics and Economics 1924–1936*, Oxford, 1986.

James, Harold, *Rambouillet, 25. November 1975. Die Globalisierung der Wirtschaft*, Munich, 1997.

Jankowski, Martin, *Der Tag, der Deutschland veränderte. 9.Oktober 1989*, Leipzig, 2007.

Jansen, Christian et al., eds. *Von der Aufgabe der Freiheit. Politische Verantwortung und bürgerliche Gesellschaft im 19. und 20. Jahrhundert. Festschrift für Hans Mommsen*, Berlin, 1995.

Jansen, Christian, *Professoren und Politik. Politisches Denken und Handeln der Heidelberger Hochschullehrer 1914–1935*, Göttingen, 1992.

Jansen, Christian and Weckbecker, Arno, *Der 'Volksdeutsche Selbstschutz' in Polen 1939–40*, Munich, 1992.

Jarausch, Konrad H., ed., *Amerikanisierung und Sowjetisierung in Deutschland 1945–1970*, Frankfurt am Main and New York, 1997.

Jarausch, Konrad H., ed., *Das Ende der Zuversicht? Die siebziger Jahre als Geschichte*, Göttingen, 2008.

Jarausch, Konrad H., *After Hitler: recivilizing Germans, 1945–1995*, Oxford, 2006.

Jarausch, Konrad H. and Sabrow, Martin, eds., *Weg in den Untergang. Der innere Zerfall der DDR*, Göttingen, 1999.

Jasper, Gotthard, *Von Weimar zu Hitler 1930–1933*, Cologne and Berlin, 1968.

Jaspers, Karl, *Freiheit und Wiedervereinigung. Über Aufgaben deutscher Politik*, Munich, 1960.

Jastrzebski, Włodzimierz, *Der Bromberger Blutsonntag. Legende und Wirklichkeit*, Poznań, 1990.

Jena, Kai von, 'Versöhnung mit Israel? Die deutsch-israelischen Verhandlungen bis zum Wiedergutmachungsabkommen von 1952', *VfZ* 34 (1986), pp. 457–80.

Jenke, Manfred, *Verschwörung von rechts. Ein Bericht über den Rechtsradikalismus in Deutschland nach 1945*, Berlin, 1961.

Jenkins, Helmut Walter, *Ursprung und Entwicklung der gemeinnützigen Wohnungswirtschaft. Eine wirtschaftliche und sozialgeschichtliche Darstellung*, Bonn, 1973.

Jescheck, Hans-Heinrich, *Das Menschenbild unserer Zeit und die Strafrechtsreform*, Tübingen, 1957.

Jeserich, Kurt G.A., ed., *Deutsche Verwaltungsgeschichte. Das Deutsche Reich bis zum Ende der Monarchie*, Stuttgart, 1984.

Joachim, Hans A., 'Romane aus Amerika', *Neue Rundschau* 412 (1930), pp. 396–409.

Joas, Hans, ed., *Vielfalt der Moderne—Ansichten der Moderne*, Frankfurt am Main, 2012.

Joas, Hans, 'Die Demokratisierung der Differenzierungsfrage', *Soziale Welt* 41 (1990), pp. 8–27.

Jochmann, Werner, *Gesellschaftskrise und Judenfeindschaft in Deutschland 1870–1945*, Hamburg, 1988.

Jochmann, Werner, *Im Kampf um die Macht. Hitlers Rede vor dem Hamburger Nationalklub von 1919*, Frankfurt am Main, 1960.

Joetze, Günter, *Der letzte Krieg in Europa? Das Kosovo und die deutsche Politik*, Stuttgart and Munich, 2001.

John, Hartmut, *Das Reserveoffizierskorps im Deutschen Kaiserreich 1890–1914*, Frankfurt am Main and New York, 1981.

Joll, James, *The Origins of the First World War*, London, 1984.

Jordan, Pascual, *Atomkraft, Drohung und Versprechen*, Munich, 1954.

Jörke, Dirk, 'Auf dem Weg zur Postdemokratie', *Leviathan. Berliner Zeitschrift für Sozialwissenschaft* 33 (2005), pp. 482–91.

Juchler, Ingo, *Die Studentenbewegungen in den Vereinigten Staaten und der Bundesrepublik Deutschland der sechziger Jahre. Eine Untersuchung hinsichtlich ihrer Beeinflussung durch Befreiungsbewegungen und—theorien aus der Dritten Welt*, Berlin, 1996.

Judt, Tony, *Postwar: a history of Europe since 1945*, London, 2005.

Jung, Edgar J., *Die Herrschaft der Minderwertigen. Ihr Zerfall und ihre Ablösung*, Berlin, 1927.

Jung, Edgar J., 'Neubelebung von Weimar?', *Deutsche Rundschau* 58.9 (1932), pp. 153–62.

Jung, Otmar, *Plebiszit und Diktatur. Die Volksabstimmungen der Nationalsozialisten: Die Fälle 'Austritt aus dem Völkerbund' (1933), 'Staatsoberhaupt' (1934) und 'Anschluß Österreichs' (1938)*, Tübingen, 1995.

Jünger, Ernst, *Der Kampf als inneres Erlebnis*, Berlin, 1922.

Jünger, Ernst, *Storm of Steel*, London, 2004.

Jungk, Robert, *The Nuclear State*, London, 1979.

Jungk, Robert and Mundt, Hans Josef, eds., *Der Griff nach der Zukunft. Planen und Freiheit*, Munich, 1964.

Jureit, Ulrike, *Generationenforschung*, Göttingen, 2006.

Jürgensen, Johannes, *Die bittere Lektion. Evangelische Jugend 1933*, Stuttgart, 1984.

Kaack, Heino, *Geschichte und Struktur des deutschen Parteiensystems*, Opladen, 1971.

Kaelble, Hartmut, ed., *Der Boom 1948–1973. Gesellschaftliche und wirtschaftliche Folgen in der Bundesrepublik Deutschland und in Europa*, Opladen, 1992.

Kaelble, Hartmut, ed., *Sozialgeschichte der DDR*, Stuttgart, 1994.

Kaelble, Hartmut, *Kalter Krieg und Wohlfahrtsstaat. Europa 1945–1989*, Munich, 2011.

Kaelble, Hartmut, *A Social History of Europe 1945–2000*, Oxford, 2013.

Kahl, Wilhelm, Meinecke, Friedrich and Radbruch, Gustav, *Die deutschen Universitäten und der heutige Staat. Referate erstattet auf der Weimarer Tagung deutscher Hochschullehrer am 23. und 24. April 1926*, Tübingen, 1926.

Kaiser, Gert and Frie, Ewald, eds., *Christen, Staat und Gesellschaft in der DDR*, Frankfurt am Main and New York, 1996.

Kaiser, Josef H., *Planung*, 6 vols., Baden-Baden, 1965–72.

Kaiser, Karl, ed. *Deutschlands Vereinigung. Die internationalen Aspekte*, Bergisch Gladbach, 1991.

Kaiser, Karl and Becher, Klaus, *Deutschland und der Irak-Konflikt. Internationale Sicherheitsverantwortung Deuschlands und Europas nach der deutschen Vereinigung*, Bonn, 1992.

Kaminsky, Annette, '"Mehr produzieren, gerechter verteilen, besser leben". Konsumpolitik der DDR', *APuZ* 28 (1999), pp. 12–20.

Kant, Hermann, *Das Impressum: Roman*, Neuwied, 1972.

Karády, Viktor, *Gewalterfahrung und Utopie. Juden in der europäischen Moderne*, Frankfurt am Main, 1999.

Karczewski, Johannes von, *'Weltwirtschaft ist unser Schicksal'. Helmut Schmidt und die Schaffung der Weltwirtschaftsgipfel*, Bonn, 2008.

Karl, Michaela, *Die Münchener Räterepublik*, Düsseldorf, 2008.

Karlauf, Thomas, *Stefan George. Die Entdeckung des Charisma*, Munich, 2008.

Karlsch, Rainer, *Allein bezahlt? Die Reparationsleistungen der SBZ/DDR 1945–1953*, Berlin, 1993.

Karlsch, Rainer, Laufer, Jochen and Sattler, Friederike, eds. *Sowjetische Demontagen in Deutschland 1944–1949. Hintergründe, Ziele und Wirkungen*, Berlin, 2002.

Kaschuba, Wolfgang, ed., *Der deutsche Heimatfilm. Bildwelten und Weltbilder. Bilder, Texte, Analysen zu 70 Jahren deutscher Filmgeschichte*, Tübingen, 1989.

Kasten, Bernd, *'Gute Franzosen'. Die französische Polizei und die deutsche Besatzungsmacht im besetzten Frankreich 1940–1944*, Sigmaringen, 1993.

Kater, Michael H., *Different Drummers: jazz in the culture of Nazi Germany*, Oxford, 2003.

Kater, Michael H. 'Wähler und Mitglieder der NSDAP. Neue Forschungsergebnisse zur Soziographie des Nationalsozialismus 1925 bis 1933', *GG* 19 (1993), pp. 155–77.

Kater, Michael H. *Hitler Youth*, Cambridge, Mass., 2004.

Keck, Otto, *Der Schnelle Brüter. Eine Fallstudie über Entscheidungsprozesse in der Großtechnik*, Frankfurt am Main and New York, 1984.

Keegan, John, *The First World War*, London, 1998.

Keegan, John, *The Second World War*, London, 1990.

Keiderling, Gerhard, ed., *'Gruppe Ulbricht' in Berlin April bis Juni 1945. Von den Vorbereitungen im Sommer 1944 bis zur Wiedergründung der KPD im Juni 1945. Eine Dokumentation*, Berlin, 1993.

Keller, Rolf, *Sowjetische Kriegsgefangene im deutschen Reich*, Göttingen, 2011.

Kemper, Peter, ed., *'Postmoderne' oder Der Kampf um die Zukunft. Die Kontroverse in Wissenschaft, Kunst und Gesellschaft*, Frankfurt am Main, 1988.

Kennan, George F., *The Decline of Bismarck's European Order. Franco-Russian Relations 1875–1890*, Princeton, 1979.

Kent, Bruce, *The Spoils of War. the Politics, Economics and Diplomacy of Reparations 1918–1932*, Oxford, 1989.

Kernig, Claus D., ed., *Sowjetsystem und demokratische Gesellschaft. Eine vergleichende Enzyklopädie*, 7 vols., Freiburg im Breisgau, Basle and Vienna, 1966–72.

Kershaw, Ian, *The End: Hitler's Germany, 1944-45*, London, 2011.

Kershaw, Ian, *Fateful Choices: ten decisions that shaped the world, 1940–1941*, London, 2007.

Kershaw, Ian, *Germany's Present, Germany's Past*, London, 1992.

Kershaw, Ian, *Hitler, 1889–1936: Hubris*, London, 1999.

Kershaw, Ian, *Hitler, 1936–1945: Nemesis*, London, 2000.

Kershaw, Ian, *The 'Hitler Myth': image and reality in the Third Reich*, Oxford, 2001.

Kershaw, Ian, *The Nazi Dictatorship: problems and perspectives of interpretation*, 4th edn., London, 2000.

Kershaw, Ian, *Popular Opinion and Political Dissent in the Third Reich: Bavaria 1933–1945*, Oxford, 1983.

Kessemeier, Gesa, *Sportlich, sachlich, männlich. Das Bild der 'Neuen Frau' in den Zwanziger Jahren*, Dortmund, 2000.

Khrushchev, Nikita S., *Khrushchev Remembers*, translated and edited by Strobe Talbott, London, 1971.

Kielmansegg, Peter, *Nach der Katastrophe. Eine Geschichte des geteilten Deutschland*, Berlin, 2000.

Killick, John, *The United States and European Reconstruction 1945–1960*, Edinburgh, 1999.

Kilz, Hans-Werner and Preuss, Joachim, *Flick. Die gekaufte Republik*, Reinbek bei Hamburg, 1984.

Kindleberger, Charles, *The World in Depression: 1929–1939*, London, 1973.

Kindler, Holger, Regelmann, Ada-Charlotte and Tullney, Marco, eds., *Die Folgen der Agenda 2010. Alte und neue Zwänge des Sozialstaates*, Hamburg, 2004.

Kingreen, Monica, ed., *'Nach der Kristallnacht'. Jüdisches Leben und anti-jüdische Politik in Frankfurt am Main, 1938–1945*, Frankfurt am Main, 1999.

Kirste, Knut, *Rollentheorie und Außenpolitikanalyse: Die USA und Deutschland als Zivilmächte*, Frankfurt am Main, 1998.

Kitchen, Martin, *The German Offensives of 1918*, Stroud, 2005.

Klages, Helmut, *Wertorientierungen im Wandel. Rückblick, Gegenwartsanalyse, Prognosen*, Frankfurt am Main and New York, 1985.

Klages, Ludwig, *Sämtliche Werke*, 9 vols., Bonn, 1974.

Klein, Markus, and Falter, Jürgen W., *Der lange Weg der Grünen. Eine Partei zwischen Protest und Regierung*, Munich, 2003.

Kleinmann, Hans-Otto, *Geschichte der CDU 1945–1982*, Stuttgart, 1993.

Kleist, Dietrich, 'Kritische Notizen zum Jugendschutz', *Unsere Jugend* 17.6 (1965), pp. 270–3.

Klenke, Dietmar, *'Freier Stau für freie Bürger'. Die Geschichte der bundesdeutschen Verkehrspolitik 1949–1994*, Darmstadt, 1995.

Kleßmann, Christoph, *Arbeiter im 'Arbeiterstaat' DDR. Deutsche Traditionen, sowjetisches Modell, westdeutsches Magnetfeld (1945 bis 1971)*, Bonn, 2007.

Kleßmann, Christoph, *Die doppelte Staaatsgründung. Deutsche Geschichte 1945–1955*, Göttingen, 1991.

Kleßmann, Christoph, *Polnische Bergarbeiter im Ruhrgebiet 1870–1945. Soziale Integration und nationale Subkultur in der deutschen Industriegesellschaft*, Göttingen, 1978.

Kleßmann, Christoph, *Zwei Staaten, eine Nation. Deutsche Geschichte 1955–1970*, Bonn, 1997.

Klingler, Walter, *Nationalsozialistische Rundfunkpolitik 1942–1945. Organisation, Programm und Hörer*, Mannheim, 1983.

Klönne, Arno, *Gegen den Strom. Bericht über den Jugendwiderstand im Dritten Reich*, Hanover and Frankfurt am Main, 1957.

Klönne, Arno, *Jugend im Dritten Reich. Die Hitler-Jugend und ihre Gegner*, Munich and Zürich, 1995.

Kloth, Hans Michael, *Vom 'Zettelfalten' zum freien Wahlen. Die Demokratisierung der DDR 1989/90 und die 'Wahlfrage'*, Berlin, 2000.

Klotzbach, Kurt, *Der Weg zur Staatspartei. Programmatik, praktische Politik und Organisation der deutschen Sozialdemokratie 1945 bis 1965*, Berlin and Bonn, 1982.

Kluge, Ulrich, ed., *Zwischen Bodenreform und Kollektivierung. Vor und Frühgeschichte der 'sozialistischen Landwirtschaft' in der SBZ/DDR vom Kriegsende bis in die fünfziger Jahre*, Stuttgart, 2001.

Kluge, Ulrich, *Agrarwirtschaft und ländliche Gesellschaft im 20. Jahrhundert*, Munich, 2005.

Kluge, Ulrich, *Die Weimarer Republik*, Paderborn etc., 2006.

Kluge, Ulrich, *Soldatenräte und Revolution. Studien zur Militärpolitik in Deutschland 1918/19*, Göttingen, 1975.

Kluge, Ulrich, *Vierzig Jahre Agrarpolitik in der Bundesrepublik Deutschland,* 2 vols., Hamburg and Berlin, 1989.

Kluge, Ulrich, 'Wandel ohne Entschädigung. Staatliche Agrarpolitik in der Bundesrepublik 1949–1986', *ZAA* 35 (1987), pp. 160–93.

Klump, Rainer, *Wirtschaftsgeschichte der Bundesrepublik Deutschland. Zur Kritik neuerer wirtschaftshistorischer Interpretationen aus ordnungspolitischer Sicht*, Stuttgart, 1985.

Kniep, Jürgen, *Wiederaufbau und Wirtschaftswunder. Bildband zur Bayerischen Landesausstellung 2009,* Augsburg, 2009.

Kniesche, Thomas W and Brockmann, Stephen, eds., *Dancing on the Volcano. Essays on the Culture of the Weimar Republic,* Columbia, 1994

Knipping, Franz, *Rom, 25 März 1957. Die Einigung Europas*, Munich, 2004.

Knipping, Franz and Matthias Schönwald, eds., *Aufbruch zum Europa der zweiten Generation. Die europäische Einigung 1969–1984,* Trier, 2004.

Knöbl, Wolfgang, *Die Kontingenz der Moderne. Wege in Europa, Asien und Amerika*, Frankfurt am Main, 2007.

Knock, Thomas J., *To End All Wars. Woodrow Wilson and the Quest for a New World Order*, New York and Oxford, 1992.

Köchling, Martina, *Demontagepolitik und Wiederaufbau in Nordrhein-Westfalen*, Essen, 1995.

Kock, Gerhard, *'Der Führer sorgt für unsere Kinder'. Die Kinderlandverschickung im Zweiten Weltkrieg*, Paderborn, 1997.

Kocka, Jürgen, ed., *Bürger und Bürgerlichkeit im 19. Jahrhundert*, Göttingen, 1987.

Kocka, Jürgen, ed., *Bourgeois Society in Nineteenth-Century Europe*, Oxford, 1993.

Kocka, Jürgen, *Arbeitsverhältnisse und Arbeiterexistenzen. Grundlagen der Klassenbildung im 19. Jahrhundert*, Bonn and Berlin, 1990.

Kocka, Jürgen, *Die Angestellten in der deutschen Geschichte 1850–1980*, Göttingen, 1981.

Kocka, Jürgen, *Vereinigungskrise. Zur Geschichte der Gegenwart*, Göttingen, 1995.

Koebner, Thomas, ed., *Deutschland nach Hitler. Zukunftspläne im Exil und aus der Besatzungszeit 1939–1949*, Opladen, 1987.

Koebner, Thomas, ed., *Mit uns zieht die neue Zeit. Der Mythos Jugend*, Frankfurt am Main, 1985.

Koebner, Thomas, Sautermeister, Gert and Schneider, Sigrid, eds., *Deutschland nach Hitler. Zukunftspläne im Exil und aus der Besatzungszeit*, Opladen, 1987.

Koehl, Robert Lewis, *RKFDV. German Resettlement and Population Policy 1939–1945. A History of the Reich Commission for the Strengthening of Germandom*, Cambridge, Massachusetts, 1957.

Koenen, Gerd, *Das rote Jahrzehnt. Unsere kleine deutsche Kulturrevolution, 1967–1977*, Cologne, 2001.

Koenen, Gerd, *Vesper, Ensslin, Baader. Urszenen des deutschen Terrors*, Frankfurt am Main, 2011.

Koenen, Gerd, *Was war der Kommunismus?*, Göttingen, 2010.

Koepf, Hans et al., eds., *Stadtbaukunst. Stadterhaltung, Stadtgestaltung, Stadterneuerung*, Sigmaringen, 1985.

Kogel, Jörg-Dieter, *Neues Deutschland. Innenansichten einer wiedervereinigten Nation*, Frankfurt am Main, 1993.

Köglmeier, Georg, *Die zentralen Rätegremien in Bayern 1918/19*, Munich, 2001.

Köhler, Joachim and van Melis, Damian, eds., *Siegerin in Trümmern. Die Rolle der katholischen Kirche in der deutschen Nachkriegsgesellschaft*, Stuttgart, Berlin and Cologne, 1998.

Kolb, Eberhard, *Bergen-Belsen. From 'Detention Camp' to Concentration Camp*, Göttingen, 1985.

Kolb, Eberhard, *Der Frieden von Versailles*, Munich, 2005.

Kolb, Eberhard, *Die Arbeiterräte in der deutschen Innenpolitik 1918–1919*, Frankfurt am Main, Berlin and Vienna, 1978.

Kolb, Eberhard, *The Weimar Republic*, London, 2007.

König, Wolfgang, *Geschichte der Konsumgesellschaft*, Stuttgart, 2000.

König, Wolfgang, *Kleine Geschichte der Konsumgesellschaft. Konsum als Lebensform der Moderne*, Stuttgart, 2008.

König, Wolfgang, and Weber, Wolfhard, *Netzwerke Stahl und Strom: 1840 bis 1940* (Propyläen Technikgeschichte, vol. 4), Berlin, 1990.

Königseder, Angelika and Wetzel, Juliane, *Lebensmut im Wartesaal. Die jüdischen DPs (Displaced Persons) im Nachkriegsdeutschland*, Frankfurt am Main, 1994.

Konrad, Helmut and Schmidlechner, Karin, eds., *Revolutionäres Potential in Europa am Ende des Ersten Weltkrieges. Die Rolle von Strukturen, Konjunkturen und Massenbewegungen*, Vienna and Cologne, 1991.

Körner, Heiko and Mehrländer, Ursula, eds., *Die 'neue' Ausländerpolitik in Europa. Erfahrungen in den Aufnahme- und Entsendeländern*, Bonn, 1986.

Korte, Karl-Rudolf, *Der Standort der Deutschen. Akzentverlagerungen der deutschen Frage in der Bundesrepublik Deutschland seit den siebziger Jahren*, Cologne, 1990.

Korte, Karl-Rudolf, *Deutschlandpolitik in Helmut Kohls Kanzlerschaft. Regierungsstil und Entscheidungen 1982–1989*, Stuttgart, 1998.

Kosok, Lisa and Jamin, Mathilde, eds., *Viel Vergnügen. Öffentliche Lustbarkeiten im Ruhrgebiet der Jahrhundertwende*, Essen, 1992.

Kossert, Andreas, *Kalte Heimat. Die Geschichte der deutschen Vertriebenen nach 1945*, Munich, 2008.

Kössler, Till, *Abschied von der Revolution. Kommunisten und Gesellschaft in Westdeutschland 1945–1968*, Düsseldorf, 2005.

Kössler, Till, 'Kaderpartei oder Milieupartei? Die KPD in Westdeutschland 1945 bis 1960', *Jahrbuch für historische Kommunismusforschung* (2004), pp. 131–55.

Kotek, Joël and Rigoulot, Pierre, *Das Jahrhundert der Lager. Gefangenschaft, Zwangsarbeit, Vernichtung*, Berlin and Munich, 2001.

Kowalczuk, Ilko-Sascha, *Endspiel. Die Revolution von 1989 in der DDR*, Munich, 2009.

Kowalczuk, Ilko-Sascha, Mitter, Armin and Wolle, Stefan, eds., *Der Tag X—17. Juni 1953. Die 'Innere Staatsgründung' der DDR als Ergebnis der Krise 1952/54*, Berlin, 1995.

Krabbe, Wolfgang R., *Die deutsche Stadt im 19. und 20. Jahrhundert. Eine Einführung*, Göttingen 1989.

Krafft-Ebing, Richard von, *Nervosität und neurasthenische Zustände*, Vienna, 1899.

Kramer, Alan, *Die britische Demontagepolitik am Beispiel Hamburgs 1945–1950*, Hamburg, 1991.

Krammer, Arnold, *Nazi Prisoners of War in America*, New York, 1979.

Kramper, Peter, *Neue Heimat. Unternehmenspolitik und Unternehmensentwicklung im gewerkschaftlichen Wohnungs- und Städtebau 1950–1982*, Stuttgart, 2008.

Krause, Michael, *Flucht vor dem Bombenkrieg. 'Umquartierungen' im Zweiten Weltkrieg und die Wiedereingliederung der Evakuierten in Deutschland*, Düsseldorf, 1997.

Kraushaar, Wolfgang, ed., Frankfurter *Schule und Studentenbewegung. Von der Flaschenpost zum Molotowcocktail 1946–1995*, Hamburg, 1998.

Kraushaar, Wolfgang, *1968 als Mythos, Chiffre und Zäsur*, Hamburg, 2000.

Kraushaar, Wolfgang, *1968. Das Jahr, das alles verändert hat*, Munich and Zürich, 1998.

Krausnick, Helmut, 'Denkschrift Himmlers über die Behandlung der Fremdvölkischen im Osten', *VfZ* 5 (1957), pp. 194–8.

Krausnick, Helmut, *Hitlers Einsatzgruppen. Die Truppen des Weltanschauungskrieges 1938–1942*, Frankfurt am Main, 1985.

Krausnick, Helmut and Broszat, Martin, *Anatomy of the SS State*, London and New York, 1970.

Kretschmer, Winfried, *Geschichte der Weltausstellungen*, Frankfurt am Main, 1999.

Kreuzer, Helmut, ed., *Jahrhundertende—Jahrhundertwende*, Wiesbaden, 1976.

Kronenbitter, Günther, Pöhlmann, Markus and Walter, Dierk, eds., *Besatzung, Funktion und Gestalt militärischer Fremdherrschaft von der Antike bis zum 20. Jahrhundert*, Paderborn etc., 2006.

Krüger, Peter, *Die Außenpolitik der Republik von Weimar*, Darmstadt, 1985.

Krumeich, Gerd, ed., *Nationalsozialismus und Erster Weltkrieg*, Essen, 2010.

Krumeich, Gerd, ed., *Versailles 1919. Ziele, Wirkung, Wahrnehmung*, Essen, 2001.

Kruse, Wolfgang, *Krieg und nationale Integration. Eine Neuinterpretation des sozialdemokratischen Burgfriedensschlusses 1914/15*, Essen, 1993.

Krzoska, Markus, 'Der "Bromberger Blutsonntag" 1939. Kontroversen und Forschungsergebnisse', *VfZ* 60.2 (2012), pp. 237–48.

Kubina, Michael and Wilke, Manfred, eds., *'Hart und kompromisslos durchgreifen.' Die SED contra Polen 1980/81*, Berlin, 1995.

Küchler, Falk, *Die Wirtschaft der DDR. Wirtschaftspolitik und industrielle Rahmenbedingungen 1949 bis 1989. Wirtschaftshistorische Studien*, Berlin, 1997.

Kuhn, Axel, *Die deutsche Arbeiterbewegung*, Stuttgart, 2004.

Kühn, Hartmut, *Das Jahrzehnt der Solidarność. Die politische Geschichte Polens 1980–1990*, Berlin, 1999.

Kulka, Otto Dov and Mendes-Flohr, Paul, eds., *Judaism and Christianity under the Impact of National Socialism*, Jerusalem, 1987.

Kuller, Christiane, *Bürokratie und Verbrechen. Antisemitische Finanzpolitik und Verwaltungspraxis im nationalsozialistischen Deutschland*, Munich, 2013.

Kundrus, Birthe, ed., *Phantasiereiche. Das Kaiserreich im Spiegel seiner Kolonien*, Cologne, Weimar and Vienna, 2003.

Kunz, Andreas, ed., *Die Akte Neue Heimat. Krise und Abwicklung des größten Wohnungsbaukonzerns Europas 1982–1998*, 2 vols., Frankfurt am Main and New York, 2003.

Kurz, Jan, *Die Universität auf der Piazza. Entstehung und Zerfall der Studentenbewegung in Italien 1966–1968*, Cologne, 2011.

Kurzman, Charles, *The Unthinkable Revolution in Iran*, Cambridge, Massachusetts, 2004.

Küsters, Hanns Jürgen, *Der Integrationsfriede. Viermächte- Verhandlungen über die Friedensregelung mit Deutschland 1945–1990*, Munich, 2000.

Küsters, Hanns Jürgen, *Die Gründung der Europäischen Wirtschaftsgemeinschaft*, Baden-Baden, 1982.

Laak, Dirk van, *Gespräche in der Sicherheit des Schweigens. Carl Schmitt in der politischen Geistesgeschichte der frühen Bundesrepublik*, Berlin, 1993.

Laak, Dirk van, *Über alles in der Welt. Deutscher Imperialismus im 19. und 20. Jahrhundert*, Munich, 2005.

Lamprecht, Karl, *Deutsche Geschichte*, 5 vols., Berlin, 1891–5.

Landfried, Christine, *Parteifinanzen und politische Macht. Eine vergleichende Studie zur Bundesrepublik Deutschland, zu Italien und den USA*, Baden-Baden, 1990.

Lang, Barbara, *Mythos Kreuzberg. Ethnographie eines Stadtteils (1961–1995)*, Frankfurt am Main and New York, 1998.

Langewiesche, Dieter, ed., *Arbeiter in Deutschland. Studien zur Lebensweise der Arbeiterschaft im Zeitalter der Industrialisierung*, Paderborn etc., 1981.

Langewiesche, Dieter, ed., *Universitäten im nationalsozialistisch beherrschten Europa*, Göttingen, 1997.

Langewiesche, Dieter, 'Politik—Gesellschaft—Kultur. Zur Problematik von Arbeiterkultur und kulturellen Arbeiterorganisationen in Deutschland nach dem 1. Weltkrieg', *AfS* 12 (1982), pp. 359–402.

Langewiesche, Dieter and Tenorth, Heinz-Elmar, *Handbuch der deutschen Bildungsgeschichte 1918–1945. Bd.5. Die Weimarer Republik und die nationalsozialistische Diktatur*, Munich, 1989.

Langkau-Alex, Ursula, ed., *Was soll aus Deutschland werden? Der Council for a Democratic Germany in New York 1944–1945*, Frankfurt am Main and New York, 1995.

Lappenküper, Ulrich, *Die deutsch-französischen Beziehungen 1949–1963. Von der Erbfeindschaft zur 'Entente élémentaire'*, vol.2, Oldenburg, 2001.

Lappenküper, Ulrich, *Mitterrand und Deutschland. Die enträtselte Sphinx*, Munich, 2011.

Laqueur, Walter Z., *Young Germany: a history of the German Youth Movement*, London, 1962.

Large, David Clay, *Munich 1972. Tragedy, Terror and Triumph at the Olympic Games*, Lanham, Maryland, 2012.

Latham, Michael E., *Modernization as Ideology. American Social Science and 'Nation Building' in the Kennedy Era*, Chapel Hill, North Carolina, 2000.

Latzel, Klaus, *Deutsche Soldaten—nationalsozialistischer Krieg? Kriegserlebnis—Kriegserfahrung 1939–1945*, Paderborn etc., 1998.

Läufer, Thomas, ed., *Europäische Gemeinschaft—Europäische Union. Die Vertragstexte von Maastricht mit den deutschen Begleitgesetzen*, Bonn, 1992.

Layritz, Stephan, *Der NATO—Doppelbeschluß. Westliche Sicherheitspolitik im Spannungsfeld von Innen-, Bündnis- und Außenpolitik, eine Fallstudie zur Entwicklung und Implementation sicherheitspolitischer Programme*, Kiel, 1991.

Leffler, Melvyn P., and Westad, Odd Arne, eds. *The Cambridge History of the Cold War. Volume 2 Crises and Détente*, Cambridge, 2010.

Lehmann, Axel, *Der Marshall-Plan und das neue Deutschland. Die Folgen amerikanischer Besatzungspolitik in den Westzonen*, Münster etc., 2000.

Lehmann, Hartmut and Oexle, Otto Gerhard, eds., *Nationalsozialismus in den Kulturwissenschaften*, Göttingen, 2004.

Lehnert, Detlef and Megerle, Klaus, eds., *Politische Teilkulturen zwischen Integration und Polarisierung. Zur politischen Kultur in der Weimarer Republik*, Opladen, 1990.

Leif, Thomas, *Die strategische Ohnmacht der Friedensbewegung. Kommunikations- und Entscheidungsstrukturen in den achtziger Jahren*, Opladen, 1990.

Lemke, Michael, *Die Berlinkrise 1958 bis 1963. Interessen und Handlungsspielräume der SED im Ost-West-Konflikt*, Berlin, 1995.

Leo, Per, *Der Wille zum Wesen. Weltanschauungskultur, charakterologisches Denken und Judenfeindschaft in Deutschland 1890–1940*, Berlin, 2013.

Leonhard, Jörn, and Hirschausen, Ulrike von, *Empires und Nationalstaaten im 19. Jahrhundert*, Göttingen, 2009.

Lepsius, Mario Rainer, *Demokratie in Deutschland. Soziologisch-historische Konstellationsanalysen*, Göttingen, 1993.

Lethen, Helmut, *Cool Conduct: the culture of distance in Weimar Germany*, Berkeley, Cal., 2002.

Lewek, Peter, *Arbeitslosigkeit und Arbeitslosenversicherung in der Weimarer Republik 1918–1927*, Stuttgart, 1992.

Lewy, Guenther, *The Nazi Persecution of the Gypsies*, New York, 2000.

Leyendecker, Hans and Rickelmann, Richard, *Exporteure des Todes. Deutscher Rüstungsskandal in Nahost*, Göttingen, 1990.

Lieber, Hans-Joachim, *Kulturkritik und Lebensphilosophie. Studien zur Deutschen Philosophie der Jahrhundertwende*, Darmstadt, 1974.

Liebing, Yvonne, *'All you need is beat.' Jugendkultur in Leipzig 1957–1968*, Leipzig, 2005.

Lillteicher, Jürgen, *Raub, Recht und Restitution. Die Rückerstattung jüdischen Eigentums in der frühen Bundesrepublik*, Göttingen, 2007.

Linden, Marcel van der, ed., *Kriegsbegeisterung und mentale Kriegsvorbereitung. Interdisziplinäre Studien*, Berlin, 1991.

Lindenberger, Thomas and Wildt, Michael, 'Radikale Pluralität. Geschichtswerkstätten als praktische Wissenschaftskritik', *AfS* 29 (1989), pp. 393–411.

Lindlar, Ludger, *Das mißverstandene Wirtschaftswunder. Westdeutschland und die westeuropäische Nachkriegsprosperität*, Tübingen, 1997.

Linnenkohl, Hans, *Vom Einzelschuß zur Feuerwalze. Der Wettlauf zwischen Technik und Taktik im Ersten Weltkrieg*, Bonn, 1996.

Linse, Ulrich, *Barfüßige Propheten. Erlöser der zwanziger Jahre*, Berlin, 1983.

Linse, Ulrich, *Ökopax und Anarchie. Eine Geschichte der ökologischen Bewegungen in Deutschland*, Munich, 1986.

Linz, Juan J., *Totalitarian and Authoritarian Regimes*, Boulder, Colorado, 2000.

Liulevicius, Vejas G., *War Land on the Eastern Front. Culture, National Identity, and German Occupation in World War I*, Cambridge, 2000.

Löffler, Bernhard, *Soziale Marktwirtschaft und administrative Praxis. Das Bundeswirtschaftsministerium unter Ludwig Erhard*, Stuttgart, 2002.

Löffler, Günter, *Die Agrarwirtschaft im 20. Jahrhundert*, Cologne, 2002.

Lohalm, Uwe, *Völkischer Radikalismus. Die Geschichte des Deutschvölkischen Schutz- und Trutz-Bundes 1919–1923*, Hamburg, 1970.

Longerich, Peter, *'Davon haben wir nichts gewusst!' Die Deutschen und die Judenverfolgung 1933–1945*, Bonn, 2006.

Longerich, Peter, *Deutschland 1918–1933. Die Weimarer Republik*, Hanover, 1995.

Longerich, Peter, *Die braunen Bataillone. Geschichte der SA*, Munich, 1989.

Longerich, Peter, *Holocaust. The Nazi Persecution and Murder of the Jews*, Oxford, 2010.

Longerich, Peter, *The Unwritten Order: Hitler's Role in the Final Solution*, Stroud, 2003.

Lönnendonker, Siegward, Rabehl, Bernd and Staadt, Jochen, *Die antiautoritäre Revolte. Der Sozialistische Deutsche Studentenbund nach der Trennung von der SPD, 1960–1967*, vol. 1, Wiesbaden, 2002.

Loquai, Heinz, *Der Kosovo-Konflikt—Wege in einen vermeidbaren Krieg. Die Zeit von Ende November 1997 bis März 1999*, Baden-Baden, 2000.

Lorenz, Hilke, *Kriegskinder. Das Schicksal einer Generation*, Munich, 2003.

Lösch, Niels C., *Rasse als Konstrukt. Leben und Werk Eugen Fischers*, Frankfurt am Main etc., 1997.

Lösche, Peter, *Der Bolschewismus im Urteil der deutschen Sozialdemokratie 1903–1920*, Berlin, 1967.

Lösche, Peter, *Die FDP. Richtungsstreit und Zukunftszweifel*, Darmstadt, 1996.

Lösche, Peter and Walter, Franz, *Die SPD. Klassenpartei,—Volkspartei—Quotenpartei. Zur Entwicklung der Sozialdemokratie von Weimar bis zur deutschen Vereinigung*, Darmstadt, 1992.

Loth, Wilfried, *Building Europe: a history of European unification*, Berlin, 2015.

Loth, Wilfried, ed., *Deutscher Katholizismus im Umbruch zur Moderne*, Stuttgart, Berlin and Cologne, 1991.

Loth, Wilfried, 'Helmut Kohl und die Währungsunion', *VfZ* 61 (2013), pp. 455–80.

Loth, Wilfried, *Helsinki, 1. August 1975. Entspannung und Abrüstung*, Munich, 1998.

Loth, Wilfried, *Katholiken im Kaiserreich. Der politische Katholizismus in der Krise des wilhelminischen Deutschlands*, Düsseldorf, 1984.

Loth, Wilfried, *Ost-West Konflikt und deutsche Frage. Historische Ortsbestimmungen*, Munich, 1989.

Loth, Wilfried, *The Division of the World, 1941–1955*, London, 1988.

Löw, Andrea, *Juden im Getto Litzmannstadt. Lebensbedingungen, Selbstwahrnehmung, Verhalten*, Göttingen, 2006.

Lowenstein, Steven M., et al., *Integration in Dispute, 1871–1918*, (German-Jewish History in Modern Times, vol.3), New York, 1997.

Lubrich, Oliver, ed., *Berichte aus der Abwurfzone. Ausländer erleben den Bombenkrieg in Deutschland 1939–1945*, Frankfurt am Main, 2007.

Lucas, Erhard, *Märzrevolution im Ruhrgebiet. Vom Generalstreik gegen den Militärputsch zum bewaffneten Arbeiteraufstand,* 3 vols., Frankfurt am Main, 1970–8.

Lüders, Carsten, *Das Ruhrkontrollsystem. Entstehung und Entwicklung im Rahmen der Westintegration Westdeutschlands 1947–1953*, Frankfurt am Main and New York, 1988.

Ludewig, Hans-Ulrich, *Arbeiterbewegung und Aufstand. Eine Untersuchung zum Verhalten der Arbeiterparteien in den Aufstandsbewegungen der frühen Weimarer Republik 1920–1923,* Husum, 1978.

Ludlam, Steven and Smith, Martin J., eds., *New Labour in Government*, New York, 2001.

Lüdtke, Alf, ed., *The History of Everyday Life: reconstructing historical experiences and ways of life*, Princeton, New Jersey, 1995.

Lüdtke, Alf, ed., *Amerikanisierung. Traum und Alptraum im Deutschland des 20. Jahrhunderts*, Stuttgart, 1996.

Ludz, Peter-Christian, *The Changing Party Elite in East Germany*, Cambridge, Mass., 1972.

Lumley, Robert, *States of Emergency. Cultures of Revolt in Italy from 1968 to 1978*, London and New York, 1990.

Lundgreen, Peter, *Wissenschaft im Dritten Reich*, Frankfurt am Main, 1985.

Luther, Hans, *Der französische Widerstand gegen die deutsche Besatzungsmacht und seine Bekämpfung. Ein Beitrag zur Erforschung der völkerrechtlichen Praxis während des Zweiten Weltkriegs*, Tübingen, 1957.

Lux, Anna, *Demokraten im Unrechtsstaat. Das politische System der SBZ/DDR zwischen Zwangsvereinigung und Nationaler Front*, Leipzig, 2006.

Lyotard, Jean-François, *The Postmodern Condition: a report on knowledge*, Minneapolis, 1984.

Maase, Kaspar, ed., *Die Schönheiten des Populären. Ästhetische Erfahrung der Gegenwart*, Frankfurt am Main and New York, 2008.

Maase, Kaspar, *Grenzenloses Vergnügen. Der Aufstieg der Massenkultur 1850–1970*, Frankfurt am Main, 2007.

MacDonald, Lyn, *Somme*, New York, 1989.

Madaiczyk, Czesław, *Die Okkupationspolitik Nazideutschlands in Polen 1939–1945*, Cologne, 1988.

Mai, Gunther, ed., *Arbeiterschaft in Deutschland 1914–1918. Studien zu Arbeitskampf und Arbeitsmarkt im Ersten Weltkrieg*, Düsseldorf, 1985.

Mai, Gunther, *Das Ende des Kaiserreichs. Politik und Kriegführung im Ersten Weltkrieg*, Munich, 1987.

Mai, Gunther, *Der Alliierte Kontrollrat in Deutschland 1945–1948. Alliierte Einheit—deutsche Teilung?*, Munich and Vienna, 1995.

Mai, Gunther, 'Die agrarische Transition', *GG* 33 (2007), pp. 471–514.

Mai, Gunther, *Europa 1914–1939. Mentalitäten, Lebensweisen, Politik zwischen den Weltkriegen*, Stuttgart, Berlin and Cologne, 2001.

Mai, Uwe, *Rasse und Raum. Agrarpolitik, Sozial- und Raumplanung im NS-Staat*, Paderborn etc., 2002.

Maier, Charles S. *Dissolution: the Crisis of Communism and the End of East Germany*, Princeton, New Jersey, 1997.

Maier, Charles S., ed., *The Marshall Plan and Germany: West German development within the framework of the European Recovery Progràmme*, New York and Oxford, 1991.

Mallmann, Klaus-Michael, 'Gehorsame Parteisoldaten oder eigensinnige Akteure? Die Weimarer Kommunisten in der Kontroverse—eine Erwiderung', *VfZ* 47 (1999), pp. 401–15.

Mallmann, Klaus-Michael, *Kommunisten in der Weimarer Republik. Sozialgeschichte einer revolutionären Bewegung*, Darmstadt, 1996.

Mallmann, Klaus-Michael and Musiał, Bogdan, eds., *Genesis des Genozids. Polen 1939–1941*, Darmstadt, 2004.

Mallmann, Klaus-Michael and Paul, Gerhard, eds., *Karrieren der Gewalt. Nationalsozialistische Täterbiographien*, Darmstadt, 2005.

Mann, Gunter, ed., *Medizin, Naturwissenschaft, Technik und das Zweite Kaiserreich*, Göttingen, 1977.

Mann, Reinhard, *Protest und Kontrolle im Dritten Reich. Nationalsozialistische Herrschaft im Alltag einer rheinischen Großstadt*, Frankfurt am Main and New York, 1987.

Mann, Thomas, *Gesammelte Werke*, vol. 10, Frankfurt am Main, 1956.

Manoschek, Walter, *'Serbien ist judenfrei'. Militärische Besatzungspolitik und Judenvernichtung in Serbien 1941/42*, Munich, 1993.

Marcuse, Herbert, *Das Ende der Utopie. Vorträge und Diskussionen in Berlin 1967*, Frankfurt am Main, 1980.

Marschalck, Peter, *Bevölkerungsgeschichte Deutschlands im 19. und 20. Jahrhundert*, Frankfurt am Main, 1984.

Marsh, David, *The Euro: the Politics of the New Global Currency*, New Haven, Connecticut and London, 2009.

Marßolek, Inge and Saldern, Adelheid von, eds., *Zuhören und Gehörtwerden. Radio im Nationalsozialismus. Zwischen Lenkung und Ablenkung*, Tübingen, 1998.

Marwick, Arthur, *The Sixties*, Oxford and New York, 1998.

Marx, Christian, *Paul Reusch und die Gutehoffnungshütte. Leitung eines deutschen Großunternehmens*, Göttingen, 2013.

Maschmann, Melita, *Fazit. Kein Rechtfertigungsversuch*, Munich, 1983.

Maschmann, Melita, *Account Rendered: a dossier of my former self*, London, 1965.

Matschke, Werner, *Die industrielle Entwicklung in der Sowjetischen Besatzungszone Deutschlands (SBZ) von 1945 bis 1948*, Berlin, 1988.

Mattioli, Aram, *Experimentierfeld der Gewalt. Der Abessinienkrieg und seine internationale Bedeutung 1935–1941*, Zürich, 2005 (Kultur—Philosophie—Geschichte 3).

Maurer, Trude, *Ostjuden in Deutschland 1928–1933*, Hamburg, 1986.

Mausbach, Wilfried, *Zwischen Morgenthau und Marshall. Das wirtschaftspolitische Deutschlandkonzept der USA 1944–1947*, Düsseldorf, 1996.

May, Ernest R., *Strange Victory. Hitler's Conquest of France*, New York, 2000.

May, Lary, ed., *Recasting America. Culture and Politics in the Age of Cold War*, Chicago, 1989.

Mayer, A., 'Der Betrieb als Lebensgemeinschaft', *Ruf ins Volk. Monatsschrift für Volksgesundung und Jugendschutz* 8 (1956), pp. 17–18.

Mazower, Mark, *Dark Continent: Europe's Twentieth Century*, London, 1998.

Mazower, Mark, *Hitler's Empire. Nazi Rule in Occupied Europe*, London, 2008.

Mazower, Mark, *The Balkans. A Short History*, New York, 2000.

McClelland, Charles E, *State, Society and University in Germany 1700–1914*, Cambridge and New York, 1980.

Meadows, Donella H., Meadows, Dennis L., Randers, Jørgen and Behrens, William W.III, *The Limits to Growth. A Report for the Club of Rome's Project on the Predicament of Mankind*, London, 1972.

Meier-Braun, Karl-Heinz, *Integration und Rückkehr? Zur Ausländerpolitik des Bundes und der Länder, insbesondere Baden-Württembergs*, Mainz, 1988.

Meinecke, Friedrich, *The German Catastrophe: Reflections and Recollections*, Boston, Massachusetts, 1963.

Meinecke, Friedrich, *Werke*, ed. by Hans Herzfeld, 10 vols., Stuttgart, 1957–79.

Meister, Rainer, *Die große Depression. Zwangslagen und Handlungsspielräume der Wirtschafts- und Finanzpolitik in Deutschland 1929–1932*, Regensburg, 1991.

Melčić, Dunja, ed., *Der Jugoslawien-Krieg. Handbuch zu Vorgeschichte, Verlauf und Konsequenzen*, Wiesbaden, 2007.

Mende, Silke, *'Nicht rechts, nicht links, sondern vorn'. Eine Geschichte der Gründungsgrünen*, Munich, 2011.

Mergel, Thomas, *Großbritannien seit 1945*, Göttingen, 2005.

Merkel, Ina, *Utopie und Bedürfnis. Die Geschichte der Konsumkultur in der DDR*, Cologne, Weimar and Vienna, 1999.

Merker, Reinhard, *Die bildenden Künste im Nationalsozialismus. Kulturideologie, Kulturpolitik, Kulturproduktion*, Cologne, 1983.

Merseburger, Peter, *Der schwierige Deutsche. Kurt Schumacher. Eine Biographie*, Stuttgart, 1995.

Merseburger, Peter, *Willy Brandt, 1913–1992. Visionär und Realist*, Stuttgart, 2002.

Messerschmidt, Manfred and Wüllner, Fritz, *Die Wehrmachtjustiz im Dienste der Nationalsozialismus. Zerstörung einer Legende*, Baden-Baden, 1987.

Metzler, Gabriele, *Der deutsche Sozialstaat. Vom bismarckschen Erfolgsmodell zum Pflegefall*, Stuttgart and Munich, 2003.

Metzler, Gabriele, *Konzeptionen politischen Handelns von Adenauer bis Brandt. Politische Planung in der pluralistischen Gesellschaft*, Paderborn etc., 2005.

Meuschel, Sigrid, *Legitimation und Parteiherrschaft. Zum Paradox von Stabilität und Revolution in der DDR 1945–1989*, Frankfurt am Main, 1992.

Meyer, Ahlrich, *Das Wissen um Auschwitz. Täter und Opfer der 'Endlösung' in Westeuropa*, Paderborn etc., 2010.

Meyer, Ahlrich, *Die deutsche Besatzung in Frankreich 1940–1944, Widerstandsbekämpfung und Judenverfolgung*, Darmstadt, 2000.

Meyer, Ahlrich, *Täter im Verhör. Die 'Endlösung der Judenfrage' in Frankreich 1940*, Darmstadt, 2005.

Meyer, Beate, *'Jüdische Mischlinge'. Rassenpolitik und Verfolgungserfahrung 1933–1945*, Hamburg, 2002.

Meyer, Beate, *Tödliche Gratwanderung. Die Reichsvereinigung der Juden in Deutschland zwischen Hoffnung, Zwang, Selbstbehauptung und Verstrichung (1939–1945)*, Göttingen, 2011.

Meyer, Bettina, *Staatliche Förderungen der Atomenergie im Zeitraum 1950–2008. FÖS-Studie*, Berlin, 2009.

Meyer, Kurt, *Geweint wird, wenn der Kopf ab ist. Annäherungen an meinen Vater—'Panzermeyer', Generalmajor der Waffen-SS*, Freiburg im Breisgau, Basle and Vienna, 1998.

Meyer, Kurt, *Grenadiere*, Zweibrücken, 2006.

*Meyers Enzyklopädisches Wörterbuch*, Stuttgart, 1976.

Miard-Delacroix, Hélène, *Im Zeichen der europäischen Einigung 1963 bis in die Gegenwart (Wissenschaftliche Buchgesellschaft, Deutsch-Französische Geschichte* vol.11), Darmstadt, 2011.

Michalka, Wolfgang, ed., *Der Erste Weltkrieg. Wirkung, Wahrnehmung, Analyse*, Munich and Zürich, 1994.

Michalka, Wolfgang, ed., *Die nationalsozialistische Machtergreifung*, Paderborn etc., 1984.

Michalka, Wolfgang and Kater, Michael H., 'Wähler und Mitglieder der NSDAP. Neue Forschungsergebnisse zur Soziographie des Nationalsozialismus 1925 bis 1933', *GG* 19 (1993), pp. 155–77.

Middendorf, Stefanie, *Massenkultur. Zur Wahrnehmung gesellschaftlicher Modernität in Frankreich 1880–1980*, Göttingen, 2009.

Militärgeschichtliches Forschungsamt, *Anfänge westdeutscher Sicherheitspolitik 1945–1956*, 4 vols., Munich and Vienna, 1982–97.

Militärgeschichtliches Forschungsamt (ed.), *Das Deutsche Reich und der Zweite Weltkrieg*, 10 volumes, Stuttgart, 1979–2008.

Militärgeschichtliches Forschungsamt (ed.), *Germany and the Second World War,* 9 volumes (in progress) Oxford,1990–.

Miller, James, *Democracy in the Streets. From Port Huron to the Siege of Chicago*, Cambridge, Massachusetts, 2000.

Miller, Susanne, *Burgfrieden und Klassenkampf. Die deutsche Sozialdemokratie im Ersten Weltkrieg*, Düsseldorf, 1974.

Mink, Andreas, *Zwangsarbeiter. Der Streit um die Entschädigung von NS-Zwangsarbeitern um 1950–1999*, Hamburg, 2001.

Mintzel, Alf, *Die CSU-Hegemonie in Bayern. Strategie und Erfolg. Gewinner und Verlierer*, Passau, 1998.

Miquel, Marc von, *Ahnden oder amnestieren? Westdeutsche Justiz und Vergangenheitspolitik in den sechziger Jahren*, Göttingen, 2004.

Mitscherlich, Alexander, *Die Unwirtlichkeit unserer Städte. Anstiftung zum Unfrieden*, Frankfurt am Main, 1965.

Mitter, Armin and Wolle, Stefan, *Untergang auf Raten. Unbekannte Kapitel der DDR-Geschichte*, Munich, 1993.

Mitterauer, Michael, *Sozialgeschichte der Jugend* Frankfurt am Main, 1986.

Mittermaier, B. and Rusinek, Bernd-A., *Leo Brandt (1908–1971. Ingenieur—Wissenschaftsförderer—Visionär* Jülich, 2009.

Mlynarczyk, Jacek Andrzej, *Judenmord in Zentralpolen. Der Distrikt Radom im Generalgouvernement 1939–1945*, Darmstadt, 2007.

Moch, Leslie Page, *Moving Europeans. Migration in Western Europe since 1650*, Bloomington, Indiana and Indianopolis, Indiana, 1992.

Moeller, Robert G., ed., *Peasants and Lords in Modern Germany. Recent Contributions to Agricultural History*, Boston, Massachusetts, 1986.

Moeller, Robert G., ed., *West Germany under Construction. Politics, Society and Culture in the Adenauer Era*, Ann Arbor, Michigan, 1997.

Moeller, Robert G., *Protecting Motherhood: women and the family in the politics of postwar West Germany*, Berkeley, Cal., 1993.

Mohr, Markus, *Die Gewerkschaften im Atomkonflikt*, Münster, 2001.

Möller, Horst, *Die Weimarer Republik. Eine unvollendete Demokratie*, 7th edn., Munich, 2004.

Möller, Sabine, *Die Entkonkretisierung der NS-Herrschaft in der Ära Kohl. Die Neue Wache, das Denkmal für die ermordeten Juden Europas, das Haus der Geschichte der Bundesrepublik Deutschland*, Hanover, 1998.

Mombauer, Annika, *Helmut von Moltke and the Origins of the First World War*, Cambridge and New York, 2001.

Mommsen, Hans, *Germans against Hitler: the Stauffenberg Plot and resistance under the Third Reich*, London, 2009.

Mommsen, Hans, *The Rise and Fall of Weimar Democracy* Chapel Hill, North Carolina, 1996.

Mommsen, Hans, 'Suche nach der "verlorenen Geschichte"? Bemerkungen zum historischen Selbstverständnis der Bundesrepublik', *Merkur* 40 (1986), pp. 864–74.

Mommsen, Hans, *Zur Geschichte Deutschlands im 20. Jahrhundert. Demokratie, Diktatur, Widerstand*, Munich, 2010.

Mommsen, Theodor, 'Was uns noch retten kann', *Die Nation* (1902), pp. 163–4.

Mommsen, Wolfgang J., *Bürgerstolz und Weltmachtstreben. Deutschland unter Wilhelm II. 1890 bis 1918*, Berlin, 1995.

Mommsen, Wolfgang J., *Der autoritäre Nationalstaat. Verfassung, Gesellschaft und Kultur im deutschen Kaiserreich* Frankfurt am Main, 1990.

Mommsen, Wolfgang J., *Imperial Germany, 1867–1918: politics, culture and society in an authoritarian state*, London and New York, 1995.

Mommsen, Wolfgang J., 'Die deutsche Revolution 1918–1920. Politische Revolution und soziale Protestbewegung', *GG* 4 (1978), pp. 326–91.

Mommsen, Wolfgang J., *Die Urkatastrophe Deutschlands. Der Erste Weltkrieg 1914–1918*, Stuttgart, 2002.

Moore, Bob, ed., *Resistance in Western Europe*, Oxford, 2000.

Mooser, Josef, *Arbeiterleben in Deutschland 1900–1970*, Frankfurt am Main, 1984.

Morin, Edgar, *L'an zéro de l'Allemagne*, Paris, 1946.

Morsch, Günter, *Eisenheim. Die älteste Arbeitersiedlung im Ruhrgebiet*, Cologne, 1990.

Möser, Kurt, *Geschichte des Autos*, Frankfurt am Main and New York, 2002.

Moses, Dirk A., 'Die 45er. Eine Generation zwischen Faschismus und Demokratie', *Die Neue Sammlung* 40 (2000), pp. 211–32.

Mosse, George L., *The Crisis of German Ideology: Intellectual Origins of the Third Reich*, London, 1966.

Mosse, George L., *Nationalism and Sexuality: respectability and abnormal sexuality in modern Europe*, New York, 1985.

Mosse, George L., ed., *Deutsches Judentum in Krieg und Revolution 1916–1923*, Tübingen, 1971.

Motte, Jan, Ohliger, Rainer and Oswald, Anne von, eds., *50 Jahre Bundesrepublik—50 Jahre Einwanderung. Nachkriegsgeschichte als Migrationsgeschichte*, Frankfurt am Main and New York, 1999.

Müggenburg, Andreas, *Die ausländischen Vertragsarbeitnehmer. Bericht der Beauftragten der Bundesregierung für die Belange der Ausländer*, Berlin, 1997.

Mühle, Eduard, *Für Volk und deutschen Osten. Der Historiker Hermann Aubin und die deutsche Ostforschung*, Düsseldorf, 2005.

Müller, Claus M., *Relaunching German Diplomacy. The Auswärtiges Amt in the 1950s*, Münster, 1996.

Müller, Hans-Harald, *Intellektueller Linksradikalismus in der Weimarer Republik*, Kronberg im Taunus, 1977.

Müller, Helmut L., *Die literarische Republik. Westdeutsche Schriftsteller und die Politik*, Weinheim and Basle, 1982.

Müller, Karl Alexander von, 'Vorwort', *HZ* 162 (1940), pp. 229–30.

Müller, Klaus-Jürgen, *Armee und Drittes Reich 1933–1939. Darstellung und Dokumentation*, Paderborn etc., 1987.

Müller, Klaus-Jürgen, *The Army, Politics and Society in Germany 1933–1945: Studies in the Army's Relation to Nazism*, Manchester, 1987.

Müller, Klaus-Jürgen, *General Ludwig Beck. Studien und Dokumente zur politisch-militärischen Vorstellungswelt und Tätigkeit des Generalstabschefs des deutschen Heeres 1933–1938*, Boppard am Rhein, 1980.

Müller, Rolf-Dieter, ed., *Der Zusammenbruch des Deutschen Reiches 1945*, Munich, 2008.

Müller, Rolf-Dieter et al., eds., *Die Zerstörung Dresdens am 13./15. Februar 1945. Gutachten und Ergebnisse der Dresdner Historikerkommission zur Ermittlung der Opferzahlen*, Göttingen, 2010.

Müller, Rolf-Dieter, *Der Bombenkrieg 1939–1945*, Berlin, 2004.

Müller, Rolf-Dieter, *Handbuch der deutschen Geschichte, Bd.21. Der Zweite Weltkrieg 1939–1945*, Stuttgart, 2004.

Müller, Rolf-Dieter, *Hitlers Ostkrieg und die deutsche Siedlungspolitik. Die Zusammenarbeit von Wehrmacht, Wirtschaft und SS*, Frankfurt am Main, 1991.

Müller, Rolf-Dieter, *Kriegsende 1945. Die Zerstörung des Deutschen Reiches*, Frankfurt am Main, 1994.

Müller, Rolf-Dieter and Volkmann, Hans-Erich, *Die Wehrmacht. Mythos und Realität*, Munich, 1999.

Müller, Sven Oliver and Torp, Cornelius, eds., *Imperial Germany Revisited: Continuing Debates and New Perspectives*, New York, 2011.

Müller-Armack, Alfred, *Das Jahrhundert ohne Gott. Zur Kultursoziologie unserer Zeit*, Münster, 1948.

Müller-Armack, Alfred, *Wirtschaftslenkung und Marktwirtschaft*, Munich, 1990.

Münch, Ursula, *Asylpolitik in der Bundesrepublik Deutschland. Entwicklung und Alternativen*, Opladen, 1992.

Münch, Ursula, *Familienpolitik in der Bundesrepublik Deutschland. Maßnahmen, Defizite, Organisation familienpolitischer Staatstätigkeit*, Freiburg im Breisgau, 1990.

Münger, Christof, *Kennedy, die Berliner Mauer und die Kubakrise. Die westliche Allianz in der Zerreißprobe 1961–1963*, Paderborn, 2003.

Münkel, Daniela, ed., *Der lange Abschied vom Agrarland. Agrarpolitik, Landwirtschaft und ländliche Gesellschaft zwischen Weimar und Bonn*, Göttingen, 2000.

Münkel, Daniela, 'Bäuerliche Interessen versus NS-Ideologie. Das Reichserbhofgesetz in der Praxis', *VfZ* 44 (1996), pp. 549–80.

Münkler, Herfried, *Machtzerfall. Die letzten Tage des Dritten Reiches dargestellt am Beispiel der hessischen Kreisstadt Friedberg*, Berlin, 1985.

Munting, Roger and Holderness, Bryan A., *Crisis, Recovery and War. An Economic History of Continental Europe*, New York and London, 1991.

Münz, Rainer, Seifert, Wolfgang and Ulrich, Ralf E., *Zuwanderung nach Deutschland. Strukturen, Wirkungen, Perspektiven*, Frankfurt am Main, 1999.

Murray, Williamson, *War in the Air, 1914–1945*, London, 2002.

Musiał, Bogdan, 'Bilder einer Ausstellung. Kritische Anmerkungen zur Wanderausstellung "Vernichtungskrieg. Verbrechen der Wehrmacht 1941 bis 1945" ', *VfZ* 47 (1999), pp. 563–91.

Musiał, Bogdan, *Deutsche Zivilverwaltung und Judenverfolgung im Generalgouvernement. Eine Fallstudie zum Distrikt Lublin 1939*, Wiesbaden, 1999.

Musiał, Bogdan, 'The Origins of "Operation Reinhard". The Decision-Making Process for the Mass Murder of the Jews in the Generalgouvernement', *Yad Vashem Studies* 28 (2000), pp. 113–53.

Naasner, Walter, *Neue Machtzentren in der deutschen Kriegswirtschaft 1942–1945. Die Wirtschaftsorganisation der SS, das Amt des Generalbevollmächtigten für den Arbeitseinsatz und das Reichsministerium für Bewaffnung und Munition, Reichsministerium für Rüstung und Kriegsproduktion im nationalsozialistischen Herrschaftssystem*, Boppard am Rhein, 1994.

Nadav, Daniel S., *Julius Moses (1969–1942) und die Politik der Sozialhygiene in Deutschland*, Gerlingen, 1985.

Nagel, Irmela, *Fememorde und Fememordprozesse in der Weimarer Republik*, Cologne and Vienna, 1991.

Nägler, Frank, ed., *Die Bundeswehr 1955 bis 2005. Rückblenden, Einsichten, Perspektiven*, Munich, 2007.

Naimark, Norman M., *Fires of Hatred. Ethnic Cleansing in Twentieth-Century Europe*, Cambridge, Massachusetts, 2001.

Naimark, Norman, M., *The Russians in Germany: a history of the Soviet Zone of occupation 1945–1949*, Cambridge, Massachusetts and London, 1995.

Narr, Wolf-Dieter, ed., *Wir Bürger als Sicherheitsrisiko. Berufsverbot und Lauschangriff. Beiträge zur Verfassung unserer Republik*, Reinbek bei Hamburg, 1977.

Naumann, Friedrich, *Central Europe*, London, 1916.

Naumann, Klaus, ed., *Nachkrieg in Deutschland*, Hamburg, 2001.

Nave-Herz, Rosemarie, ed., *Wandel und Kontinuität der Familie in der Bundesrepublik Deutschland*, Stuttgart, 1988.

Neebe, Reinhard, *Großindustrie, Staat und NSDAP 1930–1933. Paul Silverberg und der Reichsverband der Deutschen Industrie in der Krise der Weimarer Republik*, Marburg, 1979.

Neebe, Reinhard, *Weichenstellung für die Globalisierung. Deutsche Weltmarktpolitik, Europa und Amerika in der Ära Ludwig Erhard*, Cologne, 2004.

Neillands, Rob, *The Bomber War: Arthur Harris and the Allied Bomber Offensive, 1939–1945*, London, 2001.

Neitzel, Sönke, *Weltmacht oder Untergang. Die Weltreichslehre im Zeitalter des Imperialismus*, Paderborn etc., 2000.

Neu, Alexander, *Die Jugoslawien-Kriegsberichterstattung der Times und der Frankfurter Allgemeinen Zeitung—ein Vergleich*, Baden-Baden, 2004.

Neubert, Ehrhart, *Geschichte der Opposition in der DDR 1949–1989*, Berlin, 1997.

Neumaier, Christopher, 'The Escalation of German Reprisal Policy in Occupied France 1941–1942', *Journal of Contemporary History* 41 (2006), pp. 113–31.

Neumann, Franz, *Behemoth. The Structure ànd Practice of National Socialism 1933–1944*, New York, 1963.

Neutatz, Dietmar, *Träume und Alpträume. Eine Geschichte Russlands im 20. Jahrhundert*, Munich, 2013.

Niclauß, Karlheinz, *Kontroverse Deutschlandpolitik. Die politische Auseinandersetzung in der Bundesrepublik Deutschland über den Grundlagenvertrag mit der DDR*, Frankfurt am Main, 1977.

Niedhart, Gorrfried and Bange, Oliver, 'Die "Relikte der Nachkriegszeit" beseitigen. Ostpolitik in der zweiten außenpolitischen Formationsphase der Bundesrepublik Deutschland im Übergang von den Sechziger zu den Siebzigerjahren', *AfS* 44 (2004), pp. 415–48.

Niehuss, Merith, *Familie, Frau und Gesellschaft. Studien zur Strukturgeschichte der Familie in Westdeutschland 1945–1960*, Göttingen, 2001.

Niethammer, Lutz, ed., *Der 'gesäuberte' Antifaschismus. Die SED und die roten Kapos von Buchenwald*, Berlin, 1994.

Niethammer, Lutz, ed., *Lebensgeschichte und Sozialkultur im Ruhrgebiet 1930 bis 1960*, 3 vols., Berlin and Bonn, 1983–6.

Niethammer, Lutz et al., *Bürgerliche Gesellschaft in Deutschland. Historische Einblicke, Fragen, Perspektiven*, Frankfurt am Main, 1990.

Niethammer, Lutz, *Angepaßter Faschismus. Politische Praxis der NPD*, Frankfurt am Main, 1969.

Niethammer, Lutz, 'Anmerkungen zur Alltagsgeschichte', *Geschichtsdialektik* 5 (1980), pp. 231–42.

Niethammer, Lutz, *Deutschland danach. Postfaschistische Gesellschaft und nationales Gedächtnis*, ed. by Ulrich Herbert and Dirk van Laak, Berlin and Bonn, 1999.

Niethammer, Lutz, *Die Mitläuferfabrik. Die Entnazifizierung am Beispiel Bayerns*, Berlin and Bonn, 1982.

Niethammer, Lutz, *Kollektive Identität. Heimliche Quellen einer unheimlichen Konjunktur*, Reinbek bei Hamburg, 2000.

Niethammer, Lutz, 'Zum Verhältnis von Reform und Rekonstruktion in der US-Zone am Beispiel der Neuordnung des öffentlichen Dienstes', *VfZ* 21 (1973), pp. 177–88.

Niewyk, Donald L., 'Solving the "Jewish problem". Continuity and Change in German Antisemitism, 1871–1945', *Leo Baeck Year Book* 35 (1990), pp. 335–70.

Niewyk, Donald L., *The Jews in Weimar Germany*, Baton Rouge, Louisiana, Los Angeles, California and London, 1980.

Nipperdey, Thomas, *Deutsche Geschichte 1866–1918*, 2 vols., Munich 1990–2.

Nitschke, August, Ritter, Gerhard and Peukert, Detlev J.K., eds., *Jahrhundertwende. Der Aufbruch in die Moderne 1880–1930*, 2 vols., Reinbek bei Hamburg, 1990.

Noll, Chaim, *Der Abschied. Journal meiner Ausreise aus der DDR*, Hamburg, 1984.

Nolte, Ernst, *Das Vergehen der Vergangenheit. Antwort an meine Kritiker im sogenannten Historikerstreit*, Berlin and Frankfurt am Main, 1988.

Nolte, Ernst, *Der europäische Bürgerkrieg 1917–1945. Nationalsozialismus und Bolschewismus*, Frankfurt am Main, 1987.

Nolte, Ernst, *Die faschistischen Bewegungen. Die Krise des liberalen Systems und die Entwicklung der Faschismen*, Munich, 1982.

Nolte, Ernst, *Streitpunkte. Heutige und künftige Kontroversen um den Nationalsozialismus*, Berlin and Frankfurt am Main, 1994.

Nolte, Paul, *Was ist Demokratie? Geschichte und Gegenwart*, Munich, 2012.

Nooteboom, Cees, *Paris, Mai 1968*, Frankfurt am Main, 2003.

Notermans, Ton, *Money, Markets, and the State. Social Democratic Economic Policies since 1918*, Cambridge, 2000.

Notz, Gisela, 'Die autonomen Frauenbewegungen der Siebziger Jahre. Entstehungsgeschichte—Organisationsgeschichte—politische Konzepte', *AfS* 44 (2004), pp. 123–48.

Nowak, Kurt, *'Euthanasie' und Sterilisierung im 'Dritten Reich'. Die Konfrontation der evangelischen und katholischen Kirche mit dem Gesetz zur Verhütung erbkranken Nachwuchses und der 'Euthanasie' Aktion*, Halle, 1977.

Nützenadel, Alexander, *Stunde der Ökonomen. Wissenschaft, Politik und Expertenkultur in der Bundesrepublik 1949–1974*, Göttingen, 2005.

Oberkrome, Willi, *Ordnung und Autarkie. Die Geschichte der deutschen Landbauforschung. Agrarökonomie und ländlichen Sozialwissenschaft im Spiegel von Forschungsdienst und DFG (1920–1970)*, Stuttgart, 2009.

Oberkrome, Willi, *Volksgeschichte. Methodische Innovation und völkische Ideologisierung in der deutschen Geschichtswissenschaft 1918–1945*, Göttingen, 1993.

Oetzel, Günther, *Die geplante Zukunft. Die bundesdeutsche Schnellbrüterentwicklung in den 1960er Jahren*, Frankfurt am Main etc., 1999.

Oexle, Otto Gerhard, '"Zusammenarbeit mit Baal". Über die Mentalität deutscher Geisteswissenschaftler 1933—und nach 1945', *Historische Anthropologie* 8 (2000), pp. 1–27.

Offner, Avner, *The First World War. An Agrarian Interpretation*, Oxford, 1989.

Ohse, Marc-Dietrich, *Jugend nach dem Mauerbau. Anpassung, Protest und Eigensinn (DDR 1961–1974)*, Berlin, 2003.

Oldenburg, Fred, 'Neues Denken in der sowjetischen Deutschlandpolitik?', *DA* 20.2 (1987), pp. 1154–1160.

Oldenburg, Jens, *Der Deutsche Ostmarkenverein 1894–1934*, Berlin, 2002.

Oltmer, Jochen, ed., *Kriegsgefangene im Europa des Ersten Weltkrieges*, Paderborn etc., 2006 (Krieg in der Geschichte 24).

Oltmer, Jochen, *Migration im 19. und 20. Jahrhundert*, Munich, 2009.

Opitz, Reinhard, ed., *Europastrategien des deutschen Kapitals 1900–1945*, Cologne, 1977.

Oppenländer, Karl-Heinrich, ed., *Wiedervereinigung nach sechs Jahren. Erfolge, Defizite, Zukunftsperspektiven im Transformationsprozeß*, Berlin, 1997.

Orth, Karin, *Das System der nationalsozialistischen Konzentrationslager. Eine politische Organisationsgeschichte*, Hamburg, 1999.

Orth, Karin, *Die Konzentrationslager-SS: sozialstrukturelle Analysen und biographische Studien*, Munich, 2004.

Orth, Karin and Oberkrome, Willi, eds., *Die Deutsche Forschungsgemeinschaft 1920–1970. Forschungsförderung im Spannungsfeld von Wissenschaft und Politik*, Stuttgart 2010 (Beiträge zur Geschichte der Deutschen Forschungsgemeinschaft 4).

Osterhammel, Jürgen and Petersson, Niels, *Globalization. A Short History*, Princeton, N.J., 2005.

Otte, Max, 'Die Finanzkrise und das Versagen der modernen Ökonomie', *APuZ* 52 (2009), pp. 9–16.

Ottmer, Hans-Martin, *'Weserübung'. Der deutsche Angriff auf Dänemark und Norwegen im April 1940*, Munich, 1994.

Otto, Helmut and Schmiedel, Karl, eds., *Der erste Weltkrieg*, Berlin, 1983.

Overmans, Rüdiger, *Deutsche militärische Verluste im Zweiten Weltkrieg*, Munich, 1999.

Overmans, Rüdiger, *Soldaten hinter Stacheldraht. Deutsche Kriegsgefangene des Zweiten Weltkriegs*, Berlin and Munich, 2000.

Overy, Richard J., et al., eds., *Die 'Neuordnung' Europas. NS-Wirtschaftspolitik in den besetzen Gebieten*, Berlin, 1997.

Overy, Richard J., '"Blitzkriegswirtschaft"? Finanzpolitik, Lebensstandard und Arbeitseinsatz in Deutschland 1939–1942', *VfZ* 51 (1988), pp. 379–455.

Overy, Richard J., *Russia's War*, London, 1998.

Overy, Richard J., *The Air War 1939–1945*, London, 1980

Overy, Richard J., *The Nazi Economic Recovery 1932–1938*, London, 1982.

Overy, Richard J., *War and Economy in the Third Reich*, Oxford and New York, 1994.

Overy, Richard J., *Why the Allies Won*, London, 1995.

Papke, Gerhard, *Liberale Ordnungskraft, nationale Sammlungsbewegung oder Mittelstandpartei? Die FDP-Landtagsfraktion in Nordrhein-Westfalen 1946–1966*, Düsseldorf, 1998.

Patel, Kiran Klaus, *Europäisierung wider Willen. Die Bundesrepublik Deutschland in der Agrarintegration der EWG 1955–1973*, Munich, 2009.

Paterson, William E. and Smith, Gordon, eds., *The West German Model. Perspectives on a Stable State*, London, 1981.

Paucker, Arnold, *Die Juden im nationalsozialistischen Deutschland 1933–1945*, Tübingen, 1986.

Pauer, Jan, *Prag 1968. Der Einmarsch des Warschauer Paktes. Hintergründe—Planung—Durchführung*, Bremen, 1995.

Paul, Gerhard and Mallmann, Klaus-Michael, *Die Gestapo im Zweiten Weltkrieg: 'Heimatfront' und besetztes Europa*, Darmstadt, 2000.

Paul, Gerhard and Mallmann, Klaus-Michael, *Die Gestapo: Mythos und Realität*, Darmstadt, 1996.

Paul, Jens Peter, *Zwangsumtausch, Wie Kohl und Lafontaine die D-Mark abschafften*, Frankfurt am Main, 2010.

Pawlita, Cornelius, *'Wiedergutmachung' als Rechtsfrage? Die politische und juristische Auseinandersetzung um Entschädigung für die Opfer nationalsozialistischer Verfolgung (1945 bis 1990)*, Frankfurt am Main etc., 1993.

Paxton, Robert O., *The Anatomy of Fascism*, London, 2004.

Paxton, Robert O., *Vichy France. Old Guard and New Order 1940–1944*, New York, 1972.

Pehle, Walter H. and Adam, Uwe Dietrich, eds., *November 1938. From 'Reichskristallnacht' to Genocide*, Oxford, 1991.

Peisert, Hansgert, *Soziale Lage und Bildungschancen in Deutschland*, Munich, 1967.

Peschel-Gutzeit, Lore Maria, ed., *Das Nürnberger Juristen-Urteil von 1947. Historischer Zusammenhang und aktuelle Bezüge*, Baden-Baden, 1996.

Peters, Butz, *RAF. Terrorismus in Deutschland*, Stuttgart, 1991.

Peters, Butz, *Tödlicher Irrtum. Die Geschichte der RAF*, Frankfurt am Main, 2007.

Petrow, Richard, *The Bitter Years. The Invasion and Occupation of Denmark and Norway, April 1940-May 1945*, New York, 1974.

Petzina, Dietmar, *Die deutsche Wirtschaft in der Zwischenkriegszeit*, Wiesbaden, 1977.

Petzina, Dietmar, Abelshauser, Werner and Faust, Anselm, *Materialien zur Statistik des Deutschen Reiches 1914–1945*, Munich, 1978.

Petzina, Dietmar and Euchner, Walter, eds., *Wirtschaftspolitik im britischen Besatzungsgebiet 1945–1949*, Düsseldorf, 1984.

Peukert, Detlev J.K., 'Die Erwerbslosigkeit junger Arbeiter in der Weltwirtschaftskrise in Deutschland 1929–1933', *VSWG* 72 (1985), pp. 305–28.

Peukert, Detlev J.K., *Die KPD im Widerstand. Verfolgung und Untergrundarbeit an Rhein und Ruhr 1933–1945*, Wuppertal, 1980 (Düsseldorfer Schriften zur neueren Landesgeschichte und zur Geschichte Nordrhein-Westfalens, 2).

Peukert, Detlev J.K., *Jugend zwischen Krieg und Krise*, Cologne, 1987.

Peukert, Detlev J.K., '"Mit uns zieht die Neue Zeit". Jugend zwischen Disziplinierung und Revolte', in Nitschke, Ritter and Peukert, eds., *Jahrhundertwende*, vol.1. pp.176–202.

Peukert, Detlev J.K., *The Weimar Republic. The Crisis of Classical Modernity*, London, 1991.

Pfeil, Elisabeth, *Die Berufstätigkeit von Müttern. Eine empirisch-soziologische Erhebung an 900 Müttern aus vollständigen Familien*, Tübingen, 1961.

Pfieger, Klaus, *Die Rote Armee Fraktion—RAF. 14.5.1970 bis 20.4.1998*, Baden-Baden, 2004.

Philippi, Klaus-Peter, *Volk des Zorns. Studien zur 'poetischen Mobilmachung' in der deutschen Literatur am Beginn des Ersten Weltkrieges, ihren Voraussetzungen und Implikationen*, Munich, 1979.

Picht, Georg, *Die deutsche Bildungskatastrophe. Analyse und Dokumentation*, Olten and Freiburg im Breisgau, 1964.

Pierson, Paul, *Dismantling the Welfare State? Reagan, Thatcher and the Politics of Retrenchment*, Cambridge, 1996.

Pies, Ingo and Leschke, Martin, eds., *Milton Friedmans ökonomischer Liberalismus*, Tübingen, 2004.

Pingel-Schliemann, Sandra, *Zersetzen. Strategie einer Diktatur*, Berlin, 2004.

Piore, Michael J. and Sabel, Charles F., *The Second Industrial Divide: possibilities for prosperity*, New York, 1984.

Pirker, Theo et al., eds., *Der Plan als Befehl und Fiktion. Wirtschaftsführung in der DDR. Gespräche und Analysen*, Opladen, 1995.

Plato, Alexander von, *The End of the Cold War?: Bush, Kohl, Gorbachev, and the Reunification of Germany*, Basingstoke, 2015.

Plaul, Hainer, *Landarbeiterleben im 19. Jahrhundert. Eine volkskundliche Untersuchung über Veränderungen in der Lebensweise der einheimischen Landarbeiterschaft in den Dörfern der Magdeburger Börde unter den Bedingungen der Herausbildung and Konsolidierung des Kapitalismus in der Landwirtschaft*, Berlin, 1979.

Plenge, Johann, *1789 und 1914. Die symbolischen Jahre in der Geschichte des politischen Geistes*, Berlin, 1916.

Pohl, Dieter, *Die Herrschaft der Wehrmacht: Deutsche Militärbesatzung und einheimische Bevölkerung in der Sowjetunion 1941–1944*, Munich, 2008.

Pohl, Dieter, *Nationalsozialistische Judenverfolgung in Ostgalizien 1941–1944. Organisation und Durchführung eines staatlichen Massenverbrechens*, Munich, 1996.

Pohl, Dieter, *Verfolgung und Massenmord in der NS-Zeit 1933–1945*, Darmstadt, 2003.

Pohl, Hans, ed., *The Concentration Process in the Entrepreneurial Economy since the Late Nineteenth Century*, Stuttgart, 1988.

Poiger, Uta G., *Jazz, Rock and Rebels. Cold War Politics and American Culture in a Divided Germany*, Berkeley, California, Los Angeles and London, 2000.

Pollack, Detlef, *Kirche in der Organisationsgesellschaft. Zum Wandel der gesellschaftlichen Lage der evangelischen Kirchen in der DDR*, Stuttgart etc., 1994.

Pollard, Sidney, *The Development of the British Economy 1914–1990*, London, 1996.

Potthoff, Heinrich, *Die 'Koalition der Vernunft'. Deutschlandpolitik in den 80er Jahren*, Munich, 1995.

Prantl, Heribert, *Rot-Grün. Eine erste Bilanz*, Hamburg, 1999.

Prantl, Heribert, *Wehrmachtsverbrechen. Eine deutsche Kontroverse*, Hamburg, 1997.

Preller, Ludwig, *Sozialpolitik in der Weimarer Republik*, Stuttgart, 1949.

Priemel, Kim Christian, *Flick. Eine Konzerngeschichte vom Kaiserreich bis zur Bundesrepublik*, Göttingen, 2007.

Priemel, Kim Christian, and Stiller, Alexa, eds., *Reassessing the Nuremberg Military Tribunals. Transitional Justice, Trial Narratives, and Historiography*, New York, 2012.

Prieß, Lutz et al., *Die SED und der 'Prager Frühling' 1968. Politik gegen einen 'Sozialismus mit menschlichem Antlitz'*, Berlin, 1996.

Priewe, Jan and Hickel, Rudolf, *Der Preis der Einheit. Bilanz und Perspektiven der deutschen Vereinigung*, Frankfurt am Main, 1991.

Prinz, Michael, ed., *Der lange Weg in den Überfluss. Anfänge und Entwicklung der Konsumgesellschaft seit der Vormoderne*, Paderborn etc., 2003.

Prollius, Michael von, *Deutsche Wirtschaftsgeschichte nach 1945*, Göttingen, 2006.

Proske, Rüdiger, *Wider den Missbrauch der Geschichte deutscher Soldaten zu politischen Zwecken. Eine Streitschrift*, Mainz, 1996.

Przyrembel, Alexandra, *'Rassenschande'. Reinheitsmythos und Vernichtungslegitimation im Nationalsozialismus*, Göttingen, 2003.

Puhle, Hans-Jürgen, *Agrarische Interessenpolitik und preußischer Konservatismus im wilhelminischen Reich*, Bonn-Bad Godesberg, 1975.

Pulzer, Peter G.J., *The Rise of Political Anti-Semitism in Germany and Austria*, London, 1988.

Pyta, Wolfram, *Dorfgemeinschaft und Parteipolitik 1918–1933*, Düsseldorf, 1996.

Pyta, Wolfram, *Hindenburg. Herrschaft zwischen Hohenzollern und Hitler*, Munich, 2007.

Radkau, Joachim, *Aufstieg und Krise der deutschen Atomwirtschaft 1945–1975. Verdrängte Alternativen in der Kerntechnik und der Ursprung der nuklearen Kontroverse*, Reinbek bei Hamburg, 1983.

Radkau, Joachim, *Das Zeitalter der Nervosität*, Munich, 1998.

Radkau, Joachim, *Die deutsche Emigration in den USA. Ihr Einfluß auf die amerikanische Europapolitik 1933–1945*, Düsseldorf, 1971.

Radkau, Joachim, *The Age of Ecology: a global history*, Cambridge, 2014.

Radke, Frank-Olaf, 'Multikulturalismus. Ein postmoderner Nachfahre des Nationalismus?', *Vorgänge. Zeitschrift für Bürgerrechte und Gesellschaftspolitik* 117 (1992), pp. 23–30.

Radlmaier, Steffen, ed., *Der Nürnberger Lernprozess. Von Kriegsverbrechern und Starreportern*, Frankfurt am Main, 2001.

Ragnitz, Joachim, 'Transferleistungen für die neuen Länder—eine Begriffsbestimmung', *Wirtschaft im Wandel* 10 (2004), pp. 288–9.

Raithel, Thomas, *Das 'Wunder' der inneren Einheit. Studien zur deutschen und französischen Öffentlichkeit bei Beginn des Ersten Weltkrieges*, Bonn, 1996.

Raphael, Lutz, *Imperiale Gewalt und mobilisierte Nation. Europa 1914–1945*, Munich, 2011.

Raphael, Lutz, 'Radikales Ordnungsdenken und die Organisation totalitärer Herrschaft. Weltanschauungseliten und Humanwissenschaften im NS-Regime', *GG* 27 (2001), pp. 5–40.

Raschke, Joachim, *Die Zukunft der Grünen*, Frankfurt am Main, 2001.

Rass, Christoph, *'Menschenmaterial'. Deutsche Soldaten an der Ostfront. Innenansichten einer Infanteriedivision 1939–1945*, Paderborn etc., 2003.

Rathfelder, Erich, *Kosovo. Geschichte eines Konflikts*, Berlin, 2010.

Rauch, Malte J and Schirmbeck, Samuel H., *Die Barrikaden von Paris. Der Aufstand der französischen Arbeiter und Studenten*, Frankfurt am Main, 1968.

Raulff, Ulrich, *Kreis ohne Meister. Stefan Georges Nachleben*, Munich, 2009.

Rauscher, Anton, ed., *Nationale und kulturelle Identität im Zeitalter der Globalisierung*, Berlin, 2006.

Räuscher, Josef, 'Berlin', *Hochland* 281 (1930), pp. 15–26.

Reckendrees, Alfred, *Das 'Stahltrust'-Projekt. Die Gründung der Vereinigte Stahlwerke A.G. und ihre Unternehmensentwicklung 1926–1933/34*, Munich, 2000.

Recker, Marie-Luise, *Die Außenpolitik des Dritten Reiches*, Munich, 1990.

Recker, Marie-Luise, *Nationalsozialistische Sozialpolitik im Zweiten Weltkrieg*, Munich, 1985.

Rees, Goronwy, *The Great Slump. Capitalism in Crisis 1929–1933*, New York, 1970.

Rehbein, Franz, *Das Leben eines Landarbeiters*, Jena, 1911.

Reichardt, Sven, 'Authentizität und Gemeinschaftsbindung. Politik und Lebensstil im linksalternativen Milieu vom Ende der 1960er bis zum Anfang der 1980er Jahre', *Neue Soziale Bewegungen* 21 (2008), pp. 118–130.

Reichardt, Sven, *Faschistische Kampfbünde. Gewalt und Gemeinschaft im italienischen Squadrismus und in der deutschen SA*, Cologne, 2002.

Reichardt, Sven and Siegfried, Detlef, eds., *Das alternative Milieu. Antibürgerlicher Lebensstil und linke Politik in der Bundesrepublik Deutschland und Europa 1968–1983*, Göttingen, 2010.

Reiche, Danyel and Krebs, Carsten, *Der Einstieg in die ökologische Steuerreform. Aufstieg, Restriktionen und Durchsetzung eines umweltpolitischen Themas*, Frankfurt am Main, 1999.

Reichel, Peter, Schmid, Harald, and Steinbach, Peter, eds., *Der Nationalsozialismus—die zweite Geschichte. Überwindung, Deutung, Erinnerung*, Bonn, 2009.

Reichel, Peter, *Der schöne Schein des Dritten Reiches. Faszination und Gewalt des Faschismus*, Frankfurt am Main, 1993.

Reichel, Peter, *Politik mit der Erinnerung. Gedächtnisorte im Streit um die nationalsozialistische Vergangenheit*, Munich, 1995.

Reichel, Peter, *Vergangenheitsbewältigung in Deutschland. Die Auseinandersetzung mit der NS-Diktatur in Politik und Justiz*, Munich, 2007.

Reich-Hilweg, Ines, *Männer und Frauen sind gleichberechtigt. Der Gleichberechtigungsgrundsatz (Art. 3 Abs. 2 GG) in der parlamentarischen Auseinandersetzung 1948–1957, und in der Rechtsprechung des Bundesverfassungsgerichts 1953–1975*, Frankfurt am Main, 1979.

Reif, Heinz, ed., *Ostelbische Agrargesellschaft im Kaiserreich und in der Weimarer Republik*, Berlin, 1994.

Reif-Spirek, Peter and Ritscher, Bodo, eds., *Speziallager in der SBZ. Gedenkstätten mit 'doppelter Vergangenheit'*, Berlin, 1999.

Reinhold, Otto, 'Otto Reinhold im Radio DDR, 19.8.1989', *Blätter für deutsche und internationale Politik* 34 (1989), p. 1,175.

Rentschler, Eric, *The Ministry of Illusion. Nazi Cinema and its Afterlife*, Cambridge, Massachusetts, 1996.

Retallack, James N., ed., *Imperial Germany 1871–1918*, Oxford, 2008.

Reulecke, Jürgen, ed., *Generationalität und Lebensgeschichte im 20. Jahrhundert*, Munich, 2003.

Reulecke, Jürgen, *Geschichte der Urbanisierung in Deutschland*, Frankfurt am Main, 1985.

Reusch, Ulrich, *Deutsches Berufsbeamtentum und britische Besatzung. Planung und Politik 1943–1947*, Stuttgart, 1985.

Reuter, Jens and Clewing, Konrad, *Der Kosovo-Konflikt*, Klagenfurt, 2000.

Riches, William Terence Martin, *The Civil Rights Movement. Struggle and Resistance*, Basingstoke, 2004.

Richter, Hans Werner, ed., *Bestandsaufnahme. Eine deutsche Bilanz 1962*, Munich, Vienna and Basle, 1962

Riha, Ortrun, ed., *'Die Freigabe der Vernichtung lebensunwerten Lebens'. Beiträge des Symposiums über Karl Binding und Alfred Hoche*, Aachen, 2005.

Ritscher, Bodo, ed., *Das sowjetische Speziallager Nr.2, 1945–1950. Katalog zur ständigen historischen Ausstellung*, Göttingen, 1999.

Ritschl, Albrecht, 'Aufstieg und Niedergang der Wirtschaft der DDR. Ein Zahlenbild 1945–1989', *JbWG* (1995), no. 2, pp. 11–46.

Ritschl, Albrecht, *Deutschlands Krise und Konjunktur 1924–1934*, Berlin, 2002.

Ritschl, Albrecht and Spoerer, Mark, 'Das Bruttosozialprodukt in Deutschland nach den amtlichen Volkseinkommens- und Sozialproduktsstatistiken 1901–1995', *JbWG* (1997), no. 2, pp. 27–54.

Ritter, Eva-Maria, *Deutsche Telekommunikationspolitik 1989–2003. Aufbruch zu mehr Wettbewerb. Ein Beispiel für wirtschaftliche Strukturreformen*, Düsseldorf, 2004.

Ritter, Gerhard A., ed., *Deutsche Parteien vor 1918*, Cologne, 1973.

Ritter, Gerhard A., *The Price of German Unity: Reunification and the Crisis of the Welfare State*, Oxford, 2011.

Ritter, Gerhard A., *Der Sozialstaat. Entstehung und Entwicklung im internationalen Vergleich*, Munich, 1989.

Ritter, Gerhard A. and Miller, Susanne, eds., *Die deutsche Revolution 1918–1919*, Frankfurt am Main, 1983.

Ritter, Gerhard A. and Tenfelde, Klaus, *Arbeiter im Deutschen Kaiserreich 1871 bis 1914*, Bonn, 1992.

Ritter, Robert, 'Primitivität und Kriminalität', *Monatsschrift für Kriminalbiologie und Strafrechtsreform* 31 (1940), pp. 198–210.

Rödder, Andreas, ed., *Weimar und die deutsche Verfassung*, Stuttgart, 1999.

Rödder, Andreas, *Deutschland, einig Vaterland. Die Geschichte der Wiedervereinigung*, Munich, 2009.

Rödder, Andreas, *Die Bundesrepublik Deutschland 1969–1990*, Munich, 2004.

Roerkohl, Anne, *Hungerblockade und Heimatfront. Die kommunale Lebensmittelversorgung in Westfalen während des Ersten Weltkrieges*, Stuttgart, 1991.

Roesler, Jörg, 'Kombinate in der Geschichte der DDR. Von der ersten VVB bis zur durchgängigen Kombinatsbildung', *Jahrbuch fur Geschichte* 31 (1984), pp. 221–71.

Rogers, Daniel E., *Politics after Hitler. The Western Allies and the German Party System*, Basingstoke, 1995.

Rohe, Karl, *Wahlen und Wählertraditionen in Deutschland. Kulturelle Grundlagen deutscher Parteien und Parteiensysteme im 19. und 20. Jahrhundert*, Frankfurt am Main, 1992.

Rohkrämer, Thomas, *Der Militarismus der 'kleinen Leute'. Die Kriegervereine im Deutschen Kaiserreich 1971–1914*, Munich, 1990.

Rohkrämer, Thomas, *Eine andere Moderne? Zivilisationskritik, Natur und Technik in Deutschland 1880–1933*, Paderborn etc., 1999.

Röhr, Werner, ed., *Okkupation und Kollaboration (1938–1945). Beiträge zu Konzepten und Praxis der Kollaboration in der deutschen Okkupationspolitik*, Berlin and Heidelberg, 1994.

Rohrkamp, René, *'Weltanschaulich gefestigte Kämpfer': die Soldaten der Waffen-SS 1933–1945. Organisation, Personal, Sozialstrukturen*, Paderborn, 2010.

Rohwedder, Detlev Karsten, *'Schnell privatisieren, entschlossen sanieren, behutsam stilllegen': ein Ruckblick auf 13 Jahre Arbeit der Treuhandanstalt und der Bundesanstalt fur Vereinigungsbedingte Sonderaufgaben. Abschlussbericht der Bundesanstalt für Vereinigungsbedingte Sonderaufgaben (BvS)*, Berlin, 2003.

Rombeck-Jaschinski, Ursula, *Das Londoner Schuldenabkommen. Die Regelung der deutschen Auslandsschulden nach dem Zweiten Weltkrieg*, Munich, 2005.

Romein, Jan, *The Watershed of Two Eras. Europe in 1900*, Middletown, Connecticut, 1978.

Römer, Felix, *Der Kommissarbefehl. Wehrmacht und NS-Verbrechen an der Ostfront 1941/42*, Paderborn etc., 2008.

Roon, Ger van, ed., *Europäischer Widerstand im Vergleich. Die internationalen Konferenzen, Amsterdam*, Berlin, 1985.

Röpke, Andrea and Speit, Andreas, *Blut und Ehre, Geschichte und Gegenwart rechter Gewalt in Deutschland*, Berlin, 2013.

Roseman, Mark, *The Villa, the Lake, the Meeting: Wannsee and the Final Solution*, London, 2003.

Rosenkötter, Bernhard, *Treuhandpolitik. Die 'Haupttreuhandstelle Ost' und der Raub polnischer Vermögen 1939–1945*, Essen, 2003.

Rosenstock, Werner, 'Exodus 1933–1939. A Survey of Jewish Emigration from Germany', *The Leo Baeck Institute Year Book* 1.1 (1956), pp. 272–90.

Rosenthal, Jacob, *'Die Ehre des jüdischen Soldaten'. Die Judenzählung im Ersten Weltkrieg und ihre Folgen*, Frankfurt am Main and New York, 2007.

Rosenzweig, Beate, *Erziehung zur Demokratie? Amerikanische Besatzungs- und Schulreformpolitik in Deutschland und Japan*, Stuttgart, 1998.

Rosh, Lea and Jäckel, Eberhard, *Die Juden, das sind doch die anderen. Der Streit um ein deutsches Denkmal*, Berlin and Vienna, 1999.

Rossellini, Roberto, 'Germania anno zero', Italian-German cinema film, 1948.

Rossino, Alexander B., *Hitler Strikes Poland. Blitzkrieg, Ideology, and Atrocity*, Lawrence, Kansas, 2003.

Rössler, Mechtild and Schleiermacher, Sabine, eds., *Der 'Generalplan Ost'. Hauptlinien der nationalsozialistischen Planungs- und Vernichtungspolitik*, Berlin, 1993.

Rostow, Walt W., *The Stages of Economic Growth: a non-communist manifesto*, Cambridge, 1960.

Roth, Dieter, 'Was bewegt die Wähler?', *APuZ* 11/1994, pp. 3–13.

Roth, Joseph, 'Die Vereinigten Staaten von Amerika. Eindrücke und Gedanken beim 28. Eucharistischen Weltkongreß in Chicago', *Gelbe Hefte* 3/1 (1927), pp. 337–61.

Roth, Markus, *Herrenmenschen. Die deutschen Kreishauptleute im besetzten Polen. Karrierewege, Herrschaftspraxis und Nachgeschichte*, Göttingen, 2009.

Roth, Roland and Rucht, Dieter, eds., *Die sozialen Bewegungen in Deutschland seit 1945. Ein Handbuch*, Frankfurt am Main and New York, 2008.

Roth, Roland and Rucht, Dieter, eds., *Neue soziale Bewegungen in der Bundesrepublik Deutschland*, Bonn, 1987.

Rothenbacher, Franz, *Soziale Ungleichheit im Modernisierungsprozeß des 19. und 20. Jahrhunderts*, Frankfurt am Main and New York, 1989.

Rouette, Susanne, *Sozialpolitik als Geschlechterpolitik. Die Regulierung der Frauenarbeit nach dem Ersten Weltkrieg*, Frankfurt am Main and New York, 1993.

Rougemont, Denis de, *Journal aus Deutschland 1935–1936*, Vienna, 1998.

Ruck, Michael, *Die freien Gewerkschaften im Ruhrkampf 1923*, Cologne, 1986.

Rückerl, Adalbert, ed., *NS-Vernichtungslager im Spiegel deutscher Strafprozesse. Belzec, Sobibór, Treblinka, Chelmno*, Munich, 1977.

Ruedorffer, J.J. (pseudonym of Kurt Riezler), *Grundzüge der Weltpolitik der Gegenwart*, Stuttgart, 1914.

Rupieper, Hermann-Josef, *Der besetzte Verbündete. Die amerikanische Deutschlandpolitik 1949–1955*, Opladen, 1991.

Rusinek, Bernd-A., *Das Forschungszentrum. Eine Geschichte der KFA Jülich von ihrer Gründung bis 1980*, Frankfurt am Main and New York, 1996.

Rusinek, Bernd-A. *Gesellschaft in der Katastrophe. Terror, Illegalität, Widerstand—Köln 1944/45*, Essen, 1989.

Rüß, Hartmut, 'Wer war verantwortlich für das Massaker von Babij Jar?', *MGM* 57 (1998), pp. 483–508.

Sabrow, Martin, ed., *Geschichte als Herrschaftsdiskurs. Der Umgang mit der Vergangenheit in der DDR*, Cologne, 2000.

Sabrow, Martin, ed., *Wohin treibt die DDR-Erinnerung? Dokumentation einer Debatte*, Göttingen, 2007.

Sabrow, Martin, 'Bundesrepublik und DDR in der Doppelkrise europäischer Industriegesellschaften. Zum sozialökonomischen Wandel in den 1970er Jahren', *Zeithistorische Forschungen/Studies in Contemporary History* 3 (2006), pp. 343–62.

Sabrow, Martin, *Die verdrängte Verschwörung. Der Rathenau-Mord und die deutsche Gegenrevolution*, Munich, 1994.

Sabrow, Marin, Jessen, Ralph and Große Kracht, Klaus, eds., *Zeitgeschichte als Streitgeschichte. Große Kontroversen nach 1945*, Munich, 2003.

Sachse, Carola, Siegel, Tilla and Spode, Hasso, eds., *Angst, Belohnung, Zucht und Ordnung. Herrschaftsmechanismen im Nationalsozialismus*, Opladen, 1982.

Saldern, Adelheid von and Hachtmann, Rüdiger, '"Gesellschaft am Fließband". Fordistische Produktion und Herrschaftspraxis Deutschland', *Zeithistorische Forschungen/Studies in Contemporary History* 6 (2009), pp. 186–208.

Saldern, Adelheid von and Hachtmann, Rüdiger, 'Das fordistische Jahrhundert. Eine Einleitung', *Zeithistorische Forschungen/Studies in Contemporary History* 6 (2009), pp. 174–85.

Salewski, Michael, *Der Erste Weltkrieg*, Paderborn, 2004.

Salin, Edgar, *Ökonomik der Atomkraft. Vor einer neuen Etappe der industriellen Revolution*, Cologne-Marienburg, 1955.

Sammons, Jeffrey L., ed., *Die Protokolle der Weisen von Zion. Die Grundlage des modernen Antisemitismus—eine Fälschung*, Göttingen, 1998.

Sandgruber, Roman, *Strom der Zeit. Das Jahrhundert der Elektrizität*, Linz, 1992.

Sandkühler, Thomas, *'Endlösung' in Galizien. Der Judenmord in Ostpolen und die Rettungsaktionen von Berthold Beitz 1941–1944*, Bonn, 1996.

Sarotte, Mary Elise, *Dealing with the Devil. East Germany, Détente, and Ostpolitik 1969–1973*, Chapel Hill, North Carolina, 2001.

Sauer, Bernhard, *Schwarze Reichswehr und Fememorde. Eine Milieustudie zum Rechtsradikalismus in der Weimarer Republik*, Berlin, 2004.

Saul, Klaus et al., eds., *Arbeiterfamilien im Kaiserreich. Materialien zur Sozialgeschichte in Deutschland 1871–1914*, Königstein im Taunus, 1982.

Sawyer, James E., *Why Reaganomics and Keynesian Economics Failed*, Basingtoke, 1987.

Schabert, Tilo, *How World Politics is Made. France and the Reunification of Germany*, Columbia, Mo., 2009.

Schäfer, Hans Dieter, *Das gespaltene Bewusstsein. Vom Dritten Reich bis zu den langen Fünfziger Jahren*, Göttingen, 2009.

Schallmeyer, Wilhelm, *Vererbung und Auslese im Lebenslauf der Völker*, Jena, 1903.

Schanetzky, Tim, *Die große Ernüchterung. Wirtschaftspolitik, Expertise und Gesellschaft in der Bundesrepublik 1966 bis 1982*, Berlin, 2007.

Scheer, Joseph, *Deutschland, Deutschland, alles ist vorbei. Alternatives Leben oder Anarchie? Die neue Jugendrevolte am Beispiel der Berliner 'Scene'*, Munich, 1982.

Scheiper, Stephan, *Innere Sicherheit. Politische Anti-Terror-Konzepte in der Bundesrepublik Deutschland während der 1970er Jahre*, Paderborn etc., 2010.

Schelsky, Helmut, *Die Soziologen und das Recht. Abhandlungen und Vorträge zur Soziologie von Recht, Institution und Planung*, Opladen, 1980.

Schelsky, Helmut, *Die skeptische Generation*, Düsseldorf, 1960.

Schelsky, Helmut, *Wandlungen der deutschen Familie in der Gegenwart. Darstellung und Deutung einer empirisch-soziologischen Tatbestandsaufnahme*, Dortmun, 1953.

Scherf, Harald, *Enttäuschte Hoffnungen—vergebene Chancen. Die Wirtschaftspolitik der Sozial-Liberalen Koalition 1969–1982*, Göttingen, 1986.

Scheuch, Erwin K., Gräf, Lorenz and Kühnel, Steffen M., *Volkszählung, Volkszählungsprotest und Bürgerverhalten. Ergebnisse der Begleituntersuchung zur Volkszählung 1987*, Stuttgart, 1989.

Schildt, Axel, '"Mach mal Pause". Freie Zeit, Freizeitverhalten und Freizeitdiskurse in der westdeutschen Wiederaufbau-Gesellschaft der 1950er Jahre', *AfS* 33 (1993), pp. 357–406.

Schildt, Axel, *Deutschlands Platz in einem 'christlichen Abendland'. Konservative Publizisten aus dem Tat-Kreis in der Kriegs- und Nachkriegszeit*, Opladen, 1987.

Schildt, Axel, *Die Sozialgeschichte der Bundesrepublik Deutschland bis 1989/90*, Munich, 2007.

Schildt, Axel, *Militärdikatur mit Massenbasis? Die Querfrontkonzeption der Reichswehrführung um General von Schleicher am Ende der Weimarer Republik*, Frankfurt am Main and New York, 1981.

Schildt, Axel, *Moderne Zeiten. Freizeit, Massenmedien und 'Zeitgeist' in der Bundesrepublik der 50er Jahre*, Hamburg, 1995.

Schildt, Axel, 'Vor der Revolte. Die sechziger Jahre', *APuZ* 22–23/2001, pp. 7–13.

Schildt, Axel, *Zwischen Abendland und Amerika. Studien zur westdeutschen Ideenlandschaft der 50er Jahre*, Munich, 1999.

Schildt, Axel and Siegfried, Detlef, eds., *Between Marx and Coca-Cola. Youth Cultures in Changing European Societies 1960–1980*, New York and Oxford, 2006.

Schildt, Axel and Siegfried, Detlef, *Deutsche Kulturgeschichte. Die Bundesrepublik—1945 bis zur Gegenwart*, Munich, 2009.

Schildt, Axel, Siegfried, Detlef and Lammers, Karl Christian, eds., *Dynamische Zeiten. Die 60er Jahre in den beiden deutschen Gesellschaften*, Hamburg, 2000.

Schildt, Axel and Sywottek, Arnold, eds., *Massenwohnung und Eigenheim. Wohnungsbau und Wohnen in der Großstadt set dem 1. Weltkrieg*, Frankfurt am Main and New York, 1988.

Schildt, Axel and Sywottek, Arnold, eds., *Modernisierung im Wiederaufbau. Die westdeutsche Gesellschaft der 50er Jahre*, Bonn, 1993.

Schiller, Kay, *The 1972 Munich Olympics and the Making of Modern Germany*, Berkeley, Los Angeles and London, 2010.

Schivelbusch, Wolfgang, *Three New Deals: Reflections on Roosevelt's America, Mussolini's Italy, and Hitler's Germany, 1933–1939*, New York, 2006.

Schlotter, Peter, *Die KSZE im Ost-West Konflikt. Wirkung einer internationalen Institution*, Frankfurt am Main and New York, 1999.

Schmädecke, Jürgen, Bahar, Alexander and Kugel, Wilfried, 'Der Reichstagsbrand in neuem Licht', *HZ* 269 (1999), pp. 603–51.

Schmidt, Manfred G., *Das politische System der Bundesrepublik Deutschland*, Munich, 2005.

Schmidt, Manfred G., *Sozialpolitik in Deutschland. Historische Entwicklung und internationaler Vergleich*, Wiesbaden, 2005.

Schmidt-Gernig, Alexander, 'Die gesellschaftliche Konstruktion der Zukunft', *Welttrends* 18 (1998), pp. 63–84.

Schmitt, Carl, 'Der Führer schützt das Recht', *Deutsche Juristenzeitung* 39 (1934), pp. 945–50.

Schmitt, Carl, *Der Hüter der Verfassung*, 4th edn., Berlin, 1996.

Schmitt, Carl, *Political Theology. Four chapters on the concept of sovereignty*, Chicago, Illinois, 2005.

Schmitt, Carl, *Positionen und Begriffe. Im Kampf mit Weimar—Genf—Versailles 1923–1939*, Hamburg, 1940.

Schmitt, Carl, *The Tyranny of Values*, ed. and trans. by Simona Draghici, Washington, DC, 1996.

Schmitt, Carl, *Völkerrechtliche Großraumordnung mit Interventionsverbot für raumfremde Mächte. Ein Beitrag zum Reichsbegriff im Völkerrecht*, Berlin, 1939.

Schmitz, Walter et al, eds., *Völkische Bewegung, konservative Revolution, Nationalsozialismus. Aspekte einer politisierten Kultur*, Dresden, 2005.

Schmoeckel, Reinhard, and Kaiser, Bruno, *Die vergessene Regierung. Die große Koalition 1966–1969 und ihre langfristigen Wirkungen*, Bonn, 1991.

Schmuhl, Hans-Walter, *Rassenhygiene, Nationalsozialismus, Euthanasie. Von der Verhütung zur Vernichtung 'lebensunwerten Lebens' 1890–1945*, Göttingen, 1987.

Schneehain, Alexander W., *Der Atomausstieg. Eine Analyse aus verfassungs- und verwaltungsrechtlicher Sicht*, Göttingen, 2005.

Schneider, Andrea H., *Die Kunst des Kompromisses. Helmut Schmidt und die Große Koalition 1966–1969*, Paderborn etc., 1999.

Schneider, Gerhard, *In eiserner Zeit. Kriegswahrzeichen im Ersten Weltkrieg*, Schwalbach am Taunus, 2013.

Schneider, Irmin, *Die deutsche Rußlandpolitik 1890–1900*, Paderborn etc., 2003.

Schneider, Michael, *Demokratie in Gefahr?Der Konflikt um die Notstandsgesetze: Sozialdemokratie, Gewerkschaften und intellektueller Protest (1958–1968)*, Bonn, 1986.

Schneider, Michael, 'Die "Goldhagen-Debatte". Ein Historikerstreit in der Mediengesellschaft', *AfS* 37 (1997), pp. 67–83.

Schneider, Michael, *Unterm Hakenkreuz. Arbeiter und Arbeiterbewegung 1933 bis 1939*, Bonn, 1999 (Geschichte der Arbeiter und der Arbeiterbewegung in Deutschland seit dem Ende des 18. Jahrhunderts, 12).

Schneider, Michael, *Unternehmer und Demokratie. Die freien Gewerkschaften in der unternehmerischen Ideologie der Jahre 1918 bis 1933*, Bonn-Bad Godesberg, 1975.

Schneider, Wolfgang, ed., *'Vernichtungspolitik'. Eine Debatte über den Zusammenhang von Sozialpolitik und Genozid im nationalsozialistischen Deutschland*, Hamburg, 1991.

Schoenbaum, David, *Ein Abgrund von Landesverrat. Die Affäre um den 'Spiegel'*, Vienna, Munich and Zürich, 1968.

Schoeps, Julius H., ed., *Ein Volk von Mördern? Die Dokumentation zur Goldhagen-Kontroverse um die Rolle der Deutschen im Holocaust*, Hamburg, 1996.

Scholder, Klaus, *The Churches and the Third Reich*, vol. 1, London, 1987.

Schöne, Jens, *Frühling auf dem Lande? Die Kollektivierung der DDR-Landwirtschaft*, Berlin, 2005.

Schönhoven, Klaus, *Wendejahre. Die Sozialdemokratie in der Zeit der Großen Koalition 1966–1969*, Bonn, 2004.

Schörken, Rolf, *Luftwaffenhelfer und Drittes Reich. Die Entstehung eines politischen Bewusstseins*, Stuttgart, 1984.

Schrader, Bärbel and Schebera, Jürgen, *The 'Golden' Twenties: Art and Literature in the Weimar Republic*, New Haven, Connecticut and London, 1988.

Schregel, Susanne, *Der Atomkrieg vor der Wohnungstür. Eine Politikgeschichte der neuen Friedensbewegung in der Bundesrepublik 1970–1985*, Frankfurt am Main and New York, 2011.

Schreiber, Gerhard, *Der Zweite Weltkrieg*, Munich, 2002.

Schremmer, Eckart, ed., *Wirtschafts- und Sozialgeschichte. Gegenstand und Methode*, Stuttgart, 1998.

Schröder, Gerhard and Blair, Tony, 'Der Weg nach vorne für Europas Sozialdemokraten', *Blätter für deutsche und internationale Politik* 44 (1999), pp. 887–96.

Schröder, Hans Eggert, *Ludwig Klages. Die Geschichte seines Lebens*, Bonn, 1972.

Schroeder, Klaus, *Der Preis der Einheit. Eine Bilanz*, Munich and Viennà, 2000.

Schroeder, Klaus, *Der SED-Staat. Partei, Staat und Gesellschaft 1949–1990*, Munich and Vienna, 1998.

Schroeder, Klaus, *Die veränderte Republik. Deutschland nach der Wiedervereinigung*, Munich, 2006.

Schroeder, Wolfgang, ed., *Die Gewerkschaften in Politik und Gesellschaft der Bundesrepublik Deutschland. Ein Handbuch*, Wiesbaden, 2003.

Schröter, Harm G., 'Die Amerikanisierung der Werbung in der Bundesrepublik Deutschland', *JbWG* 1997/1, pp. 93–115.

Schubert, Klaus von, ed., *Sicherheitspolitik der Bundesrepublik Deutschland, Dokumentation 1945–1977*, 2 vols., Cologne 1978–9.

Schui, Herbert and Blankenburg, Stephanie, *Neoliberalismus. Theorie, Gegner, Praxis*, Hamburg, 2002.

Schulman, Bruce J., *The Seventies. The Great Shift in American Culture, Society and Politics*, New York, 2001.

Schulte, Jan Erik, ed., *Die SS, Himmler und die Wewelsburg*, Paderborn, 2009.

Schulte, Jan Erik, *Zwangsarbeit und Vernichtung. Das Wirtschaftsimperium der SS. Oswald Pohl und das SS-Wirtschafts-Verwaltungshauptamt 1933*, Paderborn etc., 2001.

Schulz, Gerhard, *Aufstieg des Nationalsozialismus. Krise und Revolution in Deutschland*, Frankfurt am Main, Berlin and Vienna, 1975.

Schulz, Gerhard, *Revolutions and Peace Treaties, 1917–1920*, London, 1972.

Schulz, Günther, ed., *1949–1957, Bundesrepublik Deutschland. Bewältigung der Kriegsfolgen, Rückkehr zur sozialpolitischen Normalität*, Baden-Baden, 2005.

Schulz, Günther, *Die Angestellten seit dem 19. Jahrhundert*, Munich, 2000.

Schulz, Günther, *Wiederaufbau in Deutschland. Die Wohnungsbaupolitik in den Westzonen und der Bundesrepublik von 1945 bis 1957*, Düsseldorf, 1994.

Schulz, Kristina, *Der lange Atem der Provokation. Die Frauenbewegung in der Bundesrepublik und in Frankreich 1968–1976*, Frankfurt am Main and New York, 2002.

Schulze, Hagen, *Freikorps und Republik 1918–1920*, Boppard, 1969.

Schulze, Hagen, *Otto Braun: oder, Preußens demokratische Sendung: Eine Biographie*, Frankfurt am Main, Berlin and Vienna, 1977.

Schumann, Dirk, *Political Violence in the Weimar Republic, 1918–1933. Fight for the Streets and Fear of Civil War*, Oxford, 2009.

Schumann, Otto and Haverstein, Martin, *Deutsche Bildung?Briefwechsel zweier Schulmänner. Otto Schumann—Martin Haverstein, 1930–1944*, ed. by Notker Hammerstein, Frankfurt am Main, 1988.

Schuster, Armin, *Die Entnazifizierung in Hessen 1945–1954. Vergangenheitspolitik in der Nachkriegszeit*, Wiesbaden, 1999.

Schwabe, Klaus, ed., *Die Ruhrkrise 1923. Wendepunkt der internationalen Beziehungen nach dem Ersten Weltkrieg*, Paderborn etc., 1984.

Schwabe, Klaus, *Deutsche Revolution und Wilson-Frieden. Die amerikanische und die deutsche Friedensstrategie zwischen Ideologie und Machtpolitik 1918/19*, Düsseldorf, 1971.

Schwabe, Klaus 'Ursprung und Verbreitung des alldeutschen Annexionismus in der deutschen Professorschaft im Ersten Weltkrieg', *VfZ* 14 (1966), pp. 105–38.

Schwartz, Michael, '"Proletarier" und "Lumpen". Sozialistische Ursprünge eugenischen Denkens', *VfZ* 42 (1994), pp. 537–70.

Schwartz, Thomas Alan, 'Die Begnadigung deutscher Kriegsverbrecher. John McCloy und die Häftlinge von Landsberg', *VfZ* 38 (1990), pp. 375–414.

Schwarz, Hans-Peter, ed., *Die Bundesrepublik Deutschland. Eine Bilanz nach 60 Jahren*, Cologne, 2008.

Schwarz, Hans-Peter, ed., *Die Legende von der verpassten Gelegenheit. Die Stalin-Note vom 10. März 1952*, Stuttgart and Zürich, 1982.

Schwarz, Hans-Peter, ed., *Konrad Adenauers Regierungsstil*, Bonn, 1991.

Schwarz, Hans-Peter, *Die Ära Adenauer: Epochenwechsel 1957-1963* Wiesbaden, 1983.

Schwarz, Hans-Peter, *Die Ära Adenauer: Gründerjahre der Republik 1949-1957* Wiesbaden, 1981.

Schwarz, Hans-Peter, *Konrad Adenauer: a German Politician and Statesman in a Period of War, Revolution and Reconstruction*, 2 vols., Oxford, 1995–8.

Schwarz, Hans-Peter, *Helmut Kohl. Eine politische Biographie*, Munich, 2012.

Schwarzkopf, Dietrich, ed., *Rundfunkpolitik in Deutschland*, 2 vols., Munich, 1999.

Schwarzmeier, Jan, *Die Autonomen zwischen Subkultur und sozialer Bewegung*, Göttingen, 2001.

Seibel, Wolfgang, *Persecution and Rescue. The Politics of the Final Solution in France, 1940–1944*, Ann Arbor, Michigan, 2016.

Seibel, Wolfgang, *Verwaltete Illusionen. Die Privatisierung der DDR-Wirtschaft durch die Treuhandanstalt und ihre Nachfolger 1990–2000*, Frankfurt am Main and New York, 2005.

Seidel, Hans, *Jugendgefährdung—heute*, Hamburg, 1952.

Seidel, Hans-Christoph and Tenfelde, Klaus, eds., *Zwangsarbeit im Europa des 20. Jahrhunderts. Bewältigung und vergleichende Aspekte*, Essen, 2007.

Seidel, Robert, *Deutsche Besatzungspolitik in Polen. Der Distrikt Radom 1939–1945*, Paderborn etc., 2006.

Seifert, Jürgen, ed., *Der Spiegel-Affäre*, 2 vols., Olten and Freiburg im Breisgau, 1966.

Sekretariat des Lokalkomitees, ed., *Die 68. Generalversammlung der Deutschen Katholiken zu Freiburg im Breisgau. 28.August bis 1.September 1929*, Freiburg im Breisgau, n.d.

Showalter, Dennis E., *Tannenberg. Clash of Empires 1914*, Hamden, Connecticut, 1991.

Siebs, Benno Eide, *Die Außenpolitik der DDR 1976–1989. Strategien und Grenzen*, Paderborn etc., 1999.

Sieburg, Friedrich, *Die Lust am Untergang. Selbstgespräche auf Bundesebene* Hamburg, 1955.

Sieder, Reinhard, *Sozialgeschichte der Familie*, Frankfurt am Main, 1987.

Siegfried, Detlef, *Time is on my Side. Konsum und Politik in der westdeutschen Jugendkultur der 60er Jahre*, Göttingen, 2006.

Siegrist, Hannes, Kaelble, Hartmut and Kocka, Jürgen, eds., *Europäische Konsumgeschichte. Zur Gesellschafts- und Kulturgeschichte des Konsums (18. bis 20. Jahrhundert)*, Frankfurt am Main and New York, 1996.

Siemens, Werner von, 'Das naturwissenschaftliche Zeitalter', *Tageblatt der Versammlung Deutscher Naturforscher und Ärzte* 59 (1886), pp. 92–6.

Silies, Eva-Maria, *Liebe, Lust und Last. Die Pille als weibliche Generationserfahrung in der Bundesrepublik 1960–1980*, Göttingen, 2010.

Sinn, Hans-Werner, *Kasino-Kapitalismus. Wie es zur Finanzkrise kam, und was jetzt zu tun ist*, Berlin, 2010.

Smelser, Ronald M., *The Sudeten Problem, 1933–1938. Volkstumspolitik and the Formulation of Nazi Foreign Policy*, Folkestone, 1975.

Smelser, Ronald and Syring, Enrico, eds., *Die SS: Elite unter dem Totenkopf. 30 Lebensläufe*, Paderborn, 2000.

Smith, Arthur L., *Die vermißte Million. Zum Schicksal deutscher Kriegsgefangener nach dem Zweiten Weltkrieg*, Munich, 1992.

Smith, Arthur L. *Heimkehr aus dem Zweiten Weltkrieg. Die Entlassung der deutschen Kriegsgefangenen*, Stuttgart, 1985.

Smith, Michael L., *Occupation, Collaboration and Resistance. Nazism and Western Europe, 1939–1945: books and materials held at the University of Hull*, Hull, 1984.

Snyder, Jack, *The Ideology of the Offensive: Military Decision Making and the Disasters of 1914*, Ithaca, New York and London, 1984.

Soell, Hartmut, *Helmut Schmidt*, 2 vols., Munich, 2003–8.

Sommer, Theo, ed., *Reise ins andere Deutschland*, Reinbek bei Hamburg 1986.

Sorge, Martin K., *The Other Price of Hitler's War. German Military and Civilian Losses Resulting from World War II*, New York, 1986.

Soutou, Georges-Henri, *L'or et le sang*, Paris, 1989.

Spannuth, Jan Philipp, *Rückerstattung Ost: Der Umgang der DDR mit dem 'arisierten' und enteigneten Eigentum der Juden und die Gestaltung der Rückerstattung im wiedervereinigten Deutschland*, Essen, 2007.

Später, Jörg, *Vansittart. Britische Debatten über Deutsche und Nazis 1902–1945*, Göttingen, 2003.

Spengler, Oswald, *The Decline of the West*, vol. 2, London, 1928.

Spilker, Rolf and Ulrich, Bernd, eds., *Der Tod als Maschinist. Der industrialisierte Krieg 1914–18*, Bramsche, 1998.

Spoerer, Mark, *Zwangsarbeit unter dem Hakenkreuz. Ausländische Zivilarbeiter, Kriegsgefangene und Häftlinge im Deutschen Reich und im besetzten Europa 1939–1945*, Stuttgart and Munich, 2001.

Staak, Michael, ed., *Aufbruch nach Gesamteuropa. Die KSZE nach der Wende im Osten*, Münster, 1993.

Staas, Dieter, *Migration und Fremdenfeindlichkeit als politisches Problem*, Münster and Hamburg, 1994.

Stachura, Peter D., ed., *Unemployment and the Great Depression in Weimar Germany*, Basingstoke, 1986.

Stahr, Gerhard, *Volksgemeinschaft vor der Leinwand? Der nationalsozialistische Film und sein Publikum*, Berlin, 2001.

Stambolis, Barbara, *Mythos Jugend—Leitbild und Krisensymptom*, Schwalbach, 2003.

Stapel, Wilhelm, 'Der Geistige und sein Volk', *Deutsches Volkstum* 1 (January 1930), pp. 1–8.

Stargardt, Nicholas, *Witnesses of War. Children's Lives under the Nazis*, London, 2005.

Staritz, Dietrich, *Die Gründung der DDR. Von der sowjetischen Besatzungsherrschaft zum sozialistischen Staat*, Munich, 1995.

Staritz, Dietrich, *Geschichte der DDR*, Frankfurt am Main, 1996.

Staud, Toralf, *Moderne Nazis. Die neuen Rechten und der Aufstieg der NPD*, Cologne, 2006.

Stavginski, Hans-Georg, *Das Holocaust-Denkmal. Der Streit um das 'Denkmal für die ermordeten Juden Europas' in Berlin (1988–1999)*, Paderborn, 2002.

Stedman, Michael, *The German Spring Offensive*, London, 2001.

Steege, Paul, *Black Market, Cold War, Everyday Life in Berlin 1946–1949*, Cambridge and New York, 2007.

Stein, Harry, *Konzentrationslager Buchenwald 1937–1945. Begleitband zur ständigen historischen Ausstellung*, Göttingen, 1999.

Steinbach, Peter and Tuchel, Johannes, eds., *Widerstand in Deutschland 1933–1945. Ein historisches Lesebuch*, Munich, 2000.

Steinbacher, Sybille, *Wie der Sex nach Deutschland kam. Der Kampf um Sittlichkeit und Anstand in der frühen Bundesrepublik*, Munich, 2011.

Steinbacher, Sybille, *Auschwitz, a history*, London, 2005.

Steiner, André, ed., *Überholen ohne einzuholen. Die DDR-Wirtschaft als Fußnote der deutschen Geschichte?*, Berlin, 2006.

Steiner, André, 'Bundesrepublik und DDR in der Doppelkrise europäischer Industriegesellschaften. Zum sozialökonomischen Wandel in den 1970er Jahren', *Zeithistorische Forschungen* 3 (2006), pp. 343–62.

Steiner, André, *The Plans that Failed. An Economic History of the GDR*, Oxford, 2010.

Steinert, Marlis, *Hitler's War and the Germans. Public Mood and Attitude during the Second World War*, Athens, Ohio, 1977.

Steingart, Gabor, *Deutschland. Abstieg eines Superstars*, Munich, 2004.

Steininger, Rolf, ed., *Die doppelte Eindämmung. Europäische Sicherheit und deutsche Frage in den Fünfzigern*, Munich, 1993.

Steininger, Rolf, *Deutsche Geschichte seit 1945*, 4 vols., Frankfurt am Main, 1996–2002.

Steininger, Rolf, *Eine Chance zur Wiedervereinigung? Die Stalin-Note vom 10. März 1952. Darstellung und Dokumentation auf der Grundlage unveröffentlichter britischer und amerikanischer Akten*, Bonn, 1986.

Stern, Fritz Richard, *The Politics of Cultural Despair. A Study in the Rise of the Germanic Ideology*, Garden City, New York, 1965.

Sternberger, Dolf, *Verfassungspatriotismus*, Frankfurt am Main, 1990.

Stevenson, David, *Armaments and the Coming of War. Europe 1904–1914*, Oxford and New York, 1996.

Stoltenberg, Gerhard, *Politische Strömungen im schleswig-holsteinischen Landvolk 1918–1933*, Düsseldorf, 1962.

Stölzl, Christoph, ed., *Die Zwanziger Jahre in München. Katalog zur Ausstellung im Münchner Stadtmuseum, Mai-September 1979*, Munich, 1979.

Stone, Norman, *The Eastern Front*, London, 1975.

Storz, Dieter, *Kriegsbild und Rüstung vor 1914. Europäische Landstreitkräfte vor dem Ersten Weltkrieg*, Herford, Berlin and Bonn, 1992.

Stöss, Richard, ed., *Parteien-Handbuch. Die Parteien der Bundesrepublik Deutschland seit 1945*, 4 vols., Opladen 1983–6.

Stöver, Bernd, *Der Kalte Krieg*, Munich, 2003.

Strachan, Hew, *The First World War: a New Illustrated History*, London, 2003.

Strachan, Hew, *The First World War. Volume One: To Arms*, Oxford, 2001.

Straßner, Alexander, *Die dritte Generation der 'Roten Armee Fraktion'. Entstehung, Struktur, Funktionslogik und Zerfall einer terroristischen Organisation*, Wiesbaden, 2003.

Straub, Eberhard, *Kaiser Wilhelm II in der Politik seiner Zeit. Die Erfindung des Reiches aus dem Geist der Moderne*, Berlin, 2008.

Strauss, Herbert A., 'Jewish Emigration from Germany. Nazi Policies and Jewish Responses', *The Leo Baeck Institute Year Book* 25 (1980), pp. 313–61, and 26 (1981), pp. 343–409.

Strazhas, Abba, *Deutsche Ostpolitik im Ersten Weltkrieg. Der Fall Ober Ost 1915–1917*, Wiesbaden, 1993.

Streeck, Wolfgang, and Höpner, Martin, eds., *Alle Macht dem Markt? Fallstudien zur Abwicklung der Deutschland AG*, Frankfurt am Main, 2003.

Stümke, Hans-Georg, *Homosexuelle in Deutschland. Eine politische Geschichte*, Munich, 1989.

Südbeck, Thomas, *Motorisierung, Verkehrsentwicklung und Verkehrspolitik in der Bundesrepublik Deutschland der 1950er Jahre. Umrisse der allgemeinen Entwicklung und zwei Beispiele: Hamburg und das Emsland*, Stuttgart, 1994.

Suhrkamp, Peter, 'Söhne ohne Väter und Lehrer. Die Situation der bürgerlichen Jugend', *Neue Rundschau* 431 (1932), pp. 681–96.

Süß, Dietmar, *Kumpel und Genossen. Arbeiterschaft, Betrieb und Sozialdemokratie in der bayerischen Montanindustrie 1945 bis 1976*, Munich, 2003.

Süß, Dietmar, *Death from the Skies. How the British and Germans survived bombing in World War II*, Oxford, 2014.

Süß, Dietmar and Süß, Winfried, *Das 'Dritte Reich'. Eine Einführung*, Munich, 2008.

Süß, Werner, ed., *Deutschland in den neunziger Jahren. Politik und Gesellschaft zwischen Wiedervereinigung und Globalisierung*, Opladen, 2002.

Süß, Werner, ed., *Die Bundesrepublik in den achtziger Jahren. Innenpolitik, politische Kultur, Außenpolitik*, Opladen, 1991.

Süß, Winfried, *Der Volkskörper im Krieg. Gesundheitspolitik, Gesundheitsverhältnisse und Krankenmord im nationalsozialistischen Deutschland 1939–1945*, Munich, 2003.

Tannenbaum, Edward R., *1900: The Generation Before the Great War*, Garden City, NY, 1976.

Taylor, Frederick, *Dresden: Tuesday, 13 February 1945*, London, 2004.

Tenfelde, Klaus, ed., *Arbeiter im 20. Jahrhundert*, Stuttgart, 1991.

Tenfelde, Klaus, ed., *Arbeiter und Arbeiterbewegung im Vergleich*, Munich, 1986.

Tenfelde, Klaus, ed., *Arbeitseinsatz und Zwangsarbeit im besetzten Europa*, Göttingen, 2005.

Tenfelde, Klaus and Seidel, Hans-Christoph, eds., *Zwangsarbeit im Bergwerk. Der Arbeitseinsatz im Kohlenbergbau des Deutschen Reiches und der besetzten Gebiete im Ersten und Zweiten Weltkrieg*, 2 vols., Essen, 2005.

Tennstedt, Florian and Sachße, Christoph, eds., *Geschichte der Armenfürsorge in Deutschland. Bd.3. Der Wohlfahrtsstaat im Nationalsozialismus*, Stuttgart, Berlin and Cologne, 1992.

Thamer, Hans-Ulrich, 'NS-Vergangenheit im politischen Diskurs der 68er-Bewegung', *Westfälische Forschungen* 48 (1998), pp. 39–53.

Thamer, Hans-Ulrich, *Verführung und Gewalt. Deutschland 1933–1945*, Berlin, 1986.

Therborn, Göran, *European Modernity and Beyond: the trajectory of European societies 1945–2000*, London, 1995.

Thiel, Jens, *'Menschenbassin Belgien'. Anwerbung, Deportation und Zwangsarbeit im Ersten Weltkrieg*, Essen, 2007.

Thiele, Hans-Günther, ed., *Die Wehrmachtsausstellung. Dokumentation einer Kontroverse*, Bonn, 1999.

Thiemeyer, Guido, *Europäische Integration. Motive—Prozesse—Strukturen*, Cologne, Weimar and Vienna, 2010.

Thomas, Frank, *Telefonieren in Deutschland. Organisatorische, technische und räumliche Entwicklung eines großtechnischen Systems*, Frankfurt am Main and New York, 1995.

Thomas, Georg Richard, *Geschichte der deutschen Wehr- und Rüstungswirtschaft (1918–1943/45)*, Boppard am Rhein, 1966.

Thoß, Bruno, *Der Ludendorff-Kreis 1919–1925*, Munich, 1978.

Tietmeyer, Hans, *Herausforderung Euro. Wie es zum Euro kam and was er für Deutschlands Zukunft bedeutet*, Munich and Vienna, 2005.

Tille, Alexander, *Volksdienst*, Berlin and Leipzig, 1893.

Tille, Alexander, *Von Darwin bis Nietzsche. Ein Buch Entwicklungsethik*, Leipzig, 1895.

Timm, Helga, *Die deutsche Sozialpolitik und der Bruch der großen Koalition im März 1930*, Düsseldorf, 1952.

Timmermann, Heiner, ed., *Das war die DDR. DDR-Forschung im Fadenkreuz von Herrschaft, Außenbeziehungen, Kultur und Souveränität*, Münster, 2004.

Tippelt, Rudolf, *Bildung und sozialer Wandel. Eine Untersuchung von Modernisierungsprozessen am Beispiel der Bundesrepublik Deutschland seit 1950*, Weinheim, 1990.

Tomaszewski, Jerzy, *Auftakt zur Vernichtung. Die Vertreibung polnischer Juden aus Deutschland im Jahre1938*, Osnabrück, 2002.

Tooze, Adam, *Die Herausforderung der Globalisierung. Wirtschaft und Politik in Deutschland 1916–1923*, Göttingen, 2005.

Trachtenberg, Marc, *Reparation in World Politics. France and European Economic Diplomacy 1916–1923*, New York, 1980.

Traube, Klaus, *Plutonium-Wirtschaft? Das Finanzdebakel von Brutreaktor und Wiederaufarbeitung*, Reinbek bei Hamburg, 1984.

Treue, Wolfgang, *Deutsche Parteiprogramme 1861–1954*, Göttingen, 1954.

Trittel, Günter J., *Hunger und Politik. Die Ernährungskrise in der Bizone (1945–1949)*, Frankfurt am Main and New York, 1990.

Troeltsch, Ernst, *Spektator-Briefe. Aufsätze über die deutsche Revolution und die Weltpolitik 1918–1922*, Aalen, 1966 [1924].

Trunk, Isaiah, and Shapiro, Robert M., *Łódź Ghetto. A History*, Bloomington, Indiana and Indianapolis, Indiana, 2006.

Tsukerman, Mosheh, ed., *Zwischen Politik und Kultur. Juden in der DDR*, Göttingen, 2002.

Tucholsky, Kurt, *Gesammelte Werke*, 3 vols., Reinbek bei Hamburg, 1960.

Turner, Henry Ashby, *German Big Business and the Rise of Hitler*, Oxford, 1985.

Twain, Mark, *The £1,000,000 Bank-Note and Other New Stories*, Oxford, 1996.

Ueberhorst, Horst, ed., *Geschichte der Leibesübungen. Bd.3.2: Leibesübungen und Sport in Deutschland von Ersten Weltkrieg bis zur Gegenwart*,, Berlin, Munich and Frankfurt am Main, 1982.

Ueberschar, Gerd R., ed., *Der Nationalsozialismus vor Gericht. Die alliierten Prozesse gegen Kriegsverbrecher und Soldaten 1943–1952*, Frankfurt am Main, 2000.

Ueberschar, Gerd R. and Müller, Rolf-Dieter, *1945. Das Ende des Krieges*, Darmstadt, 2005.

Ueberschar, Gerd R and Wetter, Wolfram, eds., *'Unternehmen Barbarossa'. Der deutsche Überfall auf die Sowjetunion 1941*, Paderborn, 1984.

Uhl, Matthias, *Krieg um Berlin? Die sowjetische Militär- und Sicherheitspolitik in der zweiten Berlin-Krise 1948 bis 1962*, Munich, 2008.

Ullmann, Hans-Peter, *Der deutsche Steuerstaat. Geschichte der öffentlichen Finanzen vom 18. Jahrhundert bis heute*, Munich, 2005.

Ullmann, Hans-Peter, *Politik im Deutschen Kaiserreich 1871–1918*, Munich, 1999.

Ullrich, Christina, *'Ich fühl' mich nicht als Mörder'. Die Integration von NS-Tätern in die Nachkriegsgesellschaft*, Darmstadt, 2011.

Ullrich, Sebastian, *Der Weimar-Komplex. Das Scheitern der ersten deutschen Demokratie und die politische Kultur der frühen Bundesrepublik 1945–1959*, Göttingen, 2009.

Ullrich, Volker, 'Der Januarstreik 1918 in Hamburg, Kiel und Bremen. Eine vergleichende Studie zur Geschichte der Streikbewegungen im Ersten Weltkrieg', *Zeitschrift des Vereins für Hamburgische Geschichte* 71 (1985), pp. 45–74.

Ullrich, Volker, *Die Hamburger Arbeiterbewegung vom Vorabend des ersten Weltkrieges bis zur Revolution 1918–19*, Hamburg, 1976.

Ullrich, Volker, *Die nervöse Großmacht. Aufstieg und Untergang des deutschen Kaiserreichs 1871–1918*, Frankfurt am Main, 1997.

Ungváry, Chrisztián, 'Echte Bilder—problematische Aussagen. Eine quantitative und qualitative Fotoanalyse der Ausstellung "Vernichtungskrieg. Verbrechen der Wehrmacht 1941–1944"', *GWU* 10 (1999), pp. 584–95.

Vanden Berghe, Yvan, *Der Kalte Krieg 1917–1991*, Leipzig, 2002.

Védrine, Hubert, *Les mondes de François Mitterrand. À l'Élysée 1981–1995*, Paris, 1996.

Verhey, Jeffrey, *The Spirit of 1914. Militarism, Myth and Mobilization in Germany*, Cambridge, 2000.

Veser, Reinhard, *Der Prager Frühling 1968*, Erfurt, 2008.

Vincent, Charles Paul, *The Politics of Hunger. The Allied Blockade of Germany 1915–1919*, Athens, Ohio and London, 1985.

Volger, Helmut, *Geschichte der Vereinten Nationen*, Munich and Vienna, 2008.

Volkmann, Hans-Erich, 'Zur nationalsozialistischen Aufrüstung und Kriegswirtschaft', *MGM* 1 (1990), pp. 133–77.

Volkov, Shulamit, ed., *Deutsche Juden und die Moderne*, Munich, 1994.

Vollnhals, Clemens, ed., *Der Schein der Normalität. Alltag und Herrschaft in der SED-Diktatur*, Munich, 2002.

Vollnhals, Clemens, *Der Fall Havemann. Ein Lehrstück politischer Justiz*, Berlin, 2000.

Vollnhals, Clemens and Schlemmer, Thomas, eds., *Entnazifizierung. Politische Säuberung und Rehabilitierung in den vier Besatzungszonen 1945–1949*, Munich, 1991.

Volze, Achim, 'Die gespaltene Valutamark. Anmerkungen zur Währungspolitik und Außenhandelsstatistik der DDR', *Das Freie Wort* 31 (1999), pp. 232–41.

Wachsmann, Nikolaus, *Hitler's Prisons. Legal Terror in Nazi Germany*, New Haven, Conn., 2004.

Wagner, Bernd, ed., *Kulturelle Globalisierung. Zwischen Weltkultur und kultureller Fragmentierung*, Essen, 2001.

Wagner, Jens-Christian, *Produktion des Todes. Das KZ Mittelbau-Dora*, Göttingen, 2001.

Wagner, Patrick, *Bauern, Junker und Beamte. Lokale Herrschaft und Partizipation im Ostelbien des 19. Jahrhunderts*, Göttingen, 2005.

Wagner, Patrick, *Volksgemeinschaft ohne Verbrecher. Konzeptionen und Praxis der Kriminalpolizei in der Zeit der Weimarer Republik und des Nationalsozialismus*, Hamburg, 1996.

Wagner, Patrick, *Hitlers Kriminalisten. Die deutsche Kriminalpolizei und der Nationalsozialismus zwischen 1920 und 1960*, Munich, 2002.

Wagner, Peter, *A Sociology of Modernity: liberty and discipline*, London, 2002.

Walk, Joseph and Leo Baeck Institute, *Kurzbiographien zur Geschichte der Juden 1918–1945*, Munich and Jerusalem, 1988.

Walkenhorst, Peter, *Nation, Volk, Rasse. Radikaler Nationalismus im Deutschen Kaiserreich 1890–1914*, Göttingen, 2008.

Walker, Mark, *German National Socialism and the quest for nuclear power, 1939–1949*, Cambridge, 1989.

Wall, Richard and Winter, Jay, eds., *The Upheaval of War. Family, Work and Welfare in Europe, 1914–1918*, Cambridge and New York, 1988.

Walter, Dirk, *Antisemitische Kriminalität und Gewalt. Judenfeindschaft in der Weimarer Republik*, Bonn, 1999.

Walter, Franz, *Die SPD. Biographie einer Partei*, Reinbek bei Hamburg, 2011.

Walther, Joachim, *Sicherungsbereich Literatur. Schriftsteller und Staatssicherheit in der DDR*, Berlin, 1996.

Wandel, Eckhard, *Die Entstehung der Bank deutscher Länder und die deutsche Währungsreform 1948*, Frankfurt am Main, 1980.

Weber, Hermann, *Geschichte der DDR*, Munich, 1985.

Weber, Hermann, *Kommunismus in Deutschland 1918–1945*, Darmstadt, 1983.

Weber, Max, *Die Lage der Landarbeiter im ostelbischen Deutschland*, Tübingen, 1984.

Weber, Petra, *Justiz und Diktatur. Justizverwaltung und politische Strafjustiz in Thüringen 1945–1961*, Munich, 2000.

Wee, Herman van der, *Der gebremste Wohlstand. Wiederaufbau, Wachstum und Strukturwandel der Weltwirtschaft seit 1945*, Munich, 1984.

Wegner, Bernd, *The Waffen-SS: organization, ideology and function*, Oxford, 1990.

Wegner, Bernd, ed., *From Peace to War. Germany, Soviet Russia and the World, 1939–1941*, Oxford, 1997.

Wehler, Hans-Ulrich, *Deutsche Gesellschaftsgeschichte*, vols. 3, 4 and 5, Munich, 1995–2008.

Wehler, Hans-Ulrich, *Nationalismus. Geschichte, Formen, Folgen*, Munich, 2001.

Weichlein, Siegfried, *Sozialmilieus und politische Kultur in der Weimarer Republik. Lebenswelt, Vereinskultur, Politik in Hessen*, Göttingen, 1996.

Weidenfeld, Werner, *Europa-Handbuch*, Gütersloh, 2002.

Weidenfeld, Werner and Korte, Karl-Rudolf, eds., *Handbuch zur deutschen Einheit*, Bonn, 1993.

Weiland, Ruth, *Die Kinder der Arbeitslosen*, Berlin, 1933.

Weinberg, Gerhard L., *A World at Arms: a global history of World War II*, Cambridge, 1994.

Weindling, Paul, *Nazi Medicine and the Nuremberg Trials. From Medical War Crimes to Informed Consent*, Basingstoke, 2004.

Weingart, Peter, Kroll, Jürgen and Bayertz, Kurt, *Rasse, Blut und Gene. Geschichte der Eugenik und Rassenhygiene in Deutschland*, Frankfurt am Main, 1988.

Weinhauer, Klaus, ed., *Terrorismus in der Bundesrepublik. Medien, Staat und Subkulturen in den 1970er Jahren*, Frankfurt am Main and New York, 2006.

Weinke, Annette, *Die Nürnberger Prozesse*, Munich, 2006.

Weinke, Annette, *Eine Gesellschaft ermittelt gegen sich selbst. Die Geschichte der Zentralen Stelle Ludwigsburg 1958–2008*, Darmstadt, 2009.

Weisbrod, Bernd, ed., *Akademische Vergangenheitspolitik. Beiträge zur Wissenschaftskultur der Nachkriegszeit*, Göttingen, 2002.

Weisbrod, Bernd, ed., *Historische Beiträge zur Generationsforschung*, Göttingen, 2009 (Göttinger Studien zur Generationsforschung 2).

Weisbrod, Bernd, 'Gewalt in der Politik. Zur politischen Kultur in Deutschland zwischen den beiden Weltkriegen', *GWU* 43 (1992), pp. 391–404.

Weisbrod, Bernd, *Schwerindustrie in der Weimarer Republik. Interessenpolitik zwischen Stabilisierung und Krise*, Wuppertal, 1978.

Weitz, Eric D., 'From the Vienna to the Paris System. International Politics and the Entangled History of Human Rights, Forced Deportations, and Civilizing Missions', *AHR* 113 (2008), pp. 1,313–43.

Weizsäcker, Richard von, *Zum 40. Jahrestag der Beendigung des Krieges in Europa und der nationalsozialistischen Gewaltherrschaft. Ansprache am 8. Mai 1985 in der Gedenkstunde im Plenarsaal des Deutschen Bundestages*, Bonn, 1985.

Wellner, Gabriele, 'Industriearbeiterinnen in der Weimarer Republik. Arbeitsmarkt, Arbeit und Privatleben 1919–1933', *GG* 7 (1981), pp. 534–54.

Welsh, Helga A., *Revolutionärer Wandel auf Befehl? Entnazifizierungs- und Personalpolitik in Thüringen und Sachsen*, Munich, 1989.

Welskopp, Thomas, *Das Banner der Brüderlichkeit. Die deutsche Sozialdemokratie vom Vormärz bis zum Sozialistengesetz*, Bonn, 2000.

Welskopp, Thomas, 'Klasse als Befindlichkeit? Vergleichende Arbeitergeschichte vor der kulturhistorischen Herausforderung', *AfS* 38 (1998), pp. 301–36.

Wember, Heiner, *Umerziehung im Lager. Internierung und Bestrafung von Nationalsozialisten in der britischen Besatzungszone Deutschlands*, Essen, 1991.

Wendt, Bernd-Jürgen, *Deutschland 1933 bis 1945: Das Dritte Reich, Handbuch zur Geschichte*, Hanover, 1995.

Wendt, Gerald, *The Prospects of Nuclear Power and Technology*, London, 1957.

Wenzel, Rüdiger, *Die große Verschiebung? Das Ringen um den Lastenausgleich im Nachkriegsdeutschland von den ersten Vorarbeiten bis zur Verabschiedung des Gesetzes 1952*, Stuttgart, 2008.

Werkentin, Falco, *Politische Strafjustiz in der Ära Ulbricht*, Berlin, 1995.

Wernecke, Klaus, *Der Wille zur Weltgeltung. Außenpolitik und Öffentlichkeit im Kaiserreich am Vorabend des 1. Weltkrieges*, Düsseldorf, 1970.

Wernecke, Klaus, *Die Weltstellung Deutschlands in der deutschen öffentlichen Meinung 1911–14. Ein Beitrag zu Presse und Pressepolitik vor dem ersten Weltkrieg*, Hamburg, 1970.

Werner, Michael, *Die 'Ohne-mich' Bewegung. Die bundesdeutsche Friedensbewegung im deutsch-deutschen Kalten Krieg*, Münster, 2006.

Werner, Wolfgang F., *Bleib übrig! Deutsche Arbeiter in der nationalsozialistischen Kriegswirtschaft*, Düsseldorf, 1983.

Werth, German, *Verdun. Die Schlacht und der Mythos*, Bergisch Gladbach, 1979.

Wertheimer, Jack, *Unwelcome Strangers. East European Jews in Imperial Germany*, New York and Oxford, 1987.

Wesel, Uwe, *Die verspielte Revolution. 1968 und die Folgen*, Munich, 2002.

Westerhoff, Christian, *Zwangsarbeit im Ersten Weltkrieg. Deutsche Arbeitskräftepolitik im besetzten Polen und Litauen 1914–1918*, Paderborn etc., 2012.

Wettig, Gerhard, *Chruschtschows Berlin-Krise 1958 bis 1963. Drohpolitik und Mauerbau*, Munich, 2006.

Wettig, Gerhard, *Entmilitarisierung und Wiederbewaffnung in Deutschland 1943–1955. Internationale Auseinandersetzungen um die Rolle der Deutschen in Europa*, Munich, 1967.

Wetzel, Walter, *Naturwissenschaften und chemische Industrie in Deutschland. Voraussetzungen und Mechanismen ihres Aufstiegs im 19. Jahrhundert*, Stuttgart, 1991.

Weyrauch, Wolfgang, ed., *Ich lebe in der Bundesrepublik. Fünfzehn Deutsche über Deutschland*, Munich, 1960.

Widera, Thomas, *Dresden 1945–1948. Politik und Gesellschaft unter sowjetischer Besatzungsherrschaft*, Göttingen, 2004.

Wiechert, Ernst, *Rede an die deutsche Jugend, 1945*, Munich, 1945.

Wiegand, Lutz, *Der Lastenausgleich in der Bundesrepublik Deutschland 1949 bis 1985*, Frankfurt am Main etc., 1992.

Wiehn, Erhard Roy, ed., *Die Schoáh von Babij Jar. Das Massaker deutscher Sonderkommandos an der jüdischen Bevölkerung von Kiew 1941. 50 Jahre danach zum Gedenken*, Konstanz, 1991.

Wierling, Dorothee, *Geboren im Jahr Eins. Der Jahrgang 1949 in der DDR. Versuch einer Kollektivbiographie*, Berlin, 2002.

Wiggershaus, Rolf, *The Frankfurt School. Its History, Theories and Political Significance*, Cambridge, 1994.

Wildt, Michael, *Am Beginn der 'Konsumgesellschaft'. Mangelerfahrung, Lebenshaltung, Wohlstandshoffnung in Westdeutschland in den fünfziger Jahren*, Hamburg, 1995.

Wildt, Michael, *Der Traum vom Sattwerden. Hunger und Protest, Schwarzmarkt und Selbsthilfe*, Hamburg, 1986.

Wildt, Michael, *An Uncompromising Generation: the Nazi Leadership of the Reich Security Main Office*, Madison, Wis., 2009.

Wildt, Michael, *Volksgemeinschaft als Selbstermächtigung. Gewalt gegen Juden in der deutschen Provinz 1919 bis 1939*, Hamburg, 2007.

Wilentz, Sea, *The Age of Reagan. A History, 1974–2008*, New York, 2008.

Wilhelm, Hans-Heinrich, *Rassenpolitik und Kriegführung. Sicherheitspolizei und Wehrmacht in Polen und in der Sowjetunion 1939–1942*, Passau, 1991.

Wilke, Jürgen, ed., *Mediengeschichte der Bundesrepublik Deutschland*, Cologne, Weimar, Vienna, 1999.

Willeke, Eduard, 'Der Arbeitseinsatz im Kriege', *Jahrbücher für Nationalökonomie und Statistik* 154 (1941), pp. 117–201 and 311–48.

Willett, John, *The New Sobriety: Art and Politics in the Weimar Period*, London, 1978.

Willgerodt, Hans, 'Der Neoliberalismus—Entstehung, Kampfbegriff und Meinungsstreit', *Ordo* 57 (2006), pp. 47–89.

Williamson, John G., *Karl Helfferich 1872–1924. Economist, Financier, Politician*, Princeton, New Jersey, 1971.

Winkler, Dörte, *Frauenarbeit im 'Dritten Reich'*, Hamburg, 1977 (Historische Perspektiven 9).

Winkler, Gunnar, ed., *Frauenreport '90*, Berlin (GDR), 1990.

Winkler, Gunnar, ed., *Sozialreport '90, Daten und Fakten zur sozialen Lage in der DDR*, Berlin (GDR), 1990.

Winkler, Heinrich August, *Arbeiter und Arbeiterbewegung in der Weimarer Republik*, 3 vols., Berlin, 1985–8.

Winkler, Heinrich August, *Germany: The Long Road West*, 2 vols., Oxford 2006–7.

Winkler, Heinrich August, *Geschichte des Westens. Bd.1: Von den Anfängen in der Antike bis zum 20. Jahrhundert*, Munich, 2009.

Winkler, Heinrich August, *The Age of Catastrophe: a history of the West, 1914–1945*, New Haven, Connecticut, 2015.

Winkler, Heinrich August, *Revolution, Staat, Faschismus. Zur Revision des historischen Materialismus*, Göttingen, 1978.

Winkler, Heinrich August, *Weimar 1918–1933. Die Geschichte der ersten deutschen Demokratie*, Munich, 2005.

Winter, Jay M., and Robert, Jean-Louis, eds., *Capital Cities at War. Paris, London, Berlin 1914–1919*, 2 vols., Cambridge 1997–2007.

Wirsching, Andreas, '"Stalinisierung" oder entideologisierte "Nischengesellschaft"? Alte Einsichten und neue Thesen zum Charakter der KPD in der Weimarer Republik', *VfZ* 45 (1997), pp. 449–66.

Wirsching, Andreas, *Abschied vom Provisorium 1982–1990*, Munich, 2006.

Wirsching, Andreas, *Der Preis der Freiheit. Geschichte Europas in unserer Zeit*, Munich, 2012.

Wirsching, Andreas, *Deutsche Geschichte im 20. Jahrhundert*, Munich, 2011.

Wojak, Irmtrud, ed., *Auschwitz-Prozeß 4 Ks 2/63 Frankfurt am Main*, Frankfurt am Main, 2004.

Wolf, Friedrich, 'Auch wir können nicht schweigen', *Aufbau* 1.3 (1945), pp. 201–4.

Wolfrum, Edgar, *Die geglückte Demokratie. Geschichte der Bundesrepublik Deutschland von ihren Anfängen bis zur Gegenwart*, Stuttgart, 2006.

Wolfrum, Edgar, *Geschichte als Waffe. Vom Kaiserreich bis zur Wiedervereinigung*, Göttingen, 2001.

Wolfrum, Edgar, *Geschichtspolitik in der Bundesrepublik Deutschland. Der Weg zur bundesrepublikanischen Erinnerung 1948–1990*, Darmstadt, 1999.

Wolfrum, Edgar, *Rot-Grün an der Macht. Deutschland 1998–2005*, Munich, 2013.

Wolle, Stefan, *Die heile Welt der Diktatur. Alltag und Herrschaft in der DDR 1971–1989*, Berlin, 1998.

Woller, Hans, *Rom, 28. Oktober 1922. Die faschistische Herausforderung*, Munich, 1999.

Woller, Hans, *Geschichte Italiens im 20 Jahrhundert*, Munich, 2010.

Woller, Hans, *Gesellschaft und Politik in der amerikanischen Besatzungszone. Die Region Ansbach und Fürth*, Munich, 1986.

Woller, Reinhard, *Aufbruch ins Heute. Entwicklungen, Erkenntnisse, Leistungen in Chemie, Biowissenschaften, Medizin, Physik, Technik und Wirtschaft in synoptischer Darstellung 1877–1977*, Düsseldorf, 1977.

Wolter, Heike, *'Ich harre aus im Land and geh, ihm fremd.' Die Geschichte des Tourismus in der DDR*, Frankfurt am Main, 2009.

Wright, Lawrence, *The Looming Tower: Al-Qaeda and the Road to 9/11*, London, 2006.

Wuermeling, Franz-Josef, *Demokratie und Jugendschutz*, Cologne, 1959.

Wulf, Peter, *Hugo Stinnes. Wirtschaft und Politik 1918–1924*, Stuttgart, 1979.

Wyman, Mark, *DPs. Europe's Displaced Persons, 1945–1951*, Ithaca, New York, 1998.

Yahil, Leni, *The Holocaust. The Fate of European Jewry, 1932–1945*, Oxford, 1991.

Yergin, Daniel, *The Prize: the Epic Quest for Oil, Money and Power*, New York and London, 1991.

Yergin, Daniel, *Shattered Peace: the Origins of the Cold War and the National Security State*, Boston, Massachusetts, 1977.

Zapf, Wolfgang, *Individualisierung und Sicherheit. Untersuchungen zur Lebensqualität in der Bundesrepublik Deutschland*, Munich, 1987.

Zatlin, Jonathan R., *The Currency of Socialism. Money and Political Culture in East Germany*, Washington, DC, 2007.

Zayas, Alfred de, *Nemesis at Potsdam: the Anglo-Americans and the Expulsion of the Germans: Background, Execution and Consequences*, London, 1979.

Zechlin, Egmont, *Die deutsche Politik und die Juden im Ersten Weltkrieg*, Göttingen, 1969.

Zelikow, Philip, and Rice, Condoleezza, *Germany Unified and Europe Transformed: a Study in Statecraft*, Cambridge, Massachusetts and London, 1995.

Zentralinstitut für Jugendforschung: *Frauenstudie 1984*, Leipzig, 1984.

Ziebura, Gilbert, *Die deutsch-französischen Beziehungen seit 1945. Mythen und Realitäten*, Pfullingen, 1970.

Ziebura, Gilbert, *World Economy and World Politics, 1924–1931: from reconstruction to collapse*, Oxford, 1989.

Ziegler, Dieter et al., eds., *Zwangsarbeit im Nationalsozialismus in den besetzten Gebieten*, Berlin, 2004.

Ziegler, Dieter, *Großbürger und Unternehmer. Die deutsche Wirtschaftselite im 20. Jahrhundert*, Göttingen, 2000.

Ziemann, Benjamin, ed., *Peace Movements in Western Europe, Japan and the USA during the Cold War*, Essen, 2008.

Ziemann, Benjamin, *War Experiences in Rural Germany 1914–1923*, Oxford, 2007.

Zierenberg, Malte, *Stadt der Schieber. Der Berliner Schwarzmarkt 1939–1950*, Göttingen, 2008.

Zimmerer, Jürgen, ed., *Genocide in German South-West Africa. The Colonial War of 1904–1908 and its Aftermath*, London, 2006.

Zimmerer, Jürgen and Zeller, Joachim, eds., *Genocide in German South-West Africa. The Colonial War (1904–1908) in Namibia and its Aftermath*, Monmouth, 2008.

Zimmermann, Ludwig, *Frankreichs Ruhrpolitik. Von Versailles bis zum Dawesplan*, Göttingen, 1971.

Zimmermann, Michael, *Rassenutopie und Genozid. Die nationalsozialistische 'Lösung der Zigeunerfrage'*, Hamburg, 1996.

Zimmermann, Michael, ed., *Zwischen Erziehung und Vernichtung. Zigeunerpolitik und Zigeunerforschung in Europa des 20. Jahrhunderts*, Stuttgart, 2007.

Zohlnhöfer, Reimut, *Die Wirtschaftspolitik der Ära Kohl, 1982–1989. Eine Analyse der Schlüsselentscheidungen in den Politikfeldern Finanzen, Arbeit und Entstaatlichung*, Opladen, 2001.

Zohlnhöfer, Reimut, *Globalisierung der Wirtschaft und finanzpolitische Anpassungsreaktionen in Westeuropa*, Baden-Baden, 2009.

Zollitsch, Wolfgang, *Arbeiter zwischen Weltwirtschaftskrise und Nationalsozialismus. Ein Beitrag zur Sozialgeschichte der Jahre 1928 bis 1936*, Göttingen, 1990.

Zschaler, Frank, 'Die vergessene Währungsreform. Vorgeschichte, Durchführung und Ergebnisse der Geldumstellung in der SBZ 1948', *VfZ* 45 (1997), pp. 191–223.

Zuber, Terence, *Inventing the Schlieffen Plan. German War Planning 1871–1914*, New York and Oxford, 2002.

Zuckermann, Moshe, *Zwischen Politik und Kultur—Juden in der DDR*, Göttingen, 2002.

Zweig, Arnold, 'Die antisemitische Welle', *Die Weltbühne* 15 (1919), pp. 381–5.

# Acknowledgements

I began writing this book at the end of 2003 at the Berlin Institute for Advanced Study and I finished it at the School of History of the Freiburg Institute for Advanced Studies, which was obliged in 2013 to close its doors. I am indebted to many people, certainly most of all to my colleagues in our institute's research groups, as well as my students at Freiburg, with whom I have discussed the idea of the book and its interim findings in lectures and seminars over the past ten years. I would like to express my particular thanks to Hans Woller and Jan Eckel, and also to Patrick Wagner and Jörg Später, who took the trouble to work through the whole manuscript with painstaking thoroughness. I am very grateful to them for their advice and criticism. I also thank Dieter Pohl, Thomas Zimmer, Ella Müller and Jörn Leonhard, who read sections of the text. If I have not been sufficiently successful in putting their advice into effect, this is entirely the fault of the author. The book also benefited from the outset from Detlef Felken's encouragement. He read the texts that came in to him with unvarying attentiveness and his stoic composure was an incentive to the author not to abandon the project. The professionalism of Verlag C.H. Beck has been impressive, and it is a pleasure to publish with them. Catharina Hofmann, Christoph Sprich, Clemens Huemerlehner, Patrick Lang, Katia-Maria Günther, Lisa Kiechle, Vera Marstaller, Darya Romanenko, Lisa Fauth, Anastasiya Kazhan and Tobias Schmitt, as well as Agnes Schuler, Janna Rösch and Jan Dreßler, were involved in putting the manuscript in finished form. I thank them, as also all the people who have helped me to procure literature and sources in past years. I am especially grateful to Cosima Götz and Helena Barop, who not only scrutinised the author's quotations, footnotes and bibliographical references, but also read various versions of the manuscript in proof and made criticisms and comments on them. They also made clear to me that the burning historical questions posed by their generation are often different from those of my own.

Above all else, however, I should like to express my thanks to my wife, Jutta Blank, for supporting me personally and intellectually in so many different ways during the years of my involvement with this book.

Freiburg, January 2014

# Index